Dedicated to the memory of five individuals:

GERARD LEBEAU—A truly good person, collector of art

WALTER OLLER—A polyglot scholar and musician

ED MANWELL—A lover of golf and the law, and a grudging Francophile

HAL BARNELL—The vagabond illustrator, alumnus of the Figaro Café

and DIANA FRANCES HECHTER—A life too short

Introduction

Don Quixote is the most translated work of fiction. In fact, four other English translations have come out during the ten years preceding this one (Burton Raffel, John Rutherford, Edith Grossman, James Montgomery). So, why in the world would I take on yet another translation? The reason I felt justified in doing it is that translations are frequently based on Spanish editions that have taken too many liberties with the original text, fixing perceived errors, changing chapter titles, even adding words to the work. That their translations reflect the defects of the Spanish editions is, of course, not the fault of the translators. Read on, and you'll discover why these so-called errors and wrong chapter titles really should be left as written by Cervantes. My translation is based on the original Spanish edition of 1605 (Part I) and 1615 (Part II) and will be free from the "corrections" made over the ages. Also, this introduction will help, I hope, to set the record straight about a number of misconceptions about the work.

But First, the Life of Cervantes as It Relates to This Work

Miguel de Cervantes, the fourth of seven children, was born on September 29, 1547, in Alcalá de Henares, a university town about twenty miles east of Madrid. His father,

Rodrigo, was a barber-surgeon. The family had little money and moved frequently. When Miguel was three and a half years old, they moved to Valladolid, which was the capital, then on to Cordova in 1553, when Miguel was seven. In 1564, the family was in Seville. Next to nothing is known about Miguel's education, although it had to be both intense and broad, whether in schools or on his own. There is a record that he attended the Estudio de la Villa de Madrid for about six months when he was a rather old twenty, under the humanist priest Juan López de Hoyos. Cervantes contributed four poems (one sonnet, two short poems, and an elegy) to the volume put together by López de Hoyos to honor the dead queen Isabel de Valois. Although not celebrated as a poet, Cervantes could handle many poetic forms adroitly, and used a large number of poetic formats in the *Quixote* (there are forty-five of his poems in the book). Don Quixote's own poems are not very good, and his young admirer, Altisidora, writes like the fourteen-year-old she is, but these bad poems are not Cervantes' fault. He is just giving us what we should expect from an old man, hardly a poet, and from an immature girl.

On September 15, 1569, an arrest warrant was issued in Madrid for Cervantes, who had wounded a rival in a duel. The warrant said that Cervantes' right hand was to be cut off and he was to be in exile from Madrid for ten years. He fled to Andalusia—the southern part of Spain—and shortly thereafter made his way to Rome, where he worked in the household of Cardinal Giulio Acquaviva, whom he may have met the previous year in Madrid. During his stay in Italy, he learned Italian and was initiated into Italian literature. You will see many references to Italy, and writings in Italian, in the *Quixote*, particularly the Italian continuations of the French *Song of Roland*. The novella of the *Ill-Advised Curiosity* (in chapters thirty-three through thirty-five in Part I) is also based on Italian models.

In the summer of 1570, Cervantes joined a Spanish regiment in Naples and went off to war as a naval gunner. He fought against the Turks in the Battle of Lepanto (at Náfpaktos, Greece) on October 7, 1571, a critical battle on which the future of Europe as a Judeo-Christian continent hinged. After another battle in Tunis, and a stay in Naples, as Cervantes was finally returning to Spain in 1575, his galley was attacked by Barbary pirates and he was taken to Algiers, where he was held for five years waiting to be ransomed. His time in Algiers is reflected in the Captive's Tale (Part I, chapters thirty-nine through forty-one).

Once back in Spain, twelve years after he had left, he had to set about earning money, and got some work from the king. Miguel married Catalina de Salazar—eighteen years his junior—in 1584, in what turned out to be an unhappy marriage. They lived in Esquivias in La Mancha, where he came to know the types of people who would later populate his *Quixote*.* The following year, he published the first—and, as it turns out, the *only*—part of his pastoral novel *La Galatea*. The novel was not successful enough to support him for long, but he liked the pastoral genre well enough to write a number of pastoral narrations in the *Quixote* (starting with Part I, chapter twelve).

For about ten years he had a job as a buyer and tax collector for the crown, and traveled all around Andalusia. His knowledge of the geography of that region is frequently seen in the *Quixote*. In 1590 he applied for one of several positions in the New World—Guatemala, Cartagena [in modern Colombia], or La Paz [in modern Bolivia]—but his petition was denied, for which posterity can be grateful.

In 1604 he moved to Valladolid to a house that you can visit today. Part I of his *Quixote* was all but finished by then, and was printed on the presses of Juan de la Cuesta in Madrid in 1605. It was an instantaneous success. As the printers were taking apart the typeset pages from the first printing, a second printing was urgently needed, and what had been taken apart had to be reset. Since the original royal license (the equivalent of the modern copyright) didn't include Portugal, two enterprising printers in Lisbon

---

* For example, fifty years earlier, the local priest in Esquivias was named Pero Pérez, and he baptized the son of Mari Gutiérrez. Pero Pérez is the name of don Quixote's village priest, and Mari Gutiérrez is one of the names ascribed to Sancho Panza's wife. This is reported by Astrana Marín in his *Vida ejemplar y heroica de Miguel de Cervantes* (Madrid: Reus, 1948–1958, vol. IV, p. 29). It all may just be coincidence, of course, since neither name is remarkable in any way, but what is important is how Cervantes created his village folk partially based on his daily observations in Esquivias.

produced pirated Spanish-language editions immediately. It was reprinted in Madrid once again, this time *including* a license for Portugal, and there was also an edition in Valencia, all before the end of 1605! Then came foreign editions in Spanish and in translation.

Now that he was well-known as an author, Cervantes turned to other projects. In 1613 he published his twelve *Exemplary Novels*, several of them being in the Italian style. In 1614 he published a long poem called *Voyage from Parnassus* in which he writes about a hundred and twenty authors. Although he had hinted at a second part of his *Quixote* at the end of Part I, he waited until 1615 to finish his Part II. In the meantime, in 1614, a second author came out with *his own* continuation of Cervantes' book (more about this in the section dealing with Avellaneda later in this introduction, since the spurious *Quixote* greatly affected Cervantes' second part). Also in 1615 his *Eight New Plays and Eight Skits* was published. Cervantes was a real fan of the theater, and in chapters forty-seven through forty-eight of Part I, there is a critique of the contemporary theater. The following year, just as he was finishing his last novel, *Persiles and Sigismunda* (published in 1617), he died on April 23.

The Maligned Genius

Ever since the *Quixote* has been annotated, every editor has pointed out that the book is filled with inconsistencies, contradictions, and errors. And it is absolutely true. You will soon see that when something—*anything*—is stated, sooner or later it will be contradicted. This has led footnote writers since the erudite and vituperative Clemencín in the 1830s to proclaim that this masterwork of world literature was written by an extremely careless author who must have written at full speed without ever going over his work, and that he included hundreds of contradictions without ever realizing his terrible mistakes. That there are hundreds of inconsistencies is undeniable, but that Cervantes was a careless writer is very far from the truth.

Since there are no wholesale contradictions in his other works, the obvious conclusion has to be that Cervantes put them in the *Quixote on purpose*. But why? The answer is very simple. Cervantes' advertised objective in writing *Don Quixote* was to imitate and make so much fun of the ancient romances of chivalry—books that told tales of roaming knights in armor—that no further ones would be written. Cervantes was quite successful, since no new romances were written in Spanish after the *Quixote* came out.

In order to imitate the romances fully, Cervantes satirized not only their content but also imitated their *careless style*. It's as simple as that. In fact, this intent is clearly stated in the Prologue to Part I. There you'll see that the author's unnamed friend, who advises him about a number of things, says: "You only have to imitate the style of what you're writing [i.e., the romances of chivalry]—the more perfect the imitation is, the better your writing will be." Far from being a defect in the book, these contradictions are truly an integral part of the art of the book. No one can convince me that Cervantes, whose erudition and memory were so vast that he was able to cite, in this book alone, 104 mythological, legendary, and biblical characters; 131 chivalresque, pastoral, and poetic characters; 227 historical persons or lineages; 21 famous animals; 93 well-known books; 261 geographical locations; 210 proverbs; and who created 371 characters (230 of whom have speaking roles),* could possibly forget from one paragraph to the next the name of Sancho Panza's wife (yet she is called Juana Gutiérrez in Part I, chapter seven, and Mari Gutiérrez four lines later. And she is *also* called Juana Panza, Teresa Panza, and Teresa Cascajo). Of greater importance is the real name of don Quixote himself. Half a dozen or more variants are proposed (Quixano, Quesada, Quijana . . .). On a couple of occasions one of them is proclaimed to be the true one, each one a different variant. In the battle of the two armies, the adversaries are identified as Pentapolín or Pentapolén and Alifanfarrón or Aleanfarrón. The doctor in *Amadís de Gaula* is said to be both Elisabat and Elisabad. A soldier is referred to as Vicente de la Rosa and Roca. (Lots of editors of this work try to help out old Mr. Careless, by homogeniz-

---

* These numbers come from the very organized appendices to Américo Castro's edition of the *Quixote* (Mexico: Porrúa, 1960) prepared by José Bergúa.

ing these perceived mistakes, but in doing so, they do him and his work a disservice, since vagueness of names is a part of the work.)

So, Cervantes imitated the careless style of these romances by, in a *very carefully* planned way, making mistakes *on purpose* about practically everything, and he made sure that whatever was said was eventually contradicted.

In Part I, chapter four, when don Quixote makes an error in math and says that seven times nine is *seventy*-three, some editors and translators think that the typesetter has made a mistake—after all, there's only one letter different between *sesenta* (sixty) and *setenta* (seventy) in Spanish. But it's not a typesetter's mistake; this is *don Quixote's* math error.

On another occasion, don Quixote makes a mistake when he says that the biblical Samson removed the doors of the temple. It was really the gates of the city of Gaza that Samson tore off. Cervantes inserted this error on purpose, either to show that don Quixote's biblical knowledge was faulty, or to show that in the heat of excitement one's memory is not as acute as it should be. To state, as Clemencín does, that this is "another proof of Cervantes' lack of attention and of his carelessness in quotations" (p. 1170 of Clemencín's Castilla edition) is ludicrous. The characters are capable of making their *own* mistakes all by themselves, and when they make them we should realize that they belong to the characters and not to the author.

Cervantes, as a rule, simply does not make mistakes and he's not careless either. Indeed he had to be particularly keen and creative in order to *make sure* everything was contradicted. Every contradiction, every mistake, every careless turn of phrase is there because Cervantes wanted it exactly that way.*

---

* These ideas can be read more fully in my article "Contradictions in the *Quixote* Explained," in *Jewish Culture and the Hispanic World*, eds. Mishael M. Caspi and Samuel Armistead, published by Juan de la Cuesta in 2001, pp. 242–46. These are studies in memory of my professor at UCLA, Joseph Silverman.

A Case in Point—"Erroneous" Chapter Titles

Aside from the contradictions and inconsistencies in the
text itself, Cervantes made sure there are mistakes in the
chapter titles. Historically, in preparing romances for the
press, someone other than the author broke the text into
chapters and supplied the chapter titles, sometimes making
mistakes that the author could never make. In *El caballero del Cisne* [*The Swan Knight*] for example, the title of
chapter 114 is: "How the Swan Knight's enemies killed his
horse," yet the horse is not killed in that chapter.* What
Cervantes did was to imitate the chopping of the romances
into chapters, and the careless preparation of chapter titles
that went along with it.

Cervantes used practically every variation possible to
mess up chapter titles. One was to do exactly what the example from *El caballero del Cisne* did, which was to state in
the chapter title events that happened in the story, but *not*
in the chapter in question. In Part I, the title of chapter ten
is preposterously wrong: "Of what else happened to don
Quixote with the Basque and the danger in which he found
himself with a mob of Yangüesans." The episode with the
Basque is over, and the Yangüesans don't come for five
more chapters. Who could possibly fail to see this amusing parody? The Spanish Royal Academy of the Language
did just that in their 1780 edition, and they, "correcting
such an evident mistake," in the words of the hostile Clemencín, changed the title to: "Of the amusing conversations
that took place between don Quixote and Sancho Panza,
his squire." Exactly the same thing happens in the title to
Part I, chapter thirty-six, "Which deals with the fierce and
colossal battle that don Quixote had with some wineskins,
and other strange adventures at the inn." The "colossal
battle" has already taken place, and everybody knows it,
especially Cervantes. Many of these inconsistencies are far
from subtle.

Another variation was to switch chapter titles around.
Cervantes reversed, *on purpose*, the titles for chapters
twenty-nine and thirty of Part I. The Academy's edition

---

* I thank Bruce Fitch for this reference.

"fixed" these titles so that they corresponded to what was in the chapters.

Once, there is a false start. Part I, chapter 37 is titled "Which deals where the story of the famous princess Micomicona is continued, with other amusing adventures." In the table of contents at the end of the book, the compositors changed this to read: "Which continues the adventures of the famous Princess Micomicona. . . ." This makes sense. Because compositors pay little attention to content while they are setting type, they copied the false start exactly. But in preparing the table of contents, where they had to look up the page numbers, they paid attention to the content and "repaired" it.

The title for Part I, chapter forty-five bears the Roman numeral XXXV, *thirty-five*. This can hardly be a typesetter's mistake since it is so different from the "correct" XLV. It has to be that Cervantes once again "made a mistake" on purpose. The table of contents *does* correct it to *chapter forty-five*. A responsible typesetter simply could not allow the chapters to be numbered 44, *35*, 46 . . . in the table of contents.

The first edition also jumps from chapter forty-two to chapter forty-four. But a title for chapter forty-three *is* listed in the table of contents in the back of the book, its page number referring to the place where the poem "Ah me, Love's mariner am I" begins. This chapter title is unique in the way it ends: "Chapter Forty-three. Where the pleasant story of the mule boy is told, with other happenings at the inn. It begins: 'Ah me! Love's mariner am I.'" Since compositors are supposed to set exactly what they see, it seems reasonable that they would not skip a chapter division (if there had been one at *Ah me! Love's mariner am I*). When the compositors were preparing the table of contents, on the other hand, they must have been horrified to see that a heading had seemingly been left out (by the author), so they *made up* a title for chapter forty-three, after they determined where they thought the chapter was *supposed to* begin. (Three preceding chapters have already begun with a poem [I,1: "In a village in La Mancha" was a verse from a ballad; I,14: "Grisóstomo's Song"; I,40: a sonnet]— so this might seem a logical guess.) You might wonder why they didn't go back and put their made-up title in the text where they believed it was supposed to go. It was either because the book was already printed, or the pages were locked up and ready to be printed—you can't make a table of contents unless you know the page numbers (and that's why the table of contents is at the end of the book). To fit in this new title, the printers would have had to shuffle type all the way through the end of chapter fifty-one, where there is a bit of white space at the bottom (see folio 308r of the first printing), and that would mean ninety-six pages would have had to be reworked or reprinted.

Another Case in Point—The Robbery of Sancho's Donkey

The biggest "error" in the whole of Part I is without doubt the mysterious robbery and return of Sancho's donkey. The readers of the first 1605 edition of the work suddenly found that Sancho's donkey was not only missing, but *stolen*, as he blurts out in chapter twenty-five: "Good luck to the person who has saved us the trouble of taking the pack-saddle off the donkey." Soon, when Sancho has to do an errand for don Quixote, he says: "It'd be a good idea to resaddle Rocinante in the absence of my donkey." When don Quixote asks for bandages a bit later, Sancho says: "It was worse luck to lose the donkey . . . because when we lost him we lost the bandages and everything." And then, when Sancho calls himself a donkey, he says: "But I don't know why I'd mention 'donkey,' since 'you should never mention rope in the hanged man's house.' " In the next chapter, Sancho meets the priest and barber of his village and "he told them about the loss of the donkey." It would seem that somewhere in chapter twenty-five as many have pointed out, the donkey was stolen. Later, in chapter twenty-nine, Cervantes makes the point that when "don Quixote got onto Rocinante and the barber his pack mule," Sancho was left "on foot." After twelve chapters with no mention of the donkey, little by little, it reappears. In chapter forty-two, Sancho is found sleeping comfortably on his donkey's trappings, which had been stolen along with the animal: "Sancho Panza despaired at the lateness of the hour, and he managed to get the best accommodation of all, stretching out on the trappings of his donkey." After a few similar allusions to trappings and the donkey's halter, in chapter forty-six, there is the donkey, miraculously, standing in the stable, and the innkeeper swore that "neither Rocinante nor Sancho's donkey would leave the inn unless he was paid down to the last *ardite*." And then the story continues with Sancho on his donkey and don Quixote on his horse.

That's the way it was in the first Cuesta edition of 1605. In the second Cuesta edition of 1605, the one that included Portugal in its copyright area, we now read about the loss of the donkey in chapter twenty-three, and its recovery in chapter thirty. These additions have led some editors to believe that Cervantes went down to Cuesta's print shop and corrected his huge mistake himself. Far from the truth. The way it was in the first edition was exactly as he wanted it.

I don't know who wrote the inserted sections. I suspect it was someone in the print shop, given the other "corrections" made there, but I know it *wasn't* Cervantes. I am sure of it for several reasons. On stylistic grounds, the passage that tells about the loss of the donkey uses a Spanish expression for "to miss" that Cervantes simply does not use. It says that "Sancho Panza . . . *halló menos su rucio*" ("Sancho missed his donkey"). But whenever Cervantes wanted to say "to miss" he used "*echar menos*" and not "*hallar menos*,"* so the person who wrote that could not have been Cervantes.

Another important proof is *where* the new material was inserted. Flores, Allen, Hartzenbusch, Stagg, and others all agree that the robbery should not have been in chapter twenty-three, where it was placed, but in chapter twenty-five, since that is where we first see references to it. And the recovery was stuck in the middle of chapter thirty, where it seems an intrusion. Would the author himself have put these added sections where they now are? Clearly not. But the added sections were never supposed to be inserted at all, as the next proof shows.

Printers in Spain and in the rest of Europe used the

---

* Both expressions were used in Cervantes' time. *Echar meno*s is taken from Portuguese, where *hallar* is *achar*. The Portuguese expression *achar menos* is closer phonetically, although not semantically, to *echar menos* in Spanish.

"corrected" second Cuesta edition as a basis for their own editions until and beyond when Cervantes' Part II came out. These included the edition in Valencia (1605), one in Brussels (1607), a new one in Madrid (1608), one in Milan (1610), and yet another in Brussels (1611). So, most of the copies of the book in circulation at the time Part II came out had the inserted sections describing the theft and recovery of the donkey.

In chapter three of Part II, a new character named Sansón Carrasco arrives and says: "And some have found fault with the memory of the author since he forgot to say who the thief was who stole Sancho's donkey, because it's not mentioned there, and you can only infer from the context that it's been stolen." To most readers this would have been perplexing, since chances are their first part of the work was a copy based on the *second* Cuesta edition, where the robbery and return of the donkey are reported in chapters twenty-three and thirty. What this means is that Sansón is basing his observation on what went on in the *first* edition, the one without the added sections, the only one approved by Cervantes. If Cervantes had written the inserted sections, Sansón's observation would not have been made.

In this translation, following Martín de Riquer's model in his Spanish editions, I have put the added sections in footnotes where they were placed in the second Cuesta edition. But to play the game correctly, in the Cervantine way, you should pay little heed to added sections. The first edition is as Cervantes wanted, and the giant error of the robbery of the donkey is also *exactly* the way Cervantes wanted it.*

The Arabic Manuscript

The Arabic manuscript has caused some confusion and a lot of discussion ever since the book was published. Let me try to clear up some of the questions here. As Part I, chapter eight ends, don Quixote is in a furious battle with an enraged Basque. Don Quixote has resolved to venture

---

* There is more detail on this topic in my "*¿Por qué Cervantes no incluyó el robo del rucio?" Anales cervantinos*, 22 (1984), 207–12.

everything on one slash of his sword, and he begins his attack with his sword raised high. At this point, amazingly, the narrator claims not to have been able to discover anything further about don Quixote, not even how the battle came out a few seconds later. One day, our narrator is in the market in Toledo and there sees a boy selling notebooks written in Arabic. He can't read that language, but takes one of the notebooks and finds someone who can translate for him. It turns out, astoundingly, that the manuscript is the story of don Quixote, as he realizes when the translator reads something that caught his eye in the margin: "This Dulcinea del Toboso, which the history mentions so many times, they say that she had the best hand for salting pork of all the women in La Mancha" (Part I, chapter nine). This book has a title similar to the one we are reading in the real world: *History of don Quixote de La Mancha, written by Cide Hamete Benengeli, Arabic historian*. In the ancient books of chivalry, frequently the authorship of the book is attributed to a foreign source: Thus, within the fiction created by their real-world authors, *Don Cirongilio de Tracia* was written originally in Latin by an author named Elisabad; *The Deeds of Esplandián* was written in Greek by Frestón; *The Knight of the Cross* and *Civil Wars of Granada* were written in Arabic, and translated into Spanish. So the story of don Quixote continues this tradition. Cide Hamete Benengeli is an author of the wizard-enchanter type, like Frestón and Elisabad, just as don Quixote predicts he has to be; otherwise he could not be omniscient; that is, he could not otherwise relate what don Quixote and Sancho say and do when they are alone in the wilderness.

On the first page of this Arabic manuscript there is a miniature showing don Quixote with his sword raised. Underneath him is a caption that says DON QUIXOTE, and under Sancho Panza there is one that says SANCHO ZANCAS, because "the history sometimes calls him *Panza* and sometimes *Zancas*" (Part I, chapter nine). It is a remarkable coincidence that Cide Hamete's manuscript begins at *exactly the same point* at which our narrator's research failed him, with don Quixote attacking the Basque.

As you read this book, you will never see that comment about Dulcinea salting pork anywhere, and you will see that Sancho is always called Panza and never Zancas.

Apparently, our narrator, who promised a faithful translation from Arabic into Spanish, has edited and changed his
translated text, added to, and even omitted certain things.
This leads us to wonder how reliable the finished text is. It
is one of Cervantes' artistic triumphs that through these
levels of narration we can perceive clearly the presence of
Cide Hamete's manuscript and at times we can even recon-
struct what the manuscript must have said.

Sometimes Cide Hamete is cited directly, so there is no
question about his exact words. One time he says: "I swear
as a Catholic Christian" (Part II, chapter twenty-seven),
and another time: "'Blessed be the powerful Allah!' says
Cide Hamete Benengeli at the beginning of this eighth
chapter, 'Blessed be Allah,' he repeats three times" (Part
II, chapter eight). There are longer direct quotes, as well,
for example when Cide Hamete speaks of don Quixote's
bravery (Part II, chapter seventeen) and his poverty (Part
II, chapter forty-four), but the ironic thing about these direct quotes is that none of them furthers the story.

The narrator also cites Cide Hamete through indirect discourse. For example, in Part II, chapter one, we see: "Cide
Hamete Benengeli relates in the second part of this history, and third expedition of don Quixote, that the priest
and barber refrained from visiting don Quixote for almost
a month. . . ." Here is another example of many: "Cide
Hamete relates that after don Quixote was healed from his
scratches . . ." (Part II, chapter fifty-two).

Many times the narrator wants to emphasize that something said is Cide Hamete's opinion and not his own. For
example, the narrator wants us to know that Sancho, "according to Cide Hamete, was quite charitable . . ." (Part II,
chapter fifty-four).

One thing the narrator cannot stand is Cide Hamete's
inexactitude in matters of flora or fauna. Where Cide Hamete has given a generic term, our narrator likes to provide
an appropriate specific term. Where Cide Hamete must
have said: "As soon as don Quixote was hidden among
some trees . . ." our narrator has: "As soon as don Quixote
was hidden in the forest, wood, or grove . . ." (Part II, chapter ten). Where Cide Hamete must have written: "as night
overtook him he veered off the road among some dense
trees . . ." our narrator writes: "as night overtook him he

veered off the road among some dense oak or cork trees—for in this, Cide Hamete is not as meticulous as he is in other matters ..." (Part II, chapter sixty). And again: "Don Quixote, leaning against the trunk of a tree ..." but our narrator writes: "Don Quixote, leaning against the trunk of a beech or cork tree (for Cide Hamete Benengeli doesn't distinguish what kind of tree it was) ..." (Part II, chapter sixty-eight). What difference does it make what kind of tree it was? Our narrator insists on supplying details that do not affect the story.

When three country girls arrive on their mounts, Cide Hamete doesn't mention what kind of animals they are riding, so our narrator proposes what they might be: "He saw coming from El Toboso toward him three peasant girls on three young donkeys or fillies (for the author doesn't state which), although it seems more likely that they were she-asses ..." (Part II, chapter ten). Again, what difference does it make? Our narrator insists on exactitude where none is called for.

This Arabic manuscript presents one of the biggest contradictions in the entire work. At the end of Part I, in chapter fifty-two, Cide Hamete's manuscript runs out; there is nothing more left, and our narrator regrets he can find nothing else: "But the author* of this history, although he searched assiduously and with diligence to find don Quixote's deeds on his third expedition, he has not been able to find anything, at least in authentic documents. . . ." Then Part II begins: "Cide Hamete Benengeli relates in the second part of this history, and third expedition of don Quixote ..." If the manuscript ended, where did this come from? This is one of those blatant errors-on-purpose that Cervantes gets away with.

The Avellaneda Affair

In 1614, when Cervantes was close to finishing Part II of the *Quixote* something astonishing happened. In Tarragona, a second part of *Don Quixote* was published, written by a mysterious fellow named Alonso Fernández de

---

* Now, our narrator, the *second author*, calls himself the "author."

Avellaneda,* who claims he is from Tordesillas. Cervantes was angered because Avellaneda's work had appeared before his own second part; because Avellaneda neither possessed his inventiveness nor remotely understood the psychological subtleties of his don Quixote and Sancho; and maybe especially because of several insults that Avellaneda hurled at him in the prologue, dealing with his age and maimed hand.†

Avellaneda himself must not have thought that he was doing anything out of the ordinary. It was fairly common—and still is, for that matter—for a second author to continue a work by another. Avellaneda cites some examples of this practice in the prologue to his *Second Volume of the Ingenious* Hidalgo *Don Quixote de La Mancha, Which Contains His Third Expedition and Is the Fifth Part of His Adventures*.‡ He says: "How many have dealt with the life and loves of Angélica? Several have written about *Arcadia*; *La Diana* wasn't written by the same hand" (Riquer, p. 10). It is true that the amorous adventures of Ariosto's *Angelica* were continued by two Spanish authors, one of them being Lope de Vega.§ And that same Lope wrote his own *Arcadia* in imitation of Sannazzaro's *Arcadia* (1504) of almost a century earlier. There are two continuations of Jorge de Montemayor's *La Diana*. Many modern critics hold Gil Polo's continuation in higher esteem than Montemayor's original.¶

---

* Avellaneda is mysterious because this book is the only reference to him *anywhere*. Scholars have proposed that this was just a nom de plume, but no one has been able to identify the man behind the name.

† See Martín de Riquer's Clásicos Castellanos edition (Madrid: Espasa-Calpe, 1972), vol. I, pp. 8 and 10. All references to Avellaneda will be from this edition.

‡ Why the *fifth* part? Because Cervantes' Part I is itself divided into four parts.

§ Barahona de Soto published *The Tears of Angélica* in Granada (1586), and Lope published his *The Beauty of Angélica* in 1602. These works are based on Angelica, a major character in Ludovico Ariosto's *Orlando Furioso* (1532).

¶ Indeed, the priest in the *Quixote* shares this opinion. In Part I, chapter six, he says that they should not burn Montemayor's *Diana*, and that Gil Polo's "should be kept as if it were by Apollo himself" (page 57). The other continuation is by Alonso Pérez.

Avellaneda didn't consider it improper to write his own sequel to Cervantes' work so soon after the publication of the original. After all, both continuations of *La Diana* came out in 1564, just five years after Montemayor's original, and Avellaneda had waited *nine* years. Aside from that, Cervantes had given indications that he was never going to continue the *Quixote*. The title page of the 1605 edition read simply *The Ingenious* Hidalgo *Don Quixote de La Mancha, written by Miguel de Cervantes Saavedra,* and said nowhere that this was just the first of two volumes.* Even the division of the *Quixote* into four parts—reflecting the organization of *Amadís de Gaula*—appeared to add evidence that Cervantes considered his work complete.

At the end of the book readers in 1605 learned, perhaps to their dismay, that there really could be no sequel to *Don Quixote* because "no authentic information about his third expedition could be found, although tradition held that he went to Zaragoza to compete in a tournament there."† The hopes of those who longed for a continuation of Cervantes' work diminished with each passing year, especially since Cervantes had turned his attention to *other* projects. In 1613 he published his *Exemplary Novels*; in 1614 he published his long poem *Voyage from Parnassus*; and in 1615, about the same time that Part II of the *Quixote* came out, he published his *Eight New Plays and Eight Skits, Never Performed*. But until he published his *Novelas*, eight years after the appearance of *Don Quixote*, there was no indication that he would publish *anything* ever again, much less a sequel to *Don Quixote*.

Cervantes himself fueled the flames about a sequel in the very last line of the *Quixote*, which is a subtle dare, a challenge to *another* author to continue don Quixote's adventures. It is a slightly modified verse from canto thirty of Ariosto's *Orlando Furioso*, which reads: "*Forsi altro canterà con miglior plectro*": "Perhaps someone else will sing

---

* I mention this because Cervantes' first book, *La Galatea* (1585), states on the title page that it's just the *first part* of the work. Had he intended to write a second part of the *Quixote*, wouldn't he have said so on the title page, as he did with *La Galatea*? At least this is an impression one could have gotten.
† See Part I, the last page of chapter fifty-two.

with a better plectrum" (or *pen*, as Cervantes later inter-preted this line).

Since Cervantes hadn't published his own second part; since he dared someone else—*anyone* else—to take up his pen; and since so much time had gone by, Avellaneda accepted the challenge and wrote a continuation. In this book—and what could be more natural?—he sends don Quixote to Zaragoza to participate in the jousting tourna-ment, taking the itinerary from the end of the 1605 *Quixote* (chapter fifty-two). At the end, this second don Quixote winds up in the crazy house in Toledo. Then Avellaneda suggests an itinerary for a future author to take up. He says that when don Quixote got out of the asylum, he took on a new squire—a young lady, and pregnant as well, of all things—and went to have adventures in Ávila, Salamanca, and Valladolid. He invites yet another author to continue don Quixote's adventures, echoing Cervantes' original dare, saying that the knight's adventures would not lack "a better pen to celebrate them" (Riquer, vol. III, p. 130). No one took up this challenge.

Since he had not yet quite finished his own second part, Cervantes, with pen in hand, had ready means with which to discredit and even conquer his foe. I would like to trace here what he did, step by step, so you can see how his method developed to destroy both Avellaneda and his characters.

Almost everybody says that Cervantes learned of the Avellaneda continuation while he was writing chapter fifty-nine of his own second part, because that is where the spurious version is first mentioned. Of course, there is no reason to believe that the instant Cervantes heard of Avel-laneda's book he lashed out against it. He could have found out many chapters earlier, and continued with his original game plan while he figured out what to do, then, finally, in chapter fifty-nine, adopted the plan of how to combat Avellaneda.

So in this chapter fifty-nine, a certain don Jerónimo and don Juan come to the inn where don Quixote is staying, and don Quixote happens to overhear don Juan suggest that they read another chapter from the *Second Part of Don Quixote de La Mancha*. Needless to say, this informa-tion startles don Quixote. But when he hears that the book in question claims that don Quixote is no longer in love with his lady Dulcinea (such was indeed the case in Avellaneda's continuation), he flies into a rage and announces that *he* is don Quixote, and that he is still very much in love with Dulcinea. The two men seem to recognize instinctively that our don Quixote is indeed the real one, and that the one described in their book has to be a *fictional* entity who has merely been assigned the same name as the real person now in their presence.

The result of this astounding news is that don Quixote resolves never to go to Zaragoza, his original destination, but to go to Barcelona instead, so the two can never be confused. At this point Cervantes' stance is that his own characters are real and that Avellaneda's are pure fiction. But no one, not even Cervantes, can combat fictional beings; he had to make Avellaneda's characters real before he could attack them.

Two chapters go by before we hear of the false don Quixote again. When don Quixote enters Barcelona, he is welcomed as the real don Quixote, "not the false, not the fictional, not the apocryphal one written about in false histories" (Part II, chapter sixty-one). Even here, Avellaneda's hero is still pure fiction, still nothing more than the hero of a novel, a figment of someone's imagination.

Then something very strange happens. In the next chapter don Quixote is wandering around Barcelona and he comes across a print shop. One of the books being typeset is none other than the "*Second Part of Don Quixote de La Mancha*, written by a certain Avellaneda, a native of Tordesillas" (Part II, chapter sixty-two), which don Quixote says he recognizes and lets it go at that. It seems very odd that Cervantes would put a new second edition of Avellaneda in his own book, making it look like a very popular book. In real life, 118 years passed between its first and second printings. But whereas don Quixote just glanced at Avellaneda's book in Part II, chapter fifty-nine, Cervantes read it carefully.* In doing so, he noticed similarities in typog-

---

* For example, in Cervantes' Part II, chapter sixty-two, don Antonio, who is don Quixote's new friend and host in Barcelona, says to Sancho at the dinner table: "We have heard, good Sancho, that you are such a fan of creamed chicken and meatballs that if you have some

raphy, decorations, and typographic style, not with books printed by Felipe Roberto, the fellow from Tarragona who is listed as the printer of Avellaneda's book, but rather with books printed by Sebastián de Cormellas in Barcelona.* Cervantes would have known books from the presses of Cormellas well, since Cormellas had produced several books of interest to Cervantes.† So Cervantes is, in a subtle way, telling us that he knew that the false *Quixote* wasn't printed in Tarragona at all, but rather in Barcelona. In other words, this episode is nothing more than an elaborate messsage from Cervantes to Avellaneda just to say: "You can't fool me!"

We see a final insult to Avellaneda in chapter seventy, when a girl named Altisidora tells a tall tale about dying and seeing devils at the gates of hell playing a game resembling baseball, but instead of using balls, the devils were swinging at books. One of the volumes that gets hit flies to pieces.

"One devil said to another: 'Look and see what this book is.' And the devil answered: 'This is the *Second Part of the History of Don Quixote de La Mancha*—not the one written by Cide Hamete, but rather by an Aragonese who says he's from Tordesillas.' 'Take it away,' responded the other devil, 'and throw it into the depths of hell so my eyes won't ever see it.' 'Is it so bad?' asked the other. 'So bad,' replied the first, 'that if *I* tried on purpose to write one worse, I couldn't do it.'"

But it is in chapter seventy-two where Cervantes deliv-

---

left over, you keep them inside your shirt for the next day." Don Antonio confuses our Sancho with the other Sancho that he read about in Avellaneda. The other Sancho did love meatballs and creamed chicken breasts and stored the leftovers exactly as don Antonio said. Only those few people who knew Avellaneda's book would recognize this reference, but through this allusion Cervantes was able to show that he had studied his rival's book.

* This was well proved by Francisco Vindel in his *La verdad sobre el falso Quixote* (Barcelona: Babra, 1937).

† For example, he printed *La Araucana*, *Guzmán de Alfarache*, Lope de Vega's *Arcadia*, his *El peregrino*, and several volumes of Lope's plays; and even a book titled *The Merman Nicolao*, which don Quixote refers to in Part II, chapter eighteen, when talking to the young poet don Lorenzo.

ers the most brilliant blow in the Avellaneda affair. Our don Quixote meets don Álvaro Tarfe—who is the most important supporting character in Avellaneda's story—at an inn. When don Quixote asks him if he is the same one written about in a book, don Álvaro says: "'I'm one and the same . . . and that don Quixote, the main subject of that history, was a very great friend of mine.'" Álvaro Tarfe later signs an affidavit, at don Quixote's request, that he had never seen our don Quixote before and that he—our don Quixote—was not the one who appears in the second book.

So, now Cervantes' thrust has changed. We had thought, or had been led to believe ever since we heard of the spurious volume in chapter fifty-nine, that Avellaneda's creation was purely a work of *fiction*, that his don Quixote and Sancho were nothing but *characters in a book*, while our don Quixote was a real person (all this, of course, within the framework of Cervantes' own fiction). But now that Álvaro Tarfe enters Cervantes' book and says he knew the other don Quixote, we are invited to believe that there *really was* a second don Quixote and a second Sancho wandering about Spain, exactly as Avellaneda had described, and that they really had gone to Zaragoza for the jousts, and that the other don Quixote was now locked up in the Toledo insane asylum. Avellaneda's don Quixote and Sancho then have become as real as don Quixote and Sancho in Cervantes' *own* book. He has brought them to life and given them eternal fame. At the same time he has cast them into eternal oblivion by arguing so convincingly what a terrible book it is.*

Now that he has destroyed Avellaneda and his work, Cervantes is going to change Avellaneda's characters back into entities of fiction. When don Quixote is dictating his will, he declares that if his executors should ever meet Avellaneda, they should "pardon him as earnestly as they can for my having caused him to write so much and so great foolishness as he has written in it" (Part II, chapter seventy-four), meaning that his own *real* exploits caused Avellaneda to compose this "foolishness"—that is, fiction.

---

* But in all fairness, Avellaneda's book really isn't as bad as Cervantes makes it out to be.

There are other less obvious, but very important ways that Avellaneda's book affected Cervantes' second part. Up to the final chapter of Part II, Cervantes never reveals don Quixote's real name. I am convinced that he never would have, either, given the vagueness and contradictory information about his name, had the false *Quixote* not been published. We learn early on in Avellaneda's book that his don Quixote's real name is Martín Quixada, and that his niece is named Madalena. Knowing this, Cervantes names his hero Alonso Quixano the Good* in his final chapter, and the niece is named Antonia Quixana. Don Quixote's housekeeper, who appears frequently in Cervantes' book, is never given a name in Avellaneda's book, so she remains nameless in the final chapter of Cervantes' Part II. Thus, the pattern of vague or nonexistent names—a real part of Cervantes' book—is destroyed.

We were also more or less led to believe in Part I that don Quixote's village was Argamasilla, since that was the town where all those academicians who wrote poems and epitaphs dedicated to don Quixote, Sancho Panza, and Dulcinea were from (Part I, chapter fifty-two). That is why Avellaneda chose to make Argamasilla (which he always erroneously calls Argamesilla) don Quixote's village. At the end of Cervantes' Part II, we are told that Cide Hamete did not name don Quixote's village so that all of the towns of La Mancha could contend among themselves for the right to claim him as their own (Part II, chapter seventy-four). But there is one village in La Mancha that can *never* claim the real don Quixote, and that is precisely Argamasilla, because if the real don Quixote had also been from Argamasilla, he would have surely known that he had a neighbor, a certain Martín Quixada, who was masquerading as himself.

The last item I want to mention is don Quixote's death. Because of Avellaneda and his dare to another author to keep don Quixote's adventures going through yet another continuation, Cervantes realized that he had to have his

---

* The reason that he is *the Good* is that Avellaneda's hero is don Quixote *the Bad*. In Part II, chapter seventy-two, don Álvaro says: "And it must be that the enchanters who pursue don Quixote the Good, have tried to pursue me using don Quixote the Bad."

hero die at the end of the book so that no one else could try
to continue his own hero's adventures. No one knows how
Cervantes' Part II would have ended were it not for Avellaneda, but there is a good chance that Cervantes would
have simply sent him home to retire. It is sad that Avellaneda's book seems to have caused the death of don Quixote.

The Secular Clergy

Finally, here is a little point of interest. In the *Quixote*, soon
after don Quixote himself is introduced, we meet Pero (Pe-
*d*ro) Pérez, the village priest. Our priest never engages in
the ordinary work of priests (except in the last chapter of
Part II, and I contend that was never in the original plan—
which will be explained later). He never says a single Mass,
nor does he even say he has to prepare for one, write a
sermon, hasten off to hear confessions, or anything of the
kind.

It is equally strange that don Quixote himself never
says that he has to go to Mass, that he needs to confess,
that he needs a blessing, that he requires spiritual advice.
You would think that a Christian knight—which is what
don Quixote professes himself to be—would be in constant
need of the services of a priest. When don Quixote, or anyone else for that matter, eats, no matter in the open wilderness or in sumptuous banquets, it is strange that no one
ever says a blessing.

But what does Pero Pérez *do* to pass the time if he
doesn't engage in religious matters? We find out the instant
he is mentioned for the first time in the book: "[Don Quix-
ote] had frequent debates with the priest of his village . . .
about who had been the greater knight: Palmerín de Ingalaterra* or Amadís de Gaula" (Part I, chapter one). What
the priest does most of the time is to engage in literary discussions about secular literature. He never even *mentions*
religious literature—the Bible, lives of the saints, missals,
prayer books, and so on. He is very astute in his valuations

---

* Palmerín de Ingalaterra ("of England") is the hero of a Portuguese
romance of chivalry first published in 1547. *Ingalaterra* is an old variant of *Inglaterra*.

of secular literature and seems to have been a voracious reader in most areas.

The priest makes certain odd interjections throughout the book. At one point he makes a pagan exclamation: "since Apollo was Apollo...a more delightful or silly book as this one hasn't been written" (Part I, chapter six). Why Apollo? Why not a biblical figure? Because this priest never thinks of religious matters, never considers religious sources. He is plainly obsessed with secular life and secular literature.

In chapter thirty-two of Part I, our priest engages in a discussion of books of chivalry with an innkeeper who has just brought out a suitcase containing books of both chivalry and history, and the priest astutely explains to him the difference between fiction and nonfiction. In chapter forty-seven of Part I we meet the canon of Toledo (a canon is a priest who serves in a cathedral). The canon is taken aside by Pero Pérez and told of don Quixote's craziness. This canon states that "I've read ... the beginning of the majority of [the romances of chivalry] that have been printed, [but] I could never read one all the way through," yet he seems to know them better than that. The canon goes on to say that he has thought not of writing a *religious* work, but of writing a book of chivalry, and in fact has already written two hundred pages of one. Our priest, talking about modern plays, thinks them bad, not on religious grounds, but because they don't follow the three unities.

The Translating Adventure and Other Matters

I used lots of editions, dictionaries, and translations to help in the production of this book. The main Spanish edition used was my own (Newark, Delaware, 1997), which was based on the carefully done old-spelling edition of Schevill and Bonilla (Madrid: 1928–1942, 4 vols.), and I also consulted an original 1605 Juan de la Cuesta printing (in the photographically reproduced edition done from a copy that the Hispanic Society of America possesses). I turned frequently to other editions: Vicente Gaos' new edition of the *Quixote* is excellent textually and has very complete and very useful footnotes (Madrid: Gredos, 1987, 3 vols.).

The new edition of the *Quixote* done in Barcelona (Galaxia Gutenberg, 1998), by Silvia Iriso and Gonzalo Pontón, was most useful in helping to figure out what some otherwise obscure expressions meant, as was the new edition directed by my friend Francisco Rico (Instituto Cervantes—Crítica, 1998); volume I is the text, with *really good* notes by Joaquín Forradellas; volume II is just as large, and has all kinds of complementary information. Among the classical editions, I consulted Francisco Rodríguez Marín's ten-volume set (Madrid: Atlas, 1947–1948), and the learned and merciless one by Diego Clemencín, whose commentary exceeds the length of the *Quixote* (the modern edition is published by Castilla [Madrid, no year mentioned]). Occasionally I used the edition done by Juan Antonio Pellicer (Boston: Lee and Shepard, 1893).

Some words and expressions have fallen into disuse, and to untangle those mysteries, I used Covarrubias' *Tesoro de la lengua castellana o española* in Martín de Riquer's edition (Barcelona: Horta, 1943), which was published between Part I and Part II of the *Quixote,* and the very complete *Diccionario de la Lengua Española en CD-ROM* of the Real Academia de la Lengua (Madrid: Espasa-Calpe, 1995).

I also consulted translations into English and French. I used the former Norton Critical Edition version of Ormsby (1981), revised by my old friend Joseph R. Jones; the version by my professor, Walter Starkie (Signet Classics, 1964), which this version replaces; the Putnam translation (Modern Library, 1949); and Robinson Smith's (Hispanic Society of America, 1932). I counted on these four translations to rescue the poetry—none of the poetic translations is my own. John Bowle (London: 1781), Shelton (in the Harvard Classics), Fitzmaurice-Kelly (London: D. Nutt, 1898–99), and Martín de Riquer's edition of the false *Quixote* were also used. For translating legal matters, I relied on Ed Manwell's advice. We were old friends from our year-in-France days (1962–1963), and he was also a respected attorney in San Francisco.

I have followed the typographical style of the first edition wherever possible. The look of the title pages; the way the headings of the four parts are done; the way the parts end with lines of diminishing length; the chapter headings all in italics with indented lines starting with the second line; the two-line drop capital to begin each chapter; indenting all lines of a poetic stanza after the first one—all follow the original edition. I have also followed the first edition's Roman numeral 4, which is always IIII. Where Cervantes uses Arabic numbers, I use them as well; and "etc." is always written "&c." which I also copy. I keep foreign language quotes in the original language as well.

As the primitive version of this translation was being done, Annette Cash read and corrected it, and after it was pretty well on its way, Victoria Richardson, winner of the Cervantes Prize at the University of Delaware, read and commented on the whole work. Russ Hultgren also read almost two hundred pages of the text at different stages and taught me about the use of *which* versus *that*. None of these readers is to be held responsible for any lingering infelicities.

None of this would have ever even begun if I hadn't taken J. Richard Andrews' class dedicated to this book at UCLA in the spring of 1964. His insights put me on the road to untangling some of the important things seen in this introduction and throughout the book.

At New American Library, my editor, Tracy Bernstein, and the copy editor, Tiffany Yates, read the book with an incredibly judicious eye, and made lots of wonderful suggestions, for which I am thankful. And finally, working in the wings, my literary agent, Scott Mendel, was able to place this book in absolutely the best place. Where would I be without you, Scott?

T.L.

THE INGENIOUS
HIDALGO DON QUIXOTE
DE LA MANCHA,
Written by Miguel de Cervantes
Saavedra.

DEDICATED TO THE DUKE OF BÉJAR,
Marquis of Gibraleón, Count of Benalcázar and Bañares,
Viscount of the Puebla de Alcocer, Lord of
the villages of Capilla, Curiel and
Burguillos.

A.D. 1605

WITH COPYRIGHT
IN MADRID By Juan de la Cuesta

Prologue

IDLE READER, you can believe me when I say that I'd like this book, as a child of my intellect, to be the most beautiful, the most gallant, and most ingenious one that could ever be imagined. But I haven't been able to violate the laws of nature, which state that each one begets his like. So, what could a sterile and ill-cultivated talent such as mine engender, if not the story of a dry, shriveled-up, unpredictable child, who was filled with thoughts never before imagined by anyone else—such a book as one might dream up while in jail, where all discomfort is to be found, and where all lugubrious sounds dwell? Tranquillity, a pleasant place, the amenity of the countryside, the serenity of the heavens, the murmuring of fountains, the stillness of the soul, make even the most sterile muses appear fertile, and allow them to bear fruit that fills the world with wonder and content.

It happens that if a father has an ugly and clumsy child, love puts blinders on his eyes so that he'll see his defects as cleverness and charm, and he describes them to his friends as if they were subtleties and witticisms. But, although I seem to be don Quixote's father, I am just his stepfather, and I don't beg you, as others do almost with tears in their eyes, to forgive or overlook the defects that you see in this child of mine. You aren't his relative, or even his friend, and you have a soul in your body, you have free will like anyone else, and you're in your home, where you're lord and master—as the king is of his taxes—and

3

you know the common proverb: "under my cloak I kill the king."* All this exempts and frees you from any obligation, and you can say whatever you want about the story, without fearing reprisal for anything bad you might say about the work, nor expecting a reward for anything good you might say.

I only wanted to offer it to you plain and simple, without the embellishment of a prologue or the countless sonnets, epigrams, and eulogies that are customarily added to the beginning of books. I can tell you that, although it required enormous effort to write the book, the hardest part was writing this prologue you're reading. Time after time I took up the pen to write, and then I put it down, not knowing what I'd say. But at one of those times when I was uninspired—paper in front of me, the quill behind my ear, my elbow on the desk, and my cheek on my hand, thinking about what to say—a witty and wise friend of mine came in unexpectedly, and when he saw me so pensive, he asked me why. I told him that I was thinking about the prologue I had to write for the history of don Quixote, and not only had it gotten me in such a state that I didn't want to do it, but I was also on the verge of abandoning all the deeds of the noble knight himself.

"How can you expect me not to be fearful of the opinion of that ancient judge they call the public, when they see that after so many years of sleeping in the silence of oblivion, I'm coming out now—at this late age—with a tale as dry as mat-weed, devoid of artifice, diminished in style, poor in conceits, lacking in all erudition and doctrine, and without marginal citations and annotations at the end that I see in other books, even in the novelistic and secular ones, filled with maxims of Aristotle, Plato, and the whole multitude of philosophers, that amaze the readers and make their authors appear well-read, erudite, and eloquent? And when they cite the Holy Scripture, they're thought to be St. Thomases† and other Doctors of the Church, and they maintain such a resourceful decorum that in one line they describe an absentminded lover, and in the next, they give a

---

* In other words, all people are free to think whatever they want.

† St. Thomas Aquinas (1225–74), Italian priest who founded the accepted philosophy of Catholicism.

Christian homily that's a pleasure to hear or read. My book will be lacking in all of this because I have no citations for the margins, nor any notes to put at the end, and I know even less which authors to put at the beginning in alphabetical order, like everyone else does,* starting with Aristotle and ending with Xenophon† and Zoilus‡ or Zeuxis,§ although the second one was a slanderer and the last one was a painter. My book will also lack sonnets at the beginning, at least by authors who are dukes, marquises, counts, bishops, ladies, or celebrated poets; although if I'd asked two or three friends who are poets, I know they would have written sonnets for me, and such that the most renowned poets in this Spain of ours couldn't equal.

"In short, *señor* and friend," I continued, "I think that *señor* don Quixote will remain buried in his archives in La Mancha until heaven furnishes someone who can adorn him with all those things that are lacking, because I'm not capable of providing them owing to my deficiencies and lack of learning, and because I'm too lazy by nature to seek authorities to say what I can say without them. So, that's where the predicament in which you found me comes from, my friend—a sufficient cause for the quandary I told you about."

When my friend heard this, he slapped his forehead, gave a hearty laugh, and said: "By God, brother, I now realize how mistaken I've been about you all the time we've known each other, because I've always considered you to be enlightened and judicious in everything you did; but now I see that you're as far from being so as heaven is from earth. How is it possible that things of so little consequence, and so easy to remedy, can baffle and absorb such a mature mind as yours, which is able to break through and

---

* Cervantes was probably thinking of Lope de Vega's *Isidro* (1599), which had an alphabetical list of 267 names at the beginning—including the ones cited here—and lots of marginal citations and notes.

† Xenophon was born in 431 B.C. He was a friend of Socrates, a soldier of fortune, and a historical writer.

‡ Greek Sophist (fourth century B.C.) who wrote nine books severely criticizing the contradictions in Homer.

§ Classical Greek painter, fifth century B.C. No work of his survives, but many were described.

overcome other more difficult things? I swear it's not that you're incapable, but rather that you're excessively lazy and poverty-stricken in your thought. Would you like to see if what I'm saying is true? Well, listen to me and you'll see in the twinkling of an eye how I can overcome all your problems, and how I can fix all the defects that you say confound and intimidate you so much that you don't feel like publishing the history of your celebrated don Quixote, the light and mirror of all knight-errantry."

"Tell me," I replied, when I heard what he was saying to me, "how do you envision filling the vacuum of my fear, and converting the chaos of my confusion into light?"

To which he said: "First, with respect to the sonnets, epigrams, and eulogies written by important persons of rank missing from the front of the book, you can fix that if you write them yourself, and afterward you can baptize them with whatever name you want, attributing them to Prester John of the Indies or the Emperor of Trebizond,* who I've heard were famous poets; and even if they weren't, and if pedants and university graduates come forth to challenge and complain about it behind your back, you shouldn't care two *maravedís*† about it, because even if they discover your deception, no one is going to cut off your hand because of it.

"With regard to citing books and authorities in the margins from where you got the maxims and sayings you put in your history, all you have to do is find some aphorisms and Latin phrases that fit, and that you already know by heart, or that at least won't be hard to find. For example, when you're dealing with freedom and captivity, use: *Non bene pro toto libertas venditur auro*;‡ and then in the margin cite Horace, or whoever said it. If you're talking about the power of death, use: *Pallida Mors æquo pulsat pede pauperum tabernas regumque turres.*§ If it's friendship and the love that God commands you to have for your enemy,

---

* Both of these are fictional, legendary characters.
† These coins were worth very little.
‡ "Freedom is not wisely sold for all the gold in the world," from Walter Anglius' *Æsop's Fables* (12th century).
§ "Pale death goes equally to the hut of the poor and to the towers of kings," from Horace.

just go into Holy Scripture, which you can do with minimal research, and say the words used by God himself: *Ego autem dico vobis, diligite inimicos vestros*.* If you're dealing with evil thoughts, go to the New Testament: *De corde exeunt cogitationes malæ*.† If it's the inconstancy of friends, there's Cato, who can give you this couplet: *Donec eris felix, multos numerabis amicos, tempora si fuerint nubila, solus eris*.‡ And with these Latin phrases, and others like them, you'll at least be taken for a professor of grammar, which nowadays is of no little honor and worth.

"As far as putting notes at the end of the book goes, surely you can do it this way—if you mention some giant in your book, make sure it's Goliath, and with this, which won't take any work at all, you can say: 'The giant Goliath, a Philistine whom the shepherd David slew with a large stone in the valley of Terebinth, as cited in the Book of Kings,' in the chapter where you'll identify it's written. After this, to show that you're a scholar in human letters and geography, arrange it so that you name the Tajo River in your history, and you'll have another great citation by writing: 'The River Tajo, which was so named by a King of Spain, starting in such-and-such a place and flowing into the Ocean Sea, kissing the walls of the celebrated City of Lisbon, and it is held that it has golden sands,' &c., &c. If you speak about thieves, I'll tell you the story of Cacus,§ which I know by heart; if prostitutes, there's the Bishop of Mondoñedo,¶ who'll lend you Lamia, Laida, and Flora, the note for which will increase your reputation; if cruel people, Ovid will hand over Medea;** and if it's about enchant-

---

* "But what I tell you is this: love your enemies," Matthew 5:44.

† "From out of the heart proceed evil thoughts," Matthew 15:19.

‡ "When you are prosperous, you'll have many friends, but when your situation looks black you'll be alone," adapted from Ovid, *Tristia*, I, 9.

§ Famous bandit of Roman mythology, son of Vulcan. He stole Hercules' oxen. His story is related in Virgil's *Æneid*, Book 7.

¶ Fray Antonio de Guevara (1480–1545) was the Bishop of Mondoñedo (province of Lugo), and writes of these three prostitutes in his *Epístolas familiares*.

** Medea murdered all but one of her children by Jason (whom she helped to find the Golden Fleece), and probably killed her father as well.

ers and witches, Homer has Calypso,* and Virgil Circe;† if
brave captains, Julius Cæsar will lend himself to you in his
Commentaries,‡ and Plutarch will give you a thousand Alexanders.§ If you speak of love, with the two ounces you
know of Italian, you'll come upon León Hebreo,¶ who will
satisfy you completely. And if you don't want to go into
other countries, you have Fonseca right here, in his *Of the
Love of God*,** where you'll find everything you and the
most fastidious person could possibly desire on that subject. So, you only have to try to list these people or use
these histories I've mentioned in your own story, and by
Jove, you'll fill your margins and use up thirty-two pages at
the end of the book.

"Now, let's come to the bibliography that other books
have and yours doesn't. The cure is very simple—all you
have to do is look for a book that lists references from A
to Z, as you say. You can put this list in your book as is, and
even though the deception can be clearly seen, since you
really didn't need it in the first place, it doesn't make any
difference. And maybe some simpleton will think that you
actually *used* those sources in your simple book. And if it
serves for nothing else, that catalogue of authorities will
give instant credibility to the book. And what's more, no
one will set out to prove whether you used them or not,
since they'll have nothing to gain by doing so, and moreover, if I understand it correctly, this book of yours doesn't
need any of the things you say are lacking, because it's all a
censure of the books of chivalry, and Aristotle†† had noth-

---

* Calypso offered Odysseus eternal youth and immortality if he would
stay with her (he left after seven years).
† Circe was the mother of three of Odysseus' children. She lived alone
on the Island of Aeaea, where she turned all visitors into animals.
‡ The *Commentaries* by Cæsar (102–44 B.C.) deal with the Gallic Wars
and the civil war.
§ This is Alexander the Great, who is described among the forty-six
biographies in the *Parallel Lives* of Plutarch (A.D. 46?–120).
¶ León Hebreo (Juda Abravanel) wrote his *Dialoghi d'amore* in Italian (1535), but you didn't need to know Italian to read it since it was
translated into Spanish three times before 1605.
** Fray Cristóbal de Fonseca wrote *Treatise on the Love of God* (1592).
†† Aristotle, the greatest Greek philosopher (384–322 B.C.), studied under Plato and tutored Alexander the Great.

ing to say about them, nor did St. Basil,* nor Cicero.† The exactness of truth is not connected to the fictional nonsense found in those books, nor are the observations of astrology, nor are geometric calculations important to them, nor the confutation used by rhetoricians, nor do they have a reason to preach to anyone, since they mix the human with the divine, which is something in which no Christian intellect should be clad.

"You only have to imitate the style of what you're writing—the more perfect the imitation is, the better your writing will be. And since the intention of your writing is to destroy the favor and influence the books of chivalry have in the world and hold over the common folk, you have no reason to go around begging for maxims by philosophers, counsel from the Holy Scripture, fables by poets, orations of rhetoricians, or miracles of saints; but rather you need to try to make sure that your writing is plain, clear, and witty, using pure and well put-together words charged with meaning. Declare your thoughts without complications and without muddling them. Try also to make the melancholy person who reads your history laugh; and the mirthful to laugh even more; and be sure you don't vex the simpleton. Move the wise person to marvel at your invention, the grave not to scorn it, and the prudent not to cease in their praise of it. So, fix your attention on bringing down the ill-founded framework of these chivalresque books, despised by many, and praised by many more; for if you achieve this, you won't have achieved little."

In profound silence I listened to what my friend was telling me, and I was so impressed by his words that, without disputing them, I deemed them to be correct, and decided to use them for this prologue, in which you'll see, gentle reader, the wisdom of my friend, and my good fortune in finding such a good counselor in my time of need, and your own relief in finding the sincere and uncomplicated history

---

* St. Basil (329–379) defended the orthodox faith against the heretical Aryans. His writings include the *Address to Young Men*, in which he supports the study of pagan literature by Christians, such as that of classical Greece.

† Cicero (106–43 B.C.) was Rome's greatest orator, also a politician and philosopher.

of the famous don Quixote de La Mancha, whom all the
dwellers around the plains of Montiel believe to be the purest lover and the most valiant knight seen around there for
many a year. I don't want to overrate the service I'm doing
you by introducing you to such a noble and honored knight,
but I do want you to thank me for the acquaintance you'll
make of the remarkable Sancho Panza, his squire,
in whom, I believe, I have exemplified all the
squirely graces that are scattered throughout
the books of chivalry. And with
this, may God give you
health—and may He
not forget me.
*Vale.**

To the book about don Quixote de La Mancha

Urganda the Unknown†

If to be welcomed by the good,‡
    Oh, book! you make your steady aim,
    No empty chatterer will dare
    To question or dispute your claim.
    But if perchance you had a mind
    To win of idiots approbation,
    Lost labor will be your reward,
    Though they'll pretend appreciation.
They say a goodly shade he finds
    Who shelters 'neath a goodly tree;
    And such a one your kindly star
    In Béjar hath provided thee:

---

* Latin for "good-bye."
† Urganda was an enchantress in *Amadís de Gaula* who could change
her appearance.
‡ In the original, these verses were written with a "broken end," as
they say in Spanish, that is, with the last syllable being replaced by a
dash, creating a linguistic puzzle for the readers. All of these poems
are modified from Ormsby.

A royal tree whose spreading boughs
A show of princely fruit display;
A tree that bears a noble Duke,
The Alexander of his day.

Of a Manchegan gentleman
Thy purpose is to tell the story,
Relating how he lost his wits
O'er idle tales of love and glory,
Of ladies, arms, and cavaliers:
A new Orlando Furioso—
Innamorato,* rather—who
Won Dulcinea del Toboso.

Put no vain emblems on your shield;
All figures—that is bragging play.
A modest dedication make,
And give no scoffer room to say,
"What! Álvaro de Luna here?
Or is it Hannibal again?
Or does King Francis at Madrid
Once more of destiny complain?"

Since heaven it hath not pleased on thee
Deep erudition to bestow,
Or black Latino's gift of tongues,
No Latin let your pages show.
Ape not philosophy or wit,
Lest one who can comprehend,
Make a wry face at thee and ask,
"Why offer flowers to me, my friend?"

Be not a meddler; no affair
Of thine the life your neighbors lead:
Be prudent; oft the random jest
Recoils upon the jester's head.
Your constant labor let it be
To earn yourself an honest name,
For fooleries preserved in print
Are perpetuity of shame.

A further counsel bear in mind:
If that your roof be made of glass,
It shows small wit to pick up stones

---

* See chapter six, page 53.

To pelt the people as they pass.
Win the attention of the wise,
And give the thinker food for thought;
Whoso indites frivolities,
Will but by simpletons be sought.

AMADÍS DE GAULA*

To don Quixote de La Mancha

SONNET

You that did imitate that life of mine
    When I in lonely sadness on the great
    Rock Peña Pobre sat disconsolate,
    In self-imposed penance there to pine;
Thou, whose sole beverage was the bitter brine
    Of thine own tears, and who without a plate
    Of silver, copper, tin, in lowly state
    Off the bare earth and on earth's fruits did dine;
Live thou, of thine eternal glory sure.
    So long as on the round of the fourth sphere
    The bright Apollo shall his coursers steer,
In your renown you shalt remain secure,
    Your country's name in story shall endure,
    And your sage author stand without a peer.

DON BELIANÍS DE GRECIA†

To don Quixote de La Mancha

SONNET

In slashing, hewing, cleaving, word and deed,
    I was the foremost knight of chivalry,
    Stout, bold, expert, as e'er the world did see;
    Thousands from the oppressor's wrong I freed;

---

* Amadís de Gaula is Spain's greatest fictional knight. The first complete existing edition of his exploits was published in Spanish in 1508.
† Don Belianís de Grecia [of Greece] was the hero of a romance of chivalry that bears his name (Seville, 1545).

Great were my feats, eternal fame their meed;
In love I proved my truth and loyalty;
The hugest giant was a dwarf to me;
Ever to knighthood's laws gave I good heed.
My mastery the Fickle Goddess owned,
And even Chance, submitting to control,
Grasped by the forelock, yielded to my will.
Yet—though above yon horned moon enthroned
My fortune seems to sit—great Quixote, still
Envy of your achievements fills my soul.

THE LADY ORIANA

To Dulcinea del Toboso*

SONNET

Oh, fairest Dulcinea, could it be!
    It were a pleasant fancy to suppose so—
    Could Miraflores change to El Toboso,
    And London's town to that which shelters thee!
Oh, could mine but acquire that livery
    Of countless charms your mind and body show so!
    Or him, now famous grown—you made him grow so—
    Your knight, in some dread combat could I see!
Oh, could I be released from Amadís
    By exercise of such coy chastity
    As led thee gentle Quixote to dismiss!
Then would my heavy sorrow turn to joy;
    None would I envy, all would envy me,
    And happiness be mine without alloy.

---

* Oriana was Amadís de Gaula's lady, as Dulcinea was don Quixote's.

Gandalín, Squire of Amadís de Gaula

To Sancho Panza, squire of don Quixote

Sonnet

All hail, illustrious man! Fortune, when she
    Bound thee apprentice to the esquire trade,
    Her care and tenderness of thee displayed,
    Shaping your course from misadventure free.
No longer now doth proud knight-errantry
    Regard with scorn the sickle and the spade;
    Of towering arrogance less count is made
    Than of plain squirelike simplicity.
I envy thee your Dapple, and your name,
    And those saddlebags you were wont to stuff
    With comforts that your providence proclaim.
Excellent Sancho! Hail to thee again!
    To thee alone the Ovid of our Spain
    Does homage with the rustic kiss and cuff.

From El Donoso, the Motley Poet

To Sancho Panza and Rocinante*

I am the esquire Sancho Pan—†
Who served don Quixote de La Man—;
But from his service I retrcat—,
Resolved to pass my life discreet—;
For Villadiego, called the Si—,
Maintained that only in reti—
Was found the secret of well-be—,
According to the *Celesti*—:
A book divine, except for sin—
By speech too plain, in my opin—

---

* Rocinante was don Quixote's horse. Donoso is a made-up name meaning "witty."
† Ormsby, whose version I keep, has elected here to keep the "broken end" format. If you don't know titles of Spanish classics, you won't know *Celestina*, a tragedy written as a novel in dialogue.

To Rocinante

I am that Rocinante fa—,
    Great-grandson of great Babie—,*
    Who, all for being lean and bon—,
    Had one don Quixote for an own—;
    But if I matched him well in weak—,
    I never took short feedings meek—,
    But kept myself in corn by steal—,
    A trick I learned from Lazari—,
    When with a piece of straw so neat—
    The blind man of his wine he cheat—.

ORLANDO FURIOSO†

To don Quixote de La Mancha

SONNET

If you are not a Peer, peer you have none;
    Among a thousand Peers you are a peer;
    Nor is there room for one when you are near,
    Unvanquished victor, great unconquered one!
Orlando, by Angelica undone,
    Am I; o'er distant seas condemned to steer,
    And to Fame's altars as an offering bear
    Valor respected by Oblivion.
I cannot be your rival, for your fame
    And prowess rise above all rivalry,
    Albeit both bereft of wits we go.
But, though the Scythian or the Moor to tame
    Was not your lot, still you do rival me:
    Love binds us in a fellowship of woe.

---

* Babieca was the Cid's horse, and Lazarillo, six lines down, is an urchin antihero of the book that gave rise to the picaresque novel *Lazarillo de Tormes.*

† *Orlando Furioso* is an Italian epic poem (published in 1540) based loosely on the French Roland legend. Orlando Furioso means "Roland Insane" in Italian.

THE KNIGHT OF PHOEBUS*

To don Quixote de La Mancha

SONNET

My sword was not to be compared with thine
    Phoebus of Spain, marvel of courtesy,
    Nor with your famous arm this hand of mine
    That smote from east to west as lightning flies.
I scorned all empire, and that monarchy
    The rosy east held out did I resign
    For one glance of Claridiana's eye,
    The bright Aurora for whose love I pine.
A miracle of constancy my love;
    And banished by her ruthless cruelty,
    This arm had might the rage of hell to tame.
But, Gothic Quixote, happier you do prove,
    For you do live in Dulcinea's name,
    And famous, honored, wise, she lives in thee.

BY SOLISDÁN†

To don Quixote de La Mancha

SONNET

Your fantasies, Sir Quixote, it is true,
    That crazy brain of yours have quite upset,
    But aught of base or mean hath never yet
    Been charged by any in reproach to you.
Your deeds are open proof in all men's view;
    For you went forth injustice to abate,
    And for your pains sore drubbings did you get
    From many a rascally and ruffian crew.

---

* The "Knight of Phoebus" was the hero of a romance of chivalry published in 1555.

† No one knows who this Solisdán is. It looks like an imitation of a character from—or author of—a romance of chivalry, since the language of the sonnet—at least in Spanish—uses archaic words and pronunciation.

If the fair Dulcinea, your heart's queen,
   Be unrelenting in her cruelty,
    If still your woe be powerless to move her,
In such hard case your comfort let it be
   That Sancho was a sorry go-between:
    A booby he, hard-hearted she, and you no lover.

DIALOGUE
BETWEEN BABIECA AND ROCINANTE

SONNET

B. "How comes it, Rocinante, you're so lean?"
   R. "I'm underfed, with overwork I'm worn."
   B. "But what becomes of all the hay and corn?"
   R. "My master gives me none; he's much too mean."
B. "Come, come, you show ill breeding, sir, I believe;
   'Tis like an ass your master thus to scorn."
   R. He is an ass, will die an ass, an ass was born;
   Why, he's in love; what's plainer to be seen?"
B. "Is it foolish to love?"— R. "It doesn't make much
   sense."
   B. "You're metaphysical."— R. "From want of food."
   B. "Rail at the squire, then."— R. "Why, what's the
   good?
I might indeed complain of him, I grant you,
   But, squire or master, where's the difference?
   They're both as sorry hacks as Rocinante."

FIRST PART
OF THE INGENIOUS
Hidalgo[*] don Quixote
de La Mancha.[†]

First Chapter. Which deals with the lifestyle and pursuits
of the famous hidalgo *don Quixote de La Mancha.*

IN A village in La Mancha, which I won't name, there lived
not long ago an *hidalgo* of the kind that have a lance in
the lance rack, an old shield, a lean nag, and a fleet grey-
hound. A stew of a bit more beef than mutton, hash most
nights, bacon and eggs on Saturdays, lentils on Fridays, and
an occasional pigeon on Sundays consumed three-quarters
of his income. The rest of it went for a broadcloth tunic
with velvet undertunic[‡] for holidays, with matching slippers; and on weekdays, he adorned himself with his finest
homespun outfit.

In his house he had a housekeeper who was past forty, a
niece who was not yet twenty, and a houseboy who saddled
his horse and did the gardening. The age of our *hidalgo*

---

[*] An *hidalgo* is a member of the lesser nobility, exempt from taxes.
[†] La Mancha is a rather poor, sparsely populated area of south-central
Spain. *De la* means "of the."
[‡] Don Quixote's tunic flared out at hip length, and beneath it was the
undertunic that would be about midthigh length. His legs would be
covered by tights.

was close to fifty.* He was of sturdy constitution, but a bit thin, lean of face, a great early riser, and fond of hunting. They say that his last name was Quijada or Quesada—for there's some difference of opinion among the authorities who write on this subject—although by credible conjecture we are led to believe that he was named Quejana. But this is of little importance to our story—it's enough that in the telling of it we don't stray one iota from the truth.

It should be known that the above-mentioned *hidalgo*, during the periods when he was idle—which was most of the year—devoted himself to reading romances of chivalry† with such eagerness and pleasure that he almost completely neglected the hunt, and even the administration of his estate. His curiosity and folly got to such an extreme that he sold many acres of farmland in order to buy romances of chivalry to read, and he took home every one of them he could find. And of all of them, none of them seemed as good as those written by the famous Feliciano de Silva,‡ because the clarity of his prose and those obscure words of his seemed to be pearls, and more so when he came to read those flirtatious remarks and letters of challenge, where many times he found items such as these: "The reason of the unreasonableness which against my reason is wrought, doth so weaken my reason, as with all reason I do justly complain of your beauty." And also when he read: "The high heavens, which with your divinity doth fortify you divinely with the stars, and make you deserveress of the deserts that your greatness deserves."§ Because of this kind of nonsense the poor man lost his wits, and he spent many a sleepless night trying to understand those words and to figure out their meaning, which Aristotle himself

---

* In seventeenth-century Spain, this was considered quite old.

† These books are early fiction about the exploits and loves of knights in armor.

‡ Feliciano de Silva (1492–1558) was a prolific and not very good author. His most famous novel of chivalry is *Amadís de Grecia* (Greece) (1535), capitalizing on the well-known *Amadís de Gaula* (1508). Gaula is the Spanish name of a fictional region situated in Brittany.

§ These are not real quotations of Feliciano de Silva, but the first one resembles a passage from his *Florisel de Niquea* (1532) and the second one from his *Segunda Celestina* (*Second Celestina*) (1534). I've used Shelton's 1612 translation of these quotes.

couldn't have succeeded in doing, even if he were brought back to life for that sole purpose.

He wasn't at all comfortable with the wounds that don Belianís inflicted and received, because he thought that no matter how great the doctors were who treated him, his face and body would have been covered with scars.* Nevertheless he praised the author for the way he ended his book with the promise of more adventures, and many times he was tempted to take up his own pen and finish those endless adventures himself, exactly as it's promised there, and without a doubt he would have done so, if other more pressing matters hadn't prevented him.

He had frequent debates with the priest of his village—a learnèd man, a graduate of the University of Sigüenza†—about who had been the greater knight: Palmerín de Ingalaterra‡ or Amadís de Gaula.§ But *maese*¶ Nicolás, a barber from the same town, said that no one could touch the Caballero del Febo,** and if anyone could be compared to him it would be don Galaor, brother of Amadís de Gaula, because he was ready for anything, and he wasn't a namby-pamby knight, nor a crybaby, like his brother; and where bravery was concerned, he was his brother's equal.

In short, he became so absorbed in his reading that he spent his nights poring over his books from dusk to dawn, and his days from sunrise to sunset. Thus, from his little sleep and considerable reading, his brain dried up and he lost his sanity. Fantasy filled his mind from everything that he read in the books—enchantments, quarrels, battles, challenges, wounds, flirtations, love affairs, misfortunes, and

---

* Don Belianís is the hero of the four books entitled *History of don Belianís de Grecia* (1547–1579). The annotator Clemencín (1765–1834) counted 101 serious wounds given to don Belianís in the first half of the saga alone.
† Sigüenza's minor university was held in little esteem.
‡ Palmerín de Ingalaterra (England) is the hero of a Portuguese romance of chivalry first published in 1547. *Ingalaterra* is an old variant of *Inglaterra*.
§ Amadís de Gaula is the first and greatest hero of the Spanish romances of chivalry.
¶ *Maese* means "master."
** The Knight of Phoebus was the hero of the four books of the *Mirror of Princes and Knights* (*Espejo de príncipes y cavalleros*) (1555).

impossible nonsense. As a result, he came to believe that all those fictitious adventures he was reading about were true, and for him there was no history more authentic in the world. He said that the Cid, Ruy Díaz,* had been a very good knight, but he couldn't be compared with the Knight of the Burning Sword,† who, with one backhand slash, had cut two fierce and huge giants in half. He preferred Bernardo del Carpio because at Roncesvalles he'd killed the enchanted Roland‡ with the same deception that Hercules used when he strangled Antæus, the son of the Earth, in his arms.§

He praised the giant Morgante because, although he was of that gigantic lineage, where they're all arrogant and rude, he alone was courteous and well mannered.¶ But above all, he admired Reinaldos de Montalbán,** especially when he saw him leave his castle and rob everybody he came across; and when he was overseas, he stole that idol of Muhammad, which was made entirely of gold, as his history states.†† If he'd had the opportunity to kick that traitor Gan-

---

* The Cid is Spain's national hero (eleventh century) and the subject of the *Poem of the Cid*.

† This is the fictional Amadís de Grecia, known by this nickname because of a red sword-shaped birthmark on his chest. He never cut two giants in half, according to Clemencín.

‡ Bernardo is a legendary hero who appears only in Spanish versions of the story of Roland. Roland, Charlemagne's nephew, is the French hero sung about in the *Chanson de Roland*. Roncesvalles, the site of the massacre in which Roland was killed in 778, is in the western Spanish Pyrenees very near the French border.

§ Antæus, son of Terra or Gaia (the Latin and Greek names for "Earth"), was a mythological giant who compelled visitors to wrestle with him. When they were exhausted, he would kill them. Hercules, realizing that Antæus's strength came from his mother (the Earth), overcame him by first lifting him off the ground and then strangling him.

¶ Morgante is the giant whom Roland converts to Christianity in an Italian burlesque epic poem, *Morgante maggiore*, by Luigi Pulci, inspired by the French Roland legend. It was published in Spanish in 1535.

** The Frenchman Renaut de Montauban was one of Roland's companions, who all together were known as the Twelve Peers of France. He is well-known in the Spanish tradition.

†† This story is from *The Mirror of Chivalry* (1525), which seems to derive from an Italian version of the Roland legend.

elón* to shreds, he would have offered up his housekeeper and his niece to boot.

So, having lost his wits, he came up with the strangest idea ever concocted by a crazy man, and that was that he thought it right and necessary, both to increase his honor and to serve the republic, to roam the world on horseback, dressed in his armor, seeking adventures. He would put into practice everything he'd read that knights-errant did, redressing all kinds of wrongs, and by putting himself at risk and in harm's way, he would achieve eternal renown and fame. The poor fellow—because of the might of his arm—already saw himself crowned emperor of Trebizond† at the very least, and thus, with these very pleasing thoughts, carried away by the uncommon delight that they gave him, made haste to put his desire into effect.

The first thing he did was to clean some armor that had belonged to his ancestors, and which—now rusted and covered with mold—had lain for ages forgotten in a corner. He cleaned and repaired it as well as he could, but he saw that something was missing—the helmet had no closed front. It was just an artilleryman's open helmet. But his ingenuity solved the problem: He fashioned a kind of closed front out of cardboard, which, when it was attached to the open helmet, gave the appearance of a complete helmet. It's true that to test its durability and to see if it could withstand a slash, he took out his sword and gave it two whacks. With the first one he instantly undid what had taken him a week to make. And the ease with which he'd knocked it to pieces truly seemed inauspicious to him. To protect himself from further danger, he made it again, and this time he put some iron straps inside to satisfy himself of its battle-worthiness. And, not willing to put it to the test once again, he deemed it a very sturdy helmet.

He then went to see his nag, which *tantum pellis & ossa fuit*,‡ and although he had more cracks in his hooves than

---

* Ganelón, Charlemagne's brother-in-law, is the traitor who caused the death of Roland and the Twelve Peers at Roncesvalles.
† The Empire of Trebizond (1204–1461) covered a large part of the southern coast of the Black Sea region.
‡ "Was all skin and bones" in Latin.

there are *cuartos* in a *real** and more blemishes than Gonella's horse,† it seemed to him that neither Alexander's
Bucephalus nor the Cid's Babieca‡ could compare with
him. He spent four days thinking of a name to give him,
because—as he said to himself—it wasn't right for a charger belonging to such a famous knight, and being such a
good animal as well, not to have a celebrated name. So
he tried to think of one that would reflect both what he'd
been before he was the horse of a knight-errant and what
he'd become. It was quite reasonable that, since his master was changing professions, the horse should change his
name as well, to something noteworthy and showy, as was
befitting the new military order and profession his master
was already engaged in. Thus, after many names he created,
struck out and removed, added, erased, and made again in
his mind, he finally came to call him ROCINANTE, a name
that, in his opinion, was majestic, sonorous, and symbolic of
what he'd been—a *rocín*, a nag—before what he was now,
which was foremost among all the nags in the world.§

Having given his horse a name so much to his pleasure,
he wanted to give one to himself. These musings lasted another week, and finally he decided to call himself DON QUI-
XOTE,¶ which, as has been said, has led experts in matters of
this true history to declare that his original name must have
been Quixada, and not Quesada, as others have claimed. But
remembering that the brave Amadís was not satisfied just
with Amadís, but added the name of his country to make it
famous, calling himself Amadís de Gaula, he wanted, as a
good knight, to add the name of his region to his own, and
thus wound up calling himself DON QUIXOTE DE LA MANCHA.
This reflected very vividly, in his opinion, his lineage and his
region, and he honored the latter by taking its name.

---

* There were sixty-eight *cuartos* in a *real*. *Cuartos* is also an affliction
that causes horses' hooves to split.
† Pietro Gonella was a buffoon in the court of the Duke of Ferrara
(fifteenth century).
‡ Alexander is Alexander the Great. The Cid won Babieca in a battle
with a Moorish king.
§ The play on words in Spanish is evident in that language: *rocín* means
"nag" and *ante(s)* means "foremost" as well as "before."
¶ *Quixote* refers to a piece of thigh armor.

Having thus cleaned his armor, made the open helmet into a closed one, given a name to his horse and to himself, he convinced himself that the only thing left was to seek a lady to be in love with, because a knight-errant without a lady love was a tree without leaves or fruit, and a body without a soul. He said to himself: "If, through my misfortune or good luck, I come across a giant—as frequently happens to knights-errant—and defeat him with one blow, or split him down the middle of his body, or finally conquer and overcome him, wouldn't it be nice to have someone to send him to? He'll go in and get on his knees before my sweet lady, and will say with a meek and obsequious voice: 'I, my lady, am the giant Caraculiambro,* lord of the Island of Malindrania,† whom the never sufficiently praised knight don Quixote de La Mancha vanquished. He commanded me to appear before your greatness, to do with me whatever you will.'"

Oh, how it pleased our good knight when he'd made this speech, and particularly when he found the one to designate as his lady love! It happened—it is generally thought—that in a nearby village there was a good-looking peasant lass with whom he'd been in love for some time, although she never knew or even suspected it. Her name was Aldonza Lorenzo, and it seemed fitting to him that she should have the title of mistress of his thoughts. And looking for a name for her that didn't differ much from her own, and which elevated itself and suggested and implied the name of a princess and a great lady, he came to call her Dulcinea‡ del Toboso—since she was from the village of El Toboso§—a name that in his opinion was both musical and original, charged with meaning, as were all the other names he'd given to himself and his belongings.

---

* The giant's name is quite indecent—*cara*, "face," *cul(o)*, "anus." Even today the expressions *caraculo* or *cara de culo* are used in a most deprecatory way. *Cara de hambre* ("hunger") is an expression referring to an unfortunate person. *Caraculiambro* combines both expressions. I thank Román Álvarez for these observations.
† With a switch in vowels, based on *malandrín* ("rascal"), it means "Island of the Rascals."
‡ Aldonza was associated with the name Dulce, "sweet."
§ El Toboso is a town near Toldeo. Today it has 2,300 inhabitants, mostly engaged in farming and sheep raising.

Chapter II. Which deals with the first expedition that the ingenious don Quixote made.

Having made these preparations, he didn't want to waste any time putting his plan into effect. He was distressed at how the world was suffering because of his delay, such were the wrongs he planned to right, the injustices to rectify, the abuses to mend, and the debts to settle. Thus, without telling anyone at all of his intentions, and without anyone seeing him, one morning—one of the hottest ones of the month of July—he put on all his armor, mounted Rocinante, and with his poorly mended helmet in place, he clasped his shield, took his lance, and went out into the countryside through the back gate of the corral, enormously happy and exhilarated at seeing how easily he'd begun his worthy enterprise.

But no sooner was he in the open countryside than he was assailed by a terrible thought, such that he almost gave up his just-begun undertaking, and that was that he'd not yet been dubbed a knight, and, in accordance with the laws of chivalry, he couldn't, nor shouldn't, take up arms against any knight. And even if he'd been so dubbed, as a novice knight he would have to wear plain armor—with no device on his shield—until he'd earned that right through his travails. These thoughts made him waver in his purpose, but since his madness overcame his reason, he resolved to have himself so dubbed by the first knight he came across, in imitation of many others who did exactly that, according to the books that had led him to that state. As for the plain armor, he planned to scour it when he had the time, so as to make it whiter than ermine. And with this he calmed down and continued his journey, taking the road his horse chose, believing that was what the spirit of adventure called for.

As our brand-new adventurer went ambling along, he talked to himself, saying: "Who can doubt that in years to come, when the true history of my famous exploits comes to light, the enchanter* who will write about them, when he

---

* In Spanish books of chivalry, it was common for knights to have an enchanter as the historian who recorded their deeds. How else could

comes to relate this first expedition of mine, will begin this way: 'Scarcely had the ruddy Apollo* begun to spread the golden tresses of his beautiful hair over the vast surface of the earthly globe, and scarcely had the pretty painted birds with their harmonious tongues greeted in sweet, melodious strains the fair Aurora,† who, having left her jealous husband's‡ bed, appeared at the gates and balconies of the Manchegan horizon, when the renowned knight don Quixote de La Mancha, forsaking the soft down, and mounting his famous steed Rocinante, entered the ancient and celebrated plains of Montiel.'" And it was true, because he was on those very plains!

And he went on, saying: "What a happy age and equally happy era when my famous deeds—worthy of being sculpted in bronze, carved in marble, and painted on panels—will come to light for future remembrance. Oh, wise enchanter—whoever you may be—you, who have been chosen to be the chronicler of this uncommon history, I beg you not to forget Rocinante, my constant companion along these highways and byways!"

Then he went on to say, as if he were really in love: "Oh, Dulcinea del Toboso, mistress of this captive heart! You've done me a grievous wrong in dismissing and banishing me with your harsh command, forbidding me to appear before your beauteous person. May it please you, lady, to remember this subjected heart, which suffers so many sorrows for your love." Along with this, he began stringing together more nonsense, all of it in the same style that the books of chivalry had taught him, imitating their language as much as he could. He moved so slowly, and the sun beat down upon him with such intensity, that it was enough to melt his brains, if he had any.

He traveled almost all of that day without anything happening that was worth relating, for which he despaired, because he wanted to come across someone right away to

---

their thoughts and actions be recorded when they were alone in the wilderness?
* The Greek god Apollo pulled the sun through the sky behind his chariot.
† Aurora was the Roman goddess of the dawn.
‡ Tithonus was Aurora's lover, not her husband.

whom he could prove the valor of his mighty arm. There are authorities who say his first adventure was the one in Puerto Lápice.* Others say it was the one about the windmills, but what I've been able to verify, and what I've found written in the annals of La Mancha, is that he traveled that whole day, and at nightfall his nag and he were dead tired and ravenously hungry. He looked all around to see if he could find some castle or a shepherd's hut where he could be sheltered, to remedy his considerable hunger and other needs, when he saw—not far off the road on which he was traveling—an inn, which was as if he'd seen a star leading him, not to the gates, but rather to the palaces of his relief. He picked up speed and arrived there just as it was getting dark.

By chance there were at the entrance two young women, of those that they call tarts, who were going to Seville with some muleteers who happened to be spending the night there. And since everything he thought, saw, or imagined seemed to him to be in the style of what he'd read, as soon as he saw the inn, it appeared to him to be a castle with four towers and pinnacles of shining silver, not lacking a drawbridge and a deep moat, with all the accoutrements with which such castles are depicted.

As he approached the inn, which to him seemed to be a castle, a short distance away from it he reined in Rocinante, expecting that some dwarf would appear among the battlements to announce with a trumpet that a knight was drawing near to the castle. But since he realized it was getting late, and Rocinante was anxious to go to the stable, he proceeded to the gate of the inn and saw the two wanton young women there, who—it appeared to him—were two beautiful maidens or gracious ladies taking their ease at the gate of the castle. Just then a swineherd, who by chance was gathering his pigs (I beg no pardon, since that's what they're called)† from a harvested field, sounded his horn to round them up, and this appeared to don Quixote to be exactly what he wanted—a dwarf announcing his arrival.

Thus, with enormous satisfaction, don Quixote approached the inn and the ladies. When they saw a man in

---

* Puerto Lápice is a town about twenty-five miles west of El Toboso.
† It was customary to beg one's pardon when using a taboo word—one didn't mention pigs in public.

armor like that, with lance and shield, they were filled with fear, and went to rush into the inn. But don Quixote, deducing their fear from their flight, raised his pasteboard visor, and, revealing his dry and grimy face, with gentle mien and calm voice, said to them: "Do not flee, your graces, nor fear any wrongdoing, for the order of chivalry that I profess does not allow me to wrong anyone, least of all maidens of high rank such as you show yourselves to be."

The young women looked at him, trying to make out the features of his face, which the ill-made visor was covering, but when they heard themselves being called maidens, something so far from their profession, they couldn't restrain their laughter. Don Quixote got into quite a huff because of this and said to them: "Politeness is becoming in beautiful women, and laughter that comes from a trifling cause is great folly. I'm not telling you this so that you'll be distressed or to make you angry, for my will is none other than to serve you."

This kind of language, which the ladies didn't understand, coupled with the strange aspect of our knight, increased their laughter, and his anger, and it would have gotten worse if at that moment the innkeeper hadn't appeared. He, being quite fat, was very easygoing. And seeing that strange figure, with such an odd assortment of arms and other things, such as the long stirrups, lance, shield, and torso armor, he was almost at the point of joining the damsels in their show of mirth. But fearing the mass of weaponry, he resolved to speak with him courteously, and said: "If your grace, *señor* knight, is looking for lodging, except for a bed, since there's none left at this inn, you'll find everything else in great abundance."

Don Quixote, seeing the humility of the warden of the castle, since that's what he appeared to him to be, responded: "For me, *señor castellano*,* anything will do since 'my only adornments are my armor, my only rest is the battle.'"

The innkeeper, hearing himself being called *castellano*, guessed it must have been because the knight thought he

---

* *Castellano* means both "a person from Castile" (central and northern Spain) as well as "warden of a castle," which is don Quixote's intended meaning.

was one of the good people from Castile,* although he was Andalusian, one of those from the Playa de Sanlúcar, and no less a thief than Cacus, nor less a trickster than a mischievous page.

"In that case 'the bed' of your grace will be 'hard rocks' and 'your sleep, constant vigilance.'† And that being the case, you can dismount, since you're sure to find in this humble house sufficient opportunity not to sleep in a whole year, not to mention just a single night."

And saying this, he went to hold don Quixote's stirrup. He got down with considerable difficulty and strain, like a person who had not eaten a bite all day long. He then told the innkeeper to take great care of his horse because there was no better one in the world. The innkeeper looked at the horse and it didn't seem to him to be as good as don Quixote was saying, and not even half as good, but he took him to the stable and went back to see what his guest might want. The two damsels were removing his armor, because they had since made peace with him. Although they had removed the breastplate and backplate, they couldn't figure out how to remove the gorget,‡ nor take off the badly made helmet that he was wearing, tied together with some green ribbons. They wanted to cut them since they couldn't be untied, but he wouldn't allow it, so he spent the whole night with his helmet on, and he was the funniest and strangest figure imaginable. And while they were removing his armor, since he imagined that those prostitutes were important ladies in that castle, he said to them with considerable grace:

> There never was on earth a knight
> so waited on by ladies fair,
> as once was he, called don Quixote,

---

* In underworld jargon, "good people from Castile" meant "cunning thieves." The Playa de Sanlúcar (near Huelva), which follows, was a place where rogues and thieves congregated, waiting to embark for the Americas.

† The innkeeper is continuing the verses from the ballad that don Quixote began.

‡ The gorget is a piece of armor to protect one's neck and upper chest.

> when first he left his village dear;
> Damsels to undress him ran with speed,
> and princesses to dress his steed.*

"Or Rocinante, for this, my ladies, is the name of my horse, and mine is don Quixote de La Mancha. Although I didn't want to reveal my name until the deeds done in your service and on your behalf made me known, but adapting that ancient ballad about Lancelot seemed so *à propos* that I let you know who I am before I should have. But a time will come when your graces will command me and I'll obey, and the strength of my arm will make my desire to serve you known."

The young women, who were not accustomed to hearing such rhetoric, said nothing. They only asked him if he wanted something to eat.

"I'll eat anything," responded don Quixote, "because I feel that it would do me a lot of good."

By chance, that day happened to be Friday, and there was nothing in the inn but a couple of servings of fish that in Castile they call *abadejo*, in Andalusia *bacalao*, in some areas *curadillo*, and in other areas *truchuela*.† They asked him if he would eat some *truchuela*, since there was no other fish to give him to eat.

"If there is a lot of *truchuelas*," responded don Quixote, "it will be the same as a full-size trout. It's all the same to me if you give me eight *reales* in coins or one piece of eight. And it may even be that these *truchuelas* are like veal, which is better than beef; and kid, which is better than goat. But be that as it may, serve me right away, because the ordeal of the weight of armor cannot be borne on an empty stomach."

They set a table for him near the door of the inn in the fresh air. The innkeeper took him a serving of badly marinated and worse-cooked codfish, and a piece of bread

---

* The original well-known ballad has "Lancelot" (*Lanzarote* in Spanish) for "*don* Quixote" and "Britain" for "his village." This version was taken from Ormsby, whose third line originally said: "as once was he, don Quixote hight." "Hight" (rhymes with "knight") is archaic for "called."

† All of these refer to variations of codfish. *Truchuela* has a double meaning of "small trout" and "smoked codfish."

that was as black and grimy as his armor. It was really very amusing to see him eat because, since he had his helmet on and had to use his two hands to keep the visor up, he couldn't put anything in his mouth, and had to depend on someone else to feed him. One of the ladies did this service for him. But it would have been impossible for him to drink anything if the innkeeper hadn't bored out a reed. He put one end of it in his mouth and poured wine down the other. He ate and drank very patiently so that he wouldn't break the ribbons of the helmet.

While this was going on, by chance there arrived at the inn a gelder of pigs, and as soon as he arrived, he played four or five notes on his panpipes, which confirmed to don Quixote that he was in a famous castle and that they were serving him accompanied by music; the codfish was trout; the bread of whitest flour; the prostitutes, ladies; the innkeeper, the warden of the castle; and he felt that his resolve to go out into the world was the right thing to do. But what bothered him was that he'd not yet been dubbed a knight, and he felt that he couldn't legitimately undertake any adventure without receiving the order of knighthood.

Chapter III. *In which is recounted the amusing way that don Quixote came to be dubbed a knight.*

THUS, TROUBLED by this thought, he cut short his skimpy dinner, typical of inns, and when he finished, he called the innkeeper, and behind the closed doors of the stable, got down on his knees before him, saying: "I won't rise from where I am, brave knight, until you grant me a boon I want to ask of you and will redound to your fame and to the benefit of mankind."

When the innkeeper saw his guest at his feet and heard those words, he was perplexed, looking at him without knowing what to do or say. He insisted that his guest get up, but don Quixote refused until the innkeeper promised to grant the boon that he had requested.

"I expected no less of your great magnificence, *señor mío*,"* responded don Quixote, "and the boon that I've

---

* *Mío* means "my, mine." *Señor mío* means "my good man."

asked of you and that you've accorded me is that tomorrow you will dub me a knight. And this night I'll watch over my armor in your castle, and tomorrow, as I've said, what I want so much will be fulfilled, so that I, as is fitting, may roam the four corners of the earth seeking adventures to favor the needy, as is the duty of knighthood and of knights-errant such as myself who are destined for such deeds."

The innkeeper, who, as has been said, was a bit of a jokester, and already had some suspicion about his guest's lack of sanity, became convinced of it when he heard these words. In order to have some entertainment that night, he decided to humor him, so he said that don Quixote was very correct in what he wanted and asked for, and that his goal was proper and natural for knights as important as he appeared to be, and as his gallant presence proved. He also said that he, in his youth, had devoted himself to that same honorable activity, traveling through different parts of the world looking for adventures, having visited the Percheles of Málaga, the Islas of Riarán, the Compás of Seville, the Azoguejo of Segovia, the Olivera of Valencia, the Rondilla of Granada, the Playa de Sanlúcar, the Potro of Córdoba, the Ventillas of Toledo,* and other places, showing the fleetness of his feet, and the light-fingeredness of his hands, doing many wrongs, courting many widows,† deflowering maidens, deceiving orphans, and finally, making himself known in courtrooms throughout Spain. He'd ended up retiring to this castle, where he lived on his income and that of others, welcoming all knights-errant of any rank and condition, only because of the fondness that he had for them, and so that they would share with him some of their money in payment for his benevolence.

He also told him that there was no chapel in his castle where he could watch over his armor, since it had been torn down so that a new one could be built. But he knew that in case of great need, it could be watched over anywhere, and that night he could watch over it in a courtyard of the castle.

---

* These places form what Clemencín called "a picaresque map of Spain." The Islas of Riarán are in Málaga, and they're not islands, but rather city blocks.

† "Courting," yes; but the Spanish also implies "soliciting sexual favors."

In the morning, if it pleased God, they would perform the proper ceremonies, and he would become a knight-errant, and such a knight that no one in the world could be more of one.

The innkeeper asked if he had any money. Don Quixote said that he didn't have a *blanca*,* because he'd never read in the histories of knights-errant that any one of them had taken money with him. To this, the innkeeper said that he was mistaken, because although the histories didn't specify something as obvious and necessary as money and clean shirts, there was no reason to believe that they didn't have them. Thus he could consider it certain and proven that all knights-errant—of which so many books of chivalry are filled—carried well-stocked purses for any contingency, and that they also took clean shirts and a small chest filled with ointments for healing injuries they received, because in the open country where they battled, there was not always someone to treat their wounds—unless they had some wise enchanter as a friend who could instantly come to their aid, bearing a maiden or dwarf on a cloud with a flask of magic elixir of such potency that, just by taking a single drop of it, they would be immediately cured of their wounds, as if they had never been injured. But when this wasn't the case, the knights of old certainly had squires who were provided with money and other necessities such as bandages and healing ointments. And when it happened that those knights didn't have squires, which was rarely the case, they themselves carried everything on the crupper of their horse, in small, practically invisible saddlebags that were made to look like they contained something of greater importance, because, except for such emergencies, having saddlebags was frowned on by knights-errant. For this reason, the innkeeper advised him—but he could even have commanded him as his soon-to-be godson—that he shouldn't venture forth from that day forth without money and the other provisions that he'd mentioned, and that he would see how useful they could be when he least suspected it.

Don Quixote promised he would do exactly what he was

---

* The *blanca* was a coin worth half a *maravedí*, that is, worth practically nothing.

advised, and so the order was given for him to watch over his arms in a large corral at the side of the inn. Don Quixote collected all his armor and put it on a trough next to a well. He clasped his shield and he grasped his lance, and with gentle mien started to pace back and forth as night fell.

The innkeeper told everyone at the inn about the craziness of his guest, the watching over of the armor, and his expectation to be dubbed a knight. Everyone was amazed at his rare kind of madness and they all went to look from a distance, and saw him with his calm demeanor, sometimes pacing, sometimes leaning against his lance, but always fixing his eyes on his armor for long periods of time. It was now night, but the moon shone so bright that it seemed to compete with the star that gave it its light, and in this way everything the novice knight did could be clearly seen by everyone.

At this point, one of the muleteers felt that it was time to water his mules, and to do it, he had to remove don Quixote's armor, which was on the trough. When don Quixote saw this, he said in a loud voice: "Oh, you knight, whoever you are, who dare to touch the armor of the most valiant errant who ever girded a sword, watch what you're doing! Don't touch it, unless you want to lose your life as a consequence of your boldness!"

The muleteer paid no heed to these words, and it would have been better for him if he had, because it would have let him keep his health. But instead, he seized the straps of the armor, and threw it a long way away. When don Quixote saw this, he raised his eyes to heaven, and directing his thoughts, so it seemed, to Dulcinea, said: "Help me, my lady, in this first affront done to your enslaved heart. May your favor and protection not fail me in this initial trial!"

And saying these and other similar words, he dropped his shield, raised his lance with both hands, and discharged such a blow to the muleteer's head that it knocked him to the ground and left him in such bad shape that if don Quixote had done it a second time, there would have been no need to try to treat the muleteer's wounds. Having done this, he collected his armor and continued pacing back and forth as before.

A while later, without realizing what had happened—since the first muleteer was still dazed—another one came with the same intention of watering his mules. When he

went to remove the armor so that he could use the trough,
don Quixote, without saying a word or asking anyone's
permission, dropped his shield again, and again raised
his lance and smashed, not his lance, but rather the muleteer's head, in more than three places, because he cracked
it open in four. Hearing this disturbance, everyone from
the inn—among them the innkeeper—ran to see what had
happened. When don Quixote saw this, he picked up his
shield, put his hand on his sword, and said: "Oh, mistress of
beauty, strength of my weakened heart, now is the time to
look down upon this, your captive knight, who stands facing such a great ordeal!"

This gave him so much courage that if all the muleteers
in the world were to attack him, he wouldn't have retreated
a single step. The wounded men's companions saw the sorry
state the two were in, and began to rain stones on don Quixote, who protected himself as well as he could with his
shield, but he wouldn't leave the trough so as not to abandon his armor. The innkeeper shouted for them to stop because he'd already told them that the fellow was crazy, and
would be set free on account of it, even if he killed everyone.
Don Quixote shouted even louder, calling them all traitors,
and said that the warden of the castle was a rogue and a
baseborn knight for having allowed a knight-errant to be
treated in this way, and he would make him accountable for
his treachery. "But for you, vile rabble, I couldn't care less!
Throw stones, come and attack me however you want—
you'll see what your foolishness and insolence get you!"

He said this with so much fearlessness that he instilled a
terrible dread in those who were attacking him, and for this
reason they stopped casting stones. Don Quixote allowed
them to remove the wounded men, and continued the vigil
of his armor, with the same tranquillity and calmness as
before.

The pranks of the innkeeper's guest weren't to his liking, so he decided to cut everything short and give him the
cursed order of knighthood right then, before any other
terrible thing happened. He went up to him and apologized
for the effrontery those two vile men had shown him—he
certainly had had no part in it—but they were well punished for their rash acts. He said to him, repeating what
he'd said earlier, that in that castle there was no chapel, and

also that there was no need to continue the vigil, since the important thing in becoming a knight consisted of laying the sword on the neck and shoulders, according to what he had learned from his book that described the ceremonies of the order, and that could be done even in the middle of a field. He had also fulfilled the requirements of the vigil, which directed him to watch over his armor for only two hours, and he now had done so for more than four.

Don Quixote believed everything he was told and said that he was ready to obey him, and that the ceremony should be done as soon as possible, because if he were attacked again when he was a full-fledged knight, he would leave no one in the castle alive, except for those whom the warden of the castle told him to spare, which he would do out of respect.

Forewarned and now a bit afraid, the warden brought a book in which he recorded the straw and barley furnished to the muleteers, and with the stub of a candle that a boy held for him, and also with the damsels mentioned earlier, he went to where don Quixote was, and told him to kneel down. He read from his account book as if he were saying a devout prayer, and in the middle of his discourse, he raised the sword and gave him a stout thwack on his neck followed by a spirited slap on the shoulder, all the while murmuring, as if he were praying. Having done this, he had one of those ladies fasten his sword on him, which she did with great poise and tact, because not a little was needed so as not to burst out laughing throughout the ceremony. But the feats of the novice knight kept their laughter at bay.

As she fastened his sword, the good lady said: "May God make you a very successful knight and bring you good fortune in battle."

Don Quixote asked what her name was, so that he would know henceforth to whom he was beholden for the favor received, because he planned to share with her the glory that he would achieve by the strength of his arm. She responded with great humility that she was called La Tolosa and that she was the daughter of a clothes-mender from Toledo, who lived near the marketplace of Sancho Bienhaya, and that she would serve him and consider him her lord wherever she might be. Don Quixote replied that, given her love for him, she should do him the favor of accepting the title of DON* and call herself DOÑA TOLOSA. She promised she would. The other lady then put his spurs on him, and he had almost the same conversation with her that he'd had with the one who put on his sword. He asked her what her name was, and she said she was La Molinera, the daughter of an honorable miller from Antequera.† Don Quixote asked her to take the DON as well and to call herself DOÑA MOLINERA, offering her further services and favors.

Once these unprecedented ceremonies were hurriedly done, don Quixote was most impatient to see himself on horseback, seeking adventures. He saddled Rocinante and mounted him, and embracing his host, he said such strange things to him when he thanked him for having dubbed him a knight that it's impossible to relate them all. The innkeeper, eager to see him leave the inn, responded with no less extravagance, although with fewer words; and without asking him to pay for the lodging, let him go.

Chapter IIII. *About what happened to our knight when he left the inn.*

IT WAS just about sunrise when don Quixote left the inn, so happy, so gallant, so exhilarated at seeing himself knighted, that the girths of his horse were bursting with joy. But remembering his host's counsel about the necessary provisions he should take with him, especially concerning money and clean shirts, he decided to return home and supply himself with everything, and to find a squire. He planned to hire a peasant, a neighbor of his who was poor and with children, but who was very well suited for the occupation of squire to a knight. With this thought he guided Rocinante toward his village. The horse, realizing he was heading back to the stable, began a brisk trot with such enthusiasm that his feet hardly seemed to touch the ground.

Don Quixote hadn't gone very far when he thought he heard a faint voice off to the right, as if from a person in dis-

---

* Only those who had a right to it could be called *don*. Knights could confer this title.

† *Molinero* means "miller." Antequera is a city near Málaga.

tress, coming from the dense part of a grove. As soon as he heard it, he said: "I give thanks to heaven for the favor it has done me, since it has so soon given me a chance to live up to what my profession demands, and an opportunity to reap the fruit of my worthy desires. This voice is doubtless coming from a person in trouble who requires my protection and aid."

And turning his reins, he led Rocinante toward where it seemed to him the voice was coming. A bit into the grove he saw a mare tied to an oak tree, and tied to another oak was a boy about fifteen years old, naked from the waist up, who was the one crying out, and not without reason, because a good-sized peasant was whipping him with a belt, and each lash was accompanied by a reprimand and reproof, because he was saying: "Keep quiet and be more vigilant."

And the boy responded: "I won't do it again, master. By the passion of God, I won't do it again; and I promise to take better care of the flock from now on!"

When don Quixote saw what was going on, he said with an angry voice: "Ill-bred knight, it's unjust to take someone on who cannot defend himself. Get on your horse and pick up your lance"—because there was one leaning against the tree where the horse was tied—"and I'll make you see that you're acting like a coward!"

The peasant, seeing the armored figure above him brandishing a lance over his face, gave himself up for dead, and with humble words he replied: "*Señor* knight, this boy I'm punishing is one of my hired hands who watches over a flock of sheep I have in these parts, and he's so careless that he loses one every day. And because I'm punishing his negligence—or roguery—he says that I'm doing it out of stinginess, so as not to pay him the salary I owe him, and by God and my soul, he's lying."

"You say that someone is lying, in *my* presence,* you wretched rustic!" said don Quixote. "By the sun that shines on us, I'm about to run you through with this lance. Pay him right now without saying another word! And if you don't, by the God who rules over us, I'll finish you off and annihilate you on the spot. Untie him right now!"

---

* To claim that another person was lying—and not only in the books of chivalry—was considered an affront to the person being spoken to as well as the person spoken about.

The peasant hung his head, and without responding, untied his hired hand, whom don Quixote asked how much he was owed. He said that it was nine months at seven *reales* per month. Don Quixote did the math and found that it came to seventy-three *reales*, and told the peasant to pay him immediately, unless he wanted to die because of it. The fearful rustic replied, on the word of one who was about to die, and on the oath he'd sworn—and he hadn't sworn anything yet—that it wasn't that much, because three pairs of shoes and one *real* for two bloodlettings when he was sick should be deducted and credited.

"All that is very good," responded don Quixote, "but let the shoes and bloodlettings pay him back for the lashes that you've given him without his being to blame. If he broke the leather of his shoes you paid for, you've broken the skin of his body; and if the barber let blood from him when he was sick, you've taken it from him when he was healthy. Thus, on this account, he owes you nothing."

"The trouble is, *señor* knight, that I have no money on me. Let Andrés come home with me and I'll pay him one *real* on top of another."

"Go with him, again?" said the boy. "No way, *señor*, not in a million years, because when he has me alone, he'll flay me like St. Bartholomew."*

"He'll do nothing of the kind," said don Quixote. "It's enough for me to command him and he'll do what I ask; and provided that he swears by the laws of knighthood that he has received, I'll release him on his own recognizance, and I'll guarantee your pay."

"Your grace, *señor*, consider what you're saying," said the boy. "This master of mine is not a knight, nor has he received any order of knighthood. This fellow is Juan Haldudo, the Rich, who lives in El Quintanar."†

"That's not very important," responded don Quixote, "because there can be Haldudos who are knights, especially since every person is the child of his works."

"That's true enough," said Andrés, "but this master of

---

* Bartholomew was one of the twelve apostles, and tradition has it that he was flayed and beheaded by King Astyages of Babylonia.
† El Quintanar de la Orden is in the modern province of Toledo, only ten miles northwest of El Toboso.

mine, of what works is he the child, since he denies me my pay, my sweat, and my work?"

"I don't deny you anything of the kind, brother Andrés," responded the peasant. "Do me the pleasure of coming with me. I swear by all the orders of knighthood in the world to pay you, as I've said, one *real* on top of another, and I'll even throw in a bit extra."

"You don't need to give him any extra," said don Quixote. "Pay him the *reales* and I'll be satisfied. And make sure you do what you swore. If you don't, by the same oath, I swear I'll come back and punish you, and I'll find you even if you conceal yourself better than a chameleon. And if you want to know who has given you this command, so that you'll be even more obliged to fulfill it, I'm the valiant don Quixote de La Mancha, the redresser of wrongs and injustices. Don't forget what you've promised and sworn, under the penalty of what has been said."

When he said this, he spurred Rocinante, and in a moment he was gone. The peasant followed him with his eyes, and when he saw that he'd left the grove and was no longer in sight, he turned to his hired hand Andrés, and said: "Come here, my son. I want to pay you what I owe, as that righter of wrongs commanded me."

"I swear," said the boy, "that your worship will do well to obey the command of that good knight—may he live a thousand years!—because he's so courageous and such an upright judge; and by San Roque, if you don't pay me, he'll come back and do what he said!"

"I swear as well," said the peasant, "but because I love you so much, I want to increase the debt so I can increase the pay."

And grabbing the boy by his arm, he tied him back up to the oak, where he gave him so many lashes that he left him for dead.

"*Señor* Andrés," said the peasant, "call that righter of wrongs back now, and you'll see how he won't right this one. In fact, I may not be finished yet, because I feel like flaying you alive, just like you feared."

But finally he untied him and said he could go looking for the judge so that he could carry out the sentence. Andrés went away a bit mournful, swearing he would look for the brave don Quixote de La Mancha and tell him exactly what had happened, and that he would have to pay seven-fold. But for all that, he went away crying, and his master stayed behind laughing.

And in this way the brave don Quixote redressed that wrong. He was very delighted with the way things had turned out. It seemed to him that he'd given a very auspicious and noble beginning to his chivalric venture, and with great self-satisfaction, he ambled back toward his village, saying softly: "You can well call yourself the most fortunate of women—oh, fairest of the fair, Dulcinea del Toboso!—since it befell your destiny to have subjected and surrendered to your will such a famous knight as is don Quixote de La Mancha, who, as everyone knows, just yesterday received the order of knighthood, and today has redressed the greatest injury that injustice ever created and cruelty ever committed. Today he took the whip from that heartless enemy who was lashing that helpless boy so unjustly."

At that point, he came to a place where the road divided into four, and remembered the crossroads where knights-errant would consider which road to take; and to imitate them, he paused quietly for a while. After having deliberated about what to do, he released the reins, leaving it up to Rocinante to decide on the route, and the horse stuck to his original plan, which was to head for the stable. After traveling about two miles, don Quixote saw a crowd of people who, as it was later learned, were Toledan merchants on their way to buy silk in Murcia.* There were six of them, each one with a parasol, and there were four other servants on horseback, and three mule boys on foot.

Hardly had don Quixote sighted them when he fancied a new adventure was at hand. And to imitate the exploits he'd read about in his books as closely as possible, what he planned to do seemed made to order. Thus, with graceful bearing and boldness, he firmly planted himself in his stirrups, clutched his lance, put his shield at his chest, and in the middle of the road waited for those knights-errant—for that's what he judged them to be—to arrive; and when they were at a distance where they could see and hear, don Quixote raised his voice and shouted arrogantly: "Everyone stop right now and confess that there's no more beautiful

---

* Murcia is an important city in southeastern Spain.

a maiden in the world than the empress of La Mancha, the peerless Dulcinea del Toboso!"

The merchants stopped when they heard what was being said so they could look at the strange figure who was speaking, and because of his appearance and words, they deduced his craziness. But they wanted to see where that confession they were being asked to give was leading. One of them, who was something of a jokester, and very witty, said to him: "*Señor* knight, we don't know who this good lady you're talking about is. Show her to us, and if she's as beautiful as you declare, we'll confess the truth you've asked of us, with pleasure and without any compunction."

"If I were to show her to you," replied don Quixote, "what good would there be in confessing such an obvious truth? The important thing is for you to believe, confess, affirm, swear, and defend it, without having seen her. If not, you'll be in battle with me, monstrous and arrogant people. You can attack one at a time, as the laws of chivalry have ordered, or all at once, as is the custom and wicked practice of people of your breed. Here I stand, waiting for you, confident that I have right on my side."

"*Señor* knight," replied the merchant, "I beg your grace, in the name of all these princes, to save us from burdening our consciences by confessing something that we haven't seen or heard, and something so prejudicial to the empresses and queens of La Alcarria and Extremadura.* Would you please show us a portrait of this lady, even though it's only as big as a grain of wheat, because 'by the yarn we can judge the skein'; and we'll be satisfied and assured, and you'll be content and appeased. And I believe that we're in such agreement with you that—even if the portrait shows that she's blind in one eye and from the other she oozes vermilion and sulfur—to please you, we will say everything in her favor that you wish."

"She doesn't ooze, despicable rabble," responded don Quixote, aflame with rage. "She doesn't ooze, I say, anything that you mention, except ambergris and civet packed

---

* La Alcarria is a region made up of parts of the modern provinces of Cuenca, Guadalajara, and Madrid in central Spain. Extremadura is a region composed of the provinces of Mérida and Badajoz in western Spain.

in cotton, and she isn't one-eyed or hunchbacked—she's straighter than a spindle from Guadarrama.* But you'll pay for this blasphemy you've committed against such great beauty as is that of my lady!"

And saying this, he attacked the man who had said it with his lance lowered, so filled with fury and anger that, if good fortune hadn't arranged for Rocinante to trip and fall in the middle of the road, the impudent merchant would have had a bad time of it. Rocinante fell, and his master went rolling over and over on the ground. He tried to get up but couldn't, such was the encumbrance that the lance, shield, spurs, and helmet caused, together with the weight of his ancient armor. And while he struggled to get up and couldn't, he was saying: "Do not flee, cowardly and wretched people; wait! It wasn't my fault that I'm sprawled out on the ground; it was my horse's!"

One of the mule boys, who must not have been very good-natured, when he heard the poor fallen man say so many arrogant things, couldn't stand it without giving his ribs an answer. He went up to him and took the lance, broke it into pieces, and with one of those pieces began to give our don Quixote so many blows that, in spite of his armor, he thrashed him like milled wheat. His masters shouted at him not to beat him up so much and to leave him alone, but the lad was irate and didn't want to leave the game until he'd vented the rest of his anger. He went back for more pieces of the broken lance and broke them all on the wretched downed man, who, even with that storm of blows raining down on him, never shut his mouth, threatening heaven and earth, and the brigands, because that's what they appeared to him to be.

The lad finally got tired, and the merchants continued their journey, taking with them stories to tell about the drubbed fellow for the rest of the trip. After don Quixote found himself alone, he tried to get up once again, but if he couldn't do it when he was hale and hearty, how could he do it when he was beaten up and almost broken to pieces? But he still thought he was fortunate, deeming that what

---

* The reference to the Guadarrama range is hard to explain. Iriso says it may deal with the beech groves found there, the wood from which provided the best utensils to the court.

had happened to him was an appropriate misadventure for knights-errant, and he blamed it all on his horse. Even so, it was impossible for him to get up, because his whole body was battered.

Chapter V. Where the narration of the misfortune of our knight continues.

SEEING THAT he could indeed not stir, he decided to resort to his usual remedy, which was to dredge up some passage from one of his books, and his madness brought to mind the one about Valdovinos and the Marqués de Mantua when Carloto left Valdovinos wounded in the forest,* a story that's known to children, not unfamiliar to young people, venerated and even believed by the older generation, and, for all that, is no truer than the miracles of Muhammad. He thought this would fit just right in his current situation, so, in a lot of pain, he began to wallow around on the ground and say with a debilitated voice the same thing that the wounded Knight of the Wood said:

> Where canst thou be, beloved heart
> That for my plight thou dost not grieve
> Either in ignorance thou art
> Or thou art false and dost deceive.

In this way he continued as far as the lines:

> Oh, noble Marqués de Mantua
> Mine uncle and lord in the flesh.†

---

* This is a popular subject from the old ballads. According to the ballad, Carloto, son of Charlemagne, falls in love with the princess Sevilla, Valdovinos' wife. In order to possess her, Carloto wounds Valdovinos and leaves him in a forest. The Marqués de Mantua, Valdovinos' uncle, finds him there while hunting.

† The weakened don Quixote makes a mistake: It should be *señor* ("lord") and *tío carnal* ("paternal uncle"). By saying it backward, *tío* and *señor carnal*, it comes out very odd-sounding in English. I used Robinson Smith's translation of these verses.

As luck would have it, when he got to this verse, a peasant from his own village, a neighbor of his who was returning home after taking a load of wheat to the mill, happened to be passing by, and seeing that man stretched out, he approached him and asked him who he was and what had happened that made him lament so sadly.

Don Quixote believed without a doubt this fellow was the Marqués de Mantua, his uncle, and so he responded only by continuing the ballad where it told of his misfortune and of the affair between his wife and the emperor's son, word for word as the ballad relates. The peasant was amazed hearing this foolishness, and removing his visor—which was already in pieces because of the blows—cleaned his face, which was covered with dirt,* and he'd hardly done so when he recognized him, and said: "*Señor* Quijana!"—for that must have been his name when he was sane and hadn't yet changed from a peaceful *hidalgo* to a knighterrant—"How did your grace get into this condition?"

But he just kept on reciting his ballad to everything that he was asked.

When the good man heard this, he took don Quixote's breastplate and backplate off to see if there were any wounds, but he saw no blood or bruises. He tried to lift him off the ground, and with no little struggle put him onto his own donkey because it seemed like a calmer mount. He gathered all the armor, and even the splintered fragments of the lance, tied it all up, and put it all on Rocinante. He then took the reins of the horse and the donkey and headed toward their village, troubled by the nonsense that don Quixote was uttering. And don Quixote was no less troubled, since he was so beaten up and pounded, he couldn't sit up on the donkey. From time to time he heaved sighs that must have reached heaven; and once again it compelled the peasant to ask him to say what ailed him. And it seems that the devil brought stories to his mind that fit what had happened to him, because at that very moment he forgot about Valdovinos and remembered the Moor Abindarráez, when the governor of Antequera, Rodrigo de

---

* Readers of the time would realize that don Quixote's neighbor does exactly what the Marqués de Mantua did with Valdovinos in cleaning off his face.

Narváez, arrested him and took him captive to his fortress. So, when the peasant asked him how he was and how he felt, don Quixote now responded with the same words that the captive Abencerraje used with Rodrigo de Narváez, in the same way he'd read the history in *La Diana* by Jorge de Montemayor, where it's written.* And he applied it so aptly to his own situation that the peasant went along cursing his fate for having to hear such a lot of nonsense, and through all this he came to realize that his neighbor was crazy, and he hurried to get to the village so that he wouldn't be further vexed by the long tirade. Finally don Quixote said: "I want your grace to know, *señor* don Rodrigo de Narváez, that this beautiful Jarifa I mentioned is now the beauteous Dulcinea del Toboso, for whom I've performed, do perform, and will perform the most famous deeds of chivalry that have ever been, are being, and will ever be seen in the world."

To this the peasant responded: "Look, your grace, *señor*, sinner that I am, I'm not don Rodrigo de Narváez nor the Marqués de Mantua, but rather Pedro Alonso, your neighbor. And you're neither Valdovinos nor Abindarráez, but rather the honorable *hidalgo señor* Quijana."

"I know who I am," responded don Quixote, "and I know that I can be not only those whom I've mentioned, but also the Twelve Peers of France† and the Nine Worthies,‡ since my deeds will surpass all of theirs put together and of each one individually."

Engaged in these and similar conversations, they arrived at their village as night was falling, but the peasant waited until it was dark so that the villagers wouldn't see

---

* This legend is found in the *Seven Books of la Diana* (1561 edition). It is the story of the Moor Abindarráez (also called Abencerraje) who, on his way to get married to Jarifa, is put in prison by Rodrigo de Narváez, governor of Antequera. The governor befriends the Moor and lets him go to get married, provided he come back within three days, which he does, with his new wife. The governor finally lets them both go free.

† The Twelve Peers were Charlemagne's men, all equal in valor, therefore "peers."

‡ The "Nine Worthies," as they're known in English, are Joshua, David, and Judas Maccabee (Jews); Hector, Alexander, and Cæsar (pagans); Arthur, Charlemagne, and Godefroy de Bouillon (Christians). Godefroy was the leader of the First Crusade.

the beaten-up *hidalgo* sorrily mounted on a donkey. When the time came, they went into the village and to don Quixote's house, which they found in an uproar. The priest and village barber—don Quixote's great friends—were there and the housekeeper was saying to them in a loud voice: "What does your grace think, *señor licenciado** Pero Pérez," for that was the name of the priest, "of my master's misfortune? It's been three days and we haven't seen hide nor hair of him, his nag, shield, lance, or armor! Woe is me! I'm beginning to understand—and it's the truth, just as I was born to die—that these cursed books of chivalry he's been and is constantly reading have made him crazy. Now I remember having heard him say to himself many times that he wanted to become a knight-errant and seek adventures in the world. May these books, which have caused the ruination of the most sensitive mind that there was in all of La Mancha, be commended to Satan and Barabbas."†

The niece said the same thing and added: "Believe me, *maese* Nicolás"—for this was the name of the barber—"that my uncle would frequently read those soulless books of misadventures two days and nights straight through, after which he'd throw the book down and grab his sword and go around stabbing at the walls, and when he was tired, he'd say that he'd killed four giants as tall as towers, and that the sweat caused by his labors was the blood from wounds he'd received in battle. Then he'd drink a pitcher of cold water, which made him feel better and calmed him down, and he'd say that the water was a most precious beverage that had been brought to him by the wise Esquife,‡ an enchanter and great friend of his. But I'm to blame for all of this, since I didn't tell your graces of my uncle's foolish acts earlier, so that you could have prevented him from getting into his present condition, and burned all those excommunicated books. He has lots of them that deserve to be burned as if they were heretics."

---

* *Licenciado* is a university title equivalent to the master's degree, cumbersome to translate.
† Barabbas was the thief released instead of Christ (Matthew 27:15–21).
‡ The niece probably means Alquife, who appears in several books dealing with Amadís and his offspring.

"That's what I say as well," said the priest. "In truth, to-morrow we'll condemn those books to the inquisitorial fire so that what happened to my good friend won't happen to whoever else might read them."

The peasant and don Quixote were listening to all of this, and the peasant finally understood the nature of his neighbor's illness, and so he began to shout: "Open up, your graces, to *señor* Valdovinos and *señor* Marqués de Mantua, who is coming badly wounded; and also to *señor* Moor Abindarráez, whom the governor of Antequera, the brave Rodrigo de Narváez, is bringing as a prisoner."

At these shouts everyone went out, and as soon as some recognized their friend and others their uncle and master—who still hadn't gotten off the donkey because he couldn't—they ran to take him in their arms.

Don Quixote said: "Everyone stop! I've come badly injured through the fault of my horse. Take me to bed, and summon the wise Urganda, if you can, who will take care of my wounds."*

"May I be cursed," exclaimed the housekeeper, "if I didn't know in my heart what foot my master limped on! Let's get you upstairs in a hurry, *señor*, and without that *señora* Hurgada† we'll know how to fix you up. Damn those books a hundred more times, I say, which have gotten your grace in such a state!"

They took him to bed, and trying to find his wounds, they saw none. He said he got a pounding from a tumble he took with Rocinante, his horse, while battling ten of the hugest and most fearless giants that could be found in this part of the world.

"Aha!" said the priest, "so there are giants in the dance? By the sign of the cross, I'll burn those books tomorrow before nightfall."

They asked don Quixote a thousand questions, which he refused to answer, but rather asked for something to eat and to be allowed to sleep because that was what was most important. That's what they did; and the peasant told the priest in great detail how he'd found don Quixote. He told

---

* Urganda the Unknown was an enchantress in *Amadís de Gaula*.
† *Hurgada* is an obscene term meaning "sexually overused."

him everything, including the foolish things he said when he found him and while he brought him back home. All this increased the priest's wish to do what he did the next day, which was to fetch Nicolás, the barber, who went with him to don Quixote's house.

Chapter VI. Of the amusing and great inquisition that the priest and barber conducted in the library of our ingenious hidalgo.

DON QUIXOTE was still sleeping. The priest asked the niece for the keys to the room where the books—the authors of the damage—were kept, and she gave them to him most willingly. Everyone went in, including the housekeeper, and they found more than a hundred very large and well-bound books* and some other smaller ones. As soon as the housekeeper saw them, she ran out of the room and returned immediately with a bowl of holy water and a sprinkler and said: "Take this, your grace, *señor licenciado*. Sprinkle the room so that one of the many enchanters that lurk in these books won't put a spell on us, to punish us for trying to banish them from the world."

The credulousness of the housekeeper made the priest laugh, and he had the barber give him those books one by one to see what they were, because it might be they would find some that didn't deserve punishment by fire.

"No," said the niece, "there's no reason to pardon any of them because all of them have done damage. It'd be best to toss them all out the window onto the patio and make a pile of them there, and set fire to them; or take them to the corral and make a fire there so the smoke won't bother anyone."

The housekeeper echoed the same thing, such was the ardent wish they both had for the death of those innocents. But the priest wouldn't agree to it without at least reading

---

* The word used for *book* here is *cuerpo*, which means "body" as well as "oversize volume." The use of *cuerpo* identifies the books with people who underwent the inquisitorial process.

the titles. The first one that *maese* Nicolás put in his hands was *The Four Books of Amadís de Gaula.**

The priest said: "This is very curious, because I've heard that this book is the first book of chivalry published in Spain, and all the rest derive from it. So it seems to me that since it's the founder of such a bad sect, we ought to condemn it to the flames without a second thought."

"No, *señor*," said the barber, "for I've heard that it's the best of all the books of that type that were ever written, and so, as something unique in its art, it ought to be pardoned."

"That's the truth," said the priest, "and for that reason its life will be spared for the time being. Let's see what's next to it."

"This one," said the barber, "is *The Heroic Deeds of Esplandián*,† legitimate son of Amadís de Gaula."

"In truth," said the barber, "the goodness of the father won't save the son. Take this, *señora* housekeeper; open the window, throw it into the corral, and start the mound of books for the bonfire."

The housekeeper did it with pleasure, and the good Esplandián went flying into the corral, patiently awaiting his fiery doom.

"Let's move on," said the priest.

"This next one," said the barber, "is *Amadís de Grecia*,‡ and I believe all the rest in this section are of that same lineage of Amadís."

---

* Don Quixote's library is well organized. The first section contains his favorite books, the romances of chivalry. The first several books all belong to the "Amadís cycle"—*Amadís de Gaula* and its continuations. The first extant edition of *Amadís de Gaula* is that of 1508, as you learned (if you read the initial poems earlier). There were nineteen other editions preceding the publication of *Don Quixote*. Information about these books comes from Dan Eisenberg's incredible research.

† This is the fifth book in the Amadís cycle, published in 1510 (the first four are the four volumes of *Amadís de Gaula*).

‡ *Grecia* is Greece. This is book nine of the Amadís cycle, written by Feliciano de Silva (1530). Book six, *Florisando*, by Páez de Ribera (1510), is not in the library because it was hard to come by. Also not mentioned are books seven and eight of the cycle—the popular *Lisuarte de Grecia*, part one, by Feliciano de Silva (1514) and the rare part two by Juan Díaz (1526). In all, there were twelve books in the Amadís cycle.

"Well, throw them all into the corral," said the priest. "Rather than spare Queen Pintiquiniestra* and the shepherd Darinel, I'd burn up the father who begat me, if he went around masquerading as a knight-errant."

"I share your opinion," said the barber.

"Me, too," said the niece.

"Since that's the way it is," said the housekeeper, "let me gather them up, and to the corral with them!"

They gave them to her. She spared the stairs, and tossed them down from the window.

"Who's that big one?" asked the priest.

"This is," said the barber, "*Don Olivante de Laura.*"†

"The author of that book," said the priest, "is the same one who wrote *The Garden of Flowers*, and in truth I can't tell which of the two books is more true, or rather, less lying. I can only say that this one will go to the corral because it's so absurd and arrogant."

"This next one is *Florimorte de Hyrcania*,"‡ said the barber.

"So, that's Florimorte?" replied the priest. "Then by my faith he'll soon be in the corral, in spite of his strange birth and resounding adventures, because the stiffness and dryness of his style deserve nothing else. To the corral with this one and the next one, *señora* housekeeper."

"My pleasure, my good *señor*," responded the housekeeper, and with great gusto, she did what she was told.

"This is *The Knight Platir*,"§ said the barber.

"That is an old book," said the priest, "but I see nothing in it that deserves forgiveness; let it join the rest without reprieve." And it was done.

Another book was opened, and they saw that it had as its title *The Knight of the Cross*.¶

---

* The priest doesn't quite remember right: it's "Pintiquinestra," without the fourth *i*.

† By Antonio de Torquemada, published in Barcelona, 1564.

‡ In the real world the book is called *Felixmarte de Hyrcania* (1556). Felixmarte's "strange birth," to be mentioned in a moment, was that his mother was midwifed in a forest by a wild woman. And his "resounding adventures" include wiping out singlehandedly an army of 1,600,000.

§ A rare book, published in 1533.

¶ *Lepolemo or the Knight of the Cross* was first published in 1521.

"Since this book has such a holy name, we might pardon its ignorance, but it's also said that 'behind the cross lurks the devil.' Away to the fire with it!"

The barber, taking another book, said: "This is *The Mirror of Chivalry*."*

"I already know his grace," said the priest. "In it are Reinaldos de Montalbán with his friends and companions—worse thieves than Cacus—and the Twelve Peers, along with the historian Turpin; in truth, I favor condemning it only to perpetual exile, just because those characters were in part responsible for Matteo Boiardo's work, from which the poet Ludovico Ariosto wove his cloth.† And if I find him here speaking a language that's not his own, I'll show him no respect, but if he's in his original language, I'll put the book on top of my head."‡

"I have him in Italian," said the barber, "but I don't understand him."

"And it's just as well you don't,"§ said the priest. "We might forgive the *señor* captain if he hadn't brought him to Spain and made him Spanish,¶ because he took away quite a bit of his original worth. And those who try to translate books in verse into another language will do the same thing—no matter how careful and skillful they are, they cannot make those works as good as when they were born. I say, therefore, that this book and all of them that deal with France should be placed in a dry well until we figure out what to do with them, except *Bernardo del Carpio*, which

---

* Published in three parts (1525, 1527, and 1547) by two authors. The first complete edition of all three parts together dates from 1586.

† Jean Turpin, archbishop of Reims, had already been dead two hundred years when the false history of Charlemagne was attributed to him. The Italian Matteo Boiardo wrote a semiburlesque poem called *Orlando Innamorato* (*Roland in Love*) (1486–1495). Another Italian, Ludovico Ariosto, published *Orlando Furioso* (*Roland Insane*) in 1532. It continues Boiardo's work.

‡ To show respect.

§ To prove the priest's point, in 1612 the Inquisition would expurgate parts of the poem for the Spanish audience. If the barber could read the original, the priest realized, he would see things the Inquisition eventually wasn't going to want him to see.

¶ Captain Jerónimo Jiménez de Urrea translated Ariosto's work into Spanish (1549), taking great liberties with it.

must be around here somewhere, and another called *Roncesvalles**—if I ever get these into my hands, they will soon be in those of the housekeeper, and from there into those of the flames, without any possibility of reprieve."

The barber approved all this, and he thought it was both good and proper, because he knew the priest was such a good Christian, and such a friend of the truth, he wouldn't say anything untrue for the world. And when he opened another book, he saw that it was *Palmerín de Oliva*, and the one next to it was *Palmerín de Ingalaterra*.† When the *licenciado* saw this, he said: "That Olive should be torn to shreds right now and burned, and not even the ashes should remain. The Palm of England should be kept and conserved as a unique item, and a box should be made for it like the one Alexander found among the spoils of Darius, and chose it to hold the works of the poet Homer.‡ This book, *señor compadre*,§ deserves veneration for two reasons: First, it's very good in itself, and second, because it's said that an ingenious king of Portugal wrote it.¶ All the adventures of the Castle of Miraguarda are very good and artfully done, the dialogues are courteous and clear, and they maintain and reflect the decorum of the person who is speaking with great propriety and understanding. I say this so that, unless you have a different opinion, *maese* Nicolás, this one and *Amadís* should stay free from the fire, and all the rest, without further examination, should perish."

---

* "History of the Deeds of the Invincible Knight Bernardo of el Carpio," a poem in octaves (1585), and "The True Outcome of the Famous Battle of Roncesvalles, with the Death of the Twelve Peers of France" (1555).

† *Palmerín de Oliva*, of uncertain authorship, had twelve editions before the publication of *Don Quixote*, beginning with Salamanca, 1511. *Palmerín de Ingalaterra* was written by Francisco Moraes Cabral in Portuguese. The earliest Spanish version was published in Toledo (Part I, 1547; Part II, 1548).

‡ Plutarch says, in his *Life of Alexander*, that when Alexander found the jewel-encrusted box among King Darius' effects, he resolved to store Homer's *Iliad* in it.

§ *Compadre*: "friend."

¶ People erroneously thought the book was by King João II of Portugal.

"No, *señor compadre*," replied the barber, "for this one I have here is the famous *Don Belianís*."*

"Well, even he," replied the priest, "together with his second, third, and fourth parts, needs a bit of rhubarb to purge his excess bile,† and all that business of the Castle of Fame and other bigger blunders should be excised. For this reason he should be given plenty of time to mend his ways, and thus both mercy and justice will be dealt him. Meanwhile, you can keep him at your house, but don't let anyone read him."

"That's fine with me," responded the barber.

And not wanting to bother reading books of chivalry anymore, the priest had the housekeeper take all the large volumes and throw them into the corral. He said this to a person who was neither stupid nor deaf, but rather someone who was more eager to do it than to weave a piece of fine cloth,‡ no matter how fine and large it might be, and she took six or eight at a time and threw them out the window. Because she'd taken so many at once, one of them fell at the feet of the barber, who was curious to see what it was, and he saw that it said *History of the Famous Knight Tirante el Blanco*.§

"God bless me!" cried the priest. "So this is *Tirante el Blanco*! Give him to me, *compadre*, because I can safely say that I've found it to be a treasury of enjoyment and a mine of entertainment. Here is don Quirieleisón¶ de Montalbán, a brave knight, and his brother, Tomás de Montalbán, and the knight Fonseca, with the fight that the brave Tirante had with the Great Dane, and the astute comments of the maiden Placerdemivida,** with the affairs and tricks of the

---

* Parts one and two were first published in Seville, 1554, and parts three and four were published in Burgos, 1579.

† Roots of the rhubarb plant were prescribed specifically for this.

‡ This doesn't seem to make much sense until you know that it also meant "to make love."

§ This was originally a Catalan work called *Tirant lo Blanch* ("the White") (Barcelona, 1490). It was translated and published in Spanish anonymously in 1511 and was a rare item, hence the priest's surprise in finding it. Earlier the priest had said that *Amadís de Gaula* was the first romance of chivalry, but the 1490 Catalan *Tirant*, which he didn't know of, preceded it.

¶ *Kyrie Eleison* (Greek for "Lord have mercy") is part of the Roman Catholic Mass.

** "Joy of my life."

widow Reposada, and the *señora* empress, who was in love with Hipólito, her squire. I'm telling you the truth, *señor compadre*, that because of its style, this is the best book in the world. Here knights eat, sleep, and die in their beds; and they make wills before their death, with lots of other things that the other books of this kind lack. So, I tell you that the person who wrote it deserves, since he didn't produce so much foolishness intentionally, to be kept in galleys for all the days of his life.* Take it home and read it, and you'll see that everything I told you about it is true."

"I'll do it," said the barber, "but what'll we do with these small books that are left over?"

"These," said the priest, "are probably not about chivalry, but rather contain poetry."

And opening one of them, he saw that it was *La Diana* by Jorge de Montemayor, and he said, thinking that they were all of the same type: "These don't deserve to be burned like the rest because they don't do the damage that the books of chivalry have done. They're intellectual books that can't hurt anyone."

"Oh, *señor*," said the niece, "you can certainly have those books burned like the rest, because it's not hard to believe that once my *señor* uncle is cured of the chivalresque infirmity, by reading these he might feel like becoming a shepherd and traipsing through the forests and fields, singing and playing music, and the worst thing is that he might become a poet, which—they say—is an incurable disease and is contagious."

"The young lady is right," said the priest, "and it'd be a good idea to clear his path of stumbling blocks and risks. Since we began with *La Diana* of Montemayor, I'm of the opinion that it should not be burned, but rather that all that material about the wise Felicia and the enchanted water should be expurgated, as well as almost all the poetry; let its prose stay as it is, and let it have the honor of being the first book of its kind."

"This one that comes next," said the barber, "is *La Di-*

---

* This has been called "the most obscure passage of the *Quixote*." It seems to refer to the galleys that are rowed, but modern opinion is that it refers to printers' galleys, thus meaning that it should be constantly reprinted. It has actually had very few editions.

ana called *The Second*, by the Salamantine; then this one is another with the same name, whose author is Gil Polo."*

"Well, the one from Salamanca," said the priest, "should accompany those of the condemned in the corral and increase their number, but the one by Gil Polo should be kept as if it were by Apollo himself. Let's keep going, *señor compadre*; and let's hurry, since it's getting late."

"This book," said the barber, opening another one, "is *The Ten Books of the Fortunes of Love*, by Antonio de Lofraso, a Sardinian poet."†

"By the orders I've received," said the priest, "since Apollo was Apollo and the muses muses, and the poets poets, a more delightful or silly book than this one hasn't been written, and in its own way it's the best and most unique book of its kind that has ever come to light in the world, and anyone who hasn't read it may be sure that he hasn't read anything so delightful. Give it to me, *compadre*, because I prize having found it more than if they gave me a cassock of fine Florentine cloth."

He put it to one side with enormous pleasure, and the barber continued: "The ones that come next are *The Shepherd of Iberia*, *Nymphs of Henares*, and *The Disillusionment of Jealousy*."‡

"Well, there's nothing else to do," said the priest, "but put them into the secular arm§ of the housekeeper, and don't ask me why, because I'd go on and on forever."

"This one coming up is *The Shepherd of Fílida*."¶

"He's not really a shepherd," said the priest, "but a very discreet courtly knight. Keep it as you would a precious jewel."

---

* Both continuations of *Diana* were published in Valencia in 1564. The *Second Diana* is by the Salmantine author Alonso Pérez, and is not considered good; the other one, known as *Diana in Love*, by Gil Polo, is thought by many to be superior to Montemayor's.

† Published in 1573.

‡ Three not so good pastoral novels, published in 1591, 1587, and 1586 respectively. The first one is the most recently published book in Don Quixote's library. The Henares River flows through Alcalá, twenty miles east of Madrid, where Cervantes was born.

§ After the Inquisition condemned a person, he or she was given to the *secular arm* of the government for execution of sentence.

¶ Published in 1582.

"This big one is called *Treasury of Various Poems*,"* said the barber.

"If there just weren't so many of them," said the priest, "they would be held in greater esteem. They should really weed it out and get rid of some of the lesser verses that are included among its great poems. You keep it, because its author is a friend of mine, and also out of respect for other more heroic and lofty works that he's written."

"This is," said the barber, "*Poems Collected by López Maldonado*."†

"The author of this book," replied the priest, "is also a great friend of mine, and when he reads his verses aloud, they fill all those who hear them with wonder, and the mellowness of his voice is enchanting. He's a bit long-winded in his eclogues, but you can't have everything. . . . What's that book next to it?"

"*La Galatea*‡ by Miguel de Cervantes," said the barber.

"For many years that Cervantes has been a great friend of mine, and I know that he's more versed in misfortunes than verses. His book has some originality—he proposes something but concludes nothing. We have to wait for the second part that he promises. Maybe after he does his penance, he'll receive the compassion that has been denied him so far.§ While we wait for this to happen, keep it in seclusion at your house, *señor compadre*."

"That's fine with me," replied the barber, "and here come three all together—*La Araucana* by don Alonso de Ercilla; *La Austríada* by Juan Rulfo, magistrate of Córdoba; and *El Monserrato*, by Cristóbal de Virués, a Valencian poet."¶

---

* The remainder of the books are of poetry, except for the misplaced *Galatea*, a pastoral novel. The *Treasury* is an anthology of poetry published in 1582.

† Published in 1586. Cervantes wrote two poems for this collection.

‡ This was Cervantes' first novel. Part I was published in 1585. Part II was never published.

§ This is a tongue-in-cheek reference to the sacrament of confession (Rico's note).

¶ Three long poems. The first deals with the Spanish conquest of the Chilean Araucanian Indians (1569). The second is about don Juan of Austria (1584), and the third talks about the founding of the monastery of Monserrat, near Barcelona (1587). The book is called *El Monserrate* in the real world.

"All three of these books," said the priest, "are the best ones that have ever been written in heroic verse in Spanish, and they can be compared favorably with the most famous ones from Italy. Keep them as you would Spain's finest jewels."

The priest got tired of passing judgment over more books, and so, without examining any others, he wanted all the rest of them burned. But the barber had already opened one called *The Tears of Angélica*.*

"I'd cry similar tears," said the priest when he heard that title, "if that book had been sent to the flames, because its author was one of the most famous poets in the world, not just in Spain, and he made truly fine translations of some of Ovid's fables."

Chapter VII. *About the second expedition of our good knight don Quixote de La Mancha.*

ALL OF a sudden, don Quixote began to shout, saying: "Gather 'round, brave knights! Here is where you must show the strength of your mighty arms, for the courtly knights are prevailing in the tournament!"

To see what the boisterous shouting was all about, the inquisition of the remaining books came to an end, and it's believed that *La Carolea* and *Lion of Spain*, together with *The Deeds of the Emperor*,† by don Luis de Ávila, went to the flames without being seen nor heard, because these books doubtless must have been among those that were left. Perhaps the priest wouldn't have passed such a rigorous sentence on them if he'd seen them.

When they got to don Quixote, he was out of bed, and kept on both with his shouting and with his absurdities, thrusting his sword everywhere, and wide-awake as if he'd never been asleep. They grappled with him and forced him

---

* A long poem by Barahona de Soto, from 1586, continuing *Orlando Furioso*.
† The first of these books (1560) is an epic poem about Carlos I of Spain; the second one is also about Carlos I (1586). This third one (1585) is a history of the Spanish city of León in verse, but it wasn't written by Luis de Ávila.

back into bed; and after he calmed down a bit, he began to speak with the priest and said: "It's certainly a great discredit, *señor* Archbishop Turpin, to those of us who call ourselves the Twelve Peers, to let the courtly knights be victorious in this tournament, just like that, since we knights-errant won the prize the first three days."

"Hush, your grace, *señor compadre*," said the priest, "because God will change your luck, and 'what is lost today is won tomorrow.' Take care of your health for now, your grace, because it seems to me you're exhausted, if not badly wounded."

"Wounded, no," said don Quixote, "but there's no doubt that I'm pummeled and bruised, because that bastard don Roland pounded me with the trunk of an oak tree, and all out of envy, because he realizes that I alone rival him in his achievements. But they wouldn't call me Reinaldos de Montalbán if, when I get out of this bed, I didn't pay him back in the same coin, in spite of his enchantments. So, for the moment, bring me something to eat, because I know that's what will do me the most good. Leave it to me to avenge myself."

They fed him, and he went back to sleep, and his lunacy astounded them.

That night the housekeeper burned all the books that were in the corral and in the whole house, and some must have burned that deserved to be kept in permanent archives. But their luck, and the sloth of the inquisitor, didn't allow it, and so the old saying came true that "the pious sometimes suffer for the sinners."

One of the remedies the priest and barber thought of to try to cure the illness of their friend was to wall up the library, so that when he got up he wouldn't find any books—perhaps by taking away the cause, the effect would cease. They'd say that an enchanter had taken away both the books and the room. And they had it done with great haste.

Two days later, don Quixote got up, and the first thing he did was to go looking for his books, and when he couldn't find the room where he'd left it, he tried to find it everywhere. He went to where the door used to be and probed the area with his hands, and looked all around without saying a word. But after a while, he asked the housekeeper the whereabouts of his library.

The housekeeper, who was well instructed in what she was supposed to say, told him: "What room, or what nothing is your grace looking for? There's no room or books anymore because the devil himself took them away."

"It wasn't the devil," replied the niece, "but rather an enchanter who came on a cloud one night after your grace left. He got off a serpent he was riding and went into the room. I don't know what he did there, but after a while he flew out through the roof, leaving the house filled with smoke, and when we went to see what he'd done, neither the books nor the room were anywhere to be seen. The housekeeper and I know only that when that evil old man left, he shouted that, because of a secret hatred he bore the owner of those books and that room, he'd done something to the room that would be seen later. He also said that he was called the sage Muñatón."

"'Frestón'* he must have said," said don Quixote.

"I don't know," responded the housekeeper, "if his name was Frestón or Fritón; I only know that his name ended in *-tón*."

"That's it," said don Quixote. "That fellow is a wise enchanter, a great enemy of mine who bears me ill will because he knows through his cunning and learning in the course of time I'll come to fight a singular battle with a knight he favors, and I'll conquer that knight without his being able to prevent it. For that reason, he does his best to give me all the misery he can. But I assure him he can't oppose nor prevent what heaven has ordained."

"No doubt about it," said the niece. "But who is it who gets you into these quarrels? Wouldn't it be best to stay quietly at home and not roam about the world seeking impossible adventures, without considering that 'many go out for wool and come back shorn'?"

"Niece of mine!" responded don Quixote. "How little you understand of any of this! Before they shear me, I'll have plucked out the beards of anybody who imagined he could touch a single hair of mine."

The two didn't want to argue with him anymore, because they saw that his anger was rising. He stayed at home in

---

* Don Quixote probably means Fristón. In *Belianís de Grecia*, Fristón is the wizard author who tells the story of Belianís.

peace and quiet for two weeks, without giving any indication that he would continue his mad pursuits. In those days he had delightful conversations with his two *compadres*, the priest and the barber, in which he said that what the world most needed was knights-errant, and that through him knight-errantry would be reborn. Sometimes the priest disagreed with him and sometimes he agreed, because if he didn't use this ploy, there was no way to reason with him. During this period, don Quixote made overtures to a neighbor of his, a peasant and an honest man—if that can be said about one who is poor*—but not very smart. In short, he said so much to him, persuaded and promised him so much that the poor rustic decided to go with him and be his squire.

Don Quixote said to him, among other things, that he should get ready to go with him gladly, because at any time, in the twinkling of an eye, an adventure might arise during which he'd win some *ínsula*—some ISLAND—and leave him behind to be its governor. With these and other promises, Sancho Panza—for that was the peasant's name—left his wife and children and became his neighbor's squire. Don Quixote then set about to raise money, and by selling one thing and pawning another, and making a bad deal every time, he accrued a reasonable amount. He also acquired a small iron shield that he borrowed from a friend, and, repairing his old helmet as best he could, told his squire Sancho the day and time he planned to start out, so that Sancho could supply himself with what he thought he most needed. Above all, he ordered him to take saddlebags, and Sancho said he would take them without fail, and also he planned to take a very fine donkey that he had, because he was not accustomed to walking very much.

Don Quixote considered the matter of the donkey for a bit, trying to think if he could remember whether any knight-errant had taken a squire on donkey-back, but none came to mind. Even so, don Quixote thought it was all right for him to take it, since he planned to get him a more honorable mount by appropriating the horse of the first discourteous knight he should run across.

He supplied himself with shirts and all the other things

---

* There's a Spanish proverb: "Poor man and honest, that cannot be."

he could think of, in accordance with the advice the inn-keeper had given him. Everything having been done, and without Panza bidding farewell to his children and wife, nor don Quixote to his housekeeper and niece, they left the village one night without anyone seeing them. They went so far that night that by daybreak they were sure they couldn't be found, even if people went searching for them.

Sancho Panza rode his donkey like a patriarch with his saddlebags and wineskin, very eager to see himself already a governor of the *ínsula* his master had promised him. Don Quixote happened to take the same path that he'd taken during his first foray, which was through the plains of Montiel, and it was much less unpleasant than the previous time because, since it was morning and the rays of the sun shone on them from a low angle, neither one was affected by the heat.

Just then Sancho Panza said to his master: "Look, your grace, *señor* knight-errant, don't forget about the *ínsula* you promised me. I'll be able to govern it no matter how big it is."

To which don Quixote answered: "I want you to know, Sancho Panza, my friend, that it was a very common custom for the knights-errant of old to make their squires governors of *ínsulas* or kingdoms they won, and I've decided to keep that pleasing custom; and I even plan to do better, because many times, and possibly even most of the time, they waited until their squires were old, and after serving them so many years of bad days and worse nights, they gave them the title of count, or at most of marquis of some valley or province of little importance. But if you live and if I live, it may well be that before six days go by I'll win a kingdom that has others dependent on it, and it will be perfect to crown you king of one of them. And don't consider it to be much, because things like this happen to those knights by such unheard-of means, that it may easily be that I can give you even more than I've promised."

"So," responded Sancho Panza, "if I became king by one of those miracles your grace has mentioned, Juana Gutiérrez, my wife, would be no less than a queen and my children princes."

"Who doubts it?" responded don Quixote.

"I do," replied Sancho Panza, "because I think that, even if God rained kingdoms onto the earth, none would fit on the head of Mari Gutiérrez. Look, *señor*, she's not worth two *maravedís* as a queen—countess would suit her better, and even then, God help her."

"Leave everything in God's hands, Sancho," responded don Quixote, "for He'll do what's best. But don't underestimate yourself to the point that you'll be content with anything less than being a provincial governor."

"I won't do that, *señor mío*," responded Sancho, "especially since I have such an important master as your grace, who'll be able to give me everything that's good for me, and that I can manage."

Chapter VIII. Of the excellent outcome that the brave don Quixote had in the frightening and never-imagined adventure of the windmills, with other events worthy of happy memory.

JUST THEN, they discovered thirty or forty windmills that were in that plain. And as soon as don Quixote saw them, he said to his squire: "Fortune is guiding our affairs better than we could have ever hoped. Look over there, Sancho Panza, my friend, where there are thirty or more monstrous giants with whom I plan to do battle and take all their lives, and with their spoils we'll start to get rich. This is righteous warfare, and it's a great service to God to rid the earth of such a wicked seed."

"What giants?" said Sancho Panza.

"Those that you see over there," responded his master, "with the long arms—some of them almost two leagues long."*

"Look, your grace," responded Sancho, "those things that you see over there aren't giants—they're windmills; and what seems to be arms are the sails that rotate the millstone when they're turned by the wind."

"It seems to me," responded don Quixote, "that you aren't well versed in adventures—they *are* giants; and if you're afraid, get away from here and start praying while I go into fierce and unequal battle with them."

---

* A Spanish league is about three and a half miles.

And saying this, he spurred his horse Rocinante without heeding what his squire Sancho was shouting to him, that what he was attacking were windmills and not giants. But he was so certain they were giants that he paid no attention to his squire Sancho's shouts, nor did he see what they were, even though he was very close. Rather, he went on shouting: "Do not flee, cowards and vile creatures, for it's just one knight attacking you!"

At this point, the wind increased a bit and the large sails began to move, which don Quixote observed and said: "Even though you wave more arms than Briaræus,* you'll have to answer to me!"

When he said this—and commending himself with all his heart to his lady Dulcinea, asking her to aid him in that peril, well covered by his shield, with his lance on the lance rest†—he attacked at Rocinante's full gallop and assailed the first windmill he came to. He gave a thrust into the sail with his lance just as a rush of air accelerated it with such fury that it broke the lance to bits, taking the horse and knight with it, and tossed him rolling onto the ground, very battered.

Sancho went as fast as his donkey would take him to help his master, and when he got there, he saw that don Quixote couldn't stir—such was the result of Rocinante's landing on top of him.

"God help us," said Sancho. "Didn't I tell you to watch what you were doing, that they were just windmills, and that only a person who had windmills in his head could fail to realize it?"

"Keep still, Sancho, my friend," responded don Quixote. "Things associated with war, more than others, are subject to continual change. Moreover, I believe—and it's true— that the sage Frestón—he who robbed me of my library— has changed these giants into windmills to take away the glory of my having conquered them, such is the enmity he bears me. But in the long run, his evil cunning will have little power over the might of my sword."

---

* Briaræus was one of the "hecatoncheires"—the hundred-handed— of Greek mythology. He had, obviously, a hundred arms.
† The rest was a part of the chest area of the armor to put the lance on.

"God's will be done," responded Sancho Panza.

Sancho helped don Quixote get back onto Rocinante, who was half-dislocated himself, and while they talked about the adventure just finished, they continued toward Puerto Lápice, because don Quixote said that it was impossible to fail to find many different adventures there, since it was a place frequented by travelers; but he was also very sad for having lost his lance, and he said to his squire: "I remember having read once that a Spanish knight named Diego Pérez de Vargas,* when he broke his lance in a battle, tore a heavy branch from an oak tree and with it performed many feats that day, and pounded so many Moors, that he took the surname 'Machuca,'† and so he and his descendants called themselves Vargas y Machuca from that day on. I've told you this because I plan to rip another such branch from the very first oak we come across, as good as the one I just mentioned, and I plan to do such deeds with it that you'll consider yourself fortunate to have been worthy to see them and to be an eyewitness to things that can hardly be believed."

"Be that as God wills," said Sancho. "I believe everything your grace says. But straighten yourself up a bit. It looks like you're listing, doubtless because of the injuries from your fall."

"That's true," responded don Quixote, "and if I don't fuss about the pain it's because knights-errant aren't allowed to complain of any wound, even though their intestines are oozing from it."

"If that's the way it is, I have nothing to say," responded Sancho, "but God knows I'd be glad if your grace complained when something hurts you. As far as I'm concerned, I can safely say that I'll complain about the least little pain I have, unless this business of not complaining also applies to squires of knights-errant."

Don Quixote couldn't help but laugh at the simplicity of his squire, and so he said that he could complain however and whenever he wanted, as often as he liked. He hadn't

---

* Diego Pérez de Vargas was a real person who fought under Fernando III in the thirteenth century. He ripped off an olive branch to use as a weapon.

† This Spanish word means "pounded."

ever read anything to the contrary in the laws of chivalry. Sancho said that he thought that it was now time to eat. His master responded that he didn't need to eat right then, but that Sancho could eat whenever he felt like it.

With this permission, Sancho made himself as comfortable as he could on his donkey, and, taking from the saddlebags what he'd put in, he ambled along, eating comfortably behind his master, and once in a while he raised his wineskin with such pleasure that the keeper of the most well-stocked tavern in Málaga might have envied him. And as he went along, taking swallow after swallow, he forgot completely about the promises his master had made him, nor did he consider going around looking for adventures as toil, but rather as great recreation, no matter how dangerous they might be.

In short, they spent that night among some trees, and from one of them don Quixote tore off a dead branch to serve him as a lance, and he put the lance head on it that he'd taken from the one that had broken. That whole night don Quixote never slept, thinking about his lady Dulcinea, in order to conform with what he'd read in his books about the many sleepless nights knights spent in the forest and wilderness, sustained by memories of their ladies.

Sancho didn't spend it that way. Since his stomach was full, and not of chicory water, he slept the whole night through, and if his master hadn't called him, neither the rays of the sun on his face nor the song of the many birds who rejoiced for the coming of the day would have woken him. When he got up, he took a swig from the wineskin and found it somewhat flatter than the night before, and he was grieved in his heart because it seemed to him that there wasn't going to be a remedy for it anytime soon. Don Quixote didn't want to break his fast because he could sustain himself with pleasant memories.

They took the route to Puerto Lápice that they had already begun, and at about three in the afternoon they saw the village.

"Here," said don Quixote when he saw it, "we can put our arms up to our elbows into what they call adventures. But let me remind you that even if you see me in great danger, you must not take your sword to defend me unless you see that those attacking me are common rabble—if they are, then you can help me. But if they're knights, the laws of chivalry forbid you to aid me in any way, until you're dubbed a knight yourself."

"There's no question, *señor*," responded Sancho, "that you'll be obeyed in this, especially since I'm peaceable by nature and an enemy of getting mixed up in other people's disputes. It's true that insofar as defending myself is concerned, I won't pay much attention to those laws, since laws both human and divine allow each person to defend himself from anyone who wants to harm him."

"And I don't say any less," responded don Quixote, "but where helping me against knights is concerned, you have to contain your natural impulses."

"I pledge I'll do it," responded Sancho, "and I'll observe this precept as well as I observe the Sabbath."

While they were having this conversation, two friars of the Benedictine order appeared along the road on two dromedaries, because the mules on which they were traveling were no smaller than that. They were wearing traveling masks, and were holding parasols. Behind them was a coach accompanied by four or five men on horseback, and two servants on foot. Inside the coach, as was later found out, there was a Basque lady who was going to Seville, where her husband was waiting to go to the New World to take a prestigious position. The friars were not in her party, although they were on the same road. But as soon as don Quixote saw them, he said to his squire: "Either I'm mistaken, or this will be the most famous adventure ever seen, because those dark shapes over there must be, and doubtless *are*, enchanters who have kidnapped a princess in that coach. I have to right this wrong with all my might."

"This will be worse than the windmills," said Sancho. "Look, *señor*, those men are Benedictine friars, and the coach is probably just carrying a couple of passengers. Consider what you're doing—don't let the devil deceive you."

"I've already told you, Sancho," replied don Quixote, "that you know little about the subject of adventures. What I've told you is the truth, as you'll soon see."

And saying this, he went forward and placed himself in the middle of the road where the friars were coming, and when they got close enough where it seemed to him he could be heard, he said in a loud voice: "Diabolical and

monstrous people! Release immediately the highborn princesses that you're holding against their will. If you don't,
prepare yourselves to receive a swift death as a just punishment for your evil deeds!"

The friars pulled in their reins, and were startled at the
figure of don Quixote, as well as at his words, to which
they responded: "*Señor* knight, we're neither diabolical
nor monstrous, but rather two friars of St. Benedict minding our own business, and we don't know if there are kidnapped princesses in that coach or not."

"For me there are no feeble excuses—I know who you
are, you lying rabble," said don Quixote.

And not waiting for an answer, he spurred Rocinante,
and with his lance lowered, he attacked the first friar with
such fury and daring that, if the friar hadn't dropped down
from his mule, don Quixote would have made him fall to the
ground much against his wishes, perhaps badly wounded,
and possibly lifeless.

The second friar, who saw the way his companion was
being treated, put his heels to his large mule, and began to
race across the countryside, swifter than the wind itself.

When Sancho saw the downed friar, he nimbly got off
his donkey and rushed over to him and began removing his
habit. The two servants of the friars went over and asked
why he was doing that. Sancho said that it was his legitimate right since it was among the spoils that his master don
Quixote had won in battle. The servants, knowing nothing about spoils nor battles, and seeing that don Quixote
wasn't looking—since he was talking with the women in
the coach—wrestled Sancho to the ground, and leaving his
beard without a hair, they kicked him senseless, knocked
the wind out of him, and left him stretched out on the
ground. Then, without waiting a second, the fearful, intimi-
dated, and pale friar leapt back onto his mule and spurred
on toward his companion, who was waiting for him a good
distance away to see where that frightening encounter was
leading, and without waiting for its end, they continued on
their way, crossing themselves more times than if they had
the devil chasing them.

Don Quixote was, as has been said, talking with the lady
of the coach, saying to her: "You are free to go about your
business, beauteous lady, because your arrogant kidnap-

pers are lying in the dust, overwhelmed by my strong arm. And so that you won't be tormented trying to discover the name of your liberator, I want you to know that I'm called don Quixote de La Mancha, knight-errant and adventurer, and captive of the beautiful Dulcinea del Toboso. All I ask for the favor you received from me is for you to go to El Toboso and present yourself before this lady, and tell her what I did to set you free."

Everything that don Quixote said was overheard by a Basque squire accompanying the coach, and when he heard that don Quixote didn't want the coach to proceed, but rather said that it had to turn back to El Toboso, he went to don Quixote and, grabbing his lance, said to him in bad Spanish and worse Basque: "Go on, knight, who acts badly. By the God who created me, that, if you not leave coach alone, you kill yourself as I am Basque."

Don Quixote understood him very well, and with great calm said to him: "If you were a knight, as I see you're not, I would have already punished your folly and insolence, you wretched creature."

To which the Basque answered: "I not knight?* I swear to God as you lie, as a Christian. If you throw lance and take sword, to the water you'll see how fast you take the cat. Basque on land, *hidalgo* on sea, *hidalgo* by the devil, and you lie, and watch out if you say anything else."†

"'Now you'll see!' said Agrajes,"‡ responded don Quixote. And throwing his lance to the ground, he drew his sword, clasped his shield, and attacked the Basque, determined to take his life.

When the Basque saw don Quixote coming toward him, he tried to get off the mule, since it was a bad rented one and couldn't be counted on, but he could do nothing ex-

---

* Just being Basque gave the Basques the right to consider themselves noble, given their ancient lineage in the Iberian Peninsula; thus the insult.

† The Basque's speech means something like this: "I swear to God as a Christian that you're lying. If you throw down your lance and draw your sword, we'll see who wins. A Basque on land, an *hidalgo* by sea, *hidalgo* by the devil, and you're lying if you say anything else."

‡ This was a proverbial expression. Agrajes was a character in *Amadís de Gaula*, and he never said these exact words in the book.

cept draw his own sword. He was lucky to be next to the coach, from which he could take a cushion to be his shield, and then the battle really began, as if they were two mortal enemies. The rest of the people tried to get them to stop, but they couldn't, because the Basque said in his badly put-together words that if they didn't let them finish their battle, he himself would kill his mistress and anyone else who opposed him.

The woman in the coach, dumbfounded and alarmed by what she was seeing, had the driver move some distance away and from there she saw the mighty struggle, in the course of which the Basque gave don Quixote a blow directly onto his shield, which was protecting his shoulder. If it had landed on him instead of the shield it would have split him down to his waist. Don Quixote felt the force of that massive blow and cried loudly: "Oh, *señora* of my soul, Dulcinea, flower of beauty, succor your knight in this severe peril for the sake of your great goodness!"

At the same instant he said this, he grasped his sword, covered himself with his shield, and attacked the Basque, determined to venture everything on a single blow. The Basque, when he saw himself being assaulted, quickly understood don Quixote's anger through his daring, and resolved to do the same as don Quixote. So the Basque waited for his opponent, well covered by his cushion, without being able to move his mule one way or the other, because the poor thing—from pure exhaustion, and not used to childish nonsense—couldn't take a step.

Don Quixote began his attack, as has been said, against the cautious Basque with his sword held high, bent on splitting him in two; the Basque waited for him as well, protected by his cushion and with his sword raised. All those present were apprehensive and in suspense about the result of the enormous blows with which they threatened each other. The lady of the coach and her other maids were saying a thousand prayers and supplications to all the holy images and shrines in all of Spain so that God would save their squire, as well as themselves, from the great danger in which they found themselves.

But the dreadful thing is that, at this point, the author of this history leaves the battle pending, apologizing that he couldn't find anything else written about the

deeds of don Quixote other than what he's already related. It is true that the second author of this work refused to believe that such a curious history would be
relegated to oblivion, or that the good minds of La
Mancha would be so uninquisitive that they wouldn't have
in their archives or in their desk drawers some documents
that dealt with this famous knight. Thus, with this
thought in mind, he didn't despair of finding
the end of this pleasant story, which,
since heaven was kind to him,
he found in the way that
will be related in
the Second
Part.

SECOND PART
OF THE INGENIOUS
Hidalgo Don Quixote
de La Mancha.

Chapter IX. Where the stupendous battle that the gallant Basque and the brave don Quixote had is concluded and brought to an end.

IN THE first part of this history, we left the brave Basque and the celebrated don Quixote with their unsheathed swords raised and ready to deliver two raging slashes that, if they had landed squarely, would at the very least have cleft them both from top to bottom and opened them up like a pomegranate. And at this perilous point the delicious history was cut off, and the author was unable to tell us where we could find what was missing. This caused me considerable distress, because the pleasure I'd gotten from reading this little bit turned into vexation when I considered how practically hopeless it would be to find what, in my opinion, seemed to be the larger part that was left to tell of this delectable history. It seemed to me that it was impossible—and so contrary to the usual custom—that such a good knight wouldn't have a wizard who would undertake to record his unheard-of deeds, this being something that was never lacking to any knight-errant who "so people say, go to seek adventures," because every one of them had one or two wizards who not only wrote of their deeds, but also described their most secret thoughts and childish acts. Such a good knight just couldn't have been so unfortunate as to lack what Platir and others had in excess. I couldn't bring myself to believe such a lively story would remain truncated and mutilated, and I blamed the perversity of time, which devours and consumes everything, and which had either hidden or destroyed it.

On the other hand, it seemed to me that since they'd found in his library such modern books as *The Disillusionment of Jealousy* and *Nymphs of Henares*, don Quixote's story must also be modern; and if it wasn't written down, at least it would still be remembered by people in his village and from neighboring ones. This was quite a perplexing thought and it left me wanting more than ever to find out, really and truly, about the life and miracles of our famous Spaniard don Quixote de La Mancha, shining light and mirror of Manchegan chivalry, and the first person in our age and in these very calamitous times to take on the profession of errant arms, and the burden of redressing wrongs, succoring widows, and protecting maidens—those who rode on palfreys with whips, and with their virginity intact, from mountain to mountain and from valley to valley, unless it happened that some rustic with a hatchet and hood, or some enormous giant, ravished them. Some maidens of yesteryear, after eighty years of never sleeping under a roof, went to their graves as virginal as the mothers who bore them.

So, as I was saying, for these and many other reasons, our gallant don Quixote is worthy of continual and memorable praises, as I am, too, for my work and diligence in searching for the end of this pleasant story. I know very well that if heaven, chance, and good fortune hadn't helped me, the world would be without the pastime and pleasure that the attentive reader will have for almost two hours. The way I found it, then, happened this way:

One day when I was in the Alcaná of Toledo,* a boy selling notebooks and papers to a silk merchant walked by me, and since I enjoy reading so much—even scraps of paper

---

* This was an ancient Jewish commercial street in Toledo, near the cathedral.

that I find in the street—I was taken by my natural curiosity and took one of the notebooks the boy was selling, and
I saw that it was written in Arabic characters. I recognized
them but I couldn't read them, so I went looking for some
Spanish-speaking Moor who could, and it wasn't hard to
find such an interpreter, because even if I'd been looking
for someone to translate from a better and more ancient
language,* I'd find one there. In short, Fortune provided
me with one. After I told him what I wanted, and put the
book in his hands, he opened it up in the middle, and when
he'd read a little of it he began to laugh.

I asked him what he was laughing at, and he told me
it was something written in the margin as a note. I asked
him to tell me what it was and he, still laughing, said: "As I
said, here's what's written in the margin: 'This Dulcinea del
Toboso, which the history mentions so many times, they say
she had the best hand for salting pork of all the women in
La Mancha.'"

When I heard Dulcinea del Toboso mentioned, I was
dumbfounded and amazed, because I realized immediately
that those notebooks contained the history of don Quixote.
With this thought, I told him to hurry and read the beginning, which he did; and translating on the fly from Arabic
to Spanish, he said that it read: HISTORY OF DON QUIXOTE DE
LA MANCHA, WRITTEN BY CIDE HAMETE BENENGELI, ARABIC
HISTORIAN. †

I needed a lot of discretion to conceal the joy I felt when
the title of the book came to my ears. I managed to keep
the notebooks and papers out of the hands of the silk merchant and bought them all from the boy for half a *real*. If
he'd only known how much I wanted them, he could have
easily asked for and gotten six *reales*‡ from the deal.

I went away with the Moor to the cloister of the cathedral and begged him to translate all those notebooks that
dealt with don Quixote into Spanish, without taking anything away or adding anything, and I offered him whatever
pay he wanted. He was satisfied with fifty pounds of raisins
and three bushels of wheat, and he promised to translate

---

* Hebrew.
† *Cide* means "Mr."
‡ Still, not very much money.

well and faithfully—and in a short time. But I, to make
things easier, and so as to not let my treasure out of my
sight, took him to my house, where, in a little more than six
and a half weeks, he translated everything, exactly as it's
written here.

On the first notebook there was painted, in a most natural way, the battle between don Quixote and the Basque.
They were in the same position as the history relates:
swords raised on high, one of them protecting himself with
his shield and the other with the cushion, and the Basque's
mule so lifelike that you could see it was a rental animal
from a crossbow shot away. At the feet of the Basque there
was a caption that read, DON SANCHO DE AZPETIA,* which
must have been his name, and at the feet of Rocinante
there was another one that read, DON QUIXOTE. Rocinante
was marvelously depicted, so long and lean, with such a
pronounced backbone, so far gone in consumption, that it
showed clearly with what acuity and good reason he'd been
called Rocinante. Next to him was Sancho Panza, who was
holding the halter of his donkey, and at his feet there was
another caption that read SANCHO ZANCAS, and that must
have been because he had—as the miniature showed—a
large belly,† a short waist, and long shanks,‡ and for that
reason the history sometimes calls him *Panza* and sometimes *Zancas*.

Other little details could be mentioned, but all of them
are of little importance and they're not critical to the true
telling of the story, because no story is bad as long as it's
true. If there's any objection to its truth, the only one could
be that its author is Arabic, and it's a very common trait for
people of that origin to be liars, although, because they're
such enemies of ours, it can be understood that he would
have fallen short of the truth rather than exaggerated it.
So it seems to me that on occasions when he could, and
should have outdone himself in praise of such a fine knight,
he passes them over in silence on purpose; this is a bad
and ill-conceived practice, since historians should be—

---

* Azpeitia is a village in the Basque country between San Sebastián
and Bilbao.
† That's what *panza* means in Spanish.
‡ That's what *zancas* means in Spanish.

indeed must be—accurate, truthful, and free from passion, and neither interest nor fear, hate nor friendship, should make them stray from the path of truth, whose mother is history—emulator of time, storehouse of deeds, witness to the past, example and counsel to the present, and caveat for the future. In this story, I know that you'll find everything that you could possibly desire in any such pleasant tale. If something is lacking in it, I hold that its dog of an author is to blame, rather than a deficiency in the subject.

In short, the second part—according to the translation—began this way:

"With their trenchant swords raised on high, the two brave and enraged combatants seemed to defy heaven, earth, and the bottomless pit, such was their courageous mien. The wrathful Basque was the first one to strike a blow, which was delivered with such force and fury that if it had not gone off course a bit, it alone would have been enough to end the bitter struggle as well as all the adventures of our knight. But good fortune, which was keeping him for greater things, deflected the sword of his opponent so that, although it hit him on the left shoulder, it did no more damage than to knock off the armor on that side, taking with it a good portion of his helmet and half his ear, and it all tumbled frightfully to the ground, and left him in a terrible plight."

Good God! Who can possibly describe the rage that entered the heart of our Manchegan, seeing himself end up that way! The only thing that can be said is that he raised himself high in his stirrups, clutched his sword in both hands, and with great fury brought it down onto the Basque, and struck him with the flat side squarely on his cushion—which was really not a good defense—and then his head, as if a mountain had fallen on him, and he began to bleed through his nostrils, mouth, and ears, and he looked like he was going to fall from his mule, which he doubtless would have done, if he hadn't been clutching its neck. But even so, his feet slipped from his stirrups; then he released his hands; and the mule—frightened by the terrible blow—began to dash across the field, and with a few bucks threw its master to the ground.

Don Quixote was watching this with great calm, and when he saw the Basque fall, he jumped nimbly from his horse and approached him, and then, putting the point of his sword right between the man's eyes, told him to surrender. If not, he would cut off his head. The Basque was so confused that he couldn't answer a word, and he would have fared badly (such was the blind rage of don Quixote), if the women in the coach—who up to that point had been watching the struggle with great dismay—hadn't gone over and asked him very fervently to do them the favor of sparing the life of their squire.

Don Quixote responded with haughty composure: "By all means, beauteous *señoras*, I'm very happy to do what you ask. But it has to be on one condition, which is for this knight to promise me he'll go to the village of El Toboso and present himself on my behalf before the peerless Dulcinea, so that she can do with him whatever she wants."

The terrified and grief-stricken women, without any idea of what don Quixote was asking, and without finding out who Dulcinea was, promised him that the squire would do everything he'd commanded.

"On the faith of that promise, I'll do him no further harm, although in my opinion, he well deserves it."

Chapter X. Of what else happened to don Quixote with the Basque and the danger in which he found himself with a mob of Yangüesans.*

B Y THIS time Sancho had risen, somewhat beaten up by the servants of the friars, and had seen the battle of his master don Quixote, and had prayed to God in his heart to make him victorious so that he might win an *ínsula* of which he'd make him governor, as he'd been promised. Seeing that the battle was over and that his master was going over to mount Rocinante, he went over so that he could hold his stirrup. Before his master mounted, he got down on his knees in front of him, took him by the hand, kissed it, and said to him: "If it pleases you, *señor* don Quixote *mío*, give me the government of the *ínsula* your grace has won

---

* Yangüesans are people from Yanguas in the province of Soria, north of Madrid.

in this rigorous battle. No matter how big it is, I feel able to govern it as well as anyone else has governed *ínsulas* in the whole world."

To this don Quixote responded: "I want you to know, brother Sancho, that this adventure, and others like it, aren't the kind that lead to winning *ínsulas* but rather are just crossroad skirmishes in which your only reward is a broken head or an ear less. Be patient, because adventures will arise from which I can make you not only a governor, but much more."

Sancho thanked him profusely, and after he kissed his hand once again, as well as the undertunic of his mail armor, he helped him mount Rocinante, and he went back to his donkey and began to follow his master, who, without saying anything else to or taking leave of the women in the coach, took off at a brisk pace and went into a forest nearby. Sancho followed him at his donkey's fastest trot, but Rocinante was going so fast that Sancho, seeing himself being left behind, had to shout to his master to wait for him. Don Quixote drew in Rocinante's reins and waited for his fatigued squire to catch up, and the latter said to him as he approached: "It seems to me, *señor*, that the best thing to do would be to take refuge in some church, given the bad shape in which you left that fellow you fought. It's likely that they'll tell the Holy Brotherhood,* who will arrest us. And I swear that before we get out of jail, we'll have a very bad time of it."

"Hush," said don Quixote, "and where did you ever hear or read that a knight-errant has been thrown in jail, no matter how many homicides he might have committed?"

"I don't know anything about ama-sighs," responded Sancho, "nor in all my life have I ever heard them mentioned; I only know that the Holy Brotherhood deals with those who fight in rural areas, and I don't meddle in that other business."

"Well, don't worry, friend," responded don Quixote. "I'll save you from the hands of the Chaldeans,† not to mention

---

* This was Spain's rural police force.

† The Chaldeans were an ancient people living in Mesopotamia, mentioned in the Old Testament. The expression means, "I'll save you from harm."

those of the Holy Brotherhood. But tell me, on your life, have you ever seen a braver knight than me in the whole world? Have you read in the histories about any other who was more spirited in his attack, showed more vigor in his perseverance, more skill in wielding his sword, or more dexterity in unhorsing his opponent?"

"If the truth be known," responded Sancho, "I haven't read any history like that because I can't read or write; but I'll venture to bet that your grace is the most daring master I've ever served. I only hope to God that your daring deeds won't be paid for in the way I've mentioned. I beg you, though, to tend to your ear because it's bleeding a lot. I have some bandages and ointment in my saddle-bag."

"All that would be unnecessary," responded don Quixote, "if I'd remembered to prepare a flask containing the Balm of Fierabrás,* because with a single drop we'd save time and medicine."

"What flask and what balm is that?" asked Sancho Panza.

"It's a balm," responded don Quixote, "the formula for which I've memorized, by means of which one needn't fear death, nor worry about dying from any wound. Thus, when I make it and give it to you, when you see me cleft in two—and this frequently happens—you have only to take the part that has fallen to the ground and position it deftly, before the blood coagulates, on the other part, being careful to make sure it sits just right; then give me two gulps of the balm that I mentioned, and you'll see me sounder than an apple."

"If that really exists," said Panza, "I renounce the government of the *ínsula* that you promised me, and I don't want anything else for my many good services than for your grace to give me the formula for that wonderful elixir. I think it must be worth more than two *reales* per ounce anywhere in the world, and I don't need anything else to live honorably and at my ease. But first I have to know if it costs very much to make it."

---

* Fierabrás was a giant Saracen written about in a French epic poem. When he sacked Rome, he stole two containers with the remainder of the embalming fluid used in Christ's body. This is what is known as the Balm of Fierabrás.

"For less than three *reales* you can make a gallon and a half of it," responded don Quixote.

"Sinner that I am," replied Sancho, "what are you waiting for to make it and show me how?"

"Keep still, my friend," responded don Quixote, "for I plan to reveal even greater secrets to you. For now, let's try to make my ear feel better. It hurts me more than I'd like."

Sancho took the bandages and ointment from his saddlebag, but when don Quixote noticed that his helmet was crushed, he thought he would lose his mind. He took his sword in his hand and raised it toward heaven, saying: "I swear to the Creator of everything, and to the four holy gospels in all their fullest meaning,* to live the life of the great Marqués de Mantua when he swore to avenge the death of his nephew Valdovinos—which was 'not to eat bread off a tablecloth, nor sport with his wife,'† and other things that, although I don't recall them, I consider to have been stated—until I avenge completely the outrage that was done to me."

Hearing this, Sancho said: "Listen, your grace, *señor* don Quixote—if the knight fulfills what he was ordered to do, which was to appear before my lady Dulcinea del Toboso, he'll have done what was necessary, and he doesn't deserve any more punishment unless he's committed another crime."

"You've made an excellent point," responded don Quixote, "so I rescind the oath as far as taking fresh vengeance on him goes. But I reaffirm the oath to live the life that I mentioned until I take a helmet, at least as good as this one, by force from some knight. And don't think I'm making idle threats, Sancho, since the same thing happened to Mambrino's helmet, which cost Sacripante so dearly."‡

"You can give such oaths to the devil, *señor mío,*" replied Sancho, "since they're so detrimental to one's health and so prejudicial to one's conscience. If I'm wrong, just tell me—if we don't come across a man in armor with a helmet

---

* "In all their fullest meaning" is a legalistic phrase.

† This derives from verses from two different sources, one about the Cid and the other about the Marqués de Mantua.

‡ In *Orlando Furioso*, it was Dardinel and not Sacripante whom it cost so dearly.

for many days, what'll we do then? Are you going to fulfill your oath in spite of so many obstacles and annoyances, such as sleeping fully dressed and not spending the night in a town* and a thousand other penances in the oath of the crazy old Marqués de Mantua that you want to revive now? Look, your grace, there are no men in armor on these roads, only muleteers and cart drivers, and they not only don't have helmets, but have probably never even heard of them in all the days of their lives."

"You've been misled in this," said don Quixote, "because we won't have been at these crossroads two hours before we see more men in armor than those who stormed Albraca trying to rescue Angélica the Beautiful."†

"So be it," said Sancho. "May it please God to make everything turn out fine, and may the time come when that *ínsula* can be won that's costing me so dearly, and may I die right then."

"I've told you, Sancho, not to worry at all. If the *ínsula* doesn't work out, why, there's the Kingdom of Denmark, or of Soliadisa,‡ which will fit you like a ring on your finger, and even better—since because it's not an *ínsula,* it should make you even happier. But let's save this for another time. Look and see if you have anything to eat in those saddlebags, because we'll need to go looking for a castle soon where we can put up for the night and make the balm that I mentioned. I swear to God this ear is hurting me a lot."

"I've brought an onion and a bit of cheese, and some scraps of bread," said Sancho, "but they're hardly appropriate food for such a valiant knight as your grace."

"How little you understand," responded don Quixote. "I'll have you know, Sancho, that the pride of knights-errant is to not eat for a whole month, and when they do, it should be whatever is at hand. This would be clear to you if you had read as many histories as I have. Among the

---

* Sancho also knows the oral poetic tradition. He refers here to verses that don Quixote didn't mention from the ballad about the Marqués de Mantua.

† In *Orlando Innamorato*, the Albraca castle was assaulted by 2,200,000 armed soldiers, stretching over four leagues.

‡ Soliadisa may be don Quixote's error for Sobradisa, the fictional kingdom ruled by Amadís' brother.

great number of them I've read, I haven't found it said that knights ate, except at sumptuous banquets given in their honor—and the rest of the time they practically fasted. Although it's understood that they couldn't go without eating, or without doing all the other natural functions—because they were in fact men like us—you have to understand also that, spending most of their lives in forests and the wilderness, without a cook, their most usual fare would be rustic food such as what you're offering me now. So, Sancho, my friend, don't be distressed thinking about what pleases me, nor try to make the world over, nor knock knight-errantry off its hinges."

"Pardon me, your grace," said Sancho, "since I don't know how to read or write, as I've said before, I don't know whether I understand all the rules of the profession of chivalry; from now on I'll have plenty of dried fruits and nuts in my saddlebag for your grace, since you're a knight; and for me, since I'm not one, I'll take poultry and more substantial things for myself."

"I don't say, Sancho," replied don Quixote, "that knights-errant *have to* limit themselves to eating these fruits and nuts you mentioned; that was just their ordinary sustenance, as well as some herbs that they knew about—as I do—that are found in the countryside."

"It's a good thing," responded Sancho, "to know about those herbs, since, the way I look at it, one day we might have to use that knowledge."

And taking out what he had, the two ate in good fellowship and company. But since they wanted to look for a place to stay, they ate their scanty and dry dinner quickly. They got back on their mounts and hurried to get to a town before dark, but the sun went down—along with the hope of finding what they wanted—near some huts belonging to goatherds, so they decided to spend the night there. As much as it caused grief to Sancho, it gave gladness to his master to sleep in the open air, since it seemed to him that everything that happened to him tended to confirm his knighthood.

Chapter XI. About what happened to don Quixote with some goatherds.

H E WAS warmly received by the goatherds, and after Sancho had taken care of Rocinante and the donkey as well as he could, he followed the aroma that came from certain chunks of goat meat that were boiling in a cauldron. He wanted to see if they were ready to be transferred from the cauldron into his stomach, but he didn't need to, since the goatherds removed them from the fire, spread some sheepskins onto the ground, quickly set their rustic table, and with a show of goodwill invited the two of them to join them to share their meal. Six goatherds sat around the skins, and with their best country manners they invited don Quixote to sit on a trough they had turned upside down especially for him. Don Quixote sat down, with Sancho standing behind to serve him his cup made from a horn.

When don Quixote saw him standing, he said: "So that you can see, Sancho, the greatness embraced by knight-errantry, and that those who practice it in any capacity are soon honored and esteemed by everyone, I want you to sit down here next to me—your master and natural lord—and in the company of these good people, eat from my plate and drink from my cup, so that it can be said of knight-errantry what is said of love: that it makes all things equal."

"It's a great honor," said Sancho, "but I can tell you that as long as I have plenty to eat, I can eat as well, and even better, standing up alone than seated at the feet of an emperor. And if the truth be told, food that I eat in a corner somewhere, without all that fussing and table manners—even though it's only bread and onions—tastes better to me than turkeys served on tables, where I have to chew slowly, drink little, use my napkin a lot, and not sneeze or cough if I feel like it, nor do any of the other things that freedom and privacy guarantee. So, *señor mío,* concerning these honors that you want to offer me, since I, as your squire, am a servant and aide to knight-errantry, I'd rather have you swap them for other things that might be of more use and benefit to me. Therefore, although I appreciate the offer, I renounce it from now until the end of the world."

"Even so, you must sit with me, because 'he who humbles himself is exalted by God.'"* And grabbing Sancho by his arm, he forced him to sit at his side.

The goatherds didn't understand all that gibberish about squires and knights-errant; they only sat there and ate quietly as they looked at their guests, who were stowing away chunks of meat the size of your fist with great gusto and pleasure. After the meat course they spread quite a few dry acorns on the skins and added half a wheel of cheese, which was as hard as if it were made of cement. And the horn was hardly idle, because it circulated so frequently— now full, now empty, like the buckets of a waterwheel— that it easily emptied one of the two wineskins that were visible.

After don Quixote had satisfied his stomach, he took some acorns in his hand, and, examining them with great care, raised his voice to speak words like these: "What a happy time and a happy age were those that the ancients called GOLDEN! And not because gold—which in this our Age of Iron is so valued—was gotten in that fortunate time without any trouble, but rather because the people who lived then didn't know the two words YOURS and MINE! In that holy age all things were commonly owned. To find their daily sustenance, they had only to raise their hands and take it from the robust oaks, which liberally offered their sweet and ripe fruit to them. Crystal-clear fountains and running rivers, in magnificent abundance, offered them their delicious and transparent water. In the fissures of boulders and in the hollows of trees, the diligent and prudent bees formed their republics and offered to any hand, without recompense, the fertile harvest of their very sweet work. The robust cork trees shed their lightweight bark without any artifice other than their own courtesy, with which people began to cover their rustic houses, built only for protection against the rigors of the heavens. Everything then was friendship; everything was harmony. The heavy plow had not yet dared to open nor visit the pious bowels of our

---

* Luke 18:14.

first mother, for she, without being forced, gave everywhere from her fertile and broad bosom which could fill, sustain, and delight the children that possessed her then.

"It was then that the simple and beautiful young shepherdesses could travel from valley to valley and from hill to hill, either in braids or with their hair flowing behind, with only enough clothing to cover modestly what decency requires, and has always required. And their ornamentation was not like the Tyrian purple and silk woven in a thousand different ways that women esteem nowadays, but rather it was of intertwined green-dock and ivy, with which they carried themselves with perhaps as much dignity and composure as our courtesans do nowadays, strutting about in extravagant dresses. In those days, literary expressions of love were recited in a simple way, without any unnatural circumlocution to express them.

"Fraud, deceit, and wickedness had not as yet contaminated truth and sincerity. Justice was administered on its own terms and was not tainted by favor and self-interest, which now impair, overturn, and persecute it. Arbitrary law had not yet debased the rulings of the judge, because in those days there was nothing to judge, nor anyone to be judged.

"Young women, with their chastity intact, traveled about on their own anywhere they wanted, as I've said, without fearing the damaging boldness or lust of others, and if they suffered any ruination, it was born of their own pleasure and free will. Nowadays, in our detestable age, no young woman is secure, even though she be hidden and locked in a new labyrinth of Crete, for even there, through the cracks or borne in the air, the plague of lust finds its way in with the zeal of cursed importunity, and brings her to ruin in spite of her seclusion. As time went by and as wickedness grew, the order of knight-errantry was instituted to defend young women, protect widows, and help orphans and needy people.

"I am a member of this order, brother goatherds, and I'm grateful for the hearty welcome and reception you've given me and my squire. For, although under natural law all living souls are obliged to show favor to knights-errant, it's still fitting that—knowing as I do you received and entertained me with no knowledge of this obligation—I should acknowledge your goodwill with utmost gratitude."

All of this long speech, which could well have been spared, was given by our knight because the acorns brought to his memory the Golden Age. And he was moved to give that useless speech to the goatherds, who, without saying a single word, were listening to him openmouthed and amazed. Sancho also remained silent as he snacked on some acorns and visited very frequently a second wineskin that had been suspended from a cork tree to make the wine cool.

But don Quixote took longer to finish his speech than his dinner, and when he'd finished, one of the goatherds said: "So that your grace, *señor* knight-errant, can say with even greater truth that we entertained you well with ready goodwill, we want to give you solace and pleasure by having one of our *compañeros* sing for you, and he'll be here pretty soon. He's a very smart goatherd and is very much in love and, above all things, he can read and write and can play the rabel,* and you can't want more than that."

As soon as the goatherd had said this, notes from a rabel came to his ears, and a little while later the one who was playing it arrived, a lad about twenty-two years old and quite good-looking. His *compañeros* asked him if he'd eaten and he said that he had. The one who had suggested that the lad might sing said: "In that case, Antonio, you can do us the pleasure of singing a little bit, so that our *señor* guest can see that we have in these mountains and woods people who can make music. We've told him about your skills and we're anxious for you to show them off and prove us true. So we'd like you to sit down and sing the ballad about your love that your uncle the priest wrote for you, and which was well received in town."

"I'd be very pleased," said the young man. And without any further urging, he sat on the trunk of a felled oak tree, tuned his instrument, and in a little while began to sing in a very spirited way:

---

* The rabel is an old Arabic bowed musical instrument with three strings tuned in fifths. It had a flat top and a rounded bottom.

ANTONIO*

Thou dost love me well, Olalla;
    Well I know it, even though
    Love's mute tongues, thine eyes, have never
    By their glances told me so.
For I know my love thou knowest;
    Therefore thine to claim I dare:
    Once it ceases to be secret,
    Love need never feel despair.
True it is, Olalla, sometimes
    Thou hast all too plainly shown
    That thy heart is brass in hardness,
    And thy snowy bosom stone.
Yet for all that, in thy coyness,
    And thy fickle fits between,
    Hope is there—at least the border
    Of her garment may be seen.
Lures to faith are they, those glimpses,
    And to faith in thee I hold;
    Kindness cannot make it stronger,
    Coldness cannot make it cold.
If it be that love is gentle,
    In thy gentleness I see
    Something holding out assurance
    To the hope of winning thee.
If it be that in devotion
    Lies a power hearts to move,
    That which every day I show thee,
    Helpful to my suit should prove.
Many a time thou must have noticed—
    If to notice thou dost care—
    How I go about on Monday
    Dressed in all my Sunday wear.

---

* The Spanish ballad form, called *romance*, is written in eight-syllable
lines with vowel-rhyme used only in the even-numbered lines. More
strictly speaking, the Spanish count to the last stressed syllable then
add one; thus the second line is seven syllables long, stressed on the
seventh, so it counts as eight. I've used Ormsby's good version here, in
which he mimics the Spanish stress, but uses full rhyme, since English
doesn't commonly use vowel rhyme.

Love's eyes love to look on brightness;
    Love loves what is gaily dressed;
    Sunday, Monday, all I care is
    Thou shouldst see me in my best.
No account I make of dances,
    Or of strains that pleased thee so,
    Keeping thee awake from midnight
    Till the cocks began to crow;
Or of how I roundly swore it
    That there's none so fair as thou;
    True it is, but as I said it,
    By the girls I'm hated now.
For Teresa of the hillside
    At my praise of thee was sore;
    Said, "You think you love an angel;
    It's a monkey you adore;
"Caught by all her glittering trinkets,
    And her borrowed braids of hair,
    And a host of made-up beauties
    That would Love himself ensnare."
'Twas a lie, and so I told her,
    And her cousin at the word
    Gave me his defiance for it;
    And what followed thou hast heard.
Mine is no high-flown affection,
    Mine no passion *par amours*—
    As they call it—what I offer
    Is an honest love, and pure.
Binding cords the holy Church has,
    Cords of softest silk they be;
    Put thy neck beneath the yoke, dear;
    Mine will follow, thou wilt see.
Else—and once for all I swear it
    By the saint of most renown—
    If I ever quit the mountains,
    'Twill be in a friar's gown.

With this the goatherd ended his song. Although don Quixote begged him to sing something else, Sancho wouldn't hear of it, because he favored going to sleep over hearing more songs, and so he said to his master: "Your grace should arrange to find a place to sleep now, since the labors these good men do all day long don't let them spend all night singing."

"I understand you, Sancho," responded don Quixote. "I easily infer that your visits to the wineskin demand compensation more in sleep than in music."

"It tasted good to us all," responded Sancho.

"I don't deny that," replied don Quixote, "but you can sleep wherever you want. Those of my profession do better keeping guard than sleeping. But, all things considered, it would be a good thing if you'd try to dress this ear, since it's causing me more pain than it should."

Sancho began to do what he was asked. When one of the goatherds saw the wound, he told don Quixote not to worry, that he would apply a remedy that would make him better. He took some rosemary leaves—from a bush that grew wild there—chewed them and combined them with a little salt, then applied them to the ear, bandaged it well, and assured don Quixote that he would need no further treatment, and it turned out to be true.

Chapter XII. About what a goatherd told those who were with don Quixote.

At that point, a boy, whose job was to bring supplies from the village, arrived and said: "Do you know what's going on in the village?"

"How can we know?" responded one of them.

"Well," he continued, "this morning that famous student-shepherd named Grisóstomo died, and the word is that he died because of his love for that bedeviled girl of Marcela— the daughter of Guillermo the Rich—the one who wanders about these parts dressed like a shepherdess."

"You mean Marcela?"* said one.

"That's the one," responded the goatherd. "And the strange thing is that he stipulated in his will that he be buried in the wilderness, as if he were a Moor, and that

---

* "That bedeviled girl of Marcela" is just an awkward way of saying "that devilish Marcela," but in Spanish it could be interpreted "Marcela's girl (servant)"; thus the clarification.

it be at the foot of a boulder where the spring flows by
the cork tree, because, as the story goes—they say he said
it—that's the place where he saw her for the first time.
He stipulated other things as well, things the parish priest
in town says don't need to be complied with since they
smack of paganism. His great friend Ambrosio, the other
student who dresses like a shepherd, responds by saying
that everything must be done exactly as Grisóstomo specified, and because of this, the whole town is in an uproar.
But according to what they say, they'll do what Ambrosio
and all the other shepherds want, and tomorrow they'll
bury him with great ceremony where I said. And it's my
opinion that it'll be something really worth seeing; at least
I'll make sure to go see it, if I don't have to return to my
village tomorrow."

"We'll all do the same," responded the goatherds, "and
we'll draw straws to see who will stay to watch over everyone's goats."

"Well spoken, Pedro," said one, "but it won't be necessary to resort to that because I'll stay. And don't attribute
it to righteousness or lack of interest on my part, but rather
to the fact that I can't go because of a thorn that pierced my
foot the other day."

"We thank you all the same," responded Pedro.

And don Quixote begged Pedro to tell him more about
the dead man and the shepherdess. Pedro responded that
what he knew was that the dead man was a rich *hidalgo*
who lived in a village in those same mountains. He'd been
a student for many years at Salamanca* and had then returned to his village, and people thought he was very wise
and learned. "Mainly, they said he knew the science of the
stars and what goes on in the heavens with the sun and the
moon, because he told us exactly when clipses of the sun
and moon would take place."

"It's called *eclipse*, my friend, and not *clipse*, when those
two great luminaries grow dark," said don Quixote.

But Pedro, not fretting over trifles, continued his story,
saying: "He also foretold whether the year would be fruit-
ful or virile."

---

* Salamanca was Spain's premier university, with about seven thousand students. It ranked with Paris, Oxford, and Bologna.

"*Sterile* is what you mean to say, not *virile*, my friend," said don Quixote.

"*Sterile* or *virile*, it's all the same. And I can tell you that in this way, his father and friends who believed him became very rich because they did what he advised them to do when he said: 'This year sow barley and not wheat; this year you can sow chickpeas but not barley; next year will be a good harvest of olive oil and the three following years there won't be a drop.'"

"That science is called astrology," said don Quixote.

"I don't know what it's called," replied Pedro, "but I do know that he knew all this and more. Finally, not many months after he came home from Salamanca, one day he showed up dressed like a shepherd, with a crook and sheepskin jacket replacing his long student's robe. Along with him, another great friend of his named Ambrosio, who had been a fellow student, also dressed up as a shepherd. I forgot to say that Grisóstomo, the dead man, had quite a hand at making up verses. He was so good that he even wrote the carols for Christmas Eve and little plays for Corpus Christi, which the boys of our town put on and which everybody said were really good. When the townspeople saw the two scholars suddenly changed into shepherds, they were astonished, and they couldn't guess what had moved them to make that odd change. By this time Grisóstomo's father had died and he'd inherited great wealth in goods as well as property, and not a few head of cattle, large and small,* and a lot of money; and the young man became the absolute owner of all this, and in truth he deserved it— he was a good *compañero*, a charitable fellow, a friend of the good people, and his face was like a blessing. Afterward, we learned that his change of clothing was for no other reason than to wander in the wilderness to be near the shepherdess Marcela, whom that young fellow mentioned earlier, and whom poor Grisóstomo had fallen in love with. And I want to tell you now, because it's important for you to know, who this young girl is. Perhaps, and even without 'perhaps,' you won't have heard anything like it in all the days of your life, even though you live longer than *sarna*."†

---

* Cows and sheep.

† *Sarna* in Spanish means the "itch."

"You mean 'Sarah,'"* replied don Quixote, not being able to stand the goatherd's confusion of words.

"*Sarna* lives long enough," responded Pedro, "and, *señor*, if you're going to try to fix all my words, we won't finish in a year."

"Forgive me, my friend," said don Quixote. "It's only because there's so much difference between *sarna* and Sarah that I mentioned it to you. But you responded very well, because the itch does live longer than Sarah. So, go on with your story, and I won't correct anything else."

"I say, then, *señor mío* of my soul," said the goatherd, "that in our village there was a peasant even richer than Grisóstomo's father named Guillermo, to whom God gave—aside from his great wealth—a daughter whose mother died in childbirth, and she was the most respected woman in these parts. I can just see her now, with that face that had the sun on one side and the moon on the other. She was hardworking and charitable with the poor, and that's why I think that her soul must be enjoying God at this very moment in the other world. Out of grief over the death of such a good wife, her husband, Guillermo, died, leaving his daughter, Marcela, young and rich, in the care of an uncle of hers, a priest in our village. The girl grew into such a beauty that she reminded us of her mother, who was very beautiful, and it was thought that her own beauty would surpass that of her mother.

"And so, when she got to the age of fourteen or fifteen, no one could look at her who didn't praise God, who had made her so beautiful, and most men fell hopelessly in love with her. Her uncle secluded her, but even so, the fame of her great beauty spread so that young men not only from our own village, but also the best men for leagues around, begged, entreated, and importuned her uncle to give her to them as their bride. But he, as should be the case, is a good Christian, and although he wanted to marry her off as soon as he saw she was of age, he wouldn't do it without her consent, without regard for the income that he'd get as long as she didn't marry. And I must say that even the gossipers in our village said this in praise of the priest. I want you to know, *señor* errant, that in these little villages everything

---

* Abraham's wife, Sarah, lived to be 110 years old.

is discussed and everything is gossiped about. And rest assured, as I do, that a priest has to be exceptionally good for his parishioners to say good things about him, especially in villages."

"That's the truth," said don Quixote. "Now go on with your story, because it's very good, and, Pedro, you're telling it with such grace."

"May the grace of our Lord not fail me, since that's the most important thing. And getting back to the story, although the uncle presented each suitor to his niece and told her of the qualities of every one who asked to marry her, begging her to marry and to choose as she pleased, she responded only by saying that she didn't want to get married right then and that, since she was still so young, she didn't feel able to take on the responsibility of being married. With these seemingly proper excuses, her uncle stopped pestering her, and waited for her to get older and choose a husband who would please her. He said—and he was right, too—that parents shouldn't marry off their children against their wishes. But here's the thing—when I least expected it, that persnickety Marcela showed up one day dressed as a shepherdess; and even though her uncle and the rest of the townspeople advised against it, she went into the countryside with the rest of the girls of the village and took to tending her own flock of sheep. And as soon as she came out into the open and everybody could see how beautiful she was, I can't begin to tell you how many rich young men—*hidalgos* and peasants—have taken up the same costume as Grisóstomo, and roam about these fields trying to court her. One of them, as has been said, was our deceased friend, about whom they say that he didn't just love her—he worshiped her.

"And don't think that just because Marcela took on that free and independent lifestyle with so little privacy—or rather no privacy at all—that she's given the slightest indication of anything that would discredit her chastity or virtue. She rather is so vigilant in the way she looks after her honor that of all those who court her, none has been able to boast, nor in truth will be able to boast, that she's ever given the least hope of fulfilling his desire. She doesn't flee from or disdain the company and conversation of the shepherds, and she treats them courteously and in a friendly way, but when any of them reveals his intention, even though it's the pure and holy one of matrimony, she rejects him as if he were shot from a catapult. With this behavior of hers, she does more damage in this country than the plague, because her graciousness and beauty attract the hearts of those who come into contact with her to serve and love her, but her scorn and reproofs drive them to despair, and so they're baffled about what to say to her except to call her cruel and ungrateful to her face, and other similar things that attest to her character. And if you stayed here, *señor*, one day you'd hear these mountains and valleys resound with the lamentations of these rejected suitors.

"Not far from here is a place where there are about two dozen beech trees, and every one of them has Marcela's name carved into its bark, and over the name you'll sometimes see a crown, as if her would-be lover is saying that Marcela wears the deserved crown of human beauty. Over here a shepherd might sing, over there another complains, way over there you hear love songs, and back over here, despairing dirges. One fellow spends the night at the foot of an oak tree or a boulder and stays there without ever closing his tearful eyes, bemused and carried away by his thoughts until he's found by the rays of morning sun. Another one, stretched out on the burning sand and continually sighing during the hottest part of the most vexatious midafternoon heat of summer, sends his appeal to the most merciful heavens. And Marcela conquers freely and without embarrassment this one and that one, and these and those; and all who know her are wondering how far her haughtiness can go and who will finally succeed in taming such a terrible nature and enjoying such an incredible beauty. Since everything I've said is such a proven truth, I can well believe that what our young friend has just told us of the cause of Grisóstomo's death is also true. And so I advise you, *señor*, to make sure you come tomorrow to his burial, which will be something to see, because Grisóstomo has a lot of friends, and it's not half a league from this place to where he's to be buried."

"I'll make a point of it," said don Quixote, "and I thank you for the pleasure you've given me in the narration of such a delightful story."

"Oh," replied the goatherd, "I don't know even half of

the things that have happened to the lovers of Marcela; it could be that tomorrow we'll come across some shepherd who could fill you in, but for now it'd be good for you to sleep inside, because the night air could make your wound worse, although the medicine they put on it is so good that you don't need to fear any infection."

Sancho Panza, who by this time was cursing the long-windedness of the goatherd, begged his master to find a place to sleep in Pedro's hut. That's what he did, but he spent all or most of the night thinking about his lady Dulcinea, in imitation of Marcela's lovers. Sancho Panza made himself as comfortable as he could between Rocinante and his donkey, and he slept—not like an injured lover, but rather like a man half beaten to death.

Chapter XIII. In which the end of the story of the shepherdess Marcela is revealed, along with other occurrences.

THE FIRST rays of dawn could just be seen along the balconies of the east when five of the six goatherds got up and went to waken don Quixote, and to tell him that if he still felt like going to see the anticipated burial of Grisóstomo, they would accompany him. Don Quixote, who wanted nothing else, got up and told Sancho to saddle the horse and donkey right away, which he did very quickly, and with that same speed they got on the road. They hadn't gone a quarter of a league when, at a place where two paths crossed, they saw as many as six shepherds coming toward them dressed in black jackets and with garlands of cypress and oleander on their heads. Each one had a sturdy staff made of holly. Two men on horseback, well equipped for travel, came along with them, with another three servants accompanying them on foot. When they met, they all greeted each other courteously, and, asking which way each party was going, they found out that they were all headed toward the funeral, and so they began to ride together.

One of those on horseback said: "It seems to me, *señor* Vivaldo, that we should consider any delay well spent to see this celebrated burial, which can't help but be remarkable, if the bizarre things these shepherds have told us are true about the dead shepherd as well as the murderous shepherdess."

"That's the way it seems to me," responded Vivaldo, "and I'd delay not just one day, but four, to witness it."

Don Quixote asked them what they'd heard about Marcela and Grisóstomo. The traveler said that early that morning they'd met those shepherds and, seeing them in such sad garb, they'd asked them why they were dressed that way. One of them explained about the odd behavior and beauty of a shepherdess named Marcela, and about how many men loved and courted her, together with the death of that fellow Grisóstomo, whose funeral they were going to witness. In short, he told them everything that don Quixote had learned from Pedro.

The man who was called Vivaldo changed the subject and asked don Quixote what had caused him to travel about in armor through such a peaceful countryside.

To this don Quixote responded: "The calling that I practice neither allows nor permits me to go about any other way. A life of ease, pleasure, and repose was invented for insipid courtly knights. But toil, anxiety, and arms were invented and made for those the world calls knights-errant, of whom I, although unworthy, am the least."

When they heard this, everyone took him to be crazy. But to delve further and find out exactly what kind of madness don Quixote suffered from, Vivaldo asked him what he meant by "knights-errant."

"Haven't your graces read," responded don Quixote, "in the annals and histories of England where it deals with the famous deeds of King Arthur, whom we always call 'Rey Artús' in Spanish, about whom there's an ancient and well-known tradition in the whole kingdom of Great Britain that this king didn't die, but rather, through the art of enchantment, changed into a raven and that, with the passage of time, he'll come back to rule and will recover his kingdom and scepter? That's the reason it cannot be proven that any Englishman from that day until this has ever killed a raven. So, during the times of that good king, the celebrated order of chivalry known as the Knights of the Round Table, and the love between Lancelot of the Lake and Queen Guinevere, came about exactly as written, and their go-between,

who was also the queen's confidante, was that honored lady
Quintañona,* from whom derived that well-known ballad
that's so prized in our Spain:

Oh, never surely was there a knight
    So served by hand of dame,
    As served was he, Sir Lancelot
    When from Britain he came

and it continues by telling in a sweet and graceful way of
his deeds in love and battle. Since then the order of chivalry has expanded and been handed down, extending and
spreading itself to different parts of the world. And through
this order the famous acts of Amadís de Gaula were made
known, with all his children, grandchildren, up to the fifth
generation; and of the brave Felixmarte de Hyrcania; and
of the never sufficiently praised Tirante el Blanco; and in
our days, why, it's as if we've actually seen, talked with, and
listened to the invincible and brave knight don Belianís de
Grecia. This is, *señores*, what it is to be a knight-errant, and
what I've described is the order of knighthood that I, as I've
said, although I'm a sinner, have made my profession. The
same things that these knights of old that I've mentioned
professed, I also profess. Thus, I travel about this wilderness and these unpopulated areas seeking adventures, and
I'm committed to offering my arm and my person in any
perilous adventure that comes my way to help the weak
and needy."

From what he said, the travelers figured out that don
Quixote was indeed crazy, and they saw the kind of madness that he had. They were as amazed as everyone else
was who came into contact with him for the first time. As
they were approaching the foot of the mountain where the
burial was to take place, Vivaldo, who was a very witty and
clever person, and of a merry disposition, wanted to give
don Quixote a chance to go further with his nonsense, to
relieve the tedium of the remaining distance that they had
to travel, so he said: "It seems to me, *señor*, that your grace
has undertaken one of the most austere professions in the

---

* Quintañona does not appear in the English Arthurian legend, but
rather is exclusive to the Spanish versions.

whole world, and I tend to think that even the Carthusian monks don't have a more rigorous one."*

"It might be as austere," responded don Quixote, "but as to the Carthusian order being as necessary in the world, I'm very close to doubting, because, if the truth be known, the soldier who carries out what the captain orders does no less than the captain who gives the orders. What I mean is that the people of the Church, in all peacefulness and tranquillity, ask heaven for goodness on earth. But we soldiers and knights put into action what they ask for, defending the world through the strength of our arms and the edges of our swords, not under a roof, but rather out in the open, and targeted by unbearable rays of the sun in the summer and the rigorous freezing of winter. We are thus God's ministers on earth, and we're the arms by which heaven's justice is administered. But since war and things pertaining to it can't be carried out without sweat, travail, and labor, it follows that those who engage in it have, without a doubt, a greater task than those who in calm peacefulness and repose beg God to favor those who can't defend themselves. I don't mean, or even think for a moment, that a knight-errant is somehow better than a cloistered monk. I only want to infer from what I undergo that knights doubtless work harder, get more beaten up, suffer more hunger and thirst, and are more miserable, ragged, and covered with lice. And there's no doubt that the knights-errant of old endured much misfortune in the course of their lives. And if some of them rose to be emperors through the strength of their arm, it cost them a good deal of blood and sweat; and if those who rose to such a level lacked enchanters and wizards to help them, they would have been deprived of their desires and quite deceived in their hopes."

"I agree completely," replied the traveler, "but one thing, among many others, to which I take exception regarding knights-errant is this—when they find themselves on the brink of a great and dangerous adventure in which it's clear

---

* In the Carthusian monasteries, monks live in cells and devote their time to prayer, study, and agriculture. They never speak to one another. Paintings in the Carthusian monastery of Granada show the monks with cleavers, among other things, embedded in their heads as they toil, doubtless an exaggeration.

that they may lose their lives, as they begin their attack, it never occurs to them to commend themselves to God, as every Christian should do when at such risk. Instead, they commend themselves to their ladies with as much longing and devotion as if these ladies were their god, something that seems to me to smack of paganism."

"*Señor*," responded don Quixote, "that cannot be otherwise, and the knight-errant who did anything else would fare ill. It's the custom in knight-errantry for the knight about to undertake a great feat of arms, if his lady is present, to turn his eyes softly and lovingly toward her, as if his eyes were pleading for her favor and protection in the perilous battle he's about to undertake. And even if she's not there to hear him, he's obliged to say a few words under his breath in which he commends himself to her with all his heart. We have an infinite number of examples of this in the histories. But this doesn't mean that they fail to commend themselves to God as well, since there's ample time and opportunity to do so as the adventure develops."

"Even so," replied the traveler, "I do have a qualm, and it's this: Many times I've read that an argument arises between two knights-errant, and from one word to the next their anger grows and they wheel their horses around, face each other, and then without further ado, they rush toward each other at full tilt, and in the middle of their course they commend themselves to their ladies. And what typically happens is that one of them tumbles over the back of his horse, having been run through by his opponent's lance, and the other, too, if he hadn't held on to the horse's mane, couldn't have avoided crashing to the ground. I just don't see how the dead man had time to commend himself to God in the course of this hurried battle. It would be better if the words he spoke during the run commending himself to his lady were used instead to discharge his duties and obligations as a Christian, especially since, at least in my opinion, not every knight-errant has a lady to whom he can commend himself, because not everyone is in love."

"That's impossible," responded don Quixote. "I say it's impossible for there to be a knight-errant without a lady, because it's as proper and natural for them to be in love as it is for the sky to have stars. And it's certain that a history has not been found where there's a knight who's not in love, for the simple reason that if he were without a love he wouldn't be considered legitimate, but rather counterfeit, one who entered the fortress of chivalry not through the front door, but over the walls, like a robber and a thief."

"Nevertheless," said the traveler, "it seems to me, if I remember right, I read that don Galaor, the brother of the brave Amadís de Gaula, never had a particular lady to whom he could commend himself, and he certainly wasn't esteemed any less, because he was a brave and famous knight."

To which our don Quixote responded: "'One swallow doesn't make a summer,' especially since I know that he was secretly very much in love; aside from that, his propensity for falling in love with all who seemed attractive to him was a natural tendency he couldn't control. But, in short, it's certain that there was one special lady whom he made the mistress of his heart, to whom he commended himself very frequently and very much in secret, because he prided himself on being a discreet knight."

"So, if it's essential for every knight-errant to be in love," said the traveler, "it can be assumed that your grace also is, since you belong to that order. And if you don't take pride in being as secretive as don Galaor, as earnestly as I can, I beg you, on behalf of all these people and myself, to tell us the name, birthplace, rank, and beauty of your lady, because she'll consider herself fortunate for everyone to know that she's loved and served by such a knight as you appear to be."

Don Quixote heaved an enormous sigh at this point and said: "I can't affirm whether my sweet enemy is pleased or not for everyone to know I serve her. I can only say, to answer what has so politely been asked, that her name is Dulcinea; her place of birth, El Toboso, a village in La Mancha; her rank must be at least that of princess, since she's my queen and mistress; her beauty superhuman, since in her are made real all the impossible and chimerical attributes of beauty that poets give to their ladies: Her hair is gold, her forehead is the Elysian Fields, her eyebrows rainbows, her eyes suns, her cheeks roses, her lips coral, pearls her teeth, alabaster her neck, marble her bosom, ivory her hands, her whiteness snow, and the parts that decency has hidden from human view are such, according to what I think and understand, as only circumspect contemplation can extol but not compare."

"We would like to know about her lineage, ancestry, and family," replied Vivaldo.

To which don Quixote responded: "She's not of the Curtii, Caii, or Scipiones of Ancient Rome; nor of the modern Colonas or Ursinos; nor of the Moncadas or Requesenes of Catalonia; and certainly not the Rebellas or Villanovas of Valencia; nor Palafoxes, Nuzas, Rocabertis, Corellas, Lunas, Alagones, Urreas, Foces or Gurreas of Aragón; nor Cerdas, Manriques, Mendozas, or Guzmanes of Castile; nor Alencastros, Pallas, or Meneses of Portugal; but rather of those from El Toboso de La Mancha, a lineage that, although modern, can give a generous beginning to the most illustrious families for centuries to come. And let no one contradict me in this, except on the conditions that Cervino put at the bottom of the trophy of Orlando's armor, which said: 'Let no one move them who doesn't want to battle with Roland.' "*

"Although my lineage is of the Cachopines de Laredo,"† responded the traveler, "I wouldn't dare compare it with El Toboso de La Mancha, although, to tell the truth, I've never heard that name before."

"What do you mean you've *never heard it before*!?" retorted don Quixote.

Everyone listened attentively to the conversation of the two of them, and even the shepherds and goatherds themselves perceived our don Quixote's delusion. Only Sancho Panza thought that everything his master said was true, knowing who he was, and having known him since his own birth. What he had lingering doubts about was that business about the fair Dulcinea del Toboso, because neither that name nor anything about that princess had ever come to his attention, even though he lived so close to El Toboso.

They were still conversing when they saw about twenty shepherds coming through a mountain pass, all dressed in black woolen jackets and crowned with garlands of, as it

---

* From canto twenty-four of *Orlando Furioso*. Cervino found Orlando's armor and hung it from a tree with that inscription.

† Laredo is a seaside town near Santander in northern Spain.

later appeared, yew and cypress. Six of them carried a litter covered with many different flowers and bouquets.

When one of the goatherds saw this, he said: "Those people coming from over yonder are bringing Grisóstomo's body, and at the foot of that mountain is the place where he asked to be buried."

Accordingly, they hurried to get there, and arrived soon after the shepherds had laid the litter on the ground. Four of them with sharp pickaxes were digging the grave near a boulder. They all greeted each other courteously, and then don Quixote and those with him went to look at the litter, and on it they saw a dead body covered with flowers. He was dressed as a shepherd and appeared to be thirty years old. And although he was dead, his body showed that when he was alive he'd been quite handsome, with a gallant appearance. Some books and many papers were strewn all around him on the litter.

All the onlookers, as well as those who were digging the grave and everyone else, were keeping perfectly quiet, until one of the litter bearers said to another: "Ambrosio, make sure that this is the place that Grisóstomo specified, since you want to comply strictly with the provisions of his will."

"This is the place," responded Ambrosio, "where he told me the story of his misfortunes many times. He told me that this is where he saw the mortal enemy of the human race for the first time, and here is also where he declared his intentions, as pure as they were filled with love. And this is where Marcela finally rebuked and disdained him, which ended the tragedy of his wretched life. And here, in testimony of so much misfortune, is where he wanted us to bury him, in the depths of eternal oblivion."

And turning toward don Quixote and the other travelers, he went on, saying: "*Señores*, this body you're looking at with pious eyes was the repository of a soul in which heaven put an infinite share of its bounty. This is the body of Grisóstomo, who was unequaled in wit, stood alone in courtesy, extreme in refinement, a phœnix in friendship, generous without measure, grave without being vain, jovial without vulgarity, and second to none in misfortune. He loved with devotion and was hated in return; he adored and was disdained. He courted a beast, he implored a block of marble, he chased the wind, he shouted to deaf ears, he served ingratitude, and as a reward all he got was the spoils of death in the prime of life, murdered by a shepherdess whom he tried to immortalize so that she would live on in the memory of all people. These papers that you see could well prove it, if he hadn't told me to commit them to the flames once we placed his body in the ground."

"You would deal with them more harshly and cruelly," said Vivaldo, "than their owner himself, since it's not right to comply with the will of someone who goes contrary to all that's reasonable in what he orders. Cæsar Augustus wouldn't have acted within reason if he'd consented to do what the Divine Mantuan had ordered in his will.* So, *señor* Ambrosio, you're consigning his body to the earth, but please don't consign his writings to oblivion. If he ordered it as a person aggrieved, don't comply with it in a moment of folly. Rather, give life to these papers so that Marcela's cruelty will serve as an example to future generations of the living, so that they'll know to flee from such dangerous undertakings. I, and the rest of us who have come here, know the tale of your loving and despairing friend, and we know of your friendship and the cause of his death and what he asked to be done after his death. And from that lamentable history we can gather the extent of Marcela's cruelty, Grisóstomo's love, your faithful friendship, and the end that's in store for those who ride recklessly along the path of unrestrained love. Last night we learned of Grisóstomo's death and that he'd be buried in this place, and out of curiosity and compassion, we detoured from our planned itinerary and decided to see with our eyes what had aroused our pity when we heard it. In recompense for our compassion and the desire we had to relieve yours, we beg you, discreet Ambrosio, at least *I* beg you on my own, not to burn these papers, and let me take some of them."

And without waiting for the shepherd to respond, he reached out and took some of the papers that were closest by. When Ambrosio saw this he said: "Out of courtesy, I'll

---

* When Virgil, born near Mantua, died, he willed that his *Æneid* be burned because it wasn't yet fully revised, but this was countermanded in the way that Vivaldo has stated.

let you keep what you've taken, but it's futile to think that I won't burn the rest, *señor*."

Vivaldo wanted to see what the papers said, so he opened one of them right away and saw that it was titled "Song of Despair." When Ambrosio heard the title he said: "That's the last thing that the unfortunate fellow wrote, and so that you can see the extent to which his misfortunes had brought him, read it so that you can be heard. You'll have time while the grave is being dug."

"I'll do it with pleasure," said Vivaldo.

And since everyone present had the same wish, they gathered around him, and reading in a clear voice, he saw that it said:

Chapter XIIII. Wherein the dead shepherd's verses of despair are set down, with other unexpected incidents.

Grisóstomo's Song*

Since thou dost in thy cruelty desire
   The ruthless rigor of thy tyranny
   From tongue to tongue, from land to land
      proclaimed,
   The very hell will I constrain to lend
   This stricken breast of mine deep notes of woe
   To serve my need of fitting utterance.
   And as I strive to shape the tale
   Of all I suffer, all that thou hast done,
   Forth shall the dread voice roll, and bear along
   Shreds from my vitals torn for greater pain.
   Then listen, not to sweet harmony,
   But to a discord wrung by mad despair
   Out of my bosom's depths of bitterness,
   To ease my heart and plant a sting in thine.

---

* I've again used Ormsby's version. In Spanish, this poem is written in eleven-syllable lines, but Ormsby uses only ten (in some verses I've replaced some archaic words, so lines will vary in length). The themes of the poem—the severity of the woman and the pain of the lover—are quite clear in the first stanza.

The lion's roar, the fierce wolf's savage howl,
    The horrid hissing of the scaly snake,
    The awesome cries of monsters yet unnamed,
    The crow's ill-boding croak, the hollow moan
    Of wild winds wrestling with the restless sea,
    The wrathful bellow of the vanquished bull,
    The plaintive sobbing of the turtledove,*
    The envied owl's† sad note, the wail of woe
    That rises from the dreary choir of hell,
    Commingled in one sound, confusing sense,
    Let all these come to aid my soul's complaint,
    For pain like mine demands new modes of song.
No echoes of that discord shall be heard
    Where Father Tajo‡ rolls, or on the banks
    Of olive-bordered Bætis;§ to the rocks
    Or in deep caverns shall my plaint be told,
    And by a lifeless tongue in living words;
    Or in dark valleys or on lonely shores,
    Where neither foot of man nor sunbeam falls;
    Or in among the poison-breathing swarms
    Of monsters nourished by the sluggish Nile.
    For, though it be to solitude remote
    The hoarse vague echoes of my sorrows sound
    Thy matchless cruelty, my dismal fate
    Shall carry them to all the spacious world.
Disdain hath power to kill, and patience dies
    Slain by suspicion, be it false or true;
    And deadly is the force of jealousy;
    Long absence makes of life a dreary void;
    No hope of happiness can give repose
    To him that ever fears to be forgot;
    And death, inevitable, waits in hell.

---

* The 1609 Spanish dictionary by Covarrubias says that the turtledove is the symbol of a widow who never remarries and keeps chaste.

† Ormsby's note: "The owl was the only bird that witnessed the Crucifixion and it became for that reason an object of envy to the other birds, so much so that it cannot appear in the daytime without being persecuted." There are other interpretations as well.

‡ This is the river that flows through Toledo on its way to the ocean at Lisbon.

§ Bætis is the Latin name for the Guadalquivir River, which flows through Seville and into the Atlantic Ocean.

But I, by some strange miracle, live on
A prey to absence, jealousy, disdain;
Racked by suspicion as by certainty;
Forgotten, left to feed my flame alone.
And while I suffer thus, there comes no ray
Of hope to gladden me athwart the gloom;
Nor do I look for it in my despair;
But rather clinging to a cureless woe,
All hope do I abjure forevermore.
Can there be hope where fear is? Were it well,
When far more certain are the grounds of fear?
Ought I to shut my eyes to jealousy,
If through a thousand heart-wounds it appears?
Who would not give free access to distrust,
Seeing disdain unveiled, and—bitter change!—
All his suspicions turned to certainties,
And the fair truth transformed into a lie?
Oh, thou fierce tyrant of the realms of love,
Oh, Jealousy! Put chains upon these hands,
And bind me with thy strongest cord, Disdain.
But, woe is me! Triumphant over all,
My sufferings drown the memory of you.
And now I die, and since there is no hope
Of happiness for me in life or death,
Still to my fantasy I'll fondly cling.
I'll say that he is wise who loveth well,
And that the soul most free is that most bound
In bondage to the ancient tyrant Love.
I'll say that she who is mine enemy
In that fair body hath as fair a mind,
And that her coldness is but my desert,
And that by virtue of the pain he sends
Love rules his kingdom with a gentle sway.
Thus, self-deluding, and in bondage sore,
And wearing out the wretched shred of life
To which I am reduced by her disdain,
I'll give this soul and body to the winds,
All hopeless of a crown of bliss in store.
Thou whose injustice hath supplied the cause
That makes me quit the weary life I loathe,
As by this wounded bosom thou canst see
How willingly thy victim I become,

Let not my death, if haply worth a tear,
Cloud the clear heaven that dwells in thy bright eyes;
I would not expect thee to atone
The crime of having made my heart thy prey;
But rather let thy laughter gaily ring
And prove my death to be thy festival.
Fool that I am to bid thee! Well I know
Thy glory gains by my untimely end.
And now it is the time; from hell's abyss
Come thirsting Tantalus, come Sisyphus
Heaving the cruel stone, come Tityus
With vulture, and with wheel Ixion* come,
And come the sisters of the ceaseless toil;†
And all into this breast transfer their pains,
And (if such tribute to despair be due)
Chant in their deepest tones a doleful dirge
Over a corpse unworthy of a shroud.
Let the three-headed guardian of the gate‡
And all the monstrous progeny of hell
The doleful concert join: a lover dead.
I think I can have no fitter obsequies.
Song of despair, grieve not when thou art gone
Forth from this sorrowing heart: my misery
Brings fortune to the cause that gave thee birth;
Then banish sadness even in the tomb.

---

* Tantalus was the mythological king of Sipylus, consigned to eternal torture. He stands in a lake with water to his chin, but he can't drink because when he tries, the water recedes. There's also fruit just out of reach. Sisyphus was the mythological king of Corinth whose punishment was to forever roll a large stone up a hill. It rolls down again before reaching the top. Tityus was killed by Zeus or Apollo and was sent to Tartarus, where his regenerating liver was eaten daily by vultures. Ixion, mythological king of Thessaly, was the first murderer. Zeus struck him with thunder and tied him to a perpetually rotating wheel in Hades, surrounded by snakes.

† Refers to the fifty Danaids, all sisters, who married sons of the same father (Egyptus). The new husbands murdered their wives on their wedding night and their punishment was to eternally fill leaking vessels with water.

‡ Cerberus, the watchdog of Hades. In addition to his three heads, he had a dragon's tail and snakes springing from his neck. He ate people who tried to escape.

Those who heard Grisóstomo's song thought it was good, although the one who read it said that it didn't quite agree with what he'd heard of Marcela's modesty and goodness, because in it he complained of jealousy, suspicion, and absence, all to the detriment of Marcela's reputation and good name. Ambrosio responded, since he knew the most hidden thoughts of his friend: "So that you'll be freed from these doubts, *señor*, I want you to know that when this unfortunate fellow wrote this song he was away from Marcela—he'd absented himself from her of his own free will, to see what effect this absence would have on him. And since there's nothing that doesn't trouble the absent lover, and no fear that doesn't haunt him, this imagined jealousy and these feared suspicions tortured him as if they were real. So, the truth that fame proclaims about the goodness of Marcela isn't diminished, and with her, envy shouldn't, indeed cannot, find any fault, although she's cruel and a bit arrogant, and very disdainful."

"That's true," responded Vivaldo. And just when he was at the point of reading from another paper that he'd kept from the flames, he was prevented from it by a wondrous vision that suddenly appeared before their eyes, because that's what she appeared to be: There was Marcela herself at the top of the boulder where the grave was being dug. She was so beautiful that her beauty exceeded her fame. Those who until then hadn't seen her gazed at her speechless and with wonder, and those who were accustomed to seeing her were no less amazed than those who had never seen her before.

But as soon as Ambrosio saw her, he said with obvious indignation: "Have you come, you fierce basilisk* of these mountains, to see if blood will start to flow from the wounds of this wretch slain by your cruelty?† Or have you come to boast of your cruel deeds, or to survey from those rocky heights, like another Nero, the flames of your burning Rome,‡ or to trample this ill-fated body, like Tarquinius' ungrateful

---

* The basilisk was a mythological creature, sort of a poisonous dragon, that could kill with its looks alone.

† There was a belief that the body of a murder victim would bleed from its wounds in the presence of the murderer.

‡ Supposedly Nero (37–68) watched Rome burn from the Tarpeian Rock.

daughter did?* Tell us quickly what you've come for, or what your pleasure is. Since I know that in his thoughts Grisóstomo never failed to obey you while he was living, even now that he's dead, I'll make everyone who called themselves his friends obey you."

"I haven't come, Ambrosio, for any of the reasons that you've listed," responded Marcela, "but rather to defend myself and to make you understand how unreasonable are those who, out of their grief, blame me for Grisóstomo's death. And I beg all those present to listen to me. It won't take much time or many words to persuade sensible people of the truth.

"Heaven made me beautiful—according to you—so that, in spite of yourselves, my beauty moves you to love me. And you insist that I, in return, am bound to love you back. With the natural understanding that God has given me, I recognize that what is beautiful is worthy of love. But what I don't understand is that just because a woman is loved because of her beauty, she's obliged to reciprocate this love. And furthermore, it could happen that the one who loves the beautiful woman is himself ugly, and since ugliness is worthy of being despised, it would be silly for him to say: 'I love you because you're beautiful; now you must love me, even though I'm ugly.' But supposing each one is equally good-looking, it doesn't necessarily mean that their yearnings will be the same, because not every kind of beauty inspires love—some are pleasing to the eye but don't overcome the will. If every type of beauty caused love and overcame the will in the same way, everyone's will would wander about confused and perplexed, not knowing which way to go, because—since there's an infinite array of beautiful things—yearnings would be equally infinite. And according to what I've heard, true love cannot be divided, and must be voluntary and not forced. If that's true, as I believe it is, why do you want to force me to yield my free will simply because you say that you love me? Tell me—what if heaven, which made me beautiful, had made me ugly instead? Would it have been right for me to complain

---

* Tarquinius Superbus was the last king of Rome, a horrible despot, from 534–510 B.C. Tarquinius' wife, Tullia (according to the legend), ran over the cadaver of her father, Servius Tullius, with a carriage.

because you didn't love me? What's more, consider this: I didn't choose to be beautiful—heaven made me that way without my asking or choosing to be. So, just as a snake doesn't deserve to be blamed for the venom given to it by nature—even though it uses the venom to kill—I don't deserve to be blamed for being beautiful. Beauty in a virtuous woman is like a distant flame or a sharp sword—the one won't burn and the other won't cut anyone who doesn't draw near. Honor and virtue are adornments of the soul, but without them the body shouldn't seem beautiful, even though it may appear to be. So, if purity is one of the virtues that must adorn both body and soul to make them beautiful, why should the woman who's loved for her beauty sacrifice her purity by yielding to the wishes of the man who, for his selfish pleasure only, seeks with all his might and wiles to cause her to lose it?

"I was born free, and in order to live free, I chose the solitude of the outdoors. The trees of these mountains are my company; the clear water of these streams are my mirrors. I communicate my thoughts and share my beauty with the trees and water. I'm the distant fire and the sword placed far away. Those whom I've caused to fall in love with me by letting them see me, I've enlightened with my words. And if desires are kept alive by hope, since I never gave any such hope to Grisóstomo—or to any other man—you could say that his obstinacy killed him rather than my cruelty. And if I'm reproached because you say that his desires were honorable, and for that reason I was obliged to yield to him, I say that in this same place where his grave is being dug and he revealed the worthiness of his intentions to me, I told him that mine were to live in perpetual solitude, and that only the earth would enjoy the fruits of my chastity and the spoils of my beauty. And, if after having been set right, he hoped against hope, and tried to sail against the wind, it's no surprise that he drowned in the middle of the sea of his recklessness. If I'd encouraged him, I would have been false; if I'd gratified him, it would have been against my better instinct and judgment. He persisted though he was turned down; he despaired without being despised. Consider now whether I'm to blame for his grief! Let the man I deceived complain, let him despair whose promised hopes were not fulfilled, let him be filled with hope whom I beckon, let him brag whom I've welcomed. But let no one call me cruel and murderous to whom I've promised nothing, upon whom I've practiced no deception, whom I've neither beckoned nor welcomed.

"Heaven has not yet ordained that I should love by fate and it's vain to think that I shall love by choice. Let this general warning be given to each one of those who try to court me for his own advantage—let it be understood from now on that if anyone dies for me, it won't be because of jealousy or rejection, since she who loves no one cannot make anyone jealous. Discouragement must not be taken for disdain. Let the man who calls me a beast and a basilisk leave me alone as he would something harmful and bad; let the man who calls me ungrateful not serve me; let him who calls me unfeeling shun me; he who calls me cruel, let him not follow me—for this beast, this basilisk, this ingrate, this cruel and unfeeling woman will not seek, serve, know, or follow them in any way. If Grisóstomo was killed by his impatience and bold desire, why should you blame my virtuous behavior and modesty? If I preserve my purity in the company of trees, why should a man want me to lose it in the company of men? I, as you know, am independently wealthy, and I don't covet anyone else's fortune. I'm free and I take no pleasure in submitting to anyone. I neither love nor hate anyone. I don't deceive this one nor court that one. I don't dally with one nor play with another. Virtuous conversation with the country girls of these villages and the care of my goats entertain me. My desires are bounded by these mountains, and if they ever stray, it's only to contemplate the beauty of the heavens, the steps by which the soul is shown the way to its first dwelling place."

Having said this, without waiting to hear any response, she turned on her heels and went into the densest part of the forest nearby, leaving everyone there astonished, as much by her mental acuity as by her beauty. Some of those who were wounded by the mighty arrow from the rays of her eyes looked as if they wanted to follow her, without heeding the very clear admonition they'd heard.

When don Quixote saw this, it seemed to him that here was a good place to use his chivalry to rescue needy damsels, so he put his hand on the hilt of his sword and in a loud and clear voice said: "Let no one whatsoever dare to pursue the beautiful Marcela, under the penalty of incurring my furious wrath. She's shown with clear words and solid reasons that she has had little or no blame in the death of Grisóstomo, and how distant she is from yielding to the desires of any of her suitors. Far from being pursued, she should be honored and revered by all good people in the world, since she shows that she's the only person who lives by such virtuous intentions."

Either because of the threats of don Quixote or because Ambrosio told everyone to finish what their good friend had asked, none of the shepherds stirred or left the place until the grave was dug, the papers burned, and Grisóstomo's body was interred—not without many tears on the part of the onlookers. They closed the grave with a large stone until a formal tombstone could be made, which Ambrosio planned to have carved and would say:

BENEATH THIS STONE BEFORE YOUR EYES
THE BODY OF A LOVER LIES:
IN LIFE HE WAS A SHEPHERD LAD,
IN DEATH A VICTIM TO DISDAIN.
UNGRATEFUL, CRUEL, COY, AND FAIR
WAS SHE THAT DROVE HIM TO DESPAIR,
AND LOVE HATH MADE HER HIS ALLY
FOR SPREADING WIDE HIS TYRANNY.*

They then scattered flowers and boughs on the grave, conveyed their sympathy to his friend Ambrosio, and bade him farewell. Vivaldo and his companion did the same, and don Quixote took leave of his hosts and the travelers, who begged him to go with them to Seville—it being a wonderful place to find adventures, since on every street and around every corner one can find more than in any other place.

Don Quixote thanked them for the information and the good intentions they showed in offering him that favor, and he said that for the moment he didn't want to, nor should he

---

* This is Ormsby's version. In the third line he wrote "shepherd swain." "Swain" means "country boy."

go to Seville, until he'd cleared those mountains of bandits,
since it was well-known that there were plenty of them there.
Seeing his resolve, the travelers didn't want to pester him
further, but rather said good-bye once again, and they left
him and continued on their way, where they didn't lack for
things to talk about regarding both the story of
Marcela and Grisóstomo and the madness
of don Quixote. Don Quixote decided to
go look for Marcela and offer her all
that he could in her service. But
it didn't happen the way he
planned, as will be seen
in the course of this
true history, where
the Second
Part ends
here.

THIRD PART
OF THE INGENIOUS
Hidalgo Don Quixote
of La Mancha.

Chapter XV. Where the unfortunate adventure is related that happened to don Quixote when he came across some soulless Yangüesans.

T HE WISE Cide Hamete Benengeli recounts that as soon as don Quixote took leave of his hosts and everyone else at the burial of Grisóstomo, he and his squire went into the same forest where they had seen that Marcela had gone. And after they had traveled a bit more than two hours looking for her without being able to find her, they came upon a grassy green meadow surrounded by a cool and pleasant stream that invited, and even forced, them to spend the siesta hours, which were fast approaching.

Don Quixote and Sancho let the donkey and Rocinante graze freely on the abundant grass while they raided the saddlebags without ceremony, and in good peace and fellowship, master and servant ate what they found. Sancho didn't bother to hobble Rocinante, since he knew him to be meek, and so lacking in lust that all the mares in the pasture of Córdoba couldn't lead him astray. But fate, and the devil (who doesn't sleep all the time), arranged for a number of Galician mares to be grazing nearby. They belonged to some Galician* muleteers who usually spent their siesta with their teams in places where there was plenty of grass and water. And that particular place where don Quixote happened to be was ideal for the Galicians. It happened that Rocinante got into his head to have some recreation with the *señoras* mares, and departing from his usual demeanor and custom, as soon as he smelled them, and without his master's permission, he set off on a jaunty little trot to communicate his need with them. But they, the way it looked, seemed more interested in grazing than anything else, and received him with their horseshoes and teeth, so that in a short time, Rocinante's saddle was knocked off. But what he must have bemoaned even more was that the muleteers, seeing the outrage being done to their mares, came with stakes, and whacked him so many times that they made him fall to the ground, badly battered.

At this point, don Quixote and Sancho, who had seen the beating Rocinante was getting, came running, out of breath. Don Quixote said to Sancho: "What I see here, Sancho, my friend, is that these aren't knights, but rather lowlifes and rabble. I say this because you can help me to take proper vengeance on the affront done to Rocinante right in front of our very eyes."

"What the devil kind of vengeance are we going to take," responded Sancho, "if they're more than twenty and we're no more than two, or maybe only one and a half?"

"I'm worth a hundred," replied don Quixote. And without any further words, he seized his sword, and Sancho did the same, moved by the example of his master. At the first exchange, don Quixote slashed at one of them and ripped open his leather tunic together with a large portion of his shoulder. The Galicians, seeing themselves abused by those two men only, since they were so many, went for their stakes, and hemming the two of them in, they began to rain blows with great zeal and fury.

It's true that with the second blow they knocked Sancho to the ground, and the same thing happened to don Quixote, so their skill and courage were of no avail. Fortune

---

* The chapter title leads us to believe that these muleteers are from Yanguas, in the province of Soria, around two hundred miles from Galicia, where these muleteers hail from.

ordained that they should fall at the feet of Rocinante, who hadn't gotten up yet. From this you can gauge the pounding force of stakes wielded by hands of angry rustics.

When the Galicians saw the injuries they had done, they gathered their team as quickly as they could and went along their way, leaving the two adventurers a sad sight and in a sorrier mood. The first to recover was Sancho Panza. Finding himself next to his master, with a feeble and doleful voice he said: "*Señor* don Quixote! Ah, *señor* don Quixote!"

"What do you want, brother Sancho?" responded don Quixote with the same weak and pained tone of voice as Sancho.

"I'd like, if it's possible," responded Sancho Panza, "for your grace to give me two gulps of that Feo Blas'* brew, if you have some handy. Maybe it'll be as good for fractures as it is for wounds."

"If I had any here, unlucky fellow that I am, what more could we want?" responded don Quixote. "But I swear to you, Sancho Panza, on my word as a knight-errant, that before two days have gone by, if Fate doesn't ordain otherwise, I'll have made some, or I'll be very unlucky indeed."

"How many days does your grace think it'll be before we'll be able to budge?" replied Sancho Panza.

"For my part," said the beaten-up knight don Quixote, "I don't know how long it'll be. But I'm to blame for everything, since I shouldn't have raised my sword against anybody who hasn't been dubbed a knight. And I think as punishment for having transgressed the laws of chivalry, the god of battles has allowed me to be punished for it. So, Sancho Panza, let me tell you something, because it's important for the health of both of us, and that is that when you see such rabble trying to beat us up, don't wait for me to take up my sword against them, because I won't, but rather take your own sword and punish them to your heart's content. And if some knights-errant come to assist and defend them, I'll be able to defend you and attack them with all my might, and you've had a thousand proofs how far the might of my arm extends." Such was the arrogance the poor *señor* had after he conquered the brave Basque.

---

* Sancho's recollection for Fierabrás is this form, which means "Ugly Blas" (*Blas* being a man's name in Spanish).

But the proclamation of his master didn't seem so good to Sancho that he should fail to respond, saying: "*Señor*, I'm a peaceful man, meek and calm, and I can overlook any injury whatsoever, because I have a wife to support and children to raise. So, let me make this suggestion—since I can't give you a command—that in no way will I take up my sword, either against a peasant or a knight. And from now until I die, I forgive any offenses done to me, or have yet to be done to me, whether he who did, does, or will have done them is of the upper or lower classes, rich or poor, *hidalgo* or commoner, not excepting any rank or condition whatsoever."

When his master heard this, he responded: "I wish I had the breath to speak, and less pain in my ribs, so I could make you see, Panza, the error into which you've fallen. Look here, you sinner, if the winds of Fortune, until now so contrary, should blow in our favor, filling our sails of desire so that inexorably and without any opposition we could reach port in one of the *ínsulas* I've promised you, what would become of you if I won it and made you lord of it? Why, it'd all come to nothing, since you aren't a knight and you don't want to become one, nor do you have the courage or intention of avenging injuries or defending your dominion. You should know that in newly conquered kingdoms and provinces, the inhabitants are never as peaceable nor as well-disposed toward their new lord so that they might not be afraid to start an uprising to change things once again, and, as they say, 'try their luck.' Thus, the new possessor has to have the understanding to govern, and the courage to fight and defend himself in any situation."

"In what has just happened to us," replied Sancho, "I wish I'd had that understanding and courage you mention. But I swear to you, on the word of a poor man, that I'm more ready for bandages than for conversation. See if you can get up, and help me with Rocinante, though he doesn't deserve it since he was the main cause of this drubbing. I never considered Rocinante would do anything like that—I always thought him to be a chaste person and as peaceable as I am. Oh, well—they say 'you need a lot of time to come to know people,' and 'nothing is certain in this life.' Who would have said, after those great slashes that your grace gave that unfortunate knight-errant, that such a tempest of blows on our backs would follow so soon in its wake?"

"Your back," replied don Quixote, "should be used to such tempests. But mine, which is accustomed to soft cloth and fine linen, will clearly feel more pain from this misfortune. And if I didn't suspect—what do I mean suspect? I know for sure!—that these discomforts are closely aligned with the practice of arms, I'd die on the spot from pure vexation."

To which the squire responded: "*Señor*, since these misfortunes are the natural harvest of knighthood, tell me if they happen very frequently or if there are specific times when they happen, because it seems to me that with two such harvests we'll be useless for a third, if God in His infinite mercy doesn't come to help us."

"You know, Sancho, my friend," responded don Quixote, "that the life of knights-errant is subject to a thousand perils and reverses, and it's just as likely for knights-errant to become kings and emperors, as has been shown by experience through many diverse knights whose histories I know thoroughly. And I could tell you now, if this pain would abate, about some who, all alone, through the strength of their arm, have risen to the high positions that I've told you about. And these same men found themselves, both before and after, in great misfortunes and misery, because the great Amadís de Gaula fell into the power of his mortal enemy Arcaláus the enchanter, who—and it's an incontrovertible fact—gave him, tied to the column of a patio, holding him as a prisoner, more than two hundred lashes with the reins of a horse. And there's an anonymous author who can be believed, who says that when they caught the Knight of Phœbus through a certain trapdoor that crumbled under his weight in a certain castle, he found himself in a deep pit under the ground, tied hand and foot, and there they gave him an enema of water and sand that almost finished him off. And if he hadn't been saved from that great peril by a wizard who was a great friend of his, the poor knight would have had a bad time of it. So, I can well suffer among such good company, for they have undergone greater affronts than we've just now undergone.

"I want you to know, Sancho, that wounds that are given by instruments that just happen to be in one's hands don't constitute an affront. This is already in the laws of the duel, written with these express words: If a shoemaker hits another person with a last that he has in his hand, since, after all, it's just a piece of wood, the other person is not to be considered affronted. I say this so you won't think that we're affronted even though we've been beaten up, because the weapons those men had with which they pounded us were nothing else but stakes, and none of them had a rapier, sword, or dagger."

"They gave me no time," responded Sancho, "to see very much, because hardly had I grabbed my sword when they put the sign of the cross on my shoulders with their clubs, so that they took the sight from my eyes and the strength from my feet, throwing me on the ground where I'm lying right now, and I couldn't care less if the blows with the stakes were an affront or not, but I do care about the pain from the blows themselves, which will remain as imprinted on my memory as on my back."

"I'll have you know, brother Panza," replied don Quixote, "that there's no memory that time doesn't erase, nor pain that death doesn't consume."

"What greater misfortune can there be," replied Panza, "than one that waits for time to consume or death to end? If our disaster were of the kind that's healed with a couple of bandages, it wouldn't be so bad. But I'm beginning to think that all the plasters in a hospital won't be enough to fix them up."

"Enough of that, and take strength from weakness, Sancho," replied don Quixote. "That's what I'll do. Let's see how Rocinante is, because the way I look at it, the poor thing hasn't gotten the least of this misfortune."

"There's no surprise in that," responded Sancho, "since he's such a good knight-errant. But what surprises me is that my donkey managed to stay free and unhurt, whereas we've been left without ribs."*

"Fortune always leaves one door open in misfortunes to remedy them," said don Quixote. "I say that because that little creature can make up for the lack of Rocinante by carrying me from here to some castle where my wounds can be treated. And further, I won't consider such a mount to be a dishonor because I remember having read that the old man Silenus, governor and tutor to the happy god of

---

* The pun here is between *costas*—"expense"—and *costillas*—"ribs."

laughter, when he entered into the city of the hundred gates, he entered quite happily on the back of a beautiful donkey."*

"It may be true that he went mounted as your grace says," responded Sancho, "but there's a big difference between going mounted that way and slung across like a sack of garbage."

To which don Quixote responded, "Wounds received in battle confer honor rather than take it away. So, friend Panza, no more arguments; but, as I said, get up as well as you can, and put me on your donkey however it pleases you, and let's leave before nightfall overtakes us in this wilderness."

"But I've heard your grace say," said Panza, "that it is very common for knights-errant to sleep in the wilderness most of the year, and they held it as good fortune."

"That is," said don Quixote, "when they can't help it or when they're in love. And this is so true that there have been knights who lived on a boulder for two years, in the sun, in the shade, withstanding all the inclemencies of the heavens, without their ladies knowing about it. And one of these was Amadís when he was known as Beltenebros, who went to stay on Peña Pobre,† I don't know if it was for eight years or eight months—I'm just not sure. It's enough that he was there doing penance for I don't know what bad thing the lady Oriana had done to him. But let's drop this, Sancho, before some misfortune happens to the donkey like the one suffered by Rocinante."

"That would be the work of the devil," said Sancho.

And emitting thirty ows and sixty sighs and a hundred twenty curses and execrations on the person who had brought him to this point, he got in the middle of the road, all bent over like a Turkish bow, unable to straighten up. Yet with all this, he was able to prepare the donkey, who had wandered off a bit what with so much freedom accorded him on that day. He then was able to get Rocinante up, and

---

* Don Quixote makes a mistake. Bacchus is from Thebes of Greece, with seven gates. The Thebes with a hundred gates was in Egypt.

† This was a small, barren island where Amadís, scorned by Oriana, went to do penance with a hermit. Amadís never said exactly how long his stay there was.

if the horse had had a language with which to lament, he wouldn't have been far behind Sancho or his master.

Finally, Sancho got don Quixote onto the donkey and tied Rocinante behind. He took the donkey by the halter and headed toward the main road. And Fortune was guiding their affairs better and better, because after they had gone only half a league, Sancho saw a road leading to an inn, which, to his own grief, and to the pleasure of don Quixote, was judged to be a castle. Sancho swore it was an inn, and his master said it wasn't an inn, but rather a castle. The dispute was still going strong when they arrived, and Sancho entered with his retinue, without further confirmation.

Chapter XVI. About what happened to the ingenious hidalgo *in the inn that he imagined to be a castle.*

THE INNKEEPER, who saw don Quixote slung across the donkey's back, asked Sancho what the matter with him was. Sancho responded that it was nothing—he'd just fallen down from a boulder and his ribs were a bit bruised.

The innkeeper had a wife who was not of the usual kind in that business, because she was by nature kindhearted and was concerned about the misfortunes of her fellow creatures, so she immediately attended to don Quixote and had her daughter, a very good-looking girl, help. An Asturian* girl served in the inn as well, wide in the face, flat at the back of her head, with a wide nose, blind in one eye, and not very sound in the other. The truth is that the gracefulness of her body made up for her other defects: She was only seven palms† tall from head to foot, and her shoulders weighed her down a bit, making her look at the ground more than she would like.

This graceful servant girl assisted the maiden, and the two of them prepared a very bad bed for don Quixote in a garret that, in bygone times, so it seemed, had been a hayloft for many years. There was a muleteer in the same loft who

---

* Asturias is a seaside region of northern Spain corresponding to the modern province of Oviedo.
† A palm is eight inches.

had his bed on the other side of don Quixote's. Although it was made of the packsaddles and blankets of his mules, it was much better than don Quixote's, which was made of only four not-very-smooth planks on two not very even trestles, and a mattress that seemed to be a quilt, because it was so thin. It was filled with lumps, which, if you didn't otherwise know they were wool, you would think were pebbles, because they were so hard. There were two sheets made of shield leather* and a cover that was so threadbare that if you wanted to count every thread, you wouldn't miss a single one.

On this wretched bed don Quixote lay down. Then the innkeeper's wife and her daughter applied bandages to him from head to foot. Maritornes—that's what the Asturian girl's name was—held the light. As she was putting the dressings on, the innkeeper's wife noticed that parts of don Quixote were very bruised, and she said that it looked more like bruises from blows than from a fall.

"Those weren't blows," said Sancho, "but rather the boulder had sharp edges and protrusions, and each one left a black-and-blue mark." And he went on to say: "Make sure that there's a few bandages left over, since there'll be someone else who needs them, because my back hurts me, and not a little."

"So," responded the innkeeper's wife, "did you fall as well?"

"I didn't fall," said Sancho Panza, "but the fright I got when I saw my master fall made my whole body hurt, as if they'd given me a thousand whacks."

"That can easily be," said the maiden. "It's happened to me that I dreamed that I was falling down from a tower and never hit the ground, and when I awoke, I was as beaten up and pounded as if I'd really fallen."

"But the funny thing is, *señora*," responded Sancho Panza, "that I wasn't dreaming, but more wide-awake than I am right now, and I have almost as many bruises as my master don Quixote."

"What's the name of that fellow?" asked Maritornes.

---

* Light frames covered with leather were common as shields since they were easy to wield. Shield leather was hard, like that used for soles of shoes (Rico's note).

"Don Quixote de La Mancha," responded Sancho Panza. "He's a knight-errant, and one of the best and strongest that the world has seen in a very long time."

"What's a knight-errant?" replied the servant.

"Are you so young that you don't know?" responded Sancho Panza. "Well, sister, a knight-errant in two words is this: First he gets cudgeled; then he gets to be a king. Today he's the most unfortunate and neediest creature in the world, and tomorrow he'll have two or three kingdoms to give his squire."

"Well, how come you—since you're the squire of this good man—" said the innkeeper's wife, "aren't even a count yet?"

"It's still too soon," responded Sancho, "because it's just been a month since we've been out looking for adventures, and up to now we haven't run across any that has been a true adventure. And it sometimes happens that you look for one thing and find another. The truth is that if my master don Quixote gets healed from this wound or fall, and I'm not crippled from it, I wouldn't exchange my aspirations for the best title in Spain."

Don Quixote was listening very attentively to all of this conversation, and sat up in his bed as well as he could. Taking the hand of the innkeeper's wife, he said to her: "Believe me, beautiful *señora*, that you can call yourself fortunate for having me in this your castle, and if I don't praise myself, it's because they say that self-praise demeans, but my squire will tell you who I am. I'll just say that I'll have eternally etched in my memory the service you've done me, and I'll be grateful to you as long as I live. And if the laws of heaven hadn't bound me to that beautiful ingrate whom I mention under my breath, the eyes of this maiden would now be ruling over my freedom."

The innkeeper's wife and her daughter, as well as the good Maritornes, were baffled when they heard these words, which they understood about as well as if he'd been speaking Greek, although they gathered that he was offering them services and flattering them. Since they weren't used to such language, they stared at him in astonishment, because he seemed to them to be a different type of man from those they were accustomed to. They thanked him in the words innkeepers use, and left, but the Asturian Maritornes stayed behind to tend to Sancho, who needed no less help than his master.

Now, the muleteer had arranged to sleep with her that night, and she'd given her word that when everyone was fast asleep, including her master and mistress, she would come to him to satisfy his pleasure in whatever way he might ask. They say of this good lass that she never made a promise she didn't keep, even though she might give it in the forest and without any witnesses, because she prided herself on being well-bred; and she wasn't ashamed to work as a servant in the inn, because she said that certain misfortunes had brought her there.

Don Quixote's hard, narrow, inadequate, and unreliable bed came first in the middle of this starlit stable, and then next to it Sancho made his own bed, which consisted of only one rush mat and a cover that seemed to be more a piece of threadbare canvas than wool. After these two beds came the one belonging to the muleteer, which was made, as has been said, of the packsaddles and all the trappings of two of his best mules—he had twelve in all. They were sleek, well fed, and fine, because he was one of the rich muleteers of Arévalo,* according to the author of this history. He mentions this muleteer particularly because he knew him well, and there are those who say he was a distant relative of his. Besides, Cide Mahamate Benengeli was very careful and diligent in everything, and this is easy to see because those things already related, as small and trivial as they are, are not passed over in silence. Let this be an example to those grave historians who report actions in so few words that we hardly get a taste of them, and they leave the most substantial parts of the history in the inkwell, either by carelessness, mischievousness, or ignorance. A thousand blessings on the author of *Tablante de Ricamonte* and on him who wrote that other book where the deeds of Count Tomillas are related.† They describe everything so accurately!

---

* Arévalo is a town in the province of Ávila (population today of 6,400), about thirty miles north of Ávila proper.

† *The Chronicle of the Noble Knights Tablante de Ricamonte and Jofre, Son of Count Donasón* (1513). Count Tomillas is a character in *History of Enrique, Son of Oliva, King of Jerusalem, Emperor of Constantinople* (1498).

So, as I was saying, after the muleteer took care of his mules and gave them their second feeding, he stretched out onto the packsaddles and began to wait for his very punctual Maritornes. Sancho was already in bandages and in bed, and although he tried to sleep, the pain in his ribs wouldn't let him. And don Quixote, because of the pain in his own ribs, had his eyes wide open like a hare. The whole inn was still and there was no light other than what came from a hanging lamp burning over its entrance. Owing to this marvelous stillness and the thoughts our knight always had about the goings-on in the books responsible for his plight, one of the strangest delusions that can be imagined came to him: He thought that he'd come to a famous castle (since—as has been said—castles are what he considered all the inns that lodged him to be), and that the daughter of the innkeeper was the daughter of the lord of the castle; and that she—overcome by his graces—had fallen in love with him, and had promised that that night, without her parents knowing, she would come and lie with him a good spell. And being convinced that all this chimera—which he'd dreamed up—was true, and starting to get worried, and thinking of the dangerous crisis his virtue was about to face, he resolved in his heart not to betray his *señora* Dulcinea del Toboso, even if Queen Guinevere herself with her lady Quintañona placed themselves in his hands.

As he was mulling over this nonsense, the fatal moment—for him—came as the Asturian girl arrived. She was barefoot and in a nightshirt and her hair was gathered in a hairnet, and with very quiet and careful little steps she went into the room where the three were lodged, looking for the muleteer. When she got to the door, don Quixote heard her and sat up in bed, in spite of his bandages and the pain in his sides, and opened his arms wide to receive the beautiful maiden. The Asturian, crouching over and keeping very quiet, was moving forward with her hands in front, trying to find her lover, when she ran into the arms of don Quixote, who seized her firmly by the wrist and drew her toward him. Without her daring to utter a word, he made her sit on the bed. He felt her nightshirt, and although it was made of burlap, it seemed to him to be of the finest silk. She was wearing some glass beads on her wrist, but he thought they were Oriental pearls. Her hair, which seemed quite like the mane of a horse, in his mind was dazzling threads of Arabian gold, the luminescence of which outshone the sun. And her breath, doubtless reeking of yesterday's stale cold cuts, to him seemed to be a sweet and aromatic fragrance. Finally, he painted her in his imagination in the same way he'd read in his books, just like the other princesses who went to visit the badly wounded knight, madly in love with them, adorned the way he'd imagined. And such was the blindness of the poor *hidalgo* that neither the touch, nor the smell, nor anything else about the girl was enough to make him see how she really was, which was that she would make anyone but a muleteer vomit. He thought he had in his arms the goddess of beauty. And still clutching her, he began to say in a soft, amorous voice: "I'd like to have found myself in a position, beautiful and highborn lady, to respond to the favor that you've done me just by letting me see you. But Fortune, which never tires of persecuting good people, has placed me in this bed, where I lie beaten up and broken, so that even if my inclinations would allow me to satisfy yours, it would be impossible. And what makes this impossibility even more impossible is that I've promised fidelity to the peerless Dulcinea del Toboso, the only lady of my most hidden thoughts. If all this didn't prevent me, I wouldn't be so foolish as to let such a wonderful opportunity as this one that your great goodness has given me pass me by."

Maritornes was very distressed and sweating profusely, seeing herself so firmly grasped by don Quixote. Not understanding or paying attention to the words he was saying, she tried, without uttering a word, to get herself free. The good muleteer, whose lascivious desires kept him awake, heard his concubine as soon as she came through the door. He was listening attentively to everything don Quixote was saying and, suspicious that the Asturian had broken her word with him for another, went over to don Quixote's cot and remained still until he saw where those words—which he couldn't understand—were leading. But since he realized that the girl was struggling to get away, and don Quixote was doing his best to restrain her, he thought the caper had gone far enough. He raised his fist high in the air and gave such a terrible punch on don Quixote's narrow jaw that he bathed his whole mouth in blood. And not content with this, the muleteer got on top of don Quixote's ribs, and with his feet he stomped all over them faster than a trot. Now the bed, which was a bit weak and didn't have a very firm foundation, unable to withstand the additional weight of the muleteer, came crashing to the floor, the noise of which woke the innkeeper up. He immediately figured that it must have had something to do with Maritornes, because she didn't answer when he called her name. So he got up and lit a lamp and went to where he'd heard the scuffle. The girl, afraid and agitated, seeing that her master was coming and in a very bad mood, took refuge in Sancho Panza's bed—he was still sleeping—where she curled up into a ball.

The innkeeper came in saying: "Where are you, you whore? All this has got to be your doing!"

At this point Sancho woke up, and feeling that bulk on top of him, thought it was a bad dream and began to punch in all directions and hit Maritornes I don't know how many times. When she felt the pain, casting aside her modesty, she returned so many of them to Sancho that, to his dismay, she woke him up, and, seeing himself being beaten up in that way and not knowing by whom, he sat up and wrestled with Maritornes, and they began the most hard-fought and amusing skirmish in the world.

When the muleteer saw by the light of the innkeeper's lamp what was happening to his lady, he left don Quixote and went to give her whatever help he could. The innkeeper went to her as well, but with an entirely different intention, because he went to punish the girl, believing that she alone was the reason for that harmony. So, as the saying goes, "the cat to the rat, the rat to the rope, the rope to the stick"—the muleteer hit Sancho, Sancho hit the girl, the girl hit him, the innkeeper hit the girl, and everybody was punching so hard and fast that there wasn't a moment of rest. And the best part was that the innkeeper's lamp went out, and since they were all in the dark, they punched so fiercely and all at once that wherever their punches landed they left nothing sound.

It happened that there was an officer of the ancient Holy Brotherhood of Toledo staying there that night, and when he heard the extraordinary commotion caused by the fight, he took his staff of office and tin box of warrants, and went in the darkened room, saying: "Stop in the name of justice! Stop in the name of the Holy Brotherhood!"

And the first person he happened upon was the pummeled don Quixote on his collapsed bed, stretched out on his back, utterly senseless. The officer felt his beard, and kept saying: "Help in the name of justice!" But seeing that the person he was grasping didn't stir, he figured that he was dead, and that those who were in that room were his killers. With this suspicion, in a loud voice he said: "Close the gates of the inn! Make sure no one leaves—they've murdered someone here!"

This news terrified everyone, and everyone stopped fighting when they heard that shout. The innkeeper went back to his room, the muleteer back to his packsaddles, and the girl to her room. The unfortunate don Quixote and Sancho couldn't move from where they were. The officer then released don Quixote's beard and went to look for a lamp so he could find and arrest the culprits. But he didn't find a lamp because the innkeeper had put it out on purpose when he returned to his room, and the officer had to go to the fireplace, where it took him a long while and quite a bit of effort to light another lamp.

Chapter XVII. Where the innumerable travails that the brave don Quixote and his faithful squire, Sancho Panza, had in the inn that, to his sorrow, he thought was a castle.

B Y THIS time don Quixote had come to, and with the same tone of voice that he'd used the previous day with his squire when he was stretched out in the "valley of the stakes,"* he began to call out, saying: "Sancho, my friend, are you asleep? Are you sleeping, friend Sancho?"

"How can I be sleeping, for God's sake," responded Sancho, filled with grief and dismay. "It seems like all the devils in hell have been after me tonight."

"You can well believe it without a doubt," responded

---

* This derives from an old ballad about the Cid that everyone would have recognized.

don Quixote, "because either I know very little, or this castle is enchanted. I want you to know ... but what I'm going to tell you now, you have to swear to me you'll keep secret until after my death."

"I swear," responded Sancho.

"I say this," replied don Quixote, "because I don't like it if anyone loses his reputation."

"I say that I swear," Sancho said again, "that I'll keep quiet about it until after the days of your grace; and may it please God that I can reveal it tomorrow."

"Do I treat you so badly, Sancho," responded don Quixote, "that you want to see me dead so soon?"

"No, it's not that," responded Sancho. "I just hate to keep things for a long time, and I wouldn't want them to go rotten for having kept them too long."

"Be that as it may," said don Quixote, "I'm confident enough of your love and respect that I can tell you that tonight one of the strangest adventures that can be imagined happened to me. I'll tell it to you in a few words. Just a little while ago the daughter of the lord of this castle came to me. She's the most elegant and beautiful maiden in this part of the world. How can I describe the way she was dressed? How can I describe her brilliant mind? How can I describe her other hidden charms that—to keep the faith I have for Dulcinea del Toboso—I'll leave intact and unsaid? I'll only say that either heaven was jealous of the marvels that Fortune had placed in my arms, or—and this seems more likely—as I said, this castle is enchanted. While I was immersed in a sweet and loving dialogue with her, without my seeing or finding out where it came from, a hand connected to an arm belonging to some enormous giant struck me on the jaw, and now it's all bathed in blood. After that he beat me up so that I'm worse than yesterday when the Galicians, through the excesses of Rocinante, mauled us in the way you know. I conjecture from all this that the treasure of beauty belonging to this maiden must be guarded by some enchanted Moor, and must not have been meant for me."

"Nor for me," responded Sancho, "because more than four hundred Moors walloped me, so that the beating with the stakes was nothing in comparison. But, tell me, *señor*, what sort of adventure do you call this fine and rare one that has left us in this condition? For your grace it wasn't so bad since you had that incomparable beauty you mentioned in your arms. But in my case, what did I have, if not the hardest punches I ever expect to get in my whole life? Unlucky me and the mother who bore me! I'm not a knight-errant nor do I ever plan to be one, yet I get the better part of all these misfortunes."

"So, you're beaten up, too?" responded don Quixote.

"Didn't I say that I was, curses on my family!?" said Sancho.

"Don't be troubled, my friend," said don Quixote, "because I'll make the precious balm right now, and we'll be healed in the twinkling of an eye."

The officer at this point had finally lit his lamp and returned to see what he thought would be the dead man, and as soon as Sancho saw him, with this nightshirt and cap, and lamp in his hand, and with a very sour expression, he asked his master: "*Señor*, is this the enchanted Moor who has returned to punish us some more, just in case he left any ink in the inkwell?"

"He can't be the Moor," responded don Quixote, "because the enchanted never let anyone see them."

"If they don't let themselves be seen, they sure let themselves be felt," said Sancho, "as my back will bear witness."

"Mine could say a few things, too," responded don Quixote, "but this isn't reason enough to believe this is the enchanted Moor."

The officer came in and since he found them talking in such quiet tones, he was quite surprised. It's true that don Quixote was still on his back, unable to move, since he was so beaten up and covered with bandages. The officer approached and said: "Well, how are you, my good man?"*

"I'd speak more respectfully," responded don Quixote, "if I were you. Is this the way they speak to knights-errant in these parts, you blockhead?"

The officer, seeing himself mistreated by a man of such wretched appearance and doubtful sanity, couldn't take it, and, raising his lamp with all its oil, he smashed don

---

* Although this was said seemingly in innocence, don Quixote takes offense because he thinks it's used in its meaning, "poor fellow." Clemencín says that is a form of address that implies great superiority.

Quixote on the head with it, making quite a wound; then he left the darkened room.

Sancho said to him: "That doubtless was the enchanted Moor who is keeping treasures for other people, but he has only punches and whacks with lamps for us."

"That's right," responded don Quixote, "and there's no reason to be vexed by these enchantments, nor should you get mad or angry over them, since the enchanters are invisible and unreal, and we won't find anyone to take vengeance on, no matter how hard we look. Get up, Sancho, if you can, and call the warden of the castle, and get a bit of oil, wine, salt, and rosemary with which to make that curative balm, because I truly feel that I need some now, since a lot of blood is flowing from the wound this phantom gave me."

Sancho got up, with enormous pain in his bones, and went off in the darkness to look for the innkeeper, and along the way met up with the officer, who was listening to see what was happening with his enemy, and said to him: "*Señor*, whoever you are, please do us the kindness of giving us a bit of rosemary, oil, salt, and wine, which we need to heal one of the best knights-errant in the world, who is lying in that bed badly wounded by the hand of the enchanted Moor who is in this inn."

When the officer heard those words, he took him for a crazy person. And because day was beginning to break, he opened the door of the inn and called the innkeeper to tell him what that good man wanted. The innkeeper gave him everything he wanted, and Sancho took it to don Quixote, whom he found with his hands on his head, groaning from the pain of the lamp blow, which had done nothing more than raise two lumps, and what he thought was blood was just sweat from the anguish caused by the latest misfortune.

He took the ingredients, which he mixed together, and then cooked them for a long time, until he felt that they were ready. He then asked for a flask to put it all in, but there was none at the inn, so he resolved to put it in a cruet or tin oil container the innkeeper gave him. Then don Quixote recited over the cruet more than eighty Our Fathers and the same number of Hail Marys, *Salve Reginas*, credos, and with every word he crossed himself by way of a blessing. Sancho, the innkeeper, and the officer witnessed all this, but the muleteer was calmly attending to the welfare of his mules.

Once he was finished, he wanted to sample some of the precious balm to see about the curative qualities he imagined it had, so he drank some of what hadn't fit into the cruet from the pot that he'd used to cook it in—almost a full quart. And no sooner had he drunk it when he began to vomit so violently that absolutely nothing remained in his stomach, and with the nausea and spasms caused by the vomiting, he began to sweat profusely, so he asked that he be covered and left alone. They covered him and he slept for three hours, after which he woke up feeling like a new man, and his bruises felt so much better that he thought he was completely healed. He truly felt that the balm of Fierabrás had really worked and that he could engage in fights from then on without any fear of disasters, battles, or clashes, no matter how perilous they might be.

Sancho Panza, who also thought the recovery of his master was a miracle, begged him for what was left over in the pot, which was not a little amount. Don Quixote let him have it. Sancho took it in both hands, in good faith and with better will, and gulped down not much less than his master. As it happened, poor Sancho's stomach must not have been as delicate as that of his master, so before he could throw up, he suffered so much nausea and so many swoons, with so much sweating and fainting spells, that he truly thought that his final hour had come. Seeing himself so afflicted and distressed, he cursed the balm and the thief who had given it to him.

When don Quixote saw what had happened to him, he said: "I think, Sancho, that all this trouble comes from your not having been dubbed a knight. I'm convinced that this balm shouldn't be taken by those who aren't so dubbed."

"If your grace knew this all along," replied Sancho, "—woe is me and all my kindred!—why did you let me drink it?"

At this point the brew started to act, and the poor squire began to discharge from both ends with such force that neither the mat on which he was lying, nor the canvas cover that was on top of him were of further use. He sweated and sweated with such seizures and paroxysms that not only he, but everyone else, thought that his life was ending. This tempest and misfortune lasted almost two hours, after which he wasn't in good shape like his master, but rather too beaten up and weak to stand up.

But don Quixote, who, as has been said, felt relieved and hale, wanted to leave immediately to seek adventures, because it seemed to him that all the time he delayed was depriving the world and those needy people in it of his favor and assistance. The self-assurance he got from the balm instilled even more confidence in him, so, armed with this desire, he saddled Rocinante himself and put the packsaddle on his squire's donkey, and he also helped Sancho to get dressed and get on the donkey. He then got on his horse and went over to a corner of the yard and picked up a short lance to use.

Everyone in the inn—and there were more than twenty— was watching him. The daughter of the innkeeper was among those looking on, and he never took his eyes from hers. Once in a while he heaved a great sigh that seemed to be coming from the depths of his bowels, but everyone interpreted it as being due to the pain he felt in his ribs, at least those who had seen him being bandaged the night before.

As soon as the two of them were mounted and at the gate of the inn, don Quixote called the innkeeper over, and with a very calm and grave voice said: "*Señor* warden, many and very great are the favors I've received in this castle, and I remain very much in your debt. I'll be thankful to you all the days of my life. If I can repay you by avenging an injury done to you by some arrogant person, I want you to know that my profession is none other than to help those not very able to help themselves, to settle accounts for those who have been wronged, and to punish treacheries. Think back and tell me if there's anything of this kind to charge me with. All you have to do is ask and I promise you, by the order of chivalry that I've received, to satisfy you completely."

The innkeeper responded with the same tranquil air: "*Señor* knight, I don't need you to avenge any injury because I know how to take any vengeance I see fit, when necessary. I only need for you to pay me for the expenses you incurred at the inn last night, such as the straw and barley for your mounts, and for the dinner and the beds."

"You mean this is an *inn*?" replied don Quixote.

"And a very reputable one," responded the innkeeper.

"I've been deceived until now," responded don Quixote. "In truth I thought it was a castle, and not a bad one. But since it's an inn and not a castle, the only thing you can do is forgive the payment, because I can't contravene the laws of knight-errantry. I know for a fact—and I haven't read anything to the contrary—that knights never paid for lodging or anything else in an inn where they stayed, because appropriate shelter is accorded them by law and by right in payment for the insufferable toil they endure while seeking adventures night and day, in winter and in summer, on foot and on horseback, suffering hunger and thirst, in heat and cold, subject to all the inclemencies of the heavens and all the discomforts of the earth."

"I don't know anything about that," responded the innkeeper. "Just pay me what you owe me, and let's hear no more about stories and chivalry. The only thing I care about is getting what is due me."

"You're a foolish man and a bad innkeeper," responded don Quixote.

And putting his spurs to Rocinante, and brandishing his lance, he left the inn without anyone stopping him; and he, not looking back to see if his squire was following, went quite a distance away. The innkeeper saw him leave without paying, so he went to collect from Sancho Panza, who said that since his master had refused to pay, he wouldn't pay either. Being the squire of a knight-errant, as he was, the same rule and principle applied to him as for his master in not paying for anything in inns. This irritated the innkeeper, who threatened him, saying that if he didn't pay, he'd collect in a way that Sancho wouldn't like. To which Sancho responded that by the laws of chivalry his master had received, he wouldn't pay even a single *cornado*,* even though it might cost him his life, because he didn't want the good and ancient traditions of knights-errant to be lost through him, nor did he want the squires of other knights who had yet to come into the world to complain about him, reproaching him for having broken such an exemplary law.

---

* This coin was worth a sixth of a *maravedí*, itself not worth very much.

As the unfortunate Sancho's bad luck would have it, among the people who were at the inn were four wool carders from Segovia, three needle makers from the Plaza del Potro in Córdoba, and two men who lived near the Marketplace of Seville,* jovial, good-hearted, mischievous, and playful fellows, who were incited and moved by the same spirit, and who went to Sancho and pulled him off his donkey. Meanwhile one of them went to fetch a blanket from the innkeeper's bed. They put Sancho on the blanket, looked up and saw that the ceiling was a bit lower than they needed for what they were going to do, so they decided to go to the corral, where the ceiling was the sky. And there, with Sancho in the middle of the blanket, they began to toss him in the air, having fun with him like they do with dogs at carnival time.

The shouts the wretched person being blanketed gave out were so loud they were heard by his master, who stopped to listen attentively, and believed that a new adventure had come his way, until he realized that the person who was bellowing was his squire. So he turned around and, with a laborious gallop, went back to the inn. When he arrived at the walls of the corral, which were not very high, he saw the joke they were playing on his squire. He saw him go up and down in the air with so much grace and nimbleness that—if his anger had allowed him—I think he would have laughed out loud. He tried to climb from the horse onto the walls, but he couldn't even get off his horse, so from the saddle he began to hurl so many insults to those who were blanketing Sancho that it's impossible to write them all down. The blanketers didn't stop their laughing or their labor on account of them, nor did the flying Sancho stop his complaints, mingled sometimes with threats and sometimes with supplications. But all this did little good until they stopped from utter exhaustion. They took him to his donkey and put him onto it, and draped his cloak over him. The compassionate Maritornes, seeing him suffering so, went to get a pitcher of water, which she got from the well so it would be cold, and took it to him. She was just

---

* The Plaza del Potro in Córdoba was already mentioned in a note in chapter three as being a place where rogues gathered. The same with the Marketplace of Seville.

at the point of giving it to him to drink when his master shouted to him: "Sancho, my son, don't drink water—it'll kill you! Look here. I have the holy balm," and he held up the cruet so Sancho could see. "With two drops of it you'll be whole again."

Sancho rolled his eyes when he heard these shouts and shouted back even louder: "Has your grace forgotten by chance that I'm not a knight-errant, or do you want me to vomit my guts out from what I have left over from last night? To the devil with that beverage, and leave me alone!"

When he finished talking, he began to drink right away. But with the first swallow he realized it was water and wouldn't take any more. He begged Maritornes to get him some wine. She did so very graciously, and paid for it with her own money, because it's said about her that, although she was just a serving girl, she was still something of a Christian.

As soon as Sancho drank, he put his heels to the donkey. They opened the gate of the inn, and he left, very content at not having had to pay anything and having gotten his way, although it had been at the expense of his usual guarantor, his back. It's true that the innkeeper kept his saddlebags in payment for what he owed, but Sancho didn't miss them, since he was in such a tizzy. The innkeeper wanted to bar the gate as soon as he saw him outside, but the blanketers wouldn't hear of it, because even if don Quixote were truly one of the knights of the Round Table, they couldn't have cared less.

Chapter XVIII. Where the words that Sancho Panza said to his master don Quixote are recorded, with other adventures worthy of being told.

SANCHO REACHED his master so exhausted and faint that he could hardly drive his donkey. When don Quixote saw him in that state, he said: "I believe now, good Sancho, that that castle or inn is enchanted without any doubt, since those men so cruelly had fun at your expense. What could they have been but phantoms and people from the other world? And I can confirm this for having seen that when I was near the walls of the corral witnessing the unfolding of your sad tragedy, I couldn't get over the walls, much less get off Rocinante, because they must have enchanted me. I swear to you, on the faith of who I am, that, if it had been possible for me to get over the walls or get off my horse, I would have avenged you so that those rogues and brigands would remember that joke forever, even if it meant that I'd have to go against the laws of chivalry, since, as I've already told you many times, they don't allow a knight to raise his hand against anyone who is not one himself, except in self-defense, and then only in the case of pressing and urgent need."

"I would have avenged myself if I could have, dubbed a knight or not, but I couldn't. But I do firmly believe that those who were having such a good time at my expense weren't phantoms or enchanted men, as your grace says, but rather men of flesh and blood like us. And all of them had names—I heard them call each other by name. One of them was called Pedro Martínez, and the other was Tenorio Hernández, and the innkeeper was called Juan Palomeque, the Left-Handed. So, *señor*, not being able to climb over the fence of the corral or get off your horse had to do with something other than enchantment. And what I conclude from all this is that these adventures we go looking for, in the end will bring us nothing but misfortune, so we won't even know which is our right foot. And what would be the best thing for us to do, in my limited understanding, is to return to our village now, since it's harvesttime, and tend to the farm, and stop going 'from Ceca to Mecca,'* and 'from a rock to a hard place,' as they say."

"How little you know, Sancho, about chivalry!" responded don Quixote. "Keep quiet and be patient, for the day will come when you'll see with your own eyes what an honorable thing it is to engage in this profession. If not, tell me, what greater content can there be in the world, or what pleasure can rival that of winning a battle and of triumphing over your enemy? None, without any doubt."

"It must be that way," responded Sancho, "although I

---

* Ceca is the name of the mosque at Córdoba and Mecca is the holy Muslim city. The expression means "from one place to another."

have no way of knowing. I only know that since we've been knights-errant, or rather since your grace has been—there's no reason to count me among such an honorable group—we've never won any battle except the one with the Basque, and even there your grace left it with only half an ear and half a helmet gone, and since then it's been whacks and more whacks, punches and more punches; and in addition to all that, I've been blanketed by enchanted persons who I can't take vengeance on, so I can't know the pleasure you get when you conquer an enemy, as you say."

"This bothers me, and must bother you as well, Sancho," responded don Quixote, "but as soon as I can, I'll try to get a sword made with such powers that whoever has it with him cannot suffer any kind of enchantment. And it may even be that good fortune will bring me the sword of Amadís, when he was called THE KNIGHT OF THE BURNING SWORD. It was one of the best swords that any knight ever had, because—aside from the powers I just mentioned—it cut like a razor, and there was no armor, no matter how sturdy and enchanted it might be, that could withstand it."

"My luck is such," said Sancho, "that when this came to pass, and you found such a sword, it would only be of use to knights, as with the balm, and as for squires . . . they'll be out in the cold once again."

"Don't worry about that, Sancho," said don Quixote, "because heaven will treat you better."

Don Quixote and his squire were having this conversation, when don Quixote saw on the road they were on an enormous thick cloud of dust. When he saw it, he turned to Sancho and said: "This is the day, Sancho, that Fate has reserved for me. This is the day on which will be demonstrated, more so than on any other day, the strength of my arm, and on which I'll do deeds that will be written in the *Book of Fame* for all future ages. Do you see that cloud of dust swirling up over there, Sancho? Well, it has been churned up by a colossal marching army consisting of innumerable soldiers from many different places."

"In that case, there must be two armies," said Sancho, "because from the other side there's a similar cloud of dust."

Don Quixote turned to see it, and he saw that it was true. It gladdened him beyond measure, since he thought that there were doubtless two armies that had come to attack and do battle in the middle of that spacious plain, because his imagination had filled him at all times with combats, enchantments, incidents, follies, romances, and challenges recounted in the romances of chivalry, and everything he said, thought, or did was along those lines. It turns out that the clouds of dust he'd seen were made by two large flocks of sheep that were coming from two different directions along that same road, and because of the dust, the sheep themselves couldn't be seen until they drew near. Don Quixote insisted with such ardor that they were armies that Sancho came to believe him and said: "*Señor*, what should we do?"

"What?" said don Quixote. "Why, help the needy and weak side. I want you to know, Sancho, that the army coming toward us is led by the great Emperor Alifanfarón, lord of the great island of Trapobana.* This other army marching at our backs is the one belonging to his enemy, the king of the Central African Garamantans, Pentapolén of the Rolled-up Sleeve, because he always goes into battle with his right arm bared."

"So why do they hate each other, these two *señores*?" asked Sancho.

"They hate each other," responded don Quixote, "because this Alefanfarón† is a raging pagan, and is in love with the Pentapolín's daughter, a very beautiful and very graceful *señora*. She's Christian, and her father doesn't want to let the pagan king have her unless he first leaves the law of the false prophet Muhammad and adopts his own religion."

"By my beard," said Sancho, "Pentapolín is quite right, and I'll help him as much as I can."

"In this you'll be doing what you should," said don Quixote, "because to enter into such battles, you don't need to be dubbed a knight."

"I understand that," responded Sancho. "But where can we put the donkey so that we can find him after the fray is

---

* Trapobana is a switched-around Taprobana, the old name for Sri Lanka.
† Translator's note: Variations in names are part of the work (Quejana, Quesada, Quijano), and I hesitate to change this one (or any other).

over? I don't think that such an animal has been used in a battle up to now."

"That's the truth," said don Quixote, "but you can just let him roam free, whether he comes back or not, because we'll have so many horses after we win the battle that even Rocinante runs the risk of being exchanged for another. But listen carefully, and look, because I want to tell you about the most important knights of both armies. And so that you can see and observe better, let's go up to that little hill over there, from where we can see both armies."

They went onto the hill from where they could see both flocks well—which don Quixote thought were armies because the clouds of dust they caused had obscured the flocks and blinded his eyes. But in spite of all this, seeing in his imagination what he didn't see with his eyes and wasn't there, he began to say in a loud voice: "That knight you see over there with the yellow armor with the shield that has a lion wearing a crown subdued at a maiden's feet, is the brave Laurcalco, Lord of the Silver Bridge;* the other one with golden flowers on his armor, who has a shield with three silver crowns on a field of blue, is the feared Micolembo, the Grand Duke of Quirocia. The other one to Micolembo's right, with gigantic arms and legs, is the ever-dauntless Brandabarbarán de Boliche, lord of the three Arabias, who is protected by that serpent skin, and uses a gate for a shield, which, fame has it, is one from the temple that Samson† pulled down, when he took vengeance on his enemies through his own death.

"But look at the other side now and you'll see in front of the other army the always conquering and never conquered Timonel of Carcajona, Prince of New Biscay, who wears armor divided into four colors—blue, green, white, and yellow—and holds a shield with a golden cat on an orangeish background with a caption that says MIAU, which is almost like the beginning of the name of the lady who, so they say, is the peerless Miulina, daughter of Duke Alefeñiquén de Algarve. The other one, who sits on and squeezes

---

* There's an old Spanish proverb: If your enemy flees, give him a silver bridge.

† In Judges 16:3, Samson removed the doors of the gates of the city of Gaza, not of the temple.

the loins of that powerful horse and wears armor white
as snow and wields a white shield without any motto, is a
novice knight from France, called Pierres Papín, Lord of
the Baronies of Utrique. The other one, who is spurring the
flanks of a striped and light-footed zebra, and has a shield
with alternating bars of blue and white, is the powerful
Duke of Nerbia, Espartifilardo of the Forest, who has an
asparagus plant on his shield with a caption in Spanish that
says My LUCK DRAGS BEHIND."

And in this way he went along naming many knights
from both squadrons that he imagined, and he improvised
the armor, colors, devices, and mottoes of them all, and without stopping, he continued: "This squadron in front is made
up of people from different nations. Here are those that
drink the waters of the famous Xanthus River;* the woods-
men who tread the Massilian Plains;† those who sift the
fine gold dust of Felix Arabia;‡ those who enjoy the famous
and cool shores of the clear Thermodon River;§ those who
drink from the golden Pactolus River;¶ the Numidians,**
who hesitate in their promises; Persians, famous for their
bows and arrows; Parthians and Medes who fight as they
flee;†† Arabs, of movable houses; Scythians, as cruel as they
are fair of skin;‡‡ Ethiopians with bored lips; and an infinite
number of other peoples, whose faces I know but I don't
remember their names.

"In this other squadron there are those who drink the
crystalline running water of the olive-bearing Bætis River;

---

* The Xanthus is the river of ancient Troy (located in modern south-
west Turkey), sung about by both Homer and Virgil. It flows into the
Mediterranean Sea.
† The Massilian Plains were in ancient Numidia, modern Algeria.
‡ Felix Arabia is one of the three Arabias mentioned above.
§ The Thermodon is a minor river in the Roman province of Pontus, on
the south shore of the Black Sea, now in Turkey.
¶ The Pactolus River, a tributary of the ancient Hermus River (mod-
ern Gediz in western Turkey), was called golden because King Midas,
who turned everything he touched into gold, reputedly bathed there.
** The Numidians lived in what is now Algeria, as you gather from the
second note above.
†† Parthia and Media were ancient kingdoms in what is now Iran.
‡‡ The Scythians were cruel because they were cannibals. They flourished before the Christian era in what is now southern Russia.

those who wash their faces with the liquid from the always rich and golden Tajo River; those who enjoy the health-restoring waters of the Genil River;* those who tread upon the Tartessian fields† with their abundant pasture; those who delight in the Elysian Fields near Jérez;‡ Manchegans, whose rich fields are covered with golden wheat; those dressed in iron, ancient remnants of Gothic blood; those who bathe in the Pisuerga River,§ famous for the gentleness of its current; those who graze their cattle on the extensive pastures of the twisting Guadiana River,¶ celebrated for its underground flows; those who shiver in the cold of the sylvan Pyrenees Mountains** and in the white snowflakes of the Apennine Mountains.†† In short, you'll find represented every nation that Europe's borders hold."

Goodness, gracious! How many provinces he mentioned, how many nations he named, ascribing to each one, with marvelous speed, its attributes, based entirely on what he'd read in his lying books.

Sancho Panza was hanging on every word, not saying a single one himself, and once in a while he turned his head to see if he could make out the knights and giants his master was describing, and since he didn't see any, he said to him: "*Señor*, I don't see any man or giant or knight of the many that you've mentioned. Maybe it's just enchantment, like the phantoms of last night."

"How can you say that?" responded don Quixote. "Don't you hear the neighing of the horses, the sounding of bugles, the rolling of the drums?"

"I don't hear anything," responded Sancho Panza, "except the bleating of sheep."

And it was the truth, because the flocks were drawing near.

---

* The Genil River flows through Granada. The remaining soldiers, except the very last ones, are all Spaniards.
† Tartessos was an ancient city along the Guadalquivir River.
‡ Refers to Jérez de la Frontera, a southern Spanish city near Cádiz.
§ This river flows north through Valladolid and exits near Santander.
¶ The Guadiana River starts in La Mancha and goes west to the border with Portugal until it exits into the Atlantic Ocean. At some places in Spain it does flow underground.
** The Pyrenees separate France from Spain.
†† The Apennines extend the length of Italy.

"It's your fear," said don Quixote, "that makes you unable to see or hear things the way they are. One of the effects of fear is to confuse one's senses and make things not seem like what they are. And if you're so afraid, step aside and leave me alone, for I alone can give victory to the side I favor."

And saying this, he spurred Rocinante, braced his lance, and went down the slope like a bolt of lightning.

Sancho shouted after him, saying: "Come back, your grace don Quixote! I swear to God that it's rams and ewes that you're about to attack! Come back! Woe to the unfortunate father that bore me! What kind of lunacy is this? Look, there are no giants or knights, nor coats of armor, nor divided, nor shields, nor blue or bedeviled bars! What are you doing, sinner that I am!?"

These words had no effect on don Quixote. Instead, he went forward, shouting: "Ho, knights who follow and do battle under the standards of the valorous Emperor Pentapolín of the Rolled-up Sleeve, follow me, all of you. You'll see how easily I take vengeance on his enemy Alefanfarón of Trapobana!"

Saying this, he dashed into the middle of the squadron of sheep and began to attack them with his lance with as much ire and daring as if he were really fighting his mortal enemies. The shepherds with the flock shouted at him to stop, but since it was doing no good, they took out their slingshots and began to greet his ears with stones as big as your fist. Don Quixote paid no attention to the stones, but scurried in all directions, saying: "Where are you, arrogant Alifanfarón? Come to me! One knight alone wants to test your strength in singular combat and take your life to punish you for the grief you've caused the brave Pentapolín the Garamantan."

At that moment a stone from a streambed hit him in the side, caving in two ribs. Seeing himself so abused, he thought he was dead or badly wounded, and remembering his potion, he took out the cruet and put it to his mouth, and began to drink the liquid. But before he could take what he thought was enough, another smooth stone struck both his hand and the cruet squarely, breaking it to pieces, taking along with it three or four teeth from his mouth, and smashing badly two fingers of his hand.

The first blow was such, and the blow from the second was such, that the poor knight couldn't help but fall from his horse to the ground. At this point the shepherds arrived and thought they had killed him, so they herded their live-stock with great haste, picked up more than seven dead sheep, and fled without further ado.

Sancho was on the hill, all the while watching his mas-ter's mad acts, pulling at his beard and cursing the moment when Fate had brought them together. Seeing him fall to the ground, and that the shepherds had departed, he went down the hill and found his master in very bad shape, but still conscious, and said to him: "Didn't I tell you, *señor* don Quixote, to come back, and you were not attacking armies but flocks of sheep?"

"That thieving necromancer, my enemy, can falsify and make such things as these vanish. Sancho, I want you to know that it's very easy for those sorcerers to make us be-lieve whatever they want, and this wicked one who perse-cutes me, envious of the glory that he foresaw I'd garner from this battle, changed those squadrons of enemies into flocks of sheep. If you want to find out for yourself, San-cho, do this: Get on your donkey and follow them stealth-ily, without their noticing, and you'll see that, when they get some distance away, they'll change back from sheep into the men they originally were, exactly as I described to you. . . . But don't go just now—I need your help. Come over here and see how many teeth are missing, because it seems to me I don't have any left in my mouth."

Sancho got so close to him that his eyes were almost inside his mouth, and it happened that it was at that very instant that the balm in don Quixote's stomach began to have its effect; and just when Sancho was about to look inside his mouth, don Quixote—like a bullet from a rifle—discharged everything from his stomach onto the beard of his compassionate squire.

"Holy Mary!" said Sancho. "What has happened to me? This sinner is doubtless mortally wounded since he's vom-iting blood through his mouth." But when he examined it a bit more, he discovered through its color, taste, and smell that it wasn't blood, but rather the balm from the cruet that he'd seen him drink, and the nausea that it brought him was so great that his stomach began to churn, and he vomited out his whole insides onto his master, and both of them were a sight to see. Sancho went to his donkey to get something from his saddlebags to clean himself with and to treat his master's wounds, and when he didn't find the saddlebags, he was on the verge of losing his mind. He cursed himself again and resolved in his heart to leave his master and return home, even though he'd lose the salary for the time he'd served, and all hopes of governing the promised *ínsula*.

Don Quixote managed to get up, his left hand on his mouth so that the rest of his teeth wouldn't fall out, and with the other hand, he took the reins of Rocinante (who never had moved an inch from the side of his master, so loyal and well trained was he) and went over to his squire. He found him leaning against his donkey with his hand on his cheek, like a very pensive man. Seeing him in that posture, looking so unhappy, don Quixote said to him: "Sancho, no man is more than another unless he does more than another. All of these little storms that overtake us are signs that very soon the weather will clear up and good things will start happening to us, because neither good nor bad can last forever. Thus it follows that, since the adversity has lasted such a long time, good luck must be around the corner. So don't take my humiliations to heart since none of them befalls you."

"How do you figure that," responded Sancho. "By chance, yesterday was it someone other than the son of my father who was blanketed? And the saddlebags missing today with all my stuff, did they belong to another or to myself?"

"You mean the saddlebags are missing?" said don Quixote.

"Yes, they are," responded Sancho.

"That means we won't eat today," responded don Quixote.

"That would be true," responded Sancho, "only if there were no herbs in these fields that your grace knows about, which unfortunate knights-errant, such as yourself, eat when there's nothing else around."

"Even so," responded don Quixote, "I'd prefer a loaf of bread, or even half a loaf, and the heads of two herrings to all the herbs that Discorides describes, even from the commentated edition by Dr. Laguna.* But anyway, get on your donkey, good Sancho, and follow me. God, who provides everything, won't fail us, and more so since we're so much in His service. Since He doesn't fail the gnats in the air, nor the worms in the earth, nor the tadpoles in the water, and is so merciful that He makes the sun shine on the good and the bad, and rains on the unjust and the just."

"Your grace might be," said Sancho, "a better preacher than a knight-errant."

"Knights-errant knew, and have to know everything, Sancho," said don Quixote, "because there were knights-errant in past centuries who would stop to give a sermon or a discourse in the middle of a military camp, as if they were graduates of the University of Paris, and from this we learn that the lance never dulled the pen, nor the pen the lance."

"All right, let it be just as your grace says," responded Sancho. "Let's get on our way and try to find a place to stay tonight, and may it please God that it not be where there are blankets or blanketers or phantoms or enchanted Moors, because if there are, may the devil take it all away."

"Ask it of God, son," said don Quixote, "and you can lead us wherever you like. I'll let you find a place for us to stay. But first give me your hand, and feel inside my mouth with your finger, and see how many teeth are missing from this upper right side of my jaw since that's where it hurts."

Sancho put his fingers in and felt around and said: "How many molars did your grace used to have on this side?"

"Four," responded don Quixote. "Except for the wisdom tooth, all of them were whole and healthy."

"Consider carefully what you're saying, *señor*," responded Sancho.

"There were four, if not five," responded don Quixote, "because no molar was ever extracted in my whole life, nor has any fallen out, nor been damaged by cavities or abscesses."

"Well, on the bottom part," said Sancho, "your grace has only two and a half, and in the upper part, neither half

---

* Pedanius Dioscorides (A.D. 40–90) was a Greek physician who wrote *De Materia Medica*, a pharmacological text that was the standard for sixteen hundred years. Dr. Andrés de Laguna's Spanish edition was published in Antwerp in 1555.

a molar nor any at all. It's as smooth as the palm of my hand."

"Woe is me," said don Quixote, hearing the sad news that his squire gave him, "I'd have preferred that they rip off an arm, as long it wasn't the one I use for my sword, because I'll have you know, Sancho, that a mouth without molars is like a mill without a millstone; and a tooth should be more treasured than a diamond. But all of us who profess the rigorous order of knighthood are susceptible to all this. Mount your donkey, my friend, and lead on, and I'll follow at whatever pace you want."

Sancho did exactly that, and went toward where he thought they could find a place, never leaving the highway, which was very straight at that point. Going slowly, since the pain in don Quixote's jaws kept him in discomfort and didn't allow him to go very fast, Sancho wanted to entertain and amuse him by telling him something, and among the things he said was what will be recounted in the next chapter.

Chapter XIX. About the tactful conversation that Sancho Panza had with his master, and of the adventure of what happened with a dead body, with other famous occurrences.

"IT SEEMS to me, *señor mío*, that all of these misadventures that have been happening to us doubtless have been to punish your grace for sinning against the order of chivalry—since you didn't comply with your oath not to eat bread on a tablecloth nor sport with the queen, and all the rest of that stuff you swore to fulfill until you took Malandrino's helmet from him, or whatever his name is—I don't remember too well."

"You're very right, Sancho," said don Quixote. "But to tell you the truth, it had slipped my mind, and you can bet that your not having reminded me of it in time is what caused your blanketing. But I'll make it up to you, because there are ways to fix everything in the order of chivalry."

"Well, did I swear anything, by chance?" responded Sancho.

"It's not important for you to have sworn anything," said don Quixote. "It's enough for me to understand that you're not entirely free from blame. Just in case, it would be a good idea to provide ourselves with a remedy."

"Well, if that's the way things are," said Sancho, "be careful not to forget this as you did the oath, since it may cause the phantoms to come back and have more fun at my expense, and maybe even yours, too, if they see you're so stubborn."

In these and other conversations, night overtook them while on the road, without being able to find a place to lodge that night. And what was worse was that they were dying of hunger, because when they lost the saddlebags, they lost their larder and all their provisions. And the icing on the cake was that an adventure—it seemed to be a real adventure, at least, and not one that involved make-believe—befell them. That night turned out to be very dark, but they still moved along, Sancho believing that, since it was a main highway, they could reasonably expect to find an inn within a league or two.

As they went along—the night being dark, the squire hungry, and the master feeling like a bit to eat—they saw that along the road, coming toward them, was a great number of torches, which looked like roving stars. Sancho was petrified when he saw them and his master was uneasy. The one pulled on the halter of his donkey and the other on the reins of his nag and they stayed quite still, trying to figure out what it could all mean, and they saw that these torches were approaching them, and the more they drew near, the bigger they appeared. When Sancho saw this, he began to shake like a leaf, and don Quixote's hair stood on end, but he plucked up some courage and said: "This, Sancho, doubtless has to be an enormous and very dangerous adventure in which I'll have to show all my courage and strength."

"Woe is me," responded Sancho, "if this adventure is one with phantoms—and it looks to me as if it might be— how will my ribs be able to stand it?"

"No matter how many phantoms there might be," said don Quixote, "I won't allow any one of them to touch a single thread of your clothing. The last time they played tricks on you I couldn't get over the walls of the corral.

Now that we're in the countryside, I can wield my sword however I like."

"And if they enchant and paralyze you, as happened the other time," said Sancho, "what good will it be to be in the countryside?"

"Nevertheless," replied don Quixote, "be of good courage, because this experience will prove to you what kind of bravery I have."

"I'll try to, if it pleases God," responded Sancho.

The two of them went to the side of the road to see what those roving torches could be. And soon after, they made out many men dressed in white. This frightening vision took away all of Sancho Panza's courage, and his teeth began to chatter as if he had the chills. His heart beat faster and the chattering became worse when they saw what the whole scene was— they beheld up to twenty men dressed in white surplices, all of them on horseback, and with burning torches in their hands. Behind them came a litter draped in mourning, followed by six other men on mules, mantled in black down to their hooves—you could tell they weren't horses because of their lazy pace. The surplice wearers were murmuring softly among themselves, in doleful tones. This strange vision, at such a late hour, and in such a desolate place, was enough to instill fear in Sancho's heart, and even in his master's. But his master instantly saw in his imagination one of the adventures from his books coming to life. He imagined that a badly wounded or a dead knight must be lying on the litter, and whom he alone was destined to avenge.

And so, without further ado, he couched his lance, sat up firmly in his saddle, and with a gentle mien and disposition planted himself in the middle of the road where the surplice wearers had to pass, and when he saw that they were near, he raised his voice and said: "Stop, you knights, or whoever you may be, and tell me who you are, where you're coming from, and what you're bearing on that litter—because it looks to me like either you've done some outrage to someone, or someone has done some outrage to you, and I need to know what happened so that I can either punish you for the bad things you've done or avenge the injury done to you."

"We're in a hurry," responded one of the surplice wearers, "and the inn is still far away, and we can't stop to tell you everything you want to know." And spurring his mule, he continued on. Don Quixote was quite offended by this answer, and grabbing the mule by its bridle, said: "Stop, and be more courteous, and tell me what I want to know. If not, you all have a fight on your hands."

The mule was skittish, and when it was seized by the bridle, it got scared and rose onto its hind legs and threw its rider to the ground. A lad who was on foot, when he saw the surplice wearer fall, began to revile don Quixote, who was now so angry that—without waiting a moment— he assailed one of the men in black, and knocked him to the ground, badly hurt. He then turned around and moved swiftly among those remaining, and the speed with which he attacked and made them flee was marvelous to behold. It looked like Rocinante had sprouted wings at that moment, he was so light on his feet and so majestic. All the surplice wearers were fainthearted and unarmed, so they left the fray immediately and began running through the countryside with their torches still lit, much in the way masqueraders run about on nights of merriment and festival. The ones dressed in mourning, encumbered and wrapped up as they were in their skirts and cassocks, found it hard to move, so don Quixote, with no danger at all to himself, could maul them all, and made them all flee, much against their will. They all thought that he was not a man, but a devil from hell, who had come to snatch away the dead body they were transporting on the litter.

Sancho was watching it all, surprised at the undaunted courage of his master, and said to himself: "Without a doubt this master of mine is as brave and valiant as he says."

There was a burning torch on the ground next to the man that the mule had thrown, and in its light don Quixote could see him. He approached him and aimed the point of his lance at the man's face, telling him to surrender or he'd put him to death.

The fallen man responded: "I've already surrendered—I can't move because my leg is broken. I beg you, if you're a Christian knight, not to kill me, since you'd be committing a great sacrilege—I'm a *licenciado*, and I've already taken the first orders of the Church."

"Well, who the devil has brought you here," said don Quixote, "since you're a man of the Church?"

"Who, *señor*?" replied the fallen man. "My misfortune."

"A greater misfortune awaits you," said don Quixote, "if you don't tell me everything I want to know."

"I can easily satisfy your grace," responded the *licenciado*. "I should tell you that although I said I'm a *licenciado*, I only hold a bachelor's degree, and my name is Alonso López. I'm from Alcobendas and I'm coming from Baeza with eleven other priests, who are those who fled with their torches. We're going to the city of Segovia* with a dead body on that litter, a knight who died in Baeza where he'd been entombed, and now, as I say, we're taking his bones to his sepulchre in Segovia, where he was born."

"And who killed him?" asked don Quixote.

"God did, by means of a pestilential fever."

"In that case," said don Quixote, "Our Lord has spared me the trouble of avenging his death if he'd been killed by anyone else. But since he was killed by the One who killed him, I'll just have to keep quiet and shrug my shoulders, and I'd do the same if He killed me. I want you to know that I'm a knight from La Mancha named don Quixote, and my profession is to wander about the world righting wrongs and redressing injuries."

"I don't see how you can call this 'righting wrongs,'" said the bachelor, "because you've wronged me, leaving me with a broken leg that will never be right in all the days of my life. And in trying to redress an injury, you've left me injured forever. You seek adventures, but my running into you has been a great misadventure for me."

"Not everything," responded don Quixote, "happens the same way. The trouble was, *señor* bachelor Alonso López, that you were coming the way you did, at night, dressed in those surplices, with lit torches, praying, dressed in mourning, and you really looked like something evil from the other world. I had to fulfill my obligation by attacking you, and I would have attacked you even if I had known that you were devils from hell, and that's exactly what I took you to be."

"Since my fate has willed it," said the bachelor, "please,

---

* Alcobendas is a small city just north of Madrid; Baeza is in the south of Spain, about eighty miles north of Granada; Segovia is sixty miles northwest of Madrid.

señor knight-errant—who have erred so much toward me—help me to get out from under this mule, because he's pinned my leg between the stirrup and the saddle."

"I could have kept talking until tomorrow," said don Quixote. "How long were you going to wait to tell me of your distress?"

He then called to Sancho Panza to come. But Sancho couldn't go right then, because he was quite busy plundering a pack mule those good men had with them, and was well stocked with things to eat. Sancho made an impromptu sack from his overcoat and filled it with everything he could, loaded his donkey, and only then attended to his master's shouting, helping to extricate the *señor* bachelor from the weight of his mule, putting him back onto his mount, and handing him his torch. Don Quixote told him to follow the same route his companions had taken, and to beg their pardon for him for any damage, but he was powerless to do anything other than what he'd done.

Sancho also said: "If by chance those *señores* want to know who the brave man was who put you in such a state, tell them that it was the famous don Quixote de La Mancha, otherwise called THE WOEBEGONE KNIGHT."

With this the bachelor went away and don Quixote asked Sancho just what had moved him to call him the Woebegone Knight at that precise moment.

"I'll tell you," responded Sancho, "because I've been looking at you for a while by the light of the torch that poor fellow was carrying, and truly you've recently taken on the most woebegone face I've ever seen. It must have been caused either by the exhaustion brought about by this battle or maybe the loss of so many teeth."

"It's not that," responded don Quixote, "but rather it must have seemed to the wizard who is charged with writing the history of my deeds that it would be a good idea for me to have a nickname, as all the knights of yore had; one was called OF THE BURNING SWORD, another OF THE UNICORN, that one, OF THE MAIDENS, this one, OF THE PHŒNIX, the other one, OF THE GRIFFIN, that other one, OF DEATH,*

---

* The first and last mentioned refer to Amadís de Grecia. The other four are Belianís de Grecia, Floriando de Macedonia, Floriarlán de Tracia (Thrace), and the historic Count of Arenberg (Belgium).

and by these names and designations they were known all over the world. So, I say that the wizard just mentioned must have made you think of and say right now that I'd call myself the Woebegone Knight, as I plan to from now on. And so this name will be very clear, I'll have a very woebegone face painted on my shield as soon as I can."

"Your grace need not waste any time or money having that done," said Sancho, "for all you have to do is show your face for everyone to see, and without any picture or shield, they'll all call you the Woebegone One. And believe me, I'm telling the truth, because I promise you, *señor*—and this is said as a jest—that your hunger and missing teeth give you such a lamentable look, you don't need a painting to show it."

Don Quixote laughed at Sancho's joke. But, even so, he proposed to call himself by that name as soon as he could have his shield painted, as he'd planned.

"I forgot to say that you should be advised that your grace is now excommunicated for having laid hands violently on something holy: *Juxta illud, si quis suadente diabolo, &c.*"*

"I don't understand that Latin," responded don Quixote, "but I know very well that I didn't use my hands, but rather this lance; and in any case I didn't realize I was attacking priests or things of the Church—which I respect and adore, as the Catholic and faithful Christian that I am—but phantoms and monsters from the other world. And even so, I remember what happened to the Cid Ruy Díaz, when he broke the chair of the ambassador of that king in the presence of His Holiness the pope,† and was excommunicated for it, and yet he acted like a very honorable and fine knight that day."

When the bachelor heard this, he left, as has been said,

---

* "After that, if anyone, at the devil's instigation, &c." But the Latin isn't the problem. The problem is how the bachelor suddenly returns. Schevill's edition includes a new sentence to indicate that the bachelor has returned and said this—and practically all editions since then include that sentence—but the original edition has no such information.

† This is from a late ballad about the Cid, not from the original *Poem*. [Clemencín's note]

without uttering another word. Don Quixote wanted to see if the body on the litter was bones or not, but Sancho wouldn't allow it, saying to him: "*Señor*, your grace has come out of this adventure more safely than from any that I've seen. These people that you routed may just realize that it was only one person who defeated them. They'll be embarrassed and ashamed because of it, and might rally and come back looking for us, and give us all kinds of trouble. The donkey is loaded with food, the foothills are near, our hunger is great, so all we have to do is leave at our leisure, and, as they say: 'let the dead go to the grave and the living to the loaves.'"

Leading his donkey, he begged his master to follow, and it seemed to his master that he was right; and without saying a word he followed him. In a little while they were between two hills, and found themselves in a spacious hidden valley, where they dismounted, and Sancho took the donkey's load off. They lay down on the green grass, and, seasoned by the sauce of hunger, they ate breakfast, lunch, and dinner all at the same time with provisions the *señores* clerics of the dead man had with them on the pack mule— for it's only rarely that they fail to provide themselves with lots of things to eat.

But another misfortune befell them that Sancho held for the worst one of all, and that was that they had no wine, or even water to drink. They were parched with thirst, but seeing that the field where they were was liberally bestowed with fine green grass, Sancho said what will be told in the next chapter.

Chapter XX. About the never-before-seen and unheard-of adventure accomplished by the brave don Quixote de La Mancha, with less danger than any ever accomplished by any other famous knight in the world.

"THE PRESENCE of this grass, *señor mío*, shows there has to be some spring or brook nearby that waters it, so it would be good for us to go on a bit, and we'll soon come to where we can quench this terrible thirst tormenting us, because without a doubt, thirst is worse than hunger."

Don Quixote considered this to be good advice, so he took Rocinante's reins, and Sancho—after he loaded his donkey with the leftovers from dinner—took its halter, and they began to go up the meadow, feeling their way, because the blackness of the night prevented them from seeing anything. But they hadn't gone two hundred paces when the roar of falling water—as if it were rushing over immense lofty cliffs—came to their ears. This sound made them extraordinarily happy, and when they stopped to try to distinguish exactly where it was coming from, they heard a most unexpected noise that diluted their joy at having discovered water, especially Sancho, who was by nature a coward and quite fainthearted. I mean, they heard what sounded like rhythmic clanking of iron and chains, which, when accompanied by the furious din of the water, would instill fear in any heart, other than that of don Quixote.

As has been said, the night was dark, and they happened to have penetrated into a forest of tall trees, whose leaves, stirred by the mild wind, made a frightening but gentle noise, so that the solitude, the site, the darkness, the noise of the water, coupled with the rustling of the leaves, caused them dread and fright, and more so when they realized that the clanking wasn't diminishing, nor the wind subsiding, nor was it getting light, and added to this, they didn't know where they were.

But don Quixote, spurred on by his dauntless heart, leapt onto Rocinante, took his shield, leveled his lance, and said: "Sancho, my friend, I want you to know that I was born by the will of heavens in our Age of Iron to revive in it the Age of Gold, or the Golden Age, as it's commonly known. I'm the one for whom dangers, great exploits, and valiant deeds are reserved. I am, I say again, the one who will revive the Knights of the Round Table, the Twelve Peers of France, the Nine Worthies; the one who will cast into oblivion all the Platires, the Tablantes, the Olivantes, and Tirantes, the Febos, and Belianises, along with the whole throng of famous knights-errant of bygone days; accomplishing in this age in which I find myself such great deeds, unusual things, and feats of arms that will outshine the brightest ones that they all performed. You observe, my faithful squire, the darkness of this night, its odd silence, the quiet and indistinct rustling from these trees, the fearful noise of that water we came looking for, which seems to be falling headlong from the Mountains of the Moon,* and that unceasing hammering that deafens our ears. All these things together, and each one on its own, are sufficient to instill fear in the heart of Mars himself, not to mention in him who is not accustomed to such events and adventures. Everything I've said incites me and awakens my soul, and makes my heart burst inside my chest with the desire it has to undertake this adventure, no matter how difficult it might be. So, tighten Rocinante's cinches a bit, may God be with you, and wait for me no more than three days. If I don't return by then, you can go back to our village, and from there, as a favor to me, and as a good deed, go to El Toboso, where you'll tell the incomparable lady of mine, Dulcinea, that her captive knight died doing a deed that would make him worthy to be called hers."

When Sancho heard his master's words, he began to weep tenderly, and said: "I don't know why your grace would want to take on this fearful adventure. It's night now, no one can see us here, and we can easily turn away and avoid this danger, even though we may not drink for three days; and since no one can see us, no one will call us cowards. What's more, I've heard the priest in our village—and your grace knows him very well—preach that he who seeks danger perishes in it.† So, it's not a good idea to tempt God by taking on such a foolhardy undertaking from which one cannot escape unless it's by a miracle; and heaven has already given you plenty of miracles in sparing your grace from being blanketed (as I was), and in making you come out victorious and without a bruise from among so many enemies such as those who accompanied the dead body. And if all this won't serve to soften your resolve, consider that as soon as you've left, I, out of pure fear, will yield my soul to whoever would take it. I left my village and my wife to come to serve you, thinking I'd be worth more and not

---

* This alludes to the headwaters of the White Nile River in the Rwenzori Mountains bordering on Uganda and the République du Congo. Ptolemy (A.D. 150) called them the "Mountains of the Moon."
† This is a quote from Ecclesiasticus 3:26 in the Apocrypha: ". . . the man who flirts with danger will lose his life."

less. But just as 'greed bursts the sack,' it has torn up my hopes, because just when I thought I was on the verge of getting that cursed and ill-fated *ínsula* that your grace has promised me many times, I see that instead, you want to leave me now in this place, so far from contact with mankind. In the name of the one true God, *señor mío*, don't let such a detestable thing be done to me! If you're determined not to give up this undertaking, put it off, at least until tomorrow, because—according to what I learned while I was a shepherd—sunrise must only be three hours away, since the Little Dipper is overhead, and it's midnight when the handle stretches to the left."*

"How can you, Sancho," said don Quixote, "see where that handle or where that dipper is, since the night is so dark and you can't see any stars at all?"

"That's true," said Sancho, "but fear has many eyes, and sees things buried in the earth—not to mention what's in the sky—but if you think about it, it's reasonable that dawn isn't far off."

"No matter how much time there may be before dawn," responded don Quixote, "let it not be said of me, now, or at any time, that neither tears nor pleas dissuaded me from doing what I am compelled to do as a knight. So I beg you, Sancho, to keep still, for God, who has put the notion in my heart to take on this unheard-of and frightening adventure, will watch out for my well-being and will console your sadness. What you must do is tighten the cinches on Rocinante and stay here, for I'll return soon, dead or alive."

When Sancho saw the final resolve of his master and how little his tears, advice, and pleas were being heeded, he determined to use his ingenuity to make him wait until daybreak, if he could. So, while he was tightening the cinches on the horse, he neatly, and without being heard, hobbled Rocinante's rear hooves, so when don Quixote tried to ride away, he couldn't, because the horse could move only by hops.

When Sancho Panza saw how well his trick had worked,

---

* In Spain in August, the handle of the Little Dipper does indeed stretch to the left of the North Star at midnight. Clemencín offers a more complex explanation.

he said: "You see, *señor*, heaven, having been moved by my tears and supplications, has made it so Rocinante can't budge, and if you insist on spurring and whipping him, it will only enrage Fortune, and you'll be 'kicking against the pricks,' as they say."

Don Quixote despaired, and the more he spurred his horse, the less he would move. And without catching on to the hobbling, he thought it prudent to calm down and wait, either for the sun to rise, or for Rocinante to be able to move, believing that the impediment derived from something other than Sancho's inventiveness, and so he said to him: "Well, since that's the way it is, and Rocinante can't stir, I'm happy to wait until the dawn smiles upon us, although I may cry about its delay in coming."

"No reason to cry," responded Sancho, "for I'll entertain you, telling stories from now until daylight, unless you want to dismount and stretch out to sleep a bit on the green grass, as knights-errant do, so you'll be more rested when day comes and ready to take on this incomparable adventure that awaits you."

"What do you mean 'dismount and sleep'?" said don Quixote. "Am I by chance one of those knights who takes a rest when there's danger ahead? *You* should sleep, since you were born to sleep, or do whatever you want, and I'll do what I see best fits my character."

"Don't get angry, *señor mío*," responded Sancho. "I didn't mean it that way."

He approached his master and put one hand on the front pommel of his saddle, and the other on the other, so that he was tight against the left thigh of his master, and didn't dare move back an inch, such was the fear he had of the unceasing rhythmic clanging.

Don Quixote told him to relate a story to pass the time, as he'd promised, and Sancho said that he would, if the fear caused by what he was hearing would allow him to.

"Even so, I'll try to tell a story which, if I can, and no one interferes, is the best one ever. Pay attention, your grace, because I'm beginning now: Once upon a time—and may the good that's coming be for everyone, and misfortune for those who go looking for it. And let me tell you, *señor mío*, that the way the ancients began their tales wasn't just any old thing, but rather a maxim of Cato Zonzorino,* the Roman, who says: 'Misfortune for those who go looking for it,' which 'fits us like a ring on your finger,' meaning that your grace should stay quiet and not go looking for trouble anywhere, but that we should slip away down another road, since no one is forcing us to stay on this one, where so many fears assault us."

"Go on with your story, Sancho," said don Quixote, "and leave the road we should take to my care."

"So I say," Sancho continued, "that in a village in Extremadura† there was a goatherd, and this goatherd, as I say in my story, was called Lope Ruiz, and this Lope Ruiz was crazy about a shepherdess who was called Torralba, and this shepherdess named Torralba was the daughter of a rich cattleman, and this rich cattleman . . ."

"If you tell stories that way, Sancho," said don Quixote, "repeating everything you say, you won't finish in two days. Tell it in a straightforward way like an intelligent man, or else don't say anything."

"Where I'm from," responded Sancho, "everybody tells these tales the same way. I can't tell them any other way, and it's not right for you to ask me to do things in a different way."

"Tell it however you like, then," responded don Quixote, "since Fate insists that I have to listen to you. Go on."

"So, *señor mío*," Sancho continued, "as I've already said, this goatherd was in love with La Torralba, the shepherdess, who was a plump, wild girl who was a bit mannish because she had a little teeny mustache. I can almost see her now."

"You knew her, did you?" said don Quixote.

"I didn't know her," responded Sancho, "but the person who told me this story said it was so factual and true that when I told it to someone else, I could affirm and even swear that I'd seen it all take place. So, as days came and went, the devil—who never sleeps and who confounds

---

* Cato Censorino (the Censor) (234–149 B.C.) was the first important Roman writer. Among other things he produced *Præcepta* ("maxims") for his son. Since this does not survive, the sayings attributed to him are doubtless apocryphal. *Zonzorino* means "stupid rogue."
† Extremadura is a poor region made up of the modern provinces of Cáceres and Badajoz in the west of Spain, bordering on Portugal.

everything—arranged it so that the love that the goatherd had for the shepherdess turned into hatred and ill will, and this was caused—as gossip has it—by a bit of jealousy that she stirred in him that was such that it overstepped the bounds of reason, and encroached on what is forbidden. And it was such that the goatherd came to hate her so much that from then on, so as not to see her, he was determined to leave that place and go where he would never set eyes on her again. La Torralba realized that Lope had scorned her, so immediately came to love him, although she never had before."

"That's the natural condition of women—" said don Quixote, "to scorn whoever loves them and to love whoever hates them. Continue, Sancho."

"It happened," said Sancho, "that the goatherd put his decision into effect, and gathering his goats, he started off through the fields of Extremadura to go into the kingdom of Portugal. La Torralba found out about it and followed him from a distance on foot and shoeless, with a staff in her hand and a knapsack hanging from her neck, and in it she had—at least this is what they say—a broken piece of a mirror and part of a comb, and some kind of canister of face powder; but whatever it was she carried, I couldn't care less for the moment. I'll just say that they say that the goatherd arrived with his flock to cross the Guadiana River,* and at that time the river was almost overflowing, and there was no boat to take him and his flock across. This distressed him to no end because he saw La Torralba was going to arrive soon and would give him a lot of trouble, what with her pleas and tears. But he looked around until he found a fisherman who had a small boat that could only hold one person and a single goat. He talked with the fisherman, who agreed to transport him and the three hundred goats he had with him. The fisherman went into the boat and took one goat; he came back and took another; he came back again and took another. Now, your grace should keep a careful tally of the goats that the fisherman is taking across, because if you miss one, the story will end and it won't be possible to say another word about it. I'll continue, saying that the landing place on the other side of the

---

* This river forms the border with Portugal for long stretches.

river was full of mud and was slippery, and it took a long time to go and come back. Nevertheless, he came back for another goat, and another, and another. . . ."

"Let's just say that he finally got them all across," said don Quixote, "and don't keep coming and going like that. Otherwise you won't finish in a year."

"How many have been taken across so far?" said Sancho.

"How the devil should I know?" responded don Quixote.

"Well, there you are! I told you to keep a tally, and you didn't. So, by God, that's the end of the story, and there's no way to go on."

"How can that be?" responded don Quixote. "Is it so important to the story to keep track of the goats that have been taken over, so that if one of them is not counted you can't go on with the story?"

"That's right, *senor*," responded Sancho, "because as soon as I asked you to tell me how many goats had gone over and you said you didn't know—at that very second, I instantly forgot what remained to be told of the story, and I swear there were worthwhile and amusing things in it."

"So," said don Quixote, "the story is finished?"

"It's as finished as my mother is," said Sancho.

"To tell you the truth," responded don Quixote, "you've told one of the most original tales or stories that anyone in the world has ever contrived, and your way of telling it and cutting it short has never been seen nor will ever be seen in a lifetime, although I expected no less from you. But I'm not surprised, since this eternal pounding must have confused your judgment."

"Anything is possible," responded Sancho, "but I know that there's nothing of my story left since it ends where the error in the tally of the goats begins."

"Let it end where you will," said don Quixote, "and let's see if Rocinante can stir." He tried his luck with the spurs again, and Rocinante gave a few hops and then stopped, so well was he hobbled.

At this point it seems—whether it was the coolness of the morning, or that Sancho had eaten something that acted like a laxative, or that it was just something natural (and this is the most believable thing)—he suddenly felt like he needed to do what no one else could do for him. But there was so much fear in his heart he didn't dare separate himself one millimeter from his master. To consider not doing what he needed to was also not possible. So what he did was to release his right hand from the rear pommel and with it he neatly and noiselessly untied the bowknot that held up his pants, without using his other hand, and when he untied it, his pants fell down and were like fetters. After this he raised his shirt as well as he could, and stuck out his rear end—which was far from small. This having been done, which was all he thought he needed to do in order to get out of that terrible bind and anguish, another thought came to him, greater than the first one, and that was that it seemed to him that he couldn't relieve himself without making some kind of noise, and he clenched his teeth and squeezed his shoulders together, holding his breath as well as he could. But even with all these precautions, he was so unlucky that he made a bit of noise, very different from the one that had made him so afraid.

Don Quixote heard it and said: "What noise is that, Sancho?"

"I don't know, *señor*," he responded. "It must be something new. Adventures and misfortunes never begin for no reason."

Again he tried his luck, and he had such success that, without any further noise or turmoil that had troubled him the previous time, he found himself free of the burden that had caused him so much discomfort. But since don Quixote had a sense of smell as keen as his sense of hearing, and Sancho was so close to him, the fumes rose practically straight up and it was impossible for them not to reach his nose; and just after they arrived, he alleviated the problem by pinching his nose between two fingers and said with something of a twang: "It seems to me, Sancho, that you're quite afraid."

"Yes, I am," responded Sancho, "but why would your grace say that at this particular moment?"

"Because you smell worse than ever, and not of perfume," responded don Quixote.

"That may easily be," said Sancho, "but I'm not to blame—*you* are, rather, since you bring me to these strange places at such odd hours."

"Go back three or four paces, friend," said don Quixote—

still holding his nose—"and from now on be more careful with your person and show me more respect. I fear that all my dealings with you have bred contempt."

"I'll bet," replied Sancho, "that your grace thinks that I've done something I shouldn't have."

"The less said, the better," responded don Quixote.

In this and other similar conversations, master and servant spent the night. But when Sancho saw how soon morning was going to arrive, he quickly unhobbled Rocinante and fastened his pants. As soon as Rocinante felt he was free, even though he was not normally very spirited, it seems that he felt better, and began to paw the ground since bucking (begging his pardon) he couldn't do. Seeing that Rocinante was moving about, don Quixote took it as a good omen and thought it was a sign that he should take on that fearful adventure. Just then daybreak arrived and things suddenly looked different. Don Quixote saw that he was among some tall trees, and that they were chestnuts that gave a very dark shade. He also was aware that the pounding hadn't stopped, but couldn't see what was causing it. And without further delay he made Rocinante feel his spurs, and bidding farewell to Sancho once again, he told him to wait three days at the longest, as he'd already told him, and at the end of that time, if he didn't return, Sancho could be sure that it had pleased God that his days should end in that dangerous adventure. He mentioned the message that he was to take to his lady Dulcinea; and insofar as getting paid for his services, he shouldn't worry because he'd made his will before he left their village, where his salary was set down, to be prorated for his length of service. But if God would guide him through that peril unscathed he could be more than certain that the promised *ínsula* would be his.

Once again Sancho shed tears, hearing the doleful words of his good master, and he resolved not to leave his side until the very end of the event at hand.

From Sancho's such honorable tears and determination, the author of this history concludes that he must have been wellborn, or at least an Old Christian,* and his feelings

---

* An Old Christian is from a family that has always been Catholic, that is, no one was or is a converted Jew.

moved his master somewhat, but not enough so he might show any weakness. On the contrary, hiding his feelings as well as he could, he began to ride toward where it seemed to him the noise of the water and the pounding were coming from. Sancho followed on foot, holding, as was his custom, the halter of his donkey, his constant companion in his good and bad times. And having gone a good distance among those chestnuts and other shady trees, they came upon a meadow that was at the foot of a towering cliff from where a mighty torrent of water plunged. At the foot of the cliff were some shacks that seemed to be more ruins than edifices, from where the noise and clatter of that pounding—which still was not letting up—was clearly coming.

Rocinante became very agitated with the noise of the water and the pounding. Don Quixote calmed him down and slowly approached the shacks, commending himself with all his heart to his lady, begging her favor in that fearful expedition and undertaking, and along the way he also commended himself to God, asking not to be forgotten by Him. Sancho never left his side, and with an outstretched neck peered between Rocinante's legs to see if he could find out what held him so much in suspense and made him so fearful.

They went another hundred paces and rounded a promontory, where they saw right in front of them the unmistakable cause (it couldn't have been anything else) of that terrifying noise that had them so much in suspense and frightened all night. And it was—if you won't consider it, dear reader, too irritating or maddening—six fulling mills* that caused all that clatter with their rhythmic pounding.

When don Quixote saw what it was, he became silent and was utterly abashed. Sancho saw that his head was bowed over his chest, showing that he was quite mortified. Don Quixote also looked at Sancho, and he saw that his cheeks

---

* In order to make homespun cloth usable, the freshly woven material had to go through the fulling process, which was to beat the cloth in water (and fuller's earth) until it shrank, thickened, and got soft. From antiquity until the Middle Ages, this was done by hand with two wooden hammers. In the thirteenth century, waterwheels provided the hard labor, and the person in the mill just kept the cloth moving. Nowadays, fulling is a combination of mechanical and chemical processes.

were puffed out and his mouth was full of laughter, almost to the point of bursting. His melancholy was not so great that at the sight of his squire he couldn't help but laugh himself. And since Sancho saw that his master had begun to laugh, he released the dam of laughter in such a way that he had to hold his sides so he wouldn't split. Four times he was able to compose himself, and another four times his fit of laughter returned with the same intensity as the first, and all of this made don Quixote angry, and more so when he heard Sancho say in jest: "I want you to know, Sancho, my friend, that I was born by the will of heaven in our Age of Iron to resuscitate in it the Age of Gold, or Golden Age. I'm the one for whom are reserved the dangers, the great deeds, the brave acts . . ." and he continued repeating all or most of the words that don Quixote had said when they first heard that terrible pounding.

Don Quixote, seeing that Sancho was making fun of him, was quite offended, and he became so angry that he raised his lance and whacked him twice, and if those blows had been on his head instead of his back, he would have been freed from paying his salary, unless it was to his heirs. When Sancho saw what little benefit there was in his joke, and fearing his master might take it further, he said with great humility: "Calm down, your grace, because, as God is my witness, I was just joking."

"Well, if you were joking, I am not," responded don Quixote. "Come here, my merry friend. Do you think that if these fulling mills had been some other dangerous adventure, I wouldn't have shown the same courage necessary to take it on and see it to its end? I'm a knight, and am I by chance supposed to be able to distinguish sounds and know which are from a fulling mill and which aren't? What's more it might be—and it is true—that I haven't seen any such mills in my whole life, unlike you—like the vile rustic you are—who must have seen them, since you were raised and born among them. Why, just change these six fulling mills into six giants, and toss them into my beard singly or all at once, and if I don't kill them all, you can make as much fun as you want to of me."

"No more, *señor mío*," replied Sancho. "I confess I've been smiling a bit too much. But tell me, your grace, now that we've made peace—and may God see you through all future adventures as safe and sound as he's seen you through this one—wasn't it really something laughable? And isn't the great fear that we had something that should be told about? At least I was afraid—I know that your grace doesn't have any notion of what fear or dread is."

"I don't deny that what happened to us is something worthy of laughter. But it's not worthy of telling others about, since not everyone is astute enough to put these points in perspective."

"At least," responded Sancho, "your grace put the point of your lance in perspective, aiming it at my head and thwacking me on my back, and I thank God I was able to veer away. But, come on, 'everything will come out in the wash,' because I've heard it told that 'the one who loves you the most will make you cry,' and what's more, I know that great men, after saying a harsh word to a servant, give him a pair of pants, but I don't know what they give them after they whack them a couple of times; unless it is that knights-errant give their squires *ínsulas* or kingdoms on terra firma after they whack them."

"That's the way the dice may fall," said don Quixote. "Everything you said may come true, and pardon me for what happened; since you're a sharp fellow, I hope you realize that first impulses are not controllable. And let me tell you—from now on you should abstain and refrain from talking too much with me because in all the romances of chivalry that I've read—and they're infinite—I've never read that any squire spoke so much with his master as you do with yours. And in truth, I consider it a great defect—both yours and mine: yours, in that you have so little respect for me; and mine, because I don't command greater respect. In fact, Gandalín, Amadís de Gaula's squire, was count of *Ínsula Firme*. You read about him that he always spoke to his master with his cap in his hand, his head bowed, and his body bent double *more turquesco*.* And what can we say of Gasabal, squire of don Galaor, who was so reserved that to show you the excellence of his wonderful silence, he's mentioned only one time in that so great and true history? From all of this, you can infer, Sancho, that it's nec-

---

* Clemencín says that Gandalín did none of this, including bending over in the "Turkish way" "in a deep bow."

essary to show a difference between master and servant, and between knight and squire. So, from now on we should treat each other with more respect, with no joking around, because if I should get angry with you, 'it'll be bad for the pitcher.'* The favors and benefits I've promised you will come in due time. And if they don't come, your salary at least won't be lost, as I've told you."

"Everything your grace has said is all right," said Sancho, "but I'd like to know, in case these favors don't come in due time and it becomes necessary to resort to a salary, just how much did a squire of a knight-errant earn in those days, and if they were paid by the month, or on a daily basis, like hod carriers."

"I don't believe," responded don Quixote, "that such squires were ever salaried, rather they worked for favors. And if I've named you in my sealed will that I left at home, it was because of what may happen, since I don't know yet how chivalry will fare in these such calamitous times of ours, and I don't want my soul to agonize in the other world because of trifles. I want you to know, Sancho, that there is in the world no more dangerous a profession than that of knights."

"That's the truth," said Sancho, "since all it takes is the noise of fulling mills to upset and disturb the heart of such a brave knight adventurer as your grace is. But you can be sure, from now on, I'll not open my mouth to make a joke about anything dealing with you, but rather to honor you as my natural lord."

"In that way," replied don Quixote, "you'll live in peace on the face of the earth, because after one's own parents, one should respect one's master as if he were a parent."

---

* There's a Spanish saying: "If the rock hits the pitcher or if the pitcher hits the rock, it'll be bad for the pitcher."

Chapter XXI. Which deals with the high adventure and priceless acquisition of Mambrino's helmet, with other things that happened to our invincible knight.

A T THAT moment, it began to rain a bit and Sancho suggested that they go into one of the fulling mills, but because don Quixote had developed such a loathing of them owing to the bad joke, he refused to go in under any circumstance. So, as the road twisted off to the right, they came upon a new one similar to the one they had taken the day before.

In a little while don Quixote saw a man riding along wearing something on his head that glittered as if it were made of gold, and hardly had he seen it when he turned toward Sancho and said: "It seems to me, Sancho, that there's no proverb that is not true, because they're all maxims taken from experience, the mother of all sciences, especially the one that says: 'where one door closes another opens.' I say this because if last night Fortune closed the door on the adventure we were seeking by deceiving us with the fulling mills, it has opened wide another better and more certain adventure now; and if I don't undertake it, it will be my own fault, and I won't be able to blame either my lack of experience with fulling mills or the darkness of the night. I say this because, if I'm not mistaken, a man is coming toward us who is wearing Mambrino's helmet on his head, about which I made the oath you know about."

"Watch what you're saying, your grace, and even more what you're doing," said Sancho. "I don't want it to be more fulling mills that will get the better of us and knock us senseless."

"The devil take you," replied don Quixote. "What does the helmet have to do with fulling mills?"

"I don't know anything," responded Sancho, "but I swear if I could talk as much as I used to, maybe I'd say things so that your grace would see that you're mistaken in what you're saying."

"How can I be mistaken in what I'm saying, you frightened traitor?" said don Quixote. "Tell me, don't you see that knight coming toward us on a dappled silver-gray horse who is wearing a golden helmet on his head?"

"What I can make out," responded Sancho, "is nothing more than a man on a dark gray donkey, like mine, who is wearing something on his head that's shining."

"Well, that's Mambrino's helmet!" said don Quixote. "Step to one side and let me at him by myself. You'll see how, to save time, I can finish off this adventure without uttering a single word, and the helmet I wanted so much will be mine."

"I'll be careful to get out of the way," responded Sancho, "but I'll say again, 'may God make it oregano,' and not turn it into fulling mills."*

"I've told you, brother, never even to consider mentioning fulling mills to me again," said don Quixote, "because I swear to . . . and I won't say any more; and may God hammer your very soul."

Sancho stopped talking, fearing that his master would fulfill the vow that he'd just made, in no uncertain terms.

Here's what the situation was with the helmet, the horse, and the rider that don Quixote saw: In that region there were two villages, one so small it had neither an apothecary's shop nor a barber, and another one nearby that did. So, the barber from the larger village served the smaller one; and in the latter village there was a sick person who needed to be bled and another who needed a shave, and for that reason the barber had a basin made of brass with him. As luck would have it, just as he was passing by, it began to rain. So that he wouldn't spoil his hat (which was probably new), he put the basin on his head, and since it was polished, it shone from half a league away. He was riding a gray donkey, as Sancho said. This was the circumstance that led don Quixote to believe that it was a dappled silver-gray horse, with a knight wearing a golden helmet, since everything he saw he easily tailored to his nonsensical notions of chivalry. When he saw that the poor man was approaching, without exchanging any words with him, he set Rocinante to gallop and lowered his lance, intending to split him in

---

* There's a Spanish saying: "May God make it oregano and not turn it into caraway seed." Caraway seed was held in less esteem than oregano.

two. But as he got near, maintaining the furious pace of his attack, he shouted to him: "Defend yourself, you vile creature, or hand over of your free will what so rightly belongs to me!"

The barber, who so unexpectedly saw that phantom bear down on him, couldn't do anything to prevent his being run through with the lance but to drop from his donkey, and hardly had he touched the ground when he jumped up more agile than a deer, and began to run through that field faster than the wind. His basin fell onto the ground, which pleased don Quixote, who said that the pagan had been prudent to imitate the beaver, who, when pursued by hunters, bites and tears out with his teeth what he knows by instinct he's being hunted for.* He told Sancho to pick up the helmet, and taking it in his hands, he said: "By God, this is a nice basin! It must be worth a *real* if it's worth a *maravedí*!"

When he gave it to his master, he put it on his head right away, turning it about to examine it, and looking for the visor. Seeing that it was missing, he said: "The pagan for whom this helmet was fitted doubtless had a very large head, but what's worse is that half of it's missing."

When Sancho heard the basin being called a helmet, he couldn't contain his laughter. But when he remembered his master's anger, he stopped laughing immediately.

"What are you laughing about, Sancho?" said don Quixote.

"I'm laughing," responded Sancho, "thinking about the big head belonging to the pagan owner of this helmet, which looks perfectly like a barber's basin."

"Do you know what I think, Sancho? I think this famous fragment of this enchanted helmet, by some strange accident, must have come into the hands of someone who couldn't recognize or appreciate its value, and without realizing what he was doing, seeing that it was cast from purest gold, he must have melted the other half for what it

---

* There was an old wives' tale that the male beaver, knowing he was being hunted for the castoreum found in his genitals, would castrate himself and leave his genitals behind to save his life. In truth, this substance is found in the perineal glands near the anus of *both* sexes, and is impossible to remove with the creature's own teeth.

might be worth, and from this half he made what looks like a barber's basin, just as you say. But no matter, since I recognize what it is, the transformation makes no difference. I'll have it repaired in the first village with a blacksmith, so that the one that the god of smithies* made and forged for the god of battles won't surpass it or even come close; and until I can have it fixed, I'll wear it as well as I can, because something is better than nothing, and what's more, it'll be enough to protect me from a shower of stones."

"That's only," said Sancho, "if they're not shot from a sling, like the ones that were hurled in the battle with the two armies, when they made the sign of the cross on your molars and broke the cruet that contained the very blessed brew that made me vomit my guts out."

"It doesn't bother me that I lost it, because, as you know, Sancho," said don Quixote, "I have the recipe for it in my head."

"I do, too," responded Sancho. "But if I ever were to make it or taste any more of it in my life, may I die right then. In any case, I don't plan to get into a situation where I'll need any, because I'll use all of my five senses to prevent myself from getting hurt by anybody. About getting blanketed again, I won't say anything, since such misfortunes can scarcely be prevented; and if they do happen, the only thing you can do is shrug your shoulders and go wherever luck and the blanket take you."

"You're a bad Christian, Sancho," said don Quixote when he heard this, "because you never forget an injury once it's been done to you. Don't you know that noble and generous hearts pay no attention to such foolishness? Are you lame? Do you have a broken rib? Did your head crack open? Why can't you just forget that jest? When you think about it, it was just a joke and entertainment, and if I'd not seen it just that way, I would have gone back and done greater damage in avenging you than the Greeks did when Helen was kidnapped.† If she lived in these times, or my Dulcinea lived in hers, you could be quite sure that she wouldn't be as famous for her beauty as she is." And here he heaved a sigh toward the clouds.

---

* This refers to Vulcan, who forged the armor for Mars.
† This resulted in the Trojan War.

And Sancho said: "It was just a prank then, since I can't do anything about it—but I do know the difference between what is in earnest and what is a joke, and I also know that it will stay in my memory and imprinted on my back. But all this aside, what should we do with this dappled silver-gray horse that looks like a gray donkey, abandoned by that fellow Martino, who you overcame when he took to his heels? It looks to me like he doesn't ever plan to come back for it, and it's a really nice donkey."

"I'm not accustomed," said don Quixote, "to despoiling those whom I conquer, nor does chivalric law allow us to take their horses and leave them on foot. Now, if the victor loses his horse in the fray, it's legitimate to take the horse belonging to the conquered one as a lawful prize of war. So, Sancho, leave this horse or donkey, or whatever you want it to be, alone, since its owner, when he sees us go away, will come back for it."

"God knows that I'd like to take it," replied Sancho, "or at least exchange it for mine, who doesn't seem quite as good. Truly the laws of chivalry are strict, since they don't even allow you to exchange one donkey for another. But I'd like to know if I can at least take the trappings."

"I'm not sure about that," responded don Quixote, "and in this case, until I can read up on the subject, I think it's all right for you to exchange them, but only if you're in great need of them."

"So great is the need," responded Sancho, "that if they were for my own use, my need wouldn't be greater."

So then, armed with this permission, he did the *mutatio capparum** and made his donkey look uncommonly handsome, bettering its looks severalfold.

Once this was done, they ate lunch using the spoils that they got from the pack mule, and they drank water from the brook downstream from the fulling mills, never looking back at them, such was the abhorrence they had of them, owing to the fear that the mills had instilled in them. Having ministered to their hunger and even their melancholy, they got back onto their mounts and, with no special destination in mind—imitating the knights-errant who took no

---

* *Mutatio capparum* was when cardinals of the Church exchanged leather hoods for ones of red silk annually on Easter.

particular road—they began to travel where Rocinante's will led them. Rocinante led his master and also Sancho's donkey, who always followed him no matter where he led, out of devotion and companionship. They wound up on the main highway, and continued along letting Fortune guide them without further thought.

As they went along, Sancho said to his master: "*Señor*, would your grace give me permission to speak with you a bit? Since you imposed that harsh commandment of silence on me, more than four things have turned rotten in my stomach, and I have yet another on the tip of my tongue that I don't want to waste."

"Say it all," said don Quixote, "and be brief in what you say, since nothing is pleasing if it's long."

"I'll say, *señor*," responded Sancho, "that for some days now I've been thinking how little one earns by wandering about and seeking the adventures your grace is looking for in these deserted areas and at these crossroads, where, though the most dangerous ones are met and overcome, no one is around to see or hear of them, so they'll be sunk into eternal silence, to the detriment of your ambition and contrary to the fame that they deserve. So, it seems to me that it would be better, unless you have a better idea, for us to try to serve some emperor, or an important prince who is at war, in whose service you can show your courage, your enormous strength, and great intelligence. And when the lord we serve sees all this, he'll just have to compensate each one according to his merits, and there will be no lack of scribes to write down your deeds for eternal remembrance. Of my own deeds I won't say anything, since they won't exceed the bounds of squirely duties, although I'll tell you, if it's chivalric custom to record the deeds of squires, I don't think mine should be passed over in silence."

"Not a bad idea, Sancho," responded don Quixote, "but before a knight can get to that point, he'll have to wander throughout the world, as if on probation, seeking adventures so that, after he's had a good number of them, he'll have such renown that when he arrives at the court of some great monarch, his fame as a knight will be known through his deeds, and hardly will the boys of the city have seen him enter through the city gates when all of them will follow and surround him, shouting: 'This the Knight of the Sun,' or 'of the Serpent,' or some other insignia under which he'll have done so many deeds. 'This is,' they will say, 'the one who conquered in a singular battle the giant Brocabruno of the Enormous Strength; he who liberated the great Mameluco of Persia from the enchantment that had gripped him for almost nine hundred years.' So from mouth to mouth his deeds will be proclaimed, and then in the midst of the tumult of the boys and the rest of the people, he'll stop before the windows of the castle belonging to the king of that kingdom. And when the king sees him, he'll recognize him immediately because of his armor or the emblem on his shield, and he'll have to say: 'All my knights! Stand up and go out to greet the flower of knighthood who is coming this way!' And at this command they'll all go out, and the king will go halfway down the stairs and will embrace him and will kiss him on the cheek, and will take him by the hand to meet the queen, where the knight will find her with the princess, their daughter, who will certainly be one of the most beautiful and perfect maidens to be found in the entire world. What will happen then is that the princess will cast her eyes on the knight and his on her, and each one will appear to the other more divine than human, and without knowing how, they will become prisoners of and be bound in the inextricable net of love, and with great affliction in their hearts because they won't know how they are to speak with each other to reveal their longings and feelings. From there he'll be taken to some richly adorned room in the palace, where, once they have removed his armor, they'll bring him a rich mantle of scarlet to wear, and if he looked good in his armor, he'll look as good or even better in his doublet.

"When the night comes, he'll dine with the king, queen, and princess, and he'll never take his eyes off of her, looking at her on the sly so others won't notice, and she'll do the same with similar circumspection, because, as I said, she's a very discreet maiden. The tables will be whisked away, and through the door of that room an ugly little dwarf will enter unannounced, followed by two giants flanking a beautiful lady-in-waiting, and she'll have with her a certain difficult trial devised by an old wise man who is an expert in matters of chivalry, and the one who does best in the trial will be deemed the best knight in the world. The king will then command all those present to attempt it, and no one will be able to do it except the guest knight, much to the enhancement of his fame, and to the contentment of the princess, all the more so for having placed her thoughts so high. And the best part is that this king or prince, or whatever he is, is engaging in a very savage war with another as powerful as himself, and the guest knight asks his permission—after a few days at his court—to serve him in that war. The king will grant it very willingly, and the knight will kiss his hands for the favor done him.

"And that night he'll go to the garden to bid farewell to the princess through the grating of the room where she sleeps, through which he's spoken to her many times, through the wiles of a maiden whom she trusts as the go-between and confidante in everything. He'll sigh, she'll faint, the maiden will bring her water and will be distraught, because the morning is coming and she doesn't want to sully the honor of her lady if they're found out. Finally the princess will come to, and will give the knight her white hands through the grating, and he'll kiss them a thousand and a thousand times more and will bathe them in tears. They will then plan how they should exchange news about their good or bad fortune, and the princess will beg him to stay away as short a time as he can, which he'll swear to do. He'll then kiss her hands again, and say GOOD-BYE with such emotion that he'll almost die. He goes to his room and throws himself onto his bed and cannot sleep because of this painful farewell, and gets up early in the morning. He goes to say his good-byes to the king and queen, and to the princess. They tell him, when he has bidden farewell to the two of them, that the princess is indisposed and cannot receive visitors. The knight figures it's because of the grief caused by his leaving, which pierces his heart, and he all but betrays his own anguish. The maiden go-between is present. She notices this and runs off to tell her mistress about it, and she receives this news with tears, and she says that one of her greatest sorrows is that she doesn't know who her knight is, or if he's of royal lineage or not. The maiden assures her that so much courtesy, gentle bearing, and valor such as her knight possesses could only be found in a royal and important person. The afflicted girl is consoled by this and tries to rally so that she won't arouse her parents' suspicion, and at the end of the second day she again appears in public. By now the knight has gone off to fight in the war, conquers the enemy of the king, sacks many cities, triumphs in countless battles. He returns to court, sees his lady in the usual place, and they agree that he'll ask her father for her hand in marriage as a reward for his services. The king refuses to give his permission because he doesn't know who he is. But by kidnapping her or otherwise, the princess comes to be his wife, and her father comes to consider it good fortune, because they have now found out that the knight is the son of a brave king of some kingdom or other—I don't think it's on the map. The father dies, the princess inherits the kingdom, and in a few words, the knight becomes king. Now is when he can do favors for his squire, and for all those who helped him rise to his present state. He marries off his squire to a maiden of the princess, who must have been the go-between in their love, and she'll be the daughter of a very important duke."

"That's what I want, no doubt about it!" said Sancho. "That's what I'm waiting for, because everything has got to turn out that way, now that you're known as the Woebegone Knight."

"Don't doubt it, Sancho," replied don Quixote, "because in precisely that way, and by those very steps I've told you about, knights-errant rise, and have risen, to become kings and emperors. All we need to do now is find out which Christian or pagan king is at war and has a beautiful daughter. But there'll be plenty of time for all this, since, as I've told you, before going to court, we have to become famous. But there's one thing more: Let's say that there's a king who is at war who has a beautiful daughter, and that I'll be incredibly famous throughout the universe; I just don't know how it can be verified that I'm of royal lineage, or at least second cousin to an emperor. The king won't hand me his daughter to be my wife unless he's informed about this, no matter how much my famous deeds make me deserving. So, I fear that because of this, I'll lose what my arm has made me worthy of. It's true that I'm an *hidalgo* of recognized lineage and have an income of five hundred *sueldos*, and it may be that the wizard who is writing my story can clear up my ancestry and origin so that I'll turn out to be the great-grandson of a king.

"I'll have you know, Sancho, that there are two kinds of lineages in the world: those that trace theirs to princes and monarchs and, little by little, taper off with time and wind up like a pyramid turned upside down; and the others that start out low-class, and rise a bit at a time, until they get to be great lords. The difference is that some people were what they now are not, and others are now what they weren't at first. I may be of those whose origin, after investigation, will prove to have been great and renowned, and the king who is to be my father-in-law will have to be content with that. And if he isn't, the princess will be so much in love with me that in spite of her father, even though she finds out that I'm the son of a water carrier, she will receive me as her lord and husband. And if that doesn't work, here's where I abduct her and take her wherever I want, and either time or death will put an end to the wrath of her parents."

"And here also fits," said Sancho, "what some mischievous people say: 'don't ask as a favor what you can take by force,' although this next one is better: 'a leap over the hedge* is better than good men's prayers.' I say this because if the king, your grace's father-in-law, doesn't want to hand over my lady the princess to you, all that needs to be done, as your grace says, is to kidnap her and take her away. But the bad part is that until peace is made and you come to enjoy the peaceful possession of your kingdom, your poor squire is left out in the cold insofar as favors go, unless the confidante who is to be his wife comes with the princess and he shares his misfortune with her, until heaven ordains something else; for it may well be, I think, that his master will give her to him right away to be his wife."

"Don't worry. No one will take her away from you," said don Quixote.

"Well, if that's the way it is," responded Sancho, "there's nothing to do but commend ourselves to God and let Fortune take whatever road it will."

"May God work it out," responded don Quixote, "as I want, and you require, and 'let him lie who will not rise.'"

"May it be God's will," said Sancho, "because I'm an Old Christian, and to be a count, that's plenty."

---

* That is, escaping.

"It's more than enough," said don Quixote, "and if it's not, it would make no difference, because since I'd be king, I could give you a noble title without your having to buy it or by your doing any particular service. Because when I make you a count, just imagine yourself there, now a knight, and say what they will. By my faith they'll have to address you as YOUR LORDSHIP, whether they like it or not."

"And just watch how well I perform my duties with this new title of mobility!" said Sancho.

"*Nobility* you should say, and not *mobility*," said his master.

"Whatever it is," responded Sancho, "I say that I'll be able to do it well, because I once served as a summoner in a brotherhood, and the robes of the summoner looked so good on me that everyone said that I could be the steward of that brotherhood. Well, what'll happen when I put on the robe of a duke, or dress up in gold and pearls, as foreign counts do? I believe they'll come from a hundred leagues just to look at me."

"You'll look good," said don Quixote, "but you'll have to keep your beard trimmed, because the way you have it now, so thick, tangled, and unkempt, if you don't have it taken care of every other day at least, they'll be able to tell what you are from a musket shot away."

"All that's needed," said Sancho, "is to keep a salaried barber at home. And if it becomes necessary, I'll have him follow me around like a groom does a grandee."

"How do you know," asked don Quixote, "that grandees have grooms that follow them around?"

"I'll tell you," responded Sancho. "Some years ago I spent a month at court, and I saw a little fellow walking around there—who they said was very *grande**—a man followed him around on horseback every turn he took, and he seemed to be this fellow's tail. I asked why this man never traveled next to the other, but always behind him. They said he was his groom, and it was the custom of the grandees to have those fellows follow them. I've always remembered it and have never forgotten it."

"You're quite right," said don Quixote, "so you can have your barber follow you. Customs weren't invented all at

---

* *Grande* is the adjective "big" as well as the noun meaning "grandee."

once, nor were they established in a single day. You can be the first count to have a barber following him around, and it requires more trust to have one's beard shaved than to have one's horse saddled."

"Leave the barber to me," said Sancho, "and your grace should just take care to become a king and make me a count."

"That's the way it'll be," responded don Quixote.

And when they raised their eyes, they saw what will be told in the next chapter.

Chapter XXII. About the freedom that don Quixote gave to many unfortunates who, much against their will, were being taken where they did not want to go.

CIDE HAMETE Benengeli, the Arabic and Manchegan author, relates in this most serious, high-sounding, meticulous, delightful, and imagined story, that, after that conversation between don Quixote de La Mancha and Sancho Panza, his squire, recorded at the end of Chapter Twenty-one, don Quixote raised his eyes and saw coming toward him as many as twelve men, strung together by their necks like beads, with a long chain, and all of them wearing handcuffs. Coming with them were two men on horseback and two on foot. Those who were on horseback had muskets and those on foot had pikes and swords, and as soon as Sancho Panza saw them, he said: "This is a chain of galley slaves, men sentenced by the king and forced to row in his galleys."

"What do you mean *forced*?" asked don Quixote. "Is it possible that the king is forcing anyone?"

"I'm not saying that—" responded Sancho, "only that these are people who, because of their crimes, are sentenced to serve the king in galleys, by force."

"So, no matter," replied don Quixote, "these people are being taken away by force and not of their free will."

"That's right," said Sancho.

"In that case," said his master, "here's where I can do what my profession requires: to set forced actions right and to succor and aid poor wretches."

"Be careful, your grace," said Sancho, "for Justice, which is the king himself, isn't using force or striking out against these people, but rather is punishing them for their crimes."

Just then, the chain of galley slaves arrived, and don Quixote, with very courteous words, asked their guards please to inform and tell him the cause, or causes, for which they were escorting those people in that way.

One of the guards on horseback responded that they were prisoners whom His Majesty was sending to the galleys, and that there was nothing more to say, nor did he have a right to find out anything else.

"Even so," replied don Quixote, "I'd like to hear from each one of them the cause of his particular misfortune."

He added to these further polite words to persuade them to tell him what he wanted to know, and the other guard on horseback said to him: "We have the registry book and the sentencing certificates for each one of these unfortunates, but this just isn't a good time to stop to take them out and read them. If your grace wants, you can ask each one individually, and they'll tell you if they want to; and they certainly will want to, since they all enjoy doing villainous acts and then talking about them."

With this license, which don Quixote would have taken even if it had not been given, he approached the chain and asked the first one what sins he'd done to wind up that way. He responded that it was because he was in love.

"Only that?" replied don Quixote. "If being in love gets you thrown into the galleys, I would have been rowing in them for many days now."

"That isn't the kind of love your grace is thinking about," said the galley slave. "Mine was that I loved a wicker basket filled with freshly washed clothes so much and hugged it to myself so hard that if the authorities hadn't taken it from me by force, I wouldn't have let it be taken away, even now, of my free will. I was caught in the act, so no torturing was necessary. When the trial was over they gave me a hundred lashes, and added three precious years in the *gurapas*, and that was that."

"What are *gurapas*?" asked don Quixote.

"*Gurapas* are galleys," responded the galley slave, a young man of not more than twenty-four years of age, and said he was from Piedrahíta, near Ávila.

Don Quixote asked the same of the second one, who didn't answer a word, since he was so sad and despondent. But the first one answered for him: "This one, *señor*, is here because he's a canary—I mean, a musician and a singer."

"What?" repeated don Quixote. "Musicians and singers go to the galleys, too?"

"Yes, *señor*," responded the galley slave. "There is nothing worse than singing under duress."

"Why, I've heard," said don Quixote, "that 'he who sings scares away his troubles.'"

"Here it's the opposite," said the galley slave, "for he who sings once cries the rest of his life."

"I don't understand," said don Quixote.

But one of the guards said: "*Señor* knight, 'to sing while in torment' means in the slang of these *non santa** people 'to confess under torture.' They tortured this sinner and he confessed his crime, which was that he was a cattle rustler, and since he confessed, they sentenced him to six years in the galleys, not to mention the two hundred lashes that he carries on his back. And he's always pensive and sad because the other thieves, both those we left behind and these here, taunt and humiliate him; and they ridicule and hold him to be of no account because he confessed and didn't have the courage to say NO, because they say that NAY has as many letters as YEA, and that a criminal is very lucky when his life or death depends only on his tongue, and not on witnesses or other proof, and I kind of think that they're not far off the mark."

"That's what I think, too," responded don Quixote, who went on to the third one, and asked him what he'd asked the others, and he answered in a carefree way, saying: "I'm going to their majesties the galleys for five years because I didn't have ten ducats."†

"I'll give you twenty," said don Quixote, "if that'll get you out of trouble."

"That's like," responded the galley slave, "the person who has money on the high seas and is dying of hunger with no place to buy what he needs. I say that because if I'd had

---

* *Non santa*: antique Spanish for leading bad lives.

† The ducat was a coin worth from ten to thirty *reales* in Cervantes' time.

those twenty ducats then that you're offering me now, I would have used them to grease the scribe's pen, and to encourage my lawyer's cleverness, so that I'd be in the Plaza de Zocodover in Toledo today, and not on this road, on a leash like a dog. But God is great: patience, and that's enough."

He moved on to the fourth, a man with a venerable face, with a white beard that extended beyond his chest, who, when he heard himself asked the cause for his being there, began to sob and didn't say a word. But the fifth convict acted as his tongue and said: "This honorable man is going for four years, having been paraded through the streets on the way to jail, wearing a dunce cap and on a burro, with a constable at his side crying out his crimes."

"That is," said Sancho, "what I think is known as being shamed in public."

"That's right," said the galley slave, "and they're giving him this punishment for having been a stockbroker, or rather, a body broker. I mean that this man was a procurer, and it's also said that he was something of a sorcerer."

"If you hadn't mentioned that sorcerer business," said don Quixote, "just being a procurer wouldn't warrant his rowing in galleys, but rather commanding them and being their admiral, because being a procurer is not an ordinary profession—it should be for discreet individuals, and is very necessary in a well-ordered state. Those who engage in it should be highborn, and there ought even to be an officially appointed inspector and overseer of them, with only a specific number of them licensed and recognized, as there is for the other professions, such as stockbrokers. In this way society could avoid the bad results that are caused when this profession is handled by stupid people of little understanding, such as mindless women, immature pages, and scoundrels, who, just when an important occasion arises and the greatest tact is required, hesitate and miss the boat because they don't know what they're doing. I'd like to continue, and give reasons why it's important to choose those who should take up this most necessary profession. But this is not the right place to do it—one day I'll tell it to the right person. I'll just say for now that my heartache caused by seeing his white hair and venerable face suffering such distress as a pimp is lessened by the fact that he was a sorcerer, for I know that there are no spells in the world that can force a person to do what he doesn't want to, as some simpletons think—our will is free, and there are no herbs or enchantments that can control it. All these silly women and roguish impostors do is mix some compounds and potions that make men crazy, causing everyone to believe that they have the power to induce love. But, as I said, it's impossible to force one's free will."

"That's true," said the honorable old man, "and in truth, *señor*, I wasn't guilty of being a sorcerer. In the matter of being a procurer, I couldn't deny it. But I never thought that I was doing anything bad. My only intention was for everyone to be happy, and live in peace and quiet, without quarrels or sorrow. But all these good intentions have come to naught, since I'm going to where I have no hope of returning, since my years are weighing down on me, and I now have a urinary infection that doesn't give me a moment's comfort."

And he began his sobbing as before. Sancho had such compassion for him that he took a *real* from his shirt pocket and gave it to him as alms. Don Quixote moved on to the next one and asked him what his crime was, and he responded with not less, but much more enthusiasm, than the previous one: "I'm here today because I joked around too much with a couple of sisters, first cousins of mine, and a couple of sisters who weren't my relatives; finally, my joking around was such that it resulted in increasing my kinfolk in such a labyrinthine way, that not even the devil can figure it out. The evidence was all against me, favor was lacking, I had no money, and saw myself at the point of being hanged. They sentenced me to the galleys for six years; I consented: It's the punishment for my guilt. I'm still young and life is long, and 'where there's life, there's hope.' If your grace has anything to help out these poor fellows, God will repay you in heaven, and we on earth will make sure to pray for your life and health; and may it be as long and as good as your generous good presence merits."

This one was dressed in the garb of a student, and one of the guards said that he was a very great talker and a good Latin scholar (which is student slang for trickster).

Behind all of these came a good-looking man who was a bit cross-eyed and thirty years of age. He was bound in a different way from the others because he had a long chain that wound around him from head to foot with two rings around his neck, one connected to the chain, and from the other hung iron bars down to, and secured at, his waist, each one connected to handcuffs that were held together by a padlock. In this way he couldn't raise his hands to his mouth, nor lower his mouth to his hands. Don Quixote asked why he had so many more fetters than the others. The guard responded because that man alone had more crimes than all the rest combined, and that he was so daring and such a great rogue, that even though he was being taken in that way, they still feared he could get away.

"What crimes can he have committed," said don Quixote, "if they have only gotten him put into the galleys?"

"He's going for ten years," replied the guard, "which is the same as what they call CIVIL DEATH.* All you need to know about this good fellow is that he's the famous Ginés de Pasamonte, who is also known as Ginesillo de Parapilla."

"*Señor* commissioner," said the galley slave, "take it easy, and let's not start getting into first and last names. Ginés is my name and not Ginesillo, and Pasamonte is my ancestry, and not Parapilla, as you suggest. And let everyone mind his own business, and that'll be a major accomplishment."

"Speak with a more civil tongue," said the commissioner, "*señor* arrogant thief, unless you want me to make you keep quiet, much to your grief."

"'Man proposes, but God disposes,'" said the galley slave. "But one day it will be known if I'm named Ginesillo de Parapilla or not."

"Well, don't they call you that, you liar?" said the guard.

"Yes, they do," responded Ginés, "but if I can't make them stop calling me that, I'll pull out my . . . Never mind. *Señor* knight, if you have something to give us, give it to us now, and go with God, because all these questions about other people's lives are bothersome. And, if you want to know, I'm Ginés de Pasamonte, whose life has been written by these fingers."

"He's telling the truth," said the commissioner. "He's

---

* This is a punishment that includes losing all of one's rights, except the right to make a will. But a ten-year sentence in the galleys would doubtless lead to the death of the convict.

written an autobiography—it's as good as can be, too. He
left the book pawned in jail in the amount of two hundred
reales."

"Is it that good?" said don Quixote.

"It's so good," responded Ginés, "that it means trouble
for *Lazarillo de Tormes** and for all other books of that
type that have been or will be written. What I can tell you
is that it deals in facts that are so true and so delightful that
there are no lies that can match them."

"And what is the title of the book?" asked don Quixote.

"*The Life of Ginés de Pasamonte*," he responded.

"And is it finished?" asked don Quixote.

"How can it be finished," he responded, "if my life is not
yet over? What is written so far goes from my birth to the
last time I entered the galleys."

"So, have you been in them already?"

"To serve God and the king, I was in them before, for
four years, and I know what sea biscuits are, and what the
whip tastes like," responded Ginés, "and it doesn't bother
me to go to them, because I'll have time to finish my book;
and I have a lot more to say—in Spanish galleys it's much
more tranquil than you might think—but I don't need much
time to write what I have to, since I know it all by heart."

"You seem clever enough," said don Quixote.

"And unfortunate," responded Ginés, "because misfortune always pursues geniuses."

"It pursues scoundrels," said the commissioner.

"I already told you to take it easy," said Pasamonte.

"Those men didn't give you that staff so you could mis-
treat us poor fellows, but rather to guide us and take us
where His Majesty commands. Otherwise, by the life of . . .
but that's enough! It may be that one day that stuff that
happened at the inn† will come out in the wash, so everyone can hold his tongue, and live well and speak even

---

* The first novel of the picaresque genre, which appeared anonymously
in Burgos, 1554. Its hero, Lázaro, is a street urchin who ekes out an
existence with several masters, and learns about life.
† "What happened at the inn" is an incident not mentioned anywhere
in this book.

better, and let's get on with it, because we've had enough joking around."

The commissioner raised his staff to strike Pasamonte in answer to his threats, but don Quixote put himself between them and begged the commissioner not to hit him, since it was quite natural for a person with his hands tied to have a loose tongue. And turning to all those who were chained together, he said: "From everything that you've told me, dear brothers, I conclude that although they're punishing you for your offenses, the punishment that you've been given doesn't please you very much, and you're going to it reluctantly, and much against your will; and it could even be that the man who lacked fortitude while being tortured, and this one's want of funds, and the other one's lack of favor, and finally, the magistrate's perverted sense of justice, caused your downfall, and your not having gotten the fair treatment due you. Everything is quite clear to me now, and it's telling, persuading, and even forcing me to show you why heaven placed me on earth and made me take up the order of knight-errantry that I profess, and the vow I took to help the needy and those oppressed by those in authority. But since I know that one of the qualities of prudence is 'what can be done by fair means ought not be done by foul,' I'll beg of these *señores* guards and commissioner to release you and let you go in peace. There will be others who can serve the king in more worthy battles, because it seems unjust to make slaves of those whom both God and Nature made free. Especially, *señores* guards," added don Quixote, "since these poor fellows haven't committed any crime against *you* personally, let each one answer for his own sins. God is in His heaven, and He won't fail to punish the bad and reward the good. It's not proper for honorable men to punish other men for something that doesn't concern them. I ask you this in all gentleness and calmness so that I may, if you do what I ask, have something to thank you for. And if you don't do it willingly, this lance and this sword, through the strength of my arm, will make you do it by force!"

"What nonsense!" responded the commissioner. "That's a good joke to end his speech with! He wants us to release the king's slaves, as if we had the authority to do it, or he had the authorization to demand it. Go on your way, your grace, and straighten up the basin on your head, and don't go looking for three feet on the cat."

"You're the cat and the rat and the rogue!" responded don Quixote. And going from words to action in an instant, he attacked with such speed that the commissioner couldn't defend himself and was thrown to the ground badly wounded by the lance; and it was fortunate for don Quixote, since he was the one with the musket. The other guards were astonished and in shock because of the unexpected situation. But those on horseback gathered their wits and raised their swords; and those on foot clutched their pikes and attacked don Quixote, who awaited them with great calm. And he would have gotten the worst of it if the galley slaves, seeing that they could use this opportunity to get their freedom, didn't do so by breaking the chain that bound them together. The confusion was such that the guards, at times racing to prevent the galley slaves from escaping, then trying to fight off don Quixote, who was attacking them, couldn't do anything useful. Sancho, on his part, helped Ginés de Pasamonte, who was the first one to rush into battle free and unencumbered. He attacked the commissioner and took his sword and musket, and by aiming it at one guard and pointing it at another, without firing a shot, soon there was not a guard to be seen in the countryside because they all fled, not only because of Pasamonte's musket, but also because of the stones that the galley slaves threw at them.

These events disturbed Sancho because he could see that those who were fleeing would tell the Holy Brotherhood about what happened, and they would sound the alarm and go looking for the delinquents. He told this to his master, and begged him to leave right then, and retreat to the forest in the neighboring hills.

"You're right," said don Quixote, "but I know what the best thing to do right now is."

He summoned together all the galley slaves, who were in an uproar after they had stripped the commissioner, leaving him virtually naked, and they all gathered together around him to hear what he had to say: "It's expected of those of good birth to render thanks for benefits received, because ingratitude is one of the sins that most offends God. I say this because you, *señores*, can bear witness by firsthand experience to the favors received at my hands, in payment for which I want—in fact, it's my will—that you go immediately to the city of El Toboso, laden with that chain that I removed from your necks, and present yourselves before the lady Dulcinea del Toboso, and tell her that her knight, the Woebegone One, sends her his compliments, and recount everything about this remarkable adventure in detail, until the part where I gave you your yearned-for freedom. Once this is done, you can go wherever you want, and good luck to you."

Ginés de Pasamonte answered for them all and said: "What you're commanding us, our lord and liberator, is of all impossible things the most impossible to comply with, because we can't travel together along the roads, but rather alone and separately, each one trying to hide in the bowels of the earth, so as not to be found by the Holy Brotherhood, which, no doubt, will come looking for us. What your grace can and should do is change this tribute to the lady Dulcinea del Toboso into a series of Hail Marys and credos, which we can recite for you, and it's something we can do by day and by night, fleeing or resting, in peace or in battle. But to think that we have to go back to the captivity of the fleshpots of Egypt, I mean, to take our chain and get on the road to El Toboso, is to think that it's night right now, even though it isn't yet ten o'clock in the morning, and asking us to do it is like trying 'to get blood from a turnip.' "

"Well, I swear," said don Quixote, now in a rage, "you whoreson, don Ginesillo de Paropillo, or whatever your name is, you alone will go, tail between your legs, with the whole chain on your back!"

Pasamonte, who was not at all patient, having figured out that don Quixote was not very sane, since he'd taken on such an outrageous thing in wanting to set them free, seeing himself being commanded that way, winked at his companions, who dropped back a bit, and began to rain so many stones on don Quixote that he could hardly cover himself with his buckler, and poor Rocinante paid as much attention to the spurs as if he'd been made of stone. Sancho got behind his donkey so he could shield himself against the shower of stones coming down on both of them. Don Quixote couldn't defend himself well enough, so that many stones couldn't help but hit him, and with such force that they knocked him to the ground. Hardly had he fallen when the student snatched his basin from his head and thwacked him on the back three or four times, then smashed it to the ground as many times, denting it severely. They took a doublet he was wearing over his armor, and would have taken his stockings if his shin armor hadn't prevented it. They took Sancho's coat and left him with hardly a stitch on, dividing up amongst themselves the booty from the battle; then they scattered in all directions, more eager to escape the Holy Brotherhood than to take the chain on their shoulders to present themselves before the lady Dulcinea del Toboso.

The donkey, Rocinante, Sancho, and don Quixote were left all alone: the donkey, head bowed low and pensive, twitching his ears once in a while, thinking that the storm of stones was not yet over; Rocinante, stretched out on the ground next to his master, because he'd also fallen to the ground in the shower of stones; Sancho, practically naked, and fearful of the Holy Brotherhood; don Quixote, very mournful, seeing himself in such bad shape caused by the very ones for whom he'd done so much good.

Chapter XXIII. About what happened to the famous don Quixote in the Sierra Morena, which was one of the strangest adventures in this true history.

Don Quixote, seeing himself in such bad shape, said to his squire: "I've always heard tell, Sancho, that doing something nice for boors is like throwing water into the sea. If I'd believed what you told me, I would have avoided all this grief. But it's over and done with—patience, and let's learn something from this."

"If your grace learns anything, then I'll become a Turk,"* responded Sancho. "But since you say that if you had believed me you would have avoided all this, believe me now, and you'll avoid further and greater trouble, because I'll tell you that the Holy Brotherhood has no use for chivalry, and wouldn't give two *maravedís* for all the knights-errant

---

* The Turks were Spain's enemies of that period.

in the world; and it seems to me that their arrows are already buzzing past my ears."

"By nature you're a coward, Sancho," said don Quixote, "but so you won't say that I'm obstinate and that I never do what you advise me to do, this time I'll heed your warning and retreat from the fury you fear so much. But it has to be on one condition: that you'll never tell anyone, in life or in death, that I withdrew from this peril because of fear, but rather only to go along with your wishes; and if you say anything else, you'll be lying, from now until then, and from then until now,* and I'll deny it, and will say that you're lying, and will lie every time you think it or say it. And don't dispute any of this, because just by thinking that I retreat from danger, especially from this one that carries with it the suspicion of the shadow of fear, I'm about to say I'll stay here and await, not only the Holy Brotherhood you mentioned, but also the brothers of the Twelve Tribes of Israel,† the Seven Maccabees,‡ Castor and Pollux,§ and all the brothers and brotherhoods there are in the world."

"*Señor*," responded Sancho, "withdrawing is not fleeing, nor is waiting around considered prudent when there's more danger than hope. Wise men save themselves for tomorrow, and don't risk everything in one day. And although I'm ignorant and a rustic, I still know something about what they call common sense. So, don't change your mind about taking my advice; get up onto Rocinante if you can, and if not, I'll help you—and follow me, for my head tells me now we need to use our feet more than our hands."

Don Quixote mounted his horse without saying another word, and with Sancho leading him on his donkey, they entered the Sierra Morena. It was Sancho's intention to go all the way across it and come out in El Vigo or in Almodóvar del Campo, and hide for a few days in that rugged terri-

---

* This is a legal formula used by scribes.
† These were the people who took possession of the Promised Land after the death of Moses, named after the sons and grandsons of Jacob.
‡ These were the seven martyred brothers who were scalped, skinned, mutilated, and roasted alive in front of their mother. It can be read in 2 Maccabees 7—the last book of the Apocrypha.
§ Castor and Pollux were mythological athletic twin half brothers [!] who, after their deaths, became the constellation Gemini.

tory, so they would not be found if the Holy Brotherhood was looking for them. He was encouraged when he saw the provisions on his donkey had escaped detection in the fray, which he considered miraculous considering everything the galley slaves had taken.*

As soon as Don Quixote went into the mountains, his heart gladdened, because it seemed to him that the place

---

* At this point in the *second* 1605 edition of *Don Quixote*, Sancho's donkey is stolen, using the words recorded here. Occasional changes were then made throughout the text, in order to keep the donkey stolen until the donkey is officially returned.

That night they reached the heart of the Sierra Morena, where it seemed to Sancho they could spend the night and maybe even a few more days, at least until they ran out of their provisions, and so they spent the night between two boulders and among some cork trees. But Fate—in the opinion of those who have not received the light of the true faith—which guides, devises, and fixes everything according to its own whims, arranged for Ginés de Pasamonte, the famous trickster and thief who had escaped from the chain gang through don Quixote's mettle and folly, and spurred on by his not-uncalled-for fear of the Holy Brotherhood, thought he would hide in those mountains, and his luck and fear took him to where don Quixote and Sancho Panza had taken refuge, while there was still sufficient light to recognize them, and waited until they went to sleep. And since bad people are always ungrateful as well, and need forces men to do what they must, and a remedy at hand is better than what might be gotten in the future, Ginés, who was neither grateful nor good-intentioned, resolved to steal Sancho's donkey, paying no attention to Rocinante since he could neither be pawned nor sold. Sancho slept, and Ginés stole the donkey, and before the sun came up, was long gone.

Aurora came, gladdening the earth, and saddening Sancho, because when he saw his donkey was missing, he began the saddest and most tender lament in the world, such that it awakened don Quixote, and he heard Sancho express: "Oh, child of my loins, born in my own house, plaything of my children, pleasure for my wife, envy of my neighbors, relief of my burdens, provider of half of my income, for with the twenty-six *maravedís* you earned every day, I paid half of my expenses."

Don Quixote, who witnessed the lament and realized the cause, comforted Sancho with the best words he could muster up, and begged him to be patient, promising to give him a letter of exchange so that he'd be given three donkeys of the five that he'd left at home. Sancho was consoled with this, dried his tears, controlled his sobs, and thanked don Quixote for his kindness.

was ideal for the adventures he was seeking. In his memory, there swirled about marvelous things that had happened to knights-errant in similar secluded, rugged places. As he went along thinking about these things, he was so engrossed and transported by them that he paid no attention to anything else; nor did Sancho, sitting sidesaddle on his donkey, following his master,* have any worries, except that of satisfying his hunger with the leftovers from the clerical spoils, taking tidbits from the bag and stowing them in his stomach; and while he was traveling that way, he wouldn't have given an *ardite*† to stumble across another adventure.

At this point he raised his eyes and saw that his master had stopped, trying to lift I don't know what kind of object lying on the ground. He hurried over to help him, as he should. And he got there just when his master was attempting to lift a saddle cushion and a valise attached to it, half rotted—or completely rotted—and falling apart. But they weighed enough so that Sancho had to dismount to pick them up, and his master told him to see what was in the valise.

Sancho did this very quickly, and although the valise was fastened with a chain and a padlock, he could see what was inside through the torn and rotted sections: four shirts of fine linen and some other items of linen no less neat than clean, and in a handkerchief, he found a heap of gold *escudos*,‡ and as soon as he saw them he said: "Praise be to heaven, because it has given us a profitable adventure!"

And looking further, he found a diary that was richly decorated. Don Quixote asked for it, and told Sancho to take the money and keep it for himself. He kissed don Quixote's hands for the favor. He took out all the linen clothes and put them in the saddlebag.

All this was seen by don Quixote, who said: "It seems to me, Sancho—and it's impossible that it can be anything

---

* Oops. Not only would Sancho not have been sitting on his donkey at this point, but the saddlebags would also be gone. The passages dealing with Sancho's donkey in this translation come from the second edition. In the third edition, made three years later, Sancho is on foot at this point. It was important to keep these inconsistencies, as will be seen later.

† The *ardite* was a practically worthless coin.

‡ *Escudos* were gold coins valued the same as *ducados*.

else—that some traveler got lost and came through these hills, and some brigands robbed and killed him, and brought him here in this hidden place to bury him."

"That can't be," responded Sancho, "because if they were thieves, they wouldn't have left this money here."

"You're right," said don Quixote, "and so I can't figure out what it's all about. But wait—we'll see if there is something written in this diary that will help us find out and come to know what we want."

He opened it and the first thing in it was a draft of a sonnet, written in a very fine hand, and reading it aloud so that Sancho could hear it as well, he saw that it read this way:

Or Love is lacking in intelligence,
        Or to the height of cruelty attains,
        Or else it is my doom to suffer pains
        Beyond the measure due to my offense.
But if Love be a God, it follows thence
        That he knows all, and certain it remains
        No God loves cruelty; then who ordains
        This penance that enthralls while it torments?
It were a falsehood, Fili, thee to name;
        Such evil with such goodness cannot live;
        And against Heaven I dare not charge the blame,
I only know it is my fate to die.
        To him who knows not whence his malady
        A miracle alone a cure can give.*

"The poem," said Sancho, "doesn't tell us much, and I can't even understand what a fillip has to do with love."

"What fillip are you talking about, Sancho?"

"It seems to me that you said something like 'fillip' somewhere there."

"What I said was *Fili*," responded don Quixote, "and this is doubtless the name of the lady about whom the author of this sonnet is complaining. And I swear he must be a pretty good poet or I know little about poetry."

"So," said Sancho, "your grace knows something about poetry?"

---

* This is Ormsby's translation, except that the name *Fili* is *Chloe* in his, and several other translations.

"And more than you think," responded don Quixote. "You'll see when you take a letter written entirely in verse to my lady Dulcinea del Toboso, because I want you to know, Sancho, that all, or most, knights-errant of bygone days were great troubadours and musicians, and that these skills, or graces—to be more accurate—are typical of errant lovers. It's true that the poems of the past knights are more passionate than beautiful."

"Read a bit more," said Sancho, "since you'll doubtless find something revealing."

Don Quixote turned the page and said: "This is prose, and appears to be a letter."

"A personal letter?"* asked Sancho.

"It seems to be more of a love letter," responded don Quixote.

"So, read it aloud," said Sancho, "because I like things dealing with love."

"I'd be pleased to do it," said don Quixote.

And reading it aloud, as Sancho had asked, he saw that it went like this:

> *Your false promise and my certain misfortune*
> *are taking me to a place where you'll hear*
> *of my death before you hear my words of*
> *complaint. You rejected me—oh, ungrateful*
> *one!—for a man who has more than I do,*
> *rather than who is worth more than I am.*
> *But if virtue were something that was valued,*
> *I wouldn't envy anyone else's happiness nor*
> *my own misfortunes. What your beauty has*
> *built, your works have torn down—through*
> *the former, I considered you to be an angel;*
> *and through the latter, I realize that you are a*
> *woman. May you remain in peace—you, who*
> *have put me at war—and may heaven fix it*
> *so your husband's deceits stay hidden, so you*
> *won't have to repent for what you did, nor will*
> *I have to take vengeance I don't want to.*

---

* There were other types of letters (credit, payment, diplomatic) so it made sense for Sancho to ask which kind.

On finishing this letter, don Quixote said: "This tells us even less than the verses, except that the person who wrote it is a disdained lover."

And glancing through most of the diary, he found other verses and letters—some he could read, others not. But all of them contained complaints, laments, jealousies, likes, dislikes, support, and scorn, some extolling, others lamenting.

While don Quixote was looking through the book, Sancho was investigating the contents of the valise and the saddle cushion without leaving a corner unsearched, uninspected, or uninvestigated, nor was there any seam he didn't undo, nor tuft of wool he didn't comb out, so he wouldn't miss anything through lack of diligence or carelessness, such was the greed that finding the *escudos*—and there were more than a hundred of them—awakened in him. And even though he found no more than he'd already found, he admitted that the flight in the blanket, the vomiting caused by the balm, the blessings from the stakes, the punches by the muleteer, and the loss of the saddlebags, the robbery of the coat, and all the hunger, thirst, and exhaustion he'd suffered in the service of his good master seemed to him to be well worth it, owing to the favor he got by being able to keep the treasure.

The Woebegone Knight greatly desired to know who the owner of the valise was, imagining—because of the sonnet and the letter, the money in gold, and the fine shirts—that he must be some upper-class lover whom disdain and bad treatment by his lady had made decide to kill himself. But since no one appeared in that uninhabitable and craggy place who could tell him what he wanted to know, he thought only of going on, taking the road that Rocinante chose (which was where he could find the surest footing), always considering that he couldn't fail to find a strange adventure in that wilderness.

As he rode along with this thought in mind, he saw on the top of a hill directly in front of him a man jumping from crag to crag and from shrub to shrub, with uncommon agility. It seemed to him that this fellow was scantily clothed and his beard was thick and black, with long, matted hair. His feet were bare and he had nothing on his legs below the knee. His thighs were covered by pants, apparently of tan velvet, but so ragged that his flesh showed through here and there. He had no hat, and was as nimble as has already been related. The Woebegone Knight saw and noted all these details. Although he tried to, he couldn't follow him, since it wasn't possible for Rocinante to travel through those rugged places, especially since he was by nature slow-footed and sluggish. At that instant don Quixote figured that fellow must be the owner of the saddle cushion and valise, and he resolved to look for him, even though he might have to wander about in those mountains for a year until he found him. So he told Sancho to get off his donkey and cut across the hill in one direction, and he would go in another, and it might be that by using this artifice they'd run across that man who so quickly had disappeared.

"I can't do that," responded Sancho, "because when I'm separated from your grace, I'm assailed by fright, and attacked by a thousand kinds of anxieties and apprehensions. And let this serve notice to you, because from now on I won't stray an inch from your presence."

"That's fine," said the Woebegone One, "and I'm very happy you want to rely on my courage, which will never fail you, even though your own soul deserts you. So, follow me, step by step, as well as you can, and turn your eyes into beacons, and we'll circle this little hill and maybe we'll find that man we saw who, without any doubt, is none other than the owner of what we found."

To which Sancho responded: "It would be a lot better not to look for him, because if we find him, and he turns out to be the owner of the money, it's very clear we'll have to give it back; so it would be appropriate, without using this useless artifice, to keep it in good faith, until by some other less meddlesome and diligent way we run across its true owner, and maybe it'll be after I've spent it all, and then the king will hold me blameless."

"You're wrong there, Sancho," responded don Quixote, "for now that we suspect who the owner is—and we're pretty sure it's the fellow who is practically in front of us— we're duty-bound to look for him and return it. And if we don't look for him, the keen suspicion we have that he's truly the person we're looking for makes us as guilty as if he were. So, Sancho, my friend, let our search for him give you no distress; rather, weigh it against the distress that will be taken from me if I *do* find him."

So he spurred Rocinante, and Sancho followed him on his donkey. And when they had gone around the hill, they found a dead mule that was saddled and bridled at the bank of a stream, half-eaten by dogs, and pecked by crows. All this confirmed their suspicion that the man who was fleeing was the owner of the mule and the saddle cushion. While they were looking at the scene, they heard a whistle like the ones shepherds use. And suddenly, on their left, there appeared a large number of goats, and behind them, on the top of a little hill, the one who kept them came into view— an old man. Don Quixote shouted to him and begged him to come down. He called back, asking who had brought them to that place so rarely trod upon except by the feet of goats or wolves, or other wild animals that inhabited that area. Sancho responded that he should come down and they would explain everything he wanted to know.

The goatherd came down to where don Quixote was, and said to him: "I'll bet you're looking at that dead pack mule that lies in that ravine, and by my faith, he's been lying there for six months. Tell me, have you found its owner?"

"We haven't run across anything," responded don Quixote, "except we did find a saddle cushion and a little traveling bag not far from here."

"I found them as well," responded the goatherd, "but I never picked them up or even went near them, fearing some mishap, and someone would claim I stole them, because the devil is sly, and something pops up that you stumble and fall on without knowing how."

"That's exactly what I say," responded Sancho. "I also found them and I wouldn't go within a stone's throw of them. I left them there, and there it sits just like it was, since I don't want any trouble either."

"Tell me, my good man," said don Quixote, "do you know who the owner of these things might be?"

"What I can tell you," said the goatherd, "is that about six months ago, a little more or less, a well-groomed and handsome young man came to a shepherd's hut about three leagues from where we are, riding on that mule now dead over there, and with the same saddle cushion and suitcase you say you found but didn't touch. He asked us where the harshest and most hidden place in these mountains was. We told him it was this place where we are right now; and it's the truth, because if you go in a half league farther you may never get out. I'm surprised you could have gotten this far, since there is no road or path that leads here.

"So, as I was saying, when he heard our response, he turned and rode to where we told him, leaving everybody charmed with his good looks, astonished at what he planned to do, and the speed with which we saw him dash into the mountains. And after that we didn't see him for a few days, when he came out into the road and went up to one of our goatherds, and without saying a word, began punching and kicking him; then he went over to the donkey with provisions, and took all the bread and cheese it was carrying. After he did what I said, he went back among the trees very nimbly to hide in the mountains. Since a few of us goatherds knew about him, we went looking for him in the densest part of the mountains for two days, at the end of which we found him reclining in the hollow part of a robust cork tree. He came out to greet us very meekly, his clothing all tattered and his face so disfigured and sunburned that we hardly recognized him. But his clothing, although it was in shreds from the way we remembered it, proved to us that he was the one we were looking for.

"He greeted us courteously, and in a few well-chosen words he told us not to marvel at seeing him going about like that because he had to so that he could complete a certain penance imposed on him for his many sins. We begged him to tell us who he was, but we could never find out what his name was. We also begged him that when he needed food—without which he couldn't stay alive—he should tell us where to find him, because we would take him some out of charity and caring. And if this wasn't to his liking either, the least he could do is ask for it and not snatch it away from the goatherds. He thanked us for our offer and begged our pardon for his past attacks, and said he would ask for food from then on in God's name, without assailing anybody. As to where he lived, he said that he had no place in particular except where night overtook him, and he ended his discourse with such a sad lament that we'd have to have been made of stone not to join him in his tears, especially considering what he had looked like when we'd first seen him, compared with the way he looked then. Because, as I've said, he was a very gentle young man, and in his courteous and well-chosen words he showed himself to be wellborn and a very courtly person and, although we who were listening to him were rustics, his refinement was such that even we could recognize it very clearly.

"And when he got to the best part of his speech, he stopped and went silent, and began staring at the ground for a long time, during which time we were quiet and in suspense, waiting anxiously to see how that spell would turn out. It was a pitiful sight to see him that way, because he'd been staring at the ground for a long time, eyes wide open without moving an eyelash, and other times closing his eyes tightly, squeezing his lips together and arching his eyebrows, and it seemed to us that a sudden fit of madness had overtaken him. And he proved to us very soon that what we suspected was correct, because he jumped up from the ground where he lay and attacked the first person he found nearby with such fierceness and rage that if we hadn't pulled them apart, he would have killed him with his punches and bites, and saying all the while: 'Ah, Fernando, you traitor! Now, now you'll pay for the outrage you did to me! These hands will pluck out your heart where all wickedness—particularly fraud and deceit—reside and have their abode.' And to these he added other words, all of them to defame that fellow Fernando, and to charge him with treachery.

"We separated them with no little trouble, and he— without saying another word—retreated into the forest, running through these brambles and other underbrush, making it impossible to follow him. Through all this, we figured that these fits of madness came only from time to time, and that someone named Fernando must have played a dirty trick on him so offensive that it had led him to the state he was in. All of this was confirmed since then, because on many occasions he would come out onto the road, sometimes to ask the goatherds for something to eat, and other times to take it by force during a fit of madness— and even though the goatherds offer him food willingly, he won't accept it, but rather beats them up and takes it away. And when he's in his right mind, he asks for it in God's name very courteously, and thanks us profusely, and with no lack of tears. And in truth, I tell you, *señores*," continued the goatherd, "that yesterday four locals and I—two of them servants and two friends of mine—resolved to look

for him until we found him. And after we find him, whether
by force or with his permission, we'll take him to the town
of Almodóvar, which is eight leagues from here, and there
we'll try to cure him, if his illness has a cure, or we'll find
out who he is when he's in his right mind, and if he has relatives who we can notify about his misfortune. This, *señores*,
is all I can tell you of what you asked me about, and I want
you to understand that the owner of the items you found is
the same one you saw racing by, as agile as he was ragged,"
for don Quixote had already told him how he'd seen that
man leaping about in the mountains.

Don Quixote was astonished to learn what he'd heard
from the goatherd, and was even more eager to find out
who the unfortunate crazy man was; and he decided to do
what he'd planned: to comb the mountainside looking for
him, leaving no corner or cave unexplored until he found
him. But his luck was better than he could have planned or
hoped, because at that moment the young man he was looking for appeared through a narrow pass that led to where
they were. He came muttering to himself, saying things
they couldn't have understood if they had been nearby,
much less when he was distant. He was dressed as has been
described, except that when he drew near, don Quixote saw
that the ragged jacket he was wearing still smelled of perfume, by means of which he could tell that the person who
wore such clothing was not of low rank.

When the young man went over to them, he greeted
them with a humble and hoarse voice, but still very courteously. Don Quixote returned his greeting no less courteously, and getting off Rocinante, with gentle demeanor and
grace, went over to embrace him, and he held him for a
long while in his arms, as if he'd known him for a long time.
The other, whom we might call the RAGGED ONE OF THE
STRICKEN FACE (as don Quixote was the Woebegone One),
after allowing himself to be embraced, pulled back and put
his hands on don Quixote's shoulders, and looked at him
to see if he recognized him, and was no less astonished at
seeing the face, figure, and armor of don Quixote than don
Quixote was at seeing him. Finally, the first one who spoke
after the embrace was the Ragged One, and he said what
will be told next.

Chapter XXIIII. Where the adventure in the Sierra Morena is continued.

THE HISTORY says that it was with great attention that don Quixote listened to the ragged knight of the sierra, who, beginning his conversation, said: "*Señor*, whoever you are, for I don't know you, I thank you for the courtesy you've shown me, and I'd like to be in a position to repay the courtesy you've shown me by the reception you've given me with something more than just goodwill. But my fate doesn't give me anything to repay your favors except with my will to do so."

"My desire," responded don Quixote, "is only to serve you, so much so that I'd resolved not to leave this sierra until I located you and learned from you if any relief can be found for the pain shown by the life you lead; and if it had been necessary to search for you, I would have looked with all diligence. And if your misfortune were of the kind for which all doors of consolation were closed, I would have accompanied you in your weeping and grieving as well as I could, because it's always a comfort to find someone with whom to share one's misfortunes. And if my good intentions deserve to be acknowledged by any kind of courtesy, I entreat you, *señor*—by the great courtesy that you possess, and by the thing in this life that you've loved or love –to tell me who you are, and the cause that brought you to live and die in this lonely place like a brute animal, since you dwell in a place so far from your social status, as your attire and person bear out. And I swear," don Quixote added, "by the order of chivalry I've received, although unworthy and a sinner, and by the profession of knight-errantry, if you, *señor*, accommodate my request, I'll serve you earnestly as being who I am obliges me, either by trying to remedy your misfortune, if it has a remedy, or by helping you to lament it, as I promised."

The Knight of the Forest, who heard the Woebegone One speak in that way, could only stare at him, and stare at him again, and once again look at him from top to bottom. And after he'd studied him well, he said: "If you have something I can eat, for the love of God, give it to me. After

I eat, I'll do whatever you ask, in recompense for the good-will you've shown me."

Sancho from his bag and the goatherd from his pouch took out some food with which the Ragged One satisfied his hunger, eating what they gave him like a half-witted person who takes no time between bites, gorging rather than taking mouthfuls, and while he ate, neither he nor those who were looking on spoke a word. Once he'd fin-ished eating, he indicated to them by signs that they should follow him. He led them around a boulder to a little green meadow, and when he got there, he lay on the grass, and the others did the same. All this was done in silence, until the Ragged One, after getting settled in his place, said: "If it's your pleasure, *señores*, for me to relate to you in a few words the immensity of my misfortune, you must promise me that you'll not interrupt the thread of my tormented story, because as soon as you do, at that point it will come to an end."

These words by the Ragged One brought back to don Quixote's memory the story his squire had told, and when he didn't know the correct number of goats that had gone across the river, it was over. But going back to the Ragged One, he continued by saying: "I've imposed this condition because I want to spend as little time as I can on the narra-tion of my misfortunes, since bringing them to mind serves only to add other ones, and the less you ask me the sooner I'll finish telling them, although I'll not leave out anything important, so as to satisfy your curiosity fully." Don Quixote promised him in the name of all the others; and he, with that assurance, began in this way: "My name is Cardenio, my home is one of the best cities in Andalusia,* my lineage noble, my parents rich, my misfortune so great that my parents must have lamented, and my relatives must have grieved that their riches couldn't redress it; for to remedy the misfortunes imposed by heaven, wealth is of no use. In my same town there lived paradise, where Love placed all the glory I could have desired, such was the beauty of Luscinda, a maiden as noble and rich as I, more fortunate but less constant than my honorable thoughts deserved.

---

* Andalusia is the southernmost region of Spain. Its three main cities are Seville, Córdoba, and Granada.

I loved and adored this Luscinda from my tenderest and earliest years, and she loved me with that simplicity and sincerity that her young age permitted. Both of our parents knew our desires and it didn't trouble them because they saw that as our intentions grew, they could only end in marriage—something that harmonized with the equality of our lineage and wealth. As our age grew, so did the love we had for each other, so that it eventually seemed to Luscinda's father that, for propriety's sake, he was forced to prohibit me from going into their house, almost imitating in this the parents of Thisbe,* who is so exalted by the poets. This denial only fanned the flames and piled one desire on another, because, although it silenced our tongues, it couldn't silence our pens, which, more freely than our tongues, made the beloved one understand what is locked inside the heart, because frequently the presence of the loved one confuses and makes silent the most determined desire and the most daring tongue. Heavens, how many love letters I wrote her! What delicate and chaste responses I got back! How many songs and how many loving verses I composed, in which my soul proclaimed and translated its feelings, painted its burning desires, delighted in its recollections, and luxuriated in its affection! So, seeing myself in dire straits, and that my soul was consumed with the desire to see her, I determined to put into action and resolved to carry out what seemed to me to be the best way to win my desired and deserved prize, which was to ask her father for her hand in marriage, and I did. He responded by thanking me for the wish I showed to honor him, and to aspire to honor myself with his jewel, but since my father was alive, it was *his* duty to make this request, because if it wasn't his will and pleasure, Luscinda was not one to be given or taken surreptitiously.

"I thanked him for his kindness, and it seemed to me that he was right in what he said, and that my father would request Luscinda's hand as soon as I asked him. With this in mind, at that very instant I went to tell my father what I wanted, and as soon as I went into the room where he was,

---

* Pyramus and Thisbe were two Babylonian lovers, as Ovid relates, who were neighbors separated by a common wall. They came to a tragic end.

I found him with a letter in his hand. Before I could say a single word to him, he handed it to me and said: 'By means of this letter, Cardenio, you'll see the affection that Duke Ricardo has for you.' Now this Duke Ricardo, as you must know, *señores*, is a grandee of Spain who has his estate in the best part of Andalusia. I took the letter and read it, and it was so flattering that even I thought it would be bad if my father didn't comply with the duke's request, which was that I be sent to him right away, because he wanted me to be the companion, not the servant, of his oldest son. He took it upon himself to put me in a position worthy of the esteem in which he held me. I read the letter and became speechless as I read it, and more so when I heard my father say: 'Two days from now you'll leave, Cardenio, to do what the duke asks; give thanks to God, because this will pave the way for you to achieve what I know you deserve.' To these words he added others of fatherly counsel.

"The day of my departure came. I spoke with Luscinda the night before, and I told her what had happened. I told her father as well, begging him to wait a few days, and not give her away until I found out what Duke Ricardo wanted of me. He promised me he would wait, and she also confirmed it with a thousand oaths and swoonings. I finally went to Duke Ricardo, and was cordially welcomed and well treated, but right away, envy began to do its work—the old servants felt that their master's inclination to favor me was an injury to themselves. But the one who took the most pleasure in my arrival was the second son of the duke, named Fernando, a charming fellow, liberal in love, and who made me such a fast friend of his in such a short time that everyone talked about it. Although the oldest one liked me well enough, it was his younger brother who liked me more, and treated me better.

"As happens between friends, there is no secret they don't communicate; the closeness I had with don Fernando quickly turned into a real friendship, and he told me all his thoughts, especially about an affair of the heart that brought him a bit of anxiety. He loved a country girl, a vassal of his father, whose parents were very rich. And she was so beautiful, modest, discreet, and virtuous that no one who knew her could determine which of these qualities was her best one, or the one that shone the most. These such good endowments of the beautiful peasant so inflamed the passions of don Fernando that he resolved, in order to achieve his end and overcome her virtue, to pledge to be her husband, because any other way would be to attempt the impossible. I felt forced by his friendship, with the best words I knew, and with the clearest examples I could find, to try to prevent and dissuade him from his intention. Seeing that they were to no avail, I planned to tell Duke Ricardo, his father, about it. But don Fernando, a crafty and discreet fellow, suspected and feared this, rightly assuming that I was obliged, in my capacity as a good servant, not to keep a thing secret that was so much to the prejudice of my lord the duke's honor. So, to mislead and deceive me, he told me he could see no better way to erase from his mind the beauty that had held him in thrall than to go away for a few months, and that he wanted us to go to my father's house on the pretext that he wanted to buy some very good horses in my city, which is the mother of the best ones in the world.

"As soon as I heard this, moved by my love, even if his intent hadn't been so good, I would have hailed it as one of the best ideas that could be imagined, because it would give me the opportunity to see my Luscinda again. With this thought and desire I agreed to his idea and backed his proposal, telling him that he should put it into effect as soon as possible, because absence would surely do its job, no matter how strong his feelings had been. When he made this suggestion, as it later turned out, he'd already enjoyed the country girl, having promised to be her husband, and he was waiting for the appropriate time to reveal the truth with safety to himself, because he was fearful of what his father might do when he learned of his rashness.

"It happened, then, that since love in young men mostly isn't really love, but only appetite, which, since its ultimate goal is gratification, when that goal is realized, it is curbed, and what seemed to be love tends to fade away, because it can't go beyond the limit imposed by nature, this limit not having been imposed by what is true love . . . what I mean is that as soon as don Fernando enjoyed the girl, his desires diminished and his zeal cooled, and if at first he pretended that he wanted to go away in order to cure his love, now in truth he wanted to go away in order to avoid his obligations.

"The duke gave his permission, and ordered me to go with him. We went to my city and my father gave him the reception due a person of his rank. I went to see Luscinda right away, and my passion for her came to life again, although it had never died or been dulled. To my sorrow, I told don Fernando about my feelings for her, since it seemed to me that, because of the great friendship he showed me, I shouldn't keep anything to myself. I lauded Luscinda's beauty, wit, and discretion in such a way that my praises made him want to see a maiden adorned with so many good qualities. To my misfortune, I gave in, letting him see her one evening by the light of a candle through a window where we used to talk to each other. She was in a simple dress, and was so beautiful that she cast into oblivion all other beautiful women he'd seen until then. He was speechless, he lost his senses, he was spellbound, and finally fell very much in love, as you'll see as the story of my misfortunes unfolds. And to increase the flames of his desire—which he concealed from me, and only told heaven when he was alone—fate arranged it so that he would find a love letter from her asking me to request her hand in marriage from her father. It was so circumspect, so chaste, and so loving that, when he read it, he told me that in Luscinda alone were to be found all of the gifts of beauty and understanding that were distributed among all other women in the world.

"It's true I want to confess now that, although I saw don Fernando praised Luscinda with just cause, it grieved me to hear those praises come from his mouth, and I began to fear and become suspicious of him, because a moment didn't go by that he didn't want us to talk about Luscinda, and he would even start conversations about her even though he had to drag them in by the hair, something that awakened in me a bit of jealousy. I didn't fear any change in the goodness and fidelity of Luscinda, yet I began to fear the same thing she reassured me about.* Don Fernando always wanted to read the letters that I sent to Luscinda, and her responses, on the excuse that our keenness of mind

---

* That is, she assured him so much that everything was all right that he began to suspect there was some danger. This is Clemencín's explanation of this "obscure expression."

gave him pleasure. It happened one day that Luscinda, having asked me for a romance of chivalry to read—and she was very fond of them—which was *Amadís de Gaula* . . ."

Don Quixote had hardly heard the title of that book when he blurted out: "If your grace had told me at the beginning of your story that her grace *señora* Luscinda was fond of reading romances of chivalry, you wouldn't have had to use any exaggeration to convince me of the superiority of her intellect, because it couldn't have been of the excellence you describe if she didn't have a taste for such delightful reading. So, with me you don't have to waste any more words in telling me about her beauty, worth, and intelligence, for, just by having learned what her interest is, I dub her the most beautiful and most circumspect woman in the world. And I'd like, *señor*, for you to have sent her, together with *Amadís de Gaula*, the good *Don Rugel de Grecia*,* because I know that *señora* Luscinda would enjoy Daraida and Geraya, and the shrewd remarks of the shepherd Darinel and those admirable verses of his pastoral poems, sung and set forth by him with such grace, wit, and ease. But a time will come when I can make good on this, for all you need to do whenever you want is come with me to my village, and there I can give you more than three hundred of them—and they are the joy of my soul and the entertainment of my life . . . although now that I think of it, I don't have any at all, thanks to the wickedness of bad people and evil enchanters. Please pardon me for having violated what we promised about not interrupting your discourse. But when I hear things about chivalry and knights-errant, I can't help talking about them, just as the rays of the sun cannot help but give warmth, and those of the moon give moisture. So, pardon me, and go on with your story, for that's the important thing."

While don Quixote was saying what is recorded here, Cardenio's head fell upon his chest, showing that he was plunged in deep thought. And although don Quixote asked

---

* *Don Rugel de Grecia* (1535) is the eleventh book in the Amadís cycle, written by Feliciano de Silva. Daraida and Garaya, mentioned in a moment, are indeed characters from that book. This book must have been in don Quixote's collection—many were tossed into the corral without stating which they were.

him twice to continue his story, he neither raised his head nor said a word. But after a while he looked up and said: "I can't get it out of my head, nor will anyone be able to convince me otherwise, and only a blockhead could hold or believe the contrary, that the scoundrel maestro Elisabat was sleeping with Queen Madésima."*

"That's not true, I swear," don Quixote shot back very angrily, "and that's monstrous libel or—to be more accurate—pure villainy. Queen Madásima was a great lady, and one shouldn't suppose that so exalted a princess should lie with a quack, and whoever says the contrary is lying like a knave. And I'll uphold this on foot or on horseback, in armor or not, by night or by day, or any way he prefers."

Cardenio was looking at him very attentively, because a bout of madness had overtaken him, and he was not about to continue his story, nor was don Quixote in any mood to listen to it, so much had he been disgusted by what he heard about the matter of Madásima. This was a very unusual thing because he'd defended her as if she'd been his true and natural lady, such was the state in which his excommunicated books had him. I say, then, that since Cardenio was mad, and heard himself called a liar, and a knave to boot, and other similar insults, it seemed like a bad jest to him, so he picked up a stone he found nearby, and hit don Quixote's chest so hard it made him fall backward. Sancho Panza, seeing his master being treated in that way, attacked the poor crazy fellow with closed fist, but the Ragged One was ready, and with one punch knocked Sancho off his feet, then jumped on top of him and crushed his ribs to his heart's content. The goatherd, who wanted to help him, suffered the same fate. And after Cardenio had subdued and beaten them all up, he went back calmly to his forest home.

Sancho got up and, so enraged at seeing himself so ill-treated without deserving it, went to take vengeance on the goatherd, telling him that *he* was to blame for not having warned them the fellow was sometimes mad—if they had known, they would have been on guard to defend them-

---

* In *Amadís de Gaula* Queen Madásima had no relations with the surgeon/priest Elisabat. The first Spanish edition shows Madésima, which seems all right here, in the mouth of this crazy young man.

selves. The goatherd responded that he *had* told them and if Sancho hadn't heard, it wasn't his fault. Sancho Panza replied, and the goatherd answered back, and finally they grabbed each other's beards and gave each other such punches that if don Quixote hadn't made peace between them, they would have torn each other to pieces. Sancho, while still holding on to the goatherd, said: "Leave me alone, your grace, *señor* Woebegone Knight, because this fellow is a rustic like myself and isn't dubbed a knight, so I can satisfy myself without injury for the offense this fellow has done me, fighting with him hand to hand, like a man of honor."

"That's true," said don Quixote, "but I know he's not to blame for what happened."

With this, they made peace, and don Quixote asked the goatherd again if it would be possible to find Cardenio, because he was still very interested in finding out the end of his story. The goatherd told him what he had told him at first, that there was no knowing for sure where his lair was, but if he wandered about that area enough, he couldn't help but find him, sane or crazy.

Chapter XXV. Which deals with the strange things that happened to the valiant Knight of La Mancha in the Sierra Morena and about the imitation that he did of the penance of Beltenebros.

D ON QUIXOTE bade farewell to the goatherd and, mounting Rocinante once again, he ordered Sancho to follow him, and he did this on his donkey most unwillingly. They entered cautiously into the most desolate part of the mountain. Sancho was dying to talk with his master, but wanted him to start the conversation so as not to contravene what he'd been ordered, but finally he couldn't stand the silence any longer, and said: "*Señor* don Quixote, give me your grace's blessing, and permit me to return home to my wife and children, with whom at least I can talk all I want, because your wanting me to go with you through these desolate places day and night, without being able to talk with you when I feel like it, is burying me alive. If Fortune would have it so that animals could talk, as they did in the time of Æsop, it wouldn't be so bad, because I could talk with my donkey whenever I felt like it, and in this way I could tolerate my turns of Fortune. It's hard to bear— it's something that can't be borne patiently, this business of going around seeking adventures one's whole life, and not finding anything except kicks and blanketings, flying brick-bats and punches, and through it all, we have to sew our mouths closed, as if we were mute."

"I understand you, Sancho," responded don Quixote. "You're dying for me to lift the interdiction I imposed on your tongue. Consider it lifted and say what you will, on the condition that you understand that this revocation will only last as long as we're wandering in this sierra."

"All right," said Sancho, "let me speak now, and God knows what'll happen later. And I'll begin to take advantage of this permission by asking what led your grace to stand up for that Queen Magimasa, or whatever her name is? What difference did it make if that abbot* was her boy-friend or not? If your grace had let it slide, since you're not her judge, I really think the crazy fellow would have gone on with his story, and you could have been spared being hit with the stone and even more than half a dozen punches."

"By my faith, Sancho," responded don Quixote, "if you knew, as I do, what an honorable and prominent lady Queen Madásima was, I know that you would say that I showed enormous restraint, since I didn't smash the mouth that uttered such blasphemies. Because it *is* a great blas-phemy either to say or think that a queen would lie with a surgeon. The truth is that maestro Elisabad, whom the crazy fellow mentioned, was a very prudent man who gave very good advice, and served as governor and doctor to the queen. But to think that she was his girlfriend is nonsense, worthy of severe punishment. And so that you can see that Cardenio didn't know what he was saying, you have to real-ize that he said it when he was out of his wits."

"That's what I'm saying—" said Sancho, "that your grace shouldn't pay attention to the words of a crazy man, because if good luck hadn't favored you, and the stone, instead of

---

* Abbot is *abad* in Spanish, which Sancho confuses with the last syl-lables of Elis*abad*, which sounds like *Elisabat*.

hitting you on the chest, had hit you on the head, we'd have been in fine shape for your having stood up for my lady, and may God confound her. And by golly, Cardenio would be set free for being crazy!"

"Against crazy men and sane ones, every knight-errant is obliged to stand up for the honor of women, no matter who they are. And more so for queens of the station and dignity of Madásima, for whom I have particular affection because of her excellent qualities. She was not only beautiful, but possessed wisdom and fortitude in her misfortunes. And the friendship and advice of maestro Elisabad were of great aid and comfort to her, so that she could withstand her travails with reason and patience. And because of this, the ignorant and low-minded public took the opportunity to say and think that she was his mistress. And anyone who thinks or says anything else lies, I say again."

"I don't say it or think it," responded Sancho. "It's their affair, and 'let 'em eat it with their bread.' If they were living together or not, they'll have to give God an accounting. 'I'm coming from my vineyards and I don't know anything.' I don't like to meddle in anyone else's business, and 'the person who buys and lies, in his purse he'll feel it.' 'Naked I was born, and naked I am: I don't win or lose.' But even if they *were* living together, what's it to me? And 'many think that there is bacon where there are no stakes.'* And 'who can put up doors in the countryside?' And, what's more, 'they even spoke ill of God.'"

"My God," said don Quixote, "what absurdities you're stringing together. What do the proverbs you're linking together have to do with what we were talking about? Sancho, stop talking, and from now just spur your donkey and don't meddle in what doesn't concern you. And try to understand with all your five senses that everything I've done, do, and may do is well-founded on reason, and very much in conformity with the rules of chivalry, and I know them better than any other knight in the world who professed them."

"*Señor*," responded Sancho, "are there rules of chivalry that say we're supposed to run around these mountains,

---

* That is, no bacon will be hanging up if there are no stakes to hang it from. You may see an application for this proverb, but not here!

without a path or a road, looking for a crazy man, who, after we find him maybe will feel like finishing what he started— not his story, but rather your grace's head and my ribs—by thrashing us completely?"

"Keep quiet, I tell you again, Sancho," said don Quixote, "because I'll have you know I'm here not only to find the crazy man, but also because I plan to do a deed that will make me eternally famous throughout the known world, and because of it, I'll put the seal on everything that can make a knight-errant famous and perfect."

"And is this deed very dangerous?" asked Sancho.

"No," responded the Woebegone One, "although we may get an unlucky throw of the dice instead of a lucky one. But everything depends on your diligence."

"On *my* diligence?" said Sancho.

"Yes," said don Quixote, "because if you come back quickly from where I plan to send you, my grief will come to an end immediately, and my glory will begin. So you won't be in suspense any longer, wondering where my words are leading, I want you to know, Sancho, that the famous Amadís de Gaula was one of the most perfect knights. That's not what I mean—he was the one and only, the first, the lord of all knights throughout the world who lived in his time. Too bad for don Belianís, and anyone who says that he equaled Amadís in anything, because he's mistaken, I swear. I also say that when a painter wants to become famous in his art, he tries to imitate the works of the greatest known painters. And this same rule goes for all—or most—professions or crafts of importance that make republics better. Thus he who would become famous for being prudent and long-suffering imitates Ulysses, in whose person Homer paints us a living portrait of those qualities; just as Virgil, in the person of Æneas, showed the goodness of a pious son and the sagacity of a brave and masterly captain. Those poets didn't paint or reveal them as they were, but rather as they should have been, so that those who came after them can emulate their virtues. In this same way, Amadís was the North Star, the evening star, and the sun of brave and en- amored knights, whom all those of us who go to war under the standard of love should imitate. Being this as it is, I find, Sancho, my friend, that the knight-errant who imitates him the best will be closest to reaching perfection in knight-

hood. And one of the things in which this knight showed
his prudence, worth, bravery, long suffering, constancy, and
love was when he went off, after he was spurned by the lady
Oriana, to do penance at Peña Pobre, changing his name
to Beltenebros, a name that was certainly meaningful* and
appropriate for the life he'd chosen of his free will. Thus
it's easier for me to imitate him in this than in cleaving giants, decapitating serpents, slaying dragons, putting armies
to flight, scattering fleets, and undoing enchantments. And
since remote places like these are so suitable for such purposes, there's no reason to let this Opportunity go by, since
he now offers me so conveniently his forelock."†

"So," said Sancho, "what is it your grace wants to do in
this desolate place?"

"Didn't I tell you already?" responded don Quixote.
"I want to imitate Amadís, playing the role of the desperate, wild, raving person, and I want to imitate the valiant
don Roland‡ as well, when he found evidence next to a
fountain that Angélica the Beautiful had committed a vile
act with Medoro,§ and the grief that it caused him made
him go crazy. He uprooted trees, muddied the waters of the
transparent streams, slew shepherds, destroyed their flocks,
burned their huts, leveled houses, dragged mares behind
him, and did a hundred thousand other infamies worthy
of record and eternal fame. And although I don't intend to
imitate Roland, Orlando, or Rotolando—for he was known
by these three names—item by item, in all the mad acts
that he performed, said, and thought, I'll at least do a rough
sketch of what seems to me to be the most essential things
as well as I can. And it may be that I'll content myself imitating only Amadís, who achieved as much fame as the best

---

* This is an old Provençal name meaning "beautiful gloom."
† This refers to the Roman god of opportunity, bald except for a lock
in front. You had to seize the lock when you saw it coming, since when
it passed by there was nothing left to take hold of.
‡ This Roland is not from the French *Chanson de Roland*, but rather
the Italian epic *Orlando Furioso* (1532) by Ludovico Ariosto (mentioned in chapter six). After his lady Angelica leaves him for the Moor
Medoro, he does all of the insane acts mentioned above. Roland had
found something next to a fountain that Medoro had written.
§ In *Orlando Furioso* 13, 105ff., we learn that Angelica slept "more
than two siestas" with Medoro.

of them by weeping and showing his feelings instead of doing crazy acts that can be harmful."

"It seems to me, *señor*," said Sancho, "that those knights were motivated and had reasons to perform these foolish acts and penances, but what reason does your grace have to go crazy? What lady rejected you? What evidence did you find that proves that your lady Dulcinea del Toboso has committed some childish nonsense with a Moor or a Christian?"

"That's the point," responded don Quixote, "and that's the beauty of my plan. If a knight goes crazy for a reason, there is no thanks or value attached to it. The thing is to go crazy *without* a reason, and to make my lady understand that if I do this when dry, what will I do when drenched? Moreover, I already have sufficient reason, owing to my long absence from the always-mine Dulcinea del Toboso, and remember what that shepherd of bygone days, Ambrosio, said: 'He who is absent has all ills and fears.' Thus, Sancho, my friend, don't waste time in counseling me not to do such a rare, such a happy, and such an unheard-of imitation. I'm mad, and mad I'll stay until you come back with an answer to a letter that I plan to send with you to my lady Dulcinea. And if it's as my devotion deserves, my madness and penance will come to an end. And if it's not, I'll be mad in earnest, and being in that state I'll feel nothing. So, no matter how she responds, I'll be freed from the conflict and travail in which you leave me—either enjoying the good fortune that you'll bring me as a sane man, or not feeling the bad fortune that you'll bring me as a crazy man. But tell me, Sancho, have you been protecting Mambrino's helmet? I saw you pick it up off the ground when that ungrateful fellow tried to smash it to pieces. But he couldn't do it, and that proves how finely tempered it is."

To which Sancho responded: "By God, *señor* Woebegone Knight, I can't fathom some of the things you say. And because of them, I'm beginning to wonder if everything you've been saying about chivalry, and winning kingdoms and empires, of giving *ínsulas*, and doing other favors and great things, as is the custom of knights-errant, is nothing but hot air and falsehoods, and just fables. Because anyone who hears you say that a barber's basin is Mambrino's helmet—and that you don't realize your mistake for more than four days running—must think that a person who says such a thing and sticks to it must be vacant in the area of sanity. I have the basin in my saddlebag, all dented up, and I'm taking it back home to repair and use when I shave, if God gives me the grace one day to be again with my wife and children."

"Look, Sancho, by the same God to whom you swore, I also swear," said don Quixote, "that you have the dullest understanding that any squire in the world has or ever had. How is it possible that all the time you've been riding with me you haven't realized that everything dealing with knights-errant seems implausible, foolish, and bewildering, and that everything seems the opposite of what it is? And not because it really *is* that way, but because there is always a multitude of enchanters who accompany us and who change things any way they want to, whether to favor or destroy us, and so, what seems to you to be a barber's basin to me seems like Mambrino's helmet, and to someone else it will seem like something different. And it was just providential on the part of the enchanter who favors me to make what really and truly is Mambrino's helmet appear to be a basin, because since it's so sought after, everybody would pursue me for it; but when they see that it appears to be nothing more than a barber's basin, they don't try to snatch it away. You could tell this when that fellow tried to smash it to bits and left it on the ground, because, if he'd recognized what it was, he never would have left it behind. Keep it, my friend—for the moment I have no need of it because I must first take off all my armor and get as naked as when I was born; that is, if I want to follow Roland more than Amadís in my penance."

They arrived at the foot of a high mountain, almost like a cliff, which stood alone among others that surrounded it. At one side, a slow-moving stream ran by, and all around there was a verdant and lush meadow, enchanting to the eye. There was a forest nearby, and other plants and flowers that made the place very pleasant. The Woebegone Knight chose this site to do his penance, and thus, when he saw it, he began to say in a loud voice, as if he were crazy: "This is the place, oh, heavens! that I designate and choose to cry away the misfortune in which you've placed me. This is the site where the liquid from my eyes will increase the waters of this stream, and my unceasing and deep sighs will continually rustle the leaves of these wild trees, as a testimony to the grief of my persecuted heart. Oh, you rustic gods, whoever you may be, who have made your home in this uninhabitable place, hear the complaints of this spurned lover whom long absence and imagined jealousy have brought to this rugged area to lament the cruel nature of that fair ingrate, the summit and quintessence of human beauty! Oh, you wood nymphs and dryads, who typically live in the densest parts of these forests, with wanton and lascivious satyrs by whom you are loved in vain, don't let them disturb your sweet repose, so that you can help me lament my misfortune, or at least not weary of hearing it! Oh, Dulcinea del Toboso, day of my night, glory of my grief, Polaris of my travels, star of my fortune—may heaven grant all that you seek from it—consider the place and condition to which your absence has brought me, and be moved to some favor commensurate with my deserving loyalty! Oh, solitary trees, who from today on will keep me company in my loneliness—show me by gently moving your boughs that my presence doesn't displease you! Oh, you, my squire, welcome comrade in prosperous and even adverse fortune, remember well what you see me do, so that you can relate and report it to its cause."

And, saying this, he got off Rocinante, and in a flash removed his bridle and saddle and, slapping him on the rump, said to him: "Liberty is yours, given to you by him who has none, oh, you steed, as consummate in deeds as you are plagued by your ill luck! Wander where you will, because on your forehead is written that neither the hippogriff of Astolfo, nor the renowned Frontino, which cost Bradamante so dear, can equal you in swiftness."*

When Sancho saw this, he said: "Good luck to the person who has saved us the trouble of taking the packsaddle off the donkey.† There would have been plenty of little pats to

---

* "The hippogriff was a winged horse with the head of an eagle on which Astolfo went in quest of information about Orlando. Frontino was the name of the horse belonging to Ruggiero, Bradamante's lover. All appear in Ariosto's *Orlando Furioso* [Canto IV]." (Ormsby's note)
† This is the first allusion to the theft of Sancho's donkey in the first edition.

give him and things to say in his praise. But if he were here, I wouldn't let anyone take off his packsaddle, since there is no reason to, since matters of love and despair don't apply to him because they didn't apply to his master, who was me, while it pleased God. And in truth, *señor* Woebegone Knight, if my departure and your insanity are really going to take place, it'd be a good idea to resaddle Rocinante in the absence of my donkey so that we can save time on my trip, because if I do it on foot, I don't know when I'll get there nor when I'll come back. When all is said and done, I don't take very much to walking."

"All right, Sancho," responded don Quixote, "do what you want. Your idea seems good. Stay here three days before you leave, because I want you to see what I do and say on her account, so that you can tell her about it."

"Well, what more do I have to see," responded Sancho, "other than what I've already seen?"

"How much more do you need to see?" responded don Quixote. "I need to rip up my clothes, scatter my armor, bash my head against these boulders, and other things like these that will amaze you."

"For the love of God," said Sancho, "your grace should be careful how you bash your head, because you may just bash it against a certain boulder in a certain spot, so that the first blow may be the end of your penance. I'm of the opinion that since you consider these bashings to be essential and that you can't do this feat without them, that you content yourself—since all this is pretend and bogus anyway—by bashing your head in the water or on something soft like cotton, and leave the rest to me, because I'll tell my lady that you bashed it on the edge of a rock harder than a diamond."

"I appreciate your good intentions, friend Sancho," responded don Quixote, "but I want you to know that nothing of what I do is done in jest, but very seriously, because any other way would contravene the order of chivalry, which commands us never to lie; otherwise I'd have to suffer the punishment of apostasy,* and doing one thing instead of another is the same as lying. So, my head bashing must be

---

* Apostasy is the renunciation of religious faith. This refers to certain crimes prosecuted by the Inquisition.

genuine, hard, and worthy, with nothing fallacious or imaginary about it. You'll have to leave me bandages to dress my wounds, since bad luck has seen to it that we don't have the balm that we lost."

"It was worse luck to lose the donkey," responded Sancho, "because when we lost him we lost the bandages and everything, and I beg your grace not to remind me of that damned brew, because just hearing it mentioned turns my whole insides, not just my stomach. And I ask you one thing more—let's just say that the three days for me to see the mad things that you want to do have now gone by, because I consider them all seen and done irrevocably, and without possibility of appeal. And I'll tell wondrous things to my lady. Write the letter and send me off right away because I'm anxious to take you out of this purgatory where I'm leaving you."

"You call it purgatory, Sancho?" said don Quixote. "Wouldn't it be better to call it hell, or even worse, if there is something worse than hell?"

"Whoever is in hell," responded Sancho, "'*nulla es retencio*,'* according to what I've heard tell."

"I don't understand what you mean by *retencio*," said don Quixote.

"*Retencio* is," responded Sancho, "when someone is in hell, he never leaves it, nor can he. And this is just the opposite in our case; if I'll have spurs to encourage Rocinante, let me get to El Toboso at once, and when I'm before my lady Dulcinea, I'll tell her such things about the follies and frenzies—for they're both the same—that your grace has done and is doing, and I'll make her softer than a glove even though I find her harder than a cork tree; and with her sweet and honeyed response I'll return through the air like a sorcerer, and I'll take your grace out of this purgatory—which seems like hell but isn't, since there is hope of getting out, and there is no hope of escape, as I said, for those in hell, and I don't think your grace will disagree with me."

"That's the truth," said the Woebegone One, "but just how will we write the letter?"

---

* What Sancho heard was doubtless "*Quia in inferno nulla est redemptio*," from the funeral Mass: "Because in hell there is no redemption."

"And the bill of exchange for the donkeys, too," added Sancho.

"Everything will be there," said don Quixote, "and it would be good, since there is no paper, to write it, as the ancients did, on leaves from trees or on wax tablets, although these would be as hard to find as paper.... But now I remember that it will be good, and even more than good, to write it in Cardenio's diary. You'll make sure to have it copied onto regular paper, in nice handwriting, in the first village where there is a schoolteacher or some sexton who can copy it—but don't give it to a notary, since they never remove the pen from the paper when they write, and Satan himself can't understand that style of writing."

"But what about the signature?" said Sancho.

"Amadís' letters are never signed," responded don Quixote.

"That's fine," responded Sancho, "but the bill of exchange must be signed, and if it's copied, they'll say the signature is forged, and I won't get the donkeys."

"The bill of exchange will be signed in the diary, and when my niece sees it, she'll do what it says. And regarding the love letter, you'll have it signed YOURS UNTIL DEATH, THE WOEBEGONE KNIGHT. And it won't make much difference if it's in someone else's handwriting, because as far as I remember, Dulcinea can't read or write, and she's never seen my handwriting nor any letter of mine in her whole life, because my love and her love have always been Platonic, no more than a modest glance. And this, so seldom, that I'll swear in truth that in the twelve years that I've been loving her more than the light of these eyes, which one day the earth will devour, I haven't seen her more than four times, and it may also be that of those four times she didn't notice once that I was looking at her—such is the modesty and seclusion with which her father, Lorenzo Corchuelo, and her mother, Aldonza Nogales, have raised her."

"Aha!" said Sancho. "So the daughter of Lorenzo Corchuelo is the lady Dulcinea del Toboso, also known as Aldonza Lorenzo?"

"That's the one," said don Quixote, "and she deserves to be mistress of the whole universe."

"I know her well," said Sancho, "and I can tell you that she's as good a man as the strongest lad in the village. By

God, she has plenty of common sense, she's strong as an ox, with hair on her chest, and she can get any knight-errant—present or future—who would have her as his lady, out of any bind. Oh, son of a bitch, what strength she has, and what a voice! I can tell you that one day she went up to the bell tower of the village to call some of her father's field hands, and even though they were more than half a league away, they heard her as if they'd been at the foot of the tower. And the best thing is that she's not at all prudish because she's been around the block, and she smiles at everyone and jokes with everybody. I now say, *señor* Woebegone Knight, that not only can you and should you do these crazy acts in her honor, but you have every right to despair and hang yourself on her account, and anyone who hears about it will say you did the right thing, even though the devil carries you off. And I'd like to get on the road right now just to see her because I haven't seen her for many days—she must have changed a bit, since being in the fields and in the sun and wind always spoils a woman's complexion. And I confess, *señor* don Quixote, until now I've been in the dark, and thought all the while that the lady Dulcinea must be some princess who you were in love with, or some person who deserved the rich presents that your grace has sent her, such as the Basque and the galley slaves, and many others, because you must have had many victories before I came to be your squire. But upon consideration, what good can it do the lady Aldonza Lorenzo—I mean, the lady Dulcinea del Toboso—when those conquered people who you send will kneel before her? Because it might be that just when they arrive, she might be combing flax, or threshing in the barn, and they'll be mortified, and she'll just laugh or lose her temper."

"I've told you many times, Sancho," said don Quixote, "that you're a great babbler, and although you have a dull wit, you sometimes show smatterings of sharpness. But so you'll see what a fool you are and how shrewd I am, I want you to listen to a little story: A beautiful widow—young, unattached, rich, and above all carefree—fell in love with a young lay brother, plump and corpulent. His superior found out about it, and one day told the good widow, as a friendly reproof: 'I'm amazed, *señora*, and not without cause, that a woman of your rank—so beautiful, and so rich—has fallen in love with a man who is so coarse, so low, and so stupid as is So-and-So, since there are so many teachers in this community, so many divinity students, and so many theologians that you could choose from as if they were pears, and say: "I'd like this one and not that one."' But she responded with great grace and ease: 'Your grace, *señor mío*, is very mistaken and behind the times if you think that I've chosen poorly in So-and-So, as stupid as he looks, because what I want him for, he knows as much and maybe more philosophy than Aristotle.' Thus, Sancho, what I want Dulcinea del Toboso for, she's worth as much as the greatest princess in the world. It's true that not all poets who praise ladies under fictitious names actually have these women as lovers. Do you think that the Amaryllises, the Phyllises, the Sylvias, the Dianas, the Galateas, the Alidas,* and others who fill books, ballads, barbershops, and theaters, were really women of flesh and blood and really belonged to those who praise and praised them? No, certainly not, because most of them are fictional, and serve only to give a subject for their poems, and so that they themselves might be taken for lovers, and worthy to be so. So, it's enough for me to think and believe that the good Aldonza Lorenzo is beautiful and chaste; her lineage matters little, since no one is going to investigate her background to give her an honorary degree—the only thing that matters is that I believe she's the greatest princess in the world. I want you to know, Sancho, if you don't know it already, that there are two things that stimulate love more than anything else: great beauty and a good reputation, and these two things are conspicuously exemplified in Dulcinea, because in beauty, no one can rival her, and in good reputation few can. To sum up, I make myself believe that everything I say about her is the absolute truth, neither more nor less, and I portray her in my imagination as I like her, so that in beauty and rank, Helen† cannot match her, nor can Lucretia‡ come near, nor any other of the famous women of ages past: Greek, barbarian, or Roman. Let anyone say what he wants—even

---

* "Alidas" is in the first edition and is usually changed to Fílidas since there is no known Alida. All the other women are characters in fiction.
† Helen of Troy, legend says, was the most beautiful woman in Greece.
‡ Lucretia was a virtuous and beautiful Roman woman.

if uninformed people criticize me, I'll not be condemned by those who are discerning."

"I say that your grace is very right in all this," responded Sancho, "and that I'm a donkey. But I don't know why I'd mention 'donkey,' since 'you should never mention rope in the house of the hanged man.' So give me the letter, goodbye, and I'm on my way."

Don Quixote took out the diary, and going off to one side, he began to write calmly, and when he finished, he called Sancho and said to him that he wanted to read it aloud so that he could memorize it, just in case he lost it along the way, because with his misfortunes, anything could happen. To which Sancho responded: "Write it, your grace, two or three times in the book and give it to me, and I'll take good care of it, but to think I can memorize it is foolish. My memory is so bad, sometimes I can't remember my own name. But in any case, recite it to me since I'm bound to take pleasure in it, and it ought to be just the ticket."

"Listen—here's what it says," said don Quixote:

Letter from don Quixote to Dulcinea del Toboso

Sovereign and highborn lady,

He who is pierced by the dart of absence, he who is wounded to his heart's core, sends you, sweetest Dulcinea del Toboso, the health that he does not possess. If your beauty scorns me, if your worthiness does not favor me, if your contempt attacks my ardor, although I'm patient as I can be, I can hardly sustain this affliction, which, aside from being overpowering, is long lasting. My good squire, Sancho, will give you a complete account—oh, beautiful ungrateful beloved enemy mine!—of the condition I am in because of you. If it pleases you to rescue me, I am yours, and if not, do whatever it may please you to do, for in finishing my life I will have satisfied your cruelty and my desire.

Yours until death,

The Woebegone Knight

"On the life of my father," said Sancho when he heard what the letter said, "this is the loftiest thing I ever heard. I'll be damned! How well your grace says everything exactly as you want, and how neatly you tuck in your signature, THE WOEBEGONE KNIGHT! I'm speaking the truth when I say you're the devil himself, and there's nothing you don't know."

"One needs to know everything," responded don Quixote, "in my profession."

"All right," said Sancho, "now put the order for the three donkeys on the other side, and sign it clearly so that they'll recognize it when they see it."

"That I will," said don Quixote.

And once it was written, he read it to him, and it went like this:

> *Your grace, señora niece, will deliver to Sancho*
> *Panza by means of this order, three of the five*
> *young donkeys that I left in your care. These*
> *three donkeys shall be delivered and have*
> *been paid for by an appropriate amount that I*
> *received from him here and is on account, and*
> *by means of this letter and his receipt they can*
> *be delivered. Given in the depths of the Sierra*
> *Morena this twenty-second of August in this*
> *current year.*

"Good," said Sancho. "Now sign it, your grace."

"I don't need to sign it," said don Quixote. "I just have to use my flourish,* which is the same as a signature, and for three donkeys, and even for three hundred, it will suffice."

"I'll trust you on this," responded Sancho, "and now let me put the saddle on Rocinante, and get ready to give me your blessing, because I plan to leave without seeing the crazy things that your grace plans to do—I'll tell her I saw so many that she'll have her fill."

"At least, Sancho, since it's really essential, I want you to see me naked doing a dozen or two crazy acts. It'll only take half an hour, and then having seen some with your

---

* The flourish, a stylized design that may or may not represent letters of the person's name, is still used in Spain.

own eyes, you can safely swear to having seen any that you want to add. And I can assure you that you won't be able to describe as many as I plan to do."

"For the love of God, *señor mío*, don't force me to see your grace naked! It'll make me sad and I won't be able to stop crying. I did so much crying over the loss of my donkey that I'm in no shape for more. If you want me to see you do some crazy acts, do them fully dressed, don't draw them out, and just do the best ones. What's more, for me none of this is required, and as I said, without them it would save time on the road and hasten my return, which will be with the news that your grace wants and deserves. And if the news isn't good, *señora* Dulcinea had better watch out, because I'm making a solemn vow to you-know-who that I'll get the right answer out of her stomach by kicks and punches. I mean, how can it be that a knight-errant as famous as your grace has to go crazy without a reason, for a . . . ? Let the lady not force me to say it, because, by God, I'm liable to say everything that comes to mind, not caring about the consequences! That's the way I am! She doesn't know me very well, because if she did, she'd have respect for me."

"Upon my soul, Sancho," said don Quixote, "it looks like you're no saner than I am."

"I'm not crazy," responded Sancho, "but I *am* angry. But, this aside, what is your grace going to eat while I'm away? Are you going to jump out into the road and rob shepherds?"

"Don't worry about that," responded don Quixote, "because, even if I had other things to eat, I would only eat the herbs and fruits of this meadow and from these trees. The beauty of this is in fasting and undergoing other similar hardships."

"Good-bye, then; but I'm afraid that I won't be able to find my way back to this place, since it's so hidden."

"Take your bearings well, and I'll try not to leave this area," said don Quixote, "and I'll even try to climb onto those highest cliffs to see if I can spot you when you return. What I think would even be better, so you won't make a mistake and get lost, is for you to cut off some broom branches of the many that there are around here, and drop them at intervals until you get out into the open. They will serve as landmarks and signs, so you can find me when you come back, imitating the cord that Perseus used in the labyrinth."*

"That's what I'll do," responded Sancho, and after cutting off some broom branches, he asked for his master's blessing, and not without many tears on both sides, he bade farewell to his master. When he mounted Rocinante—whom don Quixote put in Sancho's care and told him to look out for his horse as he would himself—Sancho set out for the plain, dropping broom branches once in a while as his master had advised. And so he went away, his master still begging him to witness at least two crazy acts. He hadn't traveled more than a hundred paces when he said: "All right, *señor*, your grace is right. So that I can swear that I've seen you cavorting about, without nagging my conscience, it would be good for me to see just one, although I've seen a very crazy act just in your staying here."

"Didn't I tell you?" said don Quixote, "Wait a second, Sancho. In the time it takes to say a credo† I'll do one."

Don Quixote took off his pants and was naked in shirt-tails, and then, without further ado, cut two capers in the air and did two somersaults, revealing things that—so that he wouldn't have to see them a second time—prompted Sancho to turn Rocinante around, quite satisfied that he could swear that his master was crazy. Thus we'll let him go his way until his return, and it was soon.

Chapter XXVI. *Where the antics that don Quixote, in the role of a lover, did in the Sierra Morena are continued.*

WHEN THE history comes to relate what the Woebegone One did after he found himself alone, it goes on to say that as soon as don Quixote did those somersaults, naked from the waist down and dressed from the waist up, and saw that Sancho had gone without waiting to see more capers,

---

* It wasn't *Per*seus, the slayer of Medusa, but rather *The*seus who found his way out of the labyrinth of Crete. This is don Quixote's mistake.
† Credo refers to the Apostle's Creed—maybe it takes fifteen seconds to say it.

he climbed to the top of a tall boulder, and there began to think about what he'd thought about many times, without having resolved the matter; namely, would it be more fitting to imitate Roland in the outrageous crazy acts he performed, or Amadís in his more sedate, melancholy ones? Talking to himself, he said: "If Roland was as good and as valiant a knight as everyone says, what's so wonderful about that? He was enchanted after all, and he couldn't be killed except by piercing the front of his foot with a large straight pin, and he always wore shoes with seven iron soles, although this device didn't do him any good against Bernardo del Carpio, who saw through it, and squeezed the life out of him in Roncesvalles.* But setting aside the matter of his courage, let's move on to the question of his loss of sanity—because it's certain he went crazy owing to the signs his destiny led him to find, and also the news that the shepherd gave him that Angélica had slept two siestas with Medoro, the little Moor with curly hair, Agramante's page. And if he understood this was the truth and his lady had committed an outrage, it was not surprising that he was driven crazy. But I—how can I imitate him in his crazy acts unless I share the same circumstances? My Dulcinea del Toboso, I'll dare to swear, has never seen a Moor in traditional garb in all the days of her life,† and she's as chaste today as the mother who bore her. I would do her a grave injustice if I, imagining anything else about her, let myself go crazy in the style of Roland.

"On the other hand, I see that Amadís de Gaula, without going mad and without doing crazy acts, became famous as a lover like the best of them, for what he did—according to his history—when he saw himself spurned by his lady Oriana, who commanded him not to appear before her until she let him, was to go to Peña Pobre in the company of a hermit, and there got his fill of weeping and commending himself to God, until heaven intervened in the midst of his greatest affliction and need. And if this is true—as it cer-

---

* Don Quixote is supposed to be an expert in these matters, yet it was not the front of his foot but rather the *sole* that had to be punctured with the pin, and the shoe of seven iron soles was worn by someone other than Roland. All of this is from the Spanish versions of the Italian Roland tradition.

† Most of the population of El Toboso was of Moorish origin.

tainly is—why should I want to get undressed, and spoil these trees, which haven't done me any harm at all; nor do I have a reason to muddy these clear streams, which have to provide me with something to drink when I feel the need? Long live the memory of Amadís, and let him be imitated by don Quixote de La Mancha in every way he can, and they'll say about him what they said about another person,* that if he didn't attain great things, at least he died trying, and if I'm neither rejected nor spurned by Dulcinea del Toboso, all I need to do, as I said, is absent myself from her. All right, let's get at it! Oh, deeds of Amadís, come to my memory now and show me how to imitate you! But now I remember, what he did the most was to pray and commend himself to God. But what'll I do for a rosary? I don't have one."

It then occurred to him how to make one. He tore off a strip of cloth from his shirttails, and he made eleven knots, one larger than the rest, and this served him as a rosary while he was there, where he prayed a million Hail Marys. What nagged at him was that there was no hermit there to whom he could confess and through whom he could be consoled. He whiled away the time strolling about in the little meadow, writing and carving poems on barks of trees and on the fine sand, each one appropriate to his sorrow, and some of them praising Dulcinea. Those that could be found whole and could be read after they found him there were only these that follow:

Ye on the mountainside that grow,
    Ye green things all, trees, shrubs, and bushes,
    Are ye weary of the woe
    That this poor aching bosom crushes?
    If it disturb you, and I owe
Some reparation, it may be a
    Defense for me to let you know
    Don Quixote's tears are on the flow,
    And all for distant Dulcinea
      DEL TOBOSO.

---

* This other person is probably Phæton of Greek mythology, who asked to drive the chariot of the sun through the heavens and couldn't control his horses. Zeus killed him with a thunderbolt to prevent damage to the earth. See Ovid's *Metamorphoses* II, 327–28.

The loyal lover time can show,
    Doomed for a lady-love to languish,
    Among these solitudes doth go,
    A prey to every kind of anguish.
    Why Love should like a spiteful foe
Thus use him, he hath no idea,
    But hogsheads full—this doth he know—
    Don Quixote's tears are on the flow,
    And all for distant Dulcinea
      DEL TOBOSO.

Adventure-seeking doth he go
    Up rugged heights, down rocky valleys,
    But hill or dale, or high or low,
    Mishap attendeth all his sallies:
    Love still pursues him to and fro,
And plies his cruel scourge—ah me! a
    Relentless Fate, an endless woe;
    Don Quixote's tears are on the flow,
    And all for distant Dulcinea
      DEL TOBOSO.*

The added "del Toboso" caused no little laughter on the part of those who found the verses transcribed above, because they thought that don Quixote figured that if he just said "Dulcinea" and didn't include "del Toboso," you couldn't understand the stanza, and it was the truth, as don Quixote later confessed. He wrote many other poems, but, as has been said, none could be made out in its entirety except these three stanzas. He occupied himself writing poetry, sighing, calling on fauns and satyrs of those forests, as well as the nymphs of the rivers, the sorrowful and tearful Echo, to respond, console, and listen to him, and in looking for some herbs for sustenance until Sancho returned (and if Sancho had delayed three weeks instead of just three days, the Woebegone Knight would have had his looks so altered even his own mother wouldn't have recognized him).

He can now be left with his sighs and verses so we can say what happened to Sancho Panza in the course of his errand. On reaching the highway he went toward El To-

---

* This is Ormsby's version of this poem.

boso, and the following day he came to the inn where he'd suffered the disgrace of the blanketing. As soon as he saw it, it seemed to him that he was flying in the air once again, and he didn't want to go inside, although it was the time of day when he could have and should have, since it was lunchtime, and he was longing for something hot, since all he'd eaten for days on end were cold cuts. This need caused him to approach the inn, but he still was wondering if he should go in or not. And while he was in thought, two people came out of the inn who recognized him immediately, and one said to the other: "Tell me, *señor licenciado*, that man on horseback, isn't that Sancho Panza, the fellow who the housekeeper of our adventurer said had left with her master to be his squire?"

"It most certainly is," said the priest, "and he's on don Quixote's horse."

They knew him well because they were the priest and the barber of his village, and the ones who had tried and condemned the books. As soon as they saw Sancho Panza and Rocinante, since they wanted to find out about don Quixote, they went toward him, and the priest called him by name, saying: "Friend Sancho Panza, where is your master?"

Sancho recognized them immediately and resolved not to reveal either his master's whereabouts or his plight, or in what state he was in. So he answered them that he was engaged in a certain place on certain important business that he couldn't tell them about for anything in the world.

"No, no," said the barber, "Sancho Panza, if you don't tell us where he is, we'll think—and we're already thinking it—that you killed and robbed him, since you're riding his horse. In short, you must produce the owner of the nag or you're in trouble."

"There's no need to threaten me, since I'm not the kind of fellow who goes around robbing or killing anyone— let everyone be killed by his fortune or by the God who made him. My master is doing penance in the heart of these mountains and all of it very much to his liking."

And then, all at once and without stopping, he told them all about his present errand and past adventures, and how he was carrying a letter to the lady Dulcinea del Toboso, who was really the daughter of Lorenzo Corchuelo, with whom don Quixote was in love up to his eyes. The two were amazed at what Sancho Panza told them, and although they were aware of don Quixote's madness, every time they heard something new about it, they were more and more astonished. They asked Sancho Panza to show them the letter he was taking to the lady Dulcinea del Toboso. He said it was in a diary, and that his master had told him to have it copied onto good paper in the first village he came to. The priest asked him to show it to them, because he himself would copy it in a very fine hand. Sancho Panza put his hand inside his shirt looking for the little book, but couldn't find it, nor would he have found it if he'd kept looking for it until now, because it was still with don Quixote, who hadn't given it to him, nor did Sancho have the presence of mind to ask for it.

When Sancho realized that he couldn't find the book, his face became deathly pale, and he began to search himself furiously, and when he confirmed that he didn't have it, he began clutching his beard with both hands and yanked out half of it, then gave himself half a dozen punches on his face and nose, bathing them in blood. The priest and barber witnessed all this and asked him what had happened to cause such a frenzy.

"What has happened," responded Sancho, "is that from one second to the next, in an instant, I've lost three donkeys, each one worth a castle."

"How's that?" replied the barber.

"I've lost the diary," responded Sancho, "where the letter for Dulcinea and the bill of exchange signed by my master were written, and in which he directed his niece to give me three donkeys of the four or five that he owns."

He then related about the loss of his own donkey. The priest consoled him and told him that when they found his master, they would ask him to prepare a new order, because those in diaries were never accepted or honored in any case. Sancho was consoled by this and said since that was the case, it didn't grieve him for having lost the letter to Dulcinea, because he knew it almost by heart, and he could have it written down wherever and whenever they wanted.

"Recite it, then, Sancho," said the barber, "and afterward, we'll copy it down."

Sancho hesitated and scratched his head to bring the letter to mind, and he switched his weight first to one foot, then to the other. Sometimes he looked up; then he looked down, and after he'd gnawed off half of the tip of his finger, holding in suspense those who had asked him to recite it, at long last, he said: "My God, *señor licenciado*, may the devil take me if I can remember anything from the letter, but it started this way: 'High and slobbering *señora*.'"

"He probably didn't say 'slobbering,'" said the barber, "but rather 'sovereign *señora*.'"

"That's it," said Sancho, "and then, if I remember correctly, it went on ... if I remember correctly, 'the wounded, the wanting of sleep, and the pierced, kisses the hands of your grace, hateful and ungrateful one,' and some such stuff about health and sickness he was sending her; then it went along until it ended in 'Yours until death, the Woebegone Knight.'"

The two took no little pleasure in the good memory of Sancho Panza, and they praised him very much, and asked him to recite the letter twice more, so that they also could learn it by heart, and he recited it again three more times and again said three thousand more foolish things. After this, he told them other things about his master, but didn't mention anything about his own blanketing at that inn, which he refused to enter. He also said that his master, if he received a favorable reply from Dulcinea, would immediately get on the road to becoming an emperor, or at least a monarch, because that's what the two of them had decided. And it would be very easy for him to become such a ruler, owing to his courage and the might of his arm. And once he was an emperor, don Quixote would marry him off—because by then he would doubtless be a widower—to a lady-in-waiting to an empress, who would inherit a rich and large estate on the mainland (no *ínsulas* this time, since he didn't want one anymore).

Sancho said this with such serenity, wiping his nose from time to time, and with so little sense, that the two were astonished anew at the intense nature of the madness of don Quixote and how it took along with it the sanity of that poor man. They didn't try to free him from his delusion, considering that since it didn't hurt his conscience, it would be better to leave him alone, and for them it would be more fun to hear his foolish remarks. So they told him to pray to God for the health of his master, and that it seemed possible and likely that with the passage of time he could get to be an emperor, as he'd said, or at least an archbishop-errant, or other similar office.

To which Sancho replied: "*Señores,* if Fortune arranged things so that my master wouldn't get the idea to be an emperor, but rather an archbishop, I'd like to know now how archbishops-errant reward their squires."

"They usually give them," responded the priest, "a simple church-related job, or a curate, or the office of sexton, which brings in a good income, not to mention altar fees that bring in as much."

"But for this," replied Sancho, "the squire will have to be unmarried and be able to help out at Mass, at least, and if this is true, woe is me! I'm married and I don't know the first letter of the ABCs. What will become of me if my master fancies becoming an archbishop and not an emperor, as is the custom with knights-errant?"

"Don't worry, friend Sancho," said the barber. "We'll implore and advise your master—in fact, we'll put it before him as a matter of conscience—that he should become an emperor and not an archbishop, because it'll be easier for him since he's more a soldier than a student."

"That's what it seems like to me," responded Sancho, "even though I always say that he's good at anything. What I think I'll do on my part is to pray to our Lord to do what is best for him, and to place him where he can do me the most good."

"You're talking like an astute man," said the priest, "and you'll do it like a good Christian. But what we must do now is figure out how we can get your master out of that useless penance you say he's doing; and in order to consider what we have to do—and also to have something to eat, because it's time—it'd be good to go into this inn."

Sancho told them to go in, but he would wait outside, and afterward he'd tell them why he wouldn't go in, and why it wasn't fitting that he should. But he asked them to bring him something hot to eat, and also some barley for Rocinante. They went in, leaving him behind, and a bit later, the barber took him something to eat. After that, when the two of them had thought about what they should

do in order to accomplish their intent, the priest hit upon
an idea admirably suited both to don Quixote's taste and to
their own motivation. He told the barber what he came up
with: that he—the priest—would dress up as a wandering
maiden, and that he—the barber—would dress up as well
as he could as a squire, and they would go to don Quixote,
the one pretending to be a distressed and needy maiden,
and she would ask him for a boon, and he—being a brave
knight-errant—couldn't refuse. The boon that he planned
to ask for would be for him to go with her wherever she
would take him, to right a wrong that an evil knight had
done her, and that she would entreat him not to ask her to
lift her veil, or ask anything about her state of affairs until
he'd avenged her on that scoundrel of a knight. He firmly
believed that don Quixote would go along with anything
she would ask along these lines, and in this way, they would
be able to take him from where he was and lead him back
to his village, where they would try to see if there was any
cure for his madness.

Chapter XXVII. How the priest and barber carried out their scheme, together with other things worthy of being revealed in this great history.

THE BARBER didn't think that the priest's idea was bad—
indeed, he thought it was so good that they resolved to
put it into effect immediately. They asked the innkeeper's
wife for a skirt and some veils, leaving a new cassock belonging to the priest for security. The barber made a long beard
from a graying red oxtail in which the innkeeper kept his
comb. The innkeeper's wife asked them why they needed
those things. The priest told her in a few words about the
madness of don Quixote and how that disguise was necessary to take him out of the mountains where he was at that
time. The innkeeper and his wife immediately recognized
that the crazy man had been their guest—the fellow with
the balm, and the master of the blanketed squire. They then
told the priest everything that had happened to don Quixote, and didn't keep quiet about what Sancho so earnestly
didn't want to reveal.

So the innkeeper's wife dressed the priest in a way that left nothing to be desired: She put a woven skirt on him, decorated with borders of black velvet a palm wide, slit at intervals to reveal the color underneath, and a bodice of green velvet decorated with trimmings of white satin, and both of them looked like they had been made during the reign of King Wamba.* The priest wouldn't let them fix his hair like a woman's. Instead, he put a quilted nightcap over his hair, and bound his forehead with a black silk strip. He used the other strip to secure a veil over his beard and face. He put on a hat that was so large that it could have served as a parasol and, putting his cloak around him, got onto a mule, sitting sidesaddle, and the barber got onto his, with his graying red beard flowing around his waist, since it was, as has been said, made from the tail of a reddish ox. They bade farewell to everyone and to the good Maritornes, who, although she was a sinner, promised to say a rosary so that God would grant success for their arduous and Christian enterprise.

But hardly had the priest left the inn when it struck him that it wouldn't become him as a priest to be seen in such garb, even though much might depend on it, so he asked the barber to exchange outfits, since it was better for the barber to play the part of the damsel in distress and that he—the priest—would be the squire, and any dishonor to his dignity would thus be greatly reduced. If the barber didn't want to do it, he was determined not to proceed, even though the devil himself carried off don Quixote.

Sancho arrived at that moment, and seeing the two of them dressed that way he couldn't contain his laughter. Meanwhile, the barber agreed to everything the priest wanted, and once their disguise was changed, the priest informed him about how to act, and the proper words to use with don Quixote in order to move and even force him to accompany the barber and leave the haunts he'd chosen for his useless penance. The barber responded that without any further instruction, he would do just fine. He didn't want to get dressed up right then, but rather wanted to wait until they were near where don Quixote was, and so he folded up the garments, the priest put away the beard, and they

---

* King Wamba reigned from 672–680.

continued their journey, with Sancho Panza leading, and as they went along, he told them about the crazy man they found in the sierra, but concealed how he'd found the suitcase, and what was inside it—for, although he was a simple fellow, he was a bit greedy.

The next day they arrived at the place where Sancho had placed the last of the broom branches to find his way back to his master, and when he saw it, he told them that was the way in and suggested that they get into costume if it was really necessary for his master's deliverance—they had told him earlier the reason for their plan to dress up that way was enormously important to take his master away from that wretched way of life he'd chosen, and they charged him not to tell his master who they were, or that he knew them. And if he asked—as they expected he would—if he'd given the letter to Dulcinea, he should say that he had, and that she, since she didn't know how to write, had responded orally, telling him that she'd commanded him to go to see her immediately because it was very important to her, and if he failed to appear before her he would incur the consequences of her wrath. With this, and with other things they planned to tell him, they were certain they could restore him to a better life, and would start him on the road to becoming an emperor or monarch right away (and that there was no reason to fear his becoming an archbishop).

Sancho heard all of this and committed it all to memory, and thanked them for their plan to urge his master to become an emperor and not an archbishop, because he was convinced that emperors could do more favors for their squires than archbishops-errant. Also, he told them that it would be good if he went first to give him the response from his mistress, since that would be sufficient to draw him away from that place without their going to so much trouble. The others thought what Sancho said was good and agreed to wait until he returned with the news of his having found his master.

Sancho proceeded into the mountain gorge, leaving the two in a ravine through which a small, gentle stream flowed. Nearby boulders and trees offered a pleasant and cool shade. The intense heat when they arrived in the midafternoon was typical of August days, so the shade made it all the more pleasant, and invited them to wait there for Sancho's return, which is what they did.

The two were resting in the shade when a sound came to their ears. It was a singing voice without accompaniment, and sounded most sweet and pleasant, which caused them to marvel not a little, since it seemed to them a most unlikely place to come across someone who sang so well. Although it's said that in forests and fields one finds shepherds with wonderful singing voices, that's more an exaggeration of poets than the truth. They were even more surprised when they realized that what they were hearing was verses, not of rustic cattle herders, but of refined courtiers. And this was confirmed when they heard these verses:

What makes my quest of happiness seem vain?
 Disdain.
What bids me to abandon hope of ease?
 Jealousies.
What holds my heart in anguish of suspense?
 Absence.
If that be so, then for my grief
  Where shall I turn to seek relief,
  When hope on every side lies slain
  By Absence, Jealousies, Disdain?

What the prime cause of all my woe doth prove?
 Love.
What at my glory ever looks askance?
 Chance.
Whence is permission to afflict me given?
 Heaven.
If that be so, I but await
  The stroke of a resistless Fate,
  Since, working for my woe, these three,
  Love, Chance, and Heaven, in league I see.

What must I do to find a remedy?
 Die.
What is the lure for love when coy and strange?
 Change.
What, if all fail, will cure the heart of sadness?
 Madness.

If that be so, it is but folly
    To seek a cure for melancholy:
    Ask where it lies; the answer saith
    In Change, in Madness, or in Death.*

The time of day, the heat, the solitude, and the skill of the person singing caused wonder and delight to the listeners, who remained still, waiting to see if there was more to hear. When they thought the silence would continue, they resolved to look for the musician who sang so well—and just when they were ready to do so, the same voice stopped them, because at that moment it took up again to sing this sonnet:

SONNET

When heavenward, holy Friendship, you did go
    Soaring to seek your home beyond the sky,
    And take your seat among the saints on high,
    It was your will to leave on earth below
Your semblance, and upon it to bestow
    Your veil, wherewith at times hypocrisy,
    Parading in your shape, deceives the eye,
    And makes its vileness bright as virtue show.
Friendship, return to us, or force the cheat
    That wears it now, your livery to restore,
    By aid whereof sincerity is slain.
If thou wilt not unmask your counterfeit,
    This earth will be the prey of strife once more,
    As when primeval discord held its reign.

The song ended with a deep sigh, and the two hoped that he would sing more, but seeing the music had turned into sobs and heartrending moans, they decided to find out who that unfortunate person was whose voice was as unique as his sobs were piteous, and they had not walked very far when they went around a boulder and saw a man of the appearance Sancho Panza had described when he told the story of Cardenio. When he saw them he was not startled, but remained still with his head bowed down onto

---

* Ormsby's version here and below.

his chest, like one deep in thought, without raising his eyes to look at them after his first glance, when they had arrived so unexpectedly.

The priest, who was an eloquent man, as one who had heard of his misfortune—since by Sancho's description he'd recognized him—approached him and, with a few well-chosen words, begged and tried to persuade him to leave that wretched life, so that he wouldn't lose it, which was the worst misfortune. Cardenio was completely sane at that moment, free from the raving lunacy that so often carried him away. Seeing them in such unaccustomed dress for that wild area, he couldn't help being a bit amazed, and especially when he heard them talk about his affairs as if they were something well-known, because that's what the priest's words communicated, so he answered them in this way:

"Whoever you may be, *señores*, I see clearly that heaven, which is careful to rescue the good and sometimes even the wicked, without my deserving it, has sent people to me in this remote and out-of-the-way place to prove to me with vivid and lively arguments how irrational the life I'm leading is, and seek to take me away from it and put me on the road to a better one. But since you don't realize that I know that if I leave this bad situation, I'll fall into an even worse one, perhaps you'll take me for a man of diminished capacity or—what's worse—devoid of reason. And it wouldn't be off the mark for you to think that, since it seems to me that the effect of remembering my misfortune is so great and so powerful that, without my being able to help it, I become like a stone at times, without feeling or consciousness. And I realize this truth when I'm told, and shown proof of things I've done when this terrible fit overcomes me. So all I can do is to bewail and uselessly curse my fate and excuse my madness by revealing its cause to anyone willing to listen, because when people with all their faculties hear the cause, they won't wonder at its effects, and if they can't help me, at least they won't blame me, and the anger they feel for my brazen acts might turn into pity for my misfortunes. And if you, *señores*, have come for the same reason that has led others, before you start in with your wise counsel, I beg you to listen to the unending story of my misfortunes, because perhaps once you've heard it, you'll spare yourselves the trouble of trying to offer solace for an anguish which allows none."

Since neither of them wanted anything else but to find
out from his own lips the cause of his sorrow, they begged
him to tell it to them, promising that they would do nothing
for his relief or comfort that he didn't desire, and so the sad
young man began his touching story using almost the same
words and in the same way he'd related it to don Quixote
and the goatherd a few days earlier, when, owing to the affair of master Elisabad and don Quixote's upholding of the
precepts of chivalry, the story remained unfinished, as the
history has related. But good fortune prevented a second
mad fit and allowed him to finish the story and tell it to its
end. So, when he got to the point about the incident where
don Fernando had found the love letter stuck between the
pages of *Amadís de Gaula*, Cardenio said that he'd memorized it, and it went like this:

Luscinda to Cardenio

*Every day I discover qualities in you that
oblige and force me to esteem you more, so
if you want to relieve me of this debt without
prejudice to my honor, you can easily do it. I
have a father who knows you and loves me,
and he—without forcing my free will—will
grant what you would request of him, if you
value me as you say you do, and as I believe.*

"Through this letter, I was moved to ask for Luscinda
to be my wife, as I've already told you, and it also caused
don Fernando to consider Luscinda one of the most discreet and clear-sighted women of her time. And this letter
was what kindled in him the desire to destroy me before
I could put my wishes into effect. I told Fernando that all
Luscinda's father was waiting for was for my father to ask
him for her on my behalf, which I was afraid to do, fearing
that he wouldn't go along—not because he wasn't familiar
with Luscinda's quality, goodness, virtue, and beauty, and
that she had qualities that would do honor to any family in
Spain—but rather because I was aware that he didn't want
me to contract marriage until he found out what Duke Ricardo ultimately was going to do with me. So, I told him that

I didn't dare speak to my father about it, not only because of that obstacle, but there were others that terrified me—and I didn't even know what they were—but it seemed to me that what I wanted would never be fulfilled.

"Fernando said that *he* would talk to my father for me and arrange for him to talk to Luscinda's. Oh, covetous Marius! Oh, cruel Catiline! Oh, wicked Sulla! Oh, deceiving Ganelón! Oh, treacherous Vellido! Oh, vengeful Julián! Oh, greedy Judas!* Traitor, cruel, vindictive, and deceitful! What disloyalty has this poor wretch done you, he who revealed the secrets and joys of his heart? What offense did I do you? What words did I say, or what advice did I give you that was not all aimed at the advancement of your honor and interest? But woe is me! Why do I complain? It's certain that when bad luck falls from the stars, since it comes from on high, flinging itself down with such fury and violence, there is no force on earth that can alter its course, nor human ingenuity that can prevent its coming. Who could imagine that don Fernando, an illustrious gentleman, sharp-witted, bound to me by gratitude for my services, able to win the object of his affections wherever he might want, should take so treacherously from me a single lamb that wasn't even mine yet? But, let's leave these considerations aside, considering them to be useless, and let's continue the broken thread of my unfortunate story.

"So, since it seemed to don Fernando that my presence was an obstacle to the design of his treacherous and wicked plan, he resolved to send me to his brother under the pretext of asking him for some money to pay for six horses that he'd bought—only so that he could achieve his wicked intention—on the very day he'd volunteered to speak with my father. Could I predict this treason? Could I, by chance, have suspected it? No, certainly not. And with greatest pleasure I offered to go immediately, glad for the fine purchase he'd made. That evening I spoke with Luscinda and told her what I'd arranged with don Fernando, and that she should have firm hope that our good and proper desires

---

* These are all famous traitors: Marius, Catiline, and Sulla are Romans, Ganelon sold out Roland, Vellido Dolfos murdered King Sancho II of Castile, Julián handed the Iberian Peninsula over to the Moors in 710, and Judas was the treacherous apostle.

would be fulfilled. She told me, as unsuspecting as I was about the treason of don Fernando, to come back soon because she believed that our desires would be culminated as soon as my father spoke to hers. I don't know why it was, when she finished telling me this, her eyes welled up with tears and a lump in her throat prevented her from uttering another word of the many that I thought she was trying to tell me.

"I was surprised at this new emotion that I'd never seen in her until then, because we always talked, when good luck and my cleverness allowed, with great joy and happiness, without mixing tears, sighs, jealousy, or fear in our conversations. I was always extolling my happiness that heaven had made her my lady. I extolled her beauty and praised her worth and intelligence. She reciprocated, praising in me what, in her loving way, seemed worthy of praise. We also talked about a thousand trifles dealing with our neighbors and acquaintances, and my boldness extended to take, almost by force, one of her beautiful white hands and bring it to my lips, as well as the narrow grating that separated us allowed. But the night that preceded the sad day of my departure, she cried, moaned, and sighed, and left me confused and terrified, frightened at having seen such strange and sad signs of grief and tenderness in Luscinda. But so as not to dash my hopes, I attributed it all to the power of the love she had for me and to the pain that absence usually causes in people in love.

"In short, I left, sad and pensive, my heart filled with illusions and suspicions, without knowing what I suspected or what the illusions were—clear omens predicting the sad event that was awaiting me. I arrived where I was sent, and gave the letter to don Fernando's brother. I was well received, but not quickly sent back because he told me to wait a week—much to my distress—in a place where the duke, his father, wouldn't see me, because his brother had asked him to send a certain amount of money without the duke's knowledge. All this was a scheme of the treacherous don Fernando, since his brother didn't lack the money to send back with me immediately. I risked not obeying this order since it seemed impossible to me to endure so many days of my life absent from Luscinda, especially since I'd left her so sad, as I told you. But, as a dutiful servant, I obeyed, although I thought it would be at the expense of my health.

"Four days after my arrival, a man came looking for me with a letter that he gave me. I recognized Luscinda's handwriting on the outside, and I opened it, frightened and distressed, believing that it had to be something very important for her to write me while I was away, since when I was there, she wrote only infrequently. I asked the man, before I read it, who had given it to him, and how long he'd been on the road. He told me that he happened to be in the street one day at noon, and a very beautiful lady called him from a window, her eyes filled with tears, and told him in great haste: 'Brother, if you're a Christian, as you seem to be, for the love of God, I beg you to take this letter with no delay to the village and to the person on the envelope—they're both well-known—and you'll be doing a great service to Our Lord. And so that you'll have the means to be able to do it, take what is in this handkerchief.' And after she said that, she threw out of the window a handkerchief that contained a hundred *reales* and this gold ring I have right here, along with the letter that I've brought you. And then, without waiting for my answer, she left the window, but first she saw that I had the letter and the handkerchief, and I communicated to her by signs that I would do what she wanted. And so, seeing myself so well paid for the labor it would take to bring it to you, and recognizing that it was you to whom it was being sent—because I know very well who you are, *señor*—and unable to resist the tears of that beautiful lady, I decided to trust no one else, and to come myself to give it to you. And in the sixteen hours since she gave it to me I've made the journey, which, as you know, is eighteen leagues.

"While the grateful and impromptu courier was telling me this, I was hanging on every word, and my legs were shaking so much, I could hardly stand up. Finally I opened the letter that had these words:

> *The promise Don Fernando gave you that he*
> *would urge your father to speak to mine, he has*
> *fulfilled much more to his own pleasure than*
> *to your advantage. I have to tell you, señor,*
> *that he has asked for me to be his wife, and*
> *my father, swayed by what he considers don*

*Fernando's superiority over you, has agreed to
what he wanted with such conviction that two
days from now the marriage is to take place in
secret and privately, so that the only witnesses
are to be heaven and a few members of the
household. You can imagine the state I'm in.
If it's important for you to return, see to it. The
outcome of the affair will show you whether I
love you or not. God grant this letter comes to
your hand before mine is forced to unite itself
with the one who keeps the faith that he has
pledged so poorly.*

"These, in substance, were the words that the letter contained and made me get on the road right away, without
waiting for another reply or any money, because I realized
then that it was not the purchase of horses but rather his
own pleasure that had moved don Fernando to send me
to his brother. The anger that I felt toward don Fernando,
coupled with the fear of losing the prize I'd won by so many
years of love and devotion, gave me wings, since almost as
though I'd flown I arrived in my village the next day just
at the right time to see Luscinda. I got there without being
seen and left the mule on which I'd come at the house of
the good man who had brought me the letter, and my good
fortune was such that I found Luscinda sitting behind the
grating, the witness to our love. She recognized me right
away and I her, but not as we should have recognized each
other. (But who is there in the world who can boast that
he's fathomed or come to know the confused mind and un-
stable nature of a woman? No one, for sure.) So, as I was
saying, as soon as Luscinda saw me she said: 'Cardenio, I'm
in my wedding dress. The traitorous Don Fernando and my
greedy father and a few witnesses are waiting for me in the
hall, but they'll witness my death before they witness my
marriage. Don't be troubled, my dear, but try to be present at this sacrifice, and if I can't prevent it by my words, I
have a hidden dagger that can stop that wicked intention
by causing an end to my life and a beginning of your knowledge of the love that I've borne and still bear you.'

"I was troubled and responded hastily, fearful that I
wouldn't have time to answer her: 'May your words, *señora*,

be validated by your deeds. If you have a dagger to affirm your honor, I have a sword either to defend you with or to kill myself, if Fortune should be against us.' I don't think she heard all these words because I could tell she was being called away in haste—the groom was waiting. With this, the night of my sorrow arrived and the sun of my happiness set. I was suddenly without the light of my eyes, unable to speak, and didn't know what was going on. I couldn't go into the house, nor could I move at all. But when I considered how important my presence was for what might happen in that house, I roused myself as much as I could, and finally went into the house. Since I knew all the ways of getting into and out of it, and owing to the chaos caused by that secret ceremony going on inside, no one noticed me; so, without being seen, I could slip into a recess covered by the edges of two tapestries, and between them I could see everything that was happening.

"How can I describe the palpitations of my heart while I was there, the thoughts that assailed me, or the reflections that passed through my mind? They neither can nor should be told. It's enough for you to know that the groom came into the hall without any adornment other than what he usually wore. His best man was one of Luscinda's first cousins, and in the whole hall no one other than family was present—except for servants from the household.

"After a little while Luscinda came out, accompanied by her mother and two of her maids, as richly dressed and adorned as her rank and beauty deserved, like one who was the pinnacle of fashion and courtly splendor. My anxiety and distraction didn't allow me to see and take note of the details of her dress. I could only see that it was scarlet and white, and gems and jewels on her headdress and all over her dress glittered. All this was surpassed by the rare beauty of her blond hair, which competed with the gems she was wearing, and the light of the four torches that burned in the hall made her beauty shine brilliantly before my eyes. Oh, memory, mortal enemy of my peace! What good does it do now to picture the incomparable beauty of my adored enemy? Wouldn't it be better, cruel memory, to remind me and present me what she did next, so that I may strive—moved by a such a great wrong—if not for vengeance, at least to rid myself of life?

"Please don't tire of hearing these digressions that I make, *señores*, for my grief is not of the kind that can nor should be told in few words and briefly, since each incident seems worthy of a long discourse."

To this, the priest responded that not only were they not tired of listening to him; on the contrary, the details that he recounted pleased them greatly, and they were such that they deserved not to be passed over in silence, and warranted the same attention as the main part of the story.

"So, then," Cardenio went on, "the ceremony was to be in the hall. The parish priest came in, and took both of them by the hand to do what the ceremony requires, and said: 'Do you, *señora* Luscinda, take *señor* don Fernando, here present, as your legitimate husband, as the Holy Mother Church prescribes?' I thrust my head and neck out from between the tapestries, and with very attentive ears and with a tormented soul I listened for what Luscinda would say, expecting from her answer either my death sentence or renewed life. Oh, if I'd only leapt out at that moment and shouted: 'Luscinda, Luscinda, watch what you're doing! Consider what you owe me, remember that you're mine and you cannot belong to another! Bear in mind that your saying I DO and my death will be simultaneous. Ah, you traitor, don Fernando! Robber of my glory, death of my life! What do you want? What do you seek? Consider that you can't, as a Christian, achieve your goal, since Luscinda is already my wife and I her husband.' Ah, fool that I am—now that I'm away and far from any danger—I'm saying what I should have done and didn't. Now that I've allowed my precious treasure to be stolen from me, I curse the robber on whom I might have wrought vengeance if only I'd have had the same heart for it that I'm using now to complain. In short, I was a coward and a fool, and no wonder I'm dying of shame now, filled with remorse, and crazy.

"The priest was waiting for Luscinda's answer—and she waited a while before giving it—and just when I was thinking she was going to take out her dagger to preserve her honor, or to say some truth, or confess something on my behalf, I heard her say in a faint and feeble voice, 'I do,' and don Fernando said the same, and when he gave her a ring, they were bound by a knot that cannot be untied.

As the husband went to embrace his wife, she placed her hand on her heart and fell fainting into her mother's arms. All that remains is to say how I felt, since in that I DO I saw all my hopes mocked, the words and promises of Luscinda proven lies, and myself without means of ever recovering the good that I'd lost at that instant. I stood stupefied, completely abandoned by heaven, it seemed to me, and made an enemy of the earth that sustained me, denying me air to breathe, and tears for my eyes. Only a fire grew within me, so that I was consumed by rage and jealousy.

"Everyone was thrown into confusion by Luscinda's fainting spell, and when her mother unfastened her bodice to give her air, a sealed letter was discovered that don Fernando took and began to read by the light of one of the torches, and when he finished reading it, he sat in a chair, and put his hand to his cheek, appearing to be a very pensive man, without taking part in the efforts to help his wife out of her swoon. When I saw the household in such confusion, I ventured to come out, whether I was seen or not; and if I was seen, I was determined to do some crazed deed, such that everyone would come to realize the righteous indignation of my heart in the punishment of don Fernando, and even on that of the fainted traitoress. But my fate, which had greater misfortunes in store for me, if it's possible that there be greater ones—ordered that my reason—which has since failed me—would prevail. And so, without wreaking vengeance on my greatest enemies, which would have been easy to do, since they were not expecting me to be there, I resolved to take it on myself, and to inflict on myself the pain they deserved, and perhaps with greater severity than I would have used on them if I'd killed them right then, since sudden death causes little pain. But the death that's drawn out with torture always kills without ending one's life.

"In short, I left that house and went to the home of the man with whom I'd left the mule, had him saddle it for me, and without saying good-bye, I got on and rode out of the city, without daring, like another Lot,* to look back. When I found myself alone, out in the open country, and the dark of night had enveloped me, and its stillness invited me to la-

---

* In Genesis 19:17, the Lord advises Lot and others to flee and not look back at the destruction of Sodom and Gomorrah.

ment my misfortune without fear of being heard or recognized, I raised my voice and untied my tongue in so much cursing of Luscinda and don Fernando as if that could avenge the wrong they had done me. I called her cruel, ungrateful, false, and thankless, but above all, greedy, since the wealth of my enemy had closed the eyes of her affection, transferring it from me to the one with whom Fortune had been more liberal. And yet in the midst of this torrent of maledictions and reproaches, I made excuses for her, saying that it wasn't surprising that a maiden, secluded in her parents' home, trained and accustomed to obey them always, would have submitted to their wishes, since they were giving her a husband—a gentleman of such distinction, so rich, and of such noble birth—that if she'd refused him, one could think either she'd lost her mind or her affections lay elsewhere, something that would besmirch her honor and good name.

"Then again, I mused, even if she'd said I was her husband, they would have seen that when she chose me, she hadn't made such a bad choice that they wouldn't have freed her, because before don Fernando offered himself to them, they themselves—if their desires were well reasoned—couldn't have wanted a better choice for their daughter's husband than me. And she could very well, before that critical moment of giving her hand, have said that I'd already given her mine, and I would have come forth to confirm what she said.

"In a word, I concluded that a bit of love, little judgment, a lot of ambition, and a yearning for rank had made her forget the words with which she'd deceived, encouraged, and supported me in my firm hopes and chaste desires.

"After all that shouting and in this troubled state I traveled the rest of the night, and at daybreak I wound up at one of the passes of this sierra, through which I roamed three days, without a path or any road, until I came to a meadow on I don't know what side of the mountain, and I asked some herdsmen where the most rugged part of this sierra lay. They told me that it was in this area, and I came in this direction right away, intending to end my life here. When I got to this harsh territory my mule fell dead of weariness and hunger, or, it may have been—and this is what I believe—to rid itself of such a useless burden. I found myself on foot, worn out, overcome by hunger, and having no one to help me.

"I was in that state for I don't know how long, stretched out on the ground, after which I got up and was no longer hungry. I found near me some goatherds who doubtless were those who relieved my need, because they told me how they had found me, how I was saying so many foolish things that plainly showed I'd lost my sanity. And since then I've felt that I don't always have my complete sanity, and I'm impaired and weak, and I do a thousand absurdities, tearing my clothes, crying aloud in these solitary places, cursing my fate, and repeating in vain the beloved name of my enemy, and only seeking to end my life in lamentation. And when I recover my senses I'm so exhausted and drained that I can hardly move.

"My usual dwelling is the hollow area of this cork tree, which is big enough to shelter my wretched body. The cowherds and goatherds who work in these mountains, moved by charity, give me things to eat by putting provisions in the roads or on rocks where I'm likely to pass by and find them. So, even when my sanity fails me, the needs of nature make me understand what I require, and awaken my cravings and give me the will to satisfy them. Other times, they tell me after I've recovered my wits, I go into the road and take food from the shepherds by force when they're coming from the village on their way to the herds, even though they would willingly give me some of the food they have with them.

"This is the way I'm spending my wretched life until heaven is pleased to take it to its ultimate end, or to cause my mind to forget the beauty and the treachery of Luscinda, and the wrong done me by don Fernando. If heaven does this without depriving me of life, I'll turn my thoughts to some better course of action, and if not, I can only beg it to have mercy on my soul, because I feel neither strength nor courage in myself to release my body from this plight in which I've chosen to place it of my own free will.

"This is, *señores*, the bitter story of my misfortune. Tell me if it can be told with less emotion than you've seen in me. And don't bother to persuade or counsel me about whatever Reason might tell you will be good for my relief, because it will do me as much good as medicine prescribed by an esteemed physician will do a sick man who will not take it. Health is meaningless without Luscinda, and since she chose to belong to someone else, even when she was or should have been mine, let me savor misery when I might have had happiness. She wanted, through her fickleness, to ruin me. I will, by seeking my own destruction, attempt to gratify her. And my case will be an example to all those in the future that I alone lacked what other unfortunate people have in abundance, which is the possibility of being consoled. This is a cause for even greater emotions and sufferings, because I believe that even after death they will not come to an end."

Here Cardenio ended his long discourse and his woeful and passionate story. And just when the priest was about to offer a few words of consolation, he was stopped by a voice that came to his ears, which said in plain-tive tones what will be told in the Fourth Part of this narrative, because right here the sage Cide Hamete Benengeli brought the Third to an end.

FOURTH PART OF THE INGENIOUS *Hidalgo* don Quixote de La Mancha.

Chapter XXVIII. Which deals with the strange and delightful adventure that the priest and barber had in the same sierra.

How very happy and fortunate were the times when that most daring knight don Quixote de La Mancha went out into the world, since because of his desire to resuscitate and restore the now lost and almost defunct order of knight-errantry to the world, we now enjoy in this, our own age, which is so lacking in light entertainment, not only the pleasure of his true history, but also that of the stories and episodes that are added to it and are scarcely less agreeable, ingenious, and filled with truth than the main story itself, which, resuming its carded, twisted, and reeled thread,* related that, as soon as the priest began to get ready to console Cardenio, he was prevented from doing so by a voice that came to his ears with pitiful tones, saying these words: "Oh, God! Can it be possible that I've found a place that can serve as a secret grave for the weary burden of this body

---

* The narrator's bad play on words detailing processes used in spinning thread.

251

that I carry against my will? Yes, it is, if the solitude of these mountains doesn't deceive me. Ah, woe is me! How much better companions will these cliffs and bushes be, since they give me the opportunity to complain of my misfortune to heaven—than the company of any man, because there is no one on earth from whom I can expect counsel in doubt, comfort in sorrow, or relief in distress!"

The priest, and those with him, heard and understood those words, and seeming to them—as it was—that all these words came from very nearby, they got up to see who had said them. They hadn't gone twenty paces when they saw from behind a large rock, seated at the foot of an ash tree, a lad dressed as a peasant. Since his head was leaning forward, and he was washing his feet in the stream that flowed past, they couldn't see his face. And they approached so silently he didn't hear them, nor was he aware of anything else other than washing his feet, which were so fair that they looked like two pieces of white crystal born of the stones of the brook. The whiteness and beauty of those feet filled them with awe, because they didn't seem made to crush clods of earth, nor drive a plow and oxen, as the lad's costume suggested.

Seeing that they had not been heard, the priest, who led the group, gave signs to the other two to crouch down or hide behind a nearby boulder. They all did this, looking closely at what the lad was doing. He was wearing a short, loose gray jacket, tightly bound to his body with a white cloth. He also was wearing pants and leggings made of a gray cloth, and on his head he wore a gray cap. His leggings were pulled halfway up his legs, which looked just like white alabaster. When he finished washing his beautiful feet, he wiped them off with a white kerchief that he took from beneath his cap. But when he took out the kerchief, he raised his face, and those who were looking at him could see in it an incomparable beauty, so much so that Cardenio said to the priest under his breath: "This person, since he's not Luscinda, cannot be a human being, but rather someone divine."

The young man took off his cap, and as he shook his head, his hair—that the rays of the sun might envy—started to cascade and spread out. By this, the observers came to realize that the person who seemed to be a peasant man was really an exquisite woman, and the most beautiful one that the eyes of the priest and barber had ever seen, and even those of Cardenio, if they hadn't seen and known Luscinda—for he declared afterward that only the beauty of Luscinda could compete with hers. Her long blond hair not only covered her shoulders, but it was so long and blond that it also hid the rest of her, because except for her feet, no other part of her body was visible. Just then she drew her hands through her hair, and if her feet looked like they were made of crystal when they were in the water, her hands seemed to be made of driven snow among her locks, all of which caused even more wonder, and made the three who were observing her even more curious to find out who she was.

With this in mind, they resolved to make themselves known, and as they went to stand up, the beautiful lass raised her head, and, parting her hair from in front of her eyes with both hands, she saw the people who had made that rustling noise, and hardly had she seen them when she got up, grabbed a bundle of clothing next to her, and without stopping to put her shoes on or gather her hair, tried to flee, filled with confusion and alarm. But she hadn't gone six paces before her delicate feet could no longer withstand the sharpness of the stones, and she fell to the ground. The three went to see if they could help her. The priest was the first to speak: "Stop, *señora*, whoever you are, because our intention is only to serve you. There is no reason for you to take to this fretful flight that your feet cannot withstand, nor can we allow it."

Bewildered and confused, she didn't respond a word to all this. They approached her, and taking her by the hand, the priest continued: "What your garb would hide, *señora*, your hair reveals: clear proof that a cause not of little consequence has disguised your beauty in such unworthy clothing and has brought you to a solitary place such as this, where we've had the good fortune to find you; and if we can't relieve your anguish, at least we can offer you comfort, since, as long as life lasts, no anguish can be oppressive or so far beyond the reach of human compassion as to make the sufferer refuse to listen to words of comfort offered with good intentions. So, *señora mía*, or *señor mío*—whichever you please—forget the fear that the sight of us has caused you, and reveal to us your good or bad fortune, and you'll find sympathy in your misfortunes from all of us together or from each of us individually."

While the priest was telling her this, it was as if the disguised young woman were spellbound, looking at each one, without moving her lips or saying a single word, just like a village rustic to whom is shown something that he's never seen before. But the priest said more words to the same effect, and, heaving a great sigh, she broke her silence and said: "Since the solitude of these sierras has not been sufficient to conceal me, and the letting down of my disordered tresses has not allowed my tongue to lie, it would be in vain to pretend once again to be what I am not, and if you were to believe me, it would be only out of courtesy and nothing else. This being so, I thank you, *señores*, for the offer you've made me, and it has made me feel I should comply with your request, although I fear the story of my misfortunes is liable to cause you as much grief as compassion, because you'll not find a way to remedy it, nor advice to alleviate it. But even so, in order for my honor not to be left a matter of doubt in your minds, since you've recognized that I'm a woman, and seeing me young, alone, and in this clothing—any of these things taken together or separately would be enough to tear down my good reputation—I'll tell you what I wanted to keep to myself if I could have."

All of this was said by the beautiful woman without hesitation and with such a sweet voice that her circumspection captivated them as much as her beauty. And they again repeated their offers and made fresh entreaties to her to tell them her story. Without further coaxing, she first put on her shoes to cover her feet, and gathered in her hair; then she sat upon a stone with the three of them surrounding her. She forced herself to withhold tears that were coming to her eyes, and with a calm and clear voice she began her story in this way:

"In this Andalusia there is a village from which a duke takes his title, which makes him one of the grandees of Spain. This man has two sons: The older one is heir to his rank and seemingly of his good qualities as well; and as for the younger one, I don't know what he's the heir of unless it's the treachery of Vellido and the falsehood of Ganelón. My parents are vassals of this man, humble in their lineage, but so wealthy that if birth had conferred on them as much as Fortune did, they would have nothing more to desire, nor should I fear seeing myself in the trouble I'm now in, because it may well be that my bad luck stems from their not having been born noble. It's true they're not so low that they should be ashamed of their status, nor so high as to remove from my mind that my misfortune derives from their humble birth. In short, they're farmers, plain people, without any mixture of impure blood,* and, as the saying goes, Old Christians, but so rich that their wealth and magnificent way of life are gradually causing them to be considered *hidalgos* and even nobles; but what they prized as their greatest fortune and distinction was having me as their daughter. So, since they had no other heir, and being very affectionate parents, I was one of the most indulged daughters that parents ever pampered. I was the mirror in which they saw themselves, the support of their old age, the object toward which all their hopes, in accordance with heaven's rules, were directed, and my own hopes didn't differ from theirs, since theirs were so worthy. And just as I was the mistress of their hearts, so was I also of their estate. I hired and fired servants. I kept track of what was sown and harvested, olive oil mills, winepresses, head of cattle (both cows and sheep), and beehives. In sum, I had in my care everything that a wealthy farmer such as my father could and did possess, and being superintendent and mistress, with such diligence on my part and satisfaction on theirs, it would be difficult for me to exaggerate.

"The leisure time that was left to me after having directed the overseers, foremen, and laborers, I spent in activities that are proper and necessary for maidens, such as embroidery, lace making, and spinning; and to better my mind I might read a devotional book or play the harp, because experience has shown me that music soothes the troubled mind and relieves weariness of the spirit.

"This was the life I led in my parents' house, and if I've told you about it in such detail, it was not out of vanity or to let you know that I'm rich, but only so that you can see how blameless I was when I fell from this happy state to my present misery. The truth is that while I was leading

---

* That is, Jewish or Moorish.

this busy, cloistered life—you could compare it to life in a convent—I was never being seen by anyone other than the servants of our household. And when I went to Mass it was so early in the morning, I was so closely attended by my mother and the other women of the household, and I was so heavily veiled and demure, that my eyes could hardly see even the ground where my feet fell. In spite of this the eyes of love—or rather those of idleness—keener than those of a lynx, saw me, and those eyes belonged to the persistent don Fernando, because that's the name of the younger son of the duke I mentioned."

The instant the storyteller mentioned don Fernando, Cardenio's face changed color and he broke into a sweat with such agitation that the priest and barber who were observing it feared that one of his fits of madness was coming on. But Cardenio only sweated and remained still, staring at the peasant girl, suspecting who she was. Without noticing the change in Cardenio, she continued her story, saying: "And hardly had they—his eyes—seen me when (as he later confirmed) he was quite smitten by me, as his behavior soon showed. So, to come to the end of this relation of my misfortunes, which have no end, I would like to pass over in silence the clever things don Fernando used for making his love for me known. He bribed everyone in my household, he gave gifts and offered favors to my relatives. Every day was like a fiesta and a celebration on our street, and at night no one could sleep because of the music. An infinite number of love letters—I don't know how—came to me, filled with loving words and pledges of love, containing more promises and vows than there were letters in the words. Nothing of this softened me, but rather hardened my heart, as if he were my mortal enemy. Everything he did to sway me to his will had the opposite effect, not because the gallantry of don Fernando was disagreeable, because it did give me a certain pleasure to find myself so loved and prized by such an important nobleman. And it didn't displease me to see my praises in his letters, because it pleases us women, it seems to me, however ugly we may be, to hear ourselves called beautiful.

"But all this was very contrary to my chastity and the continual advice of my parents, who clearly knew of don Fernando's purpose, because he didn't care if the whole world knew. My parents told me that they trusted and confided their honor and good name to my virtue and goodness, and urged me to consider the difference that there was between me and don Fernando, from which I could infer that his intentions—whatever he said to the contrary—were directed more toward his pleasure than to my advantage, and if I wanted to discourage his advances, they would arrange a marriage with anyone I preferred, either from the upper class of our town or of any of the neighboring towns, because with their wealth and my good name, they would be able to make a fine match. With their firm promises, in light of the truth they told me, my integrity was fortified, and I refused to give don Fernando a single word that might offer any hope that he might attain his desire—far from it. All of my precautions, which he should have considered to be a rejection, only served to inflame his lascivious appetite—for that's what I call his passion for me. Had it been what it should have been, you would never have heard of it, since there would be no reason to tell you about it.

"Finally, don Fernando found out that my parents were thinking of marrying me off in order to end his hopes of possessing me, or at least so that I would have more protectors to shield me. This news, or suspicion, caused him to do what you'll now hear. It happened that one night when I was in my room in the company of a maid who serves me, with the doors locked—fearing that my honor might be compromised through negligence—in the midst of these precautions, in stillness and seclusion, I found him standing before me, a vision that so disturbed me that it robbed my eyes of sight and my tongue of speech, so I couldn't cry out, nor would he, I think, have let me, because he drew close to me, and taking me in his arms—since I didn't have the strength to resist, so overwhelmed was I, as I said—he began to say such words that I cannot imagine how it's possible for so many lies to come out sounding like the truth. The traitor made it look like his tears confirmed his words, and his sighs his sincerity. I was a poor young maiden, all alone in a house filled with family members, inexperienced in these matters, and I began to think—I don't know how—that all these falsehoods were true, but not to the point that his sighs and tears would move me to compassion.

"So, after that first shock subsided, I regained my lost

senses a bit, and with more courage than I thought I could muster up, I said: 'If I were not in your arms, *señor*, but in the claws of a fierce lion; if I had to do or say something to tarnish my virtue to be released from them, it would be no more in my power to do or say it than it would be to change the past. So, though you're clutching me in your arms, my soul is bound up by my firm resolve, which is quite different from yours, as you'll see if you try to force your desires on me. I'm your vassal but not your slave. Your nobility doesn't have the right to dishonor and degrade my humble blood, nor should it. I respect myself as a country girl and farmer's daughter, as much as you do as a lord and gentleman. Your strength will do you no good, nor will your wealth have any worth; your words will not deceive me, nor will your sighs and tears soften me. If I were to see any of these things I've mentioned in the person my parents chose to be my husband, my will would adjust to his, and I'd have no will other than his. And if my honor would be preserved, even though I had no pleasure, I would willingly yield to him what you, *señor*, are trying to take by force. I tell you all this because it's unthinkable that anyone would get anything from me except as my legitimate husband.'

"'If that's your only worry, beautiful Dorotea' (for that's the name of this unfortunate woman), said the deceitful man, 'look, I'm giving you my hand to be yours, and let heaven, from which nothing is hidden, and the image of Our Lady you have here, be witness to this pledge.'"*

When Cardenio heard her say that her name was Dorotea, his agitation began again. He could confirm his initial suspicion, but he didn't want to interrupt her story so he could find out how it would come out, because he knew only bits and pieces of it, so he only said: "So, Dorotea is your name, *señora*? I've heard about another woman with this same name who can perhaps match you in her misfortunes. Please continue, because there is plenty of time for me to tell you things that will amaze you as well as cause you pity."

Dorotea noted Cardenio's words and his strange and tattered attire, and begged him to tell her right then if he

---

* In Spanish Golden Age literature, this was a legitimate—and binding—way for people to marry each other.

knew something about her situation, because if Fortune had left her anything, it was the courage to endure any disaster that might befall her, and she was sure that nothing could happen that would increase what she'd borne already.

"I wouldn't miss the chance, *señora*," responded Cardenio, "to tell you what I think if what I suspect is the truth, but up to now there is no apparent connection, nor is it important for you to learn what it is."

"Be that as it may," responded Dorotea, "what happened next in my story is that don Fernando took a holy image that was in my room, used it as a witness to our betrothal, and with the most powerful words and vows, promised to be my husband, although, before he finished, I told him to be careful in what he said, and to consider his father's anger when he saw him married to a vassal of his. I told him not to be blinded by my beauty, such as it was, because that was an insufficient excuse for his mistake, and that if through his love for me he wanted to do me a kindness, he should rather let my fortune run its course within my own rank, because unequal marriages are never happy, nor do they maintain the same pleasure with which they begin.

"All these words that I said just now I told him, and many others that I don't remember, but it had no effect in causing him to forgo his purpose—'he who has no intention of paying does not haggle over the price.' At that moment I argued the matter with myself and said: 'I won't be the first person who has risen from a humble to a lofty social position through marriage, nor will don Fernando be the first one whom beauty, or blind desire—and this is what is most likely—has led to marry beneath his rank. Since I'm not changing established practices or trying to make a new custom, it might be good to embrace this honor that Fate has offered me, because even though his love may not last longer than the fulfillment of his desire, I will, after all, be his wife in the eyes of God. If, on the other hand, I seek to repulse him with scorn, I can see that he may easily use force, and I'll be disgraced and without an excuse for the guilt that will be laid against me by those who cannot know how guiltless I've been. What arguments will suffice to persuade my parents and others that this man came into my room without my permission?'

"All these questions and answers passed through my mind

in an instant. And I was especially moved and persuaded—to what proved to be my ruin without my suspecting it—by don Fernando's vows, the witnesses he invoked, the tears he shed, and finally, his gentle disposition that, accompanied by so many signs of real love, might easily conquer a heart as free and as innocent as mine. I called my maid in so there would be a witness on earth as well as those in heaven. Don Fernando reiterated and confirmed his vows and invoked other saints as witnesses. He wished a thousand future curses on himself if he failed to keep his promise. Tears welled in his eyes again, his sighs grew more frequent, and he pressed me closer in his arms, from which he'd never let me go. And with this, my maid left the room, and I ceased to be one, and he became a betrayer and a liar.

"The day that followed the night of my disgrace came, although I think not as quickly as don Fernando wanted, because, once his appetite was satisfied, his greatest urge was to leave the scene of where this pleasure took place. I say this because don Fernando was in a hurry to leave. Through the wiles of my maid—she was the one who had let him in—he was out of the house by daybreak. And when he bade me farewell, he told me, although without the fervor and conviction of the night before, that I could rest assured of his good faith and the sanctity and sincerity of his oaths. And to confirm his words, he removed a splendid ring from his finger and placed it on mine. So he left, and I stayed behind, and I don't know if I was sad or happy, but I can tell you that I was troubled and pensive, and almost beside myself with this new situation. Either I didn't have the will to or I forgot to scold my maid for the treason committed when she let don Fernando into my room, for as yet I couldn't make up my mind if what had befallen me was good or bad. I told don Fernando when he left that, since I was now his, he could come back on other nights that same way, until it was his pleasure to make the marriage known. But he came back no other night except the following one, nor did I see him in the street or in church for more than a month. In vain I wearied myself watching for him, although I knew that he was in town and most days he went hunting, something he was very fond of.

"I remember how sad and dreary those days and hours were for me. And I well remember how I began to doubt, as those days went by, and even lose confidence in the faith of don Fernando. And I remember that my maid finally heard those words of reproof that she hadn't heard before for her daring acts; and how it was necessary for me to restrain my tears and compose my face so that my parents wouldn't ask me why I was so unhappy and force me to make up lies in reply. But all this came to a sudden end when something happened that trampled all considerations of honor and caution, and where patience was lost and my secret thoughts were made known. And this was because in a few days it was said in the village that in a nearby city don Fernando had gotten married to a very beautiful maiden of noble parents, although not so rich that through her dowry could she aspire to such a noble marriage. They said her name was Luscinda, and that at her wedding startling things happened."

Cardenio heard the name of Luscinda, and only shrugged his shoulders, bit his lips, raised his eyebrows, and in a little while let two streams of tears fall from his eyes. Dorotea, however, didn't stop her story, but went on: "This sad news came to my ears, but instead of causing my heart to grow cold when I heard it, such a wrath and fury burned in it that I almost raced out into the city shouting about the treachery done to me. But what I planned to do, and did, that very night, tended to moderate this fury. I dressed up in the clothing of one of the farmhands, a servant of my father's. I confided in him the story of all of my misfortune and I begged him to go with me to that city where I heard the lady, my enemy, was. After he'd scolded me for my daring and condemned my decision—once he saw my resolve, he offered to go with me, he said, to the ends of the earth. At once I packed a dress, some jewels, and money for emergencies inside a pillowcase, and in the silence of that night, without telling my traitorous maid, left my house, accompanied by my servant and my many troubled thoughts, and I got onto the road to that city, on foot, borne on the wings of my desire to get there, if not to frustrate what I knew had been done, at least to ask don Fernando to tell me with what conscience he'd done it.

"I arrived in two and a half days, and when I went into the city, I asked where the house of Luscinda was, and the first person I asked told me more than I wanted to hear. He

showed me where the house was and told everything that
had happened during the marriage of the daughter, something so well-known that people gather in groups to gossip
about it. He said that the evening don Fernando married
Luscinda, after she said her I DO, she fainted, and that when
the groom unlaced her dress to give her air, he found a letter in Luscinda's own handwriting in which she said and
declared that she couldn't be don Fernando's wife because
she was already married to Cardenio, who, the fellow told
me, was a man of note in that city. And if she'd said I DO
to don Fernando it was only because she didn't want to
disobey her parents. In short, the explanations in the letter
said that she'd intended to kill herself after the ceremony,
giving her reasons, all of which was confirmed by a dagger they found I don't know where in her clothing. When
don Fernando saw this, thinking that Luscinda had made
a mockery of him, and held him in little esteem, he tried
to stab her with her own dagger, and he would have, too,
if those present hadn't prevented it. And there was more:
Don Fernando left right away, and Luscinda didn't come
out of her swoon until the next day, and told her parents
that she was the true wife of that Cardenio I mentioned.

"And I found out even more: Cardenio, they said, had
been at the wedding, and when he saw her married—
something he thought would never happen—he left the
city in despair, leaving behind a letter in which he told of
the wrong Luscinda had done him, and how he was going
away never to be seen again. All this was well-known in the
city and everyone talked about it, especially when it was
known that Luscinda went missing from her parents' house
and from the city, where she was nowhere to be found and
that her parents were going mad trying to figure out how to
find her. When I learned this, I was encouraged, and I was
more pleased not to have found him than to have found
him married, because it seemed to me that the door was
not yet completely closed to a happy solution for my situation. It occurred to me that it might be that heaven had
put this impediment in the way of the second marriage so
that don Fernando could see what his obligations to the
first were, and to make him reflect that he was a Christian,
and that he was bound to consider his soul above all things
human.

"All these thoughts whirled around in my fancy, and I tried unsuccessfully to console myself, indulging in faint and distant hopes of cherishing the life I now hate. So, while I was in the city without knowing what to do because I couldn't find don Fernando, I heard a public crier offering a large reward to whoever should find me, saying how old I was and even describing the clothing I was wearing. It was said that the lad who was with me had taken me from my parents' house, and this cut me to the quick, seeing how low my reputation had fallen—it was not enough that I would lose it for having fled, but they had to add with whom, being such a low fellow and unworthy of my chaste thoughts. The instant I heard the crier, I left the city with my servant, who was already showing signs of wavering in his fidelity to me, and that same night, fearing that we'd be found, we entered the densest parts of this mountain.

"But as they say, 'one bad thing invites another,' and 'the end of one misfortune is liable to be the beginning of a still greater one.' That's what happened to me, because my good servant who had been faithful and trustworthy until then, as soon as he saw me in that lonely spot, incited more by his villainy than by my beauty, tried to take advantage of the opportunity that these solitudes presented to him. And with little shame and less fear of God and respect for me, he began to make advances to me, and seeing that I answered his impudent proposal with severe and just reproaches, he set aside the entreaties he had used at first, and began to use force. But heaven in its justice, which seldom if ever fails to watch over and assist good intentions, favored mine so that, with a little strength on my part, I was able to push him over a precipice, where I left him—I don't know if dead or alive. And so, more swiftly than my fright and weakened state seemed to permit, I came into these mountains, without any other thought or purpose, save that of hiding myself and fleeing from my father and those who were looking for me on his behalf.

"I don't know how many months went by since I came here with this in mind, when I found a herdsman who hired me on as his servant in a remote village in these mountains, and I served him all this time, always trying to be in the fields to conceal my hair, which has now so unexpectedly betrayed me. But all my care and trouble were to no avail, since my master came to realize that I wasn't a man, and harbored the same base desire as my servant. Since Fortune doesn't always find solutions to one's troubles, I didn't find a precipice or ravine where I could fling my master down and kill him, as I did with my servant, so it was much easier for me just to leave him and hide again in these rugged parts, than to put my strength or reasoning to the test once again. So, I went into the forest to look for a place where I could, without any hindrance, beg heaven with my tears and sighs to give me the grace and strength to escape from my misfortune or to end my life in this lonely place, without leaving a trace of this unhappy being, who, while being utterly guiltless, has given occasion for others to speak badly of me at home and elsewhere."

Chapter XXIX. *Which deals with the beautiful Dorotea's discretion, with other things that will give pleasure as well as diversion.*

"This, *señores*, is the true history of my tragedy. Consider and judge whether the sighs that reached your ears, the words you heard, and the tears that fell from my eyes were more restrained than they might have been. And considering the nature of my disgrace, you'll see that any solace will be impossible, since the remedy for it is as well. I only beg you—and it's something you can easily do—to show me where I may spend my life without losing it, because of the fear and alarm I have of being found by those looking for me. I know my parents love me very much and would welcome me back, but my shame is so great that just thinking that I should appear before them in a state different from what they remember, I'd prefer to banish myself forever from their sight rather than look them in the eyes with the thought that they should see me lacking the virtue that they had a right to expect."

With these words she said no more and her face flushed with a color that clearly reflected the shame and anguish in her heart. In their own hearts, those who had heard her felt as much pity as wonder at her misfortune. Although the priest wanted to console and advise her, the first one to speak was Cardenio: "So, *señora*, you are the beautiful Dorotea, the only daughter of the rich Clenardo."

Dorotea was amazed when she heard her father mentioned by name, and at how tattered he was who mentioned it, because the wretched way he was dressed has already been stated. So she said: "And who are you, brother, who know the name of my father? Because, until now, if I remember correctly, I didn't mention his name in telling my misfortunes."

"I am," responded Cardenio, "that unfortunate fellow, whom, according to what you said, *señora*, Luscinda declared to be her husband. I'm the unlucky Cardenio, whom the wrongdoing of him who brought you to your present state has reduced to the condition you see me in—broken, practically naked, bereft of all human comfort, and what is worse, insane; for I only regain sanity when heaven is pleased to restore it to me for a short period. I'm the one who was a witness to the wrong done by don Fernando, and the one who stayed to hear the I DO uttered by Luscinda that made her his wife. I'm the one who didn't have the courage to wait until her fainting fit was over, nor for what happened when they opened the paper they found in her bodice, because my heart didn't have the fortitude to bear so many misfortunes at the same time. So I left the house and my patience behind, and also a letter I gave to an acquaintance, whom I begged to put it in Luscinda's hands. I came to this wilderness with the intention of ending my life, which I hated from then on as if it were my mortal enemy. But Fortune refused to take my life from me, contenting itself only with taking away my sanity, perhaps keeping me alive for the good luck I've had in meeting you, because if what you just told me is true, as I believe it is, it may be that heaven has reserved for both of us a better way out of our tragedies than we thought. Because, since Luscinda can't marry don Fernando because she's mine—as she's so clearly stated—and don Fernando can't marry her because he's yours, we can hope that heaven will restore what is ours, since it still exists and hasn't been taken away or destroyed. And since we have this consolation, arising from not very distant hopes or wild fancies, I beg you, *señora*, to make a resolution in your honored thoughts, as I intend to do, preparing yourself for a better fate. I swear to you, as a gentleman and a Christian, not to abandon you until I see you in the arms of don Fernando; and if I can't persuade him with words to recognize what he owes you, I'll use the privilege conferred on me as a nobleman, and with just title I'll challenge him because of the injustice he's done you, not caring about my own injuries, which I'll leave for heaven to avenge; while on earth, I'll attend to yours."

Dorotea was astonished at what Cardenio said, and since she didn't know how to repay his magnificent offer, she tried to kiss his feet, but he wouldn't permit it. The priest answered for them both, approving the worthy resolve of Cardenio, and he earnestly begged, advised, and persuaded them to accompany him to his village, where they could replenish their supplies and take measures to locate don Fernando, or restore Dorotea to her parents, or do what seemed best. Cardenio and Dorotea thanked him and accepted the kind offer he'd made to them, and the barber, who had been listening closely to everything in silence, made a gracious speech, with no less goodwill than the priest, promising to serve them in everything he could.

He also told them briefly what had brought them there, along with the odd nature of don Quixote's madness, and how they were waiting for his squire who had gone to fetch him. As if it came from a dream, Cardenio remembered the quarrel he'd had with don Quixote, and told them about it, but he had no memory of what the quarrel was about.

Just then they heard shouts, and they realized that it must be Sancho Panza, who—since he hadn't found them where he'd left them—was calling them. They went to meet him, asking about don Quixote. He said that he'd found him just wearing his shirt, emaciated, pale, dying of hunger, and sighing for his lady Dulcinea, and that, although he'd told him that she had commanded him to leave and to go to El Toboso, where she was waiting for him, he'd responded that he was determined not to appear in the presence of her beauty until he'd done deeds worthy of her favor; and if this sort of thing went on, he ran the risk of never becoming an emperor, as was his duty, and not even an archbishop, which is the least to be expected of him. For this reason, they should see what could be done about it.

The priest told Sancho that he shouldn't worry, that they would rescue him in spite of himself. He then told

Cardenio and Dorotea about their plan to cure don Quixote, or at least take him home, to which Dorotea said that *she* could play the damsel in distress better than the barber, especially since she had a dress with which she could do it most naturally, and that they should leave it to her to know how to play her part because she'd read many romances of chivalry and was quite familiar with how these unfortunate maidens acted when they asked favors from their knights-errant.

"Then there's nothing to do," said the priest, "but get on with it, because good luck is doubtless on our side, since when least you expected it, the door to the solution of your problems has begun to open, and has also supplied us with a way to solve ours."

Dorotea then took a splendid dress of fine wool and a shawl made of a very pretty green material from her bag, and from a little box she took a necklace and other pieces of jewelry, and in an instant she got dressed so that she looked like an elegant and grand lady. She had brought all these things from home, she said, for any contingency, but that this was her first opportunity to use them. Her high spirits, grace, and extraordinary beauty delighted them in the extreme, and they declared that don Fernando was stupid for rejecting such charms.

But the most charmed one was Sancho Panza, since it seemed to him—and it was the truth—that in all his days he'd never seen a more beautiful creature. And he asked the priest most emphatically to tell him who that beautiful lady was, and what she was doing in those remote parts.

"This beautiful lady," responded the priest, "brother Sancho, is simply the heiress in the direct male line of the great kingdom of Micomicón,* and she's come to ask a boon of your master, which is to avenge an outrage done to her by an evil giant, and because of the fame that your master enjoys as a knight-errant throughout the world, this princess has come from Guinea† to seek him out."

"What a lucky search, and what a lucky find!" said San-

---

* Combination of *mico* ("monkey") and *cómico* ("comical").

† Guinea is a country in western Africa. In Cervantes' time the term referred to the Western African coast at the equator, near where modern Equatorial Guinea is.

cho Panza at that point. "The more so if my master is fortunate enough to right this wrong and set this injury right
by killing that son-of-a-bitch giant who you mentioned;
and he'll certainly do it if he can find him, unless he's a
phantom—against phantoms my master is quite powerless.
But I want to ask you, *señor licenciado*, among other things,
to make sure he won't take a fancy to being an archbishop,
which is something I fear, and that you'll advise him to
marry this princess on the spot. That would prevent him
from taking orders to become an archbishop and so he can
easily get his empire, and I, the object of my desires. I've
thought the whole matter through, and I figure that it'll be
bad for me if my master becomes an archbishop, because
I'm useless for the Church since I'm married, and for me to
get dispensations to get an income from the Church, since
I have a wife and children, would be an endless task. So, *señor*, it comes down to this—my master should get married
right away to this lady, and I don't even know what she's
called yet, so I can't call her by name."

"Her name," responded the priest, "is Princess Micomicona, because since her kingdom is Micomicón, it's obvious
she'd have that name."

"No doubt about it," responded Sancho. "I've seen many
people take their last name and lineage from the town
where they were born—Pedro de Alcalá, Juan de Úbeda,
and Diego de Valladolid—and they must have the same
custom over there in Guinea, queens taking their names
from what their kingdom is called."

"That must be it," said the priest, "and insofar as seeing
that your master gets married, I'll do everything I can."

Sancho was as happy about this as the priest was astonished at his simplicity, seeing that his master's delusions had
so affected him that he thought the knight would become
an emperor. Dorotea had already gotten on the priest's
mule and the barber had fastened on the oxtail beard. They
told Sancho to guide them to where don Quixote was, and
they emphasized that Sancho shouldn't speak to him about
the priest or the barber because the whole business of his
master becoming an emperor lay in secrecy. The priest and
Cardenio hesitated to go with them—Cardenio, so that don
Quixote wouldn't be reminded of the quarrel he'd had with
him; and the priest, because his presence wasn't required

right then. So, the priest and Cardenio let the others go ahead and said they would follow slowly on foot. The priest didn't forget to instruct Dorotea as to what she was to do, to which she responded that they shouldn't worry, since she knew exactly what to do, according to the descriptions and requirements from the romances of chivalry.

They had gone about three-quarters of a league when they discovered don Quixote among some rocks and crags, fully dressed but not in his armor, and as soon as Dorotea saw him, and Sancho had told her that was don Quixote, she whipped her palfrey, with the bearded barber in tow. As they drew near him, the barber jumped from his mule and went over to take Dorotea in his arms, but she got off by herself with great self-assurance and went to kneel before don Quixote. Although he begged her to rise, she spoke to him this way, still on her knees: "I'll not rise from here—oh, brave and bold knight!—until your goodness and courtesy grant me a boon that will redound to your honor and glory, on behalf of the most inconsolable maiden the sun has ever shone upon. And if the might of your strong arm matches the splendor of your immortal fame, you'll be obliged to favor this unfortunate who from afar has sought you out to remedy her misfortunes."

"I won't reply with a single word, beautiful *señora*," responded don Quixote, "nor will I hear any more about your matter until you rise."

"I'll not rise, *señor*," responded the afflicted maiden, "if you first, by way of your courtesy, do not grant me the boon I ask for."

"I promise and grant it," responded don Quixote, "only if it's not to the detriment of my king, my country, and her who has the key to my heart and freedom."

"It will not be to the detriment of any of those things you mention, my good lord," responded the aggrieved maiden.

At this point, Sancho went to his master and whispered into his ear: "Your grace, *señor*, can grant her the boon she wants—it's really nothing at all: just to slay a great big giant. The one asking for it is the high princess Micomicona, queen of the kingdom of Micomicón, of Ethiopia."

"Be that as it may," responded don Quixote, "I'll do what I'm obliged to, and what my conscience dictates, in accordance with what I've professed." And turning to the maiden, he said: "Let your great beauty arise, since I grant whatever boon that you may ask of me."

"Well, what I ask for is," said the maiden, "that your heroic person come with me wherever I'll lead you and that you promise me that you'll not engage in another adventure or quest until you've taken revenge for me on a traitor who, against all laws, human and divine, has usurped my kingdom."

"I've said that I grant it," responded don Quixote, "and so you can, *señora*, from this day forth, put aside the melancholy that has been oppressing you, and let your wilted hopes recover their energy and strength, because with the help of God, and my arm, you'll soon see yourself restored to the throne of your ancient and great estate, in spite and in defiance of all the villains that would keep you from it. Let's get to it, because, as the proverb says, 'danger lurks in delay.' "

The afflicted damsel tried very hard to kiss his hands, but don Quixote, ever courteous and considerate, would not allow it. Rather he made her stand up and embraced her warmly, and told Sancho to saddle Rocinante, and to get him dressed in his armor. Sancho took down the armor that hung from a tree like a trophy. He put the saddle on the horse and quickly put the armor on his master.

When the knight found himself in full armor, he said: "In the name of God, let's go forth to render aid to this great lady."

The barber was still on his knees, trying valiantly to conceal his laughter and endeavoring to keep his beard on at the same time, because if it fell off, all their hopes would fall with it. And seeing that the boon had been granted, and that don Quixote was eager to set out on his quest, he got up and took his lady by her hand, and between them they helped her mount. Then don Quixote got onto Rocinante and the barber mounted his pack mule, leaving Sancho on foot, which renewed in him a sense of loss for his donkey. But he took it all in stride because it seemed to him that his master was on the road to and even on the verge of becoming an emperor, believing don Quixote would get married to that princess and be, at least, the king of Micomicón. The only thing that really troubled him was considering that that kingdom lay in the area of black Africa, and that the people they would give him to be his vassals would all be black. But soon he arrived at a good solution, and said to himself: "What difference does it make to me if my vassals are black? What have I to do other than take them to Spain, where I can sell them,* where they will pay me in cash so I can buy a title or some office in which I can lead the easy life for the rest of my days? Certainly, you can—unless you're asleep or don't know how to take care of things— sell thirty or ten thousand vassals in the twinkling of an eye. I'll sell them in a flash, in pairs, or however I can do it. And my blacks will turn into silver or gold. Come on! Do you think I'm stupid?" And Sancho trudged on so unhurriedly and happy that he forgot the discomfort of being on foot.

Cardenio and the priest witnessed all this from behind some bushes and couldn't figure out how to join them. But the priest, who was a clever fellow, decided what they could do, so he took some scissors that he had in a sheath, and very quickly cut off Cardenio's beard and dressed him in his own gray jacket and a black coat that he had, leaving himself in his pants and doublet. Cardenio was so transformed from the way he'd been that he wouldn't have recognized himself, even if he looked in a mirror. The others had already passed them by while they were disguising themselves, but the two managed to get to the highway before them, since the brambles and rough areas made it harder on horseback than on foot. They waited in the middle of the road at the bottom of the hill, and as soon as don Quixote and his companions went out into the open, the priest stared at him quite deliberately, giving signs that he recognized him, and after looking at him for a while, he ran toward him with open arms, exclaiming: "How nice it is to find the mirror of knight-errantry, my good neighbor don Quixote de La Mancha, flower and cream of elegance, savior and refuge of the needy, the quintessence of knight-errantry!"

As he said this he embraced don Quixote's left knee, leaving the knight very surprised at what he saw and what he heard that man say, but he looked at him attentively and finally he recognized him as the priest. He tried to get off

---

* There were about 37,500 black slaves in Spain in 1600, according to José Luis Cortés López, a fact of life, and that's why Sancho is so blasé about it.

his horse, but the priest wouldn't permit it, so don Quixote said: "Let me dismount, your grace—it's not right for me to be on horseback, when such a reverend person as you is on foot."

"I won't allow it," said the priest. "Stay on horseback, because it's on horseback that your excellency achieves the greatest deeds and adventures that have ever been seen in our age. For me, although I'm an unworthy priest, it would suffice for me to ride on the back of one of those mules that belong to these men traveling with you, if they don't think it a bother. And I'll even consider that I'm riding on Pegasus, or on the zebra or charger on which the famous Moor Muzaraque* rode, who to this day remains enchanted on Zulema, the high hill near Cómpluto."†

"That didn't occur to me, *señor licenciado*," responded don Quixote, "and I know that my *señora* princess will be pleased, for my sake, to have her squire offer you the saddle of his mule, and he can get on its rump, if the beast can take both of you."

"Yes, it can," responded the princess, "and I know that it won't be necessary to ask my squire, because he's too courteous and courtly to allow a cleric to go on foot when he could be riding."

"That's the truth," responded the barber, and, getting off immediately, he invited the priest to take the saddle, which he did without much urging. What didn't turn out quite right was when the barber went to mount on the haunches of the donkey, which was plainly a rented one—and to say that it was not a good one, this is all that need be known— it raised its hindquarters and kicked twice in the air, and if one of those kicks had landed on *maese* Nicolás' chest or on his head, he would have cursed the search for don Quixote. Even so, the barber was so taken by surprise that he fell backward and paid little heed to his beard, which fell onto the ground. When he found himself without it, the only thing he could think to do was to cover his face with his hands and lament that his teeth were smashed in. Don Quixote, who saw that massive beard without a jaw and

---

* About the "famous" Muzaraque nothing is known.
† Zulema is a large hill southeast of Alcalá de Henares, which was called Complutum in Roman times.

with no blood, far from the face of the fallen squire, said: "My God, what a miracle this is! The mule has kicked the beard from his face as if it had been cut off."

The priest, seeing they risked discovery, promptly picked up the beard and went to where *maese* Nicolás was lying, still shouting. And lifting the barber's head to his chest, he put it back on, murmuring certain words over it, which he said was an incantation with which to stick beards back on, as they would see. And when he was sure the beard was secure, he rose, and the barber was as well bearded and as sound as before. Don Quixote was amazed beyond measure and begged the priest to teach him the incantation when the time was right, since he figured that its power must not be limited only to restoring beards—it was evident that the fellow's jaw must have been severely wounded and in bad shape, and now it was whole again.

"That's right," said the priest, and promised to teach it to him at the first opportunity.

They all agreed that the priest, for the time being, should ride, and the other two should take turns riding, until they arrived at the inn, which would be about two leagues farther on. Now that there were three riding—to wit: don Quixote, the princess, and the priest; and three on foot: Cardenio, the barber, and Sancho—don Quixote said to the maiden: "Let your excellency, *señora mía*, lead me to wherever it pleases you."

And before she could respond, the priest said: "Toward what kingdom does your ladyship wish to lead? Is it by chance toward Micomicón? That's what it must be, or I know little about kingdoms."

She, who was ready for anything, said: "Yes, *señor*, my journey leads toward that kingdom."

"In that case," said the priest, "we have to pass through the center of my village, and from there you can get on the road to Cartagena,* where you can embark on your worthy venture. If there's a fair wind and a calm sea without storms, in a little less than nine years you can get within sight of the great lake Meona, I mean Meótides,† which lies

---

* Cartagena is a seaport in southeastern Spain.
† *Meótides* (Latin *Palus Mœoticus*) is the old name for the Sea of Azov, which is the body of water that drains into the Black Sea from the northeast. *Meona* refers to a person who constantly needs to urinate.

not much more than a hundred days' journey from your highness' kingdom."

"Your grace is mistaken, *señor mío*," she said, "because is hasn't been two years since I left there, and in truth, the weather was never very good. And even so, I've fulfilled the goal of my desires, which was to see *señor* don Quixote de La Mancha, news of whose exploits reached my ears as soon as I set foot in Spain, and I was thereby moved to seek him so that I could put myself in his care, entrusting the justice of my cause to his invincible arm."

"No more—no more praise," said don Quixote at this point, "because I'm an enemy of any kind of flattery, and whether it is or isn't flattery, even so, such talk offends my chaste ears. What I can say, *señora mía*, is that whether my arm is strong or not, whatever strength it has or doesn't have will be used for your service until I lose my life. So, leaving this for its proper moment, I'd like to ask the *licenciado* to tell me why he happens to be here—it shocks me to see him alone, without servants, and without luggage."

"I'll answer you in a few words," responded the priest. "Your grace, *señor* don Quixote, should know that *maese* Nicolás—our friend and barber—and I were going to Seville to claim a certain amount of money that a relative of mine who had gone to the New World many years ago had sent me. It was no trifling sum either—no less than sixty thousand *pesos*—and yesterday coming back through these parts, four highwaymen came out and stripped us to our beards, so much so, the barber had to get a false beard to put on. And even this young man," pointing to Cardenio, "was ill treated as well. But the odd thing is that the people who robbed us were galley slaves who, they say, were freed—almost in that same place—by a brave fellow who, in spite of the commissioner and the guards, had released them all. And it must be that this man is crazy or must be as big a rogue as they are, or some soulless man without conscience, since he deliberately released the wolf among the ewes, the fox among the hens, and the fly into the honey. He defrauded justice, and went against his king and natural lord (since he went against his just commands). He wanted, I say, to rob the galleys of their feet and stir up the Holy Brotherhood, which has been at their ease all these years.

He wanted, finally, to do a deed that may cause him to lose his soul without gaining anything for his body."

(Sancho had already told the priest and the barber about the adventure of the galley slaves, achieved by his master with such great glory, and for this reason the priest pursued the topic so eagerly, just to see what don Quixote would do or say. Well, he changed color at every word, and didn't dare to say that he'd been the liberator of all those good people.)

"These were," said the priest, "the ones who robbed us, and may God through his infinite mercy pardon him who freed them from going to their just punishment."

Chapter XXX. Which deals with the amusing inventiveness and the happy method hit upon for releasing our enamored knight from his very harsh self-imposed penance.

The priest had hardly finished when Sancho said: "On my faith, *señor licenciado*, that deed was done by my master, and it wasn't because I told and advised him beforehand to be careful what he was doing, and that it was a sin to set them free, since they were all being sent away because they were great rascals."

"Blockhead," chimed in don Quixote, "it's no affair of knights-errant to find out whether the afflicted, chained together, and oppressed that we encounter on the road in such a plight are that way because of vices or virtues. The only important thing is to help them because they're people in distress, heeding their sufferings and not their mischief. I found a rosary of unfortunate malcontents strung together and I did what my religion demands. The rest is none of my business, and whoever thinks ill of it, saving the sacred dignity of the *señor licenciado*, the honored person of our friend the priest, I say knows little of chivalry, and lies like a whoreson dog, and I'll make him understand it to the full extent with my sword."

He said this bracing himself in his stirrups and closed his helmet because the barber's basin—which he thought was Mambrino's helmet—was hanging from his front pommel until he could repair the damage done by the hands of the galley slaves.

Dorotea, being a clever and witty person—since she already knew about don Quixote's diminished capacity, and that everyone made fun of him except Sancho Panza—didn't want to be left out, and seeing him so angry said: "*Señor* knight, remember the boon that your grace has promised me, and bear in mind that you cannot undertake another adventure, no matter how urgent it might be. Calm your heart, because if the *señor licenciado* had known that it was your never conquered arm that freed the galley slaves, he would have sewn his mouth closed before saying anything disrespectful of your grace."

"I'll swear to that," said the priest, "and what's more, I'd have cut off half my mustache."

"I'll be silent, *señora mía*," said don Quixote, "and I'll repress the just rage that has risen in my heart; and I'll be calm and peaceful until I accomplish your promised boon. To reward me for my goodwill, please tell me, if it doesn't trouble you, what is distressing you, and how many, who, and what kind of persons on whom I must exact deserved and entire vengeance."

"I'll be pleased to," responded Dorotea, "if it won't weary you to hear about lamentations and misfortunes."

"It will not, *señora mía*," responded don Quixote.

To which Dorotea replied: "All right, then, your worships, be attentive."

Just as she said this, Cardenio and the barber drew up to her side, eager to see how the discreet Dorotea would make up her story. Likewise Sancho, who was as deceived about her as was his master. And she, after straightening herself up in her saddle, and prepared by giving a little cough and doing other preliminaries, began in this lively way: "First of all, I want your graces, *señores míos*, to know that my name is . . ."

And she stopped at this point because she'd forgotten the name that the priest had given her. But he rescued her when he recognized why she was hesitating, and said: "It's not strange, *señora*, that Your Highness is confused and a bit reluctant to tell of your misfortunes, because they always are of such a nature that they frequently deprive persons of their memory to the point where sometimes they can't even recall their own names, as has been the case with your ladyship, who has forgotten that you are the Princess Micomicona, lawful heiress to the great kingdom of Micomicón. And with this reminder you can easily bring to your suffering mind all that you wish to tell us."

"That's the truth," responded the maiden, "and from now on I believe it won't be necessary to prompt me in anything, because I'll reach a safe port with my true story, and here it is: My father was called Tinacrio the Wise, and was well versed in what they call the art of magic. He learned through his science that my mother, who was called Queen Jaramilla, was to die before he would, and that a short time later he would also pass from this life and I would be an orphan, with neither father nor mother. But he said that this didn't bother him as much as it grieved him that a towering giant, lord of a large island that almost borders on our kingdom, who is known as Pandafilando of the Sour Look—it's well-known that although he has his eyes in the proper place he always looks in two different directions, as if he were cross-eyed, and he does this out of perversity to instill fear in those he looks at—anyway, my father learned that this giant, when he found out that I'd be an orphan, would overrun my kingdom with a powerful army and claim it for himself, and wouldn't even leave me the smallest hamlet as a refuge. But I could avoid all this ruin and disgrace if I would marry him. He thought that it would never occur to me to enter into such an unequal marriage, and in this he was right, because I never considered marrying that giant, nor any other giant, as big and as huge as he might be.

"My father also said that after he was dead and I saw that Pandafilando was coming to overrun my country, I shouldn't try to put up any defense; he urged me instead to leave the country undefended if I wanted to save the lives of my good and loyal vassals, because it would be impossible to defend against the bedeviled force of the giant. But what I should immediately do, with a few of my people, was to go to Spain, where I would find the remedy to my troubles when I found a certain knight-errant, whose fame by that time would have extended throughout the country, and who would be named, if I remember correctly, don Azote or don Gigote."*

---

* *Azote* is a whiplash; *gigote* was a dish made of ground meat.

"He must have said QUIXOTE, *señora*," interrupted Sancho Panza," or, by another name, the Woebegone Knight."

"That's the one," said Dorotea. "And he said even more—that he was tall in stature, lean in the face, and that on his right side, beneath his left shoulder, or right nearby, he had a mole, with hairs like bristles."

When don Quixote heard this, he said to his squire: "Come, Sancho, my son, help me strip—I want to see if I'm that knight that the wise king prophesied."

"Why would your grace want to strip?" said Dorotea.

"I want to see if I have that mole your father mentioned," responded don Quixote.

"No need to strip," said Sancho. "I know that your worship has such a mole in the middle of your spine, and that's a sure sign of a strong man."

"Proof enough," said Dorotea. "Among friends one can overlook trifles, and whether it's on your shoulder or on your spine matters little. It's enough that there's a mole there, and no matter where it is, it's all the same flesh. My father doubtless was correct in everything, and I've done right in commending myself to don Quixote, who is the one my father described, since his face fits the description of the one whose fame is widely known, not only in Spain, but also in all of La Mancha, because hardly had I disembarked in Osuna when I started hearing about so many of his deeds that my heart told me that this was the one I'd come looking for."

"How could your grace have disembarked in Osuna,* *señora mía*," don Quixote asked, "since it isn't on the sea?"

But before Dorotea could respond, the priest lent a hand and said: "The *señora* princess must have meant to say that after she disembarked in Málaga, the first place she heard news of your worship was in Osuna."

"That's what I meant," said Dorotea.

"And this makes sense," said the priest. "Continue, Your Majesty."

"There's no more to tell," responded Dorotea, "except that finally my luck has been so good in finding *señor* don Quixote that I consider that I'm already queen and mistress

---

* Osuna is a city between Seville and the seaport Málaga, about sixty-five miles from the sea.

of my realm, since he—out of his courtesy and generosity—
has promised to go with me wherever I might lead him,
which will be nowhere else than directly in front of Pandafilando of the Sour Look, so that he can slay him and
restore to me what has been so unjustly taken from me; and
all of this will take place just for the asking, because it had
been foretold by Tinacrio the Wise, my good father, who
also left written in Chaldean* or Greek script that I cannot
read myself, that if this knight in the prophecy, after having
beheaded the giant, would want to marry me, I should at
once offer myself to him as his lawful wife and give him
possession of my kingdom as well as of my body."

"What do you think of that, friend Sancho," said don
Quixote at this point. "Don't you hear what is being said?
Didn't I tell you? Look, we have a kingdom to rule and a
queen to marry!"

"I believe you," said Sancho. "You should get married
the instant you open *señor* Pandahilado's windpipe! Well,
the queen isn't so bad—I wish the fleas in my bed were as
good as she is."

And after he said this he cut a couple of capers in the air
and seemed extraordinarily happy. Then he went to take
the reins of Dorotea's mule, and forced her to stop so he
could kneel before her, begging her to give him her hands
to kiss, as a sign that he acknowledged her as his queen and
mistress. And who among those present, seeing the madness of the master and the simplicity of the servant, could
refrain from laughing? So Dorotea gave him her hands and
promised to make him a great lord in her kingdom when
heaven pleased to restore it to her possession. Sancho
thanked her with words that renewed the laugher of all.

"This, *señores*," said Dorotea, "is my story. The only thing
left to say is that of all the people who came with me from
my kingdom, only this bearded squire remains, because the
others drowned in a storm that overtook us just when we
were in sight of the port. He and I were washed ashore miraculously on two planks. And so, you see, the whole of my
life is a miracle and a mystery. And if in telling it I've exaggerated a bit in some places, and have not been as accurate

---

* The Chaldean language was spoken in Urartu, near the Black Sea,
from the ninth to the sixth centuries B.C.

as I could have been in others, blame it on what the *señor licenciado* said at the beginning of my story, that continual extraordinary travails weaken the memory of those who endure them."

"No matter how many travails I undergo in your service, no matter how great and unheard-of they may be, they won't take away my memory, noble and brave *señora*," said don Quixote. "So once again I confirm the boon that I promised you and I swear to go with you to the end of the earth, until I meet your fierce enemy, whose arrogant head, with the help of God and of my arm, I intend to cut off with the sharp edges of this—and I can't say 'good sword,' thanks to Ginés de Pasamonte, who stole mine," he said under his breath, and went on, "—and after I cut it off and place you in peaceful possession of your estate, you're free to do as you would like. Because while my memory is absorbed, my will is enslaved, and my mind is possessed by that woman . . . and I say no more. . . . It isn't possible for me to contemplate marriage, not even for an instant, even if it were to the Phœnix."*

This decision of his master not to marry so provoked Sancho that he raised his voice in great anger, and said, "I swear, *señor* don Quixote, your worship is not in your right mind! How is it possible for you to hesitate to marry such a noble princess as this one? Do you think that Fortune offers such a chance under every rock? Is my *señora* Dulcinea more beautiful? No, certainly not—far from it, not by half, and I'm about ready to say that she doesn't even come up to the shoe of the one standing before us. How will I ever get the earldom I so want if you go around 'looking for delicacies to eat in the middle of the ocean'? Get married, get married right now, in the devil's name, and take the kingdom that has come *de vobis, vobis*† into your hands, and once you're king, make me a marquis or a governor right away, and may the devil take it all."

Don Quixote heard these blasphemies against his lady

---

* The Phœnix was the mythical Egyptian bird that lived for five hundred years. It built its own funeral pyre, fanned the flames with its wings, and was reincarnated. It never married anyone.

† Sancho means *de bóbilis, bóbilis*—"for nothing" (i.e., free). *Vobis* is a Latin word meaning *to you.*

Dulcinea and couldn't stand it. He raised his lance, without speaking a word to Sancho, and gave him two whacks that brought him to the ground, and if Dorotea hadn't called to him to stop, he would have doubtless taken his life.

"Do you think," he said to him after a while, "you vile rustic, that you can keep showing me such disrespect, and that I'll always pardon your blunders? Well, don't think it for a moment, you excommunicated scoundrel— that's what you are, since you've spoken ill of the peerless Dulcinea! Don't you know, you rustic, hod-carrying bum, that if it weren't for the strength she instills into my arm, I wouldn't be strong enough to kill a flea. Tell me, you viper-tongued jokester, who do you think has won this kingdom, decapitated this giant, and made you a marquis—because I consider all of this as good as already accomplished—if it isn't the strength of Dulcinea, using my arm as a tool for her deeds? She fights through me and conquers through me, and I live and breathe through her. Oh, you whoreson scoundrel, look how ungrateful you are—you see yourself risen from the dust of the earth to be a lord with a title, and in return you speak ill of the person who brought it all about."

Sancho wasn't in such bad shape that he didn't hear everything his master said to him, and scrambling up quickly and hiding behind Dorotea's palfrey, he said to his master from there: "Tell me, *señor*, if your grace is determined not to marry this great princess, it's obvious that the kingdom will not be yours, and if it's not yours, what favors can you do for me? That's what I'm complaining about. Get married once and for all to this queen—now that we have her as if she rained down upon us—and afterward you can go back to my *señora* Dulcinea, because there must have been kings in the world who kept mistresses. Insofar as beauty goes, I won't get involved, since, in truth, I've never seen *señora* Dulcinea."

"What do you mean 'you've never seen her,' you blaspheming traitor?" said don Quixote. "Didn't you just bring me a message from her?"

"What I mean is that I didn't see her long enough to have studied her beauty in all its details, but on the whole, she seemed fine."

"I forgive you now," said don Quixote, "and pardon me

for the injury I did you, because first impulses are not in the hands of man."

"I can understand that," responded Sancho, "because with me the first impulse is always to talk, and I can't prevent myself from talking once the notion gets to my tongue."

"Even so," said don Quixote, "be careful what you say, Sancho, because 'the pitcher can go to the well only so often . . . ,'* and I say no more."

"All right," responded Sancho, "God is in His heaven and He sees our tricks and He'll be the judge of who does worse: I, in not speaking well, or your grace, in not acting any better."

"No more of this," said Dorotea. "Run, Sancho, and kiss your master's hand and beg his pardon, and from now on be more attentive—both to your praise and your reproaches— and don't speak ill of the *señora* Tobosa, whom I don't know, except to serve; and have confidence in God, because you'll not lack an estate where you can live like a prince."

Sancho went with hanging head to ask for the hand of his master, who gave it to him calmly, and after Sancho kissed it, don Quixote added his blessing and told Sancho that they should go ahead of the rest because he had important things to ask and tell him. When they were alone, don Quixote told him: "Since your return, I haven't had a chance to ask you any details of the message you took and the answer you brought, but now that Fortune has given us time and opportunity, don't deny me the pleasure you can give me of hearing good news."

"Ask whatever you want," responded Sancho, "and to everything I'll find the way out as easily as I found the way in. But I beg you, *señor mío*, not to be so vindictive from now on."

"Why do you say that?" said don Quixote.

"I say it," he responded, "because these blows you just gave me were more for the quarrel that the devil stirred up between us the other night than for anything I said against my lady Dulcinea, whom I love and revere as if she were a relic—although there is nothing of that about her—just because she belongs to you."

"No more of this, Sancho, on your life," said don Qui-

---

* The saying continues: "before it leaves its handle or its spout."

xote, "for I find it offensive. I pardoned you then, and you know very well what they say: 'new sin, fresh penance.'"*

While the two of them were conversing, the priest said to Dorotea that she'd been very discreet both in the telling of her story and in its brevity and its resemblance to those in the romances of chivalry. She said that she'd often entertained herself by reading them, but she didn't know where the provinces and seaports were, and that's why she made that haphazard choice of Osuna as her landing point.

"That's what I thought," said the priest, "and that's why I broke in as I did, to set things right. But isn't it strange to see how easily this unfortunate *hidalgo* believes all of our inventions and lies, only because they're in the style of the nonsense of his books?"

"Yes, it is," said Cardenio, "and it's such a strange and unheard-of thing, that I don't know if anyone could be so keen-witted that he could try to make up such nonsense."

---

* These two paragraphs were added in the second Spanish edition to complete the loss and return of Sancho's donkey:

While this was going on they saw coming along the road on which they were traveling, a man mounted on a donkey, who, as he approached, seemed to be a gypsy. But Sancho Panza, whose eyes and heart became keen wherever he saw donkeys, no sooner had he seen the man than he knew him to be Ginés de Pasamonte; and therefore surmised that the donkey he was riding had to be his own, and it was. In order to escape recognition and to sell the donkey, he'd disguised himself as a gypsy, since he could speak the gypsy language, and many more, as well as if they were his own. So, as soon as Sancho had seen and recognized him, he shouted to him: "Ginesillo, you thief, give me back my treasure, my life, my repose, my donkey! Go away, you son of a bitch! Leave my delight, get out of here, you thief, and give up what is not yours."

There was no need for so many words or insults, because at the first one Ginés jumped down, and at a trot, which was more of a sprint, made off and went away from all of them. Sancho ran to his donkey, and embracing him he said: "How have you been, my good boy, donkey of my eyes, my companion?" He kissed and caressed him all the while as if he were a person. The donkey remained silent, and let himself be kissed and caressed by Sancho without saying a single word. They all came up and congratulated him on having found his donkey, and don Quixote especially, who told him that even in light of this, he would not rescind his order for the donkeys, for which Sancho thanked him.

"There is something else," said the priest, "and that's when this good *hidalgo* isn't talking about matters affected by his madness, if you talk with him about other things, he speaks very rationally and shows himself to have a clear understanding about everything, so that, as long as you shy away from chivalry, nobody would think anything except that he was a man of sound mind."

While they were engaged in this conversation, don Quixote continued his, and said to Sancho: "As far as our quarrels go, Panza, let's let bygones be bygones, and tell me now, without thought of grudge or grievance, where, how, and when did you find Dulcinea? What was she doing? What did you tell her? What did her face look like when she was reading my letter? Who copied it for you? Tell me everything else you think is worthy to be known, asked, and answered about all this, not adding or distorting anything to give me pleasure, nor shortening it, which would deprive me of some of it."

"*Señor*," responded Sancho, "if the truth be told, no one copied the letter for me because I didn't have any letter with me at all."

"That's right, just as you say," said don Quixote, "because two days after your departure I found the diary where I'd written it in my possession, and this caused me great concern, not knowing what you would do when you discovered you didn't have it. . . . I thought you'd come back for it as soon as you found it was missing."

"That would have been the case," responded Sancho, "if I hadn't memorized it exactly as your grace read it, so I could recite it to a sexton who copied it from my memory so accurately that he said that in all the days of his life—although he'd copied many letters of excommunication—he'd never read as beautiful a letter as that one."

"And is it still in your memory, Sancho?" said don Quixote.

"No, *señor*," responded Sancho, "because as soon as I repeated it, since I saw that I'd no longer need it, I immediately forgot it. If I remember anything it's that business of 'slobbering,' I mean, 'sovereign *señora*,' and the ending 'yours until death, the Woebegone Knight.' And in between those two items, I put in more than three hundred 'souls,' and 'lives,' and 'my eyes.'"

Chapter XXXI. About the delightful conversation between don Quixote and Sancho Panza, his squire, with other events.

"NOTHING OF what you say displeases me, Sancho, so keep talking," said don Quixote. "You got there, and what was that queen of beauty doing? I bet you found her stringing pearls, or embroidering something with golden floss for this her captive knight."

"I just found her," responded Sancho, "sifting three bushels of wheat in the yard of her house."

"You must realize," said don Quixote, "that those grains of wheat touched by her hands were transformed into pearls. Did you see if it was white wheat or brown?"

"It was just ordinary red wheat," responded Sancho.

"Well, I can assure you," said don Quixote, "that when sifted by her hands it made the whitest bread, without any doubt; but please go on. When you gave her my letter, did she kiss it? Did she put it on her head? Did she perform any ceremony befitting such a letter, or what?"

"Just when I was going to give it to her," responded Sancho, "she was right in the middle of winnowing a great deal of wheat that she had in her screen, and she told me: 'Put that letter, friend, on that sack—I can't read it until I finish winnowing everything here.'"

"What a wise lady!" said don Quixote. "That must have been so she could read it slowly and savor it. Go on, Sancho, and while she was engaged in her duties, what conversation did you have? What did she ask you about me? And you, what did you say in response? Come, tell me everything; don't leave anything in the inkwell."

"She didn't ask me anything," said Sancho, "but I told her how you were doing penance in her service, naked from the waist up, roaming the sierras as if you were a wild man, sleeping on the ground, and not eating bread from a tablecloth or combing your beard, but just weeping, and cursing your luck."

"When you said that I was cursing my luck," said don Quixote, "you did wrong, because rather I bless it and I'll always bless all the days of my life for having been worthy to love so high a lady as the *señora* Dulcinea del Toboso."

"She's so high," responded Sancho, "that I swear she's more than a palm taller than I am."

"Well, Sancho," said don Quixote, "how did you come to measure yourself against her?"

"I did it this way," responded Sancho. "When I went to help her lift a sack of wheat onto a mule, we were so close that I could see that she had quite a bit more than half a foot on me."

"It's true," responded don Quixote, "and her stature must be accompanied and adorned by a billion graces of the soul. But don't deny me this next bit of information—when you were next to her, didn't she have an exquisite aroma, a fragrance, a certain delicious *je ne sais quoi* that I find impossible to give a name to. I mean, an aroma as if you were in a fine glovemaker's shop?"*

"All I can say," said Sancho, "is that I smelled a little odor that was a bit mannish, and it must be because she was sweaty and grimy owing to the physical exercise."

"It wouldn't be that," responded don Quixote, "but rather that you must have a touch of a cold, or you were smelling yourself, because I know very well how that rose among thorns, that lily of the field, that liquid ambergris smells."

"Maybe you're right," responded Sancho, "because I've frequently noticed that smell that I thought was from *señora* Dulcinea coming from me. But that's no wonder, 'for one devil is like the next.'"

"So," continued don Quixote, "now that she'd finished sifting her wheat and sent it off to the mill, what did she do when she read the letter?"

"She didn't read it," said Sancho, "because she said she doesn't know how to read or write. Instead she tore it into small pieces, saying that she didn't want to give it to anyone to read for her, so that her secrets wouldn't be known in the village, and it was enough for me to tell her about the love that your grace professes for her and the outlandish penance that you were performing for her sake. She finally told me to tell you that she kisses your grace's hands and

---

* In olden times, glove leather was perfumed.

she was waiting there with more of a desire to see you than write to you, so she begged and even commanded you to leave these thickets and stop doing these foolish acts, and get on the road to El Toboso immediately, if nothing else more important didn't prevent you, because she was really eager to see you. She laughed quite a bit when I told her that you were called the WOEBEGONE KNIGHT. I asked her if the Basque from a long time ago had gone to her. She said that he had, and he was a very nice man. I also asked her about the galley slaves but she told me that she hadn't seen any of them yet."

"So far, so good," said don Quixote, "but tell me, what did she give you for telling her the news about me when you took leave of her? It's an ancient custom among knights- and ladies-errant to give to squires, maidens, or dwarves who take them news some rich gift in appreciation of the message."

"That may be so, and I think it's a good custom, but that must have been in the old days—nowadays the custom must be to give a piece of bread and some cheese, because that's what my lady Dulcinea gave me over the corral walls when she bade me farewell, and it seemed to be cheese made from sheep's milk."

"She's liberal in the extreme," said don Quixote, "and if she didn't reward you with gold, it's doubtless because she had none at hand to give you, but 'gratuities are good even after Easter.'* When I see her, I'll make everything right. Do you know what amazes me, Sancho? It seems to me that you went and came back through the air, since it only took you a little more than three hours to make that trip to El Toboso, and the distance is greater than thirty leagues, which convinces me that the wizard necromancer who watches over my affairs and is my friend—because there has to be one perforce, otherwise I wouldn't be a genuine knight-errant—must have sped you on your way without your realizing it. There are wizards like that who take a knight-errant sleeping in his bed and without his knowing how, he wakes up the next day more than a thousand leagues away from where he fell asleep. And if it weren't for that, knights-errant couldn't rescue each other as they do all the

---

* This is a Spanish proverb translated literally.

time. It may be that one will be fighting in the mountains of Armenia with some dragon, or with a fierce monster, or even with another knight, and is getting the worst of the struggle and is on the very verge of death; and when he least expects it, all of a sudden there arrives on a cloud or in a chariot of fire another knight, his friend, who moments earlier was in England. He succors his friend and rescues him from death, and that night is back home eating dinner very eagerly, and the distance between the two places is frequently two or three thousand leagues. It's all made possible by the cleverness and ingenuity of the wise enchanters who look over these brave knights. So, friend Sancho, it's not hard for me to believe that you went and came back from this place to El Toboso in such a short time. Well, as I've told you, some wizard who favors me must have taken you by air without your knowing it."

"That might well have been," said Sancho, "because to tell the truth it really seemed that Rocinante traveled like a gypsy's donkey with quicksilver in its ears."*

"There must have been not only quicksilver," said don Quixote, "but a legion of devils as well, for devils travel and make others travel without getting tired, however they please. But, leaving this aside for the moment, what do you think I ought to do now about my lady's command to go see her at once? Although I'm bound to comply with her command, I realize that I'm helpless because of the boon I promised the princess with us—the laws of chivalry require me to fulfill my promise rather than enjoy my pleasure. On the one hand, my desire to see my lady tortures and distresses me, and on the other hand, I'm pressured and summoned by my promise and by the glory that I'll achieve by taking on this enterprise. But what I think I'll do will be to hasten the current adventure and go to this giant, and when I'm there I'll cut off his head and will put the princess peacefully in her estate, and then immediately turn around to go see the light that illuminates my senses, and I'll explain it all in such a way that she'll come to sanction my delay, seeing that it redounds to her greater glory and fame, inasmuch as all that I've achieved, am now achieving, and

---

* Putting drops of mercury in a donkey's ears was a gypsy trick to liven up the creature to make it go faster.

will achieve in this life by arms, all come to me from the favor she gives me and by my being hers."

"Alas!" said Sancho. "And how damaged is your grace's brain? Tell me, *señor*, does your grace plan to make this voyage for nothing and let such a fine marriage as this slip through your fingers—the dowry is a whole kingdom, and in truth I've heard it's more than twenty thousand leagues around, and it has in abundance all the necessities to sustain human life. And it's bigger than Castile and Portugal combined! Say no more, for the love of God. You should be ashamed for what you said. Take my advice—forgive me—and get married right away in the first village where there is a priest, and if not, here's our own *licenciado* who can do it as fine as can be. Bear in mind that I'm old enough to give advice, and this piece of advice I'm giving you today 'fits like a glove'; and 'a bird in the hand is worth two in the bush'; and 'he that has good but chooses evil, when evil comes, he shouldn't complain.'"

"Look, Sancho," responded don Quixote, "if the advice you're giving me is that I should get married so that I can become a king as soon as I kill the giant, and then I'll be able to give you favors and bestow the promised reward on you, I want you to know that without getting married I can fulfill your desire very easily because I'll stipulate in advance that when I come out victorious from the battle, they will give me as my honorarium a part of the kingdom to give to whomever I please, and when they give it to me, whom would you have me give it to if not to you?"

"That's very good," responded Sancho, "but be careful that the part you choose is on the seacoast, because if I don't like the lifestyle, I can ship off my black vassals and do with them what I've said. And don't worry about going to see Dulcinea now; just go off to kill the giant and let's get this business over and done with, because, by God, I think it will bring a great deal of honor and profit."

"I believe you're right, Sancho," said don Quixote, "and I'll take your advice about going with the princess before seeing Dulcinea. And I warn you not to tell anything to anyone about what you and I have talked about and decided, not even those with us. Since Dulcinea is so modest that she doesn't want anyone to know her thoughts, it wouldn't be good for me or anyone else to disclose them."

"If that's the case," said Sancho, "why do you make everyone your mighty arm conquers present himself before my lady Dulcinea? Isn't that as if your loving her, and that you are her beau, were your signature? And since those sent by you to pay her respect have to go and kneel before her and say they were sent by you, how is it possible for either of you to conceal your thoughts?"

"Oh, what a fool and a simpleton you are!" said don Quixote. "Don't you see, Sancho, that all of this redounds to her greater exaltation? I want you to know that in our system of chivalry it's a great honor for a lady to have many knights-errant in her service, and their thoughts go no further than just serving her for who she is, without expecting anything in return for their many and worthy desires other than that she be pleased to accept them as her knights."

"That's the kind of love," said Sancho, "I've heard our priest say that we should use to love Our Lord, for His own sake, moved neither by hope of glory nor fear of punishment. But I would like and love to serve Him for what He can do for me."

"May the devil take you for a peasant," said don Quixote. "What shrewd things you say at times! One might think you've been a student."

"Well, on my faith, I can't even read."

At this point, *maese* Nicolás called to them to say they should delay a bit so that they could all stop to drink at a little spring that was flowing nearby. Don Quixote stopped, with no little pleasure on Sancho's part, since he was so tired of lying so much, and was afraid that his master would catch him in a lie, because, although he knew that Dulcinea was a peasant girl from El Toboso, he'd never seen her in his entire life.

By this time Cardenio had dressed up in the clothing that Dorotea was wearing when they found her, and, although it wasn't very good, it was a lot better than what he'd been wearing. They all dismounted near the spring, and with what the priest had brought from the inn, they satisfied to a limited extent the hunger they all felt.

While they were sitting there eating, a boy happened to come along the road who stopped to look closely at those who were sitting by the spring, and after a moment he ran to don Quixote and clasped him by the legs and began to weep in earnest, saying: "*Ay, señor mío*, don't you recognize me? Look carefully! I'm that boy Andrés that your grace freed from that oak tree that I was tied to."

Don Quixote recognized him and, grasping him by the hand, turned to face his companions and said: "So that your graces can see how important it is for there to be knights-errant in the world who can redress the wrongs done by insolent and evil people who dwell in it, I want you to know that a few days ago when I was going through a forest, I heard someone wailing pitifully, and it sounded like a distressed and needy person. I rushed over immediately, as I'm required, to the place where it seemed to me the heart-rending cries were coming from, and I found the boy now before you tied to an oak tree. All of this makes me rejoice in my soul, since he'll be a witness and will not let me lie about anything. I repeat, the lad was tied to the oak tree, naked from the waist up, and a peasant was whipping him with the reins of a mare. I learned afterward that he was the boy's master. As soon as I saw him, I asked him what had caused that outrageous flogging, and the coarse fellow responded that he was whipping him because he was his servant, and certain acts of carelessness on his part showed he was more of a thief than a simpleton. The boy responded to this by saying: '*Señor*, he's only whipping me because I wanted him to pay me.' The master responded with some kind of excuse that I heard but didn't entertain. In short, I had the man untie him and made him swear that he would take the boy home and pay him, *real* for *real*, and even with a bit extra added. Isn't all of this true, Andrés? Didn't you see with what authority I commanded him, and with what humility he promised to do everything I ordered and required him to do? Speak up. Don't be shy or hesitate. Tell these people what happened so they can see what a blessing it is for there to be knights-errant roaming these roads."

"Everything your grace has said is very true," responded the boy, "but it turned out quite differently from what you think."

"What do you mean 'it turned out differently'?" replied don Quixote. "You mean the peasant didn't pay you?"

"Not only did he *not* pay me," responded the boy, "but as soon as you left the forest and we were alone, he tied me up again and gave me so many lashes that I was turned into another flayed St. Bartholomew. And accompanying each lash he said some joke or jibe to make fun of you and, if I hadn't been feeling so much pain, I would have laughed at what he said. He left me in such a state that until just now I've been in a hospital trying to recover from what he did to me. And you're to blame for all this, because if you'd just kept on going and minded your own business, and not meddled in other people's affairs, my master would have been content to give me a dozen or two lashes and then would have released me and paid what he owed. But since your grace insulted him without any provocation and called him so many names, he got angrier and angrier, and since he couldn't take it out on you, when he found himself alone, he took out his anger on me to such a point that I'll never be a man again as long as I live."

"The problem was," said don Quixote, "that I went away, and I shouldn't have until I left you fully paid. I should have realized through long experience that no brute keeps his word if it's not in his interest to do so. But remember, Andrés, that I swore I would hunt him down, even though he hid in the belly of the whale."*

"That's true," said Andrés, "but it wouldn't do any good."

"You'll see whether it'll do any good," said don Quixote.

And when he said this he got up quickly and told Sancho to bridle Rocinante, who was grazing while they ate. Dorotea asked him what he planned to do. He responded that he wanted to find the peasant and punish him for his wicked acts and make him pay Andrés down to the last *maravedí*, even if all the peasants in the world stood in his way. She responded that he should remember that, in accordance with the boon he'd promised her, he couldn't take on any new project until he'd settled her affair, and since he knew this better than anyone, he should restrain himself until he returned from her kingdom.

"That's true," responded don Quixote, "so Andrés must be patient until I return, as you, *señora*, say, and I swear and promise him once again not to stop until I see him avenged and paid."

"I don't believe these oaths," said Andrés. "All I want

---

* This refers to Jonah's whale from Jonah 1:17.

now, more than all the vengeance in the world, is a way to get to Seville. Give me something to eat, if you can—a bit to take with me—and may God go with your grace and all the knights-errant, and may they be as errant with themselves as they have been with me."

Sancho took a piece of bread and some cheese from his supplies and gave them to the boy, saying: "Take these, brother Andrés, because a share of your misfortune affects all of us."

"And what share affects you?" asked Andrés.

"This share of the bread and cheese I'm giving you," responded Sancho, "and God knows if I'll need them or not, because I'll have you know, friend, that we squires of knights-errant are subject to great hunger and ill luck, and many other things that are more easily felt than said."

Andrés grabbed the bread and cheese, and seeing that no one was offering anything else, he lowered his head and took the road in his hands, as they say. It's true that as he left, he said to don Quixote: "For the love of God, *señor* knight-errant, if you should ever come across me again, even though they are chopping me up into pieces, don't try to rescue or help me. Just leave me alone to my fate, because it won't be as bad as what would result from your help, and may God damn you and all the knights-errant ever born in the world!"

Don Quixote rose to chastise him, but he took to his heels in such a way that no one dared follow. Don Quixote was very crestfallen by the story of Andrés, and the others had to hold their laughter in check so that don Quixote wouldn't be utterly crushed.

Chapter XXXII. *Which deals with what happened to don Quixote and his companions in the inn.*

THE GOOD lunch came to an end without anything else happening worthy of being recorded, and the next day they arrived at the inn that had caused Sancho Panza so much terror and dread. Although he didn't want to go in, there was no way he could avoid it. The innkeeper's wife, the innkeeper, his daughter, and Maritornes, who all saw don Quixote and Sancho coming, went out to receive them, showing great joy, and he met them with a grave mien and solemnity, and told them to prepare a better bed for him than the last time, to which the innkeeper's wife said that if he paid better than the last time, she would give him one fit for a king. Don Quixote said he would, and so they prepared a reasonable one in the same garret as before, and he went to bed right away, because he felt very debilitated both in body and spirit.

No sooner was the door shut than the innkeeper's wife assaulted the barber, grabbed him by the beard and said: "By the sign of the cross, you can't use my oxtail as a beard anymore. My husband's thing is lying around the floor, which is a disgrace—I mean his comb, which I used to put into my good tail."

The barber refused to give it to her, even though she was pulling on it, until the priest said that he should give it back, since it was no longer needed for that stratagem, and that he should show his real face and tell don Quixote that when the thieving galley slaves robbed them, he'd fled to that inn, and if he asked about the princess' squire, they would tell him that he'd been sent ahead to notify her subjects of her return and that she was bringing along the liberator of them all. With this, the barber willingly returned the tail to the innkeeper's wife, as well as the other items they had been lent to rescue don Quixote. The people at the inn marveled at Dorotea's beauty and the noble appearance of the young Cardenio. The priest arranged for a meal to be made from what was available at the inn, and the innkeeper, hoping for better pay, prepared a tolerable dinner. Don Quixote slept through it all, and the others thought it was best not to wake him, because it would be better for him to sleep instead of eat.

The innkeeper, along with his wife and daughter, Maritornes, and all the travelers, spoke over dinner about the odd madness of don Quixote, and how they had found him. The innkeeper's wife told them what had happened between don Quixote and the mulcteer. She then looked around to see if Sancho was to be found, and seeing that he wasn't, told about his blanketing, which was received with no little pleasure. And when the priest said that it was the romances of chivalry that don Quixote had read that had driven him crazy, the innkeeper said: "I don't know how that can be, because in truth, the way I understand it, there is no better reading in the world, and I have two or three of them over there along with other writings that have restored my spirits—and not only mine, but that of many others. Because when it's harvesttime, many reapers come here on their days off and there's always someone who can read and picks up one of those books, and more than thirty of us gather around him, and we listen with so much pleasure that we forget our worries. At least, for me, I can say that when I hear about those raging and terrible blows that the knights deliver, it makes me feel like doing the same thing, and I want to keep on listening, night and day."

"And I no less," said the innkeeper's wife, "because it's never still in this place, except when you're listening to what is being read, and you're so entranced that it doesn't occur to you to fight with me."

"That's the truth," said Maritornes, "and on my faith I like to hear those things, too, because they're very pretty, and especially when they tell about the lady underneath the orange trees in the arms of her knight, and a lady-in-waiting is standing guard for them, dying of envy and fright. That's about as sweet as it gets."

"And what do you think of these things, young lady?" the priest said, talking with the daughter of the innkeeper.

"I don't know, *señor*, on my soul," she responded. "I listen to them as well, and in truth I don't understand much, but I get a lot of pleasure hearing them. But I don't like to hear about the blows that my father likes so well, but rather the lamentations that the knights make when they're away from their ladies. At times they make me cry because of the compassion I have for them."

"So, would you console them, *señora* maiden," said Dorotea, "if it was for you they wept?"

"I don't know what I'd do," said the girl. "I only know that there are some of those ladies who are so cruel that they call their knights tigers and lions, and other bad things. And, Jesus, what kind of people can they be, so without soul or conscience, that they'll let an honorable man die or go crazy rather than look at him! I don't know what all this priggishness is about. If it's for their honor's sake, let them marry the knights, which is all they want anyway."

"Quiet, child!" said the innkeeper's wife. "It seems that you know a lot about these things, and it's not good for girls to know or to talk so much."

"Since this man asks me," she responded, "I feel I have to answer him."

"All right," said the priest, "bring me those books, *señor* innkeeper—I want to see them."

"I'll be pleased to," said the innkeeper.

He went into his room and brought out a small valise closed by a little chain and when he opened it, he found in it three large books and a couple of manuscripts written in a very clear hand. The first book that he opened was *Don Cirongilio de Tracia*. The next one was *Felixmarte de Hyrcania*, and the other one was *History of the Gran Capitán, Gonzalo Hernández de Córdoba, Together with the Life of Diego García de Paredes*. As soon as the priest read the first two titles, he turned to the barber and said: "What we need here and now are my friend's housekeeper and his niece."

"We don't need them," responded the barber, "because I also know how to take them to the corral or the fireplace where a nice fire is already burning."

"So, your grace wants to burn more books?"* said the innkeeper.

"Only these first two," said the priest, "the one about *Don Cirongilio* and the other one about *Felixmarte*."

"By chance you think that my books are heretical or phlegmatic so that you want to burn them?"

"'Schismatic' you mean to say, my friend," said the barber, "and not 'phlegmatic.'"

"Yes, yes," replied the innkeeper, "but if you want to burn one of them up, let it be the one about the Gran Capitán and that Diego García, because I'd rather burn a child of mine up than allow either of the two others to be burned."

"My brother," said the priest, "these two books are mendacious and are filled with nonsense and silly things, but

---

* We must assume that the innkeeper had previously learned what the priest and barber had done to the library. In Spanish the text says *más* ("more"), but a number of editions have assumed an error and changed it to *mis* ("my"), since no formal mention had been made of the Inquisition of the Books (chapter six).

this one about the Gran Capitán is true history, and it deals with the exploits of Gonzalo Hernández de Córdoba,* who, because of his many deeds, has deserved to be called by everyone the Gran Capitán—the Great Captain—a famous and illustrious epithet deserved by him only. And this Diego García de Paredes† was a knight of renown, native of the city of Trujillo in Extremadura, a very brave soldier, and was so strong that he could stop a millstone in all its fury with one finger. And once, when he stood at one end of a bridge with a broadsword, he prevented an immense army from crossing over it. He did other feats as well, and he writes about them himself, as his own chronicler, with modesty imposed by his knighthood, that if someone else had written about them, freely and dispassionately, he would have cast all the Hectors, Achilles, and Rolands into oblivion."‡

"In your hat!" said the innkeeper. "What's so astounding about stopping a millstone? By God, you should read now about what Felixmarte de Hyrcania did—with a single backslash he split five giants in two as if they had been beanpod friars little children make.§ And once he attacked a huge and powerful army of more than a million six hundred thousand men, all armed to the teeth, and he vanquished every one as if they were flocks of sheep. And what do you have to say about the good Cirongilio de Tracia, who was so valiant and intrepid, as you'll see in the book, they say when he was sailing up a river, a flaming serpent leapt from the water and as soon as he saw it, he jumped onto it astride its scaly back, and seized its neck with such force that when the serpent saw that it was being strangled, it could only plunge into the depths of the river, taking along the knight, who refused to let go? And when

---

* Gonzalo Hernández de Córdoba (Cordova) was a soldier (1453–1515) who participated in the battles leading to the fall of Granada (1492), among many other accomplishments.
† Diego García de Paredes (1466–1530) fought in Granada with, and later accompanied, the Gran Capitán in Sicily. He died at age sixty-four in Bologna, having fallen from his horse at the coronation of Carlos V.
‡ Hector was an ideal warrior of the Trojan army in Homer's *Iliad*. He was killed by Achilles, the greatest soldier in Agamemnon's army.
§ These "friars" are toys that children cut out of beanpods, the top of which resembled the hood of a priest.

they got to the bottom, he found himself in a very beautiful garden, a wonder to behold, and then the serpent turned into an old man who told him incredible things.* So, *señor*, if you heard all this, you would go crazy with pleasure. I couldn't care less about the Gran Capitán and that Diego García de Paredes."

When she heard this, Dorotea whispered to Cardenio: "Our host can almost be don Quixote's understudy."

"That's what it seems like to me," responded Cardenio, "because, the way it looks, he's convinced that everything these books describe happened exactly as written, and even the barefoot friars won't make him believe anything else."

"Look, brother," the priest said to him, "neither Felixmarte de Hyrcania nor don Cirongilio de Tracia ever existed in the real world, nor did any of the other knights described in the romances of chivalry, because it's all made-up, and fiction, created by idle minds that wrote them for the reason you mentioned—to pass the time and entertain your reapers by hearing them read. Really, I swear to you that such knights never existed in the world, nor did they do any of the deeds or foolish acts in them."

"You can't dupe me!" responded the innkeeper. "As if I didn't know how many is five and where my shoe pinches! Don't think you can fool me, because, by God, I know what's what. Here you are trying to make me believe what happens in these good books is nothing more than nonsense and lies, when they're printed with the license of the Royal Council—as if those people would permit a bundle of lies to be printed with so many battles and enchantments, enough to drive you mad!"

"I've already told you," replied the priest, "that these are written to entertain us when we have idle moments. And so just as in well-ordered states we have games, such as chess and pocket billiards, to entertain those who have finished their day's work, or cannot work, in that same way they allow such books to be printed, believing—and it's the truth—that there is no one so ignorant as to think that any of them are true histories. And if this were the appro-

---

* The adventures described here didn't happen in *Cirongilio de Tracia*.

priate time, and if the present company were to demand it, I could expound on what romances of chivalry should contain to make them good, if they are to be of profit as well as pleasure. But I hope that the time will come when I can communicate this to someone who can do something about it; meanwhile, believe what I've told you, *señor* innkeeper, and take your books and try to resolve whether they're truth or lies, and much good may they do you, and may God forbid you to limp on the same foot as your guest don Quixote."

"Never that," responded the innkeeper. "I'll never be so crazy that I'd become a knight-errant, since I see that there aren't any now like there were in those days, when they say that these famous knights roamed the world."

In the middle of this conversation Sancho came in, and he became very puzzled and pensive when he heard that there were no longer any knights-errant, and that all the romances of chivalry were nonsense and lies; and he determined in his heart to wait and see how his master's expedition turned out, and if it didn't end as happily as he thought, he would leave him and go back to his wife and children and his regular work.

The innkeeper was about to take away the valise with the books when the priest said to him: "Wait a minute. I'd like to see that manuscript that's written in such a nice hand."

The innkeeper took it out and gave it to him to look at, and he saw that it was made up of two eight-folded sheets, handwritten,* and it bore a title written in large letters: "Novella of the Ill-Advised Curiosity."† The priest read three or four lines to himself and said: "The title of this novella doesn't seem bad, and I think I'd like to read it aloud."

To which the innkeeper said: "Your reverence can well read it. It has really entertained some guests who have read it here, and some have asked me for it, but I haven't given it

---

* These eight sheets were each folded in half, to make thirty-two pages in all.

† I use Ormsby's good version of the Spanish title. The word "novella" (short novel) is Italian, because the Italians developed this type of medium-length story.

away, because I planned to give this valise with these books and papers back to the person who left them behind, since it may be he'll come back sometime, and although I know I'd miss the books, I really should give everything back, because although I'm an innkeeper, I'm still a Christian."

"You're very right, my friend," said the priest, "but if the novella pleases me, you must let me copy it."

"With pleasure," responded the innkeeper.

While the two were talking, Cardenio had taken the novella and begun to read it, and having formed the same opinion of it as the priest, begged him to read it so that everyone could hear.

"I'll read it," said the priest, "if time were not better spent in sleeping than in reading."

"Passing the time hearing a story," said Dorotea, "will be sufficient rest for me, since my spirit is not so calm that it would let me sleep, even though I should."

"In that case," said the priest, "I'd like to read it, if only out of curiosity. Maybe it'll have something enjoyable in it."

Maese Nicolás went over to ask him to read it as well, and so did Sancho. When the priest saw this, and realizing that it would please everyone including himself, he said: "If that's the case, listen attentively. The novella begins like this:

Chapter XXXIII. Where the novella of the "Ill-Advised Curiosity" is related.

IN FLORENCE, a rich and celebrated city in Italy, in the province they call Tuscany, there lived Anselmo and Lotario, two rich and noble young men who were such close friends that they were nicknamed THE TWO FRIENDS by everyone. They were unmarried, young, and of the same age and upbringing, all of which was enough to account for the friendship between them. It's true that Anselmo was a bit more inclined to amorous pastimes than Lotario, who preferred the hunt. But on occasion Anselmo would give up his pleasures to accompany Lotario, and Lotario would do the same for Anselmo. And in this way their inclinations were so similar that no clock ran smoother.

Anselmo was desperately in love with a highborn and beautiful maiden of the same city, the daughter of very respected parents—she was as respected as they—and he resolved, having asked the opinion of Lotario, without whom he did nothing, to ask her parents for her hand in marriage. He thus decided to go ahead, and the person who delivered the message was Lotario. He handled the matter to the great pleasure of his friend, who in a short time found himself in possession of what he so wanted, and Camila was so glad to have gotten Anselmo for a husband that she gave unceasing thanks to heaven and to Lotario, through whom all this benefit had come to her.

The first days were merry, as all days of wedding festivities are, and Lotario continued to visit Anselmo's house as was his custom, striving to honor, regale, and gladden him in any way he could. But when the festivities were over, and the stream of visitors and well-wishers waned, Lotario began to decrease the number of visits to Anselmo's house on purpose, since it seemed to him—as it would to all men who were discreet—that one should not frequent the houses of married friends in the same way one used to when they were single, because, although good and true friendship cannot nor should not be suspect in anything, still, a married man's honor is so very fragile that it can be injured by his own brothers, not to mention friends.

Anselmo noticed Lotario's reluctance, and he complained to him bitterly, telling him that if he'd known that getting married would mean they wouldn't see each other as much as he was accustomed to, he wouldn't have gotten married. And if the good relationship they had had while he was single had attained for them the agreeable nickname of THE TWO FRIENDS, he should not allow such a famous and gratifying title to be lost without any reason except that of being circumspect. So he begged him—if the use of that word is appropriate between friends such as they were—to be master of his house once again, and to come and go as before, assuring him that Camila had no wish nor preference other than what he wanted her to have, and that since she knew what good friends they were, she was perplexed to see such aloofness in him.

To all these words and many others that Anselmo said to Lotario to persuade him to come to his house as he used to, Lotario responded with so much circumspection, discretion, and forewarning that Anselmo was quite satisfied about his friend's good intentions, and they agreed that two days a week, and on all holidays, Lotario would join them for dinner. Although they had agreed to this plan, Lotario planned to do no more than what he considered to be appropriate for the honor of his friend, whose good name meant more to him than his own. He said, and rightly so, that the married man to whom heaven had given a beautiful wife ought to be as careful about which friends he brought home as with which women his wife socializes, because those things that are not done or arranged for in the markets, churches, public festivals, or devotions— things husbands can't always deny their wives—are easily arranged for and managed in the home of a female friend or relative in whom she has most confidence.

Lotario also said that every married man needs to have a friend who will tell him about any negligent behavior that he might be guilty of, because it frequently happens that owing to the great love the husband has for his wife, either he doesn't caution her, or—so as not to vex her—doesn't tell her to do or not to do certain things, the doing or avoidance of which may be a matter of honor or censure to him; and errors of this kind can easily be corrected if advised by a friend. But where is a friend to be found who is so discreet and so loyal and true as Lotario was describing? I certainly don't know unless it was Lotario himself, because with great care and vigilance he looked after the honor of his friend, and tried to reduce, decrease, and cut short the agreed-upon days for visits to his house, so that it wouldn't appear suspicious to the idle public and to malicious and roaming eyes that a rich, young, and wellborn gentleman such as himself frequented the house of a woman as beautiful as Camila, and although his goodness and worth might make mischievous tongues hesitate, still, he didn't want to put either his friend's or his own reputation at risk, and for this reason most of the days agreed upon, he kept away, saying he had other business he pretended was unavoidable, so that much of their time was taken up by complaints on one side and excuses on the other.

It happened, however, that one day, as the two were strolling through a meadow outside the city, Anselmo said words like these to Lotario: "You probably think, Lotario my friend, that I cannot begin to thank God sufficiently for the favors He's done me in making me the son of such parents as mine were, and endowing me with abundant gifts of nature as well as those of wealth, and especially for the gift He gave me in making you my friend and Camila my wife, two treasures that I esteem, if not to the extent that I should, at least as much as I can. And yet with all these good things that are usually all that a man needs to live happily, I'm the most despairing and dissatisfied man in the whole world, because I've been troubled and harassed I don't know for how long by a desire that's so strange that I'm astonished at myself, and I blame and scold myself when I'm alone, and I try to repress and hide it from my own thoughts, with no better success than if I'd deliberately tried to tell it to the whole world. And since it's going to be revealed one way or another, I would prefer to entrust it to the secret archives of your heart, confident that if you know about it and use your cleverness as a true friend to help me, I'll soon be free from the distress it causes me, and through your diligence, my happiness will rise to the same level that my misery has reached through my folly."

Anselmo's words struck Lotario with astonishment, and he couldn't tell where that statement or preamble was leading, and although he mulled over what the desire might be that so bothered his friend, he was far from hitting the mark. To relieve himself of the anxiety caused by this suspense, he told Anselmo that he was doing a grave injustice to their great friendship by seeking a roundabout way of telling him his secret thoughts, since he was certain that he could count on his friend either for advice about how to alleviate his situation, or help to put his desire into effect.

"This is true," said Anselmo, "and with that to rely on, I want you to know, Lotario, my friend, that what's bothering me is I'm wondering if Camila, my wife, is as perfect as I think; and I cannot verify this truth unless I test her in such a way that it proves the purity of her virtue as fire proves that of gold. Because I believe, my friend, that a woman is virtuous only to the degree that she is or isn't tempted, and that she alone is strong who doesn't submit to promises, gifts, tears, and insistent requests by earnest lovers. What thanks," he said, "does a woman deserve if no one incites her to misbehave? So what if she's reserved and modest, if no opportunity is given to her to go astray and she knows that her husband will take her life upon her first shameless act? I therefore don't esteem in the same way the woman virtuous through fear or lack of opportunity as the one who comes out of temptation and pursuit with the crown of victory. So, for these reasons and for many others that I could tell you to justify and support the opinion I hold, I would like Camila, my wife, to pass through these trials and be refined by the fire of temptation and solicitation, and by a person able to carry out his design. And if she winds up with the palm branch from this battle, I shall consider my good fortune to be unequaled. I'll be able to say that the emptiness of my desires has been filled to the top. I'll be able to say that I've been lucky to find the virtuous woman that the wise man wondered could be found.* And if it works out the opposite of what I think, I'll at least have the satisfaction of knowing that I was right in my opinion, and I shall bear without grief what such a costly experiment will cause me. And since nothing that you can tell me will dissuade me in my desire, I want you, my friend Lotario, to prepare yourself to be the instrument to bring about my wish. I'll give you the opportunity to do it, including everything that I think necessary to woo a virtuous, honorable, modest, and unsuspecting woman.

"Among other reasons, I'm led to confide to you such a delicate affair because if Camila is conquered by you, the conquest will not be taken to the extreme limits, but rather, what is supposed to be done will be considered done, out of respect, and I shall thus be wronged no more than in intention, and my injury will be hidden by the virtue of your silence, and I know that everything that affects me will remain eternally as silent as death. So, if you want me to have a life worthy of the name, you must enter in this amorous battle, not in a lukewarm way, nor lazily, but rather with the energy and zeal that my desire requires and with the loyalty that your friendship assures me of."

These were the words that Anselmo said to Lotario, who

---

* The wise man is Solomon: "Who can find a virtuous woman? Her worth is far beyond rubies. Her husband's whole trust is in her" (Proverbs 31:10–11).

listened to them so carefully that he didn't open his mouth until Anselmo had stopped, and seeing that he was not going to say any more, after staring at him fixedly for a good while, as if he were examining something he'd never seen before that had caused him wonder and astonishment, he said: "I cannot persuade myself, Anselmo my friend, that what you've told me is anything more than a jest. If I really thought it to be the truth I wouldn't have allowed you to go on, because by not listening to you I would have prevented your long speech. I suspect that you don't know me or I don't know you. But no—I know that you're Anselmo and I'm Lotario. The trouble is that I think that you're not the Anselmo you used to be, because the words you've spoken are not those of my friend Anselmo, nor is what you ask me to do something you would ask of the Lotario that you know. Good friends ought to test and use their friends only as far, as the poet says, *usque ad aras*,* by which he meant that they shouldn't use their friendship for anything that might offend God. So, if a heathen felt this about friendship, how much more should a Christian who already knows that he should not for any human friendship forsake the divine. And when the friend goes to such extremes that he puts aside his duty to heaven to fulfill his duty as a friend, it should not be for trifles and inconsequential things, but rather for those that affect the life and honor of his friend. Now tell me, Anselmo, which of these two things threatens you so that I should risk myself in order to gratify you by doing such a detestable thing as you ask? Neither, to be sure. What you're asking me, rather, is to try to take away your honor and your life, and mine as well, because if I endeavor to take away your honor, it's very clear that I'm taking away your life, since a man without honor is worse than dead; and I, being the chosen instrument of so much wrong to you, won't I be just as dishonored and consequently as lifeless? Listen, Anselmo, my friend, and don't say anything until I finish saying what has occurred to me about what your request implies, because there will be time for you to respond and for me to listen."

"All right," said Anselmo, "tell me whatever you want."

And Lotario went on saying: "It seems to me, Anselmo,

---

* "As far as the altar," from *The Moralia of Plutarch*.

that your state of mind is just like the Moors', whom you cannot convince of the error of their religion by quoting Scripture, or by reasoning involving rational speculation, or by those founded on the articles of faith, but you have to bring in examples that are palpable, easy to understand, intelligible, able to be proven, with mathematical demonstrations that cannot be denied, as when you say: 'If equals are taken from equals, the remainders are equal.' And if they don't understand it through words—which in effect they don't—you must show them with your hands and place it before their eyes, and even with all of this, no one can finally persuade them of the truths of my sacred religion. I'll have to use this same procedure with you because your wish is so far from everything that has a shadow of reason to it that it seems to me that it would waste my time to try to make you see your simplemindedness, which for the time being deserves no other name, and I'm of a mind to leave you with your folly, as punishment for your wicked desire. But the friendship I have for you doesn't allow me to use these severe means with you, and this same friendship doesn't consent for me to leave you in such manifest peril of your own undoing.

"And so you can see clearly, tell me, Anselmo, didn't you say to me that I have to woo a modest woman, decoy one who is virtuous, make overtures to one who is unsuspecting, court one who is discreet? Yes, you told me all that. But if you know that you have a woman who is modest, virtuous, unsuspecting, and discreet, what more could you want? And if you believe that she'll come out victorious from all of my attacks, as she certainly will, what higher rank can you give her other than what she already has? Or in what way will she be better than she is now? Either you don't believe her to be what you say about her or you don't realize what you're asking. If you don't believe her to be what you say about her, why bother to test her—why not, if she's bad, do with her what you think best? But if she's as virtuous as you say, it's very ill-advised to make a trial of truth itself, since after the trial it will have the same appraisal as before. So, one must conclude that attempting to do things from which harm rather than profit must spring is irrational and reckless, and especially when you try to do things that you are neither forced nor obliged to do, which show from far away that attempting them is demonstrably foolish.

"Difficult things are attempted for the sake of God or for the secular world or for both. Those undertaken for the sake of God are those done by saints, trying to live the lives of angels in human bodies; those done for the world's sake are done by men who traverse bodies of water, suffer different climates, and meet many strange peoples to attain what are called blessings of Fortune. And those that are done for the sake of both together are those of valiant soldiers, who—as soon as they see a breach in the enemy's wall as wide as a cannonball can make, casting aside all fear, without reasoning or heeding the danger that threatens them, borne on the wings of the desire to battle for their faith, for their country, and for their king—catapult themselves intrepidly into the midst of a thousand different kinds of death that lurk in wait of them. These things are those that men typically attempt, and there is honor, glory, and profit in attempting them, even though they're laden with obstacles and dangers.

"But what you're saying you want to do will win neither the glory of God, the blessings of Fortune, nor fame among men, because, although things may turn out as you wish, you won't be any happier, richer, or more honored than you are now. And if it turns out differently, you'll be in greater misery than you can imagine, because it will do no good than to think that no one knows about the misfortune that will have befallen you—because just the fact that you know it yourself will be enough to torture and crush you. And to confirm this truth, I want to recite a stanza that the famous poet Luigi Tansillo* wrote at the end of the first part of his *Tears of St. Peter*, which goes like this:

The anguish and the shame in Peter's heart
    But greater grew as morning slowly came.
    No eye was there to see him, but the shame
    Of having sinned his conscience caused to smart.
    A noble breast will feel the pang of sin
    Though only heaven and earth have a part therein.†

---

* Luigi Tansillo (1510–1568) was an Italian poet who wrote *Le Lacrime di San Pietro*, translated into Spanish in 1587, seven years after its posthumous publication in Italy.
† This is Robinson Smith's good version.

"Thus, keeping it a secret you'll not relieve your grief, but rather you'll shed tears constantly, tears of blood from your heart, like those shed by the simple doctor whom our poet sings about, who performed the 'test of the goblet' that the prudent Rinaldo refused to do.* And although it's poetic fiction, it embraces a moral lesson worthy of being noted, understood, and imitated. Moreover, with what I plan to tell you now, you'll finally be led to understand the nature of the great error that you want to commit.

"Tell me, Anselmo, if heaven or good luck had made you the legitimate owner of a very fine diamond, the worth and purity of which satisfied all the gem cutters who saw it, and all of them in a single voice and of the same opinion stated that it was of the highest level of purity, quality, and fineness, and you yourself agreed, finding nothing to the contrary, would it be reasonable for you to take that diamond and put it between an anvil and a hammer and there, by dint of blows, prove it as hard and fine as they said? And if you did, and if the stone withstood such a foolish test, it would add nothing to its value or renown, but if it got smashed into pieces, which could easily happen, wouldn't everything be lost? Yes, certainly, and it would make its owner look like a fool. Anselmo, my friend, consider that Camila is a very fine diamond, in your estimation, as well as in that of others, and that it's contrary to all reason to take the risk that she'll break, since although she might remain intact, she can't rise to a higher value than she now has, whereas if she fails and doesn't resist, just consider now how you'll be deprived of her, and with what good reason you would have to complain about yourself for having been the cause of her ruination and of your own.

"Remember that there is no jewel in the world worth more than a chaste and honored woman, and that the honor of women consists of the good opinion in which they're held, and since your wife is such that she reaches the extreme of goodness, why do you want to put this truth

---

* This "test of the goblet" also comes from *Orlando Furioso*, canto 43. ("Our" poet is thus the Italian Ariosto.) In this story, there is an enchanted goblet from which no deceived husband has the power to drink. When it's presented to Rinaldo, he does not take the test.

in question? Look, my friend, a woman is an imperfect creature, and one shouldn't put impediments in her path to make her stumble and fall, but rather they should be removed and the path made clear of any obstacle, so that without hindrance she may endeavor to run her course to try to attain the desired perfection, which consists of being virtuous.

"Naturalists tell us that the ermine is an animal that has very white fur, and that when hunters want to capture one, they use this device: Knowing the path the ermines usually take, they cover it with mud, and then they shoo and drive them toward that place, and as soon as the ermine arrives at the mud, it stops and lets itself be captured rather than going through the mud and dirtying its whiteness, which it holds in greater esteem than its freedom or its life. The virtuous and chaste woman is an ermine, and her chastity is whiter and purer than driven snow. The person who wants her not to lose it, but rather to keep and conserve it, must not treat her like the hunted ermine—he shouldn't place before her the mire of gifts and wooing of importunate lovers, because perhaps—and even without perhaps—she may not have enough natural virtue and strength that she can, all by herself, overcome and avoid these impediments, which have to be taken away and replaced by the purity of virtue and beauty, because a good reputation embraces these qualities.

"The good woman is also like a mirror of clear and shining crystal, but is subject to being tarnished and dulled by every breath that touches it. Chaste women should be treated like relics—adored but not touched. The good woman should be kept and esteemed in the same way one keeps and esteems a garden filled with flowers and roses, whose owner doesn't allow anyone to traipse through it or touch the blooms. It's enough that, from a distance and through the iron grating, its fragrance and beauty are enjoyed. Finally, I want to recite some verses to you that have just come to mind, which I heard in a modern play, and which it seems to me apply to what we're talking about. A prudent old man was giving advice to another, the father of a maiden, to lock her up, watch over her, and keep her secluded, and among other arguments, he used these:

Woman is a thing of glass
 Who would test her is an ass.
 'Tis an easy thing to shatter,
 Mending is another matter.
Breaking is an easy matter,
 And it's folly to expose
 What you cannot mend to blows;
 What you can't make whole to shatter.
This, then, all may hold as true,
 And the reason's plain to see;
 For if Danäes* there be,
 There are golden showers too.†

"Everything I've said up to now, Anselmo, has been what has to do with you, and now I should say something that regards me, and if I'm long-winded, pardon me, because the labyrinth that you've entered and from which you want me to extricate you requires it. You want me as a friend and yet you want to take away my honor, something that is contrary to friendship; and in addition to that, you also are trying to fix it so I'll take away *your* honor. That you want to take away my honor is obvious, since when Camila sees me trying to woo her as you ask, it's certain she'll take me for a man without honor, since I'd be trying to do something very contrary to what I am and what your friendship demands. That you want me to take away your own honor, there is no doubt, because when Camila sees that I'm trying to woo her, she'll think that I've found something frivolous in her that makes me bold enough to reveal my base desire to her, and since she'll consider herself dishonored, her dishonor will reflect on you. And from there arises what commonly happens: The husband whose wife is adulterous—even though he knows nothing about it, nor has he given any reason to be unfaithful, nor has it been in his power to prevent his humiliation by care and

---

* Danäe was imprisoned in a tower because an oracle said that her son would cause her father's death. Zeus visited her in the form of a golden shower and she became the mother of Perseus (who, by the way, later did cause his grandfather's death).
† I use Robinson Smith's translation for the first four lines and Ormsby's for the remainder.

prudence—people will still consider him reproachful and vile, and to a certain extent he's looked upon by those who know of his wife's guilt with eyes of contempt rather than compassion, even though they see his misfortune is not his fault, but rather due to the sin of his guilty wife.

"But I'll tell you why with good reason the husband of the bad woman is dishonored, even though he doesn't know that she's bad nor is he to blame, nor has had anything to do with it, nor has given any cause for her bad behavior. And don't get tired of listening, because everything I say will be to your advantage. When God created our first father in the earthly paradise, Holy Scripture says that God made Adam go to sleep and He took a rib from his left side from which He made our mother Eve. And as soon as Adam woke up and saw her, he said: 'This is flesh of my flesh and bone of my bones.' And God said: 'For this woman a man will leave his father and mother, and the two will be the same flesh.' And then the divine sacrament of marriage was instituted, with such ties that only death can undo. This miraculous sacrament has such force and power that it makes two different persons to be of the same flesh. And more so in the case of those who are happily married, because even though they have two souls, they have only one will. So it follows that since the flesh of the wife is the same as that of her husband, any disgraces that come to her, of the injuries that she procured for herself, fall upon the flesh of the husband, even though he, as has been said, has given no cause for the wickedness. As the pain of the foot or of any other part of the human body is felt by the whole body, because it's all one flesh, and the head feels the pain in the ankle without having caused it, so the husband is a participant in the dishonor of the wife, since he's one with her. And since all worldly honors and dishonors derive from and are born of flesh and blood, as those of the adulterous woman are, the husband will share in them and is considered dishonored, even though he's not aware of it.

"So, beware, Anselmo, of the danger in which you're putting yourself by wanting to disturb the peaceful life of your wife. Consider how on account of this futile and ill-advised curiosity you want to rouse the passions that now lie dormant in the heart of your chaste wife. Be advised that you cannot gain very much but you can lose so much that I'll leave it unexpressed, not having the right words to describe it. But if everything I've said is insufficient to turn you away from your vile purpose, you can try to find another means for your dishonor and misfortune, because I'll not consent to it, though I risk losing your friendship, which is the greatest loss I can imagine."

After he said this, the virtuous and wise Lotario stopped talking, and Anselmo was so troubled and deep in thought that for a good while he couldn't say a single word, but he finally said: "You've seen how carefully I've listened to everything you've tried to tell me, Lotario, my friend, and through your words, examples, and comparisons I've seen the great intelligence you have and the extent your true friendship has attained, and I see and confess as well that if I don't follow your advice and I do what I want to, I'm fleeing from what's good and am chasing after what's bad. Having said this, you must consider that I'm suffering from a sickness some women have, where their craving causes them to eat dirt, plaster, coal, and other worse things, revolting to look at, and much more so to eat. Help me to be cured, and this can be easily done if only you would just *begin* to court Camila, even in a lukewarm and feigned way. She won't be so frail as to surrender her virtue at the first encounter, and with this beginning I'll be content, and you'll have done what our friendship calls for, not only restoring my life, but convincing me my honor is intact. You're obliged to do this for just one reason, and that is since I'm as determined as I am to do this test, you mustn't allow me to tell my folly to someone else, because that would risk the honor that you're striving for me not to lose, and if your honor should suffer in the opinion of Camila while you're courting her, it matters little or not at all, since very soon, when you see in her the integrity we expect, you'll be able to tell her the pure truth about our stratagem, so she can recover her former high esteem of you. And since you're venturing so little and you can make me so happy by initiating it, don't refuse to do it, even though further difficulties present themselves, since, as I told you, just by initiating it, I'll consider the whole thing concluded."

When Lotario saw the determination of Anselmo, and not knowing what other examples to tell him so he wouldn't follow through, and seeing that he threatened to confide his damaging scheme to another person, in order to avoid a greater injury he resolved to gratify him and do what he asked, intending to guide the affair so as to satisfy Anselmo without corrupting the mind of Camila. So he told him not to communicate his thought to anyone else, and that he would undertake the task himself, and would begin as soon as Anselmo pleased. Anselmo embraced him warmly and affectionately, and thanked him for his offer, as if he'd done him an enormous favor. The two agreed that the very next day they would begin the undertaking, and that Anselmo would give Lotario time and opportunity so he could speak alone with Camila, and he would also give him money and jewelry to give to her. He also suggested to him that he provide music for her and that he write verses in her praise— and if Lotario didn't want to take the trouble to write them, Anselmo would compose them himself. Lotario agreed to everything, but with a much different intention from what Anselmo supposed.

And with this understanding, they returned to Anselmo's house, where they found Camila anxious and fretful, awaiting her husband, who arrived later than usual. Lotario returned to his house, and Anselmo remained at home, as contented in his mind as Lotario was troubled in his, not knowing what plan he could use to get out of that ill-advised business unscathed. But that night he thought of a way he could deceive Anselmo without offending Camila. And the next day he went to eat dinner with his friend, and was welcomed by Camila, who treated him very cordially, since she understood that was what her husband wanted.

When dinner was finished and the tablecloth removed, Anselmo told Lotario he should stay with Camila while he attended to some pressing matter, and he would return in an hour and a half. Camila begged him not to go, and Lotario volunteered to go with him, but it was of no avail with Anselmo, who insisted that he stay and wait for him, since he had a very important matter to discuss with him. He also told Camila not to leave Lotario alone until he came back. In short, he pretended the need (or foolishness) of his absence so well that no one could tell it was just invented. Anselmo went away, and Camila and Lotario stayed at the table, since the household staff had gone off to eat. Lotario

found himself on the point of this duel, as his friend had
wanted, and, facing an opponent that by her beauty alone
could conquer a squadron of knights in full armor, you can
see he had good reason to be afraid.

But what he did was just to put his elbow on the arm
of the chair and his open hand on his cheek, and, asking
Camila's pardon for his bad manners, said he wanted to
have a rest while he waited for Anselmo to return. Camila
told him that he'd rest better in the drawing room than on
the chair, and begged him to go in and sleep there. Lotario
refused, and there he remained asleep until Anselmo returned, who, finding Camila in her room and Lotario sleeping, thought that, since he'd delayed so long, there would
have been time for the two of them to talk and for Lotario
to have a rest, and he could hardly wait for Lotario to wake
up so that he could accompany him home and talk about
his undertaking.

Everything turned out as Anselmo wanted. Lotario woke
up and the two left the house, and Anselmo asked him what
he was anxious to find out, and Lotario responded that it
seemed to him that he shouldn't reveal everything the first
time, so he just praised Camila for her beauty, telling her
that in the city people talked of nothing but her beauty and
intelligence, and this seemed to him to be a good way to get
in her good graces and make her willing to listen to him the
next time, thus using the trick the devil uses when he wants
to deceive someone who is already wary about looking out
for himself, changing himself from the angel of darkness
into the angel of light, and putting forth a good appearance, so that when he finally reveals who he is, he gets his
way, if his deceit is not found out at the beginning. All this
pleased Anselmo, and he told Lotario that he would give
him the same opportunity every day, although he wouldn't
leave the house, because in it he would find things to do so
Camila wouldn't come to know his deception.

It happened, then, that many days went by and Lotario,
without uttering a single word to Camila, responded to
Anselmo that he'd talked with her but had never been able
to draw the slightest indication of any dishonorable intention, not even a sign of the shadow of hope. On the contrary, he said that she threatened him that if he didn't cease
his sinful idea, she would be forced to tell her husband.

"So far, so good," said Anselmo. "Up to now Camila has resisted your words, so we need to show how she resists actions. Tomorrow I'll give you two thousand *escudos* in gold to offer her, and even to give her, and an equal amount so you can buy jewelry to excite her passion—for women, no matter how chaste they are, if they're pretty, they're fond of dressing well and being fashionable. And if she resists this temptation, I'll be satisfied, and I won't bother you anymore."

Lotario responded that since he'd begun it, he would carry through, although he thought he would come out of it weary and exhausted. The next day he got the four thousand *escudos*, and with them four hundred thousand perplexities, because he didn't know how to lie once again, but he finally resolved to tell him that Camila was as firm against gifts as she was against words, and there was no further reason to bother any more, for all this time was spent in vain.

But Fortune guided matters differently and arranged it so that once Anselmo left Lotario and Camila alone, as on other occasions, he locked himself in a room, and stayed there looking and listening to what went on between them through the keyhole, and he saw that for more than half an hour Lotario didn't say a word to Camila, nor would he have uttered a word if he'd stayed there half a century. Anselmo then concluded that everything his friend had told him about the answers of Camila was fabrication and lies. And to find out if this was the case, he left the room, called Lotario over, and asked what news there was and what Camila's disposition was. Lotario responded that he didn't want to persist any more in that affair because she reacted so sharply and bitterly, that he had no heart to say anything else to her.

"Ah!" said Anselmo, "Lotario, Lotario, you've not fulfilled your part of the bargain, even though I put all my trust in you. I was looking at you through the keyhole and I saw that you didn't say a word to Camila, which makes me believe that you haven't told her anything yet, and if this is the case—which it must be—why are you deceiving me? Or, why do you want to deprive me of the means I would use to satisfy my longing?"

Anselmo said no more, but what he'd already said was enough to fill Lotario with shame and confusion, and taking his being caught in a lie as a point of honor, he swore to Anselmo that from that moment, he would take upon himself to satisfy him without further deception, as he would see if he chose to spy on them again; but it wouldn't be necessary to take the trouble, because what he planned to do to satisfy him would remove all suspicion. Anselmo believed him, and to give him an opportunity that was more secure and free of interruption, he resolved to be absent from his house for a week by going to a friend's house in a village not far from the city. He arranged for his friend to send for him urgently so that he would have an excuse for his departure.

Unhappy, shortsighted Anselmo! What are you doing? What are you planning? What are you engineering? Watch out what you're doing to yourself, plotting your own dishonor and devising your own ruination. Your wife, Camila, is good and you possess her in peace and quiet—no one tampers with your happiness; her thoughts don't leave the walls of your house; you're her heaven on earth, the object of her wishes, the fulfillment of her desires, and the yardstick by which she measures her will, adjusting it to your own and to that of heaven. So if the mine of her honor, beauty, virtue, and modesty gives to you, without toil, all the wealth it has, and all you could want, why do you want to dig farther into the earth and look for new veins and unseen treasure, risking the collapse of it all, because it rests on the feeble supports of its weak nature? Think for a moment that he who looks for what is impossible may be justly denied what *is* possible, as a poet better expressed it, saying:

In death life is my quest,
> In infirmity I long for health,
> And in jail freedom seems the best:
> I plan to shed my chains by stealth,
> And in a traitor to place my trust.

Alas, my envious destiny,
> Which hitherto has frowned on me,
> Has with heaven now decreed
> That possible things I shall be denied
> Since for the impossible I've cried.*

---

* I use Starkie's translation here.

Anselmo went to the village, leaving instructions with Camila that the whole time he was to be away Lotario was to come to look after the house and to eat dinner with her, and that she should be careful to treat him as she would himself. The order that her husband left with her distressed her, as a respectable and honored woman, and she told him he should remember it was not proper, when he was not present, for anyone else to occupy his chair at dinner, and if he was doing it for lack of confidence that she would be able to manage his house, he should let her try this time, and he would see that she was up to greater responsibilities. Anselmo replied it was his pleasure to have it so, and she had only to submit and obey. Camila said she would do it, but against her will.

Anselmo went away, and the next day Lotario came to his house, where he was received by Camila with a warm and modest welcome. She never put herself in a position where Lotario saw her alone because she was always surrounded by her male and female servants, especially a handmaid of hers named Leonela, to whom she was greatly attached because they had grown up together in the home of Camila's parents, and when she married Anselmo, she brought her along. In the first three days Lotario didn't say anything to her, although he easily could have when the tablecloth was removed and the servants went off to eat their dinner as quickly as they could, because those were Camila's orders. And Leonela was told to eat before Camila did, and never leave her side, but the girl had her own thoughts and ideas, and needed those hours and that opportunity for her own pleasure, and didn't always obey her mistress' commands. Sometimes she left them alone, as if they had ordered her to do so. But the virtuous presence of Camila, the seriousness in her face, the composure of her person were such that they restrained Lotario's tongue. But the influence that the many virtues of Camila exerted in imposing silence on Lotario's tongue proved mischievous for them both, because if his tongue was silent, his thoughts roamed, and he had the opportunity to contemplate, part by part, the perfections of goodness and beauty that Camila had, enough to cause a marble statue to fall in love with her, much less a heart of flesh and blood.

Lotario looked at her when he was speaking to her and

he considered how worthy she was of being loved, and this consideration began to chip away at the allegiance he owed Anselmo. A thousand times he wanted to leave the city so Anselmo would never see him again and he would equally not see Camila, but the pleasure he got by looking at her made him hesitate and held him fast. He struggled and fought with himself to get rid of and repress the enjoyment he got by contemplating her. When he was alone, he blamed himself for his foolishness, he called himself a bad friend, and even a bad Christian. He argued the matter and compared himself with Anselmo, always concluding that the folly and rashness of Anselmo were greater than his own infidelity, and if he only had an excuse before God as well as men for what he intended to do, he wouldn't fear punishment for his offense.

In short, the beauty and goodness of Camila, together with the opportunity the stupid husband had placed in his hands, overthrew Lotario's loyalty, and without caring about anything else except the pleasure to which his inclinations were leading him, at the end of three days of Anselmo's absence, in which he was in a continual battle to resist his temptations, he began to woo Camila with so much intensity and with such loving words that Camila was stunned, and could only rise from her place and go into her room without answering a word. But his hopes were not diminished by her abruptness, because hope is always borne with love, and he only prized her more. She, having seen in Lotario what she never would have suspected, didn't know what to do. And since she thought it wouldn't be safe or seemly to give him another opportunity to speak to her, she resolved to send a servant of hers that very night with a message for Anselmo, and it began with these words:

Chapter XXXIIII. Wherein the novella of the "Ill-Advised Curiosity" continues.

> JUST AS it's commonly said that the army
> without its general and the castle without its
> warden look bad, I say that a young married
> woman seems even worse off without her
> husband, unless there are very pressing reasons
> for him to be away. I'm in such a bad plight
> without you and helpless to weather your
> absence, that if you don't come back quickly,
> I'll have to return to my parents' house, even
> though I will have to leave yours unprotected,
> because the sentry you left me, if I can call
> him that, I think is more interested in his own
> pleasure than what concerns you, and since you
> are discreet, I don't have to say any more, nor is
> it a good idea to.

ANSELMO RECEIVED this letter and understood by it that
Lotario had already begun his undertaking and that
Camila must have been responding as he'd hoped. Delighted beyond measure at this news, he responded to
Camila by messenger that she should not leave his house,
since he would be back soon. Camila was astonished at
Anselmo's response, which made her even more confused
than before, because she didn't dare stay at home, nor go
to her parents' house, because if she stayed, her virtue was
in danger, and if she left, she transgressed her husband's
command.

Finally she resolved to do what was worse for her, which
was to stay at home, determined to flee from Lotario's
presence so as not to give occasion for her servants to gossip, and it already grieved her for having written what she'd
written to her husband, fearful that he would think that Lotario had seen some brazenness in her that moved him to
cast aside the respect that he owed her. But relying on her
goodness, she put her trust in God and her own good intentions, and planned to resist in silence everything that Lotario might want to tell her, without sending further word

to her husband, so as not to involve him in any quarrel or trouble.

She even thought of ways to excuse Lotario when Anselmo asked what had moved her to write that letter. With these thoughts, more honorable than logical or effective, the following day she was listening to Lotario, who pressed his suit so effectively that Camila's resolve began to waver, and her virtue had enough to do to come to the aid of her eyes, so that she would give no sign of any loving compassion that the tears and words of Lotario had awakened in her heart. Lotario was aware of all this and it inflamed him all the more.

Finally, he felt he needed, in the time and opportunity left to him by Anselmo's absence, to lay siege to that fortress. So he assailed her with praise of her beauty, because nothing will overcome and subdue towers of vanity of beautiful women than vanity itself, placed on the tongue of flattery. Indeed, with all diligence he tunneled through the rock of her integrity with such explosives that even if she'd been made entirely of brass, she would have fallen. Lotario wept, begged, promised, flattered, persisted, and feigned with so much feeling and with such earnestness that he overthrew Camila's chastity and came to triumph over what he least expected and most desired.

Camila surrendered, Camila yielded; and no wonder, if Lotario's friendship couldn't stand firm! A clear proof for us that the only way to conquer the passion of love is to flee from it, and no one should grapple with such a powerful enemy, because divine force is needed to vanquish the power of love. Only Leonela knew of her mistress' weakness, because the two bad friends and new lovers couldn't hide it from her. Lotario didn't want to tell Camila about Anselmo's scheme or that Anselmo had given him the opportunity to accomplish that outcome, so that she would hold his love in less esteem, and think it was by chance and without intention, and not on purpose that he'd courted her.

A few days later, Anselmo came back to his house and he didn't notice what was missing—the thing he treated so lightly and prized the most. He went immediately to see Lotario and found him in his house. The two embraced, and Anselmo asked for the news of his life or his death.

"The news I can give you, Anselmo," said Lotario, "is

that you have a wife who deservedly can be the example and crown of all good women. The words I told her were borne off by the air; the promises were disdained; the gifts were not accepted; at my feigned tears she jested openly. In short, just as Camila is the emblem of all beauty, she's also the archive where purity dwells, where courtesy and modesty and all the virtues that can make an honest woman praiseworthy and fortunate reside. Take your money back, my friend. I have it here without having needed to touch it, because Camila's integrity does not surrender to things as low as gifts and promises. Be content, Anselmo, and don't seek further proof. Since you've sailed through the sea of difficulties and suspicions that may be—and commonly are—held regarding women, without getting wet, don't seek to plunge once again into the deep sea of new obstacles, nor try another experiment with a new navigator to test the goodness and strength of the ship that heaven has given you for your voyage across the sea of this world, but rather you should realize you're in a safe harbor, and you should moor yourself with the anchors of sound reflection, and live in peace until they come to collect the debt no human nobility can forgive you from paying."

Anselmo was very happy with Lotario's words and believed them as if they had been said by an oracle. Nevertheless, he begged Lotario not to give up the undertaking, even if just for curiosity and pastime, though he need not be as zealous as before. He only wanted Lotario to write some verses in her praise, using the name of Clori, and that Anselmo himself would give her to understand that Lotario was in love with a woman to whom he'd given that name so that he could celebrate her with the decorum her honor demanded. And if Lotario didn't want to write those verses, he would write them himself.

"That won't be necessary," said Lotario, "since the Muses are not such enemies of mine that they don't visit me at times during the year. Tell Camila what you've said about pretended love, and I'll write the poems, and if they aren't as good as their subject deserves, they'll be at least as good as I can make them."

Thus the ill-advised one and his treacherous friend agreed, and Anselmo went home and asked Camila what she was astonished he hadn't asked before—which was what had given her the occasion to write the letter that she had sent. Camila answered that it had seemed to her that Lotario was looking at her a little more freely than when Anselmo was at home, but now she realized that it was just her imagination, because Lotario now was avoiding seeing her and being alone with her. Anselmo told her that she could rest easy on that suspicion because he knew that Lotario was in love with a noble maiden in that city, whom he celebrated under the name Clori, and that even if he weren't in love, she had no reason to doubt Lotario's loyalty and the great friendship he held for both of them. And if Camila had not been previously apprised by Lotario that the love for Clori was only pretended, and he'd told it to Anselmo so he could spend some time writing praises about Camila, she doubtless would have fallen into the despairing net of jealousy; but since she had been forewarned, that possible fright caused her no grief.

The next day, when the three were at dinner, Anselmo asked Lotario to recite something that he'd composed for his beloved Clori; since Camila didn't know her, he could certainly say whatever he wanted. "Even if she knew her," responded Lotario, "I wouldn't hide anything, because when a lover praises the beauty of his lady and calls her cruel, he casts no reproach on her and her good name, and he can surely say whatever he wants. But be that as it may, all I can say is that yesterday I wrote a sonnet about the ingratitude of this Clori that goes like this:"

SONNET

At midnight, in the silence, when the eyes
> Of happier mortals balmy slumbers close,
> The weary tale of my unnumbered woes
> To Clori and to Heaven is wont to rise.
And when the light of day returning dyes
> The portals of the east with tints of rose,
> With undiminished force my sorrow flows
> In broken accents and in burning sighs.
And when the sun ascends his star-girt throne,
> And on the earth pours down his midday beams,
> Noon but renews my wailing and my tears;
And with the night again goes up my moan.

Yet ever in my agony it seems
To me that neither Heaven nor Clori hears.*

    This sonnet pleased Camila, but more so Anselmo, and he praised it and said that the lady was too cruel if she didn't respond to such manifest sincerity, to which Camila said: "Then is everything true that poets who are in love say?"

    "As poets, they don't tell the truth," responded Lotario, "but as lovers they're not always able to express what they mean."

    "There is no doubt about that," replied Anselmo, eager to support Lotario's thoughts with Camila, who was as unaware of his plan as she was in love with Lotario. So, with the pleasure that she derived from anything of his, and more so knowing that his desires and poems were directed to her, and that she was the real Clori, she asked him if he had another sonnet or some other verses that he could recite.

    "Yes, I have," responded Lotario, "but I don't think it's as good as the first one, or, I should say, less bad. But you can judge for yourself. Here it is:

SONNET

I know that I am doomed; death is to me
  As certain as that thou, ungrateful fair,
    Dead at thy feet shouldst see me lying, ere
    My heart repented of its love for thee.
If buried in oblivion I should be,
    Bereft of life, fame, favor, even there.
  It would be found that I thy image bear
  Deep graven in my breast for all to see.
This like some holy relic do I prize
  To save me from the fate my truth entails,
    Truth that to thy hard heart its vigor owes.
Alas for him that under lowering skies,
  In peril o'er a trackless ocean sails,
  Where neither friendly port nor pole-star shows.

---

* Both this sonnet and the next one are Ormsby's translations. This one is of interest to Cervantists since it was also used in one of Cervantes' plays, beginning the third act of *La casa de los celos*.

Anselmo praised this second sonnet as he had the first, and in this way he added one link after another to the chain with which he bound and fettered his dishonor, and when Lotario dishonored him the most, Anselmo told him he was most honored. And thus each step that Camila descended toward the center of her infamy, she was ascending—in the opinion of her husband—toward the summit of virtue and good reputation.

It happened that on one occasion, when Camila was with her maid, she said to her: "I'm ashamed to think, Leonela, my friend, how little regard I have for myself, since I didn't force Lotario to wait longer in taking entire possession of what I gave him so quickly of my free will. I'm afraid that he'll consider my swiftness only, without reflecting on the pressure he used on me so that I couldn't resist him."

"Don't let this bother you, *señora mía*," responded Leonela, "for it's of no importance, nor does it diminish the preciousness of a gift to give it quickly, if what is given is valuable. And they even say that 'he who gives quickly gives twice.'"

"They also say," said Camila, "that 'what costs little is little valued.'"

"That saying doesn't apply to you," responded Leonela, "because love, the way I hear it, sometimes flies in and sometimes walks; with this one it runs and with that one it dawdles; it tempers the passions in some; it wounds others; and still others it slays. At one and the same time it might begin its race of passions and in that same moment might end and finish it. In the morning it will lay siege to a fortress and in the evening it will have taken it, because there is no force that can resist it. And since that's so, what's so surprising? What do you fear? The same thing happened to Lotario, since love took the absence of my master as the instrument of our defeat. And it was necessary that during his absence what love had ordained should be concluded, without allowing time for Anselmo to come back, and cut the affair short by his arrival. Love has no better agent to carry out what it wants than opportunity, and it makes use of opportunity in all of its endeavors, especially at their beginning. I know all of this very well, more from experience than hearsay. And one day I'll tell you about it, *señora*, because I also am young and made of flesh and blood.

Moreover, *señora* Camila, you didn't surrender so quickly that you first didn't see Lotario's whole soul in his eyes and sighs, and in his words, promises, and gifts, and seeing in his soul and in his virtues how worthy Lotario was to be loved. So, if this is true, don't let these overcritical and prudish thoughts trouble your affections, but rather rest assured that Lotario prizes you as you prize him, and he lives content and satisfied that since you fell into the amorous snare, he who caught you is of worth and honor, and he not only has the four Ss* that they say good lovers must possess, but a whole alphabet. Just listen to me and you'll see while I repeat it by heart. He is, the way I see it and the way it seems to me: 'Amiable, Brave, Courteous, Distinguished, Eager, Faithful, Gay, Honorable, Illustrious, Kind, Loyal, Manly, Noble, Open, Polite, Quick, Rich—you already know the Ss— then Tender, valiant, and warm. The X doesn't fit because it's so harsh; the Y has already been given; and the Z, zealous of your honor.' "†

Camila laughed at her maid's alphabet, and took her for more practiced in things relating to love than she'd said. In fact, she confessed as much, revealing to Camila that she was having an affair with a wellborn young man of that city. This troubled Camila, fearing this might cause her to risk her own honor. She implored her to say if their relationship had gone beyond words. Without shame and with much brazenness, she responded that they had, because it's certain that the transgressions of mistresses make servants shameless, and they, when they see their mistresses make a false step, think nothing of slipping themselves, nor do they care if it's known.

Camila could only beg Leonela not to say anything about her (Camila's) affair to the man she said was her lover, and to keep her own dealings secret, so that neither Anselmo nor Lotario would find out about them. Leonela answered that she would do it. But she kept her word in

---

* These four Ss were *sabio, solo, solicito, secreto*: "wise," "faithful," "solicitous," and "discreet/secretive."

† The letters Y and I were interchangeable, as were the X and J, and the U and V, accounting for no entries beginning with Y or U. I've used Robinson Smith's alphabet, in which he's adapted the original to make it come out in alphabetical order.

such a way that she confirmed Camila's fear that she would lose her reputation because of her maid. For this immodest and daring Leonela, after she saw that her mistress was doing things she hadn't done before, had the audacity to take her own lover inside the house, confident that, even though her mistress might see him, she wouldn't risk betraying him.

This is just one of the ways harm comes to mistresses because of their sins, because they become slaves of their own servants and are forced to conceal their maids' bawdiness and depravity, as happened to Camila, who, although once, and even many times, she saw that Leonela was with her lover in one of the rooms of the house, not only didn't she dare scold her, but she gave her opportunities to conceal him, and she removed all impediments so that he wouldn't be seen by her husband.

But she was unable to prevent him from being seen leaving once, at daybreak. At first Lotario, not knowing who he was, thought he was a phantom. But when he saw him walk away, covering his face with his cape and concealing himself carefully and cautiously, as well as he could, he went from one foolish thought to another, which would have brought the ruination of everyone if Camila hadn't found a remedy. It didn't occur to Lotario that the man whom he'd seen leave Anselmo's house at such an odd hour could have entered at Leonela's bidding, nor did he even remember that there was a Leonela. What he thought was that Camila, in the same way she'd been free and easy with him, was doing the same thing with another—such are the consequences brought about by the actions of a bad woman, because she's even mistrusted by him whose begging and persuasion has caused her to fall, and he easily believes that she gives herself to others, and believes that every trivial suspicion that enters his mind is the absolute truth.

It would seem that Lotario instantly forgot his good judgment, and all his prudent maxims escaped his memory, for, without stopping to use his reasoning, without further ado, before Anselmo woke up, impatient and blind with jealous rage, with his entrails gnawing at him, and dying to take vengeance on Camila—who had not offended him in any way—he went to Anselmo and said: "You know, Anselmo, that for many days I've been struggling with myself, trying not to tell you what it's now not possible for me to conceal. I want you to know that the fortress of Camila has surrendered to me and she'll do whatever I want her to, and if I've delayed in telling you this truth, it has been because I wanted to see if it was just a little caprice of hers, or if she was doing it to try to test me and to see if my wooing—carried out with your permission—was done in earnest. I also believed that—if she were what she should be and what we both thought she was—she would have already told you of my suit. But since I saw that she was delaying, I see that the promise she made me that—when you're away from the house again—she'll speak to me in the bedroom where your jewels are," and it's true because Camila used to speak to him there. "But I don't want you to take precipitous vengeance, since no sin has been committed yet except in thought, and it may be that she'll change her mind before that time comes, and she'll show repentance. So, since you've taken my advice in whole or in part up to now, follow and take the advice I'll give you now so that you can, with trust and confidence, satisfy yourself in this matter in whatever way you want. Pretend to go away for two or three days, as you have on other occasions, and arrange it so that you can hide in your bedroom, since there are tapestries there and other things that can conceal you, and then you'll be able to see with your own eyes, and I with mine, what Camila wants. And if it's something bad, which is more to be feared than expected, in silence, caution, and discretion, you can be the avenger of the wrong."

Anselmo was amazed, confounded, and stupefied when he heard what Lotario had to say, because it came to him when he least expected it, since he thought Camila was victorious over the feigned assaults by Lotario, and he was beginning to enjoy the glory of her victory. He remained silent for a good while, looking at the floor, and not moving even an eyelash, and then he said: "Lotario, you've acted as I expected of your friendship and I'll follow your every suggestion. Do what you must, and keep the secret as you see it should be kept in such unexpected circumstances."

Lotario promised to do so, and as soon as he left, he repented entirely for everything he'd said, seeing how foolish he'd been, since he could have taken vengeance on Camila himself in a less cruel and dishonorable way. He cursed his senselessness, condemned his hasty resolve, and didn't know what course to take to undo what he'd done, or find some reasonable way out. He finally thought he would tell Camila everything; and since there was no lack of opportunity to do it, that same day he found her alone, and as soon as she saw him, she said: "I want you to know, Lotario, my friend, that I'm grieved in my heart, and it bothers me so much that I feel that my heart will burst, and it's a wonder it hasn't already. The audacity of Leonela has reached such a point that every night she lets a beau of hers into this house, and she's with him until daybreak, at the expense of my reputation, since whoever sees him leave my house at such an unusual time will be free to make his own judgment about the situation. And what bothers me is that I can't punish or scold her. Since she's the guardian of the secret of our relationship, it has put a muzzle on my tongue about her own affair, and I fear that something bad is going to come of it."

When Camila began saying this, Lotario thought it was just a trick to fool him into thinking that the man he'd seen leaving was Leonela's lover and not her own. But when he saw how she wept and suffered, and asked him what to do, he came to see the truth, and wound up confused and filled with remorse about everything. He told Camila not to worry, that he would find a way to stop Leonela's insolence. He also told her what, driven by the unbridled rage of jealousy, he'd told Anselmo, and about the arrangement for Anselmo to hide in the bedroom to see plainly how unfaithful she was to him. He asked her to pardon him for this madness, and for advice as to how to remedy it and get out of such an intricate labyrinth that his bad conduct had placed him in.

Camila was alarmed by what Lotario was telling her, and with great anger and many just rebukes she reproached and reprimanded him for his uncalled-for suspicion and the simple and mischievous scheme he'd come up with. But since a woman has by nature a quicker mind for both good and bad things than a man does, although it fails them when they set about to reason deliberately, at that very instant, Camila found a way to remedy that seemingly irremediable affair, and she told Lotario to have Anselmo hide the very next day where he said, because she planned to take from his being hidden the means by which the two of them could enjoy each other from then on without any fear. And without revealing all her thoughts, she told him to make sure, once Anselmo was hidden, to come when Leonela called him, and that he should answer as if he didn't know that Anselmo was listening. Lotario tried to get her to tell him her plan, so that he could do whatever he thought necessary with greater confidence and caution.

"I'm telling you," said Camila, "that there is nothing to be cautious about, except to answer everything I'll ask you," for she didn't want to reveal what she was going to ask beforehand, fearing that he wouldn't want to carry out the plan that seemed so good to her, and that he would seek or try to devise something else that wouldn't be as good.

Lotario went away then, and the next day Anselmo, with the excuse that he had to go to see his friend in the village, went out and then sneaked back to hide himself, which he could easily do, because Camila and Leonela gave him the opportunity. When Anselmo was hidden, with the agitation one might imagine he would have, waiting to see with his own eyes the dissection of the entrails of his honor, and finding himself about to lose the model of goodness he thought he would find in Camila, and when Camila and Leonela were sure that Anselmo was hiding, they went into the bedroom and they had hardly stepped inside when Camila, heaving an enormous sigh, said: "Ay, Leonela, my friend, before I do the thing I want to keep secret from you lest you try to stop me, wouldn't it be better for you to take Anselmo's dagger I've asked you to get, and plunge it into my miserable heart? But don't do it, because it isn't right for me to take the punishment for someone else's guilt. First I want to know what the daring and lascivious eyes of Lotario saw in me so that it would make him dare to reveal to me so base a desire as the one he told me, in contempt of his friend and my honor. Go to the window, Leonela, and call him, since he's doubtless in the street waiting to put his evil intention into effect, but my cruel but honorable purpose will be carried out first."

"*Ay, señora mía*," responded the keen-witted and crafty Leonela, "what are you planning to do with this dagger? Do you want, perhaps, to take your own life or that of Lotario?

Either one of these things will result in the loss of your reputation and good name. It would be better to disguise your offense, and not give this immoral man the opportunity to come into this house and find us alone. Look, *señora*, we're weak women, and he's a man, and a determined one at that, and since he's coming with such a base purpose, blind with passion; maybe before you put your idea into effect, he'll do something worse to you than taking your own life. Curses on my master, Anselmo, who has made such a mistake in allowing this shameless fellow into his house! And, supposing, *señora*, you kill him—and I believe you ought to—what will we do with him after he's dead?"

"What, my friend?" responded Camila. "We'll leave him for Anselmo to bury, since it's only right that he should have the labor of putting his own dishonor beneath the earth. Summon him now, for the time I delay in taking due vengeance for my offense seems to me that I'm offending the loyalty I owe my husband."

Anselmo was listening to all of this, and with every word that Camila said his mind changed, but when he heard that she was resolved to kill Lotario, he wanted to come out and reveal himself so that she wouldn't do such a thing. But the desire to see how that bold and virtuous resolution would turn out stopped him, and he planned to come out in time to prevent that act. At that moment, Camila began to faint, and threw herself on the bed nearby, and Leonela began to weep bitterly, saying: "Woe is me! I'm so unlucky that the flower of chastity, the crown of good wives, the model of virtue, should die in my arms!" and other things similar to these, so that anyone listening to her would have taken her for the most sympathetic and faithful maid in the world and her mistress for a latter-day sought-after Penelope.*

Soon, Camila came to and said: "Why don't you go off and beckon the most loyal friend of a friend that the sun ever shone upon or the night concealed? Do it now, run, make haste, lest the delay diminish the fire of my rage, and I'll see the just vengeance I want become nothing more than threats and curses."

---

* Penelope was Ulysses' wife, the model of the perfect spouse. During her husband's twenty-year absence she had 108 (or was it 112?) suitors, all of whom she rejected.

"I'm going right now to summon him, *señora mía*," said Leonela, "but you must first give me the dagger so that you won't do anything foolhardy while I'm gone that will cause those who love you to weep for the rest of their lives."

"You can go in confidence, Leonela, my friend, that I won't do anything," responded Camila, "because though I may seem rash and foolish to you in trying to recover my honor, I won't be so much so as Lucretia, who, they say, killed herself without having committed any sin, and without first having slain the man who was the cause of her disgrace.* I'll die if I have to, but I'll first be satisfied that vengeance will be taken on him who led me to this state, to cry for his insolence, issuing from no blemish of my own."

Leonela required considerable urging to go to fetch Lotario, but she finally left, and while she was on her way, Camila continued along as if speaking to herself: "God help me! Wouldn't it have been better to have rejected Lotario, as I've done many times before, instead of putting him in the position I have, to think me lustful and wicked, even for the time I must wait to reveal the truth to him? It would doubtless be better, but I wouldn't be avenged nor the honor of my husband vindicated if he were able to wash his hands of it and get out of this pass where his vile desires have led him. Let the traitor pay with his life for what he wanted to attempt out of lustful passion. Let the world know—if it should come to know—that Camila not only maintained her faithfulness to her husband, but also that she gave him vengeance on the one who tried to offend him. Still, I think it would be best to tell Anselmo, although I hinted at it in the letter I wrote him when he was at the village, but I think that since he didn't do anything to fix the damage I pointed out to him, it must have been because he's so good and trusting that he wouldn't—he couldn't—believe that such an unwavering friend could entertain even the smallest thought that was against his honor. And I didn't believe it myself except after several days, nor would

---

* Lucretia was already mentioned in chapter twenty-five, but what wasn't said then was that she killed herself with a knife. She'd been raped by Sextus Tarquinius, the son of the Etruscan king of Rome. Because of this, she killed herself, but not before her father and husband assured her that she would be avenged.

I ever have believed it, if his insolence hadn't gone so far
as to show it by those gifts, long-winded promises, and continual tears. But why am I making this long discourse? By
chance does a bold resolve need such bolstering? Certainly
not! Away with traitorous thoughts! Let vengeance come!
Let the false friend come, approach, die and be finished,
and come what may! I was pure when I went into my marriage with the man heaven gave me to be mine, and pure
I shall leave it, even though I'll leave it bathed in my own
chaste blood and in the impure blood of the falsest friend
that friendship ever saw."

And as she said this she paced around the room with the
unsheathed dagger in her hand, with wild and enormous
strides and making such gestures that one would think she
wasn't a delicate woman, but rather a dangerous ruffian.

Anselmo witnessed all of this, covered by some tapestries where he'd hidden, and he marveled at everything, and
it seemed to him that what he saw and heard was enough to
answer even greater suspicions, and the trial caused by Lotario's arrival could be dispensed with, fearing some sudden accident; and he was at the point of showing himself
and coming out to embrace and enlighten his wife when
he saw that Leonela was returning, holding Lotario by his
hand.

As soon as Camila saw him, she drew a line on the floor
with the dagger in front of her and said: "Lotario, listen
carefully to what I'm telling you—if by chance you step
over this line, or when I see that you're even going toward
it, I'll stab myself in the chest instantly with this dagger;
and before you say a single word, I want you to listen to
some that I'll say, and afterward you can answer whatever
you please. First, I want you to tell me, Lotario, if you know
Anselmo, my husband, and what opinion you have of him.
Next, I want to know also if you know me. Answer me this,
don't be nervous, nor think very much about what you're
going to say, since the questions are not hard."

Lotario was not so dull that from the instant Camila told
him to hide Anselmo he realized what her intentions were,
so he backed up her scheme so discreetly and so promptly
that they made that lie look like more than the truth, and
he answered Camila in this way: "I didn't think, beautiful
Camila, that you had me come here to ask me things so

remote from the purpose for which I came. But if you're doing it to put off the promised favor, you could have postponed it by means of a messenger, because the longed-for reward torments us more intensively as the hope of possessing it draws nearer. But so that you won't say that I don't answer your questions, I'll tell you that I know your husband, Anselmo, and the two of us have known each other since our earliest years. I won't say anything about our friendship because you know all about it, and I have no wish to bear witness against myself for the offense that love is causing me to do to him, a powerful excuse for greater sins. I know you and I have the same opinion that he has of you, because if it weren't so, given who I am, I wouldn't have gone against who I am for a lesser reward, and also against the holy laws of true friendship, now broken and violated by an enemy as strong as love."

"If you confess that—" responded Camila, "you mortal enemy of everything that rightly deserves to be loved—how do you dare come here before me, the mirror in which Anselmo sees himself, and in which you should also see yourself, to find out with what little cause you're wronging him? But now I understand who has made you have so little respect for yourself. It must have been some flippant remark on my part—for I won't call it indecency, since it couldn't have been deliberate, but rather something careless—things we women do inadvertently when we think we don't have to be cautious. But tell me, you traitor, when did I ever respond to your entreaties with any word or sign that could awaken in you the slightest shadow of hope for your base desires? When weren't your amorous words rebuked and rejected severely and harshly by mine? When were your many promises and greater gifts believed or received by me?

"But since it seems to me that nobody can persevere in an attempt to win love when it's not backed by some hope, I'm willing to attribute the guilt of your impertinence to myself, because doubtless some carelessness on my part has sustained your presumption. Therefore I'll punish myself and give myself the blame your guilt deserves. And so you can see I won't be more cruel to myself than I would be to you, I want you to be a witness to the sacrifice I plan to make for the offended honor of my respected husband, whom both of us have offended—you with your obstinate pursuit, and me by not fleeing from any occasion I might have given you to encourage and sanction your wicked intentions. I repeat that the suspicion I have that some carelessness on my part is at the root of your extravagant thoughts is what bothers me the most, and it's that carelessness I want to punish with my own hands, because if another person were to do it, my guilt would be more widely known. But before I die, I want to satisfy my hope and desire for vengeance by killing and taking along with me the person who has reduced me to such a desperate strait; for wherever I go, be it heaven or hell, when I see the punishment that unswerving and impartial Justice has given him, I'll be quite satisfied."

And saying these words, with incredible force and speed, she attacked Lotario with her unsheathed dagger, with such determination to stab his chest that he wondered if that display was false or real, because he had to use all his skill and strength to prevent Camila from stabbing him, so vividly did she feign that deception in which, in order to make it appear even more real, she determined to shed some of her own blood. When she saw or pretended that she couldn't wound Lotario, she said: "Since Fate doesn't want to satisfy my just desire, at least it won't rob me of partial satisfaction."

And using all her strength, she was able to free her hand with the dagger, which Lotario had been holding fast, and pointing it where she could make a wound that was not too deep, she stabbed herself a little above the collarbone on the left side next to her shoulder, and then she let herself fall to the floor, as if she'd fainted.

Leonela and Lotario were amazed and astounded at what had happened, and seeing Camila stretched out on the ground and bathed in her own blood, Lotario bounded over, aghast and out of breath, to remove the dagger, and when he saw how small the wound really was, the fear he had until then left him, and he again marveled at Camila's shrewdness, acumen, and good sense. And so, to support the part he had to play, he began to make a long and sad lamentation on the body of Camila, as if she were dead, cursing not only himself, but also him who had placed him in that position. And since he knew that his friend Anselmo was listening, he said things so that he who was listening would pity him more than Camila, even though he had supposed that she was dead.

Leonela took her in her arms and placed her on the bed, begging Lotario to look for someone to attend to her in secret. She asked him as well what he advised her to tell Anselmo about her mistress' wound, if he should return before it healed. He said that they could say whatever they wanted, since he was not in a position to give useful advice. He only told her to try to stop the flow of blood, since he was going away where he would never be seen again. And showing great grief and sorrow he left the house. When he found himself alone where no one would see him, he couldn't stop crossing himself, marveling over the cleverness of Camila and the good acting on the part of Leonela. He reflected that Anselmo must consider himself to have as a wife a second Portia,* and he longed to see him so that they could celebrate together the lie and the most counterfeit truth that ever could be imagined. Leonela stopped, as has been said, her mistress' blood—which was no more than was necessary to support her deception—and washing the wound with a little wine, she bandaged it as well as she could, telling her things as she dressed the wound in a way that, even if nothing had been said beforehand, would have sufficed to convince Anselmo that he had in Camila the very image of purity.

Camila added her own words to Leonela's, calling herself a coward and wanting in courage, since she lacked it just when it was most needed, to take her own life, which she despised. She asked advice of her maid whether she should tell her husband or not about the whole matter, and the maid advised her not to, because he would then have to take vengeance on Lotario, which would have to be at great risk to himself, and a good woman was not supposed to give cause to her husband to come to blows, but rather to prevent them as best she could.

Camila responded that she was right and that she would follow her advice, but in any case they needed to find an excuse for the wound, which he couldn't fail to notice, to which Leonela responded that her mistress didn't know how to tell a lie, even in jest.

---

* Portia (b. 43 B.C.) was the wife of Brutus—Cæsar's assassin. After his death, she killed herself by swallowing hot coals.

"So, sister," replied Camila, "what can I do since I don't dare to forge or sustain a lie even if my life depended on it? And if we can't find a proper solution to this, it will be better to tell him the naked truth so that he wouldn't discover us in a lying fable."

"Don't worry, *señora*, because by this time tomorrow," replied Leonela, "I'll think of what to say, and maybe because the wound is where it is, it can be hidden from his sight, and heaven will favor our just and honorable purpose. Calm down, *señora*, and try to steady your nerves, so that my master won't find you this way, and leave the rest to me and to God, who always supports good intentions."

Anselmo was listening to and carefully watching this dramatized tragedy of the death of his honor that the actors performed so powerfully that it seemed to him that what they were playing represented the truth. He could hardly wait for night to fall and an opportunity for him to escape from his house and see his good friend Lotario, so they could congratulate themselves about the precious pearl he'd found in the test of his wife's virtue. The two women were careful to give him the chance to get away, and he—not losing that chance—went out and immediately went to find Lotario, and when he found him, one cannot count the embraces that he gave him, recount the things he said to him, or the praises that he had for Camila. Lotario listened to all this without showing any signs of gladness, because he reflected how deceived his friend was, and how cruelly he'd wronged him. Anselmo saw that Lotario did not rejoice, but he believed it was because Camila had wounded herself and that he'd been the cause.

So he told him, among other things, not to worry about what had happened with Camila, because the wound was doubtless superficial, since they were trying to find a way to conceal it from him, so he had nothing to fear; that from then on Lotario could rejoice and be glad with him, since by Lotario's cleverness, and because of him, he'd risen to the greatest level of happiness that he could hope to wish for, and he wanted for their only pastime to write poems in praise of Camila, so that they could make her famous for all time. Lotario praised his good purpose and said that he would do his part in building such a noble edifice.

And so Anselmo became the most deliciously deceived

man in the world. He himself took the destroyer of his good name to his house, leading him by the hand, believing him to be the instrument of his glory. Camila received Lotario with her face averted, although with a smiling heart. This deception lasted some time, until after a few months the wheel of Fortune turned again, and the guilt that had been so cleverly concealed came to be known everywhere, and his ill-advised curiosity cost Anselmo his life.

Chapter XXXV. Where the end of the novella of the "Ill-Advised Curiosity" is concluded.

LITTLE REMAINED to be read of the novella when Sancho Panza ran in from the garret where don Quixote had been resting, and exclaimed in a dither: "Come quickly, *señores*, and rescue my master, who is in the midst of the toughest and fiercest battle I've ever seen! By God, he's given a slash to the giant, the enemy of the *señora* princess Micomicona, and has cut his head clean off, as if it were a turnip."

"What are you saying, brother?" said the priest, interrupting the end of the story he was reading. "Are you crazy? How the devil can this be when the giant is two thousand leagues from here?"

At that moment they heard an enormous racket from the room, and don Quixote was loudly shouting: "Stop, you thief, you brigand, you rogue! Now I have you where I want you, and your scimitar will do you no good!"

It sounded as if he were giving solid slashes to the walls. Sancho said: "Don't stop to listen, but go in and stop the fight, or help my master—although that probably won't be necessary, because the giant is doubtless already dead and giving an account of his wicked life to God, because I saw blood flowing on the floor, and the chopped-off head lying on its side, and I swear it's the size of a big wineskin!"

"May they kill me," said the innkeeper right then, "if don Quixote, or don Devil, hasn't stabbed one of the skins of red wine that were hanging at the head of his bed, and the spilled wine must be what this fellow thinks is blood."

The innkeeper, and all the rest, ran into the room and

found don Quixote dressed in the strangest way in the world—he was in his shirt, which barely covered his thighs and was a hand shorter in the back. His legs were very long and thin, covered with hair and not at all clean. He was wearing a dirty red cap on his head that belonged to the innkeeper. Wound around his left arm was that blanket Sancho so despised, and he knew the reason well. In his right hand was his unsheathed sword he was thrusting in all directions, crying out as if he were truly fighting with a giant. The strange thing is that his eyes weren't open, because he was still sleeping and dreaming that he was in a battle with the giant. His imagination about the adventure that he was going to be in was so intense that it made him dream he'd already arrived in the kingdom of Micomicón and that he was already fighting with his enemy. And he'd given so many slashes to the wineskins, thinking that he was giving them to giants, that the whole room was flooded with wine. When the innkeeper saw it, he became so angry and began to rain so many blows on don Quixote that if Cardenio and the priest hadn't separated them, the innkeeper would have finished the battle with the giant himself. And the poor knight never woke up until the barber brought a large bucket of cold water from the well and threw it onto his whole body in one splash, which caused don Quixote to wake up, but not sufficiently so that he knew what was going on.

Dorotea, seeing how little he was wearing, wouldn't go into the room to witness the battle between her rescuer and her enemy. Sancho was running around, trying to find the giant's head on the floor, and since he didn't see it he said: "Now I know that everything in this place happens by enchantment. The last time, in this very room where I'm standing right now, I got a lot of punches and jabs, and I didn't know who did it, and I couldn't see anyone. And now the head I saw my master chop off with my own eyes is nowhere to be seen, and there was blood flowing from the body as if it was coming from a spring."

"What blood and what spring are you talking about, you enemy of God and all his saints?" said the innkeeper. "Don't you see, you rogue, that the blood and spring are nothing more than slashed wineskins and red wine swimming around this room, and may I see the soul of the one who slashed them swimming around in hell."

"I don't know anything," responded Sancho. "I only know that it'll be too bad if I can't find that head because my county will dissolve like salt in water." Sancho awake was worse than his master asleep, such was the effect his master's promises had on him.

The innkeeper was despairing, seeing how doltish the squire was and how much damage the master had done, and he swore it wasn't going to turn out as it had the last time, when they got away without paying. This time, the privileges of his knighthood weren't going to let him get off without paying both accounts, down to the repairs he'd have to make to fix the punctured wineskins.

The priest took don Quixote by his hands, and he, thinking that he'd successfully completed the adventure and he was in the presence of the princess Micomicona, got down on his knees before the priest and said: "Your greatness, noble and famous *señora*, can live from this day forth, sure that this ill-born creature will do you no harm, and that I, also as of today, am released from the promise I gave you, since—with the help of God in heaven, and with the aid of her for whom I live and breathe—I've fulfilled it."

"Didn't I tell you," said Sancho, when he heard this. "You see, I wasn't drunk. Come and see if my master doesn't have that giant packed in salt!* 'Here come the bulls!'† My county is a sure thing!"

Who couldn't help but laugh at the foolish remarks of both the master and the servant? Everyone laughed except the innkeeper, who was despairing. In the end, the barber, Cardenio, and the priest managed to get don Quixote back into bed with no little effort, and he went to sleep looking utterly fatigued. They let him sleep, then went out to the door of the inn to console Sancho Panza for not having found the giant's head, although they had more to do to appease the innkeeper, who was despondent about the sudden death of his wineskins, and his wife began shouting very loudly: "It was a stroke of bad luck when this knight-errant came to my house—he's cost me so much! I wish I'd

---

* A slaughtered animal is put in salt to cure the flesh; therefore the giant must assuredly be dead.

† That is, if the bulls are coming, the bullfight will take place—everything is as it should be.

never seen him. Last time he stiffed us for the bed, the dinner, the straw and barley for his hack and donkey, saying that he was a knight adventurer—and may God give a bad venture to him and to all the other adventurers there are in the world!—and for that reason he didn't have to pay anything, because it was written in the laws of knight-errantry. So now, because of him, this other fellow came and took my tail away, and returned it with two *cuartillos** of damage, virtually hairless so it's no good anymore for what my husband wants it. And to top it all off, he slashes my wineskins and spills my wine—may I see his blood spilled. But don't think—by the bones of my father and by the life of my mother—that he won't pay me for everything, every single *cuarto*,† or my name isn't what it is nor am I my parents' daughter."

The innkeeper's wife said these and other words in great anger, backed up by her good maid Maritornes. Her daughter said nothing but just smiled from time to time. The priest calmed everyone down, promising to pay for their losses as well as he could, not only for the wineskins, but also for the wine, and especially for the damage done to the tail that such a fuss was made about. Dorotea consoled Sancho Panza, telling him that if it appeared certain that his master had beheaded the giant, she promised, once she was peacefully settled in her kingdom, to give him the best county in it. Sancho was consoled with that, and he assured the princess that she could be sure that he'd seen the giant's head, and that, the way it looked, he had a beard that went down to his waist, and if it was no longer around, it was because everything happened in that place by enchantment, as he'd proven on another occasion when he'd been lodged there. Dorotea said she believed him, and for him not to worry, because everything would turn out as he wished.

Now that everyone was calm, the priest wanted to finish reading the novella because he saw very little remained. Cardenio, Dorotea, and everyone else begged him to finish it. He was willing to give them the same pleasure he had in reading it, and continued the story, which went like this:

---

* Half a *real*.
† The *cuarto* was worth four *maravedís*.

* * *

It happened, then, owing to the confidence Anselmo felt about Camila's virtue, he lived a contented and carefree life, and Camila showed herself outwardly cold, on purpose, toward Lotario, so Anselmo might think her feelings toward him were the opposite of what they were. To reinforce their scheme, Lotario asked Anselmo's permission not to come to his house because he clearly saw Camila's displeasure when she saw him. But the deceived Anselmo said that he wouldn't hear of such a thing. And in a thousand ways Anselmo was the architect of his own dishonor, while he thought he was the author of his happiness.

Meanwhile, the pleasure that Leonela had in finding herself empowered to continue her affair came to the point that, not caring about anything else, she pursued it with free rein, confident her mistress would conceal it and even tell her how she could manage it safely and with little fear.

It finally happened that one night Anselmo heard footsteps in Leonela's room, and went to see who it was, but he found that the door was barred against him, which made him all the more determined to open it. So with all his strength he finally opened it, and he went in just as a man was leaping from the window to the street. He ran over to try to catch him or at least see who he was, but could do neither because Leonela grabbed him saying: "Calm down, *señor mío*, and don't get excited or try to pursue the man who just jumped from here. It's my business; in fact, he's my husband."

Anselmo refused to believe it, and blind with rage he took out his dagger and tried to stab her, demanding that she tell him the truth or he would kill her. She was so afraid, without realizing what she was saying, she blurted out: "Don't kill me, *señor*, and I'll tell you things that are more important than you can imagine."

"Tell me right now!" said Anselmo. "If you don't, you're dead."

"For the moment it's impossible," said Leonela, "because I'm so worked up. Give me until the morning, and then you'll learn things that will astonish you, and rest assured that the man who leapt out of the window is a lad from this city who has promised to be my husband."

With this, Anselmo calmed down, and agreed to wait

until the time she requested, since he didn't expect to hear anything to the detriment of Camila, because he was so satisfied with, and certain of, her virtue. So, he went out of the bedroom and left Leonela locked inside, telling her she couldn't leave until she told him what she had to say. He then went to Camila to tell her everything that had happened with her maid, and the promise she'd given him to tell him of great and important matters. There is no need to say whether or not Camila was disturbed, because her fear was so great, believing, as well she should, that Leonela was going to tell Anselmo everything she knew about her infidelity, that she didn't have the courage to wait to see if her suspicion was false or not. And that same night, when it seemed Anselmo was sleeping, she gathered her best jewelry and some money, and without being heard by anyone, left the house and went to Lotario's, and told him what had happened, and asked him to help her find a safe place to go, or for the two of them to flee together where they might be safe from Anselmo. The perplexity into which Camila threw Lotario was such that he didn't say a single word, nor could he make up his mind what to do.

He finally decided to take Camila to a convent where a sister of his was mother superior. Camila agreed, and with the speed that the situation required, Lotario took her to the convent and left her there, and he left the city as well, not telling anyone he was going.

At daybreak, Anselmo, not noticing that Camila wasn't at his side, and wanting to find out what Leonela was going to tell him, got up and went to where he'd left her locked up. He opened the door and went in, but he couldn't find her. He only found some sheets knotted together at the window, a sure sign she'd let herself down and fled. Very sad, he returned immediately to tell Camila about it, and when he didn't find her in bed, or in any part of the house for that matter, he was dumbfounded. He asked the servants about her but no one could give him any explanation.

As he continued his search for Camila, he happened to see her open jewel boxes, and that jewelry was missing; and right then he realized his disgrace, and that Leonela was not the cause of his misfortune. And so, only half-dressed, sad and pensive, he went to tell Lotario about his sorrow. But when he didn't find him, and his servants told him that he hadn't been at home the preceding night, and had taken all his money with him, he thought he'd go crazy. To add insult to injury, when he returned home, he couldn't find any of his own servants, and the house was deserted and empty. He didn't know what to think. Little by little, his wits started to return. He considered his situation, and in an instant he realized that he was without a wife, without a friend, seemingly abandoned by heaven above, and especially without honor, because in Camila he saw his ruin.

He resolved finally to go to his friend's village, where he'd gone when he'd given the opportunity for all that misfortune to be plotted. He closed the doors of his house, mounted his horse, and with a broken spirit got on the road. He'd hardly gone halfway when, beleaguered by his thoughts, he had to dismount and tie his horse to a tree, at the foot of which he lay down, giving tender and doleful sighs, and remained there until nightfall. At that hour, he saw a man approach from the city on horseback, and after greeting him, he asked what news there was in Florence.

The man from the city replied: "The strangest news heard in town for a long time, because it's said publicly that Lotario, that great friend of Anselmo the Rich, who lives near San Giovanni,* ran off with Camila, Anselmo's wife, and *he* isn't around either. All this was revealed by a maid of Camila whom the governor found last night lowering herself by a sheet from the windows of Anselmo's house. Indeed, I don't know really how it all happened. I only know that the whole city is astonished about the affair, because it would never have been expected from the great and well-known friendship of the two of them, who were so close that they were known as THE TWO FRIENDS."

"Is it known, by chance," asked Anselmo, "what road Lotario and Camila took?"

"Not in the least," said the city dweller, "even though the governor has used great diligence to search for them."

"Godspeed to you, *señor*," said Anselmo.

With this ill-fated news Anselmo found himself almost on the verge of not only losing his wits, but also of losing his life. He got up as well as he could, and went to the house

---

* The Piazza San Giovanni in Florence was the site of the old cathedral until 1128 and is now the site of the baptistery of the same name.

of his friend, who as yet had heard nothing of his misfortune. But when he saw Anselmo arrive pale, wan, and exhausted, he realized that he'd suffered some great affliction. Anselmo asked to be put to bed and to be given something to write with. That done, he left him resting and alone, because that's the way he wanted it, and he even wanted the door closed behind him. Finding himself alone, he began to dwell on his misfortune so much that it weighed down upon him, and he clearly saw that his life was ebbing away. So he determined to leave behind the reasons for his bizarre death. He began to write, but before he could put down all he wanted to, his breath failed him, and he left his life in the hands of the pain that his ill-advised curiosity had brought upon him.

When the master of the house saw that it was getting late and that Anselmo had been so silent, he decided to go in to see if his indisposition had increased, but instead he found him facedown with a quill still in his hand, half of his body on the bed and the other half on the writing desk, on which there was a partially written message. His host approached, having called out to him first, and seizing him by the hand, seeing he didn't respond, and finding him cold, he saw that Anselmo was dead. He was astonished and, greatly grieved, he called his servants to bear witness to Anselmo's sad fate, and finally read the paper he recognized to be in Anselmo's handwriting, which had these words:

> *A foolish and ill-advised wish took my life. If the news of my death gets to the ears of Camila, I want her to know that I forgive her, because she was not bound to perform miracles, nor should I have asked her to, and since I was the author of my own dishonor, there's no reason to*

Anselmo had gotten this far, by which one could see that at that point, without completing his thought, his life ended. The next day the friend told Anselmo's relatives of his death. They already knew of his disgrace, as well as where Camila's convent was. She, too, was on the point of accompanying her husband on that inevitable voyage, not because of the news of his death, but because she'd learned that her lover had gone. They say that, although she was a widow, she didn't want to leave the convent, nor become a nun, until just a few days later, when she got news that Lotario had died in a battle that Monsieur de Lautrec* was fighting with the Gran Capitán, Gonzalo Fernández de Córdoba, in the Kingdom of Naples, where her late repentant friend had gone. And when Camila heard that news, she became a nun and a few days later she herself died at the rigorous hands of grief and melancholy. Such was the end of them all, born of such a reckless beginning.

"This novella seems good to me," said the priest, "but I'm not convinced of its truth, and if it's fiction, the author did a bad job, since one cannot imagine that there is such a foolish husband who would want to try such a costly experiment as Anselmo. If this story were between a lover and his mistress, it might pass; but between husband and wife, it smacks of being impossible. As for its style, I'm not displeased."

Chapter XXXVI. Which deals with the fierce and colossal battle that don Quixote had with some wineskins, and other strange adventures at the inn.

JUST THEN, the innkeeper, who was at the door of the inn, said: "Here comes a fine group of guests. If they stop here, we can sing *gaudeamos*."†

"Who are they?" said Cardenio.

"Four men," responded the innkeeper, "are coming on horseback, riding with short stirrups, lances, and shields, and all of them have black riding masks. And with them is a woman dressed all in white, riding sidesaddle, with her face covered as well, and then there are two attendants on foot."

"Are they near?" asked the priest.

"They're so near," responded the innkeeper, "that they're arriving now."

---

* Odet de Foix, Viscount of Lautrec (1485–1528), was a Frenchman who spent years fighting in Italy.
† Latin, meaning "Let us rejoice."

When Dorotea heard this, she covered her face, and Cardenio went into don Quixote's room. And they hardly had time to do this when all those the innkeeper had mentioned came through the gate of the inn. The four on horseback, who were all handsome and of graceful demeanor, dismounted, and went to help the lady get off her horse. One of them took her in his arms, and sat her on a chair near the door to the room where Cardenio had hidden. All the while, neither she nor any of them had taken off their riding masks, nor said a word, except that when the woman sat down she gave a deep sigh and let her arms fall to her sides, like a sick person or one who was in a faint. The attendants on foot took the horses to the stable.

When the priest saw this—wanting to find out who they were, why they were dressed that way, and the reason for their silence—he went to the attendants, and asked one of them what he wanted to find out, and the lad responded: "On my faith, *señor*, I can't tell you who those people are. I only know that they seem to be people of the upper class, especially that one who carried the lady you saw in his arms, and I say this because all the rest of the men show him respect, and nothing is done except what he orders."

"And the woman—who is she?" asked the priest.

"I don't know that either," said the attendant, "because I haven't seen her face a single time during the whole trip. I've heard her sigh many times, to be sure, and give some moans, and it seemed that with each one she was going to give up the ghost. And it's no wonder we don't know more than we've said, because my companion and I have just recently been accompanying these people. When we happened upon them along the road they asked and persuaded us to go with them to Andalusia, and offered to pay us very well."

"And did you hear the name of any of them?" asked the priest.

"No, I didn't," the lad answered, "because they all travel in such silence that it's a wonder to behold, and you only hear sighs and sobs from the poor lady, which makes us pity her. We believe she's traveling against her will, wherever they're going. And from what we can judge by her outfit, she's a nun, or she's going to be one—which is more logical—and perhaps because it wasn't her idea to become a nun she's as sad as she seems."

"Anything's possible," said the priest.

The priest left them and went back to where Dorotea was. Having heard the veiled lady sigh, moved by her natural compassion, she approached her and said to her: "What's the matter, *señora mía*? Tell us if it's something that affects us women, and we know how to cure by experience. As for me, I'll do whatever I can for you."

The sad lady responded nothing to all this, and even though Dorotea repeated her offer more earnestly, she was still silent until the masked man—the one whom the lad had said they all obeyed—came and told Dorotea: "Don't bother, *señora*, to offer anything to this woman, because she's never thankful for anything done for her, and don't try to make her answer, unless you want to hear a lie coming from her mouth."

"I never lied," said the woman who had been silent until then, "rather it's because I'm so truthful, and so loath to the ways of lying, that I find myself in this terrible circumstance. And since you witnessed it all, you know that my pure truth makes you yourself false and a liar."

Cardenio heard these words clearly and distinctly, because he was virtually next to the speaker, since only don Quixote's door separated them, and as soon as he heard her words, he exclaimed: "Good God! What am I hearing? What voice has reached my ears?"

Startled by the loud voice, the lady turned her head toward where it had come from, and not seeing who had shouted, she stood to enter the room, and when the man saw her do this, he held her back, and wouldn't let her move a step. Because of her confusion and anxiety, the veil that covered her face fell, and revealed an incomparably, miraculously beautiful face, although pale and terrified, because with her eyes she searched everywhere with such intensity that she seemed to be a person who had lost her wits. The way she was acting filled Dorotea, and all who saw her, with enormous pity. The man was holding her tightly by her shoulders, and was so busy clutching her that he couldn't tend to his mask, which was falling off, and at last it fell completely away, and Dorotea, who was also clasping the lady in her arms, saw that he who held her in his embrace was her own husband, don Fernando. And as soon as she recognized him, she emitted a long and very sad cry from the depths of her heart, and fell in a faint backward, and if the barber hadn't been there to catch her, she would have fallen to the floor.

The priest went over to take off her veil so he could splash water in her face, and as soon as he took the veil off, don Fernando, still holding the other woman, recognized her, and stood there as if death-stricken. He still didn't loosen his hold on Luscinda, who was trying to get away from him, since she'd recognized Cardenio's voice, as he'd recognized hers.

When Cardenio heard Dorotea's cry as she fell fainting, thinking it to be Luscinda, he came out of the room aghast, and the first person he saw was don Fernando, who was holding Luscinda. Don Fernando also recognized Cardenio, and all three—Luscinda, Cardenio, and Dorotea—stood in silent amazement, almost not realizing what was happening to them. They gazed at each other without saying anything—Dorotea at don Fernando, don Fernando at Cardenio, Cardenio at Luscinda, and Luscinda at Cardenio. The person who broke the silence was Luscinda, speaking to don Fernando in this way: "Release me, *señor* don Fernando, for the sake of who you are, if for no other reason. Let me attach myself to the wall of which I'm the ivy, to the protection of the one from whom your demands, threats, promises, and gifts have not been able to separate me. Look how heaven, by strange and to us mysterious ways, has delivered me to my true husband. And you well know through a thousand tribulations that only death can erase him from my memory. So let these unmistakable trials of experience convince you—and you have no alternative— to change your love into rage, your affection into hatred, and put an end to my life, because I shall consider it well lost provided I die in front of my good husband. Perhaps through my death he'll be convinced that I've kept my faith to him up to the last moment of my life."

Meanwhile, Dorotea came to, and she was listening to all the words that Luscinda said, by means of which she realized who she was, and, seeing that don Fernando still wasn't releasing Luscinda from his arms, nor responding to her words, gathering as much strength as she could, she knelt at his feet, and shed a great deal of beautiful and touching tears, and began to say to him: "If the rays of the sun that you hold eclipsed in your arms hadn't dazzled and darkened the sight of your eyes, you would have seen that at your feet is kneeling the unhappy and—as long as you want me to be that way—unfortunate Dorotea. I'm that humble girl whom you—either because of your goodness or for your pleasure—chose to raise high enough to call yours. I'm that one who, in the seclusion of chastity, lived a happy life until the voice of your supplications and seemingly true and tender affection opened the doors of her modesty and handed the keys of her freedom to you, a gift that you so thanklessly received, as is clearly shown by your having found me in the place where you've found me, and my seeing you the way I see you. But I wouldn't want you to think that I came here driven by my shame—it was only my pain and sorrow at seeing myself forgotten by you. It was your desire to make me yours and although you might wish now that it weren't so, you did it in such a way that it isn't possible for you to stop being mine. Reflect, *señor mío*, that the incomparable affection that I have for you may compensate for the beauty and nobility of her for whom you left me. You cannot belong to the beautiful Luscinda because you're mine, nor can she belong to you, because she's Cardenio's. And it will be easier, if you think about it, to love the one who adores you rather than trying to make the woman who hates you love you. You wanted me to be careless, you laid siege to my virtue, you weren't ignorant of my social class, and you know very well the way I yielded wholly to your will—so there are no grounds or reason to claim deception.

"And since this is so—as it is—and you're as Christian as you are a gentleman, why are you so reticent to make me as happy in the end as you did in the beginning? And if you don't want to love me for who I am, which is your true and legitimate wife, take me at least for your slave, because since you would still be my master, I would consider myself happy and fortunate. Don't allow me, by leaving and deserting me, to be the talk of the gossipers. Don't make the old age of my parents miserable—they don't deserve such treatment in exchange for the loyal service they, as good vassals, have always performed for your family. And if you think that it will debase your blood to mingle it with mine, consider that there is little or no nobility in the world that has not traveled this road, and that in illustrious lineages, it's not the woman's blood that's important. Moreover, true nobility consists of virtue—and if you're lacking in that, denying me what you rightly owe me, I have a claim to a nobility higher than your own. So, *señor*, ultimately it comes down to this: I'm your wife, whether you like it or not. Witnesses to the marriage are your words, which should not be false, if you pride yourself on that nobility, the lack of which you so despise in me. Your signature is also a witness,* and a witness is also heaven whom you called upon to attest to what you promised me. And if all this doesn't convince you, your own conscience will not fail to raise its voice silently in the midst of all your joy, bringing home the truth of what I'm saying, and troubling your greatest pleasures and delights."

All this and more said the suffering Dorotea, with so much feeling and so many tears that those who accompanied don Fernando, and everybody else present, joined her in them. Don Fernando listened without saying a word until she finished and began such sobs and sighs that a heart would have to have been made of bronze not to be moved at so much sorrow. Luscinda was looking at her with no less compassion than admiration for her intelligence and beauty, and would have gone to her to say some words of consolation, but the arms of don Fernando didn't allow her, because they were still holding her tight.

He was filled with shame and confusion, and after a long while during which he gazed fixedly at Dorotea, he opened his arms and released Luscinda, saying: "You have conquered, fair Dorotea, you've conquered—it's not possible to have the heart to deny so many truths together."

Luscinda was at the point of fainting as soon as don Fernando released her, and was about to fall to the floor. But Cardenio was nearby, having gone just behind don Fernando so he wouldn't be recognized. Casting fear aside and

---

* Rico says that in secret marriages, the husband typically signed a document in which his obligation was recorded. Don Fernando signed no such document in chapter twenty-eight—at least that we know of.

disregarding what might happen, he went to hold Luscinda up, and taking her by the arms, said to her: "If heaven in its mercy be pleased for you to have a rest—my true, constant, and fair lady—you'll be able to rest nowhere better than in these arms that now receive you in the same way they received you long ago, when Fortune ordained that you should be called mine."

At these words, Luscinda looked up at Cardenio, and having first recognized his voice, and assuring herself with her eyes that it was he, she was almost beside herself, and forgetting about decorum, threw her arms around his neck, and pressing her face to his, said to him: "You, *señor*, are indeed the true master of this captive of yours, although contrary Fate may try to prevent it, and threaten my life, which is sustained by yours."

This was a strange sight for don Fernando and for the bystanders, who were astonished at such an unexpected event. It seemed to Dorotea that don Fernando had lost the color in his face and looked as if he had a mind to take vengeance on Cardenio, because she saw his hand reach for his sword. And no sooner did she think it when with unheard-of speed she clutched him at his knees, kissing them, and holding them fast to prevent him from moving. Without stopping the flow of her tears she said to him: "What are you planning to do, my only refuge, in this unexpected crisis? You have your wife at your feet, and the one you want to be your wife is in her husband's arms. Consider if it's right or possible to undo what heaven has ordained, or whether it would be best for you to raise to be your equal the woman who—in spite of every obstacle, and confirmed in her faith and constancy—stands before you bathing her true husband's face and chest with her loving tears. For God's sake, I beg you, and for your own sake, I implore you, that this obvious truth not only not increase your wrath but rather may it diminish it in such a way that with calm and tranquillity you permit these two lovers to have, without impediments, all the time together that heaven may be pleased to grant them, and in this you'll show the generosity of your noble heart, and the world will see that with you, reason has more power than passion."

While Dorotea said this, although Cardenio had Luscinda in his embrace, he didn't take his eyes off don Fernando, determined that if he saw him make a hostile movement, he would try to defend himself and assault any others who might try to attack him, even though it might cost him his life. But at that point, don Fernando's friends, as well as the priest and the barber, who had been present all the while, including the worthy Sancho Panza, and everyone else, ran forward and surrounded don Fernando, begging him to consider the tears of Dorotea, and that since what she said was true (as they all doubtless thought), she should not be denied her just hopes, and that he should consider that it wasn't by chance but rather by divine providence that heaven had caused everyone to come together in a place that no one would have expected. And the priest added that only death could separate Cardenio and Luscinda, and even if the blade of a sword should cut them in half, they would regard their death as most fortunate; because in cases like this one that admitted no remedy, it would be the height of prudence to restrain and conquer himself, to show a generous heart by permitting, of his free will, the two to enjoy the happiness that heaven had granted them. He told him that he should turn his eyes toward the beauty of Dorotea and he would see that few if any could equal, much less surpass her, and to her beauty should be added her modesty and the great love she bore him. Above all, he should remember that if he valued himself as a gentleman and a Christian he could do nothing else but fulfill his pledged word, and when he fulfilled it, he would be obeying God, and would meet with the approval of sensible people who know and recognize that it's the privilege of beauty, even in one of humble birth, as long as it's accompanied by virtue, to rise to the highest social level without any discredit to the person who raises it to that level. Finally, when the laws of passion prevail, no one can be blamed for obeying them, as long as there is no sin involved.

In short, everyone else added to these words so many others that the manly heart of don Fernando, which after all was nourished by noble blood, relented and allowed itself to be vanquished by the truth, which he couldn't have denied even if he'd wanted to. He showed that he'd submitted and accepted the good advice offered him by bending over and embracing Dorotea, telling her: "Stand up, *señora mía*, because it's not right that the one I have in my heart should be kneeling at my feet, and if I haven't shown any proof of what I'm now saying, it was perhaps ordered by heaven, so that, by my seeing in you the loyalty of your love toward me, I might learn to value you as much as you deserve. I beg of you not to reproach me for my transgressions and neglect, since the same cause and force that moved me to win you as mine is what incited me to struggle against being yours. And to show you that this is true, turn and look at the eyes of the now happy Luscinda, and you'll find in them an excuse for all my transgressions. And since she found and secured what she wanted, and I've found in you what I need, may she live safe and content for many long and happy years with her Cardenio, just as I'll pray to heaven that it will let me live with my Dorotea."

And saying this, he embraced her again and pressed his face to hers with such tenderness that he needed to be careful, lest his tears give sure signs of his love and repentance. That was not the case with Luscinda and Cardenio, and almost all the others who were present, because they began shedding so many, some because they were so happy, some because of the happiness of others, it seemed as if a calamity had befallen them all. Even Sancho Panza wept, although later he said it was only because Dorotea was not the queen Micomicona, from whom he expected so many favors.

Their wonder, as well as their weeping, lasted some time, and then Cardenio and Luscinda went to kneel before don Fernando, thanking him for the kindness he'd shown them, using such polite terms don Fernando didn't know how to respond, and so he asked them to rise and embraced them with great affection and courtesy.

He then asked Dorotea to tell him how she'd come to that place, so far from where she lived. She, in a few well-chosen words, told him everything she'd told Cardenio before, and the story so pleased don Fernando and those who were with him that they wished it had lasted longer, such was the grace with which Dorotea told of her misfortunes. And as soon as she finished, don Fernando told of what had happened to him in the city after he found the letter in Luscinda's bosom that said she was Cardenio's wife and couldn't be his. He said he'd tried to kill her, and would have done so, if he hadn't been prevented by her parents.

He then left their house filled with rage and shame, determined to avenge himself when the time was right. The next day he found out that Luscinda had disappeared from her parents' house without anybody knowing where she'd gone. After some months had passed, he learned that she was in a convent and she meant to stay there for the rest of her life, since she couldn't spend it with Cardenio. As soon as he learned what had happened, he chose those three men to go with him and went to the village where she was. He didn't want to speak with her, fearing that if she knew he was there, the convent would be better guarded. So he waited a day until the gatehouse was unoccupied. He left two of his companions to guard the gate, and he and the other man went into the convent looking for Luscinda, and found her in the cloister, talking with a nun. He carried her off without giving her a chance to resist. They then went to a village where they got the provisions they needed to take her away. They were able to do this in complete safety, since the convent was in the country, at a good distance from the town. He said that as soon as Luscinda saw herself in his custody, she lost all consciousness, and after she came to, she could only weep and sigh from then on, without saying a word. And so in silence and accompanied by tears, they had arrived at that inn, which for him was like arriving at heaven, where all the misfortunes of earth are brought to an end.

Chapter XXXVII. Which deals where the story of the famous princess Micomicona is continued, with other amusing adventures.

SANCHO OVERHEARD all of this with no little pain in his heart, seeing the hopes of his title vanish into smoke, and that the beautiful princess Micomicona had turned into Dorotea, and the giant into don Fernando. His master was sound asleep, unaware of anything that had happened. Dorotea couldn't convince herself that her present happiness was not all a dream. Cardenio had the same thought, and Luscinda was on the same path. Don Fernando gave thanks to heaven for the favor he'd received and for having extracted him from that intricate labyrinth where he found himself on the point of losing his honor and his soul. Finally, all who were at the inn were happy and rejoiced at the fortunate outcome of that difficult and desperate affair.

The priest fully appreciated the situation, as a sensible man, and he gave his congratulations to each one for the good that had come to him or her, but the person who was most jubilant and delighted with the outcome was the innkeeper's wife, because of the promise that Cardenio and the priest had made to pay her for all the damage and losses thanks to don Quixote. Only Sancho, as has already been said, was distressed, unlucky, and sad. So, with a heavy heart he went to see his master, who had just woken up, and said: "Your grace, *señor* Woebegone, can sleep all you want, without worrying about killing the giant, nor restoring the princess to her kingdom, because it's all over and done with."

"I can well believe that," responded don Quixote, "because I engaged with the giant in the most monstrous and hugest battle I ever expect to have in all the days of my life. With one backslash—thwack!—I whacked his head off and it tumbled to the ground. And there was so much blood that flowed forth that the streams ran along the ground as if they were water."

"Like red wine, you might better say," responded Sancho, "because I want your grace to know, if you don't know already, that the giant was a punctured wineskin, the blood was fifty liters of wine from its belly, and the chopped-off head was the whore who bore me, and may the devil take it all!"

"What are you talking about, you fool?" replied don Quixote. "Have you lost your wits?"

"Stand up," said Sancho, "and you'll see the results of your handiwork and what we'll have to pay for, and you'll see that the queen has been changed into an individual named Dorotea, and other things that, if you come to understand them, will amaze you."

"Nothing of all this will amaze me," replied don Quixote, "because, if you remember, the last time we were here, I told you that everything here happened by enchantment, and it wouldn't be hard to believe that the same thing is happening now."

"I would believe it," responded Sancho, "if my blanketing had been like that, but it wasn't—it really and truly happened. I saw that the innkeeper who is here today held one corner of the blanket, and he tossed me toward the sky with great mirth and energy, and with as much laughter as strength. And since I could recognize people, I think, although I'm a simpleton and a sinner, it's not enchantment at all, but a lot of thwacks and bad luck."

"All right—God will make it turn out right," said don Quixote. "Help me get dressed and let me get out there. I want to find out what was going on and see the transformations you're talking about."

Sancho dressed him, and while he was being dressed, the priest told don Fernando and the others about don Quixote's madness, and of the ruse they had used to lure him away from "Peña Pobre," where he imagined that the disdain of his lady had driven him. He also told them about almost all the adventures that Sancho had related, which both amazed them and made them laugh, because it seemed to them—as it seemed to everyone—that he had the strangest kind of madness that could lay hold of a muddled mind. The priest said in addition that since Dorotea's good fortune prevented them from pursuing their original plan, it would be necessary to invent and devise another plan to take him home. Cardenio offered to continue what had been started, and Lucinda would take on and play Dorotea's part.

"No," said don Fernando, "it mustn't be that way. I want Dorotea to keep her disguise—this good knight's village isn't very far from here and I'll be pleased to help in his cure."

"It's not more than a two days' journey from here."

"Well, even if it were more, I'd be happy to make the trip for such a worthy purpose."

Don Quixote came out at this moment, in full armor, with Mambrino's helmet—although it was dented—on his head, clutching his shield and leaning on his massive lance. Don Fernando and the others were astonished at don Quixote's extraordinary presence, seeing his dry, pale face, half a league long, his odd array of armor, and his grave and courtly manner.

They waited in silence to see what he would say, and he, with great dignity and tranquillity, with his eyes directed toward the beautiful Dorotea, said: "I understand from my squire, beautiful *señora*, that your greatness has been humbled and you've been transformed from the queen and great lady you had been into an ordinary maiden. If this has been by order of the king-necromancer, your father, fearful that I couldn't give you the necessary and deserved aid, I say that he didn't know, nor does he know, half the mass,* and that he was not well versed in chivalresque histories. If he had read them as attentively and as carefully as I have, he would find at every turn how other knights of lesser fame than I had achieved more difficult outcomes. It's no great feat to slay a little giant, no matter how arrogant he is, because just a few hours ago I was battling with one and ... but it's better not to say anything, so they won't claim I'm lying. But time, which reveals all things, will make it known to me when least we expect it."

"You were battling two wineskins, and not a giant," said the innkeeper. Don Fernando told him to be silent and not interrupt don Quixote's speech in any way. Don Quixote continued, saying: "I say, noble and disinherited *señora*, if for the reason I described, your father has performed this metamorphoseos† on you, don't trust him at all, because there is no danger on earth through which my sword won't cleave a way, and with this same sword, once I've made your enemy's head topple to the ground, in just a few days I'll place the crown of your realm on your head."

Don Quixote said no more, and waited for the princess to respond, and she, since she knew don Fernando's decision that she should keep up the deception until they got to don Quixote's village, responded with great grace and gravity: "Whoever told you, brave Woebegone Knight, that I've been transformed and changed did not speak correctly, because I'm the same today as I was yesterday. It's true that certain incidents of good fortune have made some changes in me, because they have given me the best of everything I desire. But I haven't stopped being what I was on any account, and I still want to avail myself of the might of your invenerable arm,‡ as I always have. So, *señor mío*, may your

---

* That is, he doesn't know anything.

† This is a secondary Greek form for *metamorphosis*.

‡ Dorotea probably means *invulnerable* arm.

goodness again bring back the honor of the father who engendered me, and consider him wise and prudent, since with his knowledge he found such an easy and appropriate way to remedy my misfortune. And I believe that it if weren't for you, *señor*, I never would have had the good fortune I now have. In this I speak the truth, and most of these people present are faithful witnesses to it. What remains is for us to get on the road tomorrow, since we cannot travel any more today, and I'll leave to God and your heart the completion of the deliverance I expect."

The discreet Dorotea said this, and when don Quixote heard it, he turned to Sancho, and showing great anger, said: "I'm telling you now, Sanchuelo,* that you're the biggest rapscallion in Spain. Didn't you just tell me, you thieving vagabond, that this princess has turned into a maiden named Dorotea, and that the head of the giant I thought I'd cut off was the whore that bore you, along with other nonsense that made me more confused than I ever have been in all the days of my life? I swear"—and here he looked toward heaven and gritted his teeth—"that I'm about to wreak havoc on you, so it might put some sense into all the lying squires of knights-errant that there shall ever be."

"Calm down, your grace, *señor mío*," responded Sancho, "because it may easily be that I've been mistaken in regard to the transformation of the *señora* Princess Micomicona. But insofar as the giant's head goes, or at least the puncturing of the skins, and the business of blood being red wine, I'm not mistaken. By God, the wounded wineskins are still lying there at the head of your bed, and the red wine is a lake in the middle of the room, and if you don't believe me, 'it'll all come out in the wash.' I mean, you'll see when the innkeeper demands payment for the damage. As for the rest, about the *señora* queen still being the way she was, I'm gladdened in my heart, since my share will come to me as to every neighbor's son."

"I tell you now, Sancho," said don Quixote, "that you're an idiot; pardon me, and that's enough."

"That *is* enough," said don Fernando, "and let's not talk about it anymore, and since this *señora* princess says we should leave tomorrow because it's too late today, let it be

---

* *Sanchuelo* shows an added contemptuous diminutive suffix.

done that way, and we can spend this evening in pleasant conversation until tomorrow, when we'll accompany *señor* don Quixote, because we want to be witnesses to the brave and unheard-of exploits that he'll do in the course of this great undertaking."

"I'm the one who will serve and accompany you," responded don Quixote, "and I thank you for the favor done to me, and the good opinion you have of me, and I shall endeavor to justify it, or it will cost me my life, and even more, if that's possible."

Many courteous words and many offers of service flowed between don Quixote and don Fernando. But a traveler who came into the inn at that moment made them stop talking. His costume showed that he was a Christian recently returned from Moorish territory, because he was dressed in a short tunic made of blue cloth, with half sleeves and no collar. His pants were also of blue cloth and his cap of the same color. He was wearing date-colored low boots and had a short, curved sword, Moorish style, hanging from a strap across his chest. Right after him, riding on a donkey, was a woman dressed in the Moorish style, her face veiled, and with a scarf on her head. She was wearing a brocaded cap and a cloak that covered her from head to foot.

The man was robust and well proportioned, and he looked to be a little more than forty years old, his face somewhat dark complected, with a long mustache and full beard. In short, if he'd been well dressed, he would have been thought to be a person of quality and good birth.

When he came in he asked for a room, and when they said that there was none at the inn, he seemed distressed, and going over to the woman who by her dress appeared to be Moorish, he took her off her mount in his arms. Luscinda, Dorotea, the innkeeper's wife and daughter, and Maritornes, intrigued by the novelty of her dress, which they had never seen before, surrounded the Moorish lady. Dorotea, who always was kindly, courteous, and quick-witted, seeing that she as well as the man accompanying her were distressed at not finding a room, said: "Don't be grieved, *señora mía*, at the comfort that's lacking here, since you rarely find it in inns. But if you wouldn't mind spending the night with us"— pointing to Luscinda—"perhaps you'll find it more comfortable than some others in the course of your journey."

The veiled lady said nothing, but just stood up, crossed both her arms on her chest, bowed her head, and bent her body at the waist to show that she was giving thanks. By her silence, they figured that she doubtless must be Moorish and that she didn't speak Spanish. The man, who looked to have been a captive in Moorish lands, had been tending to other things until then, came up, and, seeing that all the women were surrounding the one who had come with him, and she didn't respond to what they had said to her, said: "*Señoras mías*, this maiden hardly understands my language, nor can she speak any other that isn't spoken in her country, and for this reason she didn't respond, nor will she respond, to what's asked her."

"We aren't asking her anything," responded Luscinda, "but we're offering her our company this night, and a share of the quarters we'll occupy, where she'll be made as comfortable as possible, with the goodwill we're obliged to show all strangers who are in need of it, especially since it's a woman who is to be served."

"On her part, and on my own," responded the captive, "*señora mía*, I kiss your hands, and I appreciate very much, as I should, the favor you've offered, because on such an occasion, and by such persons as you all appear to be, it's easy to see that it's surely a great favor."

"Tell me, *señor*," said Dorotea, "this *señora*, is she Christian or Moor? Her dress and her silence make us think that she is what we hope she's not."

"She's a Moor in her dress and in her body. But in her heart she's a true Christian—at least she has a great desire to be one."

"So, she hasn't been baptized?" replied Luscinda.

"There was no opportunity to have it done," responded the captive, "after she left Algiers—her hometown—and up to now she's not been in an imminent risk of death that would make it necessary to baptize her before she's been instructed in the rituals that our Mother the Holy Church dictates. But God will be pleased to see her baptized with the dignity her rank deserves, which is greater than her clothing and mine reflect."

With these words he made everyone who was listening curious to find out who the Moorish woman and the captive were. No one wanted to ask them just then, seeing that it was better to get them some rest than ask about their lives. Dorotea took the Moorish woman by the hand and led her to a seat next to herself and asked her to take her veil off. She looked at the captive as if to ask him what they were saying and what she should do. He told her in Arabic that they were asking her to take off her veil and that she should do it. So she took it off, and revealed a face that was so beautiful that Dorotea thought she was more beautiful than Luscinda, and Luscinda thought she was more beautiful than Dorotea, and all the onlookers thought that if any face could compare with these two, it was the Moorish woman's, and there were some who thought she was the most beautiful of the three. And since beauty has the power to inspire friendship and charm one's will, very soon all yielded to the desire to serve the Moorish woman and treat her with compassion.

Don Fernando asked the captive what the Moorish woman's name was, and he responded that it was *lela** Zoraida. As soon as she heard this, she understood what the Christian had asked, and she said instantly, filled with distress: "No, Zoraida, *no*—María, María," giving them to understand that her name was María and not Zoraida.

These words, coupled with the earnestness with which she said them, caused more than one tear from some of those present, especially the women, who by nature are tender and compassionatc. Luscinda embraced her with great affection, saying: "Yes, yes—María, María."

To which the Moorish woman responded: "Yes, yes, María—Zoraida *macange*!" which means NOT THAT.

Night had now fallen, and by the order of those who came with don Fernando, the innkeeper used diligence and care in cooking a dinner the best way he could. At dinnertime they sat at a long table, like servants use, because there was no round or square one available at the inn, and they gave the head of the table and seat of honor, although he initially refused, to don Quixote, who wanted Dorotea to sit at his side, since he was her defender. Luscinda and Zoraida sat next to her, and across from them, don Fernando and Cardenio, and then the captive and the other men, and next to the women, the priest and barber. They ate with

---

* *Lela* means something like Ms.

great contentment, and their pleasure was increased when they saw that don Quixote had stopped eating, moved by a similar spirit as when he spoke as he did to the goatherds, and he began to say: "Truly, when you consider it, *señores míos*, those who profess the order of knight-errantry see great and unheard-of things. Who in the world, upon entering the door of this castle and seeing us here as we are, would think that we are who we are? Who could say that this woman at my side is the great queen whom we all know, and that I'm that Woebegone Knight about whom so much is spoken by the mouth of fame? There is no doubt that this art and profession exceeds all those that man ever invented, and the more it's subject to danger, the more it should be esteemed. Away with those who say that letters surpass arms, because I'll tell them—no matter who they are—that they don't know what they're talking about. What they typically say and maintain is that the labors of the mind exceed those of the body, and the exercise of arms requires the use of the body alone, as if it were a profession of hod carriers, needing physical strength and nothing more, and as if the profession of arms didn't require acts of bravery that call for great intelligence to execute, or as if the warrior who commands an army or who defends a city under siege didn't use his mind as much as his body. How can one use bodily strength to know and conjecture the enemy's intent, designs, stratagems, and foresee the difficulties and dangers ahead—all of these are acts of intelligence in which the body plays no part.

"The fact is that arms require intelligence, as letters do. Let's see now which of the two vocations—that of the man of letters or the warrior—is the most arduous. This will be known by the goal toward which each one leads, because that endeavor that has the nobler goal will be esteemed more. The goal of letters—and here I'm not talking about divine letters, whose goal is to lead souls to heaven, and such a sublime goal cannot be matched—rather I'm talking about humane letters, whose goal is to regulate distributive justice and give to everyone his due; and to understand and make sure that worthy laws are observed—something generous and noble and worthy of great praise, but not as much as the goal of arms, which is peace—the greatest good that men can desire in this life. Thus, the first good news that the world and mankind had was what the angels gave that night that is now our day, when they sang in the sky: 'Glory in the highest, and peace on earth to men of goodwill,'* and the greeting that the master of heaven taught to His followers and chosen few when they entered a house was: 'Peace to this house.'† And many other times He said: 'My peace I leave with you. I give you my peace; peace be with you'‡—a precious reward given by such a Hand, a reward without which neither heaven nor earth can have happiness. This peace is the true goal of war, and by WAR and ARMS I mean the same thing. Given, then, this truth, that the goal of war is peace, and in this it's better than the goal of letters, let's now look at the bodily labors of the man of letters and those of the warrior, and see which is the more arduous."

Don Quixote expressed his discourse in such a way and with such words that none of those listening could have thought him to be crazy. Rather, since most of them were themselves associated with arms, they listened to him with great pleasure; and he went on: "So, I say that the travails of the student are these: mainly poverty, not because they're all poor, but rather to make their case as forceful as I can, and in saying that he suffers poverty, it seems to me that there is nothing more to say about his misfortune, because he who is poor has nothing that's good. This poverty is suffered in various ways: sometimes in hunger, sometimes in cold and in nakedness, and sometimes all of them together. Yet this hunger is not so bad that he doesn't eat, although it may be a bit later than he's accustomed to, and it may be with the leftovers of the rich; and the worst humiliation there can be is for him to go to the soup kitchen. He never lacks a *brasero*§ or a fireplace, which, if it doesn't completely warm him, at least it tempers the cold, and finally at night he sleeps under a roof. I don't want to talk about other trifles, such as lack of shirts, and the not-excessive

---

* From Luke 2:14. The original has "Glory *to God* in the highest."

† Luke 10:5.

‡ The first two are from John 14:27; the third is from John 20:19.

§ This is the old Spanish "table heater," a metal tray of red-hot coals placed under the middle of a table so that the heat rises to warm all those seated there.

number of shoes, the thin and threadbare clothing, nor the pleasurable gorging when good luck sets a banquet before him.

"But along this rough and difficult road, stumbling here, falling there, getting up over there, we've seen many of these who, having slid over the sandbars and through these Scyllas and Charybdises,* as though propelled forward on the wings of favorable fortune, wind up commanding and governing the world from their chairs, exchanging their hunger for satiety, their cold for comfort, their nudity for fancy clothing, and their sleep on a mat for resting on fine fabrics and damasks, as a just reward for their righteousness. But comparing their travails with those of the soldier, he falls far short, as I'll show now."

Chapter XXXVIII. Which deals with the Discourse on Arms and Letters that don Quixote gave.

DON QUIXOTE went on, saying: "Since we began with poverty in students and its various aspects, let's see if the soldier is any richer. We'll see that there is no one poorer in poverty, because he's dependent on his miserable wages—that arrive late or never—or whatever he can steal with his hands, with quite a bit of danger to his life and conscience. At times he's so tattered that a slashed jacket serves him both as dress uniform and a nightshirt, and in the middle of winter he has to shelter himself against the cold, in the open field, with only the breath from his mouth, and since it comes from an empty place, I can assure you that it comes out cold, contrary to the laws of nature. Just let him wait for night to come so that he can be restored from these discomforts in the bed that awaits him, which will never be guilty of being too narrow, because he can measure however much of the ground he wants, and toss and turn to his heart's content, without fearing he'll rumple his sheets.

---

* Scylla and Charybdis were two irresistible monsters who haunted the Strait of Messina in the *Odyssey*. The terms now refer to the Rock of Scylla and the ever-changing, swirling currents (Charybdis) there, both things being hazards to navigation.

"Finally the day and the hour come for him to receive the diploma; that is, finally the day of battle arrives, and there they'll put the tassel on his academic cap in the form of bandages, to treat a gunshot wound that may have pierced his temples, or will leave him crippled in his arm or leg. And if this doesn't happen, and heaven keeps him safe and sound, it may be that he'll go back to the same poverty as before. And if he's to get promoted he'll need another fight, another battle. But these miracles rarely come.

"But tell me, ladies and gentlemen, if you've thought about it—how many fewer are rewarded by war than those who have perished in it? You'll doubtless have to respond that there is no comparison—the dead cannot be counted and those who are living and have been decorated number less than a thousand. It's just the opposite with men of letters who, legally or illegally, manage to sustain themselves. So, although the labor of the soldier is greater, the reward is much less. But you may answer back that it's easier to reward two thousand men of letters than thirty thousand soldiers, because the former are rewarded by giving them appointments that have to be given to those of their profession, and the latter cannot be rewarded except from the funds of the master whom they serve, but this impossibility only serves to strengthen my argument.

"But let's let this be, because it's a labyrinth difficult to get out of, and let's go back to the superiority of arms over letters, a matter that has not yet been resolved, because the arguments advanced on both sides are so good. Letters say that arms cannot exist without them, because war also has its own laws that must be obeyed, and laws are the profession of the man of letters. Arms respond to this saying that letters cannot sustain themselves without arms, because with arms, republics are defended, kingdoms are preserved, cities are protected, highways are made safe, and the seas cleared of corsairs. Finally, if there were no arms, you can bet that republics, kingdoms, monarchies, cities, and highways of the sea and of the land would all be subject to the ruin and disorder of war.

"It's a well-known fact that what costs the most is esteemed, and should be esteemed the most. If someone achieves eminence in letters, it costs him time, loss of sleep, hunger, nakedness, headaches, indigestion, and other things associated with it. But for one to become a good soldier, it costs him everything it costs a student, but in such a larger degree that there is no comparison possible, because at every step he's in danger of losing his life. And what fear of need or poverty can threaten a student compared to what a soldier faces, finding himself surrounded in a fortress, or keeping watch at a guard post, hearing his enemy tunneling toward where he is, and he cannot leave his post under any circumstance, nor flee from the danger that threatens him so nearby? All he can do is inform his captain what is happening—so that he can try to destroy the tunnel—and stay there quietly, fearing and expecting that at any moment he'll go flying to the clouds without wings, and crash to the ground against his will.*

"And if this appears to be just a slight danger, let's see if it's equaled or surpassed when two galleys attack each other, prow to prow, in the middle of the spacious sea, locked and lashed together so that the soldier has no more room than the point of the prow to stand on. But he, seeing that there are as many ministers of death before him who threaten him as there are cannons, which are not a lance-length away, and seeing that at the first misstep he would go to visit Neptune's bottomless gulf, nonetheless, with a brave heart, impelled by the honor that inspires him, uses himself as a target for all that musketry, and tries to forge a way onto the enemy ship. And what should be admired the most is that hardly has one fallen to where he cannot be raised until the end of time, when another takes his place, and if this one also falls into the sea—which itself waits for him like an enemy—another and another follow him, without any time between their deaths. This is the greatest bravery and daring that can be found in any of the perils of war.

"Happy and blessed were those ages that lacked the dreaded fury of those devilish instruments of artillery—

---

* To destroy the walls of a fortress in those days, an enemy would tunnel to where the walls were overhead and then use explosives to make the walls crumble. To defend against this, the people being attacked would tunnel outward in the hopes of reaching the enemy's tunnel and destroying it before they could do their damage to the walls. This is Rico's good note.

whose inventor I'm convinced must be in hell as a reward for his diabolical invention—with which it's possible for a despicable and cowardly arm to take the life of a brave knight. Without knowing how or from where—just at the moment when courage and dash inflame and embolden his valiant heart—along comes a stray bullet, discharged by someone who may have fled in terror and then was startled by the flash from his infernal device, whose shot cuts short in an instant the thoughts and life of a person who deserved to live many centuries.

"So, considering this, I'm almost about to say that in my heart I'm sorry I took up this calling as a knight-errant in such a detestable age as is the one we live in, because, although I fear no danger, still it troubles me to think that powder and bullets can take my chance away to be famous throughout the known world by the might of my arm and the blade of my sword. But heaven's will be done. If I succeed in my plan, I shall be even more esteemed than the knights-errant of old because I'm subject to greater dangers."

While the others ate dinner, don Quixote delivered this long speech, forgetting to put a morsel into his mouth, even though Sancho Panza told him to eat once in a while, since he could say everything he wanted to afterward. Those who were listening to him had renewed pity for him, seeing that a man of such high intelligence and such good reasoning in everything else he spoke about should lose them so entirely when dealing with his cursed chivalry. The priest told him he was correct in everything he said in favor of arms, and he, although a man of letters and a university graduate, was of the same opinion.

They finished dining, and the tablecloth was removed; and while the innkeeper's wife, her daughter, and Maritornes were getting don Quixote de La Mancha's former loft ready—that was where they arranged for all of the women to sleep that night—don Fernando begged the captive to tell them the story of his life, because it would doubtless be exotic and pleasing, judging from the hints he'd begun to give when he arrived with Zoraida. The captive responded that he would be very pleased to do what he was asked, but he only feared it wouldn't give them as much pleasure as he wished—nevertheless, he would tell it to them so as to comply with his request. The priest and everyone else thanked him, and once again asked him to tell his story. And he, seeing himself beseeched by so many, said that so much urging wasn't necessary, since don Fernando's command carried so much weight.

"So, let your graces be attentive, and you'll hear a true story. And it may be that fictitious ones written with ingenious and studied art might not be its equal."

With this, he said that everyone should get comfortable and give him complete silence, and when he saw that everyone was quiet and was waiting to hear what he had to say, with a pleasant but quiet voice he began in this way:

Chapter XXXIX. Wherein the captive tells of his life and adventures.

IN A village in the mountains of León my family had its origins. Our family was favored more by nature than by fortune, although, since those villages were so poor, my father was still thought to be rich, and he truly would have been if he'd been as skilled in holding on to his fortune as he was in spending it. This tendency of his to be generous and wasteful came from his having been a soldier in his youth, because being a soldier is a school where the stingy person becomes generous, and the generous person becomes a squanderer; and if some soldiers are stingy they're like monsters that are rarely seen. My father went past the level of liberality and flirted with extravagance, something that is not good for a married man with children to succeed him in name and position. My father had three children, all male, and all of the age when they could choose a career. My father, seeing that he couldn't resist his propensity, wanted to abandon the instrument and cause of his profligacy, and that was to deprive himself of his wealth, without which Alexander* himself would have been considered miserly.

And so, one day he called the three of us together in a room, and with no one else present, he said words to us similar to the ones I'll say now: "My sons, to tell you that I

---

* Much of what is attributed to Alexander the Great (356–323 B.C.) is fanciful, as is his legendary generosity.

love you, it's enough to know and say that you're my children; and to convince you that I don't love you, it's enough to know that I can't restrain myself in what concerns your inheritance. So you'll understand that from now on I love you as a father and don't want to ruin you like a stepfather; I propose to do something with you I've thought about for many days, and deliberated with mature consideration. You're now old enough to choose a profession, or at least to choose a calling such that when you're older will bring you honor and profit. What I've decided is to divide my estate into four parts—three of them I'll give in equal amount to the three of you, and the fourth part I'll keep for myself to live on and sustain myself the days that heaven sees fit to allot me. But I want, once you have your part of the estate, each one to choose one of the paths I'll name. There is a saying in our Spain, which in my opinion is very true, as they all are, since they're short maxims taken from long and practical experience. The one I'll tell you is this: 'Church, sea, or the royal house,' or, to say it more clearly: Whoever wants to flourish and become rich should go into the Church; go to sea, exercising the art of commerce; or serve the king and queen in their household. They also say: 'A crumb from the king is worth more than the favor of a lord.' I say all this because I'd like, and it's my will, for one of you go into letters, the second into business, and the third into the king's service in his wars, since it's hard to serve him in his household, and even though wars don't give many riches, they do give great distinction and fame. One week hence, I'll give you your shares in cash, without cheating you out of an *ardite*, as you'll plainly see. Tell me now if you wish to go along with my idea and advice in what I've proposed to you."

He called on me as the eldest to answer, and I told him not to disburse his fortune, but rather to spend it any way he wanted, since we were young men capable of earning our own living. But I finally complied with his wish; and mine was to serve in the practice of arms, thereby serving God and my king. The second brother made the same proposal, and chose to go to the Indies, investing the part of the estate that belonged to him. The youngest, and who I think was the wisest, said that he wanted to go into the Church or to finish his already begun studies at Salamanca. As soon as we agreed and chose our professions, my father embraced us all, and in the short time he stipulated, he put into effect everything he'd promised us, and, giving each of us our share, which, the way I remember it, was three thousand *ducados* in cash—because our uncle had bought the whole estate right away to keep it in the family—on that same day the three of us bade farewell to our good father. It seemed to me on that day that it was inhuman to leave him with so little for his old age, so I induced him to take back two thousand *ducados* of my three thousand, because the rest was more than enough to provide me with all a soldier needed.

My two brothers, moved by my example, also gave him back one thousand *ducados* each. So my father kept four thousand in cash and three thousand more, which, it seems, was what his portion of the estate was worth; he didn't want to sell his part, but rather keep it as land. So, finally, we bade farewell to him and to our uncle whom I mentioned, not without great emotion and tears on everyone's part. They charged us to keep in touch whenever we could, telling them about our fortunes, good or bad. We promised to do so, and embracing us and giving us his blessing, one took the road to Salamanca, the other to Seville,* and I to Alicante,† where I had news that there was a Genoese ship that was loading wool for Genoa.‡

It has been twenty-two years since I left my father's house, and during that time, although I've written some letters, I've had no news of him or of my brothers. I'll tell you briefly what happened during this time. I embarked in Alicante, and I arrived in Genoa after an auspicious voyage, and then I went to Milan,§ where I equipped myself with arms and soldier's uniforms. I wanted to begin my service in Piedmont, and when I was on the way to Alessandria della Paglia,¶ I heard that the great Duque

---

* Seville was the major port from where ships left Spain for the New World.
† Alicante is a major Mediterranean port in southeastern Spain.
‡ Genoa is a major seaport in northwestern Italy.
§ Milan is a major manufacturing, commercial, and financial city seventy-five miles north of Genoa.
¶ Alessandria della Paglia was a fortress city about halfway between Milan and Genoa.

de Alba* was going to Flanders.† I changed my plan and went with him, to serve him in the campaigns that he was undertaking; I was present at the death of the counts of Egmont and Hoorn,‡ and rose to the rank of lieutenant under the famous captain from Guadalajara named Diego de Urbina.§ After I'd been in Flanders for some time, we got news of the confederation that his Holiness Pope Pius V¶—of happy memory—had put together with Venice** and Spain against the common enemy, the Turks. At that time the Turks had won with their armada the famous Island of Cyprus,†† which had been under the control of Venice, and was an unfortunate and lamentable loss.

It was a known fact that the most serene don Juan de Austria, natural brother of our king don Felipe II,‡‡ was the general of this league. Rumors of the great preparations for war were being spread. All of this incited and moved my spirit and desire to be in the coming campaign. Although I suspected, and even had sure promises, that in the next confrontation in Flanders that came up I'd be promoted to captain, I decided to forsake everything and go to Italy. And it was my good fortune that *señor* don Juan de Austria had just arrived in Genoa§§ on his way to Naples to join the armada of Venice, as he later did at Messina.¶¶

---

* This was, in real life, the third Duke of Alba, Fernando Álvarez de Toledo, who did enter Brussels in 1567.
† Flanders is roughly modern Belgium.
‡ The Duke of Alba had the rebellious dukes of Egmont and Hoorn beheaded in June of 1568.
§ Diego de Urbina, in real life, fought in the battle of Lepanto (1571), as did Cervantes.
¶ Pius V (1504–1572) was a great reformer who eliminated Protestantism in Italy, excommunicated Elizabeth I, and organized the battle of Lepanto.
** Venice was a republic until 1797.
†† The Turks wanted to expand their empire by invading the Venetian island of Cyprus in 1570.
‡‡ Don Juan de Austria (1545–1578) was indeed the "natural" (i.e., bastard) son of Carlos V and half brother of Felipe II.
§§ Don Juan de Austria did arrive in Genoa on July 26, 1571.
¶¶ Troops were assembled in Messina, the Sicilian port nearest to mainland Italy, on August 24, 1571.

So, finally, I took part in that glorious campaign,* promoted by that time to captain of infantry, which I came into more by my good luck than by my merits. And that day—which was so fortunate for Christendom, since the world and all its nations were disabused of the error that the Turks were invincible on the sea—on that day, I say, where Ottoman pride and arrogance were dashed, among all those who were happy—because the Christians who died there were more blessed than those who survived and triumphed—I alone was miserable. Because instead of what I could have expected in Roman times—a Naval Crown†—I found myself with chains on my feet and manacles on my wrists that night after the battle.

It happened this way: Uchalí,‡ king of Algiers, a daring and adventurous corsair, attacked and defeated the flagship of Malta (where only three knights survived the attack, and these were badly wounded), so the flagship of Juan Andrea,§ with me and my men on board, went to lend support. I did what you're supposed to do in such cases, and leapt onto the enemy galley, which immediately pulled away from ours, and prevented my soldiers from following me, so I found myself alone among my enemies, whom I couldn't overcome because there were so many of them. In short, I was taken prisoner, covered with wounds. As you doubtless have heard, *señores*, Uchalí got away safely with his whole squadron, and I remained captive in his power, being the only sad one among so many happy people, and a prisoner among so many free men, because fifteen thousand Christians—all of them rowers for the Turkish fleet—regained their longed-for freedom that day.

---

* This *glorious campaign* was the Battle of Lepanto, October 7, 1571, where the Venetian and Spanish armadas defeated the Turks. "Lepanto" is in Greece at modern Náfpaktos, east of Patras on the Gulf of Corinth. After four hours the Christian fleet won the battle and captured 117 enemy galleys. The victory boosted European morale greatly.
† The Romans awarded a Naval Crown to the first soldier who jumped across to an enemy galley.
‡ Uchalí was an Italian renegade who converted to Islam and was viceroy of Algiers in 1570. In real life, he did take part in the Battle of Lepanto.
§ Giovanni Andrea Doria commanded the right wing of the Christian armada.

They took me to Constantinople,* where the Grand Turk Selim† made my master general of the seas because he'd done his duty in the battle, having taken, as a proof of his bravery, the banner of the flagship of the Order of Malta. I found myself the next year, which was 'seventy-two, in Navarino,‡ rowing in the flagship with the three lanterns.§ I saw and noted the opportunity that was lost in not taking the whole Turkish fleet in the port, because all the Turkish marines and the janissaries—the sultan's personal guards—on board were convinced that they would be attacked in that same port, and they had their clothing and *pasamaques*—which are their shoes—ready to flee to the shore immediately, without waiting for the attack—such was the fear they had of our armada. But heaven ordered it otherwise, not for any fault or carelessness on the part of the general who was commanding our side, but rather through the sins of Christendom, and because God permits us always to have scourges to chastise us.

In the end Uchalí took refuge in Modón, which is an island¶ next to Navarino, where, putting his men ashore, he fortified the entry to the port, and lay quiet until *señor* don Juan went back. In this voyage don Juan captured the galley named LA PRESA, *The Prize*, whose captain was the son of the famous corsair Barbarossa.** LA PRESA was taken by the flagship of the Neapolitan fleet, called LA LOBA, *The She Wolf*, commanded by that lightning bolt of a warrior, that father to his men, that successful and never-conquered captain, don Álvaro de Bazán, Marqués de Santa Cruz. And I don't want to forget to mention what happened with the capture of LA PRESA. The son of Barbarossa was so cruel and treated his

---

* Constantinople, capital of the Ottoman Empire, was the old name of Istanbul, Turkey's largest city.

† This is Selim II (1524–1574), son of Süleyman I, the Magnificent (1494–1566).

‡ Navarinon (its old Greek name), officially known now as Pílos, is a port town in southwestern Greece about 110 miles south of "Lepanto."

§ The galley with the three lanterns was the admiral's flagship.

¶ Modón is the Venetian name for Methóni, which is not an island at all, and is five miles south of Pílos.

** In real life, the son of Barbarossa was not the captain, but rather a certain Mehmet Bey.

captives so badly that as soon as the rowers saw the galley LA LOBA closing in, they all dropped their oars at the same moment, and seized their captain, who was at the captain's station shouting at them to row all out, and they passed him from bench to bench, from poop to prow, and they bit him so much that he'd hardly gotten past the mast when his soul went off to hell. Such was the cruelty, as I've said, with which he treated them and the hatred they bore him.

We returned to Constantinople, and the following year, which was 'seventy-three, it was learned there that don Juan had won Tunis and taken that kingdom from the Turks and put it into the hands of Muley Hamet, thus putting an end to the hopes of his brother, Muley Hamida—the cruelest and bravest Moor the world has ever seen—to rule there again.* The Grand Turk was deeply sorry about this loss, and using the cunning that all those of his house have, made peace with the Venetians, which they wanted more than he did, and the following year, 'seventy-four, he attacked La Goleta† and the fort that *señor* don Juan had left half-constructed.

In all these battles I was at the oar, with no hope at all of being released. At least I didn't expect it by ransom, because I decided not to write my father about my misfortune. La Goleta was finally lost along with the fort—there were seventy-five thousand paid Turkish soldiers, and four hundred thousand Moorish soldiers from all over Africa, and along with this enormous number of men there were so many munitions and matériel, and there were so many diggers, that with their hands alone, they could have buried La Goleta and the fort.

La Goleta, thought until then to be impregnable, was the

---

* Muley Hassan was king of Tunis until 1542 when his son Muley Hamida blinded and dethroned him. He more or less ruled until 1573, when his brother Muley Hamet took over (on October 14), but within a year the Turks imprisoned him.

† La Goleta (now a resort and residential area, as well as a port, called Halq-al-Wadi, or its French name, La Goulette) was an island fortress that protected Tunis. On July 14, 1535, Carlos V attacked La Goleta by sea with an immense force and later overran Tunis, releasing twenty thousand Christian prisoners. After that, the Spanish occupied the fortress at La Goleta, which Muley Hassan was forced to allow. The Turks did conquer it in August of 1574.

first to fall, but it wasn't lost through any fault of the defend-
ers, who did everything they could and should have done
in its defense, but rather because it was easy to construct
earthworks using desert sand. Normally you strike water at
two palms,* but the Turks didn't hit any until six feet, and
so they could make and stack sandbags so high that they
were higher than the walls of the fort, and firing inside from
above, no one could make a stand or put up a defense. It was
commonly held that our soldiers shouldn't have been shut
up inside La Goleta, but rather should have fought in the
open, but those who say this speak with no firsthand knowledge, and with little experience in such cases, because in La
Goleta and in the fort, there were scarcely seven thousand
soldiers. How could so few, no matter how resolute they
might be, go into the open and hold their own against so
many enemies? And how could a fort not be lost when no
reinforcements are sent, and more so when many fierce enemies surround them in their own country?

But many held the opinion, as I did, that it was a special
favor and mercy that heaven did for Spain in permitting the
destruction of that lair and hiding place of wicked things,
that glutton or sponge and waster of an infinite amount of
money that was spent there without any benefit, serving no
purpose other than preserving the memory of having been
won by Carlos V, as if those stones were needed to make
his name eternal, as it is and will always be. The fort was
also lost, but the Turks had to win it inch by inch, because
those who were defending it fought so valiantly and with
such heart that more than twenty-five thousand enemies
were killed in the twenty-two general assaults that were
made. Of the three hundred survivors they captured, no
one was unwounded, a sure sign of their mettle and bravery, and how well they defended themselves and kept their
positions.

A small fort or tower in the middle of the lagoon under
the command of don Juan Zanoguera,† a Valencian knight
and famous soldier, surrendered unconditionally. They
captured Pedro Puertocarrero, commandant of La Goleta,
who had done everything he could to defend his fort, and

---

* Sixteen inches.

† Juan Zanoguera and the next three people mentioned are historical.

was so beaten for having lost it that he died of a broken heart on the way to Constantinople, where they were taking him to be a prisoner. They captured the commandant of the fort, who was named Gabrio Cerbellón, a Milanese knight, a great engineer and a very brave soldier. Many important people died in these two forts, including Pagán Doria, a knight in the Order of San Juan,* a generous man, as shown by his extreme liberality with his brother, the famous Giovanni Andrea Doria. And what made his death sadder was that he was killed by some Moors to whom he'd entrusted himself, realizing the fort was lost. They offered to take him disguised as a Moor to the Island of Tabarka,† a small fort or station on the coast held by the Genoese who deal in collecting coral. Anyway, these Moors cut off his head and took it to the commandant of the Turkish armada, who made good on the Spanish proverb that says: "Though treason pleases, the traitor is hated," since they say the commandant had the men who brought the present to him hanged, because they hadn't brought him alive.

Among the Christians who were captured at the fort, one of them was named Pedro de Aguilar, born in I don't know which village in Andalusia, who had been a lieutenant at the fort, a soldier of great repute and of rare intelligence. He also had a particular gift for what they call poetry. I say it because his fate brought him to my galley and to my bench, and to be the slave of my own master, and before we left that port, the man wrote two sonnets in the style of epitaphs, one on La Goleta and the other on the fort. I may as well recite them because I have them memorized, and I think they'll give more pleasure than annoyance.

As soon as the captive mentioned don Pedro of Aguilar, don Fernando looked at his companions, and all of them smiled, and when he was about to recite the sonnets, one of them said: "Before you continue, I'd like to know what happened to this Pedro of Aguilar that you mentioned."

---

* The Order of San Juan, founded in the eleventh century, is one of the Catholic military orders whose members are the knights of that order.
† Tabarka was a small Genoese-owned port at the time of the Battle of Lepanto, formerly Spanish. It's in Tunisia between the Algerian city of Bône and Tunis.

"All I know," responded the captive, "is that after he'd been in Constantinople for two years, he escaped with a Greek spy in the garb of an Albanian, and I don't know if he finally got free, but I suppose he did, because a year later I saw the Greek in Constantinople, but I didn't get a chance to ask him about the outcome of their journey."

"Well, it was successful," responded the man, "because this don Pedro is my brother, and he's in our village right now, in good health and rich, married, and with three children."

"Thanks be to God," said the captive, "for all the mercies He's shown him, because there is nothing on earth, in my opinion, that can equal that of recovering one's lost freedom."

"And what's more," said the man, "I know the sonnets that my brother wrote."

"Recite them, then," said the captive, "because you probably know them better than I do."

"I'll be pleased to," said the man, "and the one about La Goleta goes like this:"

Chapter XL. *Where the story of the captive is continued.*

SONNET

BLEST SOULS, that, from this mortal husk set free,
    In reward of brave deeds beatified,
    Above this lowly orb of ours abide
    Made heirs of heaven and immortality,
With noble rage and ardor glowing ye
    Your strength, while strength was yours, in battle plied,
    And with your own blood and the foeman's dyed
    The sandy soil and the encircling sea.
It was the ebbing lifeblood first that failed
    The weary arms; the stout hearts never quailed.
    Though vanquished, yet ye earned the victor's crown:
Though mourned, yet still triumphant was your fall
    For there ye won, between the sword and wall,
    In Heaven glory and on earth renown.*

---

* This sonnet and the next one are Ormsby's versions.

"THAT'S IT exactly as I remember it," said the captive. "Well, then, the one about the fort," said the man, "if my memory serves me, goes like this:

SONNET

Up from this wasted soil, this shattered shell,
    Whose walls and towers here in ruin lie,
    Three thousand soldier souls took wing on high,
    In the bright mansions of the blest to dwell.
The onslaught of the foeman to repel
    By might of arm all vainly did they try,
    And when at length 'twas left them but to die,
    Wearied and few the last defenders fell.
And this same arid soil hath ever been
    A haunt of countless mournful memories,
    As well in our day as in days of yore.
But never yet to heaven it sent, I think,
    From its hard bosom purer souls than these,
    Or braver bodies on its surface bore.

The sonnets didn't seem bad, and the captive was very happy with the news that they gave him about his friend, and he continued his story, saying:

With the surrender of La Goleta and the fort, the Turks ordered La Goleta to be demolished (for the fort was already in such bad shape, it was as good as razed). In order to do it quickly and with minimal work, they laid charges under it in three places, but they couldn't blow up the part that seemed weakest—the ancient walls—whereas all that was left standing of the new building—which had been built by El Fratín*—crumbled easily. Finally, the fleet returned to Constantinople, and a few months later my master, Uchalí, died.† They called him Uchalí Fartax, which means in Turkish "the scabby renegade," because that's the way he was. It's a custom among the Turks to take names based on some defect or virtue that they have. This is because there

---

* El Fratín was an Italian architect, Giacome Paleazzo, who worked for Charles V and Philip II.
† In real life, Uchalí died in June of 1587.

are only four surnames of families* that trace their descent
from the House of Ottoman,† and the rest, as I've said, take
their first and last names sometimes from bodily blemishes,
and sometimes from moral qualities. This scabby one had
rowed at the oar as a slave of the Great Master for fourteen
years, and when he was more than thirty-four years old, he
renounced his faith because he was so angry with a Turk
who had given him a punch while they were rowing, and to
avenge himself, he converted to Islam. His valor was such
that, without resorting to immoral ways and means‡ that
other favorites of the Grand Turk use to rise to power, he
came to be king of Algiers, and afterward general at sea,
which is the third-highest position in that realm.§ He was
Calabrian by birth,¶ and morally a worthy man, and treated
his slaves with great humanity. He finally had three thousand slaves, and after his death, they were divided, as he
stipulated in his will, between the Great Master (who is an
heir of all those who die, and shares with the children of
the deceased) and his renegades. I fell to a Venetian renegade who, when he was a cabin boy on a ship, was taken
as a slave by Uchalí, and he was so beloved by him that he
became one of his regaled youths.** This former cabin boy
had become the cruelest renegade I ever saw—his name
was Hassán Bajá,†† and he grew very rich and became the
king of Algiers. I went there with him from Constantinople,
quite content to be near Spain,‡‡ not because I planned to
write to anyone about my misfortunes, but to see if Fortune
would be better to me in Algiers than in Constantinople,
where I'd attempted a thousand different ways to escape,

---

* Annotators always point out these four names: Muhammat, Mustafá,
Murad, and Alí.
† The Ottoman Empire lasted from the fourteenth century until 1922.
‡ Gaos points out that these immoral ways and means refer to sod-
omy.
§ The highest ones are grand vizier (prime minister) and *muftí* (the
highest judicial position in the empire).
¶ Calabria is the region that forms the toe of the Italian boot.
** Refers to handsome boys used for sodomy, as Gaos explains.
†† Hassán Bajá was a Venetian originally named Andreta (born in
1545). Cervantes was his slave and was pardoned three times by him
for his three attempts to escape.
‡‡ Algiers is only 210 miles from the Spanish coast.

and none worked out. I thought that I'd find other means in Algiers of getting what I wanted so much, because I'd never abandoned hope of freedom, and when the outcome of what I devised, planned, and tried didn't turn out right, I did not despair but concealed my intentions and sought fresh hope to bolster me, no matter how faint and feeble it might be.

This is the way I spent my time, shut up in a prison or house that the Turks call a BAÑO,* where they keep their Christian slaves—those belonging to the king and to some individuals; and others that they call THOSE OF THE *ALMACÉN*,† which is the same thing as saying "prisoners of the municipality," who are employed in the public works of the city and other odd jobs. These captives have a hard time getting their freedom. Since they're held in common and have no particular master, there is no one with whom one can negotiate for their ransom, even though they may have ransom money available. Individuals often take their captives to these *baños*—mainly those eligible for ransom—since they can keep them there at their ease and in safety until their ransom comes. The captives of the king who were waiting for ransom don't go out to work with the others, except when the ransom money is delayed. When that happens, to make them write more fervently for the ransom, they're made to work and gather firewood like the rest, which is no light work.

I was one of the ones waiting for ransom. Since they knew I was a captain, even though I told them I had limited means and was far from rich, it did little good, because they placed me among those who were waiting for ransom. They put a chain on me, more as a sign that I was to be ransomed than to keep me locked up, and so I lived there with a number of other men and persons of quality, designated and held for ransom. Although hunger and nakedness troubled us at times—maybe almost always—nothing bothered us quite as much as hearing and seeing at every turn the

---

* Comes from an Arabic word meaning "building"—*banayya*. It was a patio surrounded by small rooms, where the Moors kept their prisoners. Cervantes wrote a play called *The* Baños *of Algiers*.

† *Almacén* refers to the community, as the sentence goes on to explain.

unheard-of cruelties that my master inflicted on Christians. Every day he would hang one, impale this one, rip the ear off that one, and all this for very little cause, so much so that the Turks thought he did it for amusement, and that he was murderously disposed toward the whole human race. The only one who fared well with him was a Spanish soldier named So-and-So de Saavedra,* whom he never beat, nor had beaten, nor said a harsh word to, even though the Spaniard did things that will stick in people's memory for many years—and all of them to attain freedom—and for the least of the many things he did, all of us were fearful that he would be impaled, and he feared it himself more than once. If time permitted, I'd say things now that this soldier did that would interest and astonish you much more than the narration of my own story.

So, getting on with my story, the patio in our prison was overlooked by the windows of the house of a rich and important Moor. In the Moorish tradition they were really more openings than windows, covered with thick blinds. It happened, then, that one day when I was in the patio with three companions, passing the time of day by seeing how far we could jump with our chains on—we were alone, since the other Christians had gone to work. I raised my eyes by chance and saw a stick appear through one of those little windows I mentioned, and tied to it there was a piece of cloth. The stick was being waved back and forth, almost as if someone were making signs for us to go over and take it. One of the men with me went over and stood under it to see if they would release it, or what they would do. But as soon as he got there, they raised the stick and waved it back and forth, as if they were saying no by a shake of the head. The Christian came back, and they lowered it again and waved it as before. Another of my companions went over and the same thing happened to him as happened to the first one. Finally, the third one went over, and had the same result as the first two.

When I saw this, I thought I'd try my luck as well, and as soon as I went over and stood under it, they let it drop, and it fell inside the *baño* at my feet. I hurried to untie the cloth, in which I saw a knotted handkerchief that I untied,

---

* This is, of course, Cervantes' own maternal last name.

and inside it were ten *cianís*, which are coins made of gold alloy that the Moors use, and each one is worth ten of our *reales*. That I was pleased with my find goes without saying, but my wonder was as great as my joy, curious about where that good fortune could have come to us from, to me especially, since the unwillingness to release the stick except to me clearly showed that it was for me that the favor was intended. I took my welcome money, broke the stick, and went back to the terrace. I looked at the window and saw a lily-white hand that opened and shut it quickly. From this we gathered that some woman who lived in that house must have done the good deed, and to show our thanks, we made salaams in the Moorish style, bowing our heads and bending at the waist, crossing our arms over our chests. After a little while, she extended a little cross made of reeds through the window and took it back in immediately. This sign confirmed that some Christian woman must be captive in that house, and she was the one who did us that favor. But the whiteness of the hand and the bracelets that she wore dispelled this idea. Then we imagined that it must be some Christian renegade, one of those whom their masters sometimes take as their legitimate wives, and they even do it gladly, because they prefer them to women of their own race.

In all of our speculations, we were very far from the truth of the matter. From then on about the only thing we did was to fix our gaze at the window where the cross had appeared—as if it were the North Star. But two weeks went by in which we didn't see it, or the hand, or any other sign. And during this time we made every effort to find out who lived in that house, and if there was any Christian renegade woman living there, but we never found anyone who could tell us anything except that an important Moor lived there named Hajji Murad, formerly governor of El-Batha,* which they consider a highly respected office. But when we were least thinking that more *cianís* would rain down, we suddenly saw another stick appear, with a piece of cloth tied to it and a larger knotted handkerchief inside, and this was when the *baño* was deserted just like the previ-

---

* El-Batha was a fortress five miles from Oran, which is two hundred miles west of Algiers.

ous time. We tried the original test, each of the three others
going before me, but only to me was the reed delivered,
because when I went over, they let it fall. I untied the knot
and found forty Spanish *escudos* in gold, and a paper written in Arabic, and at the end of the text was a large cross.
I kissed the cross and took the *escudos* and went back to
the terrace. We did our salaams, and the hand once again
appeared. I made signs to the effect that I'd read the paper,
and they closed the window. We were perplexed and happy
with what had happened, and since none of us understood
Arabic, we were enormously curious to find out what the
paper said, but it was going to be even harder to find someone who could read it.

Finally, I decided to confide in a renegade from Murcia*
who had said he was my great friend and pledged that he
would keep the secret I'd entrust to him—because some
renegades, when they're planning to return to Christian
lands, take with them testimonials from important captives
that attest, in whatever way they can, that the renegade is a
good man who has always treated Christians well and who
is eager to escape at the first opportunity. There are some
who use these certificates with good intentions; others use
them casually and cunningly—if they go on a plundering
raid in Christian territory, and get left behind or are captured, they take these testimonials out and say that those
papers show the reason they returned, that they want to
remain in Christian lands, and that's why they participated
in the maritime raid with the Turks. By these means they
escape the immediate consequences and get reconciled
with the Church without suffering any punishment†—
and the first chance they get they return to the Barbary
Coast.‡

So, one of the renegades I mentioned was a friend of
mine who had testimonials from all of us, in which we
vouched for him insofar as we could. If the Moors found
these papers on him, they would burn him alive. I found out

---

* A major city in southeastern Spain.

† When renegades returned to Spain, they appeared before the Inquisition, and these affidavits were useful in obtaining their release
without punishment.

‡ Moorish territory along the northern African coast.

that he knew Arabic very well—not only could he speak it but he could also write it. But before I'd reveal the whole secret to him, I asked him to read the paper I said I'd found by chance somewhere in my cell. He unfolded it and spent a good while examining and deciphering it, muttering between his teeth. I asked him if he understood it. He said that he did, and very well, and if I wanted him to read it for me word for word, I should give him some ink and a pen so he could do it properly. We gave him what he asked for, and he—a bit at a time—translated it. As he was finishing, he said: "Everything that I wrote here in Spanish, without missing a letter, is what this paper in Arabic says, but where it says LELA MARIÉN, it should read OUR LADY THE VIRGIN MARY."

We read the paper, which went like this:

When I was a girl, my father had a slave who taught me in my language about the Christian ZALÁ* and she said many things about *Lela* Marién. The Christian woman died, and I know that she didn't go into the fire, but went with Allah, because I saw her twice afterward and she told me that I should go to Christian lands to see *Lela* Marién, who loved me very much. I don't know how to go there. I've seen many Christians through this window and none has seemed a gentleman, except you. I'm very pretty and young, and have a lot of money I can take with me. See if you can find a way for us to go there, and if you want, you can be my husband. If not, it won't distress me because *Lela* Marién will provide me with someone to marry. I wrote this. Be careful to whom you give this to read—trust no Moor because they're all deceivers. I'm greatly troubled and I'd like you not to reveal this to anyone, since if my father found out, he would throw me into a well and cover me with stones. I'll tie a piece of string to a stick so you can tie your answer to it. And if you have no one who can write Arabic, tell me by signs, because *Lela* Marién will make me understand. May she and Allah, and this cross which I kiss many times, protect you.

---

* *Zalá* means prayer; doubtless the Hail Mary, says Rico.

Señores, judge if I had reason for surprise and joy at the words of this paper. Both were so great that the renegade realized that I hadn't found the paper by chance, but that it had been written to one of us. So he begged us, if it was true what he suspected, that we confide in him and tell him everything, and that he would risk his life for our freedom. And when he said this, he took out a metal cross, and with many tears swore by the God that the cross represented, in whom he—although a sinner and a bad man—truly and faithfully believed, to keep everything we might want to tell him a secret, because it seemed to him, and he almost guessed it, that through the woman who had written that letter, he and all of us could get our freedom, and he could get what he most wanted, which was to restore himself to the Holy Mother Church from which—through his own ignorance and sin—he'd been severed like a rotten limb.

He said this with so many tears and signs of repentance that we all agreed to tell him the truth of the matter, so we told him everything without concealing anything. We pointed out the window from where the stick had appeared, and he situated the house from there, and took special care to find out who lived in it. We also agreed that it would be good to answer the Moorish woman's letter, since we now had someone who could do it. The renegade wrote down the words that I dictated to him without delay, which are the exact ones that I'll repeat, because of all the important things that happened to me in this whole affair, none has left my memory, nor will they ever as long as I live. This, then, is what we responded to the Moorish woman:

May the true Allah protect you, *señora mía*, and the blessed Marién, who is the true Mother of God and is the one who put into your heart that you should go to the land of the Christians, because she loves you so much. Pray to her to be pleased to instruct you how to do what she commands, because she's so good she'll certainly do it. On my part, and on that of all the Christians with me, I promise we'll do all we can, even unto death. Don't fail to write and tell me what you plan to do, and I'll always answer you, because the great Allah has given us a captive Christian who can speak and write your language as well, as you can

see by this letter. So you can tell us everything you
want without fear. As to your saying that if you went
to the land of Christians you'd be my wife, I promise
you that I'll be your husband, as a good Christian,
and you know that Christians keep their promises
better than Moors. May Allah and Marién keep you
safe, *señora mía*.

Once the letter was written and sealed, I waited two
days until the *baño* was empty as before, and then I went to
the usual place on the terrace to see if the stick appeared,
and there was little delay before it did. As soon as I saw it,
even though I couldn't see who was holding it, I showed
the letter as a sign that the string should be lowered, and I
tied the letter to it. Soon after, our star with the white flag
of peace—the little bundle—appeared again. They let it fall
and I picked it up and found all kinds of money in gold and
silver in the cloth—more than fifty *escudos* in all—which
increased our joy fifty times and strengthened our hopes
of getting free.

That same night our renegade came back and told us
he'd learned that the Moor who lived in that house was
indeed Hajji Murad, that he was really very wealthy, and
that he had one daughter, heiress to his whole estate, and
that it was commonly held that she was the most beautiful
woman on the Barbary Coast, and that many viceroys who
had come there had asked to marry her. He also found out
that she had had a Christian slave woman who had died.
All this corresponded to what was in the letter. We then
asked the renegade what plan we should use to take the
Moorish woman and return to Christian lands, and finally
we agreed to wait for the second letter of Zoraida—for
that's what the woman who now calls herself María used to
be called—because we saw clearly that she and no one else
could find a way out of these difficulties. After we agreed to
this, the renegade said that we shouldn't worry, because he
would set us free or die trying.

For four days the *baño* was filled with people, and that's
why the stick delayed four days in its appearance, but at the
end of that time, when the *baño* was empty, the cloth again
appeared and it was so pregnant that it promised a happy
birth. The stick and cloth came down to me, and I found

another letter in it and a hundred *escudos* in gold, and no other money. The renegade was there, and we gave him the letter to read, and he said that it read this way:

> I don't know, *mi señor*, how we should plan to go to Spain, and *Lela* Marién hasn't told me anything, although I've asked her. All that can be done is for me to give you—through this window—a lot of money in gold. Ransom yourself and your friends with it; then go to Christian territory, buy a boat there, and come back for the others. You'll find me in my father's garden near the Babazón gate, near the marina, where I'll be spending the summer with my father and my servants. You can take me to the boat from there without fear. And remember, you have to become my husband, because if not, I'll ask Marién to punish you. If you cannot trust anyone to go for the boat, ransom yourself and go. I know you'll come back more surely than another man, since you are a gentleman and a Christian. Try to get to know the garden, and when you stroll under my window I'll know the *baño* is empty and I'll give you a lot of money. May Allah keep you, *señor mío*.

This is what the second letter contained, and on seeing the contents, each one said he would like to be the one ransomed, and promised with conscientious good faith to go and come back, and I offered to go as well. The renegade opposed all of this, saying that in no way would he consent for one of us to gain freedom until we all could leave together, because experience had shown how poorly those who had been set free kept their promises made in captivity. Many times some important captives used those measures to ransom someone to go to Valencia or Mallorca,* with money to equip a boat and come back for those who had ransomed him, and they never came back, because recovered freedom and the fear of going back and losing it again erased from their memory all the obligations in the

---

* Valencia is a Spanish city on the Mediterranean coast and Mallorca is a Spanish island fairly nearby; either would have been chosen because of its proximity to Algiers.

world. And to confirm this truth he was relating to us, he
told us briefly about a case that happened to certain Christians very recently—the strangest case that ever happened
in those parts—where astonishing things happen all the
time.

In short, he ended by saying what could and should
be done with the money that was supposed to be used to
ransom one of us Christians was to give the money to him
to buy a boat in Algiers, under the pretext of becoming a
merchant and trader in Tetuán* and along that coast, and
since he would be the owner of the boat, he could easily
find a way of getting us from the *baño* and putting us on
board, the more so if the Moorish woman, as she said, gave
enough money to ransom us all. Since we would be free,
it would be very easy to get on board the boat in broad
daylight; the biggest hurdle would be that Moors never allow any renegade to buy a boat, unless it's a large corsair
ship, because they're afraid that anyone who buys a boat—
particularly if he's a Spaniard—only wants it to go to Christian lands. But he could get around this by making a Moor
from Tangier his partner in the purchase of the boat, and
with this pretext he would become the master of the vessel
and considered the rest as good as done.

And although it seemed better to me and my friends
to get a boat in Mallorca, as the Moorish woman had suggested, we didn't dare oppose him, fearing that if we didn't
do what he said, he might denounce us, placing us in danger of losing our lives if the agreement with Zoraida were
revealed, and for whose life we would give our own. So
we resolved to put our fate in the hands of God and the
renegade, and we immediately responded to Zoraida, telling her that we would do everything she'd recommended
because she'd advised us as well as if *Lela* Marién had dictated it to her, and it was up to her whether we put off that
affair or did it immediately. I renewed my promise to be
her husband, and so, the next day the *baño* happened to
be empty, she gave us at different times, with the stick and
cloth, two thousand *escudos* in gold, and a letter in which

---

* Tetuán is an important Moroccan city near the Mediterranean coast.
Tangier, a few lines below, is a Moroccan seaport, a well-known tour-
ist spot.

she said that the first JUMÁ—that is, Friday—she was going
to the garden with her father, and that before she went she
would give us more money, and if that wasn't enough, we
should let her know, and she would give us as much as we
asked for—her father had so much that he wouldn't miss it,
especially since she had the keys to everything.

We then gave five hundred *escudos* to the renegade to
buy the boat. With eight hundred I ransomed myself, giving
the money to a Valencian merchant who was in Algiers at
the time. He ransomed me from the king by pledging on
his word that when the next ship arrived from Valencia he
would pay my ransom. If he'd turned over the money right
then, it would make the king suspicious that my ransom
money had been in Algiers all the time and the merchant
had kept it a secret for his own advantage—my master was
so distrustful that I dared not have the money paid right
then. On Thursday before the Friday when the beautiful
Zoraida had to leave for the garden she gave us another
thousand *escudos* and told us she was leaving, begging me
that once I was ransomed I should go to her father's garden
right away and that I should find a way to see her there. I
responded in a few words that I would, and that she should
be sure to commend herself to *Lela* Marién with all the
prayers that her slave had taught her.

Once this was done, I took steps to ransom my three
companions, because if they saw me ransomed and themselves not, even though there was money for it, they might
get worried and the devil might make them do something
to betray Zoraida. Knowing them as I did, I need not have
worried—but I was unwilling to place the whole affair at
risk, so I had them ransomed in the same way I had been,
giving all the money to the merchant so that he could with
safety and confidence offer the ransom. But we never confided our arrangement and secret to him because of the
possible danger.

Chapter XLI. Where the captive continues his adventures.

B EFORE TWO weeks had gone by, our renegade had
bought a very seaworthy boat, able to hold more
than thirty people. To make his deal secure and give it
credence, he wanted to—and did—make a trip to a place
called Cherchell,* thirty leagues from Algiers on the way
to Orán,† in which there is a lot of trade in dried figs. He
made this trip two or three times in company of the *tagarino* Moor‡ whom he'd mentioned. On the Barbary Coast
they call Moors from Aragón TAGARINOS; and Moors from
Granada they call MUDÉJARES; in the kingdom of Fez§ they
call *mudéjares* ELCHES—these are the people the king typically uses in war.

So, as I was saying, every time he went by in his boat, he
anchored in a cove not two crossbow shots from the garden
where Zoraida was waiting, and there the renegade and his
young Moorish rowers would go ashore either to pray or to
rehearse casually what he planned to execute later in earnest. So he went to the garden to ask for fruit, and her father gave him some, not knowing who he was. Although he
tried to talk with Zoraida—as he later told me—to inform
her that he'd been ordered by me to take her to Christian
lands, so that she should be happy and reassured, it was
never possible because Moorish women never let themselves be seen by any other Moor or Turk, unless their husbands or fathers command them to, whereas with Christian
captives they're allowed to have dealings and speak, even
more than is becoming. For my own part, I'd have been

---

* Cherchell was quite an active port in Cervantes' time. Today it's just
a small fishing town.

† That is, toward the west. Oran is an Algerian port, the second-most-
important one after Algiers, directly south of Cartagena.

‡ In the last chapter this man was said to be from Tangier, a *tangerino*.
Now he is a *tagarino*, that is, a Moor from the old kingdom of Aragón,
as the text goes on to say. Cervantes was perfectly aware of this contradiction, which he made on purpose.

§ The Kingdom of Fez is now a part of northern Morocco. The city of
Fez is very ancient, and its university dates from 859.

upset if he'd spoken with her. Maybe she would have been startled to hear her affair talked about by renegades.

But God, who ordered otherwise, gave our renegade no occasion for his well-meant purpose. He saw how safely he could come and go to Cherchell, anchoring whenever and wherever he wanted, and that the *tagarino*, his partner, had no other will but the renegade's. Now that I was ransomed, the only thing we needed was some Christians to row, and he told me to look for those I wanted to take with me, aside from the ransomed ones, and to have them arranged for the first Friday—that was when he'd set our departure.

I therefore spoke to twelve Spaniards, all of them powerful rowers, and those who could most easily leave the city. It wasn't easy to find so many right then, because there were twenty ships on pirating raids and they had taken most of the available rowers. And these wouldn't have been available if their master hadn't stayed behind and didn't go on raids that summer so he could finish a galliot* that was being made in the shipyards. All I told these men was that the first Friday in the afternoon they should go out casually, one by one, toward the garden of Hajji Murad and wait for me there until I arrived. I gave these directions to each one separately with orders that if they saw other Christians, not to tell them anything except that I'd told them to wait in that place.

Having taken this precaution, I needed to take one other necessary step, the most important one, which was to let Zoraida know how things stood, so she could be prepared and on the lookout, and not be alarmed if we suddenly came to take her away before the time she thought that the Christian boat could return. So I decided to go to the garden and see if I could speak to her. Under the pretense of gathering some herbs one day before our departure, I went there. The first person I met was her father, who told me in the language used among captives and Moors all over the Barbary Coast and even in Constantinople—neither Moorish nor Spanish, nor of any other nation, but a mixture of all languages, with which we all understand each other—anyway, as I was saying, he asked me what I was looking for in that garden, and whose slave I was. I told him

---

* This was a small galley, sixteen to twenty rowers per side.

that I was a slave of Arnaúte Mamí*—I said this because I knew for certain that he was a great friend of his—and that I was looking for different herbs to make a salad. He then asked me if I was up for ransom or not, and how much my master was asking for me.

While these questions and answers were going on, the beautiful Zoraida, who for some time had been watching me, came out of the house, and since Moorish women don't hesitate to let themselves be seen by Christians, nor are bashful being around them, as I have already said, she didn't hesitate to come over where her father and I were. Moreover, as soon as her father saw her coming, he called her and told her to approach.

It would be beyond my power to describe the beauty and elegance, the rich, brilliant attire in which my beloved Zoraida presented herself to my eyes. I'll only say that more pearls hung about her very lovely neck, ears, and head than she had strands of hair. On her ankles, which were visible, as is their custom, she wore CARCAJES—for that's what those bracelets or anklets are called in Moorish—of purest gold, with so many set diamonds that her father told me afterward they were valued at ten thousand doubloons,† and those that she was wearing on her wrists were worth just as much. The pearls were in profusion and very fine, because a Moorish woman's greatest elegance and splendor is to adorn herself with pearls, large and small. That's why there are more pearls among Moors than any other people, and Zoraida's father had the reputation for having the finest ones in Algiers, and more than two hundred thousand Spanish *escudos*. She who is now mine was the mistress of all that.

Whether she was beautiful or not with all that adornment, you can judge what she must have looked like in her prosperous days by what remains of her beauty after so many travails. It's well-known that the beauty of some women has days and seasons, and is diminished or augmented haphazardly, and it's natural that the emotions of

---

* In real life, Arnaúte Mamí was the Albanian pirate who captured Cervantes when he was returning from Naples to Spain in 1575.

† The doubloon was worth two *escudos*. Gaos says this amount came to more than seventy thousand *reales*.

the heart can increase or decrease it, although most frequently they destroy it. I'll just say that she looked so wonderfully attired and so exceedingly beautiful, at least to me, that she seemed the perfection of all that I'd ever seen, and when I considered all I owed her, I felt I had before me a goddess from heaven who had come to earth for my happiness and relief.

As soon as she arrived, her father told her in their language how I was a captive of their friend Arnaúte Mamí, and I had come to look for things to make a salad with. She took up the conversation and in that mixture of languages I mentioned asked me if I was a gentleman, and why I wasn't ransomed. I responded that I was already ransomed, and that she could see by the price my master set on me how much he valued me, because I'd given a thousand five hundred *zoltanís** for my ransom.

She responded to this: "If you had been my father's captive, I'd have asked double that amount, because you Christians always lie in everything you say, and you pretend you're poor to cheat the Moors."

"That may be, *señora*," I answered, "but I must say, I've dealt truthfully with my master, and I deal and will continue to deal that way with everyone."

"And when are you leaving?" said Zoraida.

"Tomorrow, I think," I said, "because there is a French ship that sets sail then, and I plan to be on it."

"Wouldn't it be better," said Zoraida, "to wait for a ship heading for Spain and go with them, and not with the French, who aren't your friends?"

"No," I responded, "although if it's true a ship is coming from Spain, I'll wait for it, but it's quite certain I'll leave tomorrow, because the desire I have to be back in my country with people that I love is so great that it won't permit me to wait for another, later opportunity, no matter how good it is."

"You're doubtless married in your country," said Zoraida, "and that's why you want to be back with your wife."

"I'm not married," I responded, "but I've promised to get married when I get back."

"And is the lady you'll marry beautiful?" said Zoraida.

---

* The *zoltaní* was worth, in gold, a Spanish crown.

"She is so beautiful," I responded, "that to tell the truth, the best way to describe her is that she looks quite a bit like you."

Her father laughed heartily at this and said, "*Gualá,** Christian, she must be really beautiful if she looks like my daughter, who is the most beautiful woman in this kingdom. Just look at her and you'll see I'm telling the truth."

Zoraida's father acted as interpreter for most of these words, since he knew more Spanish, and although she knew the pidgin language that, as I've said, they use there, she showed her meaning more by signs than by words.

While we were talking, a Moorish man came running, and shouted that four Turks had climbed over the fence of the garden and were stealing fruit, though it wasn't ripe yet. The old man was startled and so was Zoraida, because Moors have an ingrained dread of the Turks, especially the soldiers, who are so insolent with and contemptuous of the Moors, who are their subjects, and whom they treat worse than if they were their slaves. So, Zoraida's father told her: "Daughter, go inside the house and lock yourself in while I go to talk with those dogs, and you, Christian, gather your herbs and go away, and may Allah carry you safely home." I bowed toward him and he went off to look for the Turks, leaving me alone with Zoraida, who made as if she were going home as her father had commanded.

But as soon as the trees of the garden hid her, she turned toward me, her eyes filled with tears, and said: "*Ámeshi,* Christian, *ámeshi?*" which means, "Are you leaving, Christian, are you leaving?"

I answered her: "*Señora,* yes, but not without you. The first *jumá* wait for me, and don't be startled when you see us, because we'll go to the land of the Christians without fail."

I told her this in such a way that she understood everything. I put my arm around her and she began to walk toward her house with feeble steps. As Fate would have it—and it might have gone very badly for us if heaven hadn't ordained it otherwise—while we were walking as I described, with my arm around her neck, her father, who was returning after chasing away the Turks, saw what we were doing, and we realized he'd seen us. But Zoraida, who

---

* My God.

was quick-witted and shrewd, didn't let me remove my arm, but rather drew close to me and laid her head on my chest, bending her knees a bit, and giving clear signs that she might faint, and I at the same time made it seem like I was supporting her against my will. Her father came running to where we were, and seeing his daughter that way, asked her what was the matter, but since she didn't respond, he said: "Doubtless she's fainted because of the fright caused by the intrusion of those dogs," and taking her from me, he supported her on his chest, and she, giving a sigh, her eyes still wet from the tears, said again: "*Ámeshi*, Christian, *ámeshi*!" "Go away, Christian, go away!" To which her father responded: "The Christian doesn't have to leave, daughter. He's done you no harm and the Turks have gone. Don't be alarmed; there is nothing that can harm you, because, as I've told you, the Turks, at my behest, went out the same way they came in."

"They did alarm her, as you said, *señor*," I said to her father, "but since she wants me to go away, I don't want to displease her. Peace be with you, and with your permission, I'll go back and collect the herbs in this garden, because my master says that there are no better herbs for salad than those in this garden."

"Come back as often as you like," responded Hajji Murad. "My daughter didn't say that because you or any other Christian had vexed her, but either she meant that the Turks should go away, or because she thought it was time for you to collect your herbs."

At this I bade them farewell, and she, looking as if her soul had been torn from her, went with her father. And I, pretending to get my herbs, scouted the whole garden at my leisure. I noted the entrances and exits and the security of the house, and everything we might use to facilitate what we had to do. After I did this, I went back and related everything that had happened to the renegade and my companions. And I could hardly wait for when I could enjoy, without fear, the prize that Fortune offered me in the fair and beautiful Zoraida.

Time passed, and the day and hour came that we so wanted. We all followed the arrangement and plan that, with due consideration and many long discussions, we'd decided upon, so we would have the success we wanted.

The Friday that followed the day I spoke with Zoraida in the garden, our renegade anchored the boat as night fell almost in front of where the fair Zoraida lived. The Christians who were to row were ready and hidden in different places in the area. Everybody was in suspense and nervous, waiting for me, anxious to attack the vessel that was within sight, because they didn't know what the renegade's plan was and figured they were to get their freedom by force of arms and killing the Moors on board the boat.

As soon as my companions and I appeared, when those who were in hiding saw us, they came out and joined us. It was now the time when the city gates were closed and there was no one else in the countryside. When we were all together, we wondered whether it would be best to go for Zoraida first or to subdue the Moorish rowers in the boat. And while we were still wondering what to do, the renegade appeared, asking why we were delaying, because it was time to act, and all the Moors were off guard, most of them sleeping. We told him why were hesitating, and he said that what was most important was to subdue the boat, which could be done very easily and without any danger, and then we would go for Zoraida. His plan seemed good to us, and without waiting any further, with him as our guide, we approached the boat, and he leapt aboard first, put his hand on a cutlass, and said in the Moorish language: "Nobody move, if you don't want it to cost you your lives!" By this time almost all of us Christians had boarded the boat. The Moors, who showed little spirit, seeing their captain speak in that way, were taken aback. No one dared take up his sword—few had one—and they let themselves, without saying a word, be tied up by the Christians, who quickly secured them and threatened the Moors that if any one of them should raise his voice, they would all be run through.

Once this was done, half of our men stayed behind to guard the crew, and the rest of us, with the renegade as our guide, went to the garden of Hajji Murad, and Fortune ordained that when we went to open the gate, it opened as easily as if it had not been locked. With great calm and silence we arrived at the house without being heard by anybody. The beautiful Zoraida was waiting for us at a window, and as soon as she realized there were people there, she asked in a whisper if we were NIZARANI, that is to say, if we were Christians. I answered YES and told her to come down. When she recognized me she didn't delay a moment, and she opened the door and looked so beautiful and was so richly dressed that words fail me when I try to describe her. As soon as I saw her, I took her hand and began kissing it, and the renegade and my two companions did the same. The rest, who didn't know exactly what was happening, did what we were doing, thinking we were thanking her and acknowledging her as the mistress of our freedom. The renegade asked her in the Moorish language if her father was in the confines of the garden. She said he was, and that he was sleeping upstairs. "We have to wake him up," replied the renegade, "and take him with us, and everything else of value."

"No," she said, "no one is to touch him, and in this house there's nothing more than I'm taking with me, which is so much that there is enough so that you all can be rich and happy—wait and see."

And saying this, she went back inside, saying that she'd return very soon, and that we should be quiet and not make any noise. I asked the renegade what had gone on with her, and he told me. I told him we shouldn't do anything more than what Zoraida wanted. She then came back carrying a little chest filled with *escudos* in gold—it was so heavy she could hardly carry it.

As bad luck would have it, her father woke up in the interim and heard the noise from the garden, and leaning out of the window, he immediately recognized that all those who were there were Christians. He raised prodigiously loud cries and began to shout in Arabic: "Christians, Christians! Thieves, thieves!" These cries put us in an enormous and fearful confusion. But the renegade, seeing the danger we were in, since it was so important to him to do all this without being heard, with great speed went up with some of our group to Hajji Murad. I didn't dare leave Zoraida alone, for she'd fallen almost fainting into my arms.

To be brief, those who went upstairs used such skill that in a moment they came down with Hajji Murad, his hands tied and with a gag in his mouth so he couldn't speak, threatening him that if he spoke a single word they would kill him. When his daughter saw him, she covered her eyes so as not to see him anymore, while her father was frightened, not knowing how willingly she'd put herself into our hands. But since we needed to use our feet swiftly, we went with due caution and great speed to the boat, where those who had stayed behind were waiting for us, fearing that our venture had failed.

The night was but two hours old when we were all in the boat and Zoraida's father was untied and the gag removed from his mouth. But the renegade told him again that if he spoke a single word they would take his life. When he saw his daughter there, he began to sigh very tenderly, and more so when he saw that I held her close and that she lay there quietly, without resisting, complaining, or trying to get away. But through all this he remained quiet so that they wouldn't put the threats of the renegade into effect.

When Zoraida got herself into the boat and saw that we wanted to start rowing, and seeing her father and the other Moors who were tied up, she told the renegade to tell me to do her the favor of releasing the Moors and giving her father freedom, because she would rather throw herself into the sea than see her father, who had loved her so much, being carried off a prisoner on her account. The renegade translated for me, and I answered that I was happy to do so. But he said that it wasn't a good idea, because if we left them there, they would call out the local populace and stir up the city, and they'd send out swift frigates to go looking for us by land and by sea so we couldn't escape. What we could do is give them their freedom when we got to the first Christian port. This was the opinion of all of us, and we explained it to Zoraida, with other reasons that prevented us from doing what she wanted, and she was satisfied. And then, in joyful silence and with happy diligence, each one of our strong rowers took his oar, and we set out, commending ourselves to God with all our hearts, toward Mallorca, the nearest Christian region.

But because the wind was blowing from the north and the sea was a bit rough, it wasn't possible to sail the direct route to Mallorca but we had to follow the coast toward Orán. This made us quite uneasy, because we didn't want to be discovered at Cherchell, which is sixty miles from Algiers. We were also afraid of meeting one of the galliots that come with goods from Tetuán, although each one on his own and everybody all together supposed that if we ran into a commercial galliot, as long as it wasn't a pirate ship, not only wouldn't we be lost, but also we could capture a vessel in which we could more safely complete our voyage. While we were sailing, Zoraida had her head between my hands so as not to see her father, and I felt that she was calling on *Lela* Marién to help us.

We must have gone about thirty miles when the sun came up and we were about three musket shots from the shore, which was deserted and without anyone there who could see us. But for all that, by dint of strong rowing, we went out a bit more to sea, which was now a bit calmer. When we went out about two leagues farther, an order was given to row in shifts so that we might eat something, because the boat was well provided, but the rowers said that it wasn't the right time to rest and that food should be given to those who were not rowing, because they didn't want to leave the oars on any account. But right then a wind began to blow toward the side of the boat, and forced us to raise our sails and head for Orán, because no other direction was possible. Everything was done very promptly, and so the wind sped us at eight knots an hour without any fear, except that of meeting a pirate ship.

We gave the Moorish sailors something to eat, and the renegade consoled them, saying they were not going as captives, and that as soon as we could, we would set them and Zoraida's father free. He then said: "I might expect and believe anything else of your liberality and good behavior, Christians, but don't think I'm such a simpleton as to imagine that you'll set *me* free. You never would have put yourselves in so much danger to take my freedom away only to give it back so generously, especially knowing who I am, and the ransom you can get by restoring my freedom to me. Name the sum you require, and I'll give it to you for me and my unfortunate daughter, or just for her alone, since she's the greatest and most precious part of my soul."

Saying this, he began to cry so bitterly that he moved us all to compassion and forced Zoraida to look at him, and when she saw him weep, she was so touched that she stood up and went to embrace her father. As she pressed her face to his, they began such a tender flow of tears that many of us accompanied them. But when her father saw her so gaily attired and with so many jewels on her, he asked her in their language: "What's going on, daughter? Last night before this terrible thing happened to us, I saw you in your ordinary clothes, and now, without having time to get all dressed up, and without getting any joyful news to celebrate by adorning yourself with such care, I see you all dressed up in the best clothing that I could give you when our luck was kinder to us. Answer me this, because you have me in greater suspense and more astonished than this misfortune itself does."

The renegade translated everything the Moor said to his daughter, but she said nothing in reply. When he saw the little chest in which he kept his jewels at one side of the boat, which he knew he'd left in Algiers and not brought to the garden, he was even more perplexed, and he asked her how it had come into our hands, and what was inside. The renegade, without waiting for Zoraida to answer, responded: "Don't bother to ask your daughter, Zoraida, so many things, because I'll easily satisfy all your questions. You should know that she's a Christian, and she's been the file for our chains and the deliverance of our captivity. She's come along of her own free will, and is so happy—as I imagine—to see herself in this position, as a person who has come out of the darkness into light, out of death into life, and out of suffering into glory."

"Is what he says true, daughter?" said the Moor.

"Yes, it is," responded Zoraida.

"So," said the Moor, "you're a Christian, and you've placed your father into the hands of his enemies?"

To which Zoraida responded: "I'm a Christian, but I didn't put you in this position, since it was never my wish to leave you or do you harm, but just to do something good for myself."

"And what good have you done for yourself?"

"For that," she responded, "you'll have to ask *Lela* Marién—she'll be able to answer you better than I can."

The Moor had hardly heard those words when, with incredible speed, he threw himself headfirst into the sea, where he would have drowned if the long and encumbering robes he was wearing didn't buoy him in the water for a while. Zoraida shouted to us to rescue him and we all ran over and took him out by his cape, half-drowned and unconscious. Zoraida was so distressed she lamented over him so tenderly and with so much grief as if he'd died. We turned him facedown and he spit up a lot of water, and came to two hours later.

The wind changed direction and we had to go toward land, using the oars skillfully so as not to run aground. But it was our good fortune to pull into a cove that lies on one side of a promontory or cape called CAVA RUMÍA, which means THE WICKED CHRISTIAN WOMAN in our language. Tradition among the Moors has it that in that place La Cava, through whom Spain was lost, is buried, because *cava* in their language means WICKED WOMAN,* and *rumía* means CHRISTIAN, and they consider it a bad omen just to anchor there even when necessity forces them to do it—that's the only time they'll do it—but in our case it wasn't a refuge of a wicked woman but a safe harbor for our relief, so rough had the sea become.

We put our lookouts onshore, and never let the oars out of our hands. We ate what the renegade had provided, and we prayed to God and Our Lady with all of our hearts to help and protect us so that we could have a happy ending to our so fortunate beginning. At the request of Zoraida, an order was given to put her father, and the other Moors who were tied up, onshore, because her spirit was not strong enough, nor could her tender heart withstand seeing her father and her compatriots tied up before her. We promised her to do this just before our departure, since there was no danger to us in leaving them in that uninhabited place. Our prayers were not to be unanswered by heaven, because soon the wind changed in our favor, and the sea became calm, inviting us to go back joyfully to the voyage we'd begun.

When we saw this, we untied the Moors, and one by one we put them ashore, which amazed them all. But when we went to put Zoraida's father on land, now that he had his wits about him, he said: "Why do you Christians think that this wicked female is glad that you've set me free? Do you think it's because of the pity she feels for me? No, assuredly

---

* "Wicked woman" refers to a prostitute. According to the medieval tradition, La Cava, daughter of Conde Julián, was perhaps raped (the sex act is certain; the force involved is not) by Rodrigo, the last Visigothic king of Spain. Julián, her father, in the African town of Ceuta (formerly of Morocco, and now a province of Spain), got his revenge by inducing the Moors to invade the Iberian Peninsula in 711. This theme is a commonplace in Spanish literature.

not. It's only because of the hindrance my presence gives her while she puts her vile designs into effect. And don't think she changed religions because she thinks yours is better than ours, but rather because she knows that immodesty is more freely practiced in Christian lands than in our country," and turning to Zoraida, while another Christian and I restrained him, fearing he might do something crazy, he said to her: "Oh, despicable and misguided girl! Where are you going, blind and distracted, in the control of these dogs, our natural enemies? Cursèd be the moment when I engendered you, and cursèd be the luxury and pleasures in which I raised you!" It looked like he wasn't going to finish anytime soon, so I hurried to put him ashore, and from there he continued shouting his maledictions and lamentations, begging Muhammad to pray to Allah to destroy and confound us, and bring about our end. And after we set sail and could no longer hear his words, we could see what he did, which was to pluck out his beard, tear out his hair, writhe about on the ground, but once he shouted so loud we could understand what he said: "Come back, beloved daughter. Come back home. I forgive you of everything. Give these men the money, because it's theirs now, and come back to console your sad father, who will lose his life on this desolate sand if you leave him!"

Zoraida heard all this with sorrow and tears, and didn't know what to answer back to him except: "May it please Allah, my father, for *Lela* Marién, who was the reason I became a Christian, to console you in your sadness! Allah knows very well that I couldn't have done anything other than what I did, and these Christians are not to blame for my act, because even if I had wanted to stay at home, it would have been impossible, since my soul was so eager to do this thing that seems as good to me as it does bad to you." She said this when her father couldn't hear her anymore nor could we see him. While I consoled Zoraida, we turned our attention to the voyage that the wind itself facilitated, so that we were certain that at daybreak we would be on the Spanish shore.*

---

* It would be about 150 miles from the African coast to the nearest Spanish shore. At eight knots an hour they would be able to make it in a single day.

But since good things pure and simple seldom or never come without being accompanied or pursued by something bad that spoils or disturbs them, our fortune—or maybe it was the curses that the Moor had hurled at his daughter (no matter whose father says them, curses are always to be dreaded)—ordained that when we were on the high seas three hours into the night, traveling at full sail with the oars lashed down because the favorable wind made them unnecessary, we saw close to us in the brightly shining moonlight a square-rigged galley in full sail, which had adjusted its rudder to put the prow a bit into the wind and crossed in front of us. It was so close that we had to take down the sails so as not to crash into it, and it veered off to give us room to go by. They gathered on the deck of the galley and asked who we were and where we were going, but since they asked us in the French language, our renegade said: "No one answer because these are doubtless French corsairs who plunder everyone." Because of this warning, no one said a word, and we continued on a bit ahead, leaving their galley downwind. Suddenly they fired two pieces of artillery, both of them apparently loaded with chain-shot, because they cut our mast in half and it fell into the sea with its sails. At the same time they fired a cannonball into our boat amidships, opening a gaping hole but doing no other damage. Since we were sinking, everyone began shouting loudly for help and begging those on the ship to take us in because we were sinking. They took down their sails and lowered a skiff, and as many as a dozen Frenchmen, well armed with their muskets with lighted wicks,* got on board. They came to our boat and, seeing how few we were and that the boat was sinking, they took us aboard, saying that this happened to us because we were impolite in not answering their question.

Our renegade took the chest with Zoraida's treasure and dropped it into the sea without anyone noticing what he was doing. Finally, we all went on board with the French, who, after being told everything they wanted to know about us, robbed us of everything we had, even Zoraida's anklets from her feet. But the distress that they caused her didn't affect me as much as the fear I had that they would

---

* The lighted wicks were used to fire the muskets.

go from taking her richest and most precious jewels to taking the jewel that was most valuable to her, and the one she esteemed the most. But what these people want doesn't go further than money. Their greed is never sated, and it was so great that they would have taken the clothes of the captives if they had been worth anything.

Some of them thought we should be thrown overboard wrapped in a sail, since they intended to do some trade in Spain claiming they were Bretons,* and if they took us there alive, they would be punished as soon as the robbery was discovered. But the captain, who was the one who had robbed Zoraida, said that he was content with the booty that he had, and that he didn't want to go into any Spanish port, but rather go through the Straits of Gibraltar by night, or however he could, and dock in La Rochelle,† from where he'd sailed. So they decided to give us the skiff from their ship and enough supplies for the short trip that remained, as they did the following day, when we were in sight of the Spanish coast, which, when we saw it, we forgot all our troubles and privations, as if we'd never had them—such is the happiness one has on getting back one's freedom.

It must have been about noon when they put us in the boat, giving us two barrels of water and some biscuits, and the captain, moved by I don't know what compassion, just as Zoraida was about to embark, gave her almost forty gold *escudos*, and wouldn't allow his soldiers to take the clothing she's now wearing. We went into the boat, gave thanks for their kindness, and showed ourselves more grateful than angry. They went out to sea in the direction of the straits. We, looking only toward the North Star of the land that was before us, hurried to row, and by the time the sun was going down, we were so close that we could land, in our opinion, before it was too dark. But since there was no moon and the night sky was dark, and not knowing where we were, some of us thought it was not safe to go ashore right then. But many of us thought that we should do so, even if it was on the rocks and far from a town, because we would at least be free from the fear we naturally felt

---

* Bretons are the French who live in Brittany in northwestern France.
† La Rochelle is a port city in southwestern France, an independent republic at that time (until 1628), and a hangout for pirates.

of the prowling corsairs from Tetuán, who leave Barbary at nightfall and arrive at the coast of Spain at daybreak, where they take booty, and return in time to sleep at home. But of all the differing suggestions, the one we took was to go to shore cautiously, and land where we could, if the sea was calm enough.

That's what we did, and it was probably a little before midnight when we arrived at the foot of a very misshapen and high hill, not so close that it didn't give us a little room to disembark comfortably. We ran the boat ashore on the sand and got out. We kissed the ground, and with tears of great happiness we gave thanks to God, Our Lord, for the incomparable goodness He'd given us. We took the provisions from the boat, and pulled it ashore, and climbed a good distance up the hill, for even there we couldn't feel easy in our hearts, nor could we believe that we were on Christian soil. The sun came up later than we would have liked, in my opinion. We finished climbing the hill to see if there was some village or shepherds' huts to be seen, but as far as our eyes could see, we couldn't make out a village, a person, a path, or a highway.

So we thought we'd go farther inland, since it had to be that soon we would find someone who could tell us where we were. What most distressed me was to see Zoraida traveling on foot over that rough terrain. I carried her for a while on my shoulders, but she was more wearied by my weariness than rested by the rest, and so she refused to let me keep on carrying her, and she went on with patience and good cheer, with me leading her by the hand. After we'd traveled a little less than a quarter of a league, the sound of a little cowbell came to our ears, a sure sign that there were cattle nearby. We all looked around cautiously to see if anyone appeared, and we soon saw at the foot of a cork tree a young shepherd who was whittling a stick with his knife, at his ease and without a care. We called to him, and he raised his head and sprang nimbly to his feet. The first people he saw, as we learned later, were the renegade and Zoraida, and when he saw them in Moorish dress he thought that all the Moors in Barbary were upon him, and with phenomenal agility, he shot into the forest and began to give the loudest cries ever heard: "Moors, Moors! To arms, to arms!"

With this shouting, we were thrown into disarray and we didn't know what to do, but considering that the shepherd's shouts would cause a commotion in the countryside and that the coastal militia would come right away to see what was the matter, we had the renegade take off his Turkish clothing and put on a captive's jacket that one of our group gave him, even though he himself was reduced only to a shirt. And commending ourselves to God, we went down the same path the shepherd had taken, expecting that at any moment the coastal militia would be upon us. And our thoughts didn't deceive us, for within two hours after we left the underbrush to a plain, we saw almost fifty men on horseback who were swiftly cantering toward us, and we stood still and waited for them. But when they arrived, they saw—instead of the Moors they were looking for—so many poor Christians that they were taken aback. One of them asked us if we were the reason that the shepherd had called out the militia. "Yes," I said, wanting to tell him what had happened to me, where we were coming from, and who we were. But one of the Christians in our group recognized the man who had asked that question, and he said, without giving me a chance to say another word: "Thanks be to God, *señores*, who has led us to such a wonderful place, because—unless I'm mistaken—where we're standing is the area around Vélez Málaga,* and if the years of my captivity haven't effaced you from my memory, you, *señor*, who asked us that question, are Pedro de Bustamente, my uncle."

Hardly had the captive Christian said these words when the horseman jumped off his horse and ran to embrace the young man, saying: "Nephew of my heart and my life! I recognize you, and I've mourned you as dead, as have my sister—your mother—and all your relatives, who are still alive. And God has been pleased to keep them alive so they can have the pleasure of seeing you. We knew that you were in Algiers, and by the way your garments and the rest of your party look, I can see that you've had your freedom miraculously restored."

"It's true," said the young man, "and there will be time to

---

* A small city (now with 25,000 inhabitants) slightly inland and about twenty miles east of Málaga.

tell you all about it." As soon as the horsemen understood that we were captive Christians, they got off their horses, and each one of them invited us to share their mounts into the city of Vélez Málaga, which was a league and a half away. Some of them went to take the boat into town, having been told where we'd left it. Others lifted us onto the cruppers, and Zoraida rode on the horse belonging to the uncle of the Christian.

The whole town came out to welcome us, since they had learned of our arrival from someone who had gone ahead. They were not surprised to see freed captives or captive Moors, since all those people are accustomed to seeing both one and the other, but they were struck by the beauty of Zoraida, which was heightened both by the exertion of the journey and by the joy of finding herself on Christian soil, with no worries of losing her way. This brought such a glow to her face that, unless I was much deceived by my love, I'd dare to say that there wasn't a more beautiful creature in the whole world, at least none I'd ever seen.

We went directly to the church to give thanks to God for the favor we had received, and as soon as Zoraida went in, she said that there were faces who looked like *Lela* Marién's. We told her that they were statues of her, and the renegade, as well as he could, tried to make her see what they meant, so that she could adore them. As if each one of them were truly the same *Lela* Marién who had spoken to her, she, with her quick mind and clear instinct, immediately understood everything that was said to her about the statues. From there they took us and placed us in different houses in the town, but the Christian who accompanied us placed the renegade, Zoraida, and me in the house of his parents, who were fairly wealthy, and they treated us with as much kindness as they did their own son.

We stayed in Vélez six days, at the end of which the renegade, having learned what he was supposed to do, went to the city of Granada to restore himself to the scared bosom of the Church. The other freed Christians went their own way. Zoraida and I were left alone and with only the *escudos* that the courtesy of the Frenchman gave Zoraida, with which I bought this animal on which she's riding. I've been her father and squire until now, and not her husband, and we're going with the intention of seeing if my father is

alive, or to find out if either of my brothers has had better
fortune than I, although, since heaven has made me Zoraida's companion, I feel that no other piece of luck could
come my way, no matter how good, that I'd value more. The
patience with which she endures the discomforts that poverty brings with it, and the desire that she truly has to become a Christian, is so great that it fills me with admiration
and moves me to want to serve her all my life—although
the happiness I feel in seeing myself hers and in seeing her
mine is troubled and marred by not knowing if I'll find
someplace to shelter her, and whether time and death will
have made such changes in the fortune and lives of my father and brothers, that, if they're not to be found, I may not
find anyone who knows me.

I've nothing more to tell you of my story, *señores*. If it's
pleasing or exotic, let your better judgment decide. All I
know is that I wish I could have told it to you more briefly,
and the fear of boring you caused me to omit more than
four incidents.

Chapter XLII. *Which deals with what else happened at the inn together with many other things worth knowing.*

WHEN THE captive stopped talking, don Fernando said:
"*Señor* captain, the way you've told this remarkable
adventure has certainly been equal to the novelty and
strangeness of the events themselves. Everything is exotic
and exceptional, and filled with incidents that astonish and
amaze anyone who listens. And the pleasure we've found
in it is so great, we wouldn't mind hearing it again, even if
we were here until tomorrow listening to the same tale."
    And saying this, don Antonio* and the others offered

---

* The first edition does read "don Antonio," who is not mentioned before or after in the inn. Spanish editors of the work, seeing what looks
like a mistake, usually change the name to Cardenio, and translators
have followed suit. The mischievous Cervantes appears to have written don Antonio.

to be helpful in whatever way they could, using such affectionate and earnest words that the captain was quite
pleased with their goodwill. Don Fernando promised that
if he wanted to return with him, he would have the marquis,
his brother, be Zoraida's godfather at her baptism, and that
he himself would give him the means to return home with
the credit and dignity that he was entitled to. The captain
thanked him in most courteous terms, but refused to accept
any of his generous offers.

At this point night fell, and when it got dark, a coach arrived at the inn, accompanied by some men on horseback.
They asked for accommodation, and the innkeeper's wife
replied that there wasn't a hand's breadth in the inn that
wasn't occupied.

"That may be," said one of those who had entered on
horseback, "but a place must be found for the *señor* judge."

At the mention of his office, the innkeeper's wife became troubled and said: "*Señor*, the thing is, I have no beds.
If his grace, the *señor* judge, has a bed with him, as he surely
must, let him come in and be welcome—my husband and I
will vacate our room to accommodate his grace."

"Very good," said the squire.

In the meantime, a man got out of the coach whose garb
showed immediately the office he held, because the long
robe with the turned-up sleeves proved he was a judge, as
his servant had said. He was leading a maiden by her hand,
about sixteen years old, dressed for travel, and so elegant,
so beautiful, and so charming that she amazed everyone;
and if they hadn't seen Dorotea, Luscinda, and Zoraida,
who were all at the inn, they would have believed that another such beauty would be hard to find.

Don Quixote was present when the judge and the maiden
came in, and as soon as he saw them, he said: "Your worship
may certainly enter this castle and rest, because although
the accommodation is limited and poorly appointed, there
are no quarters in the world that are so cramped that there
will be no room for both arms and letters, and more so if
these arms and letters have beauty as their guide and pilot,
as your learnèd grace has in this maiden, for whom not only
castles should open their portals, but also cliffs should split,
and mountains should crumble, to welcome her. Come,
your grace, I say, into this paradise—here you'll find stars

and suns to accompany the heaven your grace is bringing with you; here you'll find arms at their perfection and
beauty in its prime."

The judge was amazed at this speech by don Quixote
and looked at him very intently. He was no less amazed
by his appearance as he was by his words, and before he
found the words to respond, he was astounded anew when
he saw Dorotea and Zoraida, who, when they heard from
the innkeeper's wife about the newly arrived guests and
the beauty of the girl, had come out to see and welcome
her. But don Fernando, Cardenio, and the priest offered a
simpler and more polite greeting. In short, he entered the
inn perplexed as much by what he saw as by what he heard,
while the beauties of the inn welcomed the beautiful girl.

The judge could see that all those present were people of
quality. But the figure, face, and appearance of don Quixote
bewildered him. All civilities having been done, and the ac-
commodations of the inn having been examined, what had
already been decided was arranged—that all the women
would go into the garret already mentioned, and the men
would stay outside, on guard. The judge was content that
his daughter (for that is who the maiden was) would go
with those women, which she did most willingly; and so,
with part of the innkeeper's bed and half of the one that
the judge brought with him, they all were accommodated
better than they had expected.

The captive's heart skipped a beat as soon as he saw the
judge, because he suspected that man was his brother. He
asked one of the servants who accompanied him what his
name was and where he was from. The servant responded
that he was the *licenciado* Juan Pérez de Viedma, and he'd
heard he was from a village in the mountains of León. From
this, and from what he himself had seen, he was positive that
man was his brother, and that he'd followed the path of letters on the advice of his father. Excited and very happy, he
took Cardenio and the priest aside and told them his suspicions, assuring them that the judge was his brother. The servant had also told him that he'd just been appointed judge in
the Indies, in the supreme court of Mexico; he also knew that
the maiden was his daughter, from whose birth the mother
had died, and he'd become very rich from the dowry left him
with the daughter. The captive asked for advice as to how

he should proceed; should he reveal himself or, before he made himself known, find out if his brother, seeing him poor, would be ashamed to receive him with a warm heart?

"Leave it to me to find out," said the priest. "But there's no reason to think that you, *señor* captain, won't be received kindly, because the worth and wisdom manifest in your brother's honorable demeanor gives no indication that he'll be arrogant or unfeeling, or that he'll not know how to put the accidents of Fortune into perspective."

"Still," said the captain, "I'd like it if I could make myself known to him in a roundabout way and not all at once."

"I can assure you," said the priest, "that I'll do it so that everyone will be satisfied."

At this point, dinner was ready, and everyone sat at the table, except the captive and the ladies, who ate alone in their room. During dinner, the priest said: "*Señor* judge, I had a friend in Constantinople, while I was captive there for some years, with your same name. This friend of mine was one of the bravest soldiers and captains in the whole Spanish infantry. But he had as much misfortune as gallantry and courage."

"And what was this man's name, *señor mío*?" asked the judge.

"He was called," responded the priest, "Ruy Pérez de Viedma, and he was from a village in the mountains of León. He told me about something that happened to his brothers and him that, if such a truthful man hadn't told it to me, I'd have thought was a tale the old women tell sitting around the fire in winter. He told me his father had divided his estate among three sons, and he'd given them certain advice, better than that of Cato. And I can tell you that the one who chose to go to war had done so well that in a few years, through his bravery and good conduct, and without any help except his own worth, he rose to the rank of captain of the infantry, and thought he would soon see himself on the road to the prestigious rank of regiment commander. But Fortune was against him, because when he could have expected its favor, he lost it, and with it his freedom, on that glorious day when so many recovered theirs,* which was at the Battle of Lepanto. I lost mine at

---

* That is, the galley slaves who were set free.

La Goleta and afterward, by various routes, we found ourselves companions in Constantinople. From there he went to Algiers, where I know that he had one of the strangest adventures in the world."

And here the priest went on to relate as briefly as he could what happened with his brother and Zoraida. The judge listened to all this very absorbed—he'd never before been such a good listener.* The priest got to the point where the Frenchmen robbed the Christians on the boat, and the poverty and need in which his friend and the beautiful Moorish woman were left, and said he didn't know what had happened to them, if they had come to Spain or been carried off to France by the French. Everything the priest said was being heard by the captain, who was standing to one side, and he studied all the movements that his brother made.

The judge, seeing that the priest had finished his story, gave a great sigh and his eyes filled with tears as he said: "Oh, *señor*, if you only knew how deeply I've been touched by the news you've given me, that I have to show it by these tears, which are flowing from my eyes in spite of my usual moderation and reserve. That valiant captain you mention is my older brother, who, being stronger and loftier-minded than my younger brother and I, chose the honorable and worthy profession of war, which was one of the three careers my father proposed to us, just as your friend told you in the old wives' tale, as you put it, that you heard from him. I chose the career of letters, in which God and my diligence have put me in the position in which you see me. My younger brother is in Peru, so rich that with what he has sent to my father and me, he paid back the part of the estate he took with him, and has even given enough to satisfy my father's natural generosity, while I was able to pursue my studies well, and have come to attain my present standing. My father is still living, dying with the desire to learn about his oldest son, and he asks God in continual prayer not to close his eyes until he sees the eyes of his son. But what surprises me is that, since he has so much common sense, he never wrote his father about his troubles and sufferings, nor his prosperity, because if he'd known—or any

---

* There is a pun here, since *oidor* means both "judge" (two lines above) and "listener."

one of us had known—he wouldn't have had to wait for the miracle of the stick to get his ransom.

"But I'm very anxious wondering if the Frenchmen gave them freedom, or if they killed them to hide their theft. This will make me continue my voyage, not with the joy in which I began it, but rather with melancholy and sadness. Oh, my good brother, if I only knew where you were, I'd go to find you and free you from your travails, even if it cost me my life! Oh, if I could only take news to our aged father that you were alive, even if you were in the most hidden dungeon in Barbary, because his wealth, together with my brother's and mine, would rescue you! Oh, beautiful and generous Zoraida, if I could only repay the good you've done my brother; if only I could witness the rebirth of your soul and your marriage, which would make us all so happy!"

The judge said these and other similar words, filled with so much emotion about the news of his brother that all those who heard him shared in it, showing their sympathy for his woe. When the priest saw how well his plan had worked, matching the captain's wishes, he didn't want him to be sad any longer, so he got up from the table and went in to where Zoraida was, and took her by the hand, and Luscinda, Dorotea, and the judge's daughter followed. The captain was waiting to see what the priest intended to do, which was to take him by the hand as well, and with both of them, he went to where the judge and the other men were, and said: "Dry your tears, *señor* judge, and may your desire for all the happiness that you could possibly want be fulfilled, because here is your good brother and your good sister-in-law. This is Captain Viedma, and this is the beautiful Moorish woman who did so much for him. The Frenchmen I told you about put them in the state of poverty that you see so that you might show the generosity of your kind heart."

The captain hastened to embrace his brother, who put both his hands on his chest to look at him at some distance. But when he recognized him, he embraced him so tightly, shedding so many tears of joy, that those who were present were forced to accompany them in their tears. I believe that the words that both brothers said to each other and the feelings they showed can hardly be imagined, much less written down. There, in a few words, they told each other of

their lives; there, they showed the true affection of brothers; there, the judge embraced Zoraida; there, he offered
them his wealth; there he had his daughter embrace her;
there, the beautiful Christian and the even more beautiful
Moorish woman made everybody weep once more.

And there, don Quixote considered these strange happenings without saying a word, attributing them all to the foibles
of knight-errantry. Finally, they made plans for the captain
and Zoraida to go with his brother to Seville and send news
to their father about his having been found, and his deliverance, so that, if he was able, he could be at the wedding and
baptism of Zoraida. It was not possible for the judge to delay
his voyage, since he had news that the fleet would set sail
from Seville for New Spain* in a month, and it would be an
enormous inconvenience for him to miss the passage.

In short, everybody was happy with the captive's good
fortune, and since two-thirds of the night was over, they
agreed to retire and take their rest during the time that
remained. Don Quixote offered to guard the castle so they
wouldn't be assaulted by some giant or other malevolent
scoundrel, covetous of the great treasure trove of beauty in
the castle. Those who knew him thanked him, and they told
the judge about don Quixote's odd manner, which gave
him no little pleasure.

Only Sancho Panza despaired at the lateness of the
hour, but he managed to get the best accommodation of all,
stretching out on the trappings of his donkey, which were
to cost him dearly, as will be told later on.

When the ladies had retired to their room and the others accommodated themselves as well as they could, don
Quixote went outside the inn's walls to be the sentinel of
the castle, as he'd promised.

A little before dawn, it happened that a very musical and
good voice reached the ears of the women, and it forced all
of them to listen closely, especially Dorotea, who was awake,
and at whose side slept doña Clara de Viedma, for that was
the name of the judge's daughter. No one had any idea who
the person could be who sang so well. It was a voice not
accompanied by any instrument. Sometimes it seemed that
the singing was coming from the patio, other times from

---

* New Spain was the viceroyalty of Mexico.

the stable. As the ladies were listening amidst the confusion of where the music was coming from, Cardenio went to the door of their room and said: "If you're not sleeping, listen! You'll hear the voice of a mule boy who sings in such a way that he enchants as he chants."

"We can hear him, *señor*," said Dorotea.

And with this, Cardenio went away, and Dorotea, listening as carefully as she could, heard that what he was singing was this:

Ah me, Love's mariner am I
    On Love's deep ocean sailing;
    I know not where the haven lies,
    I dare not hope to gain it.
One solitary distant star
    Is all I have to guide me,
    A brighter orb than those of old
    That Palinurus* lighted.
And vaguely drifting am I borne,
    I know not where it leads me;
    I fix my gaze on it alone,
    Of all beside it heedless.
But overcautious prudery,
    And coyness cold and cruel,
    When most I need it, these, like clouds,
    Its longed-for light refuse me.
Bright star,† goal of my yearning eyes
    As you above me beam,
    When thou shalt hide thee from my sight
    I'll know that death is near me.‡

When the singer had gotten to this point, it seemed to Dorotea that it wouldn't be right to allow Clara to miss such a good voice, so, jostling her a bit, she woke her and said: "Pardon me, dear, for waking you, but I'm doing it so you can take pleasure in hearing perhaps the best voice that you've ever heard in all your life."

Clara woke up, quite drowsy, and asked her to repeat

---

* Palinurus was the helmsman of Æneas' boat in the *Æneid*.
† In Spanish, "bright" is *clara*, the girl's name.
‡ This is Ormsby's translation.

what she'd said, since she hadn't understood at first what Dorotea was saying, so Dorotea said it again, and Clara pulled herself together. But as soon as she heard two verses as the singer continued, she began to tremble in such an odd way, as if she were afflicted by some sudden grave fit caused by a fever; and throwing her arms around Dorotea she exclaimed: "Oh, *señora* of my soul and of my life! Why did you wake me up? The best thing Fortune could do for me right now is to let me close my eyes and ears so I won't see or hear this unfortunate musician."

"What are you saying, girl? They say that the one singing is a mule boy."

"No—he's a magistrate of villages," responded Clara, "and the place he holds in my soul so securely will never be taken from him if he doesn't want it to be."

Dorotea was amazed at the girl's heartfelt words, since it seemed to her that they exceeded by quite a bit the maturity one would expect of someone her age. So she said to her: "You're speaking, *señora* Clara, in a way that I cannot understand. Explain yourself more clearly, and tell me about your soul, and his villages, and this musician, whose voice has made you so troubled. But don't tell me now, because I don't want to miss the pleasure I get from hearing the singer while I tend to your distress, because I think he's going to sing another song with new verses."

"All right," responded Clara.

And so as not to hear him she covered her ears with both hands, and this also amazed Dorotea, who, listening to what he was singing, heard that he continued in this way:

Sweet Hope, my stay,
    That onward to the goal of thy intent
    Dost make thy way,
    Heedless of hindrance or impediment,
    Have you no fear
    If at each step you find death is near.
No victory,
    No joy of triumph doth the faint heart know;
    Unblessed is he
    That a bold front to Fortune dares not show,
    But soul and sense
    In bondage yields up to indolence.

If Love his wares
>   Do dearly sell, his right must be contest;
>   What gold compares
>   With that whereon his stamp he hath impressed?
>   And all men know
>   What costs little that we rate but low.
Love resolute
>   Knows not the word "impossibility";
>   And though my suit
>   Beset by endless obstacles I see,
>   Yet no despair
>   Shall hold me bound to earth while heaven is there.*

Here the singer ended his song and here began renewed sobs on Clara's part. All this kindled Dorotea's desire to find out the cause of such a sweet song and such bitter weeping. So she asked her once again what she'd meant before. Then Clara, fearing that Luscinda would hear her, holding Dorotea close, put her mouth so close to Dorotea's ear that she could safely speak without being heard by anyone else, and said: "This young man who is singing, *señora mía*, is the son of a gentleman from the kingdom of Aragón, the magistrate of two villages, who lived opposite my father's house in the capital. Although my father had the windows of his house covered with curtains in the winter and blinds in the summer, I don't know how, but this young man, who was a student, saw me—in church or somewhere else, I don't know—and fell in love with me, which he made me understand from the windows of his house, with so many signs and tears that I had to believe him and even love him, without knowing what he wanted of me. Among the signs that he made was to join one hand with the other, showing that he wanted to marry me, and although I'd like that very much, since I was alone and without a mother, I didn't know who I could confide in, and so I just left it as it was, showing him no favor, except (when my father and his were away from home) to raise the curtain or blinds a bit and let him see me, which excited him so much that I thought it would drive him crazy.

"The time finally came for my father's departure, which

---

* Ormsby, once again. In Spanish there are lines of seven and eleven syllables, a standard poetic form in Spanish.

the boy found out about, and not from me, because I never could say anything to him. He fell sick from grief, the way I understand it, and so the day we left I didn't see him to say good-bye, if only with my eyes. But after we were on the road for two days, when we went into an inn at some distance from here, I saw him dressed as a mule boy, so well disguised that if I didn't have him etched in my memory, I wouldn't have recognized him. I knew it was him; I was amazed, and I was glad. He looked at me undetected by my father, from whom he always hides when he goes in front of me along the roads and in the inns where we stay. And since I know who he is, and I think that because of his love for me he's making this journey on foot and with so much hardship, I'm dying of grief; and wherever he puts his feet, I put my eyes. I don't know what his intention is or how he could have escaped from his father, who loves him beyond measure, because he has no other heir, and because his son is so worthy, as your grace will realize when you see him. And what else I can say about him is that everything he sings, he's made up out of his head, and I've heard that he's a great student and poet. And what's more, every time I see him or hear him sing, I tremble all over, and my heart skips a beat, fearing that my father will recognize him and come to know our desires. I've never spoken to him in my life, and even so, I love him and cannot live without him. This is, *señora*, what I can tell you about this musician whose voice has given you so much pleasure, and by his voice alone you'll see that he isn't a mule boy as you say, but a lord of souls and towns, as I've told you."

"Say no more, *señora* doña Clara," Dorotea said, kissing her a thousand times. "Say no more, I say, and wait for the new day to come, and I'll hope that God will arrange it so your affair might have the happy ending that such a virtuous beginning warrants."

"Oh, *señora*," said doña Clara, "what ending can I expect if his father is such an important man, and so rich that it seems that I can't even be his son's maid, not to mention his wife? And I can't get married without my father's permission for anything in the world. I only want this young fellow to go away and leave me alone. Perhaps by not seeing him, and with the great distance we are to travel, it will ease my pain, although I think the remedy I've suggested will do me little good. I don't know how the devil this has happened, nor how this love I bear him came to me, since I'm so young and so is he. In truth I believe we're the same age—I'm not yet sixteen, but I will be on St. Michael's day,* according to my father."

Dorotea couldn't help but laugh at the childish way doña Clara spoke, and she said to her: "Let's rest, *señora*, for the little that remains of the night, and 'God will send another day and we'll do fine,' provided my skill doesn't fail me."

With this they went to sleep and the whole inn was shrouded in silence. The only ones who weren't sleeping were the innkeeper's daughter and Maritornes, her maid. Since they already knew the mental state of don Quixote, and that he was outside the inn on guard, in armor and on horseback, they thought they would play a joke on him, or at least spend some time listening to his nonsense.

There happened to be no window in the inn overlooking the countryside, except for one through which they threw out straw. The two semi-maidens placed themselves at this window and saw that don Quixote was mounted on horseback, leaning on his lance, and heaving very mournful and deep sighs once in a while, as if with each one his soul was being yanked out. And they also heard him say with a soft, delicate, and loving voice: "Oh, my *señora* Dulcinea del Toboso, sum of all beauty, model of discretion, archive of grace, repository of virtue, and finally, essence of all that is worthy, chaste, and delectable in the world! What must your grace be doing now? Are you thinking, perhaps, of your captive knight, who of his free will has exposed himself to so many perils just to serve you? Give me news of her, oh, luminary of three faces!† Perhaps envying her face, you're looking at her now, either strolling through some gallery in her sumptuous palace, or leaning on some balcony to consider with no detriment to her chastity and greatness how she can tame the torment which this afflicted heart is suffering for her; what glory she can bestow on my grief, what relief to my worry; and finally, what life to my death, and what reward for my services. And you, oh, bright sun! You must be in a hurry to saddle your horses to start the

---

* This is 29 September, Cervantes' own birthday.
† This refers, of course, to the moon.

day and come out to see my lady; and when you see her, I beg you to greet her for me. But be careful when you greet her not to kiss her on the cheek, because I'll be more jealous of you than you were of that flighty woman who made you sweat so much and race through the plains of Thessaly or along the shores of Peneius*—for I don't remember too well where you were running then, all jealous and in love."

When don Quixote got to this point in his doleful speech, the daughter of the innkeeper beckoned and said to him: "*Señor mío*, come over here, if you please."

When he heard this request and this voice, don Quixote turned his head and saw by the light of the moon, which was still quite bright, that he was being called from the opening, which appeared to him to be a window, and even one with a golden grating, as rich castles ought to have and as he imagined the inn to be. And then his irrational imagination conjured up once again, as the last time, the idea that the beautiful maiden, daughter of the warden of that castle, conquered by her love for him, was trying to win his affections. With this thought, so as not to appear discourteous and ungrateful, he turned Rocinante around and went over to the window, and as soon as he saw the two young women, he said: "I'm sorry, beautiful *señora*, that you've put your amorous thoughts where it's not possible to find a response your great merit and elegance deserve, and you must not blame this wretched knight-errant, whom love has made incapable of submission to any other than her whom, from the instant his eyes fell upon her, he made the absolute mistress of his soul. Forgive me, good *señora*—go back to your room and don't reveal more of your desires to me, so that I won't show myself more ungrateful still. But if your love for me suggests to you any other way I may serve you, other than by reciprocating your yearning, just ask, and I swear by that absent enemy of mine, to give it to you immediately, even if you ask for a lock of hair from Medusa,† which was nothing but snakes, or the rays of the sun placed into a bottle."

---

* Refers to Daphne, a nymph of the plains of Thessaly, daughter of the river god Peneius. Don Quixote is making up Apollo's jealousy, and that's why he can't remember what happens next.

† Medusa, after her affair with Poseidon, had her hair turned into snakes. Anyone who looked at her head was turned to stone.

"My lady has need of nothing like that, *señor* knight," said Maritornes.

"What does your mistress need, discreet *dueña*?" responded don Quixote.

"Just one of your fair hands," said Maritornes, "to be able to satisfy the passion that brought her to this window, so in detriment to her honor, that if her father heard her, the least slice he would take from her would be her ear."

"I'd like to see that," responded don Quixote. "He'd better be careful if he doesn't want to meet the most disastrous end ever met by a father for having touched a love-stricken daughter."

It seemed to Maritornes that don Quixote would offer the hand they had asked for, and she decided what she would do. She got down from the opening and went to the stable, where she took the halter of Sancho Panza's donkey, and with great speed returned to the window, just when don Quixote stood up onto Rocinante's saddle to reach the gold-grated window where he imagined the lovelorn maiden to be, and when he gave her his hand, he said: "Take this hand, *señora*, or rather, this punisher of the evildoers of the world. Take this hand, I say, that no other woman has ever touched—not even she who has entire possession of my whole body. I'm not giving it to you so you can kiss it, but rather so you can examine the network of sinews, the complexity of its muscles, and the breadth and the capacity of its veins, from which you can infer the strength of the arm that has such a hand."

"Now, we shall see," said Maritornes. And making a slipknot with the halter, she put it around his wrist and lowered herself from the opening and tied the other end tightly to the door latch of the hayloft.

Don Quixote felt the roughness of the cord on his wrist and said: "It seems to me that you are scraping rather than caressing my hand. Don't treat it so harshly, since it's not to blame for what my will has done you, nor is it good for you to take vengeance on such a small part of me. Remember that one who loves well should not avenge so ill."

But no one heard these words of don Quixote, because as soon as Maritornes tied his wrist, she and the other one fled, dying of laughter; and they left him tied up in such a way that it was impossible for him to get loose. He was,

then, as has been said, standing on Rocinante, with his
whole arm in the window and his wrist tied to the latch
of the door, greatly fearing and worried that if Rocinante
moved a little bit, he would be left hanging by his arm. So
he didn't dare move at all, although the patience and calm
of Rocinante could be counted on, because he wouldn't
move for a whole century.

Finally, since don Quixote saw himself tied fast, and now
that the women had gone away, he began to imagine that
everything was happening by enchantment, as happened
the last time, when in that same castle that enchanted Moor
of a muleteer beat him up; and he cursed to himself his lack
of discretion and judgment, since having come out so badly
the first time, he ventured a second time, when there is a
maxim among knights-errant that says that when they have
undertaken an adventure and have come out badly, it indicates that it's not meant for them, but for someone else, and
so they shouldn't attempt it a second time. Nonetheless, he
tugged on his arm to see if he could get loose, but he was
tied so tightly all his efforts were in vain. It's true he tugged
rather delicately, since he didn't want Rocinante to move,
and although he wanted to sit on the saddle, he couldn't
and had to remain standing or have his hand pulled off.

It was then he wished he had Amadís' sword, against
which the powers of enchantment had no effect; then is
when he cursed his fortune; then is when he exaggerated
the loss the world would suffer by his absence while he was
standing there enchanted—and he doubtless thought he
was; then it was that he remembered his beloved Dulcinea
del Toboso; then it was that he called his squire, Sancho
Panza, who, buried in sleep and stretched out on the packsaddle of his donkey, was oblivious even of the mother that
bore him; then is when he called on the wizards Lirgandeo
and Alquife* to help him; then is when he invoked the
name of his good friend Urganda to rescue him; and finally,
when daybreak came, he was so desperate and disheartened that he bellowed like a bull, because he had no hope
that the new day would bring relief to his misery, which he
was convinced would last forever. And seeing that Roci-

---

* Lirgandeo is the chronicler, parallel with Cide Hamete, in the *Caballero del Febo*. Alquife was a magician in *Amadís de Gaula*.

nante didn't stir, neither much nor little, he believed that his horse and he would stay without eating, drinking, or sleeping until the bad influence of the stars passed by or another, wiser enchanter would disenchant him.

But his belief deceived him greatly, because hardly had it begun to get light when four men arrived at the inn on horseback, very well equipped, with their muskets across their saddles. They knocked loudly on the gate of the inn, which was still locked, and when don Quixote saw this, still playing the part of the guard, with an arrogant and thunderous voice, he said: "Knights or squires, or whoever you are, you have no right to knock on the gates of this castle because it's amply clear that at this time of morning either they're all sleeping inside or they don't have the custom of opening the fortress until sunlight has spread over the land. Stay outside and wait until daybreak, and then we'll see if it's fitting or not to open the gates to you."

"What the devil kind of fortress or castle is this," said one, "that forces us to observe these formalities? If you're the innkeeper, order that the gate be opened to us. We're travelers and we only want to give barley to our mounts and continue on, because we're in a hurry."

"Does it seem to you, *señores*, that I look like an innkeeper?" responded don Quixote.

"I don't know what you look like," responded the other, "but I know that you're saying nonsense when you call this inn a castle."

"Castle it is," replied don Quixote, "in fact, one of the best ones in this whole province, and there are people inside who have had scepter in their hand and crowns on their head."

"It would be better the other way around," said the traveler, "the scepter on their head and the crown on their hand.* Maybe there's a group of actors inside who have these scepters and crowns that you mention, because in such a small and quiet inn, I doubt that there are people entitled to real crowns and scepters."

"You know little of the world," replied don Quixote, "since you don't know things that happen in knight-errantry."

---

* Starkie and others point out that in Cervantes' time, criminals were branded with a crown on their hand.

The travelers got weary of this conversation with don Quixote and they began to knock again with great fury, causing the innkeeper to wake up, along with everyone else in the inn, and so he got up to ask who was knocking.

It happened then that one of the mounts on which the travelers came went over to smell Rocinante, who, melancholy and sad, with his ears drooping, was supporting his stretched-out master without moving, and since he was made of flesh and blood, although he seemed to be made of wood, he couldn't help but feel the effects, and in return smell the one who was giving him those caresses, and so he'd moved only very little when don Quixote lost his footing and slipped off the saddle. He would have fallen to the ground if he hadn't been hanging by his arm, something that caused him such great pain that he believed that either his wrist was being cut through or his arm was being torn off, because he was so close to the ground that the tips of his toes kissed the ground—all the worse for him, because he could feel how little he lacked to be able to put the soles of his feet on the ground, and he struggled and stretched as much as he could to reach the ground, much like those undergoing the strappado torture,* who caught between touching and not touching aggravate their pain with their efforts to stretch out, deceived by the hope they think they have, that with a little more effort they can reach the ground.

Chapter XLIIII. Where the unheard-of events at the inn continue.

Don Quixote roared so loudly the innkeeper opened the gates of the inn and rushed out in alarm to see who was shouting, and those who were outside went to see as well. Maritornes, whom the shouts had also awakened, figuring out what must have happened, went to the hayloft unseen and untied the halter holding don Quixote up. He fell to the ground, in full view of the innkeeper and also

---

* This is a torture just like the situation don Quixote is in: The victim is raised from the ground by a rope and then dropped almost to the ground, stopping with a jerk.

of the travelers, who approached him and asked him what had caused him to bellow so loudly. Without answering a single word, he removed the rope from his wrist, stood up, mounted Rocinante, clasped his shield, couched his lance, and after making a wide turn down the field, came back at a half gallop, saying: "Whoever says I've been enchanted with just cause, if my lady, the Princess Micomicona, grants me permission, I'll show him he's lying and challenge him to a singular battle."

The new travelers were amazed at these words of don Quixote, but the innkeeper told them that he was don Quixote, and they should ignore him, since he was out of his mind. They asked the innkeeper if by chance a boy about fifteen years old had come to that inn, dressed as a mule boy, of such and such an appearance, in effect describing doña Clara's lover. The innkeeper responded that there were so many people at the inn he hadn't noticed the one they were asking about. But one of them, having seen the coach in which the judge had come, said: "He must be here, because this is the coach they say he's following. One of us should stay by the gate and the others should go looking for him. Maybe one of us should circle around the inn so that he can't escape over the wall of the corral."

"Let's do it," responded one of them. Two of them went inside the walls, one stayed by the gate, and the other rode around the outside, as the innkeeper watched and wondered why they were taking all those precautions, although he figured they were looking for the boy they had described. At this point day was breaking, and for this reason, as well as for the racket don Quixote had made, everyone was awake and getting up, especially doña Clara and Dorotea, who had slept poorly that night, one of them agitated by having her lover so near and the other curious to see him.

Don Quixote, who saw that none of the four travelers was paying any attention to his challenge, was dying of dismay and seething with rage; and if he could have found in the rules of chivalry that a knight-errant could legally engage in another enterprise, having given his word not to do so until he'd completed the one he'd promised, he would have attacked all of them and made them take up arms in spite of themselves. But considering it wouldn't be right or proper to start a new adventure until he'd installed

Micomicona in her kingdom, he held his peace and waited to see what would happen with the travelers, one of whom found the boy he was looking for sleeping next to another mule boy, quite unaware that anyone was looking for him, much less would find him. The man took him by the arm and said: "Truly, don Luis, your attire fits who you are, and the bed I find you in rivals the comfort in which your mother raised you."

The boy rubbed his sleepy eyes and looked closely at the one who was holding him, and recognized that he was a servant of his father, and was so taken aback he couldn't say a word for a long time, so the servant continued, saying: "There is nothing you can do, *señor* don Luis, except surrender calmly and return home, unless you want your father and my master to go to the other world, because that's all that can be expected from the grief he feels at your being gone."

"But how did my father find out," said don Luis, "that I'd taken this road?"

"A student to whom you had revealed your plan was the one who told him," responded the servant, "moved by the grief that he saw in your father when he realized you were gone. So he sent four of his servants to look for you, and we're all here at your service, happier than can be imagined by the speed in which we'll be able to return, restoring you to the eyes that love you so."

"That will be as I wish, or as heaven ordains," responded don Luis.

"What can you wish or what can heaven order, except to consent to go home, because there is no other possibility."

This conversation was overheard by the mule boy who'd slept next to don Luis and he got up and went to tell what was going on to don Fernando and Cardenio and to the others, who had already gotten dressed. He said the man called the boy DON and repeated the words he'd heard, and how they wanted him to return to his father's house, and how the boy didn't want to. With this, and from what they knew about him and the fine voice that heaven had given him, they all gathered around to find out most particularly who he was, and even to try to help him, if those men tried to use any force against him. So they went over to where the boy was stubbornly arguing with his servant.

Dorotea came out of her room at this point, and behind her came doña Clara, who was quite upset. Dorotea called Cardenio aside, and told him in a few words the story of the singer and doña Clara, and he told her about what happened when his father's four servants came to look for him. He didn't say it so quietly that doña Clara couldn't hear, and she became so upset that if Dorotea hadn't gone to hold her, she would have collapsed. Cardenio told Dorotea to go back with doña Clara to their room and he would fix everything, so they went back inside.

By this time the four who had been looking for don Luis were in the inn, surrounding him, and trying to persuade him that he should, without delaying a minute longer, return to comfort his father. He responded that he would not until he resolved a piece of business on which his life, honor, and soul were at stake. The servants pressured him by saying they refused to go back without him and they would carry him off whether he wanted to go or not.

"You won't," replied don Luis, "unless you take me back dead, although no matter how you take me, I will be without life."

By this point, the rest of the people at the inn were gathered around them, especially Cardenio, don Fernando, his companions, the judge, the priest, the barber, and don Quixote, to whom it seemed that it was no longer necessary to guard the castle. Cardenio, since he knew the boy's story, asked the servants who wanted to take him away why they were doing so against his will.

"It is," said one of the four, "to give life back to his father, who is in danger of losing it because of the absence of this young man."

To this don Luis said: "There is no reason to tell anyone about my affairs. I'm free, and I'll go home if I please, and if not, none of you can force me."

"Reason will convince your grace," responded the man, "and if reason fails, it's quite enough for us to do what we came for, and what we're compelled to do."

"Let's find out what's at the bottom of this," said the judge.

But the servant, who recognized him since he lived in a neighboring house, said: "Doesn't your grace, *señor* judge, recognize this young man, who is the son of your neighbor,

and who left his father's house dressed so differently from
what his rank demands, as you can see?"

The judge looked at him more closely, recognized him,
and took him in his arms, saying: "What childish things are
you doing, *señor* don Luis? Or what cause is so powerful
that it moved you to come dressed this way, which is so different from your social class?"

Tears came to the boy's eyes, and he couldn't utter a
word. The judge told the four to calm down, and that everything would work out. Taking don Luis' hand, he drew him
aside and asked him why he'd come.

While these and other questions were being asked, they
heard loud shouts coming from the gate of the inn. What
caused the noise was that two guests who had spent the
night there, seeing everyone was busy trying to find out
what the four were after, had tried to leave without paying. But the innkeeper, who was tending to his own business more than other people's, grabbed them at the gate
and demanded his payment, and reprimanded them for
their unscrupulous intention with such words that it moved
them to respond with their fists. They began to punch him
so vigorously that the poor innkeeper needed to shout and
ask for help. The innkeeper's wife and her daughter could
see no one more in a position to help them than don Quixote, to whom the daughter cried: "Your grace, *señor* knight!
By the strength that God gave you, rescue my poor father,
whom two bad men are beating up as if they were threshing
wheat!"

To which don Quixote responded slowly and with great
calm: "Beautiful maiden, your request is inappropriate, because I'm prevented from engaging in another adventure
until I happily conclude another one that I gave my word I
would settle. But what I can do to serve you is what I'll say
now: Run over and tell your father to defend himself as well
as he can and not let himself be defeated until I get permission from Princess Micomicona to succor him in his affliction, and if she grants it, rest assured that I'll help him."

"Sinner that I am," said Maritornes, who was nearby,
"before your grace can get this permission, my master will
already be in the other world!"

"Allow me, *señora*, to get the permission I mention," responded don Quixote, "and as soon as I have it, it will make

little difference if he's in the other world; in spite of everything the other world does to prevent me, I'll pluck him out, or at least I'll avenge him on those who will have sent him there, and you'll be more than somewhat satisfied."

And without saying another word, he went over and got down on his knees before Dorotea, asking her, with knightly and errant words, to be pleased to give him permission to help and rescue the warden of that castle who was in great distress. The princess gave it to him graciously and, bracing his shield and drawing his sword, he went over to the gate, where the two guests were still mauling the innkeeper. But as he approached, he hesitated. Maritornes and the innkeeper's wife asked why he'd stopped, and told him that he should rescue their master and husband.

"I'm delaying," said don Quixote, "because it's unlawful for me to draw my sword against squires. But call my own squire over here, because this defense and vengeance is his job."

That was the way things were at the gate of the inn, and there, punches and blows to the face were exchanged with full force, all to the detriment of the innkeeper, and to the rage of Maritornes, the innkeeper's wife, and her daughter, who were despairing over the cowardice of don Quixote and the bad treatment of their husband, master, and father.

But let's leave them here, because someone will doubtless rescue him, and if not, let him suffer and hold his tongue who takes on more than his strength will permit, and let's go back fifty paces to see how don Luis answered the judge, since we left him asking the boy why he'd come on foot and in such an outfit. The boy responded, taking him earnestly by the hands, as if to show that some great sorrow was troubling his heart, and shedding tears in great abundance, said to him: "*Señor mío*, I don't know what else to tell you except that since heaven ordained that we should be neighbors and that I should see my lady doña Clara, your grace's daughter and my lady, from that instant I made her the mistress of my will, and if yours offers no objection, my true lord and father, on this very day she'll be my wife. On her account I left my father's house, and for her I dressed in this attire to follow her wherever she was going, as the arrow seeks the bull's-eye, or the sailor tracks the North Star. All she knows of my passion is what she could guess from the times she's seen me shed tears from a distance. You're familiar with the wealth and nobility of my parents, *señor*, and how I'm their only heir. If you believe this is sufficient reason for you to venture to make me totally happy, receive me right now as your son, because even though my father, who might have other intentions, may not like this good fortune that I found on my own, time has more power to affect and change things than human will."

When the enamored youth finished, he was silent, and the judge was astonished, amazed, and confused, as much by the sensible way don Luis had revealed his thoughts as at the position in which he found himself, not knowing what action to take in such a sudden and unexpected matter. So he said nothing other than that the boy should stay calm and arrange with his servants not to take him that day so that he, the judge, could consider what was best for everyone. Don Luis kissed his hands, and even bathed them with tears, something that could melt a heart of marble, not to mention that of the judge, who, as a shrewd man, had already realized how good such a marriage would be for his daughter, though he wished, if it were possible, that it should be done with the blessing of don Luis' father, who he knew wanted to bestow a noble title on his son.

By now the guests had made peace with the innkeeper, because, through don Quixote's persuasion and convincing words, more than by threats, they had paid him all that he had wanted, and the servants of don Luis were waiting for the end of the conversation between the judge and their young master, when the devil, who never sleeps, ordained that at that exact moment, the barber from whom don Quixote had taken Mambrino's helmet, and with whose donkey Sancho Panza exchanged trappings, arrived at the inn. This barber, taking his donkey to the stable, saw Sancho Panza, who was fixing something on the packsaddle, and as soon as he recognized him, he ran to attack Sancho, saying: "Hey, you thief, I've got you now! Give me back my basin and my packsaddle and all the trappings you robbed me of!"

When Sancho saw himself attacked so suddenly and heard the abuse hurled at him, with one hand he held the packsaddle, and with the other he punched the barber in the face, which bathed his teeth in blood, but even with this, the barber didn't let go of the packsaddle, but raised his voice so much that everyone in the inn went to see what the ruckus and fighting were all about.

The barber said: "Help in the name of the king and justice! While I'm trying to get my property back, this thief, this highwayman, is trying to kill me!"

"You're lying," responded Sancho. "I'm not a highwayman—my master, don Quixote, won these spoils in a fair battle." By this time don Quixote was standing nearby, very pleased to see how well Sancho fought and defended himself, and from then on he held him as a man of worth, and proposed in his heart to dub him a knight at the earliest opportunity, since it seemed to him that the order of chivalry would be well bestowed on him.

As the barber fought, among other things, he said: "*Señores*, this packsaddle is mine as surely as the death I owe God. I recognize it as if I'd given birth to it, and there is my donkey in the stable, who won't let me lie. If you don't believe me, put it on him, and if it doesn't fit perfectly, call me a liar. And there's more—the same day they took my packsaddle from me, they also took a brass basin that had never before been used, and cost one *escudo*."

Don Quixote couldn't hold back anymore, and placed himself between the two, separating them, and put the packsaddle on the ground until the truth could be cleared up, and said: "I want your graces to see clearly the obvious mistake into which this good squire has fallen, since he calls a basin what was, is, and forever will be Mambrino's helmet, which I won from him in a fair battle, and became the owner of it by right and legal possession. Insofar as the packsaddle goes, I won't get involved, but what I know about it is that my squire Sancho asked permission to take the trappings from the horse belonging to this vanquished coward, to adorn his own. I gave him permission and he took them, and if the trappings changed into a packsaddle, I can't give any other reason than the usual one, which is that these transformations happen in the ordinary business of chivalry. To confirm this, Sancho, fetch the helmet that this good man calls a basin."

"Uh-oh!" said Sancho. "If we have no other proof than what your worship says, that basin is as much Malino's helmet as the trappings of this good man are a packsaddle."

"Do what I tell you," replied don Quixote, "because not everything in this castle happens by enchantment."

Sancho went to where the basin was and brought it out, and as soon as don Quixote saw it he took it in his hands and said: "Look with what cheek this squire said that this is a basin, and not the helmet I've mentioned. And I swear by the order of knighthood I profess that this helmet was the same one I took from him, without adding or removing anything."

"In this there is no doubt," said Sancho then, "because since my master won it until now he had only one battle, when he freed the luckless chain of people, and if it weren't for this basinelmet, he would have had a bad time of it, because there were plenty of stones thrown in that battle."

Chapter XXXV.* Where the matter of Mambrino's helmet and the packsaddle are finally resolved, and other adventures that happened, all of them true.

"WHAT DO your graces think, *señores*," said the barber, "about what these gentlemen declare, since they maintain that this isn't a basin but a helmet?"

"And whoever says the contrary," said don Quixote, "I'll make him see, if he's a knight, that he's lying; or if he's a squire, that he lies a thousandfold."

Our barber, who witnessed all of this, and since he knew don Quixote's state of mind so well, wanted to reinforce his folly, and in so doing keep the joke going so that everybody might have a good laugh. He said to the other barber: "*Señor* barber, or whoever you are, I want you to know that I too am of your profession, and I've had my license to practice for more than twenty years. I'm familiar with every single implement of the barber's trade. I was equally a soldier in my youth, and I also know what a helmet is, both open and closed, and other things pertaining to the military, I mean, all types of soldiers' arms. And I say—unless there is a better opinion, and always yielding to sounder

---

* In the first edition it *does* say XXXV instead of XLV. This is no typographer's mistake, since the two Roman numbers are so different in their formulation.

judgments—that this piece this good man has in his hands is not only *not* a barber's basin, but it's so far from being one as white is from black, and the truth from a lie. I also say that, although it is a helmet, it's not whole."

"Certainly not," said don Quixote, "because it's missing half—the lower face guard."

"That's right," said the priest, who saw where his friend the barber was going with all this.

Cardenio and don Fernando and his companions confirmed all of this. And even the judge, if he were not still thinking about the affair concerning don Luis, would have helped along with the jest, but the realities of what he was considering had him so absorbed that he paid little or no attention to this tomfoolery.

"God help me!" said the barber they were making fun of. "Is it possible that so many honorable people say that this isn't a basin but rather a helmet? This is something that could astonish a whole university, no matter how wise it might be! But enough—if this basin is a helmet, then this packsaddle must be a horse's trappings, as this man has said."

"To me it looks like a packsaddle," said don Quixote, "but I've already said I don't want to get involved in that."

"Whether or not it's a packsaddle or trappings of a horse," said the priest, "don Quixote has only to say so, because in matters of chivalry all these men and I acknowledge his expertise."

"By God, *señores míos*," said don Quixote, "so many strange things have happened in this castle the two times I've stayed here, I won't dare to confirm anything asked me about what goes on here, because I think that everything here happens by enchantment. The first time I was here an enchanted Moor walloped me, and Sancho fared no better with this Moor's underlings, and last night I was hanging by this arm for almost two hours, without finding out how I came into that misfortune. So if I were to give an opinion about something that is so chaotic, it would be like falling into a rash judgment. Insofar as their saying that this is a basin and not a helmet, I've already responded. But as to declaring if this is a packsaddle or the trappings of a horse, I don't dare give an unequivocal opinion, and I leave it to your better determination. Maybe since you're not dubbed knights—as I am—the enchantments of this place will not affect you, and you can judge the things of this castle as they really and truly are and not how they appear to me."

"There is no doubt," don Fernando responded, "but that don Quixote has spoken very well today, and that we should resolve this case. And so that it will rest on a firm foundation, I'll take secret votes from these men, and I'll reveal the result clearly and fully."

For those who knew don Quixote's state of mind, this was very funny, but for those who didn't, it seemed like the greatest foolishness in the world, especially to the four servants of don Luis, and to don Luis himself, and to three other travelers who happened to come to the inn who looked like officers of the Holy Brotherhood, as, in fact, they were. But the one who was least amused was the barber, whose basin had been transformed right in front of his eyes into Mambrino's helmet, and whose packsaddle doubtless was fast becoming the elegant trappings of a horse. Everyone laughed to see how don Fernando went around collecting votes, whispering in their ears, so that they could declare whether that item was a packsaddle or trappings, over which so much fighting had been done.

After he took the votes of those who knew don Quixote, he said in a loud voice: "The fact is, my good man, that I'm tired of soliciting so many opinions, because everyone I ask immediately says that it's absurd to say that this is a packsaddle, but rather trappings of a horse, and even of a thoroughbred at that; so you'll have to live with it, because in spite of you and your donkey, these are trappings, and not a packsaddle, and you've alleged and tried to prove your case very poorly."

"May I never have a case in heaven," said the already mentioned barber, "if all your graces aren't mistaken, and may my soul appear before God the way this appears to me to be a packsaddle and not trappings, but 'laws go, &c. . . .'* and I say no more. And in truth I'm not drunk—in fact, I've eaten nothing, except sins."

The foolish talk of the barber caused no less laughter than the nonsense of don Quixote, who said at that moment: "There's nothing more to do, except for everyone to

---

* "Laws go where kings want them to" is the full proverb.

take what belongs to him, and 'to whom God has given it, may St. Peter bless.' "

One of the servants said: "Unless this a planned joke, I can't convince myself that men of such intelligence as all those here are, or appear to be, would dare to say and affirm that this isn't a basin nor that that isn't a packsaddle. But since I see that they affirm and say it, I'm led to think that there is some mystery in insisting that something is so opposite to what truth and experience themselves show us, because, by Jove," he exclaimed, "all the people living in the world today will not make me believe that this isn't a barber's basin and that isn't a donkey's packsaddle."

"It might be from a jenny," said the priest.

"It's all the same," said the servant, "for the crux of the matter is not *that*, but rather if it's a packsaddle as your graces maintain."

Hearing this, one of the officers who had come in and who had heard the controversy and the dispute, filled with anger and vexation, said: "It's a packsaddle all right, just as my father is my father, and anyone who said or says different must be drunk."

"You lie like an ill-bred rogue," responded don Quixote, and raising his lance (which he never let out of his hand), he went to strike a terrible blow on the man's head, and if the officer hadn't dodged, it would have left him stretched out on the ground. The lance broke into splinters, and the other officers who saw their companion being treated so badly raised their voice, calling for help from the Holy Brotherhood. The innkeeper, who was a member of the Brotherhood, went in for his staff of office and sword, and joined the others.

Don Luis' servants surrounded him so that he couldn't escape in the tumult. The barber, seeing everything in turmoil, grabbed the packsaddle again, as did Sancho. Don Quixote drew his sword and attacked the officers; don Luis yelled at his servants to leave him and to go help don Quixote, Cardenio, and don Fernando—for everyone had taken don Quixote's side. The priest shouted; the innkeeper's wife screamed; the daughter was grief-stricken; Maritornes wept; Dorotea was confused; Luscinda bewildered; and doña Clara in a faint; the barber pounded Sancho; Sancho mauled the barber; don Luis, whom one of his servants dared to grab by his arm so he wouldn't get away, gave him a punch that bathed his teeth in blood; the judge defended don Luis; don Fernando had an officer on the ground, kicking him very heartily; the innkeeper raised his voice again, asking for help for the Holy Brotherhood; and so the whole inn was wails, shouts, screams, confusion, fears, alarms, terrors, misfortunes, sword slashings, punches to the face, kicks, and bloodshed. In the midst of this chaos and labyrinth, don Quixote imagined that he'd been thrust into the thick of the discord of Agramante's Camp.* So he roared in a thundering voice: "Everybody stop! Sheathe your swords! Everybody calm down. Listen to me, all of you, if you want to stay alive!"

At his mighty voice they all stopped, and he continued, saying: "Didn't I tell you that this castle was enchanted, and a legion of devils must be inhabiting it? To confirm this, I want you to see with your own eyes how the strife of Agramante's Camp has been transplanted into our midst. Look how over there they fight for the sword, here for the horse, over there for the eagle, over here for the helmet,† and we're all fighting at cross-purposes. Come here, then, your grace, *señor* judge, and your grace, *señor* priest, and one of you play the role of King Agramante and the other of King Sobrino,‡ and bring peace back among us, because, by God almighty, it's a great transgression that so many people of quality as those here are slaying each other for trifling causes."

The officers—who didn't understand the way don Quixote talked and were in a sorry state because of don Fernando, Cardenio, and their companions—were not about to be pacified. The barber stopped because his beard and packsaddle had been torn to shreds in the fight. Sancho, at

---

* In *Orlando Furioso*, when Agramante is laying siege to Paris, Charlemagne manages to sow seeds of discord among Agramante's men, who begin fighting among themselves for no good reason (cantos fourteen and twenty-seven).
† The sword they were fighting for was Roland's Durendal (heroes gave names to their swords), the horse was Frontino, the eagle was on a shield belonging to Hector—but the helmet here was don Quixote's own "Mambrino's helmet."
‡ These two kings pacified the battle.

the slightest word of his master, obeyed; the four servants of don Luis also calmed down, seeing what little good it did to do otherwise. Only the innkeeper insisted they must punish that crazy man for his insolence, because at every step he caused turmoil at the inn. Finally, the uproar was quelled, the packsaddle remained a horse's trappings until Judgment Day; the basin, a helmet; and the inn, a castle, in don Quixote's imagination.

Now that everyone was calmed down and a truce made by the persuasion of the judge and the priest, the servants of don Luis insisted once again that he go back with them immediately. Meanwhile, the judge consulted with don Fernando, Cardenio, and the priest about what he should do in this matter, relating to them what don Luis had told him. They finally agreed that don Fernando should tell the servants who he was, and how it was his pleasure that don Luis should go with him to Andalusia, where his brother, the marquis, would give don Luis the honor that his rank deserved, since they all knew that don Luis wouldn't go home to his father even though they tore him to pieces. When the four servants realized the social status of don Fernando and the resolve of don Luis, they agreed among themselves that three of them should return to tell his father what was happening, and the other should stay to serve don Luis and not leave him until the three returned for him, or determined what his father wanted to do.

In this way, by the authority of Agramante and the prudence of King Sobrino, this multitude of quarrels was settled. But the enemy of harmony and the adversary of truce, seeing himself thus slighted and made a fool of, and seeing how little fruit had come from throwing them all into such a labyrinth of confusion, thought he would try his hand once more by stirring up fresh quarrels and disturbances.

It happened that the officers were pacified when they overheard the rank of those with whom they had been fighting, and they withdrew from the quarrel, since it seemed to them that no matter how it came out, they would get the worst of the battle. But one of them, who was the one who had been mauled and trampled by don Fernando, remembered that among the arrest warrants that he had for some delinquents, he had one for don Quixote whom the

Holy Brotherhood had ordered arrested because of the freedom he'd given the galley slaves, as Sancho had so astutely feared. Once he'd figured this out, he wanted to verify the description he had to see if it matched don Quixote's features. Taking a parchment from inside his shirt, he came across what he was looking for, and set about reading it slowly, since he wasn't a very skilled reader. At every word he looked over at don Quixote and compared the description on the warrant with the man's face, and he found that without a doubt he was the one the warrant described, and as soon as he was satisfied, he folded up the parchment, took it in his left hand, and with his right he took hold of don Quixote firmly by the neck so he couldn't breathe, and with loud shouts cried: "Help, in the name of the Holy Brotherhood! To prove my claim is serious, read what this warrant says about arresting this highwayman."

The priest took the warrant and saw that everything the officer said was true, and that the description was of don Quixote, who, seeing himself so badly treated by the villainous brigand, was enraged and, straining every bone in his body to the point of breaking, grabbed the neck of the officer with both hands. If the officer hadn't been saved by his companions, he would have lost his life right there before don Quixote released his grip. The innkeeper, who was required to help those of this office, ran over to help him. The innkeeper's wife, who saw her husband in a new battle, once again raised an outcry, and Maritornes and her daughter joined in, asking for the help of heaven and all of those who were there. Seeing what was going on, Sancho said: "By God, everything my master says about the enchantments in this castle must be true, since you can't have a moment's peace and quiet in it!"

Don Fernando separated the officer from don Quixote, and to the relief of both, he unlocked their hands, the one clenched firmly on the other's collar and the other on his enemy's throat. But for all this the officers didn't cease their demands for their prisoner and the company's help to tie him up and deliver him to them, because that was required for their service to the king and the Holy Brotherhood, on whose behalf they asked again for help in arresting this robber and highwayman of paths and roads.

Don Quixote laughed when he heard these words, and with great calm said: "Come here, base and lowborn people. You call the one who gives freedom to men chained together, who releases prisoners, who helps wretches, who raises the fallen, who relieves the needy, a highwayman? Ah, you despicable people, who, because of your base and vile intelligence heaven will not make known to you the virtue embraced by knight-errantry, nor will it make you see the sin and ignorance that engulfs you, when you refuse to revere the shadow, not to mention the presence, of any knight-errant! Come now, robbers in a band— not officers—highwaymen with the approval of the Holy Brotherhood, tell me: Who was the ignoramus who signed the arrest warrant against such a knight-errant as I am? Who was it who didn't know that knights-errant are exempt from all jurisdiction—their laws are their sword and their prowess and their statutes are their will? Who was the dimwit, I say again, who doesn't know that there is no title of nobility with so many privileges and exemptions as the one that knights-errant acquire on the day they're dubbed a knight and devote themselves to the arduous calling of knight-errantry? What knight-errant ever paid income or sales tax, levies, vassal's tax, customs duty, or ferry transit? What tailor ever took money from him for his clothing? What castle warden ever gave him shelter and asked him to pay for his room and board? What king never had him sit at his table? What maiden never fell in love with him? And finally, what knight-errant in the world was there, is there, and will there be, who isn't strong enough to wallop four hundred officers with four hundred punches, all by himself, if they stand in his way?"

Chapter XLVI. About the notable adventure of the officers and the great ferocity of our great knight don Quixote.

WHILE DON Quixote spoke, the priest was trying to persuade the officers that since don Quixote was out of his mind, as they could see by his deeds and words, they shouldn't proceed with the matter, since even if they arrested him and took him away, they would have to release him for being crazy; to which the one with the warrant said that it was not up to him to judge the sanity of don Quixote, but rather to execute his superior's orders, and once he was arrested, they could let him go three hundred times if they wanted.

"Even so," said the priest, "this time you must not carry him off, nor will he allow himself to be taken away, I don't think."

In short, the priest told them so much, and don Quixote did so many crazy things, that the officers would be crazier than don Quixote if they didn't recognize his affliction, and so they thought it best to leave him alone, and even act as peacemakers between the barber and Sancho Panza, who were still going at their fight with great animosity. Finally, as officers of justice, they mediated the matter and were arbitrators of it in such a way that both parties were, if not completely happy, at least somewhat satisfied, because they exchanged packsaddles, but not the girths or halters. And as far as Mambrino's helmet went, the priest surreptitiously, and without don Quixote finding out, gave the barber eight *reales* for the basin, and the barber made out a receipt and had to promise he would not claim that he was defrauded thenceforth and forever, AMEN.

These two disputes—which were the most important ones—having been settled, it only remained for don Luis' servants to consent that three of them should go back and that one would stay to accompany him where don Fernando wanted to take him. And as good luck and better fortune had begun to solve problems and remove obstacles in favor of the lovers and brave men of the inn, and wanted to give a happy ending to everything, since the servants were pleased to do what don Luis wanted, this made doña Clara very happy—and anyone who saw her face right then couldn't help but observe the joy in her heart.

Zoraida, who didn't completely understand everything she saw, was sad or happy depending on the expressions on everyone's face, especially her Spaniard, whom she followed with her eyes and clung to with her soul. The innkeeper, who didn't fail to notice the money the priest had given the barber, asked for don Quixote's portion of the bill, plus the damage to the wineskins and the loss of the

wine, swearing that neither Rocinante nor Sancho's donkey would leave the inn unless he was paid down to the last
ardite. The priest made peace and don Fernando paid, although the judge had volunteered to pay with much goodwill. In this way they were all calméd down, so that the inn
no longer looked like Agramante's Camp, as don Quixote
had said, but rather the very peace and tranquillity of Octavian's time.* For all of this, it was the general opinion they
should thank the goodwill and fine eloquence of the priest,
and the incomparable generosity of don Fernando.

When don Quixote saw himself free and unencumbered of all those disputes, both his squire's and his own, it
seemed to him that it would be good to continue the journey he'd begun, and bring an end to the great adventure
for which he'd been called and chosen.† So with resolute
determination he knelt in front of Dorotea, who wouldn't
let him say a word until he stood up; and, to obey her, he
got up and said: "It's a common proverb, beautiful *señora*,
that 'diligence is the mother of good fortune,' and in many
grave matters experience has shown that the persistence
of the negotiator brings a successful conclusion to a shaky
lawsuit. But in nothing is this truth more manifest than in
war, where speed and haste prevent the advancement of
the enemy and win the victory before the opponent can
prepare his defense. I say all this, exalted and precious lady,
because it seems to me that our stay in this castle serves
no further purpose and could cause terrible damage, as we
may see one day, because who knows if by hidden and diligent spies, your enemy, the giant, might have learned that
I'm going to destroy him, and the delay gives him the opportunity to strengthen his position in some impregnable
castle or fortress against which my preparations and the
strength of my untiring arm will be of little use. So, *señora*,
let's prevent his designs, as I've said, with our diligence, and
depart quickly, with Fortune on our side, which Your Highness is only kept from enjoying to its fullest by my delay in
attacking your enemy."

---

* The *Pax Octaviana* or *Pax Romana* refers to the period of relative
tranquillity in ancient Rome between 27 B.C. and A.D. 180.
† This seems to be a reference to Matthew 20:16: "For many are called
and few are chosen." This phrase is not in every version of the Bible.

Don Quixote stopped talking and said no more, and waited with great calm for the answer of the beautiful princess, who, with commanding dignity, simulating don Quixote's style of speech, responded in this way: "I thank you, *señor* knight, because the desire you're showing in order to relieve my affliction, so like a knight, whose duty it is to protect the orphans and the distressed. Heaven grant that your desire and mine may be fulfilled, so that you'll see that there are grateful women in the world. Insofar as my departure goes, let it be immediate, because I have no will other than yours. Order me as you will, because she who has given over the defense of her person to you and placed in your hands the recovery of her kingdom will not go against what your wisdom orders."

"It's in God's hands," said don Quixote. "Since a lady humbles herself to me thus, I don't want to miss the opportunity to raise her and place her on her ancestral throne. Let's depart at once, because my desire spurs me on, and encourages me to get on the road, and you know what they say, 'in delay lurks danger.' Since heaven has never created, nor has hell ever seen, any danger that frightens or intimidates me, saddle Rocinante, Sancho, and prepare your donkey, and the palfrey of the queen, and let's bid farewell to the warden of the castle and to these people, and let's depart immediately."

Sancho, who witnessed all of this, said, shaking his head: "Ay, *señor*, 'there's more mischief in the village than you hear of,' begging the pardon of the honorable women."

"What mischief can there be in any village, or in all the cities in the world, that can be to my discredit, you rustic?"

"If you're going to get angry," responded Sancho, "I'll keep quiet and won't say what I'm obliged to say as a good squire and as a good servant—what I should say to your grace."

"Say whatever you want," replied don Quixote, "as long as you don't try to frighten me, for if you're afraid, you're behaving like yourself, and if I'm not, I'm behaving like myself."

"It's not that," responded Sancho, "but as I'm a sinner in God's eyes, I hold as sure and proven that this lady who says she's queen of the great kingdom of Micomicón is no more queen than my mother is; because if she were what she says, she wouldn't be smooching with someone of the present company when heads are turned, and behind every door."

Dorotea turned red with Sancho's words, because it was true that her husband had now and then, when no one was looking, harvested with his lips some of the reward his love had earned, and this was seen by Sancho; and it seemed to him that this brazenness smacked more of a courtesan than a queen of such a large kingdom. She wouldn't and couldn't say a word in response to Sancho, but let him continue his discourse, and he went on, saying: "I say this, *señor*, because if after we've traveled those highways and byways, spent bad nights and worse days, the fellow now enjoying himself in this inn will come to enjoy the fruit of our labor, so there is no reason for me to run to saddle Rocinante, put the packsaddle on the donkey, or get the palfrey ready. It'd be better just to stay put, and 'let every prostitute spin, and we'll eat.'"*

Good God, can you imagine how great was the rage that came to don Quixote when he heard his squire's insolent words? I say that it was so great that with a trembling, stuttering voice, with living flames shooting from his eyes, he exclaimed: "Oh, villainous rogue, boorish, brazen, ignorant, incoherent, foulmouthed, audacious gossip and slanderer! You would use such words in front of these illustrious ladies? You would dare to put in your confused mind such gross and shameless thoughts? Get out of my presence, monster of nature, storehouse of lies, closet filled with deceits, silo filled with wickedness, inventor of evil, publisher of follies, enemy of the respect due to royalty! Go away—don't appear before me again, under the pain of my ire."

And saying this he arched his eyebrows, puffed out his cheeks, looked in all directions, and stamped his right foot on the ground, all of them sure signs of the wrath that he had in his heart. At these raging words and gestures, Sancho cowered, and was so frightened that he wished the earth would open up at his feet right then and swallow him up. He didn't know what to do except turn away and leave the angered presence of his master. But the discreet Doro-

---

* In rough times, the pimp would have the prostitutes do other types of work, such as spinning, so that they all could be supported.

tea, who understood don Quixote's frame of mind, said to him to placate his fury: "Don't get angry, *señor* Woebegone Knight, over the foolish things that your good squire said. Perhaps he had good cause to say them, and we couldn't expect that his Christian conscience would bring false witness against anyone, so we must doubtless believe that, since everything in this castle happens by enchantment, as you say, it might be that Sancho must have seen, through this diabolical medium, what he says he saw, so much to the detriment of my reputation."

"By the omnipotent God I swear," said don Quixote at that moment, "that your greatness has hit the mark, and some loathsome vision was placed in front of this sinner, Sancho, that made him see what would be impossible by any other means, for I know of the goodness and innocence of this unfortunate fellow, who doesn't know how to bring false witness against anybody."

"That's what it is and what it must be," said don Fernando, "and that's why your grace should pardon him and restore him to the bosom of your favor, *sicut erat in principio*,* before those visions drove him out of his mind."

Don Quixote responded that he did forgive him, and the priest went to fetch Sancho, who came in very humbly and, kneeling down, asked for don Quixote's hand, which he gave him, and after he'd kissed it, don Quixote blessed him, saying: "Now you'll realize, Sancho, my son, that it's true what I've told you on many other occasions, that everything in this castle happens by way of enchantment."

"I believe it," said Sancho, "except that business of the blanket, which really happened the regular way."

"Don't believe it," responded don Quixote, "because if it had been that way, I'd have avenged you right then, and would even now. But neither then nor now could I, nor did I, see whom I should wreak vengeance on for that offense."

They all wanted to know what that business of the blanket was, and the innkeeper told them, point by point, about the flight of Sancho Panza, at which they all laughed not a little, and at which Sancho would have been ashamed, if, once again, his master hadn't assured him that it had hap-

---

* "As it was in the beginning . . ." from the Latin *Gloria Patri*.

pened by enchantment, although his credulousness never got to the point where he could convince himself that it wasn't the plain and simple truth, without a reasonable doubt, that he'd been blanketed by men of flesh and blood, and not by phantoms dreamed up or imagined, as his master believed and affirmed.

That illustrious company had been at the inn for two days, and it seemed to them that it was now time to leave, so they thought of a way to allow the priest and barber to take don Quixote home to find a cure for him there without forcing Dorotea and don Fernando to trouble themselves to accompany them to their village, keeping the pretext of restoring Queen Micomicona to her throne. And what they did was to arrange for a man with an oxcart who happened by to take him in this way: They made a cage with wooden bars, large enough to hold don Quixote comfortably, and then the priest had don Fernando and his companions, with all the servants of don Luis and the officers, together with the innkeeper, cover their faces, and disguise themselves in different ways, so that don Quixote would think they were not the people he'd seen in the inn.

Once this was done, in great silence they went in to where he lay resting from his previous frays. They went over to where he was slumbering and completely unaware, and seized him forcibly and bound his hands and feet very tightly, so that when he woke up with a start, he couldn't move or do anything but be thunderstruck on seeing so many strange faces in front of him. He then came to realize what his never-ending and extravagant imagination represented to him, and he believed that those figures were phantoms from the enchanted castle, and that he was doubtless enchanted as well, since he couldn't budge or defend himself. Everything happened exactly as the priest—the inventor of this scheme—had planned. Only Sancho, of all those present, was totally sane and undisguised. Although he was not far behind having his master's affliction, he didn't fail to recognize the disguised figures. But he didn't dare open his mouth until he saw where this assault and seizure of his master were leading. Don Quixote also didn't say a word, waiting to see where his misfortune was taking him. They brought in the cage and put him inside, nailing down the bars so firmly that they couldn't be easily removed.

They lifted the cage onto their shoulders, and as they left the room, an eerie voice was heard, made by the barber (not the one with the packsaddle, but the other one), who said: "Oh, Woebegone Knight, don't let the prison where you're confined give you grief, because it is necessary in order to conclude more quickly the adventure in which your great bravery has placed you. This adventure will be finished when the fierce spotted lion* shall lie as one with the dove of Toboso, having first bowed their proud necks to the soft matrimonial yoke, from whose unheard-of union will come to the light of the world fierce cubs who will have the rampant claws of their brave father. And this will take place before the pursuer of the fleeing nymph† makes two visits around the bright images‡ in his speedy and natural course. Oh, you, the noblest and most obedient squire that ever girded a sword at his side, had a beard on his face, or a sense of smell in his nose! Be not dismayed or concerned at seeing the flower of knight-errantry being borne away thus before your eyes, because soon, if the Framer of the World is pleased, you'll be so exalted that you won't recognize yourself, and the promises your good master made you will not prove false. And I assure you, on behalf of the wise Mentironiana,§ that your salary will be paid, as you'll see in due course. Follow the steps of the brave and enchanted knight, because you both must go to where you both will go, and because I'm not allowed to say more, go with God, because I'm going where only I know."

When this prophecy was over, he raised his voice to a very high pitch, then lowered it afterward, and with such a soft sound that even the people who were party to the trick almost believed that what was said was true. Don Quixote was consoled with the prophecy that he heard, because he understood completely right away what it meant and he saw that they promised him that he would be joined in holy matrimony with his beloved Dulcinea del

---

* In Spanish there is a pun: *manchado* means "spotted," but here it obliquely hints at *manchego*—"Manchegan."
† The fleeing nymph is Daphne and her follower is Apollo, the sun.
‡ These bright images refer to the zodiac signs, thus all of this means "before two days go by."
§ *Mentir* is the Spanish verb that means "to lie."

Toboso, from whose happy womb would come forth the cubs—who were his children—for the perpetual glory of La Mancha. And believing this firmly, he raised his voice, and giving a great sigh, said: "Oh, you, whoever you are, and who have foretold such happiness for me, I beg you to ask the wise enchanter in charge of my affairs not to let me perish in this prison in which they're now taking me until I see those so happy and incomparable promises made to me realized; for if this happens, I'll consider this cell my glory and these chains that bind me my comfort, and this cot on which they have laid me not as a hard battlefield, but rather a soft and happy nuptial bed. And insofar as the consolation of Sancho Panza, my squire, goes, I trust in his good nature and conduct not to leave me either in good or bad fortune, because if it should happen—either because of his or my bad luck—that I cannot give him the *ínsula* I promised him, or something just as good, at least his salary won't be lost, because in my will, which is already made, I've declared what is to be given to him, not in proportion to his many and good services, but in accordance with my means."

Sancho Panza bowed with respect and kissed both his master's hands, because he couldn't kiss just one, since they were tied together. Then they took the cage on their shoulders and placed it on the oxcart.

Chapter XLVII. Of the strange way don Quixote de La Mancha was enchanted, with other famous events.

WHEN DON Quixote found himself locked up in a cage on a cart, he said: "I've read many solemn histories of knights-errant, but I've never read, seen, or heard of enchanted knights being carried off this way,* or with the slowness of these lazy and sluggish beasts—it has always been that they're whisked away in the air with extraordinary speed, shrouded in some dark cloud, or in a chariot of

---

* Don Quixote may not have heard of it, but Cervantes doubtless had, since this episode reflects the way Lancelot was transported in the French epic *Le Chevalier de la charrette*.

fire, or on a hippogriff* or a similar animal. To think that they're hauling me away on an oxcart! My God, it upsets me! But maybe knighthood and enchantments in our times follow a different road than they did in the old days. Since I'm a novice knight in the world, and the first one who has brought back to life the now forgotten order of knight-errantry, perhaps they have invented new kinds of enchantments and other ways of carrying enchanted knights. What do you think of this, Sancho, my son?"

"I don't know what to think," responded Sancho, "because I'm not as well-read as your grace is in writings-errant. Nevertheless, I'd venture to affirm and swear that these apparitions we see here and there are not at all catholic."†

"Catholic? What do you mean?" responded don Quixote. "How can they be Catholic if they're all devils who have taken on ghostly bodies in order to come to do this, and put me in this situation? And if you want to prove this truth, go touch and feel them, and you'll see that they have no bodies but are made of air, and they're just apparitions."

"By God, *señor*," Sancho replied, "I've already touched them, and that devil who is walking over as nice as can be is a bit plump, and he has another characteristic very different from what I've heard devils have, because, as it's said, they're supposed to smell of sulfur and other bad odors— but this one smells of perfume half a league away."

Sancho said this about don Fernando, who, as a gentleman, must have smelled the way he said.

"This is not surprising, Sancho, my friend," responded don Quixote, "because I'll have you know that devils are crafty, and although they do have odors with them, they themselves don't smell, since they're spirits, and if they do smell, they can't smell good, but rather of bad and foul-smelling things, because they take hell with them no matter where they go, and have no relief from their suffering. Since sweet smells delight and comfort, it's not possible for them to smell of anything good. And if you believe this devil smells of perfume, either you're mistaken or he wants to deceive you to make you think that he's not a devil."

As master and servant held this conversation, don Fer-

---

* The hippogriff was a clawed flying horse with the face of a griffin.
† "Not at all catholic" here means "sounds fishy."

nando and Cardenio were thinking all the while that Sancho would discover their deception—and he already had it almost figured out—so they decided to cut their good-byes short. They called the innkeeper aside, and asked him to saddle Rocinante and put the packsaddle on the donkey, which he did quickly.

The priest, meanwhile, had arranged with the officers to go with them as far as their village, paying them so much per day. Cardenio hung the shield on the saddle from one side of the pommel, and from the other the basin, and by signs had Sancho mount his donkey and take Rocinante's reins. He stationed an officer on both sides of the cage, each one with a musket. But before the cart moved out, the innkeeper's wife and daughter, and Maritornes, ran out to bid farewell to don Quixote, pretending to be crying over the grief of his misfortune, and don Quixote said to them: "Do not cry, my good ladies, for all these misfortunes are customary for those who profess what I profess, and if these calamities didn't happen to me, I wouldn't consider myself a famous knight-errant, because knights of little renown and fame never suffer such things, and none of them is remembered in the world. The valiant ones, yes, they have caused many princes and other knights to envy them because of their virtue and valor. Nevertheless, virtue is so powerful that on its own—in spite of all the necromancy that its original inventor, Zoroaster, knew*—it will triumph over every battle and will give light in the world as the sun does from the sky. Pardon me, beautiful ladies, if I've done you any wrong out of heedlessness, because I've never done so to anyone willingly or knowingly. Please pray to God to release me from this imprisonment into which some evil-intentioned enchanter has placed me, and if I get free, I'll not forget the favors you've done for me in this castle, and will respond to, reward, and repay them as they deserve."

While the ladies of the castle were thus engaged with don Quixote, the priest and barber said good-bye to don Fernando and his companions, and to the captain and his brother, and to all the happy women, especially Dorotea and Luscinda. Everyone embraced and agreed to send

---

* Zoroaster (also known as Zarathustra) (628–ca. 551 B.C.). A Persian priest who, in legend, is associated with occult knowledge and magic.

news of what happened. Don Fernando asked the priest to write him and tell him how don Quixote wound up, assuring him that nothing would give him greater pleasure to hear about, and he would equally send him word about everything he might like to know—about his marriage, as well as Zoraida's baptism, what happened to don Luis, and Luscinda's return home. The priest promised to do scrupulously everything he was asked. They embraced once again and once again renewed their promises.

The innkeeper now approached the priest and gave him a stack of papers, which he said he found in the lining of a suitcase where he found the novella of the "Ill-Advised Curiosity," and because its owner had never come back, he should take them all; since he didn't know how to read, he didn't want them. The priest thanked him, and opened some papers at once, and saw that the beginning of the manuscript said it was the novella of "Rinconete and Cortadillo,"* from which he gathered that it was a story, and presumed that, since the "Ill-Advised Curiosity" had been good, that one would be too, since it might be that they were both by the same author. So he kept it, intending to read it as soon as he could.

He got on horseback, as did his friend the barber, with their masks, so they wouldn't be recognized by don Quixote, and they started out behind the cart, and the order of the procession was as follows: the oxcart went first, driven by its owner; at the two sides were the officers, as has been said, with their muskets. Sancho Panza followed on his donkey, leading Rocinante by his reins. After this came the priest and barber on their powerful mules, their faces covered, as has been said, in a grave and serious manner, and at a speed no faster than that of the oxen. Don Quixote was seated inside the cage, his hands tied, his legs stretched out, and leaning against the bars, and so quiet and so patient, as if he weren't a man of flesh and blood but a statue of stone.

Slowly and silently they went almost two leagues, when they came to a valley where it seemed to the wagoner it was a comfortable place to rest and let his oxen graze. He com-

---

* This novella was published as the third of Cervantes' twelve *Novelas ejemplares* (1613). No one would have known in 1605 that Cervantes was its author.

municated this to the priest, but the barber thought they should go on a bit more, because he knew that behind a nearby slope there was a valley with more and better grass than where they had wanted to stop. They took the advice of the barber, and moved on again.

The priest turned his head and saw coming from behind six or seven well-equipped men on mounts. And soon they were overtaken, because they were not traveling with the ease and leisure of oxen but like men on canon's mules, intent on spending the siesta at an inn, because they could see one less than a league away. As these faster people passed the slower ones, they greeted them courteously. One of them was a canon* from Toledo and the master of the others who were accompanying them, who, seeing the orderly procession of the cart, the officers, Sancho, Rocinante, priest and barber, and most notably don Quixote in a cage and imprisoned, couldn't help but ask what they were doing conducting that man in such a way. He thought, seeing the badges of the officers, that he must be some wicked highwayman or some other delinquent whose punishment was put in the charge of the Holy Brotherhood. One of the officers whom he asked about the matter responded: "*Señor*, let him tell you himself what all this means, because we don't know."

Don Quixote heard this exchange and said: "By chance, *señores*, are your graces versed and knowledgeable in the matter of knight-errantry? Because if you are, I'll tell you about my misfortunes, and if not, there is no reason to bother."

By this time, the priest and barber, seeing that the travelers were engaged in conversation with don Quixote de La Mancha, came up to answer questions in such a way that their stratagem would not be discovered. The canon, in response to what don Quixote said, replied: "In truth, brother, I know more about romances of chivalry than I do of the *Súmulas* of Villalpando.† So, if that's the only condition, you can tell me all you wish."

---

* Canons were staff priests in a cathedral.
† Gaspar Cardillo de Villalpando was a professor of theology at the University of Alcalá, where his *Summa summularum* (colloquially the *Súmulas*), a treatise on logic, was required reading.

"As God wishes," replied don Quixote. "In that event, *señor* knight, I'd like you to know that I'm enchanted in this cage because of envy and deceit of evil enchanters—for virtue is more persecuted by evil than it is loved by good. I'm a knight-errant, and not one whose name Fame has ever bothered to immortalize, but one who, in spite of Envy itself, and of all the magicians ever born in Persia, the Brahmans of India, the gymnosophists of Ethiopia,* will manage to write his name in the temple of immortality, to serve as an example in future ages, so that knights-errant can see the steps that they have to follow if they want to reach the summit of the art of arms."

"*Señor* don Quixote de La Mancha is telling the truth," the priest broke in at that point. "He's traveling enchanted in this cart, not because it's his fault or because of his sins, but rather owing to the evil intention of those whom virtue angers and bravery peeves. This, *señor*, is the Woebegone Knight, in case you never heard of him, because his brave feats and great deeds will be written on bronze tablets or carved into marble, no matter how much Envy endeavors to erase them or Evil tries to hide them."

When the canon heard the imprisoned man and the free one speak in that way, he was on the point of crossing himself in wonder, and he couldn't figure out what had happened to him, and all his companions were similarly amazed. At this point Sancho drew near to hear what was going on and, to clarify matters, said: "All right, *señores*, love me or hate me for what I'm about to say, but the case is that my master don Quixote de La Mancha is about as enchanted as my mother is. He has all of his wits about him—he eats and drinks, and performs other necessary functions as everyone else does, and as he did yesterday before they put him in a cage. This being so, how do they expect me to believe he's enchanted? I've heard many people say that those who are enchanted don't eat, sleep, or speak, and my master, if you don't stop him, will outtalk more than thirty lawyers."

And turning to look at the priest, he went on, saying: "Ah, *señor* priest, *señor* priest! Did you think I don't rec-

---

* Brahmans are Indian priests; the gymnosophists referred to here are the chief priest caste of the ancient Ethiopians, mentioned in Heliodorus' *Ethiopian Story*, Book 10.

ognize you? And do you think that I don't understand and guess where these new enchantments are leading? I want you to know that I *do* recognize you, no matter how you disguise your face, and I want you to know that I know what you're up to, no matter how you try to cover your schemes up. In short, 'where envy reigns, virtue cannot thrive,' and 'where there is stinginess, generosity cannot live.' The devil take it all, because if it weren't for your reverence, my master would be married this very moment to the Princess Micomicona, and I'd be at least a count— you couldn't expect anything less—as much through the goodness of my master, the Woebegone One, as through the worthiness of my services. But I now see that it's true what they say, that 'the wheel of fortune turns faster than a millstone,' and 'those who were prosperous yesterday are downtrodden today.' I'm sorry for my wife and children, because, whereas they could and should have expected to see their father come home a governor or a viceroy of some *ínsula* or kingdom, he'll come home a stable boy instead. All this I've said, *señor* priest, just to make you see the bad treatment my master is getting—and watch out that God doesn't hold you responsible in the other world for making my master a prisoner, and for all the wrongs he could have righted all the time he was a prisoner."

"I don't believe it!" said the barber. "Sancho, do you belong to your master's fraternity? By God, I'm thinking that you should keep him company in the cage, and you'll be as enchanted as he is for what has rubbed off onto you from his mental state. It was unfortunate when you impregnated yourself with his promises, and equally so when that *ínsula* you set your sights on got into your brain."

"I'm not pregnant by anybody," responded Sancho, "nor am I a man who would get pregnant, not even by the king himself, and even though I'm poor, I'm an Old Christian, and I don't owe anything to anyone; and if I long for *ínsulas*, other people have yearned for much worse; and 'everyone is the child of his works,' and 'being a man, I can even get to be pope,' not to mention governor of an *ínsula*—and my master may win so many, he won't have enough people to give them to. Your grace should watch what you say, *señor* barber, because there is more to life than shaving beards, and 'not every Pedro is the same.' I say that because we all know who we are, and 'you can't trick me with loaded dice.' As for the enchantment of my master, God knows the truth, and let's leave it alone, because 'stirring it up will only make it worse.' "

The barber didn't want to respond so Sancho wouldn't reveal through his naive talk what he and the priest were trying so hard to conceal. And with this same fear the priest had told the canon they should ride ahead a bit, and he would tell him the mystery of the caged man, and other things that would give him pleasure. The canon agreed, and went ahead with his servants, and listened attentively to everything about don Quixote's disposition, life, crazy acts, and customs; and the priest told him briefly about the origin and cause of his delirium, and everything that had happened until they put him in the cage, and the plan they had to take him back home to see if there was some way to cure his madness. The canon and his servants were astonished afresh when they heard the unusual story of don Quixote, and when it was over, the canon said: "Truly, *señor* priest, I find these so-called romances of chivalry to be prejudicial to the republic. Although I've read—in idle moments, moved by an irrational desire—the beginning of the majority of those that have been printed, I could never read one all the way through, because it seems to me that they're all more or less the same, and this one has no more than that, nor that one more than the next one. The way I look at it, this style of writing and composition fall under the category of Milesian tales,* which are foolish fables designed only to entertain and not to instruct, unlike the apologue fables that entertain and instruct at the same time.† Since the main purpose of these books is only to entertain, I don't see how they can do even that, since they're filled with so many enormous absurdities.

"Since intellectual pleasure should be made up of everything that is beautiful and harmonious, as seen or imagined, and anything that is ugly or disproportionate can't give us any delight, what beauty or proportion can be presented in a book where a sixteen-year-old youth stabs a giant as big as

---

* The Greek Milesian tales were pure fiction with no moral to extract.
† In contrast with the Milesian tales, the Phrygian apologues did have some moral teaching that could be derived.

a tower, and cuts him in two as if he were made of almond paste?* And when they go to describe a battle, after telling us that the enemy camp has a million combatants, and the hero of the story is fighting against them, yet as ridiculous as it seems, we're given to understand that the knight won the battle all alone just by the might of his arm.

"And what should we say about the queen or empress who so readily puts herself in the arms of an unknown knight-errant? What imagination—unless it's one that is barbarian and uncultured—can be entertained reading that a huge tower filled with knights sets sail as if it were a ship with a favorable wind† and stops tonight in Lombardy and at daybreak it's in the land of Prester John of the Indies or in some country not discovered by Ptolemy or seen by Marco Polo?‡ And if you tell me that those books were written as fiction so their authors don't have to pay strict attention to the fine points, or the way things really are, I'd respond that fiction is better the more it resembles the truth, and it's more delightful the more it has of what is truthful and possible. Fictional tales must suit the understanding of the reader and be written in such a way that impossible things seem possible, excesses are smoothed over, and the mind is kept in suspense, so that they astonish, stimulate, delight, and entertain us in such a way that admiration and pleasure go together; and the person who flees from credibility and imitation—which is what perfect writing consists of—cannot accomplish this.

"I haven't yet seen a book of chivalry where the plot agrees in all its parts, so the middle corresponds to the beginning, and the ending to the beginning and the middle.

---

* This alludes to Belianís de Grecia, who cut a giant in half at that same age (I,18).

† You can read two such episodes in *Lisuarte de Grecia*, chapters thirty-two and seventy-one, says Robinson Smith.

‡ The first edition says "discovered," as it is here. Some editors, realizing that the Egyptian geographer Ptolemy (A.D. 127–145) was not a navigator but rather a writer of treatises, change this to *described*. I prefer to leave the error with the canon (particularly since Lombardy has no ports to receive the "huge tower" just mentioned). Ptolemy knew the earth was round, and thought it was the center of the universe. Marco Polo was the Venetian merchant (1254–1324) who traveled to China, where he spent seventeen years.

Instead, they're written with so many unrelated parts they seem more like they were intended to represent a chimera* or a monster than to form a proportioned whole. Aside from this, they're wooden in their style, unbelievable in their deeds, lascivious in their loves, uncouth in their compliments, drawn out in their battles, foolish in their conversations, outlandish in their travels, and finally, devoid of any artistic excellence, and they should be exiled from a Christian state in the same way vagabonds are."

The priest was listening with rapt attention, and the canon seemed to him to be a man of fine intelligence, and that he was correct in everything he said. So he responded that he was of the same opinion, and that he so disliked romances of chivalry that he'd burned all of them that belonged to don Quixote, and there were many. And he told him about the inquisition he had made of them, and those that he'd condemned to the fire and those he'd spared, causing no little laughter on the canon's part. And the canon told him that, along with all the bad things he'd said about those books, he did find one good thing in them, which was the opportunity they gave an author with a lively intelligence to show off, because they offered a wide and spacious field through which he could let his pen run free, discovering† shipwrecks; storms; a brave captain with all the necessary qualities, showing him to be prudent, divining the cunning of his enemies; an eloquent speaker, persuading or restraining his troops; mature in his advice; ready in his resolve; and as valiant in standing by as in attacking. He can describe a tragic and lamentable episode, then a happy and unexpected one; over there a beautiful woman, chaste, discreet, and modest; over here a Christian knight, valiant and courageous; yonder a rude and reckless barbarian; here a courteous prince, brave and respected, representing goodness and loyalty in vassals, and the greatness and generosity of lords. He can show himself to be an excellent astrologer or cosmographer; a musician; intelligent in matters of state; and on occasion he can play the role of necromancer if he wants. He can show the craftiness of Ulysses,‡

---

* In Greek mythology, a *chimera* was a fire-breathing creature with the body of a lion, the head of a goat sprouting from its back, and a tail ending in a snake.
† Most editors and translators change this to "describing," as well.
‡ Ulysses is the hero of Homer's *Odyssey*. He is the master of cunning.

the piety of Æneas, the bravery of Achilles, the misfortunes of Hector, the treason of Sinon,* the friendship of Euryalus,† the generosity of Alexander, the courage of Cæsar, the clemency and truth of Trajan,‡ the fidelity of Zopirus,§ the wisdom of Cato, and finally, all the things that go into making an illustrious man, either attributing them all to a single character, or dividing the characteristics among several.

"And if this is done with gentleness of style and with ingenious imagination, and if the author aims at the truth wherever possible, he'll doubtless weave a cloth of various and beautiful threads, which, after it's finished, will show such perfection and beauty that it attains the goal that such writing aspires to, which is to teach and delight at the same time, as I've already said, because the freedom permitted by these books allows the author to be epic, lyrical, tragic, and comic, with all the qualities that are contained in the sweet and pleasant arts of poetry and oratory—for epic can be written in prose as well as in verse."

Chapter XLVIII. Where the canon pursues the subject of books of chivalry, with other items worthy of his insight.

"I CERTAINLY agree with your grace, *señor* canon," said the priest, "and for that reason those who have written such books up to now are even more deserving of censure, since they have written without considering good taste, and without respecting the rules of literary art on which they could have modeled their work and become as famous in prose as those two princes of Greek and Latin poetry¶ are in verse."

---

* Sinon was the Greek spy who persuaded the Trojans to accept the wooden horse.
† Euryalus was Æneas' companion. He and his close friend Nisus died together at the hands of the Rutuli.
‡ Trajan was the Roman emperor who was famous for clemency. He was born in Italica, near Seville, in A.D. 53, and lived until 117.
§ Zopirus was a Persian nobleman who helped Darius I (550–486 B.C.) become king of Persia in 522 B.C.
¶ These are Homer and Virgil.

"I must say," replied the canon, "that I've been tempted to write a book of chivalry myself, trying to use the characteristics that I've indicated; and to tell the truth, I've written more than a hundred sheets.* And to see if it met my expectations, I showed it to men who were fond of such reading, learnèd and intelligent; and I showed it to ignorant people, who only want to have the pleasure of listening to nonsense; and I received flattering approval from all sides. But even so, I didn't keep going, both because I was doing something that was quite far afield from my profession and because I knew that there are more fools than wise men— and even though it's better to be praised by the few wise men than to be jeered by the many fools, I don't want to subject myself to the idiotic judgment of the moronic public who, by and large, read those books.

"But what most prevented me from completing the book, from even *contemplating* finishing it, was an argument I had with myself taken from the plays that are staged nowadays, saying: 'These plays that one sees nowadays— the ones that are purely fictional, as well as those based on history—all, or most of them, are acknowledged to be pure garbage, without rhyme or reason, yet they're relished by the common folk, who think they're good when they're so far from being so; and the authors who write them and the actors who play in them say that they have to be that way because that's what the public wants. Meanwhile, plays that are carefully crafted and follow the plot as the rules demand please only the four discerning people capable of comprehending them. The rest of the people have no way of understanding their art, but authors and producers feel it's better to earn a living with the many than to be in the good graces of the few. This is what would happen with my book—after having put in so much effort to keep the precepts I mentioned, I'd be like 'the tailor on the corner.'†

"And although I've tried to persuade producers on occasion that they're making a mistake, and that they would attract more people and become more famous if they put

---

* A hundred sheets represents two hundred pages, since each sheet was written on both sides.

† Proverb: The tailor on the corner sewed for nothing and threw in the thread.

on plays that follow the rules, instead of these nonsensical ones, they're so attached to their opinion and so obstinate that there is no reasoning or proof that will convince them otherwise. I remember one day I said to one of these stubborn people: 'Tell me, don't you remember a few years ago the three tragedies, written by a famous poet of this kingdom,* that were so good that everybody who saw them was in awe, happy, and amazed—the simple as well as the wise, the common folk as well as the educated—and those three plays brought more money to the producers than thirty of the best that have been written since.' 'Your grace doubtless means,' said the producer I'm talking about, 'the *Isabella*, the *Phyllis*, and the *Alexandra*.'† 'Those are the ones,' I replied. 'Look at how they maintained the precepts of art,‡ and in keeping them did they suffer at all or were they prevented from pleasing everyone? So the fault doesn't lie with masses who seem to want foolish plays, but rather with those who can't produce anything else. *Ingratitude Avenged* wasn't trash, nor was *Numantia*, nor was any nonsense to be found in *The Merchant Lover*, and less in *The Kind Enemy*,§ nor in several others written by some learnèd poets to increase their fame and renown, and to the profit of those who produced them.' I said other things, too, and I think I left him a bit baffled, but neither satisfied nor convinced to save himself from the error he'd fallen into."

"You've touched upon a subject, *señor* canon," said the priest, "that has aroused in me an old dislike that I have for

---

* Lupercio Leonardo de Argensola (1559–1613). The three plays are mentioned below. He isn't so famous anymore.

† These plays so praised by the canon went a long time before they were published. The first and third came out in 1772 and the second had to wait until 1889—168 and 284 years, respectively, after *Don Quixote* was published.

‡ These *precepts of art* are the three classical unities of drama: action, time, and place. In Cervantes' own plays he didn't observe all three unities.

§ *Ingratitude Avenged* (1587) is by Lope de Vega (1562–1635); *Numantia* is Cervantes' tragedy about the Roman victory over the Numantians in what is now central Spain. *The Merchant Lover*, by Gaspar de Aguilar (1561–1623), respects the three unities. *The Kind Enemy* is by a canon named Francisco Agustín Tárrega (1554?–1602), which also observes the three unities. Students of Spanish literature generally have only heard of Lope de Vega and Cervantes.

the plays that are put on nowadays, so much so that it's almost as great as my opposition to books of chivalry, because a play, according to Tully,* should be a mirror of human life, a model of customs, and an image of the truth; but those that are put on nowadays are mirrors of nonsense, models of foolishness, and images of bawdiness. What greater nonsense can there be for a character to be in diapers in the first scene of act one, and in the second act come out as a bearded man? And what greater stupidity can there be than to represent a valiant old man, a cowardly youth, an eloquent lackey, a counselor-page, a handyman king, or a dishwashing princess?

"What can I say about how much attention they pay to the locales in which actions can or could happen? I've seen a play whose first act began in Europe, the second act in Asia, the third act ended in Africa, and if there had been four acts, the last doubtless would have been set in America, and all four corners of the earth would have been accounted for. And if the main thing in drama is that it's supposed to imitate real life, how is it possible for it to satisfy an average intellect, if when we have a play that is supposed to take place during the time of Pippin and Charlemagne, the main character is Heraclius, who is seen entering Jerusalem bearing the Cross and winning the Holy Sepulcher, as Godefroy de Bouillon did,† when there were infinite years between one event and the other? And what about those plays based on pure fiction that mix in historical facts, as well as things that happened in the lives of people at different times, and none of it believable, but rather filled with errors that are wholly inexcusable? And the worst thing is that there are ignorant people who claim that all this is perfect and that everything else is superfluous.

---

* Tully is Cicero. What the Roman orator really said, slightly different from what our priest attributed to him, is: "imitation of life, mirror of customs, and image of the truth."

† Pippin, that is Pépin III, the Short, lived between 714 and 768, and Charlemagne lived between 742 and 814. Heraclius (575–641) was an emperor of the Eastern Roman Empire. He claimed to have recovered the wood from Christ's cross. Godefroy de Bouillon (ca. 1060–1100) was a leader in the First Crusade. The Holy Sepulcher is a church erected in Jerusalem where it's traditionally thought Jesus was buried.

"Next, what if we talk about mystery plays? Look at the false miracles and other apocryphal and ill-understood things they relate, attributing the miracles of one saint to another! And even secular plays dare to show miracles with so little respect that they just think that such a miracle, or 'special effect,' as they call it, would go nicely there, so that the ignorant masses will be amazed and will go to see the play. All this is in prejudice to the truth and in detriment to real history, and even to the disrepute of Spanish genius, because foreign writers—who carefully maintain the laws of playwriting—consider us barbarous and ignorant, seeing the absurdities and nonsense in the plays we write.

"And it's not enough of an excuse to say that the main reason well-ordered republics allow plays to be presented in public is to entertain the community with harmless recreation, to take one's mind off the bad humors that idleness sometimes engenders, and if it can do this with any play— be it good or bad—there's no reason for new guidelines to force writers and producers to do what they should, since— as I've said—the same object is achieved with any kind of play. But I'd respond that this goal can be achieved much better—there's no comparison—with good plays rather than the other kind. Because after they see an artistic and well put-together play, the audience will be delighted with its jokes, instructed with its truths, thoughtful about its issues, sharpened by its turns of phrase, made more aware by its ironies, wiser through its examples, angered by vice, and appreciative of virtue—for all these things will be awakened in the souls of the listener, no matter how rustic and slow he might be. Of all impossibilities, the greatest is that the play that has all of these characteristics cannot fail to entertain, satisfy, and gratify, much more than the play that lacks them—which are most of the plays you see nowadays.

"The fault doesn't lie entirely with the poets who write them, since some of them know very well that they're erring, and know very well what they should do. But since plays have become a salable commodity, they say—and rightly—that the producers won't buy them if they're not of a certain type. So the poet tries to adapt himself to what the producer—who is going to pay him for his work—demands. And to show you that this is true, just look at the infinite number of plays that a very fortunate genius* of these realms has written, so festive, with so much wit, with such elegant verses, such well-chosen words, with serious maxims, and finally with such eloquence and lofty style, that he's known throughout the world. But because sometimes he adapts to the taste of the producers, not all of his plays have achieved, as some have, the level of perfection they require.

"Other playwrights write so carelessly that after the plays are put on, the actors have to flee for fear of being punished, as they have been many times, for having appeared in plays that are prejudicial to certain kings and dishonor certain families.

"All of these annoyances—and others I haven't mentioned—would cease if there were an intelligent and sensible person at court who would examine every play before it was put on—not only those to be put on in the capital, but every one that was to be put on in Spain—without whose approval, seal, and signature no magistrate would allow any play to be produced. And in this way the directors would take care to send plays to the capital, and they could produce them without worries. And those who write plays would use greater care in what they were doing, knowing that their work would have to pass a rigorous examination by a knowledgeable person, and in this way good plays would be written, and the goals of dramatic art would be achieved—namely, entertainment of the people, the good opinion of Spain's intelligentsia, income and security of the actors, and no more bother of punishing them.

"And if they gave a similar charge to another person—or maybe the same one—of examining newly written books of chivalry, some of them would turn out with the perfection your grace has mentioned, enriching our language with a precious new treasure of eloquence, and making the old books fade away in the light of the new ones that came out to offer harmless entertainment, not only for idle people, but also for the busiest—because 'it's not possible for the bow always to be taut' and the weak human condition can't be sustained without some kind of wholesome entertainment."

---

* Reference to Lope de Vega (1562–1635), the most prolific playwright. He wrote about two thousand plays, many of them great classics.

The canon and the priest arrived at this point of their conversation when the barber came over and said to the priest: "Here, *senor licenciado*, is the place I told you about, where we can have a nap and the oxen can graze on this fresh and abundant pasture."

"It seems like a good idea to me, too," responded the priest. And turning to the canon, he told him of their plan. The canon said he would stay as well, attracted by the captivating valley that lay before them. So, in order to enjoy both the view and the conversation with the priest, to whom he'd taken a liking, and to find out more about don Quixote, he had some of his servants go ahead to the inn, which wasn't far, and bring back something to eat for everyone, because he planned to have his siesta there that afternoon. One of the servants replied that the pack mule must already be at the inn, and it had enough provisions already so all they would need from the inn was barley for the animals.

"If that's the case," said the canon, "take all of the animals there, and bring back the mule with the food."

While this was going on, Sancho saw that he could speak with his master without continual interference from the priest and barber, whom he considered suspicious, and he went to the cage in which his master was traveling, and said: "*Señor*, to relieve my conscience, I want to tell you what's going on with your enchantment. Those men who have covered their faces are the priest and the barber of our village, and I think that they dreamed up this trick to haul you off in this way out of pure envy, seeing that your worship is surpassing them in famous deeds. Assuming this truth, it follows that you're not enchanted, but deceived and made a fool of. And to prove it, I want to ask you a question, and if the answer is as I think it will be, you'll be able to put your finger on this trick, and you'll see that you're not enchanted at all, but rather have had your wits turned inside out."

"Ask what you want, Sancho, my son," responded don Quixote, "and I'll satisfy you and answer to your heart's content. Regarding those accompanying us being the priest and the barber, our fellow townsmen and friends, it may seem that they appear to be, but don't believe that they really are for a moment. What you have to believe and understand is that if they seem to be, as you say, it must be that those who enchanted me have taken on their appearance, because it's easy for enchanters to take on any form they choose, and they would have taken on the shape of our friends to make you think what you're thinking, and put you into a labyrinth of confusion from which you won't be able to find your way out, even though you had Theseus' rope.* Not to mention that they wanted to confuse me as well, so I can't figure out where this harm is coming from; because on the one hand you tell me that the barber and priest of our town are with us, and on the other, here I am in a cage, when I know that no human power, unless it were supernatural, is sufficient to keep me in a cage; so what should I say or think, except that this enchantment is more powerful than any I've read about in the histories that deal with knights-errant who have been enchanted? So, you can calm yourself in the knowledge that they're not who you say they are, because they're about as close to being what you say as I am to being a Turk. And as for asking me something, go ahead, and I'll answer you even though you ask questions from now until tomorrow morning."

"Holy Mary Mother of God!" responded Sancho in a loud voice. "Is it possible that your grace is such a numbskull and lacking in brains that you don't realize I've told you the pure truth, and that your being in a cage and your misfortune are more due to malice than enchantment? But since you don't believe me, I'll prove to you you're not enchanted. Tell me this, and may God pull you out of this ordeal and may you soon see yourself in the arms of my lady Dulcinea when least you think—"

"Stop this nonsense," said don Quixote, "and ask whatever you want. I've already told you I'd answer completely and immediately."

"What I ask," replied Sancho, "and what I want to know is that you should tell me without adding or taking away anything, but rather with the complete truth, as is to be expected from those who profess arms, as your grace does, under the title of knight-errant—"

"I've said I'll not lie about anything," responded don Quixote. "Just ask me, because in truth I'm getting tired of all your oaths, supplications, and precautions, Sancho."

---

* As the story goes, Ariadne gave Theseus a thread, not a rope, so he could find his way out of the labyrinth of Crete.

"Then I say that I'm sure about the goodness and truth of my master, and so, since it has to do with our subject at hand, I ask, speaking with respect, if perhaps after you've been put in the cage, and in your opinion enchanted, if you've felt like doing number one or number two, as they say."

"I don't understand this business of numbers, Sancho. Clarify a bit if you want me to answer properly."

"Can it be that your grace doesn't understand what 'number one' and 'number two' are? Schoolboys are weaned on that expression. Well, what I mean is have you felt like doing what no one else can do for you?"

"Now, now I understand, Sancho. Yes, frequently, and even now I feel the urge. Get me out of this plight, or we'll be in a real mess."

Chapter XLIX. Which deals with the shrewd conversation that Sancho Panza had with his master don Quixote.

"Ha!" said Sancho. "I've got you there! That's what I wanted to find out with all my heart and soul. Come, then, *señor*, can you deny what they commonly say when a person is indisposed: 'I don't know what's the matter with So-and-So, who doesn't eat or drink anything, or answer anything put to him properly—why, it seems like he's enchanted,' from which one can gather that those who don't eat or drink, or sleep, or perform those bodily functions I mentioned earlier, are enchanted, but not those who feel like doing what you do, and who drink when they're given something to drink, and eat when they can, and answer anything they're asked."

"You speak the truth, Sancho," responded don Quixote, "but I've already told you that there are many kinds of enchantments, and it may be that in time some have changed into others, and nowadays enchanted people do what I do, even though they didn't used to. So, there's no way of arguing against customs, since they change through time, or of drawing inferences either, based on the way things used to be. I know and hold to be true that I'm enchanted, and it would weigh heavily on my conscience if I weren't so, since I'd be lying in this cage out of sloth and cowardice, cheating many needy people out of the help I could be giving them, and who may be, this very minute, in need of that help."

"For all that," replied Sancho, "I say that it would be good if your grace tried to get out of this jail, and I promise to do everything I can to help, and even to get you out and see if I can put you on Rocinante once again. It seems that he's enchanted, too, since he's so sullen and sad. Once this is done, we can try our luck at more adventures, and if things don't work out right, there'll be plenty of time to return to the cage, and I promise as a good and faithful squire to lock myself up with your grace if you are so unfortunate, or I so dumb, to fail in what I've proposed."

"I'm happy to do what you say, brother Sancho," replied don Quixote, "and when you see the chance to free me, I'll obey you in every way. But you'll see, Sancho, how mistaken you are in your notion of my undoing."

The knight-errant and ill-errant squire were talking this way when they arrived where the priest, canon, and barber—who were already dismounted—were waiting. The carter had unyoked the oxen and let them graze freely in that green and peaceful place, whose coolness invited not only persons as enchanted as don Quixote, but also as rational and sensible a fellow as Sancho to enjoy it. Sancho begged the priest to allow his master to leave the cage for a while, because if they didn't, the prison wouldn't be as clean as the decency of such a knight as his master required.

The priest understood, and said that he would be pleased to grant the favor, but he feared that when his master found himself free, he might try to do what he wanted, and go off where no one would ever see him again.

"I'll guarantee that he won't flee," responded Sancho.

"Me, too," said the canon, "especially if he gives me his word as a knight not to go away until it's our pleasure."

"I so give," responded don Quixote, who was listening to everything, "and more so because a person who is enchanted—as I am—hasn't the freedom to do what he pleases, because the one who has enchanted him may make him not be able to budge for three centuries; and if he did flee, the enchanter would bring him back through the air."

This being so, they could safely set him free, since it was to everyone's advantage to do so. And if they didn't let him out, he assured them, it would offend their sense of smell unless they kept their distance. The canon shook his hand, although they were tied together, and on his good faith and promise, they took him out of the cage, which made him very happy. The first thing he did was to stretch his whole body, and then went over to Rocinante and gave him two slaps on his haunches, and said: "I still trust in God and His Blessed Mother, flower and mirror of horses, that soon we'll be back doing what we want to—you with your master on your back and I mounted on my steed—following the calling for which God placed me on the earth."

And saying this, don Quixote went off in Sancho's company to a remote area, from where he came back much relieved, and very willing to do what his squire might command. The canon looked at him and was amazed at the curious nature of his great madness, and how when he spoke and answered questions, he showed that he had a fine intellect. It was only when he dealt with chivalry that he "lost his stirrups," as has been said on occasion. So, moved by compassion, after everyone was seated on the green grass to wait for the provisions to arrive, he said: "Is it possible, *señor hidalgo*, that the bitter and idle reading of books of chivalry has been so powerful and impaired your sanity to such a degree that you believe you're enchanted and those other things, all of which are so far from the truth as are lies? And how is it possible that anyone can really believe that there existed in the world that multitude of Amadises and that horde of famous knights, emperors of Trebizond, Felixmartes de Hyrcania, palfreys, maidens-errant, serpents and dragons, giants, incredible adventures, all kinds of enchantments, battles, outrageous encounters, bizarre garb, princesses in love, squire-counts, amusing dwarves, love letters, flirting, valiant women, and finally, all the foolish things that books of chivalry contain? I'll tell you that when I read them, as long as I don't get to thinking that they're all lies and frivolity, I think they're all right. But when I realize what they are, I fling the best of them against the wall, and I'd toss them into a fire if one were nearby. They deserve such a punishment, since they're false and impostors and outside of the bounds of human nature, and as inventors of new sects and a new way of life,* and causing the ignorant masses to believe and hold as true all the foolishness that they contain.

"And they're so insolent that they dare to confuse the wits of intelligent and wellborn *hidalgos*, as can be seen by what happened to your grace, since they brought you to the point where you had to be shut up in a cage and transported on an oxcart, just like they'd haul a lion or a tiger from place to place, to earn money by letting people see them. Come on, *señor* don Quixote, take pity on yourself and return to the bosom of wisdom, and make use of what heaven gave you, using your keen intelligence for other kinds of reading that will redound to the benefit of your mind and will increase your honor. And if you still want, guided by your nature, to read books of great feats and true chivalry, read the Holy Scripture in the Book of Judges, where you'll find grandiose truths and deeds as true as they are valiant. Lusitania had a Viriathus, Rome a Cæsar, Carthage a Hannibal, Greece an Alexander, Castile a Count Fernán González, Valencia a Cid, Andalusia a Gonzalo Fernández, Extremadura a Diego Pérez de Paredes, Jérez a Garci Pérez, Toledo a Garcilaso, Seville a don Manuel de León,† whose valiant deeds can entertain, instruct, delight, and amaze even the finest

---

* Whereas to us something new tends to be attractive, in the Spain of Cervantes, something new was defined as "usually dangerous since it brings with it a change from old customs" (Covarrubias' dictionary, 1611—article: "*Novedad*"). This was pointed out by Joseph Silverman.
† Viriathus was a Celtic leader in Lusitania (modern Portugal) who fought to prevent the Romans from entering his country (he was assassinated in 140 B.C.). Hannibal (247–ca. 181 B.C.) was a great Carthaginian general who led his forces against Rome in the Second Punic War (218–201 B.C.). Fernán González (died 970) united various counties to form a unified Castile. Spain's national hero, the Cid, is here credited to Valencia (which he conquered) rather than Burgos (where he was born). Andalusia's Gonzalo Fernández was already mentioned as the Gran Capitán, Gonzalo Hernández de Córdoba. The Garcilaso de le Vega mentioned here is not the Spanish poet, but rather the soldier of the same name who participated in the conquest of Granada with Ferdinand and Isabella. Manuel Ponce de León ("lion") was a contemporary of Garcilaso—after he went into an arena with lions to retrieve his lady's glove, she slapped him with it.

of intellects who would read them. This would certainly be reading worthy of your keen understanding, my dear *señor* don Quixote, from which you'll become apprised of history, enamored of virtue, instructed in goodness, bettered in manners, brave without being rash, daring without cowardice, and all this to honor God, to your own benefit and glory of La Mancha, where—I've learned—your grace was born and has his origin."

Don Quixote was very attentive listening to the words of the canon, and when he saw that he'd finished, and after looking at him for some time, he said: "It seems to me, *señor hidalgo*, that the reason for your grace's speech was to lead me to understand that there were never any knights-errant in the world, and that all of the books of chivalry are false, full of lies, damaging, and useless in our republic; and that I've done ill in reading them, worse in believing them, and worst of all in imitating them, by taking on the difficult profession of knight-errantry that they teach; and you deny that there were ever any Amadises—either from Gaula or from Greece—or any of the other knights that those writings are filled with."

"That's exactly what I said and meant," said the canon.

And don Quixote responded: "You grace also added that these books had done me a lot of damage, since they had made me crazy and placed me in a cage, and that it would be better for me to change my reading habits by studying other, truer books that would better entertain and instruct."

"That's also right," said the canon.

"In that case," said don Quixote, "I find that *your grace* is the crazy and enchanted one, since you've blasphemed a thing so universally accepted and held as true that anyone who denies it—as your grace has—deserves the same sentence that you say the books of chivalry deserve when you read them and they annoy you. Because to argue that Amadís didn't exist in the world, nor any of the other knight adventurers of which the histories are filled, is like saying that the sun doesn't shine, or ice isn't cold, or the earth gives no nourishment. Is there an intelligent person who can convince another that the history of the princess Floripes and Guy of Burgundy wasn't true? And what happened to

Fierabrás on the Bridge of Mantible* during the time of Charlemagne, which I swear is as true as it's day right now?

"And if that's not true, it must be that there was no Hector, nor Achilles, nor a Trojan War, nor the Twelve Peers of France, nor a King Arthur of England—who still lives, changed into a raven, until the day he returns to rule. And also they will dare to say that the story of Guarino Mezquino† and the one about the quest for the Holy Grail,‡ and the love between Tristan and Iseult§ are also apocryphal, as is the love between Lancelot and Queen Guinevere, when there are people today who can almost swear they have seen duenna Quintañona, who was the best wine pourer in Great Britain.¶ I remember my grandmother on my father's side used to tell me when she saw an old nursemaid in traditional headdress: 'That woman, grandson, looks like Quintañona.' On the basis of that I argue that she must have known her, or at least she must have managed to see a portrait of her. And who can deny that the story of Pierres and the beautiful Magalona** is true? Even today one can see in the Royal Armory the peg that the valiant Pierres used to guide his wooden horse through the air—it's a bit larger than a cart pole—and next to

---

* Don Quixote is recalling two sections from the same popular book of fiction, *History of the Emperor Charlemagne and the Twelve Peers of France* (Seville, 1525), printed ten times before 1605. Floripes (the sister of the giant Saracen Fierabrás) married Gui of Burgundy. Those who wanted to pass over the marble bridge of Mantible had to pay an enormous tribute: a hundred each of maidens, horses, falcons, and dogs.

† *Chronicle of the Very Noble Knight Guarino Mezquino* (Seville, 1512, with two more editions), translated from the Italian (Padua, 1473). Juan de Valdés in his *Dialogue of the Language* says it's an exceptionally untruthful book and is poorly written to boot.

‡ The Holy Grail is the cup Christ used at the Last Supper. *The Quest for the Holy Grail* (Toledo, 1515), in which King Arthur and Lancelot go looking for it, is pure fiction.

§ The story of Tristan and Iseult came from a Celtic legend and became a well-known Old French poem. It first appeared in Spain in 1501.

¶ *Dueña* Quintañona—as explained in the first note to chapter thirteen above—is pure fiction, doubly so since she doesn't appear in the British legend—only the Spanish.

** *History of the Beautiful Magalona, Daughter of the King of Naples, and of Pierres, Son of the Count of Provence* (Seville, 1519, and five more editions before 1605), a very popular work of fiction of Provençal origin (twelfth century).

it is Babieca's saddle.* And at Roncesvalles is Roland's horn, which is as large as a beam,† from which it can be inferred that there were the Twelve Peers, that there was a Pierres, that there were Cids, and other such knights

> of those that people say
> go off to their adventures.‡

"And I suppose you'll tell me that there was no such knight-errant as the brave Portuguese Juan de Merlo,§ who went to Burgundy and fought in the city of Arras with the famous Lord of Charny called Sir Pierres, and afterward in the city of Basel, with Sir Henri de Remestan, emerging from both battles victorious and crowned with honor and fame. And do they doubt the adventures and challenges of the brave Spaniards Pedro Barba and Gutierre Quijada¶—from whose lineage I'm descended in the direct male line—vanquishing the sons of the Count St. Pol? Will they deny that don Fernando de Guevara** went off looking for adventures in Germany, where he fought with Monsieur Giorgio, a knight in the house of the Duke of Austria? Let them say that the jousts of Suero de Quiñones, the one of the 'Paso,'†† were just a joke. Will they say

---

* Pierres rode no flying wooden horse in the book about Magalona. That episode derives from *The History of the Very Valiant and Strong Clamades* . . . (Burgos, 1521). In the Royal Armory you won't see the peg next to Babieca's saddle. You won't see Babieca's saddle there either, anymore. (Babieca was the Cid's horse.)

† Roland's horn, the *oliphant*, was made from an elephant's tusk. Visitors who go to Roncesvalles in Spain, near the French border, will not see Roland's horn there.

‡ A variant of these verses is found at the beginning of chapter nine.

§ All of the people mentioned here are historic. Juan de Merlo fought with Juan II of Castile (1406–1454). Arras is the capital of the French department of Pas-de-Calais. Clemencín has astonishing notes about these people starting on p. 1474 of the Castilla edition.

¶ Both of these are mentioned in the *Crónica de Juan II*.

** Also mentioned in the chronicle just cited.

†† This *Paso* is the *paso honroso*. In 1434 Suero de Quiñones defended a bridge on the river Órbigo near León (this was his *paso honroso*). He fought and defeated sixty-eight knights there from Spain, Portugal, Britain, Italy, and France.

the same about the accomplishments of Sir Luis de Falces against don Gonzalo de Guzmán,* a Christian knight, with many other deeds done by Christian knights, of this and foreign realms; which are so authentic and true, I say once again, that anyone who would deny them lacks reason and common sense?"

The canon was amazed at the mixture of truths and fiction don Quixote concocted, as well as to see how much he really knew about all those things concerning the facts of his knight-errantry, and so he answered: "I can't deny, *señor* don Quixote, that something of what you said is true, especially in the matter dealing with Spanish knights-errant, and I also grant that there were the Twelve Peers of France, but I can't believe that they did all of those things that Archbishop Turpin writes about them, because the truth of the matter is that they were knights selected by the kings of France, and they were called PEERS because they were all equal in courage, rank, and prowess, and if they weren't, they should have been. It was like a religious order such as those of Santiago or Calatrava,† where it's assumed that those who are in those orders are, or should be, brave and valiant knights, and wellborn. And as we speak of a KNIGHT OF SAN JUAN or OF ALCÁNTARA, they spoke, in those times, of Knights of the Twelve Peers, because they were twelve of equal skill chosen for that military-religious order. As for the Cid, there is no doubt, nor is there for Bernardo del Carpio, but about the deeds attributed to them there is serious doubt. And as far as the peg that your grace says belonged to Count Pierres, and which is next to Babieca's saddle in the Royal Armory, I confess my sin, that I'm so ignorant or shortsighted that— although I've seen the saddle—I didn't notice the peg, even though it's as big as your grace says it is."

"Well, it's there, with no doubt," replied don Quixote, "and what's more, they say it's in a leather sheath so it won't rust."

"Anything is possible," said the canon, "but, by my holy orders, I don't remember having seen it. Even if I concede

---

* Two more knights from the same chronicle.
† These are Spanish religious-military orders of knights dating from the late twelfth century.

that it's there, I'm not obliged to believe the stories of so many Amadises nor of that multitude of knights they tell us about, nor should a man such as yourself, so honored and with such good qualities, and endowed with such fine intelligence, think that the extravagant nonsense in those foolish books is true."

Chapter L. About the adroit debate that don Quixote and the canon had, together with other events.

"THAT'S A good one," responded don Quixote. "Books that are printed with the license of kings, and approved by those to whom they're submitted, and are read with general pleasure, and praised by adults and young people alike, by poor and rich, by the learnèd and the ignorant, by plebeians and knights, and finally, by all kinds of people of any rank or condition—these are supposed to be lies even though they appear so much to be the truth? They say who the knight's father and mother were, and who all his relatives were, his age, where he's from, and the deeds he did, point by point, and day by day. Hush, your worship. Don't say any more blasphemies, and believe me—and I give you this advice about what you should do, since you're a man of sense—read them, and you'll see what pleasure you get.

"Tell me, can there be a greater pleasure than to see, as it were, right now in front of us a giant lake of pitch, boiling furiously, with a host of serpents, snakes, and lizards swimming here and there, as well as many other kinds of ferocious creatures? And from the middle of the lake a plaintive voice issues forth, saying: 'You, knight, whoever you are, looking at this fear-inspiring lake—if you want to find the treasure that lies hidden beneath these black waters—show the bravery in your heart by throwing yourself into the middle of its black fiery liquid, because if you don't, you won't be worthy of seeing the noble wonders that are in the seven castles of the seven fairies that lie beneath this blackness.' And as soon as the knight has heard this mournful voice, without further thought, and without considering the danger into which he's placed himself, and even without removing the weight of his heavy armor, commending himself to God and to his lady, he plunges into the middle of the boiling lake.

"And when he least expects it, and when he doesn't know where he'll wind up, he finds himself in the middle of flowering fields, with which the Elysian ones cannot be compared. There, the sky is more transparent, and the sun shines with new brilliance. In front of him he sees a quiet forest, with such green trees that provide enormous shade, and whose lushness delights his eyes, and the sweet natural singing of an infinite number of little painted birds flitting about their branches entertains his ears. Here he discovers a little brook whose fresh waters like liquid crystal run over fine sand and little white stones, which look like sifted gold and fine pearls. Over there he sees a fountain made of variegated jasper and smooth marble. Here he sees another one, decorated with small clamshells and swirling white and yellow snail shells, arranged in disordered order, with pieces of shining crystal and false emeralds, making a varied work of art that imitates nature yet seems to surpass it.

"Over yonder, suddenly, there rises before him an impregnable castle or beautiful palace, whose walls are of solid gold, battlements made of diamonds, gates of jacinth. Even though it's built of diamonds, rubies, pearls, gold, and emeralds, its workmanship is even more exquisite. And, after having seen all this, what more could you want to see? Well, here come a large number of maidens from the gate of the castle, whose elegant and beautiful dresses— if I started to describe them as the histories do, I'd never finish. The principal maiden takes the hand of the daring knight who had plunged into the lake, and leads him, without saying a word, inside that rich palace or castle, and has him strip as naked as when his mother bore him, and bathes him with warm water, then anoints him all over with sweet-smelling ointments, and dresses him in a shirt of fine silk, fragrant and perfumed; then another maiden comes and puts a cloak on his shoulders worth at least a city, and maybe more.

"Then, how wonderful is it when they tell us that after this, they lead him to another room, where he finds a table set so extravagantly that he's amazed? Look how they wash his hands with perfumed water distilled from sweet-smelling flowers! See how they have him sit in a chair made of ivory! Look how maidens, keeping absolutely silent, serve him! Watch how they take him all kinds of different foods, so deliciously prepared his appetite doesn't know which one to reach for first? And now comes some music while he eats, and he doesn't know who is singing or where it's coming from. And after dinner is over and the tables cleared, here is our knight, relaxing on his chair, perhaps picking his teeth—as is the custom—and suddenly a maiden more beautiful than the others comes in and sits next to the knight to tell him what castle he's in and how she's enchanted in it, with other details that amaze the knight and keep the readers of the history turning the pages.

"I don't want to make it too long, but you can gather that any part of any history of a knight-errant will please and cause astonishment to anyone who reads it. And believe me, your grace, as I said earlier, if you read these books you'll see that they banish any melancholy you might have, and they'll cheer you up if you're depressed. About myself, I can tell you that since I've become a knight-errant, I'm brave, polite, liberal, gracious, generous, courteous, daring, gentle, patient, and able to endure travails, imprisonment, and enchantments. Although it has been only a short time since I've been locked in a cage like a crazy man, in a few days, I plan—through the strength of my arm, and if heaven favors me and Fortune isn't contrary to me—to see myself king of some realm, where I can show the gratitude and generosity of my heart. Upon my faith, a poor man can't show himself generous to anyone, even though he may be a very generous person. And gratefulness, through desire alone, is a dead thing, as faith is dead without works. Because of this, I'd like for Fortune to give me the opportunity to be an emperor, to show the goodness of my heart by doing nice things for my friends, particularly this poor Sancho Panza, my squire, who is the best man in the world. I'd like to bestow a county on him that I promised him many days ago, but I fear he won't be able to govern his estate."

Sancho heard these words his master said, and said back to him: "Your grace, try to give me that county—which is as promised by you as it's expected by me—and I swear to you that I won't lack the ability to govern; and if I can't,

I've heard that there are men in the world who lease estates from their masters and pay them something every year, and take charge of the government while his master leans back and puts his feet up and enjoys the income that they give him, without worrying about anything. That's what I'll do, and I won't worry about the details, and will hand over the government and enjoy the income like a duke, and who cares about the rest?"

"That, brother Sancho," said the canon, "applies to enjoying the income; but the administration of justice has to be done by the master of the estate, and here is where ability and good judgment come in, and above all, an honest intention to do what is right; and if this is lacking in the beginning, the middle and the end will go astray. And God usually helps the good intentions of plain people, as He foils the bad intentions of conniving persons."

"I know nothing about those philosophies," responded Sancho Panza, "but I only know that as soon as I have a county, I'll know how to govern it, because I have as much heart as the next person, and as much body as the best of them. I'll be such a king on my estate as anyone else is on his, and being that, I'd do what I wanted, and doing what I wanted would please me, and doing what pleased me, I'd be happy, and when someone is happy, he's satisfied, and being satisfied, that's all there is to it. Let the earldom come, and 'fare thee well,' and '"Let's see," as one blind man said to the other.'"

"Those are not bad philosophies, as you say, Sancho, but even so there's a lot to be said about the business of counties."

To which don Quixote replied: "I don't know if there's more to say. I'm guided only by the example that the great Amadís de Gaula has given me, in that he made his squire the count of *Ínsula Firme*. So I can make a count out of Sancho Panza—one of the best squires that a knight-errant ever had—with a clear conscience."

The canon was astonished at the well-conceived nonsense that don Quixote said—the way he described the adventure of the Knight of the Lake, the impression made on him by the unconscionable lies of the books he'd read, and finally, he was amazed by the simplicity of Sancho, who so wanted the county his master had promised him.

The canon's servants had now come back with the provision-laden mule, and making a table of a carpet and the green grass of the meadow, in the shade of some trees, they sat down and ate right there, so that the carter could take advantage of that place, as has been said. And while they were eating, suddenly they heard a loud noise and the ringing of a cowbell that came from some nearby brambles and thick bushes, and at that same instant they saw a beautiful she-goat emerging from them, her fur speckled with black, white, and brown. Behind her came a goatherd shouting, using words they typically use to make their goats stop, or go back to the flock. The fugitive goat, fearful and terrified, ran to the people, as if for their protection, and stopped there. The goatherd arrived and, taking her by the horns, as if she could speak and understand, said: "Ah, you vagabond—Spotty, Spotty! Look how you've been limping! What wolves have frightened you, daughter? Can't you tell me what's the matter, my pretty one? But what can it be except you're a female and you can't stay still? A curse on your temperament and on all those you imitate! Come back, come back, my little friend. And if you aren't happy, at least you'll be safer in your fold, or with your companions, because if you—who should watch over and lead them— wander about like this, what'll become of them?"

The words of the goatherd entertained those who were listening to him, and especially the canon, who said: "On your life, brother, rest a bit here if you're not in such a great hurry to return this goat to its flock, because, being a female as you say, she'll follow her natural instinct no matter what you do to prevent it. Take this morsel, and drink something—you can have a bit to eat while the goat rests."

And as he said this, he gave him the loins of a cold rabbit on the point of a knife. The goatherd took it and thanked him; he drank a bit, then relaxed and said: "I don't want your graces to take me for a simpleton because I've been talking in such a serious way to this creature; but in truth the words I said to her are far from puzzling. I'm a rustic, but not so much of one that I don't know how to deal with men as well as beasts."

"I can well believe that," said the priest, "because I know from experience that the forests breed men of letters, and the huts of shepherds nurture philosophers."

"At least, *señor*," replied the goatherd, "they shelter men who have learned from experience, and so that you'll believe this truth and touch it with your hands, though it may seem that without being asked I'm inviting myself, if it wouldn't annoy you too much, and if you want, *señores*, to lend me your ears for a short time, I'll tell you a truth that will confirm what this man—" pointing to the priest—"as well as what I have said."

To which don Quixote responded: "Seeing that this carries the whiff of a knightly adventure, as far as I'm concerned, I'll hear you out very gladly, and these other men will do the same because they're intelligent and are eager to hear stories that surprise, charm, and entertain the senses, as I think your story certainly will. Begin, then, friend, because we're all listening."

"Deal me out," said Sancho. "I'm going over to that brook with this meat pie, where I plan to stuff myself for three days. I've heard my master don Quixote say that the squire of a knight-errant has to eat whenever food is offered until he can't eat any more, because it often happens that they're drawn to enter a forest so dense that they can't find their way out for six days, and if a man doesn't go in well filled or his saddlebags well stocked, he can turn into a mummy, which frequently happens."

"You're right about that, Sancho," said don Quixote. "Go wherever you want and eat all you can, for I've had enough, and now only my soul needs some nourishment, which I'll get by listening to the story of this good fellow."

"We'll all do that," said the canon, and he begged the goatherd to begin his story as he'd promised. The goatherd, who was holding the goat by its horns, slapped her on the back twice, and said: "Lie down here, next to me, Spotty. We have plenty of time to return to the flock."

It seemed like the goat understood, because when her master sat down, she nestled herself quietly beside him, and looked up at his face to show him that she was ready to hear what he would say; and the goatherd began his story in this way:

Chapter LI. Which deals with what the goatherd told all those who were taking don Quixote home.

THREE LEAGUES from this valley there's a small village that is among the wealthiest in this whole region. In it there lived a very rich farmer, and although being honored goes along with being rich, he was held in greater esteem for his virtue than for the riches he'd acquired. But what made him most fortunate, according to what he said, was that he had a daughter who was so beautiful, with such rare intelligence, charm, and virtue, that anyone who knew her and looked at her marveled at the remarkable gifts that heaven and nature had bestowed upon her. As a child, she was pretty, and kept growing in her beauty. At age sixteen she was very beautiful. The fame of her beauty began to spread throughout the nearby villages. Why do I say just the nearby villages? It spread to distant cities, and even extended into the palace of the king and queen, and went into the ears of people of all walks of life who came from all over to see her, as if she were a rare thing or a miracle-working image.

Her father watched over her, and she watched over herself —for there are no padlocks, bolts, or locks that protect a maiden better than her own chastity. The wealth of her father and the beauty of the daughter moved many men from our village, as well as outsiders, to ask for her hand in marriage. But he—just like a person whose responsibility it was to place a fine jewel with the best person—was very perplexed, not knowing how to determine to whom he should award her from among the infinite number of suitors she had. I was one among those who had this worthy desire, and because her father knew who I was, born in the same village, clean in blood,* in the flower of youth, with a large income, and no less endowed in intelligence, I had great hopes of success.

Another fellow from the same village, with similar qualities, also asked to marry her, and this was enough to cause

---

* "Clean in blood," you'll recall, meant that you had no Jewish blood in your ancestry.

her father to postpone his decision and let it hang in the balance, because it seemed to him that with either one of us his daughter would have a good marriage. To escape from this perplexing state, he resolved to tell Leandra—that's the name of that rich girl who has left me in such poverty—that since we were equal, it was better to let his beloved daughter make the choice, which is what all fathers who want to marry off their children should do. I'm not saying that they should allow them to choose bad things, but rather should propose only good things, and have them choose what they want from among them. I don't know what her choice was—I only know that her father put both of us off, saying she was too young and other things like that, which didn't obligate him, and didn't free us either. My rival is named Anselmo, and I'm Eugenio, so that you'll know the names of the actors who have a role in this tragedy, whose ending is still up in the air, though it's clear it's destined to be disastrous.

At about that time, a certain Vicente de la Rosa came to our town, the son of a poor peasant of the same village. Now, this Vicente was coming back from Italy and other places, where he was a soldier. When he was a child, maybe twelve years old, a captain—who happened to come through with his company of soldiers—took him off, and the young man came back twelve years later in a soldier's uniform, arrayed in a thousand colors and with a thousand trinkets of glass and fine steel chains. Today he'd be in one dress uniform and tomorrow in another, but all of them flimsy, showy, with little substance and less worth. Peasants—who are mischievous by nature, and when they have nothing to do can be rascality itself—noticed everything and counted all his finery and trinkets, piece by piece, and found that he had just three different outfits of different colors, with their garters and stockings, but he made so many different arrangements and combinations that if you didn't count you'd swear that he had more than ten outfits and twenty feathered hats. And don't think this business of his dress is beside the point or inconsequential, because it plays an important part in this story.

He would sit on a bench under a large poplar tree in our plaza, and there he'd keep us all agape, telling of his exploits—there was no country in the world he hadn't seen, nor any battle he hadn't engaged in. He'd killed more Moors than there are in Morocco and Tunisia combined, and had participated in more singular combats, according to him, than Gante y Luna, Diego García de Paredes,* and a thousand others that he named, and he was victorious in all of them, without shedding a single drop of blood; but on the other hand, he showed us scars, which—although we couldn't make them out—he made us think were musket wounds received in different battles and actions. Finally, with incredible arrogance, he would address his equals, and anyone who knew him, as vos,† and he said that his only father was his right arm, his lineage was his deeds, and that as a soldier he owed nothing, even to the king himself. To these pretensions it should be added that he was something of a musician, and played the guitar with *rasgueados*‡ in such a way that some said he made it speak. But his talents didn't end there, because he also fancied himself a poet and wrote a *romance*§ a league and a half long about every bit of nonsense that happened in the village.

This soldier that I've described, this Vicente de la Rosa, this brave, handsome man, this musician, this poet, was frequently seen and watched by Leandra from a window in her house that overlooked the plaza. She was enamored of the tinsel on his colorful outfits; his *romances* enchanted her (and he handed out twenty copies of every one he wrote); the deeds that he related wafted up to her ears; and, in short—and the devil must have ordained it so—she fell in love with him before he'd conceived the presumption of wooing her, and since in cases of love there is none more easily concluded than the ones in which the woman has the desire, Leandra and Vicente came to an

---

* Since Garcilaso and Diego García de Paredes are mentioned in the same sentence in chapter forty-nine above, some editors and translators have assumed that Gante y Luna is a compositor's misreading for Garcilaso and have changed the name to Garcilaso.

† This singular *vos*, meaning *you*, was generally reserved for inferiors.

‡ *Rasgueado* is a Spanish strumming technique involving from one finger to all five, typical of flamenco playing.

§ *Romance* is the typical Spanish narrative poetic form, verse lines eight syllables long, and every other line rhymes with vowels only.

understanding easily, and before any of her many suitors realized what her desire was, she'd already carried it out, having left the house of her beloved father (since she had no mother), and leaving the town with this soldier, he fared better in this enterprise than any of the others he boasted of.

The whole town was amazed, as was everyone else who heard of the matter. I was aghast, Anselmo was astonished, her father sad, her relatives offended, the forces of justice were ready, the officers prepared. They took to the roads, they scoured the forests and everywhere else, and at the end of three days, they found the wayward Leandra in a mountain cave, wearing only a slip, and stripped of the money and precious jewels she'd taken from her house. They took her back to the presence of her despondent father and questioned her about her misfortune. She confessed without hesitation that Vicente de la Roca* had deceived her, and on his word that he would become her husband, persuaded her to leave her father's house, and he would take her to the richest and most luxurious city in the whole world, which was Naples, and she—ill-advised and worse deceived—had believed him. She stole from her father, and gave him everything the night she disappeared, and he took her to a desolate mountain and shut her up in that cave where they had found her. She also related how the soldier, without robbing her of her honor, took everything else and then left her in that cave and went away— something that further astonished everyone.

It was hard for us to believe the restraint of the young man, but she confirmed it with such great sincerity that it helped to console her grief-stricken father, not caring about the valuables that had been taken, since his daughter still had that jewel that, once lost, has no hope of being recovered.

The same day Leandra came back, her father made her disappear from our eyes, and he had her placed in a convent in a town near here, hoping that time would wear

---

* The first two mentions of his name were "Rosa." The first edition has "Roca" here (folio 306v), which was a typical effort by Cervantes to confuse names *on purpose*. Most editions and translations change this instance to "Rosa"; those that don't homogenize them all to "Roca."

away part of the disgrace that she'd brought upon herself. Leandra's tender age served as an excuse for her failing, at least to those who didn't care if she was good or bad. But those of us who knew of her shrewdness and great intelligence didn't attribute her sin to ignorance, but rather to her frivolity and the natural inclination of women, who tend to be reckless and unbalanced.

With Leandra locked away, Anselmo's eyes were blinded, or anyway he had nothing to look at that made him happy. My eyes were in darkness, without the light to lead them toward anything that gives pleasure. With Leandra's absence, our sadness increased, our patience diminished, we cursed the soldier's outfits, and condemned her father's carelessness. Finally, Anselmo and I agreed to leave the village and come to this valley, where he, letting a large number of his own sheep graze, and I a large flock of goats, also mine, spend our lives among the trees, giving vent to our passions, or singing together the praises or curses of the beautiful Leandra, or sighing alone, communicating our complaints to heaven.

Many others of Leandra's suitors have imitated us and have come to this harsh place, adopting our same occupation, and there are so many of them, it seems like this area has been converted into a pastoral Arcadia, such is the number of shepherds and flocks, and there's nowhere in this area where you won't hear the name of the beautiful Leandra. This one curses her and calls her capricious, indifferent, and immodest; that one condemns her as being frail and frivolous; another absolves and pardons her; one condemns and censures her, one celebrates her beauty, another complains about her character, and finally, all of them malign and all of them adore her; and their madness goes so far that some who have never even spoken to her complain of her scorn, and some lament and feel the raging illness of jealousy, for which she never gave anyone cause, because—as I already said—her sin was discovered before her passion was known. There is no nook among the boulders, nor the bank of a brook, nor the shade of a tree, which is not prowled by some shepherd who relates his misfortune to the wind. Wherever an echo can resonate, you hear the name of Leandra—LEANDRA resounds in the forests, LEANDRA murmurs in the brooks, and LEANDRA keeps us all bewildered and enchanted, hoping without hope, and afraid, not knowing what to fear.

Among all of these fools, the one who shows the least and yet has the most sense is my competitor Anselmo, who, having so many things to complain about, only laments her absence; and accompanied by a rabel—which he plays admirably well—and in verses in which he shows his keen intelligence, sings his fate. I've taken an easier path, and, to my way of looking at things, the best one, which is to curse the fickleness of women, their inconstancy, double-dealing, their worthless promises, and finally the little judgment they show in establishing their affections and inclinations. And this is what caused me, *señores*, to say those words I said to this goat when I came here—that is, since she's a female, I hold her in little esteem, even though she's the best one of my flock.

This is the story that I promised to tell you. If I've been long in telling it, I'll not be short in serving you. Near here I have my hut, and in it I have fresh milk and very delicious cheese, which, with other various seasonal fruits, are no less pleasing to see than they are to eat.

Chapter LII. Of the quarrel that don Quixote had with the goatherd, with the strange adventure of the penitents, to which he gave a happy conclusion through his sweat.

THE GOATHERD'S story gave great pleasure to all those who had listened to it, especially the canon, who noted with particular curiosity the way he'd told it—far from seeming to be a rustic goatherd, he seemed more to be a polished courtier. He said that the priest was very astute when he said that the forests bred scholars. Everyone offered their services to Eugenio, but the one who showed himself most liberal was don Quixote, who said to him: "I'll say, brother goatherd, if I were free to initiate a fresh adventure, I'd get on the road right now to bring you good fortune, and would take Leandra from that monastery, where she's doubtless being held captive against her will, in spite of the abbess and however many might try to stop me, and I'd place her in your hands so that you could do with her whatever you pleased, but always within the laws of chivalry, which dictate that no maiden be treated harshly. But I trust in God our Lord that the might of a malicious enchanter will not overpower that of another better-intentioned one, and until that time I promise you my favor and assistance, as I'm bound to do by my profession, which is none other than to help the weak and needy."

The goatherd looked at him, and seeing don Quixote's sorry appearance, asked the barber, who was near him: "*Señor*, who is this man who looks so odd and talks in this strange way?"

"Who else," responded the barber, "but the famous don Quixote de La Mancha, the undoer of wrongs, the redresser of injuries, the rescuer of damsels, the dread of giants, and the winner of battles?"

"This looks to me," responded the goatherd, "like what you read in those books about knights-errant, who do all these things that you say this man does, although I'm convinced that either you're joking or this gentleman must have some vacant rooms in his head."

"You're a great rapscallion," don Quixote said, "and you're the empty and wretched one, and I'm fuller than that bitch of a whore who bore you ever was."*

And, changing words into action, he took a loaf of bread that was next to him, and smashed it into the face of the goatherd with so much fury that he flattened his nose.† But the goatherd, who knew nothing of jokes, seeing himself mistreated in earnest, without any respect to the carpet, tablecloth, or those who were eating, sprang onto don Quixote, and grabbing him by the throat with both hands, would certainly have throttled him if Sancho Panza hadn't come over right then and clutched him by the shoulders and thrown him onto the table, smashing plates, breaking cups, and spilling and scattering everything that was on it.

---

* Don Quixote contrasts *empty* with *full*. *Full*, in Spanish, is also used to mean *pregnant*, but only for animals, thus the insult to Eugenio's mother is increased.

† Translator's note: This is clearly not Wonder bread. I know from experience that Manchegan bread can be heavy, hard crusted, and with jagged points on the top, a weapon to be feared in close combat.

Don Quixote, who found himself free, ran back to jump on the goatherd, whose face was covered with blood and mauled by Sancho's kicks. He was on all fours, looking for a knife with which to take bloody vengeance, but the priest and canon prevented him, and the barber fixed it so the goatherd could get on top of don Quixote and rain so many blows that the poor knight's face streamed with blood as freely as his own.

The canon and the priest were bursting with laughter, the officers were dancing with joy, and several people were urging them on, like they do with fighting dogs. Only Sancho Panza was despairing, because he was being held back by a servant of the canon, and this prevented him from helping his master. Finally, with everyone rejoicing and enjoying it all, except for the two combatants who were mauling each other, they heard the sound of a trumpet, so sad that everyone turned their faces to see where the sound was coming from. But the one who was most aroused to hear it was don Quixote, who, although he was under the goatherd quite against his will, and more than somewhat beaten up, said: "Brother devil—you've got to be one, since you've had the power and strength to subdue me—I beg you to make a truce for no more than an hour, because the doleful sound of that trumpet that has come to our ears seems to be a new adventure calling to me."

The goatherd, who was already tired of beating up and of being beaten up, let him loose, and don Quixote stood up and turned his face toward the sound, and he suddenly saw a number of men dressed like penitents, in white, coming down a hill. As it happened, that year the clouds had denied the earth their showers, and in the villages in that region there were many processions, prayers, and flagellations, asking God to open His hands of mercy and rain on them. For this reason the people of a village nearby were coming in a procession to a holy shrine on one side of that valley.

Don Quixote saw the strange garb of the penitents,* without remembering he had to have seen them many times before, and imagined that it was going to be an ad-

---

* What these people are wearing is very similar to what the Ku Klux Klan wear today.

venture destined for him only—as a knight-errant—to undertake, and this thought was further confirmed when he saw a statue covered in mourning that they were carrying, and that he thought was some lady of rank being abducted by those rogues and insolent brigands.

With this in his head, he quickly went over to Rocinante, who was grazing nearby, and took the bridle and his shield from the pommel, and in an instant bridled him, and got his sword from Sancho. He then mounted Rocinante, firmed his grip on the shield, and said in a loud voice to those present: "Now you'll see, worthy friends, how important it is to have men who profess the order of knight-errantry. Now, I say, you'll see—when I free that lady held captive over there—if knights-errant should be esteemed or not."

And saying this, he squeezed his thighs against Rocinante (for he had no spurs), and at a good trot (because one never reads in this entire history that Rocinante was capable of a full gallop) went to confront the penitents. The priest, canon, and barber tried to prevent him, but that was not possible, and neither were the shouts that Sancho gave, saying: "Where are you going, *señor* don Quixote? What the devil do you have in your heart that incites you to go against our Catholic faith? Watch out—may I be damned!—that's a procession of penitents, and that woman that they're carrying on the litter is a statue of the Very Holy Virgin without blemish. Careful, *señor*, what you're up to, because this time one could say you don't know what you're doing."

Sancho did all this in vain, because his master was so determined to assault those sheet-wearing people and to liberate the woman in mourning that he didn't hear a word, nor would he have gone back even if the king himself commanded him. He went to the front of the procession and reined in Rocinante, who was eager to rest a bit, and with an angry and hoarse voice, said: "You—who hide your faces perhaps because you're evil—come here and listen to what I want to tell you."

The first ones who stopped were the statue bearers; and one of the four clerics who were singing litanies, seeing the strange expression of don Quixote, the leanness of Rocinante, and other laughable circumstances he saw and noted, responded: "*Señor* brother, if you want to tell us something, do it quickly, because these brothers are scourging themselves, and we cannot, nor is it proper to, listen to anything unless you can say it in two words."

"I'll say it in one," replied don Quixote, "and it's this: Immediately release that beautiful woman, whose tears* and sad face clearly show that she's being held against her will, and to whom you've done some terrible outrage. And I, who was born in the world to redress such wrongs, will not allow you to take a single step farther without giving her the freedom she deserves."

With these words, all those who heard don Quixote realized he must be a madman and burst out laughing, which was adding gunpowder to the anger that came over don Quixote, because without saying a single word, taking out his sword, he attacked the litter. One of those who was holding it up, giving his share of the weight to his companions, went out to meet don Quixote, brandishing a forked prop used to hold the litter up when they rested. Don Quixote slashed at the prop and cut it in two. With the remaining part his adversary gave don Quixote such a whack on the shoulder of his sword arm—because he couldn't shield himself from the tremendous blow—that he fell to the ground in very bad shape.

Sancho Panza, who came up panting, trying to follow him, when he saw him on the ground, shouted to his assailant not to hit him anymore, because he was just a poor enchanted knight who had never done any harm to anybody in all the days of his life. But what really stopped the rustic wasn't Sancho's shouts, but rather seeing that don Quixote wasn't moving either his hands or his feet. And thinking that he'd killed him, he quickly raised his habit to his waist and fled across the fields like a deer.

By this time, don Quixote's companions went to where he was lying. The people in the procession, seeing those others come running, including the officers with their muskets, surrounded the statue, fearing trouble. They raised their hoods, grasped their whips, and the clerics their candles, and waited for the assault, determined to

---

* As in this case, Spanish statues of the Virgin frequently have tears running down their cheeks.

defend themselves, or even strike their attackers offensively if they could, but Fortune made it turn out better than anyone expected, because Sancho only went over and threw himself on the body of his master, making the most pitiful and comical lament in the world, believing that he was dead.

Our priest was recognized by the other one who was in the procession, and thus the fear of both squadrons was calmed. Our priest said to the other one in a few words who don Quixote was, and so he, like the rest of the penitents, went to see if the poor knight was dead, and they heard Sancho Panza, with tears in his eyes, saying: "Oh, flower of knighthood, with only one blow from a club you ended the course of your so well-spent years! Oh, honor of your lineage, honor and glory of all of La Mancha, and even the whole world, which, with you missing from it, will be filled with evildoers who won't fear being punished for their wicked deeds. Oh, more liberal than all the Alexanders, since with only eight months of service you had given me the best *ínsula* that the sea encircles and surrounds. Oh, you, humble with the proud, and arrogant with the humble; you welcome dangers, you withstand humiliation, you love without cause, you imitate the good, you whip the bad, you're an enemy of the lowlifes; that is, you're a knight-errant, and that's all that can be said."

At these loud cries and sighs by Sancho, don Quixote revived, and the first words he said were: "He who lives absent from you, sweetest Dulcinea, undergoes worse miseries than these. Help me, my friend Sancho, to get into the enchanted cart, for I cannot sit on Rocinante's saddle because my shoulder is in pieces."

"I'll do that with great pleasure, *señor mío*," responded Sancho, "and let's go back to my village in the company of these men, who only wish you good, and there we'll plan another expedition, which will be more profitable and will bring us more fame."

"Well said, Sancho," responded don Quixote, "and it would be a good idea to allow the bad influence of the stars currently in force to pass."

The canon, priest, and barber told him it would do him good to do what he said, and, having gotten great pleasure from Sancho's naive remarks, they put don Quixote back

in the cart, as he was before. The goatherd bade farewell
to everyone. The officers didn't want to go any farther. The
canon asked the priest to write him with news of don Quixote—whether he got cured of his madness, or was still
mad—and with this, he left to continue his journey.

So they all went their separate ways, leaving only the
priest and barber, don Quixote and Sancho Panza, and the
good Rocinante, who, having witnessed everything, was
as patient as his master. The ox handler reyoked his oxen
and helped don Quixote get comfortable on a bed of hay
and, with his usual slow pace, followed the road the priest
wanted. Six days later they arrived at don Quixote's village, where they entered at noon. It happened to be Sunday
and the people were all in the plaza, through the middle
of which don Quixote's cart passed. Everyone came to see
what was in the cart, and when they recognized their fellow villager, they were astonished. A boy ran to give the
news to his housekeeper and niece that their master and
uncle was coming home, thin and pale, stretched out on a
pile of hay, and on an oxcart. It was a pitiful thing to hear
the shouts that the two women raised to heaven, the cuffs
they gave themselves, the curses they once again leveled
on those vexatious books of chivalry—all of which was
repeated when they saw don Quixote enter through the
gates.

At the news of the arrival of don Quixote, Sancho Panza's
wife came over, because she'd known that he'd gone with
don Quixote as his squire, and as soon as she saw Sancho,
the first thing she asked him was if the donkey was healthy.
Sancho said he was in better shape than his master.

"Thanks be to God," she replied, "for the good He's
done me. But tell me now, my friend, what good has come
out of your squiring? What skirt are you bringing me? What
shoes for your children?"

"I'm not bringing anything like that, my wife," said Sancho, "but I have other things that are more important and
worth more."

"That pleases me," responded the woman. "Show me
these things that are more important and worth more, because I want to see them so that my heart can be happy,
for it has been sad and upset during the centuries of your
absence."

"I'll show you when we get home," said Panza, "but for now be content, because, if God is pleased, we'll go out once again seeking adventures, and you'll soon see me a count or the governor of an *ínsula*—and not one of those run-of-the-mill ones, but the best one that can be found."

"May heaven grant it, my husband, because we do need one. But tell me, what is this business of *ínsulas*, because I don't understand?"

"'Honey was not intended for the mouths of donkeys,'" responded Sancho. "In time you'll see, woman, and you'll even be more amazed when you hear yourself being called LADYSHIP by all your vassals."

"What are you saying, Sancho, about ladyships, *ínsulas*, and vassals?" responded Juana Panza, because that was the name of Sancho's wife, not that they were related, but in La Mancha, women customarily take the name of their husbands.

"Don't be in such a hurry, Juana, to find out everything so quickly. It's enough that I'm telling you the truth. Stitch your mouth closed. I can only tell you in passing that there is nothing more pleasurable in the world than for an honest man to be the squire of a knight-errant, a seeker of adventures. It's true that most of them don't turn out as a man might like, because ninety-nine out of a hundred turn out bad and different from what you'd expect. I know from experience, because from some I've come out blanketed and from others mauled. But even so, it's nice to wonder what will happen next, crossing mountains, searching forests, climbing on rocks, being lodged in inns at will, without paying a single *maravedí*."

Sancho Panza and Juana Panza, his wife, had all this conversation while don Quixote's housekeeper and niece received him, and undressed him, and put him in his former bed. He looked at them with squinting eyes, and didn't know where he was. The priest charged the niece to take special care of her uncle, and to be careful that he not escape again, and related to them what they had had to do in order to bring him back home. The two raised new lamentations to heaven; they renewed their curses on the books of chivalry; they asked heaven to plunge the authors of such lies and foolishness into the bottom of the abyss.

Finally, they were afraid that as soon as he was better they would once again be without their master and uncle, and it turned out the way they thought.

But the author of this history, although he searched assiduously and with diligence to learn of don Quixote's deeds on his third expedition, has not been able to find anything, at least in authentic documents. There is only what tradition has preserved in the memories of La Mancha—that don Quixote, the third time he left his home, went to Zaragoza,* where he took part in some famous jousts held in that city, and things happened to him there worthy of his bravery and resolute mind. About his end, he could find nothing, nor would he ever have, if good luck hadn't presented him with an old doctor who had in his possession a leaden box that, according to what he said, had been found in the demolished foundation of an ancient hermitage that was being rebuilt. In this box there were some parchments written in Gothic letters† but in Castilian verses, which contain many of his deeds and tell about the beauty of Dulcinea del Toboso, the figure of Rocinante, the faithfulness of Sancho Panza, and the sepulcher of don Quixote himself, with different epitaphs and praises of his life and character.

Those that they could read and make out were those that the trustworthy author of this original and never-before-seen history has included here. This author doesn't ask anything of his readers in recompense for the immense amount of work it took him to investigate and search in all the Manchegan archives to bring it to light, except that they give him as much credence as sensible people do the books of chivalry that are so favored in the world, and with this he'll consider himself well paid and satisfied. And he'll be encouraged to find other histories, if not as true, at least as inventive and no less entertaining. The first words writ-

---

* A major Spanish city on the Ebro River, 185 miles west of Barcelona.
† There is some dispute as to what Gothic letters are. The writing used, for example, in Alfonso el Sabio's court (thirteenth century) is said to use Gothic letters. In any case, the parchments are old, given how they were found.

ten on the parchment that was found in the lead box were these:

THE ACADEMICIANS OF*
ARGAMASILLA,† A VILLAGE OF LA MANCHA, ON THE LIFE AND DEATH OF DON QUIXOTE DE LA MANCHA, *HOC SCRIPSERUNT*‡

MONICONGO,§ ACADEMICIAN OF ARGAMASILLA, ON THE TOMB OF DON QUIXOTE

EPITAPH

The scatterbrain that gave La Mancha more
  Rich spoils than Jason's;¶ who a point so keen
  Had to his wit, and happier far had been
  If his wit's weathercock a blunter bore;
The arm renowned far as Gaeta's shore,
  Cathay, and all the lands that lie between;
  The muse discreet and terrible in mien
  As ever wrote on brass in days of yore;
He who surpassed the Amadises all,
  And who as naught the Galaors accounted,
  Supported by his love and gallantry:

---

* I am again using Ormsby's verses, slightly modified.

† Argamasilla is a village southwest of El Toboso. Today there are 6,300 inhabitants there, mostly dealing in agriculture. There was no academy there in real life.

‡ "They wrote this," in Latin.

§ This is the old name for the Congo (modern République Démocratique du Congo, formerly Zaire). In those days, academicians would take literary pseudonyms. The burlesque names seen here would have been amusing in that light.

¶ Jason is a mythological hero who was sent on a suicide mission to find the Golden Fleece, which led to the successful expedition of the Argonauts. Since Jason had no connection with Crete, you should be immediately suspicious about the quality of these academicians.

Who made the Belianises sing small,
    And sought renown on Rocinante mounted;
    Here, underneath this cold stone, does he lie.

Paniaguado, Academician of Argamasilla, *In Laudem Dulcineæ del Doboso* *

Sonnet

She, whose full features may be here descried,
    High-bosomed, with a bearing of disdain,
    Is Dulcinea, she for whom in vain
    The great don Quixote de La Mancha sighed.
For her, Toboso's queen, from side to side
    He traversed the grim sierra, the champaign
    Of Aranjuez,† and Montiel's famous plain:
    On Rocinante oft a weary ride.
Malignant planets, cruel destiny,
    Pursued them both, the fair Manchegan dame,
    And the unconquered star of chivalry.
    Nor youth nor beauty saved her from the claim
    Of death; he paid love's bitter penalty,
    And left the marble to preserve his name.

---

* *In . . . in praise of Dulcinea del Doboso*. The first edition *did* say "Doboso." It looks like an amusing error-on-purpose by Cervantes. Virtually all editors and translators "correct" this, mostly without saying so. Eduardo Urbina's "Electronic Variorum Edition of the Quixote" at http://www.csdl.tamu.edu/cervantes/english/index.html all eight copies of the first edition show "Doboso," seemingly indicating that this wasn't a typographical error. (While books were printed in those days, proofreading continued and corrections were made.)
† Aranjuez is a city thirty miles south of Madrid. Don Quixote never got near that place.

Caprichoso, a Most Clever Academician of Argamasilla, in Praise of Rocinante, Steed of don Quixote de La Mancha

Sonnet*

On that proud throne of diamantine sheen,
    Which the blood-reeking feet of Mars degrade,
    The mad Manchegan's banner now hath been
    By him in all its bravery displayed.
There hath he hung his arms and trenchant blade
    Wherewith, achieving deeds till now unseen,
    He slays, lays low, cleaves, hews; but art has made
    A novel style for our new paladin.
If Amadís be the proud boast of Gaula,
    If by his progeny the fame of Greece
    Through all the regions of the earth be spread,
Great Quixote crowned in grim Bellona's† hall
    Today exalts La Mancha over these,
    And above Greece or Gaula she holds her head.
Nor ends his glory here, for his good steed
    Does Brillador and Bayardo‡ far exceed;
    As mettled steeds compared with Rocinante,
    The reputation they have won is scanty.

Burlador, Academician of Argamasilla, On Sancho Panza

Sonnet

The worthy Sancho Panza here you see;
    A great soul once was in that body small,
    Nor was there squire upon this earthly ball
    So plain and simple, or of guile so free.

---

* The seventeen-line sonnet is not a mistake. Adding three lines was common. You'll see that Ormsby, whose versions are used here, needed an eighteenth line.

† Bellona was the Roman goddess of war, the sister, friend, or wife of Mars.

‡ These were the horses respectively of Orlando (Furioso) and Reinaldos de Montalbán.

Within an ace of being count was he,
    And would have been but for the spite and gall
    Of this vile age, mean and illiberal,
    That cannot even let a donkey be.
For mounted on an ass (excuse the word),
    By Rocinante's side this gentle squire
    Was wont his wandering master to attend.
Delusive hopes that lure the common herd
    With promises of ease, the heart's desire,
    In shadows, dreams, and smoke you always end.

CACHIDIABLO, ACADEMICIAN OF ARGAMASILLA, ON THE TOMB OF DON QUIXOTE

EPITAPH

The knight lies here below,
    Ill errant and bruised sore,
    Whom Rocinante bore
    In his wanderings to and fro.
By the side of the knight is laid
    Stolid man Sancho too,
    Than whom a squire more true
    Was not in the esquire trade.

TIQUITOC, ACADEMICIAN OF ARGAMASILLA, ON THE TOMB OF DULCINEA DEL TOBOSO

EPITAPH

Here Dulcinea lies.
    Plump was she and robust:
    Now she is ashes and dust:
    The end of all flesh that dies.
A lady of high degree,
    With the port of a lofty dame,
    And the great don Quixote's flame,
    And the pride of her village was she.

These were all the verses that could be read; the rest, the
handwriting being worm-eaten, were handed over to one of
the academicians to conjecture their meaning. The news
is that at the cost of many sleepless nights and
much exertion he has succeeded, and that
he intends to bring them to light,
in expectation of don
Quixote's third
expedition.

*Forse altro canterà con miglior plectio.**

FINIS.

---

* This is an ill-remembered verse from *Orlando Furioso* (XXX,16):
Forsi altri canterà con miglior plettro. After having stated that don
Quixote made a third sally that took him to Zaragoza, the rather
cocky narrator dares anyone to take his pen and continue the story.
The quote means: "Perhaps another will sing with a better pick," the
pick being analogous with a pen.

TABLE OF THE
Chapters that contain this famous History of the brave knight don Quixote de La Mancha

First Part of the Ingenious *Hidalgo* Don Quixote de La Mancha.

Fourth Part of the Ingenious *Hidalgo* Don Quixote de La Mancha.

502   *Miguel de Cervantes Saavedra*

SECOND PART
OF THE INGENIOUS
KNIGHT DON
QUIXOTE DE LA MANCHA.

By Miguel de Cervantes Saavedra, author of its first part.
Dedicated to don Pedro Fernández of Castro,
Count of Lemos, of Andrade, and of Villalba;
Marquis of Sarria, Gentleman-in-waiting to His Majesty,
Commander of the Patronage of Peñafiel,
and Officer of the Order of Alcántara;
Viceroy, Governor, and Captain-General
of the Kingdom of Naples,
and President of the Supreme Council of Italy

A.D.   1615

WITH COPYRIGHT
In Madrid *by Juan de la Cuesta,*
Sold in the establishment of Francisco de Robles,
bookseller of the King, our lord.

Prologue to the Reader

GOD HELP ME, HOW anxiously you must be waiting for this prologue, illustrious or plebeian reader, expecting me to avenge myself, denounce, and reproach the author of the second *Quixote*. I mean the fellow they say was conceived in Tordesillas and was born in Tarragona.* But in truth I can't give you this satisfaction, for although injustice typically awakens wrath in the meekest of hearts, my case will be the exception to this rule. You would have me call him an ass, an idiot, or a boor, but I'm far from doing that— let his sin punish him, let him eat it on his bread, and let's say no more.

What offended me the most was his saying that I'm old and maimed,† as if I had it in my power to stop time, and as though my maimed arm was a result of some tavern brawl rather than from the noblest battle any age ever witnessed,

---

* Since you are reading the prologue, you should also read the part of the introduction that talks about Alonso Fernández de Avellaneda, the author of the 1614 continuation of *Don Quixote*. The title page of Avellaneda's book says that he is from Tordesillas, and that his book was printed in Tarragona.

† Avellaneda says that Cervantes is as old as the "Castillo de San Cervantes" in Toledo, as it was colloquially known. It's really the Castle of San *Servando*, near the Alcántara Bridge, and dates from the ninth century. Avellaneda also says that "Cervantes confesses that he has only one hand." These references can be found in Martín de Riquer's edition of Avellaneda's *Quixote*, Clásicos Castellanos 174, pp. 10 and 8.

or that current and future ages will ever witness.* If my wounds don't seem resplendent in the eyes of the man on the street, they're revered at least by those who know where they came from, since the soldier looks better dead in battle than free in flight. I'm so convinced of this that if the impossible were offered to me right now—that I could be free from my wounds by not having participated in that battle—I would refuse. Wounds that a soldier has on his face or his chest are stars that guide others to the heaven of honor and to the thirst for earned praise. Also bear in mind that you don't write with gray hairs, but rather with your intellect, which only gets better with the passage of time.

I also take offense that he calls me envious, and that he goes on to explain to me, as if I were stupid, what envy is. Of the two kinds of envy,† I know only the one that's holy, noble, and pure. And that being so—as it is—I'm not of a mind to attack any priest, especially if he's a member of the Holy Office. And if he said that for the benefit of whom I think he said it,‡ he made an enormous mistake, since I worship his genius, I admire his works, and his ever virtuous way of life.§ But I'm indeed grateful to this author when he says that my novellas are more satirical than exemplary, but good withal—because they wouldn't be good if they didn't have both qualities.

You must be saying that I'm showing great restraint and I'm containing myself within the bounds of modesty, knowing that one shouldn't add more misery to the person who is suffering; and the suffering of this man must be great, since he doesn't dare appear in an open field under the clear sky, but rather conceals his name and disguises his hometown, as if he has committed high treason. If by chance you happen to run into him, tell him for me that I don't consider

---

* This was the Battle of Lepanto. See Part I, chapter thirty-nine, page 372.

† The first type of envy is one of the seven deadly sins, together with pride, covetousness, lust, gluttony, anger, and sloth. The second type, the one Cervantes is referring to here, is what Vicente Gaos calls "noble emulation."

‡ This person is Lope de Vega, the famous playwright and Cervantes' rival.

§ Cervantes knew about Lope de Vega's scandalous private life.

myself insulted; that I know very well what temptations of the devil are, and one of the greatest ones is to make a man think that he can write and publish a book to become as famous as he is rich, and as rich as he is famous. To illustrate, I want you to tell him this witty and charming story:

In Seville there dwelled a madman who came up with the most ridiculous hobby that any madman ever dreamed up. And it was that he fashioned a tube with a sharp end, and would catch a dog in the street, or anywhere else, and with his foot he would hold down one of the dog's hind legs, and he would lift the other leg with his hand, and would fit the tube as well as he could into the place where, when he blew into it, he made the dog as round as a ball. Then, he would give it a couple of little slaps on its belly and would let it go, saying to the bystanders—and there were always a lot of them: "Do your graces think that it's not much work to inflate a dog?"

Does your grace think now that it's not much work to make a book?

And if this story doesn't seem quite right, you'll tell him, dear reader, this one, which is also about a madman and a dog:

There was in Cordova another madman who used to balance a piece of marble or other such stone—and not a light one either—on his head, and when he came across an unsuspecting dog, he went up to it and let the stone fall straight down onto it. The dog would be inordinately vexed and would go barking and yelping for three blocks.

It happened that among the dogs onto which he discharged his load was one belonging to a hatmaker, whose owner loved him very much. He dropped his stone, it hit the dog's head, the dog raised a fuss, the owner saw and heard what was going on, took a yardstick, and ran out to the madman and didn't leave a whole bone in his body. With every thwack he said: "You dog of a thief! My pointer? Didn't you see, you cruel creature, that my dog is a pointer?"

And he repeated the word POINTER many times, and sent the madman away beaten up. The madman learned a lesson from this, and he didn't go to the plaza for more than a month, but finally returned with his usual game and with a heavier weight. He would go up to a dog, and after examining it carefully, he wouldn't let the stone fall, saying: "This is a pointer, watch out!" So, every dog he saw, whether they were Great Danes or lapdogs, he said they were pointers, and never let the stone fall again.

Perhaps in this way it will happen to this storyteller that he won't dare to release the weight of his wit in books that, being bad, are harder than rocks.

Tell him as well, regarding the threat he made that he'll take away my earnings with his book, I couldn't care less, and I answer, adapting that famous comic skit named *La Peredenga*:* "I still have my patron, and peace be unto you." Long live the Count of Lemos,† whose charity and well-known liberality support me, and long live the great charity of His Eminence of Toledo, don Bernardo de Sandoval y Rojas,‡ even though there are many more printing presses in the world, and even though they may print more books against me than there are letters in the *Couplets of Mingo Revulgo*.§ These two princes, without receiving praise or any other kind of flattery from me, have of their own goodness done me a service by which I consider myself more fortunate and richer than if Fortune itself had taken me to its summit. Honor is possible for the poor person, but not for the wicked—being poor can cloud nobility, but not obscure it completely. Virtue emits light, even though it might

---

* This FAMOUS *La Peredenga* is something of a mystery. Agustín Moreto wrote a comic skit of that name—it means *prostitute*—that exists in manuscript form, but Moreto was born four years *after* Cervantes' death. Martín de Riquer suggests that since Moreto adapted earlier works by others, this could be a play, now lost, that Moreto reworked.
† This Count of Lemos, the seventh one, was don Pedro Fernández Ruiz de Castro y Osorio (1576–1622), viceroy of Naples from 1610 to 1622. Cervantes also dedicated his *Eight Plays and Eight Skits* (1615) and his *Persiles and Sigismunda* (1616) to this same person.
‡ Bernardo de Sandoval y Rojas, as archbishop of Toledo, aided Cervantes in his old age.
§ The *Couplets de Mingo Revulgo*, written around 1470, is an anonymous satiric poem consisting of thirty-two nine-verse stanzas. The meaning of the phrase beginning with *even though there are many more printing presses*... is obscure, at least to me and other translators. It seems to say that no matter how many books are published against him, Cervantes will still be protected by these two men. If LETTERS refers to letters of the alphabet, you'll have to count them to see how many books Cervantes is referring to. If it means "stanzas," which it can, then he is not afraid of thirty-two books against him.

be through straits and cracks of poverty, which comes to be valued by high and noble spirits, and consequently favored by them.

And don't tell him anything else, nor do I want to tell you anything else, except to advise you that you should consider this *Second Part of don Quixote* that I present to you as cut by the same creator and from the same material as the first, and in it I give you don Quixote at greater length and finally dead and buried, so that no one else can dare relate new stories about him since those already told are enough. And it's enough that an honorable man has related the stories of these witty follies without going into the matter again, for too much of a good thing makes one not value it as much and a scarcity—even of bad things—earns some esteem. I forgot to tell you to expect the *Persiles* soon and that I'm finishing the second part of *Galatea.**

---

* The *Persiles* was finally published posthumously in 1616. Cervantes finished it just four days before his death, and even in the prologue to that book—one day after receiving extreme unction from the Church—he said he still hoped to finish *La Galatea*, a pastoral novel (Part I of which was his first published fiction, 1585). Some people think that the second part of *Galatea* was lost. I think, given this joking reference to it, that it was never even begun.

FIRST CHAPTER
About the conversation the priest and barber had with don Quixote concerning his illness.

CIDE HAMETE Benengeli relates in the Second Part of this history, and third expedition of don Quixote, that the priest and barber refrained from visiting don Quixote for almost a month, so as not to remind him about and bring to his memory things from the past. But that doesn't mean they didn't visit the niece and housekeeper, urging them to pamper him and give him things to eat to fortify him, and that were also right for his heart and brain, from where issued—so it seemed—all of his bad fortune. They told him they were doing just that, and would continue to do so with goodwill and care, because they saw that their master at times seemed to be completely sane, which made the two men very happy, causing them to feel they were right to bring him home enchanted in the oxcart, as was related in the last chapter of the First Part of this great and factual history.

So they finally decided to visit him and judge his recovery for themselves. They thought it was almost impossible that he would have gotten better, thus they agreed not to touch on anything related to knight-errantry, so as not to put him in danger of reopening his wounds, which were very fresh.

They found him seated on his bed, dressed in a green flannel jacket, and with a red Toledan nightcap. He was so dried up that he looked like he was a mummy. He received them cheerfully, and they asked about his health. He told them very rationally and with elegant words how he was doing and the state of his health. During their conversation they got on the subject of politics and discussed their views of government, amending this abuse and condemning that one, reforming one custom and getting rid of another, each one of the three of them being transformed into a new legislator, a modern Lycurgus or a brand-new Solon.* And they so refashioned the republic that it seemed that they had put one into a forge and taken out quite another. And don Quixote spoke so sensibly about everything that the two examiners believed without a doubt that he was completely cured and quite sane.

The niece and housekeeper were present during this conversation and they couldn't thank God enough when they saw their master with such good sense. But the priest, changing his mind about not talking about matters of chivalry, wanted to try an experiment to see if don Quixote's recovery was in appearance only, or if it was genuine. So he began to relate some news that had come from the capital, where it was thought to be certain that the Turkish army was approaching with a powerful armada, though they didn't know what the Turks' plan was, or where their storm would burst. Almost every year this fear sounded the alarm, and all of Christendom was constantly on the alert, and His Majesty had provided for the defense of Naples, Sicily, and the Island of Malta.

To this responded don Quixote: "His Majesty has acted like a very prudent warrior in protecting his dominions in advance so the enemy won't find him unprepared, but if he'd take my advice, I'd tell him to try something I doubt he has thought of."

Hardly had the priest heard this when he said to himself: "May God protect you, poor don Quixote, because it seems that you're flinging yourself down from the height of your madness into the abyss of your simplicity."

But the barber, who had realized what the priest's thought was, asked don Quixote what the measure was

---

* Lycurgus (seventh century B.C.) was the lawmaker responsible for institutions in ancient Sparta, particularly the military. Solon (630–560 B.C.) was an Athenian statesman, one of the Seven Wise Men of Greece, who introduced a more humane law code and ended aristocratic control of the government.

that he thought would be so useful—it might be put onto the list of irrelevant suggestions that are typically made to princes.

"Mine, *señor* shaver, wouldn't be irrelevant, but quite to the point."

"I don't mean it that way," said the barber, "only that experience has shown that all or most advice given to His Majesty is either impossible or foolish, or is damaging to the king or to the kingdom."

"But mine," responded don Quixote, "is neither impossible nor foolish, but rather the easiest, most just, and most feasible and direct that any adviser could formulate."

"Your grace seems to be delaying in telling us what it is, *señor* don Quixote."

"I wouldn't want," said don Quixote, "to tell you this here and now, and tomorrow morning have it in the ears of the king's advisers, for which someone else would get the thanks and credit for my labor."

"As for me," said the barber, "I pledge my word in the presence of God not to reveal to king or rook or any other living man what your grace may say—an oath that I learned from the 'Ballad of the Priest,' in which the priest was able to reveal to the king about how a thief stole a hundred doubloons and his swift mule from him."*

"I don't know those stories," said don Quixote, "but I do know that your oath is good because I know that the *señor* barber is an honorable man."

"And if he weren't," said the priest, "I'll vouch for him, and he will say no more about the matter than a person who lacks the ability to speak, or he'll have to pay any judgment against him."

"And, your grace, who will vouch for you?" said don Quixote.

---

* The "Ballad of the Priest" is discussed at length in Rodríguez Marín's Atlas edition of the *Quixote* (1949), vol. IX, pp. 280–95. In this Valencian story, a priest is robbed on the road of his donkey and his money, the thief admonishing him to tell no one of the robbery. In saying Mass later in front of the king, he sees the thief beneath the pulpit and is able to denounce him within the Mass itself, and the king has the thief arrested. Sam Armistead says that this ballad is unknown in the modern oral tradition.

"My profession," responded the priest, "which is to keep secrets."

"Well, then, by God," said don Quixote, "what else should His Majesty do but have a public crier summon all the knights-errant roaming all over Spain to meet in the capital on a certain day? And even though only half a dozen of them come, there might be one of them who would be able to destroy the power of the Turk single-handedly. Listen carefully and follow along. By chance is it unheard-of for a single knight-errant to destroy an army of two hundred thousand men as if they all had one single throat or if they were made of almond paste? Tell me, how many histories are filled with these wonders? It would be to my misfortune and no one else's if the famous don Belianís de Grecia, or any other of the countless men from Amadís de Gaula's innumerable lineage were living today! For if any one of these came and confronted the Turk, I swear I wouldn't want to be in his shoes. God will look out for His people and will send one who, if not as fierce as the previous knights, at least won't be inferior in his courage. God understands me and I say no more!"

"*Ay!*" said the niece at this point. "May they kill me if my master doesn't want to be a knight-errant once again!"

To which don Quixote said: "A knight-errant I'll die! Let the Turk come or go whenever he wants, and with whatever strength he can muster—once again I say that God understands me."

At this point the barber said: "I beg your grace to permit me to tell a little story about something that happened in Seville, which I'd like to tell you because it seems most pertinent to this case."

Don Quixote gave him permission, and the priest and the others lent an ear, and he began in this way: "In the nuthouse of Seville there was a man whose relatives had put him there because he was crazy. He was a graduate in canon law from the University of Osuna,* but even if he'd been graduated by Salamanca, in the opinion of many, he still would have been crazy. This graduate, after some years in confinement, let it be known that he was sane and in

---

* This was a minor university like the priest's own University of Sigüenza mentioned in Part I, chapter one, page 21.

his right mind, and with this thought he wrote to the archbishop, begging him earnestly, with well-chosen words, to
be taken out of the misery in which he was living, since by
the compassion of God he'd recovered his lost sanity; but
his relatives, in order to hold on to and keep using his income, insisted that he stay there, and in spite of the truth,
wanted him to stay crazy until he died.

"The archbishop, persuaded by the many coherent and
sensible letters, sent one of his chaplains to find out from
the superintendent of the madhouse if it was true what the
licenciado had written, and also to speak with the crazy
man. If it seemed to him he was sane, he could take him
out and set him free. The chaplain went, and the superintendent maintained that he was still crazy. Although much
of the time he spoke like a person with great intelligence,
he finally would hurl a lot of nonsense that rivaled his
previous good sense both in quality and quantity, as the
chaplain could find out for himself by speaking with him.
The chaplain wanted to, and the superintendent took him
to the crazy man. The chaplain spoke with him for an hour
or more, and in all that time the crazy man didn't utter an
odd or foolish word, but rather spoke so intelligently that
the chaplain was forced to believe the crazy man was sane.
Among other things the crazy man said to him was that
the superintendent bore him a grudge so that he wouldn't
lose the gifts the crazy man's relatives gave him, and that's
why he would keep on saying that he was crazy but with lucid intervals; and the biggest obstacle he had was his great
income, since his enemies—in order to spend it—willfully
misrepresented him and denied the favor that Our Lord
had done by turning him from a beast back into a man.

"In the end, his reasoning was so lucid that the chaplain began to wonder about the intentions of the superintendent. The crazy man made his relatives look covetous
and soulless, and himself look so sensible that the chaplain
decided to take him away, and let the archbishop himself
determine the truth of the matter.

"In good faith, then, the chaplain asked the superintendent to have the clothing in which he'd entered the asylum
returned to the *licenciado*. The superintendent once again
said that he should be careful, because without any doubt
the *licenciado* was still crazy, but despite his precautions and

warnings, the chaplain still insisted on taking him away. The superintendent obeyed, seeing it was an order from the archbishop. They gave the *licenciado* back his clothing, which was new and decent, and when he saw himself dressed as a sane man and divested of his craziness, he asked the superintendent if he might bid farewell to his friends, the other crazy men. The chaplain said that he wanted to go along and see the crazy men who were in that asylum, so they and the others in their company went upstairs, and when the *licenciado* came to the cell of a certain raving lunatic, although at the moment he was calm and quiet, he said to him: 'My brother, tell me if there's anything I can do for you, because I'm going home. God, through His infinite goodness and mercy, has been pleased, without my deserving it, to restore my sanity. I'm healthy and sane again, because where the power of God is concerned, nothing is impossible. Maintain your hope and confidence in Him, because if He returned me to the way I was, He can do the same for you, if you trust in Him. I'll make sure to send you some good things to eat. Make sure you eat them, because I think—since I've been through all this—that much of our madness comes from having our stomachs empty and our minds filled with air. Take courage, take courage, I say, because despondency in misfortunes saps one's health and leads to death.'

"Another crazy man, who was in the opposite cell, heard all these words said by the *licenciado*, and getting up off an old mat where he lay naked, asked in a loud voice who it was that was healthy and sane.

"The *licenciado* responded: 'I'm the one, brother, who is going away. I don't need to be here anymore, for which I give infinite thanks to heaven that has favored me so.'

"'Watch what you're saying, *licenciado*; don't let the devil deceive you,' replied the crazy man. 'Don't be so anxious to leave—stay here at your ease and you'll save yourself a trip back.'

"'I know I'm cured,' replied the *licenciado*, 'and there'll be no reason to come back.'

"'*You*, cured?' said the crazy man. 'All right, we'll see about that—go with God, but I swear to Jupiter,* whose

---

* Jupiter (or Zeus in Greek) was the supreme Roman god, also the god of weather and rain, the sender of lightning.

majesty I represent on earth, that for just this one sin Seville is committing today by releasing you from this asylum and in saying that you're sane, I'll punish the city so harshly that its memory will last for all time, AMEN. Don't you know, you miserable little *licenciado*, that I can do it, since, as I say, I AM THE THUNDERING JUPITER, and I have in my hands burning lightning bolts with which I can threaten and even destroy the world? But I'll use just one punishment to chastise these ignorant people, and that is that I'll withhold rain from the city and the whole area for three whole years, and this will start as soon as I pronounce this threat. You free, healthy, and sane?—and I crazy, sick, and imprisoned? I'll feel like raining about as much as I'd consider hanging myself.'

"All those present were listening attentively to the shouts of the crazy man, but our *licenciado*, turning to face the chaplain and taking him by the hands, said: 'Don't worry, your grace, or pay attention to what that crazy man has said. For if he's Jupiter and refuses to rain, I am Neptune, the father and god of the waters, and I'll rain whenever I feel like it and wherever it's needed.'

"To which the chaplain responded: 'For all that, *señor* Neptune, it will not be a good idea to anger *señor* Jupiter. Stay here, your grace, in your house. On another day, when the time is right, we'll come back for you.'

"The superintendent and all the others who were present laughed, and their laughter embarrassed the chaplain. They undressed the *licenciado*, and he remained in the asylum, and that's the end of the story."

"So, that's your story, *señor* barber?" said don Quixote. "This is the one that was so much to the point that you just had to tell it? Ah, *señor* shaver, *señor* shaver, how blind can anyone be who can't see through cheesecloth! Is it possible that your grace doesn't know that comparisons that are made between one talent and another, one brave warrior and another, one beauty and another, or one family and another, are always odious and ill received? I, *señor*, am not Neptune, the god of the waters, nor do I try to make others think I'm sane when I'm not. I only get tired of trying to convince the world of its error in not reviving the happy time when the order of knights-errant flourished. Our depraved age is not worthy of enjoying the good fortune of those days when knights-errant undertook squarely on their shoulders the defense of kingdoms, the protection of maidens, the rescuing of orphans, the punishment of the arrogant, and the reward of the humble. Nowadays, knights dress in damasks, brocades, and other rich fabrics instead of coats of mail. Nowadays there's no knight who sleeps in the fields, exposed to the rigors of the elements, in armor from head to foot. Nowadays there's no one who, without taking his feet from his stirrups, leans against his lance to get a bit of sleep, as the knights-errant did. Nowadays no one leaves the forest and wanders through the mountains, and from there goes down to walk along a sterile and deserted beach by the tempestuous and angry sea, and finds at the shore a little vessel without oars, sail, mast, or rigging of any kind, and with an intrepid heart jumps headlong into it, at the mercy of the relentless waves of the deep sea, which throws him as high as the sky one minute and sinks him into the abyss the next, and he, heading into the invincible storm, when least he expects it, finds himself three thousand and more leagues distant from the place where he got on the boat. And going ashore in some remote and unknown territory, things happen to him that are worthy of being written, not on parchments, but etched in bronze.

"Nowadays sloth triumphs over industry, idleness over labor, vice over virtue, arrogance over valor, military theory over the practice of arms, which lived and shone only in the Golden Age of knights-errant. Tell me, who was more chaste and braver than Amadís de Gaula? Who more discreet than Palmerín de Inglaterra? Who more easily pleased and milder than Tirante el Blanco? Who more gallant than Lisuarte de Grecia? Who slashed and got slashed more than don Belianís? Who more intrepid than Perión de Gaula?* Who took on more dangers than Felixmarte de Hyrcania? Who was more sincere than Esplandián? Who bolder than Ceriongilio de Tracia?† Who fiercer than Rodamonte?‡ Who more prudent than

---

* Perión de Gaula is Amadís' father.

† This is the same *Ciron*gilio de Tracia, mentioned in Part I, chapter thirty-two.

‡ Rodamonte is a character in *Orlando Furioso* who fought against Charlemagne and was later killed by Ruggiero, soon to be mentioned.

King Sobrino? Who more daring than Reinaldos?* Who
more invincible than Roland? And who more gallant
and courteous than Ruggiero, from whom the Dukes
of Ferrara of today descend† according to Turpin in his
Cosmography?‡

"All these knights, and many others whom I could mention, *señor* priest, were knights-errant, the light and glory
of chivalry. I would want these, or men like them, to be on
my side, because if they were, His Majesty would be well
served and would spare an enormous expense, and the
Turk would be tearing his beard out. So, I don't want to remain at home, since there's no chaplain to rescue me, and if
Jupiter—as the barber has said—won't rain, here I am, and
I'll rain whenever I feel like it. I say this so that *señor* basin
will see that I understand him."

"In truth, *señor* don Quixote," said the barber, "I didn't
mean it that way; and so help me God, my intention was
good, and your grace shouldn't be offended."

"I'm the one to judge," responded don Quixote, "if I'm
offended or not."

To this the priest said: "Even though I've hardly uttered
a word until now, I don't want to be left with a slight reser-
vation that has been gnawing at me, born of what *señor* don
Quixote has said."

"For this and other things," responded don Quixote,
"the *señor* priest is permitted to vent his reservations, because it's not good to be troubled by doubts."

"With this consent," responded the priest, "my reserva-
tion is that I cannot persuade myself at all that the whole
multitude of knights-errant your grace, *señor* don Quixote,
has mentioned, were really men of flesh and blood in the
world. Rather I imagine that it's all fiction, fable, falsehoods, and dreams related by men who are wide-awake, or
better said, half-asleep."

"This is another mistake," responded don Quixote, "that

---

* This is Reinaldos de Montalbán (known as Renaut de Montauban in
the French legends), mentioned in Part I, chapter one.

† It is Ariosto's *Orlando Furioso*, canto three, where it says that the
dukes of Ferrara descend from Ruggiero.

‡ Turpin never had such a work attributed to him until don Quixote's
remark.

many who believe these knights never existed in the world have fallen into, and I have tried many times, with different people and on different occasions, to make them see the truth of this common error. Sometimes I haven't succeeded and sometimes I have, supporting what I've said on the shoulders of Truth; and this Truth is so certain that I can almost say I've seen Amadís de Gaula with my own eyes—he was a tall fellow, light complected, with a nice black beard, neither stern nor gentle in his bearing, a man of few words, slow to anger, and quickly appeased. And the way I've pictured Amadís, I could, I think, describe all the knights-errant in the world told about in the histories. Given my understanding of them through their histories, and by their deeds and characteristics, one can postulate, through sound reasoning, what their facial features, complexion, and stature were."

"How tall does your grace, my *señor* don Quixote, think the giant Morgante* was?" said the barber.

"In the matter of giants," responded don Quixote, "there are different opinions as to whether or not they existed in the world. But Holy Scripture, which cannot stray an atom from the truth, tells us the history of that big Philistine Goliath, who was seven and a half cubits tall,† which is an inordinate size. Also on the island of Sicily they've found some shinbones and shoulder blades so big that it proves their owners were gigantic,‡ as tall as towers—geometry takes away all doubt from this truth. But I can't determine with certainty just how big Morgante was, although I have to conclude he wasn't very tall. I give this opinion because in the history that makes particular mention of his deeds, it says he frequently slept under a roof, and if he could find a house to contain him, it's clear he can't have been inordinately large."

"That's right," said the priest, who, enjoying hearing him say such foolish things, asked him if he could describe the faces of Reinaldos de Montalbán and of don Roland,

---

* For Morgante, see Part I, chapter one, page 22.
† In I Samuel 17:4, Goliath is really only *six* and a half cubits tall: nine feet, nine inches.
‡ This refers to mastodon bones found in the Middle Ages on the slopes of Mount Etna.

and the other peers of France, since all of them had been knights-errant.

"About Reinaldos," responded don Quixote, "I venture to say that he had a wide, ruddy face, with twinkling—and rather protruding—eyes, excessively suspicious and wrathful, a friend of thieves and lost souls. Of Roland, or Rotolando or Orlando—for by these three names he was known in the histories—I'm of the opinion, in fact, I affirm that he was of medium height, wide in the shoulders, a bit bowlegged, dark complected and with a red beard, his body hairy, and with a menacing appearance, of few words, but very courteous and well behaved."

"If Roland was no more handsome than your grace has stated," replied the priest, "it's no wonder that *señora* Angélica the Beautiful scorned him for the elegance, dash, and wit that the little soft-bearded Moor to whom she gave herself must have had, and that she was wise in choosing to adore Medoro's* softness over the harshness of Roland."

"That Angélica," responded don Quixote, "*señor* priest, was a licentious flirt, and somewhat capricious, and left the world filled as much with her indiscretions as with the fame of her beauty. She disdained a thousand lords, a thousand warriors, and a thousand discerning men, and satisfied herself with that little dandy with no income or any reputation except what he got through loyalty to his friend.† The great singer of her beauty, the famous Ariosto, not daring or not caring to sing about what happened after her vile surrender—and it couldn't have been anything overly wholesome—bade her farewell with these lines:

> How she received the scepter of Cathay,
> another, with better plectrum, will sing someday.‡

"And this without a doubt was like a prophecy, especially since poets are also known as VATES, or fortune-tellers. One sees this evident truth because since then a famous

---

* See Part I, chapter twenty-five, page 214.
† This was the devotion that he had for his master, Dardinel.
‡ The second line of this couplet is the last line of Part I, in Italian there.

Andalusian poet wept and sang of her tears, and another famous and unique Castilian poet praised her beauty."*

"Tell me, *señor* don Quixote," said the barber, "hasn't there been—among those who have praised her—some poet who has written a satire about that *señora* Angélica?"

"Maybe," responded don Quixote, "for if Sacripante† or Roland had been poets, they would have satirized the maiden, because it's proper and natural for poets who are disdained and turned down by their ladies (imaginary or not), by those that they chose to be the mistresses of their hearts, to avenge themselves with satires and lampoons, a vengeance certainly unworthy of generous hearts. But up to now no discrediting verse has come to my notice against *señora* Angélica, who turned the world topsy-turvy."

"That's a miracle," said the priest.

And just then they heard the housekeeper and niece, who had left during the conversation, shouting in the patio, and they all went to see what it was about.

Chapter II. Which deals with the notable struggle that Sancho Panza had with don Quixote's niece and housekeeper, with other amusing matters.

THE HISTORY relates that the noises don Quixote, the priest, and the barber heard were from the niece and housekeeper, who were yelling at Sancho and barring his way at the door, while he was struggling to get inside to see don Quixote.

"What does this lowlife want in this house? Go home, brother! It's you and no one else who delude and entice my master to go away, and take him down those byroads."

To which Sancho responded: "Satan's housekeeper! The enticed and the deluded one is me, and not your master. He

---

* The Andalusian poet is Barahona de Soto, who wrote *The Tears of Angélica* (1586), a book that was in don Quixote's library (see Part I, chapter six, page 59). It was Lope de Vega who wrote *The Beauty of Angélica* (1602).

† A character in *Orlando Furioso*, referred to in error in Part I, chapter ten, page 81.

took me off through the world. You're badly mistaken; he enticed *me* away from my home with deceptions, promising me an *ínsula* I'm still waiting for."

"May you choke on bad *ínsulas*," responded the niece. "Damn you, Sancho, and what are *ínsulas*, anyway? Are they something to eat, you glutton?"

"You don't eat them," replied Sancho. "You govern and rule them, and they're better than four cities and four judge-ships."

"All the same," said the housekeeper, "you'll not come in here, you bag of misdeeds and sack of wickedness. Go govern your house and work your fields, and stop looking for *ínsulas* or *ínsulos*.*

The priest and barber were delighted to hear the conversation of the three of them, but don Quixote—fearing that Sancho would open up and spew out a pile of foolishness, and would touch on things not to his master's credit—called him and told the two women to be quiet and let him come in. Sancho went in, and the priest and barber took leave of don Quixote, despairing about his recovery, seeing how set he was in his extravagant thoughts and how immersed he was in the simplicity of his ill-errant chivalry, and so the priest said to the barber: "You'll see, my friend, how when least we expect it, our *hidalgo* will be off on another expedition."

"I don't doubt that," said the barber, "but I'm not so much amazed at the madness of the knight as I am at the simplicity of the squire, who is so confident about that *ínsula* business. No matter how we try to enlighten him, it won't be enough to get it out of his head."

"May God help both of them," said the priest, "and let's keep on the lookout. We'll see what becomes of these absurdities of the knight and squire. It looks like the two were cast from the same mold and that the master's lunacy wouldn't be worth an *ardite* without the servant's foolishness."

"That's right," responded the barber, "and I'd really like to find out what the two are talking about."

"I'm sure," responded the priest, "the niece and house-keeper will tell us afterward, because they're certainly going to listen in."

---

* *Ínsulos* is a nonsense word.

Meanwhile, don Quixote shut himself up in his room with Sancho, and when they were alone, he said: "It distresses me quite a bit, Sancho, that you've said I was the one who took you from your cottage, even though you knew that I didn't stay at home either. Together we set out, together we went off, and together we roamed—a common fortune and a common fate have befallen both of us. If they blanketed you once, they beat me up a hundred times, and this is where I've come out ahead of you."

"That seems reasonable," responded Sancho, "because, as your grace says, misfortunes are more suited to knights-errant than they are to their squires."

"You're mistaken, Sancho," said don Quixote. "According to that old saying: *quando caput dolet, &c.*"*

"I don't understand any other language but my own," responded Sancho.

"What I mean," said don Quixote, "is that when your head hurts, the rest of your body hurts along with it, and since I'm your master and lord, I'm your head and you're a part of me, since you're my servant; for this reason any suffering that may come to me has to affect you, and vice versa."

"That's the way it should have been," said Sancho, "but when they were blanketing me, as a part of your body, there was my head on the other side of the fence, watching me fly through the air, without feeling any pain at all. Since the parts of the body are supposed to feel the pain in the head, the head should feel their pain, too."

"Do you mean to say, Sancho," responded don Quixote, "that I didn't suffer when they were blanketing you? If you do say it, stop! Don't even think it, since I felt more pain in my soul than you did in your body. But let's let this go for the moment—there'll be time to consider this and settle the matter. So, tell me, Sancho, what are they saying about me in town? What do the common folk say about me? What do the *hidalgos* and knights say? What do they say about my bravery, about my deeds, and about my courtesy? What is being said about my having resuscitated and brought back to the world the now forgotten order of chivalry? I

---

* *Cuando caput dolet, cætera membra dolent* ("When the head hurts, the other members hurt"). Latin proverb.

want you, Sancho, to tell me exactly what has come to your ears, and you have to tell me without adding anything to the good or taking away anything from the bad, for faithful vassals are supposed to tell the truth to their masters as it really is, without exaggerating the good things nor diminishing the bad out of respect. And I want you to know, Sancho, that if the naked truth reached the ears of important people, without being dressed in flattery, things would be quite different, and other eras would be held more as Iron Ages, more so than ours, which I consider to be the Golden Age."*

"I'll do that with pleasure," responded Sancho, "on the condition that your grace won't be angry about what I say, since you want me to repeat it stark naked without putting more clothes on it than the way it came to me."

"In no way will I get angry," responded don Quixote. "You can speak freely without beating around the bush, Sancho."

"Well, the first thing I can say," he said, "is that the common people think you're totally crazy and that I'm no less a fool. The *hidalgos* say that you're not satisfied just being a member of their class, but have insisted on adding a *don* to your name† and have dared to call yourself a knight with just four grapevines and two yokes of land,‡ wearing a shirt that's nothing but tatters. The knights say that they don't want *hidalgos* trying to rival them, especially the squirely ones who polish their shoes with soot and darn their black socks with green thread."

"That," said don Quixote, "has nothing to do with me, since I'm always well dressed and never wear mended clothing§—threadbare, maybe, but most of that damage is

---

* There has been lots of speculation here, since don Quixote has said that he lives in the Iron Age (Part I, chapter eleven), and that the Golden Age is long past.

† In Cervantes' time only certain nobility had the right to precede their first name with *don*, equivalent to the British *sir*.

‡ A yoke of land was the area a pair of oxen could plow in one day (a yoke equals a pair of oxen).

§ It was considered bad for *hidalgos* to wear mended, patched clothing, although threadbare was all right. Mended clothing was for the working class.

due to the wear and tear caused by my armor and not by its wearing out through time."

"Insofar as your grace's bravery, courtesy, deeds, and endeavors are concerned," Sancho went on, "there are differing opinions: some say 'crazy but amusing,' others say 'valiant but unfortunate,' still others, 'courteous but ill-advised.' There are so many things being said about us that they haven't left either of us with a sound bone in our bodies."

"Look, Sancho," said don Quixote, "wherever there's a high level of virtue, it's attacked. Few or none of the famous men who passed this way have not been slandered with malice. Julius Cæsar, a very spirited, very prudent, and very brave captain, was regarded as ambitious and thought to be not very clean, either in his clothing or in his customs. Alexander, whose deeds earned him fame as being GREAT, is said to have been a bit of a drunk. About Hercules— the one of the many labors—they say that he was lascivious and effeminate. Of don Galaor, the brother of Amadís de Gaula, it's murmured that he was more than somewhat lustful, and of his brother, they say he was a whiner. So, Sancho, amidst so much slander lashed out at these good men, what has been said about me is insignificant."

"There's the rub, on my father's grave," replied Sancho.

"You mean, there's more?" asked don Quixote.

"'The tail has yet to be skinned,'" said Sancho. "You haven't heard anything yet, but if your grace wants to find out everything about the slanders they're laying on you, I'll bring over someone right now who can tell you about them all, without omitting anything. Last night Bartolomé Carrasco's son came back home—he was studying at Salamanca and is now a bachelor—and when I went to greet him, he told me that the history of your grace is circulating in books with the title *Ingenious* Hidalgo *don Quixote de La Mancha*. And he says that they mention me in it with my real name, Sancho Panza, and *señora* Dulcinea del Toboso, too, and other things that happened to us when we were alone. It made me cross myself in amazement how the historian who wrote it could have known about everything."

"I assure you, Sancho," said don Quixote, "that some wise enchanter must be the author of our history, since nothing of what they want to write about is hidden from them."

"But how," said Sancho, "can he be wise and an enchanter if—according to the bachelor Sansón Carrasco, because that's the name of the fellow I mentioned—the author is named Cide Hamete Berenjena!"*

"That's a Moorish name," responded don Quixote.

"That's right," responded Sancho, "because I've heard that the Moors are fond of *berenjenas*."

"You must, Sancho," said don Quixote, "be mistaken about the last name of that Cide, which in Arabic means *señor*."

"That may be," replied Sancho, "but if your grace wants me to have him come over here, I can go get him in a hurry."

"It will please me quite a bit, my friend," said don Quixote, "for what you told me has me very anxious, and I won't eat anything that tastes good until I've learned everything."

"All right, I'm going to get him," responded Sancho.

And leaving his master, he went to fetch the bachelor, and came back with him in a short while, and among the three of them there ensued a very amusing conversation.

Chapter III. About the laughable conversation that took place between don Quixote, Sancho Panza, and the bachelor, Sansón Carrasco.

Don Quixote was quite preoccupied while waiting for the bachelor Carrasco, from whom he hoped to hear what it was they said about him in a book, as Sancho had reported, but he couldn't persuade himself that such a history could exist, since the blood on the blade of his sword from the enemies he'd slain wasn't dry, and yet they were telling him that his high chivalric deeds were already circulating in print. With all this he imagined that some enchanter, either a friend or an enemy, through the art of magic, must have published them—if a friend, to magnify and exalt them

---

* *Berenjena* means "eggplant" in Spanish.

over the most outstanding feats of knight-errantry; if an enemy, to humble them and place them beneath the most despicable acts that had ever been written about a pathetic squire, although—he said to himself—deeds of squires were never written about. And yet if there really was such a history, since it was about a knight-errant, it had to be grandiloquent, noble, distinguished, magnificent, and true.

With this in mind, he was somewhat consoled, but it unsettled him to think that its author was a Moor, since his name was preceded by CIDE, and from the Moors you couldn't expect anything true at all, because they're all deceivers, liars, and troublemakers. He feared that the matter of his love might have been handled indecently, resulting in discredit to and detriment of *señora* Dulcinea del Toboso's chastity. He hoped that the author would have declared the faithfulness and respect that he always kept for her, scorning queens, empresses, and maidens of every rank, and holding in check the impulses of his natural inclinations. And so, immersed and wrapped up in these and other thoughts, Sancho and Carrasco found him, and don Quixote received the latter with great courtesy.

The bachelor, although he was named Sansón,* was not very big, although he was a great jokester, and his complexion was a bit pallid, but he had a keen intelligence. He was about twenty-four years old, round-faced, snub-nosed, and with a large mouth, all of these features being signs of a mischievous personality and with a liking for jokes and jests, as he showed when he met don Quixote, kneeling in front of him and saying: "Give me your hands, your greatness, *señor* don Quixote de La Mancha. By the habit of St. Peter I'm wearing,† although I only have the first four orders, I swear your grace is one of the most famous knights-errant there ever have been, or will ever be on the face of the earth. Blessed be Cide Hamete Benengeli, who wrote

---

* The biblical Samson was very strong. For example, in Judges 16:3 it says: "[Samson] rose, seized hold of the doors of the city gate and the two posts, pulled them out, bar and all, hoisted them onto his shoulders and carried them to the top of the hill. . . ."

† Swearing on your habit is like swearing on a Bible. Sansón is just a member of the secular clergy at this point, with only the first four orders.

the history of your great deeds, and blessed be once more the curious fellow who took the care to have them translated from Arabic into our common Castilian for the universal enjoyment of all."

Don Quixote made him stand up, and said: "So, it's true that there's a history about me and that it's a Moor and a sage who wrote it?"

"It's so true, *señor*," said Sansón, "that I'm convinced that as of now there are more than twelve thousand copies of that history in print. And if you don't believe it, just ask around in Portugal, Barcelona, and Valencia, where they were printed. There's even a rumor that it's being printed in Antwerp,* and it seems to me that there will be no nation or language that will not have its own translation."†

"One of the things," said don Quixote, "that must please a virtuous and eminent man the most is to see himself, while still living, spoken about with a good name by the tongues of men. I said WITH A GOOD NAME because if it were the opposite, no death would be its equal."

"If it's a question of good reputation and renown," said the bachelor, "your grace takes the palm over all other knights-errant, because the Moor in his language and the Christian in his were careful to depict in a very lively way your gallantry, your courage in facing danger, your patience

---

* In real life, editions of the *Quixote* preceding the publication of the second part were produced in Madrid, Lisbon, Valencia (1605), Brussels (1607), and Milan (1610). The first Barcelona edition was of both parts in 1617. The first edition in Antwerp was in 1673. Rodríguez Marín (volume IV, p. 82) calculated that the first ten printings done until 1610 would have totaled, conservatively, fifteen thousand copies. Let's give Sansón the benefit of the doubt for the total printed in his world.

† In this, Sansón was quite right. The *Quixote* has been translated into virtually every important Western language, and many from elsewhere: Afrikaans, Albanian, Arabic, Armenian, Basque, Bulgarian, Catalan, Chinese, Croatian, Czech, Danish, Dutch, English, Esperanto, Finnish, Flemish, French, Gaelic, German, Hebrew, Hindustani, Indonesian, Italian, Japanese, Kashmiri, Korean, Mallorquín, Norwegian, Polish, Portuguese, Provençal, Rumanian, Russian, Sanskrit, Serbian, Slovenian, Swedish, Tagalog, Tibetan, Turkish, Ukrainian, Welsh, and Yiddish (not every one of these is complete, and several languages have multiple translations).

in adversity, your sufferance in misfortunes and wounds, and the chastity and restraint of your Platonic love for your and my lady doña Dulcinea del Toboso."

"I've never," said Sancho, "heard my lady Dulcinea referred to as DOÑA, only just THE LADY DULCINEA DEL TOBOSO, and in this the story has made a mistake."

"That's not a bad mistake," responded Carrasco.

"Certainly not," responded don Quixote. "But tell me, your grace, *señor* bachelor, what deeds of mine are most praised in this history?"

"Well," responded the bachelor, "there are different opinions, as there are different tastes—some say the adventure of the windmills, which to your grace appeared Briaræuses and giants; others say it was the one of the fulling mills; this one, the description of the two armies, which appeared afterward to be two flocks of sheep; that one extols the adventure of the dead body they were taking to Segovia to be buried; one says that the best one of all was the releasing of the galley slaves; another says that none equals the one about the two giant Benedictine monks, together with the battle with the brave Basque."

"Tell me, *señor* bachelor," said Sancho, "do they include the adventure of the Yangüesans, when our good Rocinante felt like asking for impossible things?"

"The enchanter left nothing in the inkwell," responded Sansón. "He says and notes everything, even the capers that the good Sancho cut in the blanket."

"I cut no capers in the blanket," said Sancho. "In the air, yes, and even more than I would have liked."

"The way I imagine it," said don Quixote, "there's no history in the world that doesn't have its ups and downs, especially those that deal with chivalry, which are never filled only with favorable outcomes."

"Yet some readers," responded the bachelor, "who have read the history say that they'd have preferred it if the author had left out some of the infinite thwacks that *señor* don Quixote received on several occasions."

"There's where the truth of the story comes in," said Sancho.

"Out of fairness, they didn't need to mention them all," said don Quixote, "since there's no reason to write about actions that don't alter the truth of the history, if they're likely to redound to the derision of the hero. I mean, Æneas wasn't as pious as Virgil describes him, and Ulysses wasn't as judicious as Homer portrays him."

"That's right," replied Sansón, "but it's one thing to write as a poet and another thing as a historian. The poet can relate or sing things not as they were but as they should have been, but the historian must write things not as they should have been but rather as they were, without adding or taking away anything at all."

"Well, if this Moor is supposed to tell the truth," said Sancho, "it must be that among the thwacks given to my master, mine doubtless are mentioned there as well, because they never measured his grace's shoulders without measuring my whole body. But there's no reason for me to marvel at that, since, as my master says, the rest of the body has to feel the pain in the head."

"You're a jokester, Sancho," responded don Quixote. "I swear your memory doesn't fail you when you want to remember something."

"Even if I wanted to forget those thwacks with a club they gave me," said Sancho, "the welts, which are still fresh on my back, won't let me."

"Hush, Sancho," said don Quixote, "and don't interrupt the *señor* bachelor, whom I ask to continue telling me what the history tells about me."

"And about me," said Sancho, "for they say I'm one of the main parsonages in it."

"*Per*sonages, not *par*sonages, friend Sancho," said Sansón.

"Here's another critic of words," said Sancho, "and if that keeps up we won't finish in my lifetime."

"By golly, Sancho," responded the bachelor, "if you aren't the second most important person in the history, and there are people who prefer to hear you talk over the best of them, but there are others who say you were too gullible in believing that you'd become governor of the *ínsula* promised by *señor* don Quixote."

"There's still time," said don Quixote, "and as Sancho gets older, with the experience afforded by his years, he'll be more suited and able to be a governor, more so than now."

"By God, *señor*," said Sancho, "if I can't govern the *ín-*

sula now at my age, I won't be able to govern it when I'm as old as Methuselah.* The trouble is that the *ínsula* in question is out there somewhere—I don't know where—and not that I don't have the brains to govern it."

"Put it in God's hands," said don Quixote. "Everything will turn out fine, and perhaps better than you think—because the leaves on the trees don't stir unless God so wills it."

"That's the truth," said Sansón. "If God pleases, Sancho won't lack a thousand islands† to govern, not to mention just one."

"I've seen governors," replied Sancho, "who, in my opinion, don't reach the sole of my shoe, and even so they're called LORDSHIP, and they're served on silver plates."

"Those aren't governors of *ínsulas*," replied Sansón, "but rather of other more manageable realms—governors of *ínsulas* at least need to know grammar."

"I know something about GRAMS, said Sancho, "but I don't have any idea about MYRRH, because I don't know what it is. But leaving the matter of the government in the hands of God, who can send me wherever He pleases. I say, *señor* bachelor Sansón Carrasco, it pleases me infinitely that the author of the history has spoken about me in a way that what is told about me offends no one. I swear as a good squire that if he'd said things unbefitting the Old Christian that I am, the deaf would have heard about it."

"That would be working miracles," responded Sansón.

"Miracles or not," said Sancho, "everyone should be careful with what they say or write about people, and not say willy-nilly the first thing that comes to mind."

"One of the blemishes they say the story has," said the bachelor, "is that its author included a novella called 'The Ill-Advised Curiosity.' Not that it's bad or poorly written, but because it's out of place and doesn't have anything to do with the history of *señor* don Quixote."

"I'll bet," replied Sancho, "that the son of a dog has mixed everything up."

"I think," said don Quixote, "that the author of my his-

---

* In Genesis 5:27 we read that Methuselah lived 969 years.

† Whereas up to now everyone has used the old literary term for island (*ínsula*), here Sansón uses the standard word.

534 *Miguel de Cervantes Saavedra*

tory wasn't an enchanter but some ignorant chatterbox who just began writing willy-nilly and without any plan, no matter how it would turn out, like Orbaneja,* the painter from Úbeda,† who, when they asked him what he was painting, would say: 'Whatever turns out.' Perhaps he'd paint a rooster in such a way and so badly that he'd have to print next to it in Gothic letters:‡ 'THIS IS A ROOSTER.' That's what my history must be like—it'll need commentary to understand it."

"No, not that," responded Sansón, "because it's so clear that there isn't anything difficult in it. Children rummage through it, young people read it, adults understand it, and old people praise it. Finally it's so well-worn, so widely read, and so well-known by all types of people, that hardly will they see some skinny nag when they'll say: 'There goes Rocinante,' and those who have read it the most are the pages. There's no antechamber of a lord where a *Don Quixote* isn't found. Some take it when others put it down; these grab it and those ask for it. That history is among the most pleasurable and least harmful entertainments that has ever been seen, because in the whole thing you won't find even a hint of an unchaste word or a thought that isn't Catholic."

"Writing any other way," said don Quixote, "wouldn't be writing truths, but lies—and historians who use lies should be burned like counterfeiters. I don't know what moved the author to use irrelevant novellas and stories when he had so much to write just about me. He doubtless was thinking of the proverb 'whether with straw or with hay, &c.'§ In truth, just to record my thoughts, my sighs, my tears, my good intentions, and my undertakings, it would take a volume of work larger than, or at least as big as, the works of El Tostado.¶ Indeed, what I think, *señor* bachelor, is that

---

* Nothing is known about this painter Orbaneja.

† Úbeda (pop. 28,000) is the commercial center for the surrounding agricultural area. It is north of Granada.

‡ Gothic letters here, according to Gaos, were large capital letters. These would be different from the Gothic letters mentioned in Part I, chapter fifty-two, page 492.

§ The proverb continues: 'my stomach is full either way.'

¶ Alonso de Madrigal (El Tostado) (1400–1455) was bishop of Ávila. His complete works total thirty-one volumes, twenty-one of which are biblical commentaries in Latin.

it requires fine judgment and a mature understanding to write histories and books of any kind—and to write with grace and wit requires great talent. The shrewdest character in a play is the fool, because the person who wants to be taken for a fool must not be one himself. History is like a sacred thing, because it has to be true, and where truth is, God is as well, insofar as the truth goes. Aside from this, there are some who write books and crank them out like doughnuts."

"There's no book so bad," said the bachelor, "that it doesn't have something good in it."*

"There's no doubt about that," replied don Quixote. "But frequently it happens that authors who have deservedly won and attained great reputation through their manuscripts, when they have them published, they lose their reputation, or at least damage it somewhat."

"The reason for this," said Sansón, "is that since printed works can be read slowly, it's easy to see their defects. And the more famous the author is, the more his works are scrutinized. People who are famous through their talent—great poets, illustrious historians—are always, or most of the time, envied by those who get both pleasure and entertainment from critiquing the writings of others without having brought any of their own to the light of day."

"This is not surprising," said don Quixote, "because there are many theologians who are not good in the pulpit, but are very good at seeing the defects or excesses of those who do preach."

"All that is correct, *señor* don Quixote," said Carrasco, "but I'd like for censors to be more merciful and less hypercritical, without stressing the spots on the brilliant sun they're criticizing, because if *aliquando dormitat Homerus*,† they should consider how much time he spent awake to give light to his work with as little shadow as he could, and

---

* This is a maxim of Pliny the Elder (A.D. 23–79) found in his *Epistles*, III, 5.

† Sansón misquotes Horace very slightly (*Ars Poetica*, A.D. 359), which has *quandoque* instead of *aliquando*. It means "Sometimes Homer dozes ("makes mistakes"). Modern scholarship holds that "Homer," instead of being a single poet, is really a series of poets in the oral tradition; thus inconsistencies do crop up in the *Iliad*.

perhaps it might be that what seems bad to them could be moles that at times increase the beauty of the face that has them. And I say therefore that the person who decides to publish a book puts himself at great risk, since it's impossible to write one in such a way that will satisfy and please everyone who reads it."

"The book about me," said don Quixote, "must have pleased few."

"On the contrary, since *Stultorum infinitus est numerus*,* there're an infinite number who like that history. And some have found fault with the memory of the author, since he forgot to say who the thief was who stole Sancho's donkey, because it's not mentioned there, and you can only infer from the context that it's been stolen. Then a while later we see Sancho riding on his donkey's back, before it was returned. They also say that the author failed to set down what Sancho did with those hundred *escudos* he found in the Sierra Morena, because he never mentions it, and many want to know what he did with them, or what he spent them on, and that's one of the serious omissions in the work."

Sancho replied: "I, *señor* Sansón, am not about to get into accountings or explanations. My stomach is growling, and if I don't take care of it with a couple of swallows of wine, I'll get punctured by St. Lucy's thorn.† I have some at home; my wife is waiting for me. And after I eat I'll come back and will answer all your questions about the loss of the donkey as well as what I spent the hundred *escudos* on."

And without waiting for a response or saying another word, he went home. Don Quixote asked and even begged the bachelor to stay and take potluck with him. The bachelor accepted the invitation and stayed. A couple of pigeons

---

* "There is an infinite number of stupid people," Ecclesiastes 1:15, in the Latin Vulgate Bible. Your copy of the Bible probably will not contain this phrase, which is the second half of the verse and is eliminated in most versions.

† This is an odd expression referring to getting weak from hunger. St. Lucy (A.D. 304), patron saint of Sicily. She was martyred by being stuck in the neck with a sword—could this sword be St. Lucy's thorn? In any case, what her life and works have to do with the meaning of the expression is obscure.

were added to the usual lunch. They spoke about chivalry over the meal, Carrasco indulging his state of mind, they slept the siesta, Sancho came back, and the previous conversation continued.

Chapter IIII. Where Sancho Panza satisfies the bachelor Sansón Carrasco's doubts and questions, with other events worthy of being known and told.

S ANCHO RETURNED to don Quixote's house, and going back to the conversation they were having, he said: "To answer what señor Sansón said he wanted to know about who, or how, or when my donkey was stolen: In response I'll say that the same night we were fleeing from the Holy Brotherhood, we went into the Sierra Morena. After the unfortunate adventure of the galley slaves and of the dead body that was being taken to Segovia, my master and I went into a dense forest, where my master, leaning against his lance and I on my donkey, beaten up and weary from the recent frays, went to sleep as if we were on four feather mattresses. I especially slept with such a deep sleep that whoever he was found it possible to come and prop me up on four stakes that he put under the four corners of the packsaddle, in such a way that he left me propped up in the saddle and was able to slip the donkey out from under me without my noticing it."

"That's an easy ruse and nothing new.* The same thing happened to Sacripante, when he was at the siege of Albraca and the famous thief Brunelo was able to take his horse from under him using this same device."†

"At dawn," Sancho went on, "hardly had I stretched when the stakes gave way and I fell to the ground. I looked for the donkey and when I didn't see him, tears came to my eyes and I made such a lamentation that if the author of our history didn't include it, he left out something good,

---

* This quote is not attributed to either don Quixote or to Sansón, so editors and translators attribute it variously to one or the other. You decide.

† This is from stanza eighty-four of the twenty-seventh canto of *Orlando Furioso*.

trust me. I don't know how many days later, when I was going along with the Princess Micomicona, I recognized my donkey, and riding it was that trickster and rogue that my master and I had set free from his chains, Ginés de Pasamonte, dressed as a gypsy."

"That's not the mistake," replied Sansón, "but rather that before the donkey came back, the author says that Sancho was riding it."

"I don't know how to respond to that," said Sancho, "except that maybe the historian made a mistake or the printer was careless."

"That must be it," said Sansón, "but what happened to the hundred *escudos*? Did they disappear?"

Sancho responded: "I spent them for the benefit of myself and my wife and my children,* and they're the reason that my wife is patient while I travel the highways and byways serving my master, *señor* don Quixote. If I'd come home after so much time without a *blanca* and without my donkey, it would have been rough going. And if you want to find out anything else, here I am, and I'll answer to the king himself in person, though it's nobody's business if I brought or didn't bring, if I spent or didn't spend. If the thwacks I got on these trips were to be paid in money, even if they were paid at the rate of four *maravedís* each, another hundred *escudos* wouldn't cover even half. Let each one put his hand over his heart and not try to say that 'white is black and black is white,' because 'everyone is as God made him, and even worse at times.'"

"I'll make sure," said Carrasco, "to tell the author if he prints it again, not to forget what good Sancho has said, and the book will be enhanced by a great deal over what it is."

"Is there anything else to fix in the text, *señor* bachelor?" asked don Quixote.

"There must be," he answered, "but none is as important as what was already mentioned."

---

* Sancho says later, in chapter twenty-eight of Part II, that he earned two *ducados* a month when he worked for Bartolomé Carrasco, which must have been enough to support his family. The *ducado* and the *escudo* were equivalent, so you can imagine how much money these one hundred *escudos* represented—more than what he would earn in four years toiling for Sansón's father.

"And, by chance," said don Quixote, "does the author promise a second part?"

"Yes, he does," responded Sansón, "but he says that he hasn't found it, nor does he know who has it, and so we don't know if it will come out or not. For that reason, and also because, as some say: 'Sequels are never good' and others say: 'What has been written about don Quixote is enough,' it's doubtful that there will be a second part, although some, more jovial than saturnine,* say: 'Let's have more Quixoteries, let don Quixote charge and let Sancho Panza talk, and whatever comes of it, we'll be content.'"

"And, what is the author waiting for?"

"He's waiting," responded Sansón, "to find the story he's looking for with such diligence, and when he finds it he'll take it to the printer right away, moved more by the profit he'll make than from any praise that might come."

To which Sancho said: "The author is just looking for profit and income? It'll be a wonder if he can succeed, because he'll just work fast like the tailor the night before Easter, and work you do in a hurry is never done with the perfection that it requires. Let this *señor* Moor, or whatever he is, take his time, and be careful about what he's doing, and me and my master will give him such an abundance of adventures and different incidents that he'll be able to write not only a second part, but a hundred of them. The good fellow must doubtless be thinking that we're just loafing—well, just 'let him hold up our hooves to be shod and he'll see which one we limp on.'† What I know is that if my master would take my advice we should be out in the open right now redressing grievances and righting wrongs, as is the custom with knights-errant."

Sancho had barely said these words when the neighs of Rocinante reached their ears. Don Quixote took them as a very good omen, and he resolved to initiate another expedition in three or four days. Declaring his intention to the bachelor, he asked his advice where he should begin his

---

* More jovial than sad. From the astrological signs of Jove and Saturn.

† Sancho mixes two proverbs: "You didn't hold his foot while he was being shod?" and "I know which of my feet is lame." It means something like: "Let him get to know us and he'll see who we are."

journey. The bachelor answered that he thought he should go to the kingdom of Aragón and to the city of Zaragoza, where a few days hence they were going to hold some very solemn jousts for the festival of St. George,* in which he could gain renown over all the Aragonese knights, which would be like gaining it over all the knights in the world. He praised don Quixote's very honorable and very valiant resolve, and told him to be careful when he engaged in dangerous undertakings, since his life was not his own, but rather belonged to those who needed him so he could protect and rescue them in their misfortunes.

"That's what I'm complaining about, *señor* Sansón," Sancho said at this point, "for my master will attack a hundred men in armor just like a sweet-toothed boy will attack half a dozen watermelons. By golly, *señor* bachelor, there are times to attack and times to withdraw. And not everything has to be 'St. James, and close in, Spain!'† And there's more, because I've heard tell, and I believe it was my master who said it, if I'm not mistaken, that between the extremes of cowardice and recklessness is the middle ground of valor, and if this is so, he shouldn't attack when the odds are against him. But above all if my master wants me to go with him, it has to be on the condition that *he* has to do all the fighting, and that I'm obliged only to look after his person in matters of cleanliness and comfort, and in this I'll see that his desires are taken care of. But to think that I'll put my hand on my sword, even against rustic brigands with hatchets and wearing leather helmets, is to think the unthinkable. I, *señor* Sansón, don't plan to get famous as a brave person, but rather as the best and most loyal squire that ever served a knight-errant. And if my master don Quixote, obliged by my many and good services, should want to give me an *ínsula* from the many he said he's bound to come across out there, I'll get great pleasure in it. And if he doesn't give me one, I'm alive, and a man shouldn't live under another's protection, only God's; and what's more, my

---

* St. George is the patron saint of Zaragoza; his feast day is April 23, but the knights of Zaragoza held jousts in his honor three times a year in the bullring.

† This is the old Spanish battle cry, used in wars against the Moors. In Spanish, "close in" means "attack."

bread will taste as good, if not better, without a government than if I'm a governor, for do I know, by chance, if the devil hasn't planted some stumbling block where I'll trip and fall and break my teeth? I was born Sancho and Sancho I plan to die—but with all this, suddenly, without a lot of bother and risk, if heaven should present me with some *ínsula* or something like it, I'm not so stupid that I wouldn't accept it. They also say: 'when they give you the heifer, go fetch the halter' and 'when good luck comes, take it home.' "

"You, Sancho," said Carrasco, "have spoken like a professor, but still, trust in God and in *señor* don Quixote, who will give you a kingdom, not just an *ínsula*."

"It's all the same to me," responded Sancho, "although I can tell *señor* Carrasco that my master won't be putting the kingdom that he might give me into a bag with a hole in the bottom. I've taken my pulse and I find that I'm healthy enough to govern kingdoms and *ínsulas*, and I've told this to my master on other occasions."

"Listen, Sancho," said Sansón, "professions change one's customs, and it might be that when you see yourself a governor, you would even shun the mother who bore you."

"That may be true," responded Sancho, "with those of low birth, but not with those who have three inches of Old Christian fat on their souls, as I do. Look at me—would I be ungrateful to anyone?"

"Let's put it in God's hands," said don Quixote. "We'll see when the governorship comes—I can practically see it now right in front of my eyes."

After he said this, he asked the bachelor, if he was a poet, to do him the favor of writing some farewell verses he hoped to deliver to his lady Dulcinea del Toboso, and told him that each verse should begin with a letter from her name, so that, when it was all written, the first letters would spell out Dulcinea del Toboso.

The bachelor answered that although he was not one of the famous poets in Spain—for there were only three and a half such—he wouldn't fail to write those verses; although there was one difficulty about its composition, and that was that there were seventeen letters in her name,* and if

---

* But note the seventeen-line sonnet at the end of chapter fifty-two of the first part. And it's already dedicated to Dulcinea, too.

he made four stanzas of four lines each, it would be one letter short, and if they were of five lines, such as *décimas* or *redondillas*,* there would be three letters left over. But even so he promised to try to remove a letter somewhere so that four four-line stanzas would work out for the name Dulcinea del Toboso.

"That has to be done no matter what," said don Quixote, "because if the name isn't obvious and clear, there's no woman who would believe those verses were written for her."

They settled on this and agreed that the departure would be a week hence. Don Quixote charged the bachelor to keep it a secret, especially from the priest and *maese* Nicolás the barber, and from his niece and the housekeeper, so they wouldn't thwart his honorable and brave resolve. Carrasco so promised and took his leave, requesting that don Quixote keep him apprised of his good or bad fortunes when he could, and so they all said good-bye, and Sancho went to get things in order for their journey.

Chapter V. About the wise and amusing conversation between Sancho Panza and his wife, Teresa Panza, and other events worthy of happy remembrance.

WHEN THE translator of this history begins to write this fifth chapter, he says that he thinks it's apocryphal, because in it Sancho Panza speaks in a way quite different from what could be expected from his limited intelligence, and he says such subtle things that the translator thinks it's impossible that he could know them. But he didn't want to refuse to translate it, to comply with the obligations of his profession, and so he continued, saying:

Sancho went home so joyful and jubilant that his wife could see how happy he was from a crossbow shot away, so much

---

* At the time, *décimas* were made up of two five-line stanzas. The *redondilla* is typically associated today with a four-line stanza, but there were other possibilities. This is not a mistake.

so that she felt she should ask: "What's happened, Sancho, my friend, that makes you so happy?"

To which he answered: "Wife, if God so wished, I would be pleased not to be as happy as I seem."

"I don't understand you, husband," she replied, "and I don't know what you mean when you say you would be pleased, if God wished, if you weren't so happy, because, even though I'm not very smart, I don't know who it pleases not to be happy."

"Look, Teresa," responded Sancho, "I'm joyful because I've decided to serve my master once again. He wants to go out on a third expedition to seek adventures, and I'm going with him because I really want to go and I hope I'll find another hundred *escudos* like the ones already spent, although I'm sad to have to leave you and my children. And if God wanted to supply me with food in the comfort of my home, without my having to trudge along rough trails and pass through crossroads—and he could do it easily, just by willing it—it's obvious that my joy would be more lasting and certain, since it's mixed with the sadness of having to leave you. Thus I said well that I would be pleased, if God so wished, for me not to be so happy."

"Look, Sancho," replied Teresa, "since you've been a part of a knight-errant, you speak in such a roundabout way no one can understand you."

"It's enough for God to understand me, wife," responded Sancho. "He understands all things, and that's it. Be advised, sister, it's your job to look after the donkey these next three days so he'll be ready to bear arms. Double his feed, prepare the packsaddle and the other gear, because we're not going to a wedding, but rather to roam the world and to have it out with giants, dragons, and horrible monsters, and to hear whistles, roars, bellowing, and shouts. All this would be trivial if we didn't have to deal with Yangüesans and enchanted Moors."

"I believe, husband," replied Teresa, "that squires-errant earn the bread they eat, and so I'll stay here praying to Our Lord to deliver you from such misadventures."

"I tell you, wife," responded Sancho, "that if I didn't think I'd be a governor of an *ínsula* before long, I'd keel over."

"Not that, husband," said Teresa. "'Let the chicken live,

even with the pip.'* Live on, I say, and let the devil haul
off all the governments in the world. Without a government you came from your mother's womb, and you've
lived without a government until now, and without a government you'll go—or they'll carry you—to your grave,
when God pleases. How many are there in the world who
live without a government, yet don't cease to exist or be
counted among the living? 'The best gravy in the world
is hunger,' and since hunger is never lacking among the
poor, they always eat with pleasure. But look, Sancho, if
you by chance come into a government, don't forget me
and your children. You know that Sanchico is already fifteen years old and it's only right that he should start going to school, if his uncle the abbot is going to bring him
into the Church. And look, Mari Sancha, your daughter,
wouldn't die if we married her off—she gives me hints
that she'd like to have a husband, just like you want that
government, and when all is said and done, 'a daughter
who's an unhappy wife is better than one who's a happy
mistress.'"

"By my faith," responded Sancho, "if God should give
me something of a government, my wife, I'll marry Mari
Sancha so high that she'll have to be called LADYSHIP."

"Not that, Sancho," responded Teresa. "Marry her to her
equal, that's the best thing. If you take her out of her clogs
and put her in fine shoes, and from her gray flannel into
hoop skirts made of silk, and from MARICA and a simple
YOU to DOÑA and LADY SO-AND-SO, the poor girl won't
know where she is, and will commit a hundred gaffes at
every step, showing the thread of the coarse cloth she's cut
from."

"Hush, ninny," said Sancho. "She'll only have to practice
it for two or three years, and after that her rank and dignity
will fit her like a glove, and if not, what's the difference? It's
going to be LADYSHIP, and that's final!"

"Measure yourself, Sancho, against your equals," responded Teresa. "Don't try to raise your social level, and
remember the saying: 'clean off the nose of your neighbor's
child and take him to your house.' How would it be to marry

---

* This is a proverb meaning that it is better to live with a handicap than
not live at all. The pip is a tumor on the tongue.

our María to a big old count or to a fancy knight who would put her in her place whenever he felt like it by calling her a country girl, daughter of a clodhopper, and a thread spinner. Not while I'm alive, husband! I certainly didn't raise her for this! You bring home some money, and as for marrying her off, leave it to me. There's Lope Tocho, the son of Juan Tocho, a plump and healthy lad, and we know him, and I know that he has given her some interested glances, and with him, who's our equal, she'd be well married, and we'd always have them nearby, and we'll be a big family, parents and children, grandchildren and children-in-law, and the peace of God and His blessing would be among us. I won't have you marrying her off in those courts and in those big palaces where they won't understand her and where she won't fit."

"Tell me, you fool and Barabbas' wife," replied Sancho, "why do you want—for no reason—to prevent me from marrying my daughter to someone who will give me grandchildren who'll be known as YOUR LORDSHIP? Look, Teresa, I've always heard my elders say that anyone who doesn't catch hold of opportunity when it comes his way shouldn't complain when it passes him by. It wouldn't be good, now that it's knocking at our door, to slam the door in its face. Let's let ourselves be carried by this favorable wind at our backs." (It's this way of talking, and what Sancho says below, that made the translator of this history say that he thought this chapter was apocryphal.)

"Doesn't it seem to you, creature," Sancho went on, "that it'll be good for me to get myself into some profitable governorship that'll take our feet out of the mud? Let Mari Sancha marry whoever I want and you'll see that they'll call you DOÑA TERESA PANZA, and in church you'll sit on a pew cushion nestled in pillows and brocades, despite all the highborn ladies in the village. No, you just want to stay as you are, without growing larger or smaller—just like a tapestry figure! We won't talk of this again, because Sanchica will be a countess no matter what you say."

"Do you know what you're saying, husband?" responded Teresa. "With all this, I think that my daughter's count will be her ruination. Do what you want—make her a duchess or princess! But I can tell you that it will be against my will and without my consent. I always favored equality, brother, and I don't like to see people putting on airs for no reason. They called me Teresa at my baptism, a plain and simple name, without additions or trimmings, and without the adornment of DOÑA. Cascajo was my father's name, and they call me—being your wife—Teresa Panza, but by rights they should call me Teresa Cascajo. But 'kings go where laws want,'* and with this name I'm satisfied without their putting a DOÑA on top of it that will weigh so much you can hardly carry it. I don't want to give anyone the occasion to say, when they see me walking down the street dressed like a countess or a governor's wife: 'Look how conceited that repulsive woman is! Only yesterday she was spinning flax and went to Mass with her head covered by the tail of her skirt instead of a shawl, and today she goes with a hoopskirt and brooches, and haughty as well, as if we didn't know her.' If God lets me keep my seven or five senses, or however many I've got, I never plan to let myself get into such an awkward situation. You, brother, go and get to be governor, and be as conceited as you like, and my daughter and I won't move a step from our village, not on the life of my mother. 'The reputable woman has a broken leg and stays at home,' and 'the virtuous girl's recreation is keeping busy.'† Go with your don Quixote and with your adventures and leave us to our misfortune, because God will help us if we're good. . . . And I don't know who gave him the right to use DON, since his parents and his grandparents didn't use that title."

"I say now," replied Sancho, "that you have a devil inside your body! God help you, woman, how many things have you been stringing together without head or tail! What do gravel,‡ brooches, sayings, and haughtiness have to do with what I've been saying? Come, now, you ignorant blockhead—for that's what I should call you, since you don't understand my words and you seem to be fleeing from happiness—if I told my daughter to leap from a tower, or

---

* Teresa mixes this up: Laws go where kings want.
† The first part of this saying really means that a married woman, to be honorable, should stay at home. Here Teresa uses it to mean that she should not leave her village. The second part of the saying is more usual as: "The maiden should have a broken leg and a half."
‡ Teresa's maiden name, *Cascajo*, means "gravel."

to roam the world like the princess doña Urraca* wanted to, you'd be right in not yielding to my wishes. But, if in an instant and in the twinkling of an eye I give her a DOÑA and a LADYSHIP, taking her out of the fields and putting her under a canopy and on a dais in a drawing room with more velvet cushions than the Almohadas† in Morocco, why do you refuse to consent and not want what I also want?"

"Do you know why, husband?" responded Teresa. "Because of the proverb that says: 'he that covers you, discovers you.' All eyes pass the poor man by, but they stop on the rich man, and if that rich man was once poor, the gossiping and the cursing start. There's no stopping those backbiters, because there are lots of them in the streets, like swarms of bees."

"Look, Teresa," responded Sancho, "and listen to what I'm going to tell you, something you may have never heard in all the days of your life, and I'm not talking about me this time. All I'm going to say are maxims from the priest who was preaching last Lent in this town, and he said, if I remember correctly, that all things our eyes see as they are now remain in our memory much more than things we saw in the past do."

(All these words that Sancho is saying are the second reason that the translator holds this chapter to be apocryphal, because they exceed the mental capacity of Sancho, who went on saying:)

"So when we see a person decked out in rich clothing and with a show of servants, it seems that by force we're moved and invited to have respect for him, even though at that moment we recall a time when we saw him in a low state. That low condition—maybe due to poverty or lineage—since it's in the past, doesn't exist anymore, and there's only what we see right now. And if this person who

---

* This is from an old ballad that everyone knew, dealing with doña Urraca, Fernando I of Castile's daughter, who was so upset when she learned that only her brothers would inherit from their father that she said: "I'll roam these lands / like a bad woman / and this my body I would give / to whomever I wanted— / to Moors for money / and to Christians for free."

† *Almohadas* means "cushions." Sancho means Almohades, who held power starting in the twelfth century in Morocco and Spain.

Fortune raised from his low level—these were the priest's very words—to the heights of prosperity, assuming he's well mannered, liberal, and courteous with everyone, and doesn't try to vie with those who are noble by birth, be certain, Teresa, that no one will remember the way he was but will respect the way he is, if they aren't envious, from which no good fortune is safe."

"I don't understand you, husband," replied Teresa, "but do whatever you want and don't break my head with your harangues and rhetoric. And if you're revolved to doing what you say . . ."

"Re*solved*, you mean to say, wife," said Sancho, "and not re*volved*."

"Don't begin arguing with me, husband," said Teresa. "I speak the way God pleases and I don't beat around the bush. I say if you're fiercely determined to have that government, take your son, Sancho, with you and teach him right now how to govern, because it's a good thing for children to inherit and learn their professions from their parents."

"When I have my government," said Sancho, "I'll send for him right away, and I'll send you money—which I won't lack, since governors always have people to lend them money when they're short, and dress them in a way that hides what they are and makes them look like what they're going to be."

"You send the money," said Teresa, "and I'll put lots of clothing on him."

"So, we're agreed," said Sancho, "that our daughter will be a countess?"

"The day I see her a countess," responded Teresa, "I'll think I'm burying her. But once again I tell you to do whatever you want, because we women are born with this burden of being obedient to our husbands, even though they're blockheads."

And with this she began to cry with so much emotion that it was as if her daughter had died and was buried. Sancho consoled her, telling her that though he was bound to make her a countess, he'd postpone it as long as he could. With this their conversation ended, and Sancho went back to see don Quixote to arrange for their departure.

Chapter VI. About what happened to don Quixote with his niece and his housekeeper—one of the most important chapters in the entire history.

WHILE SANCHO Panza and his wife were having that irrelevant conversation, don Quixote's niece and housekeeper weren't idle, because by a thousand signs they began to suspect that their uncle and master wanted to escape for a third time and return to the profession of his—to them—illerrant chivalry. They tried every way they could think of to dissuade him from such a bad plan, but it was all preaching in the wilderness and pounding on cold iron. With all this, among other things, the housekeeper told him: "In truth, *señor mío*, if your grace doesn't behave and stay quietly at home, and if you go wandering about mountains and valleys, like a soul in torment, seeking what they say are called adventures—which I call misadventures—I'll complain loudly to God and the king so they can send some help."

To which don Quixote responded: "Housekeeper, I don't know how God will respond to your complaints, nor His Majesty either, and I only know that if I were the king, I would avoid responding to such an infinity of inconsequential petitions as they give him every day—for one of the annoyances that kings have to put up with is hearing and responding to every one of them, and I don't want my affairs added to his burden."

To which the housekeeper said: "Tell us, *señor*, are there knights in His Majesty's court?"

"Yes," responded don Quixote. "There are many of them, and it's proper for there to be, as an adornment to the greatness of princes, and for glory of royal majesty."

"So, shouldn't your grace," she replied, "be one of those who, without moving a step, serves the king in his court?"

"Look, my friend," responded don Quixote, "not all knights can be courtly, nor can—or should—the courtly knights be errant. In the world there must be both kinds, and although we're all knights, there's a lot of difference between the one and the other, because the courtly ones, without leaving their rooms or stepping over the threshold of the court, travel the world by looking at a map, without it costing them a *blanca*, or suffering cold, hunger, or thirst. But we true knights-errant—in the sun, in the cold, in the inclemencies of the skies, by night or by day, on foot or on horseback—measure the earth with our own feet. And we don't know our enemies just through paintings, but in the flesh, and in every battle we attack them, without minding trifles or laws of the duel—checking to make sure both have swords or lances of equal length, to see if one is wearing holy relics for good luck or is concealing some ploy, or to verify that the sun affects both combatants equally, and other formalities of that kind used in duels—something you don't know about, but I do.

"And here's something else for you to know—the good knight-errant, even though he sees ten giants whose heads not only touch but pierce the clouds, and each one of whom has enormous towers for legs, and whose arms look like immense masts taken from huge and powerful ships, and every eye like a huge millstone, and burning hotter than a glass furnace—these giants must not frighten him; rather, with an easy bearing and intrepid heart he has to attack, and if possible, vanquish and rout them in an instant, even though their armor is made of scales of a certain fish they say are harder than diamonds, and in place of swords they bring sharp Damascus knives or clubs studded with sharp steel protrusions, which I've seen more than twice. I've said all this, my housekeeper, so that you could see the difference there is between some knights and others, and it would be good if princes esteemed this second kind of knights, or maybe I should have said first kind of knights, which are the knights-errant—some of which, according to their histories, have been the salvation not only of one kingdom but of many—"

"*Ay, señor mío*," the niece interrupted, "don't you know that everything you've said about knights-errant is fiction and lies, and their histories—those that aren't burned— deserve at least to have a *sambenito** put on them, or some other marking, which clearly shows that they're infamous and corruptors of good customs?"

"By the God who sustains me," said don Quixote, "if you

---

* This is a folk version of *saco benedicto*, a yellow woolen shirt with a red cross in front worn by penitents sentenced by the Inquisition.

weren't my own niece, the daughter of my sister, I'd have to punish you for the blasphemy you've uttered in such a way that it would echo through the whole world. How can it be that a girl who can hardly manage twelve lace bobbins can open her mouth to disapprove of the histories of knights-errant? What would *señor* Amadís say if he heard you say that? But he surely would have pardoned you because he was the most humble and courteous knight of his time, and besides, he was a great protector of damsels; but there are some who could have heard what you said and it wouldn't have sat so well with them. Not all of them were courteous and well mannered—some were rude and insolent. Not all those who call themselves knights are gentlemen—some are of gold, others of fool's gold—yet all of them look like knights, but not all of them can withstand the touchstone.* There are base fellows who pride themselves on looking like knights, and there are highborn knights who, it seems, are dying to appear to be common folk. The former rise through either ambition or virtue, and the latter sink through sloth or vice, and you have to use knowledge and discretion to distinguish between the two types, so similar in name but so different in actions."

"God help me," said the niece, "you know so many things, *señor*, that if it were necessary, you could climb up into a pulpit and start preaching through the streets, and yet with all this, you fall into a blindness so enormous and into an absurdity so obvious that you believe that you're courageous when you're old; strong when you're sick; that you redress wrongs when you're bent over with age; and above all, that you're a knight when you're not one, because although *hidalgos* can be knights, the poor ones can't be."

"You're quite correct, niece, in what you say," responded don Quixote, "and I could tell you things about lineages that would amaze you—but so as not to mix the divine with the human, I won't. Look, my friends, and listen carefully—you can reduce all the families in the world into four types, which are these: Some had humble beginnings and gradually extended and expanded until they achieved the height

---

* The touchstone was used to grade the purity of gold. Purity was judged by the nature of the streak left on it when rubbed with the gold being tested.

of greatness; others had high beginnings and have preserved and maintained the greatness that they began with;
still others, although they had great beginnings, wound up
like the point of a pyramid, having diminished from what
they originally were until they came to an end with nothing, which, when compared to its base, is insignificant; and
those—and these are the most common—which never had
either a fine beginning, nor a reasonable middle, and that's
the way they'll end up, nameless, like the plebeian and ordinary class.

"Of the first type, which had humble origins and rose
to greatness and still exist, the Ottoman House will serve
as an example, for from a humble and low shepherd who
initiated it, it's in its present glory.* An example of the
second type of family, which started out in greatness and
continues that way, would be the princes who, having inherited titles, preserve their greatness as they were, content to live within their borders peacefully. Of those who
began great and wound up as nothing, there are thousands of examples, because the pharaohs† and Ptolomys
of Egypt,‡ the Cæsars§ of Rome, and all the multitude—
if you can use that term with them—of infinite princes,
monarchs, lords, Medes, Assyrians, Persians, Greeks, and

---

* Don Quixote believes that Osman (1258–1324), Uthmān in Arabic,
the founder of the empire, was a shepherd and a highwayman, but in
reality he was a prince from a part of what is now northwestern Turkey.
He conquered the remainder of northwestern Turkey. The Ottoman
Empire went on to conquer most areas around the Mediterranean and
Black seas in a clockwise circle from Trieste to the Moroccan border,
achieving its maximum size in 1683. The name Ottoman ultimately
derives from the name Uthmān.

† The pharaohs ruled in Egypt from 1570 to 945 B.C.

‡ Ptolemy I (367–282 B.C.) became ruler of Egypt in 323 B.C. and
founded the Ptolemaic Dynasty, which lasted until 30 B.C. The last
Ptolemy was number fifteen. Ptolemy, the astronomer and geographer
(ca. A.D. 100–170), is not related to this dynasty.

§ There was, with one exception, a continuum of fifteen Cæsars, from
Julius (100–44 B.C.) through Antoninus Pius (that is, *Cæsar* Titus Ælius
Hadrianus Antoninus Augustus Pius), who reigned from A.D. 138–161.
Titus, who was not called Cæsar, reigned from A.D. 79–81.

barbarians*—all these lineages and dominions have ended in nothing, themselves and their founders as well, since none of their descendants can be found anywhere, and even if we did find some, they would be in a low and humble circumstance. Of the plebeian lineage I've nothing to say except that it serves to increase the number of people who are living, and their importance deserves no other fame or praise.

"From all that I've said, I want you to deduce, my silly ones, that there's great confusion among the various lineages, and that those that are great and illustrious are so only because of the goodness, bounty, and generosity of their members. I said 'goodness, bounty, and generosity' because a grandee who is evil will be an evil grandee; the rich man who is not generous will be a miserly beggar—for the pleasure in possessing is not in hoarding one's riches, but rather in sharing them, and not spending them in just any old way, but knowing how to spend them well. The poor knight has no way of showing that he's a knight except by virtue, by being affable, well mannered, courteous, considerate, and obliging; not proud, not arrogant, not backbiting. Above all he must be charitable, since two *maravedís* gladly given to the poor will make him seem as generous as the man who gives out alms accompanied by the clanging of bells. All who see him—even those who don't know him—adorned with these virtues will recognize his good breeding. And it would be a miracle otherwise, since praise has always been a reward for virtue, and virtuous people will always be praised.

"There are two roads, daughters, for men to become rich and honored. One is through letters and the other is through arms. I was born under the influence of the planet

---

* Medes were related to the Persians and settled in northeastern Iran as early as the seventeenth century B.C. The ancient kingdom of Assyria, which flourished in the seventh century B.C., was originally located in what is now northern Iraq, and it expanded greatly. Persians lived in what is now Iran. Barbarians generally are peoples you consider inferior: For the Greeks, non-Greeks were barbarians; for the Romans, anyone who lived outside their Empire was a barbarian.

Mars,* so I'm inclined to the latter. I'm bound to stick to that road, in spite of the whole world, and it would be fruitless for you to wear yourselves out trying to persuade me not ·to want what heaven wants me to do, what Fortune orders, and what reason demands, and especially what my will desires. Knowing as I do the innumerable travails associated with knight-errantry, I also know the multitude of blessings that go along with it. And I know that the path of virtue is very narrow, and the road of vice is broad and ample. And I know that the goals of both are different, because the goal of vice, though wide and easy, is death; and the goal of virtue, narrow and laborious though it is, leads to life, and not in life that ends, but rather the one that has no end. And I know, as our great Castilian poet says:

It is by rugged paths like these they go
    That scale the heights of immortality,
     Unreached by those that falter here below."†

"*Ay*, woe is me," said the niece. "My uncle is a poet as well. He knows everything; he understands everything. I'll bet that if he wanted to be a bricklayer, he'd know how to make a house as easily as he could a cage."

"I promise you, niece," responded don Quixote, "that if these thoughts of chivalry didn't consume all my faculties, there would be nothing I couldn't do, nor craft I couldn't learn, especially birdcages and toothpicks."‡

At this point there were knocks at the door, and when they asked who was there, Sancho said it was him. The moment the housekeeper recognized his voice, she ran to hide, so much did she despise him. The niece opened the door for him, and his master don Quixote went to receive him with open arms. They went together into his room, where they had a conversation that the previous one couldn't match.

---

* Mars was the Roman god of war. Thus, being under the influence of the planet Mars carries with it that don Quixote is a warrior by nature.
† Garcilaso de la Vega (1501?–1536), in his *Eclogue I*, verses 202–204.
‡ These toothpicks are of the fancy kind, sculpted from ivory or fancy woods.

Chapter VI.* About what don Quixote said to his squire, with other very famous events.

As soon as the housekeeper saw that Sancho Panza was closed up with his master, she figured out what they were talking about, and concluded that the conversation would result in their third expedition. Taking her shawl, and filled with anguish and grief, she went to look for the bachelor Sansón Carrasco, thinking that since he was so well-spoken and a new friend of her master, he could persuade him to abandon such a ludicrous proposition.

She found him pacing on the patio of his house, and when she saw him, she fell at his feet, flushed and distressed. When Carrasco saw her looking so doleful and terrified, he said to her: "What's this, *señora* housekeeper? What has happened—it looks like you're about to give up the ghost."

"It's nothing, *señor* Sansón, except my master is breaking out, he's surely breaking out."

"Where's he breaking out, *señora*?" asked Sansón. "Has he eaten something that has caused him to break out?"

"He's breaking out," she responded, "through the door of his madness. I mean, my dear *señor* bachelor, that he's about to make another expedition—and this will be the third time—to roam the world to seek what he calls adventures. I don't understand how he can give them that name. The first time they brought him back stretched across a donkey, beaten to bits. The second time he came in an ox-cart, shut up in a cage, where he said he was enchanted. He was so pathetic, the mother who bore him wouldn't have recognized him—gaunt, yellow, his eyes sunken into the deepest recesses of his brain. And to help him get restored it took more than six hundred eggs, as God and everyone knows, and my chickens won't let me lie."

"I can well believe it," responded the bachelor. "They're so good and well trained that they won't say one thing for another even though they might burst. So then, *señora*

---

* The original edition does say VI here at the beginning of chapter seven.

housekeeper, there's nothing else—no other misfortune has happened—except that you fear what *señor* don Quixote will do."

"No, *señor*," she responded.

"Then don't worry," responded the bachelor, "and go back home, fix me something hot to eat for lunch, and along the way say the prayer to St. Apolonia,* if you know it. I'll come over right away and you'll witness miracles."

"Woe is me," replied the housekeeper. "You say I should say the prayer to St. Apolonia—this would be if my master had a toothache, but where he aches is in his brain."

"I know what I'm talking about, *señora* housekeeper— go on and don't argue with me, since you know I'm a bachelor of arts from Salamanca, and there's no better bachelor than that."†

And with this, the housekeeper went away, and the bachelor immediately went to look for the priest to tell him what will be reported in due time.

While don Quixote and Sancho were alone, this is the conversation they had, as recorded accurately in the true account of the history:

Sancho said to his master: "*Señor*, I've dissuaded my wife to let me go with your grace wherever you want to lead me."

"*Per*suaded, you should say, Sancho," said don Quixote, "and not *dis*suaded."

"Once or twice," responded Sancho, "if I remember correctly, I've asked your grace not to fix my words if you understand what I mean, but when you don't understand, just say, 'Sancho, I don't understand you,' and if I'm not yet clear, I'm fossil enough to let you correct me."

"I don't understand you, Sancho," said don Quixote, "since I don't know what 'fossil enough' means."

"*Fossil enough* means," responded Sancho, "I'm *sufficiently that way.*"

"I understand *that* even less," replied don Quixote.

"Well, if your grace doesn't understand me," responded Sancho, "I don't know how else to say it. I don't know anything else, and may God be with me."

---

* This prayer is still used for relief from toothaches.
† *To be a bachelor* also meant "to lie with aplomb."

"Now I catch on," responded don Quixote. "You mean that you're so *docile*—accommodating and meek—that you will go along with what I tell you to do, and you'll do what I instruct you to do."

"I bet," said Sancho, "that since I began, your grace understood me, but you just wanted to embarrass me to hear me say another two hundred stupid things."

"That may be," replied don Quixote, "but indeed, tell me—what does Teresa say?"

"Teresa says," said Sancho, "that I should 'tie a string around my finger' with your grace,* and that 'documents speak, not beards,'† because 'he who cuts doesn't shuffle' and 'a bird in the hand is worth two in the bush.' And I say that 'the advice of a woman is not worth very much and he who doesn't heed it is crazy.'"

"I agree, too," responded don Quixote. "Tell me, Sancho, move along, because you're saying real gems."

"It happens," replied Sancho, "as you know better than I do, we're all subject to death, and 'here today and gone tomorrow,' and 'the lamb goes to the slaughter just as the sheep does,' and 'no one can have more time in this world than God wants to give him,' because 'death is deaf,' and when he comes to knock on the door of our life, he's always in a hurry and won't stop for entreaties, nor resistance, nor scepters, nor miters.‡ This is all common knowledge and we also hear it preached from the pulpits."

"All that is true," said don Quixote, "but I don't know where it's all leading."

"It's leading," said Sancho, "to asking you to tell me what salary you intend to pay me every month of the time that I serve you, and that the salary be paid from your income. I don't want to be dependent on favors, which come late or never—may God help me with what I hope to earn. In a word, I want to know what I am to earn—as little or as much as it may be, because 'the hen will sit on only one egg,' and 'many littles make a big,' and 'if you're earning something you're not losing anything.' The truth is, if it should happen—and I don't think it will, nor are my hopes

---

* That is, "I should be careful with you."
† That is, "don't speak when you can use documents instead."
‡ Miters are liturgical headdresses worn by bishops and abbots.

up—that you give me the *ínsula* you promised me, I'm not so ungrateful, nor do I take things to such extremes, that I won't allow the income that would come from the *ínsula* to be appraised and taken out of my salary, procreated."

"Sancho, my friend," responded don Quixote, "sometimes it's better to rate something instead of creating it."

"I see," said Sancho. "I'll bet I was supposed to say *pro*-rate and not *pro*create. But this isn't important at all, since you understood me."

"And so well," responded don Quixote, "that I've penetrated to the very bottom of your thoughts, and I know the target of the innumerable arrows of your proverbs. Look, Sancho, I would fix a wage if I had found in any one of the histories of knights-errant an example that would show a glimmering of what squires would earn every month or every year. But I've read all or most of their histories, and I cannot recall that a single knight-errant had given a fixed salary to his squire. I only know that they all served in expectation of favors, and when least they expected it, if their masters had been lucky, they found themselves regaled with an *ínsula*, or something similar, and in any case they were given a title or made a lord. If with these hopes and inducements you, Sancho, want to serve me again, well and good—because to consider that I would knock the ancient custom of knight-errantry off its hinges is to think the unthinkable. So, Sancho *mío*, go back home and declare my intent to your Teresa, and if she wants, and you want to be dependent on my favors, *bene quidem*,* and if not, we'll be friends as always—for 'if the pigeon house doesn't lack grain, it won't lack pigeons either.' And again, my son, 'a favorable hope is better than a bad possession' and 'a good claim is better than bad pay.' I'm speaking this way, Sancho, to make you see that I, like you, know how to hurl proverbs as if they were rain. Finally, I want to say, and I will say, that if you don't want to work for favors and take the same risks I take, may God stay with you and make you a saint—for I won't lack squires more obedient and more diligent, and not so awkward and loquacious as you."

When Sancho heard his master's firm resolution, his sky clouded over and the wings of his heart drooped, because

---

* Latin: "agreed."

he'd believed his master wouldn't go without him for all the money in the world, and while he was crestfallen and pensive, Sansón Carrasco came in with the niece, the latter wanting to hear what Sansón would say to her master to prevent him from going out to seek more adventures. Sansón—the famous jokester—went up to him and embraced him as before, and with a raised voice said: "Oh, flower of knight-errantry! Oh, shining light of arms! Oh, honor and mirror of the Spanish nation! May it please God Almighty to grant that any person or persons who try to hinder your third expedition be mired in the labyrinth of their desires, and may their wicked design never be realized!"

And turning to the housekeeper, he said: "You needn't recite the prayer to St. Apolonia any longer, because I know that heaven has clearly ordained that *señor* don Quixote should go out to put his high-minded and new intent into effect. I would wrong the dictates of my conscience if I didn't suggest and even urge this knight not to let the strength of his arm and the virtue of his very brave spirit be confined and detained any longer, because through his delay he neglects the righting of wrongs, the protection of orphans, the honor of maidens, the favoring of widows, the support of married women, and other similar endeavors, all of which deal with, pertain to, depend on, and are associated with knight-errantry. Come, don Quixote *mío*, handsome and fierce, right this moment rather than tomorrow let your grace and greatness get on the road, and if you need anything to help your endeavor, here I am to supply it with my person and financial support; and if you need me, I'll even be your squire, and I'll consider it to be very good fortune."

Don Quixote then said, turning to Sancho: "Didn't I tell you, Sancho, there would be an abundance of squires? Look who has offered to be mine—none but the phenomenal bachelor Sansón Carrasco, perpetual joker and merrymaker of the patios of the schools of Salamanca, sound of body, fleet of foot, endurer of both heat and cold, and hunger and thirst, with all the requisite qualities to be a squire of a knight-errant. . . . But heaven forbid that I should shatter this column of letters and vessel of knowledge, or fell the lofty palm of good and liberal arts. Let the new Samson remain at home, and by honoring it he'll bring honor to the white hair of his agèd parents, because I'll be content with any squire, since Sancho doesn't care to come with me."

"Yes, I *do* care," responded Sancho, deeply moved and with eyes filled with tears, and he went on: "Let it not be said of me, *señor mío*, 'the bread partaken, the company forsaken.' I don't come from an ungrateful stock—everybody knows, especially in my town, who the Panzas were who I come from. Moreover, I know and understand through your good deeds and kind words that your grace wants to show me favor, and if I've fussed a bit about my salary, it was to humor my wife, because when she has a mind to press a point, there's no mallet that drives the hoops of a barrel the way she drives you to do what she wants. But, let's face it, a man has to be a man, and a woman, a woman; and since I'm a man wherever I please, which I can't deny, I'll be one in my own house, no matter what. And there's nothing left to do except for your grace to add a codicil to your will that cannot be provoked, and let's get on the road right away, so that the soul of *señor* Sansón won't suffer, since he says that his conscience dictates him to persuade your grace to go out a third time through the world. And I once again offer myself to serve your grace faithfully, and as well as, or better than, all the squires who ever served knights-errant in past and present times."

The bachelor was amazed to hear Sancho Panza's way of talking, and, although he'd read the first part of the history of his master, he never believed that Sancho was as amusing as they describe him; but hearing him say just now "codicil to your will that cannot be provoked," instead of "codicil to your will that cannot be revoked," he came to believe everything that he'd read about him, and he deemed him one of the most celebrated idiots of our times, and he said to himself that two such crazy men as this master and servant had never been seen before in the world.

Finally, don Quixote and Sancho embraced and made up once again, and on the advice and with the blessing of the great Carrasco, who was at that point their oracle, it was ordered that three days hence they would leave, during which time they had to prepare for the journey and to find a covered helmet, which don Quixote said he needed to have. Sansón offered this to him because he had a friend who had one and wouldn't refuse his request, although it was rusty and moldy rather than clean and brightly polished steel.

The curses that both the housekeeper and niece heaped upon the bachelor had no end; they pulled out their hair, they scratched their faces, and they raised a lamentation about the departure the same way hired mourners do, as if their master were dead. The plan that Sansón drew up to persuade him to go out a third time will be revealed later in the story, all of which was approved by the priest and barber, with whom he'd discussed it beforehand.

In short, in those three days they gathered what they thought they'd need, and Sancho, having appeased his wife, and don Quixote, having done the same with his niece and housekeeper, at dusk, without anyone seeing them except the bachelor, who wanted to go with them out of town for half a league, got on the road toward El Toboso—Don Quixote on his good Rocinante and Sancho on his regular donkey, the saddlebags filled with food and their purse with money, which don Quixote gave Sancho for whatever might come up. Sansón embraced him and begged him to write of his good or bad fortune, to sadden him with the former, or gladden him with the latter, as the laws of friendship demanded. Don Quixote promised him he'd do it, Sansón went back to their village, and the two got on the road toward the great city of El Toboso.

Chapter VIII. Where what happened to don Quixote on the way to see his lady, Dulcinea del Toboso, is recounted.

"BLESSED BE the powerful Allah!" says Cide Hamete Benengeli at the beginning of this eighth chapter. "Blessed be Allah," he repeats three times, and says that he offers this thanksgiving because he sees don Quixote and Sancho on the road, and that the readers of this pleasant history can rest assured that at this point the deeds and drolleries of don Quixote and his squire will begin. He urges his readers to forget the ingenious *hidalgo*'s past acts of chivalry and to turn their eyes toward those that are to come, since they're beginning now, on the road to El Toboso, on the plains of Montiel; and it's not much to ask, considering what he promises. He begins this way, saying:

Don Quixote and Sancho were alone, and hardly had Sansón gone back when Rocinante began to neigh and the donkey to break wind,* and all this was held as a very fine sign and a good omen by knight and squire, although if the truth be told, the donkey broke more wind and brayed more than the nag neighed, from which Sancho deduced that his good fortune would surpass that of his master, based on I don't know what astrological prediction he knew, since the history doesn't clarify. He was only heard to say that when he tripped or fell,† he would prefer not to have left home, because all he got from tripping or falling was a ripped shoe or broken ribs, and even though he was unlettered, on this point he wasn't far off the mark.

Don Quixote said to him: "Sancho, my friend, night is falling fast and it's getting too dark for us to reach El Toboso by morning; and I'm determined to go there to get the blessing and gracious leave of the peerless Dulcinea del Toboso before starting any adventure. With that license I plan to—in fact I'm certain I will—take on and emerge victorious from every dangerous adventure, because nothing in this life makes knights-errant more valiant than to see themselves favored by their ladies."

"I believe that, too," responded Sancho, "but I think it will be hard for your grace to speak with her, or see her alone, at least in a place where you can get her blessing, unless she tosses it to you over the walls of the corral where I saw her the first time, when I took her the letter that had the news of the follies and crazy acts you were doing in the heart of the Sierra Morena."

---

* The primary meaning of the Spanish word used here, *sospiros*, is "sighs." Donald McGrady, in his 1973 article "The *Sospiros* of Sancho's Donkey" (*Modern Language Notes*, 88 [1973], 335–37) shows clearly that this secondary meaning is correct. I thank the encyclopedic Dan Eisenberg for this reference.

† That is, when he suffered physically because of one of don Quixote's adventures. I thank Dan, once again, for his help with this passage.

"You thought those were the walls of a corral, Sancho," said don Quixote, "where you saw that never sufficiently praised gentle breeding and beauty? Weren't they galleries, corridors, or porticoes—or whatever they're called—of a rich and royal palace?"

"Anything is possible," responded Sancho, "but they looked like corral walls to me, if memory serves."

"In any case, let's go there, Sancho," replied don Quixote. "As long as I see her, it's all the same to me if it's over walls or through windows, or even through chinks or garden grates—any ray of the sun of her beauty that comes to my eyes will enlighten my understanding and fortify my heart so that I'll be unique and without equal in sagacity and in valor."

"But in truth, *señor*," responded Sancho, "when I saw this sun of Dulcinea del Toboso, it wasn't bright enough to emit rays at all, and it must have been because her grace was winnowing the wheat I mentioned, and the wheat dust that was flying around gathered like a cloud around her face and obscured it."

"You still insist, Sancho," said don Quixote, "in saying, thinking, and arguing that my lady Dulcinea was winnowing wheat, when that's a task at variance with what persons of quality are supposed to do, born and bred as they are for other activities and pastimes that show their high birth from a crossbow shot away? Did you forget, Sancho, those verses by our poet* where he describes the handwork of the four nymphs in their crystal houses? They rose from their beloved Tajo River,† and in the green meadow they embroidered that rich material our ingenious poet describes for us, everything made of gold, silk, and pearls, all woven together. And this is what my lady must have been doing when you saw her, but the envy some evil enchanter harbors toward me corrupts everything that would give me pleasure and changes its appearance, and that's why I fear that in the history they say is circulating about my deeds, if by chance the author was an enchanter who is my en-

---

* "Our poet" again is Garcilaso, and the poem is his third *Eclogue*, starting at verse fifty-three.

† This river flows through Toledo and leaves the Iberian Peninsula at Lisbon, as you know.

emy, he may have written one thing for another, mixing one truth with a thousand lies, and amusing himself by telling idle tales that are not related to the truth of the history. Oh, envy, root of infinite wickedness and destroyer of virtue! All vices, Sancho, take along with them a bit of pleasure, but envy brings only disgust, animosity, and rage."

"That's what I say, too," responded Sancho, "and I think that this legend or history that the bachelor Sansón Carrasco has seen must have dragged my honor through the dirt, as they say, from pillar to post, here and there, sweeping the streets with it. But on the faith of an honest person, I've said nothing ill about any enchanter, nor do I have so much wealth that they can envy me for. It's true that I'm a bit mischievous and that I have traces of rascally qualities, but it's all concealed under the cape of my simplicity, always natural and never affected. If for no other reason than that I believe, firmly and truly, in God, and in everything that the Holy Roman Catholic Church holds and teaches, and that I'm a mortal enemy of the Jews, the historian should have shown mercy on me and treated me well in his writings. But say what they will, 'naked I was born and I'm still naked—I neither lose nor gain.' But since I see myself in books and traveling throughout the world from hand to hand, I couldn't care less—let 'em say what they want about me."

"That reminds me, Sancho," said don Quixote, "of what happened to a famous poet of these times who wrote a malicious satire about all the courtesans* of the court except one, since he didn't know if she was one or not. And she, when she saw that she wasn't on the list with the others, complained to the poet, asking him what he'd seen in her that caused him to leave her out, and demanded that he should add to his satire and put her in the appendix, and if not, beware the consequences. The poet did as she asked, and described her in a way that even a duenna wouldn't repeat, and she was quite satisfied to see herself famous, even though she was now infamous. And this brings to mind what they say about the shepherd who set fire to and

---

* This is a probable reference to Vicente Espinel's 1578 work *Satire Against the Ladies of Seville*. Courtesans were prostitutes with a high-class clientele.

burned down the famous temple of Diana, hailed as one of the seven wonders of the world, only because he wanted his name to stay alive in future centuries. And although it was ordered that no one should utter or write his name, so that he wouldn't get the fame he wanted, it was still known that he was called Herostratus.*

"This reminds me, too, of what happened to the great Emperor Carlos V† with a gentleman in Rome. The emperor wanted to see the famous Temple of the Rotunda,‡ which in ancient times was known as the Pantheon, and nowadays, with a Catholic name, as All Saints. It's the best-preserved building erected by the pagans in Rome, and the one that conserves best the grandeur and magnificence of its founders. It has the shape of half an orange and is extremely large and well lit, its only illumination coming from a window, or better said, a round skylight in the top, from which the emperor was looking down into the building, and at his side was a Roman gentleman who was telling him about the fine points and subtleties of that great building and its memorable architecture. Once they had left the skylight, the man said to the emperor: 'Holy Majesty, I was tempted a thousand times to grab you and hurl myself through that skylight to achieve eternal fame throughout the world.'

"'I thank you,' responded the emperor, 'for not having succumbed to such a wicked impulse, and from now on I won't give you the opportunity to put your loyalty to the test, and so I forbid you to speak to me or appear in my

---

* Herostratus was an Ephesian who set fire to the Temple of Artemis (Diana) in 356 B.C. to immortalize himself. Although the Ephesians passed a decree condemning his name to oblivion, it only increased his notoriety and helped him achieve what he wanted. The temple measured 350 by 180 feet. Of the Seven Wonders of the World, only the Pyramids of Giza still stand.

† Carlos V of the Holy Roman Empire was also Carlos I of Spain (1500–1558). He did go to Rome in 1536 and delivered an address before Pope Paul III. The anecdote that follows is reported nowhere else. Schevill thinks that Cervantes heard about it when he was in Italy.

‡ This is the Pantheon in Rome, which took its final shape in about A.D. 120 in the form of a dome 142 feet in diameter, rising to a height of 71 feet. The 27-foot round opening at the top is its only source of illumination. It was dedicated as a church in 609.

presence ever again,' and after he said that, he gave him a nice gift.

"I mean, Sancho, that the desire to be famous is a powerful incentive: What was it that made Horatius* throw himself from the bridge, in full armor, into the depths of the Tiber?† What is it that caused Mucius to burn his arm and hand?‡ What was it that caused Curtius§ to throw himself in the deep burning pit that appeared in the middle of Rome? What was it that, despite all the bad omens shown to him, made Cæsar cross the Rubicon?¶ And with some modern examples, what was it that caused the very courteous Cortés** to scuttle his ships and strand and isolate his brave Spaniards in the New World? All these and other great and varied deeds are, were, and will be monuments to mortal men's desire for fame as a reward and part of the immortality that their actions merit, although Christians, Catholics, and knights-errant should rather aim for future glory in heaven than to the vanity of fame attained in this transitory life—this fame, no matter how long it lasts, will come to an end when the world ends at its appointed time. So, Sancho, our deeds will not pass beyond the limit imposed by the Christian religion we profess. We will kill pride when we slay giants; envy, through generosity and goodness of

---

* This is Horatius Cocles, who is said to have held back the Etruscans from a wooden Roman bridge until it could be demolished; then he is supposed to have swum across the Tiber to safety, despite his wounds. One record states that he drowned.

† The Tiber is the river that flows through Rome.

‡ This was Gaius Mucius Scævola, a Roman hero in the sixth century B.C. who held his right hand in a flame to show his indifference to pain.

§ Marcus Curtius was a fourth-century A.D. Roman hero who, to save his country, leaped, armed and on horseback, into a chasm that suddenly opened in the Forum, after which, we're told, it closed and all was well. That this chasm was flaming, as don Quixote says in a moment, is doubtful.

¶ On January 10, 49 B.C., Julius Cæsar crossed the Rubicon (a river that flows into the Adriatic Sea a bit south of modern Ravenna) with very few soldiers to go against an army of sixty thousand, and won.

** Hernán Cortés landed in Veracruz in 1519 with about six hundred soldiers and sailors on eleven ships. To prevent desertion, he secretly had his ships scuttled. Later they went to Tenochtitlán, the Aztec capital, which they conquered.

heart; anger, through a calm and quiet mind; gluttony and drowsiness, by eating little and through long vigils; lust* and lasciviousness, through faithfulness to those we have made mistresses of our thoughts; sloth, by wandering through all parts of the world seeking opportunities that will make us, in addition to being Christians, into famous knights.† Can you see, Sancho, that these are the means by which we can win the highest praise that fame will allow?"

"Everything your grace has said up to now," said Sancho, "I've understood very well, but even so, I would like you to revolve a doubt that has come to mind just now."

"*Resolve*, you mean, Sancho," said don Quixote. "Tell me, and I'll respond as well as I know how."

"Tell me, *señor*," Sancho went on, "those Julys or Augusts, and all those industrious knights that you've mentioned who are now dead, where are they now?"

"The pagans," responded don Quixote, "are doubtless in hell. The Christians, if they were good ones, are either in purgatory or in heaven."

"That's fine," said Sancho, "but let's see now—those graves where those bigshots lie, do they have silver lamps in front of them, or are the walls of their chapels decorated with crutches, shrouds, locks of hair, or legs and eyes made of wax? And if this isn't so, what are they decorated with?"

To which don Quixote responded: "The sepulchers of gentiles were usually sumptuous temples. The ashes from the body of Julius Cæsar were put in a pyramid of stone of inordinate size in Rome, which they call St. Peter's Needle.‡ A castle as large as a small town, which they called Moles Hadriani, served as the sepulcher for the Emperor Hadrian, and is now called Castel Sant'Angelo in Rome.§

---

* Actually, the first edition says *injuria* ("injury") instead of *lujuria* ("lust"), but since *lasciviousness* follows, *lujuria* may have been what Cervantes wrote.

† Don Quixote has listed six of the seven cardinal sins. Greed is missing.

‡ St. Peter's Needle in St. Peter's Square in Rome is an obelisk, not a pyramid. It doesn't have Cæsar's ashes inside of it, either.

§ When the Roman emperor Hadrian (A.D. 76–138) died, his burial place was what is now called the Castel Sant'Angelo, the famous round fortress at the Tiber River in Rome overlooking the Ponte Sant'Angelo.

Queen Artemesia* entombed her husband, Mausolus, in a sepulcher that was one of the seven wonders of the world—but none of these sepulchers, nor any other of the many used by pagans, was decorated with shrouds or other offerings and tokens to show that those buried there are saints."

"I'm coming to that," replied Sancho. "Tell me now which is greater, to bring a dead person back to life or to kill a giant?"

"The answer is obvious," responded don Quixote. "It's greater to bring a dead person back to life."

"I've got you there!" said Sancho. "So the fame of the person who brings the dead back to life, gives sight to the blind, makes the cripple whole, and restores health to the sick, and in front of whose sepulchers lamps burn, and their chapels are full of devout people who adore their relics on their knees—their fame will be greater both for this world and the next than what was achieved by all the pagan emperors and knights-errant who have ever lived."

"I confess that's the truth as well," responded don Quixote.

"So, this fame, these favors, these prerogatives, or whatever you call them," responded Sancho, "deal with the bodies and relics of the saints, which, with the approval of the Holy Mother Church, have lamps, candles, shrouds, crutches, paintings, locks of hair, eyes, and legs, which increase devotion to them and enhance their Christian fame. Kings carry the bodies of saints or their relics on their shoulders. They kiss fragments of their bones, and use them to adorn and embellish their chapels and their most valued altars. . . ."

"And what should I be getting out of all you've said?" said don Quixote.

"What I'm getting at," said Sancho, "is that we should try to become saints and we'll get the fame we're after much sooner. Did your grace know, *señor*, that just yesterday or the day before—it was such a short time ago it seems like yesterday—they canonized or beatified two barefoot friars, and now it's considered great good luck just to be able

---

* Artemesia II (died ca. 350 B.C.) reigned in Anatolia (Asian Turkey). She built the tomb for her husband Mausolus in Halicarnassus (modern Bodrum, Turkey).

to kiss or touch the iron chains with which they had been bound and tortured, and those chains are more revered, the way I hear, than Roland's sword in the armory of the king our lord, may God protect him? So, *señor*, it's better to be a humble friar of any order whatsoever than to be a valiant knight-errant. Two dozen lashes go farther with God than two thousand lance thrusts, whether to giants or monsters or dragons."

"All that is so," responded don Quixote, "but not everybody can be a friar, and there are many roads by which God leads His own to heaven. Chivalry is a religion, and there are knightly saints in heaven."

"Yes," responded Sancho, "but I've heard that there are more friars in heaven than knights-errant."

"That's right," responded don Quixote, "because there's a greater number of those of the religious vocation than of knights."

"There are many adventurers," said Sancho.

"Many," responded don Quixote, "but few are those who deserve to be called knights."

In these and other similar conversations they spent the whole night and the following day, without anything worthy of being reported happening to them, which disturbed don Quixote more than a little. Finally, the next day at nightfall, they saw the great city of El Toboso,* which gladdened the spirits of don Quixote and saddened Sancho, because he didn't know where Dulcinea's house was, nor had he ever seen it in his whole life, any more than his master. Both were agitated, the one because he was eager to see her and the other because he'd never seen her, and Sancho had no idea what he was going to do when his master sent him into El Toboso. Finally, don Quixote said they would enter the town at nightfall, and they waited among some oak trees near El Toboso. And at the proper time they entered the city, where important things happened to them.

---

* The "great city of El Toboso" was just a small village then.

Chapter IX. Where is told what will be seen.

"IT WAS at the stroke of midnight,"* a little more or less, when don Quixote and Sancho left the forest and went into El Toboso. The town was very still because everyone was sleeping and stretched out, as they say. The night was fairly bright, although Sancho wished it were completely dark so the darkness might give him an excuse for his folly. In the whole town the only sound was the barking of dogs that deafened the ears of don Quixote and upset Sancho's heart. Once in a while a donkey brayed, the pigs grunted, the cats meowed—the different animal noises being intensified by the stillness of the night, all of which seemed to be a bad omen to the enamored knight, but even so he said to Sancho: "Sancho, my son, lead me to Dulcinea's palace. Perhaps we'll find her awake."

"What palace am I to lead you to, by golly," responded Sancho, "because the one in which I saw her greatness was nothing more than a very small house."

"She must have withdrawn," responded don Quixote, "to a small apartment in her palace, taking her ease with her maidens, as such noble ladies and princesses are wont to do."

"Señor," said Sancho, "since your grace insists, in spite of me, that Dulcinea's house is a palace, do you suppose we'll find an open door at this hour? And will it be good to start knocking loudly until they hear us and open the doors to us, upsetting everyone? Are we lovers, who knock on the door of our mistresses and go in at any hour, no matter how late?"

"In any case, Sancho, let's find the palace," replied don Quixote, "and then I'll tell you what would be appropriate for us to do. And, look, Sancho, either my eyes are deceiving me, or that large shadowy mass over there must be Dulcinea's palace."

"All right, you lead me, then," responded Sancho. "Maybe it is. Even if I were to see it with my eyes and touch it with my hands, I'd believe it as I believe that it's day right now."

---

* These first words are from a poem that everyone would have recognized.

Don Quixote went ahead, and having gone two hundred paces, he came to the shape that caused the silhouette, and saw a great tower, and recognized right away that it wasn't the palace, but the main church in town, and he said: "We've come across the church, Sancho."

"I see it," responded Sancho, "and may it please God that we don't find our graves as well—because it's not good to rummage about cemeteries at such hours, and the more so since I told your grace, if I remember correctly, that the house of this lady was on a dead end."

"May God curse you, you fool!" said don Quixote. "Where did you learn that royal palaces are built on dead ends?

"*Señor*," responded Sancho, "every region has its own customs. Maybe in El Toboso they build palaces and large buildings on dead ends. I would ask your grace to let me search these streets to see what I can find. It may be that in some spot I'll find this palace; and may I see it eaten by dogs for having put us on this wild-goose chase."

"Speak with respect, Sancho, about things dealing with my lady," said don Quixote, "and let's not argue or 'get to the point of no return.'"

"I won't say anything more," responded Sancho, "but how am I going to be patient if your grace expects me to remember where our lady's house is—I saw it only once—and find it at midnight, when *you* can't even locate it, and you must have seen it thousands of times?"

"You're making me despair, Sancho," said don Quixote. "Listen, you heretic, haven't I told you a thousand times that I haven't seen the peerless Dulcinea in all the days of my life, nor have I once crossed the threshold of her palace, and that I'm in love with her only by hearsay, owing to her fame as a beauty and woman of discretion?"

"I hear you," responded Sancho, "and I'll tell your grace that since you haven't seen her, neither have I."

"That can't be," replied don Quixote, "because you told me that you saw her winnowing wheat when you brought me the response to the letter I sent with you."

"Don't believe that, *señor*," responded Sancho, "because I can tell your grace that my visit was also by hearsay, as was the response I brought you. I know who the *señora* Dulcinea is about as well as I can punch the sky."

"Sancho, Sancho," responded don Quixote, "there are times to joke around, and times when jokes are not appropriate. Just because I said I haven't seen or spoken to the lady of my soul doesn't mean that you, too, haven't spoken to or seen her either, when the opposite is true, as you know."

While they were conversing thus, they saw a man with two mules approaching, and by the noise of the plow being dragged on the ground, they figured it must be a peasant who had gotten up before sunrise to go do his farming, and it was the truth. The peasant came singing that ballad that says:

> You fared ill, men of France,
> in what happened at Roncesvalles*

"May I die, Sancho," said don Quixote when he heard this, "if anything good happens to us tonight. Don't you hear what this rustic is singing?"

"Yes, I hear it," responded Sancho, "but what does the hunt at Roncesvalles† have to do with our business at hand? He might as well be singing the 'Ballad of Calaínos,'‡ which would make no difference as far as we're concerned."

At this moment the farmhand arrived, and don Quixote asked him: "Can you tell me, my good friend, and may God give you good luck, where the palaces of the peerless Dulcinea del Toboso are?"

---

* The ballad goes on: "Don Carlos [Charlemagne] lost his honor / and the Twelve Peers died."

† Very interesting phenomenon here. Ballads exist in about as many versions as there are people who sing them. The farmhand sang one version, but Sancho automatically remembers the version he knows that refers to the "*hunt at* Roncesvalles," and not "*what happened* at Roncesvalles." Sancho knows a more common version of this "Ballad of Conde Guarinos."

‡ When Sancho says that the farmhand could sing the "Ballad of Calaínos" (where the Moor Calaínos, in order to marry the daughter of the ruthless Almanzor, had to first cut off the heads of three of the Twelve Peers of France), it really means that it doesn't make any difference what he's singing. "Verses from Calaínos" was a proverbial reference to inconsequential statements.

"*Señor*," responded the young man, "I'm not from around here, and I've only been here a few days working for a rich farmer in his fields. The priest and sexton of this village live in this house right in front of us. One or both of them can tell your grace about this princess because they have the list of all the people who live in El Toboso. I think, though, that there's no princess living here at all—but there *are* many important women, and each one may be a princess in her own home."

"The one I'm asking you about," said don Quixote, "must be among those."

"It might be," responded the young man, "and good-bye, because the sun is coming up."

And putting the whip to his mules, he didn't wait for any more questions.

Sancho, who saw that his master was perplexed and quite ill at ease, said to him: "*Señor*, I know that it'll soon be day, and it won't be right to have the sun find us in the street. It'll be better for us to leave town and for you to hide in a nearby thicket, and I'll come back when it's daytime, and I'll leave no stone unturned in the whole town looking for the house, castle, or palace of my lady. And I'll be pretty upset if I can't find it; and when I do find it I'll speak with her grace and will tell her where you are and how you're hoping she'll tell you how to visit her without damaging her honor and reputation."

"You've said, Sancho," said don Quixote, "a thousand wise thoughts within those few words. I enthusiastically accept the advice you've just given me. Come, my son, let's look for a place among the trees where I can hide. You'll come back, as you say, to see and speak with my lady, from whose discretion and courtesy I expect more than miraculous favors."

Sancho was desperately eager to take his master out of the town so that he wouldn't discover the lie about Dulcinea's response that he'd taken to him in the Sierra Morena, and he made sure they left in a hurry. Two miles from town they found a thicket or forest where don Quixote hid while Sancho returned to the city to speak with Dulcinea, and on this errand things befell him that require of the reader both attention and suspension of disbelief.

*Chapter X. Where the deception Sancho used to en-
    chant the lady Dulcinea is revealed, as are other
    events as ridiculous as they are true.*

WHEN THE author comes to relate what happens in this
chapter, he says he wanted to pass over it in silence,
fearful that he wouldn't be believed, because the madness
of don Quixote not only reaches the limits of the most extreme case that can be imagined, but goes two crossbow
shots beyond. Nevertheless, albeit with fear and trepida-
tion, he wrote about don Quixote's crazy acts exactly as
they were performed, without adding or taking away an
atom of the truth, not caring at all that people might call
him a liar. And he was right, because truth may stretch but
it will not break, and it always floats over lies, like oil on
water. Continuing with his story, he says that as soon as don
Quixote was hidden in the forest, wood, or grove near the
great city of El Toboso, he told Sancho to return to the city,
and not to come back until he'd spoken on his behalf to
his lady, asking her if she would receive her captive knight,
and deign to bestow her blessing on him, so that he could
expect happy outcomes in all his endeavors and difficult
undertakings. Sancho said he would do just as he'd been
told, and would take back as good a response to him as he
did the first time.

"Go, my son," replied don Quixote, "and don't be
blinded by the light of the sun of beauty that you're seeking. You're more fortunate than all other squires in the
world. Remember how she receives you and let nothing escape your notice—if she blushes while you're giving her my
message; if she's unsettled and confused when she hears my
name; if she can hardly sit still on her cushion, if you find
her in her drawing room; or if she's standing, watch carefully to see if she first stands on one foot, then the other; if
she repeats the answer she gives you two or three times;
if she changes from soft to harsh, or from harsh to amorous; if she raises her hand to primp her hair, even though
she's perfectly coiffed; in other words, my son, take note of
all her actions and movements, because if you can relate
to me what they were like, I can tell what she has hidden

in the depths of her heart regarding my love for her. You should know, Sancho, if you don't already, that between two lovers, the actions and physical movements they show are certain indicators that tell about what is going on inside their hearts. Go, my friend, and may better luck than mine guide you, and may it bring you a better outcome than the one I'm fearing or expecting in this bitter solitude in which you're leaving me."

"I'll go and come back quickly," said Sancho, "and cheer your heart, *señor mío*, for it must be no larger than a hazelnut. Consider what they say, 'a stout heart breaks bad luck' and 'where there's no bacon there are no stakes.'* And also they say 'when you least expect it, up pops the hare.' I say this because if last night we didn't find the palaces of my lady, now that the sun is out, I think I'll find them when I least expect it, and once I find them, just let me at her!"

"Sancho," said don Quixote, "your proverbs are always so pertinent to the situation at hand—I hope God will give me better luck in what I wish."

After don Quixote said this, Sancho turned to go and whipped his donkey, and don Quixote stayed behind, resting on his stirrups and leaning on his lance, filled with sad and confused thoughts. Here we will leave him in order to follow Sancho Panza, who was no less confused and pensive than his master. He'd hardly gone out of the forest when, first having turned around to see if don Quixote was in sight, he got off his donkey, and sitting down at the foot of a tree, began to talk to himself, saying: "'Let's see now, brother Sancho, where are you going? Is your grace looking for a donkey that got lost?' 'No, not that.' 'Well, what *are* you looking for?' 'I'm looking for a princess, that's all, and she's the sun of beauty and heaven combined.' 'And where do you plan to find what you're looking for, Sancho?' 'In the great city of El Toboso.' 'All right, and on whose behalf are you looking for her?' 'On behalf of the knight don Quixote de La Mancha, who rights wrongs and feeds those who are thirsty, and gives something to eat to those who are thirsty.' 'All this is very good. And do you know where her house is, Sancho?' 'My master says it has to be a royal

---

* The usual form of this saying is "Where you think that there is bacon, there are no stakes." You've seen the normal version several times.

palace or splendid castle.' 'And did you see her one day by chance?' 'Neither I nor my master has ever seen her.' 'And do you think it'd be wise if the people of El Toboso knew you're going there intending to entice away their princesses and disturb their ladies, and won't they come after you and pound your ribs until you don't have a sound bone left in your body?' 'In truth they would be right, unless they realized that I'm only the messenger, and that

> Friend, as a messenger you came,
> and therefore shall not meet with blame.*

"'Don't put any trust in that, Sancho, because the people from La Mancha can be as angry as they are honorable and won't put up with anything from anybody, and if they suspect something, I promise you'll have bad luck.' Get out of here! 'Let the lightning bolt hit someone else!' 'I'm not going to look for three legs on the cat.' Furthermore, looking for Dulcinea in El Toboso is like looking for Marica in Ravenna† or a bachelor in Salamanca. The devil, the devil himself has gotten me into this and no one else."

Sancho said this soliloquy to himself, and the upshot of it was that he continued, saying: "All right, everything can be fixed except death, under whose yoke everyone must pass when our life ends, even though we don't like it. Now, this master of mine from all appearances I've seen is as mad as a hatter, and I'm not far behind; in fact I'm more of an idiot than he is, since I follow and serve him, and the saying is true that says: 'Tell me the company you keep, and I'll tell you who you are,' and the other one that says: 'Not with whom you're bred but with whom you're fed.' But being crazy as he is, and his madness being of the kind where he takes one thing for another, and says that white is black and black is white, such as when it seemed to him that the windmills were giants, and the mules of the friars dromedaries, and the flocks of sheep enemy armies, and many other things of that sort, it wouldn't be hard to make

---

* This is from a ballad where Bernardo del Carpio rejects a message from the king, but doesn't blame the messenger for its contents.
† Ravenna is in northern Italy, near the Adriatic Sea, south of Venice and east of Bologna. *Marica* is an affectionate diminutive for *María*.

him believe that a peasant girl—the first one that happens along—is the lady Dulcinea, and if he doesn't believe it, I'll swear it's her; and if *he* swears, I'll swear even more; and if he argues, I'll argue more, and in this way I'll always come out on top, no matter what. Maybe through my stubbornness I can put an end to his sending me on this kind of errand, seeing the bad news I bring back; or perhaps he'll think—as I believe he will—that some evil enchanter who he says has it in for him will have changed this woman to do him a wrong turn and cause him grief."

With what Sancho Panza dreamed up, his spirit became more relaxed, and he considered the job as good as done. He waited there until the afternoon to allow sufficient time for don Quixote to think he'd been away long enough to go and come back from El Toboso. But things happened better than he expected, because, when he got up to mount his donkey, he saw coming toward him from El Toboso three peasant girls on three young donkeys or fillies (for the author doesn't state which, although it seems more likely that they were she-asses, since those are what village girls typically ride). But, since this isn't very important, there's no reason to stop to try to verify the truth of the matter.

So, as soon as Sancho saw the three peasant girls, he raced back to fetch his master don Quixote, whom he found sighing and saying a thousand love lamentations. As soon as don Quixote saw him, he said: "What's going on, my friend? Should I mark this day with a white stone or a black one?"*

"It would be better," responded Sancho, "for your grace to mark it with red paint like they do to show professorships† so that everyone will be able to see it."

"So," replied don Quixote, "you have good news."

---

* Pliny the Younger, Book VII, Chapter XL, said that the Thracians put a white stone to indicate a good day, or a black stone to indicate a bad one, in an urn. On their death, the stones would be counted and the proportion would reveal how happy their lives had been. From there came the Roman custom of saying that happy days were identified with a white stone and unhappy ones with a black one. This is Gaos' note.

† At that time, successful candidates for professorships at universities painted their names on the university walls with red paint.

"So good," responded Sancho, "that all your grace has to do is spur Rocinante and ride into the open to see the lady Dulcinea del Toboso, who is coming with two of her maidens to see you."

"Holy God, what are you saying, Sancho, my friend?" said don Quixote. "I hope you aren't deceiving me, nor trying to ease my true sorrow with false joy."

"What good would it do me to deceive you," responded Sancho, "especially since you're so near to finding out my truth? Spur on, *señor*, and come along, and you'll see the princess, our mistress, coming, all dressed up and covered with jewels, like the lady she is. Her maidens and she are a glowing ember of gold. They look like clusters of pearls and diamonds, rubies, brocades more than ten layers thick.* Their hair hangs loose on their shoulders, like so many rays of the sun playing in the wind, and above all they're mounted on three spotted weldings, a sight to see."

"You mean *geldings*, Sancho."

"There's not much difference between *weldings* and *geldings*—but no matter what they're riding, they're the handsomest women you could ever want to see, especially the princess Dulcinea, my lady, who stuns the senses."

"Let's go, Sancho, my son," responded don Quixote, "and as a reward for such news, as unexpected as it is good, I'll give you the best spoils that I win in my first encounter; and if this doesn't please you, I'll give you the colts that my three mares will bear me this year, and you know that they're about ready to foal in the common meadow of our town."

"I'll take the colts," responded Sancho, "because I'm not sure that the spoils of the first encounter will be good."

At this point they left the forest and saw that the three village girls were approaching. Don Quixote surveyed the road leading from El Toboso, and since he could see only the three peasant girls, he became quite flustered, and asked Sancho if he'd left them just outside the city.

"What do you mean, 'just outside the city'?" he responded. "By chance are your eyes in the back of your head? Don't you see that they're these three women, as resplendent as the sun itself at midday?"

---

* This type of working of brocaded fabric had a maximum of *three* layers, not more than ten, as Sancho exaggerates.

"I only see, Sancho," said don Quixote, "three peasant girls on three donkeys."

"May God save me from the devil," responded Sancho. "Is it possible that three geldings—or whatever they're called—as white as fallen snow, appear to you to be donkeys? As God lives, may they pluck out my beard if that's true."

"Well, I tell you, Sancho, my friend," said don Quixote, "that it's as true they're donkeys as I am don Quixote de La Mancha and you are Sancho Panza. At least that's what it looks like to me."

"Hush, *señor*," said Sancho, "and don't say such things. Open your eyes and come and make obeisance to the lady of your thoughts, who is drawing near."

Having said this, he went to receive the three village girls, and getting off his donkey, he took the halter of the donkey of one of the three peasants, and went down on both knees, saying: "Queen and princess and duchess of beauty, may Your Highness and greatness be pleased to receive in your grace and goodwill your captive knight, who stands in your presence as if made of stone, disturbed, and without a pulse, to find himself before your magnificent presence. I'm Sancho Panza, his squire, and he's the overwrought knight don Quixote de La Mancha, also known as the Woebegone Knight."

By this time, don Quixote had gotten down on his knees next to Sancho, and looked with wild and bewildered eyes at the person Sancho called "queen" and "lady," and since he could see only a village girl, and not a very good-looking one, because she was round faced and flat nosed, he was confused and amazed, and he didn't dare say a word. The peasant girls were equally startled, seeing those two men so different from each other and both kneeling before them, and who wouldn't let their companion get by. This girl, who was surly and annoyed, broke the silence, saying: "Get the devil out of the way and let us move on. We're in a hurry."

To which Sancho responded: "Oh, princess and universal lady of El Toboso! How is it that your magnanimous heart doesn't become tender seeing kneeling before your sublime presence the pillar and support of knight-errantry?"

When one of the two others heard this, she said: "Whoa, look how these two little men come to make fun of us country girls, as if we don't know how to joke around just like they do. Go on your way and let us move on, and you'll be better off."

"Stand up, Sancho," said don Quixote. "I see that Fortune, which is not sated with my sorrows,* has blocked all roads that might comfort this wretched soul that I bear in my flesh. And you, summit of all perfection that could be desired, limit of all human refinement, the only relief for this afflicted heart that adores you; since the wicked enchanter who pursues me has placed clouds and cataracts over my eyes, and has changed your peerless beauty and features into those of a poor peasant for my eyes only, unless he has changed me into some horrible monster to make me hateful in your eyes, don't refuse to look at me tenderly and lovingly, witnessing in my submission on bended knees, which I'm making before your deformed beauty, the humility with which my soul adores you."

"Get out of here!" said the village girl. "I'm not one to listen to this flattery nonsense! Move away and let us go by, and thank you very much."

Sancho moved away and let her pass by, very pleased with the way his deception was working out.

As soon as the village girl who had played the part of Dulcinea found herself free, she spurred her "welding" with her pointed stick and started to race across the meadow. And since the donkey felt the prick much more than usual, it began to buck in such a way that it threw the lady Dulcinea to the ground, and when don Quixote saw what happened, he went over to help her get up, and Sancho went to tighten the packsaddle that had slipped beneath the animal's stomach. He adjusted the packsaddle, and as don Quixote went to lift his enchanted lady onto the donkey, she relieved him of that chore by getting up by herself, and taking a couple of steps back, took a little run, slapped both hands on the rear of the donkey, and vaulted astride onto the packsaddle like a man, as light as a falcon. Sancho exclaimed: "By golly, that lady, our mistress, is as light as a hawk, and can show the most skillful Cordoban or Mexican a thing or two about mounting a horse. She went over the

---

* Starting with *Fortune*, this is a verse taken directly from Garcilaso's *Third Eclogue*.

back of the saddle in a single leap, and without spurs she makes a welding run like a zebra, and her maidens are not far behind, for they're all running like the wind."

And it was true, because as soon as Dulcinea got mounted, they all pricked their donkeys and shot off running, without looking back for half a league. Don Quixote followed them with his eyes, and after they disappeared, he turned to Sancho and said: "Sancho, what do you think of those enchanters who despise me so? Look to what point their evil and dislike extends, since they wanted to deprive me of the joy I could have had seeing my lady in her proper form. Truly, I was born to be an example of the unfortunate— to be the bull's-eye where the arrows of bad luck are aimed and shot. And you must also be aware, Sancho, that these traitors were not content just with having changed and transformed my Dulcinea, but rather having changed and transformed her into a figure so low and ugly as that of a village girl, and what's more they took from her something that ladies of rank have, which is a pleasant aroma, since they're always scented by perfume and flowers. I'll have you know, Sancho, that when I went to help Dulcinea get onto her gelding, as you call it, which seemed to be a donkey to me, she smelled of raw garlic, which made me gag and poisoned my soul."

"Oh, the vile creatures!" Sancho shouted. "Oh, ill-fated and evil-minded enchanters, if only I could see you all strung up by your gills like sardines on a stick! You know much, you are empowered to do much, yet you do even more. It should have been enough, you rascals, to have changed the pearly eyes of my lady into cork tree gall* and her hair of purest gold into the reddish hair of an oxtail, and finally, all of her features from good to bad, not to mention her smell, because by it alone we would see what was hidden by that ugly bark. Although, to tell the truth, I never saw her ugliness, only her beauty, which was enhanced by a mole she had above her lip on the right side, kind of like a mustache, with seven or eight red hairs longer than a half a foot growing out like golden locks."

---

* Spanish uses the same word, *agalla*, in two meanings. It was just used to mean "fish gill," and here, it is repeated in the meaning of "gall," which is an abnormal growth of plant tissue owing to infection.

"According to the way bodily moles correspond," replied don Quixote, "she must have another one on the side of her thigh where she has the one on her face. But hairs of the length you describe are very long for moles of the size you've mentioned."

"Well, I can tell your grace," responded Sancho, "that they were there as plain as day."

"I believe it, my friend," responded don Quixote, "because nature didn't put anything on Dulcinea that was not perfect, and so, if she had a hundred moles as you describe, on her they wouldn't be moles, but shining moons and stars. But tell me, Sancho, that thing that seemed to me to be a packsaddle that you adjusted, was it a plain saddle or a sidesaddle?"

"It was neither," responded Sancho. "It was one with high pommels and short stirrups, with a decorated saddle blanket worth half a kingdom, so rich did it seem."

"And I didn't see any of it, Sancho!" said don Quixote. "I say once again and I'll say a thousand more times that I'm the most unfortunate of men."

The jokester Sancho had a hard time concealing his laughter, hearing the foolishness of his master, so exquisitely deceived was he. Finally, after further conversation between them, they got back on their mounts and headed again toward Zaragoza, where they planned to arrive in time for the solemn jousts that take place in that illustrious city. But before they arrived, certain things happened to them, and because they were so many, so important, and so unusual, they deserve to be written down and read, as will be seen.

Chapter XI. About the strange adventure that happened to don Quixote with the wagon or cart of the Parliament of Death.

DON QUIXOTE was lost in thought as he rode along the road, considering the mischievous turn the enchanters had done him, changing his lady Dulcinea into the lowly village girl, and he couldn't figure out a way to change her back. These thoughts upset him so that without being aware of it, he let his reins drop, and Rocinante—realizing he could amble freely—stopped to graze on the green grass, which was abundant in those fields. Sancho Panza roused him from his reverie, telling him: "*Señor*, sadness was not made for beasts, rather for men, but if men dwell on it too much they become beasts. Perk up, your grace, and be yourself once again and pick up Rocinante's reins. Take heart, and show that gallantry knights-errant possess. What the devil is this? Why are you in such low spirits? 'Are we here or in France?' Let the devil carry off as many Dulcineas as there are in the world, because the well-being of a single knight-errant is worth more than all the enchantments and transformations on earth."

"Hush, Sancho," responded don Quixote with a voice not too faint. "Hush, I say, and say no blasphemies against that enchanted lady—for I alone am responsible for her misfortune. Her ill luck is born of the envy that the wicked bear me."

"That's what I say," responded Sancho. "'He who saw her then and sees her now, what heart wouldn't weep?'"*

"You can say that, Sancho," replied don Quixote, "since you saw her in the wholeness of her beauty. The enchantment didn't extend to the point of changing your sight or disguising her beauty. Their venom is aimed against me and my eyes alone. But I realize even so, Sancho, that in one detail you described her beauty poorly, because—if I'm not remembering incorrectly—you said that she has pearly eyes. Eyes that look like pearls belong rather to a fish than to a lady, and the way I see it, the eyes of Dulcinea must be almond-shaped green emeralds, with two heavenly rainbows that serve as eyebrows. Take these pearls away and give them to her teeth. Doubtless you were mixed up and took her eyes for her teeth."

"Anything is possible," responded Sancho, "because I was as much dazed by her beauty as you were vexed by her ugliness. But let's commend it all to God, because He's the knower of all things that will happen in this vale of tears, in this evil world we live in, where you can hardly find anything not tainted by iniquity, tricks, and mischief.

---

* Sancho adapts an old proverb here, where "you" is used instead of "her."

One thing distresses me, *señor mío*, more than all the others, and that is thinking about what will happen when your grace conquers a giant or another knight and sends them to present themselves before the beauty of the lady Dulcinea—where will the poor giant or the poor, miserable defeated knight go to find her? I can imagine them wandering around El Toboso like idiots looking for my lady Dulcinea, and although they might see her in the middle of the street they won't recognize her more than they would my father."

"Perhaps, Sancho," responded don Quixote, "the enchantment will not prevent the conquered people and the giants and knights that I send from recognizing Dulcinea. We'll try an experiment with one or two of the first people I conquer and send to her—if they see her, I'll command them to come back and tell me exactly what they saw."

"*Señor*," replied Sancho, "what you've said seems good to me, and with this ploy we'll find out what we want to know, and if it turns out that her beauty is hidden only from you, the misfortune will be more yours than hers. But since Dulcinea will be healthy and happy, we can adapt and make the best of it, and we'll continue looking for adventures, letting time run its course, because time is the best doctor for these and other greater maladies."

Don Quixote wanted to answer Sancho Panza, but a cart that was crossing the road prevented him. It was carrying the most diverse and strange characters that one could imagine. The person driving the cart and serving as carter was an ugly demon. The cart itself was open, without a canopy. The first figure who presented himself to don Quixote's eyes was that of Death, with a human face; next to him was an angel with some large painted wings. To his side was an emperor with a crown, seemingly of gold, on his head. At the feet of Death was the god they call Cupid, without a blindfold over his eyes, but with his bow, quiver, and arrows. There was also a knight in armor from head to foot, without a closed helmet, but wearing a plumed hat of several colors. With these came other persons of different dress and makeup. All this, seen so suddenly, startled don Quixote, and instilled fear in the heart of Sancho. But soon don Quixote became happy again, believing that he was being handed a new and dangerous adventure, and with this thought in mind, and with a heart resolved to meet any danger, he placed himself in front of the cart and, with a loud and menacing voice, said: "Carter, driver, devil, or whatever you are, tell me right now who you are, where you're coming from, and who the people are that you're taking on your wagon, because this appears more like Charon's boat* than a regular cart."

To which the devil on the cart responded meekly: "*Señor*, we're actors of the company belonging to Angulo el Malo.† This morning, since it's the Sunday following Corpus Christi,‡ we performed a play called *The Parliament of Death* in a village on the other side of that hill, and we have to perform it again in that village you can see over yonder, and since the distance is so short, we're going in costume so we won't have to undress and dress up again. That young fellow is dressed as Death, the other as an angel. That woman, who is the manager's wife, is the queen, the other fellow is a soldier, that one an emperor, and I'm the devil, one of the main characters in the play, because I always play the important roles in this company. And if you want to know anything else, just ask me, and I'll be able to answer in detail—since I'm the devil I know everything."

"On the faith of a knight-errant," responded don Quixote, "when I saw this cart, I thought that some great adventure was awaiting me, but now I say that you have to touch appearances with your hand to let the truth come through. Go with God, good people. Prepare your performance. And if there's anything I can help you with, I'll do it with pleasure and goodwill, because since I was a boy I've been a fan of the theater, and in my youth I thought I would become an actor."

While this conversation was going on, as luck would

---

* Charon was the ferryman who transported the dead across the River Styx into hell.

† There was such a theater manager, as Clemencín well explains on p. 1570 of his edition, who would have been seventy-six years old in 1615.

‡ Corpus Christi celebrates the presence of the body of Jesus in holy communion. It takes place on the Thursday following the first Sunday after Pentecost, or Whitsunday, which is itself fifty days after Easter. Typically it is in June or July. As part of the celebration, sacred plays were performed, such as this one.

have it, another member of the company arrived dressed as
a jester, with many jingle bells, and at the end of a stick he
had three cow bladders inflated with air. This young fellow,
when he approached don Quixote, began to brandish his
stick and beat the ground with the bladders and leapt in the
air, making the bells ring. Rocinante was so startled at this sight
that, without don Quixote being able to stop him, taking the
bit between his teeth, he began to race across the countryside
with greater speed than one would have thought the bones
of his body would allow. Sancho, who thought that his master was in danger of being thrown off, jumped down from
his donkey and ran at full speed to rescue him. But when he
got to him, he was already on the ground with Rocinante
next to him, because he'd fallen along with his master. This
was the usual outcome of the horse's exuberance and his
master's daring acts.

But hardly had Sancho left his mount to tend to don
Quixote when the demon jester jumped onto the donkey
and began beating him with the bladders. The donkey,
more from fear and the noise than from the pain caused
by the blows, flew along the countryside toward where they
were going to perform. Sancho saw the racing donkey and
the fall of his master and didn't know which of the two situations to take care of first. But as with a good squire and
a good servant, the love for Sancho's master was stronger
than the care of his donkey, although every time he saw
the bladders rise in the air and fall upon the haunches of
his donkey, they were for him anguish and fright of death,
and he would have preferred that those blows had fallen
on his own eyes than on the least hair of the donkey's tail.
With this perplexing tribulation he got to where don Quixote was, more beaten up than he would have liked, and,
helping him back onto Rocinante, said to him: "*Señor*, the
devil has taken the donkey."

"What devil?" asked don Quixote.

"The one with the bladders."

"Well, I'll get the donkey back," replied don Quixote,
"even if that fellow should lock himself up with the donkey
in the deepest dungeon of hell. Follow me, Sancho, because
the cart is going slowly, and with one of its mules I'll make
up for the loss of your mount."

"There's no need, *señor*," responded Sancho. "Calm

down, because it looks like the devil has left the donkey, and he's coming back."

And it was true, because the devil had fallen from the donkey to imitate don Quixote and Rocinante and was heading on foot to the village while the donkey returned to his master.

"Even so," said don Quixote, "it's a good idea to punish someone on the cart for the rudeness of that devil, even though it's the emperor himself."

"Don't even consider it, your grace," replied Sancho, "and take my advice—never mess with actors, since they're a privileged group. I've seen an actor arrested for two murders and be set free. Your grace should know that they're merry people and give pleasure, and everyone is on their side, everyone protects, helps, and treasures them, and all the more since that troupe is among those that have official charters from the crown, and all or most of them in their costumes and demeanor seem like princes."

"No matter," responded don Quixote. "That devil actor is not going to get away boasting, even if the whole human race is on his side."

And saying this, he went over to the cart that was on its way to the town. He rode along shouting: "Stop, wait, you merry and festive mob, because I want to make you see how you should treat donkeys and other animals that serve as mounts to knights and squires of knights-errant!"

Don Quixote's shouts were so loud that the people in the cart heard and understood them, and, judging his intention by his words, Death leapt down from the cart in an instant, and after him the emperor, the devil cart driver and the angel, joined by the queen and Cupid. All of them picked up stones and waited in a line, expecting to receive don Quixote with the sharp edges of their stones. Don Quixote, who saw them form a lively squadron with their arms raised showing their intention to throw the stones, pulled back on Rocinante's reins, and began to consider how he could attack with the least danger to himself. Sancho arrived, and seeing him ready to attack the well-formed squadron, said: "It would be foolhardy to try to take on such a venture, because there's no defensive armor in the world to keep your hat on amidst flying stones, unless you hide under a bronze bell. You also have to consider that it's more recklessness than bravery for a single man to attack an army led by Death, where emperors fight in person, and where good and bad angels lend assistance. And if this consideration doesn't make you pause, you should realize that among all those there you see kings, princes, and emperors, but there's no knight-errant."

"Now," said don Quixote, "you've hit upon the point that can and should make me change my mind. I can't nor should I unsheathe my sword, as I've told you many times, against anyone who has not been dubbed a knight. It's up to you, Sancho, to avenge the offense they did to your donkey, and I'll lend support from here with shouts to offer sound advice."

"There's no need, *señor*," responded Sancho, "to take vengeance on anyone, since good Christians shouldn't avenge offenses. Furthermore I'll arrange with my donkey to submit his offense to my own will, which is to live peacefully all the days of life that heaven has allocated me."

"If that's your decision," replied don Quixote, "good Sancho, discreet Sancho, Christian Sancho, sincere Sancho, let's abandon these phantoms and seek better and worthier adventures. I believe that this area won't fail to offer us many and very miraculous ones."

He turned his reins, and Sancho went to get his donkey. Death and all of his renegade squadron went to their cart and continued their journey. This was the happy ending of the fearful adventure of the Cart of Death, and may thanks be given to the upright counsel given by Sancho Panza to his master, to whom the next day came an adventure with another enamored and errant knight, with no less suspense than the preceding one.

Chapter XII. About the strange adventure that happened to the brave knight don Quixote with the brave Knight of the Mirrors.

DON QUIXOTE and his squire spent the night that followed the encounter with Death under some tall, shady trees, and Sancho persuaded don Quixote to eat some of what was in the donkey's saddlebags. During dinner, Sancho said to his master: "*Señor*, I would have been a fool to have chosen the spoils of the first adventure that your grace had instead of the colts of the three mares. It's really true that a 'bird in the hand is worth two in the bush.'"

"Still," responded don Quixote, "if you, Sancho, had let me attack as I wanted to, you would have at least gotten the empress' crown of gold, and Cupid's painted wings, which I would have taken against their will and placed into your hands."

"Crowns and scepters of actors," responded Sancho Panza, "never are of real gold but rather of foil and tin."

"That's true," replied don Quixote, "because props shouldn't be real, but pretend and make-believe, just like the play itself, toward which I would like you, Sancho, to be well-disposed; and by the same token toward those who perform and write them, because all of them are instruments of great good to the republic, placing a mirror before us at every step, where we see a live representation of human life. There's nothing that portrays so vividly what we are and what we should strive to be than plays and their actors do. Tell me, haven't you been at plays where you see kings, emperors, and popes; knights, ladies, and other diverse characters? One plays the ruffian, another the trickster, this one the merchant, that one the soldier, another the idiot, and another the fool in love. And when the play is over and the actors take off their costumes, they're all equal."

"Yes, I've seen them," said Sancho.

"Well, the same thing," said don Quixote, "that happens in plays happens in life—some are emperors, others popes, and all the characters that there are in a play. But when the end comes, which is when life ends, Death takes away all the clothing that differentiates them and they become equal in the grave."

"A fine comparison," said Sancho, "although not so new that I haven't heard it many, *many* times, like the business of the game of chess—while it's being played, each piece has its particular function, and when the game is over, they're all mixed up and jumbled together, and they're put into a bag, which is like finishing one's life in the grave."

"Every day, Sancho," said don Quixote, "you're becoming wiser and less of a dolt."

"Yes, because something of your grace's wisdom has rubbed off," responded Sancho. "Land is barren and dry by itself, but by spreading manure on it and cultivating it, it gives good fruit. I mean that my conversations with you have been the manure that has fallen on the dry soil of my barren intellect. The cultivation of this land is the time that I've been serving and talking with you, and I hope all this will bear fruit that will not be unworthy and will not slip off the path of good breeding on which your grace has been guiding my infertile understanding."

Don Quixote laughed when he heard Sancho's stilted words, but what he said about his improvement seemed true enough, because once in a while Sancho spoke in a way that amazed him, although most of the time when Sancho wanted to talk in a learnèd or in a courtly way, his speech wound up tumbling from the mountain of his simplicity to the abyss of his ignorance. His strongest suit was bringing in proverbs, whether or not they were to the point, as will have been seen and noticed throughout the course of this history.

In these and other conversations they spent most of the night, and Sancho felt like closing the floodgates of his eyes, as he used to say when he wanted to go to sleep. After he took the packsaddle off the donkey, he let him graze freely on the abundant pasture. He didn't take the saddle off Rocinante, since he was expressly told by his master not to remove it when they were roaming the countryside or not sleeping under a roof—an ancient custom established and kept by knights-errant. It was all right to take the bridle and hang it from the pommel, but take the horse's saddle off—never! And that's what Sancho did, and gave him the same freedom as the donkey, whose friendship with Rocinante was so unique and strong that tradition from father to son says that the author of this true history devoted particular chapters to it, but that, in order to maintain the dignity and decorum such a heroic history deserves, he didn't include them, although once in a while he strayed from this resolve, and writes when the two animals were together they scratched one another, and after they were finished scratching each other and were satisfied, Rocinante would cross his neck half a yard beyond the neck of the donkey, and the two of them would look attentively at the ground, and would stay that way for three days, at least, except when hunger made them look for something to eat.

They say that the author had written that he'd compared them with the friendship between Nisus and Euryalus, and Pylades and Orestes,* and if this is true, one can notice— for universal wonder—how solid the friendship of these two peaceful animals was, to the shame of men who know so little about keeping friends.

And don't think that the author went far astray in comparing the friendship of these animals with that of men, because from the beasts men have gotten many lessons and have learned several important things, as, for example: from storks the enema;† from dogs, vomiting and gratitude; from cranes, vigilance; from ants, foresight; from elephants, chastity; and loyalty from the horse.

Finally, Sancho went to sleep at the foot of a cork tree and don Quixote dozed next to a robust oak. But little time had gone by when don Quixote was wakened by a noise he heard behind him. He got up with a start and began to look and listen in the direction of where the noise came from, and saw there were two men on horseback. One of them, as he got off his horse, said to the other: "Dismount, my friend, and take the bridles from the horses, because I think this site abounds in grass for them; and in silence and solitude, which my amorous thoughts require."

He said this at the same time he stretched out on the ground, and when he lay down, his armor clanked, a sure sign that revealed to don Quixote that he must be a knight-errant. He approached Sancho, who was sleeping, took his arm, and with no little struggle roused him, and with a quiet voice said: "Brother Sancho, we've got an adventure."

---

* These are two pairs of male friends from mythology. Nisus and Euryalus have already been mentioned in Part I, chapter forty-eight, page 457. Both were companions of Æneas, and were killed together while raiding a Latin camp. Pylades and Orestes were boyhood friends. Pylades married Electra, Orestes' sister.

† All of these traits about animals come from Pliny, except that the reference to the stork here is the Egyptian ibis in Pliny (*Natural History*, book eight, chapter twenty-seven). You can read there how this autoenema is administered. Clemencín gives all the references on p. 1578 of his edition.

"May God grant that it be a good one," responded Sancho, "and where is her grace, Madam Adventure?"

"Where, Sancho?" replied don Quixote. "Turn your eyes and look over there, and you'll see a knight-errant stretched out. The way it looks to me, he must not be too happy, because I saw him slide off his horse and stretch out on the ground with some show of despair, and when he went to the ground, his armor clanked."

"So, how can your grace tell," said Sancho, "this is an adventure?"

"I don't mean it's an adventure at all, but the beginning of one—all adventures begin this way. But listen—it sounds like he's tuning a lute or a vihuela,* and the way he's spitting and clearing his throat, he must be getting ready to sing something."

"I'll bet that's what he's going to do, all right," responded Sancho, "and he must be a knight in love."

"There are no knights who aren't in love," said don Quixote. "Let's listen to him; if he sings, we'll get a clue to his thoughts, because the tongue speaks from the outpouring of the heart."†

Sancho was of a mind to reply, but the voice of the Knight of the Forest, which was neither good nor bad, prevented him, and the two of them were astonished as they heard him sing this sonnet:

SONNET

Your pleasure, please, lady mine, unfold;
> Declare the terms that I am to obey;
> My will to yours submissively I mold,
> And from your law my feet shall never stray.

---

* The lute was originally a Moorish fretted stringed musical instrument. The Spanish lute has a teardrop-shaped body and typically has six pairs of strings. The striking feature is that the mechanical head to which the strings are attached is bent back almost ninety degrees owing to the pressure of the strings. The vihuela was a Hispanic instrument, usually with six strings, tuned like a lute, thus don Quixote's confusion.

† Matthew 12:34: "For the words that the mouth utters come from the overwhelming of the heart."

Would you I die, to silent grief a prey?
  Then count me even now as dead and cold;
  Would you I tell my woes in some new way?
  Then shall my tale by Love itself be told.
The unison of opposites to prove,
  Of the soft wax and diamond hard am I;
  But still, obedient to the laws of love,
Here, hard or soft, I offer you my breast,
  Whatever you grave or stamp thereon shall rest
  Indelible for all eternity.*

With an *AY!* yanked, seemingly, from the deepest part of his heart, the Knight of the Forest finished his song, and a moment later, with a doleful and lamenting voice, said: "Oh, you most beautiful and ungrateful woman in the world! How can it be, most serene Casildea de Vandalia,† that you allow your captive knight to be consumed, and persist in continual wanderings and in harsh and difficult travails? Isn't it enough that I've made all of the knights of Navarre, all the Leonese, all the Tartessian,‡ all the Castilian, and finally, all the Manchegan knights confess that you're the most beautiful woman in the world?"

"That can't be," said don Quixote. "*I'm* from La Mancha and I never confessed anything like that, nor could nor should I confess something so prejudicial to the beauty of my lady. That knight is talking nonsense, as you see, Sancho. But let's listen—maybe he'll say something else."

But that didn't happen, because the Knight of the Forest, having overheard them, without continuing his lamentation, stood up and said in a loud but courteous voice: "Who goes there? Is it perhaps one of the happy or one of the distressed?"

"One of the distressed," responded don Quixote.

"Well, come here," responded he of the Forest, "but un-

---

* Ormsby's translation.
† Casildea is a variant of Casilda. Vandalia is Andalusia.
‡ Navarre was the kingdom bordering on France between Castile and Aragón. The ancient kingdom of León bordered on Castile to the west. The Tartessians were the Andalusians in Phœnician times.

derstand that you're approaching sadness and distress personified."

Don Quixote, who saw that he was answered so kindly and courteously, drew near, as did Sancho as well. The mournful knight took don Quixote by the arm, saying: "Sit here, *señor* knight; it's enough for me to have found you in this desolate place, with only the solitude and night breeze to keep you company, to prove to me that you're among the distressed and among those who profess knight-errantry."

To which don Quixote responded: "A knight I am, and of the profession you mention, but even though sadness and misfortune properly dwell in my soul, the compassion I have for other people's misfortunes has not been banished from it. From what you sang a moment ago I gather that your misfortune derives from love; I mean, the love of that beautiful ingrate you mentioned in your lament."

And while the two were talking, they were sitting next to each other on the hard ground in good peace and fellowship, and not at all as if when day broke, they weren't going to have to crack each other's heads open.

"By chance, *señor* knight," asked he of the Forest to don Quixote, "are you in love?"

"By misfortune I am," responded don Quixote, "although loss that's born of good intentions should rather be held as favors than misfortunes."

"That's the truth," replied he of the Forest, "if disdain didn't upset our reason and understanding; but too much disdain smacks of vengeance."

"I was never disdained by my lady," responded don Quixote.

"No, certainly not," said Sancho, who was sitting nearby, "because she's like a tame lamb, and is softer than butter."

"Is this your squire?" asked he of the Forest.

"Yes, he is," responded don Quixote.

"I've never seen a squire," replied he of the Forest, "who dares to speak when his master is talking. At least, there's mine, and he's as tall as his father, yet no one can prove that he has ever opened his mouth when I'm speaking."

"Well, I swear," said Sancho, "that I've spoken and can speak before another such . . . and let it drop, because it'll be worse to stir it up."

The Squire of the Forest took Sancho by the arm, saying to him: "Let's go the two of us where we can speak as squires as much as we want, and let's leave these two masters of ours to quarrel about the stories of their loves. I'm pretty sure they won't have finished by sunup."

"All right," said Sancho, "and I'll tell your grace who I am so that you'll see if I can join the most talkative squires."

With this, they went away, and had as amusing a conversation as the one their masters had was serious.

Chapter XIII. Where the adventure of the Knight of the Forest is continued, with the discreet, novel, and delicious conversation that took place between the two squires.

THE KNIGHTS and squires were now separated, the former telling about their loves and the latter about their lives. But the history first tells of the conversation between the servants and then moves on to that of the masters, and so it says that, separating themselves a bit from their masters, the one of the Forest said to Sancho: "It's a difficult life we lead and live, *señor mío*, those of us who are squires of knights-errant. In truth we eat bread by the sweat of our brows,* which is one of the curses God laid on our original parents."

"You can also say," added Sancho, "that we eat it in the chill of our bodies, because who suffers more heat and more cold than those wretched squires of knight-errantry? It wouldn't be as bad if we ate well, since 'sorrows grow less when accompanied by food.' As it stands, we sometimes go a day or two without eating anything, unless it's the wind that blows."

"But we can put up with all that," said the one of the Forest, "in the expectation we have of getting the reward, because if the knight-errant whom the squire serves is not too unfortunate, at least, after a while, he will be rewarded with a nice *ínsula*, or with a pretty good earldom."

---

* Genesis 3:19: "You shall earn your bread by the sweat of your brow."

"I," replied Sancho, "have already told my master that I'll be happy with the government of an *ínsula*, and he's so noble and liberal that he has promised it to me many times."

"I," said he of the Forest, "I will be satisfied with a canonry in exchange for my services, and my master has already promised it to me, and such a one it is, too!"

"It must be," said Sancho, "that your grace's master is an ecclesiastical knight and can offer these favors to his good squire, but mine is just a lay knight, although I remember when certain wise—but I thought ill-intentioned—people wanted to advise him to try to be an archbishop. He only wanted to be an emperor, but it made me nervous at the time, because if he felt like going into the Church, I wasn't up to having an ecclesiastical job. I'll tell your grace that although I look like a man, I'm a beast as far as a job in the Church is concerned."

"But in truth your grace is mistaken," said the one of the Forest, "because islands aren't all they're touted to be. Some of them are corrupt, some poor, some gloomy, and even the proudest and healthiest one carries with it the ponderous weight of woes and lack of comfort, which the unfortunate person to whose lot it falls must bear on his shoulders. Much better would be for those of us who profess this cursèd servitude to go to our homes and there tend to lighter duties, such as hunting or fishing. I mean, what squire in the world is so poor that he doesn't have a horse, a couple of greyhounds, and a fishing pole to pass the time of day in his town?"

"I lack none of those items," responded Sancho. "Well, I don't have a horse, but I have a donkey worth twice as much as my master's horse. And I'll tell you the truth—I'd never switch my mount for his, even if they gave me six bushels of wheat to boot, though your grace may think that the value I place on my silver-gray—that's his color—is a joke. As for greyhounds, they abound in my town. And what's more, hunting is more fun when it's done at someone else's expense."*

"Really and truly," responded the one of the Forest, "*se-*

---

* That is, if it's not clear to you, Sancho enjoys using someone else's dogs to hunt with.

ñor squire, I'm determined to leave the absurdities of these knights and retire to my home to raise my little children—I have three, as precious as Oriental pearls."

"Two is how many I have," said Sancho, "worthy of being presented to the pope in person, especially the girl, who I'm training to be a countess, if God is so pleased, in spite of her mother."

"And how old is this lady being trained to be a countess?" asked he of the Forest.

"Fifteen, two more or less," responded Sancho, "but she's as tall as a lance, and fresh as an April morn, and she's as strong as a porter."

"Those are qualities," responded he of the Forest, "that not only can make her a countess but the nymph of the green forest. What a whore daughter of a whore, how strong that one must be!"

To which Sancho responded, somewhat annoyed: "She's no whore, nor was her mother before her, and neither ever will be, God willing, while I'm alive. Speak more courteously. Since your grace was trained by knights-errant—who are courtesy personified—your words don't seem very well chosen."

"Oh, how little your grace understands," replied he of the Forest, "about the nature of praise, *señor* squire! How is it you don't know that when a knight gives a good thrust with his lance in the bullring, or when someone does something really good, the common folk typically say: 'Son of a bitch! How well he did that!' and what might at first seem to be a rebuke in that circumstance turns out to be particular praise? You should disown, *señor*, any children who don't do deeds that deserve that kind of praise from their parents."

"Yes, I'll disown them," responded Sancho, "and in that way for that same reason, your grace can heap upon me, my children, and my wife any of those insults, because everything they do and say is worth such praise in the extreme. And so I can return home to see them again, I pray to God to save me from mortal sin,* which is just the same as saving me from this profession, into which I've fallen a second

---

* A mortal sin is a sin of the worst kind. If a Catholic dies with a mortal sin not yet absolved, that person will go to hell.

time, baited and enticed by a purse with a hundred *ducados* I found one day in the heart of the Sierra Morena. The devil puts a sack of doubloons* before my eyes, here, there, everywhere—not quite within reach, so that I can almost touch it with my hand and embrace it at every step, and hug it and take it home, and invest it, set up an income and live like a prince. And while I'm thinking about this, it makes tolerable all the travails that I endure with this imbecile master of mine—who I know is more of a crazy man than a knight."

"That's why they say," responded he of the Forest, "'greed bursts the bag,' but if you're talking about crazy men, there's no greater one in the world than my master— he's of those about whom it's said: 'other people's cares killed the donkey,'† because he has turned himself into a crazy man so that another person might recover his lost sanity, and he's seeking something that, when he finds it, is liable to blow up in his face."

"And is he in love, by chance?"

"Yes," said he of the Forest, "with a certain Casildea de Vandalia, the rawest and the cruelest woman‡ who can be found in the whole world. But her cruelty isn't bothering him right now—he's got other schemes growling inside him, as will be seen in a few hours."

"'There's no road so flat,'" replied Sancho, "'that it doesn't have bumps and obstacles.' 'In other houses they boil beans, but in mine they boil by the cauldronful.'§ Madness has more followers and servants than wisdom does. But if it's true what they commonly say, that 'misery loves company,' with your grace I can be consoled, since you serve a master as crazy as mine."

"Crazy, but brave," responded he of the Forest, "and more of a scalawag than crazy and brave."

---

* The doubloon was a gold coin of varying value, from two to eight *escudos*.
† This saying refers to meddling in other people's business and suffering the consequences.
‡ There is a pun here. The Spanish word *cruda* means "cruel," which is what we expect the woman to be, but it also means "raw."
§ This saying means that the speaker thinks his troubles are greater than the next person's.

"Mine's not that way," responded Sancho. "I mean, there's nothing of the rogue about him. He's as kind as can be. He doesn't know how to harm anybody, but does good to all. A child can make him believe that it's night at noontime, and because of this simplicity I love him with all my heart and I can't leave him, no matter how many foolish things he does."

"But, brother and *señor*," said he of the Forest, "'if the blind lead the blind, both run the risk of falling into the pit.' It's better for us to return soon to our homes, because those who seek adventures don't always find good ones."

Sancho was spitting frequently, and his spit was viscous and somewhat dry, which was seen and noted by the charitable Squire of the Forest, who said: "It seems to me that we have spoken so much, our tongues are sticking to the roofs of our mouths. But I have an unsticker hanging from the pommel of my horse, and it's really good."

He got up and came back a moment later with a large wineskin and a meat pie half a yard wide (and this is no exaggeration, because there was a white rabbit inside that Sancho, when he felt it, thought was a goat, and not just a kid), and when he saw it he said: "Is this the kind of thing your grace takes along, *señor*?"

"What do you think?" said the other. "Am I by chance one of those poor-relation squires? I have better provisions on the haunches of my horse than a general takes with him when he goes on a campaign."

Sancho ate without any urging and he drank wine in the darkness in large gulps, and said: "Your grace is certainly a faithful, loyal, perfect, magnificent, and great squire, as can be seen by this banquet, which if it didn't come here by enchantment, at least it seems like it. Unlike me, wretched and unfortunate that I am—all I have is some cheese hard enough to brain a giant, together with four dozen carob beans and as many hazelnuts and walnuts, thanks to the stinginess of my master. It's his opinion, and the rule he keeps, that knights-errant have to feed and sustain themselves only with nuts and herbs from the fields."

"On my faith, brother," replied the one of the Forest, "my stomach wasn't made for thistles or wild pears, nor for roots from the forest. Let our masters keep their rules and laws of chivalry, and eat whatever they want. I have

lunch baskets and this wineskin hanging from the pommel
of my saddle, just in case. I'm so devoted to it and I love
it so much that few moments pass without my giving it a
thousand kisses and hugs."

And saying this, he put it in the hands of Sancho, who,
raising it to his mouth, sat there looking at the stars for
a quarter of an hour, and when he finished drinking, he
cocked his head to one side and gave a great sigh, and said:
"Oh, the son-of-a-bitch rascal, how good it is."

"You see," said he of the Forest, "how you've praised
that wine by calling it a son of a bitch."

"I confess," responded Sancho, "that I realize that it's
not an insult to call anyone a son of a bitch when it's intended to praise him. But tell me, *señor*, on your mother's
life, isn't this wine from Ciudad Real?"*

"What a wine taster!" responded he of the Forest. "In
truth it's from nowhere else, and it has been aging a few
years."

"No need to tell me," said Sancho. "Don't think that it's
beyond me to recognize that wine. I have such a good and
natural instinct in matters of knowing wines, because just
by the bouquet I can tell you the origin, type, flavor, vin-
tage, and how it was decanted, and everything else about
the wine. But it's no wonder, since I had on my father's
side of the family two of the best wine tasters La Mancha
has had in a long time. To prove it, here's something that
happened to them one day. They gave both of them some
wine to taste from a barrel, asking their opinion of the
condition, characteristics, and goodness or badness of the
wine. One of them put a drop of it on the tip of his tongue,
and the other did no more than smell it. The first one said
that it tasted of iron and the second said that it tasted
more of Cordovan leather. The master said that the barrel
was clean and that the wine had nothing added to it that
would have given it the flavor of iron or of leather. Even
so, the two famous wine tasters maintained what they
had said. As time went by, the wine was sold, and when
the barrel was cleaned they found a small key attached
to a strap of leather inside. And that'll show your grace

---

* This would be a logical guess, since Ciudad Real is the nearest re-
gional wine center.

if someone from that lineage can give his opinion about such things."

"That's why I say," said he of the Forest, "we should stop wandering about seeking adventures. 'We have loaves. Let's not look for cake.' Let's go home, and that's where God will find us, if He wants."

"I'll serve my master until he goes to Zaragoza; then we'll see."

Finally, the two squires spoke and drank so much that sleep had to come to tie their tongues and moderate their thirst—eliminating it would have been impossible. And the two of them, still holding on to the almost empty wineskin, with partially chewed food still in their mouths, went to sleep, and that's how we'll leave them for the time being so we can relate what the Knight of the Forest said to don Quixote.

Chapter XIIII. Where the adventure of the Knight of the Forest continues.

AMONG THE conversations held between don Quixote and the Knight of the Forest, the history states that he of the Forest said to don Quixote: "So, *señor* knight, I would like you to know that my destiny, or, better said, my choice, led me to fall in love with the peerless Casildea de Vandalia. I say that she's peerless because she had no equal either in the size of her body or in the degree of her rank or beauty. This Casildea de Vandalia that I'm talking about rewarded my pure thoughts and gallant desires by making me, as Hercules' stepmother did, engage in many diverse and dangerous labors,* promising me after each one was finished that I would get what I hoped for at the conclusion of the following one. So one labor led to the next and I don't know how many have been done nor which will be the last one—the beginning of the fulfillment of my pure desires. Once, she made me challenge that famous giantess

---

* Juno was Hercules' stepmother, and made him perform the famous Twelve Labors, from killing a lion to bringing the three-headed dog Cerberus up from the underworld.

in Seville called La Giralda.* She's so robust and strong, as if she were made of bronze, and, without moving from where she stands, is the most changeable and fickle woman in the world. I went, I saw her, I conquered her, and I made her stay still because for more than a week only north winds blew.†

"There was another time when she made me go to weigh the ancient stones of the massive Bulls of Guisando,‡ an undertaking more suited to porters than to knights. Once she made me plunge into the pit of Cabra,§ an unheard-of and fearful danger, telling me that I should bring her a description of what is enclosed in those dark depths. I stopped the movement of La Giralda, I weighed the Bulls of Guisando, I plunged into the pit and brought to light what was hidden in its abyss, and my hopes are still as dead as can be, and her orders more alive than ever.

"To conclude, she recently commanded me to roam through all the provinces in Spain and make all knights-errant wandering through them confess that she is superior in beauty to any others living today, and that I'm the bravest and most enamored knight in the world. In pursuit of this quest I've combed most of Spain, and have vanquished many knights who have dared to contradict me. But the one that I'm proudest to have vanquished in battle is that so-famous knight don Quixote de La Mancha, and I made him confess that my Casildea is more beautiful than his Dulcinea, and by this victory alone I consider that I've vanquished all the knights in the world, because this don

---

* The Moorish bell tower beside Seville's cathedral is known as La Giralda today (340 feet tall, built as a minaret in the late twelfth century), but technically *giralda* refers only to the weather-vane statue of a woman at its top. The statue is made of bronze, as the knight goes on to say.

† That is, because only north winds blew, the weather vane remained still.

‡ The four famous "bulls" of Guisando near El Tiemblo (province of Toledo) are pre-Christian representations carved from granite of four-legged animals—they do look more like bulls than anything else. They bear Iberian and Roman inscriptions.

§ The bottomless pit of Cabra is a cave about five miles outside of Cabra (province of Cordova). Supposedly it is one of the entrances to hell.

Quixote that I mention has conquered them all, and since I defeated him, his glory, fame, and honor have been transferred to me:

> The more the vanquished boast of fame,
> so much the more the victors claim.*

"So, all of his innumerable deeds of this already mentioned don Quixote belong to me."

Don Quixote was amazed when he heard what the Knight of the Forest had to say; a thousand times he was about to tell him that he was lying, and the denial was on the tip of his tongue, but he refrained from doing so in order to make him confess his lie from his own mouth: "That your grace, *señor* knight, has conquered most of the knights-errant in Spain, I cannot comment about, but that you conquered don Quixote de La Mancha, I doubt it very much—perhaps it was another one who looked like him, although few do."

"What do you mean?" said he of the Forest. "I swear in heaven's name, I fought with don Quixote and conquered and overcame him—he's a tall man with a withered face, his limbs are lanky and tanned, hair turning gray, an aquiline nose with a bit of a hook, and with a long drooping black mustache. He battles under the name of the WOEBEGONE KNIGHT, and has as his squire a peasant named Sancho Panza. He mounts and holds the reins of a famous horse named Rocinante, and finally he has as the mistress of his will a certain Dulcinea del Toboso, called Aldonza Lorenzo, as mine, whom, since she's named Casilda and being from Andalusia, I call Casildea de Vandalia. If all these features don't suffice to establish the truth, here's my sword, that will make incredulity itself believe it."

"Calm down, *señor* knight," said don Quixote, "and listen to what I want to tell you. I want you to know that this don Quixote that you've mentioned is my best friend in the whole world, so much so that I can say that I respect him as much as I do myself, and by the features that you've

---

* These two verses are adapted from *The Araucana*, I: 2, of Alonso de Ercilla (1533–1594), the epic poem about the conquest of the Chilean Indians by the Spaniards.

described to me, so accurate and solid, I have to believe that he was the same one that you've vanquished. On the other hand, what I see with my eyes and touch with my hands is that it cannot be true, unless it's that since he has many enemy enchanters—especially one who pursues him regularly—one of them may have taken on his appearance and let himself be vanquished so as to defraud him of the fame that his chivalric deeds have won and earned for him throughout the known world. And to confirm this, I want you also to know that the enchanters, his enemies, transformed the figure and person of Dulcinea del Toboso into a coarse and low village girl, and in this same way they must have changed don Quixote. And if this doesn't suffice to convince you, here's don Quixote himself who will maintain it with weapons, on foot or on horseback, or in whatever way pleases you."

As he said this, he stood up and took his sword in hand, waiting to find out what decision would be taken by the Knight of the Forest, who, with a calm voice, responded: "'Leaving a pledge doesn't bother a good payer.' He who once, *señor* don Quixote, could vanquish you in a transformed state, can certainly expect to conquer you in your original state. But since it isn't a good idea to take up arms in the dark, like highwaymen and thugs, let's wait for the day to arrive so the sun can witness our combat. And the condition of our battle must be that the conquered one must submit to the will of the victor and do whatever he's told, provided that what is commanded is proper for a knight to obey."

"I'm more than happy with this agreement on terms," responded don Quixote.

Once they had said this, they went over to where their squires were, and they found them snoring and in the same position they were when sleep overtook them. They awakened them and told them to prepare their horses, because when day broke, the two of them were going to have a bloody, single, and arduous battle, at which news Sancho was astonished, and fearful for the well-being of his master because of the brave acts of the Knight of the Forest he'd heard his squire relate. But, without saying a word, the two squires went to fetch their mounts, because by this time the three horses and the donkey had smelled one another and were close together.

On the way over the Squire of the Forest said to Sancho: "I want you to know, brother, that there's a custom in Andalusian duels—when the principals are fighting, their seconds don't just stand around with their arms folded. I mention this because while our masters are fighting, we also have to fight and smash each other to bits."

"That custom, *señor* squire," responded Sancho, "may be true among ruffians and the combatants that you mention, but among squires of knights-errant it's quite unheard-of. At least, I've never heard my master mention such a custom, and he knows all the rules and regulations of knight-errantry. Even if I recognize that it's true and a legitimate regulation that squires are supposed to fight while their masters do, I won't go along with it, but rather I'll pay the fine imposed on all the peaceful squires. I'm pretty sure it won't be more than two pounds of wax,* and I'd rather pay those couple of pounds, because I know that it'd cost me more in bandages to mend my head, because I can see it now split in half. Moreover, it's impossible for me to fight, since I have no sword and never put one on in my whole life."

"I have a good solution for that," said he of the Forest. "I have two linen sacks of the same size—you'll take one and I'll take the other, and we'll fight with those equal weapons."

"In that case, it's all right," responded Sancho, "because that kind of fight will dust us off more than it will wound us."

"It won't be that way," said the other, "because we'll put half a dozen nice smooth rocks that all weigh the same into those bags—to give them heft—and in that way we can whack each other without harm."

"Look," responded Sancho, "put sable fur or cotton balls into the sacks so that our brains won't get beaten out of us or our bones pulverized! But even if they were filled with silkworm cocoons, *señor mío*, I won't fight. Let our masters fight and have it out, and let's drink and live, because time will fin-

---

* This sounds like an unusual fine to pay, but the old religious brotherhoods would demand wax to make candles with. Sancho knows what such penalties would be, since he had been a summoner in a local brotherhood (Part I, chapter twenty-one).

ish us off without us looking around for reasons to end our lives before their time, when they'll fall like ripe fruit."

"Even so," said he of the Forest, "we must fight, even if it's only for half an hour."

"No, we won't," responded Sancho. "I won't be so rude or so ungrateful that I'd pick even a small fight with someone with whom I've eaten and drunk. And what's more, not being angry, who the devil would start a fight just like that?"

"For that," said he of the Forest, "I'll create a reason, and that is before we begin to fight, I'll walk up to your grace as nice as can be and give you three or four punches that will make you crumble at my feet, and with them I'll arouse your anger, even if it's sleeping like a dormouse."

"I know another plan to counter that one," responded Sancho, "which is just as good. I'll take a club and before your grace can arouse my anger I'll send your anger to sleep with such thwacks of my club that it won't be awakened unless it's in the other world, where it's known that I don't let my face be touched by anyone. 'Let everyone look out for himself,' because 'no one knows the soul of another,' and sometimes 'you go out for wool and come back shorn,' and 'God blessed peace and cursed dissension.' Because 'if a cat is shut up and cornered it turns into a lion,' God knows what I can turn into being a man, so I'll tell your grace, *señor* squire, all the harm and damage that comes from our fight will be on your shoulders."

"All right," said he of the Forest. "'God will send the new day and we'll prosper.'"

Just then a thousand kinds of multicolored birds began to chirp in the trees and through their various happy songs it seemed as if they were welcoming and greeting the fresh Aurora, who was beginning to show her beautiful face through the doors of the Orient, shaking from her hair an infinite number of liquid pearls. Grass was bathed in this gentle liquor and from it rained tiny pearls. Willows distilled delicious manna,* fountains laughed, streams murmured, the

---

* This is not the biblical manna, the food that kept the Hebrews alive during the forty years between the Exodus from Egypt and their arrival in the Promised Land, but rather a sweet liquid that's harvested from trees and then dried. The only thing is, this manna comes from the flowering ash tree, and not from the willow.

forest rejoiced, and the meadows gloried in her coming. But hardly had the new light made it possible to see things, when the first thing that Sancho Panza saw was the nose of the Squire of the Forest, which was so big that it almost cast a shadow over his whole body. It's said, in effect, that it was enormously large, hooked in the middle, and all covered with purple warts, like an eggplant. It drooped below his mouth by the width of two fingers, and when Sancho saw it, his feet and hands began to tremble like a child with epilepsy. He resolved in his heart to take two hundred punches before he would let his wrath be aroused to fight this monster.

Don Quixote looked at his adversary, and found that he'd already put his helmet on and closed it so that he couldn't see his face, but he saw that the man was burly and not very tall. Over his armor he had a tunic or coat made of a material that shone like very fine gold, and attached to it there were many little moons cut from shining mirrors that made him look very handsome. Fluttering on top of his helmet were a great number of green, yellow, and white feathers. The lance that was leaning against the tree was very long and stout, with a steel tip more than a span wide.

Don Quixote looked at and noted all this, and he judged from what he saw that the knight must be very strong. Not for this was he afraid like Sancho Panza—rather with calm courage he said to the Knight of the Mirrors: "If your eagerness to fight, *señor* knight, hasn't taken away your courtesy, to it I appeal that you raise your visor a bit so that I can see if the gallantry of your face corresponds with that of your adornment."

"Whether you come out of this undertaking vanquished or victor, *señor* knight," said the Knight of the Mirrors, "you'll have plenty of time and opportunity to see me, and if I don't satisfy your curiosity now, it's because it seems to me that I'm doing a notable disservice to the beautiful Casildea de Vandalia in wasting the time it would take to raise my visor before I made you confess what you know that I want you to."

"But while we're mounting our horses," said don Quixote, "you'll surely be able to tell me if I'm that don Quixote you said you vanquished."

"I'll respond to that," said he of the Mirrors. "You look

like the knight I conquered like one egg looks like another. But the way you say you're persecuted by enchanters, I won't dare affirm that you're that same one or not."

"That's enough," responded don Quixote, "to convince me of your mistake. However, to rid you completely of your error, let our horses be brought. In less time than it would take you to raise your visor, if God, my lady, and my arm prevail, I'll see your face, and you'll see that I'm not the conquered don Quixote that you think."

With this, they cut off their conversation, got on their horses, and don Quixote turned Rocinante around so he could pace off what he needed of the field in order to come back to attack his adversary, and he of the Mirrors did the same. But don Quixote had not gone twenty paces when he heard him of the Mirrors call him, and as they turned to face each other he of the Mirrors said: "Don't forget, *señor* knight, that the condition of our battle is that the vanquished one, as I've said before, will be at the disposal of the conqueror."

"I'm aware of that," responded don Quixote, "provided what is imposed on the conquered one must be things that are within the bounds of chivalry."

"Understood," said he of the Mirrors.

Don Quixote then saw the strange nose of the squire, and he was no less astonished than Sancho, so much so that he thought he was some monster, or some new kind of man not from this world. Sancho, who saw his master readying to begin his run, didn't want to be alone with that big-nosed fellow, fearing that with just one slap of that nose on his own, his battle would be over, and from that one blow, or just from fright, he would be knocked to the ground. He ran after his master, grabbing onto one stirrup strap, and when he thought it was time for him to turn around, said: "I beg your grace, *señor mío*, before you go into battle, help me to climb into that cork tree from where I can see the gallant combat that your grace will have with this knight more comfortably and better than from on the ground."

"I rather think," said don Quixote, "that you want to climb to a higher place 'to see the bulls without danger.'"

"If I have to tell the truth," responded Sancho, "the enormous nose of that squire has me astonished and filled with fear, and I don't dare stay near him."

"It's such a nose," said don Quixote, "that if I weren't who I am, it would terrify me as well, so come, and I'll help you to climb where you want."

While don Quixote delayed in order to help Sancho go up into the tree, he of the Mirrors was pacing off what he thought he needed of the field, and thinking don Quixote had done the same, without waiting for the blare of a trumpet or any other sound to advise them, he wheeled his horse around—and he was no swifter or better-looking than Rocinante—and at the horse's full speed (which was nothing more than a half trot), went to attack his enemy. But seeing him busy helping Sancho, he pulled back on the reins and stopped in the middle of his course, for which the horse was extremely thankful, since he could no longer budge. But it seemed to don Quixote that his enemy was flying toward him, and he kicked his spurs into the skinny flanks of Rocinante and made him race in such a way that the history says that this was the only time that he was known to run a bit—for all the other times he just trotted— and with this unheard-of fury he ran toward where he of the Mirrors was digging into his horse up to the buttons,* without being able to move him an inch from where he'd stopped his course.

At this opportune moment don Quixote found his adversary encumbered with his horse and fiddling with his lance, which he never, or couldn't, or didn't, have time to put in the lance rest. Don Quixote, who wasn't paying attention to these hindrances, without risk and without any danger whatsoever, attacked him of the Mirrors with so much force that, much against his opponent's will, he toppled him to the ground over the haunches of his horse. From the fall he could move neither hand nor foot, and gave the impression that he was dead.

As soon as Sancho saw that he'd fallen, he slipped down from the cork tree and went to where his master was. Don Quixote got off Rocinante and placed himself over him of the Mirrors, and unlaced the helmet to see if he was dead, or to give him air, if he happened to still be alive, and he saw ... Who can say what he saw without causing astonish-

---

* Old spurs were simple spikes, with knobs to prevent too much penetration.

ment, wonder, and awe in those who hear it? He saw, so says the history, the face, the figure, the aspect, and the effigy of the bachelor Sansón Carrasco, and as soon as he saw him, he shouted: "Come, Sancho, and look at what you will see but not believe. Hurry, my son, and see what magic can do; what sorcerers and enchanters can do."

Sancho got there and when he saw the face of the bachelor Carrasco, he began to cross himself a thousand times at this totally unexpected sight. All the while, the flattened knight gave no sign of life, and Sancho said to don Quixote: "I'm of the opinion, *señor mío*, that your grace should get down on one knee and plunge your sword into the mouth of this fellow who looks like the bachelor Sansón Carrasco. Maybe you'll kill some of your enemies, the enchanters."

"Not a bad idea," said don Quixote, "because the fewer enemies, the better."

After don Quixote took out his sword to put Sancho's advice into effect, the squire of him of the Mirrors, now without the nose that had made him look so ugly, shouted loudly: "Watch what you're doing, *señor* don Quixote, because that fellow at your feet *is* the bachelor Sansón Carrasco, your friend, and I'm his squire."

When Sancho saw him without that which caused his ugliness, he said: "And what happened to your nose?"

To which he answered: "Here it is, in my pocket."

And putting his hand into his right-hand pocket, he took out a nose made of pasteboard and varnish in the shape that has been described, and after Sancho had looked at him very carefully, he said in a very surprised voice: "Holy Mary, help me! If it isn't Tomé Cecial, my neighbor and pal."

"Of course!" responded the un-nosed squire. "Tomé Cecial I am, Sancho Panza's friend and pal, and I'll tell you right now the secrets, tricks, and scheming that brought me here. Meanwhile, ask and beg your master not to touch, abuse, wound, or kill the Knight of the Mirrors whom he has at his feet, because he is without any doubt the daring and ill-advised bachelor Sansón Carrasco, our fellow townsman."

Just then, he of the Mirrors came to, and when don Quixote saw it, he placed the point of the sword above his face and said: "You're dead, knight, unless you confess that the peerless Dulcinea del Toboso is more beautiful than your

Casildea de Vandalia. And in addition, you must promise to go to the city of El Toboso and appear before her on my behalf so that she can do with you whatever she pleases. And if she lets you go free you must come looking for me—for the trail of my deeds will guide you—and tell me what transpired with her. These conditions, in accordance with what we agreed to before our combat, are within the bounds of the rules of chivalry."

"I confess," said the fallen knight, "that the tattered and dirty shoe of the lady Dulcinea del Toboso is more worthy than the unkempt but clean beard of Casildea, and I promise to go and come back from her presence to yours and relate in minute detail what you're asking of me."

"You must also confess and believe," added don Quixote, "that the knight you conquered was not and could not have been don Quixote de La Mancha, but someone who looked like him, just as I confess and believe that you, although you look like the bachelor Sansón Carrasco, are not him, but rather another who looks like him, and that my enemies have given you his features to restrain and moderate the intensity of my wrath, so that I wouldn't use the glory of my conquest to its fullest extent."

"I confess, judge, and feel everything that you believe, judge, and feel," responded the battered knight. "Allow me to stand up, I beg you, if the pain of my fall will let me, because I'm pretty bad off."

Don Quixote helped him get up, as did Tomé Cecial, his squire, whom Sancho stared at, asking him things the answers to which proved that he really was the Tomé Cecial he said he was. But the apprehension caused by what his master had said—that enchanters had changed the features of the Knight of the Mirrors to make him look like the bachelor Carrasco—prevented him from believing what his eyes were seeing. In the end, the master and servant remained deceived, and he of the Mirrors and his squire, angry and in bad shape, left don Quixote and Sancho with the intention of finding a village where they could get bandages applied to his ribs. Don Quixote and Sancho continued on their way to Zaragoza, where the history leaves them in order to explain who the Knight of the Mirrors and his nosed squire were.

Chapter XV. Where the identity of the Knight of the Mirrors and his squire is revealed and made known.

D ON QUIXOTE was extremely happy, proud, and swelled-up for having achieved a victory over such a brave knight as he thought him of the Mirrors to be, from whose chivalric promise he hoped to find out whether the enchantment of his lady persisted, since the vanquished knight was obliged to return and relate what had transpired between the two of them; otherwise he'd be stripped of his knighthood. But don Quixote was thinking one thing, and he of the Mirrors was thinking something else entirely, since his only thought was to find someplace to have bandages applied, as has been said.

The history says that when the bachelor Sansón Carrasco advised don Quixote to return to his curtailed chivalry, it was only after he'd had a secret meeting with the priest and barber about how they could make sure don Quixote would stay calmly at home and not be moved to go out on further ill-advised adventures. What was determined by common vote of all, and particularly the persuasion of Carrasco, was that they should encourage don Quixote to go out again, because stopping him seemed impossible, and that Sansón would follow him disguised as a knight-errant. He would then do battle with him, since a pretext would be easy to find, and vanquish him—thinking it would be very easy— and they would have made a pact that the conquered one would be at the mercy of the victor; thus with don Quixote defeated, the bachelor knight would command him to go to his town and home and not leave for two years, or until he was told otherwise. It was very clear that the conquered don Quixote would do what he was commanded without question, so as not to contravene and break the laws of chivalry, and it might be that during the time of his forced retirement, he would forget his foolishness, or there would be an opportunity to find a reasonable cure for his madness.

Carrasco accepted the idea, and Tomé Cecial, friend and neighbor of Sancho Panza, and a jovial and lively fellow, volunteered to be his squire. Sansón put on the armor already described and Tomé Cecial put the false nose over his own, as already mentioned, so he wouldn't be recognized by his friend when they saw each other, and they followed the same trail as don Quixote and almost found themselves involved in the adventure of the Cart of Death. They finally met them in the forest, where everything happened that the careful reader has learned, and if it weren't for don Quixote's outlandish thoughts, where he was deluded into believing that the bachelor was not the bachelor, the *señor* bachelor would have forever been prevented from being graduated as a *licenciado*, "not finding nests where he expected to find birds."*

Tomé Cecial, who saw how badly their plan had turned out, and the sorry ending to their journey, said to the bachelor: "Surely, *señor* Sansón Carrasco, we got what was coming to us. It's easy enough to plan and take on an undertaking, but most of the time it's hard to succeed in it. Don Quixote is crazy and we're sane, yet he's on the road laughing and safe, and your grace is beaten up and sad. Let's ponder this—who is crazier: the person who can't help it or the person who goes crazy of his own free will?"

To which Sansón answered: "The difference between these two crazy people is that he who is crazy by nature will always be that way, and he who has chosen to be can stop being so whenever he wants."

"That being so," said Tomé Cecial, "I was crazy of my free will when I agreed to be your grace's squire, and with that same free will I want to stop being one and go home."

"Do what you want," responded Sansón, "but if you think I'll go home before I've thrashed don Quixote you're very wrong. And it's not my vow anymore to try to find him so that he'll recover his sanity, but rather for revenge. The great pain in my ribs won't allow me to have a more charitable thought."

They talked about this until they got to a town where by chance there was a bonesetter who mended the unfortunate Sansón. Tomé Cecial turned back and left him, and Sansón stayed behind to plan his vengeance. The history will speak of him again at the right time, but for the time being it must share don Quixote's joy.

---

* This saying means that things turned out the opposite of what was planned.

Chapter XVI. About what happened to don Quixote with a discerning gentleman of La Mancha.

WITH JOY, happiness, and vanity that have been mentioned, don Quixote continued his journey, thinking his recent victory was over the most valiant knight-errant the world had at that time. He considered all the adventures that might befall him from then on as happily concluded. He cared little about enchantments or enchanters, and he forgot the infinite thwacks laid on him during the course of his chivalric career, as well as the hailstorm of stones that knocked out half his teeth, and the ungratefulness of the galley slaves, and even the Yangüesans and their shower of stakes. Finally, he said to himself that if he could find a method, way, or means to break the spell on Dulcinea, he wouldn't envy the greatest adventure that the bravest knight-errant of ancient times ever performed.

He was engrossed in these thoughts when Sancho said to him: "Isn't it something, señor—I still can see before my eyes the enormous and strange nose of my pal Tomé Cecial?"

"And do you still think, Sancho, that the Knight of the Mirrors was the bachelor Sansón Carrasco, and his squire, Tomé Cecial, your friend?"

"I don't know what to say about that," responded Sancho. "I only know that what he told me about his house, wife, and children, no one else could have told me except him, and his face, once his nose was taken off, was the same as Tomé Cecial's, just like I frequently saw it in my town, since he lives next door to my own house; and the tone of his voice was the same."

"Let's be logical," replied don Quixote. "How can it be that the bachelor Sansón Carrasco would come dressed as a knight-errant with offensive and defensive arms to fight me? Have I been his enemy? Have I ever given him rise to bear me a grudge? Am I his rival, or has he taken up arms out of envy of the fame that I've won through my own arms?"

"What can we say, *señor*," responded Sancho, "about the appearance of that knight, whoever he was, which jibed perfectly with that of the bachelor Sansón Carrasco, and

that of his squire, my pal Tomé Cecial? And if it's enchantment at work, as your grace has said, weren't there two others in the world they might look like?"

"It's all artifice and tricks," responded don Quixote, "of
the perverse magicians that pursue me. Foreseeing that I
would be victorious in the fray, they arranged for the vanquished knight to have the face of my friend the bachelor,
so that the friendship I have for him would get between the
point of my sword and the severity of my arm, and moderate the righteous ire in my heart, and in this way I spared
the life of him who wanted to take mine through deceit
and fraud. For proof of all this, Sancho, you know by experience, which will not allow you to lie or deceive, how
easy it is for enchanters to change faces of others, turning a
beautiful one into an ugly one, since just two days ago you
saw with your own eyes the beauty and fine appearance of
Dulcinea in their entire and natural form, and I saw only
an ugly, low, and coarse peasant girl, with cataracts over her
eyes, and with a bad smell in her mouth. So, if there's an enchanter so perverse as to perform such a bad transformation, it's no wonder that he has produced those with Sansón
Carrasco and your friend in order to snatch the glory of the
victory from my hands. But there's consolation in any case,
because no matter what form he was in, I still vanquished
my foe."

"God knows the truth about everything," responded Sancho.

Since the transformation of Dulcinea had been his own
trick and deception, the wild ideas of his master didn't convince him. But he couldn't answer back, or his hoax might
be discovered.

They were in the midst of this conversation when a
man who was riding a gray mare behind them on the same
road passed by dressed in an overcoat made of fine green
material, with appliqués of tan triangles made of velvet,
and with a cap of the same velvet. The trappings of the
mare were for country riding, with a short-stirruped saddle, likewise of purple and green. He wore a short curved
Moorish sword suspended from a wide green-and-gold
strap. His spurs were not golden, but coated with a green
lacquer, so shiny and burnished that when they were
taken with his outfit as a whole, they seemed better than

if they had been made of purest gold. When the traveler drew up to them, he greeted them courteously, and spurring his mare on, passed them by. But don Quixote called to him: "*Señor*, if it happens that you're taking the same road we are, and you're not in a hurry, I would be pleased if we could travel together."

"In truth," responded he of the mare, "I wouldn't have sped by if I weren't afraid that the company of my mare would excite your horse."

"You can," responded Sancho, "rein in your mare, *señor*, because our horse is the most chaste and best-behaved one in the world. On similar occasions he has never done any vile deed, and the one time he behaved badly, my master and I paid sevenfold for it. I say once again that you can join us, if you want, because even if your mare were given to him on a silver platter, he wouldn't look at her."

The traveler pulled on his reins, astonished at the appearance and face of don Quixote, who was traveling without a helmet, since Sancho had placed it over the pommel of his donkey's packsaddle, and if the man in green studied don Quixote, don Quixote studied the man in green much more, seeming to him to be a man of good sense. He looked about fifty years old, with few gray hairs and an aquiline face, his expression somewhere between merry and grave. All in all, in his dress and appearance he gave the impression of being a man of worth.

What the man in green thought about don Quixote de La Mancha was that he'd never before seen a man of that type and appearance. He marveled at the length of his horse, the size of his body, the leanness and sallow aspect of his face, his armor, his gestures and demeanor—a person whose appearance hadn't been seen in that area for a very long time. Don Quixote noticed the way the traveler was inspecting him, and since he could tell what he wanted to know by means of the man's astonishment, and since he was so courteous and fond of pleasing everyone, before the man asked him anything, he anticipated it by saying: "I don't wonder that you're surprised at the way I look, since my appearance is so different from what one ordinarily sees. But you won't be surprised any longer when I tell you, as I'm doing now, that I'm a knight 'of those that people say / go off adventuring.'

"I departed from my house, pawned my estate, left the comforts of home, and turned myself over to the arms of Fortune so they could take me wherever they pleased. I tried to resuscitate the now dead order of knight-errantry, and for many days now, stumbling here, tripping there, falling headlong over here, but getting up over there, I've fulfilled most of my wishes, rescuing widows, protecting maidens, and sheltering married women and orphans— which is the natural occupation of knights-errant. Owing to my brave, numerous, and Christian deeds I've been rewarded by being in print in almost all or most of the nations of the world. Thirty thousand copies have been printed of my history, and thirty thousand times a thousand more are on their way to being printed, if heaven doesn't put a stop to it. To summarize it in a few words, or in just one, I say that I'm don Quixote de La Mancha, also called the Woebegone Knight. Although 'he who praises himself spatters himself,' I'm forced to do it at times, such as when no one else is present who can do it for me. So, *señor*, neither this horse, this lance, nor this shield, nor squire, nor all of my armor, nor the sallowness of my face, nor my lean figure need surprise you anymore, having learned who I am and the profession I follow."

Don Quixote remained silent after he said this, and the man in green, since he took so long in answering, seemed unable to respond. But after a while he said: "You were exactly right in figuring out by my astonishment what I wanted to know. But you haven't been able to mitigate the wonder caused in me just by seeing you. As you say, *señor*, finding out who you are should have lessened my wonder, but it hasn't done that at all, since now that I know who you are, my fascination and amazement are only increased. How is it possible that there are knights-errant in the world today, and that there are histories published about real chivalric deeds? I cannot persuade myself that there are people today who help widows, protect maidens, honor married women, or rescue orphans, and I wouldn't have believed it until I saw it with my own eyes. Thank heaven, because with this history your grace says has been published dealing with your high and true chivalric deeds, the innumerable ones about fictional knights-errant—which the world was filled with and which have so corrupted good manners and have so deprecated the true histories—can now be cast into oblivion."

"There's much to be said," responded don Quixote, "as to whether or not the histories of knights-errant are fictional or not."

"Well, is there anybody who doubts," said the Green One, "that those histories are not false?"

"I doubt it," responded don Quixote, "and let's leave it at that for the moment. If our journey lasts, I hope to make your grace see that you haven't done well in going along with the stream of those who maintain they're not true."

From this last remark, the traveler began to suspect that don Quixote must be some half-wit, and he expected other remarks to confirm it. But before they engaged in other conversations, don Quixote begged him to say who he was, since he himself had already revealed who he was and told something of his own life. To which he of the Green Coat responded: "I, *señor* Woebegone Knight, am an *hidalgo* from a village where we will eat lunch today, if God is pleased. I'm more than moderately rich and my name is don Diego de Miranda. I live with my wife and my children. My pastimes are those of hunting and fishing. I don't have a hawk or any greyhounds, but rather a tame partridge* and a daring ferret. I have as many as six dozen books, some in Spanish and some in Latin, mostly dealing with history, but some are devotional. Those about chivalry have not come over the threshold of my door. I turn pages more in the secular books than the devout ones, as long as they're appropriate entertainment, delight with their language, and maintain interest by their invention, although of these there are very few in Spain. I eat sometimes with my neighbors and friends, and I frequently invite them to dine. My banquets are neat and well stocked. I don't like to gossip, nor do I allow anyone to gossip in my presence. I don't meddle in the lives of others, nor do I spy on other men's actions. I go to Mass daily and share my wealth with the poor, without making too much of my charitable works, so as not to allow hypocrisy or boastfulness to enter my heart, because they are enemies that can subtly take possession of

---

* These tame partridges were, and are still, used as hunters' decoys.

the most modest heart. I try to reconcile those who are at odds with each other. I'm a devotee of Our Lady and trust in the infinite mercy of Our Lord."

Sancho was listening very carefully to the life and pastimes of the *hidalgo*, and they seemed to him good and holy, and that whoever lived such a life must be able to work miracles, so he threw himself from his donkey with great speed and went to grasp his right stirrup and with a devout heart and almost in tears he kissed his feet again and again. When the *hidalgo* saw what was going on, he asked Sancho: "What are you doing, brother? Why all those kisses?"

"Let me keep kissing," responded Sancho, "because it seems to me that your grace is the first saint on horseback that I've seen in all the days of my life."

"I'm not a saint," responded the *hidalgo*, "but a great sinner. You, certainly, brother, must be good, as your simplicity demonstrates."

Sancho went back to his mount, having brought out a laugh from the profound melancholy of his master, and caused fresh astonishment in don Diego.

Don Quixote asked him how many children he had, and went on to say that one of the things that the philosophers of old—who lacked the true knowledge of God—considered very important was in the area of possessing the gifts of nature and of Fortune, in having many good friends, and many good children.

"I, *señor* don Quixote," responded the *hidalgo*, "have one son, and if I didn't have him, I might consider myself more fortunate than I am—not because he's bad, but because he isn't turning out quite as good as I had wished. He's about eighteen years old, and for six has been in Salamanca, learning Greek and Latin, and when I wanted him to go on to study other sciences, I found he was so engrossed in poetry—if you can call that a science—that it wasn't possible to persuade him to take up the study of law, or the queen of them all, theology. I would like him to be an honor to his family, since we're living at a time when the crown prizes a good and virtuous education—an education without virtue being pearls on a dung heap. He spends all day studying whether Homer succeeded or not in a cer-

tain verse of the *Iliad*, if Martial* was indecent or not in a
particular epigram, or how you have to understand certain
verses of Virgil. In short, his life is devoted to the books of
those poets I mentioned, and those of Horace,† Persius,‡
Juvenal,§ and Tibullus.¶ He holds the people who write in
Spanish in little esteem, and even though he seems to dislike poetry in Spanish, he's now racking his brain trying to
gloss a quatrain they sent him from Salamanca**—I think
it's some kind of literary joust."

To all this don Quixote responded: "Children, *señor*, are
part and parcel of the bowels of their parents, thus they
are to be loved, no matter how good or bad they are, as
much as we love our life-giving souls. The job of parents
is to guide them from when they're small, along the path
of virtue, good upbringing, and good Christian customs, so
that when they grow up, they can be a comfort to the old
age of their parents and a glory to their descendants. And
insofar as forcing them to study this or that science, I don't
believe it's a good idea, although trying to persuade them
seems harmless enough. And if they don't study with an
aim to *pane lucrando*,†† when the student is lucky enough

---

* The Roman epigramist Martial was born in Bibilis, near modern Ca-
latayud in Spain, about fifty-five miles southwest of Zaragoza. He is
faulted for his gushy adulation of emperors and his obscenity. Interesting for understanding don Diego de Miranda's son are these epigrams
by Martial: "Nothing is more confident than a bad poet" (Book II: 63);
"He does not write at all whose poems no man reads" (Book III: 9).
† Horace was a famous Latin poet (65 B.C.–A.D. 8). He wrote about
friendship, love, philosophy, and the art of poetry in his *Epistles* and
Odes.
‡ Persius (A.D. 34–62) was a Latin Stoic poet whose satires had a high
moral tone. He was a precursor of Juvenal.
§ Juvenal (A.D. 55?–127?) was the best-known of the Latin satiric poets. His sixteen *Satires* deal with daily life in Rome under good and
bad emperors. They attack the corruption of society in Rome and the
brutalities and follies of mankind.
¶ Tibullus (55–19 B.C.) was a Roman elegiac poet considered by
Quintilian to be the best of them all. His clear and unaffected style is
marked by simplicity, grace, tenderness, and exquisiteness of feeling.
** The contest consists of taking a four-line poem and composing a
new, longer poem of four stanzas, each one ending with a line from the
original, as you will soon see.
†† "To earn a living" in Latin.

for heaven to have given him parents who will permit it, I'd be of the opinion that they should allow him to study anything that they see he's most inclined to, and although poetry is less useful than pleasure-giving, it isn't among those pursuits that will dishonor the person who possesses them.

"Poetry, *señor hidalgo*, in my opinion, is like a tender young maiden who is beautiful beyond all measure, and whom other maidens are trying to enrich, polish, and beautify. These maidens are the other sciences, and she's served by them all and they all find their worth through her. But this maiden doesn't want to be handled or dragged through the streets, nor paraded about in the corners of the plaza or into the corners of palaces. She's made of an alchemy of such virtue that he who knows how to use it can turn her into purest gold of inestimable value. But he who possesses her must keep her within bounds, not allowing her to get into clumsy satires or soulless sonnets. Nor should she be merchandised, unless it's in heroic poems, in moving tragedies, or in merry, well-crafted plays. She shouldn't be allowed to fall into the hands of buffoons or the ignorant masses, who are not capable of understanding or appreciating the treasures she encompasses. And don't think, *señor*, that I mean that only the masses are ignorant—for anyone who is ignorant, even though he be a lord or a prince, can and should be counted among them. So, if the poet possesses the requirements I've mentioned, he'll be famous and appreciated in all civilized nations of the world.

"Insofar as what you say, *señor*, about your son not appreciating poetry written in Spanish, I don't think he's right, and this is the reason: The great Homer didn't write in Latin because he was Greek, nor did Virgil write in Greek because he was a Roman. So, all the ancient poets wrote in the language they were born into, and they didn't seek foreign languages in which to declare their lofty conceits. And this being so, it's reasonable that all nations should rightly follow this custom; the German poet should not be thought less of because he writes in his own language, nor the Castilian, nor even the Basque who writes in his.

"But your son, *señor*, the way I see it, isn't so much at odds with Spanish verse as he is with poets who know only Spanish, without knowing other languages or other branches of knowledge to embellish, awaken, and nurture their natural inspiration. Even in this he may be wrong, because—if it's true as they say—'the poet is born.'* That is, the natural poet is born a poet out of his mother's womb. And with this propensity that heaven gave him, without further study or discipline, he writes things that prove what the man said: *Est deus in nobis,* &c."† I also say that the natural poet who makes use of art will be better than and will surpass the poet who strives to be one through art alone. The reason is that art doesn't surpass nature; it just perfects it, and when nature is combined with art, and art with nature, they will bring out the most perfect poet.

"Let this be the conclusion of my speech, *señor*—your grace should allow your son to travel the road on which his star leads him, and since he's as good a student as he should be, and having risen happily to the first step of the essential disciplines, which is that of languages, with them he shall rise to the height of humane letters, which greatly complement a secular knight, and adorn, honor, and elevate him, as miters do bishops, or as robes do learnèd judges. Scold your son if he writes satires that damage other people's honor—punish him and tear them up. But if he writes discourses in the style of Horace, where he condemns vices in general, which Horace did so well, praise him, because the poet is allowed to write against envy and to speak ill of the envious in his verses, and the same with the other vices, provided that he not single out any individual. But there are poets who—just to say one spiteful thing—risk being exiled to the islands of Pontus.‡ If a poet is virtuous in his way of life, he also will be in his verses. The pen is the tongue of the soul—and if his conceits are engendered with virtue in his soul, his writings will reflect that virtue. And

---

* The first part of a Latin adage, *Poeta nascitur, non fit,* "A poet is born, not made."

† *Est deus in nobis: agitante calescimus in illo* ("There is God in us: he stirs and we get warm"), from Ovid's *Fasti,* vi, 5.

‡ This is Ovid (43 B.C.–A.D. 17), exiled in A.D. 9, to the shores (*not* islands) of Pontus Euxinus on the Black Sea, because he had written *Ars Amatoria,* a poem dealing with the art of love. The Emperor Augustus was particularly annoyed because he was trying to foster moral reforms when Ovid's masterpiece of witty impropriety appeared.

when kings and princes discover the miraculous art of poetry in wise, earnest, and good citizens, they will honor, appreciate, and enrich them, and they will even crown them with leaves from the tree that lightning never strikes,* to show that people with such crowns adorning their heads are to be respected."

The Man in the Green Coat was amazed at the discourse of don Quixote—so much so that he was losing the opinion that he formed that the other was a half-wit. But in the middle of this speech, Sancho—since he found it a bit tedious—had gotten off the road to get a little milk from some shepherds who were milking sheep nearby. Just as the *hidalgo* was getting ready to continue the conversation, extremely satisfied with don Quixote's intelligence and reasoning, don Quixote looked up and saw, coming along the road toward them, a cart flying royal pennants. And thinking that it must be some new adventure, he shouted to Sancho to come and give him his helmet. Sancho, hearing himself being called, left the shepherds, and as quickly as he could, returned to his master, to whom a frightening and reckless adventure happened.

Chapter XVII. Wherein is declared the height and extreme to which the unheard-of bravery of don Quixote reached or could ever reach, with the very fortunate conclusion of the Adventure of the Lions.

THE HISTORY relates that when don Quixote was calling to Sancho to take him his helmet, he was purchasing some cottage cheese the shepherds were selling him, and pressed by the haste of his master, didn't know what to do with it, nor how he could carry it back. So as not to waste it, since he'd already paid for it, he thought he would put it in his master's helmet, and with these good provisions, he returned to his master to see what he wanted.

"My friend, give me my helmet—for either I know little

* The tree that lightning never strikes, according to an ancient superstition, is the laurel, whose leaves were used to make wreaths to place on the heads of heroes and poets.

about adventures, or I can see one over there that will and does need me to take up arms."

He of the Green Coat heard this and looked everywhere and found nothing other than a cart coming toward them with two or three small pennants, which were intended to show that the cart was carrying something belonging to His Majesty, and that's exactly what he told don Quixote.

But don Quixote didn't believe it, firmly convinced that everything that happened to him had to be adventures and more adventures, so he replied to the *hidalgo*: "'Forewarned is forearmed.' Nothing is lost by my being prepared. I know from experience that I have visible and invisible enemies, and I don't know when, where, at what moment, nor in what shape they will attack me."

And turning to Sancho, he asked for his helmet, and since Sancho hadn't had time to take the cottage cheese out, he had to hand it over as it was. Don Quixote took it, without noticing what was in it, and quickly put it onto his head. Since the cottage cheese was squeezed, the whey began to trickle down all over don Quixote's face and beard, which startled him so much that he said to Sancho: "What can this be, Sancho? You'd think my brain was softening or I'm sweating from head to foot. And if it's sweat, in truth it's not from fear. Doubtless this is a terrible adventure that is about to happen to me. Give me, if you can, something to wipe my face with, because the copious sweat is blinding my eyes."

Sancho said nothing and handed him a piece of cloth, and gave with it thanks to God that his master hadn't discovered the truth of the matter. Don Quixote cleaned off his face and took off the helmet to see what it was that, in his opinion, was cooling off his head, and when he saw that white mush inside his helmet, he brought it to his nose, and when he'd smelled it he said: "On the life of my lady Dulcinea del Toboso, this is *cottage cheese* that you put in my helmet, you traitor, scoundrel, and ill-bred squire!"

To which with great calm and dissimulation Sancho responded: "If it's cottage cheese, give it to me, your grace, and I'll eat it. But let the devil eat it, since he must have put it there. Would I dare dirty your grace's helmet? Do you think I'm to blame? On my faith, *señor*, God makes me think that I also must have enchanters who pursue me, as a part of your grace, and they must have put that slop there to change your patience to anger and to cause my ribs to be pummeled as usual. But in truth they're off the mark this time. I trust in the good sense of my master, who will have considered that I don't have any cottage cheese, nor milk, nor anything of the kind, and if I had any, I'd put it in my stomach rather than in the helmet."

"Anything is possible," said don Quixote.

The *hidalgo* saw everything, and everything left him amazed, especially when, after don Quixote cleaned off his head, face, beard, and helmet, which he put back on his head, made himself fast in his stirrups, girded his sword, and grasped his lance, he said: "Now, come what may, because I have enough courage to take on Satan himself."

At that moment the cart with the pennants drew near, on which there were no people other than the carter on one of the mules and another man sitting on the front of the cart. Don Quixote placed himself in front of the cart and said: "Where are you going, brothers? Whose cart is this? What are you transporting in it and whose pennants are those?"

To which the carter responded: "The cart is my own; what I'm transporting is two fierce lions in cages, which the general of Orán is sending to the court as presents for His Majesty; the pennants are His Majesty's own, to show that this is something of his."

"And are the lions big?" asked don Quixote.

"So big," responded the man who was on his way back to the door of the cage, "that larger ones, nor even as large, have never been transported before between Africa and Spain. I'm the lion keeper and I've brought others over, but none like these. They're a female and a male. The male is in this first cage, the female in the one behind. They're hungry because they haven't eaten today. So, your grace, get out of the way, because I have to find a place soon where I can feed them."

To which don Quixote said with a half smile: "Little lions for me? For me, little lions, and at this time of day? Well, by God, those men who sent them to me will see if I'm a man to be frightened by lions or not. Get down, my good man, and since you're the lion keeper, open those cages and send those beasts out—for in the middle of this field I'll show them who don Quixote de La Mancha is, in spite of all the enchanters who have sent them to me."

"Aha," the *hidalgo* said to himself at this point. "At last, this good knight has shown who he is. The cottage cheese has doubtless softened his brain."

At his point, Sancho went to the *hidalgo* and said: "For God's sake, your grace, see that my master doesn't take on these lions, because if he does, they'll tear us all to bits."

"Is your master so crazy," responded the *hidalgo*, "that you fear and believe he'll take on such fierce animals?"

"He's not crazy," responded Sancho, "just daring."

"I'll see that he doesn't do it," replied the *hidalgo*.

And approaching don Quixote, who was pressing the lion keeper to open the cages, he said: "*Señor* knight, knights-errant should undertake adventures that promise a favorable outcome, and not engage in those that cannot. Courage that invades the territory of recklessness smacks more of foolhardiness than bravery. Moreover, these lions are not here to do battle with you, nor are they even dreaming about it. They're presents for His Majesty and it's not a good idea to stop them nor hinder their progress."

"Get out of the way, your grace, *señor hidalgo*," responded don Quixote, "and tend to your tame partridge and your daring ferret, and leave everyone to his own business. This is mine, and I know whether these *señores* lions are really meant for me or not."

And turning to the lion keeper, he said: "I swear, you knave, if you don't open the cages right now, I'll pin you to this cart with my lance!"

The carter saw the resolve of that phantom in armor and said: "*Señor mío*, if your grace pleases, out of charity, let me unyoke the mules and put them and myself where we'll be safe before the lions are released, because if they kill my mules, I'll be ruined for the rest of my life—I have no property other than this cart and these mules."

"Oh, man of little faith!"* responded don Quixote. "Get down and unyoke the mules and do whatever you want. Soon you'll see that your trouble was in vain and that you didn't have to take that precaution."

The carter got down and unyoked the mules in great

---

* This echoes what Christ says in Matthew 14:31.

haste, and the lion keeper cried out: "All those who are here, be my witnesses that against my will and having been forced, I'm opening the cages and releasing the lions, and that I'm warning this man that all the harm and damage they may do are his responsibility, including my wages and fees. Your graces, *señores*, take cover before I open the cages. I'm sure they won't harm me."

Once again the *hidalgo* tried to persuade him not to do that mad act, because taking on such a foolish thing was tempting God, to which don Quixote responded that he knew what he was doing. The *hidalgo* told him to consider it carefully, and that he was convinced he was mistaken.

"Now, *señor*," replied don Quixote, "if your grace doesn't want to witness this act you think will be a tragedy, spur your gray mare and go where it's safe."

When Sancho heard this, with tears in his eyes he begged him to stop that perilous undertaking, compared to which the windmills, the fearful adventure of the fulling mills, and all the other deeds he'd attempted in his entire life had been a piece of cake. "Look, *señor*," said Sancho, "there's no enchantment here nor anything of the kind. I saw the real claw of a lion between the bars of the cage, and I judge by the size of the claw that the lion itself must be bigger than a mountain."

"Fear, at least," responded don Quixote, "will have made it seem larger than half the world. Stand back, Sancho, and leave me alone, and if I should die here, you know our long-standing agreement—you'll go to Dulcinea . . . and I'll say no more."

He added further comments that made Sancho realize that he was not about to give up his foolish intent. The Man in the Green Coat would have tried to thwart him, but he was not nearly as well armed, and he realized that it was not prudent to take on a crazy man—for that's exactly what don Quixote appeared to be. The knight again pressed the lion keeper and renewed his threats, all of which inspired the *hidalgo* to spur his mare, Sancho his donkey, and the carter his mules, all of them trying to get as far away from the cart as they could before the lions were released.

Sancho was weeping over the impending death of his master, for he believed without any doubt he was going directly into the claws of the lion. He cursed his luck and thought it was a very ill-fated moment when he got the idea to serve him again. But even though he was crying and lamenting, he managed to whip his donkey to get away from the cart. The lion keeper, seeing that those who were fleeing were a good distance away, tried again to dissuade and warn don Quixote the same way he'd tried to already. He responded that he had heard him and didn't care to hear any more dissuasions or warnings, for they would all have little effect, and also the lion keeper shouldn't waste any more time. During the time the lion keeper took to open the first cage, don Quixote considered whether it would be better to do the battle on foot rather than on horseback, and finally decided to do it on foot, fearing that Rocinante would be spooked when he saw the lions. For this reason, he jumped off the horse, threw down his lance, clasped his shield, and, unsheathing his sword, step by step, with marvelous courage and with a brave heart, placed himself in front of the cart, commending himself to God with all his heart, and then to his lady Dulcinea.

And it should be said that when the author got to this point in this true history, he exclaims: "Oh, strong and beyond all exaggeration dauntless don Quixote de La Mancha, mirror in which all of the valiant men in the world may see themselves, a second and new Manuel de León,* who was the glory and honor of Spanish knights! What words can I use to describe this so frightening deed, or with what words can I make future ages believe it, or what praise is there that will not be fitting, no matter how much exaggeration is used? You on foot, alone, intrepid, heroic, with a single sword—and not one of those really sharp ones from Toledo—with a none too shiny or clean steel shield, are waiting for the two fiercest lions that were ever born in the African jungles. Let your own deeds serve as praise, you brave Manchegan—for here I'll leave your deeds at their height, lacking the words to describe them."

Here the exclamation of the author ends and he continues, getting back to the thread of his story, saying:

Now that the lion keeper saw that don Quixote was ready, and that he couldn't avoid releasing the male lion

---

* See Part I, chapter forty-nine, page 468.

for fear of the enmity of the indignant and daring knight, he opened wide the door of the first cage, where the lion, as has been said, was. This lion seemed inordinately large and had a fearful and ugly face. The first thing the lion did was to turn around in the cage, where he'd been lying, extend his claws, and stretch all over. He opened his mouth wide and yawned very slowly, and with a tongue almost a foot long, he licked the dust from his eyes and washed his face. Then he stuck his head out of the cage and looked in all directions, with eyes that seemed to be red-hot coals, and with a gaze and an attitude that would instill fright in fear itself. But don Quixote watched him with great intent, hoping he'd jump out of his cage and attack, at which point he planned to tear the poor creature to shreds.

His unheard-of madness reached this height. But the generous lion, more courteous than arrogant, indifferent to all this childishness and bravado, after having looked all around, as has been said, turned back, showing his rear end to don Quixote, and with great apathy and sluggishness, returned to lie down in his cage.* When don Quixote saw this, he commanded the lion keeper to give him a few whacks and provoke him so he'd come out.

"I'll not do that," responded the lion keeper, "because if I do, the first one he'll claw to pieces will be me. Be content, your grace, *señor* knight, with what you've done, since nothing more can be said of your bravery. Don't tempt Fortune a second time. The lion has his door open before him. Let him decide if he wants to come out or not. But since he hasn't come out yet, he won't come out all day. The greatness of your bravery has been well proven. No courageous fighter, the way I understand it, is obliged to do any more than challenge his enemy and wait for him in the field of battle, and if his contrary doesn't show up, in him lies the infamy, and the person who waits ready to fight wins the crown of victory."

"That's true," responded don Quixote, "so close the door, my friend, and write me an affidavit in as good a form as you can, about what you saw me do—to wit: You opened the door

---

* Translator's note: It took me a long time to figure out why the hungry lion didn't leap out and rip don Quixote apart. The truth of the matter is that male lions *never* kill the prey they eat—it's only the female who hunts.

of the lion's cage; I waited for him; he didn't come out; I kept waiting; he remained in the cage and went back to lie down. There's nothing more I can do, and there's no enchantment. And may God let reason, truth, and true chivalry prosper. So close the cage while I signal those who fled so they can find out from your own mouth what transpired here."

The lion keeper did what he was asked, and don Quixote attached to the point of his lance the cloth he'd used to wipe the trickles of cottage cheese from his face, and began to call those who were still fleeing while still looking back at every step, with the *hidalgo* in green bringing up the rear. But when Sancho saw the signal with the white cloth, he said: "May they kill me if my master didn't vanquish the fierce beasts—he's summoning us."

The others reined in and realized that the person who was waving the cloth was don Quixote, and with their fear partially relieved, they cautiously returned to where they could hear don Quixote calling them. Finally, they returned to the cart, and when they got there, don Quixote said to the carter: "You can yoke up your mules and go your way, and you, Sancho, give two *escudos* in gold to him and the lion keeper in recompense for the delay I've caused them."

"I'll give them with great pleasure," responded Sancho, "but what happened to the lions? Are they dead or alive?"

Then the lion keeper related in great detail the course of the combat, exaggerating the bravery of don Quixote as well as he could and knew how—how the lion was unnerved at the sight of don Quixote and refused to leave his cage, although the cage was left open more than enough time. He also said that he'd told that knight that it was tempting God to irritate the lion in order to force him out against the lion's wishes, and that don Quixote, contrary to his own will, had permitted him to close the cage.

"What do you think of that, Sancho?" said don Quixote. "Are there enchantments that can have any effect against true bravery? Enchanters may well be able to rob my good fortune—but my resolve and courage, never!"

Sancho gave them the *escudos*, the carter yoked up his mules, the lion keeper kissed don Quixote's hand for the favor received, and promised to tell the king himself about the brave deed when he saw him in court.

"If His Majesty should ask who did that deed, you will

tell him it was the KNIGHT OF THE LIONS, for that's what I want my old name, the WOEBEGONE KNIGHT, to be changed, altered, transformed, and made over into from now on, and in this I'm following the ancient custom of knights-errant, who changed their names whenever they wanted, or whenever it seemed appropriate."

The cart went on its way, and don Quixote, Sancho, and the Man in the Green Coat went theirs. In all this time don Diego de Miranda had not said a word, being absorbed in looking at and noting the deeds and words of don Quixote, for it seemed to him that he was a sane crazy man and a crazy man who was leaning toward being sane. The first part of his history had not yet come to his notice. If he'd read it, his wonder would have disappeared, since he would have known what kind of madness he suffered from. But since he didn't know, sometimes he took him for sane and other times for crazy, because what he said was well put together, elegant, and well stated, and what he did was foolish, reckless, and stupid. He said to himself: "What can be crazier than to put on a helmet filled with cottage cheese and believe that enchanters were softening his brains, and what greater recklessness and foolishness can there be than to want to fight lions?"

Don Quixote roused him from these thoughts and this soliloquy, when he said: "Who doubts, *señor* Diego de Miranda, that your grace must hold me as a fool and a crazy man? And it wouldn't be too far off the mark, since my deeds seem to point to nothing else. But I want your grace to be aware that I'm not as crazy and diminished as I must have appeared. A gallant knight who gives a fortunate lance stroke to a fierce bull in the middle of the plaza must look good in the eyes of the king. A knight dressed in shining armor who competes in animated jousts must look good to the ladies. And all those knights who engage in military exercises, or exercises that look military in nature, entertain and gladden people, and, if I may say so, honor the court of their princes. But above all of these, a knight-errant is the best, for he wanders through deserts, wilderness, crossroads, forests, and mountains, seeking dangerous adventures with the intention of bringing them to a happy conclusion, for the sole purpose of achieving glorious and lasting fame. A knight-errant rescuing a widow in some barren place, I say, seems better than a courtly knight wooing a damsel in the city. Every knight has his particular function: Let the courtly knight serve the ladies, glorify his king at court with his handsome uniforms, feed the poor knights with splendid food at his table, arrange jousts, take part in tournaments, and show himself to be liberal and magnificent, and above all a good Christian—in this way he'll fulfill his precise obligations.

"But let the knight-errant scour the corners of the earth, penetrate into the most intricate labyrinths, attack impossible things every step of the way, resist the burning rays of the desert sun in the middle of summer, and in winter, the cruel bitterness of the winds and snows. He won't let lions terrify, nor monsters frighten, nor dragons daunt him, for seeking these, attacking those, and vanquishing all of them are his main and true exercise. I, then, since it was my fate to be among the knights-errant, can't help but take on everything that seems to me to fall under the purview of my profession; so attacking lions, which I just did, was something I had to do, even though it seemed to be foolhardy recklessness. I well know what bravery is—it's a virtue somewhere between the two vices of cowardice and foolhardiness. But it will be better for the brave man to rise to the point of recklessness rather than to lower to the point of cowardice. So just as it's easier for the generous person to be more liberal than the miser, it's easier for the reckless man to be truly brave than for the coward. Insofar as taking on adventures is concerned, believe me, *señor* don Diego, it's better to lose by a card too many than one too few, because 'that knight is reckless and daring' sounds better to the ear than 'that knight is timid and cowardly.'"

"I agree, *señor* don Quixote," responded don Diego, "that everything you've said is proven by reason itself, and I can see that if the rules and laws of knight-errantry were lost, they could be found in your grace's heart as they would be in their own storehouse and archive. Now let's hurry, because it's getting late. We'll go to my village and house, where your grace can rest from your travails, which—if these weren't of the body, they certainly were of the spirit—frequently result in fatigue of the body."

"I accept your offer as a great favor and kindness, *señor* don Diego," responded don Quixote.

And spurring their horses more than they had before, they arrived at about two in the afternoon at the village and house of don Diego, whom don Quixote called the KNIGHT OF THE GREEN COAT.

Chapter XVIII. About what happened to don Quixote in the castle of the Knight of the Green Coat, with other extravagant things.

DON QUIXOTE found the house of don Diego to be as large as a village. The coat of arms, carved in soft stone, above the door leading to the road; the wine cellar on the patio, and the underground food-storage area at the gate; and many clay vats all around (since they were made in El Toboso) renewed his memory of the enchanted and transformed Dulcinea. And, giving a sigh, without realizing what he was saying, nor in whose presence he was, he said:

Oh, you sweet treasure, to my sorrow found!
Once sweet and welcome when it was heaven's goodwill.*

"Oh, you Tobosan vats, who have brought to mind the sweet treasure of my greatest bitterness!"

The student-poet, son of don Diego, who had come out with his mother, heard him say this as they went out to receive him, and both the mother and son were amazed to see the strange figure of don Quixote, who, when he got down from Rocinante, went over to take the lady's hand and kiss it. Don Diego said: "*Señora*, receive with your accustomed affability *señor* don Quixote de La Mancha, who is the person before you, a knight-errant, and the bravest and shrewdest one in the world."

The lady, who was named doña Cristina, received him with great affection and courtesy, and don Quixote offered his services politely. He used almost the same polite expres-

---

* These are the first two lines of Garcilaso de la Vega's *Sonnet X*. The treasure in the case of the sonnet is a lock of hair from his deceased lady, Isabel de Freyre.

sions with the student, who, when he heard don Quixote talk, considered him to be sharp and keen witted.

Here the author describes all the details of don Diego's house, depicting everything that a house belonging to a rich country gentleman contains. But the translator of this history thought he would pass over these and similar details in silence, because they didn't fit in with the main purpose of the history, which derives its strength from the truth rather than from boring digressions.

They ushered don Quixote into a room, where Sancho took his armor off, leaving him in his knickers and chamois doublet, all stained with the rust of armor. The collar was of the unadorned flat kind, like students wear, without starch or lace; his leggings were date-colored, and his shoes were waxed. His worthy sword hung from a sealskin strap, for it's held that he'd suffered from a kidney infection for many years.* He also put a cape of good gray material on. First of all, he washed his head and face with five—or maybe six (because there's a difference of opinion about the number)—buckets of water, and even with that, the water was still the color of whey, thanks to the gluttony of Sancho and the purchase of his black† cottage cheese that made his master so white.

With the attire as described and with a gentle and gallant appearance, don Quixote went out into another room, where the student was waiting to entertain him while the tables were being set. Since such a noble guest had arrived, doña Cristina wanted to show she knew how to entertain people who might come to her house.

While don Quixote was removing his armor, don Lorenzo (for that was the name of don Diego's son) had the opportunity to say to his father: "Who in the world is this knight that you have brought home? His name, looks, and saying that he's a knight-errant have astonished my mother and me."

"I don't know what to tell you, son," said don Diego. "I can say only that I've seen him do things that only the .

---

* Clemencín says that sealskin was supposed to be good for kidney infections.

† *Black* here in Spanish means "cursèd." It is kept as "black" because of the pun at the end of the sentence.

craziest man in the world would do, and I've heard him say things that were so keen they overshadow and efface his deeds. Go speak to him and take the pulse of his knowledge, and, since you're sharp, you can judge for yourself what seems most reasonable regarding his sagacity or foolishness, although, to tell the truth, I judge him to be crazy rather than sane."

With this, don Lorenzo went to entertain don Quixote, as has been said, and among the conversations they had, don Quixote said to don Lorenzo: "*Señor* Diego de Miranda, your grace's father, has told me of the rare skill and subtle genius you possess, and especially that you're a great poet."

"Poet, possibly," responded don Lorenzo, "but great, certainly not. It's true that I'm a bit fond of poetry and of reading good poets, but in no way do I deserve my father calling me great."

"This humility doesn't seem bad to me," responded don Quixote, "because there's no poet who isn't arrogant and doesn't think he's the best one in the world."

"'There's no rule without an exception,'" responded don Lorenzo, "and there must be some who are fine poets but don't think so."

"Very few," responded don Quixote, "but tell me, your grace, what verses are you working on now? Your *señor* father has told me that you have a project that is making you nervous and pensive. And if it's a gloss, I know something about the subject of glosses, and I'd like to see it. And if it's a literary joust, try to take second prize, because the first prize is awarded as a favor to a person of rank, and the second is awarded on the basis of merit alone, and by this reasoning the third becomes the second, and the first prize becomes the third, just like degrees that they give at universities. But even so, it's great to be first."

"So far," said don Lorenzo under his breath, "I can't say that you're crazy—but let's move on." And he said aloud: "It seems to me that you've studied at the university. What was your major?"

"It was knight-errantry," responded don Quixote, "which is as good as poetry, and even a bit better."

"I don't know what that branch of knowledge is," replied don Lorenzo, "and until this moment I've never heard of it."

"It's an area," replied don Quixote, "that encompasses all or most of the sciences in the world, because he who professes it must be expert in legal matters and know laws of distributive and commutative justice, so as to give every person what he's due and what is fitting. He has to be a theologian so he can communicate clearly and distinctly the Christian faith that he professes whenever he's asked. He has to be a doctor, mainly an herbalist, so that he can recognize—in unpopulated areas and the wilderness—which herbs have the property to heal wounds, since knights-errant cannot go looking for someone to treat them at every step of the way. He has to be an astronomer to be able to tell by looking at the stars how many hours have gone by at night, and to tell what part of the world he is in. He has to know math because he'll need it all the time, not to mention that he should be endowed with all of the virtues, theological and cardinal.* Coming down to lesser details, he has to be able to swim as they say the merman Nicolás or Nicolao did.† He has to know how to shoe a horse and repair a saddle and a bridle. And coming back to more important matters, he has to be faithful to God, and to his lady. He has to be chaste in his thoughts, pure in his words, liberal with others, valiant in his deeds, patient in his travails, charitable with the needy, and finally, keeper of the truth, even though it may cost him his life to defend it. Of all these great and small parts is made the good knight-errant. Now your grace can judge for yourself, *señor* don Lorenzo, if what the knight studies and professes is a puerile field, or if it can equal the most elevated ones that schools teach."

"If that's what it is," replied don Lorenzo, "I say it exceeds all others."

"What do you mean, '*if* that's what it is'?" responded don Quixote.

"What I mean," said don Lorenzo, "is that I doubt that there ever were nor are there now knights-errant endowed with so many virtues."

---

* The theological virtues are faith, hope, and charity; the cardinal virtues are prudence, justice, temperance, and fortitude.

† This was a legendary fifteenth-century Sicilian merman, the masculine version of the mermaid.

"I've said many times what I'll repeat now," responded don Quixote, "that most people think that there were and are no knights-errant in the world, and since it seems to me that if heaven cannot miraculously make them understand the truth that there were and are such people, no matter what is done, it will be in vain, as experience has shown me many times; so I don't want to take the time to correct your error, which you share with many others. What I plan to do is pray that heaven will correct this mistake, and make you understand how beneficial and how necessary knights-errant of past centuries were, and how useful they'd be in the present one, if they were in fashion. But nowadays—because of man's sins—sloth, laziness, idleness, gluttony, and lust triumph."

"Our guest has shown his colors," don Lorenzo said to himself, "but he's an odd madman, and I'd be an idiot if I didn't believe it."

Here their conversation ended, because they were called to eat lunch. Don Diego asked his son what he'd learned about the wits of their guest, to which he responded: "All the doctors and scribes in the world won't be able to fix the first draft of his craziness. He's a crazy man with periods of lucidity."

They went to eat, and the lunch was just as don Diego had described while they were on the road—clean, abundant, and delicious. But what delighted don Quixote the most was the marvelous silence that reigned in the whole house, which seemed like a Carthusian monastery. Once the table was cleared, thanks were given to God, and hands were washed, don Quixote begged don Lorenzo to recite the verses of the literary joust. To which he responded that he didn't want to be like those poets who, when you ask them to recite their verses, refuse, and when you don't ask them, they vomit them out. "I'll recite my gloss, from which I expect no prize at all—I did it only for the intellectual exercise."

"A learnèd friend of mine," responded don Quixote, "thought that no one should bother glossing verses, and the reason, he said, was that the gloss could never be as good as the original text, and that most or much of the time, the gloss strayed from the intention and scope of what was being glossed, and further, that the rules of the gloss were too stringent—barring questions, expressions such as 'he said' and 'I'll say,' making verbs of nouns, or changing meaning, along with other restrictions and constraints that bind and hamper those who gloss, as your grace must know."

"Truly, *señor* don Quixote," said don Lorenzo, "I'd like to catch you in some error but I can't, because you slip through my hands like an eel."

"I don't understand," responded don Quixote, "what you mean about my slipping through your hands."

"I'll tell you later," responded don Lorenzo, "but now let your grace listen attentively to the verses to be glossed, which I'll recite now:*

If my "was" should be turned to "is"
    Without the hope of what shall be,
    Or that the time should come again
    Of what hereafter is to be.

THE GLOSS

As all things fade and pass away,
    So Fortune's favors will not stay;
    And though once she gave me all,
    Now she will not heed my call.
    For ages at your feet I've lain,
    Stern Fortune, hoping, but in vain;
    What happiness for me, what bliss
    IF MY "WAS" SHOULD BE TURNED TO "IS."

I wish no other prize or glory,
    No other victory or palm,
    But to regain once more the calm
    Where lack disturbs my memory;
    If you will give me back your boon,
    My restless craving will be spent,
    The more, if you will give it soon,
    For then I'll rest and be content
    WITHOUT THE HOPE OF WHAT SHALL BE.

---

* I have used the Starkie translation for this poem and for the sonnet that follows.

Like a fool I call upon the past,
    And beg it to return in vain:
    No power on earth can call back Time,
    For it will never come again.
    It races on with nimble wing;
    And he is wrong who hopes to bring
    By his cries all the past again,
    OR THAT THE TIME SHOULD RETURN AGAIN.

To live in such perplexity,
    Forever poised between hope and fear,
    Is not life; better death in verity;
    If by this way I could get clear
    Of all my woes, then this were bliss;
    But reason whispers in my ear
    OF WHAT HEREAFTER IS TO BE.

When don Lorenzo finished reciting his gloss, don Quixote stood up and in a very loud voice—almost a shout—he went to clasp don Lorenzo's right hand and said: "By the highest heaven, noble young man, you're the best poet on earth, and you deserve do be crowned with laurel not by Cyprus or Gaeta, as a poet said (and may God pardon him for it), but rather by the Academies of Athens,* if they were still flourishing, and by those that are in Paris, Bologna, and Salamanca today. If the judges refuse you first place may Phœbus shoot them with arrows,† and the Muses never pass over the thresholds of their houses.‡ Recite for me, *señor*, if you will, some longer verses,§ for I want to take the pulse of every aspect of your admirable genius."

Is it necessary to say that don Lorenzo was pleased to hear himself praised by don Quixote, even though he con-

---

* The Academy of Athens was founded in 387 B.C. by Plato and lasted until A.D. 529. It is the ancestor of Western universities.

† Phœbus is the Roman name for Apollo, who, with Artemis, killed eleven of Amphion's children with arrows.

‡ The nine Muses, daughters of Zeus, provided inspiration for poetry, theater, music, and other endeavors.

§ That is, the gloss was in eight-syllable lines, known as "lesser art" (*arte menor*). Don Quixote wants to hear some eleven-syllable verses, "greater art" (*arte mayor*), such as the verses of a sonnet.

sidered him crazy? Oh, power of flattery! How wide you cast your net and how vast are the boundaries of your satisfying dominion! Don Lorenzo confirmed this truth, because he agreed to don Quixote's request and desire, reciting to him this sonnet about the fable of Pyramus and Thisbe:*

SONNET

The fair maiden the cruel wall does break
    That had been cleft by Pyramus' manly heart.
    Straightway from his Cyprian home does Cupid start
    To see the prodigious rift that love did make.
There no voice enters, only silence spake,
    For souls though dumb may not be kept apart,
    Perforce they'll speak, and Love has still the art
    A crafty enemy to subjugate.
But the rash maiden's passion goes awry,
    And haste makes her woo death instead of love.
    The hapless pair together: tragic story!
Are both united in their common doom:
    One sword, one sepulcher, one memory
    Slays, covers, crowns with immortality.

"Blessed be God!" said don Quixote, having heard don Lorenzo's sonnet, "among the infinite number of consumed poets, I've seen a consummate poet,† and that's you, *señor mío*, for your sonnet has convinced me of it."

Don Quixote was well-entertained for four days in don Diego's house, at the end of which he begged permission to leave, saying that he thanked them for the kindness and attention he'd received in their home, but since it didn't seem right for knights-errant to spend too much time at leisure and in comfort, he wanted to discharge the duties of his profession by seeking adventures, which he'd been informed abounded in that region, and where he expected to spend time until the day came for the jousts in Zaragoza, for that was his destination. But first he wanted to go into the Cave of Montesinos, about which were told so many

---

* See Part I, chapter twenty-four, page 24.
† There is a pun here between *poetas cunsumidos* ("wretched poets") and consummate poets.

and such wondrous things throughout that area, to investigate and try to find the origin and true source of the seven Lagoons of Ruidera, as they're known.

Don Diego and his son praised his honorable resolve and told him that he should take anything he wanted from their home and estate, and that they would help him in any way they could, because his valor and honored profession obliged them to do so.

Finally the day of his departure arrived, as happy a one for don Quixote as it was sad for Sancho Panza, who was very content with the abundance in don Diego's house, and was loath to go back to the hunger that's so common in the woods and wilderness, and to the skimpiness of their badly provisioned saddlebags. But he stuffed them with what seemed to him to be most necessary. And when he bade farewell, don Quixote said to don Lorenzo: "I don't know if I already said this to you or not, and if I did, I'll repeat it—if your grace wants to cut short the paths and travails to get to the height of the temple of fame, all you have to do is leave the path of poetry, which is a bit narrow in itself, and take the even narrower one of knight-errantry, which will suffice to make you an emperor in the twinkling of an eye."

With these words don Quixote proved his madness beyond a reasonable doubt, and gave further proof when he said: "God knows I'd like to take *señor* don Lorenzo with me to teach him how to spare the humble and subdue and trample on those who are arrogant—these being functions of my profession. But because your tender age will not allow it, and your praiseworthy endeavors will not consent to it, I'll content myself by telling your grace that by being a poet you can come to be famous, if you're guided more by the opinion of others than your own, since no child seems ugly in the eyes of his parents, and this deception is even more prevalent when it comes to children of one's intellect."

Once again father and son marveled at don Quixote's words, sometimes wise, sometimes foolish, and at his passion and resolve to go back headlong into his questionable quests, the target of his desires. The promise of services and courtesies was reiterated, and with the final permission of the lady of the castle, don Quixote and Sancho left, one on Rocinante and the other on the donkey.

Chapter XIX. Where the adventure of the enamored shepherd is recounted, together with, in truth, other amusing events.

D ON QUIXOTE had traveled just a short distance from don Diego's village when he met with what seemed to be two priests or students* along with two peasants, riding on four donkeys. One of the students was carrying something like a traveling bag made out of a piece of green buckram containing some white linen and two pairs of ribbed stockings. The other one had nothing but two new fencing foils with buttons on the tips. The peasants were carrying other things that indicated that they were coming from a large town, where they had made their purchases and were taking them back to their village. Both the students and peasants were as astonished as everyone was who saw don Quixote for the first time, and they were all dying to find out who that man was who looked so different from other men.

Don Quixote greeted them courteously, and after finding out what road they were taking, which was the same as his, he offered to keep them company, and asked them to slow down a bit because their young donkeys were going faster than his horse. To convince them to do so, he told them in a few words who he was, and that his profession was that of a knight-errant, and that he traveled the world searching for adventures. He said that his true name was don Quixote de La Mancha, but that he was known as the Knight of the Lions. To the peasants this all was as if he were talking Greek or gibberish, but not so for the students, who recognized the weakness in don Quixote's brain right away. But even so, they looked at him with wonder and respect, and one of them said to him: "If your grace, *señor* knight, is not taking any particular road, as is the custom with those who seek adventures, you should come with us and you'll witness one of the best and richest weddings ever celebrated in La Mancha, or for many leagues around."

Don Quixote asked him if it was the marriage of some

---

* The confusion is natural, since both dressed in black.

prince that they were praising in that way. "No," the student responded, "but of a peasant lad and a peasant girl—he's the richest man in this whole area and she's the most beautiful woman anyone has ever seen. The festivities that accompany the marriage will be extraordinary and unheard-of, because they'll take place in a meadow near the town of the bride, whom they call, because of her qualities, QUITERIA THE BEAUTIFUL, and him they call CAMACHO THE RICH. She's eighteen years old and the bridegroom is twenty-two, and they're a well-matched couple, although some meddlesome people, who know everyone's lineage by heart, say that the beautiful Quiteria's surpasses Camacho's.* But this isn't important, since 'wealth can solder many cracks.' This Camacho is generous and he had the idea to screen the whole field with branches overhead in such a way that the sun will have a hard time of it if it wants to shine on the green grass covering the meadow. He has also arranged for dancers—both with swords and those who ring jingle bells as they dance—because in his village there are those who can ring them to perfection. Of the *zapateadores*† I won't say anything, because he'll have a multitude of them. But none of the things I've mentioned, nor many others that I haven't, will make the wedding more memorable than what the despairing Basilio will do there.

"This Basilio is from the same village as Quiteria—he's her next-door neighbor—and Cupid had a chance to renew in the world the now forgotten love of Pyramus and Thisbe, because Basilio fell in love with Quiteria when he was a tender child, and she responded with a thousand innocent signs of affection, so much so that the whole town, for pleasure, talked about the love of the two children, Basilio and

---

* The ballets about don Quixote, both Russian, are based on this episode. The first was choreographed by the French-born Marius Petipa in 1869, music by Ludwig Minkus. A modern version by Mikhail Baryshnikov, subtitled *Kitri's Wedding* ("Kitri" is the Russian "Quiteria"), also using Minkus' music, was done in 1984. Both are available on DVD. Petipa's version was revised by Rudolf Nureyev, who also played Basilio, a barber, in the 1973 version. You'll meet Basilio later, and he's not a barber. In each one, don Quixote somehow manages to attack windmills.

† Covarrubias in his 1611 dictionary says that these are rustic dancers who slap their shoes rhythmically as they dance.

Quiteria. As they grew older, Quiteria's father decided to bar Basilio from his house—Basilio used to come and go as he pleased—so as not to arouse fear or suspicion. He ordered his daughter to marry the rich Camacho. It didn't seem a good idea to marry her to Basilio, who is less endowed with material wealth than by nature, for if the truth be known, and without envy, he's the most nimble fellow we know—a great hurler of the bar,* an incomparably good wrestler, and a great ballplayer. He runs like a deer, jumps better than a goat, and is a magician at ninepins. He sings like a lark, and when he plays the guitar, it's like he's making it speak, and above all he wields the sword like the best of them."

"On the basis of this skill alone," said don Quixote, "this fellow deserves not only to marry the beautiful Quiteria, but Queen Guinevere herself if she were alive today, in spite of Lancelot and everyone else who might try to prevent it."

"Tell that to my wife," said Sancho Panza, who until then hadn't said anything, but was still listening. "She wants everyone to marry his equal, sticking to the saying 'every ewe to its mate.' What I'd like is for this Basilio—and I'm beginning to like him already—to marry this lady Quiteria, and may those who prevent those who love each other from getting married have a good life and good death (I really mean the opposite)."

"If all those who were in love should get married," said don Quixote, "parents would lose their option to choose to whom and when their children marry, and if left to the will of the daughters to choose their husbands, one would choose to marry her father's servant; another would pick someone she saw walking down the street who seemed elegant and haughty even though he might be a degenerate bully. Love and fondness easily blind the eyes of one's understanding, which is so necessary to choose a mate, and it's very easy to make a mistake in this area. You need to use great discretion, and get help from heaven to do it right. When you want to make a long voyage, if you're prudent, before starting out, you'll choose a faithful and

---

* This sport consists of throwing a metal bar as far as you can, but it has to land sticking in the ground, like a javelin.

pleasant companion. So, why shouldn't the person who has to travel his whole life until the destination of death is reached do the same thing, especially when the companion is with him in bed, at the table, and everywhere else, as a wife is with her husband? The company of one's wife is not like merchandise that, after you buy something, you can return it, because it's an unbreakable bond that lasts one's whole life. It's a noose that, once it's around your neck, is like the Gordian knot,* which, unless it's cut by the scythe of death, is not untieable. I could say many other things on this subject, but I won't, since I want to find out if there's anything more the *señor licenciado* has to say about Basilio."

To which the bachelor, or *licenciado*, as don Quixote called him, replied: "The only thing that I have left to say is that since Basilio found out that the beautiful Quiteria was getting married to Camacho the Rich, he's never been seen to laugh, nor said anything that made sense, and he always walks around pensive and sad, muttering to himself, which gives clear and unmistakable signs that he's gone crazy. He eats and sleeps very little. When he does eat, it's only fruits, and when he sleeps, it's in the countryside on the hard ground like a wild animal. Once in a while he looks at the sky, and at other times he stares at the ground in such a reverie that he seems to be a statue dressed in clothing that the wind flutters. So, he appears so heart-stricken that all of us who know him fear that when Quiteria says I DO tomorrow, that will be his death sentence."

"God will do better than that," said Sancho, "for 'if God gives the wound he'll provide the remedy.' 'No one knows what is to come,' and 'from now until tomorrow there are many hours,' and 'in one of them—or even in a moment—a house can tumble down.' 'I've seen it rain and be sunny at the same time.' 'A man goes to sleep sound as an apple and can't get out of bed in the morning.' And tell me, 'is there

---

* In 333 B.C., Alexander the Great went into Gordium, the capital of Anatolia, and was shown a chariot lashed to a pole by means of a knot with a hidden end. Only the conqueror of Asia would be able to untie it. Legend says that he just cut the knot, but early versions say that he found a way to untie it. In any case, the Gordian knot was supposed to be impossible to untie, thus the allusion here.

anyone who can boast that he put a nail into the wheel of
Fortune?' No, certainly not, and 'between a woman's YES
or NO I wouldn't try to put the point of a pin' because it
wouldn't fit. Tell me that Quiteria loves Basilio with all
her heart and will, and I'll give him a sackful of good luck.
'Love—as I've heard tell—looks through glasses that make
copper look like gold; poverty, wealth; and the sleep from
one's eye, pearls.' "

"When are you going to stop, Sancho, damn you?" said
don Quixote. "When you begin to string proverbs and an-
ecdotes together, no one can put up with you but Judas,*
and may he haul you away. Tell me, creature, what do you
know about nails, or wheels, or anything else?"

"Oh, well, if you don't understand me," responded
Sancho, "it's no wonder that you consider my maxims
nonsense—but no matter, I understand myself and I know
that I haven't said much foolishness, but your grace, *señor mío*, is always the cricket of my sayings and also my
deeds."

"You mean *critic*," said don Quixote, "and not *cricket*,
you prevaricator of good language, and may God confound
you!"

"Don't get angry with me, your grace," responded Sancho, "since you know I wasn't raised at court, nor have I
studied at Salamanca, so that I'd know if my words have
an extra letter or not. God help me, there's no way you
can ask a Sayagués to talk like someone from Toledo,† and
maybe there are some Toledans who aren't so skilled in
their language."

"That's right," said the *licenciado*, "because those who
were bred in the tanneries and in the Plaza de Zocodover
can't talk as well as those who spend almost all day long in
the cloister of the cathedral, yet they're all Toledans. Pure
and proper, elegant and clear language belongs to enlight-

---

* This Judas is not the treacherous apostle, but rather the legendary
wandering Jew who is waiting for the coming of the Messiah. Only this
person would have the patience to suffer Sancho's string of proverbs,
in don Quixote's view.
† Sayagués was the Aragonese dialect that epitomized rustic speech
in the Golden Age theater. Toledan represented the cultured standard
language.

ened courtiers, even if they were born in Majalahonda.* I
said *enlightened* because many of them aren't, and enlight-
enment is the grammar of good language that comes from
practice. I, *señores*, for my sins, have studied canon law at
Salamanca, and I pride myself a bit on having my say using
clear, plain, and meaningful words."

"If you didn't pride yourself more in wielding the foils you
have with you than your language," said the other student,
"you would have been first in your class instead of last."

"Look, bachelor," responded the *licenciado*, "you hold
the most mistaken opinion in the world about skill with
swords when you say that they're of no use."

"As far as I'm concerned, it's not an opinion, but rather a
well-established fact," replied Corchuelo, "and if you want
me to prove it to you, you've got the swords, we've got the
opportunity, I've got steady hands and am strong, and fortified by my heart, which is not small, and I'll make you confess that I'm not mistaken. Dismount, position your feet,
calculate your circles and angles, and use your knowledge,
and I'll try to make you see stars at noon with my modern
and coarse skills in which I put my trust. After God, the
man has yet to be born who will make me turn my back,
and there's no one in the world whom I cannot make give
ground."

"In this matter of turning your back or not, I'm not concerned," replied the swordsman, "although the spot where
you begin this sword fight will be where they dig your grave.
I mean that there you will be killed by the skill you hold in
such low esteem."

"We'll see," responded Corchuelo. And getting off his
donkey, he furiously snatched one of the swords that the
licenciado's donkey was carrying.

"It must not be that way," said don Quixote instantly. "I
want to be the referee of this fencing bout and judge of this
often disputed matter."

And getting off Rocinante and taking his lance, he placed
himself in the middle of the road just when the *licenciado*,
with a graceful gait, moved toward Corchuelo, who was coming at him shooting flames from his eyes, as they say. The two

---

* This formerly sleepy rustic town, now called Maja*d*ahonda, is about
ten miles northwest of Madrid.

peasants who were accompanying them didn't dismount, but remained as spectators at this mortal tragedy. The sideways slashes, straight thrusts, downward thrusts, diagonal slashes from the left, and two-handed slashes that Corchuelo dealt were infinite, like falling hail. He attacked like a provoked lion, but he was met with a little hit on his mouth by the button of the *licenciado*'s foil, which checked his fury and made him kiss it as if it were a relic (but not with the same devotion with which relics should be and are customarily kissed).

Finally, the *licenciado* wound up cutting off all the buttons on the cassock he was wearing and systematically tearing the bottom of it into strips, making it look like the tentacles of an octopus. He knocked his hat off twice and tired him so much that, in dismay, anger, and rage, Corchuelo took his sword by the hilt and threw it into the air with so much force that one of the peasants in attendance, who was a scribe, went to fetch it, and later made a deposition stating that he had thrown it almost three-quarters of a league, and this affidavit serves and served to prove that beyond a doubt force is conquered by skill.

The exhausted Corchuelo sat down and Sancho went over to him and said: "On my faith, *señor* bachelor, if you'd take my advice, from now on, you shouldn't challenge anyone to a fencing duel, but rather to wrestle or hurl the bar, since you're both strong and experienced enough for that. Those people that are called fencing masters can put the point of their sword through the eye of a needle."

"I'm satisfied," responded Corchuelo, "to have seen the error of my ways, and that experience has shown me the truth that was so elusive to me."

And getting up he embraced the *licenciado*, and they became better friends than before. They didn't want to wait for the scribe to return with the sword, figuring it would delay them too much, so they decided to continue on in order to arrive early at Quiteria's village, where they all were from.

For the remainder of the journey, the *licenciado* elaborated on the wonders of swordsmanship, together with so many conclusive arguments, and with so many figures and mathematical demonstrations, that everyone was convinced of the worth of the science, and Corchuelo was cured of his obstinacy.

It was now nightfall, but before they arrived, it seemed

to everyone that on their side of the village the sky was filled with innumerable shining stars. They heard the soft sound of many instruments such as flutes, drums, psalteries, cymbals, tambourines, and small drums all mingled together, and when they went over they saw a bower of trees at the entrance to the village that was filled with lanterns that were not affected by the breeze, which didn't even stir the leaves of the trees. The musicians were the merrymakers of the wedding, and in different groups in that pleasant site were wandering, some dancing, some singing, and others playing the various instruments already mentioned. Indeed, it seemed that throughout the whole meadow mirth and revelry leapt in frolic and joy.

Many others were busy erecting platforms from where people could see the performances and dances that were going to be put on in that place the following day to celebrate the wedding of the rich Camacho, and the funeral rites of Basilio. Don Quixote refused to go into the town even though both the peasant and the bachelor asked him to. He gave as an excuse one that seemed sufficient to him, and that was that it was the custom of knights-errant to sleep in the fields and forests rather than in towns, even though it might be under golden roofs; and with this he turned off the road, much against Sancho's will, remembering well the good lodging he had in the castle or house of don Diego.

Chapter XX. Where the wedding of Camacho the Rich is recounted together with what happened to poor Basilio.

Hardly had the fair Aurora given the shining Phœbus time to dry the liquid pearls from her hair with his warming rays* when don Quixote, shaking off the stiffness from his limbs, stood up and called his squire, Sancho, who

---

* Liquid pearls are dew. Phœbus, recently mentioned in chapter eighteen of Part II, was the Roman name for Apollo, the god of the sun. Aurora was the Roman goddess of the dawn. This passage reflects the language don Quixote used to describe the outset of his own first expedition (Part I, chapter two, page 27).

was still snoring. When don Quixote saw him sleeping so peacefully, before waking him up, he said: "Oh, most fortunate of all who live on the face of the earth, since without envying or being envied, you sleep with a calm spirit, and enchanters don't pursue you, nor do enchantments overwhelm you! Sleep on, I say once again, and I'll say it a hundred more times, without the jealousy of your lady keeping you constantly watchful, nor thoughts of debts to keep you awake, nor how you have to provide for your small and needy family tomorrow, nor does ambition disturb you, nor the pomp of the world bother you, since the limits of your desires go no further than feeding your donkey; and you have put on my shoulders the responsibility of providing for you, a weight and a charge that nature and custom have imposed on masters. The servant sleeps while the master stays awake, thinking how he has to sustain him, better him, and grant him favors. The distress in seeing that the sky darkens and keeps needed dew from the earth doesn't bother the servant, but rather the master, who has to support, in barren times and famine, the one who served him in times of fertility and abundance."

If Sancho answered nothing to all this, it was because he was sleeping, and he wouldn't have woken up anytime soon if don Quixote hadn't roused him with the point of his lance. He finally woke up, sleepy and lethargic, and, looking all around, said: "From that bower, if I'm not mistaken, is coming the aroma and smell more of roasted bacon than of rushes and thyme. Weddings that begin with such smells, by the sign of the cross, must be abundant and generous."

"Stop, you glutton," said don Quixote. "Come, let's go see this marriage to find out what the disdained Basilio will do."

"Let him do whatever he wants," responded Sancho. "He can't be poor and marry Quiteria. Imagine not having two bits and wanting to marry in the clouds. By my faith, *señor*, I think the poor fellow ought to content himself with whatever he can find, and not 'go around asking for delicacies in the middle of the sea.' I'll bet an arm that Camacho can smother Basilio with *reales*, and this being so, Quiteria would be foolish to throw away the jewels that Camacho has given her, and can keep on giving her, for all of Basilio's hurling the bar and fencing. You can't get a pint of wine in a tavern for a good throw of the bar or a subtle feint with the sword. Leave those skills to Count Dirlos.* But when such dexterity falls to a person who has lots of money, let my life be like his. 'On a solid foundation you can erect a good building,' and 'the best foundation in the world is money.'"

"In the name of God, Sancho," said don Quixote, "finish your speech. I think that if you were allowed to keep on talking, you'd have no time left to eat or sleep, because you'd spend all your time talking."

"If your grace has a good memory," replied Sancho, "you would remember the provisions of our agreement before we left home the last time. One of them was that you had to let me say anything I wanted, provided it wasn't to the detriment of anyone or your authority, and up to now I don't think I've overstepped this provision."

"I remember no such provision, Sancho," responded don Quixote, "and even though there may be such a one, I want you to stop talking and come, for the instruments we heard last night are making the valleys rejoice, and doubtless the nuptials will take place in the cool of the morning and not in the heat of the afternoon."

Sancho did what his master bade, and putting the saddle on Rocinante and the packsaddle on the donkey, the two mounted, and one step at a time they entered into the bower. The first thing that Sancho caught sight of was a whole young bull on a spit made of an elm tree, and on the fire where it was going to be roasted there burned a good-sized mountain of firewood, while six pots surrounding the fire were not ordinary ones, since they were the size of wine vats, and each one contained a veritable slaughterhouse of meat, and they swallowed up whole sheep as if they were young pigeons. The skinned rabbits and plucked chickens hanging in the trees to be submerged into the pots were without number. Game birds of different types were infinite, hanging from trees so the air would cool them. Sancho counted more than sixty wineskins of more than six gallons apiece and all of

---

* Count Dirlos was a well-known character in the Spanish ballads, and was the brother of Durandarte (see if you can remember this man's name for a couple of chapters).

them full, as it later appeared, of full-bodied wines. There
were great piles of the whitest bread, like mounds of wheat
on the threshing room floor. Wheels of cheese, positioned
in stacks like bricks, formed a wall, and two oil-filled cauldrons, larger than those in a dyer's shop, served to fry the
pastries, which, with two large shovels, were then taken out
and plunged into another vat of prepared honey nearby.
The cooks—both male and female—numbered more than
fifty, all of them clean, all of them busy, and all of them
happy. In the distended stomach of a bullock there were
twelve tender and small suckling pigs sewn inside to give it
flavor and make it tender. Spices of many kinds seemed to
have been bought not by the pound, but by the bushel, and
they were all on display in a large chest. The preparations
for the wedding were rustic, but in such abundance that
they could have fed an army.

Sancho saw it all and contemplated it all, and took a liking to it all. He was initially captivated by the stew pots, of
which he would have willingly taken an average-sized one.
Then the wineskins started to appeal to him, and finally the
contents of the frying pans, if that's the right term for those
cauldrons. And so, without being able to stand it any further, and not being able to help himself, he approached one
of the diligent cooks, and with courteous and hungry words
he begged him to be allowed to dip a crust of bread into
one of those pots. To which the cook responded: "Brother,
this is not one of those days when hunger rules, thanks to
the rich Camacho. Dismount and see if there's a ladle, and
skim off a chicken or two, and *bon appétit.*"

"I don't see any ladle," responded Sancho.

"Wait," said the cook. "Sinner that I am! How helpless
you must be!" And saying this, he grabbed a pot, immersed
it into one of the cauldrons, and scooped out three chickens
and two geese, and said to Sancho: "Eat, my friend, and
break your fast with these skimmings while you wait for
dinner."

"I don't have anything to put it in," responded Sancho.

"Well, then, take everything," said the cook, "the ladle
and all, for the wealth and generosity of Camacho supplies
everything."

While this was going on with Sancho, don Quixote was
watching twelve peasants on twelve beautiful mares in an-

other part of the bower, with rich and flamboyant country trappings and with many jingle bells on their front straps, and all of them festively dressed. They ran in an orderly rush not once but many times through the meadow, and with their elated uproar shouted: "Long live Camacho and Quiteria. He's as rich as she is beautiful, and she's the most beautiful woman in the world!"

When don Quixote heard this he said to himself: "It's clear that these fellows haven't seen my Dulcinea del Toboso, for if they had, they would have been more restrained in their praise of this Quiteria."

Right then, from several places in the bower there entered many different dancers, among them about twenty-four sword dancers, young handsome men, all of them dressed in fine white linen, with their headdresses embroidered with silk thread of different colors. One of the mare riders asked the leader of the sword dancers, a nimble lad, if any of the dancers ever got hurt.

"Up to now, thanks be to God, no one has been wounded—we're all unhurt." And then he joined his companions and they made so many turns with such skill that, although don Quixote was accustomed to seeing similar dances, none seemed to him as good as that one. Another dance that he liked was done by twelve very beautiful maidens—none was younger than fourteen nor older than eighteen—dressed in a fancy green material, with their hair partly in braids, and partly flowing, and all of them so blond that they rivaled the rays of the sun. On their hair they were wearing garlands woven of jasmine, roses, amaranth, and honeysuckle. They were led by a venerable old man and an old matron, but stronger on their feet and more agile than their years would lead one to believe. They danced to the music of a Zamoran *gaita*,* and with modesty in face and eyes, and nimbleness of feet, revealed themselves to be the best dancers in the world.

After this dance, another one—an artistic one they call a "spoken dance"—began. It was made up of eight nymphs in two rows. The first row was led by the god Cupid and the second by Wealth; the former was adorned with wings, quiver, and arrows, and the latter dressed in different colors

---

* The Zamoran *gaita* is a kind of hurdy-gurdy, played with a crank.

of silk. The nymphs lined up behind Love had their names written on their backs, on white parchment: POETRY was the title of the first one, the second was INTELLIGENCE, on the third GOOD LINEAGE, and the fourth VALOR. The same method was used with those following Wealth: It said GEN-EROSITY on the first one, BOUNTY on the second, TREASURE on the third, and on the fourth, PEACEFUL POSSESSION. In front of them was a castle made of wood pulled by four wild men, all of them dressed in ivy and burlap dyed green, looking so natural that Sancho was almost startled. In front of the castle and on each of its four sides was written THE CASTLE OF MODESTY. Music was being made by four players of drum and flute. Cupid began by dancing two figures; then he raised his eyes and aimed his arrow at a maiden who was between two battlements of the castle, to whom he recited this:

I am the mighty god whose sway
    Is potent over land and sea.
    The heavens above us own me; nay,
    The shades below acknowledge me.
I know not fear, I have my will,
    Whatever my whim or fancy be;
    For me there's no impossible,
    I order, bind, forbid, set free.

The little poem ended and he shot an arrow above the castle and went back to his place. Then Wealth came out and did his two figures. The drums ceased and he said:

But mightier than Love am I,
    Though Love it be that leads me on,
    Than mine no lineage is more high,
    Or older, underneath the sun.
To use me rightly few know how,
    To act without me fewer still,
    For I am Wealth, and I vow
    Forevermore to do your will.

Wealth retired, and Poetry came forward, and when she'd gone through her figures like the others, fixing her eyes on the maiden of the castle, she said:

With many a fanciful conceit,
    Fair Lady, winsome Poetry
    Her soul, an offering at your feet,
    Presents in sonnets unto thee.
If you my homage will not scorn,
    Your fortune, watched by envious eyes,
    On wings of poetry upborne
    Shall be exalted to the skies.

Poetry withdrew, and from the side of Wealth, Generosity came forth, and after having gone through her figures, said:

To give, while shunning each extreme,
    The sparing hand, the over-free,
    Therein consists, so wise men deem,
    The virtue Generosity.
But you, fair lady, to enrich,
    Myself a prodigal I'll prove,
    A vice not wholly shameful, which
    May find its fair excuse in love.

In this way all of the dancers of the two sides came out and withdrew, and each one did her figures and recited her verses—some of them elegant and some ridiculous—but don Quixote remembered only those already mentioned, even though his memory was very good. And then they all came together, weaving in and out with grace and ease, and when Love passed in front of the castle he shot his arrows on high, while Wealth smashed against it clay spheres painted gold and filled with coins.

Finally, after he danced for quite a while, Wealth took out a large purse made of the skin of a large striped cat that seemed to be filled with coins, and threw it at the castle, and with the impact, the boards loosened and fell off, leaving the maiden inside exposed and helpless. Wealth approached her along with his companions and threw a golden chain around her neck, and they pretended to take, subdue, and capture her. When Love and his companions saw this, they went over to try to take her back, and everything they did was accompanied by the rhythm of drums and dancing in harmony. The wild men made peace between them, and then put the castle back together, and the maiden went back in, and with this the dance was over, to the enormous pleasure of those who witnessed it.

Don Quixote asked one of the nymphs who had composed and put that show together. She answered that it was a priest in that town who was gifted in that type of production.

"I'll bet," said don Quixote, "that the bachelor or priest is more Camacho's friend than Basilio's and that he's better at satire than saying vespers—see how he juxtaposed the skills of Basilio and the wealth of Camacho in one dance."

Sancho Panza, who was listening to all of this, said: "'The king is my rooster'* and I'll stick to Camacho."

"Indeed," said don Quixote, "it looks like you're one of those rustics who say 'long live the winner.'"

"I don't know which group I favor," responded Sancho, "but I know that from Basilio's pots I'll never get as elegant skimmings as these that I got from Camacho's."

And he showed him the pot filled with geese and chickens; then, taking a chicken, he began to eat with great spirit and zest, and said: "I could care less about Basilio's skills. 'You're worth as much as you have,' and 'you have as much as you're worth.' 'There are two lineages in the world,' a grandmother of mine used to say: 'the HAVES and the HAVE-NOTS,' and she always stuck with the Haves. And today, my dear *señor* don Quixote, people prefer owning to knowing. 'A donkey covered with gold seems better than a horse with a packsaddle.' So, I say again, I'll stick to Camacho, from whose pots we have skimmings that include geese and chickens, hares and rabbits, while those of Basilio, if it ever comes to hand, or even if it only comes to foot, will be nothing but dishwater."

"Have you finished your speech, Sancho?" said don Quixote.

"I must have finished it," responded Sancho, "since I see your grace is annoyed by it. If you hadn't stopped me I'd have gone on for three days."

"I pray to God, Sancho," responded don Quixote, "that I'll see you speechless before I die."

---

* This comes from cockfighting to indicate which is the favored bird.

"The way we're going," responded Sancho, "before you die I'll have kicked the bucket, and then I'll be so speechless that I won't say a word until the end of the world, or at least until Judgment Day."

"Even if that happens, Sancho," responded don Quixote, "your silence will never match how much you've spoken, speak, and will speak during your lifetime, and moreover, it's very likely that the day of my death will precede yours, and thus I'll never see you not talking, not even when you're drinking or sleeping, which is the most I can say."

"In truth, *señor*," responded Sancho, "you don't have to depend on the fleshless one. I mean Death, who eats lambs as well as sheep, and I've heard our priest say that she treads with equal feet in the high towers of kings as she does the humble huts of the poor.* This lady has more power than reluctance, and she's not at all squeamish. She eats everything and fills her saddlebags with people of all ages and rank. She's not a reaper who takes *siestas*, because she reaps all the time, and she cuts dry grass as well as green, and it seems that she doesn't chew, but just gorges and swallows everything placed before her, because she has the hunger of a dog, and they never stop eating. And though she has no stomach, she still swells up, and thirsts for the lives of all living creatures, just like a person would drink a jug of cold water."

"No more, Sancho," said don Quixote. "Stand pat and don't risk falling down, for in truth what you've said about death in your rustic terms is what a good preacher could have said. I tell you, Sancho, that since you have a natural wit and wisdom, you could take a pulpit in your hand and wander about the world preaching beautiful things."

"'He who lives well preaches well,'" responded Sancho, "and I know no other theology."

"Nor do you need to," said don Quixote, "but what I can't fathom nor understand is that since the fear of God is the beginning of wisdom, you—who are more afraid of a lizard than of Him—know so much."

"Just judge your chivalry, *señor*," responded Sancho,

---

* The priest's citation is from the pagan Roman poet Horace, and not from the Bible. See the Prologue to Part I, page 6.

"and don't get involved in judging other people's fears or bravery. I'm as fearful of God as the next fellow. Let me eat up these skimmings, because everything else that we're liable to account for in the other world is idle banter."

And saying this, he began to assault his pot once again with such energy that he inspired the same in don Quixote, who would have joined him if he hadn't been prevented by what will be told later.

Chapter XXI. Where the wedding of Camacho is continued, together with other delightful events.

WHILE DON Quixote and Sancho were in the midst of the conversation reported in the previous chapter, loud voices and a deafening clamor were heard, made by the people riding the mares, who at a gallop and with loud cries raced to receive the bridal couple. The two were surrounded by a thousand kinds of instruments and people carrying festive placards. They were accompanied by the priest, their relatives, and the most distinguished people from neighboring towns, all in gala attire. As soon as Sancho saw the bride he said: "I swear she's dressed not like a peasant but like an elegant lady from the court. Golly, the necklace she's wearing looks to be made of fine coral and the green Cuenca cloth is made of velvet that's thirty piles high.* And look at the trimming of white cloth, which I declare must be satin. Just look at her hands decorated with bracelets made of jet. May I never prosper if those aren't rings made of gold—and pure gold—set with pearls as white as cottage cheese, and each one must be worth an eye. And, son of a bitch, what hair—if it's not a wig, I've never seen longer and blonder hair in my whole life. And try to find something the matter with her dash and the way she carries herself. Wouldn't you compare her to the swaying of a palm tree laden with dates—that's what the trinkets hanging from her hair and throat look

---

* Velvet had a maximum of three piles, not thirty: two warps and one woof.

like. I swear she's a spirited girl who can pass through the banks of Flanders."*

Don Quixote laughed at the rustic praise of Sancho Panza. But it seemed to him that, except for Dulcinea del Toboso, he'd never seen a more beautiful woman. The beautiful Quiteria was a bit pale, and must have had the bad night that brides always have getting ready for the next day when they'll get married. They went to a platform at the side of a meadow, decorated with carpets and branches, where the wedding ceremony was to take place, and from where they were to see the dances and placards. And just when they got to that place, they heard loud shouts behind them, one of which was: "Wait, you inconsiderate and hasty people!"

At these words everyone looked back and they saw a man dressed in a black robe with crimson patches in the shape of flames. As was quickly seen, he was wearing a crown of funereal cypress on his head, and in his hand he held a large staff. As he approached everyone recognized that it was the spirited Basilio, and everyone was in suspense, waiting to see where his words were leading, and fearing some kind of trouble from his arrival at such a time.

He finally arrived, tired and out of breath, and stuck his staff into the ground—for it had a point of steel. He turned pale and looked into Quiteria's eyes, and with a trembling and hoarse voice said these words: "You know, ungrateful Quiteria, that by the holy law that we profess, while I'm alive you cannot take a husband. And you know as well that while I was waiting for time and my diligence to improve my finances, I never failed to maintain the respect due your honor. But you, turning your back on what my love deserves, want to give what is mine to another, whose wealth not only serves him as material fortune but also makes him

---

* The "banks of Flanders" have caused a lot of interpretations. Rodríguez Marín devotes a chapter in his appendix to it (see volume ten of his 1949 Atlas edition, pp. 22–30), in which he shows that *banks* refers to the nuptial bed and *Flanders* refers to the wood the bed is made of (pine of Flanders). But "banks of Flanders" also refers to shoals along the Belgian coast that are difficult to navigate (and this is well documented), as well as simply Flemish banks (financial institutions). Thus Gaos proposes the triple play on words, that she is a spirited woman who can pass through the nuptial bed, confront the difficulties of marriage, and marry a banker if she wants.

fortunate. And so that his happiness will be fulfilled—not that I think he deserves it, but because it's heaven's will—I, with my own hands, will rid the obstacle in his way, taking myself from between you. Long live, long live the rich Camacho with the ungrateful Quiteria, long and happy ages; and die, die poor Basilio, whose poverty clipped the wings of his happiness and placed him in his tomb!"

And saying this, he seized his staff, which was stuck in the ground, and pulled off the top half, which served as a sheath for a half rapier that had been hidden inside. With what might be called the hilt still stuck in the ground, with ease and a resolved determination, he leapt onto the blade, and instantly the bloody point and half the steel edge appeared at his back, and the sad fellow was bathed in blood and stretched out, pierced by his own weapon.

His friends ran over to help him, overcome by his wretched and piteous misfortune, and don Quixote dismounted from Rocinante, went over to him, took him in his arms, and saw that he'd not yet expired. They wanted to take the rapier out, but the priest, who was present, said that they shouldn't do it until he'd confessed, because he would die as soon as it was removed. Basilio began to come to a bit, and with a sorrowful and faint voice said: "If you would, cruel Quiteria, give me your hand as my wife in this last mortal moment, I would think that my rashness would be forgiven, since through it I'd have the incredible happiness of being yours."

The priest, hearing this, said that he should attend to the care of his soul rather than the pleasures of his body, and he should fervently ask pardon of God for his sins and his desperate act. Basilio responded that he wouldn't confess unless Quiteria first gave him her hand to be his wife. That joy would restore his will and would give him the strength to confess.

When don Quixote heard the injured one's request, he exclaimed that Basilio was asking for a righteous and very reasonable thing, and besides, it was very easy to accomplish, and señor Camacho should be honored to receive *señora* Quiteria as the widow of the brave Basilio just as if he received her from her father: "Here there will be no more than an I DO, which consists only of saying the words, since the nuptial bed of this wedding will be the grave."

Camacho heard all of this and was left hesitant and confused, and he didn't know what to do or say. But the outcries of Basilio's friends were so profuse, asking him to allow Quiteria to offer her hand in marriage so that he wouldn't lose his soul, leaving this life in such despair, that he felt compelled to say that if Quiteria wanted to do it, it was all right with him, since it was just putting off fulfilling his own desires for a moment.

Then they all went over to Quiteria, and some of them with entreaties, others with tears, and still others with powerful arguments, persuaded her to give her hand to poor Basilio, and she—harder than marble and more unmovable than a statue—was utterly baffled and couldn't say a word. And she wouldn't have said anything if the priest hadn't told her to decide in a hurry because Basilio's soul was already between his teeth and this was no time for indecisiveness.

The beautiful Quiteria then, without saying anything, notably disturbed and seemingly filled with grief, went to Basilio. His eyes were already upturned and he was breathing with difficulty, murmuring Quiteria's name under his breath, dying almost like a heathen and not like a Christian. Quiteria knelt down and by signs and not with words asked for his hand. Basilio opened his eyes and looked at her fixedly and said: "Oh, Quiteria, you've become merciful at a time when your mercy will be the knife that takes away my life; I no longer have the strength to enjoy the glory you've given me in choosing me to be yours, nor to stop the pain that is so quickly covering my eyes with the frightening shadow of death! The only thing I ask you, my fatal star, is that the hand you ask of me and the one you want to give me will not be just out of courtesy, nor to deceive me once again, but rather that you confess that, of your own free will, you're giving me your hand as you would to your legitimate husband, for it's not right that you should deceive me in such a desperate crisis as this, nor use deception with a person who always dealt truthfully with you."

While he said these words he fainted periodically and all those present thought that each fainting spell would take his soul along with it.

Quiteria, quite earnest and bashful, took Basilio's hand in her right hand, and said to him: "No force can bend my free will, so with my freest possible will I give you my hand as your legitimate wife and I receive yours, if you give it of your free will, without the tragedy into which you've plunged yourself clouding or confusing your judgment."

"Yes, I give it to you," responded Basilio, "neither clouded nor confused, but rather with clear understanding with which heaven saw fit to endow me, and I thus give myself to you as your husband."

"And I as your wife," responded Quiteria, "whether you live many years or whether they take you from my arms to your grave."

"For being in such bad shape," said Sancho Panza, "this fellow talks a lot. They should make him stop all this courting and tend to his soul. It seems to me it's more on his tongue than between his teeth."

While Basilio and Quiteria clasped each other's hand, the priest, tender and in tears, blessed them and asked heaven to grant sweet repose to the soul of the bridegroom, who, as soon as he received the blessing, leapt to his feet with incredible nimbleness and with unheard-of boldness removed the rapier for which his body had been the sheath.

All those present were dumbfounded, and some who were more credulous than knowing began to shout: "It's a miracle! A miracle!"

But Basilio responded: "No, not a miracle; it's just a trick, a neat trick!"

The priest, who was disturbed and astonished, ran over to feel the wound with both hands, and discovered that the point had passed, not through Basilio's flesh and ribs, but rather through a tube that had been fitted in place, and had been filled with blood that had been treated so that it wouldn't coagulate (as later was found out).

Finally, the priest and Camacho, with most of those present, realized that they had been tricked and deceived. The bride gave no indication that the trick displeased her, but rather, hearing that the marriage, being fraudulent, was not binding, she said that she confirmed it again. From this it became clear that the whole thing had been planned beforehand with consent and knowledge of both parties. Camacho and his companions were very embarrassed and they sent their vengeance to their hands, unsheathing

many swords, and went to attack Basilio, who was instantly
defended by just as many others. Don Quixote, taking the
lead on horseback, with his lance couched and shield in
place, made them all give way. Sancho, who never liked
such mischief, went over to the stew pots where he'd gotten
those agreeable skimmings, since that place seemed sacred
to him and would be held inviolable.

Don Quixote shouted: "Stop, *señores*! It's not right to
avenge the offenses that love causes. Consider that love
and war are the same thing; and just as in war it's lawful
and even customary to use ruses and stratagems to conquer
the enemy, it's the same thing in battles and competitions
dealing with love. Tricks and intrigues that are used to ob-
tain the desired goal are considered legitimate, as long as
they don't result in discredit and dishonor to the person
loved. Quiteria belonged to Basilio and Basilio to Quiteria
through the just and favorable will of heaven. Camacho is
rich and can buy whatever he wants, whenever, and however he wants. Basilio has only this lamb, and no one can
take her away, no matter how strong he is. Those whom
God has joined together cannot be separated by man, and
anyone who tries to do it will have to pass through the
point of this lance first."

And he brandished it so deftly and decisively that he
frightened all those who didn't know him. And Quiteria's
rejection made such an intense impression on Camacho's
mind that he erased her from his memory in an instant, and
the persuasions of the priest, who was a prudent and well-
intentioned man, were such that Camacho and his group
calmed down, sheathing their swords and blaming Quiteria's ready compliance more than Basilio's cleverness.
Camacho reasoned that if Quiteria loved Basilio while unmarried, she would also love him after she was married,
and that he should give thanks to heaven for having taken
her away from him, rather than for allowing her to be given
to him.

Once Camacho and his followers were consoled, Basilio's followers also calmed down, and the rich Camacho,
to show that he didn't resent the trick, insisted that the
festivities continue, as if he'd really married her himself.
But Basilio and his wife and their followers declined to
stay, and so they went to Basilio's village, and from this it

can be seen that poor people who are virtuous and astute have those who follow, honor, and aid them, just as the rich have those who flatter and accompany them. They took don Quixote with them, considering him to be a man of worth and stout of heart. It was only Sancho whose soul was darkened, since it was now impossible for him to enjoy Camacho's splendid food and festivities, which lasted until nightfall. And so, overwrought and sad, he followed his master, who was going with Basilio's retinue, and thus he left the fleshpots of Egypt, although he carried them in his soul. The almost consumed skimmings from the kettle represented the glory and abundance he was losing, and so, with an aching heart, although not at all hungry, without getting off his donkey, he followed Rocinante's hoofprints.

Chapter XXII. Wherein is related the great adventure of the Cave of Montesinos, which is in the heart of La Mancha, which the brave don Quixote de La Mancha brought to a happy conclusion.

THE BRIDAL couple treated don Quixote most warmly, obliged by his defense of their cause. On a par with his bravery they valued his wisdom, holding him for a Cid in arms and for a Cicero* in eloquence. Good Sancho enjoyed three days at the expense of the newlyweds, who revealed that the deception of the false wound hadn't been communicated to Quiteria, but rather it was Basilio's cleverness alone, who had hoped it would have the effect we have seen. It's quite true that he'd told his plan to some of his friends so that they could further his purpose at the right moment and support his deception.

"You cannot and should not call deceptions those that lead to honorable ends," said don Quixote, and he went on to say that the marriage of those who love each other was the most excellent end, pointing out that the greatest enemy that love has is hunger and continual need, because

---

* Cicero (106–43 B.C.) was Rome's greatest orator, also a politician and philosopher, as already mentioned in the Prologue to Part I, page 9.

love is all happiness, joy, and contentment, especially when the lover is in possession of the person he loves, against whom need and poverty are determined enemies. And he said all this to show Basilio that he should stop practicing the talents that, although they gave him fame, didn't bring in money, and that he should try to earn a living by legal and industrious means, which the prudent and diligent never lack.

"The poor but honorable man—if a poor person can be honorable—has a jewel when he has a beautiful wife, and when she's taken away, his honor is also taken away and obliterated. The beautiful and honorable woman whose husband is poor deserves to be crowned with laurel and palm branches of victory and triumph. Beauty alone attracts desire in all beholders, just as a tasty morsel causes royal eagles and other high-flying birds to swoop down to it, but if this beauty is mingled with need and poverty, crows and kites and other birds of prey will attack it, and the woman who remains firm amidst all this can be called the crown of her husband.*

"Look here, Basilio, my clever friend," added don Quixote, "I don't know which philosopher held that there was just one good woman in the world, but he advised every man to think and believe that it was his own wife, and thus he would live content. I'm not married and up to now I've never planned to get married, yet I would be so bold as to advise anyone who asked the way one should look for a woman whom he would like to marry. First, I'd advise him to look more into her reputation than her income, because the good woman doesn't attain a good reputation just by being good, but by appearing to be so. Wanton acts and scandals done in public are much more damaging than misdeeds done in secret. If you take a good woman to your house, it will be easy to keep her and better her in that virtue. But if you bring a bad one, it will be difficult to correct her because it isn't very easy to go from one extreme to the other. I don't mean it's impossible; I just mean it's difficult."

Sancho heard all this and said to himself: "This master of mine, when I say things of pith and substance, usually says

---

* This comes from Proverbs 12:4: "A capable wife is her husband's crown."

that I could take a pulpit in my hands and wander about the world preaching beautiful things; but I say about him that when he begins to link maxims together and give advice, not only could he take a pulpit in his hands, but two on each finger and roam through the plazas and be treated royally. May the devil take you, you knight-errant—you know so much! I thought in my soul that he only knew about things relating to knight-errantry, but there's nothing he doesn't nibble on and he puts his spoon into everything."

Sancho muttered this and his master overheard him and asked: "What are you mumbling about, Sancho?"

"I'm not saying or mumbling anything," responded Sancho. "I was just saying to myself that I would have liked to have heard what your grace has said here before I got married, and maybe I'd be saying now: 'The untethered ox licks himself well.' "

"Is your Teresa that bad?" said don Quixote.

"She's not bad," responded Sancho, "but she's not very good, either. At least, she's not as good as I'd like."

"You do wrong, Sancho," said don Quixote, "in saying bad things about your wife. She is, after all, the mother of your children."

"We don't owe each other anything," responded Sancho, "because she also says bad things about me whenever she feels like it, especially when she's jealous. Then, even the devil can't put up with her."

So, they spent three days with the newlyweds, where they were entertained and served like royalty. Don Quixote asked the fencing *licenciado* if he'd provide a guide to lead him to the Cave of Montesinos, because he was quite eager to descend into it and see with his own eyes if the wonders they told about it throughout the region were true. The *licenciado* told him he'd ask his cousin, a famous student and very keen about reading books of chivalry, who would be very willing to put him in the mouth of the cave itself and would show him the Lagoons of Ruidera, famous throughout La Mancha and even all of Spain; and he said that he would find him quite entertaining, because the fellow knew how to write books and dedicate them to princes. The cousin came riding a pregnant donkey whose packsaddle was placed over a rug or saddlecloth of many colors. Sancho saddled Rocinante and got his donkey ready, put their provisions as well as the cousin's in his saddlebags, and they all commended themselves to God, and bidding farewell to everyone, they got on their way, taking the road toward the famous Cave of Montesinos.

On the road, don Quixote asked the cousin what his pastimes, profession, and studies were. To which he responded that he was by profession a humanist, and his pursuits and studies were writing books to be published, all of them of enormous benefit to and no less entertaining for the republic. One of them was called *The Book of Liveries*,* where he described seven hundred three uniforms with their colors, mottos, and emblems, from which courtly knights could pick and choose those that they wanted for festivals and holidays, without asking others or racking their brains, as they say, to find the ones suited to their tastes and desires.

"I offer the jealous, the disdained, the forgotten, and the absent, garb that's appropriate and fits them to a tee. Another book I have, which I'll call *Metamorphoseos, or the Spanish Ovid*,† also a new and clever creation, because in it I parody Ovid, and I describe who Giralda of Seville and the Angel of Magdalena‡ were; I explain who the sewer called Vecinguerra in Cordova was named after;§ I say who or what

---

* These liveries are the outfits and ornaments worn by knights for their jousts and tournaments.

† Ovid has been referred to before (Part II, chapter sixteen, page 622) for his *Ars Amatoria*. His other most famous work is the *Metamorphoses*, written in fifteen books, all in verse. In it is a series of mythological and legendary stories in which transformation (*metamorphosis* in Latin) plays a role, starting with the creation of the world and ending with the deification of Julius Cæsar. The Spanish title, *Metamorfóseos*, unlike Ovid's title, reflects a Greek genitive singular form, meaning something like "what is characteristic of Metamorphosis," which is a clever transformation in itself. I thank Nik Gross for his interpretation of the Greek case.

‡ La Magdalena here is one of the lesser parish churches in Salamanca. This angel weather vane no longer exists. The old weather vane represented the woman sinner who anointed Jesus' feet, bathed them with her tears, then dried them with her hair (Luke 8:37–38).

§ This is a sewer that flowed from Cordova into the Guadalquivir River. Vicente Guerra, in whose honor this sewer takes its name, was a Cordovan hero during the Reconquest.

the Bulls of Guisando were; the Sierra Morena; the fountains of Leganitos and Lavapiés in Madrid, not forgetting the ones called 'Piojo,' the 'Caño Dorado,' and the 'Priora'*—all this, with their allegories, metaphors, and transformations, in such a way that they will delight, amaze, and edify all at the same time. Another book I have I call *The Supplement to Polydore Virgil*,† which deals with the invention of things, and shows great erudition and study, because I elucidate and explain in an elegant style the significant things Polydore failed to say, such as who the first person who had a cold was, and the first one to use ointments to cure the French pox‡—and I clarify all this, using more than twenty-five authorities, so your grace can see that I've worked assiduously and that the book will be useful to everyone."

Sancho had listened attentively to what the cousin said, and replied: "Tell me, *señor*—and may God give you good fortune in publishing your books—who was the first person to scratch his head? I think it must have been our father, Adam."

"Yes, it must have been," responded the cousin, "because there's no doubt that Adam had a head and hair, and this being so, since he was the first man in the world, sometime or other he must have scratched it."

"That's what I think," responded Sancho, "but tell me now, who was the first acrobat in the world?"

"In truth, brother," responded the cousin, "I won't be able to answer that until I study the matter, which I'll do when I get back to where my books are, and I'll give you a report when I see you again, since this won't be the last time we'll meet."

"Well, look, *señor*," responded Sancho, "you don't need to go to that trouble, because I've just hit on the answer.

---

* These three others are or were fountains in Madrid as well.

† Polydore Virgil (ca. 1470–1555), as he was known in England, was an Italian-born humanist whose history of England became required reading in British schools. His *De rerum inventoribus* (1499), a popular treatise on various inventions, is the book that the cousin has supplemented. It was translated from Latin into Spanish in 1550 by Francisco Thámara and published first in Antwerp. Several editions followed.

‡ Attributing syphilis to the French seems unfair, since it is generally believed that the disease came back from the New World with Columbus' crew.

The first acrobat in the world must have been Lucifer,* when they threw him out of heaven and he went tumbling into the abyss."

"You're right, my friend," said the cousin.

And don Quixote said: "This question and answer aren't yours, Sancho. You must have heard someone else say them."

"Hush, *señor*," replied Sancho. "If I start asking and answering questions, I won't finish in a week—as if I need help from my neighbors in asking foolish things and answering with nonsense."

"Sancho, you've said more than you know," said don Quixote, "for there are some people who tire themselves trying to figure things out that, once they're learned and proven, turn out to be worthless knowledge."

They spent the day in these and other pleasurable conversations, and that night they lodged in a small village where the cousin said to don Quixote that the Cave of Montesinos was no more than two leagues away, and if he decided to go into it, they should provide themselves with rope so that he could tie it to himself and be lowered into its depths.

Don Quixote said that even though the cave reached the abyss, he had to see how deep it was, and so he bought six hundred feet of rope, and the next day at two in the afternoon, they arrived at the cave, whose mouth is spacious and wide, but filled with thorny bushes, wild fig trees, brambles and briars, and so thickly overgrown that they obscure and conceal the cave. When they saw it, the cousin dismounted first, then Sancho, and then don Quixote, whom they tied firmly with the rope. While they were making him fast, Sancho said to him: "Be careful, your grace, and don't bury yourself alive, nor get yourself in a position where you're like a bottle they hang in a well to get cold. It's none of your grace's affair to investigate into what must be worse than a dungeon."

"Just keep tying and stop talking," responded don Quixote, "because such an undertaking as this, Sancho, my friend, is reserved for me."

---

* There is only one biblical reference to Lucifer ("light bearer" in Latin) in Isaiah 14:24.

The guide then said: "I beg your grace, _señor_ don Qui-xote, to look carefully and examine with a hundred eyes what there is inside. Perhaps there'll be things that I can put in my book of transformations."*

"'The tambourine is in the hands of him who knows how to play it well,'" responded Sancho Panza.

This having been said, when they finished tying don Quixote, not over the armor, but rather over the doublet, he said: "We should have also gotten a little cowbell that could be tied next to me on this very rope, by the ringing of which you could tell if I still was being lowered and was still alive. But this isn't possible now, so it's in God's hands, and may He guide me."

And then he got onto his knees and offered a prayer quietly to heaven, asking God to help him and give him a happy outcome to this seemingly dangerous and novel adventure, and in a low voice he said: "Oh, mistress of my actions and movements, bright and peerless Dulcinea del Toboso! If the prayers and entreaties of this, your fortunate lover, reach your ears, by your unparalleled beauty I beg you to listen. They are only to beg you not to deny me your favor and protection now when I need them the most. I'm going to plunge, engulf, and sink myself into the abyss I have in front of me, only so that the world might know that if you favor me, there's no impossible feat that I cannot take on and accomplish."

Once he'd said this, he approached the pit and saw that it wasn't possible to let himself down nor find a way to enter, except by hacking a passage away by force of arms, so he took his sword and began to chop away and cut the brambles at the mouth of the cave, the noise and commotion from which caused a multitude of crows to fly out, so thick and so fast that they knocked don Quixote to the ground. And if he'd been as superstitious as he was a Catholic Christian, he would have taken it to be a bad omen and wouldn't have entered such a place. Finally, he got up, and seeing that there were no further crows or other night birds such as bats (which also flew out with the crows), he gave the rope to the cousin and Sancho, and let himself be lowered into the depths of the fearful cavern.

---

* That is, in his _Metamorfóseos._

As he went down, Sancho offered a blessing accompanied by a thousand signs of the cross, and said: "May God, and the Peña de Francia,* together with the Trinity of Gaeta† guide you, flower and cream of knights-errant! There you go, the bravest man in the world, heart of steel, arms of bronze! God guide you, once again, and may He bring you back safe, sound, and unscathed, to the light of this life that you're leaving in order to bury yourself in the darkness you seek!"

The cousin made almost the same prayers and petitions.

Don Quixote shouted to them to give him more and more rope, and they gave it to him a bit at a time, and when the shouts coming up the cave as if through a pipe were no longer audible and they had let down the six hundred feet of rope, they felt they should bring don Quixote back up, since they couldn't give him more rope. Even so, they waited about half an hour, at the end of which they pulled the rope up and it was very light and there was no tension, seemingly indicating that don Quixote was left inside, and when Sancho realized that, he began to cry bitterly and pulled even faster to find out the truth. But when they had pulled up, in their opinion, a bit less than five hundred feet, they felt some weight and they rejoiced heartily. At sixty feet they saw don Quixote distinctly, and Sancho shouted to him, saying: "Welcome back, your grace, *señor mío*. We thought you were going to stay there for a generation."

But don Quixote said nothing in response, and when they had taken him completely out, they saw that his eyes were closed, revealing that he was asleep. They stretched him out on the ground and untied him, yet with all this he didn't wake up. But they turned him from side to side and shook him for a good while until he came to, stretching as if he'd been woken out of a very deep and heavy slumber.

---

* This is Nuestra Señora de la Peña de Francia, a monastery that was built at the summit of a mountain on the site of where an image of Holy Mary was discovered in 1409. It is located between Ciudad Rodrigo and Salamanca.

† This is another monastery, founded by Fernando de Aragón, at Gaeta, a town in the kingdom of Naples, already mentioned in Part II, chapter eighteen.

Looking all around as if he were distressed, he said: "May God forgive you, my friends, for you've plucked me from the most delicious and agreeable life and spectacle that any human being has ever seen or lived. Now I finally understand that all of the joys of this life are just shadows and dreams, or wither like a wildflower. Oh, unfortunate Montesinos! Oh, badly wounded Durandarte!* Oh, unfortunate Belerma! Oh, tearful Guadiana and you unfortunate daughters of Ruidera,† whose waters are the tears that your beautiful eyes cried!"

The cousin and Sancho listened to don Quixote's words, which he imparted as if he'd pulled them from his entrails with enormous pain. They begged him to help them understand what he was saying, and tell what he'd seen in that hell.

"'Hell,' you call it?" said don Quixote. "Don't call it that, because it doesn't deserve it, as you'll see soon enough."

He asked them to give him something to eat, for he was ravenous. They spread the cousin's pack cloth on the green grass and went to the saddlebags for provisions, and once the three of them were seated in good fellowship and company, they ate lunch and dinner all at the same time. Once the cloth was removed, don Quixote de La Mancha said: "Nobody rise, and listen carefully, my sons."

---

* *Durandarte* is the Spanish equivalent of *Durendal*, the name of Roland's sword. At Roncesvalles, where Roland was slain, he had Durendal with him. Over the ages, the sword became transformed into a person in the Spanish tradition. None of what happens at Roncesvalles involving Durandarte, Montesinos, and Belerma—all of which you will soon find out—is part of the French *Song of Roland* tradition.

† Since the Guadiana River begins in this area and the Lagunas de Ruidera are nearby, Guadiana and Ruidera take on human form in don Quixote's account of his adventure, as if they would later be transformed into the river and the lakes in the same way mythological characters were similarly changed.

Chapter XXIII. About the marvelous things that the incomparable don Quixote said he had seen in the deep Cave of Montesinos, the impossibility and magnitude of which have led to this adventure being held as apocryphal.

Iᴛ ᴡᴀꜱ about four in the afternoon. The sun was partially covered by clouds, and with diminished and mild rays allowed don Quixote to relate to his illustrious listeners, without heat or discomfort, what he'd seen in the Cave of Montesinos, and he began like this: "At about twelve or fourteen times a man's height down this pit, on the right-hand side there's a recess and ledge large enough to put a cart with its mules. A bit of light trickles in through some fissures or holes far above on the surface. I saw this recess and ledge at a moment when I was dangling on the rope, tired of descending through that dark region without any specific destination, so I decided to stop there and rest a while. I shouted to you, saying you shouldn't let down any more rope until I told you to, but you must not have heard me. I pulled in the rope you were lowering and made a coil of it and sat on it, deep in thought, considering what I needed to do to get to the bottom, since there was now no one to suspend me.*

"And while I was in these thoughts and confusion, suddenly, and without wanting to, I was overcome by a deep sleep; then when least I expected it, not knowing how, I woke up and found myself in the middle of the most beautiful, pleasant, and delightful meadow that Nature could have created, nor could the most ingenious human imagination dream it up. I opened my eyes and rubbed them and saw that I was not dreaming, but was wide awake. Even so, I felt my head and chest to assure myself it was really me who was there, and not some kind of bodiless and false

---

* The cave, as described by don Quixote, is quite like the rabbit hole in *Alice in Wonderland*, which goes straight down. In reality, this cave consists of a series of "rooms" connected by an easy-sloping trail. Clemencín describes this cave on p. 1641 of the Castilla edition.

phantom. But my sense of touch, my emotion, and the well-ordered reasoning I did with myself convinced me I was there as I'm now here.

"Then I saw a sumptuous royal palace or castle, whose ramparts and walls seemed to be transparent and made of clear glass, and when its great doors opened, I saw coming out toward me a venerable old man dressed in a cloak made of purple flannel that dragged behind him. On his shoulders and chest was a scholar's hood of green satin, and on his head he was wearing a black Milanese cap, and his very white beard extended below his waist. He was unarmed except for a rosary in his hand whose small beads were the size of walnuts and the large ones* the size of an average ostrich egg.† His demeanor, mien, and the dignity of his stately presence, individually and together, amazed me and filled me with wonder. He approached me and the first thing he did was to embrace me tightly, and then said: 'It's been a long time, brave knight don Quixote de La Mancha, that those in this lonely place have been waiting to see you so you can tell the world what is in this deep cave—called the Cave of Montesinos—that you've entered, and it's a deed that has been reserved for your invincible heart and your stupendous courage only. Come with me, most illustrious *señor*, for I want to show you the wonders hidden in this transparent palace, of which I'm the governor and perpetual chief guardian, because I'm Montesinos himself, from whom the cave takes its name.'

"Scarcely had I heard him say that he was Montesinos when I asked him if it was true what they told about him in the world above, that he'd removed his great friend Durandarte's heart with a small dagger from the middle of his chest and taken it to the *señora* Belerma, as he'd requested just before he died.

"He told me they said the absolute truth, except for the dagger business, because it was neither a dagger nor was it small, but rather a sharp poniard with a point like an awl."

---

* The Catholic rosary is essentially five sets of eleven beads, but the beads are small—the large ones are generally smaller than a pea.
† An ostrich egg is six inches across and three inches wide. It weighs about three pounds.

"That poniard must have been made by Ramón de Hoces in Seville,"* said Sancho.

"I don't know," don Quixote went on, "but it can't have been made by this poniard maker, since Ramón de Hoces was alive yesterday, and what happened in Roncesvalles— where this misfortune occurred—was many years ago,† and this is of no importance, nor does it affect or alter the truth or context of the story."

"That's the truth," responded the cousin. "Go on with your story, *señor* don Quixote, for I'm listening with the greatest pleasure in the world."

"And I'm telling it with no less pleasure," responded don Quixote. "I was saying that the venerable Montesinos took me into the crystal palace, where, in an excessively cool room on the ground floor, there was an exquisitely made marble sepulcher constructed of alabaster, on top of which was a knight stretched out full-length, not made of bronze, marble, or jasper, but of pure flesh and blood. His right hand—which seemed to me to be a bit hairy and sinewy, proof that its owner was very strong—was placed over his heart. And before I could ask Montesinos anything, seeing me amazed at the sight of the man on the sepulcher, he said: 'This is my friend Durandarte, flower and mirror of the enamored and brave knights of his time. That French enchanter that they say is the child of the devil, Merlin, has him held enchanted here, as he has me and many others. And I'd say he's not the child of the devil, but rather he knows a bit *more* than the devil. How, and for what reason, he has us enchanted, no one knows, but it will be revealed in time, and I imagine that time is not far off. What most has me in wonder is that I know, just as it's day right now, that Durandarte finished his life in my arms, and after his death I removed his heart with my own hands. In truth it must have weighed two pounds,‡ and according to the natural philosophers, the man who has a large heart is endowed with a greater courage than he who has a small one. This

---

* No one knows if there was a real Ramón de Hoces who worked in Seville.

† "Many years ago" is an understatement. Roland was slain at Roncesvalles in A.D. 778.

‡ The human heart typically weighs only about ten and a half ounces.

being so, and since this knight really died, how is it he's able to lament and sigh from time to time, as if he were alive?'

"After this had been said, the poor Durandarte, in a very loud voice, said:

Oh, cousin Montesinos!
　'Twas my last request of you,
　When my soul had left my body,
　And that lying dead I be,
　Whether with thy poniard or thy dagger
　Cut the heart from out my breast,
　And bear it to Belerma.
　This was my last request.*

"When the venerable Montesinos heard that, he got on his knees before the doleful knight, and with tears in his eyes, he said: 'Señor Durandarte, dear cousin of mine, I did what you commanded me to do on that fatal day of our loss.† I removed your heart as well as I could and didn't leave the least bit of it in your chest. I cleaned it with a handkerchief trimmed with lace, and I raced off to France with it, having first put you in the bosom of the earth, with so many tears that they sufficed to wash my hands and cleanse away the blood from having opened you up. Then, cousin of my soul, in the first village I came to when I left Roncesvalles, I put a pinch of salt on your heart so it wouldn't smell bad, and so it would be, if not fresh, at least cured when in the presence of *señora* Belerma, who, together with you and me and Guadiana, your squire, and with the duenna Ruidera and her seven daughters and two nieces, and many other friends and acquaintances, are held enchanted here by the sage Merlin these many years, and although more than five hundred have gone by,‡ not one of us has died. Only Ruidera and her daughters and nieces are no longer here. Out of the compassion Merlin must have had for their tears, he changed them into as many lakes, which in the world of the living and in the province of La Mancha are known as

---

* Modified from Ormsby.
† This was the French loss at the battle of Roncesvalles.
‡ It would have been a bit more than eight hundred years since the battle at Roncesvalles.

the Lagoons of Ruidera. The seven belong to the monarchs of Spain, and the two nieces to the very holy order of San Juan.* Guadiana, your squire, who bewailed your fate as well, was changed into a river bearing his same name, and when he got to the surface of the earth and saw the sun of another sky, his grief was so great when he realized that he was leaving you, he submerged into the bowels of the earth.† But since it isn't possible for him to curb his natural flow, from time to time he comes out and shows himself where the sun and people can see him. The lagoons already mentioned along with many other sources supply him with their water and so he enters into Portugal, magnificently, and very wide.‡ But even so, wherever he goes, he shows his sadness and melancholy and doesn't care to raise in his waters good-tasting and worthy fish, but rather coarse and bad-tasting ones, quite unlike the fish from the golden Tajo River. And what I'm telling you now, my cousin, I've told you many times, and since you don't answer me, I deduce that either you don't believe me, or you don't hear me, and the grief all this gives me only God knows.

"'I want to give you some news that, although it may not relieve your pain, at least won't increase it in any way. I want you to know that you have in your presence—open your eyes and you'll see him—that great knight don Quixote de La Mancha, who has revived anew and with greater success than in former ages the now forgotten order of knight-errantry, and by whose means and favor we may break our enchantment—for great deeds are reserved for great men.'

"'And if it doesn't come to pass,' responded the doleful Durandarte, with a faint and low voice, 'if it doesn't come to pass, my cousin, I say, "Patience and shuffle the cards."'"

---

* According to Ferreras, two of these lakes were assigned to the Order of San Juan de Jerusalén and the remainder belonged to the kingdom.

† The Guadiana River does originate in La Mancha, and some sections of it do flow underground, as much as twenty-five miles.

‡ The Guadiana flows west to Badajoz, then turns toward the south, where it forms the border with Portugal for about thirty miles. Then it goes into Portugal, and about thirty miles before it enters the sea, once again it is the border between the two countries. By the time it gets to Badajoz, it is a very wide river.

And turning on his side, he went back to his accustomed silence without saying another word.

"Just then I heard loud howls and lamentations, accompanied by profound sighs and pathetic sobs. I turned my head and saw through the walls of glass a procession of two rows of very beautiful maidens, all of them dressed in mourning, with white turbans in the Turkish fashion on their heads. At the end of the two rows came a lady, for in her dignity she appeared to be one, also dressed in black, with a white veil so long that it kissed the ground. Her turban was twice the size of the biggest one worn by the others. She had eyebrows that grew into each other, and her nose was a bit flat, but her lips were red. Her teeth, when she showed them, had gaps, and were not very straight, although they were as white as peeled almonds. In her hands she was carrying a piece of linen and in it I could see a mummified heart, so dry it was. Montesinos told me that all those people in that procession were servants of Durandarte and Belerma, who were enchanted along with their master and mistress, and the last person, who was carrying the heart wrapped in linen, was *señora* Belerma herself, who, with her maidens, made that procession four times a week, and sang—or rather cried—dirges over the body and the piteous heart of her cousin. And if she seemed a bit ugly to me, or at least not as beautiful as her fame would lead you to believe, it was because of the bad nights and worse days she spent in that enchantment, as you could see in the bags under her eyes and in her sallow complexion.

"'And don't think that her yellow complexion and the bags under her eyes are due to the monthly ailment common to women—because it has been many months and even years since she has had it, nor has it even appeared at her gates—but rather because of the pain she feels in her heart for the one she always has in her hands, which brings to her memory the misfortune of her unlucky lover. If it weren't for this, the great Dulcinea del Toboso, so celebrated in these parts and even throughout the world, wouldn't equal her beauty, grace, and dash.'

"'Careful,' I said, '*señor* don Montesinos. Tell your story as you should, since you know that 'all comparisons are odious,' and that's why there's no reason to compare anyone with anyone else. The beautiful Dulcinea del Toboso is who she is, and *señora* Lady Belerma is who she is and has been, and let's leave it at that.'

"To which he responded: '*Señor* don Quixote, forgive me, your grace. I confess I was wrong when I said that *se-ñora* Dulcinea would hardly equal Belerma, since it was enough for me to have understood through I don't know what kind of hunch that your grace is her knight, for which I'd bite my tongue rather than compare her to anything but heaven itself.'

"With this apology that the great Montesinos gave me, my heart calmed down from the distress I got when I heard that my lady was being compared with Belerma."

"And I'm astonished," said Sancho, "that your grace didn't jump on that old guy and kick his bones to bits and yank his beard clean off his face."

"No, Sancho, my friend," responded don Quixote. "It wouldn't have been right for me to do that, because we're all supposed to show respect for old people even if they aren't knights, but especially to those who are knights and are enchanted. I know very well neither of us owed each other anything after the many questions and answers that passed between us."

At this point, the cousin said: "I don't know, *señor* don Quixote, how your grace in the short time you were down there saw so many things and conversed so much."

"How long ago did I go down?" asked don Quixote.

"A little more than an hour ago," responded Sancho.

"That cannot be," replied don Quixote, "because night came upon me, then morning arrived; then night and morning came again three times. So by my count I've been in that remote area, hidden from our sight, for three days."

"My master must be telling the truth," said Sancho. "Since everything that happens to him is by enchantment, maybe what to us seems to be an hour must seem to be three days and nights down there."

"That's what it must be," responded don Quixote.

"And did your grace eat during all that time, *señor mío*?" asked the cousin.

"I didn't eat a bite," responded don Quixote, "nor was I hungry—I didn't even think about it."

"And do enchanted people eat?"

"They don't eat," responded don Quixote, "nor do they

have bowel movements, although it's thought that their fingernails, beards, and hair do grow."

"And do the enchanted people sleep, *señor*?" asked Sancho.

"Certainly not," responded don Quixote. "At least in the three days that I was with them, none of them closed an eye, and neither did I."

"Here's where that proverb fits in well," said Sancho, "that says: 'tell me the company you keep and I'll tell you who you are.' Your grace joins enchanted people who are fasting and always awake, and you see how easy it is for you not to eat or sleep while you're with them. But excuse me, your grace, *señor mío*, if I tell you that of everything you've said here, may God carry me off—I was going to say THE DEVIL—if I believe a single thing."

"How not?" said the cousin. "Is *señor* don Quixote going to lie, and even if he wanted to, there hasn't been enough time to invent and dream up so many millions of lies."

"I don't believe that my master is lying," responded Sancho.

"If not, what *do* you believe?" asked don Quixote.

"I believe," responded Sancho, "that Merlin, or those who enchanted the crowd of people that your grace says you saw and spoke with down there, put into your head or memory all that rubbish that you've told us, and everything that remains to be told."

"That *might* be the case, Sancho," replied don Quixote, "but it really isn't, because what I told you, I saw with my own eyes and touched with my own hands. What will you say when I tell you right now that among an infinite number of other things that Montesinos showed me—which at our leisure and at appropriate moments I'll tell you during the course of our travels, since they would be out of place here—he pointed out to me three peasant girls in those fields who went frisking and flitting about like goats, and hardly had I seen them when I recognized that one of them was the peerless Dulcinea del Toboso, and the other two were those same peasant girls accompanying her, with whom we spoke outside of El Toboso. I asked Montesinos if he knew them. He told me that he didn't, but that they must be some enchanted upper-class ladies, and for me not to be surprised, because there were many other ladies from past and present times, enchanted in various strange ways; I even saw Queen Guinevere and her duenna Quintañona, pouring wine for Lancelot 'when from Britain he came.'"

When Sancho Panza heard his master say this, he thought he would lose his mind or die of laughter. Since he knew the truth of the faked enchantment of Dulcinea, of whom he'd been the enchanter and the inventor of the whole thing, he realized that his master was undoubtedly out of his mind and totally crazy, and so he said: "It was a bad moment and a worse time, and on an ill-fated day that your grace, my dear master, went down into the netherworld, and at an unfortunate moment that you came into contact with *señor* Montesinos, who sent you back to us in such a state. You were better off here when you were fully sane, just as God made you, saying maxims and giving advice at every turn, and not as you are now, telling the greatest absurdities that can be imagined."

"Since I know you, Sancho," responded don Quixote, "I know not to pay heed to what you say."

"And I won't heed what your grace says either," replied Sancho, "not even if you hit or even kill me for what I've said or plan to say, unless you correct and emend what you said. But tell me, your grace, now that we have made up, how was it that you recognized the lady our mistress? And if you spoke with her, what did she say back?"

"I recognized her," responded don Quixote, "because she was wearing the same outfit as when you first pointed her out to me. I spoke to her, but she didn't answer a word, but rather turned her back on me and went off at full speed, so that even a dart wouldn't have caught her. I tried to follow her, and would have, if Montesinos hadn't advised me not to bother because it would be futile, especially since the time was approaching for me to leave the cave. He told me also that the time would come when he would tell me how he and Belerma and Durandarte, and all the others who were there, could be disenchanted. But what most distressed me of everything I saw there was that while Montesinos was saying those words, one of the companions of the unfortunate Dulcinea came up to me without my noticing her, and with her eyes filled with tears, and with a troubled and muted voice, told me: 'My lady Dulcinea del Toboso kisses your grace's hands and begs you to tell her how you are; and that, since she's in great need, she begs you, as earnestly as she can, please to lend her, against this new cotton shawl I have with me, a half dozen *reales*, or whatever your grace might have. She promises to pay it back to you very soon.'

"That request shocked and stunned me, and I turned to *señor* Montesinos and asked him: 'Is it possible, *señor* Montesinos, that these enchanted upper-class people suffer from need?' To which he responded: 'Believe me, your grace, *señor* don Quixote de La Mancha, this thing they call NEED is found anywhere and everywhere and affects everyone, and even the enchanted are not spared from it. And since *señora* Dulcinea del Toboso has sent someone to request those six *reales* and the collateral is good, it would seem that there's nothing to do but lend them to her. She must be in a real bind.'

"'I won't take any collateral,' I responded, 'nor can I give her what she requests, because I have only four *reales*.' I gave them to her, and they were the ones that you, Sancho, gave me the other day to give as alms to poor people we might meet along the road—and I said to the girl: 'Tell your mistress, my friend, that her travails grieve me in my soul, and I wish I were a Fugger* so I could alleviate them. And I want her to know that I can't, nor should I enjoy good health while I'm lacking her company and conversation, and I beg her grace as earnestly as I can to see and talk with her humble servant and overwrought knight to see and talk with her. You will also tell her that when she least expects it, she'll hear that I've made an oath and a vow, in the style of the one that the Marqués de Mantua made to avenge his nephew Valdovinos when he found him on the point of dying on the mountain, which was that he wouldn't eat bread off a tablecloth, and other trifles† that he added, until he avenged him. So I'll not rest, but will roam the seven

---

* The Fuggers formed a banking and mercantile dynasty that not only dominated European business in the fifteenth and sixteenth centuries, but also affected European politics. Through their wealth they were able to get rid of François I of France and finance the election of Carlos V of Spain as Holy Roman Emperor.

† You can see in Part I, chapter ten, page 81, what these "other trifles" were. The Marqués de Mantua and Valdovinos are also mentioned in Part I, chapter five, several times.

parts of the world even more diligently than don Pedro de Portugal,* until I disenchant her.' 'All this and more your grace owes my mistress,' responded the maiden. And taking the four *reales*, instead of bowing to me, she jumped for joy two full yards in the air."

"Oh, Holy God!" Sancho shouted at that point. "Is it possible that enchanters and enchantments have so much power that they have made my sane master crazy? *Señor, señor*, for God's sake, your grace, look out for yourself and consider your honor, and don't believe this nonsense that has impaired you and taken away your wits."

"You're talking this way, Sancho, because you love me," said don Quixote, "and since you're not experienced in things of the world, everything that is a bit difficult seems impossible to you. But the time will come, as I've told you before, when I'll tell you about the things that I've seen down there, and they'll make you believe the things I've just told you, the truth of which doesn't allow an objection or dispute."

Chapter XXIIII. Where a thousand trifles, as irrelevant as they are necessary to the true understanding of this great history, are recounted.

THE PERSON who translated this great history from the original that its first author, Cide Hamete Benengeli, wrote, says that when he got to the chapter about the adventure of the Cave of Montesinos, he found in the margin and in Hamete's own handwriting, these words:

I cannot convince or persuade myself that what the previous chapter relates about what happened to the brave don Quixote really happened exactly as writ-

---

* The known world had only four parts then, Asia, Europe, Africa, and America. Don Pedro de Portugal (1392–1449) was the subject of a book (*Book of the Prince don Pedro de Portugal, who Traveled the Four Parts of the World* [Salamanca, 1547]). The number was increased to seven—and there is a lot of discussion about this—perhaps because of the general influence of the magic number seven.

ten. The reason is that all the other adventures met with so far have been possible and credible; but I can find no way I can accept this one about the cave as true because it's so far beyond the bounds of reason. But to think that don Quixote would lie, being the most truthful gentleman and the noblest knight of his time, is not possible, even if they were shooting him with arrows. On the other hand, considering that he related and told it with all those details, he couldn't make up such a mass of nonsense in so short a time. If this adventure seems apocryphal, I'm not to blame; I write it without confirming it as either true or false. You, reader, since you're discerning, can judge for yourself. I shouldn't try to and can't do more— although it's said that at the time of his end and death, he retracted it and said that he'd invented it all, since it seemed to him that it was appropriate and fit in well with the adventures that he'd read in his histories.

And he goes on, saying:

The cousin was amazed both at Sancho's boldness and with the forbearance of his master, and he judged that his happiness at seeing his lady Dulcinea del Toboso, though she was enchanted, was responsible for his good mood; otherwise the words that Sancho said would have earned him a beating, because it really seemed to him that Sancho had been quite impudent with his master, and the cousin said to him: "*Señor* don Quixote de La Mancha, I consider the trip I've made with your grace as time well spent, for I've gained four things. The first is that I've met your grace, which makes me very happy. The second is having learned what is in the Cave of Montesinos, with the transformations of Guadiana and the Lagoons of Ruidera, which will be useful for my Spanish *Ovid* that I'm working on now. The third is how old playing cards are, since they were already used in the times of Charlemagne in France, from which one can deduce from the words that you relate that Durandarte said, when at the end of Montesinos' long speech, he awakened and said: 'Patience and shuffle the cards,' and he couldn't have learned this expression while he was enchanted, but rather when he wasn't, during the time of the already mentioned Charlemagne, and this discovery goes perfectly into the other book I'm writing, which is the *Supplement to Polidore Virgil, on the Invention of Antiquities*. I believe in his own book he didn't remember to put in anything about playing cards, as I'll now do, and it'll be of considerable importance, especially since I can quote an authority as serious and truthful as *señor* Durandarte. The fourth is having learned with certainty where the Guadiana River originates, something people have not known until now."

"Your grace is right," said don Quixote, "but I'd like to know, if God grants that they allow you to print those books of yours—which I doubt—to whom will you dedicate them?"

"There are lords and grandees in Spain to whom they can be dedicated," said the cousin.

"Not many," responded don Quixote. "Not because they don't deserve the renown, but rather because they don't want to be bound by the debt of gratitude due the author, so that they won't be obliged to reward him for his labors and courtesy. I know a prince* who can make up for the lack of the others in such good measure that if I daresay what they are, it would awaken envy in more than four noble hearts. But let's put this off for a better time, and let's look for a place where we can spend the night."

"Not far from here," responded the cousin, "is a hermitage where a hermit makes his abode, and they say he was a soldier and is held to be a good Christian, and is very wise and charitable besides. Next to the hermitage, he has a little house that he built at his own expense, and although it's small, it can still lodge guests."

"Does this hermit have chickens?" asked Sancho.

"Few hermits are without them," responded don Quixote, "because the ones nowadays are not like the ones from the deserts of Egypt, who dressed in palm leaves and ate roots from the ground. And don't think that because I speak well of the latter, I disparage the former, but rather

---

* Editors usually say that this prince is the Conde de Lemos to whom Part II was dedicated. Don Quixote, of course, couldn't know any flesh-and-blood count, since he himself is fictional. Nonetheless, it would seem that Cervantes put this in to bring a smile to the count's face.

I mean that the penance endured by the modern hermits does not come close to the severity and poverty suffered by those of Egypt. But that doesn't mean they cease to be good men—at least, I judge them to be good—and if worse comes to worst, the hypocrite who pretends to be good does less harm than the shameless sinner."

While they were saying these things, they saw a man on foot coming toward them, walking quickly and whipping a mule carrying lances and halberds. When he reached them, he greeted them and kept going. Don Quixote said to him: "Good fellow, slow down! It looks like you're going faster than that mule can stand."

"I can't stop now, *señor*," responded the man, "because the weapons that I have must be used tomorrow, so it's imperative for me not to stop. Good-bye. But if you want to know why I have them, the inn that's a bit beyond the little hermitage is where I plan to spend the night, and if you're going along this same road, you'll find me there, where I'll tell you amazing things, and good-bye again."

He pricked his mule, and so don Quixote had no chance to ask him what the amazing things were that he was going to tell them, and since he was somewhat curious and always eager to learn new things, he had his party leave and go to spend the night at the inn, without stopping at the hermitage where the cousin had wanted to spend the night.

So they all mounted and went along the quickest road to the inn, where they arrived a little before nightfall. The cousin said to don Quixote that they should go there to drink a swallow of wine. As soon as Sancho heard this, he turned his donkey toward the hermitage,* and don Quixote and the cousin did the same. But to Sancho's bad luck it seems that the hermit was not at home, as the female subhermit that they found at the hermitage told them. They asked her for some good wine, and she responded that her master had none, but if they wanted some cheap water, she would be happy to provide some.

---

* Another obvious contradiction. They just decided to skirt the hermitage and go to the inn. And now they are at the hermitage? Nothing new, just some more imitation of the careless style of the books of chivalry. Many editors and translators change the inn just mentioned into a hermitage.

"If I wanted to drink water," responded Sancho, "there are wells along the way where I could have quenched my thirst. Ah, Camacho's wedding and the abundance at don Diego's house, how often I miss you!"

So they left the hermitage and spurred on to the inn, and after a while they came across a young man who was walking rather slowly in front of them and so they overtook him. He was carrying on his shoulder a sword from which was dangling a bundle, seemingly containing his clothing, which must have been some pants or breeches, a cape, and a shirt. He was wearing a jacket made of velvet, parts of which were so worn they were as shiny as satin, and his shirt was untucked; his stockings were of silk and his shoes square-toed like they wear at court. He must have been eighteen or nineteen years old, with a pleasant face, and was light on his feet. He was singing *seguidillas* to pass the tedium of the journey. When they got to him he'd just finished singing one that the cousin memorized, and they say it said:

> For want of cloth and bread
> To the wars I must go;
> If I were rich instead,
> This would never be so.*

The first to speak to him was don Quixote, who said: "Your grace is traveling very lightly, young man. Where are you going? We'd like to know, if you would be willing to tell us."

To which the young man responded: "Traveling lightly is due to the heat and poverty, and where I'm going is off to war."

"How due to poverty?" asked don Quixote. "The heat is easy to understand."

"*Señor*," replied the young man, "I'm carrying in this bundle some pants made of velvet that go with this doublet. If I wear them on the road, I won't be able to wear them in the city, and I have nothing to buy other ones with. So, as if to air myself, I'm traveling this way until I get to some

---

* In those days, the *seguidilla* was a lively, happy song. Nowadays, at least in the flamenco version, they are sad, emotional songs. I have used Robinson Smith's translation here.

infantry companies that are not quite twelve leagues from here, where I'll begin my military service, and there'll be no lack of packhorses to take me from there to the port, which they say should be Cartagena. I'd prefer to have the king as my master and serve him in the war rather than some worthless person at court."

"And does your grace have some bonus pay for entering the service, by chance?" asked the cousin.

"If I had served some grandee of Spain or some titled person," responded the young man, "I certainly would have that bonus, for by serving good people you become a lieutenant or captain or rise from servants' tables to have a good pension. But I, unfortunately, always served worthless people and upstarts of such miserable and lean income that it took half their pay to get their collar starched, and it would be a miracle if a page-adventurer could ever come by reasonably good luck from that."

"And tell me on your life, friend," asked don Quixote, "is it possible that in the years you served you never wore a livery?"

"I had two," said the page, "but just like when you leave a religious order before being ordained, they take away your habit and return your old clothes, my masters returned mine to me, when, having finished their business at court, they returned home and took back the liveries, which they used only for show."

"Such *spilorceria*,* as they say in Italian," said don Quixote, "but even so, you should consider it good luck that you left court on such a worthy quest, because there's nothing on earth of greater honor or of greater value than to serve God first, and next to serve your king and natural lord, especially in the profession of arms, by means of which you acquire, if not riches, at least greater honor than you would have through letters, as I've said many times. Although letters have created more great lineages than arms, still, the lineages created by arms have a certain edge over those created by letters, since they have a special splendor with which nothing else compares.

"And what I'm about to tell you now, learn it well, for it will be of great use and comfort to you in your travails, and

---

* "Stinginess."

it is that you should put out of your mind the adversities that may befall you. The worst of these is death, and if it's a good one, it's the luckiest of all. They asked Julius Cæsar, that brave Roman emperor, what the best death was, and he answered that it was the unexpected one, one that came suddenly and not foreseen, and although he answered like a pagan and without knowledge of the true God, he spoke well, as far as sparing human suffering goes. Though they may kill you in the first battle and fray, or with an artillery shot, or if you're blown up by a mine, what difference does it make? It's all dying, and it's over and done with. And according to Terence, a soldier seems better dead in battle than alive and safe in flight.* The good soldier achieves fame insofar as he's obedient to his captains and those who can give him orders. And be aware, my son, that it's better to smell of gunpowder than civet, and if old age finds you in this honorable profession, even though you may have many wounds and you're crippled or lame, at least it won't find you without honor that poverty will not be able to diminish. Right now they're making laws that old and crippled soldiers be given care and relief,† because it's not good that they be treated like slaves, who are freed when they're old and can no longer work, and they're released and are told they're free, making them slaves to hunger, from which only death will liberate them. For the moment I have nothing more to tell you except I'd like you to ride with me on my horse as far as the inn, and there you will dine with me. Tomorrow you'll continue your journey, and may God make it as successful as your worthy desires deserve."

The page didn't accept the invitation to ride, but he did agree to eat dinner at the inn, and they say Sancho said to himself right then: "May God bless you as a master! And

---

* No one has been able to find this reference in Terence. Clemencín ascribes this wrong attribution to *Cervantes'* faulty memory, but this is really don Quixote's error. Cervantes makes a similar statement in the second paragraph of the Prologue to this part, but cites no source.

† This order was not forthcoming during Cervantes' lifetime, although a petition was presented in 1598 recommending a hospital and pension for old and crippled soldiers. Starkie says that the soldiers' pension was not introduced until the mid-1700s.

is it possible that a man who can say so many and such good things as he has said, should also say that he has seen the foolish and impossible things that he related about the Cave of Montesinos? Well, then, time will tell. . . ."

At this point they arrived at the inn, just when night was falling, and not without Sancho's pleasure, since he saw that his master judged it to be a real inn and not a castle, as was his custom. They had just entered when don Quixote asked the innkeeper about the man with the lances and halberds, and he responded that he was in the stable attending to his mule. The nephew* and Sancho also went to the stable, giving Rocinante the best manger and the best stall.

Chapter XXV. Where the adventure of the braying is set down along with the amusing one about the puppeteer and the prophecies of the divining monkey.

DON QUIXOTE's bread wouldn't bake, as the saying goes, until he heard about and learned of the marvels promised by the man carrying the weapons. He went to look for him where the innkeeper said he was, and when he found him, he told him to relate immediately what he'd planned to tell him later, about what he'd asked him along the road. The man responded: "The story of my wonders has to be told at leisure and not standing up. Your grace, good *señor*, let me finish feeding my mule, and I'll tell you things that will astound you."

"Don't let that stop you," responded don Quixote, "because I'll help you."

And that's what he did, giving him the barley and cleaning out the manger—humility that compelled the man to tell amenably what was asked of him—and sitting down on a bench with don Quixote next to him, having for his audience the cousin, the page, Sancho Panza, and the inn-

---

* *Nephew* has been *cousin* to this point. Schevill keeps it, but says that it is "carelessness on the part of Cervantes for *cousin*." It is not carelessness at all, but rather just another contradiction built into the work in imitation of books of chivalry.

keeper, he began his story as follows: "In a village four and a half leagues from this inn, it happened that an alderman from the town, through the deception and deceit of one of his servant girls—and this is too long to tell about—lost one of his donkeys, and although he did everything possible to find it, he couldn't. About two weeks went by, it's said, after the donkey went missing, and the alderman who had lost the donkey was in the plaza when another alderman of the same town told him: 'Good news, *compadre*. Your donkey has turned up.' 'That *is* good news, *compadre*,' responded the other, 'but tell me, where did he show up?' 'In the forest,' responded the finder. 'I saw him this morning without a packsaddle and without any other trappings, and so thin that it made me sad just to look at him. I wanted to catch him and take him to you, but he's so wild and skittish that when I approached him, he ran away into the deepest part of the forest. If you want, we can go back and look for him. Let me put this she-ass in the stable and I'll be right back.' 'It will give me great pleasure,' said the one with the lost donkey, 'and I'll try to pay you back in the same coin.'

"Everyone privy to the truth of this matter tells this story with these same particulars and in the same way that I'm telling it. So, the two aldermen, on foot and hand in hand, went to the forest, and when they got to where they thought they'd find the donkey, he wasn't there, and they couldn't find him anywhere, no matter how much they looked. Seeing, then, that he wasn't there, the alderman who had seen the donkey said to the other: 'Look, *compadre*, I've just thought of a plan we can use to find this animal even though he's buried in the bowels of the earth, not to mention the forest, and it's this: I know how to bray wonderfully, and if you know how to bray a bit as well, we can consider the business concluded.'

"'A bit, you say, *compadre*,' said the other. 'By God, no one can surpass me, not even the donkeys themselves.'

"'We'll see,' responded the other, 'because my plan is for you to go around one side of the forest, and I'll go around the other, so that we'll walk completely around it, and once in a while you'll bray and I'll bray, and the donkey will be sure to hear us and will bray back, if he's in the forest.' To which the owner of the donkey responded: 'I say, *com-

padre, that the idea is excellent and worthy of your great intellect.'

"So they separated, the way they agreed, and it happened that they brayed at almost the same time, and each one, deceived by the braying of the other, went looking, thinking that it was the donkey. And when they saw each other, the donkey loser said: 'Is it possible, *compadre*, that it wasn't my donkey who brayed?'

"'It was just me,' responded the other.

"'I must say,' said the owner, 'that there's no difference at all between you and a donkey where braying is concerned, because in my entire life I've never seen nor heard anything more natural.'

"'This praise and exaltation,' responded the fellow who had devised the plan, 'are better used for you than for me, *compadre*, because by the God who created me, you can give a handicap of two brays to the greatest and best brayer in the world—your tone is loud, your voice is sustained both in meter and rhythm, and your cadences are many and rapid. In short, I give up and I yield the palm, and give you the banner for this rare skill.'

"'Now I can say,' responded the owner, 'that I'll think better of myself from now on and will consider that I can do something worthwhile, since I have this talent. Although I always thought I brayed well, I never considered that I was as good as you say.'

"'I'll tell you now as well,' responded the second man, 'that there are rare gifts that are lost in the world and many are wasted on those who don't know how to use them.'

"'Ours,' responded the owner, 'is not likely to be handy except on occasions such as this, but still, may it please God, I hope it'll be useful.'

"Having said this, they split up again and went back to their braying, and at every step they fooled each other and came together, until they decided to use a device—to bray twice in succession—so they would know it was the other one braying and not the donkey. With this double braying, they went around the forest again but the lost donkey didn't respond once, not even by signs. But how could the poor illfated animal respond, since they finally found him in the deepest part of the forest, eaten by wolves? And when they saw him, the owner said: 'It's no wonder he didn't respond.

If he hadn't been dead, he would have responded if he'd heard us, or he wouldn't have been a donkey. But by reason of having heard you bray with such grace, I consider the effort I used to find him well spent, even though I found him dead.'

"'I toast you, my friend,' responded the other. "'If the abbot sings well, the acolyte can't be far behind.'"

"So, disconsolate and hoarse, they returned to their village, where they told their friends, neighbors, and acquaintances what had happened to them while searching for the donkey, each one exaggerating the talent of the other. All of this was made known in neighboring villages, and the devil, who never sleeps, since he delights in sowing quarrels and discord wherever he can, swirling gossip in the wind and making great confusion out of nothing, arranged it so that people from other villages, when they saw people from ours, would bray, as if to rub our noses in the braying of our aldermen. Finally the boys started up with it, which was the same thing as putting it in the hands and mouths of all the demons of hell, and the braying spread from one village to another, so that natives of the braying village are known and differentiated as blacks are from whites, and the disgrace of this prank has reached the point where those mocked have gone out armed in squadrons against the jokesters to do battle. I think that tomorrow or the next day those of my village, which is the braying town, are going to do battle with another town two leagues from ours—one of the ones that taunts us the most. In order to be well prepared, I've bought these lances and halberds that you've seen. These are the wonders I said I would tell you about, and if they didn't seem that way to you, I don't know any others."

And with this, the good fellow ended his speech, and at the same moment a man came in through the gate of the inn dressed in chamois skin, stockings, breeches, and doublet, and in a loud voice said: "*Señor* innkeeper, is there any room? The divining monkey and the puppet show about the rescue of Melisendra are coming."

"By my faith," said the innkeeper, "here's *señor maese* Pedro. We've got a fine night ahead of us!"

I forgot to say that this *maese* Pedro had his left eye and almost half his cheek covered with a patch of green taffeta,

an indication that something was the matter with that side
of his face. And the innkeeper went on, saying: "Welcome
your grace, *señor maese* Pedro. Where're the monkey and
the puppet theater? I don't see them."

"They're coming," responded the fellow dressed in
chamois. "I came ahead to find out if there was room."

"I'd throw the Duke of Alba* out to make room for *señor
maese* Pedro," responded the innkeeper. "Let the monkey
and the puppet theater come, for there are people here who
will pay to see the show and the talents of the monkey."

"Good," responded the man with the patch. "I'll lower
my price and if I get back my expenses I'll consider myself well paid. I'll go get the cart with the monkey and the
show." And then he went out of the inn.

Don Quixote asked the innkeeper who *maese* Pedro was,
and what monkey and what puppet theater he was bringing.

To which the innkeeper responded: "This fellow is a
famous puppeteer who has been wandering through this
Mancha de Aragón† putting on performances about the
rescue of Melisendra by the famous don Gaiferos, one
of the best shows—and best performed, too—to be seen
in this area of the kingdom for many years. He also has
a monkey with him with the strangest talent ever seen
among apes, or even among men for that matter, because, if
you ask him something, he listens carefully; then he jumps
on his master's shoulder and whispers in his ear the answer
to what has been asked, and *maese* Pedro then repeats it.
He can say more about things that have already happened
than about things yet to come. He doesn't get it right every
time, but most of the time he doesn't make a mistake, and
it makes us think that he has the devil inside him. *Maese*
Pedro charges two *reales* for each question, if the monkey
answers—I mean, if his master answers for him after having heard the response in his ear. It's believed that this
maese Pedro is very rich, and he's a *uomo galante*, as they
say in Italy, and *buon compagno*,‡ and he enjoys the best

---

* The Duke of Alba is a title passed from generation to generation—
there is one today.
† This is the eastern La Mancha, not related to the ancient kingdom
of Aragón.
‡ A *uomo galante* is a man who is attentive to women, and a *buon*

life in the world. He talks more than six men and drinks more than twelve—and all this is paid for by his tongue, his monkey, and his puppet show."

Just then, *maese* Pedro came back, followed by a cart carrying the puppet show and the monkey—a big tailless one with a calloused rear end, but his face was pleasant enough. And as soon as don Quixote saw him, he asked: "Tell me, your grace, *señor* diviner, *che pesce pigliamo*?* What's to become of us? Here are my two *reales*."

And he told Sancho to give them to *maese* Pedro, who answered for the monkey, saying: "*Señor*, this animal doesn't foretell things that have yet to happen. Of the past he knows certain things, and of the present a bit."

"I swear," said Sancho, "I won't give an *ardite* for anyone to tell me what happened to me, because who can know it better than me? And paying to find out what I already know would be really foolish. But since he knows things that are going on, here are my two *reales*. Have the *señor* monkey tell me what my wife, Teresa, is doing right now."

Maese Pedro refused payment, saying: "I don't want to take money in advance without first having rendered service."

After he gave his left shoulder a couple of pats, the monkey leapt up to it in one bound, and putting his mouth to his master's ear, he chattered rapidly, for about the time it would take to say a credo, and then jumped back to the floor. And at that same instant, *maese* Pedro raced over to kneel before don Quixote, clutched his legs, and said: "I embrace these legs as if I were embracing the Pillars of Hercules,† illustrious reviver of the forgotten profession of knight-errantry, never sufficiently praised knight don Qui-

---

compagno means he is a good companion. The Spanish original has Hispanified the Italian forms a bit.

* Again, I have used standard Italian, but the Spanish transcription comes quite close to the Italian pronunciation of *Che pesce pigliamo?* ("What fish will we catch?"), which, in effect, means what don Quixote goes on to say.

† The Pillars of Hercules refer to two peaks at the Straits of Gibraltar (the Rock of Gibraltar on the Iberian Peninsula and Mount Hacho in Ceuta on the African coast). The ancients believed that these were originally one mountain and Hercules split them to open the Mediterranean Sea.

xote de La Mancha, restorer of the faint, prop to those who are about to fall, helping hand for those who have fallen, support and counsel of all unfortunate people!"

Don Quixote was dumbfounded, Sancho amazed, the cousin astounded, the page stupefied, the person from the braying village spellbound, the innkeeper perplexed, and, finally, everyone flabbergasted at the words of the puppeteer, who went on to say: "And you, good Sancho Panza! The best squire of the best knight in the world! Be happy, for your wife, Teresa, is fine, and right now she's combing a pound of flax, and it looks like there's a cracked pitcher at her side that has a good bit of wine, which she takes a nip from once in a while as she works."

"I can believe that very well," responded Sancho, "because she's very fortunate, and if she weren't jealous, I wouldn't trade her for the giant Andandona,* who, according to my master, was a very clever and worthy woman, and my Teresa is one of those who don't let themselves be deprived of anything, even at the expense of her heirs."

"Now I say," said don Quixote, just then, "that the person who reads and travels a lot comes to see and know many things. I say this because what could have made me believe that there are apes in the world who can divine, as I've seen here with my own eyes? I'm the same don Quixote de La Mancha that this animal has named—although he has gone too far in my praise—but whatever kind of person I might be, I thank heaven, which endowed me with a gentle and compassionate nature, disposed to do good to all and ill to none."

"If I had any money," said the page, "I'd ask *señor* monkey what will happen to me in the pilgrimage I'm on."

To which *maese* Pedro, who was no longer kneeling at don Quixote's feet, responded: "I've already said that this little creature doesn't predict what will happen, but if he

---

* Andandona was the sister of the giant Madarque in *Amadís* (chapter 65, vol. ii, p. 39, of the Edwin Place translation), where she is described as "the fiercest and harshest woman in the world. She was excessively large and swift of foot. Her hair was entirely white and so kinky that she couldn't comb it; she was so very ugly of countenance that she resembled a devil. . . . She was very hostile to Christians and did them great harm."

did, having money wouldn't matter—because to be of service to don Quixote, here present, I'd forgo all the earnings in the world. Now, because I owe him something and want to please him, I'll set up my puppet theater and entertain all those in the inn at no charge."

When the innkeeper heard this, he was overjoyed and showed him where the theater could be set up, and this was done in an instant. Don Quixote wasn't very happy with the divinations of the monkey, since it didn't seem appropriate for a monkey to divine either future things or past things. And so, while *maese* Pedro set up the puppet theater, don Quixote withdrew with Sancho to a corner of the stable, where, without being heard by anyone, he told him: "Look, Sancho, I've been thinking about the extraordinary ability of this monkey, and I have to conclude that this *maese* Pedro without a doubt has made a pact, tacit or expressed, with the devil."

"If the pack is sent express and by the devil, I'm not going to open it. But what good are these packs to *maese* Pedro?"

"You don't understand me, Sancho. I only want to say that he must have made some deal with the devil, who has given the monkey this ability so he can earn a living, and when he gets rich, he'll give his soul to the devil, which is what humankind's universal enemy wants. And what makes me believe this is that the monkey can tell only past or present things, and the knowledge of the devil doesn't go beyond that, since he doesn't know the future except by conjecture, and doesn't hit the mark every time. To know all is reserved only for God, and for Him there's no past or future—everything is in the present, and that being so, as it is, it's evident that this monkey speaks the way the devil might. I'm shocked he hasn't been denounced yet to the Inquisition and scrutinized by them to find out through whose power the monkey is able to divine. Because it's certain that this monkey is not an astrologer, nor can his master cast those figures that they call a horoscope, which is so common in Spain nowadays that there's no serving girl, page, or cobbler who doesn't pride himself on being able to make one up, as easily as picking up the jack of spades from the floor, bringing the wondrous truth of science to ruin through their lies and ignorance. I know of one woman who asked one of these astrologers if her little lapdog would get pregnant and give birth, and how many puppies and of what color they would be. To which the astrologer, after casting the horoscope, responded that the dog would get pregnant and would deliver three puppies—one green, one red, and one of mixed color, provided that the dog mated between eleven and twelve o'clock of the day or night on Monday or Saturday. And what happened was that the dog died two days later of overeating, and the astrologer was confirmed as being very astute, as happens to all or most of them."

"Even so," said Sancho, "I'd like your grace to tell *maese* Pedro to ask his monkey if what happened to you in the Cave of Montesinos is true. As for me, begging your pardon, I think it was all deceit and lies, or at best something dreamed up."

"Anything is possible," responded don Quixote. "I'll do what you advise even though I have some qualms about it."

As they were finishing this conversation, *maese* Pedro came over to get don Quixote and tell him that the theater was prepared, and that he should come see the show because it was worthwhile. Don Quixote communicated his thought and begged him to ask the monkey right then if certain things that happened to him in the Cave of Montesinos were dreamed up or true, because it seemed to him they could go either way. To which *maese* Pedro, without saying a word, brought back the monkey, and in front of don Quixote and Sancho said: "Look, *señor* monkey, this knight wants to know if certain things that happened to him in a cave called 'of Montesinos' were false or true."

And giving the usual sign, the monkey jumped on his left shoulder, and seemingly spoke into his ear, and then *maese* Pedro said: "The monkey says that some of the things that happened to your grace in that cave were imagined, and some seem to be true, and that's all he knows, and nothing else, insofar as that question goes. And if your grace wants to know more, next Friday he'll answer anything asked him, because for the time being his powers have left him and they won't return until Friday, as he has said."

"Didn't I say," said Sancho, "that I couldn't believe everything your grace, *señor mío*, has said about the events of the cave, not even half of them?"

"Events will show, Sancho," responded don Quixote, "for time, the revealer of all things, leaves nothing that's not brought to the light of day, even if it hides in the bosom of the earth; and for the moment we'll let it go at that. Let's go see the puppet show of the good *maese* Pedro, because I believe it'll reveal something novel."

"What do you mean *something*?" responded *maese* Pedro. "This show of mine has sixty thousand new things in it. I tell you, my *señor* don Quixote, that it's one of the best things to see in the world today, so *operibus credite & non verbis*.* And let's get to it, because it's getting late, and we have lots to do, say, and show."

Don Quixote and Sancho obeyed, and went to where the show was going to be, and the theater was set up and ready, lighted on every side by little candles, which made it fine-looking and bright. When *maese* Pedro got there, he went behind it, since he was going to work the puppets, and outside the puppet theater there was a boy, *maese* Pedro's servant, who was going to narrate the mysteries of the show. He had a little wand in his hand to point out the various characters as they came out. With everyone at the inn, some standing, some sitting, in front of the theater, and don Quixote, Sancho, the page, and the cousin settled in the best seats, the narrator began to say what will be heard and seen by whoever hears or reads the next chapter.

Chapter XXVI. Where the delightful adventure of the puppeteer is continued, together with other things that are in truth quite good.

A SUDDEN silence fell on them all;† I mean, all those who were watching the show were hanging on the words of the narrator about its wonders, when they heard the sound of drums and trumpets and the noise of artillery emerge from the theater, the thunder of which soon faded away, and

---

* This is similar to John 10:38: "Though you believe me not, believe the works."

† The Spanish begins with the start of the 1555 Spanish translation of the first verse of Book II of the *Æneid*: *Conticuere omnes, intentique ora tenebant*. The words I have used come from an English translation of Virgil.

then the boy raised his voice and said: "This true history being performed for your graces is taken word for word from
French chronicles and from Spanish ballads. It depicts the
rescue by señor don Gaiferos of his wife, Melisendra,* who
was being held captive in Spain, in the city of Sansueña,
which it was called in those days and we call Zaragoza today. And look, your graces, how don Gaiferos is playing
backgammon, as is sung:

Gaiferos is playing backgammon
    and his Melisendra is forgotten

"And that character just coming out now with the crown
on his head and the scepter in his hands is the emperor
Charlemagne, the supposed father of Melisendra, who,
annoyed with the idleness and neglect of his son-in-law,
comes over to scold him. And look with what vehemence
and insistence he reprimands him, and it even looks like
he would like to knock him on the head a half dozen times
with his scepter, and some authorities say that he did, and
well deserved they were, too. And after having said many
things about the risk to his honor for not trying to rescue
his wife, they say that he said:

See to it—I have said it too many times.

"Look, your graces, also how the emperor turns his back
and leaves don Gaiferos despairing, whom you can now see,
impatient with anger, casting the board and the pieces away

---

* There is nothing in French history or literature about this. Gaiferos,
in the Spanish tale, is Charlemagne's nephew and Melisendra is his
daughter. The way the story is told here follows the Spanish ballads of
the sixteenth century. In the story, before they got married, Melisendra
was kidnapped and Gaiferos stayed in Paris for seven years before he
went to rescue her. This is where *maese* Pedro's dramatization begins.
   Menéndez Pidal proposes that this story derives from legends
about a Visigothic hero named Walter de España, who rescued his
betrothed, Hiltgunda, in a similar fashion (you can read about it in
his *La epopeya castellana a través de la literatura española* [Madrid:
Espasa-Calpe, 1959, p. 25]). If you squint at the name Walter and apply
a couple of philological rules to it, you can develop "Gaiter" from it,
which is pretty close to Gaiferos.

from him, and quickly asks for his weapons, and how he asks
don Roland, his cousin, if he can borrow his sword, Durendal, and how don Roland refuses to lend it to him, offering
him instead his own services for this difficult undertaking
before him. But the brave angered man refuses to accept,
and says that he alone will suffice to bring back his wife,
even if she were hidden in the center of the earth. And with
this, he goes in for his armor so he can get on the road.

"Now, your graces, turn your attention to that tower
over there, which we suppose is one of the towers of the
castle of Zaragoza that is known today as the Aljafería,
and that lady on that balcony, dressed in the Moorish fashion, is the peerless Melisendra, who goes there frequently,
looking toward the road leading to France, and by thinking
about Paris and her husband, she's able to console herself during her confinement. Look at something else that's
happening now, perhaps never before seen. Don't you see
that Moor who, keeping very quiet, on tiptoe, with a finger
to his lips, comes behind Melisendra? Well, look how he
gives her a kiss right on her lips, and how she makes haste
to spit and clean her mouth off with the white sleeve of
her smock, and how she begins to lament, and pulls out
her hair in grief, as if it were to blame for the insult. Look
also at that stately Moor in the corridor, who is King Marsilio of Sansueña, who—having seen the insolence of the
other Moor, even though he was a relative of his and a
favorite—has him arrested right away and they sentence
him to two hundred lashes, and to be taken through the
streets of the city,

with town criers in front
    and constables behind

"And see here, where they're about to give him his punishment, though the crime has just been committed, because
there are no indictments or remands as there are with us."

"Child, child," shouted don Quixote at this moment,
"follow your story in a straight line and don't lead us down
curves or side streets. To establish a truth clearly, many
proofs are necessary."

Maese Pedro also said from within: "Boy, stay on track,
do what that man says, and that'll be the best thing. Keep

to your plainsong and don't use any counterpoint, since it tends to break down from being too subtle."

"I will," responded the boy, and he went on saying: "This figure coming out on horseback, wearing a hooded cape, is don Gaiferos himself. Here his wife, now avenged for the daring of the enamored Moor, and, more at her ease, is on the battlements of the castle, and she begins to speak with her husband, thinking he's just some traveler, and she uses the words from that ballad that begins this way:

Horseman, if you are going to France,
    Ask about don Gaiferos,

and I won't repeat any more of it, since verbosity begets boredom. It's enough to see how don Gaiferos makes himself known, and by the joyous gestures of Melisendra, we see that she has recognized him, and now we see her climbing over the balcony so she can jump onto the haunches of her husband's horse.

"But, alas! The poor thing gets her skirt caught on the railing, and she's left hanging in the air, without being able to get down. But now look how pious heaven aids us in the greatest need, for don Gaiferos, without caring if he tears her rich skirt, grabs onto her, and by force brings her to the ground, and in one heave, he puts her astride, like a man, on the haunches of his horse and he tells her to hold on to him tight by putting her arms around him so she won't fall, since *señora* Melisendra is not used to such horseback riding. Look also how the neighs of the horse show how happy he is to be carrying his brave and beautiful master and mistress. Look how they turn their backs and are off, and happily and joyfully they take the road toward Paris.

"May you leave in peace, peerless pair of true lovers! May you arrive safely in your beloved fatherland, unimpeded by bad luck along your happy journey! May the eyes of your friends and relatives see you enjoy the days that remain of your lives—and may they be as long as Nestor's."*

Here *maese* Pedro's voice rose again and said: "Be

---

* Nestor participated in the Trojan War, took part in the Greek war councils, and ruled as king of Pylos for three generations. The oral tradition augmented the three generations into hundreds of years.

plain, boy, and don't be bombastic, because all affectation is bad!"

The narrator didn't respond to this, but continued, saying: "There was no lack of idle eyes—those that notice everything. They saw Melisendra slide down and get on the horse, and they ran to tell King Marsilio, who then ordered the alarm to sound, and see with what speed! Now the city is deluged with the sound of bells that ring in all the towers of the mosques."

"That can't be," said don Quixote. "In the business of bells *maese* Pedro is not correct, because among the Moors bells aren't used, but rather drums and *dulzainas*,* like our *chirimías*.† To have bells in Sansueña is a great absurdity."

When *maese* Pedro heard this, the playing stopped, and he said: "Don't bother about trifles, *señor* don Quixote, nor look for perfection where none is possible. Don't they put on a thousand plays every day with a thousand inaccuracies and idiocies, and still those plays have a complete run, and the people who attend them not only applaud but also admire them? So, go on, boy, and let them say whatever they want. As long as I fill my purse, let there be as many improprieties as there are rays of the sun."

"You're right," said don Quixote.

And the boy went on: "Look at how many magnificent horsemen race from town pursuing the two Catholic lovers; how many trumpets sound, how many *dulzainas* are being played and drums resound. I'm greatly afraid that they will catch them and take them back tied to the tail of their own horses, and what a horrendous spectacle that would be."

When don Quixote saw such a multitude of Moors and heard all that noise, it seemed to him that he should render assistance to the fleeing couple, and, standing up, with a loud voice he said: "I'll not allow, while I'm alive and present, for such *soperchieria*‡ to be done to such a famous knight and daring lover as is don Gaiferos. Stop, you ill-

---

* This was a double-reeded Renaissance folk wind instrument, an indirect predecessor of the oboe.

† This was a double-reeded instrument that looked like a clarinet, with ten finger holes.

‡ "Outrageous behavior" in Italian.

bred rabble. Stay and pursue no more! If you do, you're in battle with me!"

As soon as he said that he went into action, and taking out his sword, in one leap he was in front of the puppet theater and with incredible speed and fury he began raining slashes onto the Moorish horsemen, knocking some over, demolishing others, decapitating still others, mutilating this one, smashing that one, and gave such a downward thrust amidst many of them that if *maese* Pedro hadn't lowered himself, hunched up, and ducked, don Quixote would have chopped off his head more easily than if he were made of almond paste.

Maese Pedro shouted from inside, saying: "Stop, your grace, don Quixote—these things you're knocking over, smashing, and killing aren't real Moors, but rather little figurines made of pasteboard. Look, sinner that I am, you're wrecking my entire livelihood!"

But don Quixote didn't stop raining his thrusts, backhands, slashes, and lunges on this account. Finally, in less than the time that it takes to say the credo twice, he destroyed the whole puppet theater, cutting to bits all the equipment and figures, leaving King Marsilio badly wounded and the Emperor Charlemagne with his crown and head split in two. The whole audience was in an uproar, the monkey fled over the roof of the inn, the cousin was afraid, the page cowered down, and even Sancho Panza himself was very fearful, because, as he swore after the storm was over, he'd never seen his master so recklessly angry.

With the general destruction of the theater, now that don Quixote was settled down a bit, he said: "I'd like to have before me right now all those who don't and even *refuse* to believe how useful it is to have knights-errant in the world. Consider what would have happened to the good don Gaiferos and the beautiful Melisendra if I hadn't been here. I'll bet that those dogs would have caught them by now and would have done something dreadful to them. So, long live knight-errantry over all other things on the earth!"

"Long may it live and good luck to it!" said *maese* Pedro in a very tired voice. "And may I die, since I'm so unfortunate that I can say what don Rodrigo said:

Yesterday I ruled over Spain.
> and today I don't have a single fort
> that I can say belongs to me.*

"It hasn't yet been a half hour, nor even half a moment, when I was the master of kings and emperors, my stables and chests and sacks filled with an infinite number of horses, and liveries without number. Now I'm devastated and disheartened, poor, and a beggar, and especially without my monkey, because I swear that before he comes back to me my teeth will have to sweat,† and all of it because of the ill-considered fury of this *señor* knight, of whom it's said that he rescues orphans and rights wrongs, and does other charitable things; it's only in my case that his generous intention failed—praise heaven, where the highest thrones are found. I guess the Woebegone Knight was destined to make my puppets so woebegone."

Sancho Panza was moved to compassion by *maese* Pedro's lament, and said to him: "Don't cry, *maese* Pedro, and don't grieve anymore, because you're breaking my heart. I'll have you know that my master don Quixote is so Catholic, and such a staunch Christian, that if he realizes that he has done you ill, he'll insist on paying for it and making it up to you."

"If *señor* don Quixote would pay me back for some part of the figures that he has broken, I'd be content, and his grace would have a clear conscience, because 'he cannot be saved who has what belongs to someone else against the will of the owner and refuses to give it back.'"

"That's right," said don Quixote, "but as of now I have no idea that I have anything of yours, *maese* Pedro."

"What do mean you have NO IDEA?" responded *maese* Pedro. "And these remains on the hard and sterile floor? Who scattered and annihilated them if not the invincible power of that mighty arm? And whose bodies were they except mine? And how will I earn a living without them?"

"Now I'm convinced," said don Quixote, "what I've

---

* These verses are taken from the "Ballad about how don Rodrigo lost Spain." It was Rodrigo who lost Spain to the Moors in A.D. 711.
† Meaning that it'll cost him a lot of labor.

believed on many other occasions—that these enchanters who pursue me do it only to place people as they really are in front of my eyes, and then change them and turn them into whatever they want. Really and truly I tell all who are listening to me that it appeared to me that everything that happened here was really going on exactly as it seemed— that Melisendra was Melisendra; don Gaiferos, don Gaiferos; Marsilio, Marsilio; Charlemagne, Charlemagne. For this reason, I got angry, and to comply with my profession of knight-errantry, I had to give aid to those who were fleeing, and with this upright goal in mind I did what you saw me do. If it has turned out differently, I'm not to blame— the evil people who pursue me are. Nevertheless, for this mistake, although there was absence of malice, I want to sentence myself to pay. Let *maese* Pedro tell me what he wants for the broken figures, and I'll pay for them immediately, in good and valid Castilian currency."

Maese Pedro bowed acknowledgment, and said: "I expected no less from the unheard-of Christianity of the valorous don Quixote de La Mancha, the true helper and protector of all those in need and of needy vagabonds. The innkeeper and the great Sancho Panza will be mediators and assessors between your grace and myself concerning what each of the broken figures is or may be worth."

The innkeeper and Sancho said that they would do it, and then *maese* Pedro picked King Marsilio of Zaragoza up from the floor, with the head missing, and said: "You can see how impossible it will be to restore this king to his original state, so it seems to me, barring better judgment, that I'm owed four *reales* and a half for his death, end, and destruction."

"Move on," said don Quixote.

"Well, for this one, which is split down the middle," said *maese* Pedro, taking in his hands the cleft Emperor Charlemagne, "it wouldn't be unreasonable to ask five *reales* and a quarter."

"That's not little," said Sancho.

"Nor much," said the innkeeper. "Let's split the difference and say five *reales*."

"Let him be given the full five and a quarter," said don Quixote. "This notable misfortune is not worth quibbling over a quarter more or less, and let's finish quickly, *maese* Pedro—dinnertime is approaching and I'm getting hungry."

"For this figure," said *maese* Pedro, "whose nose has been chopped off and who has an eye poked out, which is the beautiful Melisendra, and I think this figure is appropriate, two *reales* and twelve *maravedís*."

"How can that be?" said don Quixote. "Melisendra must already be with her husband, at least as far as the French border, since her horse, it seemed to me, was flying more than running, and so don't try to pull the wool over my eyes by trying to make me think this is Melisendra without a nose, when the real one is relaxing in France with her husband. May God help everyone, *señor maese* Pedro, and let's play fair and square and move on."

Maese Pedro could see that don Quixote was beginning to talk nonsense and was going back to his old ways, which he didn't want to happen, so he said to him: "Right, this can't be Melisendra—it has to be one of the maidens who served her—with sixty *maravedís* I'll be content and well paid."

In this same way he went along pricing many other destroyed figures, which the arbitrating judges adjusted, to the satisfaction of both sides, to forty *reales* and three quarters, and in addition to this—which Sancho paid him immediately—*maese* Pedro asked for an additional two *reales* for catching the monkey.

"Give them to him," said don Quixote, "not for the monkey, but rather for the she-monkey,* and I'd reward two hundred more to the person who could tell me with certainty the good news that *señora* doña Melisendra and *señor* Gaiferos were back in France with their families."

"No one can tell you that better than my monkey," said *maese Pedro*, "but now there's no devil that can catch him. Although I imagine that his affection for me and hunger will force him to look for me tonight, and 'tomorrow is another day, and we'll see.'"

So, the storm of the puppet theater blew over, and everyone ate dinner in peace and good fellowship at don Quixote's expense, because he was generous in the extreme.

---

* "She-monkey" refers to getting drunk; thus don Quixote offers this extra money for him to get drunk with.

Before sunup the fellow with the lances and halberds left, and just after dawn the cousin and page came to say good-bye to don Quixote, one to return home, and the other to continue his journey, and don Quixote helped him on his trip by giving him a dozen *reales. Maese* Pedro didn't want to have any more disputes with don Quixote, whom he knew very well, and so he got up early before the sun came up, and, taking the remnants of his puppets and his monkey, also went away in search of adventures. The innkeeper, who didn't know don Quixote, was as much in wonder at his crazy acts as he was at his generosity. Sancho paid him well on orders of his master, and bidding him farewell, at about eight o'clock in the morning they left the inn, where we will let them go on by themselves so that we can have the time to relate things dealing with the telling of this famous history.

Chapter XXVII. Where it is revealed who maese *Pedro and his monkey were, together with the unfortunate outcome don Quixote had in the Adventure of the Braying, which didn't turn out as he wanted and planned.*

CIDE HAMETE Benengeli, chronicler of this great history, begins this chapter with the words: "I swear as a Catholic Christian," to which his translator adds that when Cide Hamete swears "as a Catholic Christian," as a Moor, which he doubtless was, he only wanted to say that when a Catholic Christian swears, he swears or ought to swear the truth and speak the truth in whatever he says; so he's saying that he was telling the truth as a Catholic Christian might when he wrote about don Quixote, especially when he said who *maese* Pedro was, along with his divining monkey—who caused people so much wonder with his miraculous guesses.

He says, then, that the person who read the first part of this history will remember a certain Ginés de Pasamonte, whom don Quixote liberated along with the other galley slaves in the Sierra Morena—a reward that was ill thanked and poorly repaid by those ungrateful and ill-mannered people. This Ginés de Pasamonte, whom don Quixote called Ginesillo de Parapilla, was the fellow who stole Sancho Panza's donkey, which, since it wasn't explained in the first part—a printer's error—has baffled many readers, who attributed it to the author's bad memory rather than the mistake of the print shop. So, Ginés stole it when Sancho Panza was sleeping on the saddle, with the trick that Brunelo used at the siege of Albraca, when he removed Sacripante's horse from between his legs. Later, Sancho recovered his donkey as has been described. This Ginés, then, fearful he would be discovered by the law that was looking for him to punish him for his infinite number of tricks and crimes—which were so many and so bad that he himself wrote a large volume about them—resolved to go to the kingdom of Aragón and cover his left eye, and became a puppeteer. He knew how to do this and also perform sleight of hand extremely well.

It happened, then, that he bought the monkey from a recently freed Christian coming from the Barbary Coast, and he taught the monkey to come up on his shoulder when he made a certain signal, and to murmur—or at least pretend to murmur—into his ear. Once the monkey knew how to do this, before he would go into a village where he was going with his puppet theater and monkey, he'd find out in the nearest village, or from an appropriate individual, what things had happened in that village and to which persons. He would keep all these things in his memory, and the first thing he'd do was put on his show, sometimes using one story, sometimes another, but all of them lighthearted, cheerful, and well-known. When the show was over, he would mention the skill of his monkey, telling the people that he could divine the past and the present, but couldn't tell the future. For every correct answer he would get two *reales*. Sometimes he would discount his price, depending on what he felt about the people asking questions. Once in a while he was in the house of people whose doings he knew, and although they didn't ask anything so as not to have to pay him, he gave the monkey the signal, and then he would say that the monkey had told him such-and-such things, which jibed perfectly with what had happened. With this he got incredible credit and everyone flocked to him. Other times, since he was so clever, he would make his answers fit the questions very well, and since no one investigated or pressed him to say how his monkey divined, he made monkeys out of them all and filled his purse.

The instant he went into the inn, he recognized don Quixote and Sancho, and since he knew them, it was easy to amaze them and all those who were there. But it would have cost him dearly if don Quixote had lowered his hand a little more when he cut off King Marsilio's head and destroyed his cavalry, as has been said in the previous chapter.

This is what there is to say about *maese* Pedro and his monkey. And going back to don Quixote de La Mancha, I'll say that after he left the inn, he resolved to see the shores of the Ebro River* and that whole area before he went into the city of Zaragoza, since there was quite a bit of time before the jousts were to begin. With this intention he went along his way and for two days nothing happened to him worthy of setting down in writing, until the third day, when he was going up a hill, he heard a great din of drums, trumpets, and muskets.

At first, he thought some regiment of soldiers was moving through the area, and to see them better, he spurred Rocinante and went higher on the hill, and when he was at its highest point, he saw at the foot of the hill what seemed to him to be more than two hundred men armed in different ways—with lances, crossbows, large and small halberds, pikes,† and some muskets, and many round shields. He went down the slope, approached the squadron, and could easily see their banners, distinguish their colors, and note their devices. There was a banner or pennant in particular made of white satin on which a very lifelike small donkey was painted, his head in the air, his mouth open and tongue sticking out, in the act and posture of braying. Surrounding it were written these verses in large letters:

They didn't bray in vain,
      the one and the other magistrate.

---

* The Ebro is Spain's longest river (565 miles), and the least navigable of the major ones. It flows through Zaragoza on its way to the Mediterranean coast, south of Barcelona.
† The pike was a long-handled halberd.

By this, don Quixote gathered that those persons must be from the braying village and that's what he told Sancho, repeating to him what was written on the banner. He told him also that the person who had told them the story was mistaken when he referred to the two aldermen who had brayed, since according to the verses on the banner they were magistrates.

To which Sancho Panza responded: "*Señor*, that doesn't matter, because the two aldermen who brayed then with time might have become magistrates of their town, and thus they can be called both ways, but in any case it makes no difference to the truth of the story whether or not the brayers were aldermen or magistrates, since they did bray, and it's just as likely for a magistrate to bray as it is for an alderman."

They soon figured out that the ridiculed town was going out to fight with another village that had offended them more than was called for, and more than neighborly decency should allow. Don Quixote went over to them, not without some distress on Sancho's part, since he never liked to be in such situations. The men of the squadron surrounded him, thinking he must be a person favoring their cause. Don Quixote lifted his visor, and with a certain dash and demeanor went to the banner with the donkey, and the leaders of the army gathered around to see him, astonished in the same way all who see him for the first time are.

Don Quixote, who saw them looking at him so attentively, none of them saying a word, wanted to take advantage of that silence, and breaking his own, raised his voice and said: "Good men, I earnestly ask you not to interrupt a speech I want to deliver to you until you see that it bores or annoys you. If this is the case, at the least sign you give me, I'll seal my lips and will put a gag on my tongue."

They all told him to say what he wanted, and they would be happy to hear what he had to say. With this license, don Quixote continued, saying: "I, *señores míos*, am a knight-errant, whose profession is that of arms, and whose occupation is to help the needy and to relieve the oppressed. Some days ago I learned of your misfortune and the reason that you've taken up arms on occasion to take vengeance on your enemies. And having mulled over your situation once and even many times in my mind, I find that—according to the laws of the duel—you're mistaken in considering yourselves insulted, because no individual can insult a whole population, unless it is to call the whole population traitorous because he doesn't know the individual who committed the treason. An example of this we have in don Diego de Ordóñez de Lara, who challenged the whole city of Zamora because he didn't know that only Vellido Dolfos had committed the treason of killing the king,* so he challenged everyone, and the task of answering him and vengeance concerned everyone. Although it's true that *señor* don Diego went a bit far and even exceeded the limits of the challenge, since he had no reason to challenge the dead, nor the water, nor the bread,† nor those who were still unborn, nor other trivialities that are mentioned there. But, alas! when anger overflows its banks, it's almost impossible to stop it. This being the case, since a single person cannot offend a kingdom, province, city, republic, nor an entire population, it follows that there's no reason to go to war to avenge such an insult, because there was no insult to begin with. It would really be unfortunate if the town known as the Clockers went around killing those who called the town that, and the same with the Casserolers, Eggplanters, Whalers, Soapers,‡ or any

---

* Sancho II (the Strong) of Castile and León (1038?–1072) was laying siege to Zamora in 1072 when Vellido Adolfo, also known as Vellido Dolfos, sneaked out of Zamora on October 7 and treacherously murdered him while he was relieving himself (see Menéndez Pidal's edition of the *Primera Crónica General*, chapter 836, p. 511, col. 1, ll. 24–30). Vellido Adolfo then returned to Zamora. Diego Ordóñez de Lara, knowing full well (despite what don Quixote thinks) that Vellido Adolfo murdered the king, in order to make the Zamorans release the culprit, challenged the whole city, past, present, and future: "I challenge the Zamorans, the adult as well as the child, the dead as well as the living, and the one who has yet to be born as well as the water they drink and the clothing they wear" (*Primera Crónica General,* translated, p. 513, col. 2, ll. 15–19).

† Why would Diego Ordóñez challenge their *bread*? The Spanish *panes* ("bread") seems to be a misconstrued *paños* ("clothes"), mentioned in the same breath as water in the example from the *Primera Crónica General* in the previous note. On the other hand, why would he have challenged their *clothes*? Hm . . .

‡ Clockers (people from Espartinas, near Seville), casserolers (people from Valladolid), eggplanters (people from Toledo), whalers (people from Madrid), and soapers (people from Seville). Rodríguez Marín, in appendix 30 to his 1948 edition (vol. X, pp. 49–56), explains these references. Why are the people from Madrid called "whalers"? See his p. 53.

of those other names that circulate in mouths of boys and the rabble in general. Wouldn't it be lovely if all these notable cities were offended and wanted to take vengeance, and always went around taking their swords out over every little quarrel! No, no, God won't allow it, nor does He want it.

"Men of discretion and well-ordered republics should take up arms and unsheathe their swords and put themselves, their lives, and their estates at risk for four reasons: first, to defend the Catholic faith; second, to defend themselves, and this obeys laws both natural and divine; third, in defense of their honor, their family, and their estate; and fourth, in service of their king in a just war; and if we want to add a fifth one, which fits into the second, it is in defense of their country. To these five causes, as the main ones, you might add a few other reasonable ones that might make you take up arms, but to take them up on account of trifles, and because of things that are more laughable and amusing than offensive, it seems that anyone who would take up arms in those situations lacks logic—more so since there can be no just vengeance that is unjust—and goes directly against the holy law that we profess, which requires us to do good to our enemies and to love those who hate us, a commandment that, although it seems hard to comply with, is only so for those having less of God than the world, and more of flesh than spirit. Jesus Christ—God, and true man, who never lied, nor could He lie—since He was our Lawgiver, said that His yoke was easy and His burden was light,* and so He wouldn't command us to do anything that was impossible to obey. So, *señores míos*, your graces are obliged by divine and human laws to go in peace."

"May the devil carry me off," said Sancho, to himself, "if this master of mine isn't a theologian, and if he isn't, he seems like it, 'as one egg is like the next one.'"

Don Quixote took a breath, and seeing that they were still quiet, tried to go on in his talk, and would have if the astute Sancho hadn't seen that he'd stopped, and took the floor, saying: "My master, don Quixote de La Mancha, who was known as the Woebegone Knight for a while and now is known as the Knight of the Lions, is an *hidalgo* of great intelligence, who knows Latin and Spanish like a bachelor,

---

* Matthew 11:30: "His yoke was easy and his burden light."

and everything he talks about and advises comes from his being a good soldier, and he has all the laws and ordinances at his fingertips, so there's nothing to do but take his advice, and you can blame me if it's bad advice—especially because it's foolishness to be offended by a single bray.

"I remember, when I was a boy, I brayed whenever I felt like it, without anybody stopping me, and with such grace and propriety that when I brayed, all the donkeys of the village brayed too, and yet for this I didn't stop being the son of my parents, who were very honorable people. And even if I was envied for this skill by more than four snooty boys from my town, I couldn't have cared less. And to show I'm telling the truth, wait a second and listen. This is just like swimming—once you learn it, you never forget it."

And then he put his hand to his nose and began to bray so loudly that all the nearby valleys resounded. One of the fellows next to him, thinking he was making fun of them, raised the staff he held in his hand and gave Sancho such a thwack that he couldn't help but fall to the ground. Don Quixote, who saw Sancho in such bad shape, attacked the person who had hit Sancho with his lance. But so many people intervened that he couldn't avenge his squire. Seeing the shower of stones raining down on him and that a thousand crossbows were aimed at him and no fewer muskets, he turned Rocinante around and, at the fastest gallop he could muster, shot away, commending himself to God with all his heart to free him from that danger, fearing at every step that a bullet would go in through his back and come out his chest, and he constantly drew breath to make sure he could still breathe.

But the squadron was content for him to flee without shooting at him. They put Sancho—who was barely conscious, and couldn't yet ride properly—across his donkey, and let him follow his master. The donkey followed the trail of Rocinante, from whom he was never separated.

After don Quixote had traveled a good distance, he turned his head back and saw that Sancho was coming along, and waited for him, seeing that no one else was following. The people of the squadron waited until nightfall, and since their adversaries didn't show up, they returned to their town joyful and happy, and if they had known the ancient Greek custom, they would have erected a monument in that field.

Chapter XXVIII. About things that Benengeli says that whoever reads them will learn, if he reads attentively.

IF THE brave man flees, foul play is at its root, and prudent men save themselves for future battles. This truth was manifested in don Quixote, who, giving time for the fury of the braying town and the bad intentions of that indignant squadron to settle down, made haste to get away. Without thinking about Sancho or of the danger in which he left him, he went far enough away so he would be safe. Sancho followed him, slung across the donkey's back, as has been mentioned, now having come to more or less, and when he got to his master, he let himself slide off the donkey at Rocinante's feet, in anguish, battered, and beaten up.

Don Quixote got off Rocinante to examine his wounds, but as he found him sound from head to foot, with some anger said to him: "It was most unfortunate when you learned how to bray, Sancho! Where did you get the idea that it was a good idea to 'mention rope in the house of the hanged man'? And to the music of braying, what counterpoint could there be but that of a beating? Give thanks to God, Sancho, that they crossed your back with a stake and that they didn't make the *per signum crucis** with a scimitar."

"I'm in no condition to answer," responded Sancho, "because I feel like I'm talking through my back. Let's mount our animals and get out of here, and I won't bray again, but I won't keep silent about knights-errant who flee and leave their good squires ground up like a sack of wheat, in the hands of his enemies."

"'He who retires doesn't flee,'" responded don Quixote, "because you should know, Sancho, that courage that's not based on prudence is called recklessness, and the deeds of the reckless person can more be attributed to good luck than to bravery. So, I confess that I retired but not that I fled, and in this I've imitated many brave men who have

---

* This *per signum crucis* ("the sign of the cross") refers to a slash on the face, reflecting the small sign of the cross that many Catholics perform on their foreheads.

saved themselves for better occasions, and the histories are full of this. I won't tell you what histories I'm referring to now, since it won't do you any good and it won't give me any pleasure."

By this time, Sancho was sitting on his donkey, having been helped up by don Quixote, who then got on Rocinante all by himself, and they headed off slowly toward a poplar grove a quarter of a league away. Once in a while Sancho gave deep sighs and painful groans. Don Quixote asked him what was causing him such bitter distress, and he responded that from the base of his spine to the nape of his neck it was so painful he thought it would drive him crazy.

"The cause," said don Quixote, "must doubtless be that since the stake they were pounding you with was long and straight, and they hit you all over your back, that's the area where you hurt. And if they hit you elsewhere, it'd hurt you there, too."

"By God," said Sancho, "your grace has cleared up a great doubt I had and you've revealed the truth to me in brilliant terms. I swear, was the cause of my pain so hidden that you had to tell me that the areas that hurt me are where I was pummeled with the stake? If my ankles hurt me it'd be worthwhile to try to find out why they hurt. But to tell me that it hurts me where they pounded me is no great feat to guess. On my faith, *señor* our master, 'other people's grief doesn't affect us,' and every day I'm finding out how little I can expect from keeping company with you, because if this time you let me get beaten up, another and a hundred more times we'll go back to the blanketings and other pranks of bygone days, and if it's my back that pays the price this time, next time it may be my eyes. I'd do a lot better—but I'm a barbarian and I'll never do anything good in my whole life—I'd do a lot better, I repeat, to go home to my wife and children, supporting her and raising them with what God was pleased to give me, and not go running around following you along nonexistent roads and paths that aren't there, drinking poorly and eating worse. And as for sleeping, 'measure off six feet of ground, brother, and if you need more, take double that amount, for you can take as much as you like, and stretch out as much as you want,' and may I see the first person who started knight-errantry burned up and made into dust—or at least the first person who wanted to be a squire to those dimwits, as all the ancient knights-errant must have been. About the contemporary knights, I say nothing, because, as your grace is one of them, I respect them, and because I know that your grace knows a bit more than the devil when you talk and think."

"I bet, Sancho," said don Quixote, "that now that you're talking without anyone stopping you, your body doesn't hurt anywhere. Keep on talking, my son, and say anything that comes to your mind or your mouth, because in exchange for relieving you of your pains, I'll consider the vexation that your impudence causes me to be a pleasure, and if you want to go back home so much to be with your wife and children, may God not prevent me from stopping you. You have my money—figure out how long we've been on this third quest since we left our town, and calculate how much you can and should earn every month, and pay yourself with your own hand."

"When I worked for Tomé Carrasco," responded Sancho, "the bachelor Sansón's father, who your grace knows well, I earned two *ducados* every month, in addition to lunch. With your grace I can't figure out how much I should earn, since I know it's more work to be a squire to a knight-errant than it is to work for a farmer. So, in sum, those of us who work for farmers, no matter how much we work by day, no matter what happens, at night we eat stew and sleep at home. I haven't slept in a bed since I started working for your grace, except the short time we were in Diego de Miranda's house, during the banquet I had with the skimmings that I got from Camacho's stew pots, and what I ate and drank in Basilio's house. The rest of the time I've slept on the hard ground in the open air, subject to what they call inclemencies of the heavens, feeding myself on pieces of cheese and crumbs of bread, and drinking water from streams or fountains that we come across along the by-roads of our travels."

"I concede," said don Quixote, "that everything you've said may be true. How much more should I give you than what Tomé Carrasco gave you?"

"In my view," said Sancho, "if your grace adds two *reales* more per month, I'll consider myself well paid. This is insofar as the salary for my labor goes. But as for your promise that your grace made to give me the government of an *ínsula*, it would be proper to add six more *reales*, and that would bring the total to thirty."

"That's fine," replied don Quixote, "and in accordance with the salary that you've calculated, it's been twenty-five days since we left our town. Figure out how much I owe you prorated and pay yourself, as I've said, with your own hand."

"Oh, good God!" said Sancho. "You're very mistaken in your numbers, because insofar as the promise of the *ínsula* goes, you have to count from the day you promised it to me up to the present moment."

"So, how long has it been since I promised it to you?" said don Quixote.

"If I remember correctly," responded Sancho, "it must have been more than twenty years—three days more or less."

Don Quixote gave himself a slap on the forehead and began to laugh heartily and said: "But I didn't go to the Sierra Morena—indeed I didn't begin any of my adventures at all—until just two months ago. And you say, Sancho, that I promised the *ínsula* to you twenty years ago? I say that you want to take all my money that you have, and if that's so and that's your pleasure, I give it all to you right now—and may it do you good—because in exchange for seeing myself without such a bad squire, I'll be pleased to become poor and without a penny. But tell me, you corruptor of all squirely laws of knight-errantry, where have you ever seen or read that any squire of a knight-errant has bargained with his master for 'you'll give me so much every month so that I'll serve you'? Go, go, you brigand, you rogue, you monster—for you seem to be all three—set sail, I say, into the *mare magnum** of their histories, and if you find that some squire has said or thought what you've said, I'd like you to nail it to my forehead, and you can give me four slaps on the face to boot. Turn your reins on the donkey and go back home, because you won't go one step farther with me. Oh, ungrateful person! Oh, promises ill placed! Oh, man more beast than human! You're leaving just when I was getting ready to set you up, and in such a way that in spite

---

* "Great sea," in Latin.

of your wife they would call you LORDSHIP? You're quitting now, when I had the firm and worthy intention of making you the lord of the best *ínsula* in the world? As you've said many times, 'honey wasn't meant, etc.'* A donkey you are and a donkey you'll remain, and a donkey you'll be when the course of your life ends, since I maintain that it'll come to an end before you realize you're a beast."

Sancho looked steadily at don Quixote while he was saying those reproaches, and he was pierced with remorse and tears came to his eyes. With a doleful and feeble voice he said: "*Señor mío,* I confess that the only thing I lack to turn me into a donkey is a tail. If your grace wants to put one on me, I'll accept it and will serve you as a beast of burden for the remaining days of my life. Pardon me, and take pity on my inexperience, and be aware that I don't know very much, and if I talk a lot, it comes more from weakness than from malice. But 'he who errs and mends, to God himself commends.'"

"I would be surprised, Sancho, if you didn't mix a proverb into your speech. All right, I forgive you provided that you do mend your ways and from now on show yourself less interested in money, and that you try to open your heart a bit and take hope in waiting for my promise to be fulfilled, for even though it may be late, it isn't impossible."

Sancho responded that he would, although he'd have to draw strength from weakness. With this, they went into the poplar grove, and don Quixote made himself comfortable at the foot of an elm tree and Sancho at a beech, for these and similar trees always have feet but not hands. Sancho spent the night in pain because the effects of the beating were more acute in the night air. Don Quixote spent the night with a succession of memories, but even so did finally sleep, and at dawn they continued their journey looking for the banks of the famous Ebro, where what happened to them will be told in the next chapter.

---

* The only time we witness Sancho saying, "Honey wasn't meant for the mouths of donkeys," is to his wife in Part I, chapter fifty-two. This does not preclude other times, of course, that have not been recorded. But even though don Quixote didn't say the remainder of the proverb, he is reminded of *donkey*, and that's why that word begins the next phrase.

Chapter XXIX. About the famous adventure of the Enchanted Boat.

Two DAYS after leaving the poplar grove, don Quixote and Sancho came upon the Ebro River, and seeing it gave great delight to don Quixote, because he could see in it the pleasantness of its banks, the clarity of its waters, the calmness of its current, and the abundance of its liquid crystal. This refreshing sight caused a thousand amorous thoughts to course through his memory. He especially thought about what he'd seen in the Cave of Montesinos, and although *maese* Pedro's monkey had told him that part was fact and part fiction, he thought more was true than false, quite the reverse of what Sancho thought, for he held that everything was lies, and nothing but.

As they continued along in this way, there came into view a small boat without oars or any other rigging, tied to the trunk of a tree near the bank. Don Quixote looked all around and saw no one, and then just like that, he got off Rocinante and told Sancho to get off the donkey as well, and secure both animals to a poplar or a willow that was nearby. Sancho asked the reason for dismounting and having the animals tied up so suddenly.

Don Quixote responded: "I'll have you know, Sancho, that this boat you see right here is enchanted—it can't be anything else—and is beckoning and inviting me to board it and rescue some knight or some other noble person who must be in great danger, because this is what happens in books that deal with histories of knights and of enchanters who act and perform their dark arts. When some knight is in great difficulty, and he cannot be helped except by another certain knight, even though they're separated by two or three thousand leagues, or even farther, either the knight is carried off on a cloud, or is given a boat to get into, and in the twinkling of an eye he's taken—either through the air or on the sea—wherever his help is needed. So, Sancho, this boat has been put here for the same effect, and this is as true as it's day right now, and before this day is over, tie the donkey and Rocinante together, and let the hand of God guide us, for I must sail away, even if barefoot friars asked me not to."

"All right," responded Sancho, "and since your grace wants to give in to these things, which I don't know if I should call nonsense, I guess I just have to obey and lower my head, heeding the saying: 'do what your master tells you to and sit with him at his table.' But just so I can unburden my conscience, I want to tell your grace that to me, it doesn't look like this boat is enchanted, but rather belongs to some fishermen who work this river, because in it you catch the best shad in the world."

Sancho said this while he tethered the animals, leaving them to the protection of the enchanters, with a great grief in his soul. Don Quixote told him not to worry about abandoning the animals, because the one who would take them to such *longinquous* regions would make sure they were taken care of as well.

"I don't understand this business of *logicual*," said Sancho, "and I've never heard that word in all my life."

"*Longinquous*," responded don Quixote, "means *remote*, and I'm not surprised you don't understand it because you aren't supposed to know Latin, as some who think they do, but don't."

"Well, they're tied up," replied Sancho. "What do we have to do now?"

"What do we have to do?" responded don Quixote. "Just cross ourselves and weigh anchor—I mean, get on board and cut the rope that's securing this boat."

And jumping into it, followed by Sancho, don Quixote cut the line and the boat began to drift away slowly from the bank, and when Sancho saw that the boat had gone about six feet into the river, he began to tremble, fearing for his life. But nothing gave him more grief than to hear his donkey bray and to see Rocinante struggling to get loose, and he said to his master: "The donkey is braying, grieving over our absence, and Rocinante is trying to get free to jump in after us. Dear friends, stay there in peace, and may the madness that takes us away from you change to sanity and allow us to return to your presence."

And then he began to cry so bitterly that don Quixote, annoyed and angry, said to him: "What are you afraid of, cowardly creature? What are you crying about, heart of butter? Who is pursuing or harassing you, you who have the courage of a mouse? Or what do you lack—you think you're needy while you're amidst abundance? By chance are you shoeless and on foot in the Rhiphæian Mountains,* and not sitting on a bench like an archduke, floating along the silent current of this delightful river, where in a short time we'll flow into the vast sea? But by now we must have gone out into it and traveled at least seven or eight hundred leagues; and if I had an astrolabe† with which to tell the longitude, I would tell you how far we've traveled, although either I know little or we have crossed or are about to cross the equator that divides the two opposite poles into equal halves."

"And when we arrive at the quaker your grace has mentioned," asked Sancho, "how far will we have gone?"

"Quite a distance," replied don Quixote, "because of the three hundred sixty degrees that the globe of water and earth encompasses, according to the computation of Ptolemy,‡ who was the best cosmographer ever known, we will have traveled half of it when we arrive at the line I mentioned."

"God help us," said Sancho, "your grace has brought in an odd witness to what you're saying, what with the amputation of Tully-Me who was a good cause-monger. What does that mean?"

Don Quixote laughed heartily at the way Sancho interpreted COMPUTATION, PTOLEMY, and COSMOGRAPHER, and said to him: "You know, Sancho, that when Spaniards embark for the East Indies from Cádiz,§ one of the ways they can tell that they have passed the equator that I've told you about is that all the lice on the sailors die, without a single one surviving, and you can't find a one of them on board, even if they'd pay for them in gold. So, Sancho, you can

---

* Refers to the Rhiphæi Montes, as the ancients called them, at the headwaters of the Tanais River (now the Don, which flows through southern Russia). This area is just south of Moscow, now known as the Central Russian Upland.

† The astrolabe was a very old navigational instrument, dating from the second century A.D., which was used to tell sailors their latitude, distance, and the time of day. It was replaced by the more accurate sextant.

‡ Ptolemy (fl. A.D. 127–145) considered that the earth was the center of the universe.

§ Cádiz is Spain's most important Atlantic port city.

slide your hand over your thigh, and if you find any living thing, we'll have no further doubt, and if not, we'll have passed the equator."

"I don't believe any of that," responded Sancho, "but I'll do what your grace asks me to do, although I don't know why we need to do those experiments, since I can see with my eyes that we're not yet fifteen feet from the bank, nor have we gone too far from the animals, because there are Rocinante and the donkey in the same place we left them, and looking around me, I swear that we're not moving faster than an ant."

"Do the demonstration I told you to do and don't worry about anything else, because you don't know what colures, lines, parallels, zodiac signs, ecliptics, poles, solstices, equinoxes, planets, astrological signs, points of the compass, and measurements are, of which the celestial sphere and the terrestrial sphere are composed.* If you knew all these things, or even some of them, you would see clearly which parallels we have crossed, or which signs of the zodiac we've left behind, and which we're crossing right now. So, I say once again that you should do that search. As for me, I'm convinced that you're cleaner than a smooth sheet of white paper."

Sancho slid his hand neatly toward his left knee, then raised his head and looked at his master and said: "Either the test doesn't work, or we haven't gotten to the place your grace has mentioned, not by a long shot."

"What?" asked don Quixote. "Have you come across something?"

"Several somethings," responded Sancho.

And shaking his fingers, he rinsed his whole hand in the river, along which the boat was gently drifting in the middle

---

* Don Quixote is referring to pre-Copernican astronomical terms. People had thought that the sky was a celestial sphere, like the inside of a basketball, with the earth in the middle. Colures are the equinoctial and solstitial lines of the celestial sphere, intersecting at the poles. The ecliptic is the projection on the celestial sphere of the orbit of the Earth around the Sun, and the constellations of the zodiac are arranged along this ecliptic. When Copernicus (1473–1543, born and died in Poland) revolutionized astronomy, most of these terms were no longer useful.

of the stream, and it wasn't some unknown power or some hidden enchanter guiding it, but rather the current of the water, which was still calm and smooth.

Just then they saw some large water mills in the middle of the river, and as soon as don Quixote saw them, he shouted to Sancho: "Don't you see over there, my friend, a city, castle, or fort where there must be some oppressed knight or some queen or wronged princess, for whose assistance I've been summoned?"

"What the devil kind of city, fort, or castle are you talking about, *señor*?" said Sancho. "Can't you see that they're water mills in the river, where flour is milled?"*

"Hush, Sancho," said don Quixote. "Although they appear to be water mills, they are *not*, and I've told you that enchantments change things from their natural state. I don't mean that the enchanters really change the form of things, but rather it just looks that way, as experience has shown in the transformation of Dulcinea, the sole refuge of my hope."

At this point the boat, having gone into the middle of the river's current, began to travel less slowly. Some millers in the water mills, who saw the boat coming toward them down the river, realized that it was going to enter into the millrace leading to the waterwheels, and jumped out with poles to prevent it, and since their faces and clothing were covered with flour, they were a menacing sight. They shouted loudly: "You devils! Where are you going? Are you depressed and want to kill yourselves and be crushed to pieces by these waterwheels?"

"Didn't I tell you, Sancho," said don Quixote, "that we have come to a place where I must show the strength of my arm? Look at how those brigands and rogues have come to attack us. Look how many monsters are against me. Look at the ugly grimaces they're making at us. Well, now you'll see, you scoundrels!"

He stood up in the boat and with a very loud voice began to threaten the millers, saying: "Evil and ill-advised rabble, set the oppressed person free that you're keeping in this fort or prison, whether he be noble or plebeian, of whatever condition or station in life. I'm don Quixote de

---

* Since the current is strongest in the middle of a river, these floating mills were anchored there to make the milling of flour more efficient.

La Mancha, also called the Knight of the Lions, for whom the happy conclusion of this adventure is reserved."

And saying this, he clapped his hand on his sword and began to brandish it in the air toward the millers, who, hearing but not understanding his foolish banter, tended to the business of stopping the boat with their poles, so it wouldn't go into the torrent of the channel leading to the mill wheels. Sancho got on his knees and was praying devoutly to heaven to free him from such imminent danger. The millers, with great skill and speed, pushed against the boat with their poles and stopped it, but not without turning it over and causing don Quixote and Sancho to be thrown overboard into the water. It came out all right for don Quixote, who knew how to swim like a goose, although the weight of the armor he was wearing took him to the bottom twice, and if it weren't for the millers, who plunged in after them and took them out as deadweight, it would have been another Troy* for the two of them.

When they were onshore, more drenched than dying of thirst, Sancho, once again on his knees and his hands joined in prayer, asked God, through a long and devout supplication, to free him starting right then from the daring plans and assaults of his master. At this point arrived the fishermen, owners of the boat that the waterwheels had smashed to bits, and when they saw it in pieces, they attacked Sancho, tearing at his clothes, and demanded payment from don Quixote, who, with great calmness, as if nothing had happened to him, told the millers and fishermen that he would pay for the boat very willingly, provided that they set free the person or persons who were languishing in that castle.

"What person or castle are you talking about, you crazy man?" replied one of the millers. "Do you want to carry off the people who bring wheat to grind in these mills?"

"That's enough," said don Quixote to himself. "It would be like preaching in the wilderness to persuade this rabble to do anything good. In this adventure there must have been two fierce enchanters—one of them prevents what the other attempts. One of them presented me with the boat and the other threw me overboard. May God provide

---

* From Virgil's *Æneid*; "Troy" symbolizes disaster.

the remedy, for the world is filled with plots and tricks, all contrary to each other. I can't do any more."

And raising his voice, looking toward the mills, he continued: "Friends, whoever you may be who remain locked up in that prison, pardon me, for by my misfortune and yours, I cannot remove you from your afflictions. This adventure is doubtless reserved for some other knight."

After he said this, the fishermen and he came to an agreement on the price, and don Quixote paid fifty *reales* for the boat, which Sancho disbursed much against his will, saying: "Two more boat trips like this one, and all our wealth will have sunk to the bottom."

The fisherman and millers were amazed at those two figures, so uncommon and different from other men. They never did understand where don Quixote's words and questions were leading, and considering the two of them to be crazy, they left them; the millers went back to their mills and the fishermen to their huts. Don Quixote and Sancho returned to their animals, and this was the end of the adventure of the enchanted boat.

Chapter XXX. About what happened to don Quixote with a beautiful huntress.

THE KNIGHT and his squire were of downcast spirits when they got to their mounts, especially Sancho, for when something touched his money, it also touched his soul, since it seemed to him that everything taken from his supply of money was the same as taking away his very eyes. So, without saying a word, they mounted their animals and went away from the famous river, don Quixote buried in thoughts of love and Sancho in his advancement, which just then seemed far from attainable, because, although he was unlettered, he realized that all or most of the actions of his master were foolhardy, and he was hoping to find an occasion whereby, without explanations or farewells to his master, he might one day escape and go home. But Fortune ordered it so things turned out quite the reverse of what he feared.

It happened, then, the next day at sunset, when they were

emerging from a forest, don Quixote looked out onto a green meadow, and at the far side of it he saw some people, and as he approached he realized that they were hunting with falcons. As he drew even closer, he saw among them a handsome woman riding a snow-white palfrey or hackney, caparisoned with green decorations and a sidesaddle made of silver. The woman was also dressed in green, and so beautifully and richly that elegance itself was personified in her. On her left hand she held a falcon, which meant to don Quixote that she must be a great lady and the mistress of all the hunters (as was the truth), and so he said to Sancho: "Go, my son, and tell that lady with the falcon on the palfrey that I, the Knight of the Lions, kiss her grace's hands and that if Her Highness grants me permission I'll kiss them in person and will serve her to the best of my ability, and for as long as she commands me to do so. Watch, Sancho, how you speak, and be careful not to insert any of your proverbs in your message."

"Would I go inserting proverbs?" responded Sancho. "Honestly! As if this were the first time I've taken messages to noble and important ladies in this life."

"Except for the one you took to señora Dulcinea," replied don Quixote, "I'm not aware that you've taken another, at least while you've been working for me."

"That's the truth," responded Sancho, "but 'a trustworthy payer doesn't mind leaving security' and 'in a well-provisioned house, dinner is soon served.' What I mean is that you don't have to tell me anything or give me admonitions. I know a bit about everything and am ready for whatever happens."

"And I believe it, Sancho," said don Quixote, "so go, good luck, and may God guide you."

Sancho rode away at top speed, going faster than usual on his donkey, and went to where the beautiful huntress was. He got off his donkey and knelt before her, saying: "Beautiful lady, that knight over there, called the Knight of the Lions, is my master, and I'm a squire of his, who they call Sancho Panza at home. This Knight of the Lions, who not long ago was called the Woebegone Knight, sends me to ask Your Highness to be pleased to give him your consent, permission, and blessing, to put his desire into effect, which is none other—the way he says and I think—than to serve Your lofty Highness and beauty. With this permission you will be doing something that will redound to your benefit, and he'll consider it a great favor and a source of great satisfaction."

"Good squire," responded the lady, "you've certainly given your message with all the details required for such missions. Get up from the ground, for a squire of such a great knight as is the Woebegone Knight, about whom we have heard quite a bit, shouldn't be on his knees. Arise, my friend, and tell your master to come and be the guest of myself and of the duke, my husband, in a country home we have nearby."

Sancho got up, astonished by the beauty, courtesy, and quality of the woman, and more so by what she said about having heard of his master, the Woebegone Knight; and if she didn't call him the Knight of the Lions, it must be because it was such a newly acquired name. The duchess—whose domain was never learned—asked him: "Tell me, brother squire, this master of yours, isn't he the one circulating in a history called *The Ingenious* Hidalgo *don Quixote de La Mancha*, who has for his lady a certain Dulcinea del Toboso?"

"The very same, *señora*, and that squire of his who appears, or should appear in the same history, who they call Sancho Panza, is me, unless they changed me in the cradle— I mean, unless they changed me in the print shop."

"I'm very pleased about all of this," said the duchess. "Go, brother Panza, and tell your master that he's welcome at my estate, and that nothing would make me happier."

Sancho, with this most gratifying response, and with greatest pleasure, went back to his master, to whom he told what the great lady had said to him, praising to the skies in his rustic terms her great beauty, charm, and courtesy. Don Quixote straightened up in his saddle. He firmed himself in his stirrups, adjusted his visor, put the spurs to Rocinante, and with a gallant mien went to kiss the hands of the duchess, who, having sent for the duke, her husband, told him while don Quixote was approaching all about his message. The two of them waited for him—since they had read the first part of his history and through it knew about don Quixote's absurd behavior—with greatest pleasure, and eager to meet him, having decided to humor him and go along with whatever he might say, treating him like a knight-errant during the days he might stay with them, with all the usual ceremonies that they had read about in the books of chivalry, of which they were still quite fond.

Don Quixote arrived just then with his visor raised, and made to dismount. Sancho was about to go over and hold his stirrup but his luck was so bad that when he went to get off his donkey, his foot got caught in a rope of the pack-saddle in such a way that he couldn't get it free, and found himself hanging with his chest and face on the ground. Don Quixote, who was not accustomed to dismounting without his stirrup being held, and thinking that Sancho had come over to hold it for him, got off all at once, and took Rocinante's saddle (which must have been loose) with him, and both he and the saddle fell to the ground, with no little embarrassment on his part, and many curses directed under his breath to Sancho, whose foot was still trapped.

The duke told his hunters to help the knight and his squire. They picked up the bruised don Quixote from his fall, and he went limping over as well as he could and knelt before the two people. But the duke wouldn't allow it. Rather, getting off his horse, he went over to embrace don Quixote, saying to him: "I'm sorry, *señor* Woebegone Knight, that the first thing that happened to you on my estate has turned out as unfortunately as this. But carelessness on the part of squires sometimes results in even worse things happening."

"My luck in meeting you, worthy prince," responded don Quixote, "cannot be bad, even if my fall had taken me to the depths of the abyss, since the glory of having seen you would have lifted me up and taken me out. My squire—may God damn him!—is much better at loosening his tongue to say mischievous things than tying and cinching a saddle so it'll stay up. But no matter how I find myself, fallen or standing up, on foot or on horseback, I'll always be at your service, and that of my lady, your worthy companion, mistress of beauty, and universal princess of courtesy."

"Careful, *señor* don Quixote de La Mancha," said the duke, "for where my lady Dulcinea del Toboso is, it's not right to praise other beauties."

By this time, Sancho Panza was free from the rope, and since he was nearby, before his master could respond, he said: "You cannot deny, but rather confirm, that my lady

Dulcinea del Toboso is very pretty. But 'when least you expect it the hare leaps up' and I've heard that this thing they call nature is like a potter who makes vessels from clay; if she can make one, she can make two, three, even a hundred. I say it because I swear my lady the duchess isn't at all behind my lady Dulcinea del Toboso."

Don Quixote turned toward the duchess and said: "Your Highness should imagine that no knight-errant in the world has ever had such a talkative nor a more amusing squire as the one I have, and he'll prove me right if your great loftiness would accept my service for a few days."

To which the duchess responded: "Because the good Sancho is amusing, I hold him in higher esteem, since that means he's quick-witted. Wit, *señor* don Quixote, as you know, isn't found in dunces, and since he's witty, from now on I'll hold him as quick-witted."

"And talkative," added don Quixote.

"So much the better," said the duke, "because many clever things cannot be said with few words; and not to waste time with words, so let the great Woebegone Knight come along with us."

"'Of the Lions,' Your Highness should say," said Sancho, "for there's no more 'Woebegone,' just 'He of the Lions.' "

The duke went on: "So I say, let the Knight of the Lions come to a castle of mine near here, where he'll be received as the noble person he is, and in the same way the duchess and I typically receive all knights-errant who go there."

By this time Sancho had adjusted and tightened the saddle well on Rocinante, and once don Quixote had mounted him, and the duke his own beautiful steed, they placed the duchess between them and rode toward the castle. The duchess had Sancho ride next to her because she enjoyed his witticisms immensely. Sancho needed no further urging, and inserted himself among the three, and the four of them engaged in conversation, to the great pleasure of the duchess and duke, who considered themselves very lucky to receive in their castle such a knight and such a squire.

Chapter XXXI. Which deals with many and great things.

Sancho was extremely happy seeing himself seemingly in the duchess' favor, because it appeared to him that he would find in her castle what he'd found in the houses of don Diego and Basilio, ever a friend of the good life, and so he took opportunity by the forelock* whenever good hospitality was offered.

The history relates, then, that before they arrived at the country house or castle, the duke went on ahead and told all his servants how they were to treat don Quixote. As soon as he arrived with the duchess to the portals of the castle, two grooms or stableboys, dressed from head to foot in what they call house robes, made of exquisite crimson satin, hurried over and took don Quixote's arm, and quietly said to him: "Your greatness, go over and help my lady the duchess dismount."

Don Quixote went over, and there was a long exchange of polite remarks between them about what should be done, but the duchess prevailed, and refused to get off her palfrey except in the arms of the duke, saying that such a useless weight was not worthy of such a great knight. The duke then came over to help her down, and when they went into a large patio, two beautiful maidens came and placed a cloak of very fine scarlet cloth over don Quixote's shoulders, and instantly the galleries of the patio were crowded with servants of the duke and duchess, both male and female, shouting: "Hail to the flower and cream of knights-errant!"

And almost everyone began sprinkling sweet-smelling water from vials onto don Quixote and the duke and duchess, which amazed don Quixote. That was the first day that he thought and believed himself to be a true knight-errant

---

* The Roman god of opportunity, Cærus, was bald except for a lock of hair in the middle of his forehead. When you saw opportunity coming, you had to grab him by the forelock before he went by; otherwise it was too late. The same opportunity was more or less mentioned in the Prefatory Verses to Part I, in the sonnet of Belianís dedicated to don Quixote.

and not a make-believe one, seeing himself being treated in the same way he'd read that knights-errant wère treated in earlier ages.

Sancho, having left his donkey outside, had latched onto the duchess and gone into the castle, but since his conscience caused him some remorse for leaving the donkey all alone, he approached a reverend duenna, and said to her very quietly: "Señora González, or whatever your grace's name is . . ."*

"Doña Rodríguez de Grijalba† is my name," responded the duenna. "What do you want, brother?"

To which Sancho responded: "I would like your grace to do me the favor of going out of the gates of the castle, where you'll find a gray donkey of mine. Would your grace please have him put, or put him yourself, in the stable, because the poor thing is a bit timid, and he can't stand being left alone."

"If the master is as sharp as the servant," responded the duenna, "we're in trouble. You go yourself, brother, and bad luck not only to you but also to the man who brought you here—take care of your donkey yourself, because duennas in this house don't do those things."

"In truth," responded Sancho, "I've heard my master, who is quite knowledgeable about history, tell about Lancelot:

When from Britain he came
ladies took care of him
and duennas took care of his horse,‡

and as for my donkey, I wouldn't trade him even for *señor* Lancelot's horse."

---

* Walter Starkie points out that Sancho's calling her by this name is far from arbitrary, since duennas were often given thc name González and pages, Álvarez.

† Grijalba is a very small town in the province of Burgos. A recent census showed it with 158 inhabitants.

‡ Sancho never heard don Quixote say this in the narrative. In Part I, chapter two, don Quixote recited a variant, but this was before Sancho was in the picture. In any case, the typical version was: "duennas took care of him / maidens took care of his horse . . ."

"Brother, if you're a troubadour," replied the duenna, "keep your songs for when they're appropriate and you'll get paid for them, because from me you'll only get a fig."*

"It would be a ripe one," responded Sancho, "and where years count, you won't lose the game by a point too few."

"Whoreson!" said the duenna, burning with rage. "If I'm old or not, I'll give an accounting only to God, and not to you, you garlic-stuffed knave."

And she shouted this so loudly that the duchess heard her and, turning around to see the duenna so worked up and with her eyes flashing, asked why she was quarreling.

"I'm quarreling," responded the duenna, "with this good fellow who has so courteously asked me to put a donkey of his at the gate of the castle into the stable, giving as an example that some ladies from I-don't-know-where took care of a certain Lancelot, and duennas looked after his horse—and he wound up by calling me old."

"I'd be more insulted by that," said the duchess, "than anything else that could be said to me."

And turning to Sancho she said: "You should be aware, Sancho, my friend, that doña Rodríguez is quite young, and she wears that hood more to show her position, and more because it's a custom, than because of her age."

"May the remaining years of my life be bad," responded Sancho, "if I meant it as an insult. I only said it because of the great affection I have for my donkey, and it seemed to me that I could do no better than to put him in the charge of a person as charitable as doña Rodríguez."

Don Quixote heard everything and said to him: "Is this type of conversation appropriate for a place such as this?"

"*Señor*," responded Sancho, "everybody has to talk of his needs wherever he happens to be. I remembered the donkey right here, and right here I spoke about him. If I had remembered in the stable, I would have spoken about him there."

To which the duke answered: "Sancho is very right and we can't fault him for anything. We'll give the donkey all the feed he wants, and Sancho need not worry, for we'll treat the donkey as well as we'll treat him."

---

* The "fig" is a vulgar sign made with the fist, where the thumb is inserted between the index and middle fingers.

With these words, savored by all except don Quixote, they arrived at the top of the stairs, and escorted don Quixote into a room lined with rich brocaded material with gold strands. Six maidens removed his armor and served him as pages, all of them instructed and forewarned by the duke and duchess about what they had to do and how they were to treat don Quixote, so he might think and see they were treating him like a knight-errant. After they had removed his armor, don Quixote was dressed in his tight breeches and chamois doublet; he was withered, lank, and long, with cheeks that kissed each other on the inside, a figure at which—if the maidens hadn't known they should hide their amusement (which was one of the strict orders their masters had given them)—they would have burst out laughing.

They asked him if he would let them undress him so he could put on a shirt, but he wouldn't consent, saying that modesty became knights-errant as much as courage.

So, he asked them to give the shirt to Sancho, and shutting himself up in a room where there was a richly decorated bed, he stripped and put on the shirt, and seeing himself alone with Sancho, said to him: "Tell me, you modern scoundrel and old-fashioned blockhead, did it seem like a good thing to you to offend such a venerable duenna so worthy of respect as that one is? Was it the right moment to remember your donkey? Or are these people who will let an animal be mistreated when they entertain their owners so elegantly? In the name of God, Sancho, restrain yourself, and don't show your true character so they'll see that you're woven of coarse country stuff. Look, you sinner, a master is held in greater respect the more he has honored and well-mannered servants, and one of the advantages that princes have over other men is that they have servants who are as good as they are. Don't you know— you who are as wretched as I am unfortunate—if they see that you're a coarse bumpkin or an amusing idiot, they'll think that I'm some charlatan or some fraudulent knight? No, no, Sancho, my friend. Flee, flee from these obstacles, for once you stumble into being a chatterbox and a jester, when you trip the first time, you'll turn into a most unfortunate buffoon. Bridle your tongue, and consider and meditate on each word that leaves your mouth, and be aware that we're now in a place where, with the help of God and by the strength of my arm, we will leave greatly enriched in fame and fortune."

Sancho promised him most earnestly that he would stitch his mouth closed or bite his tongue before he'd say a word that wasn't pertinent and well thought-out, as he was commanded, and that don Quixote shouldn't worry about it any further. Through his behavior it would never be known who they were.

Don Quixote got dressed and put on his sword, threw the scarlet cloak on his back and put a cap of green satin— which the maidens had given him—on his head, and in this outfit he went into the great hall, where he found the maidens arranged in two equal outstretched lines, all with vessels with which to wash his hands, which they did with proper respect and ceremony. Then came twelve pages with the steward, to escort him to dine, for his hosts were waiting for him. They put him in the middle, and with full pomp and majesty took him into the next room, where there was a rich table set only for four. The duchess and duke went to the door to receive him, and with them there was a solemn ecclesiastic of the kind that rules the houses of princes—of those who, since they weren't born princes, don't succeed in instructing those who are in how to behave; of those who want the greatness of the great to be measured against the pettiness of their spirits; of those who, trying to teach those they govern how to be thrifty, succeed only in making them miserable; of those, I say, that the solemn ecclesiastic who went with the duke and duchess to receive don Quixote must have been. They said a thousand courteous things and finally, surrounding don Quixote, they went in to sit at the table.

The duke invited don Quixote to sit at the head of the table, and although he refused, the insistent requests by the duke were so many that he finally relented. The ecclesiastic sat opposite him, and the duke and duchess were at either side. Sancho witnessed all this and was amazed and, dumbfounded seeing the honor those noble people had shown his master and noting the great respect shown and entreaties that passed between the duke and don Quixote to invite him to sit at the head of the table, said: "If your graces will allow me, I'll tell a little story about something that happened in my village, about the matter of seating."

Scarcely had Sancho said this when don Quixote began to tremble, believing without any doubt that he was about to say something foolish. Sancho looked at him and understood what he was thinking, and said: "Don't worry, your grace, *señor mío*, that I'll behave poorly or that I'll say something that isn't pertinent. I haven't forgotten the advice your grace gave me a little while ago about speaking a lot or a little, or well or badly."

"I don't remember anything of the kind, Sancho," responded don Quixote. "Say whatever you want, as long as you don't take too long."

"Well, what I have to say is very true," said Sancho, "and my master don Quixote, who is here, won't let me lie."

"As far as I'm concerned," replied don Quixote, "you can lie, Sancho, as much as you want and I won't stop you. But be careful in what you say."

"I'll be really careful, and 'he who sounds the alarm is safe,' as you'll soon see."

"It'd be a good idea," said don Quixote, "for Your Highnesses to have this idiot ejected from here, because he's going to say a thousand stupid things."

"On the life of the duke," said the duchess, "Sancho won't leave my side one single bit. I like him very much because I know he's wise."

"May your holiness live wise days," said Sancho, "for the confidence you have in me, even though I don't deserve it. And the story that I want to tell you goes like this: An *hidalgo* in my town, who was very rich and from the upper class, since he came from the Álamos of Medina del Campo,* who married doña Mancía de Quiñones, the daughter of Alonso de Marañón, a knight of the Order of Santiago who drowned in the battle of Herradura,† about whom there was that dispute in our town years ago, which I understand my master don Quixote had something to do with, and from which that mischievous Tomasillo, the son

---

* Medina del Campo (current population approximately 20,000) is about 105 miles northwest of Madrid and was an important commercial and economic center in Cervantes' time.
† This refers to the loss of twenty-two galleys, which took the lives of four thousand men due to a storm near Herradura (a port on the southern coast of Spain), in 1562.

of Balbastro the blacksmith, wound up wounded.... Isn't all of this true, *señor* master? Say it's so, as you live, so that these people won't take me for a talkative liar."

"Up to now," said the ecclesiastic, "I think you're more talkative than a liar, but from now on I don't know what I'll think of you."

"You've cited so many witnesses, Sancho, and given so much proof, that I have to agree you must be telling the truth. Go on, and shorten your story, because you're carrying on so much, you won't finish in two days."

"He is not to shorten it," said the duchess, "to please me. Rather he should tell it the way he knows it even though it takes him six days to finish. If it takes that long, those will be the best days of my life."

"So, I say, *señores míos*," Sancho went on, "that this *hidalgo*, who I know like the back of my hand, because his house isn't a bow shot from mine, invited a poor but honorable peasant ..."

"Move along, brother," said the religious man at that point, "because the way you're going, you won't finish until we get to the other world."

"I'll stop less than halfway there, if it pleases God," responded Sancho, "and, I say, when the peasant got to the house of the *hidalgo* I mentioned who invited him, and may his soul rest in peace because he's dead now, and the way they tell it, he had the death of an angel. I wasn't there since I had to do some harvesting at Tembleque ..."*

"For the love of Mike, son, come back soon from Tembleque, and without burying the *hidalgo*, if you don't want to bore us to death, and finish your story."

"So, what happened," replied Sancho, "is that just as the two of them were getting ready to sit down—and it's as if I can see them now ..."

The duke and duchess were really amused at the religious man's vexation over the length of and pauses in Sancho's story, and at how don Quixote was quite consumed with anger and rage.

"So, as I was saying," said Sancho, "when the two of them were about to sit down, the peasant begged the *hidalgo* to

---

* Tembleque (population 2,000) is a farming and cattle-raising community about sixty miles south of Madrid.

sit at the head of the table and the *hidalgo* begged the peasant to sit at the head of the table, because in his house you
were supposed to do what he asked. But the peasant, who
considered himself very courteous and well-bred, refused
until the *hidalgo*, who was quite annoyed, putting his hands
on the other's shoulders, forced him to sit, saying: 'Sit down,
you stupid boor, for wherever I sit, it will be the head of
the table.' And that's the story, and in truth I think that it's
quite pertinent."

Don Quixote turned a thousand colors, and his tanned
skin looked quite mottled. The duke and duchess concealed
their laughter so that don Quixote wouldn't be totally
abashed, since they understood Sancho's mischievousness;
so to change the subject and prevent Sancho from continuing his foolishness, the duchess asked don Quixote what
news he had of *señora* Dulcinea, and if he'd sent her presents of giants or brigands in recent days, since he must have
conquered many of them.

To which don Quixote responded: "*Señora mía*, my misfortunes, although they had a beginning, will never have an
end. I've vanquished giants and I've sent her rogues and
brigands. But where will they find her, since she has been
enchanted and turned into the ugliest peasant girl you can
imagine?"

"I don't know," said Sancho, "because to me she appeared to be the most beautiful creature in the world. At
least, in her lightness of foot and in frisking about, a tum-
bler couldn't surpass her. I swear, *señora* duchess, she jumps
onto a she-ass as if she were a cat."

"And have you seen her in her enchanted form, Sancho?" asked the duke.

"What do you mean *have I seen her*?" responded Sancho. "Who the devil was it, if not me, who first thought of
this enchantment business? She's as enchanted as my father is."

The ecclesiastic, who heard all this about giants, rogues,
and enchantments, realized that this must be don Quixote
de La Mancha, from whose history the duke frequently
read, and he'd chastised him many times for it, saying that
it was foolish to read such nonsense. When he was sure that
what he suspected was true, he spoke to the duke and with
great anger said: "Your excellency, *señor mío*, will have to

account to our Lord about what this good fellow is doing. This don Quixote, or don Stupid, or whatever he's called, I imagine must not be as idiotic as your excellency thinks, since you're encouraging him to carry out his follies and nonsense." And turning his attention to don Quixote, he said: "And you, you numbskull, who put it in your brain that you're a knight-errant and that you conquer giants and take on brigands? Be on your way, and let me tell you: Go home and raise your children if you have any, and take care of your estate, and stop wandering through the world wasting time and being the laughingstock of all those who meet you and even those who don't. Where in heaven's name have you heard that there were or are now knights-errant? Where are there giants in Spain or brigands in La Mancha, or enchanted Dulcineas, or anything else from the pack of nonsense that they report about you?"

Don Quixote was quite attentive to the words of that venerable man, and seeing that he was now silent, without respecting the presence of the duke and duchess, with a furious expression of indignation on his face, he stood up and said . . . But his answer deserves a chapter to itself.

Chapter XXXII. About the response don Quixote gave his reprimander, with other grave and amusing events.

DON QUIXOTE stood up, trembling from head to foot, and said in a rapid-fire and irritated voice: "The place where I stand, in whose presence I find myself, and the respect I've always had and continue to have for your grace's profession hold and tie the hands of my just anger. So, because of what I've just said, and because everyone knows that the weapon of gown wearers* is the same as that of a woman, which is the tongue, that's what I'll use to enter into fair battle with your grace, from whom I should have expected good counsel instead of vile reproaches. Pious and good-intentioned reprimands require different circumstances and demand grounds other than these. The

---

* These are people such as academics and priests.

least thing I can say is that being rebuked in public, and so harshly, has gone beyond all limits of fair reprimand, since initial reproofs should be based on gentleness rather than on harshness, and it's certainly not a good idea for you, if you don't know what the sin in question is, to call the sinner an idiot and a fool.

"So, tell me, your grace, which idiotic acts have you seen me perform for which you condemn and censure me, and thus command me to return to my home and take care of it, and of my wife and children, without knowing if I have a wife or children? Do you simply have to enter willy-nilly into someone else's house and govern its masters; and after having been raised in the spartan fare of a university boardinghouse, without having seen more of the world than what is found within twenty or thirty leagues of the area, you would rashly dare to give laws to knighthood and judge knights-errant?

"Is it in fact a waste of time to wander through the world, not seeking its comfort, but rather the austerity through which good people rise to the seat of immortality? If knights, grandees, nobles, or honorable, magnanimous people thought I was a moron, it would be an irreparable affront. But if students who never entered into or traveled along the paths of knighthood think that I'm foolish, I couldn't care less. I'm a knight and I'll die a knight, if it pleases God.

"Some travel the broad field of arrogant ambition, others use base and groveling adulation, still others use deceitful hypocrisy, and others use the path of true religion. But I, led by my star, have taken the narrow path of knighthood, and in doing so I scorn wealth, but not honor. I've satisfied grievances, righted wrongs, punished impudence, conquered giants, and trampled monsters. I'm in love, only because it's required for knights-errant to be in love; and although I'm in love, I'm not one of those depraved lovers, but rather of the Platonic kind. My intentions are always directed toward meritorious ends, to do good to all and ill to none. If the person who understands this and labors toward these goals, if the person who does this deserves to be called a fool, let Your Highnesses, the duke and duchess, declare me to be one."

"That's good, by God," said Sancho. "Say no more on your behalf, your grace, *señor* and master of mine, because there's nothing more to say, to think about, or insist on. And what's more, since this man denies that there ever were or are now knights-errant, I'll bet he doesn't know what he's talking about."

"By chance, brother," said the ecclesiastic, "are you that Sancho Panza they talk about, to whom your master has promised an *ínsula*?"

"Yes, I am," responded Sancho, "and I deserve it as much as the next fellow. I'm one who says 'stay near the good folk and you'll be one of them' and of those who say 'not with whom you're bred but with whom you're fed' and of those that say 'he who leans against a good tree is protected by good shade.' I've been leaning against my master, and it's been many months I've been in his company, and I'm going to be just like him, God willing. And if he lives and if I live, there won't fail to be empires for him to rule, nor *ínsulas* for me to govern."

"Certainly not, Sancho, my friend," interrupted the duke, "because I, in the name of don Quixote, grant you the governorship of one I happen to have, and that's not of poor quality."

"Kneel down, Sancho," said don Quixote, "and kiss his excellency's feet for the favor he has done you."

Sancho obeyed, but the ecclesiastic stood up from the table inordinately angry, saying: "By the habit I wear, I'm tempted to say that your excellency is as foolish as these sinners. No wonder they're lunatics, if the sane bolster their lunacy. Your excellency can stay with them, and while they're in this house I'll be in mine, and I'll condemn no further something I cannot remedy."

And without saying another word, or eating anything else, he went out, despite the entreaties of the duke and duchess, although the duke couldn't say much due to the laughter that the cleric's high dudgeon had caused him. He finished laughing and said to don Quixote: "*Señor* Knight of the Lions has defended himself so well that there's no need for further action, for although it appears to be an insult, it really isn't, because just as women cannot insult anyone, ecclesiastics cannot either, as your grace well knows."

"That's true," responded don Quixote, "and the reason is that he who cannot be insulted cannot insult anyone else. Women, children, and ecclesiastics, since they cannot defend themselves, even though they may be *offended*, can't be *insulted*, because between an offense and an insult there's this difference, as your excellency knows. An insult comes from someone who can give it, and when he gives it he can maintain it. An offense can come from anywhere without any insult. Here's an example—a man is in the street minding his own business, and ten armed men come and beat him up. He grabs his sword and does what he has to. But his many opponents prevent him from achieving what he intends, which is to avenge himself. This man is offended but not insulted, and the same thing will be confirmed by another example. A man has his back turned and another one comes up and gives him a punch, then runs away, and the other runs after him but can't catch him. This man who was punched receives an offense but not an insult, because an insult has to be maintained. If the man who punched him, even if it was on the sly, should put his hand on his sword and stay there, the one punched would be insulted as well as offended—offended because he was punched treacherously, and insulted because his attacker maintained it and didn't run away. So, according to the laws of the cursèd duel, I consider myself offended but not insulted, because just as children don't insult, and women cannot either flee or stand their ground, the same thing with those ordained to our holy religion, because these three types of people lack offensive and defensive weapons, and so, although they're obliged by nature to defend themselves, they cannot insult anyone. A moment ago I said I might be offended—now I say not, in no way, because he who cannot receive any offense cannot give one. And for these reasons I shouldn't, and don't, resent what this good fellow has said. I only wish he'd stayed a bit longer so that I could make him see the error he committed in thinking and saying that there have never been knights-errant in the world. Why, if Amadís were to hear that, or any one of the infinite men of his lineage, I know it wouldn't go well with his grace."

"I can vouch for that," said Sancho. "They would have given him a slash that would have opened him up from top to bottom like a pomegranate or a very ripe cantaloupe. They wouldn't stand for such nonsense! By my faith, I'm positive that if Reinaldos de Montalbán had heard these words from this little fellow, he would have given him such

a punch in the mouth that he wouldn't have been able to
speak for three years. Let him take them on and he'll see he
won't escape from their hands!"

The duchess was dying of laughter hearing Sancho speak,
and in her opinion he was more amusing and crazier than
his master, and many at that time were of the same opinion. Finally, don Quixote calmed down and they finished
their dinner, and the tablecloth was taken away. Then four
maidens came, one of them with a silver basin, another with
a pitcher of water, the next one with two very white, thick
towels on her shoulder, and the fourth had her arms bared
to her elbows, and in her white hands—because certainly
they were white—a round cake of Neapolitan soap.* The
one carrying the basin approached, and with gentle grace
and much confidence placed the basin beneath don Quixote's beard. Astonished at such a ceremony, he supposed
it to be a custom in those parts to wash the beard instead
of the hands. So without saying anything he extended his
beard as far forward as he could, and at the same moment
the girl began to pour from the pitcher and the one with
the soap scrubbed his beard very vigorously, creating snowflakes (because the lather was no less white) not only on his
beard but all over the obedient knight's face and eyes, so
that he was forced to close his eyes tight.

The duke and duchess hadn't expected any of this and
were waiting to see how this extraordinary washing ceremony would end. The maiden in charge of the beard, when
she had his face covered with a very thick lather, pretended
that her water had run out and told the girl with the pitcher to
fetch some more. While she was doing that, don Quixote sat
there, the strangest and most laughable sight anyone could
imagine. All those present, and there were many, when they
saw his tanned stretched-out neck, more than half a yard
long, his eyes closed and his beard covered with soap, found
it very hard, and required immense self-control, to hide their
laughter. The girls who'd organized the prank kept their eyes
turned down and didn't dare look at their masters. The latter

---

* Neapolitan soap, says Rodríguez Marín, was really "homemade"
soap that the upper classes had made for them. The basis was Valencian soap, to which was added wheat bran, poppy juice, goat milk, deer
marrow, bitter almonds, and even sugar.

thought they should be angry and at the same time had to repress their laughter, and they didn't know what to do—to punish the boldness of the girls or reward them for the pleasure they got seeing don Quixote in that state.

Finally, the maiden with the pitcher came back and they finished washing don Quixote's beard; then the one with the towels wiped and dried him carefully, and then the four of them curtsied in an aristocratic way all together and were on their way out when the duke—so don Quixote wouldn't realize that it had been a jest—called the maiden with the basin and said to her: "Come here and wash my beard, too, and make sure you don't run out of water."

The girl, who was quick-witted and knew what to do, went over and put the basin under his beard as they had done with don Quixote, and the four of them washed and lathered him quickly, and leaving him clean and dried off, and curtsying once again, they went away. Afterward it was learned that the duke had sworn that if they hadn't washed him as they had done don Quixote, he would have punished their brazenness, which they cleverly avoided by washing his beard.

Sancho was a witness to this washing ritual and said to himself: "My God, I wonder if it's customary in this region to wash the beards of the squires of knights-errant, because God knows, and I know in my heart, that I have great need of it myself, and if they shaved it completely off, I would like it even better."

"What are you saying, Sancho?" asked the duchess.

"I'm saying, *señora*," he responded, "that in the courts of other princes I've always heard that when the tablecloths were taken away, water was brought out to wash one's hands, and not soap for one's beard. And for that reason, it's nice to live a long time to see many things, although they also say that 'the person who lives a long life undergoes much suffering,' but having one's beard washed seems more like a pleasure than pain."

"Don't worry, friend Sancho," said the duchess. "I'll have the maidens wash your beard, and even put *you* in the washtub, if need be."

"The beard will be enough," responded Sancho, "for now, at least; God has ordained what will take place with the passage of time."

"See to it, steward," said the duchess, "and do what the good Sancho asks to the letter."

The steward answered that *señor* Sancho would be attended to in everything, and with this he went off to eat and took Sancho with him, leaving the duke, duchess, and don Quixote at the table, talking about many different things, but all dealing with the practice of arms and of knight-errantry. The duchess begged don Quixote to outline and describe— since he seemed to have happy memories—the beauty and features of the lady Dulcinea del Toboso, who, according to the fame circulating about her beauty, must be the most beautiful creature in the world, and even in all of La Mancha.

Don Quixote sighed at what the duchess asked him to do and said: "If I could only pluck my heart out and place it here on a plate on this table in front of your greatness, it would spare my tongue the travail of having to say what can hardly be imagined, because your excellency would be able to see her in all of her beauty. But why should I try to outline and describe her beauty feature by feature and part by part, since it would be a task worthy of shoulders other than my own, work that should be done by the brushes of Parahassius, Timanthes, Apelles; the chisels of Lysippus* to paint and carve her on tablets, marble, and bronze; and Ciceronian and Demosthenian† rhetoric to praise her?"

"What does *Demosthenian* refer to, *señor* don Quixote?" asked the duchess. "It's a word that I've never heard in all my life."

---

* These are three ancient Greek painters and a sculptor. Parrhasius worked in the fifth century B.C. in Athens. None of his works or copies of them survives. Timanthes was a painter of human passions, born around 400 B.C. Apelles (fl. fourth century B.C.) was a painter whose work was held in such high esteem that he continues to be regarded, even though none of his works have survived, as the greatest painter of antiquity. Lysippus (fl. fourth century B.C.) was a Greek sculptor famous for the slender proportions of his figures and for their lifelike look. Alexander the Great wouldn't let any other sculptor portray him.

† Demosthenes (384–322 B.C.) was the greatest of ancient Greek orators, who roused Athens to oppose Philip of Macedon and, later, his son Alexander the Great. His speeches provide valuable information about the political, social, and economic life of Athens in the fourth century B.C.

"*Demosthenian rhetoric*," responded don Quixote, "is the same as saying *the rhetoric of Demosthenes*, as *Ciceronian* is of Cicero, and they were the two best rhetoricians in the world."

"That's right," said the duke, "and you've shown your ignorance through such a question. But even so, it would give us great pleasure if *señor* don Quixote would describe her for us. I'll bet that even if it's just a rough sketch and an outline, she'll be such that the most beautiful women will envy her."

"I would willingly do it," responded don Quixote, "if the recent misfortune that happened to her hadn't erased her from my mind. I'm more ready to cry over her than describe her, because I must tell you that a few days ago when I was on the road to kiss her hands and receive her blessing, approval, and permission to do this third expedition, I found her quite different from the way I expected. I found her enchanted and changed from a princess into a peasant, from a beautiful woman to an ugly one, from an angel to a devil, from sweet-smelling to noxious, from well-spoken to a rustic, from a woman of peaceful leisure to one who goes leaping about, from light to darkness, and finally, from Dulcinea del Toboso to a country girl from Sayago—"*

"God help me," interrupted the duke with a shout. "Who could have done such a bad thing to the world? Who has snatched from it the beauty that gave it joy, the grace that soothed it, the virtue that was a credit to it?"

"Who?" responded don Quixote. "Who else can it be other than one of the wicked enchanters who persecute me? This cursèd race, born in the world to obscure and spoil the deeds of good people and to bring forth and heighten the deeds of the bad. Enchanters have persecuted me, enchanters still persecute me, and enchanters will persecute me until they finally sink me and my high chivalric deeds into the abyss of oblivion. And they do me the most harm and wound me where they see I'll feel it the most, because to

---

* Don Quixote doesn't mean that she is literally "a country girl from Sayago," but rather reminds him of one. Sayago is a district in the province of Zamora, bordering on Portugal, about 235 miles from El Toboso. Its inhabitants and their dialect epitomized what "rustic" meant in the Golden Age (see Part II, chapter nineteen, page 646).

take his lady away from a knight-errant is to take the eyes away with which he sees, the sun that gives him light, and the nutrition that sustains him. I've said this many other times, and I'll repeat it now, that a knight without a lady is like a tree without leaves, a building without a foundation, and a shadow without the body that casts it."

"There's nothing more to be said," said the duchess, "but if we're to believe the history about *señor* don Quixote that came out a few days ago, to general applause by everyone, one deduces from it, if I'm not mistaken, that your grace has never seen the lady Dulcinea, and that this lady really doesn't exist in the world, but is rather an invented lady that you created and gave birth to in your imagination and described with all the charms and perfections you wanted."

"There's much to be said about this," responded don Quixote. "God knows if there's a Dulcinea in the world or not, or if she's imagined or not. This is not the type of thing that can be fully verified. I neither created nor gave birth to my lady, although I contemplate her as a lady who has all those qualities that can make her famous throughout the world, which are: beautiful without blemish, distinguished but without pride, loving yet modest, gracious through courtesy, courteous through good breeding, and finally, noble of lineage, since beauty shines and flourishes most perfectly because of good breeding than does beauty that's humbly born."

"That's right," said the duke, "but *señor* don Quixote must allow me to say what the history of your deeds that I read forces me to suggest, and that is that one infers, although one concedes that there's a Dulcinea in El Toboso (or outside of that town), and that her beauty is at the high level that your grace has described, that insofar as her *lineage* goes, it doesn't compare with that of the Orianas, the Alastrajareas, and the Madásimas,* nor with others like them that abound in the histories that your grace knows well."

"To this I can say," responded don Quixote, "that

---

* Alastrajarea was the wife of Prince Folanges de Altrea in *Florisel de Niquea*; Oriana was Amadís' lady; and Queen Madásima is another character in *Amadís de Gaula* already referred to in Part I, chapter twenty-four, with a variant spelling of her name.

Dulcinea is the daughter of her works, and that virtue makes up for blood, and that a humble but virtuous person is more to be esteemed than a depraved noble. What's more, Dulcinea has within her a quality that can make her a queen with a crown and scepter, since the worth of a beautiful and virtuous woman allows her to work great miracles, and she has the potential within herself for greater fortune."

"I grant, *señor* don Quixote," said the duchess, "that in everything your grace says he's very circumspect and, as they say, prudent, and that from now on I will believe and will tell everyone else in this household to believe, and even the duke, my lord, if it were to be necessary, that there is a Dulcinea del Toboso and that she lives today, and she is beautiful and wellborn and deserving that a knight such as *señor* don Quixote serve her, which is the greatest thing I can say of her. But I can't help feeling a certain qualm and a grudge against Sancho Panza. The qualm is that the history says that Sancho Panza found Dulcinea, when he was sent to her by your grace with a letter, winnowing a sack of wheat, and it was red wheat, which makes me doubt the nobility of her lineage."

To which he responded: "*Señora mía*, you must know that everything, or most everything, that happens to me falls beyond the usual experience of other knights-errant, being so directed by the inscrutable will of the Fates or by the malice of some envious enchanter, and since it's a proven fact that all or most famous knights-errant have particular powers—one of them cannot be enchanted, another has impenetrable skin that will prevent his being wounded, such as the famous Roland, one of the Twelve Peers of France, of whom it was said he couldn't be wounded except through the sole of his left foot,* and this only with a large straight pin and not with any other weapon. So when Bernardo del Carpio killed him at Roncesvalles, seeing that he couldn't injure him with a weapon, he lifted him up in his arms and throttled him, recalling the death that Hercules gave Antæus, that ferocious giant who is the son of the Earth—I want to infer by what I said that I might have one of the gifts that I mentioned. It can't be the one of being invulnerable

---

* In Part I, chapter twenty-six, don Quixote said that the pin had to be stuck into the *front* of his foot—*now* he is right.

to wounds, because experience has shown me many times that my flesh is soft and not at all impenetrable, nor that of being immune to enchantment, for I've seen myself put in a cage, where—if I hadn't been enchanted—there would be no force on earth capable of locking me up otherwise. But since I freed myself from that enchantment, I'd like to think that no other one can stop me, so I feel sure these enchanters who can't use their power against *me* anymore are taking their vengeance on what I love the most, and they try to take away my life by mistreating Dulcinea, for whom I live. And so, I believe that when my squire took her my message, they changed her into a country girl busying herself with so low an activity as winnowing wheat. But I've already said that that wheat wasn't red or even wheat at all, but rather grains of Oriental pearls. And to prove this truth I want to say to your excellencies that as we were going a while ago to El Toboso, I couldn't find Dulcinea's palaces. And the next day, after Sancho, my squire, saw her the way she really looks, which is the most beautiful woman in the world, she seemed to me to be an ill-bred peasant, ugly, and not at all well-spoken, whereas she's really the most well-spoken person in the world. And since I'm not enchanted, nor can I be, it seems *she's* the enchanted, the offended, and the transformed one—transformed and changed again—and on her my enemies have avenged themselves, and for her I'll live in perpetual tears until I see her in her pristine state again.

"I've said all this so that no one will take seriously what Sancho said about Dulcinea's sifting and winnowing. Since they changed her on me, it's no wonder that they would change her on him as well. Dulcinea is noble and wellborn and from one of the best families in El Toboso, of which there are many, ancient and very fine.* Certainly none can compare with the peerless Dulcinea, for whom her village will be famous and celebrated in future centuries, as Troy has been for Helen, and Spain for La Cava,† although her rank and fame will be greater. On the other hand, I want you to

---

* In those times, El Toboso was mostly populated by people of Moorish origin; thus there was little room for noble families, although Clemencín did find *one*.

† This is a most unfortunate comparison, since Spain was *lost* because of La Cava.

understand that Sancho Panza is one of the most amusing squires that ever served a knight-errant. At times his naïveté is so great that it's hard to tell whether he's simple or wise. He does mischievous things that condemn him as a rascal, and has an absentmindedness that confirms him as a fool. He doubts everything and he believes everything. Just when I think he's going to topple into something foolish, he comes up with something wise that raises him to the heavens.

"In the end I wouldn't trade him for any other squire, even if they threw in a city to boot. So, I wonder if it would be a good idea to have him govern the *ínsula* your grace has awarded him, although I see in him a certain aptitude for the business of governing, and if you smooth out his intellect a bit, he'll manage as well in any government as the king does his taxes. And we know through long experience that one doesn't need much ability or education to be a governor, because there are a hundred out there who can hardly read, and they govern very well indeed. The important thing is to have good intentions and want to succeed in everything; and there will never be a lack of people to advise him and put him on the right track, just like other uneducated men who pass judgment with the help of a legal adviser. I would counsel him not to take bribes, or surrender the law, and other little things on my mind, which I'll bring to light at the right moment for Sancho's use and for the benefit of the *ínsula* he'll govern."

At this point in the conversation among the duke, duchess, and don Quixote, they heard shouts and voices of the palace help, and all of a sudden Sancho came dashing into the room, looking quite apprehensive, with a heavy cloth as a bib, followed by many young men—or better said, kitchen boys and other riffraff, one of them with a basin of water, which looked to be dirty dishwater. The fellow with the basin chased him, trying to put it under his beard, and another boy was trying to wash it.

"What is going on, brothers?" asked the duchess. "What is this? What are you doing to this man? Don't you know he has been made a governor?"

To which one of the kitchen boys answered: "This fellow won't let us wash his beard as is the custom, and as was done with the duke, my master, and with his master."

"Yes, I will," responded Sancho angrily, "but I would like

for it to be done with cleaner towels, clearer soapy water, and with hands that are not so dirty. There's not so much difference between my master and myself that they should wash him with perfumed water and me with the devil's dishwater. The customs of countries and palaces are only good if they aren't unpleasant; the washing custom that's practiced here is worse than whipping penitents. My beard is clean enough, and I don't need such grooming, and if anyone comes over to wash or even touch a hair on my head, I mean, on my beard—speaking with due respect— I'll punch him so hard that I'll leave my fist inside his skull. Such cirimonies and soapings seem more to be practical jokes than the polite reception of guests."

The duchess was dying of laughter seeing Sancho's anger and hearing his words. But it didn't please don Quixote very much to see him in the stained towel and surrounded by so many pranksters from the kitchen, and, giving a deep bow to the duke and duchess, with a calm voice he said to the rabble: "Hey! Sir knights! Your graces should release this young man and go back where you came from, or anywhere else you please. My squire is as clean as the next man, and those basins are nothing more than a practical joke to him. Take my advice and let him go, because neither he nor I put up with nonsense."

Sancho saw where don Quixote was going and he continued: "Just let 'em try to put one over on this unsuspecting fellow, and I'll put up with it as much as it's night right now. Bring a comb or whatever you want, and curry my beard, and if you find anything that appears unclean, let 'em shear the whole thing off."

Without stopping her laughter, the duchess then said: "Sancho Panza is perfectly right in everything he has said, and he always will be in whatever he says. He's clean, and as he says, he has no need to wash his beard, and if our custom offends him, let him do what he wants, especially since you ministers of cleanliness have been remiss and careless, not to mention impudent, to bring to such a personage with such a beard dishrags and basins made of wood, instead of imported towels and basins and pitchers of pure gold. You are wicked and lowborn, and like the brigands you are you cannot help showing the grudge you hold against squires of knights-errant."

The mischievous servants, and even the steward who came with them, thought that the duchess was speaking in earnest, and so they removed the cloth from Sancho's chest, and, quite perplexed and almost ashamed, they went away and left him. Sancho, seeing himself liberated from that great danger, went over to kneel before the duchess, and said: "From great women great favors are expected. The one your grace has done me today cannot be repaid except with the desire to see myself dubbed a knight-errant so I can spend all my days in serving such a noble lady. But I'm a peasant. I'm called Sancho Panza. I'm married, have children, and serve as a squire. If I can serve your greatness in any of these capacities, I'll obey quicker than you can command."

"It's quite obvious," responded the duchess, "that you've learned to be courteous in the school of courtesy itself. It's quite evident, I mean, that you've been nurtured at the side of don Quixote, who doubtless is the cream of politeness and the flower of ceremonies, or 'cirimonies,' as you say. Blessings on such a master and such a servant—the one, because he's the polestar of knight-errantry, and the other, because he's the star of squirely faithfulness. Stand up, Sancho, my friend. In return for your courtesy, I'll make sure that the duke, my lord, bestows the favor of a governorship on you as soon as he can."

With this, the conversation ended, and don Quixote retired for his *siesta*, and the duchess asked Sancho, unless he felt very much like sleeping, to come to spend the afternoon with her and with her maidens in a very cool room. Sancho responded that, although it was true that he customarily had a *siesta* of four or five hours during the summer, to serve her goodness, he would try with all his might to do without one and that he would be obedient to her command, and he went along with her. The duke gave new orders as to how don Quixote should be treated as a knight-errant, without straying from the way it's said that they treated knights-errant of old.

Chapter XXXIII. About the delicious conversation that the duchess and her maidens had with Sancho Panza, worthy of being read and noted.

THE HISTORY states, then, that Sancho didn't have that siesta, but rather, in order to keep his word, after eating, he went to visit the duchess. Given the pleasure she got by listening to him, she asked him to sit next to her in a low chair, although Sancho, being such a good servant, didn't want to sit. But the duchess told him to sit down as a governor and speak as a squire, and that he deserved even the bench that belonged to the Cid, Ruy Díaz, the Warrior.*

Sancho shrugged his shoulders, obeyed, and sat down, and all the duchess' maidens and duennas surrounded him and were quite attentive, and were absolutely still so they could hear what he would say.

The duchess was the one who spoke first, saying: "Now that we're alone and no one can hear us, I would like the *señor* governor to resolve a few doubts I have, born of the history that has been printed about the great don Quixote. One of these is that since the good Sancho never saw *señora* Dulcinea—I mean, *señora* Dulcinea del Toboso— nor did he take don Quixote's letter, because it stayed behind in the diary in the Sierra Morena, how was it that he dared to fabricate an answer and say that he found her winnowing wheat when it was all a trick and a lie, to the detriment of the reputation of the peerless Dulcinea, and quite out of keeping with the character and loyalty of good squires?"

Without giving any answer, Sancho stood up from his chair, and with quiet steps, his body hunched over, and his finger placed on his lips, walked all around the room looking behind the drapes, and then went back and sat down again and said: "Now, *señora mía*, that I've seen that no one is listening to us on the sly, outside of those present, I'll answer what has been asked and everything else that may be asked me without fear or distress. And first I want

---

* The Cid won this marble bench in Valencia (verse 3115 of the *Poema de mío Cid*).

to say that I'm convinced that my master, don Quixote, is completely mad, although sometimes he says things that, in my opinion and even of those who listen to him, are so wise and on the right track that Satan himself couldn't say them any better. But even so, truly and without any doubt, it strikes me that he's a half-wit.

"So, with this in mind, I dare to make him believe things that have no sense, as was the case with the response to that letter, and that business of maybe six or eight days ago, which isn't yet in the history—I'm talking about the enchantment of my lady Dulcinea. I've led him to believe that she's enchanted although she's no more so than 'the hills of Úbeda.' "*

The duchess begged him to tell her about that enchantment or ruse, and Sancho told it exactly as it had happened, from which his listeners derived no little pleasure.

And continuing Sancho's thought, the duchess said: "What the good Sancho has told me causes a little qualm to flit about in my soul, and there's a whisper in my ear saying, 'If don Quixote de La Mancha is crazy, witless, and an idiot, and Sancho Panza, his squire, knows it, and even so serves and follows him, and believes in his vain promises, he doubtless must be crazier than his master. And if this is so, as it is, it'll be bad for you, *señora* duchess, if you give an *ínsula* to this Sancho Panza to govern, for if he cannot govern himself, how can he govern others?' "

"Before God, *señora*," said Sancho, "this qualm is well-founded. But you can tell it that it doesn't need to whisper because I know that what it says is true. If I were wise, I should have left my master days ago. But this was my luck and misfortune. I can't help it—I have to follow him. We're from the same town, I've eaten at his table, I like him a lot, he's grateful, he gave me his donkey colts, and above all, I'm faithful. So it's impossible for us to be separated, except by the one who has the pick and shovel. If Your Highness doesn't wish to give me the promised office, well, God made me for less, and it might be that not giving it to me would be better for my conscience, for although I'm dull, I

---

* "To go over the hills of Úbeda" is a proverbial expression meaning to stray, as from the point. There are no hills at Úbeda (a Spanish city seventy-five miles north of Granada).

understand the proverb that says: 'to its detriment the ant grew wings.'*

"And it may even be that Sancho the squire will enter heaven before Sancho the governor. 'They make as good bread here as they do in France' and 'at night all cats are black.' 'Unlucky is the man who hasn't broken fast by two in the afternoon.' 'There's no stomach that's half a foot bigger than another,' and 'it can get full,' as they say, 'with straw or hay,'† and 'the little birds of the field have God as their provider.' And 'four yards of Cuenca flannel warms better than four yards of fine silk from Segovia.' And 'when we leave this world and get put into the ground, the prince has to travel a path as narrow as the day laborer,' and 'the body of the pope takes up no more feet of earth than the sexton,' even though one may be taller than the other, because when we enter the grave we all have to adjust and scrunch up, or rather they make us adjust and scrunch up, even though we may not like it, and good night. And I say again that if your ladyship doesn't want to give me the *ínsula* because I'm dull, I'm smart enough not to let it bother me. And I've heard it said that 'behind the cross lurks the devil,' and 'not all's gold that glitters' and that they took the farmer Wamba from between two oxen, plows, and yokes and made him king of Spain, and that from his brocades, pastimes, and riches they took King Rodrigo to be eaten by snakes, if the old ballads don't lie—"

"How can they lie?" interrupted doña Rodríguez, the duenna, who was one of the listeners. "There's a ballad that says that they put King Rodrigo alive—I mean, *alive*—in a tomb filled with toads, snakes, and lizards, and two days later the king said from inside the tomb, with a pitiful voice:

"'They're eating me, they're eating me
   where I sinned the most.'‡

---

* Since it will get eaten by birds, as Gaos points out. In other words, it doesn't pay to rise above your station.

† Alluded to already in Part II, chapter three, page 534.

‡ Rodrigo was the last of the Gothic kings in what was to be Spain. Because of his sexual escapade with La Cava, "Spain" was lost to the Moors. So the ballad refers to the eating of his genitals by the creatures. (Historically, though, Rodrigo died in the Battle of Guadalete [July 711] fighting the Moors.)

"And according to this, this fellow is very correct in saying that he prefers to be a peasant than a king, if vermin are going to eat him."

The duchess couldn't contain her laughter, hearing the simplicity of her duenna, nor could she cease to wonder at the words and wisdom of Sancho, to whom she said: "The good Sancho knows that once a knight makes a promise, he endeavors to keep it, even though it might cost him his life. The duke, my lord and husband, although he's not among the errants, he's still a knight, and he'll keep his word about the promised *ínsula*, in spite of all the envy and malice of the world. Let Sancho be of good cheer, and when least he's thinking about it he'll see himself sitting on the throne of his domain, and will grasp his office, which he can trade in for a brocade of three layers.* What I charge him to do is take care how he governs his vassals, remembering that they're all wellborn and loyal."

"Regarding the matter of governing well," responded Sancho, "there's no need to charge me with anything, because I'm charitable by nature and I have compassion for the poor and 'don't steal bread from the person who kneads and bakes.' And by the Holy Cross, 'they won't use loaded dice on me.' 'I'm an old dog and I understand "here, boy!"' and I know how to wake up at the right time, and no cobwebs will be spun over my eyes, because 'I know where my shoe pinches.' I say this because with me the good people will have help and flavor—I mean, favor—and the bad people won't even be able to put their foot in the door. And it seems to me that in this business of governments 'a good beginning is everything,' and it may be that after two weeks I'll really like the office and I'll know more about governing than the way I was raised to till the soil."

"You're quite right," said the duchess, "because 'no one is born educated' and 'bishops come from men, not from rocks.' But going back to the conversation we were having about the enchantment of the lady Dulcinea, I happen to know for certain and from a reliable source that what Sancho thought was a joke on his master—making him think

---

* That is, he can move to an even better position from there. The duchess knows more about brocade than Sancho (see his erroneous comment in Part II, chapter ten, page 578).

that the peasant girl was Dulcinea, and that the reason
his master didn't recognize her was because she was enchanted, and it was the work of one of the enchanters who
persecute him—well, I know *for certain* that the peasant
girl who leapt onto the she-ass *was* and really *is* Dulcinea
del Toboso, and that Sancho, thinking he was the deceiver,
turns out to be the deceived one, and there's no reason to
doubt this any more than to doubt other things that we
have never seen.* Also, Sancho should know that we also
have enchanters who favor us and tell us what is happening
in the world, purely and simply, and without circumlocu-
tions and deceptions. And may Sancho believe me when
I say that the leaping peasant girl was and is Dulcinea del
Toboso, and she's about as enchanted as the mother who
bore her. And when we least expect it, we'll see her in her
real form, and then Sancho will be rid of the delusion under
which he lives."

"All this may easily be," said Sancho Panza, "and now
I want to believe what my master tells me about what he
saw in the Cave of Montesinos, where he says he saw lady
Dulcinea del Toboso in the same outfit and habit that I said
I had seen her in when I enchanted her for my own pleasure. Everything must be the reverse, as your grace says,
because with my limited intelligence, one cannot expect
me to make up in an instant such a clever trick, nor do I
believe that my master is so crazy that with my weak and
feeble persuasion he would believe something that's so unlikely. But, *señora*, I hope you won't think I'm mischievous
because of this, because a blockhead such as myself can't
be expected to penetrate the thoughts and evil acts of bad
enchanters. I made that up to escape my master's scolding
and with no intention of doing him harm. And if it turned
out the opposite way, 'God is in His heaven and He judges
our hearts.'"

"That's the truth," said the duchess, "but tell me now,
Sancho, what's this business about the Cave of Montesinos? I'd like to find out about it."

So Sancho told her, point by point, what has been said
about that adventure. When she heard it, the duchess said:

---

* Those who know the Catholic catechism will realize this is referring
to believing things by faith, things you never saw.

"From this, one can infer that since the great don Quixote says he saw the same peasant girl there that Sancho had seen leaving El Toboso, she's doubtless Dulcinea, and it appears we have some clever and quite curious enchanters around here."

"That's what I say," said Sancho Panza, "and if my lady Dulcinea del Toboso is enchanted, too bad for her; I won't take on my master's enemies, who must be many and evil. The truth of the matter is that the person I saw was a peasant girl, and if that was Dulcinea, it's not my fault, and they can't blame me. Let them not come at me every step of the way saying: 'You tell me and I'll tell you; Sancho said it, Sancho did it, Sancho went and Sancho came back,' as if I were a nobody, and not the same Sancho Panza who circulates in books throughout the world, according to what Sansón Carrasco told me, and he has, at least, been bachelored by Salamanca. And graduates from there cannot lie, except when they feel like it, or it suits their purpose. So there's no reason for anyone to pick a fight with me, and the way I heard my master say it, 'a good name is worth more than great wealth,' so let them put this governorship on me and they'll see miracles, because whoever has been a good squire will be a good governor."

"Everything that the good Sancho has said here," said the duchess, "is Catonian maxims,* or at least taken from the very soul of Micael Verino, *florentibus occidit annis*.† Indeed, indeed, speaking the way he does,‡ 'under a bad cloak you can find a good drinker.'"

"In truth, *señora*," responded Sancho, "I've never in my life used drinking as a vice. When I'm thirsty, maybe, because there's nothing of the hypocrite about me. I drink when I feel like it, and when I don't but it's offered to me

---

* This refers to "Dionysius Cato" (third century A.D.) whose 164 moral maxims (each one written as a two-line hexameter), called *Disticha moribus ad filium*, were used as a schoolbook in the Middle Ages.

† This quote, by Angelo Poliziano, means "who died in the flower of his youth." The Florentine Micael Verino, in fact, did die at age seventeen in the 1480s. He wrote a series of two-line maxims to help instruct children. Because of their similar nature, his maxims and those by "Dionysius Cato" were frequently published together.

‡ That is, the way Sancho does.

(so as not to appear prudish or ill-bred). When it comes to toasting a friend, what heart can be so hard as not to raise a glass? But although 'I do wear shoes, I don't get mud on them.' And what's more, squires of knights-errant usually just drink water because they're always running around forests, fields, mountains, and cliffs, without finding a drop of wine, even if they were willing to trade an eye for some."

"That's what I think, too," responded the duchess, "and in the meantime, let Sancho go rest, and afterward we'll speak further and we'll see how we'll 'put this government on him,' to use his expression."

Sancho kissed the duchess' hands again, and begged her to do him the favor of taking good care of his gray, because he was the light of his eyes.

"What gray is this?" asked the duchess.

"My donkey," responded Sancho. "Since I don't want to refer to him just as a 'donkey,' I often call him THE GRAY, and I begged this duenna when I came into the castle to take care of him, and she got quite upset, as if I had said she was ugly or old, but duennas are better suited to feed donkeys than swagger about halls. I swear to God, a man from my village really had it in for these ladies!"

"He must have been a real lowlife," said doña Rodríguez. "If he were an *hidalgo* and wellborn, he would have praised them to high heavens."

"All right," said the duchess, "no more of this. Let doña Rodríguez keep still and *señor* Panza calm down and leave the comfort of the donkey in my care, because since he belongs to Sancho, I'll consider him the light of my own eyes."

"It's enough for him to be put in the stable," responded Sancho, "because neither he nor I am worthy of being the light of the eyes of Your Highness. And I would no more consent to it than I would to stab myself a couple of times; although my master says that where courtesy is concerned, 'it's better to lose by a card too many than one too few,' in matters of donkeys one should be prudent and take the middle road."

"Let Sancho take him to his government," said the duchess, "and there he can pamper him as much as he wants, and even put him out to pasture."

"Your grace shouldn't think she has exaggerated," said Sancho. "I've seen more than two jackasses go to governments, and taking mine with me wouldn't be anything new."

Sancho's words renewed the duchess' laughter and delight, and after she sent him off to rest, she went to tell the duke what had transpired between them. And the two of them made a plan to play a joke on don Quixote that would be in the chivalresque style, and they later played many more on him, so inventive and ingenious that they're the best adventures in this great history.

Chapter XXXIIII. Which tells how the peerless Dulcinea del Toboso was to be disenchanted, which is one of the most famous adventures in this history.

GREAT WAS the pleasure the duke and duchess got from their conversations with don Quixote and with Sancho Panza, and since they were eager to carry out pranks that would give the appearance and semblance of adventures, they chose as a theme what don Quixote had told them about the descent into the Cave of Montesinos, thinking it would make a good jest. But what the duchess marveled at most was that Sancho was so gullible that he'd come to believe it was true that Dulcinea del Toboso was enchanted, when he was the enchanter and the trickster of the affair himself. So, having told her servants what they had to do, six days later the duke and duchess took don Quixote on a hunting expedition, with an array of hunters and beaters worthy of a crowned king.

They gave don Quixote a hunting outfit and another one to Sancho, green in color and made of very fine cloth. But don Quixote didn't want to wear his, saying that one day he'd have to return to the rigorous profession of arms and he couldn't take a wardrobe or luggage with him. Sancho, on the other hand, took the one they gave him, with the intention of selling it as soon as he could.

When the designated day came, don Quixote put on his armor, Sancho got dressed, and, riding his donkey—for he refused to leave him behind, even though they offered him a horse—the two of them joined the company of hunters. The duchess came out dressed very elegantly, and don Quixote, showing great courtesy, led her palfrey by the reins, although the duke tried to object. Finally they arrived at a forest between two high mountains, and once the sites, blinds, and paths were assigned, and people were stationed at different spots, the hunt began with a lot of noise, shouts, and yelling so loud they couldn't hear one another speak, all this amidst the barking of dogs and the sounding of huntsmen's horns. The duchess dismounted and, with a sharp spear in her hands, placed herself where she knew wild boars usually came through. The duke and don Quixote also dismounted and placed themselves at her sides. Sancho got behind everyone else, without getting off his donkey, whom he didn't dare leave alone so that he wouldn't be harmed in any way.

And no sooner had they settled and fanned out with many of their servants than a huge wild boar ran out, pursued by dogs and hunters, gnashing his teeth and tusks, with foam streaming from his mouth. When don Quixote saw him, he clutched his shield, clasped his sword, and started to go out to receive him. The duke did the same with his spear. But the duchess would have gotten in front of everyone if the duke hadn't prevented her. Only Sancho, seeing the fierce animal, abandoned his donkey and started to run as fast as he could. He found it impossible to climb all the way up a tall oak, but when he was halfway up, holding on to a branch, trying to get to the top, owing to his bad luck and misfortune the branch broke off and he got caught on a snag before he reached the ground. When Sancho saw himself in that plight, and he realized that the suit was tearing, it seemed to him that if the animal attacked, he was hanging low enough for the animal to reach; so he began to shout so loudly and yell for help with such insistence that everyone who heard him thought he was already in the jaws of some wild beast.

Finally the tusked boar was pierced by the several pointed spears that he faced. Don Quixote turned his head toward Sancho's shouts—for he recognized whose they were—and saw him dangling from the oak, headfirst, and the donkey, who wouldn't abandon his master in his misfortune, standing next to him. And Cide Hamete says that he rarely saw Sancho Panza without also seeing the donkey, nor the donkey without seeing Sancho, such was the friendship and loyalty the one had for the other. Don Quixote went over and helped Sancho down. Once he was free and on the ground he looked at his torn hunting outfit and it grieved him in his heart, because he felt that the garment was worth a fortune.

Then they placed the powerful boar on a pack mule and, covering it with sprigs of rosemary and myrtle branches, they took it as the spoil of victory to some large field tents erected in the middle of the forest, where they found the tables set and a meal already prepared, which was so sumptuous and enormous that it was easy to see the greatness and magnificence of those who offered it.

Sancho, showing the rents of his torn outfit to the duchess, said: "If this hunt had been for rabbits or little birds, my suit would have never ended up in this state. I don't know what pleasure anyone can get waiting for an animal who can snatch away your life if he gets you with one of his tusks. I remember hearing an ancient ballad sung, which goes like this:

> The bears may gulp you down
> Like Favila of renown.*

"He was a Gothic king," said don Quixote, "who, when he went off to hunt, was eaten by a bear."

"That's what I said," responded Sancho, "for I think it's wrong for princes and kings to run such a risk just for a little pleasure, which seems like it's no pleasure at all, since it involves killing an animal that has committed no crime."

"You're quite mistaken," responded the duke, "because the hunt is the best and most necessary activity for kings and princes. It is the image of war. In it there are stratagems, skills, and snares to conquer one's enemy safely. During the hunt one endures bitter cold and insufferable heat; laziness and listlessness are cast aside; and finally, it's an activity that can be done with no injury to anyone, and gives pleasure to many. And the best thing about it is that this kind of hunting

---

* Favila was the king of Asturias from A.D. 737 to 739, when he was indeed killed by a bear.

is not for everyone, as are other types of hunting, except falconing, which is also reserved for kings and great lords. So, Sancho, change your opinion, and when you're governor, engage in the hunt and you will benefit from it."

"I don't think so," responded Sancho, "because the good governor should have 'a broken leg and stay at home.' A pretty predicament if people with business came to see him all tired out and he's off in the forest hunting. Why, the government would go to pot. On my faith, *señor*, hunting and pastimes should be reserved for lazy people and not for governors. What I think I'll do for entertainment is to play cards on religious holidays and ninepins on Sundays and holidays. Hunting doesn't jibe with my temperament or agree with my conscience."

"May it please God that's the way it'll be, Sancho, because 'there's a big difference between saying and doing.'"

"No matter," replied Sancho, "because 'the person who pays on time doesn't worry about leaving security' and 'him who God helps is better off than he who gets up early' and 'it's the stomach that carries the feet and not the feet that carry the stomach.' I mean that if God helps me, and I do what I should with a good purpose, I'll doubtless govern perfectly. 'Let them put their finger in my mouth and see if I bite.'"

"May God and all his saints confound you, cursèd Sancho!" said don Quixote. "And when will the day come, as I've said on many other occasions, when I'll see you say a whole speech, well put together and coherent, without proverbs? Your Highnesses should pay no attention to this idiot, because he'll grind up your souls, not just between two but amidst two thousand proverbs, which he drags in, and if they're ever to the point and timely, may God give him salvation, and to me as well, if I ever should listen to them."

"The proverbs of Sancho Panza," said the duchess, "although he knows more of them than the Greek commander,* are to be prized for the brevity of the maxims. For myself I can say they give me more pleasure than others that are more to the point and more aptly introduced."

---

* This is El Pinciano (1475?–1553), who collected three thousand *Sayings or Proverbs in Spanish* (Salamanca, 1555). He was a commander in the Order of Calatrava and a professor of Greek, thus the nickname.

With these and other entertaining conversations they left the tent and went into the forest, where they visited some hunting blinds, and soon the day was over and night overtook them, which was not as clear or as calm as might have been expected, since it was the middle of summer. But a certain chiaroscuro that it brought with it helped the duke and duchess' plan. So, when night began to fall, just before dusk, suddenly it appeared as if the whole forest were aflame everywhere. And then an infinite number of bugles and other musical instruments of war were heard here and there in all four directions, as if many mounted troops were coming. The blaze of the fire and the blare of military horns almost blinded the eyes and numbed the ears of all those present and even of all those who were in the forest.

Then an infinite number of war cries was heard, in the style of Moors entering into battle.* Trumpets and bugles blared, kettledrums resounded, fifes whistled, all almost at the same time, continuously, and without ceasing, and anyone who was sane would lose his sanity on hearing so many instruments. The duke was stunned; the duchess amazed; don Quixote stood in wonderment; Sancho Panza trembled; even those privy to what was happening were astonished. Fear reduced them to silence, and a messenger dressed as the devil on horseback rode past, playing, not a bugle, but a long, hollow ox horn that emitted a hoarse, frightful sound.

"Ho, brother courier," said the duke, "who are you, where are you going, and what warriors are these who are marching through the forest?"

To which the messenger replied in a terrifying voice: "I'm the devil. I'm looking for don Quixote de La Mancha. The people who are coming are six groups of enchanters, who are bringing on a triumphal carriage the peerless Dulcinea del Toboso. She's enchanted along with the gallant Frenchman Montesinos, who is to instruct don Quixote in how that lady is to be disenchanted."

"If you were the devil, as you say and as your appearance reveals, you should have already recognized that

---

* This Moorish war cry is made by moving your tongue from [u] (as in "S*u*e") to [e] (as in "see") two or three times a second. It produces a startling effect.

knight don Quixote de La Mancha, since here he is right in front of you."

"Before God and my conscience," responded the devil, "I wasn't paying attention—I have so many different things to think about that the reason I came slipped my mind."

"Doubtless," said Sancho, "this demon must be a good man and a good Christian, because if he wasn't, he wouldn't have sworn 'before God and my conscience.' Now I believe that in hell itself there must be good people."

Then the devil, without dismounting, looking over to don Quixote, said: "The unfortunate but brave knight Montesinos has sent me to you, Knight of the Lions—and may I see you in their claws—to tell you to wait for him in whatever place I should find you, because he's bringing the one they call Dulcinea del Toboso with him, to instruct you how to disenchant her. Since this is all I came for, I won't stay any longer. May demons such as I remain with you and good angels with these others."

And when he said this, he sounded his huge horn, and turned around and left without waiting for anyone's response.

Wonder once again fell on everyone, especially Sancho and don Quixote. Upon Sancho because he saw that, in spite of the truth, they would have it that Dulcinea was enchanted; upon don Quixote because he couldn't be sure if what had happened to him in the Cave of Montesinos was true or not. And while he was absorbed in these thoughts, the duke asked him: "Does your grace plan to wait, *señor* don Quixote?"

"Most certainly," he responded. "I'll wait here dauntless and strong, even if all hell comes to attack me."

"If I see another devil and hear another horn like that one, I'll as much wait here as in Flanders," said Sancho.

By this time, it was getting very dark, and many lights began to flicker in the forest, just as dry exhalations from the earth dart across the sky, which seem like shooting stars to us.* At the same moment a terrifying sound was heard, like the noise made by the solid wheels of an oxcart, whose

---

* References to "dry exhalations" derive from the way the ancients thought the universe was organized, these being a result of either the region of fire above the Earth or from a ball of fire within.

harsh and continual creaking, it is said, causes wolves and bears to flee, if there are any around. Adding to this flurry, another storm of noise arose that gave the impression that in the four corners of the forest there were four battles going on, because over there was the din of frightening artillery; in another corner they were firing infinite muskets; nearby you could hear the shouts of the combatants; and far away there were more Muslim war cries.

Finally, the cornets, the ox horns, the huntsman's horns, the bugles, the trumpets, the drums, the artillery, the muskets, and especially the frightful sound of the carts, all together made such a cacophonous and horrendous noise that don Quixote had to pluck up all his courage to be able to withstand it. But Sancho's heart fell to earth and sent him half fainting to the skirts of the duchess, who received him and had water brought right away to throw in his face. It was done and he came to just as a cart with creaking wheels was arriving. It was pulled by four sluggish oxen, all covered with black caparisons, and each one had a blazing wax torch tied to each horn. On top of the cart there was a high seat on which was seated a venerable old man with a beard that was whiter than fallen snow itself, and so long that it extended below his waist. He was clad in a long black robe of buckram. Since the cart was coming with a great many torches it was easy to perceive and discern everything that was on it. It was driven by two ugly demons dressed in the same fine buckram, and their faces were so ugly that Sancho, as soon as he saw them, closed his eyes so he wouldn't have to see them again. When the cart came up to them, the venerable old man stood up from his seat, and said in a loud voice: "I'm the wizard Lirgandeo." Without another word, the cart continued along.

After this one, another similar one came, with another old man enthroned on top, who, making the cart stop, with a voice that was no less grave than the other, said: "I'm the wizard Alquife, the great friend of Urganda the Unknown,"* and he went by as well.

Then, in the same way, another cart arrived. But the person who was seated on the throne was not an old man like

---

* Urganda was an enchantress and Amadís' friend, mentioned in Part I, chapter five. She was also the wife of Alquife.

the others, but a big robust man with an evil eye, and he, when he came, stood up as the others did, and said with an even more hoarse and even more devilish voice: "I'm Arcaláus, the enchanter, the mortal enemy of Amadís de Gaula and all his kinfolk." And he passed by.

These three carts moved to one side and the distressing noise made by their wheels ceased. Then what was heard wasn't a noise, but rather the sound of sweet and harmonious music that made Sancho glad, and he took it as a good omen. And so he said to the duchess, from whom he dared not move an inch: "*Señora*, where there's music, there can't be anything bad."

"Nor where there's light and brightness," responded the duchess.

To which Sancho replied: "The fire gives light and the bonfire gives brightness, as we can see in those that surround us, but they may scorch us. But music always indicates joy and festivity."

"We'll see soon enough," said don Quixote, who was listening to it all, and he was correct, as the next chapter will show.

Chapter XXXV. Where the information that don Quixote received about Dulcinea's disenchantment was continued, together with other astonishing events.

FOLLOWING THE rhythm of the pleasing music, they saw coming toward them a cart of the kind they call triumphant, pulled by six gray mules draped in white linen, and on each one there was a penitent of light, also dressed in white, with a burning wax torch in his hand. This cart was two or even three times the size of the other ones, and on its sides and on top there were twelve more penitents dressed in robes as white as snow, all of them with burning torches—a sight that caused wonder and fear at the same time.

On a raised throne was a nymph clad in a thousand layers of silvery gauzelike material on which shone an infinite number of gold sequins, which made her look, if not richly, at least splendidly dressed. Her face was covered by a

transparent and delicate silk veil through which a beautiful
maiden's face could be seen. And the many lights permitted
one to distinguish her beauty and her age, which was not
more than twenty but not less than seventeen years. Next
to her was a figure in a flowing robe that went to his feet,
and his head was covered with a black veil. At the instant
that the cart arrived in front of the duke and duchess and
don Quixote, the music made by the horns stopped, and
then the music of harps and lutes that were being played on
the cart also stopped. The figure stood up and opened his
robe and removed his veil, revealing clearly the fleshless
and ugly face of Death. Don Quixote felt apprehensive,
Sancho felt fear, and the duke and duchess were also a bit
afraid. This living Death, with a listless voice that appeared
sleepy and with a tongue not quite awake, begin to speak
in this way:*

I am that Merlin who the legends say
    The devil had for father, and the lie
    Hath gathered credence with the lapse of time.
    Of magic prince, of Zoroastric lore
    Monarch and treasurer, with jealous eye
    I view the efforts of the age to hide
    The gallant deeds of doughty errant knights,
    Who are, and ever have been, dear to me.
    Enchanters and magicians and their kind
    Are mostly hard of heart; not so am I;
    For mine is tender, soft, compassionate,
    And its delight is doing good to all.
    In the dim caverns of the gloomy Dis,†
    Where, tracing mystic lines and characters,
    My soul abides now, there came to me
    The sorrow-laden plaint of her, the fair,
    The peerless Dulcinea del Toboso.
    I knew of her enchantment and her fate,
    From highborn dame to peasant wench transformed
    And touched with pity, first I turned the leaves

---

* The translation of the poem is Ormsby's. If you are tempted *not* to
read the whole thing, the last eight lines are the critical ones.
† The Roman god Dis is known more commonly as Pluto, the god of
the underworld.

Of countless volumes of my devilish craft,
And then, in this grim grisly skeleton
Myself encasing, hither have I come
To show where lies the fitting remedy
To give relief in such a piteous case.
Oh thou, the pride and pink of all that wear
The adamantine steel! Oh shining light,
Oh beacon, North Star, path and guide of all
Who, scorning slumber and the lazy down,
Adopt the toilsome life of bloodstained arms!
To you, great hero whom all praise transcends,
La Mancha's luster and Iberia's star,
Don Quixote, wise as brave, to thee I say—
For peerless Dulcinea del Toboso
Her pristine form and beauty to regain,
'Tis needful that thy squire, Sancho, shall,
On his own sturdy buttocks bared to heaven,
Three thousand and three hundred lashes lay,
And that they smart and sting and hurt him well.
Thus have the authors of her woe resolved.
And this is, gentle people, why I have come.

"Oh, no!" said Sancho instantly. "Never mind the three thousand lashes; I'll no more give myself three than I'd stab myself three times. What the devil kind of disenchantment is this? I don't see what my rear end has to do with enchantments. By God, if *señor* Merlin can't find another way to disenchant Dulcinea del Toboso, she'll have to go to her grave enchanted."

"You garlic-stuffed hayseed," said don Quixote. "I'll take you myself and tie you to a tree, naked as when your mother bore you, and I don't say three thousand three hundred, but rather I'll give you six thousand six hundred lashes, and so well laid on you won't be able to pull them off with three thousand three hundred tugs.* And don't say a word or I'll tear your soul out."

When Merlin heard this, he said: "It cannot be that way,

---

* There is a pun here in Spanish, where the word for "stuck on" also means "pulled off." These lashes will be so well stuck on he won't be able to take them off with as many tugs. Not a very good pun, but then again, Don Quixote is livid.

because the lashes that the good Sancho is to receive have to be voluntary and not by force, and in the period of time that he chooses. There's no time limit imposed. But if he wants to cut his whipping in half he can let another's hand administer them, even though they might be a bit weightier than he'd like."

"Neither another's hand nor my own, nor weighty, nor to be weighed," replied Sancho. "No hand at all will touch me. Did I give birth to *señora* Dulcinea del Toboso so that my rear end should pay for the sins of her eyes?* My master, yes, for she's a part of him; he's always calling her 'my life, my soul,' his mainstay and support—he's the one who can and should whip himself for her and do everything necessary for her disenchantment. But as for my whipping myself, *abernuncio.*"†

Hardly had Sancho said this when the silvery nymph who was next to Merlin stood up, and taking away the light veil from her face she revealed a face that seemed exceedingly beautiful to everyone, and with manly confidence and a not very ladylike voice, speaking directly to Sancho Panza, she said: "Oh, contemptible squire, you fool, heart of a cork tree, guts as hard as rocks! If they commanded you, you thief and shameless fellow, to leap from a high tower to the ground; if they asked you, you enemy of the human race, to eat half a dozen toads, two lizards, and three snakes; if they persuaded you to kill your wife and children with a huge, trenchant sword, it wouldn't be surprising that you would be squeamish and reticent. But to make a big deal over three thousand three hundred lashes—there's no orphan, no matter how puny he may be, who doesn't get that many every month—it would amaze, stun, and astonish all those pious souls who learn of it and those who will eventually learn of it with the passage of time.

"Cast, you wretched and hardened animal, cast, I say, your skittish mule eyes on these eyes of mine, which you can compare to shining stars, and you'll see them cry thread

---

* Translator's note: "Why should my rear end pay for the sins of her eyes?" doesn't make sense to me. Some translate it something like, "Why should my rear end pay for her mistakes?"

† Deformation of *abrenuncio* ("I renounce"), a Latinism used during the sacrament of baptism to reject the devil.

by thread and skein by skein, making furrows, roads, and paths along the beautiful fields of my cheeks. I hope you will be moved, you rogue and evil-intentioned monster, by my flowering youth—still in its teens, for I'm nineteen and not yet twenty—which is fading and withering under the crust of a rustic peasant. And if I don't appear that way right now, it's because of a special favor by *señor* Merlin, here present, only so that my beauty can move you. May the tears of a distressed beauty turn stones into cotton and tigers into sheep.

"Smack, smack those hams of yours, you untamed brute, and cast away that sluggishness caused by your nature that makes you inclined only to gorge yourself and eat some more. Free the smoothness of my flesh, the gentleness of my nature, and the beauty of my face. And if you don't want to relent for my sake, nor adhere to some reasonable time limit, do it for this poor knight standing next to you— for your master, I mean—whose soul, I can plainly see, is stuck in his throat, just a few inches from his lips, and he waits only for your harsh or mild answer, either for his soul to emerge from his mouth or return deep inside him."

When don Quixote heard this, he felt his throat and said, facing the duke: "By God, Dulcinea has spoken the truth, for here's my soul lodged in my throat like the nut* of a crossbow."

"How are you going to respond to this, Sancho?" asked the duchess.

"I'll answer, *señora*," responded Sancho, "what I've already said—that where the lashes are concerned, *abernuncio*."

"*Abrenuncio*, you should say, Sancho, and not as you've said," said the duke.

"Leave me alone, Your Highness," responded Sancho, "for I'm not going to look for subtleties nor one letter more or less, because these lashes that are supposed to be given to me or I'm supposed to give myself have so upset me that I don't know what I'm doing or saying. But I would like to find out from the lady, my *señora* Dulcinea del Toboso, where she learned this way of seeking favors. She comes to

---

* The *nuez* ("nut") is where the cord releases the arrow from the crossbow. There is also a play on words with *nuez de garganta* ("Adam's apple").

ask me to open my flesh with lashes, then calls me a fool, and an untamed beast, with a series of bad names that the devil can haul off. Is my flesh made of bronze by any chance? Or do I care if she's disenchanted or not? What basket of clothes, shirts, handkerchiefs, socks (not that I wear them) does she send ahead to soften me up—she brings reproaches instead, knowing the proverb that they say around here that 'a donkey loaded with gold goes up a mountain easily' and 'gifts break stones,' 'pray devoutly and hammer stoutly,' and 'one TAKE is better than two I'LL GIVE YOUS'?

"Then there's my master, who should have taken me by the hand and treated me tenderly to gain my favor, and he says that he'll tie me naked to a tree, and will double the ante. And these sad people should consider that not only are they asking a squire to whip himself, but a governor as well. Like they say, they're 'piling one good thing on top of another.' Let them learn, let them learn how to seek favors, to ask politely, and behave themselves. Everything has its proper time and men aren't always in a good humor. Right now I'm about to burst with grief over my torn green suit, and they come and ask me to whip myself of my free will, which I'm as far from doing as I am turning into an Indian chief."

"Well, in truth, my friend Sancho," said the duke, "if you don't soften yourself more than a ripe fig, you'll not get your hands on the governship. A fine thing it would be if I sent a cruel, hard-hearted governor to my islanders, one who doesn't acquiesce to the tears of distressed maidens or to the requests of wise, powerful, and aged enchanters and wizards. So, Sancho, either you whip yourself, or you get whipped, or you cannot be a governor."

"*Señor*," responded Sancho, "won't you give me two days to make up my mind about what is best for me?"

"No, in no way," said Merlin, "right now, at this instant and in this place, decide how this business will turn out—either Dulcinea will return to the Cave of Montesinos and to her former state as a peasant, or be taken as she is to the Elysian Fields, where she'll wait for the number of whip-lashes to be completed."

"Come, good Sancho," said the duchess, "chin up, and show yourself grateful for the bread you've received from *señor* don Quixote, whom we are all obliged to serve and please, owing to his noble character and his worthy chivalry. Say YES to this whipping, and let the devil go to hell, and leave fear to the wretched. 'A stout heart breaks bad luck,' as you well know."

To these words, Sancho responded with these foolish ones of his own, and he asked Merlin: "Tell me, your grace, *señor* Merlin—when the devil courier came and gave my master a message from *señor* Montesinos, he commanded him to stay because he was coming with instructions how to disenchant the lady Dulcinea del Toboso. Well, up to now we haven't seen Montesinos or the likes of him."

To which Merlin responded: "The devil, friend Sancho, is an ignoramus and a great rogue. *I* sent him to look for your master, but not with a message from Montesinos, but rather from me, because Montesinos is in his cave, waiting, or rather, hoping for his disenchantment, and on that matter the 'tail has yet to be skinned.' If he owes you anything, or if you have anything to negotiate with him, I'll fetch him and put him down wherever you want. For now, just say YES, and believe me, it will be to the advantage of your soul as well as to your body—to your soul, through the love by which you'll do it, and for your body, because I know you're of a sturdy constitution, and losing a little blood won't do you any harm."

"There are so many doctors in the world, even enchanters are doctors," replied Sancho. "All right, since everyone tells me to, although I don't quite understand why, I agree to give myself the three thousand three hundred lashes, on the condition that I'll give them whenever I choose, without any limit on the time. I'll try to get out of debt as quickly as I can so that the world can enjoy the beauty of the lady doña Dulcinea del Toboso, since the way it appears, quite different from what I thought, she is beautiful. Another condition is that I'm not obliged to draw blood with the whip, and if some of the lashes are only hard enough to whisk flies away, they're to be counted. Moreover, if I make a mistake in my count, *señor* Merlin, since he knows everything, will have to tell me how many are left or how many I'm ahead."

"As for your being ahead of the count, I won't have to tell you," responded Merlin, "because the instant you get to the correct number, lady Dulcinea will be disenchanted at that very moment and will come, gratefully, to the good Sancho to thank him and even reward him for his good works. So there's no reason to have any reservations about the excess or shortage, nor will heaven permit me to deceive anyone, even though it's just by a single hair on one's head."

"All right then, it's in God's hands now," said Sancho. "I consent to my bad luck—that is, I accept the penitence with the conditions duly noted."

Hardly had Sancho said these words than the music began once again and an infinite number of muskets was fired, and don Quixote threw himself around Sancho's neck, giving him a thousand kisses on his forehead and cheeks. The duchess and the duke and everyone else appeared to be very happy, and the cart began to move, and when it went by Dulcinea bowed slightly to the duke and duchess and gave a deep bow to Sancho.

By this time the happy and smiling sunrise was fast approaching. The little flowers in the fields stood up and the liquid crystal of the streams, murmuring among the brown and white pebbles, ran to pay tribute to the expectant rivers. The happy earth, the clear sky, the clean air, the serene light, each on its own and all together gave unmistakable signs that the day, which was treading on the skirts of the dawn, was going to be fine and clear. And the duke and duchess, satisfied with their hunt and with having succeeded in their plan so cleverly and happily, returned to their castle with the object of continuing their pranks, which gave them more delight than anything else.

Chapter XXXVI. Where is narrated the extraordinary and never-before-imagined adventure of the Distressed Duenna, otherwise known as the Countess Trifaldi, together with a letter that Sancho Panza wrote to his wife, Teresa Panza.

THE DUKE had a steward who had a very jovial and carefree wit, and he had played the part of Merlin, arranged everything for the last adventure, wrote the verses, and had a page play Dulcinea. And then, with the collaboration of the duke and duchess, he prepared another one, of the rarest and most amusing kind imaginable.

The duchess asked Sancho the next day if he'd begun the labor of the penance he had to perform to disenchant Dulcinea. He said that he had, and that the previous night he'd given himself five lashes. The duchess asked with what he'd given himself those lashes. He answered that he'd used his hand.

"That," replied the duchess, "is more like giving yourself slaps than lashes. I'm convinced that the wizard Merlin will not be satisfied with such gentleness. The good Sancho will have to make some kind of whip with metal thorns, or a cat-o'-nine-tails, which can be felt. 'Misfortunes make us wise,'* and the liberty of such a great lady as is Dulcinea cannot be achieved at such a small price. Sancho should know that works of charity that are done tepidly and half-heartedly have no merit and are worthless."

To which Sancho responded: "Your ladyship, give me an appropriate scourge or rope, and I'll whip myself with it, as long as it doesn't hurt me too much. I'll have your grace know that, although I'm a peasant, my flesh is more cotton than hemp, and it wouldn't be good for me to do myself damage for someone else's gain."

"All right," said the duchess, "tomorrow I'll give you a scourge that will be just right and will suit the tenderness of your flesh, as if your flesh were your own sister."

To which Sancho said: "I want you to know, *señora mía* of my soul, that I've written a letter to my wife, Teresa Panza, telling her everything that has happened to me since I left her. I have it here inside my shirt, and all it needs is to be addressed. I would like you to read it because is seems to me to be in line with a governor—I mean, in the style of what governors ought to write."

"And who wrote it?" asked the duchess.

"Who would write it if not me, sinner that I am?" responded Sancho.

"And did you write it down?"

"Not in a million years," responded Sancho, "because I don't know how to read or write, although I can sign my name."

---

* The original Spanish—*La letra con sangre entra* ("Learning [letters] comes by means of blood")—is typically said to schoolchildren regarding the effort necessary to learn, and has an ironic flavor here.

"Let me see it," said the duchess, "because it must be that you show the quality and capacity of your wit in it."

Sancho took out the letter from his shirt and when the duchess took it, she saw that it read this way:

Letter from Sancho Panza to Teresa Panza, his wife

*"If they gave me solid lashes, at least I had a
fine mount";* if I got a good governship, it's
costing me hearty lashes. You won't understand
this, Teresa, for now—you'll find out about
it soon. You should know, Teresa, that I've
determined that you'll ride in a coach, for that's
the appropriate thing to do, for anything else
would be like crawling on all fours. You are a
wife of a governor, so see if they'll talk about
you behind your back now. I'm sending you a
green hunting outfit that my lady the duchess
gave me. Turn it into a skirt and bodice for our
daughter. Don Quixote, my master, the way I
heard it said in this region, is a crazy sane man
and an amusing idiot, and that I'm not too
far behind him. We have been in the Cave of
Montesinos, and the wizard Merlin has selected
me for the disenchantment of Dulcinea del
Toboso, known as Aldonza Lorenzo in those
parts, and with three thousand three hundred
lashes that I have to give to myself, less five,
she'll be as disenchanted as the mother who
bore her. Don't tell any of this to anyone
because "if you take a piece of business to the
town council, some will call it white, others
black."*

*In a few days I'll leave for the governorship,
where I'm going with a great desire to make
some money, because they've told me that all*

---

* It is assumed that this refers to an unattested proverb dealing with the lawbreaker who is whipped, then put on the back of a donkey and paraded through town. See Part I, chapter twenty-two, where Sancho speaks of prisoners being shamed in public. Sancho is being ironic in a couple of ways, particularly in reference to his whiplashes.

*novice governors go with that same desire. I'll
take the pulse of the place and I'll tell you if
you have to come to be with me or not. The
donkey is fine, and he sends you his regards,
and I won't leave him behind, even if they
make me the Grand Turk.* My lady, the duchess, kisses your hands a thousand times. Send
her back two thousand, for there's nothing that
costs less or comes cheaper, according to my
master, than good manners. God hasn't been
pleased to offer me another valise with another
hundred escudos like the last time. But don't
worry, Teresa, dear, for "the one who sounds
the alarm is safe," and "everything will come
out in the wash" with this governorship. One
thing that bothers me is that they told me that
once I taste it, I'll eat my hands after it, and if
this is true, it'll cost me dearly, although those
who are maimed or one-armed have benefits in
the alms they beg for. So, one way or another,
you're to be rich and will have good fortune.
May God give it to you as well as He can, and
may He keep me healthy to serve you. From
this castle, on the 20th of July, 1614.*

Your husband the Governor,

Sancho Panza

Once the duchess finished reading the letter, she said
to Sancho: "The good governor is a bit off the track in two
places—the first is when he says or gives her to understand
that this government is being given to him in exchange for
the lashes he is to give himself, when he knows full well,
and cannot deny, that when the duke, my lord, promised it
to him, no one in the world had yet dreamed of any lashes.
The second thing is he shows himself to be very greedy in
the letter, and I wouldn't want him to look like a seeker of
gold, because 'greed bursts the bag' and a greedy governor
makes for ungoverned justice."

* This was the sultan of Constantinople. See Part I, chapter forty, page 379.

"I didn't mean it that way, *señora*," responded Sancho, "and if your grace thinks that the letter shouldn't be sent as it is, we can just tear it up and start again, and it might prove to be a worse one if it's just left up to me."

"No, no," replied the duchess, "this one is fine, and I want the duke to see it."

With this they went into a garden where they were to have lunch that day. The duchess showed Sancho's letter to the duke, from which he derived great pleasure. They ate, and after the cloths were removed and they had enjoyed a delicious conversation with Sancho for a while, suddenly they heard the sad notes of a fife and the hoarse beating of an unharmonious drum. They all seemed to be agitated because of the confused, military, and sad harmony, especially don Quixote, who was so excited he could hardly stay seated. As for Sancho—no need to mention it—his fear took him to his accustomed refuge, which was next to or behind the skirts of the duchess, because really and truly the sounds they were hearing were very sad and melancholic. And when they were all in such suspense, they saw two men enter the garden dressed in mourning that trailed on the ground. They were playing two large drums, also draped in black. To their side came the fife player, clad in black as the others were. Following these three came a person of gigantic proportions, draped rather than dressed in a very black long robe, whose train likewise was enormously large. Over the gown was a wide strap, also black, on which hung an inordinately large scimitar set with stones in a black scabbard. His face was covered with a transparent black veil through which one could glimpse a very long beard that was as white as snow. With great gravity and composure he moved in time with the drums. His immense size, his affected gait, his blackness, and his retinue could and did amaze everyone who looked at him and was unaware of who he was.

He went with the already mentioned slowness and pomposity to kneel before the duke, who, with the others, awaited him standing, and wouldn't allow him to speak until he stood up. The frightening and monstrous apparition did so, and once he was standing, he removed the veil from his face, revealing the most horrendous, longest, whitest, and fullest beard that human eyes had ever seen up to that point, and then, fixing his gaze on the duke, he drew from his wide and expanded chest a grave and sonorous voice, and said: "Very high and powerful lord, I'm known as Trifaldín of the White Beard. I'm the squire of the Countess Trifaldi, also known as the Distressed Duenna, on whose behalf I'm bringing to your greatness a message, and it's that your magnificence be pleased to allow her to enter and tell you of her affliction, which is among the most unusual and astonishing ones that the most anguished imagination in the world could dream up, but first, she wants to know if the brave and never conquered don Quixote de La Mancha is present, whom she has come on foot to seek, without eating, from the kingdom of Candaya* to your estate, something that should be held as a miracle, or as the result of enchantment. She's at the gate of this castle or country estate, and is waiting only for your blessing to enter. I have spoken."

And then he coughed, smoothed his beard from top to bottom with both hands, and with great calm waited for the answer from the duke, which was: "Yes, good squire Trifaldín of the White Beard, we have known of the misfortune of my lady the Countess Trifaldi, whom the enchanters have named the Distressed Duenna, for some days. You can well tell her to come in, stupendous squire, where she'll find the brave don Quixote de La Mancha, whose generous qualities will surely provide all protection and assistance, and you can also tell her that if she needs my help, it won't be lacking, since I'm obliged to give it to her, being a knight, whose duty it is to help all kinds of women, especially widowed, injured, and distressed duennas, as your mistress must be."

When Trifaldín heard this, he knelt on one knee and signaled to the fife and drum players to begin playing, and with the same music and tempo in which he'd entered, he went out of the garden, leaving everyone astonished by his appearance and demeanor.

And the duke, turning toward don Quixote, said: "So, famous knight, neither the darkness of wickedness nor ignorance can conceal and dim the light of courage and of virtue. I say this because it has been just six days since your

---

* Candaya seems to be an island that the squire later situates near modern Sri Lanka. Don't try to find it on the map, since it is fictional.

goodness has been in this castle and already sad and distressed people come here looking for you—not in coaches or on dromedaries—but on foot and fasting, confident that they will find in this very strong arm the remedy for their afflictions and travails, thanks to your great deeds, which are celebrated far and wide over the known world."

"I would like, *señor* duke," responded don Quixote, "for that holy ecclesiastic, who showed such prejudice and ill will toward knights-errant at dinner the other night, to be here now to see with his own eyes whether knights are necessary in the world. He could actually touch with his own hands those people who are extraordinarily distressed and who, when they're in dire straits and in enormous misfortune, don't go looking for relief from the houses of men of letters, nor of village sextons, nor from the knight who has never left the city limits of his town, nor from the lazy courtly knight, who goes looking for news to tell others rather than trying to do works and deeds for others to tell and write about. Relief from distress, rescue from need, protection of maidens, solace of widows, can be sought in no better type of person than knights-errant, and because I'm one of them, I give infinite thanks to heaven, and I consider any misfortune and labor that I may undergo along the way well worth it in this so honorable profession. Let this duenna come and ask whatever she wants, and I'll find relief for her through the might of my arm and in the intrepid resolve of my dauntless will."

Chapter 37.* Where the famous adventure of the Distressed Duenna is continued.

THE DUKE and duchess were extremely delighted to see how well don Quixote was responding to their plan, but just then Sancho said: "I don't want this duenna to put some stumbling block in the way of my promised government, because I heard from an apothecary from Toledo—and he spoke as beautifully as a goldfinch sings—that when

---

* Arabic numbers are used here in the first Spanish edition instead of Roman.

duennas interfere, nothing good can come out of it. So help me God! How that apothecary bore a grudge against duennas, and since they are all vexatious and troublesome, no matter what their rank and disposition, I have to wonder about the distressed one, as they've called this Countess Three Skirts* or Three Trains—because in my region skirts and trains, trains and skirts, it's all the same."

"Hush, Sancho, my friend," said don Quixote. "Since this *señora* duenna has come from such a long way to seek me, she must not be one of the ones whom the apothecary was thinking of. Moreover this one is a countess, and when countesses serve as duennas, it must be they're serving queens and empresses, for countesses are great ladies who are waited upon by other duennas."

To this doña Rodríguez responded: "My lady the duchess has duennas in her service who could have been countesses if Fortune had favored them. But 'laws go as kings will' and no one should speak ill of duennas, especially of the old maids, for, although I'm not one of them myself, I can understand and appreciate the advantage that a maiden duenna has over a widowed one, and 'he who sheared us still has the shears in his hand.'"†

"Even so," replied Sancho, "there's so much to shear in duennas, according to my barber, that 'it would be better not to stir the rice, even though it sticks.'"

"Squires always," responded doña Rodríguez, "are our enemies, since they're imps of antechambers, and they see us all the time. The times that they're not praying—and there are many such—they spend gossiping about us, digging up our bones,‡ and burying our good name. Well, I'd like to send them to the galleys, because, even though they don't like the idea, we too have to live in the world and in noble houses, though we may die of hunger and we may cover our delicate or not so delicate flesh with nun's habits, as one covers a dung heap with a tapestry on the day of the procession. I swear that if I were allowed and the occasion demanded, I would make not only those present but

---

* *Trifaldi* implies "three skirts" in Spanish.

† That is, "he who treated one of us badly can also treat another one badly."

‡ That is, "gossiping about our shortcomings."

everyone understand that there's no virtue that duennas don't possess."

"I believe," said the duchess, "that my good doña Rodríguez is right, very right, but she must wait for some other time to defend herself and the other duennas, to refute the bad opinion of that apothecary, and take away the one that the great Sancho Panza holds in his heart."

To which Sancho responded: "Since I've tasted a bit what it's like to be a governor I've lost something of the pettiness of being a squire and I don't care a wild fig for all the duennas in the world."

The conversation about duennas would have continued if the music of the fife and drums hadn't started up again, from which they understood that the Distressed Duenna was coming. The duchess asked the duke if it would be good to go out to welcome her, since she was a countess and a noble person.

"For what she has of a countess," responded Sancho before the duke could say anything, "I agree we should go out to welcome her, but for what she has of a duenna, I'm of the opinion that we shouldn't move a muscle."

"Who brought you into this, Sancho?" said don Quixote.

"Who, *señor*?" responded Sancho. "I brought myself, and I can, too, as a squire who has learned courtesy in your grace's school, since you're the most courteous and best-mannered knight in the realm of courtesy, and in these matters, according to what I've heard your grace say, 'you can lose as much by a card too many as by a card too few' and 'a word to the wise is sufficient.'"

"It's as Sancho says," said the duke. "We'll see first what the countess is like and then we can gauge the courtesy due her."

The fife and drums players appeared again as they had the first time.

And here the author ended this short chapter and began the next one dealing with the same adventure, which is one of the most notable ones in the history.

Chapter XXXVIII. Where the story of the misfortune of the Distressed Duenna is told.

FOLLOWING THE sad musicians, as many as twelve duennas entered the garden in two columns, all dressed in roomy nuns' habits made of what looked like fine lightweight wool, with white headdresses of fine muslin. These were so long that only the hems of the habits were visible. Following them came the Countess Trifaldi, whom Trifaldín of the White Beard was leading by the hand. She was dressed in a high-quality and very dark un-napped flannel (for if it had been napped, each tuft would have been the size of a chickpea from Martos*). The tail, or skirt, or whatever you might want to call it, ended in three trains, each of which was being held in the hands of three pages, also dressed in mourning, making a handsome and mathematical figure with those three acute angles formed by the three trains, and all of them realized when they saw the three-pointed dress that that was why she was called the COUNTESS TRIFALDI, as if we were saying the COUNTESS OF THE THREE SKIRTS. And Benengeli says that it was true and that her real name was COUNTESS LOBUNA because many wolves were bred in her county, and, if instead of wolves they were foxes, they would have called her the COUNTESS ZORRUNA,† because it's the custom in those parts for people to take the names of things that abound on their estates. However this countess, to favor the novelty of her skirt, dropped LOBUNA and took up TRIFALDI.

The twelve duennas and the lady came in slowly, their faces covered with black veils, and not of the kind you could see through, like the squire's, but so dense that nothing could be seen behind them.

As soon as the squadron of duennas appeared, the duke,

---

* Martos is an Andalusian town in the province of Jaén. The indefatigable Rodríguez Marín found documents showing that Cervantes went to Martos in 1592 and collected 150 bushels of chickpeas for use in galleys (volume six, p. 153, note 1).

† *Lobo* means "wolf" and *zorro* means "fox."

the duchess, don Quixote, and everyone else who was looking at that slow procession stood up. The twelve duennas
stopped and made a passage, through the middle of which
the Distressed Duenna came forward without releasing
Trifaldín's hand, and when the duke, the duchess, and don
Quixote saw them, they strode out a dozen paces to welcome her.

She, kneeling on the ground, with a voice that was more
coarse and rasping than soft and delicate, said: "May it
please your greatnesses not to show so much courtesy to
this your manservant—I mean, to this your maidservant!
I'm so distressed that I can't speak properly, since my
strange and never-before-seen misfortune has carried away
my senses. I don't know where they are, and they must be
a long way away, for the more I search for them, the less I
find of them."

"A person would be senseless," responded the duke,
"*señora* countess, who couldn't see how worthy you are
and that you're deserving of the cream of courtesy and the
flower of politest ceremonies."

And taking her by the hand, he led her to sit next to the
duchess, who received her with great courtesy as well.

Don Quixote said nothing and Sancho was dying to see
Trifaldi's face and also the faces of some of her many duennas, but it was not possible until they revealed them at their
pleasure and free will.

Once they all settled down and were quiet, everyone
was waiting to see who would break the silence, and it was
the Distressed Duenna, with these words: "I'm confident,
most powerful lord, most beautiful lady, and very discreet
company, that my great affliction will find in your worthy
hearts a no less attentive than generous and sympathetic
reception. This affliction is such that it can make marble
tender, soften diamonds, and mollify the steel of the hardest hearts in the world. But before I announce it to your
sense of hearing, not to mention your ears, I would like you
to make known to me whether in this fellowship, group,
and company is to be found the very unblemished don Quixote de La Manchísima, and his squirísimo,* Panza."

---

* They are misusing these Latin suffixes, meaning "very," in an attempt
to sound lofty.

"The Panza," Sancho said, before anyone else could respond, "is here, and don Quixotísimo as well. So you can, needy duennísima, say what you would likísimo. We're all ready and preparedísimo to be your servantísimos."

At this, don Quixote stood and, directing his words to the Distressed One, said: "If your afflictions, needy *señora*, can offer some hope of relief by the bravery or strength of some knight-errant, here are mine, which, although feeble and limited, can be used in your service. I'm don Quixote de La Mancha, whose business is to help all kinds of people in need, and that being so, as it is, you need not, *señora*, beg for favors nor use preambles, but in plain terms and without beating around the bush state what your afflictions are. Listeners will hear you, and if they can't help you, at least they will commiserate with you."

When she heard this, the Distressed Duenna gave every indication that she would throw herself at the feet of don Quixote, and in fact she did so, and struggling to embrace them, she said: "Before these feet and legs I throw myself, unconquered knight, since they're the pedestals and columns of knight-errantry. I want to kiss these feet, on whose footsteps hangs the entirety of my relief, brave errant, whose deeds leave behind and dim the fabled ones of the Amadises, Esplandianes, and Belianises!"

And turning away from don Quixote, she faced Sancho Panza and, grasping him by the hands, said to him: "Oh, you, the most loyal squire that ever served a knight-errant in modern or in ancient times, whose goodness is more expansive than the beard of Trifaldín, my companion present here! You can well pride yourself that in serving the great don Quixote you're serving in effect the whole multitude of knights who have ever borne arms in the world. I beg you, by what you owe to your most loyal goodness, to be a just intercessor for me with your master, so that he'll aid this most humble and most unfortunate countess."

To which Sancho responded: "*Señora mía*, that my goodness is as long and large as the beard of your squire doesn't matter very much to me. What is important is that my soul has a beard and a mustache when I leave this life. I care little or not at all about beards here on earth. But without these schemes or supplications, I'll beg my master—who I know loves me, and more so now that he needs me for a certain favor—to help you insofar as he can. Disclose your affliction and tell it to us, and leave it to us, for we'll all understand."

The duke and duchess were bursting with laughter at these things, as were the others who had figured out the truth of this adventure, and they praised among themselves the shrewdness and ingenuity of Trifaldi, who sat down and said: "Queen Maguncia,* widow of King Archipiela,† her lord and husband, from whose marriage was born the princess Antonomasia,‡ heiress of the realm, reigned over the famous kingdom of Candaya, which lies between Trapobana and the Southern Sea, two leagues away from Cape Comorín.§ Antonomasia was raised and grew up under my protection and instruction, since I was the most important duenna, and the one of longest service to her mother. It happened, then, as days came and went, the girl Antonomasia came to be fourteen years old and with such a perfection of beauty that Nature couldn't improve on it. And should we think she had the mind of a child? Her mind was as great as her beauty, and she was the most beautiful girl in the world, and still is, if the envious Fates and the Three Sisters¶ haven't cut the yarn of her life. But they haven't yet, for heaven will not allow such a bad thing to happen on earth. It would be like plucking a bunch of premature grapes from the best grapevine.

---

* *Maguncia* is the Spanish name for Mainz, the city on the Rhine River in Germany, where Gutenberg set up his printing press.
† Abbreviated form of *archipiélago*, a series of islands.
‡ *Antonomasia* is the rhetorical device of using a proper name to represent a class of persons or a specific trait, such as "Juan is a real Solomon" ("wise ruler").
§ Trapobana refers to modern Sri Lanka. See Part I, chapter eighteen, page 140. Cape Comorín is the southern tip of India. The Southern Sea is the Indian Ocean.
¶ The Three Sisters in classical mythology control life and death. Clotho spins the thread of life at birth; Lachesis, the disposer of lots, determines the length of life; and Atropos cuts off life. The Three Sisters were well-known in Spain because they appear in *Eclogue II* by Garcilaso, Spain's most renowned poet.

"An infinite number of princes, both foreign and domestic, fell in love with this beauty whom I hardly have the words to describe—among whom a certain knight at court dared to raise his eyes to this heaven of so much beauty, trusting in his youth, elegance, and in his many skills, gallantry, accomplishments, and charm. I'll have you know, if it won't bore you, that he played the guitar and could almost make it speak, and what's more he was a poet and a great dancer, and he could make birdcages, so well that he could have earned a living at it, if he should find himself in great need. All of these skills and graces are sufficient to demolish a mountain, not to mention to move a delicate maiden. But all his elegance and charms, and all his skills and abilities, were of little or no use to subdue the fortress of my girl, if that shameless thief hadn't gotten to me first. At the outset, the brigand and soulless vagabond made sure to win my will over and overcome it, so that I, a bad governess, would give him the keys to the fortress I was supposed to be guarding.

"At length he flattered my senses and overcame my will with I don't know what trinkets and headdress pins. But what most humbled me and brought my downfall was the verses that I heard him sing one night from the window that looked out onto a narrow street where he stood, and if I don't remember badly, they were these:

From that sweet enemy of mine
  My bleeding heart hath had its wound;
  And to increase the pain I'm bound
  To suffer and to make no sign.*

"The verses seemed like pearls to me, and his voice sweet as syrup; and afterward, ever since then, looking at the misfortune into which I've fallen, I've thought that poets, as Plato admonished,† should be banished from all well-ordered states—at least the lascivious ones, for they

---

* This is a translation from the fifteenth-century Italian poet Serafino dell'Aquila (1466–1500), annotated by editors since Juan Antonio Pellicer put it in his 1797 edition of the *Quixote*.
† In his *Republic*, III.

write verses, not like those dealing with the Marqués de Mantua, that entertain and draw tears from women and children, but subtleties of the kind that pierce your heart like soft thorns, and like the lightning bolts that strike you there, without tearing your dress. And he sang another one:

Come, Death, so subtly veiled that I
    Thy coming know not, how or when,
    Lest it should give me life again
    To find how sweet it is to die.*

"And other little verses in this same style, and refrains that sung were enchanting and when written would amaze. Well, what happens when they humble themselves to write a type of verse common in Candaya, and which was called SEGUIDILLAS? There's where souls would dance about, laughter would ring out, and bodies would become restless, and finally agitate all the senses. And so I say, *señores*, that they should rightly exile troubadours to the Islands of Lizards. But they're really not to blame—those who praise them and the foolish women who believe them are. And if I'd been as good a duenna as I should have been, his stale conceits wouldn't have moved me, nor should I have believed his statement to the effect: 'I live dying, I burn up in the ice, I shiver in the fire, I hope without hope, I leave and I stay' along with other impossible things of that kind that his writings were full of. What should I do when they promise the Phœnix of Arabia,† the Crown of Aridiana,‡ the horses of the Sun,§ pearls from the Southern Sea, the gold

---

* This is modified from a popular four-verse poem by Comendador Escrivá (fifteenth century) and published in the *Cancionero general* in Valencia (1511).

† Mentioned in the *Natural History* X, 2, of Pliny the Elder (A.D. 23–79).

‡ *Aridiana* is a rustic way in Spanish of referring to Ariadna (Ariadne, in Greek mythology). When she married Dionysus, he gave her a crown, now among the stars, known as the Corona Borealis.

§ The Roman god Sol (Helios in Greek) drove his four-horse chariot across the sky every day. These are the horses referred to here.

of Tíbar,* the balm of Pancaya?† In these promises they let their pens run free, since it costs them little to promise what they have no intention of delivering, nor could they deliver. But I wander. Woe is me, unfortunate one! What crazy act or what folly leads me to tell of the defects of others when I have so much to say about my own? Woe is me, once again, luckless person that I am! The verses didn't overcome me—my foolishness did. The music didn't make me soft—my frivolity did. My great ignorance and my lack of caution opened the way and cleared the path for the footsteps of don Clavijo, for this is the name of the knight I mentioned. And with me as the go-between, he found his way many times into the bedchambers of that deceived— not by him but by me—Antonomasia, under the title of her lawful husband, because, although I'm a sinner, I wouldn't consent to his getting even as far as the welt of the sole of her slippers unless he was her husband. No, no! Marriage has to precede any affair like this that I have anything to do with! But there was a flaw in this business, and it was that there was no equality, since don Clavijo was an ordinary knight and Antonomasia was a princess, heiress, as I said, to the kingdom.

"This intrigue continued, concealed and hidden by the cleverness of my prudence, until I noticed a certain swelling growing swiftly in the tummy of Antonomasia, the fear of which made the three of us go into a secret meeting and the result was that before this bad news was made public, don Clavijo would ask to marry Antonomasia before the vicar to fulfill a contract that the princess had made agreeing to be his wife, and was written at my insistence in such a binding way that even Samson's strength couldn't break it. The preparations were made, the vicar saw the contract and he heard the confession of the lady. She confessed openly, and he placed her in the custody of a very honorable bailiff—"

Just then Sancho interrupted, saying: "So, there are bai-

---

* Many think that Tíbar is a river. Rodríguez Marín maintains that it comes from the Arabic *tibr*, meaning "pure"; thus it refers to pure gold.
† Pancaya refers to Felix Arabia, modern Yemen, a fertile region, celebrated for its spices, among other things.

liffs, poets, and *seguidillas* in Candaya, too. It seems to me
that the world is the same everywhere. But hurry up a bit,
your grace, *señora* Trifaldi, because it's getting late and I'm
dying to find out the end of this long history."

"All right," responded the countess.

Chapter XXXIX. *Where Trifaldi continues her stupendous and memorable history.*

THE DUCHESS got as much pleasure from anything Sancho said as don Quixote despaired at it, and after he
told him to be quiet, the Distressed One continued, saying:
"So, after many questions and answers, since the princess
persisted in not varying her original answer, the vicar found
in favor of don Clavijo and gave her to him as his legitimate
wife, which so upset the queen, doña Maguncia, that within
three days we buried her."

"Without a doubt, she must have died," said Sancho.

"Evidently," responded Trifaldín. "In Candaya living people aren't buried—only dead ones."

"It's a known fact, *señor* squire," replied Sancho, "that
people who have just fainted have been buried, having
been thought to have died, and it seems to me that Queen
Maguncia would have fainted instead of died. 'Where
there's life, there's hope,' and the princess' foolishness was
not so great as to be felt so deeply. If this woman had gotten married to some page or some servant from the house,
as many others have done, according to what I hear, it
would have been past remedy. But having married a knight
who was such a gentleman, and one so accomplished as
this one has been described, in truth, in truth, although it
was foolish, it was not as bad as you might think, because
according to the precepts of my master, who is here and
won't let me lie, just as educated men can become bishops,
knights—and especially errant ones—can become kings
and emperors."

"You're quite right, Sancho," said don Quixote, "because
a knight-errant, if he has just a bit of luck, is always at the
threshold of being the greatest lord in the world. But let
señora Distressed go on with her story. It seems to me that

what remains to be told is the bitter part of what has been up to now a sweet tale."

"The bitter part indeed remains to be told," responded the countess, "and so bitter is it that in comparison with it, bitter apples* are sweet, and oleander† is tasty. Now that the queen was dead, and not just in a faint, we buried her, and we had hardly covered her with dirt and said our last farewell when *quis talia fando temperet a lachrymis*?‡ Who should appear on the grave of the queen, riding a wooden horse, but the giant Malambruno, Maguncia's first cousin, who, aside from being cruel, was also an enchanter, and who, with his magic, to avenge the death of his cousin, and to punish the daring of don Clavijo, as well as the excesses of Antonomasia, left them enchanted on top of the grave itself. She has been changed into an ape made of bronze and he into a crocodile of some unknown metal, and between them is a column, also made of metal, on which is written in the Syriac language§ some letters that, having been translated into Candayan, and now into Spanish, read as follows:

THESE TWO DARING LOVERS WILL NOT RETURN TO THEIR ORIGINAL FORM UNTIL THE WORTHY MANCHEGAN DOES SINGULAR BATTLE WITH ME. FOR HIS VALOR ALONE THE FATES HAVE RESERVED THIS UNPARALLELED ADVENTURE.

"Once this was done, he took from its sheath a wide and very large cutlass, and, taking me by the hair, he threatened to slit my throat and cut off my head. I became alarmed and my voice stuck in my throat and I was mortified in the extreme. But with a trembling and mournful voice, I told him so many things that I forced him to put off the execution of his severe sentence. Finally, he had all the duennas of the palace brought before him—and they were these present—

---

* These "bitter apples" aren't apples at all, but rather a kind of Mediterranean squash.

† The oleander has a poisonous milky juice.

‡ From Virgil's *Æneid*, II, 6 and 8: "Who, on hearing this, can contain his tears?"

§ The Syriac language, based on East Aramaic, flourished from the third through the seventh centuries.

and after having exaggerated our guilt and condemned the character of duennas in general, and their bad customs and worse tricks, and heaping the guilt onto all of them that I alone had, he said that he didn't want to impose the death penalty on us but rather other prolonged sentences that would give us a cruel and continuous death, and at the very instant he spoke those words, we all felt the pores of our faces opening up and it felt like our faces were being pricked with needles. We raised our hands to our faces, and we found them to be the way you'll now see."

And then the Distressed One and the others removed the veils they had been wearing, and revealed their faces populated with beards, some of them red, others black, some white, and some brown, at which sight the duke and duchess were astonished, don Quixote and Sancho were stunned, and all the others astounded. Trifaldi continued: "In this way that rogue and malevolent Malambruno covered the softness and smoothness of our faces with the roughness of these hog's bristles. It's a shame heaven didn't ordain him to chop off our heads with his great cutlass rather than darken the light of our faces with this fur that covers them. If we consider it, *señores míos*—and what I'm about to say should be said with eyes turned into fountains, but the thought of our misfortune, and the seas of tears that have already rained down, has them without fluid, and dry as chaff, so I'll say it without tears ... So, as I was saying, where can a duenna who has a beard go? What father or mother will have compassion for her? Who will help her? Even when she has a smooth complexion and her face is tortured with a thousand kinds of cosmetics and makeup, she can hardly find anyone to like her; what will she do when she shows a face that looks like a forest? Oh, duennas and my companions, we were born at a bad time, and at a cursèd instant our parents begat us!"

At this, she looked like she was about to faint.

Chapter XL. About things that appertain and pertain to this adventure and to this memorable story.

REALLY AND truly all those who take pleasure in histories such as this one should be grateful to Cide Hamete, its first author, because of the care he took in telling us the least details of it, omitting nothing—no matter how small—that he didn't bring to the light of day. He imparts thoughts, reveals intentions, answers unasked questions, clarifies doubts, and resolves arguments. Finally, he satisfies and explains the tiniest details that the most curious mind might desire to know. Oh, most celebrated author! Oh, fortunate don Quixote! Oh, famous Dulcinea! Oh, amusing Sancho Panza! May they all together and each one individually live infinite centuries for the pleasure and universal enjoyment of all those alive.

So, the history says that as soon as Sancho saw the Distressed One in a faint, he said: "I swear on the faith of a good man and by the life of all of my Panza ancestors that I've never heard of nor seen, nor has my master told me anything about, nor even in his mind has he ever considered, an adventure such as this one. Malambruno, may a thousand devils haul you away—not just curse you, since you're both an enchanter and a giant! Couldn't you have found another way of punishing these sinners other than putting beards on them? Wouldn't it have been better for them, and more appropriate, if you had just cut off half their noses, even if it made them speak with a twang, rather than giving them beards? I'll wager they don't have enough income to pay someone to shave them off."

"That's the truth, *señor*," said one of the twelve. "We don't have the income to have ourselves shaved, and so some of us have been saving money by using sticky patches or plasters and applying them to our faces and yanking them off, and then we're as smooth as the bottom of a mortar made of stone.* Although there are in Candaya women who go from house to house to remove hair and pluck eyebrows and provide cosmetics for women, we duennas of my lady

---

* A stone mortar, such as the kind used with pestles by pharmacists to grind medicines, would become very smooth after long use.

always refused to let them in because most of them smack
of go-betweens, no longer being prime prostitutes. And if
señor don Quixote doesn't help us, they'll take us bearded
to our graves."

"I would shave off my own," said don Quixote, "in Moorish lands, if I couldn't relieve you of yours."

At this point, Trifaldi came out of her faint and said:
"The resonance of this promise, brave knight, came to my
ears in the middle of my fainting spell and has brought
me back to my senses, and so once again I ask, illustrious
knight and unconquerable *señor*, if you'll turn your promise into action."

"There will be no delay because of me," responded don
Quixote. "Tell me, *señoras*, what I should do. My courage is
ready to serve you."

"The thing is," responded the Distressed One, "from
here to the kingdom of Candaya, if you go on foot, is five
thousand leagues, but if you go by air in a direct line, it's
three thousand two hundred twenty-seven. You should
know that Malambruno told me that when fate should locate the knight, our liberator, he would send a mount that
is a lot better and with fewer defects than those you rent,
because it's a horse made of wood, the same one on which
Pierres carried off the abducted Magalona.* This horse is
guided by a peg in its forehead, which serves as a bridle,
and it flies through the air so swiftly that it seems like the
devils themselves are carrying it. This horse, according to
ancient tradition, was made by the wizard Merlin. He lent it
to Pierres, who was his friend, and with it he took great voyages and kidnapped, as has been said, the pretty Magalona,
carrying her on the horse's crupper through the air, leaving
all those on the ground who saw them dumbfounded. And
he never lent it to anyone except those he liked or who
paid him well. Since the great Pierres until now, we know
that no one else has ridden him. But by magic, Malambruno

---

* Martín de Riquer, the person who knows Old French and medieval Spanish heroic literature best, says that this episode of the flying wooden horse derives from an Old French source (ca. 1290) called
Cléomadés, which was related in prose in the Spanish *History of the
Very Valiant and Strong Clamades* ... (Burgos, 1521, and reprinted
many times). See also Part I, chapter forty-nine, pages 470–71.

has gotten possession of him and uses him for his voyages he makes once in a while to different parts of the world—today he's here, and tomorrow he's in France, and the next day in Potosí;* and the good part is that the animal neither eats nor sleeps nor uses horseshoes, and without wings zips through the air, and he who rides him can have a cup of water in his hand and not a drop will spill over, such is the smoothness of his gait, and that's why Magalona liked to ride him so much."

To this Sancho said: "For a smooth ride, there's my donkey, although he doesn't fly. But on the ground, I'll match him against any beasts of burden in the world."

Everyone laughed, and the Distressed One continued: "And this horse, if Malambruno wants to bring our misfortune to an end, will be in front of us before the night is half an hour old. Because he told me that the signal that he would give me, by which I would be able to tell that I had found the proper knight, would be that he'd send me the horse wherever I might be, opportunely, and with dispatch."

"And how many people fit on this horse?" asked Sancho.

The Distressed One responded: "Two people—one in the saddle, and one on the crupper—and these people are mostly a knight and his squire, when there's no kidnapped maiden."

"I would like to know," said Sancho, "*señora* Distressed, what the name of this horse is."

"His name," responded the Distressed One, "is not like Bellerophon's,† called Pegasus; nor like Alexander the Great's Bucephalus; nor like Brilladoro belonging to Roland;‡ nor Bayarte that belonged to Reinaldos de Montalbán; nor Frontino like the one of Ruggiero; nor Boötes, nor Peritoa, that they say belonged to the Sun,§ nor is he called Orelia, on

---

* Potisí is in Bolivia, and here refers to faraway places in general.

† Bellerophon captured the flying horse Pegasus and used him on many adventures. When he tried to fly to heaven, the gods sent a gadfly to sting the horse, and Bellerophon was thrown and killed.

‡ This Roland is the Orlando of *Orlando Furioso.*

§ The horses of the Sun (see Ovid's *Metamorphoses*, II, III) are Pyrœis, Eous, Æton, and Phlegon, and *not* Boötes and Peritoa, although Pyrœsis sounds a bit like the latter. Boötes is the Plowman constellation in the northern sky. Peritoa possibly refers to Theseus' friend Peirithous, who became a perpetual prisoner of Hades for trying to abduct Persephone.

which the unfortunate Rodrigo, the last Gothic king, entered into battle and lost his life."

"I'll bet," said Sancho, "that since they haven't given him any of the names of these famous horses of such well-known knights, they probably haven't given him the name of my master's horse, Rocinante, either, even though it's such a fitting one, and exceeds all the other names given so far."

"That's true," said the bearded countess, "but his fits him well, since he's named Clavileño the Swift, whose name jibes with his being made of wood and from the peg—the *clavija*—on his forehead,* and with the speed with which he travels. So as far as the name goes, he can compete with the famous Rocinante."

"The name doesn't displease me," replied Sancho, "but by what kind of bridle or halter is he guided?"

"I already said," responded Trifaldi. "With the peg that the rider moves from side to side to make him go high in the air or almost skim the ground, or between the two, which is the mean one seeks in all well-ordered actions."

"I would like to see it," responded Sancho, "but to think that I'll get up onto him, either on the saddle or on the crupper, is to try 'to get blood from a turnip.' Why, I can hardly hold myself straight on my own donkey, on a pack-saddle softer than silk itself, and now they want me to stay on the crupper made of wood without even a cushion or a pillow! By golly, I'm not going to let myself get battered in order to remove beards from anyone! Let them shave themselves as well as they can, because I don't plan to go with my master on such a long voyage, especially since I'm not as important for the shaving off of these beards as I am for the disenchantment of Dulcinea."

"Yes, you are," said the Distressed One, "and so much so that without your presence I've been led to believe that nothing will happen."

"Help in the name of the king!" said Sancho. "What do squires have to do with the adventures of their masters? Are they supposed to get all the fame for the adventures they do while we do all the work? I swear, if historians would only say: 'Such-and-such a knight did such-and-such

---

* The *leño* part of the name means "wood."

an adventure, but only with the help of his squire, without whom it would have been impossible to complete it.' But what they really write is just this: 'Don Parlimpómenon of the Three Stars completed the adventure of the six monsters,' without mentioning the person of his squire who witnessed it all, as if he didn't exist in the world! Now, *señores*, I say again that if my master can go alone, good luck in whatever he does. I'll stay here in the company of my lady the duchess, and it may be that when he comes back he'll find Dulcinea's cause greatly improved, because in slack times I plan to give myself a bunch of lashes so severe that my hair won't grow back."

"Even so, you must go with him if it's necessary, good Sancho, because important people beg you to. It would be a terrible thing if the faces of these women remained populated because of your pathetic fear."

"Help in the name of the king once again!" replied Sancho. "If this kindness were done for some modest maidens or for some orphans, a man could risk himself in any travail. But in order to take the beards off of duennas, nothing doing—I'd sooner see all of them with beards, from the oldest to the youngest, and from the most straitlaced to the most brazen one."

"You really have it in for the duennas, Sancho, my friend," said the duchess. "You seem to share the opinion of the Toledan apothecary, but I'm convinced you're not right. There are duennas in this house who can serve as models for the rest. And here's doña Rodríguez, who won't let me say otherwise."

"Your excellency has spoken well," said Rodríguez, "and God knows the truth about everything, and no matter how good or bad, bearded or smooth-skinned, we duennas may be, our mothers bore us like all other women, and since God put us on the earth, He knows for what reason, and I cling to His grace, and not to the beards of anyone else."

"All right, *señora* Rodríguez," said don Quixote, "and *señora* Trifaldi and company, I hope that heaven will look with kind eyes on your afflictions. Sancho will do whatever I command, both when Clavileño comes and when I find myself before Malambruno. I know that no razor will shave your graces as easily as my sword will chop the head from

Malambruno's shoulders. God will permit evil ones to exist, but not forever."

"Oh!" said the Distressed One just then. "Brave knight, may all the stars in all the regions of the sky look upon your greatness with favorable eyes, and may they infuse your spirit with all prosperity and courage so you can be the shield and protection for the downtrodden and disheartened race of duennas, maligned by apothecaries, gossiped about by squires, and tricked by pages. Woe to the wretched girl who, in the flower of her youth, doesn't become a nun rather than a duenna! How unfortunate we duennas are, for although we may come in a direct male line from Hector the Trojan* himself, our mistresses still speak to us as inferiors, and that makes them feel like they're queens. Oh, Giant Malambruno, although you're an enchanter, you keep your promises! Send us right now the peerless Clavileño, so that our misfortune can come to an end. If it gets hot and we still have these beards, alas! we'll be most unlucky."

Trifaldi said this with such feeling that it caused all the onlookers to start to cry, and even Sancho's eyes welled with tears, and he resolved in his heart to go with his master to the ends of the earth, if that would help remove the wool from those venerable faces.

Chapter XLI. About the arrival of Clavileño and the end of this drawn-out adventure.

NIGHT FELL and with it the time when the famous horse Clavileño should come, and whose tardiness bothered don Quixote, since it seemed to him that if Malambruno was delaying in sending it to him, either he wasn't the knight for whom this adventure was reserved, or Malambruno was afraid to engage in single battle with him. But all of a sudden four wild men dressed in green ivy entered the garden and on their shoulders they were bearing a large horse made of wood.

---

* Hector was a great warrior, a good son, and a loving husband, and has nothing to do with duennas.

They placed him on his feet and one of the wild men said: "May the person brave enough get up onto this horse."

"Not me," said Sancho. "I'm not getting up there because I'm not brave enough nor am I a knight."

And the wild man went on: "And may the squire, if there is any, sit on the crupper, and trust in the gallant Malambruno, because nothing and no one will hurt you except Malambruno's sword. And you have only to turn the peg that has been placed on his neck, and he'll take you through the air to where Malambruno is waiting. But so that the altitude and loftiness of the way won't make you dizzy, you have to blindfold your eyes until the horse neighs, and that will be the sign that your voyage is over."

Having said this, they left Clavileño, and went back to where they had come from with a gentle demeanor. The Distressed One, as soon as she saw the horse, almost with tears in her eyes said to don Quixote: "Brave knight, the promises of Malambruno have been fulfilled, the horse has arrived, our beards are growing, and each one of us, with every hair of our beards, beg you to shave and shear us, since all you have to do is get on the horse to give a happy beginning to your novel voyage."

"I'll do it very willingly, Countess Trifaldi, without taking time to find a cushion nor put spurs on so as not to delay, so eager am I to see you, *señora*, and all these duennas smooth and shaved."

"I'll not do it," said Sancho, "either willingly or not, in no way. And if this shaving cannot be done unless I get on the crupper of this horse, my master can find another squire to go with him, and these women can find another way to smooth their faces. I'm not a wizard who likes to fly through the air. And what will my islanders think when they find out their governor goes around flying along with the wind? And here's something else—since it's more than three thousand leagues from here to Candaya, and if the horse gets tired or the giant gets vexed, it'll take us half a dozen years to go there and come back, and there won't be either an *ínsula* or islanders in the world who'll know who I am. And since it's commonly said that 'danger lurks in delay' and 'when they give you a heifer, run and fetch a halter,' let the beards of these women excuse me, for 'St. Peter is at home in Rome.' I'm quite all right in this house, where so much kindness is

shown me, and from whose owner I am to receive so great
a boon as to see myself a governor."

To which the duke responded, "Sancho, my friend, the
ínsula that I've promised you will stay put and will not
wander away. It has roots that reach into the bowels of the
earth and they cannot be yanked out of where they are,
even if you try three times to do it. And since you know
there's no kind of office of importance that's not won without some kind of bribery, large or small, the bribe I want in
exchange for this governorship is for you to go with your
master don Quixote to bring about a happy conclusion
to this memorable adventure. Whether you come back
on Clavileño with the speed his swiftness promises, or if
bad luck brings you back and you have to come back on
foot as a pilgrim, from hostelry to hostelry, and from inn
to inn, whenever you return, you'll find your *ínsula* where
you left it, and your islanders with the same desire they
always have had to receive you, and my resolve will always
be the same; and don't doubt this truth, *señor* Sancho, for
otherwise it would be quite an insult to the desire I have
to serve you."

"Say no more," said Sancho. "I'm a poor squire and I
don't know how to respond to so much courtesy. Let my
master mount and cover my eyes, and commend me to God,
and tell me if I can commend my own self to our Lord while
we're flying, or invoke the angels who watch over me."*

To which Trifaldi responded: "Sancho, you can commend
yourself to God, or to whomever you wish. Malambruno,
although he's an enchanter, is a Christian, and performs
his enchantments very wisely, and with consideration, meddling with no one."

"All right then," said Sancho, "may God and the Holy Trinity of Gaeta help me."

"Since the memorable adventure of the fulling mills,"
said don Quixote, "I've never seen Sancho as afraid as he is
now, and if I were as superstitious as some are, his cowardice might make my courage waver. But come here, Sancho.
If we can be excused for a moment from this company, I'd
like to have a couple of words with you."

---

* Since this voyage smacks of sorcery, Sancho is loath to invoke God,
fearing some kind of divine retribution.

And drawing away among some trees in the garden, and taking Sancho by both his hands, he said to him: "Now you see, Sancho, brother, the long voyage that lies ahead of us, and God only knows when we'll be back, and whether or not the business at hand will allow us some respite or opportunity for other activities. So, I would like it if you would withdraw into your room, as if you were going to look for something you need for the voyage, and right there give yourself a good portion of the three thousand three hundred lashes you're obliged to, even if it's just five hundred. Then that part will be over, because 'to have begun something is like having it half-finished.'"

"By God!" said Sancho. "Your grace must be impaired! This is like what they say: 'you see me pregnant and you want me to be a virgin?' I have to sit on a wooden plank and your worship wants me to make my rear end sore? In truth, in truth, your grace, you're not right. Let's shave these duennas now. When we get back, I promise you on the faith of who I am to speedily pay my debt so that you'll be satisfied, and I say no more."

And don Quixote responded: "Well, with that promise, good Sancho, I'm relieved, and I believe you'll fulfill it, because, in effect, although you're unlettered, you're a veracious man."

"Voracious, no, even though I do get hungry once in a while," said Sancho, "but even if I were voracious, I'd keep this promise."

So they went back to climb onto Clavileño, and when he mounted, don Quixote said: "Blindfold yourself, Sancho, and climb up. He who sends for us from such a long way away didn't do it to trick us for the sake of the little glory he'd get by misleading those who trusted in him, and although everything can turn out differently from what I imagine, no malice can dim the glory of having undertaken this deed."

"Let's go, *señor*," said Sancho, "because I have the beards of these ladies nailed to my heart, and I won't eat a bite that tastes good to me until I see their faces smooth. Climb up first, your grace, and cover your eyes. Since I have to get up on the haunches, it's obvious that the one who sits in the saddle has to go first."

"That's true," replied don Quixote.

And taking a handkerchief out of his pocket, he asked the Distressed One to cover his eyes, but once they were covered, he took the blindfold off and said: "If I remember correctly, I've read in Virgil that business of the Palladium of Troy,* a horse made of wood that the Greeks gave to the goddess Pallas, and it was filled with armed soldiers, and turned out to be the total ruin of Troy. So I'd like to see what Clavileño has inside before we go."

"There's no need," replied the Distressed One, "for I'll vouch for the horse, and I know that Malambruno is neither mischievous nor traitorous. Your grace, *señor* don Quixote, can mount without fear, and I'll be to blame if something goes awry."

It seemed to don Quixote that anything he might say about his own safety would be to the detriment of his reputation for courage, and so without further debate, he mounted Clavileño, and tried the peg, which turned easily, and since there were no stirrups and his legs hung down, he looked just like a figure on a Flemish tapestry, painted or woven, in a scene of some Roman victory.† Much against his will, Sancho slowly approached to mount, and settling himself as well as he could on the haunches, he found them to be a bit hard and not at all soft, and he asked the duke, if it was possible, to give him a cushion or pillow, even if it was from his lady the duchess' drawing room or from the cot of some page, because the haunches of that horse seemed to be made more of marble than wood.

To this Trifaldi replied that Clavileño couldn't stand any kind of trapping or adornment. What he could do was sit sidesaddle, and that way he wouldn't feel the hardness so much. That's what Sancho did, and saying good-bye, he let himself be blindfolded, but after his eyes were covered,

---

* Don Quixote here confuses Palladium with the Trojan Horse. The Greeks pretended that the Trojan Horse was an offering to Athena (Pallas) in order to make Troy impregnable. Once inside the city, Greek soldiers came out of the horse and opened the gates of the city so their army could enter. *Instar montis equum, divina Palladis arte, ædificant* ("They built a horse as large as a mountain with the divine skill of Pallas"), *Æneid*, II, 15. I thank Nik Gross for the translation.
† The stirrup wasn't invented until about the year 500, after Roman times, and thus none would be depicted in a Roman scene.

he removed the blindfold and, looking tenderly at every-one with tears in his eyes, asked them to help him in his ordeal by each one saying one Our Father and one Hail Mary apiece so that God might provide them with people to say prayers for them if they found themselves in similar straits.

To which don Quixote said: "You thief, are you on the gallows, or in the throes of death, to use such supplica-tions? Aren't you, you soulless and cowardly creature, sit-ting where the beautiful Magalona sat, and when she got down, it wasn't to lower herself into her grave, but rather to become the queen of France, if the histories don't lie? And I—who am at your side—I'll be just like the valiant Pierres who sat in this same place that I now sit in. Blindfold your-self, I say, you spiritless animal, and don't let another word about your fears come from your mouth, at least in my presence."

"Blindfold me," responded Sancho, "and since they don't want me to commend myself, nor for me to be commended to God, is it any wonder that I'm afraid that some legion of devils might be lurking around that will snatch us away to Peralvillo?"*

They blindfolded themselves again, and when don Qui-xote felt he was ready, he turned the peg a bit and hardly had he placed his finger on it when all the duennas and everyone present raised their voices and said: "May God guide you, brave knight! God be with you, intrepid squire! Now, right now, you're flying through the air, rip-ping through it faster than an arrow! You're amazing and causing wonder in all those who are looking at you! Hold on, brave Sancho, for you're tottering a bit. Be careful not to fall! Your fall would be worse than that of the daring lad who tried to drive the chariot belonging to the Sun, his father."†

Sancho heard the shouts, and clutching his master tightly with both arms, said to him: "*Señor*, how can their voices

* Clemencín points out that Peralvillo was a town near Ciudad Real where the Holy Brotherhood summarily executed criminals.
† This refers to Phæthon, son of Apollo ("Sun"), who took his father's chariot and rode across the sky. When he was about to crash into the earth, Zeus killed him with a lightning bolt.

reach us if as they say we're so high in the air? It seems as if they're right here next to us?"

"Pay no attention to that, Sancho. Since these flights are so out of the ordinary, you can see and hear anything you like from a thousand leagues away. And don't squeeze me so hard, because you'll make me fall. In truth I don't know what is upsetting you or what you're afraid of. I'll swear that in all the days of my life I've never gotten on a horse that's so smooth. It's as if we haven't moved a step. Banish your fear, my friend, for everything is turning out fine, and the wind is at our back."

"That's the truth," responded Sancho, "because from this side I feel such a strong wind that it seems like a thousand bellows are blowing at me."

And that was really so, because some large bellows were blowing toward him. The adventure was so well planned by the duke and duchess and their steward that nothing was lacking to make it perfect.

When don Quixote felt the air, he said: "Without a doubt, Sancho, we must be in the second region of air, where hail and snow come from. Thunder and lightning are engendered in the third region, and if we keep going up in this way, soon we'll be in the region of fire, and I don't know how to turn this peg so that we won't rise to where we'll get burned."*

At this point, they warmed their faces with some tow, which is easy to light and extinguish, suspended from sticks a short distance away. Sancho felt the heat and said: "May they strike me down if we aren't in the region of fire or very near, because a large part of my beard has been singed and I'm about to take off my blindfold, *señor*, to see where we are."

"You'll do nothing of the kind," responded don Quixote. "Remember the true story of the *licenciado* Torralba,† whom the devils took flying through the air, riding on a pole, with his eyes closed, and in twelve hours he arrived in Rome, where he got off at the Torre di Nona,‡ which

---

* This paragraph presents Ptolemy's thought on the nature of space.
† Dr. Eugenio Torralba was tried by the Inquisition in 1531, having been accused of going from Spain to Rome on a rod, and returned the same night. See Clemencín, p. 1756, note 38.
‡ Annotators point out that this is a jail; true, but it's also a street: Via di Torre di Nona.

is a street in the city, and he saw the defeat, assault, and death of Bourbon,* and by the next morning he was back in Madrid, where he told everything he'd seen, and he also said that when he was flying through the air the devil told him to open his eyes, and he opened them, and he saw so close to himself the body of the moon that he could have grabbed it with his hand, and that he dared not look at the earth for fear of fainting. So, Sancho, there's no reason to take our blindfolds off. He who has sent for us will take care of us. And perhaps we're going higher so that we can fall onto the kingdom of Candaya like falcons do when they descend to catch a heron, no matter how high it's flying. And although it seems to us that it hasn't been half an hour since we left the garden, believe me, we must have traveled a long distance."

"I can't tell," responded Sancho Panza. "All I know is that if the lady Magallanes† or Magalona liked this seat, she must not have had very tender flesh."

The duke and duchess were hearing all these conversations, and were extraordinarily entertained by them. And wanting to bring the strange and invented adventure to a close, they used some lighted tow to set fire to Clavileño's tail and immediately—because the horse was filled with thundering firecrackers—it erupted with a strange noise and threw don Quixote and Sancho Panza to the ground, half-singed.

By this time, the whole bearded squadron of duennas had disappeared from the garden, Trifaldi and all, and those who were in the garden were acting as if they had fainted, stretched out on the ground. Don Quixote and Sancho got up badly bruised, and, looking around in all directions, they were astonished to see that they were in the garden from where they had left, and to see a great number of people stretched out on the ground. And their astonishment grew when at one side of the garden they saw a large lance stuck in the ground, and hanging from it by two silk cords was a

---

* This is Carlos, Duke of Bourbon (1490–1527), who was killed by a bullet while Rome was being sacked by soldiers of Carlos V in May of 1527.

† Magallanes is the Spanish name for the Portuguese explorer Fernão de Magalhães (1480–1521), whom we know as Magellan.

smooth white parchment where was written what follows
in large golden letters:

> THE ILLUSTRIOUS KNIGHT DON QUIXOTE DE LA
> MANCHA FINISHED AND COMPLETED THE ADVEN-
> TURE OF THE COUNTESS TRIFALDI, ALSO KNOWN
> AS THE DISTRESSED DUENNA, AND HER COMPANY,
> JUST BY ATTEMPTING IT.
>
> MALAMBRUNO IS COMPLETELY PLEASED AND SAT-
> ISFIED, AND THE CHINS OF THE DUENNAS ARE
> SMOOTH AND SHAVED, AND THE KING DON CLAVIJO
> AND QUEEN ANTONOMASIA ARE RESTORED TO THEIR
> ORIGINAL STATE. AND WHEN THE SQUIRELY WHIP-
> PING IS FINISHED, THE WHITE DOVE WILL BE FREED
> FROM THE FOUL FALCONS THAT PURSUE HER AND
> WILL BE IN THE ARMS OF HER BELOVED FLATTERER.
> FOR THIS IS THUS ORDERED BY THE WIZARD MERLIN,
> PROTOENCHANTER OF THE ENCHANTERS.

Once don Quixote had read the words of the parchment, he understood clearly that it was speaking of the
disenchantment of Dulcinea, and giving many thanks to
heaven for having completed such a great deed with so
little danger, returning to their former complexion the
faces of those venerable ladies who were no longer there,
he went over to where the duke and duchess were, as they
hadn't come to yet, and, grasping the duke by his hand, he
said to him: "So, good *señor*, take courage, take courage—
it's all over. The adventure is finished with no danger to
anyone, as is clearly shown by the banner hanging on that
column."

The duke roused, little by little, and like someone waking from a deep sleep, and the duchess was doing the same,
as was everyone else who was stretched out in the garden,
all showing such wonder and surprise that it almost looked
like they had truly undergone what they had been able to
simulate so well. The duke read the sign with half-closed
eyes, and then with open arms went over to embrace don
Quixote, telling him that he was the best knight ever seen
in any age.

Sancho was looking around for the Distressed One, to see what her face looked like without a beard, and if she was as beautiful without it as her gallant appearance promised. But they told him that as soon as Clavileño dropped burning from the skies and fell to the ground, the whole squadron of duennas along with Trifaldi had disappeared, and they were shaven and without stubble.

The duchess asked Sancho how things had gone on that long voyage. To which Sancho responded: "I, *señora*, felt that we were flying, as my master said, through the region of fire, and I wanted to take a peek under my blindfold. But my master, who I asked if I could take my blindfold off, didn't consent. But I have some kind of spark of curiosity in me, and wanting to know everything that's put in my way or is forbidden me, I neatly, and without anyone seeing, right at my nose, lifted the blindfold that was covering my eyes ever so slightly, and through that opening I looked at the earth, which was no larger than a mustard seed, and the people were just a bit larger than hazelnuts,* so you can see how high we were then."

To this the duchess said: "Sancho, my friend, do you realize what you're saying? You must not have seen the earth but rather only the people walking on it, because if the earth seemed to be the size of a mustard seed, and every person like a hazelnut, a single person would hide the entire earth."

"That's true," responded Sancho, "but I was looking through a little slit and saw the whole thing."

"Look, Sancho," said the duchess, "when you look through a slit, you can't see the whole thing you're looking at."

"I don't know about these ways of seeing," replied Sancho. "I only know you should realize that since we were flying by enchantment, by enchantment I could see the whole earth and all the people wherever I looked. And if I'm not believed so far, neither will your grace believe that when I took a peek just above my eyebrows I was so close to the sky that I wasn't more than a palm and a half from it, and I

---

* Mustard seeds are about two millimeters in diameter. Hazel nuts are about a half inch in diameter (thirteen millimeters).

can attest that it's very large, *señora mía*. And it happened that as we passed by the place where the seven little goats* are, since I was a goatherd when I was a boy, before God and on my soul, as soon as I saw them, I felt like frisking with them for a while, and if I didn't do it, I thought I'd burst. So here I am and what do I do? Without saying anything to anyone, I got off Clavileño neatly and quietly, and I frolicked with the goats—and they're like little flowers—for almost three-quarters of an hour and Clavileño didn't budge a step from where he was."

"And while the good Sancho was frolicking with the goats," asked the duke, "what was *señor* don Quixote doing?"

To which don Quixote responded: "Since all these things and all these events don't happen in the normal way, it's easy to believe that Sancho says what he does. As for me, I can say I didn't remove my blindfold either on the way up or on the way down, nor on the ground, nor did I see the heavens, nor the earth, nor the sea, nor the shore. It's true that I felt that I was going through the region of air, and that I was near the region of fire, but I can't believe that we went past it. Since the region of fire is between the atmosphere of the moon and the highest region of air, we couldn't have gotten to where the seven goats are without getting burned. And since we weren't consumed by fire, either Sancho is lying or he was dreaming."

"I'm neither lying nor dreaming," responded Sancho. "You can even ask me what the seven goats looked like, and you'll see if I'm telling the truth or not."

"Describe them, then, Sancho," said the duchess.

"Two of them are green," responded Sancho, "two of them are red, two are blue, and one is a mixture of all three."

"That's a new breed of goat," said the duke. "In our region of the earth we don't see such colors. I mean, our goats aren't those colors."

"Of course not," said Sancho. "Certainly there are differences between the goats in the heavens and those on earth."

---

* The seven goats are in the star cluster known as Pleiades, in the constellation Taurus, about four hundred light-years from the Earth. It has several hundred stars, of which six or seven can be seen without a telescope.

"Tell me, Sancho," asked the duke, "did you see a billy goat among those goats?"

"No, *señor*," responded Sancho, "but I heard it said that none got by the horns of the moon."*

They didn't want to ask him any more about his trip because it seemed to them that Sancho was ready to wander through the whole sky, and describe everything that happened, when in reality he hadn't left the garden. So, this was the end of the adventure of the Distressed Duenna, which amused the duke and duchess, not only then, but for the rest of their lives, and it gave Sancho something to talk about for centuries, if he lived that long.

Don Quixote went over to Sancho and whispered in his ear: "Sancho, if you expect me to believe what happened to you in the heavens, I want you to believe what I saw in the Cave of Montesinos, and I say no more."

Chapter XLII. About the advice that don Quixote gave Sancho before he went to govern the ínsula, with other well thought-out matters.

AFTER THE happy and amusing outcome of the adventure of the Distressed One, the duke and duchess were so pleased they decided to keep on playing tricks, seeing that they had a perfect subject who would consider their jokes to be real. So, having instructed their servants and vassals how to behave with Sancho in his governing of the promised *ínsula*, the day after the flight of Clavileño, the duke told Sancho to prepare himself and get ready to be a governor, for his islanders were waiting for him like the showers in May.

Sancho bowed and told him: "Since I came back down from the sky, and saw the earth so small from that high place, my desire to be a governor has diminished somewhat, because what greatness is it to be in control of a mustard seed, or what dignity or power is there in governing half a dozen men—that's how many there appeared to me to be—no bigger than hazelnuts? If your lordship were able

---

* Rico can't figure this meaning out either.

to give me a piece of heaven, even though it would be no bigger than half a league, I would prize it more than the best *ínsula* in the world."

"Look, Sancho, my friend," responded the duke, "I can't give a piece of heaven to anybody, even if it's no bigger than a fingernail. These favors and privileges are reserved exclusively to God. What I can give you I am giving you—a real and true *ínsula*: a round and well-proportioned one, bounteously and abundantly fertile, where, if you're clever enough, through the riches of the earth you can gain the riches of heaven."

"All right, then," responded Sancho, "let the *ínsula* come. I'll try to be the kind of governor who, in spite of all the rascals, will go to heaven. It's not from greed that I want to go where I don't belong nor try to make myself greater than others, but rather because I want to see what it's like to be a governor."

"If you try it once, Sancho," said the duke, "you'll eat your hands off after it, because it's so sweet to be in command and to be obeyed. Certainly when your master gets to be an emperor—which he surely will be, the way things have been going his way—it won't be easy to take it away from him, and he'll lament in his soul all the time he wasn't one."

"Señor," replied Sancho, "I imagine it's nice to be in command, even if it's only over a herd of cattle."

"May they bury me next to you, Sancho, for you know everything," responded the duke, "and I hope that you'll be as good a governor as your good judgment promises. And let it rest there. I want you to know that tomorrow morning you'll leave for the government of the *ínsula*, and this afternoon they'll fit you for the proper suit to wear, and furnish all the things you'll need to take when you leave."

"Dress me," said Sancho, "however you want. No matter how I'm dressed I'll still be Sancho Panza."

"That's the truth," said the duke, "but clothing has to fit the office or title you're practicing. It wouldn't be right for a professor of law to dress like a soldier, or a soldier like a priest. You, Sancho, will be dressed partly as a man of letters and partly as a captain, because in the *ínsula* that I'm giving you, arms are as necessary as letters, and letters are as necessary as arms."

"Of letters," responded Sancho, "I have few, because I still don't know the ABCs, but it's enough for me to have the *Christus** in my memory to be a good governor. Of arms, I'll use whatever they give me until I fall, with the help of God."

"With such a good memory," said the duke, "Sancho won't err in anything."

Just then don Quixote arrived, knowing what was going on and the swiftness with which Sancho was to leave for his governorship. With the permission of the duke, he took him by the hand, and went with him to his room with the intention of advising him how he needed to comport himself in his office.

Once they were in the room, then, he closed the door after them and practically forced Sancho to sit next to him, and with a calm voice, said: "I give infinite thanks to heaven, Sancho, my friend, because before I found good luck myself, it has come to find you. I had thought that my good fortune would pay you for your services, but I still see myself at the door of advancement, whereas you, before it's time, and contrary to all the laws of reason, have found yourself rewarded with what I wanted for you. Others bribe, beg, request, get up early, plead, importune, and they never get what they hope to. And another one comes along, and without knowing why, finds himself with the position that many others wanted. And here's where the saying fits very well that says: 'merit can accomplish much, but good luck can accomplish more.' You—who as far as I'm concerned are a blockhead—without getting up early or burning the midnight oil, and without making any preparations, only with the breath of knight-errantry, find yourself a governor of an *ínsula*, just like that. I say all this, Sancho, so you won't attribute the favor received to what you deserve, but rather that you should give thanks to heaven, which quietly takes care of things; and after that give thanks to the greatness the profession of knight-errantry encompasses. Now that your heart is ready to believe what I've told you, be attentive, my son, to your Cato, who wants to be your adviser, North Star, and guide, who will place you on the road leading to

---

* This was a cross printed at the beginning of spelling books, but also— says Rico—it refers to a bit of Christian instruction.

a safe harbor in this tempestuous sea that could otherwise engulf you. Offices and great responsibilities are nothing other than a deep sea of confusion.

"First, my son, you must fear God, because in fearing Him lies wisdom, and if you're wise you will err in nothing.

"Second, you must realize who you are, and try to get to know yourself, which is the most difficult knowledge that can be imagined. When you know yourself, you will not get all puffed up like the frog who wanted to make himself as big as an ox.* If you do this, when you consider that you had been a swineherd back home it will be the ugly feet of the train of your folly."†

"That's true," responded Sancho, "but I was a lad then. Afterward, as a young man, it was geese that I kept and not pigs. But this doesn't seem to me to be pertinent. Not everyone who governs comes from royal stock."

"That's true too," replied don Quixote, "and for that reason, those not of noble descent must moderate the serious nature of their office with leniency, which, when tempered with wisdom, will save them from the malicious gossip from which no realm is free.

"Be proud, Sancho, of the humbleness of your lineage, and don't be loath to say that you come from peasants. Because when they see that you're not ashamed, no one will try to shame you; and take pride in being more humble and virtuous than an arrogant sinner. Innumerable are those who come from a low lineage and have risen to pontifical or imperial dignity, and I could bring so many examples of this truth to mind it would tire you out.

"Take care, Sancho, to guide your life on the path of virtue, and if you take pride in doing virtuous acts, there's no reason to be envious of princes and lords. Because blood is inherited and virtue is acquired. Virtue is precious in itself, and blood in itself is worth nothing.

---

* This refers to Æsop's fable about the frog who exploded while trying to expand himself to the size of an ox.

† This reflects the saying: "Look at your feet and your train will fall," referring to the peacock who haughtily spreads his train out, then looks at how ugly his feet are, and his tail falls. Don Quixote really mixes things up here.

"This being as it is, if one of your relatives should come to visit you on your *ínsula*, don't scorn or offend him; rather you must receive, honor, and entertain him, and with this you will satisfy heaven, because it will please God, who doesn't want anyone to spurn what He has made, and you will comply with what you owe to the well-ordered plan of Nature.

"If you take your wife with you—because it isn't good for those who have to attend to governments to be without their womenfolk—teach her, instruct her, and trim away her natural rough edges, because what a prudent governor attains can be ruined by a rustic and slow-witted wife.

"If you should become a widower—as can happen—and because of your position you get a better wife, don't use her as a hook and a fishing pole, and as one who says: 'I won't take a bribe—put the money in my hood instead.' Because in truth I tell you that everything the wife of a judge receives, her husband has to account for on Judgment Day, where he'll pay fourfold in death for the things he refused responsibility for in life.

"Never let yourself be guided by arbitrary law, which is favored by the ignorant who think they're so clever.

"Let the tears of the poor find in you more compassion, but no more justice, than the testimony of the rich.

"Try to discover the truth among the promises and gifts of the rich, as well as among the sobs and pleadings of the poor.

"When equity can and should find favor, don't put the whole weight of the law on the delinquent, because the fame of the severe judge is no more than that of the compassionate one.

"If you should bend the rod of justice, let it not be because of the weight of a gift, but rather because of mercy.

"If it happens you're judging the case of some enemy of yours, don't consider previous injuries, and concentrate on the truth of the case.

"Don't let your passion blind you on someone else's behalf. Errors that you make that way are often not fixable, and if they're discovered, they may be to your discredit and may even affect your position.

"If some beautiful woman comes to ask justice of you, pay no attention to her tears and her sighs and consider carefully the substance of what she's asking, if you don't want to drown your judgment in her weeping and your virtue in her sighs.

"If you have to punish someone, don't humiliate him as well, because the pain of punishment is sufficient without abusive words.

"Consider the guilty person who comes under your jurisdiction as a poor wretch, subject to the frailty of our depraved nature, and insofar as you can, without doing harm to the prosecution, show yourself to be pious and clement, because, although the attributes of God are equal, mercy flourishes and is more resplendent than justice.

"If you keep these precepts and heed these rules, Sancho, your days will be many, your fame eternal, your rewards bounteous, your happiness inexpressible; you'll marry your children however you want; they and your grandchildren will have titles, you'll live in peace and with the approval of the people, and in the last moments of your life, death will find you at a sweet and ripe old age, and tender and delicate hands of your great-grandchildren will close your eyes.

"Up to now, I've given you instructions as to how to adorn your soul. Listen now to what you should do to adorn your body."

Chapter XLIII. About the second set of advice that don Quixote gave to Sancho Panza.

WHO COULD have listened to the speech just made by don Quixote and not considered him to be a person of sound judgment and sounder intellect? But as has been set down many times in the course of this great history, he only spoke nonsense in matters of chivalry, but in other areas he had clear and confident understanding, so that at every step along the way his works contradicted his words and his words his works. But in the matter of the second set of advice that he gave to Sancho, he showed great acuity of mind and intelligence, and you could see both his wisdom and his madness at very high levels.

Sancho listened most attentively to him, and tried to store all his advice in his memory, planning to keep it, and by use of it to bring the pregnancy of his government to a happy birth.

So don Quixote went on and said: "As to how to govern yourself and your household, the first thing that I charge you to do is to be clean, and cut your fingernails without letting them grow, as some do, who through their ignorance consider that long nails beautify their hands, thinking that uncut growth was fingernails, but they're really claws of a lizard-catching hawk—a foul and unnatural abuse.

"Don't go about, Sancho, without a belt, wearing loose-fitting clothing, because slovenly attire seems to indicate a careless spirit, unless shabby appearance and negligence was intentional, as was supposedly the case of Julius Cæsar.*

"Take the pulse wisely of what your office can afford. If it will allow, give uniforms—more in good taste and useful than showy and flashy—to your servants, and divide them between your servants and the poor. I mean, if you want to give uniforms to six pages, dress just three of them and then dress three poor people. In that way, you'll have pages in heaven and on earth. This novel way of giving uniforms is not known to the arrogant.

"Don't eat garlic or onions, so people won't be able to tell your low birth by the way you smell. Walk slowly and speak with deliberation, but in such a way so that it won't appear that you're listening to yourself, because all affectation is bad.

"Eat little at lunch and eat even less at dinner because the health of the body is forged in the workshop of the stomach.

"Be restrained in your drinking, considering that too much wine keeps neither secrets nor its word.

"Be careful not to eat with food in both cheeks, nor to eruct in front of anyone."

"I don't understand this eruct business," said Sancho.

And don Quixote said to him: "To *eruct* means to *belch*. This is one of the crudest words in the Spanish language, although it's quite charged with meaning, so diligent people

---

* This is the second time Don Quixote has spoken about the carelessness of dress on the part of Cæsar (see Part II, chapter two), but in reality Cæsar was not slovenly in his dress.

have gone to Latin, and instead of saying *belch* they say *eruct*,* and instead of saying *belches* they say *eructations*. If some people don't understand these terms, it matters little, because in time they will, when usage will accustom them. This will enrich the language that custom and the common man control."

"In truth, *señor*," said Sancho, "one of the pieces of advice that I plan to keep in my memory will be that business of belching, because I do it frequently."

"*Eructing*, Sancho, and not *belching*," said don Quixote.

"Yes, *eructing* is what I'll say from now on," responded Sancho, "and I swear I won't forget."

"Also, Sancho, you must not mix the multitude of proverbs that you know into your conversation as you always do. Although proverbs distill the wisdom of the ages, you often drag them in by their hair and they seem more like foolishness than maxims."

"God will have to provide a remedy for this," responded Sancho, "because I know more proverbs than are in a book and they come to my mouth so jumbled together when I speak they fight with each other to get out. But my tongue throws out the first one it finds, even though it may not fit the situation exactly. I'll be careful from now on to say only those that conform to the gravity of my office, because 'in a full house supper is soon cooked' and 'the one who shuffles doesn't cut' and 'the man who sounds the alarm is safe' and 'to give and to retain requires a good brain.'"

"That's exactly what I mean," said don Quixote. "You insert, string together, and pile up proverbs. No one can stop you! 'My mother punishes me and I make fun of her!' I'm trying to tell you to stop using proverbs and in an instant you've tossed out a long list of them that fit into what we're talking about as well as 'over the hills of Úbeda.'† Look, Sancho, I'm not saying that an appropriate proverb isn't a good thing. But to heap and string proverbs together willy-nilly makes for a dull and coarse conversation.

"When you get on horseback, don't sit way back in the saddle, nor with your legs stiff and sticking out, away from

---

* *Eructāre* in Latin does indeed mean "to belch."
† This is a proverbial expression seen already in Part II, chapter thirty-three, page 754.

the body of the horse, nor slouch the way you do on the donkey. Riding horses makes some look like horsemen and others like stable boys.

"Be moderate in your sleep, for 'he who doesn't wake up with the sun doesn't enjoy the day.' And be aware, Sancho, that 'industry is the mother of good luck' and its contrary, laziness, never accomplishes what good desires demand.

"This last bit of advice I want to give you now—although it doesn't deal with the adornment of your body—I want you to keep it lodged in your memory, and I think it'll be no less useful than those that I've given you up to now, and it's this: Never get involved with questioning lineages; at least comparing them, since invariably one will turn out better, and you'll be hated by the person you put down, and you'll never be rewarded by the one you praised.

"You should wear long pants and a jacket, and a cape that is a bit longer. As for those loose-fitting pants, don't even consider it! They're not good either for knights or for governors.

"This is all I have to advise you about for the moment, Sancho. With the passage of time, and depending on the circumstances, if you tell me how things are going, I will give you more instructions."

"*Señor*," responded Sancho, "I see that everything you've told me is good, virtuous, and beneficial. But what good will it do me if I can't remember a single thing? It's true I won't forget the business of not letting my fingernails grow, and of getting married again if the occasion arises. But all that other tangled mishmash of things I can't remember, nor will I remember any more of them than I would the snows of yesteryear, so you'll have to give them to me in written form. Because although I can't read or write, I'll give them to my confessor so that he can pass them on to me and remind me as needed."

"Ah, sinner that I am," responded don Quixote, "how bad it seems when governors can't read or write! You should know, Sancho, that not being able to read or being left-handed indicates one of two things—either he was a child of parents who were too humble or he was so mischievous and bad that he couldn't be taught good customs or what he needed to know. It's a grave defect that you have, and I'd like you at least to learn to sign your name."

"I *can* sign my name," responded Sancho, "because when I was a steward in my town, I learned to make some letters like they use to mark on bales, and they said that it was my name. Besides, I can pretend that my right hand is maimed and I can have someone else sign for me. 'There's a remedy for everything except death,' and 'holding the power and the staff, I'll do whatever I want.' And what's more, 'he who has a bailiff for a father . . .'* And since I'll be governor, which is higher than bailiff, come on and we'll see what happens! Let them scorn and slander me! 'They'll come for wool and go back shorn' and 'the lucky man has nothing to worry about.' And 'the foolish remarks of the rich man pass for wisdom in the world.' And being governor and liberal at the same time, as I plan to be, they'll think I'm flawless. 'Make yourself into honey and the flies will eat you up.' As my grandmother used to say: 'you're worth as much as you have.' And 'you can't take vengeance on the landed gentry.' "

"May God curse you, Sancho!" said don Quixote. "May sixty thousand devils haul you and your proverbs off! It's been an hour since you started stringing them together and torturing me with each one. I can assure you that these proverbs will lead you to the gallows one day. Because of them your vassals will take away your governorship, or it will cause them to revolt against you. Tell me, you ignoramus, where do you find them? Or how do you apply them, you idiot? For me to say a single one and apply it well, I sweat and work as if I were digging a ditch."

"Before God, *señor* our master," replied Sancho, "you're complaining about very little. Why the devil do you get angry because I'm using my heritage, since it's all I have? My only wealth is proverbs and more proverbs. And right now four of them come to mind that fit the situation exactly, 'like peaches in a basket.' But I won't say them, because 'good silence is called Sancho.' "†

"That's not you," said don Quixote, "because not only

---

* ". . . goes safely to trial."

† This was originally a slightly different proverb: "Good silence is called *santo* ('holy')," but it got changed to *Sancho* sometime before Sancho said it. Of course, the best English version is "Silence is golden," but this doesn't fit in with what don Quixote says in the next line.

are you not 'good silence'—you're 'bad speech' and obstinate as well. But even so, I'd like to find out which four
proverbs just came to you that fit the situation so well. I've
been ransacking my brain, and I can't think of a single one
that's *à propos*."

"What better ones are there than 'never put your thumbs
between your wisdom teeth,' and 'to "leave my home" and
"what do you want with my wife?" there's nothing to answer,' and 'if the pitcher hits the stone or the stone hits the
pitcher, it's bad for the pitcher'? All of them fit perfectly.
No one should take on their governor, nor anyone who's
in charge, because he'll come out hurt, just like someone
who puts his finger between his wisdom teeth, and even if
they're not the wisdom teeth, as long as they're molars it
doesn't make any difference. And no matter what the governor asks, there's nothing to say, just like 'leave my house'
and 'what do you want with my wife?' And the one about
the pitcher and the rock, a blind man can see it. So, 'why
do you look at the speck in your brother's eye with never a
thought for the plank in your own?'* lest it be said of him:
'the dead woman was frightened to see another with a slit
throat.' And your grace already knows the one about 'the
fool knows more in his own house than the wise man in
someone else's.' "

"Not so, Sancho," responded don Quixote, "for the fool
in his own house or in anyone else's doesn't know anything,
because on the foundation of foolishness you can't build
the edifice of intelligence. And let's let it go here, Sancho,
because if you govern badly, 'yours will be the blame and
mine will be the shame.' But I can console myself in that
I've done what I should by advising you with truths and
with whatever discretion I could. With that I'm discharged
from my obligation and promise. May God guide you, Sancho, and may He govern you in your government, and take
from me the misgiving that I have that you might wind up
with the *ínsula* flat on its back, something that I could prevent by revealing to the duke who you are, telling him that
the little fat person that you are is nothing more than a sack
filled with proverbs and mischief."

"*Señor*," replied Sancho, "if your grace thinks that I'm

---

* This is Matthew 7:3.

not right for this government, I'll give it up right now. I love the tiniest part of my soul more than my whole body, and I'll survive simply as Sancho with bread and onions than a governor with partridges and capons. And what's more, 'when they're asleep, everyone is the same—the grandees and the little folk, the rich and the poor,' and if you think about it, you'll see that you alone made me start to think about being a governor. I don't know any more about governing *ínsulas* than a vulture does, and if you think that if I become a governor the devil will carry off my soul, I'd prefer to go to heaven as Sancho than to hell as a governor."

"By God, Sancho," said don Quixote, "with just these last words you've said, I judge that you deserve to be governor of a thousand *ínsulas*. You have a good instinct, without which knowledge is worthless. Commend yourself to God, and try not to err in your main purpose. I mean that you should always keep a firm intent and intention to do right in all things, because 'heaven supports worthy aims.' Let's go eat now, because these people are waiting for us."

Chapter XLIIII. How Sancho Panza was taken to his governorship, and the strange adventure that befell don Quixote in the castle.

THEY SAY that in the original account of this history one reads that when Cide Hamete comes to write this chapter, his translator didn't render it as written, for the Moor criticizes himself for having taken on a history that was as dry and as limited as this one about don Quixote. It seemed to him that he had to talk about nothing but don Quixote and Sancho, without daring to include digressions and more serious and more entertaining episodes, and he said that having to dedicate all his intellect and use his hand and pen to write exclusively about a single subject, and to speak through the mouths of so few characters, was an unbearable labor whose fruit yielded little in return to its author. Because of this drawback, he resorted to using the device of interspersed tales in Part I, such as the one about the "Ill-Advised Curiosity" and the one about the "Captive Captain," which are not part of the main story, although everything else that happened in that part dealt with don Quixote, and had to be recorded. Also, he says, he thought that many people who were very interested in the deeds of don Quixote wouldn't pay much attention to these novellas, and would skip over them in haste or hostility without noticing their grace and craft, which would be quite apparent if they were published by themselves, without depending on the crazy acts of don Quixote or the follies of Sancho. And so, in this Second Part he didn't introduce novellas, whether separate from the action or woven into it, but just some tales that derive from the episodes themselves, and even these are very limited and use only enough words to be related. And since he contains and confines himself within the narrow limits of the narration, even though he has sufficient ability, faculties, and intellect to embark on the whole universe, he begs no one to scorn his work, and to praise him not for what he has written but rather for what he has chosen not to write.

And then he continues his history, saying that after the midday meal on the day don Quixote gave advice to Sancho, he wrote it down and gave it to him so he could find someone to read it to him. But hardly had he given it to Sancho than Sancho dropped it and it came into the hands of the duke, who showed it to the duchess, and the two marveled at both don Quixote's madness and intellect. And so, to continue with their jests, that afternoon they sent Sancho with a large retinue to a village that was to be the *ínsula*.

It happened that the person who was in charge was a steward of the duke who was very sharp and witty—because there's no wit without intelligence—and who had played the role of the Countess Trifaldi with the charm that has been described, and with this, and the instructions he got from his master and mistress about how he had to act with Sancho, he carried out their scheme marvelously well.

I say, then, that it happened that as soon as Sancho saw that steward, he thought that his face seemed to be just like Trifaldi's, and turning toward his master, he said: "*Señor*, either the devil hauls me off from here right now, or your grace has to confess that the face of this steward of the duke, here present, is the same as the Distressed One's."

Don Quixote looked attentively at the steward and, after having examined him carefully, he said to Sancho:

"There's no reason for the devil to haul you off immediately, Sancho. The face of the Distressed One looks like the steward's, but that doesn't mean that the steward *is* the Distressed One, because if he were, it would imply an enormous contradiction. This isn't the right time to go about looking for proofs, for it would mean going into an intricate labyrinth. Believe me, my friend, what we have to do is pray to Our Lord very earnestly to free us from evil sorcerers and enchanters."

"This is no joke, *señor*," replied Sancho, "for I heard him speak a while ago and it seemed just like the voice of Trifaldi was resonating in my ears. All right, I'll keep quiet, but I'll still continue to be on the alert from now on to see if I discover any other sign that confirms or denies my suspicions."

"That's what you should do, Sancho," said don Quixote, "and you'll tell me everything you find out about this, and everything that happens to you in your government."

Sancho finally left, accompanied by many people, dressed as a man of letters, and wearing a tan cloak with a matching cap, and riding a mule with short stirrups. Behind him, on orders of the duke, came his donkey, with trappings and magnificent ornaments made of silk. Sancho turned around once in a while to look at his donkey, and he was so pleased with his company, he wouldn't have switched places with the emperor of Germany.

When he bade farewell to the duke and duchess, he kissed their hands, and received a blessing from his master, who bestowed it with tears, and Sancho received it with blubbering.

Let's let Sancho go away in peace, dear reader, and wait for two bushels of laughter when you find out how he behaved in his new position, and meanwhile, let's tend to what happened to his master that night. And if you don't laugh, at least you'll spread your lips in a monkey grin, because whatever befalls don Quixote either has to be greeted with wonder or laughter.

It's told, then, that hardly had Sancho left when don Quixote began to miss him, and if it had been possible to revoke the commission and take away his governorship, he would have done it. The duchess saw his melancholy, and asked him why he was so sad. If it was because of Sancho's absence, they had squires, duennas, and maidens in their house who could serve him perfectly.

"It's true, *señora mía*," responded don Quixote, "that I lament Sancho's absence, but that's not the main reason for my seeming so sad; and of the many offers your grace has made me, I'll accept only the spirit in which they were offered. And as for the rest, I beg you to permit me to wait upon myself inside my room."

"In truth," said the duchess, "*señor* don Quixote, this must not be. Four of my maidens will serve you, and they're as pretty as flowers."

"For me," responded don Quixote, "they won't be like flowers, but rather like thorns that pierce my soul. They'll as soon come into my room, or get anywhere near it, as they would fly. If you want to continue to do me favors—which I don't deserve—allow me to have my way so that I can erect a wall to guard my passions and my chastity. I won't forsake this precept of mine for all the liberality Your Highness wants to bestow on me. In other words, I'd rather sleep fully dressed than consent to having anyone else undress me."

"That's enough, that's enough, *señor* don Quixote," replied the duchess. "I'll give an order so that not even a fly should enter your room, not to mention a maiden. I'm not a person who would impeach *señor* don Quixote's sense of propriety, for I see clearly that the most eminent of your virtues is chastity. You may undress and get dressed alone and in your own way, however and whenever you wish. Inside your room you'll find the vessels necessary for the needs of those who sleep behind a locked door, so no call of nature should oblige you to open it. May the great Dulcinea del Toboso live a thousand centuries and may her name be known over the face of the earth, since she deserved to be loved by such a valiant and chaste knight, and may the benign heavens instill in the heart of Sancho Panza, our governor, a desire to finish his penance very soon, so the world can enjoy the beauty of such a great lady once again."

To which don Quixote responded: "Your Highness has spoken like the person she is, because worthy ladies don't speak ill of any other woman. And Dulcinea will be better known throughout the world for having been praised by your greatness than by all other praises that could be given to her by the most eloquent people on earth."

"Now, then, *señor* don Quixote" replied the duchess, "dinnertime is approaching and the duke must be waiting. Let your grace come and let's eat; then you can go to bed early, for the voyage yesterday to Candaya was not so short that it won't have fatigued you."

"I'm not tired, *señora*," responded don Quixote, "because I'll swear to your excellency that I've never in my life ridden a calmer, more even-paced animal than Clavileño, and I don't know what could have caused Malambruno to get rid of such an easy and gentle mount, and blow him up just like that."

"One can only imagine," responded the duchess, "that when he repented of the bad thing done to Trifaldi, her company, and from other bad things he must have done to others as a sorcerer and enchanter, he wanted to have done with the implements of his craft; and since Clavileño was the primary tool that took him wandering from country to country, he burned him up. Through those ashes and the monumental scroll, the bravery of don Quixote de La Mancha will be eternal."

Once again don Quixote gave thanks to the duchess, and after he ate, he returned to his room all alone, without allowing anyone else to go in with him to serve him, so much did he fear finding reasons that might cause or force him to lose the chastity he was keeping for Dulcinea, always thinking of the virtue of Amadís, flower and mirror of knights-errant. He locked his door after him, and by the light of two candles he got undressed, and when he was taking off his shoes—oh, calamity unworthy of such a person!—there burst, not sighs, or anything that might discredit the purity of his thoughts, but rather about two dozen stitches from one of his stockings, turning it into latticework. The good man grieved greatly and would have given an ounce of silver for a bit of green thread. I say green thread because his stockings were green.

Here Benengeli exclaims and writes: "Oh, poverty, poverty! I don't know what moved the great Cordovan poet to call you an 'unappreciated holy gift'!* I, although I'm a Moor, know very well through my speaking with Christians that holiness consists of charity, humility, faith, obedience, and poverty. But, with all this, I say that the person who

---

* This Cordovan poet was Juan de Mena (1411–1456), who wrote ⌐ut this in his *Labyrinth of Fortune*, 227.

can be content being poor must have much of God in him, unless it's the same kind of poverty about which one of the greatest saints said: 'Possess all things as if you possessed them not.'* This is what they call poverty of the spirit. But you, second poverty,† are the one I'm talking about. Why do you insist on victimizing *hidalgos* and the wellborn, more than other people? Why do you oblige them to apply soot to their shoes, and make them use some buttons of silk, others of horsehair, others of glass on their coats? Why must their collars be pleated and not starched?" (And by this you can see that using starch for collars is a very ancient custom, indeed.) And he went on, saying: "Ah, the wretched wellborn, who nourish their honor while eating poorly behind closed doors, then go out picking their teeth as though there were something there, making their toothpicks into hypocrites. Ah, the wretch, I say, who is so skittish he thinks that people will see the patch on his shoe, the sweat stain on his hat, his threadbare cape, and the hunger in his stomach from a league away!"

All of this was brought home to don Quixote by the run in his stocking. But he consoled himself, seeing that Sancho had left him some traveling boots he would put on in the morning.

Finally, he went to bed, pensive and sorrowful, as much from missing Sancho as from the irreparable misfortune of his stockings, which he would have darned even with thread of another color—one of the surest signs of wretchedness that can betray an *hidalgo* in the course of his lengthy poverty. He extinguished the candles. It was a hot night and he couldn't sleep, so he got out of bed and opened the window that looked out onto a beautiful garden, and when it was open, he heard people walking about and talking in the garden. He began to listen attentively.

The voices below got louder so that he could hear these words: "Don't beg me to sing, Emerencia, since you know as soon as the stranger came into this castle, and my eyes saw him, I can't sing anymore—I can only cry. And what's more, my mistress sleeps more lightly than heavily, and I wouldn't want her to find us here for all the wealth in the

---

* More or less from I Corinthians 6:30.
† That is, material poverty.

world. And even if she didn't wake up, my song would be in vain if he's sleeping and won't be awake to hear it, this new Æneas,* who has come here to leave me scorned."

"Don't worry, Altisidora, my friend," she responded, "because without a doubt the duchess and everyone else in this house is sleeping except the lord of your heart and the awakener of your soul—for I just heard the window to his room open, and he doubtless must be awake. Sing, my afflicted one, softly and smoothly, accompanied by your harp, and if the duchess hears us, we'll just blame it on the heat of the night."

"That's not the point, Emerencia," responded the one named Altisidora. "I just wouldn't want my song to reveal what's in my heart, and be judged a capricious and frivolous maiden by those who don't know about the powerful forces of love. But come what may, 'better shame on the face than sore in the heart.'"

And then he heard the harp start playing very softly, and he was astonished because at that instant, an infinite number of adventures similar to that one—of windows, grates and gardens, music, love plaints, and faintings, which he'd read about in his vacuous books of chivalry—came back to him. Then he imagined that some maiden of the duchess was in love with him, and that her modesty forced her to keep her love a secret. He feared he might be tempted, but resolved in his heart not to give in. And commending himself with all his heart and will to his lady Dulcinea del Toboso, he resolved to listen to the music, and so they would know that he was listening, he feigned a sneeze, which pleased the maidens no little, for they wanted nothing more than for don Quixote to hear them. Running her fingers over the strings and tuning the harp, Altisidora began her ballad:

Oh, you who are above in bed,
    Between the Holland sheets,
    Lying there from night till morn,
    With outstretched legs asleep;
Oh, you, most valiant knight of all
    The famed Manchegan breed,

---

* This refers to Æneas, the hero of Virgil's *Æneid*. On his way to Italy, Æneas visited Dido, the founder of Carthage, and she fell in love with him. After he left her, she committed suicide on a funeral pyre.

Of purity and virtue more
Than gold of Arabia;
Give ear unto a suffering maid,
Well grown but evil-starred,
For those two suns of yours have lit
A fire within her heart.
Adventures seeking you do rove,
To others bringing woe;
You scatter wounds, but, ah, the balm
To heal them do withhold!
Say, valiant youth, and so may God
your enterprises speed,
Did you the light mid Libya's sands*
Or Jaca's rocks first see?†
Did scaly serpents give you suck?
Who nursed you when a babe?
Were you cradled in the forest rude,
Or gloomy mountain cave?
Oh, Dulcinea may be proud,
That plump and lusty maid;
For she alone hath had the power
A tiger fierce to tame.
And she for this shall famous be
From Tajo to Jarama,
From Manzanares to Genil,
From Duero to Arlanza.‡
Fain would I change with her, and give
A petticoat to boot,
The best and bravest that I have,
All trimmed with gold galloon.
Oh, for to be the happy fair
Your mighty arms enfold,
Or even sit beside your bed

---

* In Part I, chapter fourteen, Libya was referred to as a place where wild animals are found (in Grisóstomo's Song).
† Jaca is a small city (now with about 24,000 people) in the foothills of the Pyrenees, north of Pamplona.
‡ Dulcinea isn't going to be very famous, since the Henares, Jarama, and Manzanares are all tributaries of the Tajo, and the Arlanza flows into the Pisuerga. That is, they don't represent geographical separation, as, say, the Duero and the Tajo would.

And scratch your dusty poll!
I rave,— to favors such as these
Unworthy to aspire;
Your feet to tickle were enough
For one so mean as I.
What caps, what slippers silver-laced,
Would I on you bestow!
What damask breeches make for you;
What fine long Holland cloaks!
And I would give you pearls that should
As big as oak-galls show;
So matchless big that each might well
Be called the great "Alone."
Manchegan Nero, look not down
From your Tarpeian Rock*
Upon this burning heart, nor add
The fuel of your wrath.
A virgin soft and young am I,
Not yet fifteen years old
(I'm only three months past fourteen,
I swear upon my soul).
I hobble not nor do I limp,
All blemish I'm without,
And as I walk my lily locks
Are trailing on the ground.
And though my nose is rather flat,
And though my mouth is wide,
My teeth like topazes exalt
My beauty to the sky.
You know that my voice is sweet,
That is if you do hear;
And I am molded in a form
Somewhat below the mean.
These charms, and many more, are yours,
Spoils to your spear and bow all;
A damsel of this house am I,
By name Altisidora.†

---

* This alludes to the Tarpeian Rock in Rome, from where condemned prisoners were thrown, and from which, in a Spanish ballad, Nero watched Rome burn.

† This is adapted from Ormsby.

Here the stricken Altisidora ended her song and the dread of the wooed don Quixote began. He heaved a great sigh and said to himself: "Why am I such an unfortunate errant, for there's no girl who looks at me but what she doesn't fall in love with me? Why is Dulcinea so unlucky that they won't leave her alone to enjoy my incomparable fidelity? What do you queens want of Dulcinea? For what reason do you empresses persecute her? Why do you maidens of fourteen or fifteen years of age hate her? Please let the poor girl triumph, and rejoice and boast of the good fortune that Love gave her by offering her my heart and handing her my soul. Take notice, you lovesick crew, that I'm dough and almond paste only for Dulcinea, and for everyone else I'm made of flint. For her I'm honey, and for you I'm bitterness. For me alone Dulcinea is beautiful, discreet, chaste, charming, and wellborn, and the rest are ugly, foolish, frivolous, and lowborn. To be hers alone, and not for anyone else, nature placed me on earth. Let Altisidora cry or sing, and let the lady for whom they mauled me in the castle of the enchanted Moor despair, for I belong to Dulcinea, boiled or roasted, clean, courteous, and chaste in spite of all the powerful witchcraft in the world."

And with this he slammed the window shut, and despairing and sorrowful as if some great disgrace had befallen him, he lay down on his bed, where we'll leave him for the moment, because the great Sancho Panza is beckoning to us, and is about to assume the reins of his government.

Chapter XLV. How the great Sancho Panza took possession of his ínsula *and how he began to govern.*

OH, PERPETUAL discoverer of the antipodes,* light of the world, eye of heaven, sweet shaker of wine vessels!†
Thymbræus here, Phœbus there, now archer, now doctor, father of poetry, inventor of music, you, who always come

---

* Antipodes represent the opposite sides of the earth. This and the references that follow are to the sun.

† This means that when the sun is hot, you drink frequently, thus the allusion to shaking them (i.e., taking them up and putting them down).

out but—though you seem to—never set! To you I say, oh,
sun! with whose help man engenders man.... * To you, I
say that you should favor and illuminate the darkness of
my intellect so that I can faithfully report, point by point,
the narration of what went on in the government of the
great Sancho Panza, for without you, I feel listless, dejected,
and confused.

I say, then, with all his retinue, Sancho Panza arrived at
a village of about a thousand inhabitants, which was one
of the best ones that the duke possessed. They led him to
believe that it was called THE ÍNSULA BARATARIA, either
because the village was called BARATARIO, or because of
the *barato*—the deception—by means of which he'd been
given the governorship. When he arrived at the gates of the
town, which was walled, the municipal council came out to
receive him. The bells rang and all the inhabitants showed
signs of general festivity and with great pomp they led him
to the main church to give thanks to God, and then with
ridiculous ceremonies, they handed him the keys of the
town, and declared him to be the perpetual governor of the
Ínsula Barataria.

The dress, beard, plumpness, and shortness of the new
governor amazed everyone who was not in on the secret,
and even those who were (and they were many). Finally,
when they took him from the church, they led him to the
judge's seat and placed him on it, and the steward said: "It's
an ancient custom on this *ínsula*, *señor* governor, that the
person who comes to take possession of this famous *ínsula*
is obliged to answer a question that's asked him. It's a bit
knotty and difficult, and by his answer the people take the
pulse of the cleverness of the new governor, and they either
will be cheerful or sorrowful about his arrival."

While the steward was saying this to Sancho, he was
looking at many large letters written on the wall in front of
his chair, and since he didn't know how to read, he asked
what those painted marks on the wall were. He was told:
"*Señor*, the date on which your lordship took possession is
written and noted there, and the inscription says that To-
DAY, AT SUCH-AND-SO OF SUCH A MONTH AND SUCH A YEAR,

---

* In Aristotle's *Physics* II: 2, it says: "both man and the Sun beget
men." The sun is ultimately responsible for all life.

SEÑOR DON SANCHO PANZA TOOK POSSESSION OF THIS *ÍNSULA*, AND MAY HE KEEP IT MANY YEARS."

"And who are they calling *don* Sancho Panza?" asked Sancho.

"Your grace," responded the steward, "for on this *ínsula* there's no other Panza except the one sitting in that chair."

"Then observe, brother," said Sancho. "I have no DON, nor in all my lineage was there ever any. Just plain Sancho Panza is my name, and my father's name was Sancho, and Sancho my grandfather, and they were all Panzas without adding any DONS or DOÑAS.* And I imagine that in this *ínsula* there must be more dons than rocks. But that's enough. God understands me, and it may be that if this government lasts me four days, I'll weed out these dons, because there are so many of them they must be as bothersome as mosquitoes."

At that instant, two men came into the courtroom, one of them dressed as a peasant and another as a tailor (because he was carrying scissors in his hand). The tailor said: "*Señor* governor, this peasant and I come before your grace because this good man came to my shop yesterday—begging your pardon, I'm a licensed tailor, God be praised—and putting a piece of material in my hands, asked me: '*Señor*, is there enough material here to make me one cap?' I examined the piece and answered that there was. He must have thought—the way I see it, and rightly—that I doubtless wanted to steal some of the material, founding his belief on his *own* wickedness and his bad opinion of tailors. He then asked if I could make two caps. I guessed what he was thinking, and said yes. And he, riding along on his cursèd initial thought, kept on adding caps, and I kept on saying yes, until we got to five caps, and just now he has come to pick them up. I hand them over and he doesn't want to pay for my labor. Instead, he asks me to pay him or return the material."

"Is all this true, brother?" asked Sancho.

"Yes, *señor*," responded the man, "but have him show you the five caps that he made for me."

---

* In Spanish there is a pun here. *Dones* (the Spanish term for "dons") means "gifts" and *donas* are goods that are ceded in a marriage agreement.

"Very willingly," said the tailor.

And immediately taking his hand out from under his cape, he displayed the five caps on the tips of his fingers and said: "Here are the five caps that this good man asks me for, and by God and by my conscience nothing was left over, and I'll turn over my work to be inspected by the inspectors of the guild."

All those present laughed about the number of caps and the novelty of the case. Sancho sat there considering a bit and then said: "It seems to me that this case doesn't merit long delays, since a commonsense judgment can be given right away. So, the sentence is that the tailor loses his labor and the peasant his cloth, and the caps should be taken to the prisoners in jail, and that's all there is to it."

If the previous sentence of the cattleman's purse* moved the onlookers to wonder, this one caused laughter. But in the end what the governor commanded was done. Then two old men came in before the governor, one of them walking with a tall staff; the one without a cane said: "*Señor*, I lent this good man ten *escudos* in gold some days ago as a favor to him and to do a good deed, on the condition that he give them back whenever I asked for them. Many days went by without my asking for them back, since I didn't want to cause him greater distress in giving them back than when he asked for them. But since it seemed to me that he'd forgotten to pay me back, I asked him for them, not once but many times, and not only has he not given them back, but he denies everything, and said that I never lent him those ten *escudos* in the first place, or if I really lent them, he returned them to me already. I have no witnesses either to the loan, or the payment for that matter, since he hasn't paid them back. I would like your grace to take a sworn statement from him, and if he swears that he has given them back to me, I'll forgive the debt here and before God."

"What do you have to say, good old man with a cane?" said Sancho.

"I, *señor*, confess that he lent them to me. Lower your

---

* Translator's note: Of course, the episode with the cattleman has yet to happen. Cervantes—who knows *exactly* where everything is and should go—is just pretending to be careless.

rod, * your grace, since he leaves it to my oath, and I'll swear that I gave them back and paid him really and truly."

The governor lowered his rod, and the old man with the cane gave it to the other old man to hold while he was giving his oath. He put his hand on the cross of the rod, saying that it was true, that he'd been lent the ten *escudos* that were being asked of him, but that he'd given them back from his hand to the other man's hand, and that he must have forgotten, because he was asking for them back again.

When the great governor saw this, he asked the creditor what he had to say to his adversary. And he said that without a doubt his debtor must be speaking the truth because he held him to be a good man and a good Christian, and that he must have forgotten how and when they had been returned, and that from then on he would never ask for them again. The debtor took his staff back, and bowing, left the courtroom. When Sancho saw this, and that he left without delay, and seeing also the resignation of the plaintiff, he bowed his head onto his chest, and putting his right index finger between his eyebrows, appeared pensive for a while; then he raised his head and had the old man with the staff summoned, for he'd already left. They brought him back, and when Sancho saw him he said: "Give me your staff, my good man, for I have need of it."

"Very well," responded the old man, "here it is, *señor*." And he put it in his hand.

Sancho took it and gave it to the other man and said to him: "Go with God, for you're now paid back."

"I am, *señor*?" responded the old man. "Is this staff worth ten *escudos* in gold?"

"Yes, it is," said the governor, "or if it isn't, I'm the greatest blockhead in the world, and now it'll be seen if I'm smart enough to govern an entire realm."

And he had the cane broken open in front of everyone. It was done, and in its center they found ten *escudos* in gold. Everyone marveled, and they held their new gover-

---

* The "rod of office" had a cross on it to remind the person swearing to tell the truth. But since the accused was going to tell the truth, he needed no such reminder.

nor for a new Solomon.* They asked him how he'd figured
out that the *escudos* were in the cane, and he responded
that when he saw the old man hand his cane to his adversary while he was swearing, and then swore that he'd given
them back really and truly, then when he finished swearing
he took back the cane, it occurred to him that the money
that was being asked for was inside. And from this it can be
seen that some governors, even though they're uneducated,
sometimes are led by God in their judgments. And what's
more, he'd heard a similar case reported by the priest of
his village and he had such a great memory that—if he
hadn't forgotten everything he wanted to remember—no
memory on the island would equal his. Finally, the shamed
old man and the paid-back one left, and those who were
present were in wonder. And the one who kept a record of
the words, deeds, and movements of Sancho couldn't make
up his mind if he'd consider him to be, and report him as, a
fool or a wise man.

When this case was over, a woman came into the courtroom holding tightly on to a man who was dressed as a
rich cattleman, and she was shouting loudly: "Justice, *señor*
governor, justice, and if I can't find it on earth I'll seek it
in heaven! *Señor* governor of my soul, this bad man seized
me in the middle of that field and he took advantage of my
body as if it were a dirty old rag—unfortunate me!—and he
snatched away what I had kept for twenty-three years, defending it from Moors and Christians, fellow countrymen
and foreigners. I was always as hard as a cork tree, keeping myself as pure as a salamander in a fire,† or like wool
among the brambles, and now this fellow comes along and
fondles me just like that."

"We'll find out soon enough about that," said Sancho
and, turning to the man, asked him what he had to say in
response to the complaint of that woman.

He—all flustered—responded: "*Señores*, I'm a poor pig

---

* Solomon is, of course, the biblical king, whose "wisdom excelled the
wisdom of all the children of the east country and all the wisdom of
Egypt" (I Kings 3:30–31).
† Covarrubias (p. 921, col. 2, ll. 58–60) says that the salamander is so
cold that it extinguishes hot coals if it passes through them. This is pure
nonsense, of course.

farmer, and this morning I left this village to sell—pardon me for mentioning their names—four pigs, which they took from me, what with all those taxes and their cunning, for a little less than what they were worth. As I was returning to the village I ran across this good woman along the way, and the devil (who embroils and tangles everything up) caused us to lie together. I paid her enough, and she, not content, grabbed on to me and didn't release me until we got to this place. She says that I forced her, but by the oath that I'm making, or rather plan to make, she's lying. And this is the whole truth without leaving out the least little bit."

The governor asked if he had any silver coins on him. He said that he had about twenty *ducados* inside his shirt in a leather pouch. He told him to take it out and give it to her. He did so, trembling, and the woman took it, making a thousand curtsies to everyone, and praying to God for the life and health of the *señor* governor, who looked out for needy orphans and maidens. And with this, she left the courtroom, clutching the purse with both hands, although she first made sure that the coins inside were of silver.

She'd hardly left when Sancho said to the cattleman, who was standing there in tears, and his eyes following his purse: "My good man, go after that woman and take away the purse and bring it back here along with her."

The cattleman was neither stupid nor deaf, because he shot out like a bolt of lightning as he was commanded to. Everyone present was in suspense to see how the case would turn out, and after a moment the man and the woman came back, and she was grasping him more tightly than before. Her skirt was raised, enveloping the purse, and the man was struggling to get it from her but it wasn't possible, given the way the woman was protecting it. She shouted: "Justice from God and from the law! Your grace, look, *señor* governor, at the lack of shame and little fear this soulless man has, because in the center of town—in the middle of the street—he tried to snatch away this purse you had him give me."

"And was he able to wrest it away from you?" asked the governor.

"What do you mean?" responded the woman. "I'd surrender my life before I'd let anyone take this purse away from me. They'll have to throw someone else against me, and not this hapless and disgusting fellow. Pincers, hammers, mallets, and chisels aren't enough to take it away from my fingernails, not even the claws of lions. They'd have to rip out my soul first."

"She's right," said the man. "I give up—I'm powerless. I confess that I'm not strong enough to take it away, so I'll let her be."

Then the governor said to the woman: "Let me see that purse, honorable and mighty woman."

She gave it to him right away, and the governor returned it to the man and said to the forceful but not forced woman: "My sister, if you had used the same strength—or even half—that you've shown in defending this purse to defend your body, the strength of Hercules couldn't have forced you. Go with God, and may bad luck follow you, and don't appear in this *ínsula* nor within six leagues of it, under pain of two hundred lashes. Get out of here, I say, you charlatan and shameless deceiver!"

The woman became very frightened and left crestfallen and unhappy, and the governor said to the man: "My good man, go with God to your village and with your money, and from now on, if you don't want to lose it, see to it that it doesn't occur to you to lie with anybody."

The man thanked him in a rustic way and went away and the bystanders were once again amazed with the judgments and sentences of their new governor. Everything was then written down by his chronicler and sent to the duke, who was eagerly waiting for it.

And let's leave good Sancho here, for his master, disturbed by Altisidora's music, is begging us to make haste.

Chapter XLVI. About the fearful feline bell fright that befell don Quixote in the course of the amours of the amorous Altisidora.

WE LEFT don Quixote wrapped up in thoughts caused by the music of the enamored maiden Altisidora. He went to bed thinking of them and, as if they were fleas, they—together with the stitches that had run in his stocking—didn't let him sleep or even rest. But since time is swift, and there's no obstacle that can stop it, it galloped along, and with great speed dawn came. When don Quixote saw the morning arrive, he left the soft feathers, and—not lazy in the least—dressed himself in his chamois-skin suit and put on his boots to conceal the bitter misfortune to his stocking. He flung the scarlet cape about him and put his green velvet cap edged with silver on his head, he hung the strap with his trusty trenchant sword over his shoulder, he took a large rosary he always had with him, and with a pompous air and something of an affected gait, he went into the antechamber where the duke and duchess were already dressed and looked as if they were waiting for him. When he passed by a gallery, Altisidora and the other maiden, her friend, were waiting for him on purpose. As soon as Altisidora saw don Quixote she pretended to faint, and her friend caught her in her lap, and with great speed she began unlacing the bodice of her dress. Don Quixote saw it and approached them and said: "I know why she had this fainting spell."

"I certainly don't," responded the friend, "because Altisidora is the healthiest maiden in the whole house, and I've never heard her exclaim AY! since I've known her. Curses on all the knights-errant in the world, if all of them are this ungrateful. Go away, your grace, *señor* don Quixote. This poor girl won't come to while you're here."

To which he responded: "Your grace, *señora*, please have a lute placed in my room tonight. I'll console this lovesick maiden as well as I can, because nipping amorous matters in the bud frequently works decisive and worthy remedies."

And with this he went away, so that what had gone on wouldn't be noticed by any who might see him. He hadn't gone very far when the fainted Altisidora came to and said to her companion: "We'll have to give him a lute. If don Quixote wants to give us music, I'm sure, if it's his own, it won't be bad."

They then went to tell the duke and duchess what was going on and about the lute that don Quixote had asked for. The duchess, excessively pleased, arranged with the duke and with her maidens to play a joke on him that would be more amusing than harmful, and with great joy they waited for the night, which came as quickly as the day had, and which they spent in delicious conversations with don Quixote. And the duchess that same day really and truly dispatched a page of hers—the one who had played the figure of the enchanted Dulcinea in the forest—to Teresa Panza with the package of clothing that had been left for her, and she charged him to bring back an accurate account of everything that happened with her.

Having done that, and when it was eleven o'clock at night, don Quixote found a vihuela* in his room. He tuned it, opened the grate, and could hear that people were walking in the garden. Once he'd run his fingers over the frets, and having tuned it as well as he could, he spit and cleared his throat, and then with a bit of a hoarse voice, although in tune, he sang the following ballad he'd composed that very day:

Mighty Love the hearts of maidens
    Does unsettle and perplex,
    And the instrument he uses
    Most of all is idleness.
    Sewing, stitching, any labor,
    Having always work to do,
    To the poison Love instills
    Is the antidote most sure.
    And to proper-minded maidens
    Who desire a married name
    Modesty's their marriage dowry,
    Modesty their highest praise.
    Men of prudence and discretion,
    Courtiers gay and gallant knights,
    Dally with the wanton damsels
    But take the modest ones to wife.
    There are passions, transient, fleeting,
    Declared in traveler's hostelries,
    Sun rises love with sunset ended,
    When the guest has gone his way.
    Love that springs up swift and sudden,
    Here today, tomorrow flown,
    Passes, leaves no trace behind it,
    Leaves no image on the soul.
    Painting that is laid on painting

---

* Vihuelas were tuned like lutes.

Makes no display or show;
Where one beauty's in possession
There no other can take hold.
Dulcinea del Toboso
Painted on my heart I wear;
Never from its tablets, never,
Can her image be erased.
The quality of all in lovers
Most esteemed is constancy;
'Tis by this that love works wonders,
This exalts them to the skies.*

Here don Quixote arrived at the end of his song, which
the duke and duchess, Altisidora, and almost everyone from
the castle were listening to, when all of a sudden from a
gallery above don Quixote's window more than a hundred
cowbells all tied together on a cord were lowered straight
down, followed by a large sack filled with cats—each one
with a smaller bell tied to its tail. So great was the noise of
the cowbells and the meowing of the cats that, although
the duke and duchess had been the inventors of the joke,
it gave them quite a fright, and don Quixote was stunned
and frightened as well. As luck would have it two or three
cats entered the room through the grating, and with their
running from one side to the other, it seemed like a legion
of devils was loose in that room. They went racing about,
looking for a way out, quickly extinguishing the candles
burning in the chamber. Meanwhile the shaking of the cowbells didn't stop, and most people in the castle, who didn't
know the truth of the matter, were amazed.

Don Quixote stood up and, putting his hand on his
sword, began to thrust it through the grating and shout:
"Out, you wicked enchanters! Out, you bewitched rabble!
I'm don Quixote de La Mancha, against whom your evil
intentions have no power!"

And turning toward the cats who were racing around his
room, he lunged here and there. The cats raced to the window and jumped out, although one of them, seeing himself
almost slashed by don Quixote's thrusts, jumped onto his
face and clamped down onto his nose with its claws and

---

* This has been modified from Ormsby.

teeth. Because of the pain, don Quixote shouted as loud as he could. When the duke and duchess heard this, figuring out what must have happened, they ran to his room and opened the door with their master key and saw the poor knight struggling with all his might to pull the cat from his face. They raced in with torches and saw the unequal battle. The duke ran over to stop the fight, and don Quixote shouted: "Nobody remove him! Let me fight hand to hand with this demon, with this wizard, with this enchanter! I'll make him see who don Quixote de La Mancha is!"

But the cat, paying no heed to these threats, snarled and held fast. Finally the duke removed it and threw it out the window.

Don Quixote was left with a face full of holes and a nose that wasn't very whole, and despairing that they hadn't let him finish the pitched battle he'd had with that brigand enchanter. They had some Oil of Aparicio* brought and Altisidora herself with her very white hands bandaged all the wounds, and after she applied the dressings she said in a low voice: "All these misfortunes happen to you, you hard-hearted knight, because of the sin of your harshness and stubbornness. May it please God that Sancho will forget to whip himself, so that your so beloved Dulcinea will never be disenchanted, nor will you ever enjoy her, nor will you get into the marriage bed with her, at least while I—who adore you so—am still alive."

Don Quixote responded not a word to this, except to give a deep sigh, and then he lay back on his bed, thanking the duke and duchess, not because he feared the enchanted cats and bells, but rather because he recognized the good intention with which they had come to help him. The duke and duchess let him calm down and went away, sorry about the bad outcome of the trick. They hadn't believed that adventure would prove so painful and costly for don Quixote, who spent five bedridden days in his room, where another adventure, more pleasing than the previous one, befell him, which his historian didn't want to relate for the moment in order to return to Sancho Panza, who was very diligent and amusing in his government.

---

* This was a sixteenth-century curing oil formulated by Aparicio de Zubia.

Chapter XLVII. How Sancho Panza's progress in government is continued.

THE HISTORY relates that they took Sancho Panza from the courtroom to a sumptuous palace, where a regal and very clean table was set in a large room. And as soon as Sancho entered the room, the music of *chirimías* was heard and four pages came out with water to wash his hands, which Sancho received solemnly.

The music stopped and Sancho sat down at the head of the table because there was only that one chair and no other table setting. An individual—who later proved to be a doctor—stood at his side with a little whalebone wand in his hand. They removed a rich white cloth that was covering fruits and a great diversity of dishes of different things to eat. One person who seemed to be a student gave the blessing and a page put a lace-trimmed bib on Sancho, and another who was the chief steward placed a plate of fruit in front of him, but hardly had he eaten a mouthful when the man with the wand touched the plate with it and it was taken away with great speed. The chief steward brought another plate of something else to eat. Sancho was going to try it, but even before it was placed on the table and before he could taste it, the wand had touched it and a page took it away with the same speed as the fruit plate. When Sancho saw all this, he was amazed, and asked if his dinner was going to be all sleight of hand.

To which the man with the wand replied: "Only the things, *señor* governor, that are usually eaten on *ínsulas* where there are governors will be eaten here. I, *señor,* am a doctor and I'm retained on this *ínsula* to be the personal physician of its governors. I look out for their health more than my own, studying night and day, and examining their constitution so that I can cure them if they become sick. And the main thing I do is to be present at their lunches and dinners and let them eat only what I believe will do them the most good and take away what I think will do them harm and be injurious to their stomach. The reason I had the plate of fruit removed was that it was too moist, and the other plate of food was taken away because it had too many spices, which increase one's thirst. And he who drinks much kills and consumes the radical humor* that life consists of."

"So, that plate of roasted partridges, which in my opinion look well seasoned, won't do me any harm."

To which the doctor responded: "The *señor* governor will not eat that as long as I'm alive."

"Well, why not?" said Sancho.

And the doctor responded: "Because our master Hippocrates, the North Star and shining light of medicine, in one of his maxims says: *Omnis saturatio mala, perdices autem pessima.*† It means: 'Any overeating is bad; but of partridges it's worse.' "

"If that's so," said Sancho, "examine all the food on this table and see which one will do me the most good and the least harm, and let me eat it without snatching it away. Because, on the life of the governor—and may God allow me to enjoy being one—I'm dying of hunger, and denying me food, even though it grieves the doctor, and no matter what he tells me, is more taking life away than prolonging it."

"Your grace is right, *señor* governor," responded the doctor, "and so in my opinion, you shouldn't eat any of those stewed rabbits because it's a food that is from a fine-haired animal. That veal, if it weren't marinated and roasted you could have a bit of it, but not that way."

And Sancho said: "I think that great big steaming plate over there is stew, and given the diversity of ingredients in such stews, I can't help but run across something that I'll like and will do me good."

"*Absit*,"‡ said the doctor. "May the bad thought of it flee from us. There's nothing in the world that nourishes worse than a stew. Let the canons or headmasters of schools eat stew, or save it for rustic weddings, but let's keep it away from tables of governors, where every kind of delicacy served with care should abound. And the reason is that

---

* Rico says that this radical humor is semen.
† Not only did the ancient Greek physician Hippocrates never say this, but the popular maxim refers to *panis* ("of bread") and not *perdicis* ("of partridge"). *Perdices* is not the correct Latin form, but how is Sancho to know?
‡ "Away with it" in Latin.

medicine made of simple ingredients is always more prized everywhere and by everyone than compound ones, because in the simple ones you cannot err and in the compound ones you can, by varying the amounts of the things that go into them. But I know that the *señor* governor must eat now, and to preserve his health and fortify it I'll give him a hundred wafers and a few thin slices of quince that will sit lightly in his stomach and be easy to digest."

When Sancho heard this he leaned back in the chair and looked fixedly at that doctor, and with a serious tone asked him what his name was and where he'd studied.

To which he responded: "My name, *señor* governor, is Dr. Pedro Recio de Agüero and I'm from Tirteafuera,* between Caracuel and Almodóvar del Campo, on the right-hand side,† and I have the degree of doctor from the University of Osuna."‡

To which Sancho responded, red with rage: "Well, *señor* Dr. Pedro Recio de Mal Agüero,§ native of Tirteafuera, a village on the right-hand side when you go from Caracuel to Almodóvar del Campo, graduate of Osuna, get out of here. If not, I swear to the sun that I'll get a bludgeon and, starting with you, clobber all doctors on this *ínsula*, at least those that I feel are ignorant. The wise, prudent, and intelligent doctors I'll put on my head and will honor them as I do divine persons. And I repeat that Dr. Pedro Recio should go away from here. If not, I'll take this chair that I'm sitting on, and I'll smash it over his head, and let them call me to account when I leave office. I'll clear myself, saying that I did a great service to God in killing such a bad doctor, an executioner of the republic. Get me something to

---

* This real town name means "get yourself out of here."

† If you imagine the letter V, Almodóvar is at the bottom, Caracuel is at the top right and San Quintín is on the top left. Tirteafuera is half-way up the left side, between Almodóvar and San Quintín. Tirteafuera is indeed on the right if you are going from Caracuel to Almodóvar. You'll see that Sancho is more specific when he repeats this.

‡ The crazy man in the barber's story in chapter one of this part was another graduate of this minor university. Osuna was also given as the Princess Micomicona's port of entry into Spain (Part I, chapter thirty [page 278]).

§ *Agüero* means "omen" in Spanish. *Mal agüero* is a bad omen.

eat, or else take back your government. An office that gives its chief nothing to eat isn't worth two beans."

The doctor became upset at seeing the governor so angry and was about to take his leave when a post horn sounded in the street and the steward leaned out the window and came back, saying: "A messenger is coming from the duke my master. He must have some important dispatch."

The messenger came in sweating and frightened, and taking a dispatch from his shirt he put it in the hands of the governor, and Sancho put it in the those of the steward, whom he asked to read the address, which said: "To don Sancho Panza, governor of the *ínsula* Barataria, in his own hands or those of his secretary."

When Sancho heard this, he said: "Who is my secretary?"

And one of those present answered: "I, *señor*, because I can read and write, and I'm Basque."*

"With that little addition," said Sancho, "you can be the secretary to the emperor himself. Open this sheet and see what it says."

The recently born secretary opened it and when he read all of what it said, he announced it was some private business. Sancho had the room cleared; the only ones who stayed were the stewards, and the rest—including the doctor—left; then the secretary read the letter, which went like this:

> *Notice has come to me, señor don Sancho Panza,*
> *that some enemies of mine who live on that ínsula*
> *are going to attack it furiously I don't know what*
> *night. Beware and be alert so that they won't take*
> *you unawares. I also know through spies that*
> *four disguised people have gone to that village to*
> *kill you because they fear your cleverness. Keep*
> *your eyes open and beware of those who come*
> *to speak to you, and don't eat anything they give*
> *you. I'll be sure to rescue you if you get in trouble,*
> *and please act as we expect of a person with your*
> *intellect. At this village, August 16 at 4:00 A.M.*

Sancho was dumbfounded and those around him were equally so. Turning to the steward, he said: "What must be

---

* Basques were traditionally royal secretaries, says Silvia Iriso.

done, and done immediately, is to put Dr. Recio in jail, because if anyone is going to kill me, it'll be him, and it's a slow death and terrible death, starvation is."

"Also," said the butler, "it seems to me that your grace shouldn't eat anything in this place because it has been prepared by some nuns, and, as they say, 'behind the cross stands the devil.'"

"I don't deny that," responded Sancho, "so for the moment, give me a piece of bread and about four pounds of grapes, because there can't be any poison in them, and I can't do without eating, and if we're supposed to be ready for battles that threaten us, it'll be necessary to be nourished. Because 'your stomach carries your heart and not your heart your stomach.' You, secretary, respond to the duke my lord, and tell him that we'll do exactly what he commands, and kiss my lady the duchess' hand for me, and beg her not to forget to send a messenger with my letter and package to my wife, Teresa Panza. I'll really appreciate it, and I'll take care to serve her with all my power, and on the way you can kiss my master don Quixote de La Mancha's hand, so that he'll see that I'm grateful. And you, as a good secretary and as a good Basque, can add anything you'd like and that's to the point. Take away these cloths and give me something to eat, and once I've eaten, I'll deal with as many spies and murderers and enchanters that come against me and my *ínsula*."

At this point a page entered and said: "Here's a peasant with business to discuss and he wants to talk to your lordship about a matter of great importance."

"It's odd, these people with business to discuss," said Sancho. "Are they so foolish that they don't know this is not an appropriate time to come to talk business? Are we who govern, we judges, not men of flesh and blood? We should be left alone to rest when the need requires; but instead they want us to be made of marble. By God and in my conscience, if this government lasts—and it doesn't seem likely—I'll give a whipping to more than one of these who come with business to discuss. Now, tell this good man to come in. But first make sure that he isn't one of the spies or people who have come to kill me."

"No, *señor*," responded the page, "because he seems like a good soul, and either I know little, or he's as good as gold."

"There's nothing to fear," said the steward, "since we're all here."

"Might it be possible," said Sancho, "steward, now that Dr. Pedro Recio isn't here, for me to eat something substantial, even though it's only a piece of bread and an onion?"

"Tonight at dinner we'll make up for the lack of food, and your lordship will be satisfied."

"May God grant it," responded Sancho, and just then the peasant came in. He had a nice appearance, and from a thousand leagues one could see he was good and had a good soul.

The first thing he said was: "Who is the governor here?"

"Who else can it be," said the secretary, "but the one seated in the chair?"

"I humble myself before your presence," said the peasant. And kneeling down, he asked for his hand to kiss it. Sancho wouldn't hear of it and told him to stand up and state his business.

The peasant stood up and then said: "I, *señor*, am a peasant, born in Miguelturra, a village two leagues from Ciudad Real."

"Here's another Tirteafuera," said Sancho. "I can tell you, brother, that I know Miguelturra very well and that it's not far from my own village. Tell me what's on your mind."

"The thing is, *señor*," said the peasant, "I was married in the Holy Roman Catholic Church. I have two children who are students. The younger one is studying for the bachelor's degree and the older one for the master's degree. I'm a widower because my wife died, or rather because a doctor killed her. He gave her an enema while she was with child. And had God been pleased that a boy had been born, I would have had him study to receive a doctorate so that he wouldn't envy his brothers, the bachelor and the one with the master's degree."

"So," said Sancho, "if your wife hadn't died, or if she hadn't been killed, you wouldn't now be a widower?"

"No, *señor*, in no way," said the peasant.

"So far, so good," said Sancho. "Now get on with it. It's time to have a nap rather than to conduct business."

"As I was saying, then," said the peasant, "this son of mine studying for the bachelor's degree fell in love with a girl of our same village named Carla Perlerina, daughter of Andrés Perlerino,* a very rich peasant. And this name of Perlerines doesn't come from any lineage or any other family line because they're all paralyzed, and to make the name sound better, they call them Perlerines; although to tell the truth, the maiden is like an Oriental pearl, and seen from the right-hand side she seems to be a flower in the field; on the left-hand side not so much, because she lost an eye after she had smallpox. And although the pockmarks of her face are many and large, people who love her say that those aren't pockmarks at all, but rather graves where her lovers are buried. She's so neat that she won't get her face dirty; her nose is turned up, as though it were trying to flee from her mouth. With all of this she's quite good-looking because she has a large mouth, and if she weren't lacking ten or twelve teeth, it could surpass the best-formed mouths around these parts. About her lips I can't say anything because they're so thin and delicate that if it were customary to wind lips, you could make a skein of them.† But since they're of a different color than lips typically are, they seem miraculous, because they're mottled blue, green, and deep purple. And may the *señor* pardon me if I'm describing her charms in such detail, because she'll eventually be my daughter. I love her very much and she seems just fine to me."

"Describe her in any way you wish," said Sancho, "for I'm enjoying the description, and if I had eaten, there wouldn't be any better dessert than your portrait."

"I'm about to serve the dessert," responded the peasant, "and the time will come when we'll get to it, if we're not there already. And I say, *señor*, that if I could describe her elegance and her height, it would amaze you. But I can't do this because she's all bent and hunched over, and her knees are right at her mouth, and with all this, it's easy to see that if she could stand straight, her head would touch the ceiling, and she would have already given her hand to my son the bachelor, but she can't extend it, because it's so

---

* Clemencín says that when the father's name ended in -o, daughters would use the feminine form as their last name, as in this case.

† Lips-as-yarn would be very fine, but lips-as-skein would be very oversized.

withered. Still, her long and grooved fingernails show how fine and well proportioned it is."

"All right," said Sancho, "now that you've described her from head to foot, tell me what you want. Come to the point without beating around the bush, without gaps, bits and pieces, or additions."

"I would like, *señor*," replied the peasant, "for you to write me a letter of recommendation to my son's future father-in-law asking him if he would sanction this marriage, since we're not unequal in material wealth or blessings of Nature; because, to tell the truth, *señor* governor, my son is possessed by the devil, and no day goes by that evil spirits don't torment him three or four times. And from having once fallen into a fire, his wrinkled face looks like parchment, and his eyes are quite watery and running. But he has the disposition of an angel, and if he didn't constantly punch himself, he'd pass for a saint."

"Would you like anything else, my good man?" replied Sancho.

"I would like something else," said the peasant, "but I don't dare reveal what it is; but—what the heck!—I won't let it rot in my chest. Whether it's appropriate or not, I say, *señor*, I'd like you to give me three or six hundred *ducados* to help with my bachelor's portion of the dowry; that is, to help him set up his household, because, let's face it, they have to live on their own, without the interference of their parents-in-law."

"See if there's anything else," said Sancho, "and don't hold back because of shyness or shame."

"That's all," responded the peasant.

And hardly had he said this when the governor stood up and seized the chair he was sitting in and said: "I swear, don Rustic and Ill-bred Hayseed, if you don't get out of and hide from my presence this second, I'll break your head open with this chair. You son-of-a-bitch rapscallion, devil's own mischief maker, you come here and expect me to have six hundred *ducados*? And where would I get them, you foul stench? And why would I give them to *you*, you scoundrel and idiot? And what do I care about Miguelturra or the whole line of Perlerines? Get out, I say! If not, by the life of the duke my lord, I'll do what I said! You must not be from Miguelturra, but rather some clown sent to me from hell to taunt me. Tell me, you soulless person, I haven't yet been governor for a day and a half and you think I have six hundred *ducados*?"

The butler motioned to the peasant to leave, which he did with bowed head, seemingly fearful that the governor would vent his anger on him. The rascal played his role very well, but let's leave Sancho, and may peace reign, and let's go back to don Quixote, whom we left with his face bandaged and treated with medicine from his feline wounds, from which he healed in a week. On one of those days something happened to don Quixote that Cide Hamete promises to relate with his characteristic scrupulousness and truth, no matter how trivial it might be.

Chapter XLVIII. About what happened to don Quixote with doña Rodríguez, the duenna of the duchess, with other events worthy of being written about and deserving of eternal memory.

THE BADLY wounded don Quixote lay suffering and dispirited, his face bandaged and badly wounded, not by the hand of God,* but by the claws of a cat, a misfortune not at all associated with knight-errantry. He didn't go out into public for six days, and on one of those nights, when he was wide-awake, thinking about his misfortunes and the persecutions of Altisidora, he heard someone opening the door to his room with a key, and he immediately thought that the enamored maiden had come to assail his chastity and induce him to betray his fidelity to Dulcinea del Toboso.

"The greatest beauty on earth," he said out loud, believing his thought to be right, "cannot extinguish the adoration that I have engraved and imprinted in the middle of my heart and in the most hidden recesses of my bowels, whether you are, *señora mía*, transformed into an onion-stuffed peasant, or into a nymph of the golden Tajo River,†

---

* Ferreras says that this old saying referred to a person with a bodily defect.

† This refers to the nymphs of Garcilaso's *Eclogue III* (mentioned in Part II, chapter eight, page 563).

weaving fabric of twisted silk and gold, or in whatever form
Merlin or Montesinos may have you. Wherever you are,
you're mine, and anywhere I am, I'm yours."

The end of his speech and the opening of the door were
at the same instant. He stood up on the bed, covered from
top to bottom by a quilt of yellow satin, a cap on his head,
and with a bandaged face and mustache—his face was bandaged because of the scratches, and the mustache so it
wouldn't droop and fall; and in that outfit he looked like
the most extraordinary phantom that could be dreamed
up. He kept his gaze on the door, and where he expected
to see the surrendered and love-smitten Altisidora, he saw
instead a very reverend duenna wearing a white veil that
was so long it covered her from head to foot. Between two
fingers of her left hand she carried a lighted candle and
with her right she shielded her eyes, which were covered by
a large pair of glasses. She was treading quietly and moved
her feet softly.

Don Quixote looked at her from his vantage point and
when he saw the way she was dressed and noted her silence, he thought that some witch or sorceress was coming
dressed like that to do him harm, and he began to cross
himself repeatedly. The vision drew near and when she
reached the middle of the room, she raised her eyes and
saw how don Quixote was crossing himself; and if *he* was
fearful at seeing such a figure, she was just as startled to see
him, because as soon as she saw him so tall and so yellow,
with the quilt and bandages that altered his looks, she cried:
"Jesus, what am I seeing?"

In her great distress the candle fell from her hands, and
when she realized she was in complete darkness, she turned
around to go away; and in her fear, she stumbled on her
train and fell down hard. Don Quixote, who was fearful
himself, began saying: "I implore you, phantom, or whatever you are, to tell me who you are and what you want of
me. If you're a soul in torment, tell me. I'll do everything my
strength will allow for you, because I'm a Catholic Christian and I always do good to everyone. For this reason I
took up the order of knight-errantry I profess, the practice
of which extends to doing good to souls in purgatory."

The perplexed duenna, hearing herself thus beseeched,
through her own fear could see don Quixote's, and with a

quiet, sad voice responded to him: "*Señor* don Quixote—if your grace really is don Quixote—I'm not a phantom, nor a vision, nor a soul in purgatory, as you must have thought, but rather doña Rodríguez, the principal duenna of my lady the duchess, and I have come to your grace with a need of the kind that you customarily remedy."

"Tell me, *señora* doña Rodríguez," said don Quixote, "have you perhaps come to be a go-between? Because I'll have you know that I can't be of use to anyone, owing to the peerless beauty of my lady Dulcinea del Toboso. So I say, *señora* doña Rodríguez, as long as your grace makes no mention of love messages, you can go and relight your candle, and come back, and we'll speak of anything you may ask, or whatever gives you pleasure, except, as I say, any amorous suggestion."

"Me, with a message from someone?" responded the duenna. "You don't know me very well. I'm not so old that I need to resort to such childish nonsense, since—God be praised—I'm still vigorous and full of life and I have all my teeth (except for a few I lost because of the catarrh, which is very common in this region of Aragón). But wait a moment for me. I'll go light my candle and will return in an instant to tell of my afflictions to the one who can alleviate the grief of the world."

And without waiting for an answer, she left the room, where don Quixote remained, waiting calmly and pensively for her return. But then a thousand thoughts about this new adventure befell him, and it seemed not only a bad idea, but also poorly thought out, to put himself in danger of breaking his promised faithfulness to his lady. He said to himself: "Who knows if the devil, who is subtle and clever, doesn't want to deceive me now with a duenna, since he never could deceive me with empresses, queens, marquises, or countesses? I've heard many times and from many wise people that, if he can, he'll give you a flat-nosed woman instead of one with a pretty nose.* And who knows? Maybe this night, this solitude, this occasion, and this silence will

---

* There is a proverb: "If we can provide a flat-nosed woman, let's not offer one with a pretty nose." This means, in this context, that the devil may be tempting him with an ordinary-looking woman. If the devil were to use a beautiful one, don Quixote might be more on guard.

awaken my dormant desires, and will make me fall where I never have before stumbled in all my years. And in similar cases, it's better to flee than wait for a battle.

"But I must not be in my right mind to say and think such nonsense. It's not possible that a duenna who is tall, dressed in white, and bespectacled can arouse a lascivious thought in the most lustful heart in the world. By chance is there a single duenna in the world who has a beautiful body? By chance is there a single duenna in the world who isn't arrogant, wrinkled, and prudish? Out with you, you duenna-mob, useless for any human pleasure! How well that woman did who, they say, kept statues dressed to look like duennas at one end of her drawing room—posed like they were making lace and wearing eyeglasses—and those statues were as good as real duennas for the dignity of the room!"

And once he'd said this, he leapt up from his bed with the intention of locking the door and not letting doña Rodríguez enter. But just as he went to lock the door, doña Rodríguez returned with a white candle that was lit, and when she saw don Quixote close-up, wrapped in the quilt, with his bandages and cap, she feared once again, backed up a few steps, and said: "Am I safe, *señor* knight? I don't think it's very proper that you've gotten out of your bed."

"I was going to ask you that, *señora*," said don Quixote, "and so I'll ask if *I'm* safe from being attacked and ravished."

"Who are you asking if you'll be safe, *señor* knight?" responded the duenna.

"I'm asking you," replied don Quixote, "because I'm not made of marble nor you of bronze, nor is it ten in the morning, but rather midnight, and maybe a bit later, I believe; and we're in a room that is more closed up and secret than the cave where that traitorous and daring Æneas enjoyed the fair and pious Dido.* But give me your hand, *señora*, for I need no other greater assurance than my restraint and the modesty manifest in your reverend veil."

And saying this, he kissed his right hand and after she did the same ceremony, he took her hand.† Here Cide

* See the *Æneid* IV, verses 165–66.
† What happens here is that each one kisses his/her own hand; then they shake hands, a sign of good faith.

Hamete inserts a parentheses and says that by Muhammad, he would have given the better of his two capes to have seen the two of them walk hand in hand from the door toward the bed. Don Quixote got back into bed, and doña Rodriguez sat in a chair a bit of a distance away, and kept her glasses on and her candle burning. Don Quixote curled up and covered himself completely except for his face and when they were both settled, the first one to break the silence was don Quixote, saying: "You can speak freely now, *señora mía*, and unburden yourself of what you've locked up in your afflicted heart and soul, for it will be heard by my chaste ears and rescued by pious works."

"I believe you," responded the duenna, "for from your grace's noble and amiable presence one couldn't expect anything except such a Christian response. Well, the thing is, *señor* don Quixote, that although your grace sees me seated in this chair in the heart of the kingdom of Aragón and in the habit of a humbled and downtrodden duenna, I was born in the Asturias of Oviedo* and of a lineage shared by some of the best families in that province.

"But my bad luck, and the carelessness of my parents, led to their untimely economic downfall, and without my knowing how or why, they took me to the court in Madrid, where, for the sake of peace, and to prevent further misfortune, they got me a position as seamstress to a noble lady. And I want your grace to know that in stitching hems and doing backstitches, no one has surpassed me in all my life. My parents left me working there and went back home, and a few years later they must have gone to heaven, because they were very good and were Catholic Christians. I was orphaned and dependent on the wretched salary and the dismal favors that they give to such servants in the palace. And at that time, through no fault of my own, a squire of the house, a man already on in years, bearded and good-looking, and above all an *hidalgo* like the king, because he was from the region around Santander,† fell in love with me. Our affair was not so secret that my lady didn't find out about it, and to avoid gossip, she had us get married with

---

* This refers to western Asturias, in northwestern Spain.

† People considered themselves *hidalgos* if they were from that region. Gaos gives two good references (vol. ii, p. 665, note 142).

the blessing of the Holy Mother Roman Catholic Church, from which marriage was born a daughter that killed my luck, if I ever had any—not because I died in childbirth, which was safe and on time, but rather because my husband died soon afterward of a certain fright he had, which if I had time to tell of it, would amaze you."

And then she began to cry tenderly, and said: "Pardon me, *señor* don Quixote. I can't help it, because every time I think of my ill-fated husband my eyes fill with tears. So help me God, with what dignity he would take my lady on the haunches of a powerful jet-black mule! In those days they didn't use coaches or litters as they do now, and ladies would ride on the haunches behind their squires. And there's one incident I have to tell you because it shows the upbringing and diligence of my good husband.

"As one enters Santiago Street* in Madrid, which is a bit narrow, a magistrate from court came out with two constables in front of him, and as soon as my good squire saw him, he turned the reins of the mule, giving every indication he was going to escort him.† My lady, who was on the haunches, with a muted voice said: 'What are you doing, you fool? Don't you see that I'm here?' The magistrate, out of pure courtesy, pulled the reins back on his horse, and said to him: 'Don't change your route, *señor*. I should be accompanying my lady doña Casilda,' for that was the name of my mistress. But my husband still insisted on accompanying the magistrate, cap in hand. When my lady saw this, filled with rage, she took a hatpin, or rather, I think it was an awl, from her needle case, and stuck it into his lower back, and my husband gave a huge yelp, and twisted his body so much that he knocked his mistress to the ground.

"Two of her grooms ran over to help her up, as did the magistrate and the constables. The Guadalajara Gate‡ was

---

* As you leave the Plaza Mayor going west on the Calle Mayor, this street is reached by turning right at the second street (Milaneses), then bearing left.

† This was done to show respect. Clemencín says that the custom dates from Roman times.

‡ You won't find this Puerta de Guadalajara anymore—it burned down in 1582, says Pellicer—but it was where Milaneses Street met Santiago Street.

in an uproar—I mean, the idle people who congregate there were in an uproar. My mistress finally stood up and my husband went to the barber-surgeon's shop, saying that his bowels had been pierced all the way through. The courtesy of my husband became so well-known that boys in the street ran after him, and because of it, and because he'd been a bit shortsighted, my lady the duchess* fired him, and I'm convinced that the grief that it caused was responsible for his death.

"I was left a helpless widow with a daughter to take care of, and she grew in beauty like the foam of the sea. Finally, since I was famous as a great seamstress, my lady the duchess—who had recently married the duke my master—wanted to bring me and my daughter as well to this kingdom of Aragón, where as days went by she grew up with all the grace in the world. She sings like a lark, does courtly dances well, and popular dances like a woman possessed. She reads and writes like a schoolteacher, and does math like a miser. Of her cleanliness I'll say nothing—running water is no cleaner, and she must be now, if memory serves, sixteen years, five months, and three days old, more or less.

"So, to come to the point, the son of a rich farmer who lives in one of my master the duke's villages not far from here fell in love with my daughter. In short, I don't know how, but the two of them made love, and under the promise of being her husband, he deceived my daughter and he doesn't want to keep his word. My master, the duke, knows about it because I've complained to him, not once but many times, and I've asked him to make the farmer marry my daughter. He doesn't listen, and the reason is that the father of the seducer is so rich, and lends him money, and occasionally bails him out after his mischief, and so he doesn't want to displease him or give him any grief.

"I would like, then, *señor mío*, for your grace to take charge of righting this wrong either with words or with arms, since everyone says your grace was born into the world to right wrongs, rectify injuries, and help poor wretches. Con-

---

* Several editors and translators omit "the duchess" here, thinking that "Cervantes" or "the printer" has made a mistake by confusing doña Casilda with doña Rodríguez's current mistress. But there is no reason why doña Casilda shouldn't be a duchess as well. After all, why did the magistrate say that *he* should be accompanying *her*?

sider that my daughter is an orphan, is refined, young, and has all the characteristics I said she has. I swear before God and in my conscience that of all the duennas my mistress has, none of them comes up to the sole of her shoe, and the one they call Altisidora—the one they consider to be the most free and easy and charming—in comparison with my daughter doesn't come within two leagues of her. I want your grace to know, *señor mío*, that 'all that glitters isn't gold,' because this Altisidora has more vanity than beauty, and more sauciness than modesty, and in addition she's not very healthy—she has such bad breath you can't stand to be near her for a second; and even my lady the duchess . . . I should hush, because as they say, 'walls have ears.' "

"On my life, what's the matter with my lady, the duchess, *señora* doña Rodríguez?" asked don Quixote.

"With an entreaty like that," responded the duenna, "I feel I must answer what was asked with the complete truth. Does your grace, *señor* don Quixote, see the beauty of my mistress the duchess—that complexion of her face resembles a shiny polished sword blade, those two cheeks of milk and scarlet that have the sun on one side and the moon on the other, and that gracefulness with which she walks, as if she scorns the ground, it looks like her health spills over wherever she goes? Well, I want your grace to know she can be thankful for all that first to God and then to two issues* that she has in each leg through which are carried off all the bad humors that the doctors say she's full of."

"Holy Mary!" said don Quixote. "Is it possible that my lady, the duchess, has such drains? I wouldn't have believed it if barefoot friars had told me. But since *señora* doña Rodríguez says it, it must be that way. But such issues in such places mustn't discharge humors but rather liquid ambergris. Truly, I can now see that this matter of issues must be an important thing for one's health."

Hardly had don Quixote said these words when the doors of his room flew open with a great bang, and at the frightening sound doña Rodríguez dropped her candle and

---

* These issues are made by incisions for purposes of, for example, discharging pus. But since they are on her legs, where they wouldn't be seen, it is doubtless an example of the old medicine, bloodletting to let "bad humors" drain.

the room turned as dark as the mouth of the wolf, as the saying goes. Suddenly the duenna felt two hands on her throat clutching so tightly that she couldn't scream, and someone else raised her skirt and with what seemed to be a slipper began to spank her so many times it was pitiful. Although don Quixote felt compassion, he didn't stir from his bed; he didn't know what was going on. He stayed there still and silent, fearing that the next batch of spanks would be for him. And his fear was not in vain, because when the silent tyrants left the mauled duenna—who didn't dare to open her mouth in complaint—they went to don Quixote and, removing his sheet and quilt, they pinched him so much and with such strength that he was forced to defend himself with punches; and all of this happened in an astonishing silence. The battle raged for almost half an hour; then the phantoms left, and doña Rodríguez straightened her skirt and went out through the door, moaning over her misfortune, but didn't say a word to don Quixote, who was left alone and in pain, pinched, confused, and deep in thought, where we will leave him desirous to find out who the perverse enchanter was who had placed him in that sorry state. But that will be told in time. Sancho Panza is calling us, and the structure of the history leads us to him.

Chapter XLIX. About what happened to Sancho making the rounds of his ínsula.

WE LEFT the great governor angry and annoyed with the rascal of a peasant who described those likenesses so vividly, and who—having been coached by the steward, who in turn was coached by the duke—played that joke on Sancho. But Sancho held his own with everyone, although unlettered, coarse, and pudgy, and he said to those who were with him and to Dr. Pedro Recio, who, since there was no longer a secret about the letter from the duke, had come back into that room: "Now I truly understand that judges and governors must be, or should be, made of bronze so they can withstand the demands of petitioners who come at all hours wanting to be heard and attended to, thinking only of their own affairs, no matter what. And if the poor judge doesn't listen and attend to them either because he cannot or because they don't come at the proper time to be heard, then they slander and criticize him and gnaw his bones and even gossip about his lineage. Foolish petitioner, don't rush—wait for the right time to handle your business! Don't come at lunchtime or when it's time to have a nap! Judges are made of flesh and blood and must give what Nature demands, except me, for I'm not allowed to eat, thanks to señor Pedro Recio de Tirteafuera, here present, who wants me to die of hunger, and affirms that this death is life. And may God do the same for him and all those of his kind—I mean, at least for *bad* doctors. Good doctors deserve palms and laurels."

All those who knew Sancho Panza marveled when they heard him speak so elegantly and didn't know what to attribute it to, except that positions of responsibility either sharpen or dull one's intellect. Finally, Dr. Pedro Recio Agüero de Tirteafuera promised to give him a dinner that evening, even though he would break all the aphorisms of Hippocrates. With this, the governor was happy and waited very anxiously for dinnertime to arrive, and although time, in his view, was standing still and didn't budge, the moment that he so desired finally came and they gave him beef hash with onions, and some cooked calves' feet that were a bit stale.

But he devoured these with greater pleasure than if they had been sandgrouses from Milan, pheasants from Rome, Sorrento veal, partridges from Morón, or geese from Lavajos,* and during the meal he turned to the doctor and said: "Look, Doctor, from now on don't give me dainty things to eat nor rich food; they'll knock my stomach off its hinges, seeing as it's used to goat, beef, bacon, jerky, turnips, and onions, and if you give it food from the palace, it gets queasy and even nauseous. What the butler can do is bring me some stew, and the longer it's cooked, the better it smells, and he can throw in and include anything he wants, as long as it's something to eat, and I'll be grateful and I'll pay him back one day. And let no one play jokes on me, because we all have to get along. Let's live and eat in good peace and fellowship, because 'when God starts the

---

* Morón de la Frontera is a city in the province of Seville. Lavajos is also a town in the province of Seville.

day, He starts it for everyone.' I'll govern this island without usurping any right or asking for bribes, and everyone keep a watchful eye and mind his own business, because I want you to know that 'the devil is in Cantillana,'* and if you give me a chance, you'll see marvels. 'Make yourself into honey and the flies will come.'"

"Certainly, *señor* governor," said the steward, "your grace is right in everything you've said, and I can say, in the name of all the islanders, that they'll serve you conscientiously, with love and goodwill, because your easygoing way of governing in these first days won't let them think or do anything that would be a disservice to you."

"I believe it," responded Sancho, "and they'd be foolish if they did or thought anything else. And I say again that care must be taken in my sustenance and my gray's. This is the most important thing. When it's time let's make the rounds. It's my intention to rid this *ínsula* of all kinds of filth, of idlers, and loafing bums. I want you to know, my friends, that idle and lazy people in a republic are the same as drones in a beehive who eat the honey that the worker bees make. I plan to favor the workers, keep the rights of the *hidalgos*, reward the virtuous, and above all respect the religion and honor of the ecclesiastics. What do you think of that, my friends? Am I saying something important or am I breaking my head?"

"Your grace is saying so much, *señor* governor," said the steward, "that I'm in awe that a man without education as your grace is—for I believe you have none—should say such and so many things filled with wisdom and counsel, so far beyond what was expected of your intelligence by those who sent us and those who live here. Each day one sees new things in the world, jests turn into truths, and the jesters are made fools of."

Night came and the governor ate with permission of Dr. Recio. They prepared to make the rounds and Sancho left with the steward, the secretary, the butler, the chronicler (who took care to write down his acts), and constables and

---

* Proverb: "The devil is in Cantillana and the bishop is in Brenes." Both of these are towns in the province of Seville. It means that there is a disturbance somewhere, or as we might say, after Shakespeare, "something is rotten in the state of Denmark."

scribes—so many that they could form half a squadron.
Sancho was in the middle with his staff of office—a sight
to see—and after a few blocks, they heard what sounded
like a sword fight. They hurried over and found that it was
only two men who were fighting, and they stopped as soon
as they saw the authorities. One of them said: "Help in the
name of God and the king! How is it they can rob a man
right out in the open in this town and assault him in the
middle of the street?"

"Calm down, my good man," said Sancho, "and tell me
what the cause of this quarrel is, for I'm the governor."

The other fellow said: "*Señor* governor, I'll tell about it
with just a few words. I want your grace to know that this
gentleman has just won more than a thousand *reales* in the
casino across the street, and God knows how. I was a spec-
tator and I judged more than one point in his favor,* quite
against what my conscience dictated. He picked up his winnings, and I expected him to give me at least an *escudo* as
a tip, as is customary to give important men such as myself
who are present to oversee fair or foul play, and back up
injustices and avoid quarrels. Well, he pocketed his money
and left the place. I followed him, a bit annoyed, and very
politely asked him to give me at least eight *reales*, since he
knows that I'm an honorable man and I have no job, because
my parents didn't teach me how to do anything, nor did they
leave me anything. But this unscrupulous fellow—and Cacus is no greater thief nor is Andradilla† a worse cheater—
refused to give me more than four *reales*, so you can see,
señor governor, how little shame and how little conscience
he has. But I swear that if your grace hadn't come, I would
have made him vomit his winnings and settle accounts."

"What do you have to say about this?" asked Sancho.

And the other responded that it was true what his adversary said, and he'd refused to give him more than four

---

* Translator's note: This seems like a strange custom nowadays. Covarrubias says that it was usual to share one's winnings with servants
and onlookers (such as this man is). What is strange is that the opinion
of onlookers would help decide a point. Modern casino games don't
allow for judgments, as far as I know, since all points are unambiguous;
but we don't know what the game was here.

† No one knows who this Andradilla was.

reales because he'd already tipped him many times. Those who receive a tip should be polite and accept happily whatever is given them, without arguing with the winners, unless they know for certain that they're cheaters and that their winnings are ill-gotten. And to show that he was a good man and not a thief, as the other claimed, there was no greater proof than his refusal to pay, since cheaters always pay the onlookers who know them.

"This is true," said the steward. "Now, your grace, *señor* governor, say what should be done with these two men."

"What will be done is this," said Sancho. "You, winner, by fair, foul, or indifferent means, give a hundred *reales* to this quarrelsome man, and pay thirty more for the poor in jail. And you, who have no job or inheritance and are a vagrant in this *ínsula*, take those hundred *reales* and sometime tomorrow go into exile for ten years; if you return before then, you'll finish your sentence in the next life, for we'll hang you from the gallows, or at least the executioner will, by my command. And neither of you reply, or you'll feel the weight of my hand."

The one man paid the money, the other received it; the latter then left the *ínsula*, the former went home, and the governor stood there and said: "Now, I do believe I'll get rid of these casinos. It seems to me that they're very harmful."

"This one, at least," said a scribe, "you can't get rid of, because a very important man owns it, and he loses more in card games every year than he takes in. You can exert your authority against the smaller casinos, since they do more damage and harbor the worst abuses. In the casinos that belong to noble gentlemen and lords, the cardsharps don't dare to try to cheat. Since gambling has become so popular, it's better to gamble in legitimate casinos rather than in a low-class joint where after midnight they grab any unfortunate person and take him for all he's worth."

"I see now, scribe," said Sancho, "that there's much to say about that."

Just then a constable arrived holding on to a young man, and said: "*Señor* governor, this young fellow was coming toward us, and as soon as he realized we were the authorities, he turned and began to run like a deer, a sign that he must be a delinquent. I ran after him, and if he hadn't stumbled and fallen, I would never have caught him."

"Why were you running, man?" asked Sancho.

To which the young man responded: "*Señor*, to avoid answering the many questions that the authorities ask."

"What is your line of work?"

"I'm a weaver."

"And what do you weave?"

"Iron tips for lances, by your grace's kind leave."

"An amusing fellow, are you? You consider yourself a comedian? All right. And where were you going right now?"

"*Señor*, to take the air."

"And where does one take the air on this *ínsula*?"

"Wherever it blows."

"Good. You're answering very well, and you're a witty young man. But bear in mind that I'm the wind, and I'm blowing at your back, and I'm blowing you into jail. Grab him and haul him away, for I'll make him sleep there tonight, without a breeze."

"By God," said the young man, "you can make me sleep in jail about as much as you can crown me king!"

"Why can't I make you sleep in jail?" responded Sancho. "Don't I have the power to arrest you and let you go wherever and whenever I please?"

"No matter how much power your grace may have," said the young man, "it's not enough to make me sleep in jail."

"Why not?" responded Sancho. "Take him at once to where he'll see with his own eyes how wrong he is. And just in case the jailer should solicit a bribe to let you go, I'll slap a fine of two thousand *ducados* on him if he lets you take one step away from your cell."

"All that is very laughable," responded the young man. "The thing is, no living creature can make me sleep in jail."

"Tell me, you little devil," said Sancho, "do you have some angel who can take you away and remove the shackles I plan to have put on you?"

"Now," responded the young man with great wit, "let's think about it and get to the point. Suppose, your grace, that you have me taken to jail and that they put shackles and chains on me and that they put me in a cell, and they threaten the guard with stiff fines if he lets me go, and he does what he's told. With all this, if I don't want to sleep, and stay awake all night without closing an eye, will your power be enough to make me sleep if I don't want to?"

"That's right," said the secretary. "The fellow has made his point."

"So," said Sancho, "you wouldn't sleep only because it's your free will not to, and not because you want to go against my will?"

"No, *señor*," said the young man, "I wouldn't even consider that."

"Then go with God," said Sancho. "Go sleep in your own house and may God let you sleep well. I don't want to rob you of your sleep. But I advise you from now on not to joke with the authorities, because you'll run across someone who'll take your joke and bash it against your head."

The young man went away and the governor continued his rounds. In a little while he met two constables holding on to a man and they said: "*Señor*, this person who seems to be a man is not, but rather is a woman—and not an ugly one—dressed as a man."

They held two or three lanterns near her and discovered the face of a woman, sixteen or a bit older. Her hair was gathered in a hairnet made of gold and green silk, and as pretty as a thousand pearls. They looked at her from head to foot, and saw that she was wearing some flesh-colored silk stockings, with garters made of white taffeta fringed with gold and seed pearls. Her trousers were green, with golden threads, and she wore a cape of the same material, unfastened, under which she was wearing a doublet of very fine gold-and-white fabric, and her shoes were men's style and white in color. No sword hung at her side, only a very richly decorated dagger, and on her hands there were many fine rings. The girl seemed quite attractive to all of them, and of all who saw her, no one recognized her. The natives of the town said that they had no idea what family she belonged to. The accomplices of the tricks to be played on Sancho were the most amazed of all, because they had not planned this and so they were in suspense wondering how it would turn out.

Sancho was stunned at the beauty of the girl and asked her who her family was, and what had made her dress that way. Looking at the ground, with innocent shame, she responded: "I can't say in public what was so important for me to keep a secret. One thing I want to be understood—I'm not a thief or a wicked person, just an unfortunate maiden whom the power of jealousy caused to break the laws of propriety."

When the steward heard this, he said to Sancho: "Ask the others to clear away, *señor* governor, so that this woman can state with less embarrassment whatever she wants."

The governor asked that this be done and the crowd moved away, except for the steward, the butler, and the secretary. Seeing that they were alone, the maiden went on, saying: "I, *señores*, am the daughter of Pedro Pérez Mazorca, the tax collector for woolens in this village, who visits my father's house frequently."

"That makes no sense, *señora*," said the steward, "because I know Pedro Pérez very well and I know that he's childless, having neither a son nor a daughter, and what's more, you say that he's your father and also that he visits your father's house frequently."

"I caught that, too," said Sancho.

"*Señores*, I'm upset and I don't know what I'm saying," responded the maiden, "but the truth is that I'm the daughter of Diego de la Llana, whom all of your graces must know."

"Now, that makes more sense," responded the steward, "because I know Diego de la Llana, and I know that he's a rich *hidalgo* who has a son and a daughter, and that since he became a widower, no one in this village can say that he has seen the face of his daughter. He keeps her so secluded that even the sun doesn't see her, though rumor has it that she's extremely beautiful."

"That's the truth," said the girl, "and I'm that daughter. Whether or not the rumors lie as to my looks, you, *señores*, will have to judge for yourselves, since you've seen me."

And then she began to weep tenderly. When the secretary saw this, he went to whisper into the butler's ear: "Without a doubt something important must have happened to this girl, since she's such an elegant woman, walking around so far from her home, dressed like that, and at such a late hour."

"There's no doubt about that," responded the butler, "and what's more, your suspicion is confirmed by her tears."

Sancho consoled her with the best words he could think of, and asked her to tell him, without any fear, what had happened, and that everyone would try to help her most earnestly and in any way possible.

"The thing is, *señores*," she responded, "my father has kept me in seclusion for ten years, ever since my mother's death. Mass is said at home in a magnificent chapel, and in all this time I have seen nothing but the sun by day and the moon and stars by night. I don't even know what the streets, plaza, or churches look like, or who people are, outside of my father and brother, and Pedro Pérez, the tax collector— and since he comes to my house so often, I thought I'd say he was my father, so as not to mention who my real father is. This seclusion, and not letting me go out of the house— not even to the church—for so many days and months has made me very stricken with grief. I would like to see the world, or at least the town where I was born, which I don't believe exceeds the bounds of propriety that highborn maidens ought to observe. When I heard that they fought bulls, there were mock battles, and that plays were put on, I asked my brother—who is a year younger than I am—to tell me about those things, and many others I had never seen. He told me as well as he could, but it only served to increase my desire to see them for myself. Finally, to make this story of my ruin short, I begged and asked my brother, and, oh! I should have never asked or begged him. . . ."

And once again she renewed her weeping. The steward said to her: "Continue, your grace, *señora*, and finish telling us what has happened, because your words and tears are holding us all in suspense."

"I have just a few more words left," responded the maiden, "although many more tears to shed, because my misdirected longings can only bring negative results."*

The beauty of the maiden settled over the heart of the butler, and he once again held his lantern close to see her, and it seemed to him that it wasn't tears she was shedding, but rather seed pearls or dew of the meadows—he even held them in higher esteem, comparing them to Oriental pearls, and he hoped that her misfortune wasn't as

---

* Here, the girl uses business terms, not well translatable, that she learned from her father's speech.

great as her weeping and sighs seemed to indicate. The governor was despairing at the girl's delay in finishing her story, and told her to stop keeping them in suspense, because it was late and he still had a long way to go on his rounds. Between broken sobs and half-formed sighs, she said: "My calamity and misfortune is only that I begged my brother to dress me in one of his suits, and that he take me out one night to see the whole town while our father slept.

"He was pestered by my entreaties and agreed to go along with my wish, dressing me this way, and he dressed himself in one of my outfits that fits him like a glove, and since he doesn't have any hint of a beard yet, he looks just like a beautiful girl. Tonight about one o'clock, more or less, we left our house, and led by our childish and ill-advised intention, we walked all around this town, and as we were getting ready to go home, we saw a large group of people coming and my brother said: 'Sister, this must be the night patrol. Put wings on your feet and run behind me so they won't find out who we are, for it will be bad for us if they do.'

"And saying this, he turned around and began, not to run, but to fly. I fell after six steps because of my distress, and then that minister of justice came and brought me to your graces, where I find myself humiliated and shamed in front of so many people."

"So, *señora*," said Sancho, "nothing else happened to you, and it wasn't jealousy—as you said at first—that took you out of your house?"

"Nothing happened to me, nor did jealousy take me out of my house—just the desire to see the world, even if it was only to see the streets of this village."

And this truth was confirmed by the constables with her brother in custody, whom one of them caught when he was fleeing. He was wearing only a fancy skirt and a shawl of blue damask with fine gold trim; his head had no hood, and was unadorned except by his curly blond hair, which looked like rings of gold.

The governor, steward, and butler took him away from his sister, so she wouldn't hear, and asked him why he was dressed that way, and he, with no less shame and embarrassment, told the same story his sister had related, which gave great pleasure to the enamored butler. But the governor told them: "It seems to me, *señores*, this has been nothing but a childish prank, and they didn't need so many long explanations, tears, or sighs to tell it. Just by saying: 'We're So-and-So and we left our parents' house to take a walk, only out of curiosity, and with no other intention,' we would have ended the tale, with no sighs and crying, and that's it."

"That's true," said the maiden, "but I was so upset I couldn't act rationally."

"No harm was done," responded Sancho. "All right, we'll go with your graces to your father's house. Perhaps he won't have missed you. But from now on, don't be so childish nor so eager to see the world. Because 'the honorable maiden should stay home with a broken leg' and 'by wandering about, the woman and the hen are soon lost.' And 'the one who wants to see also wants to be seen' and I say no more."

The young man thanked the governor for the favor he wanted to do them by escorting them home, and they went toward the house, which wasn't far off. When they arrived, the brother threw a pebble through the grate and in a moment the maid, who was expecting them, came down to let them in. They went in, leaving everyone amazed as much by their refinement and their beauty as by their desire to see the world at night, without leaving their village, but they attributed it all to their youth.

The butler was left with an aching heart and he resolved the next morning to ask her father for permission to marry her, certain that he wouldn't be denied, since he was a servant of the duke; and even Sancho got the idea to marry the young man to Sanchica, his daughter, and he resolved to arrange it in due time, feeling that no husband could be refused a governor's daughter. With this they ended the rounds that night, and two days later the governorship also ended, whereby all of his designs were cut off and scattered to the wind, as will be seen farther on.

*Chapter L. Where it is declared who the enchanters
and tormentors were who whipped the duenna and
pinched and scratched don Quixote, together with
what happened to the page who took the letter to
Teresa Panza, wife of Sancho Panza.*

CIDE HAMETE, the scrupulous investigator of the minut-
est details of this true history, says that when doña
Rodríguez left her room to go to don Quixote's, another
duenna who slept in the same room heard her, and since
all duennas are eager to pry into things, find out what
they're about, and sniff them out, she followed her so
quietly that the good Rodríguez didn't notice. As soon as
the duenna saw her go into don Quixote's room, in order
to prove that she was a gossip like all other duennas, she
went to tell the duchess that doña Rodríguez was in don
Quixote's room.

The duchess reported it all to the duke and asked his
permission to go with Altisidora to see what that duenna
wanted with don Quixote. The duke did so, and the two
of them, slowly and quietly, one step at a time, went to the
door of the room, so close that they could hear everything
that was said inside. And when the duchess heard doña
Rodríguez reveal the Aranjuez of her issues,* she couldn't
stand it, and neither could Altisidora; filled with anger and
wanting revenge, they burst into the room, pinched don
Quixote, and spanked the duenna as has been related,
because an insult against the beauty and pride of women
awakens enormous wrath in them and sets aflame the desire to avenge themselves.

The duchess told the duke what had happened, which
delighted him quite a bit. And the duchess, continuing with
her plan to play tricks on and have fun with don Quixote,
dispatched the page who had played the part of Dulcinea
in the artifice of her disenchantment—which Sancho had

---

* There is a pun here, since the word for "issue" and "fountain" is the
same in Spanish. Aranjuez—the Spanish Versailles—is a town near
Toledo famous for its fountains. You can figure it out from here.

completely forgotten about while he was governor—to Teresa Panza, his wife, with the letter from her husband, and another one from her, and with a long strand of elegant coral beads as a present.

The history says, then, that the page was very witty and clever, and, dedicated to serving his master and mistress eagerly, he left for Sancho's village. At the outskirts, he saw a number of women washing clothes in a stream and asked them if they might be able to tell him if a woman named Teresa Panza lived in that town, the wife of a certain Sancho Panza, squire to a knight named don Quixote de La Mancha. A young girl who was washing clothes rose and said: "That Teresa Panza is my mother, and that Sancho is my father, and that knight is our master."

"Well, then, young lady," said the page, "take me to your mother, because I'm bringing her a letter and a present from your father."

"I'll do that with great pleasure, *señor mío*," responded the young girl, who seemed to be fourteen years old, more or less. And leaving the clothes that she was washing with a friend, without covering her head or putting on her shoes, because she had nothing on her legs and her hair was uncombed, skipped in front of the page's horse and said: "Come, your grace, for our house is right near the entrance to the town, and my mother is at home and is pretty worried, since she hasn't heard from my *señor* father in many days."

"Well, I'm taking news to her," said the page, "and such good news that she'll give thanks to God for it."

So, jumping, running, and skipping, the girl got to the village, and before going into her house, she cried from the door: "Come out, mother Teresa, come out, come out! A man has come bringing letters and other things from my good father."

At these cries the mother appeared, spinning a ball of flax, and wearing a gray skirt. It seemed, because it was so short, that it had been cut in a shameful place,* with a bodice that was gray as well, and a low-cut blouse. She wasn't very old, although she seemed to be past forty, but she was

---

* This reflects a verse from an old ballad that everyone knew, too complicated to go into, that meant that the skirt was quite short.

strong, hearty, vigorous, and tanned,* and when she saw her daughter and the page on horseback, she said: "What's going on, daughter? Who is this man?"

"He's a servant of my lady doña Teresa Panza," responded the page. And as he said that, he jumped from his horse and went over with great humility to kneel before *señora* Teresa Panza, and said: "Give me your hands, my lady doña Teresa Panza, since you're the only legitimate wife of *señor* Sancho Panza, the rightful governor of the *ínsula* Barataria."

"*Ay, señor mío*, stand up. Don't do that," responded Teresa. "I'm not one of those palace women—just a poor peasant, a daughter of bumpkins, and wife of a squire-errant, and not of any governor."

"Your grace," responded the page, "is the very worthy wife of a twice-worthy governor, and to prove this truth, here's a letter and this present."

And he instantly took from his pocket a string of coral beads interspersed with ones of gold, and placed them around her neck, and said: "This letter is from the *señor* governor, and I have here another from my lady the duchess who sends it to your grace."

Teresa was dumbfounded, and her daughter was no less so, and the girl said: "May they kill me if our master, don Quixote, doesn't have something to do with this, for he must have given him the governorship or an earldom, which he promised him so many times."

"That's the truth," responded the page, "for it's through *señor* don Quixote that *señor* Sancho is now governor of the *ínsula* Barataria, as will be seen in this letter."

"Read it to me, your grace, *señor* gentleman," said Teresa, "because although I can spin, I can't read a thing."

"I can't either," added Sanchica, "but wait for me here a minute. I'll go fetch someone to read it, either the priest himself or the bachelor Sansón Carrasco, and they'll come willingly to hear news about my father."

---

* "Tanned" in Spanish is *avellanado*. Did Cervantes use this word—which is similar to the name of the person who wrote the spurious second part of *Don Quixote*, Avellaneda—to hint that he was correcting his rival, who said that she was going on fifty-three years old?

"There's no reason to call anyone, for I don't know how to spin, but I can read, and I'll read it."

And so he read the whole letter as it was set down already, so it's not repeated here, and then he took out the one from the duchess, which went this way:

My friend Teresa:

The good qualities of your husband—his kindness and cleverness—moved and obliged me to ask my husband the duke to give him the governorship of an ínsula from the many that he possesses. I hear he's governing perfectly, and this makes me very happy, as it does the duke, my master, for which I thank heaven I was not wrong in choosing him for that position, for I want señora Teresa to know that it's difficult to find a good governor in the world, and may God treat me as well as Sancho governs.

I'm sending you, my dear, a string of coral and gold beads. I would be better pleased if they could be Oriental pearls, but "he who gives you a bone doesn't want to see you dead." * The time will come when we'll get to meet and talk, God knows when. Remember me to Sanchica, your daughter, and tell her to get ready, for I plan to marry her into a high station when least she suspects it. They tell me that in your village there are large acorns. Send me about two dozen, which I'll esteem greatly, since they will have been collected by you, and write me a long letter, telling me of your health and well-being; and if you need anything, you have only to open your mouth, and whatever you ask will be done. And may God keep you for me. From this village, your friend who loves you well,

The Duchess

---

* Francisco Rico interprets this saying this way: "Even though it is not much, it is a sign of appreciation."

"Ay!" said Teresa when she heard the letter. "How good
and how open and how humble this lady is! May they bury
me with ladies like this, and not with the *hidalgas* like we
have in this town who think not even the wind should touch
them, and who go to church with such vanity as if they were
queens themselves, and consider it beneath them even to
look at a peasant. And see here where the duchess calls
me FRIEND and treats me as her equal. May I see her made
equal to the highest bell tower in all of La Mancha. And as
for the acorns, *señor mío*, I'll send her ladyship a peck of
them that will astonish her when she sees them. For now,
Sanchica, make sure this gentleman is comfortable, tend to
his horse, go to the stable for some eggs, cut a good portion
of bacon, and let's feed him like we would a prince. The
good news he brought us and his honest face deserve no
less. Meanwhile, I'll go to tell my lady friends the news of
our happiness, as well as the priest, and *maese* Nicolás the
barber, who are and have been such good friends of your
father."

"All right, Mother," responded Sanchica, "but don't you
think you should give me half of that necklace? I don't
think that the duchess is foolish enough that she would
send it all to you."

"It's all for you, daughter," responded Teresa. "But let
me wear it around my neck for a few days because it truly
gladdens my heart."

"Both your hearts will be gladdened when you see what
is in this valise—it's a suit of very fine material that the
governor wore only one time while hunting, and he's sending it to Sanchica."

"May he live a thousand years," responded Sanchica,
"and the person bringing it, may he live no more nor less,
and even two thousand years, if necessary."

Teresa left her house with the letters and with the necklace around her neck, and was slapping the letters against
her hand as if she were playing the tambourine. By chance
she ran across the priest and Sansón Carrasco, and began
to dance and say: "I swear there's no poor relation now! We
have a little government! Let the best of the *hidalgas* take
me on, and I'll show her!"

"What is this, Teresa Panza? What lunacy is this and
what papers are those?"

"It's no lunacy but rather these are letters from duchesses and governors, and these beads I have around my neck are coral for the Hail Marys and the beaten gold ones are the Our Fathers,* and I'm a governor's wife."

"No one but God can understand you, Teresa, and we don't know what you're saying."

"You'll see soon enough," responded Teresa. And she gave them the letters. The priest read them aloud for Sansón Carrasco to hear, and Sansón and the priest looked at each other astonished at what they had read. The bachelor asked who had brought the letters. Teresa responded that they should come with her to her house and they would see the messenger, who was a very charming young man, and who had brought another present worth quite a bit. The priest took the corals from her neck and examined them, and examined them again, and realized that they were of fine quality, then examined them again, and said: "By the habit I'm wearing, I don't know what to say or think about these letters and these presents. On the one hand I'm seeing and touching the quality of these corals, and on the other I'm reading that a duchess has asked for two dozen acorns—"

"What nonsense," interrupted Carrasco. "All right, let's go see the bearer of this letter. From him we'll see how to solve the problem that it implies."

So they returned with Teresa. They found the page sifting a bit of barley for his mount, and Sanchica cutting some bacon to put in scrambled eggs for the page to eat. They were pleased to see his fine appearance, and after they greeted each other courteously, Sansón asked him to relate news about don Quixote as well as about Sancho Panza. Although they had read the letters from Sancho and the duchess, they were still confused and couldn't fathom the business of Sancho's governorship, especially of an *ínsula*, since all or most islands in the Mediterranean Sea belonged to His Majesty. To which the page responded: "That *señor* Sancho Panza is governor, there's no doubt. That it's an *ínsula* or not where he governs, I'm in no position to have an opinion. But it's enough that it's a village of more than a

---

* This alludes to the rosary. The Hail Marys (smaller beads) are of coral and the Our Fathers (larger beads) are of beaten gold.

thousand inhabitants; and as far as the acorns go, well, my lady the duchess is so open and humble," he said, "that she not only asks a peasant lady to send her acorns, but she once had to borrow a comb from a neighbor of hers. I must say that the ladies of Aragón, even though they're of high birth, are not affected and presumptuous like the ladies of Castile are. They treat everyone with more consideration."

When he was in the middle of this conversation, Sanchica came in with a skirt full of eggs and asked the page: "Tell me, *señor*, does my father wear knickers since he became governor?"

"I haven't noticed," responded the page, "but I guess he does."

"*Ay!* My goodness!" replied Sanchica. "My father with those pants on must be a sight to see. Isn't it funny that since I was born I've always wanted to see my father in those pants?"

"And you will see those things, if your grace lives," responded the page. "Why, if his governorship lasts two months he'll be traveling with a beautiful warm hood."

The priest and bachelor could see that the page was speaking with great irony. But the quality of the coral necklace and the hunting outfit Sancho had sent—for Teresa had shown them the suit—made them wonder, and they couldn't help but laugh about Sanchica's wish, and more so when Teresa said: "*Señor* priest, see if anyone is going to Madrid or Toledo so they can buy me a bell-shaped skirt, ready-to-wear, and of the most fashionable kind there is. In truth, in truth, I have to honor my husband's position as much as I can; and even if it vexes me, I have to go to court and run around in a coach like the rest of them, for she who has a governor for a husband can have and maintain one."

"And why not, Mother?" said Sanchica. "Please God it should be today rather than tomorrow, even though women who see me riding around with my mother in that coach might say: 'Look at little Miss So-and-So, daughter of that garlic-stuffed fellow! Look at her sitting all stretched out in that coach as if she were a lady pope!' But let 'em walk through the mud, and let me be in my coach with my feet off the ground. A bad year and a bad month to all those gossips in the world! Let 'em laugh at me while I travel and stay warm! Am I right, Mother?"

"You certainly are!" said Teresa. "My good Sancho promised me all this good fortune and even more. And you'll see, daughter, how he won't stop until he's made me a countess. The key is to start with a little bit of luck, and as I've heard your good father say many times—just as he's your father, he's also the father of proverbs—'when they give you a heifer, run to fetch the halter' and when they give you a government, take it; when they give you an earldom, grab it; and when they offer you something nice, go get it. If not, 'go to sleep, and when good luck and good times come knocking on your door, don't answer!'"

"And what do I care," Sanchica added, "if when they see me haughty and stuck-up, they feel like saying, 'the dog put on a pair of pants,' and all the rest?"*

When the priest heard this he said: "I have to believe that every one of the whole line of Panzas was born with a bag of proverbs in his body. I've not seen any one of them who doesn't spew them out all the time in every conversation they have."

"That's the truth," said the page, "for the *señor* governor Sancho says one every minute. And even though many don't hit the mark, at least they give pleasure, and *señora mía* the duchess and the duke really praise them."

"So, your grace still affirms, *señor mío*," said the bachelor, "that it's true about Sancho's governorship, and that there's a duchess in the world who sends presents and writes to Teresa? Because we, although we touch the presents and have read the letters, don't believe it, and we think that this has something to do with don Quixote, our neighbor, who thinks that everything happens by enchantment. I almost want to touch and feel you to see if you're a phantom messenger or a man of flesh and blood."

"All I can tell you, *señores*," said the page, "is that I'm a real messenger and *señor* Sancho Panza is an actual governor, and my masters, the duke and duchess, can give, and have given him, that governorship. And I've heard that Sancho Panza has conducted himself very worthily. If there's any enchantment in that or not, your graces can decide between yourselves. I don't know anything else but

---

* The saying goes on to say: "...and now he doesn't even talk to us!"

the oath that I swear on the life of my parents, who are still alive, and whom I love very much."

"That may be," replied the bachelor, "but *dubitat Augustinus*."*

"You can doubt it if you want," responded the page, "but the truth is what I've said, and truth always floats on top of lies like oil on water. And if not, *operibus credite, et non verbis.*† Let either of your graces come with me, and you'll see with your eyes what you don't believe with your ears."

"That's for me!" said Sanchica. "Take me, *señor*, on the crupper of your horse. I'll go enthusiastically to see my father again."

"Daughters of governors must not go alone along the roads, but rather accompanied by coaches and litters, and a great number of servants."

"By God," responded Sanchica, "I can travel just as well on a donkey as in a coach. Do you think I'm so fussy?"

"Hush, child," said Teresa. "You don't know what you're talking about. This gentleman is right, for 'as the time, so the tactics.' When it's Sancho, then Sancha; and when it's the governor, it's MY LADY—do you know what I mean?"

"You've said more than you think," said the page. "Give me something to eat and let me leave right away, for I plan to get back this afternoon."

To which the priest said: "Your grace, come take potluck with me. *Señora* Teresa has more goodwill than goods to serve such a fine guest."

The page demurred, but finally he saw that he should go with the priest. And the priest led him away eagerly so he'd have the time to ask him at his leisure about don Quixote and his deeds. The bachelor offered to write letters of response from Teresa, but she didn't want the bachelor to meddle in her affairs, for she considered him to be a smart aleck. And so she gave a roll and two eggs to an acolyte who could write, and he wrote two letters—one for her husband and another for the duchess, dictated out of her head, and they're not the worst ones to be read in this great history, as will be seen later.

---

* "St. Augustine doubts it." This derives from St. Augustine's skepticism about the effectiveness of urgently confessing oneself just before death.
† "Believe my works and not my words" (John 10:38).

Chapter LI. Of the progress in the government of San-
   cho Panza, together with other events, such as they
   are.

THE DAY dawned following the night of the governor's
rounds, which the butler spent sleepless, his thoughts
dominated by the face, spirit, and beauty of the disguised
maiden. The steward used what remained of the night to
write to his masters what Sancho Panza did and said, amazed
as much by his deeds as by what he said, because his words
and actions were streaked with both wisdom and folly.

The *señor* governor finally got up, and on the orders of
Dr. Pedro Recio they served him a bit of fruit compote and
a few sips of cold water for breakfast, which Sancho would
have willingly exchanged for a piece of bread and a bunch
of grapes. But when he realized he was forced to go along
and had no choice in the matter, he submitted with grief
in his heart and a growling stomach, since Pedro Recio
had convinced him that light and delicate food quickened
the mind, and that was what was best for people who have
power or are in serious offices, where they need more intellectual prowess than physical strength.

With this deceitful nonsense, Sancho suffered such
hunger that he secretly cursed his governorship, and even
the person who had given it to him. But with his hunger
(and his compote) he began his day on the bench, and
the first case before him was a stranger who asked him a
question before the steward and the other assistants present: "*Señor*, a raging river divided two parts of the same
dominion—listen carefully, because the case is important
and thorny.

"So, then, over this river was a bridge, and on the other
side of it there was a gallows and a kind of court set up in
which there were usually four judges who administer the law
set down by the owner of the river, the bridge, and the dominion. That law read like this: 'If anyone crosses this bridge
from one side to the other, he must swear first where he's
going and why. And if he tells the truth, he should pass, and
if he lies, he should be hanged on the gallows without possibility of appeal.' Many people went over the bridge, and

since they all knew the law, it was easy to tell that what they stated was the truth, and the judges let them pass freely.

"It happened, then, that a man swore on his oath that he came to die on the gallows, and for no other reason.

"The judges considered the oath and said: 'If we let this man pass freely his oath will be proven a lie, and by law he should die. But if we hang him, he would have been telling the truth, and for that same reason should be set free.' We ask your grace, *señor* governor, what the judges should do with the fellow. Even now they're still uncertain and are quite puzzled. Having heard of your keen intellect, they sent me to beg you to give your opinion on this knotty and uncertain case."

To which Sancho responded: "Those *señores* judges should not have sent you to me, because I'm more ignorant than wise. But, even so, explain the matter to me once again so I can understand it. Maybe I'll be able to 'hit the nail on the head.'"

The petitioner repeated what he'd said, and repeated it again; then Sancho said: "In my opinion I can set this straight in an instant. Here's the problem: The man swears he's going to die on the gallows, and if he dies on the gallows he swore the truth, and by law he should go free, and pass over the bridge; while if they don't hang him, he swore falsely, and by that same law should be hanged."

"It's exactly as the *señor* governor stated," said the messenger, "and insofar as the complete understanding of the case goes, there's nothing more to ask or doubt."

"So I say, then," replied Sancho, "that the part of the man that spoke the truth be allowed to pass, and the part that told the lie be hanged, and in this way the law regarding passage over the bridge will be followed to the letter."

"But, *señor* governor," replied the petitioner, "to do this we'd have to cut the man into two parts, the lying part and the truthful part, and if he's cut in half, perforce he has to die, and neither provision of this binding law will be obeyed."

"Look, my good man," responded Sancho, "this traveler that you're talking about, either I'm a blockhead or he has just as much reason to die as he does to live and pass over the bridge. If the truth saves him, a lie condemns him. And this being so, I think you should tell these *señores* who sent you to me, since the reasons for condemning him and absolving him are exactly equal, they should let him go free, since it's more praiseworthy to do good rather than bad. I would sign my name to it if I could write; and in this case I've not spoken my own opinion, but rather it was a precept I got, among others, from my master don Quixote the night before I came to be the governor of this island, which was that when justice hangs in the balance, I should lean toward and favor mercy. And God has ordained that I should think of this right now, since it fits the case like a glove."

"That's right," responded the steward. "And I'm of the opinion that Lycurgus, who gave the laws to the Lacedæmonians,* could have given no better judgment than the great Panza has given. With this, the morning session stands adjourned, and I'll give the order that the *señor* governor should eat as much as he pleases."

"That's what I ask for, and with no deceptions," said Sancho. "Give me something to eat and let them rain their cases and doubts on me. I'll solve them instantly."

The steward kept his word, for it bothered his conscience to starve such a wise governor to death. And what was more, he planned to finish this governorship that very night by playing one last jest he'd been charged to do.

It happened, then, that when he'd eaten that day, against the rules and aphorisms of Dr. Tirteafuera, after they removed the tablecloth, a messenger came with a letter from don Quixote for the governor. Sancho had the secretary read it silently, and if there was nothing in it that needed to be kept secret, he should read it aloud. The secretary read it twice and said: "It can be read aloud. What *señor* don Quixote writes to your grace deserves to be printed in gold letters; and it says:

Letter from don Quixote de La Mancha to Sancho Panza, governor of the ínsula *Barataria*

> *Expecting news of your blunders and nonsensical acts, Sancho, my friend, I heard instead of your wise judgments, for which I give particular thanks to heaven, which can*

---

* See Part II, chapter one, page 513. Lacedæmon refers to Sparta.

raise the poor and stupid from the dunghill and
make them wise. They tell me that you govern
as a man but as a man you're like a dumb
animal, such is the humility you show in your
dealings. And I want you to know, Sancho, that
it's frequently fitting and even necessary, owing
to the importance of one's office, to go against
the humbleness of one's heart, for example in
the way one dresses, which should conform to
what the office requires rather than one's own
humble nature. Dress well since "a stick that is
well clad doesn't appear to be a stick anymore."
I don't mean you should wear jewels or a full
dress uniform, or that as a judge you should
dress like a soldier, but rather that you adorn
yourself with what your office requires, as long
as it's clean and looks good.

To win the goodwill of the people that you
govern, there are two things, among others, that
you have to do: the first, be a good servant to all,
although I have already told you this; and the
other, try to provide an abundance of things that
sustain life, for there's nothing that dampens the
heart of the people more than hunger and want.

Don't make many laws, and if you do make
any, make sure that they're good and especially
that they be kept and obeyed. For laws that
are not kept are the same thing as if there were
no such laws. Rather they give the impression
that the prince who formulated them had the
wisdom and authority to make them, but not
the strength to make sure they were obeyed—
and laws that threaten but are not obeyed are
like the log, the king of the frogs,* which at first
frightened them but which in time they came to
scorn and climbed on top of.

---

* See Æsop's fables, number forty-four. In the Spanish version, *Yso-
pete*, it is Fable 1 of Book II (see John Keller's translation [*Æsop's Fables*, Lexington: The University Press of Kentucky, 1992], p. 70). After
Jupiter sent the frogs a log to be their king and the frogs complained,
he sent a stork who ate them.

Be a father to the virtues and a stepfather to the vices. Don't always be harsh or always mild—choose a happy medium between these two extremes. Visit the jails, the butcher shops, and the marketplaces, for the presence of the governor in those places is very important. It consoles the prisoners waiting for their coming release, it's a source of dread for the butchers who, at least for the moment, will weigh their goods fairly, and it's a deterrent to the market women for the same reason. Don't show yourself to be (even if you might be, which I don't believe) greedy, a chaser of women, or a glutton, because when the people and those surrounding you learn of those inclinations, they will attack you until they knock you into the depths of ruin.

Examine and examine again, consider and consider again the advice and written documents I gave you before you left, and you'll see how, if you observe it all, you'll have something to help you get through the travails and difficulties that beset governors at every turn. Write to your masters and show them that you're grateful to them. Ingratitude is the child of pride, and one of the deadliest sins; and the person who is grateful to those who have done him favors shows that he'll be grateful to God, who has blessed him and will continue to shower many blessings on him.

The *señora* duchess sent one of her servants with your hunting outfit and another present to your wife, Teresa Panza. We're expecting a response at any moment.

I've been a bit indisposed from a cat-clawing that happened to me, and turned out to be not to the advantage of my nose; but it was really nothing. If there are enchanters who treat me ill, there are also those who defend me.

Tell me if the steward with you had anything to do with Trifaldi as you suspected; and keep me apprised of everything that happens to you,

*because the distance is so short, and I plan to
leave this life of leisure that I'm leading, for I
was not born for it.*

*Something has come up that I fear will put
me in ill grace with these people. Although I am
concerned, my feelings really mean nothing,
since after all I have to comply with my profession rather than their pleasure, in accordance
with what is said:* Amicus Plato, sed magis
amica veritas.* *I say this in Latin because I
suppose that since you've been a governor you
will have learned it. Farewell, and may God
keep you away from harm.*

> *Your friend,*
>
> *Don Quixote
> de La Mancha*

Sancho listened to the letter with great attention, and
it was praised and thought to be wise by all who heard
it. Then he got up from the table, called in his secretary,
and they shut themselves up in his room, because Sancho
wanted to respond to his master don Quixote immediately.
He told the secretary to write exactly what he said, without
adding or taking away anything. And that's what was done.
The response went like this:

Letter from Sancho Panza to
don Quixote de La Mancha

*Because I've been so busy I've not had the time
either to scratch my head or even to cut my
fingernails—they have grown so long that God
will have to fix them. I say this,* señor mío *of
my soul, so that your grace won't be surprised
that I haven't yet related my ups and downs
in this government, in which I'm hungrier*

---

* "Plato is a friend, but the truth is a greater friend." This version of
the proverb comes from the *Adagia* of the Dutch humanist Erasmus
(1469–1536).

than when we wandered through forests and wastelands.

My lord the duke wrote me the other day to warn me that certain spies had entered this island to kill me, and up to now I haven't discovered any except a certain doctor who is employed in this village to kill any governor who comes here. His name is Dr. Pedro Recio, and he is from Tirteafuera, so that your grace can judge whether or not I have reason to fear dying at his hands. This doctor himself said that he doesn't cure illnesses when one has one, but rather prevents them from coming, and the medicines he uses are diet and more diet, until he reduces the patient to gnawed bones, as though emaciation weren't worse than a fever. In other words, he's starving me to death, and I'm dying of dismay—whereas I thought I was coming to this government to eat hot food and drink cool refreshments, and enjoy the comfort of Holland sheets on feather beds—instead I have been doing penance as if I were a hermit, and since I'm not doing it of my free will, I believe that in the end the devil will carry me off.

Up to now I've not collected a fee nor taken a bribe, and I don't know where it's all leading, because they have told me here that governors who come to this ínsula, before they take office, the people in the town typically lend or give them large sums of money; and this is the usual practice for those who go to govern, and not only here.

Last night when I was making the rounds, I ran across a beautiful maiden wearing a man's clothing and a brother of hers in a woman's dress. The butler fell in love with the girl and has chosen her to be his wife—at least that's what he says—and I chose the young man to be my son-in-law. Today the two of us will tell our thoughts to their father, a certain Diego de la Llana, and as good an Old Christian as you could want.

*I do visit the marketplaces as your grace
advises and yesterday I found a market woman
who was selling fresh hazelnuts and I discovered that she'd mixed a bushel and a half
of fresh ones with a bushel and a half of old,
rotten, worthless ones. I gave them all to the
orphans, who can tell the good ones from the
bad, and sentenced her not to come back to
the market for two weeks. They told me that I
did very well. All I know is that it's said that in
this town there's no one worse than the market
women, because they're all shameless, soulless,
and pushy, and I believe it because of what I've
seen in other towns.*

*I'm very pleased that my lady the duchess
has written my wife, Teresa Panza, and sent her
the present your grace mentions, and I'll try
to show my gratitude in due course. Kiss her
hands for me, your grace, telling her that I say
she has not cast her bread upon the waters* in
vain, as she'll soon see.*

*I wouldn't want your grace to get into
trouble with my masters, because if you have a
falling-out with them it will hurt me, and since
I've been advised to be grateful, it makes no
sense for your grace not to be as well to those
who have done you all those favors, and for the
regal way you have been treated in their castle.*

*I don't understand about that cat busi-
ness, but I imagine that it must be one of the
misdeeds that the evil enchanters typically use
against you. I'll find out when we see each
other.*

*I would like to send your grace something,
but I don't know what to send, unless it's some
high-quality enema kits that they make on this
ínsula. If this office lasts, I'll look for something
to send, one way or another.*

If my wife, Teresa Panza, writes me, please

---

* Ecclesiastes 11:1: "Cast your bread upon the waters, for after many
days you will find it again."

*pay the postage and send me the letter. I really
want to find out what's going on at home with
my wife and children. And with this, may God
deliver you from evil-intentioned enchanters
and send me safe and sound from this government, which I doubt, because I think I'll leave
my life here, the way Dr. Pedro treats me.*

Servant of your grace,

Sancho Panza, governor

The secretary sealed the letter and dispatched the courier immediately, and gathering together those who were play-ing these jokes on Sancho, they figured out how to dispatch him from the governorship. Sancho spent the afternoon drawing up some ordinances dealing with the good govern-ment of the village he thought was an *ínsula*. He ordered that no one should hoard basic necessities in the republic, and that wine could be brought from anywhere they might like, with the added stipulation to state where it came from, so that it could be priced according to its appraisal, quality, and reputation, and the person who waters wine or changes the label should lose his life for it. He lowered the price of footwear, mainly shoes, because he thought that the prices were exorbitant. He fixed the rate of servants' pay, which had been increasing at an alarming rate. He imposed heavy fines on those who would sing lascivious and brazen songs, either by day or night. He ordered that no blind person sing about miracles unless he could produce authentic tes-timony that they were true, because it seemed to him that most miracles that blind people sing about are made up, in prejudice to the real ones. He created an overseer for the poor, not so that they could be persecuted, but rather to verify whether their condition was real, because "in the shadow of a feigned handicap and a false wound one finds thieves and drunks." In short, he made such good ordi-nances that they're in force even today and are called THE CONSTITUTION OF THE GREAT GOVERNOR SANCHO PANZA.

Chapter LII. Where the adventure of the second Distressed (or Afflicted) Duenna, otherwise named doña Rodríguez, is related.

CIDE HAMETE relates that after don Quixote was healed from his scratches it seemed to him that the life he was leading in that castle went against the order of knighthood that he professed, so he decided to ask permission of the duke and duchess to leave for Zaragoza, whose festival was fast approaching, and where he planned to win the suit of armor that is contested at such festivals.

One day at the table with the duke and duchess, just when he was about to make his intention known, who should enter through the great hall door but two women, as was later proved, covered in mourning from head to foot. One of them approached don Quixote and threw herself to the ground, stretched fully out, her lips sewn to his feet, and emitted sighs so sad and profound and so doleful that all who saw and heard her were put in a state of bewilderment. Although the duke and duchess thought that it must be some joke that their servants wanted to play on don Quixote, the intensity with which the woman was sighing, moaning, and crying made them doubtful, until the compassionate don Quixote had her get up from the floor and asked her to say who she was, and take the veil from her tearful face.

She did, and it turned out to be what no one would have ever expected, because she revealed the face of doña Rodríguez, the duenna of the house, and the other woman in mourning was her daughter, the one who had been taken advantage of by the rich farmer. Everyone who knew her was astonished, the duke and duchess more than anyone. Although they held her to be a fool, they didn't think she would go so far.

Doña Rodríguez, turning toward her master and mistress, said to them: "May it please your excellencies to grant me leave to speak with this knight, so that I can get out of a situation in which I've been put by the insolence of a malicious rogue."

The duke said that he gave her permission to speak with

don Quixote as much as she wanted. So, turning to face and directing her voice to don Quixote, she said: "It has been many days, brave knight, since I revealed to you the injustice and treachery that an evil peasant has done to my very dear and beloved daughter, this unfortunate girl here, and you promised to rescue her, righting the wrong done to her, but now, news has come to me that you are planning to leave this castle to search for adventures God may offer you. And I would like you, before you roam those roads, to challenge this wild rustic, and force him to marry my daughter and fulfill the promise he made to be her husband before he slept with her. To think that the duke my master will get me justice is like 'trying to get blood from a turnip,' for the reasons I've revealed to your grace in secret. And with this, may the Lord give your grace much health and may He not abandon us."

To these words don Quixote responded with much gravity and pomposity: "Good duenna, restrain your tears, or better said, dry them and spare your sighs. I'll take on the welfare of your daughter, though she would have done better if she hadn't been so easily swayed by a lover's promises, which generally are easy to give and difficult to keep. So, with the permission of my lord the duke I'll leave immediately to look for this soulless young man, and I'll find him and I'll challenge him, and I'll kill him if he fails to comply with his oath. The main thrust of my calling is to pardon the humble and punish the arrogant. I mean, to help the wretched and destroy their oppressors."

"Your grace doesn't need," responded the duke, "to go to the trouble of seeking the rustic about whom this good duenna is complaining, nor do you have to ask my permission to challenge him. I consider him challenged already and I take upon myself to make this challenge known to him, to force him to accept, and to come to answer for himself in this my castle, where I shall give you both a jousting field, keeping all the conditions usual to such deeds, and also ensuring fair play for both of you, as all noblemen must do who offer an open field to those who do battle within their dominion."

"With that assurance and with Your Highness' good leave," replied don Quixote, "from this moment I renounce my title of *hidalgo* and I lower myself to the level of the offender, and I make myself equal with him. So even though he's not here, I challenge him because he seduced this poor girl, who was a maiden, but is no longer one because of him. He must fulfill the promise he gave to be her legitimate husband, or die in the enterprise."

And then, taking off a glove, he threw it into the middle of the hall, and the duke picked it up, repeating what he'd said before, that the duke would accept that challenge in the name of his vassal, and he fixed the event for six days hence, and said that the field would be the castle yard, and that the arms would be those customary to knights—lance and shield and articulated armor with all of its pieces, without deceit, fraud, or any talisman, and overseen by field judges.

"But before anything else, it's necessary for the good duenna and this unfortunate girl to put their cause in the hands of *señor* don Quixote; otherwise this challenge cannot take place."

"I so agree," responded the duenna.

"Me too," said the daughter, all tearful and ashamed, and in a bad state.

Now that this agreement was reached, and the duke had figured out what to do, the mourning women left, and the duchess ordered that from then on they were not to be treated as servants, but rather as ladies-errant who had come to their house asking for justice. So they were given a room to themselves and were served as outsiders would be, not without astonishment on the part of the other female servants, who didn't know where the folly and brazenness of doña Rodríguez and her ill-faring daughter would end.

At that moment, to end the dinner with rejoicing, who should enter into the hall but the page who had taken the letters and presents to Teresa Panza, the wife of the governor Sancho Panza, and whose arrival caused the duke and duchess great satisfaction, for they wanted to find out what had happened on his mission. They asked him and he responded that he couldn't say with so many people around, nor with few words; that their excellencies should let it rest until they were alone, and meanwhile they could be entertained with two letters that he took out and put in the hands of the duchess. One of them was addressed: LETTER TO MY LADY THE DUCHESS SO-AND-SO, OF I-DON'T-KNOW-

WHERE, and the other: To MY HUSBAND SANCHO PANZA, GOVERNOR OF THE *ÍNSULA* BARATARIA WHO MAY GOD PROSPER MORE YEARS THAN MYSELF. The duchess' "bread wouldn't bake," as they say, until she read her letter, and after she opened it and read it to herself, seeing that she could read it aloud for the duke and the bystanders to hear, she read it in this way:

Letter from Teresa Panza to the Duchess

Señora mía, *the letter Your Highness wrote me gave me great pleasure. The coral necklace is very fine, and my husband's hunting outfit is not far behind. That your ladyship has made a governor of Sancho, my husband, has been received with great pleasure in this town, even though nobody believes it, mainly the priest and* maese *Nicolás, the barber, and Sansón Carrasco, the bachelor. But I couldn't care less—since it's a fact, as it is, let anyone say what they will, although, if the truth be known, if the coral necklace hadn't come together with the suit, I wouldn't have believed it either, because in this town everyone holds my husband to be a blockhead; and unless it was to govern a herd of goats, they can't imagine what kind of governing he'd be suited for. But may God grant it, and have him see to the needs of his children.*

With your grace's leave, señora *of my soul, I've resolved to take advantage of this situation by going to court and stretching out in a coach in order to make the eyes pop of the thousand people who envy me. So I beg your excellency to have my husband send me a bit of money, and make sure it's quite a bit, because at court expenses are hefty: A loaf of bread costs a* real, *and a pound of meat costs thirty* maravedís— *it's shocking. And if he doesn't want me to come, have him tell me quickly, because my feet are eager to get on the road. My friends and neighbors tell me that if my daughter and I go*

*around puffed up and pompous at court, my
husband will be better-known through me than
I through him, since many people will have to
ask: "Who are those two women in the coach?"
and a servant of mine will answer: "Why, it's the
wife and daughter of Sancho Panza, the governor of the ínsula Barataria," and in this way
Sancho will get to be well-known and I'll be
admired, and the sky's the limit!*

*It grieves me as much as it can that this year
there was no harvest of acorns in this town.
Even so, I'm sending Your Highness about a
quarter of a peck I went into the forest to collect, and I found no larger ones than the ones
I am sending. I wish they could be the size of
ostrich eggs.*

*Don't forget, your pomposity, to write me,
and I'll be sure to answer, telling you about my
health and everything that's going on in this
village, from where I beg God to keep your
greatness, and not forget me either. Sancha, my
daughter, and my son kiss your hands.*

*She who wants to see your ladyship more
than to write her,*

Your servant,

Teresa Panza

All those who heard Teresa Panza's letter were very
pleased, mainly the duke and duchess; and the duchess
asked don Quixote if it would be all right to read the letter that came for the governor, for she thought it would be
very good. Don Quixote said that he would open it to give
them pleasure, and he saw that it read this way:

*Letter from Teresa Panza to
Sancho Panza, her husband*

*I received your letter, Sancho mío of my
heart, and I promise you and swear to you as
a Catholic Christian that I was an inch away*

from going crazy with happiness. Listen, when
I heard that you were a governor, I thought
I'd drop dead out from joy. You know that
they say that a sudden joy can kill just like a
great sadness. Sanchica, your daughter, out of
sheer happiness, wet herself without realizing
it. Even with the suit that you sent me right in
front of me, the coral necklace from my lady
the duchess, the letters in my hands, and the
messenger who brought them standing there—
with all that, I still believed that everything I
saw and touched was all a dream. Who could
have thought that a goatherd could rise to be
the governor of ínsulas? You know how my
mother always used to say that "you have to
live a long time to see a lot"? I say this because
I plan to see more, if I live longer; in fact, I
don't plan to stop until I see you a landlord or
a tax collector, which are offices—although the
devil snatches away those who abuse them—
that always bring in lots of money. My lady
the duchess will tell you the desire I have to go
to court. Look into it, and tell me what your
pleasure is, for I plan to honor you there by
going around in a coach.

The priest, the barber, the bachelor, and even
the sexton can't believe that you're a governor,
and they say it's all a deception or something
done by enchantment, as are all things that happen to your master; and Sansón says that he's
going to come to look for you and take that
government out of your head, and the madness out of don Quixote's brain, but I just stand
there and laugh and look at my necklace and
think about the dress I'll make for our daughter
from your green suit.

I sent some acorns to my lady the duchess.
I wish they were of gold. Send me some pearl
necklaces if they're fashionable in that ínsula.

Here's some news from around town: Ber-
rueca married her daughter to a not so skilled
painter who came to this town to do odd jobs.

The town council hired him to paint the royal
arms over the door of the town hall. He asked
for two ducados and they paid him in advance.
He worked a whole week, at the end of which
he hadn't painted anything and said he couldn't
paint junk like that. He returned the money,
and with all that, he got married as if he were
a good artisan. Since then he's abandoned the
paintbrush and taken up the hoe, and he goes
to work in the fields like a gentleman. Pedro de
Lobo's son has received the minor orders of
the Church and now has a tonsure, and he intends to become a priest. Minguilla, the grand-
daughter of Mingo Silvato, found out and is
suing him for breach of promise. Evil tongues
say that she's pregnant by him, but he denies it
flatly.

This year there've been no olives, nor is
there a drop of vinegar to be found in the
whole town. A company of soldiers came
through and carried off three of the village
girls, but I don't want to tell you who they are.
Maybe they'll come back and there will be no
lack of young men who will take them as their
wives, even with their flaws—good or bad.

Sanchica is making lace and earns eight
maravedís every day free and clear, and she's
saving them in a money box to help with her
trousseau. But now that she's the daughter of a
governor, you will give her a dowry without her
having to work for it. The fountain in the plaza
dried up, a lightning bolt hit the pillory, and I
could care less.

I'll wait for an answer to this letter, and
what's to happen about me going to court.
And with this, may God keep you more years
than myself, or at least as many, because I
wouldn't want to leave you without me in this
world.

                        Your wife,

                        Teresa Panza

The letters were applauded, laughed over, approved, and admired, and to cap it off, the courier came with a letter Sancho was sending to don Quixote that they also read publicly, and it gave them some doubts as to whether the governor was really a fool.

The duchess withdrew with the page to find out what had happened in Sancho's village; he told her in great detail, and no aspect was left untouched. He gave her the acorns and some cheese that Teresa had sent that was better than Tronchón.* The duchess received it with great pleasure, and we'll leave her with that in order to relate the end of the government of the great Sancho Panza, flower and mirror of all governors of *insulas*.

Chapter LIII. About the troubled end and conclusion of Sancho Panza's government.

"To THINK things in this life will endure forever in their current state is to think the impossible. It seems rather that life is circular, I mean, goes 'round and 'round. Spring leads to summer, summer harvesttime, harvesttime the fall, fall winter, and winter spring, and time thus revolves on this ever-moving wheel. Only human life races to its end, even swifter than time itself, without any hope of renewing itself, unless it's in the other life where time has no limits to curb it." This is what Cide Hamete, the Muhammadan philosopher, says. Many people without the illumination of faith, with only their natural intelligence, have understood the swiftness and instability of earthly life and the duration of the eternal life that we strive for. But here our author says all this in regards to how quickly Sancho's government came to an end, crumbled, and vanished into the shadows and smoke.

On the seventh night of the days of his office, Sancho was in bed, not stuffed with bread and wine, but rather with judgments, legal opinions, and the making of statutes and ordinances, when sleep, in spite of his hunger, began to close his eyelids. He suddenly heard the din of bells and

---

* Tronchón is a sheep's-milk cheese made in the city of Teruel.

shouts that made it seem like the whole *ínsula* was sinking. He sat up in bed and listened attentively to see if he could figure out the cause of this uproar. Not only did he have no idea what it was, but in addition to the din of voices and bells, he heard an infinite number of trumpets and drums, and he became more bewildered and frightened. He stood up and put his slippers on (because the floor was damp) and without putting on a robe or anything else, he left his room to find more than twenty people coming toward him with lighted torches in their hands and with drawn swords, all of them shouting: "Emergency, emergency, *señor* governor, emergency! An infinite number of enemies has entered the *ínsula*, and we're lost unless your cleverness and courage can save us!" With this noise, fury, and uproar they came, while Sancho stood dumbfounded, and when they reached him, one of them said: "Arm yourself immediately, your lordship, if you don't want yourself and this whole *ínsula* to perish."

"Arm myself?" responded Sancho. "I don't know anything about arms or rescuing. This matter is better left to my master, don Quixote, who will take care of it and set it straight in a flash. I, sinner that I am, don't understand any of these troubles."

"Oh, *señor* governor!" said another. "What indifference this is! Arm yourself—we've brought offensive and defensive arms. Come out to the plaza and be our guide and our captain, because as our governor by all rights it's your responsibility."

"All right, arm me," replied Sancho. And they produced two full-length body shields and put them over what he was wearing, without letting him change into anything else— one behind and another in front. They pulled his arms out of the armholes they had cut; then they lashed the shields together with some rope so that he was bound up and splinted, as straight as a spindle, without being able to bend his knees or budge a single step. They put a lance in his hand, which he used to help keep himself upright. When he was thus armed, they instructed him to march out and guide and encourage them all, for if he was their beacon and North Star, they'd come out of the battle winners.

"How am I supposed to march out?!" responded Sancho. "I can't even bend my knees with these shields that seem sewn to my flesh. What you have to do is carry me and put me on the ground across a doorway, or even standing in one, and in that way I'll guard it with my lance or my body."

"Walk, *señor* governor!" said another. "It's fear, not the shields, that are preventing you from walking. Come on, move your feet, because it's late and the enemy force is growing, and the voices are getting louder, and the danger is mounting."

At these persuasions and reproaches, the poor governor tried to move and fell headlong onto the floor so hard he thought he was broken into pieces. He was like a tortoise, enclosed and covered by his shell, or like half a side of pork curing between planks, or rather like a ship that has run aground on the sand. Seeing him on the floor, those mischievous people showed him no compassion at all. Instead, they extinguished their torches, and their voices grew even louder as they shouted, "To ARMS!" once again. They trampled all over poor Sancho, giving an infinite number of sword thrusts to his shields, and if he hadn't hunched up inside them, the poor governor would have had a bad time of it. Shrunk up in that confinement, he sweated and sweated more, and with all his heart he commended himself to God to deliver him from this danger.

Some people stumbled over him, others fell on him, and one of them even stood on top of him for a good while, and from that vantage point, as if he were on a watchtower, commanded the armies with shouts: "Come over here, for the enemy is heaviest here! Guard that gate, close that door, bar those stairs! Bring firebombs and vats of boiling pitch. Barricade the streets with those mattresses!"

He named with great zeal all the details, instruments, and weaponry used in wars, with which one usually defends oneself in the assault of a city, and the beaten-up Sancho, who heard and endured everything, said to himself: "Oh, if only the Lord were pleased to allow the *ínsula* to be captured, or if I could be dead or relieved from this great anguish!"

Heaven heard his prayer, and when he least expected it, he heard shouts that said: "Victory is ours! Victory! The enemy is fleeing in defeat! *Señor* governor, your grace, arise! Enjoy the conquest, and divide the spoils won from the enemy through the valor of this invincible arm!"

"Help me up," said Sancho, with a doleful voice.

They helped him get up, and once he was on his feet he said: "Any enemy that I've vanquished, let them nail him to my forehead. I'll not distribute any spoils, but rather ask and beg some friend, if I have any, to give me a swallow of wine, because I'm parched; and to dry my sweat, because I'm perspiring like crazy."

They wiped him off and brought him some wine, and untied the shields, and he sat down on his bed and fainted from the shock and travail. Those who played the trick were ashamed for having pushed it so far. But when Sancho came to, it relieved the grief that his fainting spell had given them. He asked what time it was. They responded that it was dawn. He said nothing more and began to get dressed, shrouded in silence, and everyone looked at him and wondered why he was dressing so quickly. When he finished getting dressed, he went out to the stable one step at a time (since he couldn't move very fast), and all those who were there followed him. When he came to the donkey, he embraced him and gave him a kiss of friendship on his forehead, and not without tears in his eyes, said to him: "Come here, my companion and friend, fellow sufferer in my travails and miseries. When I was together with you and had no thoughts other than mending your trappings or keeping your little body fed, my hours were happy, as were my days and years. But since I left you and climbed up the towers of ambition and pride, a thousand miseries, a thousand travails, and four thousand anxieties have crowded into my soul."

While he was saying these words, he was putting the packsaddle on the donkey without anyone saying a word. Once the saddle was on the gray, with great discomfort and pain he mounted him and began to speak to the steward, the secretary, the butler, and Pedro Recio, the doctor, who were all present: "Make way, *señores míos*, and let me go back to my former freedom. Let me seek my old life to bring me back from my current death. I wasn't born to be a governor, nor to defend *ínsulas* from enemies who might want to attack them. I know how to plow and dig, to prune and to plant grapevines in the fields better than to make laws and defend provinces or kingdoms. 'St. Peter is well off in Rome.' I mean that everyone is better off doing the job he was born for. A scythe is better for me than a governor's scepter. I'd prefer to stuff myself with gazpacho than to be subject to the miseries of an arrogant doctor who starves me to death, and what's more, I want to lie down in the shadow of an oak tree in the summer and dress in a sheepskin jacket—the kind with wool on the inside—in the winter, rather than to go to bed between Holland sheets and dressed in stables* with the weight of the government on me. Stay with God, your graces, and tell the duke that 'I was born naked and I'm naked now; I neither win nor lose.' I mean, I came to this government without a *blanca* and I'm leaving without a *blanca*, quite the reverse of what happens with governors of other *ínsulas*. Make way, let me pass. I'm going to get my body bandaged, for I fear all my ribs are crushed, thanks to my enemies who this night have trampled me."

"It doesn't need to be that way, *señor* governor," said Dr. Recio, "for I'll give you a potion for falls and beatings, which will restore you instantly to your former strength and hardiness, and as for food, I promise to mend my ways, and let you eat anything you might like abundantly."

"It's too late," responded Sancho. "I'd as soon not go away as become a Turk. I'm not going to go through this twice. By God, I'd just as soon remain in this government or take on another one—even if it was served under glass—as I would fly to the sky without wings. I'm from a long line of Panzas, and all of them are obstinate, and if once they say NO, NO it stands until the end of the world. Let the wings of the ant stay in this stable, those wings that took me into the skies only to be eaten by swifts and other birds, and let's go back to walking on the ground with a sure step. If there are no fancy shoes of Cordovan leather, a person can still walk firmly with *alpargatas* made of rope.† 'Every Jack has his Jill' and 'never stretch your feet beyond the sheet' and now let me by, for it's getting late."

To which the steward said: "*Señor* governor, we would very willingly let your grace go, although it would grieve us much to lose you. Your cleverness and Christian behavior make us wish you would stay. But it's well-known that ev-

---

* Sancho means "sables."
† These are typical Spanish canvas shoes with soles made of coiled rope.

ery governor is obliged, before he leaves office, to give an accounting. Give your accounting for the ten days you were in office, and then go with God in peace."

"Nobody can ask me for that," responded Sancho, "except the duke himself. I'll be seeing him soon, and I'll tell everything to him; what's more, since I'm leaving naked, there's no other proof needed to see that I've governed like an angel."

"By God, the great Sancho is right," said Dr. Recio, "and I think we should let him go because the duke will be very pleased to see him."

Everyone agreed and they let him go, offering first to escort him on his way, and anything else he might need for his comfort and convenience during his trip. Sancho said that he only wanted a bit of barley for the gray, and a chunk of cheese and half a loaf of bread for himself. Since the road was so short, he didn't need more or better provisions. They all embraced him, and he, in tears, embraced everyone, and left them amazed as much by his words as by his unshakable resolve.

Chapter LIIII. Which deals with things about this history and no other.

THE DUKE and duchess decided that don Quixote's challenge to his vassal regarding the case already mentioned should move forward. And since the young man was in Flanders, where he'd fled so that he wouldn't have doña Rodríguez for his mother-in-law, they ordered a lackey from Gascony* named Tosilos to stand in for him, and they instructed him very carefully about everything he had to do.

Two days later the duke said to don Quixote that his opponent would arrive in four days and would present himself in the field armed as a knight, and would maintain that the maiden was lying through half her beard—even through her whole beard—if she attested that he'd given his word to be her husband. Don Quixote was pleased with this news,

---

* An area in southwestern France.

and he promised himself that he would perform wonders; and he considered it was very good fortune that he'd been offered this occasion on which people could see how far the might of his powerful arm extended. So, with exhilaration and contentment, he waited those four days, which seemed to him, given his desire, to be four hundred centuries.

Let's let these days go by, as we have let other things go by, and let's accompany Sancho, who, somewhere between happy and sad, went along on his donkey to look for his master, whose company meant more to him than being the governor of all the *ínsulas* in the world.

It happened, then, that not too far from the *ínsula* where he'd governed—and he never was able to tell if what he governed was an *ínsula*, city, town, or village—he saw coming along the road toward him six pilgrims with their staffs. They were foreigners, of the kind that ask for alms by singing, and when they drew near to him they put themselves in a row, and began to sing in a language that Sancho didn't understand, except for one word that they clearly said, which was ALMS, and since, according to Cide Hamete, he was quite charitable, he took from his saddlebags the half loaf of bread and chunk of cheese that he'd been provided with, and was willing to share it with them, telling them by signs that he had nothing else to give them. They received what he gave with appreciation and said: *"Geld, Geld!"**

"I don't understand what you're asking me for, good people," responded Sancho.

One of them then took a purse from inside his shirt and showed it to Sancho, by which he understood that they were asking for money, and he, putting his thumb on his throat, with his fingers extended skyward, indicated that he didn't have any money at all, and spurring on his gray, he broke through the line.

When he went through, one of them who had been looking at him closely ran over to him and, throwing his arms around his waist, said in a very loud and very Spanish voice: "By God, what am I seeing? Is it possible that I have in my arms my dear friend, my good neighbor Sancho Panza? Yes, I do, without a doubt, because I'm neither sleeping nor drunk."

Sancho was amazed to hear himself called by name and

---

* *Geld* is the German word for money.

to be embraced by that foreign pilgrim, and after having looked at him for some time in silence, he still couldn't recognize him. Seeing Sancho's hesitation, the pilgrim said to him: "Is it possible, Sancho Panza, my brother, that you don't recognize your neighbor Ricote, the Moor, a shopkeeper from your village?"

Then Sancho, examining him more attentively, began to recognize him, and finally he remembered him fully, and without getting off his donkey, put his arms around the other's neck and said: "Who the devil could recognize you, Ricote, in that vagabond outfit you're wearing? Tell me, who made you into a foreigner, and how did you dare to come back to Spain—if they catch you and figure out who you are, you'll be in trouble!"

"If you don't betray me, Sancho," responded the pilgrim, "I'll be safe. In this outfit no one will recognize me. Let's get off the road into that poplar grove over there, where my companions want to eat and have a rest, and you'll eat with them, for they're very good folk. I'll have time to tell you everything that's happened to me since I left our village, in order to obey His Majesty's edict* that so seriously threatened the unfortunates of my race, as you heard."

Sancho agreed, and after Ricote spoke to the other pilgrims, they went off to the poplar grove nearby, a bit off the royal highway. They threw down their staffs and took off their capes, but not their jackets; all of them were young men except Ricote, who was a man on in years. All of them had knapsacks that seemed very well stocked with things that stimulate thirst and beckon it from two leagues off.

They all lay on the ground and made the grass into tablecloths. They placed on it bread, salt, knives, nuts, slices of cheese, gnawed ham bones—which, if they couldn't be eaten, at least they could be sucked. They also had a black food that they called CAVIAR, made from fish eggs—a great awakener of thirst. There was no lack of olives, although they were dry and with no juices at all, but tasty and able to ward off hunger. But what most abounded in that rustic banquet were six *botas*† of wine that each one took from his bag. Even the

---

* The expulsion of the Moors began in 1609 and lasted until 1614.
† These are leather wine bags used to squirt wine into the mouths of those who drink it.

good Ricote, who had been transformed from a Moor into a German, or a *tudesco*,* took out his own, which in size could compete with the other five put together. They began to eat with great pleasure and very slowly, savoring each mouthful, which they ate from the point of a knife, taking a little bit of each dish. Then all six of them at one time raised their *botas* into the air. With the spouts of the wineskins pointing into their mouths, their eyes fixedly on the sky as if they were aiming at it, they spent a long time pouring the contents of their vessels into their stomachs, and by moving their heads from side to side, they confirmed their pleasure.

Sancho took it all in, and "nothing bothered him,"† but rather, in order to fulfill the proverb he knew very well: "when in Rome do as the Romans," he asked Ricote for the *bota*, and he took aim like the others, with no less pleasure than the rest. They raised their *botas* four times to drink from, but the fifth time it wasn't possible because they were drier than mat-weeds, something that dampened the happiness they had displayed until then.

Once in a while one of them took Sancho by the right hand and said: "*Español y tudesqui tutto uno—bon compagno.*"‡

And Sancho responded: "*Bon compagno, giura Di*"§ after which he burst out laughing for a whole hour, during which he didn't think at all about what had happened to him in his government, because while eating and drinking, one forgets about one's cares. Finally, once the wine was gone, slumber descended over them, and they fell asleep on the tables and tablecloths.

---

* *Tudesco* means "German" (compare Italian *Tedesco*—"German"). At that time there was a distinction made between the two—Rico cites an example from Lope de Vega, but doesn't reveal what that distinction is.
† This is another reference to Nero from a ballad: "Nero looks from the Tarpeian Rock / at Rome as it burns; / shouts from young and old, / and nothing bothered him" (see Rodríguez Marín, volume vii, p. 213, note 3). The first reference to Nero on the Tarpeian Rock is in Part II, chapter forty-four, page 828.
‡ "A Spaniard and Germans together make good company." This mock-Italian is a kind of Mediterranean pidgin that even Sancho knows.
§ Sancho continues the pidgin conversation. Editors say that *giura Di* means "I swear to God," yet Italian *giurare* ("to swear") would have as its first-person form *giuro* and not the form *giura*. Nonetheless, "I swear" seems to be the only reasonable meaning.

Only Ricote and Sancho remained alert, because they had eaten more and drunk less, and they moved away to the foot of a beech tree, leaving the pilgrims buried in sleep. Ricote, without once stumbling into his Moorish language, in pure Spanish said to Sancho: "You know very well, Sancho, my neighbor and friend, that the proclamation and edict that His Majesty had published against those of my race filled us all with terror. I, at least, was so frightened that even before the time we were supposed to leave Spain, I felt like the sentence had already been carried out on my whole family.

"I resolved, then, and I think prudently, as the way someone who knows that on a certain date they're going to take away the house he lives in goes to look for another one … I resolved, I say, to leave town alone, without my family, to look for a place to take them comfortably, and without the pressure that others who left were subjected to. Because I saw, and all our friends saw, that the proclamations weren't idle threats, as some said, but rather were real laws that would be put into effect at the appointed time.

"And what forced me to believe this truth was that I knew what vile and foolish intentions our people had, and it seemed to me it was divine inspiration that moved His Majesty to put such a bold resolution into effect. Not that we were all to blame, for there were some who were solid and true Christians. But these were so few that they couldn't compare with those who weren't, and it would have been unwise to keep enemies in one's own house, like sheltering a serpent inside one's shirt. So, with good reason we were punished with the sentence of banishment—which seemed soft and easy in the opinion of some, but to us it was the most terrible sentence that could be given to us. Wherever we are, we weep for Spain, where we were born, after all; it's our native country.

"And nowhere did we find the reception that our misfortune yearned for. Everywhere along the Barbary Coast and other places in Africa, where we expected to be welcomed, is where they hurt and mistreated us the most. 'We don't recognize good fortune until we've lost it.' And so great is the desire we all have to go back to Spain that most of those who speak the language, as I do, return, leaving their wives and children in exile unprovided for, such is the love we have for our country. And now I recognize and know by experience what they say—that the love for the fatherland is sweet.

"When I left our town, I went to France, and although they were friendly enough there, I wanted to see all possibilities. So I went through Italy to Germany, and it seemed to me that we could live there with the greatest freedom, because its inhabitants don't care about the fine points, and everyone lives however he wants, because nearly everywhere there's freedom of worship. I took a house in a town near Augsburg.* There I met these pilgrims who generally go back to Spain every year to visit the shrines and because they consider Spain to be their Indies† and a place where they can collect some money. They wander through almost the whole country, and there's no town where they aren't given food and drink and don't get at least a *real* apiece. At the end of their trip they will have earned more than a hundred *escudos* free and clear, which they exchange for gold, and keep either in their hollowed-out staffs, in the patches on their capes, or in whatever other way they can think of. They take it out of the kingdom and go to their homes, in spite of the guards who search them at the borders.

"The reason I'm here, Sancho, is to retrieve the treasure that I left buried. Since it's outside of town I can dig it up with no danger, and I'll write from Valencia to my wife and daughter, or go to them—I know they're in Algiers—and make a plan to take them to some French port, and from there I'll take them to Germany, where we'll wait and see what God has in store for us. So, Sancho, I know for certain that Ricota, my daughter, and Francisca Ricota, my wife, are Catholic Christians, and although I'm not so much a one, still I'm more Christian than Moor, and I always pray to God to open the eyes of my understanding and make me see how I am to serve Him. What I don't understand is

---

* Augsburg is a city northwest of Munich. Madariaga thinks that this city was chosen because it was where the Augsburg Confession was presented to Charles V at the Diet of Augsburg in 1530. This document explained Lutheran theology and defended Lutheranism against misrepresentations made about it.

† That is, since Spaniards went to the Indies (the New World) to get rich, these pilgrims considered Spain to be the place where they could earn lots of easy money.

why my wife and daughter preferred the Barbary Coast to France, where they could live as Christians."

To which Sancho responded: "Look, Ricote, that really wasn't left up to them, since Juan Tiopeyo, your wife's brother, took them—since he's such a good Moor—to where he thought best. And I can tell you something else I believe: You'll look in vain for what you left buried, because we heard that the officials took a great many pearls and a lot of money in gold from your brother-in-law and your wife that they were carrying when they were searched."

"That may very well be," replied Ricote, "but I know they didn't go near my hiding place, because I never told anyone where it was for fear of some misfortune. So, Sancho, if you want to come with me and help me to take it out and conceal it, I'll give you two hundred *escudos* with which you can lessen your needs, because you know I know you have many."

"I would do it," responded Sancho, "but I'm not at all greedy. In fact, just this morning I left an office that I held from which I could have covered the walls of my house with gold and eaten off silver plates before six months went by. For that reason, as well as that it seems to me I'd be committing treason to my king to help out his enemies, I wouldn't go with you even if you promised me four hundred *escudos* cash instead of two hundred."

"And what office did you leave, Sancho?" asked Ricote.

"I was governor of an *ínsula*," responded Sancho, "and such a one that I swear you couldn't find a better one no matter how hard you looked."

"And where's this *ínsula*?" asked Ricote.

"Where?" responded Sancho. "Two leagues from here, and it's called the *ínsula* Barataria."

"Come on, Sancho," said Ricote, "*ínsulas* are in the middle of the sea—there aren't any on land."

"Is that so?" replied Sancho. "I tell you, Ricote, my friend, that this morning I left, and yesterday I was governing as I pleased, like a wise man. But even so, I left it because the office of governor seemed filled with peril."

"And what did you get out of this governorship?" asked Ricote.

"I learned," responded Sancho, "that I'm no good for governing, unless it's over a herd of cattle, and that any wealth that derives from those governments comes at the cost of losing rest and sleep and even nourishment. Because in *ínsulas*, governors should eat little, especially if they have doctors looking after their health."

"I don't follow you," said Ricote. "But it seems to me that everything you've told me is nonsense. Who would give you *ínsulas* to govern? Is there such a lack of men in the world more able to govern than you are? Hush, Sancho, get ahold of yourself and see if you want to come with me, like I told you, to help me retrieve the treasure that I left hidden. It's so large that it really can be called a treasure; and I'll give you some to live on, as I told you."

"I already said that I don't want to," replied Sancho. "Just be satisfied that I don't turn you in. Continue your journey and good luck to you, and let me continue mine. I know that even honestly earned gains may be lost, but ill-earned gains may be lost *and* take their owner with them."

"I don't want to insist, Sancho," said Ricote, "but tell me—were you in town when my wife, my daughter, and my brother-in-law left?"

"Yes, I was," responded Sancho, "and I can tell you that when your daughter left, she was so pretty that everyone in town came out to see her go, and they said she was the most beautiful creature in the world. She cried and embraced all her girlfriends and acquaintances, and everyone who went to see her, and she asked everyone to commend her to God and Our Lady, His mother. And all this with such feeling that it made me cry, and I'm not usually a crybaby. I swear that many wanted to grab her on the road and hide her, but the fear of going against the command of the king stopped them. Don Pedro Gregorio, that rich young heir who you know, seemed most affected by her departure, and they say that he loved her very much; and after she left, he was never again seen in our village, and we all thought that he went after her to kidnap her, but up to now nothing more has been learned."

"I always suspected that young fellow adored my daughter," said Ricote. "But I had confidence in my Ricota, and it never bothered me knowing that he loved her. I'm sure you've heard that Moorish women seldom or never fall in love with Old Christians, and my daughter—the way I see it—who cared more about her Christian religion than being loved, wouldn't pay heed to the attentions of this young heir."

"God grant it," replied Sancho, "for it would be bad for both of them. So, let me leave now, Ricote, my friend. I want to get to where my master, don Quixote, is by nightfall."

"God be with you, Sancho, my brother. My companions are stirring and it's time for us to go as well."

And then the two embraced, and Sancho got on his donkey and Ricote took his staff and they went their different ways.

Chapter LV. About the things that happened to Sancho on the road and other things that cannot be surpassed.

BECAUSE HE'D stopped to visit with Ricote, Sancho didn't have time to get back to the duke's castle that day—although he was just half a league away when a very dark and cloudy night overtook him. Since it was summer, he wasn't much bothered, and simply veered off the road, intending to wait for morning. As his ill luck would have it, while he was looking for a place to get comfortable, both he and the donkey fell into a deep and very dark pit among some ruined buildings. As he fell, he commended himself to God with all his heart, fearing he wouldn't stop until he reached the depths of the abyss; but it wasn't to be so, because at three fathoms the donkey hit the bottom. Sancho found himself still on top and without any injury or harm. He felt his whole body and held his breath to see if he was in one piece or punctured somewhere, and, finding himself in good shape, in one piece, and with all his health, he couldn't thank God sufficiently for the favor He'd done him, because he thought that he'd be smashed into a thousand pieces. He also felt the walls of the pit with his hands to see if there was a way he could get out without anyone's help. But he found them all smooth and without any place to grab on to, and felt very upset, especially when he heard the donkey complain piteously and in such pain—and it was no exaggeration, nor did he lack cause, because in truth he wasn't in a very good situation.

"*Ay!*" said Sancho Panza just then. "What unexpected things happen at every step to those of us who live in this world! Who would have thought that someone who was enthroned as governor of an *ínsula* yesterday, giving orders to his servants and vassals, today would find himself buried in a pit, with no one—neither a servant nor a vassal—to lend a hand or come to his aid? Here we will perish of hunger, my donkey and me, unless we die first—he from his bruises and I from my sorrows.

"I probably won't be near as lucky as my master was when he went down into that enchanted Cave of Montesinos, where he found people to entertain him better than at home—with even a freshly made bed and a table laid. There he saw beautiful and peaceful visions, and here I'll probably see toads and snakes. Woe is me! Where have my folly and fantasy led me? They'll discover my bones when heaven is pleased for them to be found, gnawed, white, and scraped, and those of my good gray with them. Maybe that's how they'll be able to tell who we are—at least those who have heard that Sancho Panza was never separated from his donkey, nor his donkey from Sancho Panza. Once again I say, wretched us, because our ill luck wouldn't let us die at home, surrounded by our family, and even if no one could remedy our misfortune, at least someone would be there to mourn us, and in the last moment of our passing on, they would close our eyes!

"Oh, my companion and friend, how poorly I've rewarded you for your good service! Forgive me and ask Fortune as best as you can to deliver us from this wretched pass in which we find ourselves. And if we can get out, I promise to put a crown of laurel on your head so that you'll appear to be a poet laureate, and to double your feed."

In this way, Sancho Panza lamented and his donkey listened to him and didn't say a word back, such was the anguish and bad state in which the poor creature found himself. Finally, after a whole night of wretched complaints and lamentations, the day came, and through its light Sancho saw that it was impossible to extricate himself from that pit without help, and he began to wail and shout in case someone might hear him. But all his cries were lost in the wilderness, since in that whole area there was no one who could hear him; and at this point he gave himself up for dead. The donkey lay on his back and Sancho Panza helped him stand up, though he could hardly stay upright. And taking out of the packsaddle—which had suffered the same misfortune of the fall—a piece of bread, he gave it to his donkey, to whom it didn't taste bad, and Sancho said to him as if he understood: "'With bread all sorrows are lessened.'"

Just then, he noticed that there was a hole on one side of the pit through which a person could pass, if he bent over and hunched up. Sancho Panza went over, crouched down, and went into it, and saw that there was a spacious area on the other side, illuminated by a ray of sunlight that came through what must be called the ceiling. He could see that it extended into another large area, and when he realized that, he went back to where the donkey was, and with a stone began to dig the earth out around the hole. In a short time he'd enlarged it so that the donkey could pass through easily; so he took the halter and began to walk through that grotto to see if there was an exit on the other side. Sometimes he walked in the dark and sometimes without light, but never without fear.

"God Almighty help me!" he said to himself. "This misadventure for me would make a better adventure for my master, don Quixote. He certainly would take these depths and dungeons for flowering gardens, and for the palaces of Galiana,* and would expect to get out from this darkness and peril to some flowering meadow. But I, unfortunate man that I am, lacking in advice and poor in spirit, worry with every step that another pit, deeper than this one, will open and swallow me up. 'I welcome misfortune if it comes alone.'"

In this way, and with these thoughts, he must have traveled more than half a league, until he saw a blurred light that seemed to be coming somehow from the sun, and this suggested to him that what he had thought to be the road to the other life had an opening at the end.

Here Cide Hamete Benengeli leaves him and goes back to dealing with don Quixote, who was exhilarated and joyful as he waited for the battle with the thief of the honor of doña Rodríguez's daughter, for whom he planned to re-

---

* Galiana was the wife of the Moorish governor of Toledo, and her palace was near the banks of the Tajo River.

dress the wrong and injury that had been done to her in such a foul way.

It happened, then, that he was out one morning to train and practice for what he had to do in the battle the following day, lunging this way and attacking that way with Rocinante, when he almost drove his horse into a pit that, if he hadn't pulled up short, he would have certainly tumbled into. He went a few steps forward and without dismounting looked into the depths. He heard loud shouts coming from inside, and, listening attentively, he could make out these words: "Hello, up there! Is there some Christian who can hear me, or some charitable knight who will take pity on a sinner buried alive, an unfortunate unbegoverned governor?"

It seemed to don Quixote that he was hearing Sancho Panza's voice, which was astonishing, and raising his voice as loud as he could, he said: "Who is down there? Who is wailing?"

"Who else could it be, and who else would be wailing," the voice responded, "but the defeated Sancho Panza, governor—because of his sins and bad luck—of the *ínsula* Barataria, squire of the famous knight don Quixote de La Mancha?"

When don Quixote heard this, his astonishment grew, since he now imagined that Sancho Panza must be dead, and his soul must be in purgatory. And with this in mind he said: "I beseech you by all that I can beseech you as a Catholic Christian to tell me who you are, and if you are a soul in torment, tell me what I can do for you. Since my profession is to favor and succor needy people, it extends to succoring and helping those needy people in the other world who cannot help themselves."

"In that case," the voice responded, "your grace who is speaking to me must be my master, don Quixote de La Mancha, and even your voice belongs to none other, without a doubt."

"I am don Quixote," replied don Quixote, "the one whose profession it is to succor and help the living and the dead with their needs. Tell me who you are, for you've astonished me. If you're my squire, Sancho Panza, and you've died, since the devils haven't carried you off and by the grace of God you're in purgatory, our Holy Mother the Roman Catholic Church has services to deliver you from the torment you're in, and I'll go to the Church and plead for you with all the resources that I have. So go on, tell me who you are."

"I swear," the voice answered, "on whose ever birth you may want me to swear, *señor* don Quixote de La Mancha, that I'm your squire, Sancho Panza, and I've never died in all the days of my life, but rather, having left my government for things and reasons that will require time to explain, last night I fell into this pit where I stand, the gray with me, and he won't let me lie, because—as further proof—he's here with me."

And just then the donkey seemed to understand what Sancho said and began to bray so loudly that the whole cave reverberated.

"Excellent witness!" said don Quixote. "I recognize the bray as if I had given birth to it, and I hear your voice, Sancho *mío*. Wait for me while I go to the duke's castle nearby, and I'll get help to rescue you from this pit where your sins must have led you."

"Go, your grace," said Sancho, "and come back soon, because by the only true God, I can't stand being buried alive here, and I'm dying of fear."

Don Quixote left him and went to the castle to tell the duke and duchess what had happened to Sancho Panza, which astonished them no little, although they realized that he must have fallen into the far end of the cave that had been there from time immemorial. But they couldn't figure out how he'd left his governorship without their having heard about it. Finally, as they say, "they took rope and tackle," and with the effort of many people and with a lot of work they lifted the donkey and Sancho Panza from that darkness into the light of day.

A student who happened to be observing said: "This is how all bad governors should leave government office, just like this one coming out of the depths of the abyss: dying of hunger, pale, and without a *blanca*, by the look of him."

Sancho heard what had been said and replied: "Only eight or ten days ago, brother gossip, I went to govern the *ínsula* they gave me, during which time I never saw my stomach full even for an hour. Doctors assailed me and enemies have crunched my bones. I had no time to collect bribes or fees. So, that being the case, I don't think I deserved to leave it this way. But 'man proposes and God disposes,' and God knows best what is good for every man and 'as the time, so the tactics,' and 'let no one say "I'll not drink of that water"' and 'where you expect bacon there aren't any stakes' and God understands me, and that's enough and I'll say no more, even though I could."

"Don't get angry, Sancho, nor worry yourself over what you hear, or there'll be no end of it. Since you have a clear conscience, let them say what they want, for it's as hard to tie the tongues of backbiters as it is to 'put up doors in the countryside.' If the governor leaves office rich they'll say he was a thief; and if he leaves it poor, he's a numbskull and an idiot."

"In this case," responded Sancho, "I bet they consider me more an idiot than a thief."

While they were conversing, surrounded by little boys and many other people, don Quixote and Sancho arrived at the castle, where the duke and duchess were waiting for them in a gallery. Sancho refused to go see them until he had first put the donkey in the stable, because he'd spent such a bad night in that "lodging." Then he went up to see his masters, before whom he got on his knees and said: "*Señores*, because your greatnesses wanted it, and not because I deserved it, I went to govern your *ínsula* Barataria, in which 'I entered naked and, naked I am, I neither lose nor gain.' If I governed well or poorly, there are witnesses who will say what they want. I've clarified doubts and judged lawsuits, always dying of hunger, since that was the wish of Dr. Pedro Recio, native of Tirteafuera, the physician of the *ínsula* and specifically to the governor. Enemies attacked us by night and it was tough for a while, but the people of the *ínsula* say that we came out on top because of the might of my arm. May God give them as much health as they are truthful.

"In short, during this time I weighed the duties and obligations that being a governor brings, and I've concluded that I can't bear the burden of them on my shoulders, or my ribs; they are not arrows for my quiver. And so, before the government could hit me broadside, I hit the government broadside, and yesterday morning I left the *ínsula* as I found it, with the same streets, houses, and roofs that it had when I arrived. I asked no one for a loan, nor did I receive any profit, and although I planned to make some useful laws, I made none at all, fearful that they wouldn't be observed—which would be the same as not making them.

"I left the *ínsula*, as I say, without any retinue other than my donkey. I fell into a pit and felt my way through it, until this morning when, with the light of day, I saw a way out, but not such an easy one, and if heaven hadn't sent me my master don Quixote, I would have stayed there until the end of the world. So, my duke and duchess, here's your governor Sancho Panza, who has learned in the ten days that he governed that he wouldn't give anything to be a governor—not only of an *ínsula*, but even of the whole world. And with this idea in mind, kissing your graces' feet and imitating the game in which children say: 'you leap over then give me one,' I give a leap over the government and I go back to serving my master, don Quixote. Because, although with him I eat my bread in fear, at least I get full, and as far as I'm concerned, if I'm full, it's all the same to me if it's with carrots or partridges."

With this Sancho ended his long speech, and don Quixote, who always feared that he would say thousands of foolish remarks, gave thanks to heaven in his heart when he saw him finish with so few. The duke embraced Sancho and told him that he was very sorry that he'd left his government so soon but he would arrange for Sancho to be given another office on his estate with less responsibility and greater profit. The duchess embraced him as well, and ordered that he be very well treated, since he looked like he'd been badly beaten and worse abused.

Chapter LVI. About the colossal and unheard-of battle that don Quixote had with the groom Tosilos, in defense of the daughter of the duenna doña Rodríguez.

THE DUKE and duchess weren't sorry about the trick they'd played on Sancho Panza in the government they had given him, and even less so when that same day their steward came and gave them a blow-by-blow account of almost everything Sancho had said and done during those days, ending with the assault on the *ínsula*, and Sancho's fear and departure, which gave them no little pleasure.

After this, the history says the day agreed upon for the battle came. The duke had told his groom Tosilos time and time again how he was to deal with don Quixote in order to conquer him without killing or even injuring him. He'd ordered that the iron tips from the lances be removed, telling don Quixote that Christianity—which he valued so—didn't permit that battle to be fought with so much risk and danger to life, and that he should be glad they were giving him an open field on his grounds, even though it went against the Holy Council,* which prohibits such challenges, and not carry such a perilous contest to extremes.

Don Quixote said that his excellency should arrange things however he pleased and that he would obey him in everything. So, the dreaded day having arrived, and a spacious platform built in the courtyard of the castle where the field judges would sit along with the petitioners, mother and daughter, an infinite number of people from neighboring villages and towns came to witness the unique battle, since no one living in that region (and even those who had already died) had ever seen or heard of anything like it.

The first person on the field and dueling place was the master of ceremonies, who went over the field carefully, walking the entire length to make sure there was no deceptive spot or some concealed irregularity that might cause them to trip and fall. Then the duennas entered and sat in their seats, with veils not only covering their eyes but cascading down to their chests, showing no little emotion. After don Quixote entered the dueling area, the imposing groom Tosilos thundered into the arena from one side, heralded by many trumpets, his helmet closed, and looking serious and erect in his strong and shiny armor. The horse was a Frieslander,† broad and gray in color,

---

* The Council of Trent (1545–1563) forbade duels of all kinds, and threatened excommunication for those who engaged in them.

† This is an imposing fleecy horse with large hooves from the region of Frisia (encompassing parts of Holland and Germany).

sporting what seemed to be twelve kilos of wool at each
fetlock.*

The valiant combatant was well prepared by his master,
the duke, about how he was to conduct himself with the
brave don Quixote de La Mancha, having been cautioned
not to kill him under any circumstances, but rather try to
avoid hitting him in the first pass to avoid any danger of his
death, which would surely result if he should be met head-
on. He pranced about the courtyard and went to where the
duennas were, and for some time stood staring at the girl
who sought him to be her husband. The field judge called
don Quixote—who had already come into the courtyard—
and together with Tosilos, he spoke to the duennas, asking
them if they consented to having don Quixote de La Mancha champion their cause. They said they did, and that anything he might do for their cause they would consider well
done and binding.

By this time, the duke and duchess were seated in a gallery that overlooked the dueling place, which was crowded
with an infinite number of people anxious to see the outcome of this unheard-of battle. The condition laid down
for the combatants was that if don Quixote won, his opponent would have to marry the daughter of doña Rodríguez,
and if he were vanquished, his opponent would be freed
from his promise and any further obligation. The master
of ceremonies placed them so that the sun favored neither
one and placed each one where he was supposed to wait.
Drums rolled, the air was filled with the sound of trumpets,
the earth trembled underfoot, and the hearts of the gazing
crowd were tense, some fearful and others hopeful about
the outcome of the contest. Finally, don Quixote, commending himself with all his heart to the Lord our God
and to the lady Dulcinea del Toboso, waited for the sign to
begin the attack.

The groom, however, had different thoughts, which I'll
now reveal. It seems that when he was looking at his enemy, he found her the most beautiful creature he'd ever
seen in all his life, and the little blind boy who is commonly

---

* The horse's fetlock, just above the rear part of the foot, is character-
ized by a tuft of hair. Twelve kilos of hair (26.5 pounds), doubtless an
exaggeration, attests to the massiveness of the horse.

called Love didn't want to lose this chance to conquer the heart of a groom and put it on the list of his conquests. And so, he sidled up as nice as could be, without anyone seeing him, and shot an arrow six feet long into the groom's left side, right through his heart, which he could do in complete safety because he's invisible and comes and goes wherever he pleases without anybody asking him to account for his deeds.

As I was saying, then, when the signal to charge was given, our groom was carried away in other thoughts, thinking about the beauty of the one whom he'd already made the mistress of his freedom, and so he paid no heed to the sound of the trumpet, unlike don Quixote, who as soon as he heard it began his attack. At the fastest speed that Rocinante could muster, he shot off to meet his enemy. When his good squire, Sancho, saw him begin his run, he shouted loudly: "May God guide you, cream and flower of knights-errant! May God make you victorious, since right is on your side!"

And although Tosilos saw don Quixote racing toward him, he didn't move a step from where he was. Instead, with loud shouts, he called the field marshal, who came to see what he wanted. He said to him: "*Señor*, isn't this battle supposed to decide if I should marry that *señora* or not?"

"That's right," he was answered.

"Well," said the groom, "my conscience is bothering me and I would be placing a great burden on it if this battle were to continue; so I say that I consider myself vanquished, and I wish to marry that *señora* right now."

The field marshal was astonished when he heard Tosilos' words, and since he was in on the trick, he had no idea what to reply. Don Quixote stopped in midgallop, seeing that his enemy was not attacking. The duke didn't know why the battle wasn't continuing, but the field marshal went to tell him what Tosilos had said, which amazed him and made him extremely angry.

While this was going on, Tosilos went over to doña Rodríguez and shouted loudly: "I, *señora*, want to marry your daughter, and I don't want to gain by means of conflict and battle what I can achieve peaceably and without danger of death."

The brave don Quixote heard this and said: "Since this is

as it is, I'm freed and released from my promise. Let them marry and good luck to them. And since our Lord has given her to him, may St. Peter add his blessing."

The duke had come down to the courtyard of the castle and approached Tosilos, saying: "Is it true, *señor*, that you've conceded defeat, and that your conscience makes you want to marry this maiden?"

"Yes, *señor*," responded Tosilos.

"He's onto something," said Sancho at this point, "because 'what you were going to give to the mouse, give to the cat, and save yourself trouble.'"

Tosilos was unlacing his helmet, and begged those around him to help him remove it quickly, because he was stifling and could no longer stand to be restricted in such a cramped area. They hurriedly removed it, and the face of the groom was clearly visible. When doña Rodríguez and her daughter saw it, they shouted: "This is a trick, a trick! They put Tosilos, my master's groom, in my true husband's place. Justice in the name of the king for such malice, such a swindle!"

"Don't worry, *señoras*," said don Quixote, "for this is neither malice nor villainy, and if it is, it's not on account of the duke, but rather because of the evil enchanters who harass me. Since they're jealous that I might get the glory of this conquest, they have changed the face of your husband into the face of this fellow that you say is the duke's groom. Take my advice, and in spite of the malice of my enemies, marry him. He's doubtless the one you want for your husband."

The duke was on the point of venting his anger when this made him burst out with laughter, and he said: "The things that happen to don Quixote are so extraordinary that I'm ready to believe that this isn't my groom. But let's use this plan—postpone the wedding for two weeks, if you want, and let's lock up this person whose identity has us all wondering, during which time perhaps he'll recover his original form. The animosity that the enchanters bear don Quixote cannot last that long, especially since their deceits and transformations are of so little avail."

"Oh, *señor*," said Sancho, "it's true that these brigands are always changing things relating to my master. Just the other day a knight that he conquered, called the Knight of the Mirrors, had his face transformed into that of the bachelor Sansón Carrasco, a native of our village and a great friend of ours; and Dulcinea del Toboso was changed into a rustic peasant; so I can imagine that this groom will die and live a groom all the days of his life."

To which the daughter of Rodríguez said: "No matter who this fellow is, I'm grateful to him, for I'd rather be the legitimate wife of a groom than a gentleman's spurned mistress, though the one who deceived me is no gentleman."

So, it all ended by locking Tosilos up until they could see where his transformations would lead. Everyone acclaimed don Quixote as the victor, but most were disappointed that the eagerly awaited combatants hadn't ripped each other to shreds, just as boys are sad when the criminal is not hanged, because the accuser or justice has pardoned him. The people dispersed, the duke and duchess and don Quixote returned to the castle, Tosilos was jailed, doña Rodríguez and her daughter were very content that one way or another it would all lead to marriage, and Tosilos expected no less.

Chapter LVII. Which deals with how don Quixote bade farewell to the duke, and what happened with the clever and impudent Altisidora.

IT SEEMED to don Quixote that it was a good idea to leave the life of ease that he was leading in that castle. He imagined that he was making a great mistake in allowing himself to be cloistered in idleness among infinite distractions and delights given to him because he was a knight-errant, and that he would have to give a strict accounting in heaven for living this easy life and shunning his responsibilities. He thus asked permission of the duke and duchess to leave. This was granted to him with a show of grief because they were reluctant to let him go.

The duchess gave the letters from his wife to Sancho Panza, who wept on receiving them and said: "Who would have thought that such big hopes engendered in the heart of my wife, Teresa Panza, by the news of my government would end by me returning to the unpredictable adven-

tures of my master don Quixote? Even so, I'm happy to
see that my Teresa behaved like herself in sending the
acorns to the duchess. For if she hadn't sent them, I'd have
been sorry and she would have shown herself to be ungrateful. I'm consoled that this gift can't be considered a
bribe, since I already had the government when she sent it,
and it's reasonable that those who get some benefit should
show they're grateful, even if it's only with trifles. So, I
went to the government naked, and I came out of it naked.
I can say with sure conscience—which is no little thing—
that 'naked I was born, naked I find myself; I neither lose
nor gain.' "

This is what Sancho said to himself on the day of their
departure. And that morning as don Quixote was getting
ready to leave—for he'd bidden farewell to the duke and
duchess the previous evening—he presented himself in
full armor in the courtyard of the castle. From the galleries all the people in the castle were looking at him, and
the duke and duchess came out to see him as well. Sancho was on his donkey—with his saddlebags, suitcase, and
provisions—and was very happy, because, without don
Quixote's knowledge, the duke's steward (the one who
had played the part of Trifaldi) had given him a little purse
with two hundred gold *ducados* in it to help with the expenses of the journey.

Suddenly, while all were looking at don Quixote, from
amidst the other duennas and maidens of the duchess came
the voice of the impudent and clever Altisidora, saying in
a doleful tone:*

Give ear, cruel knight;
      Draw rein; where's the need
      Of spurring the flanks
      Of that ill-broken steed?
      From what are you fleeing?
      No dragon I am,
      Not even a sheep,
      But a tender young lamb.

---

* If you don't read the whole poem, look at the second stanza, where
Altisidora accuses don Quixote of stealing things of hers. Ormsby's
translation.

You have jilted a maiden
As fair to behold
As a nymph of Diana*
Or Venus of old.
Vireno, Æneas,† what worse shall I call thee?
Barabbas go with thee! All evil befall thee!

In your claws, ruthless robber,
You bear away
The heart of a meek
Loving maid for your prey,
Three kerchiefs you steal,
And garters a pair,
From legs than the whitest
Of marble more fair;
And the sighs that pursue thee
Would burn to the ground
Two thousand Troys,
If so many were found.
Vireno, Æneas, what worse shall I call thee?
Barabbas go with thee! All evil befall thee!

May Sancho be so obstinate
That your Dulcinea
Be left still enchanted,
May your falsehood to me
Find its punishment in her,
For in my land the just
Often pays for the sinner.
May your grandest adventures
Misadventures prove,
May your joys be but dreams,
And forgotten your love.
Vireno, Æneas, what worse shall I call thee?
Barabbas go with thee! All evil befall thee!

---

* Diana was the Greek goddess of the forests. Venus, in the next line, was the Greek goddess of love.

† Vireno is a character in *Orlando Furioso*, who, in Canto X, abandons Olympia. In the *Æneid* IV, Æneas abandons Dido. Barabbas, in the next verse, is the thief who was released instead of Christ; see, for example, Matthew 27:16.

May your name be abhorred
    For your conduct to ladies,
    From London to England,
    From Seville to Marchena;*
May your cards be unlucky,
    Your hands contain never a
    King, seven, or ace
    When you play cards;
    When your corns are cut
    May it be to the quick;
    When your teeth are pulled
    May the roots of them stick.
Vireno, Æneas, what worse shall I call thee?
Barabbas go with thee! All evil befall thee!

While the stricken maiden was voicing her complaints don Quixote stared at her, and without responding with a single word, he turned to Sancho and said: "On the lives of your forebears, Sancho *mío*, I beg you to tell me the truth. Do you, by chance, have the three kerchiefs and the garters that this enamored young woman has mentioned?"

"I have the three kerchiefs," responded Sancho, "but as for the garters, that's a bunch of nonsense."

The duchess was amazed at the brazenness of Altisidora, who, although they held her to be daring, lighthearted, and free and easy, had not seemed the type to do such an audacious thing. And since the duchess wasn't privy to this trick, her wonder grew.

The duke was eager to bolster the prank and said: "It doesn't seem right to me, *señor* knight, since you were so well received in my castle, for you to have dared to take the three kerchiefs, if not the garters of my maiden as well. This is a sign of ill will and it doesn't reflect well on you. Return the garters. If you don't, I challenge you to a mortal battle, and you need not fear that mischievous enchanters will change my form or face, as happened with Tosilos, my groom, who entered into battle with you."

"God forbid," responded don Quixote, "that I should take my sword out against your illustrious person, from whom I've received so many favors. I can return the ker-

---

* Marchena is a town in the province of Seville, east of the city.

chiefs because Sancho has them. It's impossible to give back
the garters, because neither he nor I ever had them, and if
your maiden wishes to look in her hiding places, I'm sure
she'll find them. I, *señor* duke, have never been a thief in
my entire life, as long as God holds me in his hand. As this
maiden confesses, she's speaking as a woman in love, for
which I'm not to blame, and so I don't have to beg pardon
of her or of you, who I hope will have a higher opinion of
me and give me leave once again to continue my journey."

"May God give *señor* don Quixote such a journey," said
the duchess, "that we may always hear good news of your
deeds. Go with God, for the longer you stay, you increase
the fire that burns in the hearts of the maidens who gaze at
you. And as for my maid, I'll punish her so that from now
on she'll not let either her eyes nor her tongue go astray."

"I would like you to hear just one more word, brave don
Quixote," Altisidora said, "and that is that I beg your pardon for the theft of the garters, because, before God and
my soul, I'm wearing them, and I made the blunder of the
man who, while riding his donkey, was looking for him."

"Didn't I say so?" said Sancho. "A fine one I am to hide
thefts. If I had wanted to steal, there were plenty of occasions while I was a governor."

Don Quixote bowed his head to the duke and duchess
and to all those who were in attendance, and turning Rocinante's reins, with Sancho following on his donkey, he left
the castle, on the road toward Zaragoza.

*Chapter LVIII. Which deals with how so many adven-
tures rained down on don Quixote that each one
had no room to move about.*

WHEN DON Quixote found himself in the open, free
and unencumbered from the wooings of Altisidora,
it seemed to him that he was in his element once more and
that his spirits were strong enough to pursue the business
of chivalry again. Turning toward Sancho he said: "Freedom, Sancho, is one of the most precious gifts that heaven
ever gave to man. Neither the treasures hidden in the earth
nor those the sea covers can equal it. For freedom, as well

as for honor, one can and should risk one's life. And the opposite is also true—captivity is the worst evil that can befall men.

"I say this, Sancho, because you've witnessed the pleasure and the abundance we enjoyed in the castle we just left. Well, right in the middle of those delicious banquets and beverages made of snow, it seemed to me I'd been placed in the straits of hunger, because I couldn't enjoy them with the same joy as if they had been my own. The sense of obligation imposed by the benefits and favors received are fetters that prevent one's free will from flourishing. Fortunate is he whom heaven has given a piece of bread, without his having to thank anyone other than heaven itself!"

"With all that your grace has told me," said Sancho, "we should still be grateful for these two hundred gold *escudos* I am carrying over my heart like a poultice, for any needs that may come up. We won't always find castles to welcome us, but sometimes we may find inns where we'll get beaten up."

In these and other conversations the knight and his squire went along, and after they had gone a little more than a league, they saw about a dozen men dressed as peasants eating lunch on their cloaks in a little green meadow. Next to them were what looked like white sheets covering some items spread out here and there, some of which were standing up and others lying on their sides.

Don Quixote went over to those who were eating, and after a courteous greeting, he asked them what items the sheets were covering. One of them answered: "*Señor*, under these sheets are some sculpted statues made of wood for an altarpiece we're making in our village. We're carrying them covered so they won't lose their sheen, and on our shoulders so that they won't break."

"If you please," responded don Quixote, "I'd like to see them, since statues that are carried with such care must be good."

"And are they ever!" said another one. "If not, let their cost speak for them, for none of them is worth less than fifty *ducados*. Wait a moment, and you'll see with your own eyes."

He stopped eating and stood up, and went over to remove the covering from the first statue, which proved to be of St. George* on horseback, with a serpent coiled at his feet looking as fierce as one usually sees it represented, and with the saint's lance stuck in its mouth. The whole statue seemed to be made of shining gold, as they say. When don Quixote saw it, he said: "This knight was one of the best errants that the divine militia possessed. He was called St. George, and he was, in addition, a great defender of maidens. Let's see the next one."

The man uncovered it, and it seemed to be St. Martin† on horseback who was sharing part of his cape with the poor man, and hardly had don Quixote seen it when he said: "This knight also was a Christian adventurer, and I think he was more generous than brave, as you can see, Sancho, because he's sharing half his cape with the poor man, and it doubtless was winter then, for if it weren't, he would have given it all to him, so charitable he was."

"It probably wasn't that," said Sancho, "but rather he must have been thinking of the proverb: 'to give and to retain, one needs a good brain.'"

Don Quixote laughed, and asked them to take off the next sheet, under which was seen a statue of the patron saint of Spain‡ on horseback with his bloodied sword, running over Moors and trampling heads, and when he saw it he said: "This certainly is the knight of the squadrons of

---

* St. George, the patron of England, lived in about the third century A.D. Some legends about him were extravagant, such as the one depicted here, where he rescued a maiden from a dragon.

† St. Martin of Tours (ca. 316–397) was originally a pagan and served in the Roman army. When he became a Christian, he refused to fight anymore. He was later named bishop of Tours in 371 and founded a monastery nearby. Legend has it that he tore his cape in half to share with a ragged beggar and that later he had a vision in which Christ was wearing that half cape. He was one of the first nonmartyrs to become a saint.

‡ St. James the Great, the Apostle, known as Santiago and San Diego in Spain, is Spain's patron saint. He was martyred in Jerusalem in about A.D. 44 and his bones were taken to Hispania, where he had evangelized, it was said. The tomb was discovered in 813, and the relics became a rallying point for the Christians in their battles against the Moors, during which he is said to have descended from heaven on his white horse to slay Moors. Today Spaniards still call on him before entering into battle.

Christ; this one is called St. James Moor-slayer, one of the bravest saints and knights the world, and now heaven, ever had."

Then they took off another sheet that seemed to have covered the fall of St. Paul from the horse, with all the details typically found in such representations. It was so life-like, it looked to don Quixote like Christ was talking to him and he was responding. "This man," said don Quixote, "was the greatest enemy of the Church of Our Lord in his time, and he was also the greatest defender that the Church ever had, a knight-errant in life and a steadfast saint in death. A tireless worker in the garden of the Lord, a teacher of the gentiles whose school was heaven, and whose professor and schoolmaster was Jesus Christ himself."*

There were no more statues, and so don Quixote asked that they be covered again, and said to those who were transporting them: "I consider having seen what I've seen to be a good omen, brothers, because these saints and knights professed what I profess, which is the exercise of arms. The only difference between them and me is that they were saints and battled in a heavenly way, whereas I'm a sinner and I battle in a secular way. They conquered heaven by force of arms, because heaven suffers violence,† and up until now I don't know what I'm conquering by dint of my labors. But if my Dulcinea del Toboso is able to be released from her own travails, both my luck and my mind will get better, and it may be that my steps will lead me to a better road than the one I'm on."

"'May God hear it, and sin be deaf,'" said Sancho in response.

The men were amazed at the figure and words of don Quixote, without understanding half of what he meant by them. They finished their meal, packed up their statues, bade farewell to don Quixote, and continued their journey.

Sancho once again marveled, as if he'd never before met his master, at how much he knew, for it seemed to him that there wasn't a story in the world nor an event he didn't have written on his fingernail or nailed into his memory,

---

* See Galatians 4:11–12 for the biblical reference.

† Matthew 11:12: "Ever since the coming of John the Baptist the kingdom of heaven has been subjected to violence. . . ."

and he said: "In truth, *señor* master, if what just happened to us can be called an adventure, it has been among the calmest and sweetest ones in the course of our pilgrimage. We have come out with no blows or suffering of any kind, nor have we taken up our swords, nor have our bodies been tossed to the ground, nor were we left hungry. Blessed be God for having allowed me to witness such a thing with my own eyes!"

"You're right, Sancho," said don Quixote, "but you must consider that all times are not one, nor do they all run the same course, and what the ignorant person calls a good omen, since it's not based on natural reason at all, the wise person should consider a fortunate occurence. One of these foolish soothsayers might leave his house in the morning, happen to meet a friar of the blessed order of St. Francis,* and turn right around and run back home as if he has seen a griffin. Another Mendoza† spills some salt on the table, and melancholy spills onto his heart, as if nature were obliged to give signs about upcoming misfortunes by means of such trifling things as I mentioned. The wise person and the Christian shouldn't go trying to figure out what heaven wants to do. Scipio‡ arrives on African soil, and stumbles and falls to the ground. His soldiers think it's a bad omen, but he takes the earth in his hands and says: 'You cannot get away from me, Africa, because I have you tight in my arms.' So, Sancho, having found those statues is for me a very fortunate event."

"I can believe it," responded Sancho, "and I'd like your grace to explain why Spaniards, when they're on the point of attacking in battle, invoke St. James Moor-slayer by cry-

---

* There was a superstition in Spain that running across a priest was a bad omen. The Franciscan religious order was founded by St. Francis of Assisi in the early thirteenth century. (For these superstitions, see Rodríguez Marín, vol. ix, p. 200.)

† The Mendoza family is well documented as being superstitious, to the point where *mendocino* used to mean "superstitious" in Spanish. See Gaos, vol. ii, p. 805, note 112.

‡ Scipio Africanus (263–186 B.C.) was the celebrated Roman general who defeated Hannibal in 202 B.C., thus ending the Second Punic War. The quotation that follows about holding Africa in his arms is also attributed to Cæsar.

ing, 'St. James and close Spain!' Is Spain open, somehow, and how can he close it? What kind of ceremony is that?"*

"You're very simple, Sancho," responded don Quixote. "Look! God has given Spain this great knight with the red cross† as its patron saint and protector, especially in the rigorous battles the Spaniards have had with the Moors, so they invoke him and call him to be their protector in all battles. Many times he has been visible during these battles, knocking down, trampling, destroying, and killing the Muhammadan squadrons, and one could relate many examples of this truth from true Spanish histories."

Sancho changed the subject, saying: "I'm amazed, *señor*, about the brazenness of Altisidora, that lady's maid of the duchess. She must have been cruelly wounded and pierced by Cupid, whom they say is a little blind boy who, even if he's a bit bleary-eyed, or even completely blind, when he takes aim at a heart, no matter how small it is, he hits it straight on and splits it in two with his arrows. I've heard also that timid and modest girls make the arrows of Cupid blunt. But in the case of Altisidora they seem to be sharper rather than duller."

"Remember, Sancho," said don Quixote, "that Cupid knows no respect nor follows any rules in his doings, and he's quite like Death in that he goes to castles of kings as well as the humble huts of shepherds, and when he takes entire possession of a soul, the first thing he does is to remove all timidity and shame. That's why Altisidora declared her wishes so shamelessly, and they engendered more confusion than compassion in my heart."

"What shameful cruelty!" said Sancho. "What unheard-of ingratitude! I know I would have given in at the least mention of love. Son of a bitch! What a heart of marble, what guts of bronze, what a soul of mortar! But I can't imagine what the maiden saw in you to yield and submit in that way. What grace was it, what dash, what wit, what handsome face—which of these things separately or together caused her to fall in love with you? In truth, in truth, many times I stop to look at your grace from the tips of your feet

---

* See Part II, chapter four, where Sancho uses this expression while talking with Sansón, seemingly with full understanding.
† St. James' shield is white with a red cross on it.

to the last hair on your head, and I see more things that cause fright than inspire love. I've also heard that the first and principal thing that arouses love is beauty, and since your grace has none at all, I don't see what the poor thing fell in love with."

"Listen, Sancho," responded don Quixote, "there are two types of beauty—one is of the soul and the other is of the body. The beauty of the soul flourishes and is seen through one's intellect, in one's chastity, good behavior, generosity, and good upbringing, and all of these traits can be found in an ugly man; and with this sort of beauty—and not the beauty of the body—love can arise with great suddenness and force. I realize, Sancho, that I'm not handsome, but I also know that I'm not deformed, and it's enough for a man not to be a monster to be well loved, as long as he has the qualities of the soul that I've mentioned."

With these words and conversations they rode into a forest that was off the road, and suddenly, without realizing it, don Quixote found himself entangled in a green net stretched between some trees.

Since he couldn't figure out what it could be, he said: "It seems to me, Sancho, these nets must herald one of the rarest adventures that can be imagined. I'd bet my life the enchanters who pursue me want to tangle me up in them and slow my journey, as if to avenge the harshness I showed Altisidora. Well, I guarantee them that if these nets, instead of being made of green cord, were made of hardest diamonds, or even were stronger than the material that the jealous god of blacksmiths* used to ensnare Venus and Mars,† I would break through them as if they were made of rushes or cotton thread."

As he tried to go forward and break through them, suddenly two very beautiful shepherdesses came out from among some trees—at least they were dressed up as shepherdesses, but their jackets and skirts were made of fine brocade, and their skirts were made of very elegant golden silk. Their hair, as golden as the rays of the sun itself, hung loose about their shoulders, and was crowned with interwo-

---

* The god of the blacksmiths is Vulcan.
† Vulcan was Venus' husband and captured her with her lover Mars, to the shame of both.

ven garlands of green laurel and red amaranth.* Their age
appeared to be no less than fifteen nor more than eighteen.
This was such a sight that it amazed Sancho, confused don
Quixote, and caused the sun to stop in its orbit just to see
them, and all of them stood in wondering silence.

Finally, the first one to speak was one of the country girls,
who said: "Stop, *señor* knight, and don't break our nets—
they're not there to endanger you, but rather are stretched
out for our entertainment. And because I know you're going to ask why we've put them there and who we are, I'll
tell you in a few words. In a village about two leagues from
here, where there are many rich and important people and
many *hidalgos*, some of our friends and relatives decided—
with their children, neighbors, friends and kin—to come
here and enjoy this site, which is one of the nicest in this
whole area. We have made a new pastoral Arcadia—the
girls dressing up as shepherdesses and the boys as shepherds. We have memorized two eclogues, one by the famous poet Garcilaso, and the other by the very excellent
Camões,† in his own Portuguese language, but we haven't
recited them yet. We're sleeping in field tents, as they're
called, under these branches, on the banks of a brimming
stream that nourishes these meadows. We stretched these
nets last night to deceive the simple birds who, frightened
by our noise, will get caught in them. If you would like to
be our guest, *señor*, you will be received and treated kindly,
liberally, and courteously, because for the time being, no
cares or melancholy will enter this place."

She stopped and said no more. To which don Quixote
responded: "Certainly, beautiful *señora*, Antæon‡ couldn't

---

* Amaranth is a weed with a showy flower. Silvia Iriso says that the
combination of laurel and amaranth symbolizes immortal fame or
beauty.
† Luis de Camões (ca. 1524–d. 1580) is Portugal's national poet, the
author of *Os Lusíadas*, an epic poem that tells of the major events in
Portuguese history. However, the girl in this episode is going to recite
one of his sixteen eclogues from the collection of *Rimas* (1598), and
not anything from *Os Lusíadas*.
‡ Actæon (Antæon is a frequent variant) was a hunter in Greek mythology. He spied on Artemis (Diana) when she was bathing naked,
and she turned him into a stag, whereupon he was promptly devoured
by his own hunting dogs.

have been more amazed when he saw Diana bathe herself than I am astonished to see your beauty. I praise the reason for your entertainment, and am grateful for your offer, and if I can serve you, you can be assured that I'll obey whatever you might command, for my profession is none other than to show myself grateful and to be kind to all persons, especially those of rank, which you show yourselves to be, and if these nets—instead of covering the small area that they do—covered the entire earth, I would seek new worlds to cross in order to avoid breaking them. And so that you can give some credit to my exaggeration, I want you to know that the one making this promise is none other than don Quixote de La Mancha, if that name has reached your ears."

"*Ay!* Friend of my soul," said the other country girl to the first one, "what a great stroke of luck has befallen us! You see this man before us? Well, I'll have you know that he's the most valiant, the most enamored, and the most courteous man in the world, if a history circulating in printed form dealing with his deeds doesn't lie and deceive us. And I'll bet that this good man who accompanies him is Sancho Panza, his squire, whose repartee none can rival."

"That's the truth," said Sancho, "because I'm that funny fellow and that squire that your grace has mentioned, and this man is my master, don Quixote de La Mancha himself, who is told about in histories."

"*Ay!*" said the other one. "Let's beg him to stay. Our parents, brothers, and sisters will be extremely pleased he's here. I've also heard about his bravery and elegance, just as you've said, and especially that they say that he's the most constant and loyal lover known, and his lady is a certain Dulcinea del Toboso, to whom all of Spain concedes the palm of beauty."

"And correctly so," said don Quixote, "unless your own matchless beauty clouds the issue. But don't bother to try to detain me, *señoras,* because the stringent obligations of my profession don't let me rest anywhere."

Just then a brother of one of the two shepherdesses approached the four of them, also dressed as a shepherd, with the richness and elegance that corresponded to the way the country girls were dressed. The girls told him the person with them was the brave don Quixote de La Mancha, and the other was the squire about whom he already knew for having read their history. The gallant shepherd offered his services and asked him to join them in their tents. Don Quixote felt he had to accept, so he went with them.

At this point the beating began in order to frighten the birds, and the nets filled with different ones flying into the danger they thought they were fleeing from, deceived by the color of the nets. More than thirty people gathered at that spot, elegantly dressed as shepherds and shepherdesses, and in an instant they all learned who don Quixote and his squire were, which gave them no little pleasure because they knew of him already from reading his history.

They went to the tents and found the tables nicely set and well stocked, and they honored don Quixote by placing him at the head of the table. All looked at him and were amazed at what they saw. Finally, once the tablecloths were removed, with great calm don Quixote raised his voice and said: "Among the greatest sins that men commit, although some say it's pride, I say that it's ingratitude, as in the proverb: 'hell is filled with ungrateful people.' Insofar as it has been possible for me, I've fled from this sin from the moment I had use of my faculties. And if I cannot repay the kindness that you're doing for me, I can substitute my desire to do so. And if this isn't enough, I'll make these desires known, because he who declares and makes known the kindnesses he receives would repay them in kind if he could, since those who receive are generally the inferiors of those who give. Thus God is above everyone because He's the giver of all things, and the gifts of men are infinitely far from equaling those of God. Yet this poverty and want is, in a certain way, made up for by gratitude.

"I, then, being grateful for the favor that has been thus done for me, and not being able to repay it in kind, constrained by the narrow limits of my ability, I offer what I can and what I have available to me. So, with your permission, I'll proclaim for two whole days, in the middle of the royal highway that leads to Zaragoza, that these two country girls are the most beautiful and most courteous maidens in the world—excepting the peerless Dulcinea del Toboso, the only mistress of my thoughts."

When Sancho heard this—he'd been listening with great attention—he raised his voice to say: "Is it possible that there are people in the world who dare to say and swear that my master is crazy? Tell me, your graces, *señores* shepherds, is there a village priest, no matter how wise and studious he may be, who can say what my master has just said? Nor is there a knight-errant, no matter how famous he is for his valor, who can offer what my master has offered?"

Don Quixote turned toward Sancho, his face burning with anger, and said: "Is it possible, Sancho, that there is in the whole world anyone who wouldn't say that you're an ignoramus lined with ignorance and trimmed with I don't know what kind of mischievousness and roguery? Who allows you to meddle in my affairs and proclaim if I'm wise or foolish? Hush, and don't reply, but rather saddle Rocinante, if he's unsaddled. Let's go to make good my offer. With right on my side, you can consider vanquished anyone who might try to contradict me."

And with a great fury and show of anger he got up from his chair, leaving all those present dumbfounded, and making them wonder if they should take him to be crazy or sane. They tried to persuade him not to take on such a venture, because they knew his gratitude was above reproach, and that new evidence was unnecessary to prove his valorous spirit, since those referred to in the history of his deeds were sufficient. Even so, don Quixote went ahead with his plan, mounted Rocinante, grasped his shield, took his lance, and placed himself in the middle of the royal highway not far from the green meadow. Sancho followed him on his donkey, along with all the people from the pastoral flock, eager to see where his haughty and unheard-of proposition would lead.

Once don Quixote placed himself, as I've told you, in the middle of the highway, he pierced the air with words like these: "Oh, travelers and passersby, knights, squires, men on foot and on horseback who are traveling or will travel along this road for the next two days, I want you to know that don Quixote de La Mancha, a knight-errant, is here to maintain that the nymphs who inhabit these meadows and forests surpass all of the beauty and courtesy in the world, setting aside the mistress of my soul, Dulcinea del Toboso. Anyone who believes differently, come forth. I'm waiting for you!"

He repeated these words twice, and twice they weren't

heard by any adventurer. But luck, which was guiding his
affairs better than ever, ordered that in a little while a
group of men on horseback could be seen on the highway,
many of them with lances in their hands, traveling crowded
together and moving very fast. As soon as those who were
with don Quixote saw them, they turned and went far from
the highway, recognizing that if they stayed there, something bad might happen to them. Only don Quixote, with
intrepid heart, held his ground, and Sancho Panza shielded
himself behind Rocinante's haunches.

The troop of lancers came, and one of the leaders began
to shout to don Quixote: "Get off the road, you devil, because these bulls will tear you to pieces!"*

"You rabble," responded don Quixote, "bulls mean nothing to me, not even if they're fiercer than those raised on
the banks of the Jarama!† Confess, you brigands, on faith
alone, that what I've declared here is the truth, or do battle
with me."

The cowherds had no time to respond, nor could don
Quixote get out of the way even if he wanted. The troop of
fighting bulls, along with the oxen leading them, together
with the multitude of cowherds and other people taking
them to where they would fight the next day, trampled
over don Quixote and Sancho Panza, Rocinante, and the
donkey, knocking them all to the ground, scattering them
all over the place. Sancho was beaten up, don Quixote was
frightened, Rocinante was pounded, and the donkey wasn't
in very good shape. But everyone was finally able to get up,
and don Quixote began staggering toward the herd, tripping and falling all the while, and shouting: "Stop and wait,
you cursèd rabble. Just one knight awaits you, and he isn't
one who believes or says that 'if the enemy flees, build a
silver bridge for him'!"

But the hurrying crowd didn't stop on his account, nor
did they pay more attention to his threats than to the snows
of yesteryear. Don Quixote was too drained to continue;
and more angry than avenged, he sat in the middle of the

---

* There would be six or eight bulls for a single afternoon of bullfighting.
† The Jarama River flows south into the Tajo River, a bit to the east
of Madrid. Clemencín says that it was held that the pasturage in the
Jarama Valley contributed to the fierceness of these bulls.

road, waiting for Sancho, Rocinante, and the donkey. They finally came back, and master and man mounted again and, without bidding farewell to the pretend or imitation Arcadia, and with more embarrassment than pleasure, went along their way.

Chapter LIX. Where an extraordinary incident befell don Quixote, which can be regarded as an adventure.

A CLEAR and crystalline stream that don Quixote and Sancho found in a wooded area brought relief from the discourtesy of the bulls. The beaten master and man sat down on the banks of the stream and let Rocinante and the donkey roam freely without halter or bridle. Sancho went over to his saddlebags and took out what he called "regular food." Don Quixote rinsed his mouth and washed his face, and the coolness restored his discouraged spirit somewhat, but he was too grieved to eat. Out of politeness Sancho didn't dare touch the food he had in front of him and he waited for his master to take the first bite. But seeing that his master was transported by his imagination, and was of no mind to put food into his mouth, Sancho, trampling over all table manners, began to stow away the bread and cheese that was spread out.

"Eat, Sancho, my friend," said don Quixote. "Sustain life, which means more to you than to me, and let me die by my own hands and thoughts and by the power of my misfortunes. I was born to live dying, Sancho, and you to die eating. And to demonstrate the truth of what I'm saying, consider that I'm written about in histories, famous in arms, courteous in my actions, respected by princes, and courted by damsels. And just when I was expecting palms, triumphs, and crowns, earned by and deserved through my brave deeds, I find myself this very morning stepped on, trampled, and thrashed by the feet of filthy, vile animals. This thought blunts my incisors, dulls my molars, numbs my hands, and removes completely any desire I might have to eat, so I plan to let myself die of hunger—the cruelest kind of death."

"So," said Sancho, without stopping his rapid chewing, "you won't approve the proverb that says 'let Martha die, but let her die full.' I, for one, don't plan to kill myself. I will instead do like the shoemaker, who stretches the leather with his teeth until he gets it to where he wants—I'll stretch out my life by eating until I get to the end determined by heaven. I want you to know, *señor*, that there's no greater folly than letting oneself despair, as you're doing. Believe me, after you eat and have a nap on this mattress made of green grass, you'll feel a lot better when you wake up."

Don Quixote decided to take Sancho's advice, for his words seemed to be more those of a philosopher than an imbecile, and he said: "Sancho, if you would do for me what I'm about to tell you, my relief would be more certain and my suffering not as great, and that is, while I follow your advice and go to sleep, you should go over there and, baring your flesh to the air, take Rocinante's reins and give yourself three or four hundred lashes of the three thousand odd that you owe for the disenchantment of Dulcinea. It's no little pity that the poor *señora* is enchanted through your carelessness and negligence."

"There's much to say on that subject," said Sancho. "Let's sleep for a while, the both of us, and afterward God has said what will happen. I want your grace to know that this business of whipping oneself in cold blood is hard to bear, especially on an ill-nourished and worse-fed body. One day, when you least expect it, you'll see me turned into a sieve from the lashes, and 'where there's life, there's hope,' I mean, I'm still alive, and I plan to fulfill my promise."

Don Quixote thanked him and ate a little, while Sancho ate a lot, and they both went to sleep, leaving the two friends and companions, Rocinante and the donkey, to wander freely wherever they wanted on the abundant pasture that the meadow provided. They woke up a bit later, and got on their mounts and continued their journey, hurrying toward an inn that looked to be about a league away. I say that it was an inn because don Quixote called it that, contrary to his custom of calling all inns castles.

So they arrived at the inn and asked the innkeeper if there was a place to stay. He answered that there was, and with all the comfort and luxury that could be found in Zaragoza. They dismounted, and Sancho took his provisions to a room to which the innkeeper gave him a key. He then took the animals to the stable and gave them feed, and finally went to see what don Quixote—who was seated on a stone bench—wanted him to do, giving particular thanks to heaven that his master didn't think the inn was a castle.

The dinner hour came, and they went to their rooms. Sancho asked the innkeeper what was available for dinner. The innkeeper responded that he could ask for whatever he wanted—the inn was stocked with the little birds of the air, the larger birds that live on land, and fish from the sea.

"I don't need all of that," responded Sancho. "With a couple of chickens that you could roast for us we'll have enough, because my master is delicate and doesn't eat very much, and I'm not overly gluttonous."

The innkeeper responded that he didn't have any chickens because the kites had devastated them.

"Well, then, *señor* innkeeper," said Sancho, "how about a tender pullet, broiled."

"Pullet? My father!" responded the innkeeper. "In truth, I sent more than fifty to town yesterday to be sold. Outside of pullets, ask for anything your grace might want."

"In that case," said Sancho, "there must be veal or lamb."

"At the moment," responded the innkeeper, "there isn't any in the place because our stock is exhausted. But next week, there'll be plenty to spare."

"A lot of good that'll do," responded Sancho. "I assume these deficiencies will be made up by bacon and eggs."

"By God," responded the innkeeper, "my guest seems to have a short memory, since I just told him there were no pullets or chickens, and he wants there to be eggs. Consider other delicacies, if you want, and stop asking for chickens."

"Let's get down to business, by golly, and tell me once and for all what you have, and let's stop these discussions, *señor* innkeeper."

The innkeeper said: "What I really, truly have are two cows' feet or cows' heels. They're boiled with garbanzos, onions, and bacon, and are calling, 'Eat me, eat me!'"

"In that case, they're mine," said Sancho, "and don't let anyone else touch them! I'll pay for them better than anyone else, because there isn't anything that would give me more pleasure, and it doesn't make any difference if they're feet or heels."

"No one will touch them," said the innkeeper, "because the other guests lodged here, being people of quality, have brought their own cooks, stewards, and stores with them."

"As for people of quality," said Sancho, "no one is more so than my master. But his profession doesn't allow him to bring stores or provisions. There we are in the middle of a meadow, and we stuff ourselves with acorns or crab apples."

This was the end of the conversation between Sancho and the innkeeper, for Sancho didn't want to keep on answering his questions, including what his master's profession was.

Dinnertime came, then, and don Quixote was in his room when the innkeeper brought the stew, such as it was, and he sat down to eat it with great relish. It seems that in the room next door to don Quixote's—there was no more than a slim partition between the two—don Quixote heard: "On your life, *señor* don Jerónimo, while they're bringing dinner, let's read another chapter from the *Second Part of don Quixote de La Mancha*."

As soon as don Quixote heard his name he stood up and with a very alert ear listened to what they were saying about him, and he heard that already mentioned don Jerónimo respond: "Why would your grace, *señor* don Juan, want us to read that foolishness? Anyone who's read the first part of the history of don Quixote de La Mancha can't get any pleasure from the second one."

"Even so," said don Juan, "let's read it; there's no book that's so bad that it doesn't have something good in it. What I like least about it is that it says that don Quixote is no longer in love with Dulcinea del Toboso."

When don Quixote heard this, he raised his voice filled with wrath and dismay and said: "Whoever says that don Quixote de La Mancha has forgotten or can forget Dulcinea del Toboso, I'll make him understand with equal arms that he's very far from the truth, because the peerless Dulcinea del Toboso cannot be forgotten, nor can don Quixote forget her. His glory is his constancy and his profession is keeping it with care and without any violence."

"Who is speaking?" they said from the other room.

"Who should it be," responded Sancho, "but don Quixote de La Mancha, who will make good on everything he has said and even on what he has yet to say, for 'a good payer doesn't worry about IOUs.'"

As soon as Sancho said this, two gentlemen—for that's what they appeared to be—came into their room, and one of them threw his arms around don Quixote's neck and said: "Neither your presence can belie your name, nor can your name not confirm your presence. Without a doubt, you, *señor*, are the true don Quixote de La Mancha, North Star of knight-errantry, in spite of the one who wants to usurp your good name and negate your deeds, as the author of this book—which I have here to give you—has done."

And he put the book that his companion had brought into don Quixote's hands. Don Quixote took it and, without saying a word, began to flip through the pages. After a while he gave it back, saying: "In the little bit I saw, I found three things worthy of reprimand. The first is some words I read in the prologue.* The second is that the language is Aragonese and at times it's written without articles.† The third thing—and what confirms him as ignorant—is that he errs and goes astray from the truth in the most essential thing of the history, because he says here that the wife of Sancho Panza, my squire, is named Mari Gutiérrez, and that's not what her name is—it's Teresa Panza. And if he made such an enormous error in this important matter, he must also be mistaken in the other details of the history."

To this Sancho said: "That's quite a thing for a historian to do! He must really know our affairs if he calls Teresa Panza, my wife, Mari Gutiérrez! Look at the book again, *señor*, and see if I'm mentioned there and if my name has been changed."

"From what I've heard just now, my friend," don Jerónimo said, "you doubtless must be Sancho Panza, the squire of *señor* don Quixote."

"Yes, I am," responded Sancho, "and proud of it."

"So, it seems," said the gentleman, "this modern author

---

* These gratuitous insults have already been discussed in the Prologue to Part II.

† There are really no missing articles in Avellaneda's book.

doesn't treat you with the decency your person deserves. He describes you as a glutton and a fool, not at all witty, and quite different from the Sancho described in the first part of the history of your master."

"May God forgive him," said Sancho. "He should have left me in my corner without remembering me at all! 'He who knows how should play the song' and 'St. Peter is well off in Rome.'"

The two gentlemen asked don Quixote to join them for dinner in their room because they well knew that there was nothing appropriate for him in that inn. Don Quixote, who was always courteous, accepted their invitation and ate with them. Sancho stayed back, with full power over the stew. He sat at the head of the table with the innkeeper, who was no less appreciative of cows' feet.

During dinner don Juan asked don Quixote what news he had of *señora* Dulcinea del Toboso—if she'd gotten married, had given birth, or was pregnant, or if, preserving her virtue and decorum and aware of the loving thoughts of *señor* don Quixote, her virginity was still intact.

To which don Quixote responded: "Dulcinea is a virgin, my thoughts are firmer than ever, our relationship is unfruitful as always, and her beauty has been transformed into the shape of a low peasant."

And then he began to recount, point by point, the enchantment of *señora* Dulcinea, and what had happened in the Cave of Montesinos, with the order that Merlin had given as to how to disenchant her, which was by means of Sancho's lashes.

The gentlemen got great pleasure from hearing don Quixote relate the strange events of his history, and they were as astonished at his nonsense as they were at the elegant way he had of expressing himself. Sometimes they thought he was clever and other times he seemed to slip into being a lunatic, and they couldn't tell how far he went in either direction.

When Sancho finished eating, he left the innkeeper drunk and went to the room where his master was; and when he went in he said: "May they kill me, *señores*, if the author of that book wants to get in my good graces. Now that he's called me a glutton, I hope he doesn't call me a drunk as well."

"Yes, he does," said don Jerónimo. "I don't remember exactly how, although I know that the words are offensive, and besides, they're untrue, as I can easily see on the face of the good Sancho who is here present."

"Believe me," said Sancho, "the Sancho and the don Quixote in that history must be different from those who appear in the one by Cide Hamete Benengeli, which is us—my master brave, shrewd, and in love; and me, simple, amusing, and neither a glutton nor a drunk."

"That's what I think," said don Juan, "and if it were possible, it should be ordered that no one except Cide Hamete Benengeli, its first author, should dare to write about things pertaining to don Quixote, just as Alexander the Great would have no one paint his portrait except Apelles."*

"Anyone can paint me who wants to," said don Quixote, "but let him treat me right. 'Patience often stumbles when they load it with too many offenses.'"

"There's no offense done to don Quixote that he cannot avenge," said don Juan, "unless he wards it off on the shield of his patience, which, in my opinion, is strong and great."

In these and other conversations they spent a large part of the night, and although don Juan wanted don Quixote to read more from the book, to see where there were discrepancies, they couldn't convince him to do it, since he said that he considered it already read and confirmed it to be all nonsense. And he didn't want the author—in case he heard that don Quixote had held the book in his hands—to flatter himself, thinking that he'd read it, since our thoughts should be protected from obscene things, and our eyes even more so.

They asked him where he was headed and he responded that he was going to Zaragoza to participate in some jousts held there every year and whose prize was a suit of armor. Don Juan told him that the new history related that don Quixote, whoever he was, had gone to Zaragoza to pierce the ring with his lance, an episode that was lacking in invention, poor in its vocabulary, and poorer still in style, although rich in foolishness.

"For that reason," responded don Quixote, "I'll *never*

---

* Apelles did paint a portrait of Alexander holding a lightning bolt (neither it nor any copy of it survives).

set foot in Zaragoza, and in this way I'll expose to the world the lies of this modern historian, and people will be able to see that I'm not the don Quixote mentioned there."

"That's a good idea," said don Jerónimo. "There are other jousts in Barcelona where *señor* don Quixote can show his valor."

"That's what I plan to do," said don Quixote. "Permit me, for it's late, to go to bed, and consider me among the number of your best friends and greatest servants."

"Me, too," said Sancho. "Maybe I'll be good for something."

With this they bade farewell, and don Quixote and Sancho retired to their room, leaving don Juan and don Jerónimo astonished with the mixture of wisdom and nonsense they had seen in don Quixote, and they truly believed that these were the real don Quixote and Sancho, and not those described by the Aragonese author. Don Quixote got up early, and knocked on the partition between the rooms to say good-bye to his friends. Sancho paid the innkeeper magnificently, and advised him either to praise his provisions less, or to be better stocked.

Chapter LX. About what befell don Quixote along the way to Barcelona.

THE MORNING was cool, as the day promised to be, when don Quixote left the inn, having first determined the shortest route to Barcelona without setting foot in Zaragoza, such was his desire to prove untruthful the new historian who they said had abused him so.

It happened, then, that in more than six days nothing happened to him that's worthy of writing about, at the end of which, as night overtook him, he veered off the road among some dense oak or cork trees—for in this, Cide Hamete is not as meticulous as he is in other matters. Master and man dismounted, and once they had gotten comfortable against trunks of trees, Sancho (who had had an afternoon snack) allowed himself to plunge headlong through the doors of sleep, but don Quixote (whose thoughts kept him awake much more than his hunger did) couldn't close his eyes. His thoughts wandered in all directions. Now it almost seemed to him that he was in the Cave of Montesinos; then he was watching Dulcinea, transformed into a peasant, leap onto her she-ass, and next the words of the wizard Merlin about what had to be done to disenchant Dulcinea buzzed in his ears.

He despaired at Sancho's sloth and lack of charity, because as far as he knew Sancho had given himself only five lashes—a small number, and very little in comparison with the infinite number that remained. He was so vexed and angered by this that he began this discourse: "If Alexander the Great cut the Gordian knot, saying, 'It's the same thing to cut as it is to untie it' and for all that didn't fail to become the lord of all of Asia, neither more nor less can happen now with the disenchantment of Dulcinea if I whip Sancho in spite of himself. If the condition for this remedy lies in Sancho receiving three thousand or so lashes, what difference is it to me if he gives them to himself or if someone else gives them to him, since the essential thing is that he gets them, no matter from where?"

With this in mind, he took Rocinante's reins, holding them so he could use them as a whip, went over to Sancho, and began to undo the cord—for the common opinion is that he had only one—holding up Sancho's pants.

But hardly had he begun when Sancho woke up with a start and said: "What's going on? Who's touching me and taking my pants off?"

"I am," responded don Quixote, "and I've come to make up for your deficiencies and to bring an end to my travails. I've come to whip you, Sancho, and to remove in part your debt. Dulcinea is languishing, you're living without cares, I'm dying with desire, so lower your pants of your free will, for mine is to give you at least two thousand lashes out here in this wilderness."

"No," said Sancho. "Don't move another step, your grace. If not, by God, the deaf will hear us. The lashes I agreed to must be voluntary, and not by force, and right now I don't feel like whipping myself. It's enough that I give you my promise to whip myself when I feel like it."

"There's no leaving it up to you, Sancho," said don Quixote, "because you're hard-hearted, and although rough-hewn, you have tender flesh." And so he struggled to remove his belt.

When Sancho realized what was going on, he stood up and tackled his master, gripping him on equal terms, tripped him, and threw him to the ground on his back. He then put his right knee on don Quixote's chest, and grasped his hands, so don Quixote could hardly move or breathe.

Don Quixote said: "How can you rebel against your master and natural lord, you traitor? You dare to do this to the man who gives you your bread?"

"'I neither pull down nor raise up a king,'" responded Sancho, "'I am only defending myself,' for I'm my own lord.* Your grace must promise me that you'll be still and won't try to whip me now and I'll release you; if not: 'here you will die, you traitor, enemy of doña Sancha.'"†

Don Quixote promised him, and swore that he would never again touch a hair on Sancho's head, and that he'd leave the matter of whipping himself whenever he pleased to his free will. Sancho got up and went over some distance to lean against a tree, and felt something touching his head. He raised his hands and discovered two feet of a person, with shoes and stockings. He trembled in fear, and rushed over to another tree, where the very same thing happened. He began to shout, calling don Quixote to protect him. Don Quixote went over, asking what had happened and what he was afraid of, and Sancho responded that all those trees were filled with human legs and feet.

Don Quixote felt them and realized then what it had to be, and said to Sancho: "You don't have to be afraid, because these feet and legs you can feel but can't see doubtless belong to outlaws and highwaymen who have been hanged in these trees. In this area, Justice, when it catches them, hangs them by twenties or thirties, so I'm led to believe I must be near Barcelona."

And it was just as he imagined.

With the dawn of day they raised their eyes and saw that the trees were full of clusters of bodies of highwaymen. If

---

* Sancho says the first part of the proverb correctly, which derives from an old ballad about Pedro the Cruel and his bastard brother Enrique de Trastámara, but this final part he adjusts to fit himself. Ordinarily it would just be: "but I defend my lord."

† These are two verses from an old ballad about the Seven Princes of Lara. Doña Sancha was their evil aunt.

the dead men frightened them, they were no less distressed by the sudden appearance of more than forty living ones who surrounded them, telling them in the Catalan language to make no noise and not to move until their captain arrived.

Don Quixote was on foot, his horse without a bridle, his lance leaning against a tree, and so as it turns out was without defense of any kind, so he felt it best to cross his arms and bow his head, waiting for a better time and opportunity. The highwaymen came to scrutinize the donkey, and left nothing in the saddlebag and valise. It was fortunate for Sancho that he'd put the *escudos* from the duke and the money he'd brought with him in a belt he was wearing. Yet these good folks would certainly have rummaged through and looked at everything that might be hidden between his clothing and flesh if their captain hadn't arrived just then. He appeared to be about thirty-four years old, robust, taller than average, with a stern look, and dark-complected. He was on a powerful horse and was wearing a coat of mail, and had four pistols, which in that area are called PETRO-NELS, on both sides. He saw that his squires—for that's what the people of that profession are called—were about to strip Sancho. He told them not to do it and was instantly obeyed, and that's how the belt escaped. He was amazed to see the lance resting against the tree, the shield on the ground, and don Quixote in his armor, wearing the saddest and most melancholic face that sadness itself could have fashioned.

Approaching him, he said: "Don't be so sad, my good man, because you haven't fallen into the hands of a cruel Osiris,* but rather into those of Roque Guinart,† which are more compassionate than severe."

Don Quixote responded, "I'm not sad because I fell into

---

* Osiris was the ancient Egyptian god of fertility and also the personification of the dead king. However, who is meant here is *Bu*siris, who is, in Greek mythology, an Egyptian king who annually sacrificed a foreigner (until the foreigner in question was Hercules, who killed Busiris instead of allowing himself to be sacrificed).

† There was a historical Roca Guinarda who would have been thirty-three years old in 1615. Of course, the historical Roca never met up with the fictional don Quixote.

your hands, gallant Roque, whose fame knows no bounds on this earth, but rather because I was so careless that your soldiers caught me with my horse unbridled—because I am obliged, according to the laws of knight-errantry, which I profess, to live in continual alert, being my own sentinel at all times. I'll have you know, great Roque, if they had found me on horseback with my lance and shield, it would have been difficult for them to subdue me, because I'm don Quixote de La Mancha, that same one whose deeds fill the world."

Roque realized then that don Quixote's malady was due more to madness than daring, and although he'd heard him mentioned on some occasions, he never believed that his deeds were true, nor could he be persuaded that such a condition could take over the heart of a man; and he was very pleased to meet him, to be able to touch up close what he'd heard from far away, and so he said to him: "Brave knight, don't despair, nor consider your situation to be a catastrophe of Fortune, because it may be that through these stumblings your luck will turn around. Heaven, through strange and roundabout ways, undreamed-of by men, tends to lift up the fallen and enrich the poor."

Don Quixote was just about to thank him when he heard coming behind him the pounding of horses' hooves; but there was just a single horse, on which a young man of twenty, it seemed, was racing toward them, dressed in a loose shirt and in green damask pants trimmed with gold. He was wearing a feathered hat and his tight-fitting boots were waxed. He had a golden dagger and sword, and a small musket in his hands and two pistols at his sides.

On hearing the noise, Roque turned his head and saw this handsome person, who said to him when he arrived: "I have come searching for you, brave Roque, to find in you, if not a remedy, at least some solace for my misfortune. And so that you won't be in suspense any longer, since I see you haven't recognized me, I want to tell you who I am. I'm Claudia Jerónima, the daughter of Simón Forte, your staunch friend and professed enemy of Clauquel Torrellas, who is your enemy, since he's of a rival faction. And you know that this Torrellas has a son called don Vicente Torrellas, or at least that's what his name was not two hours ago. This man—to make the story of my misfortune short,

I'll tell you in a few words about the grief he caused me—saw me, courted me, I listened to him, I fell in love with him without my father finding out, for there's no woman no matter how secluded and shy she may be who doesn't have more than enough time to put her hastily conceived desires into effect. He promised to be my husband and I to be his wife, and nothing else happened between us. I learned yesterday that he'd forgotten what he'd promised me, and was getting married to another woman. This news upset my senses and ended my patience. And since my father wasn't in town, I put on this outfit you see me in, and spurring this horse on, I overtook don Vicente about a league from here, and without bothering to complain to him or hear his excuses, I fired these muskets at him, and these two pistols as well, and I gather I must have lodged more than two bullets in his body, opening doors out of which my honor could escape, covered in his blood. I left him there among his servants, who either didn't dare or couldn't do anything in his defense. I've come looking for you so that you can help me get to France, where I have relatives with whom I can live, and also to beg you to protect my father, so that don Vicente's many relatives won't try to take vengeance on him."

Roque, astonished at the gallantry, pluck, good looks, and initiative of the beautiful Claudia, said to her: "Come, *señora*, and let's go see if your enemy is dead; then we'll figure out what is best for you."

Don Quixote was listening attentively to what Claudia Jerónima had said and what Roque Guinart responded, and said: "Let nobody take on the defense of this woman, for I'll do it on my own. Give me my horse and my arms, and wait for me here. I'll go looking for this man, and dead or alive, I'll make him keep the promise made to such a beauty."

"Let no one doubt this," said Sancho, "because my master is a very good matchmaker—not many days ago he made another fellow marry a maiden to whom he'd broken his promise, and if it hadn't been for the enchanters who pursue my master and changed the fellow's face into that of a groom, by now she would have been a maiden no more."

Roque, who was concentrating more on the beautiful Claudia's situation than on the words of the master or the man, didn't hear what was said, and commanded his squires to give back everything they had taken from the donkey and then to go back to where they had spent the night. Then he left with Claudia at full speed to find the wounded or dead don Vicente. They went to the place where Claudia had caught up to him and all they found was recently spilled blood. They raised their eyes and looked in all directions, and saw some people on the slope of a hill. They figured—and rightly so—that it must be don Vicente whom his servants were carrying, dead or alive, to treat his wounds or to bury. They sped up to overtake them, and—since the people on the hill were moving slowly—they easily did so.

They found don Vicente in the arms of his servants, whom he was asking with a weak and tired voice to let him die there because the pain of the wounds wouldn't allow him to go any farther. Claudia and Roque jumped off their horses and ran over to him. The servants were terrified by the presence of Roque, and Claudia seemed quite disturbed when she saw the state of don Vicente. She went to him, and half tenderly and half sternly, grasping his hands, she said: "If you had given me these in accordance with our agreement you would never have seen yourself in such straits."

The wounded man opened his almost closed eyes and, recognizing Claudia, he said: "I can see, beautiful and deceived *señora*, that it is you who have killed me, a punishment my intentions neither deserved nor caused, for neither with my intentions nor deeds have I ever tried to nor could I offend you."

"So, it's not true," said Claudia, "that you were going to marry Leonora, the daughter of the rich Balvastro, this morning?"

"Certainly not," responded don Vicente. "My bad luck must have given you this news, so that you would take my life in a jealous rage. But since I'm dying in your arms, I consider my luck fortunate. And to prove this truth, take my hand and receive me as your husband, if you want. I have no better way to satisfy you for the offense that you think I did you."

Claudia took his hand and pressed it against her heart and she fell into a faint on the bloody chest of don Vicente, and he was seized by a mortal convulsion. Roque was perplexed and didn't know what to do. The servants went to look for water to throw into their faces, which they did. Claudia came to, but don Vicente didn't recover from his convulsion, because his life was over. When Claudia saw this, realizing that her sweet husband was no longer living, she rent the air with her sighs, pierced the sky with her complaints, tore out her hair and threw it to the winds, scratched her face with her own hands, and showed all the pain and feeling that can be imagined of a grieving heart.

"Oh, cruel and inconsiderate woman," she said, "how rashly you put your wicked design into effect! Oh, raging power of jealousy, to what desperate lengths you lead those who welcome you into their hearts! Oh, my husband, whose unfortunate luck in being my prize has taken you from the wedding bed to the grave!"

Claudia's ravings were so sad they brought tears to the eyes of Roque, which were not accustomed to shedding them on any occasion. The servants all wept, Claudia fainted again and again, and the scene seemed like a field of sadness and a place of misfortune. Roque Guinart told don Vicente's servants to take the body to his father's village, which was nearby, so that he could be buried. Claudia told Roque that she wanted to go to a convent where an aunt of hers was the abbess, and she planned to spend the rest of her life there, accompanied by a better and more eternal Husband. Roque praised her good intention, and offered to accompany her wherever she wanted to go, and to defend her father from don Vicente's relatives and from everyone else, if they tried to harm him. Claudia refused his company and thanked him for his offer with all politeness, and bade him farewell, weeping. The servants of don Vicente carried off his body, and Roque went back to his men. And this was the end of the loves of Claudia Jerónima. And is it any surprise, considering the intrigue of her lamentable story was woven by the invincible power of jealousy?

Roque Guinart found his squires where he'd told them to go, and don Quixote was among them on Rocinante, delivering a speech to persuade them to leave that way of life, which was as dangerous for their souls as for their bodies. But since most of them were from Gascony, a rustic and lawless area, don Quixote's speech didn't sit well with them. When Roque arrived, he asked Sancho Panza if his men had returned his belongings and what precious objects they had taken from the donkey. Sancho said they had, except for the three kerchiefs, which were worth three cities.

"What do you mean by that?" asked one of those present. "I have them and they're not worth three *reales*."

"That's true," said don Quixote, "but clearly my squire prizes them because of who gave them to me."

Roque Guinart had them given back, and called his men to form a half circle around him and produce all the clothing, jewels, and money, and everything else that they had stolen since the last distribution, and after making a rough estimate, setting aside what couldn't be distributed, he calculated how much money it was worth, and divided it among all his men so equally and prudently that he didn't fail distributive justice in any way.

Having done this—leaving everyone happy, satisfied, and gratified—Roque said to don Quixote: "If I weren't so meticulous with these fellows, it would be impossible to live with them."

To which Sancho said: "By what I've seen here, justice is such a good thing that you have to practice it with thieves themselves."

One of the squires heard this, and he raised the butt of his musket with which he doubtless would have opened Sancho's head, if Roque Guinart had not shouted to him not to. Sancho was taken aback, and vowed to keep his mouth shut tight while they were with those people. At this point, one of the several squires who were positioned as sentinels along the road rushed over to tell their chief what was going on, saying: "*Señor*, not far from here, on the road to Barcelona a bunch of people are coming."

To which Roque responded: "Can you tell if they're the kind of people who are looking for us or the kind we're looking for?"

"They're the kind we're looking for," responded the squire.

"Everyone get moving," replied Roque, "and bring them to me right away, and don't let anyone escape!"

They all went away, leaving don Quixote, Sancho, and Roque alone, waiting to see what the squires would bring, and in the meantime Roque said to don Quixote: "Our way

of life—new adventures, new events, all these dangers—
must seem strange to you. And I don't wonder that it
would, because I must confess that there's no way of life
more nerve-racking or more terrifying than ours. What got
me into it was the desire for revenge, which can pervert the
calmest of hearts. I'm compassionate and good-intentioned
by nature, but as I've said, the desire to avenge myself of an
offense done to me has brought down all my good intentions. I persevere in this calling in spite and in defiance of
my better judgment. And just as one abyss calls another,
and one sin calls another, these acts of revenge have been
linking one to another so that I take not only mine, but I've
taken upon myself also those of others. But God is pleased
that, although I find myself in the middle of the labyrinth
of my perplexity, I haven't lost hope of getting out of it and
arriving at a safe port."

Don Quixote was amazed to hear Roque talk so elegantly, because he thought that among those whose profession it was to rob, kill, and plunder, there could be no
one who had sound judgment, and he responded: "*Señor*
Roque, the beginning of health is to recognize the illness
and for the sick person to take the medicine the doctor prescribes. Your grace is sick, you recognize your illness, and
heaven—or really God, who is our Doctor—will give you
medicine to cure you—a bit at a time, not quickly, or by a
miracle. And what's more, wise sinners are nearer to correcting their sins than the simpletons, and since your grace
has shown your judiciousness through your words, all you
have to do is have a good spirit and wait for the cure for
the malady of your conscience. And if your grace wants to
save time and get on the road to salvation sooner, join me.
I'll teach you to be a knight-errant, where one has so many
travails and misadventures that if they're taken as a penance, in an instant they'll have you in heaven."

Roque had to laugh at don Quixote's advice, and he
changed the subject and told him about the tragic event
with Claudia Jerónima, which grieved Sancho tremen-
dously, for the girl's beauty, boldness, and energy had very
much impressed him. At this point the squires returned
with their captives, consisting of two men on horseback and
two pilgrims on foot, a coach full of women and some half
a dozen servants who were accompanying them on foot

and on horseback, along with the mule boys the gentlemen
were bringing. The squires surrounded the captives, and
all of them stood very still, waiting for the great Roque to
speak. He asked the men who they were and where they
were going, and how much money they had with them.

One of them said: "*Señor*, we're two captains in the Spanish infantry. Our companies are in Naples and we're going to
embark on one of four galleys that they say are in Barcelona,
with orders to go to Sicily. We have between two and three
hundred *escudos*, which seems like plenty to me, since the
ordinary lot of soldiers doesn't allow greater treasures."

Roque asked the pilgrims the same question as the captains. He was answered that they were embarking for Rome,
and that between them they had about sixty *reales*. He also
wanted to know who was in the coach, where they were
going, and how much money they had. One of the men on
horseback said: "In the coach is my lady doña Guiomar de
Quiñones, the wife of the president of the court of justice in
Naples, with a small daughter, a maid, and a duenna. We're
six servants accompanying her, and our money totals six
hundred *escudos*."

"So," said Roque Guinart, "we have here nine hundred
escudos and sixty *reales*. I have about sixty soldiers. Let's see
how much that is for each one, for I'm bad at arithmetic."

When the highwaymen heard this, they said in a single
voice: "May Roque Guinart live many years, in spite of the
*lladres** who are looking for him."

The captains looked grieved, the president of the court
of justice's wife became sad, and the pilgrims weren't too
pleased either, seeing their wealth confiscated. Roque
held them all in suspense for a while, but he didn't want to
prolong their sadness, which was easy to recognize a musket shot away; and turning to the captains, he said: "Your
graces, *señores* captains, out of courtesy, please lend me
sixty *escudos*, and the *señora* president of the court of justice's wife, eighty to satisfy this squadron that accompanies
me, because 'the abbot dines on what he sings.' And then
you can continue traveling freely, with a safe-conduct pass
I'll give you, so that if you run into any other of my squadrons I've scattered around this area, they will do you no

---

* This is "thieves" in Catalan.

harm, because it's not my intention to harrass soldiers or any woman, especially one of such high social status."

The captains thanked Roque with many cordial words for being courteous and generous, for that's how they considered his having left them with their money. *Señora* Guiomar de Quiñones tried to jump out of the coach and kiss the feet and hands of the great Roque, but he wouldn't hear of it. He rather begged her pardon for the wrong done her, since he had to comply with the obligations required by his wicked calling. The lady had a servant of hers hand over the eighty *escudos* that were assessed, and the captains gave their sixty.

The pilgrims were about to hand over their pittance, but Roque told them to stay still, and, turning toward his men, he said: "Of these *escudos*, two will be given to each one of you, and that leaves twenty left over. Ten of them will be given to these pilgrims and the other ten will go to this worthy squire so that he'll have something good to say about this adventure."

Then, using the writing material he always had at hand, he produced passes addressed to the captains of his squadrons and bade them go on their way. They all left admiring his nobility, gallant demeanor, and unusual conduct, holding him to be more an Alexander the Great than a well-known thief.

One of the squires said in his Gascon/Catalan language:* "This captain of ours is better suited to be a *frade*† than a highwayman. From now on, if he wants to show how generous he is, let him do it with his own money, not ours."

The unfortunate fellow didn't speak so softly that Roque couldn't hear, and he took out his sword and almost split the fellow's head in two, saying: "This is the way I punish insolent men."

Everyone was stunned, and no one dared to say anything, such was their submission to his authority. Roque drew away and wrote a letter to a friend of his in Barcelona, ad-

---

* This linguistic mixture is far from far-fetched. Gascón is a dialect of Provençal, and Catalán is related to that language.
† Martín de Riquer, a Catalan speaker, points out that *frade* ("priest") is not Catalan or Gascón, but rather Portuguese. Is it a typesetter's error or Cervantes' error (heaven forbid)?

vising him that he was with the famous don Quixote de La
Mancha—that knight-errant about whom so many things
were being said—and that he was the most amusing and the
most intelligent man in the world, and that four days hence,
which was St. John the Baptist's day,* he would lead him
right to the waterfront, in full armor, on Rocinante, his horse,
and also Sancho on his donkey, and that he should let his
friends the Niarros know, so that they could be entertained
by them. He didn't want the Cadells,† his enemies, to enjoy
the entertainment, but realized that this would be impossible, since the crazy doings and shrewdness of don Quixote
and the witticisms of Sancho Panza couldn't fail to delight
everyone. He sent this letter with one of his squires, who
changed his outfit from that of a highwayman to that of
a peasant and delivered it in Barcelona to the person to
whom it was addressed.

Chapter LXI. About what happened to don Quixote as he entered Barcelona, with other things that are truer than they are clever.

FOR THREE days and nights don Quixote stayed with
Roque, and had he stayed three hundred years, there
still would have been new things to learn and wonder at
in his way of life. They would wake up here, eat lunch over
there, sometimes flee not knowing from whom, and other
times lie in wait without knowing for whom. They slept on
horseback, and interrupted their sleep to move from one
place to another. They spent all their time sending out spies,
listening to sentinels, and blowing on the wicks of their
muskets,‡ but they had few of these since they all used flint-

---

* The birth of John the Baptist is celebrated on June 24. The date of his
decapitation is August 29. One has to assume the latter date, given the
general chronology of this book.
† Historically, there were Nyerros and Cadells in Barcelona, of opposite political viewpoints, the former favoring the monarchy, the latter
favoring the common man.
‡ In this version of the musket, a slow-burning cord—which you
kept burning by blowing on it—was used to ignite the charge in the
breech.

pistols. Roque spent the nights separated from his men in places where they couldn't know where he was, because the viceroy of Barcelona had issued several edicts against his life, and he was nervous and fearful, and didn't dare confide in anyone, afraid that even his own men would either kill him or hand him over to the authorities—a miserable and vexing way of life to be sure.

Finally, by lesser-used roads, shortcuts, and secret paths, Roque, don Quixote, and Sancho left with six other squires for Barcelona. They arrived at the beach there the night before St. John the Baptist's day. Roque embraced don Quixote and Sancho (to whom he gave the ten *escudos* that he'd promised but hadn't yet handed over), and they took their leave, offering a thousand services to each other.

Roque went back and don Quixote stayed there waiting on horseback for daybreak. He didn't have to wait long for shining Aurora to show her face in the balconies of the East, gladdening the grass and flowers, just as at that same instant ears were gladdened by the music of *chirimías* and drums, the ringing of jingle bells, and the shouts of, "Make way, make way," given by runners coming from town. Aurora gave way to the sun, who, with a face larger than a shield, began to rise little by little over the horizon. Don Quixote and Sancho looked all around and saw the sea, which they had never seen before; it seemed very wide and vast, and considerably larger than the Lagunas de Ruidera that they had seen in La Mancha. They saw galleys along the beach that, with their awnings rolled up,* seemed covered with pennants that fluttered in the wind and at times kissed and swept the surface of the water. From inside came the music of trumpets and *chirimías*, which from near and far filled the air with military melodies. The galleys began to move about and engage in a mock skirmish in the calm waters, and almost in imitation of them a large number of knights arrived from the city mounted on horses, with handsome liveries. Soldiers on the ships shot a great deal of artillery, and those along the walls and forts of the city responded, and the shot from heavy cannons broke into the wind, and the large maritime cannons

---

* Awnings had a couple of uses on galleys—these were to protect the ships during the night. Others gave shade to passengers.

aboard the galleys responded. The sea was merry, the earth cheerful, the air clear except where darkened at times by the smoke from the artillery; and all this appeared to instill pleasure in everyone.

Sancho couldn't imagine how those hulks moving around the sea could have so many feet. Just then, all those in liveries raced up to don Quixote with shouts, Arabic war cries, and uproar, amazing and astonishing him. One of them, the person Roque had written to, said in a loud voice: "Welcome to our city, mirror, lantern, and North Star of knight-errantry, and everything else that goes along with it. Welcome, I say, to the valiant don Quixote de La Mancha, not the false, not the fictional, not the apocryphal one written about in false histories, but rather the true, real, and faithful one described to us by Cide Hamete Benengeli, the flower of historians."

Don Quixote was speechless, and the knights didn't wait for a response, but, whirling about on their horses with those who followed, began to prance all around him. He turned to Sancho and said: "These people have recognized us. I'll bet they've read *our* history, and even the one recently printed by the Aragonese fellow."

The knight who spoke first to don Quixote came back and said to him: "Your grace, *señor* don Quixote, come with us. We're your servants and great friends of Roque Guinart."

To which don Quixote responded: "If courtesy engenders courtesy, yours, *señor* knight, must be the child or close relative of that of the great Roque. Take me to wherever you want, for I've no will other than yours, especially if you want to use my desire to serve you."

With words no less courteous than these the knight answered him, and gathering him in their midst, they rode toward the city to the music of the *chirimías* and the drums. When they arrived, the devil—who makes all bad things happen—and some boys, who are worse than the devil, caused two of them, mischievous and daring, to thread themselves through the crowd and, one of them raising the donkey's tail and the other raising Rocinante's, stuck in bunches of furze.* The poor animals responded to this

---

* This is a spiny European evergreen shrub, the emphasis here being on *spiny*.

different kind of spur by pressing their tails down, but that just increased their torment so that they bucked a thousand times and threw their riders to the ground. Don Quixote, feeling embarrassed and offended, went to remove the plumage from the tail of his nag, and Sancho did the same for his donkey. Those who were leading don Quixote wanted to punish the daring of the boys, but it was impossible because they were now lost among the thousand people who were following. So Don Quixote and Sancho remounted and with the same applause and music they arrived at their guide's house, which was large and princely, that is, like that of a rich gentleman, where we will leave them for the time being, for that's what Cide Hamete wants.

Chapter LXII. Which deals with the adventure of the enchanted head, with other folderol that must be revealed.

D ON ANTONIO Moreno was the name of don Quixote's host, a rich and witty gentleman, and a lover of harmless diversions. When don Quixote was in his house, he began looking for ways to put his madness on display without harming him, because a practical joke that hurts anyone is no good, nor are there any worthy pastimes that harm anyone. The first thing he did was to have his armor removed and to put him on display in that tight chamois outfit of his—as we have described many times—on a balcony that overlooked one of the main streets of the city, visible to people and boys who looked at him as they would a monkey. Once again the liveried horsemen began to cavort about as if they were doing it especially for his benefit rather than to celebrate that festive day. And Sancho was extremely happy, since it seemed to him that they had found—he didn't know how or why—another Camacho's wedding, another house like don Diego de Miranda's, and another castle like the duke's.

Some of don Antonio's friends ate lunch with him that day, all of them honoring and treating don Quixote as a knight-errant, which made him act in a vain and pompous way, and he couldn't contain his joy. Sancho's drolleries were so many that the servants in the house, and everyone else who could hear him, hung on every word. While they were at the table, don Antonio said to Sancho: "We have heard, good Sancho, that you're such a fan of creamed chicken and meatballs that if you have some left over, you keep them inside your shirt for the next day."*

"*No, señor*, that's not true," responded Sancho, "because I'm a clean person, not a glutton, and my master, don Quixote here, knows quite well that we can live off a handful of acorns or walnuts for a week. The truth is that 'if they give me a heifer, I run for the halter.' I mean, I eat what I'm given, and take things as they come. And whoever may have said that I'm a glutton and not a polite eater, you can be sure he's wrong. I'd say they were lying if it weren't for the respect I have for those sitting at this table."

"Indeed," said don Quixote, "Sancho's moderation and cleanliness can be recorded and engraved on plaques of bronze for the lasting memory of ages to come. It's true that when he's hungry he does seem a bit of a glutton, since he eats quickly, chewing on both sides of his mouth. But his cleanliness is always as it should be; and while he was a governor he even learned to eat in a most fastidious way, eating grapes and even pomegranate seeds with a fork."

"Do you mean," said don Antonio, "that Sancho has been a governor?"

"Yes," responded Sancho, "of an *ínsula* called Barataria. I governed it perfectly for ten days, during which time I lost my peace of mind and I learned to scorn all the governments in the world. I fled from it and I fell into a cave where I thought I would die, and from which I was saved by a miracle."

Don Quixote related in detail the course of Sancho's government, which delighted the listeners greatly. Once the tablecloths were removed, don Antonio took don Quixote by the hand and led him to an out-of-the way room in which there was no furniture other than a table, seemingly

---

* Don Antonio has confused "our" Sancho here with Avellaneda's, since the other Sancho does love creamed chicken, and in chapter twelve of Avellaneda, we see the other Sancho saving meatballs just this way (see Riquer's edition, vol. I, p. 228). Whereas don Quixote refused to read any of Avellaneda's book, Cervantes has just proven *he* knew it well.

made of jasper with a base of the same material, and on top of which was a bust in the style of the Roman emperors, apparently made of bronze. Don Antonio walked with don Quixote around the table a number of times and then he said: "Now, *señor* don Quixote, that I'm confident no one is listening to us and the door is closed, I want to relate to your grace one of the rarest adventures, or better said, curiosities, that can be imagined, provided that your grace will deposit it in the innermost rooms of secrecy."

"I so swear," responded don Quixote, "and I'll even place a stone slab on top for greater security, because I want your grace to know, *señor* don Antonio"—for by then he knew his name—"that you're speaking with someone who, although he has ears to hear, has no tongue with which to speak. So you can say whatever is in your heart to mine in complete safety, and can be sure that you've flung it into the abyss of silence."

"On the faith of that promise," responded don Antonio, "I want you to marvel at what you will see and hear, and give me some relief for the heartache that not being able to communicate my secrets has given me, for they're not to be revealed to just anyone."

Don Quixote was in suspense, wondering where all these precautions were leading. Don Antonio took his hand and guided it over the bronze head, then the whole table, and even the jasper base on which it stood, and said: "This head, *señor* don Quixote, was made by one of the greatest enchanters and sorcerers the world has ever had. I think he was Polish by birth and a disciple of the famous Escotillo,* about whom so many wondrous tales are told. He was here in my house and, for the price of a thousand *escudos*, made this head, which has the properties and power to answer whatever you ask at its ear. This fellow noted the orbit of the heavenly bodies, made magic signs, observed the stars, looked at the points of the celestial sphere, and finally, made it with the perfection we'll see tomorrow, for it doesn't talk on Fridays, and because today is Friday, we have to wait

---

* There is some discussion who this Escotillo is. Pellicer, the first annotator of the *Quixote*, thinks it refers to an Italian adventurer from Parma, sixteenth century. Rico says that it may refer to a magician who worked out of Flanders a few years before the *Quixote* was written.

until tomorrow. Until then you can be thinking about what you want to ask. By experience I know that he speaks the truth in whatever he says."

Don Quixote marveled at the power and properties of the head, and almost didn't believe don Antonio. But when he considered how little time he had to wait to find out, he decided not to say anything other than to thank him for telling him such a great secret. They left the room and don Antonio locked the door with a key and they went back to the room where the others were.

In the meantime Sancho had related many of the adventures and experiences that had happened to them. That afternoon they took don Quixote out for a ride, not in armor, but in street clothes, wearing a short-sleeved cape made of tawny cloth that could have made ice itself sweat. They had the servants entertain Sancho so that he wouldn't leave the house. Don Quixote rode, not on Rocinante, but rather on a large mule with an even step, and elegantly decorated. They put the cape on his shoulders, and without him noticing it, they had attached to it a parchment on which they had written in large letters: THIS IS DON QUIXOTE DE LA MANCHA. The sign drew the eyes of all who saw them riding by and when they read THIS IS DON QUIXOTE DE LA MANCHA, don Quixote marveled that everyone who looked at him recognized him and called him by name. He said to don Antonio, who rode beside him: "Knight-errantry embraces such privileges that it makes the man who professes it known and famous all over the earth. Just look, your grace, *señor* don Antonio—even the boys of this city, who have never seen me before, recognize me."

"That's true, *senor* don Quixote," responded don Antonio, "for just as a fire cannot be concealed, virtue cannot fail to be recognized, and the kind of virtue that derives from the profession of arms shines and flourishes above all others."

It happened, then, that as don Quixote was enjoying this acclaim, a Castilian read the sign on his back, raised his voice, and said: "Don Quixote can go to hell! How did you last so long without being killed by all the maulings you had? You're crazy, and if you were just crazy alone and by yourself, it wouldn't be so bad. But you have the capacity to make all those who deal with and accompany you crazy as well. If you doubt it, look at these people with you. Go home, you idiot, and take care of your estate, your wife, and children, and leave this nonsense that eats away at your brain and skims off your intelligence."

"Brother," said don Antonio, "move on and don't give advice where it's not asked for. *Señor* don Quixote de La Mancha is quite sane and we who accompany him are not fools. Virtue is to be honored wherever it's to be found. Go away and bad luck to you, and don't meddle where you're not asked."

"By golly, your grace is right," responded the Castilian, "because to advise this good fellow is to beat your head against the wall. But even so, I think it's a pity that this good mind, which they say this fool has, should leak out through the channel of his knight-errantry. And the bad luck your grace mentioned be upon me and all my descendants, though I live longer than Methuselah, if I ever again offer advice to anybody, whether they ask me for it or not."

The "adviser" went away, and the tour continued. But the crush of people was so great, because the boys and the rest of the people were reading the sign, that don Antonio was forced to take it off, pretending he was removing something else.

When night fell, they went home, and there was a party with music to which ladies had been invited. Don Antonio's wife, who was a woman of quality, merry, beautiful, and keen-witted, invited several lady friends to come and honor their guest and enjoy his unheard-of lunacies. Some of them came, and a splendid dinner was provided. The dancing began a little before ten o'clock in the evening. Among the ladies there were two mischief makers who, although they were very virtuous, were ready for some pranks that would be fun but wouldn't humiliate anyone. These two were so persistent in inviting don Quixote to dance that they thoroughly exhausted him, both in body and in soul. It was something to see, that figure of don Quixote, long, lanky, thin, and sallow, in his tight-fitting suit, clumsy, and above all, not light on his feet.

The young ladies flirted with him discreetly, and he— also discreetly—scorned them, but when he saw himself beleaguered with so much coquetry, he raised his voice and said: "*Fugite, partes adversæ.** Leave me alone, you evil thoughts! Stay away, *señoras*, with your lustful desires, for the peerless Dulcinea del Toboso doesn't allow any desires other than her own to subdue me and hold me subject."

And having said this, he sat down in the middle of the room, thoroughly thrashed and pounded from having engaged in so much dancing. Don Antonio arranged for him to be carried off to bed, and the first one to lift him was Sancho, who said: "Why did you have to go and dance, *señor*? Do you think that all brave men and knights-errant are dancers? I say that if you think so, you're mistaken. Many men would prefer to kill a giant than to cut a caper. Now, if it were country dancing, I could have done it for you, because I can do that kind of dancing really well. But I don't know anything about ballroom steps."

With these and other words, Sancho made everyone at the party laugh, and he accompanied his master to his bed, covering him so that he could sweat out his lack of gracefulness in dancing.

The next day don Antonio thought it was a good idea to try out the enchanted head. So, with don Quixote, Sancho, two other friends of his, and the two ladies who had exhausted don Quixote at the dance (for they had spent the night with don Antonio's wife), he locked them in the room where the head was. He described for them the qualities of the head and made them pledge secrecy and told them that this was the first time he was going to put the head's powers to the test. Only don Antonio's two friends were in on the secret of the enchantment; no one else knew about it. And if don Antonio hadn't told them about it first, they would have been as astonished as the rest of them, for any other reaction was impossible, such was its appearance and the skill with which it was made.

The first one to approach the ear of the head was don Antonio himself, who asked it in a low voice—but not so low that it wasn't heard by everyone: "Tell me, head, by the power that you have, what am I thinking right now?"

And without moving its lips, the head answered in a

---

* These Latin words, meaning, "May the enemies flee," is part of the Catholic rite of exorcism.

clear and distinct voice so that everyone could hear: "I can't read minds."

Everyone was aghast when they heard this, and more so when they realized that no one else was in the room or behind the table who could have made that response.

"How many of us are there here?" asked don Antonio for his second question, and he was answered: "There are you and your wife, together with two of your friends and two friends of your wife's, and a famous knight named don Quixote de La Mancha, and a squire whose name is Sancho Panza."

Here certainly was a new cause for wonder; here their hair stood on end out of pure awe. Don Antonio moved back from the head and said: "This is enough to prove to me that I was not cheated by the person who sold you to me, wise head, talking head, responding head, and miraculous head. Let someone else come and ask a question."

And since women are usually eager to find out things, the first one who stepped up was one of the friends of don Antonio's wife, and she asked: "Tell me, head, what can I do to be more beautiful?"

And she was answered: "Be very chaste."

"That's all I wanted to find out," said the questioner.

Her friend went over and said: "I would like to know, head, if my husband really loves me or not."

And it answered: "Reflect on the things he does for you and you'll see."

She drew away, saying: "That answer didn't need a question because, in truth, what a person does clearly shows his intentions."

Then one of don Antonio's friends approached and asked: "Who am I?"

And the answer was: "You know who you are."

"I'm not asking that," responded the gentleman, "but rather for you to tell me if you know me."

"Yes, I know you," he was answered. "You're don Pedro Noriz."

"I have nothing else to ask, because this convinces me, head, that you know everything."

And when he went away, the other friend stepped up and asked: "Tell me, head, what are the desires of my son and heir?"

"I've already said," he was answered, "that I cannot tell thoughts. But even so I can tell you that your son wants to see you buried."

"That," said the gentleman, "is obvious, and I'll ask nothing more."

Don Antonio's wife went over and said: "I don't know what to ask you, head. I only would like to know if I'll enjoy many years together with my good husband."

And she was answered: "Yes, you will, because his health and his moderation in living promise a long life, which many cut short because of abuse."

Then don Quixote went over and said: "Tell me, you who give these answers, was what I say happened to me in the Cave of Montesinos real or a dream? Will Sancho, my squire, give himself the required number of lashes? And will it release Dulcinea from her enchantment?"

"Insofar as the cave goes," he was answered, "there's much to say—there's a bit of everything to it. Sancho's lashes will proceed slowly. The disenchantment of Dulcinea will come to pass."

"I don't want to know anything else," said don Quixote, "because as soon as I see Dulcinea disenchanted, I'll see that all good fortune has come my way."

The last one to ask a question was Sancho, and what he asked was: "By any chance, head, will I have another government? Will I be relieved of the toils of being a squire? Will I see my wife and children again?"

To which he was answered: "You will govern in your house, and if you return to it, you'll see your wife and children, and once you stop service, you will no longer be a squire."

"By God," said Sancho Panza, "I could have said that myself. The prophet Perogrullo* couldn't have told me more."

"That's enough," said don Quixote. "What did you expect him to say? Isn't it enough for the answers to correspond to the questions asked?"

"Yes, it *is* enough," responded Sancho, "but I would have preferred that it say something more substantial and with more details."

With this, the questions and answers came to an end, but

---

* Perogrullo was supposedly an Asturian famous for saying self-evident facts.

not the wonder that remained with everyone, except the two friends of don Antonio, who were in the know.

Here Cide Hamete Benengeli wanted to divulge the way it worked, so as not to keep the world in suspense any longer, in case it was thought that some sorcerer or some extraordinary mystery resided in that head, and so he says that don Antonio Moreno, imitating another head that he'd seen in Madrid, made by an engraver, had this one made in his house to amuse himself and dumbfound the ignorant. It was made in this way: The top of the table was of wood, painted and varnished like jasper, and the base that held it up was similarly made, with four eagle talons that stabilized the weight. The head, which was in the image of a Roman emperor and bronze in color, was completely hollow, as was the tabletop, on which the head fit so well that no sign of joining was noticeable.

The base was also hollow, and was located just below the bust, and this in turn communicated with the room immediately below the head. Through this hollowness in the base, and through the chest of that bust, there was a tube made of tin that couldn't be seen by anyone. In the room just beneath awaited the person who was to give the answers, with his mouth right at the tube so that, like an ear trumpet, voices could travel up and down clearly, and in this way no one could figure out the trick. A nephew of don Antonio, a sharp and witty student, was the person giving answers; having first been told who was going to be with him in that room, it was easy to answer quickly and correctly to the first question. To the rest he answered by conjecture, and, since he was a sharp person, in a clever way.

And Cide Hamete goes on to say that this marvelous device lasted ten or twelve days. But since it was getting to be known throughout the city that don Antonio had an enchanted head in his house that answered anyone's questions, and fearing that the news would get to the sentinels of our faith, don Antonio himself told the *señores* inquisitors about it, and they had him take it apart and not use it anymore, so that the ignorant masses wouldn't be duped. But as far as don Quixote and Sancho Panza knew, the head remained enchanted and able to answer questions, more to the satisfaction of don Quixote than of Sancho.

The knights of the city, in order to please don Antonio and entertain don Quixote (and give him a cause to reveal his follies), arranged for a tilting at the ring* to take place six days hence, but it didn't come to pass for reasons that will be explained.

Don Quixote felt like strolling about the city on foot, for he feared that if he went on horseback, the boys would pursue him, and so he and Sancho, with two servants don Antonio sent with them, went out for a walk.

It happened that when they were walking down a street, don Quixote raised his eyes and saw written above a door, in very large letters, BOOKS PRINTED HERE, which pleased him quite a bit because until then he'd never seen a print shop and he wanted to see what one was like. He and his retinue went in, and he saw a sheet of pages being printed in one area, proofs being corrected in another, type being set over here and justified over there, and in sum all the machinery seen in large printing houses. Don Quixote went over to a typesetter and asked him what he was composing. He told him what it was, and don Quixote moved on. He went over to another one and asked what he was doing. The typesetter responded: "*Señor*, that gentleman over there"—and he pointed out a handsome but rather solemn fellow—"has translated a book from Italian into our Castilian language, and I'm setting the type for it."

"What is the title of the book?" asked don Quixote.

To which the author replied: "*Señor*, the book in Italian is called *Le Bagatelle*."

"And what does *bagatelle* mean in our Castilian language?"

"*Le bagatelle*," said the author, "is as if we said THE TOYS in Castilian, and although this book has a humble title, it has in it and embraces many good and substantial things."

"I know a bit of Italian," said don Quixote, "and take

---

* The "tilting at the ring" is an event in which the knight on horseback endeavors to run his lance through a ring to demonstrate his skill. This is precisely the event that the false don Quixote engaged in at the jousts in Zaragoza (Avellaneda, chapter eleven, and referred to here at the end of chapter fifty-nine).

pride in being able to sing some stanzas of Ariosto. But tell me, your grace, *señor mío*—and I'm not saying this to test you but rather only for information—have you ever come across the word *pignatta*?"

"Yes, many times," said the author.

"And how do you translate it into Castilian?" asked don Quixote.

"How else should I translate it," replied the author, "except with the word COOKING-POT?"

"Well, I'll be!" said don Quixote. "How advanced you are in the Italian language. And I'll bet that where it says *piace* you say PLEASES; and where it says *più*, you say MORE; and the word *su* you render with ABOVE and *giù* with BELOW."

"That's what I say all right," said the author, "because those are their correct translations."

"I'll dare to assert," said don Quixote, "that your grace is not well-known in the world, which is always averse to rewarding flowering talents or praiseworthy works. How many skills are lost, how many talented persons are shoved into a corner, how many virtues despised! Still, it seems to me that translating from one language to another, unless it's from the queens of the languages—Greek and Latin—is like seeing Flemish tapestries from behind. Although you can see the figures, threads confuse the images, and they don't have the clarity and vividness of the front. And translating from easy languages doesn't show any more ingenuity or style than copying from one piece of paper to another. I don't mean to imply that the practice of translating is not praiseworthy, because there are worse and less useful things that a man can do. And I am not refering to two famous translators in this, one of them being doctor Cristóbal de Figueroa in his *Pastor Fido*,* and the other don Juan de Jáurigui, in his *Aminta*,† where they make you doubt which is the translation and which is the original. But tell me, your grace, are you printing this book

---

* Cristóbal Suárez de Figueroa (ca.1571–1639) published in 1602 his Spanish translation of Battista Guarini's *Il Pastore Fido*, a pastoral work.
† Juan de Jáuregui (1583–1641) translated Tasso's *L'Aminta* in 1607, another pastoral work.

at your own expense, or did you sell the rights to some bookseller?"*

"At my own expense," responded the author, "and I plan to earn a thousand *ducados*, at least, with this first printing, which is to be a run of two thousand copies, and will be sold for six *reales* apiece in the twinkling of an eye."

"You seem to know quite a bit about all this," responded don Quixote, "but it seems you haven't taken into account the fraudulent accounting of the printers and the tricks they play. I assure you that when you find yourself saddled with two thousand copies of your book, you'll be so exhausted you'll be horrified, especially if the book is not very satirical or amusing."

"So," said the author, "your grace expects me to turn it over to a bookseller who will give me three *maravedís* in royalties and will think he's doing me a favor? I don't publish my books to become famous throughout the world, because I'm already well-known through my books. I'm looking for monetary gain, because without it, being famous is not worth a *cuatrín*."†

"May God grant you good luck," responded don Quixote.

He went on to the next typesetter, where he saw that they were correcting a proof of a book called *The Light of the Soul*,‡ and when he saw it, he said: "Books like these, although there are many of them, are those that should be printed, because many sinners can profit from them, and an infinite number of lights are necessary for so many unenlightened people."

He went on to the next station and saw that they, too, were correcting another book. He asked what the title was, and he was told that it was called *The Second Part of the Ingenious* Hidalgo *don Quixote de La Mancha*, written by a certain fellow from Tordesillas.

"I've heard about this book," said don Quixote, "and in

---

* If the author prints the book at his own expense, he earns all of the proceeds, or incurs all of the losses. If he sells the copyright to a bookseller, as Cervantes did with Francisco de Robles for this work, he collects only a royalty.

† This is a coin of very little worth.

‡ This is *The Light of the Christian Soul* by Brother Felipe de Meneses (Valladolid, 1554, with several reprintings).

truth and in my heart I thought it had been burned up and turned into ashes because of its impudence. But its Martinmas* will come to it as it does to every pig. Fictional stories are good and delightful only insofar as they approach the truth, or the semblance of truth, and the true ones are better the truer they are."

And saying this, with a bit of consternation, he left the print shop. And that same day don Antonio had him taken to visit the galleys along the beach, which pleased Sancho quite a bit, because he'd never seen one before in his life. Don Antonio had told the commodore of the galleys to expect a guest that afternoon, the famous don Quixote de La Mancha, about whom the commodore and everyone in the city knew, and what happened there will be told in the next chapter.

Chapter LXIII. About Sancho Panza's ordeal during his visit to the galleys, and the daring adventure of the beautiful Moorish woman.

DON QUIXOTE kept meditating on the response of the enchanted head. None of these meditations led him to figure out the trick, but all of them centered around the promise—which he held as true—of the disenchantment of Dulcinea. He paced about and inwardly rejoiced that he would soon see it accomplished. And Sancho, although he abhorred being a governor, as has been said, still wanted to command and be obeyed—this is the curse that being in authority carries with it, even if it's just mock authority.

Finally, that afternoon, don Antonio and his two friends went with don Quixote and Sancho to the galleys. The commodore, who knew they were coming, was eager to see the famous don Quixote and Sancho. As they got to the shore, all the galleys drew their awnings back and *chirimías* began to play. Into the water they lowered a skiff adorned with ornate rugs and cushions and covered with crimson velvet, and as soon as don Quixote put his foot into the skiff, the

---

* On Martinmas, the feast of St. Martin (November 11), pigs are traditionally slaughtered.

flagship discharged its midship cannon, and the other galleys did the same. And when don Quixote began to mount
the starboard ladder, the crew greeted him, as they always
do when an important person arrives on deck, saying HU,
HU, HU three times.

The general—for that's what we'll call him—who was an
important Valencian knight, offered his hand, saying: "I'll
mark this day with a white stone because it's one of the
best days I think I'll ever have in my life, having met *señor*
don Quixote de La Mancha, in whom is invested and epitomized all the valor of knight-errantry."

With no less courteous words don Quixote responded,
overjoyed beyond measure at seeing himself treated in
such a lordly way. They all climbed to the poop deck at the
stern, which was lavishly decorated, and sat on the guest
benches. The bosun went amidships, and with his whistle
gave the rowers the signal to remove their shirts, which
they did in an instant. When he saw so many people naked
from the waist up, Sancho was flabbergasted, and more so
when he saw them roll up the sail so quickly, because it
seemed to him that all the devils were at work. But all this
was nothing compared to what I'll now relate.

Sancho was seated on a beam next to the principal rower
on the starboard side, who, having been told what he was to
do, grabbed Sancho and raised him in his arms. The whole
crew was now on their feet and ready, and starting with the
starboard side, they passed him from hand to hand, twirl-
ing him as they went with such speed that the poor Sancho
couldn't see, and doubtless thought the devils themselves
were carrying him off. They didn't stop until they had finished on the port side and placed him on the poop deck.
The poor fellow was beaten up, panting, and sweating, unable to fathom what had happened to him.

Don Quixote, who saw Sancho's wingless flight, asked
the general if that was a ceremony that was done with all
newcomers aboard, because if it was, he had no intention of
participating and refused to engage in such an activity, and
he swore to God that if someone came to grab him to make
him do the same rounds, he would kick his soul out. And
having said this, he stood up and brandished his sword.

At that instant they removed the awning, and with a huge
din the lateen yard crashed down. Sancho thought that the

sky was becoming unhinged and was going to fall on his head. He ducked his head between his legs in fear. Don Quixote was a bit afraid himself, since he, too, hunched up his back a bit and lost the color in his face. The crew hoisted the yard with the same speed and noise they had used in lowering it, and all this in perfect silence, as if they neither had voices nor the ability to breathe. The bosun signaled them to weigh anchor and, swiftly moving amidships, began to sting the crew's shoulders with a whip, and little by little the galley put out to sea.

When Sancho saw so many red feet moving about—because that's what he thought the oars were—he said to himself: "These must truly be enchanted things, and not of the kind my master talks about. What did these unfortunates do to deserve being whipped, and how does that man who goes around whistling dare to whip so many people? This has got to be hell, or at least purgatory."

Don Quixote saw how closely Sancho was observing what was going on and said to him: "Ah, Sancho, my friend, how quickly and with so little cost you could, if you wished, take off your shirt and sit among these men, and finish off the disenchantment of Dulcinea! Because if you shared the misery and grief of so many, you wouldn't feel yours so much. And it may be that Merlin would consider each of these lashes, since they'd be given by another's hand, as equal to ten of those that you give yourself."

The general wanted to ask what lashes and what disenchantment he was talking about when a sailor said: "Montjuich is warning us there's a galley on the western coast."

When he heard this, the general went amidships and said: "Don't let him get away, boys! The ship the watch tower has warned us about must be some brigantine of Algerian pirates."

The other three galleys caught up with the flagship to get their orders. The general commanded two of them to go out to sea while he, together with the other one, would go along the coast so that the ship couldn't escape. The crews worked the oars hard, propelling the galleys with such fury that it seemed like they were flying. When the ones that went out to sea were about two miles out, they saw a ship that appeared to have fourteen or fifteen ranks of rowers on each side. That ship, when it saw the galleys, started to flee, with the intention and hope of outrunning them with its speed.

But the ship was unlucky, because the flagship was one of the fleetest vessels that sailed the seas, and gained on it with such speed that those in the brigantine realized they couldn't escape. So the *arráez*—the Arabic captain—had them lift their oars and give up so as not to antagonize the captain who was directing our galleys.

But Fortune ruled otherwise, and ordained that as the flagship approached near enough for the other to hear the shouts admonishing them to give up, two drunken *Toraquíes*, which is the same as saying two drunken Turks, who were among the rowers, fired two muskets that killed two soldiers who were on the prow of one of our ships. When the general saw this, he swore he wouldn't leave anyone on that ship alive, and he started to ram the ship with the greatest fury, but the enemy managed to slip away, and our ship kept moving ahead. Those on the other ship realized their predicament, so while ours was turning around, they put up their sails and fled using both sails and oars. But their effort helped them less than their daring harmed them, because the flagship caught them in a bit less than half a mile, and the rowers went aboard and took them all alive.

At this point the two other galleys arrived, and all four of them with the prize returned to the shore, where a large crowd was waiting for them, eager to see what they were bringing. The general dropped anchor near land, and learned that the viceroy of the city was present. He had the skiff sent out to bring him back, and had the yard lowered so he could hang his prisoners on the spot, and the rest of the Turks that he caught as well. There were about thirty-six, all of them stouthearted, and most of them Turkish riflemen.

The general asked who the captain of the brigantine was, and was answered in Castilian by one of the captives, who later appeared to be a Spanish renegade: "This young man that you see here, *señor*, is our captain."

And he indicated one of the handsomest and most gallant young men that human imagination could describe, who looked to be not yet twenty years old. The general asked him: "Tell me, you ill-advised dog, what motivated you to kill my soldiers? Didn't you see it was impossible to escape? Don't you know that rashness is not the same as bravery? Faint hope should make men resolute, not rash."

The *arráez* was about to respond, but the general couldn't stay to listen because he had to go to receive the viceroy, who was just then entering the galley, and with him were some of his servants and some townsfolk.

"The hunting has been good, *señor* general!" said the viceroy.

"So good," responded the general, "that you'll soon see it hanging from this yardarm."

"How so?" said the viceroy.

"Because contrary to all reason and against all rules of war," responded the general, "they've killed two of my best soldiers who were on these galleys, and I've sworn to hang all those I've captured, and particularly this young fellow, who is the *arráez* of the brigantine."

And he pointed out to him the young man with his hands already tied together and a rope around his neck, awaiting his death.

The viceroy looked at him, and seeing that he was so handsome, so gallant, and so humble—his good looks giving him an instant letter of recommendation—he felt like commuting his execution, and so he asked the lad: "Tell me, *arráez*, were you born a Turk, a Moor, or are you a renegade?"

To which the lad responded in Castilian: "I'm neither a Turk, nor a Moor, nor a renegade."

"Well, then, what are you?" replied the viceroy.

"A Christian woman," responded the youth.

"A woman, and Christian, in such clothing and in such straits? That's more perplexing than believable."

"*Señores*, put off the execution," said the youth. "You won't lose too much time if you delay your vengeance until you hear the story of my life."

Who could be so hard-hearted that he wouldn't soften at least until he heard what the sad and doleful young woman wanted to say? The general told her she could say whatever she wanted, but she should not expect to be pardoned for her clear guilt.

With this permission, the youth began to speak in this

way: "Of that nation that was more unfortunate than prudent, on whom a sea of misfortune has rained in recent times, I was born of Moorish parents. In the course of their misfortunes, I was taken by two uncles of mine to the Barbary Coast, without my being able to explain that I was a Christian—and not of those feigned or make-believe ones, but of the true Catholics. Stating this truth did me no good with those who were in charge of our wretched banishment, and my uncles refused to believe it. They rather took the truth for a lie I invented so that I could stay in the country where I was born, and more by force than of my free will they took me with them.

"I had a Christian mother and a wise father who was no less Christian. I took in the Catholic faith with my mother's milk and I was raised with good habits. Neither in my language nor in my customs did I ever, in my opinion, give signs of being Moorish. Along with these virtues—which I think they are—whatever beauty I have grew. And although my modesty and seclusion were great, they were not sufficient to prevent a young man from seeing me whose name was Gaspar Gregorio, the heir of a gentleman who had a village next to our own. How he happened to see me, how we spoke with each other, and how he fell head over heels for me, and I quite the same for him, would be too long to tell here, much longer than I fear I have time left before the cruel rope will cut me off between my tongue and neck.

"And so I'll only say that don Gregorio wanted to join me in our banishment. He blended in with the Moors who were leaving from other villages, since he knew the language well, and during the voyage he came to be friends with my two uncles who were escorting me, because my father, who was prudent and cautious, had left our village as soon as he heard the first proclamation of our banishment, and went to look for a new place to live in foreign kingdoms. He left buried in a place that only I know many pearls and precious stones of great value, with some Portuguese gold coins and doubloons of gold. He commanded me not to touch the treasure if we were banished before he came back. I obeyed him, and with my uncles, as I've said, and some other relatives and close friends, we went to the

Barbary Coast. We settled in Algiers, and it was as if we were in hell itself.

"The king got wind of my beauty, and he also heard a rumor about my wealth, which in part was good luck for me. He called me before him and asked me where in Spain I was from and what money and jewels I had brought with me. I told him the name of the village, and that the jewels and money were buried there, and how easily they could be recovered if I myself went for them. I said all this so that he might be more blinded by his greed than my beauty. While we were talking, someone came and told him that among those who had come with me was one of the most gallant and handsome young men that could be imagined. I understood right away that they were talking about don Gaspar Gregorio, whose beauty is far greater than can be described. I was distressed, considering the risk that don Gregorio was in, because among those barbarian Turks, a lad or a young man is more prized than a woman, no matter how beautiful she might be.

"The king commanded that he be brought so he could see him, and he asked if it was true what they were saying about him. Then, I—as if forewarned by heaven—said that it was, but I wanted him to know that he wasn't a man, but rather a woman like me, and I begged him to allow me to dress her in her usual dress, so that her beauty could be seen and so she might appear before him with less reluctance. He told me that I could go and said that we'd speak the next day about how we could arrange for me to return to Spain to retrieve the hidden treasure.

"I spoke with don Gaspar and told him the danger he would be in if he showed that he was a man. I dressed him as a Moorish woman and that same afternoon brought him before the king, who was dazzled at the sight and decided to make a present of 'her' to the grand vizier. To escape the dangers that might befall her in the harem with his other women, and not even trusting himself, he had her placed in the house of one of the most important Moorish ladies, who would protect and serve her, and she was taken there right away. What we both felt—for I can't deny that I love him—can be left to the imagination of those who are separated from those they love.

"The king then made arrangements for me to return

to Spain in this brigantine, and that I should be accompanied by two native Turks, who were those who killed your soldiers. This Spanish renegade also came with me." She pointed out the man who had spoken initially. "And I know he's a secret Christian who would much rather stay in Spain than return to the Barbary Coast. The rest of the crew are Moors and Turks, who serve only to man the oars. The two greedy and insolent Turks ignored the orders we had to land me and this renegade as soon as we got to the Spanish coast, dressed as Christians, using the clothing we had brought with us, and wanted first to sweep the coast for booty, fearing that if we got off first and something happened to us, we might reveal where the brigantine was; and if there were any galleys on the coast, it would be taken.

"Last night we discovered this beach, and since we didn't notice the four galleys, we were seen, and you've witnessed what happened to us. So, don Gregorio remains dressed as a woman among women, in grave danger of losing his life, and I find myself with my hands tied, expecting, or rather, fearing I'll lose this life, of which I am weary.

"This is, *señores*, the end of my lamentable story, as true as it is unfortunate. What I beg of you is that you allow me to die as a Christian, since, as I've said, I've not been guilty of the error into which those of my nation have fallen."

And then she stopped talking, her eyes brimming with tears, and many of those present joined her weeping. The viceroy, who was tender and compassionate, without saying a word, went over to her and untied the cord that was binding her beautiful hands.

As the Christian Moorish woman was relating her story, an old pilgrim who had gotten onto the galley when the viceroy went aboard was staring at her, and hardly had the Moorish woman finished her narrative when the old man threw himself at her feet and clasped them in his arms, and with words interrupted by a thousand sobs and sighs, said: "Oh, Ana Félix, my unfortunate daughter! I'm your father, Ricote, who has returned to look for you since I couldn't live without you, for you're my heart and soul."

At these words, Sancho opened his eyes and raised his head—which he'd bowed while thinking about the humiliation of his recent flight—and, looking at the pilgrim, he realized that it was the same Ricote he'd come across the day he'd left his government. With her hands untied, his daughter now embraced her father, mixing her tears with his as he said to the general and viceroy: "This woman, *señores*, is my daughter, who is more unfortunate in the things that happened to her than in her name. She's named Ana Félix, her last name is Ricote, and she's famous as much for her beauty as for my wealth. I left my home to look in foreign kingdoms for a country that would give us shelter and welcome us, and having found such a place in Germany, I returned in pilgrim's clothing, in the company of three Germans, to look for my daughter and dig up the wealth I had left hidden. I didn't find my daughter, but I found the treasure, which I have with me, and now, by a strange twist of fate that you've witnessed, I've located the treasure that makes me richest, and that is my beloved daughter. I hope that our minimal guilt and our tears, through the integrity of your justice, might open the doors of mercy. Please forgive us, for we never had any intention of offending you, nor have we gone along with the intention of our people, who have been justly banished—"

Sancho interrupted: "I know Ricote well, and I know that what he says about Ana Félix, his daughter, is true. Insofar as the other trifles dealing with coming and going, having good or bad intentions, I won't get involved."

All those present were astonished at this unusual case, and the general said: "Your tears will not allow me to impose my sentence. Live out, beautiful Ana Félix, the years that heaven has allotted you, and may the insolent and daring persons suffer the punishment for what they did."

And he commanded that the two Turks who had killed his soldiers be hanged immediately from the yardarm. But the viceroy asked him as earnestly as he could not to hang them, since it was more madness than arrogance that had caused their crime. The general did what the viceroy asked, because vengeance is not well-done in cold blood.

They then sought to make a plan to rescue don Gaspar Gregorio from the danger he was in, with Ricote volunteering to contribute more than two thousand *ducados* he had with him in pearls and jewels. Many ways were suggested, but none was as good as the one the Spanish renegade mentioned. He volunteered to go back to Algiers in a small boat with up to six banks of Christian rowers, because he knew where, how, and when he could and should disembark, and he knew where don Gaspar was being kept.

The general and the viceroy were reticent to trust the renegade, or to give him the Christian rowers he wanted to man the oars. Ana Félix said she would vouch for him, and Ricote, her father, said he promised to pay the ransom for the Christians if they were caught. With this resolve, the viceroy and don Antonio Moreno left the ship and took the Moorish woman and her father with them. The viceroy directed him to entertain them and treat them as well as he could, and that he would offer anything of his own for their comfort—such was the goodwill and charity that the beauty of Ana Félix stirred in his heart.

Chapter LXIIII. Which deals with the adventure that gave don Quixote the most sorrow of any that had happened to him.

DON ANTONIO'S wife—so the history states—was very happy to welcome Ana Félix into her home. She received her very graciously, and was taken as much by her beauty as by her intelligence, because the Moorish girl was equally endowed with both, and all the people in the city were drawn to her as they would be to a tolling bell.

Don Quixote said to don Antonio that their plan to regain don Gregorio's freedom was not a good one because it was more dangerous than achievable; it would be better to put him on the Barbary Coast in his armor and on horseback, and he would rescue him in spite of all the Moors, as don Gaiferos had done with his wife, Melisendra.

"Consider, your grace," said Sancho when he heard this, "that señor don Gaiferos rescued his wife on land and took her back to France on land. But in this case, if we rescue don Gregorio, we'll have no way of getting him back to Spain, since there's a sea in the middle."

"'There's a remedy for everything except death,'" responded don Quixote, "because as soon as a boat comes to the shore, we'll hop on, even though the whole world tries to stop us."

"Your grace describes it well and makes it look easy,"

said Sancho, "but 'it's a long way between thought and deed' and I'll put my money on the renegade; he seems to be a good fellow with a stout heart."

Don Antonio said that if the renegade didn't succeed, they would send the great don Quixote over to the Barbary Coast. Two days later, the renegade left on a fleet boat with six ranks of oars, manned by a powerful crew, and two days after that, the galleys sailed for the East. The general asked the viceroy to keep him informed about the freedom of don Gregorio and the outcome of Ana Félix's situation, and the viceroy agreed to do as he was asked.

One morning when don Quixote went out for a ride along the shore, in full armor (because, as he'd said many times, "his armor was his only adornment and fighting his only rest," and he was never seen without his armor for a moment), he saw coming toward him a knight wearing white armor, and on his shield was painted a shining moon. This man, as soon as he was within earshot, said: "Renowned and never sufficiently praised don Quixote de La Mancha, I'm the Knight of the White Moon, whose unheard-of deeds have perhaps come to your attention. I come to do battle with you and test the strength of your arms, so as to make you believe and confess that my lady—whoever she might be—is incomparably more beautiful than your Dulcinea del Toboso, and if you confess this truth right now you'll avoid your death and will spare me the labor of giving it to you. But if you fight, and I conquer you, I want no other satisfaction than for you to lay down your arms and stop seeking adventures, and for you to retire to your village for the duration of one year, without putting a sword in your hand, in untroubled peace and profitable tranquillity, because that's what you need to increase your income and save your soul. And if you vanquish me, my life will be at your discretion, my arms and horse will be your spoils, and the fame of my deeds will go to you. Judge what is best, and answer me right now, because I must finish this affair today."

Don Quixote was dumbfounded and awestruck, as much by the arrogance of the Knight of the White Moon as by the reason for this challenge. With calm restraint he responded: "Knight of the White Moon, news of whose deeds has not reached me until now, I'll dare to swear you've never seen the illustrious Dulcinea, for if you had seen her, I know you wouldn't have begun this crusade; because if you saw her, you would be convinced that there has never been, nor can there be, a beauty to compare with hers. So, not saying that you're lying, but rather you're misinformed in what you've said—with the conditions that you've stated, I accept your challenge, and immediately, so the day you've reserved for this business will not pass by. I'll only exclude the provision that the fame of your deeds would become mine, because I don't know what they are and what they consist of. I'm happy with my own, such as they are. Take the side of the field you want and I'll do the same, and 'whom God shall prosper, let St. Peter bless.' "

People had seen the Knight of the White Moon in the city and had told the viceroy that the knight was talking with don Quixote de La Mancha. The viceroy, thinking that it must be a new adventure made up by don Antonio Moreno or by some other man in the city, went immediately to the waterfront with don Antonio and many other men who were accompanying him, arriving just as don Quixote was turning Rocinante about to measure the field. When he saw they were planning to face each other to attack, he went between them and asked what had moved them to such sudden combat.

The Knight of the White Moon responded that it had to do with beauty, and in a few words he told him what he'd told don Quixote, along with the agreement of the conditions of the challenge by both parties. The viceroy asked don Antonio privately if he knew who the Knight of the White Moon was, or if it was some prank they wanted to play on don Quixote. Don Antonio responded that he had no idea who the fellow was, nor if the challenge was in jest or real. This answer left the viceroy perplexed as to whether or not to allow the battle to proceed.

But since he could only persuade himself that it had to be a joke, he drew back, saying: "*Señores* knights, if there's no other recourse except to confess or die, and *señor* don Quixote stubbornly persists in this, and your grace, Knight of the White Moon, equally does, it's all in God's hands, so go to it."

He of the White Moon thanked the viceroy with courteous and thoughtful words for the permission that was given them, and don Quixote did the same. The latter then commended himself to heaven with all his heart and to his Dulcinea, as was his custom, wheeled around, and took more room in the field, because he saw that his opponent was doing the same. And without the sound of a trumpet or of any other martial instrument to give the signal to begin their attack, both of them turned their horses around at the same moment. Since the horse of the Knight of the White Moon was swifter than don Quixote's, he traveled two-thirds of the course and there, without hitting him with his lance—which he had raised, seemingly on purpose—crashed into don Quixote with such great force that both don Quixote and Rocinante tumbled to the ground in a perilous fall.

He went at once to stand above his opponent, and, placing his lance over his visor, said to him: "You're vanquished, knight—and dead, if you don't confess the conditions of our dispute."

Don Quixote, thoroughly thrashed and dazed, without raising his visor and speaking as if from within a tomb, said in a weak voice: "Dulcinea del Toboso is the most beautiful woman in the world, and I the most unfortunate knight on earth. It's not right that my weakness should forfeit this truth. Plunge your lance home, knight, and take my life, since you've taken my honor."

"I'll certainly not do that," said he of the White Moon. "Long live, long live in its flawlessness the beauty of *señora* Dulcinea del Toboso. I'll be satisfied if the great don Quixote de La Mancha retires to his village for one year, or for the length of time that I may dictate, as we agreed before entering into this battle."

The viceroy and don Antonio heard all of this, along with the others who were present, and they also heard don Quixote respond that since he was asking something that did not prejudice Dulcinea, he would comply with all the rest as a conscientious and truthful knight.

Once this promise was made, he of the White Moon turned his reins and, bowing his head toward the viceroy, rode off at a half gallop into town. The viceroy had don Antonio follow him to find out at any cost who he was. They lifted don Quixote and uncovered his face and found him pale and sweating. Rocinante couldn't move, since he was so beaten up.

Sancho, very sad and troubled, didn't know what to say

or do. It seemed to him that the whole thing had been a dream, and the result of enchantment. He saw his master conquered and forced not to take up arms for a year. He imagined the light of his glorious deeds dimmed, his hopes and new promises evaporated, like smoke in the wind. He wondered fearfully if Rocinante would be permanently injured, or if his master would be dislocated,* although it wouldn't be bad if his craziness were knocked out of him.

At last, the viceroy had don Quixote carried to the city on a litter, and returned to town eager to find out the identity of the Knight of the White Moon, who had left don Quixote in such a sorry state.

Chapter LXV. Where it is revealed who he of the White Moon was, together with the return to freedom of don Gregorio, and other events.

D ON ANTONIO Moreno followed the Knight of the White Moon, and many boys also followed and even pursued him until they caught up with him at an inn inside the city. Don Antonio went in to meet him. A squire came out to receive the knight and take off his armor, and he went into one of the rooms on the ground floor. With him went don Antonio, whose "bread wouldn't bake" until he learned who he was.

When the Knight of the White Moon saw that the man wouldn't leave him alone, he said to him: "I know, *señor*, why you have come—to find out who I am. Since there's no reason to deny you, while my servant is taking off my armor, I'll tell you the whole truth of the matter. *Señor*, I'm the bachelor Sansón Carrasco. I'm from the same village as don Quixote de La Mancha, whose madness and folly has moved all of us who know him to pity, none more than myself. I believe that his health lies in his resting, being in his own region, and at home, so I devised a plan to force him to do just that. About three months ago I left home dressed

---

* *Dislocated* doesn't make too much sense, since joints are dislocated and not people, but there is a pun with another Spanish word— *deslocado*—which can mean "with his craziness removed."

as a knight-errant, calling myself the Knight of the Mirrors, intending to fight with him and vanquish him without doing him any harm, demanding that the loser of our battle should do whatever the winner said. And what I was going to demand of him, since I thought he would lose, was that he return to his village and not leave it for a year, during which time he would be cured.

"But Fate made it turn out differently, because *he* conquered *me* and knocked me off my horse, so my plan didn't work out. He went his way and I went home vanquished, embarrassed, and hurting from the fall, which was a dangerous one as well. But this didn't dissuade me from coming back to look for him and conquer him, as has been seen today. Since he's so conscientious in keeping the rules of knight-errantry, he will without a doubt keep his word. This, *señores*, is what is going on, and I don't need to tell you anything else.

"I beg you not to reveal any of this, nor tell don Quixote who I am, so that my good plan will be complied with and a man who has such good sense will recover it as soon as he rids himself of this folly about chivalry."

"Oh, *señor*," said don Antonio, "may God forgive the injury you've done to the world in wanting to restore sanity to its most amusing lunatic. Don't you see, *señor*, that the benefit of don Quixote's sanity doesn't approach the pleasure that his insanity gives? But I imagine that your stratagem won't be enough to make a man who is so completely mad sane again. If it weren't uncharitable, I would say that I hope don Quixote never gets better, because with his cure, not only do we lose his own pleasantries, but also those of Sancho Panza, his squire, for either one of them can turn melancholy itself into merriment.

"But I'll be quiet and won't say a thing, to see if I'm right in suspecting the plan you've concocted will have no effect."

Carrasco answered that in any case the affair was having a good beginning and he expected a happy outcome. And after don Antonio offered to do anything else he was asked, Carrasco bade him farewell and had his armor tied to a pack mule. He mounted the horse he'd used for the battle right away, and left the city that very day and went home without anything happening to him that we need to report in this true history.

Don Antonio told the viceroy what Carrasco had related, from which he got little delight, because don Quixote's retirement would eliminate all pleasure from hearing about further crazy exploits.

Don Quixote was in bed for six days, under the weather, sad, pensive, and in a bad mood. Sancho tried to console him, and among other things, he said: "*Señor mío*, raise your head and cheer up if you can, and thank heaven that, although you were cast to the ground, you have no broken ribs, and you know that 'if you dish it out you can take it' and 'there's not always bacon where there's stakes,' and who cares about the doctor? You don't need one. Let's go home and stop seeking adventures in regions and villages we don't know. If you think about it, I'm the one who loses the most, although you're in worse shape. When I left my government, I also lost interest in being a governor again, but I still would like to be a count, and this will never happen if your grace fails to become a king, leaving your profession of knighthood, and thus seeing my hopes go up in smoke."

"Hush, Sancho. My retirement will be no longer than a year. After that, I'll go back to my honorable profession, and there'll be no lack of kingdoms to win and some earldom to give you."

"'May God listen,'" said Sancho, "'and may sin be deaf.' I've always heard that 'a good hope is better than a bad holding.'"

They were thus engaged when don Antonio came in saying, with a showing of great content: "Good news, *señor* don Quixote—don Gregorio and the renegade who went to rescue him are onshore! Did I say, 'onshore'? They're already in the house of the viceroy, and will be here in a moment."

Don Quixote cheered up a bit and said: "In truth, I'm almost at the point of saying that I would be better pleased if it had turned out quite the opposite, because then I'd have to go to the Barbary Coast, where with the strength of my arm I would free not only don Gregorio, but also all the captive Christians there are in Barbary. But what am I saying, wretch that I am? Am I not the vanquished one? Am I not the fallen one? Am I not the one who cannot take up arms for a year? What am I promising? What am I boasting about if I'm better suited to work a spinning wheel than to take up the sword?"

"Stop that way of talking, *señor*," said Sancho. "'Let the chicken live, even with the pip.' 'Today for you, tomorrow for me.' And pay no mind about battles and knocks, for 'he who falls today can get up tomorrow,' unless he wants to stay in bed, I mean, and allow himself to become weak, without finding new energy to fight new battles. Get up now, your grace, to welcome don Gregorio. It sounds like the household is in an uproar so he must be here already."

And it was true, because once don Gregorio and the renegade had told the viceroy about the voyage over and back, he wanted to see Ana Félix, and he went with the renegade to don Antonio's house. Although don Gregorio had left Algiers dressed as a woman, aboard the boat he changed into the clothes of a captive who'd come back with him. But no matter what he was wearing he showed himself to be a person to be prized, waited upon, and respected, because he was extremely handsome, and seventeen or eighteen years old. Ricote and his daughter went out to greet him, the father with tears, and the daughter with modesty. They didn't embrace because where there's love there don't need to be excessive gestures. Everyone present admired what a beautiful couple don Gregorio and Ana Félix were. Silence spoke for the two lovers, and their eyes were the tongues that revealed their joyful and chaste thoughts.

The renegade recounted the clever means he'd used to rescue don Gregorio. Don Gregorio told of the dangers and close calls he'd had among the women with whom he'd stayed—not with a long-winded speech, but with a few words, in which he showed his intelligence was greater than his years. Finally, Ricote paid the renegade and the crew who had manned the oars. The renegade reconciled and reconfirmed himself with the Church, and from a rotted member, he was cleansed and made whole by his penitence and repentance.

Two days later the viceroy and don Antonio discussed how they could arrange for Ana Félix and her father to stay in Spain, since it seemed to them that there was no real obstacle in allowing such a Christian daughter and such a seemingly good-intentioned father to stay. Don Antonio offered to go to the capital—where he had to go on business in any case—to try to negotiate for it, intimating that by using favors and gifts many difficult things could be resolved.

"There's no point," said Ricote, who overheard the conversation, "to try to use favors and gifts, because the great don Bernardino de Velasco, Count of Salazar,* whom His Majesty put in charge of our expulsion, will not abide pleadings, promises, gifts, or pitiful demonstrations. Although it's true that he tempers his justice with compassion, he sees the whole body of our race as contaminated and rotten, and he cauterizes our wounds rather than using a salve to soothe them. Thus with prudence, wisdom, and diligence, and by the fear that he inspires, he has carried on his broad shoulders the weight of this great challenge to its due implementation, without our ingenuity, ploys, persistence, and frauds being able to dazzle his Argus† eyes, which are continually on the alert, so that none of our nation remains hidden to one day sprout and give poisonous fruit in Spain, which is now cleansed, now free of the fears the population felt. What a heroic resolution the great Felipe III had and what unheard-of astuteness in placing it all in don Bernardino de Velasco's hands!"

"Still and yet, while I'm there, I'll do everything I can, and let heaven do what it wills," said don Antonio. "Don Gregorio will go with me to console the grief that his parents must have experienced by his absence. Ana Félix will stay with my wife at home, or in a convent, and I know that the *señor* viceroy will be pleased to have Ricote as a houseguest until it's seen how I deal with this matter."

The viceroy consented to everything that was proposed, but don Gregorio, when he heard the plan, said that he in no way wanted to leave Ana Félix. But since he did need to see his parents, and since he could come back for her, he finally agreed. Ana Félix stayed with don Antonio's wife and Ricote in the house of the viceroy.

The day came for don Antonio to leave, and don Quixote and Sancho's departure came two days later, for his

---

* The Count of Salazar was in charge of the expulsion of the Moors from various regions in Spain starting in 1609. He cleared the area where Ricote would have lived in 1614.

† Argus was a mythological monster with a hundred eyes.

fall prevented him from leaving any earlier. There were tears, there were sighs, fainting, and sobs when don Gregorio said good-bye to Ana Félix. Ricote offered don Gregorio a thousand *escudos* if he wanted them, but he didn't take any except for five that don Antonio lent him, and he promised to pay them back in the capital. With this, the two of them left, followed soon after don Quixote and Sancho, as has been said—don Quixote, not wearing his armor, but rather dressed for travel, and Sancho was on foot because the donkey was carrying the arms and armor.

Chapter LXVI. Which deals with what the person who reads it will see, or the person who listens to it will hear.

WHEN THEY left Barcelona, don Quixote stopped to look at where he'd fallen and said: "Here was Troy; here my bad luck—not my cowardice—snatched away all the glory I had achieved. Here's where Fate used its transformations and misdirections against me. Here's where my deeds faded into darkness. Here, in short, is where my fortune fell, never again to rise."

When Sancho heard this he said: "It's as important for brave hearts, *señor mío*, to bear their misfortunes as it is for them to take joy in their prosperity, and I can speak from my own experience, for if, when I was a governor I was happy, now that I'm a squire on foot, I'm not sad. I've heard that what they call Fate is a drunken and capricious woman, and above all, blind, and so she doesn't see who she tears down, nor who she raises up."

"You're being very philosophical, Sancho," responded don Quixote, "and you're speaking with great wisdom. I don't know who has educated you. What I do know is that there's no such thing as Fate in the world, and that things that happen, good or bad, don't happen by chance, but rather by particular providence of heaven. From this comes the common saying that 'every man is the architect of his own destiny.' I have been of mine, but not with the necessary prudence, and so my pride has cast me down. I should have realized that Rocinante's frailty was no match for the massive size of the horse of the Knight of the White Moon. I was daring. I did what I could, and I was knocked down. Although I lost my honor, I didn't lose, nor can I ever lose, the virtue of keeping my word. When I was a bold and valiant knight-errant, my works and hands confirmed my deeds, and now that I'm an ordinary squire I'll confirm my promise by keeping my word. Start walking, then, my friend, and let's have a year of penitence in our own village, and with our seclusion, let's recover virtue anew so we can go back to my never-forgotten profession of arms."

"*Señor*," responded Sancho, "being on foot is not so enjoyable that it makes me look forward to long days of travel. Let's leave these arms and armor hanging from a tree, like those men who were hanged, and I'll be on the back of the gray with my feet off the ground, and we'll make our daily travels as you wish, for as long as you want. To think I'm going to travel on foot all day is to think the unthinkable."

"Well said, Sancho," responded don Quixote. "Let my armor be hung as a trophy, and under or surrounding it, we'll carve into the trees what was written around Roland's armor:

THESE LET NONE MOVE
WHO DARES NOT HIS MIGHT WITH ROLAND PROVE.*

"That sounds good to me," responded Sancho, "and if it weren't that we'd miss him on our trek, I'd say we should hang Rocinante up as well."

"Well, I don't want to hang either the horse or my arms and armor," replied don Quixote, "so that no one can say 'to good service bad reward.'"

"That's well stated, your grace," responded Sancho, "because, according to the opinion of wise people, 'the fault of the donkey should not be laid on the packsaddle.' And since in this affair your grace is the only guilty party, you should punish yourself, and you shouldn't vent your wrath on your broken and bloody armor, nor on the gentleness of Rocinante, nor on the softness of my feet, since you want me to walk more than is right."

---

* This is from *Orlando Furioso*, canto twenty-four.

In these and other conversations they spent the whole day, and four more, without anything happening to them that might delay their travels, and on the fifth day, just as they were going into a village, they saw many people gathered in front of an inn, taking their leisure, since it was a holiday.

When they drew near, a peasant raised his voice, saying: "One of these two *señores* approaching, who don't know the circumstances, can tell what should be done with our wager."

"Certainly, I'll be able to judge," said don Quixote, "and with all fairness, if I can understand what the situation is."

"It happens, good *señor*," said the peasant, "that a resident of this village, who is so fat that he weighs eleven *arrobas*,* challenged a neighbor of his, who weighs no more than five, to a race of a hundred meters, on the condition that they run with equal weight. When they asked the challenger how the weight was supposed to be equalized, he said that the challenged man should carry six *arrobas* of iron on his back, and in that way the eleven *arrobas* of the thin man would equal the eleven of the fat one—"

"No, no, this is all wrong," interrupted Sancho, before don Quixote could answer. "Just a few days ago I was a governor and a judge, as everyone knows, and had to resolve doubts and render judgments in all legal cases."

"You answer, then, Sancho, my friend," said don Quixote. "I'm of no use, since my mind is shaken up and twisted around."

With this permission, Sancho addressed the many peasants who had gathered around him in anxious expectation of the ruling that would come from his mouth: "Brothers, what the fat man asks is inappropriate and shows no justice at all, because if it's true what they say that the challenged can choose the arms, it isn't fair that he should choose weapons that would prevent the other from winning the contest. So, it's my opinion that the challenger should prune, peel, scrape, pare, trim, and clear away six *arrobas* of his flesh from different parts of his body, in the best way he can think of and that suits him the best, and in this way he'll weigh five *arrobas* and will be the same weight as his opponent, and in that way they can run with equal weight."

---

* About 275 pounds (125 kilos).

"I swear," said a peasant who heard Sancho's judgment, "this man has spoken like a saint and judged like a canon. But I'm sure the fat man won't want to take off an ounce from his flesh, much less six *arrobas*."

"The best thing is for them not to race," responded another, "so that the thin one won't crumble under the load, nor the fat one go on a diet. Let half the wager go for wine, and let's take these two men to the tavern that has the best wine, and I'll take responsibility."

"I thank you, *señores*," responded don Quixote, "but I cannot delay a single second, because my deep thoughts and certain sad events rob me of my manners and force me to move on swiftly."

And so, spurring Rocinante, he moved on, leaving them in wonder at having seen his strange figure as well as the wisdom of his servant, for that's what they thought Sancho to be.

And another of the peasants said: "If the servant is so wise, what must the master be like? I'll bet if they're on their way to study at Salamanca, they'll be judges in the royal court before you know it. It's just study, and study some more, and everything else is inconsequential. And with a few favors and a bit of luck, when a man least expects it, he finds himself with a staff in his hand and a miter on his head."

Master and servant spent that night in the open countryside, and the next day, as they continued their journey, they saw coming toward them a man with a pack on his shoulders and a short lance in his hand. When he got close to don Quixote he quickened his step, and half running he came and embraced him around his right thigh (for he could reach no higher), and said joyfully: "Oh, my *señor* don Quixote, what pleasure it will be to the heart of my master, the duke, when he finds out you're returning to his castle! He's still there with his wife, the duchess."

"I don't recognize you," responded don Quixote, "nor will I know who you are unless you tell me."

"I, *señor* don Quixote," responded the messenger, "am Tosilos, the groom of the duke, my master, the fellow who refused to fight with your grace over the marriage of doña Rodriguez's daughter."

"God help me!" said don Quixote. "Is it possible that

you're the person my enemies the enchanters transformed into a groom to defraud me of the honor of that battle?"

"Hush, good *señor*," replied the messenger. "There was no enchantment at all. When I went into the fray, I was the same groom Tosilos as when I came out of it. I thought I could marry without fighting, since the girl seemed so nice. But it came out the opposite of what I planned, because as soon as your grace left the castle, the duke had me flogged a hundred times for having disobeyed the orders he gave me before I went into the battle. The girl is now a nun, and doña Rodriguez has gone back to Castile, and I'm on my way to Barcelona with a packet of letters to the viceroy that my master is sending him. If you would like a swallow, I have some of the good stuff in this gourd—it's pure, although a bit warm—and I have some slices of Tronchón cheese, which can be an appetizer and an awakener of thirst, in case yours is sleeping."

"I accept the invitation," said Sancho. "Take out everything else you have to eat, and let the good Tosilos pour out a dram in spite of all the enchanters there are in the Indies."

"Sancho," said don Quixote, "you are the biggest glutton in the world, and the greatest fool on earth, if you're not persuaded that this messenger is enchanted, and this Tosilos is counterfeit. You stay behind with him and I'll go on ahead, waiting for you to catch up with me."

The groom laughed and took out his gourd and cheese from the saddlebags, as well as some bread, and he and Sancho sat on the green grass, and in peace and good fellowship ate until they reached the bottom of the saddlebags, and with such relish that they even licked the packet of letters, since it smelled of cheese.

Tosilos said to Sancho: "Without a doubt, this master of yours, Sancho, my friend, must have a screw loose."

"What do you mean '*a* screw loose'?" responded Sancho. "Practically all his screws are loose. I know it, and I've told him so, but what good does it do? Especially now that his career is ended, since he was defeated by the Knight of the White Moon."

Tosilos asked him to explain what had happened. But Sancho responded that it was impolite to leave his master waiting for him. On another occasion, if they should meet again, there would be time enough to tell him everything. And getting up, after having shaken off his coat and removed the crumbs from his beard, he led the donkey away, and met up with his master who was waiting for him in the shade of a tree.

Chapter LXVII. Of don Quixote's resolve to become a shepherd and live in the country during the year of his vow, with other events that are truly entertaining and good.

IF MANY thoughts had troubled don Quixote before he was conquered, many more vexed him now, after his fall. He was in the shade of the tree, as has been said, and there, "like flies to honey," thoughts were attacking and stinging him. Some of these were about Dulcinea's enchantment, and others about his forced retirement. Sancho arrived, and praised the liberal nature of the groom Tosilos.

"Is it possible, Sancho," don Quixote said to him, "that you still believe he's the real groom? You must have forgotten that you saw Dulcinea converted and transformed into a peasant, and the Knight of the Mirrors into the bachelor Carrasco, all of it the work of enchanters who pursue me. But tell me, did you ask this Tosilos, as you call him, what happened to Altisidora—if she wept because of my absence, or if she's put the thoughts of love that so troubled her in my presence into the hands of oblivion?"

"I had other things on my mind," responded Sancho, "than asking dumb things. On my soul, *señor*, are you in a position to look into other people's thoughts, especially thoughts of love?"

"Look, Sancho," said don Quixote, "there's a great difference between deeds one does for love and those done out of gratitude. It may well be that a knight is not in love, but he can't be—strictly speaking—ungrateful. Altisidora loved me, apparently. She gave me the three kerchiefs that you know about, she wept at my departure, she cursed me, she called me names, and she shamelessly abused me in public—sure signs, all of them, that she adored me. A lover's rage typically ends in curses. I had no hope or treasure to give her because I've surrendered my hopes to Dulcinea, and the rewards of knights-errant are like those of elves— illusory and fanciful. I can only give her the memories I have of her, without prejudice to those I keep of Dulcinea, whom you wrong by postponing the flaying of your flesh (and may I see it devoured by wolves), which you would rather give to the worms than to the relief of that poor *señora*."

"*Señor*," responded Sancho, "to tell the truth, I can't persuade myself that the lashes on my rear end have anything to do with the disenchantment of enchanted people—it's like saying: 'if you have a headache, put ointment on your knees.' I bet that in all the histories of knight-errantry that your grace read, you've never run across an disenchantment done by means of lashes. But whether yes or no, I'll lash myself when I feel like it and when the time is right for it."

"God grant it," responded don Quixote, "and may heaven make you realize the debt you owe my lady—and she's your lady too, since you belong to me."

In conversations like this one they kept traveling until they got to the very place and spot where they were trampled by the bulls. Don Quixote recognized the spot and said to Sancho: "This is the place where we came across the elegant shepherdesses who wanted to revive and imitate the pastoral Arcadia, an idea that was as novel as it was imaginative. If you think it's a good idea, I'd like for us, Sancho, to imitate them and become shepherds, just for the period of our seclusion. I'll buy some sheep and all the other things needed to be a shepherd, and I'll call myself THE SHEPHERD QUIXOTIZ, and you will be THE SHEPHERD PANCINO, and we'll wander about the hills, woods, and meadows, singing here, lamenting there, drinking the liquid crystal from springs or clear creeks or sometimes from raging rivers. Oak trees will give us their sweet fruit with their generous hand; cork trees will provide a seat with their hard trunks; willows will furnish shade; roses, a sweet aroma; the broad fields, carpets of a thousand harmonizing colors; the stars and moon, light, in spite of the darkness of night; song will give us pleasure; weeping, happiness; Apollo, poetry; love, conceits with which we can become immortal and famous, not only in present times, but also in future ages."

"By God," said Sancho, "this type of life is square with

me—corners, in fact. And what's more, as soon as bachelor Sansón Carrasco and *maese* Nicolas the barber see us,
they'll want to follow in our footsteps and join us as shepherds themselves, and may it please God for the priest to
enter the fold as well, for he's very merry and likes to have
a good time."

"You've spoken very well," said don Quixote, "and the
bachelor Sansón Carrasco, if he enters the fraternity of
shepherds, as he'll doubtless do, can be called THE SHEP-
HERD SANSONINO, or maybe THE SHEPHERD CARRASCÓN; the
barber Nicolás can be named MICULOSO,* as Boscán of old
called himself Nemoroso;† I don't know what to call the
priest, unless it's some derivative of his name, such as THE
SHEPHERD CURIAMBRO.‡ It will be as easy as picking pears
to choose names for shepherdesses we're supposed to be in
love with. My lady's own name fits as well for a shepherdess as for a princess, so there's no need for me to trouble
myself in looking for a better one. You, Sancho, can give
yours whatever you want."

"I don't think I'll give her any other name," responded
Sancho, "than TERESONA,§ which fits in well with her stout-
ness and her own name, since she's called Teresa. And
what's more, when I celebrate her in my verses, I'll reveal
my chaste desires, since 'I don't go looking for impossible
things in other people's houses.' The priest maybe shouldn't
have a lady, to set a good example. But if the bachelor wants
to have a lady, let him do whatever he wants."

"By God," said don Quixote, "what a life we'll have,
Sancho, my friend! What music of *churumbelas*¶ will reach
our ears, what hurdy-gurdies, what tabors and flutes, what

---

* Since Micolás was a rustic variant of Nicolás, the name Miculoso
makes good sense from the poetic pastoral point of view.
† It is true that El Brocense first identified the poet Garcilaso de la Vega's
friend Boscán with the name Nemoroso, apparently erroneously, even
though the Latin *nemus* means "forest" (*bosque* in Spanish). It is more
logical that Garcilaso used that name to represent himself. But certainly
in 1615, people thought Boscán was Nemoroso, owing to El Brocense.
‡ Refer to Part I, chapter one, page 25 to see how this fits; but here,
since *cura* means "priest" in Spanish, it becomes really quite offensive
to the priest.
§ *-ona* is an augmentative suffix.
¶ This is another old double-reeded instrument.

rebecs!* And *albogues* will keep time to all this music! We'll have almost every kind of pastoral instrument there is."

"What are *albogues*?" asked Sancho. "I've never heard of them nor have I seen them in all the days of my life."

"*Albogues*," responded don Quixote, "are little brass plates that look like candleholders,† and when you strike them together it makes a noise that, if not especially agreeable or harmonious, is not too displeasing and fits in well with the rusticity of the hurdy-gurdy and the tabor and flute. The name *albogue* is Moorish, as are all those that begin in Spanish with *al-*, such as *almohaza, almorzar, alhombra, alguacil, alhucema, almacén, alcancía,*‡ and other similar words . . . there must be a few more.§ And there are only three Moorish words in our language that end in -*í,* and they are *borceguí, zaquizamí,* and *maravedí.* Also clearly Arabic are *Alhelí* and *alfaquí,*¶ as much for the initial *al-* as for the final -*í.* I mention this in passing because *albogues* made me think of it.

"I'm something of a poet, as you know, and the bachelor Sansón Carrasco is even better than I am, which will help us to perfect our new calling. About the priest I can't say anything, but I'll bet that he has smatterings of being a poet too, and I don't doubt that *maese* Nicolás does as well, because all or most barbers are also guitarists and ballad singers. I'll complain of absence, you'll praise yourself as being constant, the shepherd Carrascón of being scorned, and the

---

* Rebecs are ancient three-stringed bowed instruments from the Middle East.

† Sancho may not have heard the word *albogues* before, but he *heard* and *saw* these cymbals at Camacho's wedding, Part II, chapter nineteen. They're held by the part that looks like where the candle would be inserted and clapped together.

‡ An *almohaza* is a horse-grooming brush, *almorzar* is to eat lunch and is not Arabic in its origin, *alhombra* is "carpet" (modern *alfombra*), *alguacil* is "bailiff," *alhucema* is the lavender plant, *almacén* is a warehouse, and *alcancía* is a money box.

§ There are really hundreds of words of Arabic origin that begin with *al-* in Spanish. *Al* is the Arabic definite article, which became fused with the noun, and that's why there are so many.

¶ *Borceguí* is a low boot, *zaquizamí* is a garret, *maravedí* is an old coin, *Alhelí* is a pink flower, and *alfaquí* is an Arabic professor of jurisprudence.

priest Curiambro of whatever he pleases, and so that's the way it'll be, and it won't leave anything to be desired."

To which Sancho responded: "I am, *señor*, so unlucky that I fear that the day will never come when I'll see myself in that calling. But if I do become a shepherd, what polished spoons I'll make!* What fried bread crumbs I'll cook; what whipped cream; what garlands; what pastoral trinkets I'll put together; although they won't earn me fame as a wise man, they will make me famous as a clever fellow! Sanchica, my daughter, will bring food right to us. But hold on! She's pretty good-looking, and there are shepherds who are more mischievous than simple, and 'I wouldn't want her to go out for wool and come back shorn.' Love and evil desires just as soon roam about the countryside as in the cities, and in pastoral huts as well as in royal palaces, and 'if you take away the cause, you take away the sin,' and 'what the eyes don't see doesn't break the heart,' and 'a leap over the hedge is better than prayers of good men.'"

"No more proverbs, Sancho," said don Quixote. "Any one of them on its own is enough to make one see what your point is. I've told you many times not to be excessive in your proverbs, and to show a little restraint in using them. But it seems to me that it's like 'preaching in the desert,' and 'my mother punishes me and I mock her.'"

"It seems to me, *señor*, that your grace is like what they say: 'the pot calling the kettle black.' You're scolding me for using proverbs, and you go stringing them together two at a time."

"Look, Sancho," responded don Quixote, "I bring in pertinent proverbs, and when I say them, 'they fit like a ring on your finger.' But you drag them in by their hair, with no direction. And if I remember correctly, on another occasion I told you that proverbs are maxims taken from the experience and contemplation of the wise ancients, and a proverb that doesn't fit is more nonsense than wisdom. But let's leave all this, for night is coming, and let's get off the highway a good distance, where we can spend the night, and God knows 'tomorrow will be another day.'"

They left the road, ate late and poorly, much against the

---

* Shepherds did carve wooden spoons, but Gaos thinks this phrase refers to polishing the spoons through eating.

will of Sancho, who thought about the poverty of knight-errantry out in the forests and hills, compared to the abundance manifest in castles and homes, as in the case of don Diego de Miranda, and in Camacho's wedding, and the house of don Antonio Moreno. But he realized that "it wasn't possible for it to be always daytime," nor always nighttime for that matter, and so he spent that night sleeping, and his master watching.

Chapter LXVIII. Of the bristly adventure that happened to don Quixote.

I T WAS a somewhat dark night, for although the moon was in the sky, it was not where it could be seen. At times Diana* travels to the far ends of the earth and makes the hills black and valleys dark. Don Quixote slept his first sleep, but never accomplished his second, quite the opposite of Sancho, who never had a second one because the first lasted from the night to the morning, evidence of his sturdy constitution and few cares.

Don Quixote's own cares kept him awake, and he woke Sancho and said: "I'm amazed at how free and easy you are. I think you must be made of marble or of hard bronze, a person in whom there's no emotion or feeling of any kind. I stay awake while you sleep. I cry while you sing. I faint and fast while you're lazy and sluggish because you're so stuffed.

"Good servants share the grief of their masters and feel their emotions, if only for the sake of appearances. Look at the serenity of this night, the solitude that surrounds us, inviting us to take a break from our sleep. Stand up, by God, go over there, and with a good heart and grateful spirit, give yourself three or four hundred lashes toward the disenchantment of Dulcinea. I'm begging you—I don't want to have to grapple with you like the last time, because I know that you're strong. After you've lashed yourself, we'll spend the rest of the night singing—I about my absence

---

* The goddess Diana occupied varying roles. She was *also* the goddess of the moon, as seen here.

and you about your constancy—and we'll begin the pastoral calling right now that we'll keep doing in our village."

"*Señor*," responded Sancho, "I'm not like a friar who can wake up in the middle of the night and whip himself, nor do I think that after one extreme of the pain of the lashes I can go to the other extreme of singing. Let me sleep, your grace, and don't rush me into whipping myself. You'll force me to swear that I'll never touch even a hair on my coat, much less my flesh."

"Oh, you hard-hearted, pitiless squire! Oh, bread ill bestowed and favors ill appreciated—both those I have done and plan to do for you! Because of me you've been a governor. Because of me you have firm hopes of being a count or getting some other appropriate title, and the fulfillment of these hopes will be delayed only as long as this year lasts—for *post tenebras spero lucem*."*

"I don't understand any of that," replied Sancho. "I only understand that while I'm sleeping, I have no fear, no hopes, no work, no glory. Blessed be the person who invented sleep, the cloak that covers all human thoughts, the food that takes away all hunger, water that drives away thirst, fire that warms you when you're cold, coolness that tempers heat, and, finally, the money with which all things are bought, the scale that makes the shepherd equal to the king and the fool to the wise man. There's only one thing bad about sleep, the way I hear it, and that is that it's like death, because there's not much difference between a sleeping man and a dead one."

"Sancho, I have never heard you speak so elegantly as now," said don Quixote, "which makes me realize the truth of that proverb you frequently use: 'it's not with whom you're bred, but rather with whom you're fed.'"

"Ah, woe is me!" replied Sancho. "*Señor*, I'm not the one who's stringing proverbs together now, for they drip from your mouth two at a time, better than from mine. The difference between yours and mine is that yours hit the mark while mine are scattered all over the place. But, still, they're all proverbs."

---

* From Job 17:12, meaning "After darkness I hope for light." Also, of course, it is the Latin motto on Juan de la Cuesta's covers, which you can see at the beginning of Parts I and II in this translation.

They were discussing this when they heard a deafening thunder and a harsh dissonance resound throughout the valleys. Don Quixote got up and took out his sword, and Sancho cowered beneath the donkey, putting the bundle of armor on one side of him and the packsaddle on the other, as frightened as don Quixote was agitated. Gradually the noise increased and drew near to the two fearful men, or at least near the one fearful man, for the other's bravery is well-known.

What was going on was that some men were driving more than six hundred pigs to market at that late hour, and the noise they made, together with the pigs' grunting and snorting, deafened the ears of don Quixote and Sancho, and they didn't know what it could be. The grunting massive herd, without showing respect either for don Quixote's or for Sancho's authority, trampled them both, destroying Sancho's barricade and knocking over not only don Quixote but Rocinante along with him. The herd, the grunting, the speed with which the dirty animals arrived brought chaos to and toppled the packsaddle, the armor, the donkey, Rocinante, Sancho, and don Quixote. Sancho got up as well as he could and asked his master for his sword, saying he wanted to kill half a dozen of those rude pigs, for he'd realized what they were.

Don Quixote told him: "Let them be, my friend, for this affront is atonement for my sin, and for a conquered knight-errant to be eaten by jackals, stung by wasps, and trampled by pigs is a just punishment from heaven."

"It must also be a punishment from heaven," responded Sancho, "for flies to bite, lice to eat, and hunger to attack squires of knights-errant. If we squires were children of the knight we serve, or very close relatives, it wouldn't be unreasonable if we suffered the punishment of our masters' sins, even down to the fourth generation. But what have the Panzas to do with the Quixotes? Ah, well, let's get comfortable again and sleep what little is left of the night. 'Tomorrow is another day' and we'll get along all right."

"You sleep, Sancho," responded don Quixote. "You were born to sleep. I, on the other hand, was born to keep vigil. In the time that remains until daybreak, I'll give free rein to my thoughts, and I'll release them in a little madrigal I composed last night in my head without your knowing about it."

"It seems to me," responded Sancho, "that there must not be many thoughts that can give rise to songs. Make as many verses as you want, and I'll sleep as much as I can."

And so, taking as much of the ground as he wanted, he curled up and slept a sound sleep, without bonds, debts, or any pain at all to prevent him from it. Don Quixote, leaning against the trunk of a beech or cork tree (for Cide Hamete Benengeli doesn't distinguish what kind of tree it was), to the accompaniment of his own sighs, sang in this way:

When in my mind
    I muse, oh, Love, upon thy cruelty,
    To death I flee,
    In hope therein the end of all to find.
But drawing near
    That welcome haven in my sea of woe,
    Such joy I know,
    That life revives, and still I linger here.
Thus life doth slay,
    And death again to life restores me;
    Strange destiny,
    That deals with life and death as with a play!*

Each verse was accompanied by many sighs and not a few tears, like from one whose heart was pierced with the pain of defeat, and with the absence of Dulcinea. At this point, day came and the rays of the sun shone on Sancho's face, and he woke up and stretched his limbs and shook himself. He saw the damage done to his supplies by the pigs, and cursed the herd in no uncertain terms.

Finally, the two of them got back on the road, and at the end of the day they saw coming toward them as many as ten men on horseback and four or five on foot. Don Quixote's heart quickened and Sancho's became distressed, because the people who were approaching were bringing lances and shields and appeared ready for battle.

---

* This is an English translation by Ormsby (via Spanish) of an Italian poem by Pietro Bembo from a collection called *Gli Asolani* (1505). Cultured readers would have recognized this popular poem and its Italian source.

Don Quixote turned to Sancho and said: "If I were free to take up arms, Sancho, and my promise hadn't tied my hands, this predicament that has come upon us would be a piece of cake. But it may be something other than what we fear."

The men on horseback arrived, and, brandishing their lances, they surrounded don Quixote without saying a word and pointed their lances at his chest and back, threatening him with death. One of those on foot, with his forefinger on his lips, indicating that don Quixote should remain quiet, took Rocinante's bridle and led him from the road; the others, who were on foot, took Sancho and the donkey and, maintaining that marvelous silence, followed the steps of the man leading don Quixote, who tried two or three times to ask where he was being taken, or what they wanted. But as soon as he began to move his lips, it looked like they were going to close them with their lances. And the same thing happened to Sancho, because as soon as he opened his mouth, one of those on foot pricked him with a sharp stick, and the donkey as well, as if he too were about to speak.

When night closed in, they quickened their pace, and fear increased in the prisoners, and more so when they heard the others say at regular intervals: "Keep walking, you brutes! Keep quiet, you barbarians! Pay up, you cannibals! Don't complain, you Scythians!* Don't even open your eyes, Polyphemi,† killers, butchering lions!" And they added other similar names to these, with which they used to torment the ears of the wretched master and servant. Sancho went along, saying to himself: "They called us barbers and cannonballs? I don't like any of these names—'an ill wind is threshing this wheat.' Bad things come to us all at once, like smacks on a dog, and I hope that the threats will result in words and not the blows that this misadventure is threatening us with."

Don Quixote was stunned, unable to figure out despite all his speculations what those names meant, but he did

---

* The Scythians were cruel warriors who flourished in about the eighth century B.C. in what is now Iran.
† Polyphemus was the most famous cyclops (one-eyed giant cannibal) in Greek mythology.

surmise he couldn't expect anything good and should fear something bad. At this point they arrived, almost at night-fall, at a castle that don Quixote recognized as being the one belonging to the duke, where he'd recently stayed.

"God help me!" he said as soon as he recognized the place. "What can this be? Truly in this house all is courtesy and civility. But for the vanquished, good things turn bad, and bad things get worse."

They entered into the main courtyard of the castle, and they saw it all decorated and set up in a way that increased their wonder and doubled their fear, as will be seen in the next chapter.

Chapter LXIX. About the rarest and most unusual event that happened to don Quixote in the course of this great history.

THE MEN on horseback dismounted, and together with those on foot they took don Quixote and Sancho hur-riedly from their mounts and led them into the courtyard, around which burned almost a hundred torches in their sconces, and in the galleries surrounding the courtyard there were more than five hundred lanterns, so that even though it was night, it seemed like daylight. In the middle of the courtyard there was a bier about six feet above the ground, covered by a canopy made of black velvet, with steps leading up to it on which more than a hundred white candles burned in silver candlesticks. On top of it there lay the dead body of a maiden who was so exqui-site that she made death itself beautiful. Her head was on a brocaded cushion, crowned with a garland of several sweet-smelling flowers woven together, her hands crossed on her chest, and in them was a branch of yellowed con-quering palm.*

Along one side of the courtyard was a stage with two chairs, on which were seated two persons who, since they

---

* The palm is symbolic of virtue, and "conquering" means that she has conquered sin. It is yellow because it's been kept since Palm Sunday.

were wearing crowns on their heads and had scepters in their hands, seemed to be kings, either real or feigned. Next to this stage were two more chairs, reached by some stairs, on which those who brought the prisoners seated don Quixote and Sancho, all this done in silence, and their captors making signs to the two of them that they should also be silent. But they would have said nothing even without those signs, because their astonishment at what they were seeing had them tongue-tied.

At that point, two notable persons, followed by a large retinue, walked up onto the stage, and don Quixote recognized them immediately as the duke and duchess, his hosts. They sat on two richly decorated chairs, next to those who appeared to be kings. Who wouldn't be moved to wonder at all this, especially when don Quixote recognized that the dead body lying on the tomb was that of the beautiful Altisidora?

When the duke and duchess went over to their seats, don Quixote and Sancho stood up and bowed deeply, and the duke and duchess nodded their heads slightly in return. Next, an officer went over to Sancho and wrapped him in a robe of black buckram painted with flames. The man removed Sancho's cap and put a penitent's hat on his head of the kind worn by those condemned by the Holy Office, and whispered into his ear that he must not open his mouth or they'd gag or kill him. Sancho looked at himself from top to bottom and saw the flames licking up, but since they didn't burn him, he couldn't have cared less.

He took his hat off and saw that it was painted with devils, then put it back on and said to himself: "It's all right, because the flames don't burn me and the devils aren't carrying me off."

Don Quixote also looked at him, and although fear had numbed his senses, he couldn't help but laugh at the figure of Sancho. And now from under the bier, there began to be heard a soft and pleasant sound of flutes, unaccompanied by any human voice, for silence itself kept silent there. Then there suddenly arose next to the cushion under the body a handsome lad dressed in a toga, who, accompanying himself on a harp, sang with a smooth and articulate voice these two stanzas:

Until fair Altisidora, who the sport
    Of cold don Quixote's cruelty hath been,
    Returns to life, and in this magic court
    The dames in sables come to grace the scene,
    And while her matrons all in seemly sort
    My lady robes in baize and bombazine,
    Her beauty and her sorrows will I sing
    With defter quill than touched the Thracian sting.*
But not in life alone, I think, to me
    Belongs the office; Lady, when my tongue
    Is cold in death, believe me, unto you
    My voice shall raise its tributary song.
    My soul, from this strait prison-house set free,
    As over the Stygian lake† it floats along,
    Thy praises singing still shall hold its way,
    And make the waters of oblivion stay.‡

"No more," said one of those men who appeared to be kings, "no more, divine singer. You would never finish if you were to recount the death and graces of the peerless Altisidora—not dead in the way the ignorant world believes, but alive in the tongues of fame, and by means of the penance that Sancho Panza, here present, must undergo to return her to her lost light. And so, oh, Rhadamanthus!§ You who judge with me in the dark caverns of Lys!¶ Since you know everything the inscrutable Fates have prescribed for how to make this maiden revive, say and declare it right now, so that the happiness that will come with her return will not be delayed."

Hardly had Minos, a judge and companion of Rhadamanthus, said this when Rhadamanthus stood up and said: "Oh, officers of this house, high and low ones, big and little ones, draw near and smack Sancho twenty-four times on

---

* This refers to the death of Orpheus, who was killed by the women of Thrace.
† The Stygian lake refers to the River Styx.
‡ This second octave is by Garcilaso de la Vega (*Eclogue III*, lines 9–16). This translation once again is by Ormsby.
§ Rhadamanthus and Minos (the person talking, who will be named later) were the mythological kings of hell.
¶ Lys is Minos' confusion for Dis, the god of the underworld.

his face, give him twelve pinches, and six pinpricks on his arms and back. By means of this ceremony, Altisidora will be resuscitated."

When Sancho Panza heard this, he broke his silence and said: "I swear, I'll as much let my face be slapped or even touched as I would become a Moor! On my soul, what does slapping my face have to do with the resurrection of this girl? 'The old lady took a fancy to beets. . . .'* They enchant Dulcinea and then they whip me so she can be disenchanted. Altisidora dies of an illness it pleased God to send her, and twenty-four slaps on my face, riddling my body with pinpricks, and bruising my arms with pinches will bring her back! You can do these pranks on some other dunce. I'm an old dog, so don't try any of that 'here, doggy' stuff with me."

"You will die!" roared Rhadamanthus. "Relent, you tiger! Humble yourself, arrogant Nimrod;† endure and be silent; we're not asking impossible things of you. Don't argue about the difficulties of this affair. You will be slapped, you will see yourself pricked, you will moan with pinches. Ho, officers, do what I tell you. If not, you'll find out, on the faith of an honest man, for what reason you were born."

Just then there appeared in the courtyard about six duennas in a procession, one after the other, four of them wearing glasses, and all of them with their right hands raised high, with four inches of their forearms showing, to make their hands look longer, as is the custom nowadays.

As soon as Sancho saw them he began to bellow like a bull and said: "I'll let anyone else paw my face, but these duennas, never! Scratch my face like they did to my master in this same castle, stick pointed daggers through my body, tear at my arms with fiery pincers, and I'll bear it all patiently in deference to the duke and duchess. But I won't let duennas touch me, even if the devil hauls me off."

Don Quixote broke his silence and said to Sancho: "Be

---

* "The old lady took a fancy to the beets," and it goes on to say: "she left neither green nor dry ones." Sancho is equating the old lady's eagerness to eat with the enchanters' eagerness to make Sancho the means by which women are disenchanted, as the text goes on to confirm.
† Little is said about the warrior Nimrod in the Old Testament (Genesis 10:8–12, I Chronicles 1:10, Micah 5:6), but he had a reputation for being evil and haughty.

patient, my son, and humor these people, and give thanks to heaven for having given you the power to disenchant the enchanted and raise the dead through martyrdom."

The duennas had now reached Sancho, and, in a better temper and more persuaded, he sat down in the chair and offered his face and beard to the first one, who gave him a well-placed slap, then bowed.

"Less courtesy and not so many cosmetics, *señora* duenna," said Sancho, "because by God your hands smell of *vinagrillo*."*

So all the duennas smacked him, and others from the household pinched him. But he couldn't stand the idea of pinpricks. He stood up from the chair, looking very angry, and, seizing a lighted torch next to him, he began to pursue the duennas and all those who were tormenting him, saying: "Away with you, you infernal ministers—I'm not made of bronze, that I won't feel such extraordinary torture."

At this point, Altisidora, who must have been tired of being on her back for so long, turned onto her side. When the onlookers saw this, they said almost in unison: "Altisidora is alive! Altisidora lives!"

Rhadamanthus told Sancho to lay aside his wrath, because his task had been completed.

As soon as don Quixote saw Altisidora come to life, he got on his knees before Sancho and said: "Now is the time, child of my bowels—and not my squire—for you to give yourself some of the lashes you must endure to disenchant Dulcinea. Now, I say, is the time when your power is at its height, and you can do what is expected of you efficiently."

To which Sancho responded: "That seems to me to be one bad move on top of another, and not honey on top of a cake. A nice thing it is, after pinches, slaps, and pinpricks, to come back with lashes! All that's left is to take a big stone and tie it around my neck and throw me in the well so I can be the wedding heifer to cure other people's problems.† Leave me alone, because if you don't, by God, I'll run wild, come what may!"

---

* *Vinagrillo* was a cosmetic used to whiten the hands and face, and whose principal ingredient was vinegar.

† A heifer used to be slaughtered for rustic weddings. Sancho's allusion here is that he has to be a martyr.

At this point, Altisidora sat up on the tomb, and at the same instant, *chirimías* began to play accompanied by flutes, and everyone shouted: "Long live Altisidora, long live Altisidora!"

The duke and duchess stood up, and the kings Minos and Rhadamanthus, and all of them together with don Quixote and Sancho went to receive Altisidora and bring her down from the bier. Pretending to be faint, she bowed in the direction of the duke and duchess, and looked over at don Quixote and said: "May God pardon you, unloving knight, since by your cruelty I was in the other world for what seemed like more than a thousand years. And you, oh, most compassionate squire in the world! I thank you for the life I possess. As of today, you may take six shirts of mine that I offer you so you can have them remade for yourself, and if they're not all in good shape, at least they're clean."

Sancho kissed her hands with his pointed hat in one hand and his knees on the ground. The duke asked that the hat and flaming robe be taken back, and for Sancho's jacket to be returned to him. Sancho begged the duke to let him keep the robe and hat, saying he wanted to take them back home in memory of this unprecedented event. The duchess said they would allow it, because Sancho knew what a great friend of his she was. The duke had the courtyard cleared and told everyone to go to their rooms, and that don Quixote and Sancho should be taken to the rooms they had used before.

Chapter LXX. Which follows the sixty-ninth and deals with things necessary to the clear understanding of this history.

SANCHO SLEPT that night in a portable bed in the same room as don Quixote, which he would have liked to have avoided if possible, because he well knew his master was going to keep him awake asking him questions. He wasn't in the mood to talk a lot because he was still hurting from his recent martyrdom, and his pain wouldn't let his tongue move freely. He would have preferred to sleep in a hut by himself than in that elegant room with someone else.

His fear turned out to be well-founded and his suspicion true, because no sooner did his master get into bed than he said: "What do you think, Sancho, about what happened tonight? The might of a lover's scorn is great and powerful— you've seen Altisidora with your own eyes, dead, and not killed by arrows, nor by a sword, nor by any other instrument of war, nor by deadly poisons, but just by her brooding on the rigor and scorn with which I've always treated her."

"Let her die as much as she wants and however she wants," responded Sancho, "and let me stay at home, because I never led her to love me, nor did I ever scorn her in my entire life. I don't know, nor can I imagine, what the health of Altisidora, a girl more capricious than wise, has to do with the torments of Sancho Panza, as I've said before. Now I can certainly understand clearly and distinctly that there are enchanters and enchantments in the world, and may God free me from them, since I cannot free myself. Even so, I beg your worship to let me sleep, and not ask me anything else unless you want me to throw myself out the window."

"Sleep, Sancho, my friend," responded don Quixote, "if the pinpricks, pinches, and slaps that you received will allow you."

"No pain," replied Sancho, "comes close to the affront of the slaps, if only because they were done by duennas— may God confound them! And I ask you once again to let me sleep, because sleep soothes the miseries of those who have them when awake."

"All right," said don Quixote, "and may God be with you."

The two of them went to sleep, and while they slept, Cide Hamete Benengeli, the author of this great history, wanted to explain how the duke and duchess came to dream up the aforementioned scheme. He says that the bachelor Sansón Carrasco (having not forgotten that when he was the Knight of the Mirrors he was vanquished and knocked down by don Quixote, which erased and ruined all his plans) wanted to try again, expecting a better result than the first time. And so he found out from the page who had taken the letter and present to Teresa Panza, Sancho's wife, where don Quixote was. He found another suit of armor and a new horse, and he put a white moon on his shield. He put the shield and armor on a mule guided by a peasant (not Tomé Cecial, his former squire, so he wouldn't be recognized either by Sancho or don Quixote).

He arrived, finally, at the castle of the duke, who informed him about the road don Quixote was taking and his plan to participate in the jousts in Zaragoza. He also told him about the pranks they had played, especially about the scheme to disenchant Dulcinea at the expense of Sancho's rear end. He revealed the joke Sancho had played on his master as well, making him believe that Dulcinea was enchanted and transformed into a peasant, and how the duchess, his wife, had made Sancho believe that he was the one who was deceived, because Dulcinea was really enchanted. The bachelor laughed no little about this, reflecting on the shrewdness and simplicity of Sancho, as well as the complete madness of don Quixote.

The duke asked that if he should find him, and whether or not he vanquished him, he should come back to tell him what happened. The bachelor promised just that and went off looking for don Quixote. He didn't find him in Zaragoza, so he kept on going, and what has been recounted happened. He returned by way of the duke's castle, and told him everything that had taken place, along with the conditions of the battle, and that don Quixote was going back to keep, as a good knight-errant, the word he'd given to retire for a year in his village, during which perhaps—said the bachelor—he would regain his sanity, for that was what had moved him to take on the disguise, as it was such a pity to see an intelligent *hidalgo* as don Quixote without his wits. With this he bade farewell to the duke and went back to his village to await don Quixote, who was following along.

The duke then decided to play another trick, since he enjoyed so much the things that don Quixote and Sancho did. He sent many of his servants on foot and on horseback to comb the roads near and far from the castle, everywhere he thought don Quixote might be coming, so that they could bring him back either by force or by his free will to the castle, if they found him.

They found him, and sent word back to the duke, who had planned what to do, and as soon as he heard that they were about to arrive, had the torches and candles lit, and had Altisidora get up onto her bier, with all the other details mentioned, so well contrived and well-done that there was little difference between appearance and reality.

Cide Hamete goes on to say that personally he thinks that the jokesters were as crazy as those they played jokes upon, and that the duke and duchess were not two fingers from looking like fools themselves in making fools of real ones.

At the first rays of the sun, those two, one sleeping soundly, the other keeping vigil with unbridled thoughts, felt like getting up, for staying in bed, whether as victor or vanquished, never gave pleasure to don Quixote.

Altisidora, who, don Quixote believed, had returned from death to life, followed the orders of her masters and went into don Quixote's room crowned with the same garland that she was wearing while on her tomb, and dressed in a tunic of white taffeta, decorated with gold flowers, her hair flowing below her shoulders, and leaning on a cane made of very fine black ebony. Upset and confused, he wrapped himself in his sheets and quilts from the bed, his tongue silent, without offering her any of the usual courtesies.

Altisidora sat in a chair at the head of the bed, and after giving a great sigh, said in a weak, tender voice: "When ladies of quality and modest maidens trample their honor, and let their tongues break through every obstruction, revealing the secrets from the depths of their hearts in public, they're really in desperate straits. I, *señor* don Quixote de La Mancha, am one of those, enamored, vanquished, and in love. But, with all this, I was patient and virtuous—so much so that my soul burst through my silence and I lost my life. I was dead for two days—at least, that's what those who saw me thought—from dwelling on the severity with which you've treated me, oh, heart harder than marble to my laments, knight made of flint! And if it weren't that Love, having compassion for me, found a way to save me through the torments of this good squire, I'd still be in the other world."

"Love could have just as easily," said Sancho, "found a way to torment my donkey instead, and I would have been grateful. But tell me, *señora*—and may heaven find a kinder lover for you than my master—what did you see in the other world? What is hell like? Why is it that someone who dies of despair has to wind up there?"

"To tell the truth," responded Altisidora, "I must not have completely died, because I didn't go into hell. Once you go in, you can't get out, even if you want to. The truth is, I got to the gate, where a dozen devils were playing ball, all of them wearing pants and vests, with collars decorated with lace, and more lace at their cuffs, with four inches of their forearms showing to make their hands look longer, and in their hands they had bats made of fire.

"And what impressed me most was that instead of balls they were using books, seemingly filled with hot air and rubbish, a marvelous and novel thing to behold. But this didn't amaze me as much as seeing that, whereas usually winners are happy and losers are sad, down there in that game everyone grumbled, everyone argued, and everyone called each other names."

"That doesn't surprise me," responded Sancho, "because devils, whether they're playing or not, can never be content, win or lose."

"That's what it must be," responded Altisidora, "but there's something else that surprises me, I mean, that surprised me then, and that was that after the first thwack, no book was whole, nor was it usable again, and the way they smashed new books and old to smithereens was a marvel to see. They whacked one of those books, brand-new and well bound, which came totally apart and its pages went flying around. One devil said to another: 'Look and see what this book is.' And the devil answered: 'This is the *Second Part of the History of don Quixote de La Mancha*, not the one written by Cide Hamete, but rather by an Aragonese who says he's from Tordesillas.' 'Take it away,' responded the other devil, 'and throw it into the depths of hell so my eyes won't ever see it.' 'Is it so bad?' asked the other. 'So bad,' replied the first, 'that if *I* tried on purpose to write a worse one, I couldn't do it.' They continued their game, hitting other books, and since they mentioned don Quixote—whom I adore and love—I tried to remember that vision."

"It doubtless had to be a vision," said don Quixote, "because there's no other me in the world, and that history just goes from hand to hand, and stays in none, because they all kick it away. It makes no difference to me if I'm wandering like a ghost into the depths of hell, or in the brightness of the earth, because I'm not the person that history deals with. If it were good, faithful, and true, it would live for centuries, but if it's bad, it'll be a short road from its birth to its grave."

Altisidora was going to continue her grievances about don Quixote when he said to her: "I've told you many times, *señora*, that it distresses me that you've made me the object of your affection, since my own thoughts can do nothing in return except acknowledge yours. I was born to belong to Dulcinea del Toboso, and the Fates—if indeed there are any—pledged me to her. To think that another beauty would take her place in my heart is to think the impossible. I hope this will enlighten you sufficiently so that you can withdraw into the bounds of your modesty, since no one should take on something impossible."

When Altisidora heard this, she lost her temper and said to him: "By God, don Codfish, soul of mortar, pit of a date, you're more stubborn than a peasant when he insists he's right. If I could, I'd scratch your eyes out! Do you actually think, don Vanquished and don Cudgeled, that I died for you? Everything you saw tonight was pretend! I'm not a woman who would care the slightest bit about a camel such as you, not to mention to *die* for you!"

"I can believe it," said Sancho, "because dying on account of love is something laughable. They may say they will, but actually doing it, let Judas believe it!"*

When they were talking about these things, the singing musician came in, the fellow who had sung the two stanzas given earlier, and bowing deeply before don Quixote, he said: "Your grace can count me among your most faithful servants, because I've been a fan of yours for many days, as much because of your fame as because of your deeds."

Don Quixote responded: "Tell me who your grace is, so that my courtesy can respond properly."

The young man responded that he was the musician and poet from the night before.

"Of course," replied don Quixote. "Your grace has a wonderful voice. But what you sang didn't seem to the

---

* More or less from Horace's *Satires* I, vv. 100–1: "Let Judas believe it, *not me.*" This is not a biblical Judas, if you were wondering, since Horace lived before Christ.

point, because what do Garcilaso's stanzas* have to do with the death of this *señora*?"

"Don't wonder about that, your grace," said the musician. "Among novice poets of our age each one writes whatever he wants and steals from whomever he wants, whether or not it fits with what his point is, and there's nothing they sing or write that they don't attribute to poetic license."

Don Quixote tried to respond but the duke and duchess' arrival prevented him from doing so, and there was a long and pleasant conversation in which Sancho said so many amusing and astute things that the duke and duchess were amazed once again, as much by his simplicity as by his acuity. Don Quixote begged them to allow him to leave that very day, since vanquished knights like himself should live in a pigsty rather than royal palaces. They willingly gave him permission and the duchess asked him if Altisidora was still in his good graces.

He answered: "*Señora mía*, you should realize that this maiden's trouble comes from being idle, and the remedy is for her to have something useful to do to occupy her time. She told me that lace is used in hell, and since she must know how to make lace, let her keep doing it. If she makes the bobbins flit about, the image or images of what she desires won't flit about her imagination. And this is the truth, this is my opinion, and this is my advice."

"And mine," added Sancho, "since I've never seen a lacemaker in all my life who died from love. Busy maidens think more about finishing their work than about love. At least that's the way it is with me, because when I'm farming, I don't think about my wife, I mean, about my Teresa Panza, whom I love more than my eyelashes."

"You've spoken well, Sancho," said the duchess, "and I'll make sure my Altisidora keeps busy from now on doing handwork, which she knows how to do very well."

"There's no reason for that remedy, *señora*," responded Altisidora, "since just thinking about the cruelty this ignorant brigand has done me will erase him from my memory without any other tactic. And now with your greatness' permission, I will leave, so that I won't have to gaze on not

---

* Of course only the *second* stanza was by Garcilaso (see the previous chapter at page 1002). But give don Quixote credit for recognizing it.

only his woebegone expression, but also his ugly, abominable appearance."

"That seems to me," said the duke, "like the saying: 'he who offends is close to forgiving.'"

Altisidora pretended to wipe tears from her face with a handkerchief, and, bowing toward her masters, left the room.

"I promise you, poor girl," said Sancho, "that you're bound to have bad luck, since you were up against a soul as dry as a rush and a heart as hard as an oak tree. If you were dealing with me, another rooster would be singing to you."

The conversation ended, don Quixote got dressed and ate with the duke and duchess, then left that afternoon.

Chapter LXXI. What happened to don Quixote with his squire, Sancho, on the way to their village.

DON QUIXOTE was riding along on the one hand feeling low, and on the other hand very happy. His defeat caused his sadness, but Sancho's powers, as revealed in the resurrection of Altisidora, revived his spirits, although he did wonder if the enamored maiden had really been dead.

Sancho was not at all happy, because Altisidora had not kept her word to give him the six shirts, and as these thoughts ran to and fro in his mind, he said to his master: "In truth, *señor*, I'm the most unfortunate doctor in the world. Even when they kill the patient they're treating, physicians insist on being paid for their work, which is only to sign a prescription for some medicine, that they don't even compound—the pharmacist does—and the poor patient is out of luck! And look at me—other people's health costs me blood, slaps, pinches, pinpricks, and lashes, and they don't give me an *ardite* for it. I swear, if they bring me another sick person, before I cure him, they'll have to grease my palms. 'Where the abbot sings, he dines' and I don't think that heaven gave me these powers so that I can use them with other people *de bóbilis, bóbilis*."*

---

* This means "free of charge." See Part I, chapter thirty, page 280. He at least gets it right this time.

"You're right, Sancho, my friend," responded don Quixote. "Altisidora did ill in not giving you the shirts she promised, and even though your power is *gratis data*,* at least you didn't have to study; of course, it's worse than studying when you have to withstand torture on your body. For myself, I'll say that if you wanted to receive pay for the lashes to disenchant Dulcinea, I would have already paid you well. But I don't know if payment will affect the cure, and I wouldn't want the fee to counteract the medicine. With all this, it seems to me that it wouldn't hurt to try. Sancho, figure out the price you want, and start whipping yourself right now; then you can pay yourself in cash with your own hand, since you have my money."

Sancho opened his eyes and ears wide when he heard this offer, and resolved in his heart to whip himself lustily, and he said to his master: "All right, *señor*, I want to please you in what you want, to my profit. The love for my children and wife makes me interested. Tell me, your grace, how much you'll give me for each lash I give myself."

"If I were to pay you, Sancho," responded don Quixote, "according to the worth and quality of this remedy, the treasures of Venice and the mines of Potosí wouldn't be enough to pay you. Estimate what money of mine you have and put a price on each lash."

"There are," responded Sancho, "three thousand three hundred lashes. Of those I've given myself as many as five and the rest are left. Let's add back the five already given, and let's start with three thousand three hundred at a *cuartillo* apiece—I won't take anything less even if the whole world commanded me to—and it comes to three thousand three hundred *cuartillos*. Three thousand *cuartillos* are one thousand five hundred half *reales*, and that's seven hundred fifty *reales*. And the three hundred makes a hundred fifty half *reales* and that comes to seventy-five *reales*. These added together come to eight hundred twenty-five *reales*. I will take this amount from what I have of yours and I'll go home rich and content, though well whipped, because 'you don't catch trout . . .'† and I'll say no more."

---

* "Given free," Latin phrase.

† ". . . with dry pants on."

"Oh, blessed Sancho! Oh, amiable Sancho!" responded don Quixote. "How obliged Dulcinea and I will be to serve you all the days that heaven is pleased to give us! If she comes back to her lost self—and it's not possible that she won't—her misfortune will be turned into joy and my vanquishment will be a happy triumph. And when do you think, Sancho, you want to start this whipping, because if you do it quickly, I'll add a hundred *reales*."

"When?" replied Sancho. "I'll begin tonight without fail. Make sure we're in the countryside, beneath a clear sky, and I'll open my flesh."

The night don Quixote was waiting for finally came. It seemed to him that the wheels of Apollo's chariot had broken, and that the day was much longer than usual, as happens with people in love, who can never adjust time to their desires. Finally, they went in among some trees that were a bit off the road, and where they left the saddle and packsaddle of Rocinante and the donkey unoccupied, and they stretched out on the grass and ate a dinner from Sancho's saddlebag. He made a flexible and strong whip from the gray's halter and bridle, and went about twenty paces away among some beech trees.

Don Quixote, who saw him go off with such courage and dash, said to him: "Watch out, my friend, and don't whip yourself to pieces. Make sure that you space the lashes out. Don't hurry so much that your breath will fail you halfway through. I mean, don't whip yourself so hard that your life will be over before you get to the necessary number. And so that you won't lose track of how many lashes you will have given yourself, I'll keep count over here with my rosary. May heaven favor you as much as your good purpose deserves."

"'Pledges never bother a good payer,'" responded Sancho. "I plan to administer them in such a way that I'll hurt myself without killing myself. This must be the essence of this miracle."

Sancho then took off his clothes from the waist up, and seizing the whip he began to lash himself, and don Quixote began to count.

Sancho had given himself only six or eight lashes before it seemed that the joke was a little costly and the price for them was too cheap, so he stopped for a moment and said to his master that he'd made a bad deal, because each lash was worth a half *real* and not a *cuartillo*.

"Keep going, Sancho, and don't worry," don Quixote said to him, "because I'll double the stake."

"In that case," said Sancho, "it's in God's hands, and let it rain lashes."

But that jokester Sancho stopped lashing his back and started whipping the trees, giving moans once in a while that gave the impression that he was tearing out his soul with every lash. Don Quixote, both sympathetic and fearful that Sancho would end his life and therefore not achieve his desire through his own carelessness, said: "On your life, my friend, stop this business right now. This medicine seems harsh and it'd be a good idea to take it at intervals. 'Rome wasn't built in a day.' You've given yourself more than a thousand lashes, if I counted right. That's enough for now. 'A donkey—speaking in general terms—can carry a load, but not a double load.'"

"No, no, *señor*," responded Sancho, "I don't want anyone to say about me 'once the money's paid, the labor's delayed.' Stay away a bit longer, and let me give myself just another thousand lashes. With two of these series we'll have finished the match, and there'll be merchandise left over."

"Since you're so eager," said don Quixote, "may heaven assist you. Lash yourself and I'll go back where I was."

Sancho went back to his task with great enthusiasm and he removed the bark from many trees, so vigorously did he whip himself. Once he raised his voice and—giving an enormous lash to a beech tree—said: "'Here Samson will die, and all those with him.'"*

Don Quixote ran to where the doleful voice and terrible blow came from, and seized the halter that served Sancho as a whip. "Sancho, my friend," he said, "in order to please me, don't let Fortune let you lose your life, which has to support your wife and children. Let Dulcinea wait a bit more—I'll keep myself within the limits of my soon-to-be-realized hope, and I'll wait for you to get back some strength so you can finish this business to the satisfaction of everyone."

---

* This is Sancho's version of the popular saying: "Let Samson die, and all those with him."

"Since your grace wants it that way, *señor mío*," responded Sancho, "let it be as you say. Toss your cape over my shoulders—I'm sweating and I don't want to catch a cold. Novice flagellants run that risk."

Don Quixote did as he was asked, and he covered Sancho, who slept until the sun came up. They then continued their journey, which ended in a village three leagues down the road. They stopped at an inn, for that's what don Quixote called it, and not a castle with a deep moat, iron gratings, and drawbridge. Ever since he'd been vanquished, his mind was more lucid, as will be seen now. He was lodged in a first-floor room, where, instead of tooled leather panels, there were painted fabric hangings, commonly seen in villages. One of them showed a badly painted scene of the kidnapping of Helen, when the daring guest took her from Menelaus,* and in another one the story of Dido and Æneas, where she's in a tower, waving what looked like half a sheet at the fleeing guest, who was at sea in a frigate or a brigantine.†

Don Quixote could see in the hangings that Helen wasn't exactly going against her will, because she was laughing on the sly. But the beautiful Dido was crying tears the size of walnuts. When don Quixote saw them he said: "These two *señoras* were most unfortunate for not having been born in these times, and I, most unfortunate of all for not having been born in theirs. If I had found those two fellows, Troy wouldn't have burned, and Carthage wouldn't have been destroyed, because if I had just killed Paris, so many misfortunes would have been prevented."

"I'll bet," said Sancho, "that before much time passes there won't be a wine shop, inn, or barbershop where the history of our deeds isn't painted. But I'd prefer that a better painter do it than the one who did these."

"You're right, Sancho," said don Quixote, "because this painter is like Orbaneja, a painter from Úbeda, who, when they asked him what he was painting, he would answer: 'Whatever it turns out to be.' And if by chance he was painting a rooster, he wrote beneath it: 'THIS IS A ROOSTER,' so that

---

* The daring guest is Paris, and the kidnapping is what started the Trojan War.

† In the *Æneid*, Dido falls in love with Æneas. This scene shows Æneas abandoning her on the African coast.

they wouldn't think it was a fox. The painter or writer (for it's all the same) who brought to light this new don Quixote must have done the same thing—he painted or wrote whatever it turned out to be. Or maybe it was like a court poet years ago named Mauleón, who gave instant answers to everything he was asked, and when he was asked what '*Deum de Deo*' meant,* he said, '*Dé donde diere.*'† But, leaving this aside, tell me if you plan to do more whipping tonight, Sancho, and whether you'll do it inside or out."

"By golly, *señor*, what I plan to do I can do either inside or out. But even so, I'd prefer that it be among the trees, because it seems to me that they help me to bear my pain marvelously well."

"Well, it shouldn't be that way, Sancho, my friend," responded don Quixote. "So that you can get back some strength, we should wait until we're in our own village. We'll arrive there the day after tomorrow at the latest."

Sancho said that he'd go along with his master's wishes, but he'd prefer to finish that business "while his blood was still flowing warm" and "while the mill was still grinding," because "danger lurks in delay" and "pray to God and wield the mallet" and "one TAKE is worth two I'LL GIVE YOUS," and "a bird in the hand is worth two in the bush."

"No more proverbs, Sancho, by the only God," said don Quixote, "because it seems like you're going back to *sicut erat.*‡ Speak plainly, smoothly, and not in a roundabout way, as I've asked you many times, and you'll see how 'one loaf is as good as a hundred.'"

"I don't know what my problem is," responded Sancho, "because I don't know how to say a word without a proverb, and all of my proverbs seem to be to the point. But I'll try to mend my ways if I can."

And with this, their conversation ended.

---

* "God from God" in Latin.
† "Let him strike wherever he can" in Spanish.
‡ "As it was in the beginning" in Latin.

Chapter LXXII. How don Quixote and Sancho arrived at their village.

DON QUIXOTE and Sancho spent the whole day waiting in that village and inn, one of them to finish the tally of his whipping, and the other to see the end of it, since it meant the fulfillment of his desire. In the meantime, a traveler on horseback arrived with three or four servants, one of whom said to the man who appeared to be the master: "*Señor* don Álvaro Tarfe, your grace can have a siesta here. The place seems clean and cool."

When don Quixote heard this he said to Sancho: "Listen, Sancho, as I was looking through the second part of my history, it seems to me that I ran across that name in passing."*

"That may well be," responded Sancho. "Let's let him get off his horse and then we can ask him."

The horseman got down and the innkeeper's wife gave him a room on the first floor, decorated with fabric hangings like those in don Quixote's room.

The newly arrived gentleman changed into some cool clothes and went out onto the inn's porch, which was spacious and cool, where don Quixote was strolling, and asked him: "Where is your grace headed, *señor*?"

And don Quixote answered: "To a village near here, where I was born—and your grace, where are you going?"

"I, *señor*," replied the gentleman, "am going to Granada, my hometown."

"And a good one it is," replied don Quixote. "But tell me, for courtesy's sake, what is your name, because it might be more important to know than I can rightly state."

"My name is don Álvaro Tarfe," responded the guest.

To which don Quixote replied: "Without any doubt, you must be that don Álvaro Tarfe who appears in the *Second Part of don Quixote de La Mancha* that was recently written and published by a contemporary author."

"I'm one and the same," responded the gentleman, "and

---

* Don Álvaro Tarfe is indeed the third-most-important character in the false *Quixote*, appearing already in the first chapter (mentioned first on p. 33, l. 19 of Riquer's edition).

that don Quixote, the main subject of that history, was a very great friend of mine. I was the one who took him away from his home, or at least inspired him to go with me to Zaragoza for some jousts, and in truth, in truth, I did many things for him as his friend, and even prevented his being whipped for his great recklessness."*

"And tell me, your grace, *señor* don Álvaro Tarfe, do I look like that don Quixote you mention?"

"No, you don't," responded the guest, "not in the slightest."

"And that don Quixote," said ours, "did he have a squire with him named Sancho Panza?"

"Yes, he did," responded don Álvaro, "and although he was reputed to be amusing, I never heard him say anything remotely funny—"

"I can well believe that," interrupted Sancho, "because not everyone can say amusing things, and that Sancho that your grace has mentioned, *señor*, must be some great scoundrel, dunce, and thief, all rolled up into one. I'm the real Sancho Panza, and I have more witty sayings than there are drops of rain, and if you don't believe me, try me out and follow me around for at least a year, and you'll see that they drip off of me with every step, in such a way and so many that often without my knowing how, I make everyone who hears me laugh. And the real don Quixote de La Mancha, the famous one, the brave, the wise, the one who is in love, the righter of wrongs, the guardian of orphans, the protector of widows, the killer of maidens, he who has as the only object of his affection Dulcinea del Toboso, is this *señor* here present, and he's my master. Any other don Quixote and any other Sancho Panza are just pranks and jokes—and badly dreamed-up ones at that."

"By God, I believe it," responded don Álvaro, "because, my friend, you've said more witty things in four sentences than the other Sancho Panza did in all the times I heard

---

* This is from Avellaneda's chapter eight (starts in vol. i, p. 166, l. 11 in Riquer's edition) where don Quixote believes that a thief being taken to be whipped is really a captive knight, so he attacks the constables who are taking the criminal away. They in turn haul don Quixote off to jail. In chapter nine, don Quixote is rescued by Álvaro Tarfe.

him speak, and there were many of them. He was more
of a glutton than well-spoken, and more stupid than witty.
And it must be that the enchanters who pursue don Quixote the Good have tried to pursue me using don Quixote
the Bad. But I don't know what to say. I swear I left him
in the Asylum of the Nuncio of Toledo* for treatment, and
here's another don Quixote, although quite different from
mine."

"I don't know if I'm GOOD," said don Quixote, "but I do
know that I'm not the BAD one, proof of which, *señor* don
Álvaro Tarfe, is that I've never stepped in Zaragoza in all
the days of my life. In fact, since I was told this trumped-up
don Quixote had gone to the jousts in that city, I refused
to go there to prove his lie to the world, and went directly
to Barcelona, that treasure house of courtesy, shelter for
strangers, abode for the poor, hometown of the brave,
avenger of the offended, welcome dwelling of firm friend-
ships, and uniquely beautiful in its location. And although
what happened to me there was not much to my liking, but
rather has caused me a lot of sorrow, I left there with no
sorrow, just because I saw that city.

"In short, *señor* don Álvaro Tarfe, I'm don Quixote de
La Mancha, the same one proclaimed by fame, and not that
luckless fellow who has attempted to usurp my name and
grace himself with my thoughts. I beg you, since you're a
gentleman, to make an affidavit before the mayor of this
town, stating that this is the first time your worship has seen
me in all the days of your life until now, and that I'm not
that don Quixote written about in the second part, nor is
this Sancho Panza, my squire, the one your grace knew."

"I am very willing," responded don Álvaro, "although
it's amazing to have seen two don Quixotes and two Sanchos at practically the same time, so alike in their names
yet so different in their actions, and I'll say once again and
confirm that I didn't see what I saw nor did I experience
what I experienced."

"Your grace," said Sancho, "must be enchanted like my

---

* In the last chapter of Avellaneda (thirty-six), Álvaro Tarfe does take
don Quixote to this madhouse in Toledo. The institution was founded
by a papal nuncio (the pope's representative to civil government) in
the late 1400s, thus its name.

lady Dulcinea del Toboso. And may it please heaven that your enchantment could be undone by my giving myself three thousand–odd lashes like I'm doing for her, because I'd do it without any pay."

"I don't understand this business of lashes," said don Álvaro.

And Sancho responded that it was a long story, but he would tell it to him if they were traveling the same road.

Lunchtime came. Don Quixote and don Álvaro ate together; and by chance the mayor of the town with a scribe came into the inn. Don Quixote told him he wanted to make an affidavit, which was his legal right, that don Álvaro Tarfe, that gentleman who was there present, had not previously known don Quixote de La Mancha, who was also present, and that he was not the one who was written about in a history titled *Second Part of don Quixote de La Mancha*, written by a certain Avellaneda, a native of Tordesillas. The mayor made the affidavit, which was done with all the appropriate legal trimmings, which made don Quixote and Sancho very happy—as if such a deposition were important; as if their deeds and words wouldn't clearly show the differences between the two don Quixotes and Sanchos. Many courteous words and pledges of service passed between don Álvaro and don Quixote, in which the great Manchegan showed his wisdom, which convinced don Álvaro Tarfe that he'd been deceived; that in fact he must have been enchanted, since he'd touched two so different don Quixotes with his hand.

When late afternoon came, they left the village, and about half a league from there they came to a fork in the road, one leading to don Quixote's village, and the other the one don Álvaro needed to take. In that short time, don Quixote told of the misfortune of his defeat and Dulcinea's enchantment and remedy, all of which caused fresh wonder in don Álvaro, who, embracing don Quixote and Sancho, went on his way, as did don Quixote. They spent that night among some trees to give Sancho the chance to finish his whipping, at the expense of the bark of the beech trees, much more than his back, which he preserved so carefully that the lashes wouldn't have scared off a fly had one alighted there.

The deceived don Quixote didn't lose count of a single

lash, and found that together with the previous night, the total came to three thousand twenty-nine. It seems that the sun came up early, eager to shed light on the sacrifice, and at that light, they continued their journey once again, speaking about how don Álvaro had been deceived, and how wise it was to get an affidavit from the mayor, and one with such authority.

That day and night they traveled without anything worthy of being told, except that Sancho finished his labor, which pleased don Quixote immensely, and he could hardly wait for day to come to see if they would run across the disenchanted Dulcinea, his lady. Along the road he scrutinized every woman he came across to see if she was Dulcinea del Toboso, since he believed the promises of Merlin were infallible.

With these thoughts and desires, they went up a hill from the top of which they could see their village. As soon as he saw it, Sancho got down on his knees and said: "Open your eyes, longed-for home, and see that Sancho Panza is returning to you, if not very rich, at least well whipped. Open your arms and receive your son, don Quixote, who, if he's coming back vanquished at someone else's hand, at least he has triumphed over himself, and he says that's the victory most to be desired. I'm coming with money, because 'if they gave me lashes, at least I had a fine mount.' "*

"Stop that nonsense," said don Quixote, "and let's go into our village, right foot in front,† where we'll give free rein to our imagination, and start planning for the pastoral life we expect to lead."

With this they went down the slope and approached their village.

---

* See Part II, chapter thirty-six, page 776.
† Covarrubias says this means "for luck."

Chapter LXXIII. About the omens that don Quixote saw when he entered his village, with other events that embellish and authenticate this great history.

AT THE entrance of the village, according to Cide Hamete, don Quixote saw two boys arguing on the threshing floor, and one of them said to the other: "Don't wear yourself out, Periquillo—you'll never see her again as long as you live."*

Don Quixote heard this and said to Sancho: "Do you realize, my friend, what that boy has said: 'You'll never see her again as long as you live'?"

"So—what difference does it make what he said?" responded Sancho.

"What difference?" replied don Quixote. "Don't you see that if you apply those words to my situation, it means that I won't see Dulcinea again."

Sancho was on the point of responding when he saw a hare being pursued by many hunters and greyhounds through the countryside. The hare ran over to take shelter, and crouched under the donkey. Sancho picked it up easily and gave it to don Quixote, who was saying: "*Malum signum,*† *malum signum!* A hare flees, greyhounds pursue it, Dulcinea doesn't appear."

"Your grace is acting very strange," said Sancho. "Let's suppose that this hare is Dulcinea del Toboso and these greyhounds are the foul enchanters who transformed her into a peasant. She flees, I catch her and put her in your grace's care, and she's in your arms being petted. What bad sign is this and what bad omen can be read here?"

The boys who had been arguing came over to see the hare, and Sancho asked one of them why they were arguing. He was answered by the one who had said, "You'll

---

* Translator's note: I have had to fudge a bit here. The word "her" really should be "it," as English usage demands, since it refers to a cage, as you'll see. But since "cage" is feminine in Spanish, Spanish usage requires the pronoun "her." Why it was necessary to use "her," against English rules, will be obvious soon enough.

† "Bad omen," in Latin.

never see her again as long as you live," that he'd taken a cricket cage from the other boy that he didn't plan ever to return to him as long as he lived.

Sancho took four quarter *reales* from his purse and gave them to the boy for the cage, which he put in don Quixote's hands, saying: "Here, s*eñor*, are your omens, broken and crushed, and they have no more to do with our affairs, the way I look at it, uneducated as I am, than the clouds of yesteryear. And if I remember correctly, I've heard the priest of our village say that it's not right for wise Christian people to put any stock in such foolishness, and even your grace himself has said the same thing in recent days, giving me to understand that all those Christians who put stock in omens are stupid. There's no need to insist on this too much. Let's just keep going and enter our village."

The hunters came over to ask for their hare, and don Quixote gave it to them. Then they moved on and at the entrance to the village they came across the priest and Sansón Carrasco, praying in a little meadow. It must be said that Sancho Panza had covered the donkey and the armor with the buckram robe painted with flames—which they had given him at the duke's castle the night that Altisidora revived. He'd put the penitent's hat on the donkey's head as well, and he was now the most unusually transformed and adorned donkey in the world.

The two were immediately recognized by the priest and the bachelor, who ran to them with open arms. Don Quixote got off his horse and embraced both of them warmly. The boys, who are all-seeing lynxes, noticed the penitent's hat on the donkey and went to see him, and yelled to the others: "Come here, boys, and you'll see Sancho Panza's donkey, handsomer than Mingo,* and don Quixote's horse, thinner than ever."

So, surrounded by boys and accompanied by the priest and the bachelor, they entered the village and went to don Quixote's house, and found the housekeeper and the niece waiting at the door, for news had reached them about their arrival. Teresa Panza, wife of Sancho, had heard the same news, and with hair uncombed and without a shawl, leading

---

* Although this was a popular comparison, no one knows who this Mingo was.

her daughter, Sanchica, by the hand, she went to see her husband. And seeing him not as well dressed as she thought a governor should be, she said to him: "How is it, my husband, that you're returning on foot and footsore, looking more like a man without a government than a governor?"

"Hush, Teresa," responded Sancho, "for many times 'where there are stakes there's no bacon.' Let's go home and there you'll hear wonders. I'm bringing money, which is the important thing, earned by my cleverness, and without hurting anyone."

"You bring the money, my good husband," said Teresa, "and no matter how you earned it, you won't have invented any new ways of getting it."

Sanchica hugged her father and asked him if he'd brought anything for her, for she was waiting for him like the rains of May. And she held on to his belt, and with his wife holding his other hand, the daughter leading the donkey, they all went home, leaving don Quixote in his house in the care of his niece and housekeeper, and in the company of the priest and the bachelor.

Don Quixote, not waiting an instant, shut himself up with the bachelor and priest, and in a few words told how he had been vanquished and that he was obliged not to leave his village for a year, during which time he planned to keep his promise to the letter, without violating it the least bit, for as a knight-errant he was obliged by the rigorous order of knight-errantry; he said he planned to be a shepherd during that year, and pass his time in the solitude of the fields, where he could vent his amorous thoughts with a free rein, engaged in that pastoral and virtuous vocation, and if *they* were not prevented by urgent business elsewhere, they might want to be his companions. He would take care of buying enough sheep and other livestock so that they could be legitimately called shepherds, and the most important piece of business had already been taken care of, because he'd figured out names for them that fit them like a glove.

The priest asked him to tell them what they were. Don Quixote responded that he himself would be the shepherd QUIXOTIZ, and the bachelor, CARRASCÓN, and the priest, the shepherd CURAMBRO, and Sancho Panza, the shepherd PANCINO.

They were dumbfounded to see the new madness of don

Quixote. But so that he wouldn't leave town again on his knight-errantries, and hoping that in that year he would recover, they went along with his new plan, and approved it as wise, and offered to be his companions in his new vocation.

"And what's more," said Sansón Carrasco, "since, as everybody already knows, I'm a most celebrated poet, I'll write pastoral or courtly verses—whichever suits my fancy—to keep us entertained on those byroads on which we have to travel. And what we most need to do, *señores míos*, is choose names for the shepherdess that each one plans to celebrate in his verses, and that we not leave a single tree, no matter how hard its wood is, where we don't inscribe her name, as is the custom of enamored shepherds."

"That's exactly right," responded don Quixote. "Although I'm free to choose a name for an imaginary shepherdess, I already have Dulcinea del Toboso, the glory of these riverbanks, the adornment of these meadows, the sustenance of beauty, the cream of wit, and finally, the subject on which all praises can repose, no matter how exaggerated they may be."

"That's the truth," said the priest, "but we others will seek meeker shepherdesses, who, if they're not perfect, at least they'll approach perfection."

To which Sansón Carrasco added: "And if we don't find any, we'll use the names of those who appear in books, of which the world is full: Fílidas, Amarilis, Dianas, Fléridas, and Belisardas. Since they're on sale in the marketplaces, we can easily buy them and have them for our own. If my lady, or maybe I should say 'my shepherdess,' should be named Ana, I'll celebrate her using the name Anarda; and if it's Francisca, I'll call her Francenia; if it's Lucía, Lucinda; and that's the way it works. And Sancho Panza, if he enters our fraternity, can celebrate his wife, Teresa Panza, with the name Teresaina."

Don Quixote was amused to hear how these names were applied, and the priest praised don Quixote's chaste and honorable resolve greatly, and offered once again to keep him company, when his necessary obligations didn't keep him away. With this, they bade him farewell, and begged and advised him to be careful with his health, and to eat only those things that were good for him.

As luck would have it, the niece and housekeeper overheard the conversation of the three of them, and as soon as they left, they both went into don Quixote's room and the niece said: "What's all this, *señor* uncle? Now that we were thinking that your grace came back to stay at home to enjoy a quiet and honorable life, you want to start a new labyrinth, turning yourself into: 'Little shepherd, you who come, / Little shepherd, you who go'?* In truth, 'the barley is too hard to make flutes with.'"†

To which the housekeeper added: "Can you withstand the heat of summer, the night air of winter, the howling of wolves? Certainly not. This is a profession and calling for robust men, hardened by the weather, and raised for that job since they were in diapers. All things considered, it's better to be a knight-errant than a shepherd. Look, *señor*, take my advice—not given with a stomach filled with bread and wine, but fasting, and with fifty years under my belt—stay home and tend to your estate, confess frequently, help out the poor, and it'll be on my soul if things turn out wrong."

"Hush, my daughters," responded don Quixote. "I know what I need to do. Take me to bed—I don't feel quite right—and rest assured that whether I'm a knight-errant or a future shepherd, I'll not fail to tend to your needs, as you'll see proven out."

And the good daughters, which the niece and housekeeper were, helped him to bed, where they gave him something to eat and pampered him as much as they could.

---

* Clemencín has identified the *first* line of this *villancico* as coming from the *cancionero de Amberes* ("Antwerp") (1603). No printed source has been found for the *second* line. In the first edition, these lines are not set off (folio 276r).

† This is a musical saying. Children used this green barley, when still naturally moist, to make little pipes with which to make music, but once it was dry, it could no longer be used for that purpose. In other words, she implies don Quixote is too old to take on this new calling.

Chapter LXXIIII. *About how don Quixote fell ill, the will he dictated, and his death.*

Since no things human are eternal, but rather decline from their beginnings to their ultimate end, especially the lives of men, and since don Quixote had no privilege from heaven to stay its course, his end came when least he expected, either because of the melancholy caused by his being vanquished, or because of the will of heaven, which ordered that a fever take hold of him and put him in bed for six days, during which time he was visited many times by the priest, the bachelor, and the barber—his friends— and Sancho never left his bedside.

These men, thinking it was the grief at seeing himself vanquished and of not seeing his desire for the freedom and disenchantment of Dulcinea fulfilled that had him in that state, tried to raise his spirits through all possible means. The bachelor told him to cheer up and get out of bed to begin their pastoral calling, for which he'd already written an eclogue, and too bad for all those Sannazzaro* had written; and that he'd bought with his own money two fine dogs to guard the fold, one of them named Barcino and the other Butrón,† that a cattleman from El Quintanar had sold him. But not for all this did don Quixote come out of his sadness. His friends called the doctor, who took his pulse and was not too pleased. He said that, just in case, they should tend to the salvation of his soul, because the health of his body was in danger.

Don Quixote heard this with great calm, but not so his housekeeper, niece, and squire, who began to weep tenderly, as if he were already dead in front of them. The doctor's opinion was that grief and dejection were finishing him off. Don Quixote asked to be left alone so he could sleep a bit. They did, and he slept a stretch—as they say—of more than six hours, and it was so long that the housekeeper and niece

---

* Jacopo Sannazzaro (1456–1520), a very influential Italian writer who composed the first pastoral romance, *Arcadia* (1504).

† *Barcino* means "reddish colored," and *Butrón* is an ancient Spanish noble surname.

thought he would never come out of it. He woke up at the end of that time, crying in a loud voice: "Blessed be the Almighty God who has done so much for me! His mercies are limitless, and they're not reduced or restrained by the sins of men."

The niece heard these words of her uncle and they seemed more rational than his usual talk, at least during that illness, and she asked him: "What is your grace saying, *señor*? Is this something new? What mercies are these, or what sins of men do you mean?"

"The mercies," responded don Quixote, "are those God has just this instant given me, and He, as I said, is not swayed by my sins. I'm sane now, free and clear-minded, without the dark shadows of ignorance the detestable books of chivalry shrouded over me, owing to my bitter and continual reading of them. I now see their foolishness and their deceits, and my only grief is that this realization has come to me so late that it doesn't allow me time to compensate by reading other books that could be the light of my soul.

"I feel, niece, that I'm about to die. I would like to meet death in such a way that people know my life was not so bad that I should be remembered as a crazy man. That is, I was one, but I wouldn't like to confirm it in my death. Call to my bedside my good friends the priest, the bachelor Sansón Carrasco, and *maese* Nicolás, the barber. I want to confess and dictate my will."

But the niece didn't need to fetch them, since all three happened in right then. As soon as don Quixote saw them he said: "Good news, worthy *señores*, for I'm no longer don Quixote de La Mancha, but rather Alonso Quixano, for whom my good qualities have earned the epithet 'THE GOOD.' I'm now the enemy of Amadís de Gaula, and the whole multitude of his lineage, and now the profane histories of knight-errantry are hateful to me. I realize my folly and the danger into which my having read them has placed me. Now, by the grace of God, and having learned by my own experience, I abominate them."

When the three heard him say this, they believed that some new craziness had overcome him. And Sansón said to him: "You're telling us this now, when we have news that *señora* Dulcinea is disenchanted, *señor* don Quixote? Now that we're about to become shepherds to spend our lives singing like princes, you want to become a hermit? Don't talk like that, on your life. Collect your senses and stop this foolishness."

"What has happened up to now," replied don Quixote, "has truly been to my detriment, but my death, with the help of heaven, will set things right. I, *señores*, feel that death is coming at full speed. Leave these jests aside, and find a confessor so I can confess, and bring a notary to prepare my will, for in such critical moments as this one, a man ought not to trifle with his soul. And so I beg you, while I'm confessing, to fetch the notary."

They all looked at each other, amazed by don Quixote's words, but although they were in some doubt, they tended to believe him. One of the signs that led them to believe he was dying was that he'd gone so easily from crazy to sane, for he'd added to those words others that were so well stated, so Christian, and so sensible, that they removed all doubt and they accepted he was truly sane.

The priest made everyone leave, and he stayed behind with don Quixote and confessed him. The bachelor went for the notary and came back a short while later with him and with Sancho Panza. Sancho, who had heard news about the state of his master from the bachelor, found the housekeeper and niece in tears, and he began to whimper and weep himself. The confession ended and the priest came out, saying: "Truly he's dying, and truly Alonso Quixano, the Good, is sane. We can all go in now so that he can dictate his will."

This news started a flow of tears from the eyes of the housekeeper, the niece, and Sancho Panza, and they began to cry, accompanied by a thousand sobs from their hearts, because, truly, as has been said once, both while he was plain Alonso Quixano, the Good, and while he was don Quixote de La Mancha, he always had a gentle nature and a pleasant demeanor, and for this reason he was loved, not only in his household, but by everyone who knew him.

The notary came in with the others, and after don Quixote had dictated the opening of his will and put his soul in order, and tended to all the other required Christian details, when he came to the list of bequests, he said: "ARTICLE I: It's my will that Sancho Panza, whom in my madness I made my squire, keep certain money I have given him—

because there have been between him and me certain accountings and credits and debits—and I want no claim to be made against him nor that he be asked for any accounting at all, and if anything is left over after he's paid what I owe him, he can keep the rest, which will be very little, and may it do him much good. And if when I was crazy I was responsible in part for giving him the governship of an *ínsula*, if I could now, being sane, give him a kingdom, I would, because the simplicity of his nature and the fidelity of his services make him worthy of it."

And turning toward Sancho Panza, he said: "Forgive me, my friend, for having made you seem crazy like myself, making you fall into the same error into which I fell, of believing that there were and are knights-errant in the world."

"Ah," responded Sancho in tears, "don't die, *señor mío*, but take my advice and live many years, because the craziest thing a man can do is to let himself die just like that, without anyone killing him, nor any other hands finishing him off except those of melancholy. Look, don't be lazy— get out of bed, and let's go into the countryside dressed as shepherds, as we agreed. Maybe behind some bush we'll find the lady Dulcinea, disenchanted as nice as can be. If you're dying because of the grief of seeing yourself vanquished, let me take the blame, saying that because I didn't tighten Rocinante's saddle enough you were knocked over. Moreover, your grace probably saw in your books of chivalry that knights are always overcoming others, and he who is defeated today is a victor tomorrow."

"That's true," said Sansón. "The good Sancho Panza is quite right in this matter."

"*Señores*," said don Quixote, "not so fast, because 'in the nests of yesteryear there are no birds this year.' I was crazy, and now I'm sane; I was don Quixote de La Mancha, and now I'm Alonso Quixano, the Good. May my repentance and truth restore me to the esteem in which I used to be held. And let's move along, *señor* notary.

"ARTICLE 2: I bequeath all my estate to Antonia Quixana, my niece, here present, having first taken off the top what is necessary to fulfill the bequests that I'll have made. And the first payment I want to be made is to pay the salary I owe for the time my housekeeper has served me, plus twenty *ducados* for a dress. I appoint as my executors the priest and the bachelor Sansón Carrasco, here present.

"ARTICLE 3: It's my will that if Antonia Quixana, my niece, should wish to marry, that she marry someone about whom it will have been first learned that he doesn't know what books of chivalry are, and if it's found out that he does, and she marries him anyway, she'll lose what I've bequeathed, and my executors are free to distribute it for pious works as they see fit.

"ARTICLE 4: I ask those *señores*, my executors, that if good fortune leads them to meet the author who they say wrote a history that's circulating called *Second Part of the Deeds of don Quixote de La Mancha*, that they beg his pardon as earnestly as they can for my having caused him to write so much and such great foolishness as he has written in it, because I leave this life with the misgiving of having given him the reason to write it."

He finished his will, and was overcome by a fainting spell and lay stretched out on his bed, to the dismay of everyone, and everyone tended to his care. In the three days he lived after they say he made his will, he frequently fainted. The house was in an uproar, but even so, the niece ate, the housekeeper drank, and Sancho Panza was joyful, because inheriting something erases, or at least suppresses, the sense of grief the dead person leaves behind to the inheritor.

At last, don Quixote's final hour came, after he received all the sacraments, and after he cursed the books of chivalry with many powerful words. The notary was present, and he said that he'd never read in any book of chivalry that a knight-errant had died in his bed so calmly, and in such a Christian way as don Quixote, who, amidst the pity and tears of those surrounding him, gave up the ghost; that is, he died.

When the priest saw it, he asked the notary to write an affidavit that Alonso Quixano, the Good, commonly called don Quixote de La Mancha, had passed away from this present life, and died of natural causes. And he asked for such an affidavit to remove the possibility that an author other than Cide Hamete Benengeli might bring him back to life falsely* and write endless histories about his deeds.

---

* At the end of Avellaneda's book, it says that don Quixote continued his adventures in Old Castile—Salamanca, Ávila, and Valladolid—

This is the end of the ingenious *hidalgo* don Quixote de La Mancha, whose village Cide Hamete Benengeli refused to declare, so that all the towns and villages of La Mancha might contend among themselves to adopt him and claim his as their own as did the seven cities of Greece for Homer.*

The lamentations of Sancho, of the niece, and of the housekeeper are not included here, nor is the new epitaph for his grave, although Sansón wrote this one:

> A NOBLE GENTLEMAN LIES HERE;
> A STRANGER ALL HIS LIFE TO FEAR;
> NOR IN HIS DEATH COULD DEATH PREVAIL,
> IN THAT LAST HOUR, TO MAKE HIM QUAIL.
> HE FOR THE WORLD BUT LITTLE CARED;
> AND AT HIS FEATS THE WORLD WAS SCARED;
> A CRAZY MAN HIS LIFE HE PASSED,
> BUT IN HIS SENSES DIED AT LAST.†

And the most prudent Cide Hamete said to his quill: "Here you will rest, hanging on this rack and from this wire—whether skillfully cut or not, I don't know—where you will live long centuries, if presumptuous and rude historians don't take you down to profane you. But before they touch you, you can warn them, saying in as good a form as you can:

> Hold off! ye weaklings; stay your hands!
> Don't try it, anyone. Let no one touch it,
> For this enterprise, my lord the king,
> Was meant for me alone.‡

---

with a new name, THE KNIGHT OF THE TRAVAILS (see Riquer's edition, vol. iii, pp. 229–30). This affidavit was supposed to prevent further continuations, specifically one inspired by Avellaneda.

* These Greek cities were Smyrna, Rhodes, Colophon, Salamis, Chios, Argos, and Athens.

† This epitaph and the quatrain that follows are both from Ormsby.

‡ These verses are more or less in imitation of a ballad found in *Guerras civiles de Granada* (see Gaos, Part II, p. 1043, note 192e).

"For me alone* don Quixote was born, and I for him. He knew how to act and I how to write. Together we make a unit, in spite of the false Tordesillesque writer who dared, or may dare, to write with his coarse ostrich quill—so incapable of good writing—the deeds of my brave knight. This is no burden for his shoulders, nor a subject for his ungraceful wit. And if you meet him by chance, tell him to leave the weary and rotted bones of don Quixote alone, and that he shouldn't carry him off, against all laws of death, to Old Castile, making him leave the grave, where really and truly he lies stretched out and helpless to make a third expedition and fresh outing. The two he made already, to the pleasure and approval of people who heard of them in this country and abroad, are already sufficient to mock all those expeditions by so many knights-errant. And with this you'll fulfill your Christian calling, giving good advice to one who wishes you ill, and I'll be satisfied† and proud to have been the first one to have enjoyed the fruit of my writings as much as I could want, since my only purpose was to make men loathe the fictitious and foolish histories of the books of chivalry, which, because of this true history of don Quixote, are now beginning to stumble, and surely will fall into oblivion, without any doubt. Vale."

FINIS

---

* That this is the pen talking and not Cide Hamete Benengeli is very clear in Spanish, since the gender of "me alone" is the feminine form that "quill" would require.

† Translator's note: Oops. This "satisfied" is now masculine in Spanish, indicating that the narration has switched back to Cide Hamete Benengeli. I'm only the translator here.